# THE
# *unofficial* GUIDE®
# TO Walt Disney World®

2015

**Other Unofficial Guides**

# THE *unofficial* GUIDE®
## TO Walt Disney World®

2015

BOB SEHLINGER *and* LEN TESTA

(Walt Disney World® is officially known as Walt Disney World® Resort.)

!keen
communications

Please note that prices fluctuate in the course of time and that travel information changes under the impact of many factors that influence the travel industry. We therefore suggest that you write or call ahead for confirmation when making your travel plans. Every effort has been made to ensure the accuracy of information throughout this book, and the contents of this publication are believed to be correct at the time of printing. Nevertheless, the publishers cannot accept responsibility for errors or omissions, for changes in details given in this guide, or for the consequences of any reliance on the information provided by the same. Assessments of attractions and so forth are based upon the authors' own experiences; therefore, descriptions given in this guide necessarily contain an element of subjective opinion, which may not reflect the publisher's opinion or dictate a reader's own experience on another occasion. Readers are invited to write the publisher with ideas, comments, and suggestions for future editions.

Published by:
Keen Communications, LLC
P.O. Box 43673
Birmingham, AL 35243

Cover design by Scott McGrew

Text design by Vertigo Design and Annie Long

For information on our other products and services or to obtain technical support, please contact us from within the United States at 888-604-4537 or by fax at 205-326-1012.

Keen Communications, LLC, also publishes its books in a variety of electronic formats. Some content that appears in print may not be available in electronic formats.

ISBN 978-1-62809-020-8

Distributed by Publishers Group West

Manufactured in the United States of America

5 4 3 2

# CONTENTS

# LIST *of* MAPS *and* DIAGRAMS

# INTRODUCTION

## ■ WHY "UNOFFICIAL"?

### DECLARATION OF INDEPENDENCE

THE AUTHORS AND RESEARCHERS of this guide specifically and categorically declare that they are and always have been totally independent of the Walt Disney Company, Inc.; of Disneyland, Inc.; of Walt Disney World, Inc.; and of any and all other members of the Disney corporate family not listed.

The material in this guide originated with the authors and researchers and has not been reviewed, edited, or approved by the Walt Disney Company, Inc.; Disneyland, Inc.; or Walt Disney World, Inc.

This guidebook represents the first comprehensive *critical* appraisal of Walt Disney World. Its purpose is to provide the reader with the information necessary to tour Walt Disney World with the greatest efficiency and economy and with the least hassle.

In this guide, we represent and serve you. If a restaurant serves bad food or a gift item is overpriced or a ride isn't worth the wait, we say so, and in the process we hope to make your visit more fun and rewarding.

### DANCE TO THE MUSIC

A DANCE HAS A BEGINNING and an end. But when you're dancing, you're not concerned about getting to the end or where on the dance floor you might wind up. In other words, you're totally in the moment. That's the way you should be on your Walt Disney World vacation.

You may feel a bit of pressure concerning your vacation. Vacations, after all, are very special events—and expensive ones to boot. So you work hard to make your vacation the best that it can be. Planning and organizing are essential to a successful Walt Disney World vacation, but if they become your focus, you won't be able to hear the music and enjoy the dance.

So think of us as your dancing coaches. We'll teach you the steps to the dance in advance so that when you're on vacation and the music plays, you'll dance with effortless grace and ease.

## THE IMPORTANCE OF BEING GOOFY

EDGAR AND FRANCINE are sitting at their kitchen table. Francine is swiping maniacally at her iPad as Edgar looks on befuddled, his head in his hands. . . .

"Who knew planning a trip to Disney World was such a pain in the keister?" Edgar grouses to no one in particular. "And I thought signing up for health care was bad."

"Now, now, Edgar, let's think positive!" Francine commands. "OK, we know when we're going—now we have to decide which Disney park to visit each day!"

"What if we don't *wanna* go to a park every day?" Edgar pleads.

"Doesn't matter! Gotta choose so we can reserve our FastPass+ times for specific attractions in the park we're visiting! You can request a specific time, such as 1 p.m., or you can let the FastPass+ system give you its 'first available' reservation," chirps Francine, sounding rather like a press release.

"OK, fine," Edgar shrugs. "Monday at Epcot—let's get FastPasses for Soarin', Test Track, and Living with the Land. Those are the ones we've always gotten FastPasses for before."

Francine, suddenly serious, clasps her husband's hand meaningfully. "Edgar, *everything* has changed. Now we can only get a FastPass+ for one of those."

"But you said we could reserve FastPasses for three rides—"

"That's right—just not the three we want! We can also pick two from Journey into Imagination, *Captain EO,* or Spaceship Earth!"

"Now wait just a minute!" Edgar exclaims. "You can walk on those anytime without waiting! And what have you been smoking to think I'd wanna ride Journey into Imagination? I'd rather be forced to watch *The Monkey's Uncle* on repeat!"

"Oh, calm down, Edgar, I didn't make the rules! Now . . . if I don't make any mistakes, I can get it all squared away on the Disney website in just *eight* steps!".

"Well, I guess that doesn't sound *too* bad," Edgar concedes. "Eight steps online and we're done."

Francine looks over her glasses. "Not so fast—I have to repeat the process for every park for each day we're there. We also have to choose our restaurants and when we want to eat each day so we can make our Advance Reservations."

"For the love of Pete, Francine! How am I supposed to know where I want to eat and when I want to eat it half a year from now? What if we're too tired? What if we filled up on turkey legs and beer and we just wanna skip dinner?"

"Sorry! If we have an Advance Reservation—say, we want to meet Buell and Myrna for dinner at The Hollywood Brown Derby on Thursday—we have to decide on Wednesday whether we need to cancel. If we wait till Thursday to back out, we have to pay a no-show charge for all four of us."*

"This is *insane*!" Edgar sputters. "Next you're gonna tell me we have to book the pool at the Polynesian!"

*Everything above the asterisk is true. Below . . . not so much.*

"I was *just* getting to that—one thing at a time, please! Now, since we know we're going to Epcot on Monday, we need to apply for visas to all the different countries in World Showcase, except for Mexico and Canada, of course.

"Oops, almost forgot: When would be a good time for you to work in a BM? Let's say we eat dinner at the San Angel Inn on Monday—you know what Mexican does to your colon. If we go to the Magic Kingdom the next day, we could make you a PottyPass+ reservation for the *Tangled* restroom! Just remember they charge a "Crapper Camper" fee if you stay in there more than 10 minutes—*EDGAR, ARE YOU LISTENING TO ME???*"

And so it goes. . . .

What really makes writing about Walt Disney World fun is that the Disney people take everything so seriously. Day to day, they debate momentous decisions with far-ranging consequences: Will Pluto look silly in a silver cape? Have we gone too far with The Little Mermaid's cleavage? With the nation's drug problem a constant concern, should we have a dwarf named Dopey?

Unofficially, we think having a sense of humor is important. This guidebook has one, and it's probably necessary that you do, too—not to use this book, but to have the most fun possible at Walt Disney World. Think of the *Unofficial Guide* as a private trainer to help get your sense of humor in shape. It will help you understand the importance of being Goofy.

## HONEY, I BLEW UP THE BOOK!

THE FIRST EDITION OF *The Unofficial Guide to Walt Disney World* was fewer than 200 pages, a mere shadow of its current size. Since that edition, Disney World has grown tremendously. The *Unofficial Guide* has grown to match this expansion.

A mom from Streator, Illinois, is amazed by the size of the *Unofficial Guide,* writing not unsympathetically:

> It had been 10 years since we'd been to WDW, and I was shocked by how the size of your book grew. After going, I'm surprised that it's so small.

The good news is that we're working with leading scientists to put the entire book on a computer chip implanted directly in your brain! In the meantime, we offer a qualified apology for the bulk of this edition. We know it may be too heavy to carry comfortably, but we defend the inclusion of all the information presented. Not every diner uses ketchup, A.1. sauce, or Tabasco, but it's nice to have all three on the table.

Concerning *Unofficial Guide* content, readers have offered these suggestions for new material:

> • *I think your guide should have a list of attractions that provide (1) seats, (2) air-conditioning, and (3) at least 15 minutes off your feet.*

> • *I feel the* Unofficial Guide *should include a claustrophobia rating for each attraction.*

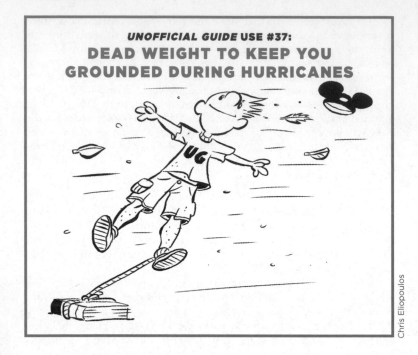

*UNOFFICIAL GUIDE* USE #37:
## DEAD WEIGHT TO KEEP YOU GROUNDED DURING HURRICANES

Chris Eliopoulos

- *I wish you'd discuss restrooms more in the next edition. I found myself constantly searching for one.*

- *We think you need a rating system regarding water [i.e., how wet you can expect to get on specific attractions]. EW = Extreme Water; SW = Some Water; M = Mist.*

These comments are representative in that many of you would like more detailed coverage of one thing or another. We've debated adding hundreds of things, but we haven't done so. Why? Because we don't have an infinite number of pages to work with, and we felt other information was more important. New ideas for book material are usually tested first at **blog.touringplans.com,** so check there to see what your fellow readers have suggested.

## YOUR *UNOFFICIAL* WALT DISNEY WORLD TOOLBOX

WHEN IT COMES TO WALT DISNEY WORLD, a couple with two toddlers in diapers need different advice than a party of seniors going to the Epcot International Flower & Garden Festival. Likewise, adults touring without children, families with kids of varying ages, and honeymooners all require their own special guidance.

To meet the varying needs of our readers, we've created the very comprehensive guide before you. We call *The Unofficial Guide to Walt Disney World,* at about 850 pages, the "Big Book." It contains the detailed information that anyone traveling to Walt Disney World needs to have a super vacation. It's our cornerstone.

As thorough as we try to make the main guide, there still isn't sufficient space for all the tips and resources that may be useful to certain readers. Therefore, we've developed four additional guides that provide information tailored to specific visitors. Although some advice from the Big Book, such as arriving early at the theme parks, is echoed in these guides, most of the information is unique.

Here's what's in the toolbox:

**The Unofficial Guide Color Companion to Walt Disney World,** by Bob Sehlinger and Len Testa, proves that a picture is indeed worth a thousand words. In the Big Book, for instance, you can learn about the best guest rooms to request at the Wilderness Lodge, but in the *Color Companion* you can *see* the rooms, along with the pool and the magnificent lobby. Full-color photos show how long the lines get at different times of day, how wet riders get on Splash Mountain, and how the parks are decked out for various holidays. The *Color Companion* will whet your appetite for Disney fun, picture all the attractions, serve as a keepsake, and, as always, help make your vacation more enjoyable. Most of all, the *Color Companion* is for fun. For the first time, we're able to use photography to express our zany *Unofficial* sense of humor. Think of it as Monty Python meets Walt Disney . . . in Technicolor.

**The Unofficial Guide to Walt Disney World with Kids,** by Bob Sehlinger and Liliane J. Opsomer with Len Testa, presents detailed planning and touring tips for a family vacation, along with more than 20 family touring plans that are exclusive to this book.

**Mini-Mickey: The Pocket-Sized Unofficial Guide to Walt Disney World,** by Bob Sehlinger, Len Testa, and Ritchey Halphen, is a portable CliffsNotes-style version of the Big Book. It distills information to help short-stay or last-minute visitors decide quickly how to plan their limited hours at Disney World.

**Beyond Disney: The Unofficial Guide to Universal, SeaWorld, and the Best of Central Florida,** by Bob Sehlinger and Robert N. Jenkins with Len Testa, is a guide to non-Disney theme parks, attractions, restaurants, outdoor recreation, and nightlife in Orlando and Central Florida.

## THE DEATH OF SPONTANEITY

ONE OF OUR ALL-TIME FAVORITE LETTERS came from a man in Chapel Hill, North Carolina:

> *Your book reads like the operations plan for an amphibious landing: Go here, do this, proceed to Step 15. You must think that everyone is a hyperactive, type-A theme park commando. What happened to the satisfaction of self-discovery or the joy of spontaneity? Next you'll be telling us when to empty our bladders.*

(We'd love to hear this reader's thoughts on FastPass+, which lets you reserve spots on popular rides two months in advance.)

As it happens, *Unofficial Guide* researchers are a pretty existential crew who are big on self-discovery. But Disney World—especially for first-time travelers—probably isn't the place you want to "discover" the spontaneity of needless waits in line or mediocre meals when you could be doing better.

In many ways, Disney's theme parks are the quintessential system, the ultimate in mass-produced entertainment, the most planned and programmed environment anywhere. Lines for rides form in predictable ways at predictable times, for example, and you can either learn here how to avoid them or "discover" them on your own.

We aren't saying that you can't have a great time at Walt Disney World. What we *are* saying is that you should think about what you want to do before you go. The time and money you save by planning will help your family have more fun.

## DON'T LET THE TAIL WAG THE DOG

SOME FOLKS BECOME SO INVESTED in their plan that it becomes the centerpiece of the vacation. Witness this Columbia, Missouri, mom:

> *Getting to the park when it opens is the key to beating the lines. To make that happen: (1) Pack breakfast on the go—you can eat your Pop-Tarts once you're on the shuttle bus, then drink your juice while you wait in line for Dumbo. (2) Send the fastest runner in your party to jump on the bus or boat; the driver will wait if he sees you coming and one of your kids is already hanging on. (3) Showering wastes precious park and rest time; the pool will do. (4) Braid your daughter's hair. Seriously. My 8-year-old never had to brush her hair in the morning. (5) Ball caps for boys also avoid hair brushing.*

The stress and doggedness of such an approach would push most of us over the edge. So remember the basics: Know thyself, nothing to excess, and concentrate on having fun.

## WE'VE GOT ATTITUDE

SOME READERS DISAGREE about our attitude toward Disney. A woman from Golden, Colorado, lambastes us:

> I read your book cover-to-cover and felt you were way too hard on Disney. It's disappointing when you're all enthused about going to Walt Disney World to be slammed with all these criticisms.

A reader from Little Rock, Arkansas, takes us to task for the opposite prejudice:

> Your book was quite complimentary of Disney, perhaps too complimentary. Maybe the free trips you travel writers get at Disney World are chipping away at your objectivity.

And from a Williamsport, Pennsylvania, mother of three:

> Reading your book irritated me before we went to Disney World because of all the warnings and cautions. I guess I'm used to having guidebooks pump me up about where I'm going. But once I arrived, I found I was fully prepared and we had a great time. In retrospect,

*I have to admit you were right on the money. What I regarded as you being negative was just a good dose of reality.*

✳ *unofficial* **TIP**
Check out experienced Disney World visitors' opinions of the parks in this book, and apply them to your own travel circumstances.

Finally, a reader from Phoenixville, Pennsylvania, prefers no opinions at all, writing:

*While each person has the right to his or her own opinion, I didn't purchase the book for an opinion.*

For the record, we've always paid our own way at Walt Disney World: hotels, admissions, meals, the works. We don't dislike Disney, and we don't have an ax to grind. Personally, we have enjoyed the Disney parks immensely over the years, both experiencing them and writing about them. Disney, however, as with all corporations (and all people), is better at some things than others. Because our readers shell out big bucks to go to Walt Disney World, we believe they have the right to know in advance what's good and what's not. For those who think we're overly positive, please understand that the *Unofficial Guide* is a guidebook, not an exposé. Our aim is for you to enjoy your visit. To that end, we report fairly and objectively. When readers disagree with our opinions, we, in the interest of fairness, publish their viewpoints alongside ours. To the best of our knowledge, the *Unofficial Guides* are the only travel guides in print that do this.

## THE SUM OF ALL FEARS

EVERY WRITER WHO EXPRESSES an opinion is accustomed to readers who strongly agree or disagree: It comes with the territory. Extremely troubling, however, is the possibility that our efforts to be objective have frightened some readers away from Walt Disney World or made others apprehensive.

A mom from Avon, Ohio, was just such a person, writing:

*After reading parts of the* Unofficial Guide, *I seriously reconsidered going to WDW at all because I felt it required too much planning— too many things that could go wrong, too many horrible outcomes (like waiting for hours in scorching heat with kids), etc. A friend convinced me it wouldn't be that bad, so I kept on with planning the trip.*

We certainly understand the reader's feelings, but the key point was that, though apprehensive, she stayed the course. Here's what she said after returning home:

*Let me tell you, your guide and touring plans were dead-on accurate! We didn't wait more than 10 or 15 minutes for almost every attraction in two days!*

For the record, if you love theme parks, Disney World is as good as it gets—absolute nirvana. If you arrive without knowing a thing about the place and make every possible mistake, chances are about 90% that you'll have a wonderful vacation anyway. The job of a guidebook is to give you a heads-up regarding opportunities and potential problems. We're certain we can help you turn a great vacation into an absolutely *superb* one.

## TOO MANY COOKS IN THE KITCHEN?

WE RECEIVED THIS QUERY from a Manchester, Vermont, reader and feel it deserves a serious response:

> I read a review on the Internet criticizing the Unofficial Guide because it was "written by a team of researchers." The reviewer doesn't say why he thinks the team approach is inferior, but the inference is along the lines of "too many cooks spoil the soup." Why do you use this approach?

There are several reasons. Most guidebooks do a reasonably good job with the what and where; *Unofficial Guides* add the how and why. Describing attractions or hotels or restaurants (the what) at a given destination (the where) is the foundation of other travel guidebooks. We know from our research, though, that our readers like to know how things work.

*unofficial* **TIP**
Researching and writing this book as a team results in a more objective guidebook for you.

However, no individual author can possibly be qualified to write about every topic in the vast range of important subjects that make up a good guide to Walt Disney World. Our team approach enables us to provide deeper explanations of Disney's operations and undertake much more sophisticated and extensive research. Creating touring plans (see page 73), for example, requires statisticians who can analyze millions of attraction wait times to predict how and why lines will build throughout any day. Another project, monitoring the Disney transportation system, requires riding and timing every bus, boat, and monorail route, a task that takes four researchers almost a week to complete. Our Walt Disney World with Kids chapter (Part Six) was developed in consultation with three nationally respected child psychologists and an advisory group of parents. Similarly, our professional culinary experts ensure, say, that the *pollo al forno* you order at Epcot's Italy Pavilion is a decent approximation of what you might get in Rome.

We also conduct extensive research on you, the reader. Your tastes, preferences, and opinions—expressed in reader surveys, e-mails, and blog comments—dictate the subjects we research and the content of our books. Other guides are researched and developed by individual authors or coauthors, the content filtered through the lens of their tastes, preferences, and opinions. Publishers of these guides hope the information is compatible with the needs of the reader—but if it is, the compatibility is largely accidental.

Known and respected in both the travel industry and academe, *Unofficial Guide* research has been recognized by *USA Today,* the BBC, *The New York Times,* the *Dallas Morning News,* the Travel Channel, Wired.com, and CNN, plus numerous academic journals. We (Bob and Len) put the fruits of our research into words, but behind us is an organization unequaled in travel publishing.

### THE *UNOFFICIAL* TEAM

SO WHO ARE THESE FOLKS? Allow us to introduce them all, except for our dining critic, who shall remain anonymous:

Steve Bloom is the voice of reason in the wilderness that is statistical analysis. Gerelyn Reaves answers e-mail better than we could

**BOB SEHLINGER** Author and publisher
**LEN TESTA** Coauthor
**RITCHEY HALPHEN** Managing editor
**FRED HAZELTON** Statistician
**SARAH KELLETH** touringplans.com webmaster, Lines developer
**KAREN TURNBOW, PhD** Child psychologist
**JIM HILL** Entertainment reporter

**PAM BRANDON** Shopping diva
**LARRY OLMSTED** Golf expert
**LAUREL STEWART** Fact-checking supervisor

**DATA COLLECTORS**
**ROB SUTTON,** *Supervisor*
Chantale Brazeau
Guy Garguilo
Shane Grizzard
Lillian Macko
Richard Macko
Kristen Mitchell
Cliff Myers
Jeff "Fred" Reisdorf
Darcie Vance
Rich Vosburgh
Kelly Whitman

**CONTRIBUTING WRITERS**
Rich Bernato
Liliane J. Opsomer
Sue Pisaturo
Laurel Stewart
Darcie Vance
Mary Waring
Deb Wills

**HOTEL INSPECTORS**
Ritchey Halphen
Kristen Helmstetter
Lillian Macko
Richard Macko
Myra E. Merkle
Darcie Vance

**ART & PRODUCTION**
**ANNIE LONG** Typesetter
**STEVE JONES, SCOTT McGREW** Cartographers
**TAMI KNIGHT, CHRIS ELIOPOULOS** Cartoonists

and generally keeps everyone in line. Morgan Crutchfield is our menu, technical, and spiritual advisor. Seth Kubersky is our Universal Orlando guru, assisted by food *consigliere* Derek Burgan. David Davies is our jack-of-all-trades; Brad Huber assists with software development. Brian McNichols does Disney bar "research" and whatever photographer Tom Bricker tells him. Todd Perlmutter skillfully debugged our touring plan software. Our Lines app was created by Henry Work, who's now trying to perfect soccer-playing animatronics for Disney. Lines' chat is moderated by the fabulous weasus.

We'd like to thank the following folks for their assistance with proofreading and fact-checking: Lines users bwalker75, Jags, JenWSU, Keithloveswaffles, LoisLane, MissingDisney, mossmacl, and onehappy sahm, along with Erin Foster, Melissa Adele Haskin, Sara Moore, and Darcie Vance. Finally, a heartfelt thanks to Frances Lennie of Indexing Research for graciously taking on this monster project at the 11th hour.

## THIS IS NOT A NOVEL!

THOUGH THIS GUIDE IS FULL OF CHARACTERS—and was created by a few more—it is at heart a reference work, and many readers do not read it cover-to-cover, as they would a piece of fiction. For some this causes problems—witness this angry reader who identified him/ herself as "None of Your Business":

*This e-mail is in regards to The Unofficial Guide to Walt Disney World, which I purchased last year for our trip to Disney World this year. I am very disappointed that the book doesn't mention that an additional fee is required to access the touring plans and crowd-level information on your website. Here is an excerpt from the book:*

If you decide to splurge and burn a pass on a half-day or less, refer to our Unofficial Guide Crowd-Level Calendar at **touringplans.com.**

**SURVEY:** *Which author do you prefer to write your guidebooks? (Guess which ones you got?)*

*The book refers to this website in other sections as well but does not mention that a fee is involved! I don't mind paying, but I am disgusted that you would not mention it in your book. Shame on me for assuming this information would be free, even though I shelled out $23.99 [Canadian] for the book.*

Don't you hate it when people hide their true feelings just to be polite? In any event, None of Your Business's complaint illustrates how readers use the guide in different ways. Here's our reply to NOYB:

*Dear None,*

*Thanks for your letter. Here's the thing:*

*The Unofficial Guide to Walt Disney World is used by many readers as a reference work as opposed to a cover-to-cover read. Consequently, a reader might miss something, say, at the beginning of the guide, that provides information necessary for understanding references to the same subject elsewhere. For several editions, we've been explaining in Part One, Gathering Information, specifically what readers can access on our website at no cost and what they can access only with a paid subscription.*

*In the last edition, this information read as follows:*

Much of our web content, including new research, book updates, resort photos and video, and up-to-date dining menus, is completely free. Access to part of the site, most notably the Crowd Calendar, additional touring plans, and in-park wait times, requires a small subscription fee (current-book owners get a substantial discount). This nominal charge helps keep us online and costs less than a sandwich at Flame Tree Barbecue in Disney's Animal Kingdom. Plus, **touring plans.com** offers a 45-day money-back guarantee—something we don't think the Flame Tree can match.

*In an 850-page book, it's unrealistic for us to think everyone will read every word. On the other hand, it's totally impractical to explain things that are mentioned multiple times each time they're referenced. So we don't blame you for being angry—you probably were using the guide as a reference and just missed the explanation.*

*All the best,*
*Bob and Len*

To sum up: If you use the guide like an encyclopedia or dictionary —for example, you look something up in one of the indexes, then go to the cited page—you may overlook information presented in previous sections that is vital to understanding the subject. Likewise, if you skip or skim over explanatory material in the introductory chapters, that might lead to a misunderstanding later on.

## CORRECTIONS, UPDATES, AND BREAKING NEWS

LOOK FOR THESE at the *Unofficial Guide* website, **touringplans.com**. See page 26 for a complete description of the site.

## THE *UNOFFICIAL GUIDE* PUBLISHING YEAR

WE RECEIVE MANY QUERIES asking when the next edition of the *Unofficial Guide* will be available. Usually our new editions are in stores by late August or early September. Thus, the 2016 edition will be on the shelves in August or September 2015.

## LETTERS AND COMMENTS FROM READERS

MANY WHO USE *The Unofficial Guide to Walt Disney World* write us to comment or share their own strategies for visiting Disney World. We appreciate all such input, both positive and critical, and encourage our readers to continue writing. Their comments and observations are frequently incorporated into revised editions of the *Unofficial Guide* and have contributed immeasurably to its improvement. If you write us or complete our reader survey, rest assured that we won't release your name and address to any mailing-list companies, direct-mail advertisers, or other third parties. Unless you instruct us otherwise, we'll assume that you don't object to being quoted.

*unofficial* **TIP**
If you're up for having your comments quoted in the guide, please be sure to tell us your hometown.

### Online Reader Survey

Our website hosts a questionnaire you can use to express opinions about your Walt Disney World visit. Access it here: **touringplans.com/walt-disney-world/survey.** The questionnaire lets every member of your party, regardless of age, tell us what he or she thinks about attractions, hotels, restaurants, and more.

If you'd rather print out and send us the survey, mail it to

Reader Survey
*The Unofficial Guides*
P.O. Box 43673
Birmingham, AL 35243

Finally, if you'd like to review this book on Amazon, go to **tinyurl .com/wdw2015reviews.**

### How to Contact the Authors

Bob Sehlinger and Len Testa
*The Unofficial Guide to Walt Disney World*
P.O. Box 43673
Birmingham, AL 35243
**unofficialguides@menasharidge.com**

When you write, put your address on both your letter and envelope; the two sometimes get separated. It's also a good idea to include your phone number. If you e-mail us, please tell us where you're from. Remember, as travel writers, we're often out of the office for long periods of time, so forgive us if our response is slow. *Unofficial Guide* e-mail isn't forwarded to us when we're traveling, but we'll respond as soon as possible after we return.

# WALT DISNEY WORLD:
## *An* OVERVIEW

IF YOU'RE CHOOSING A US TOURIST DESTINATION, the question is not whether to visit Walt Disney World, but how to see its best offerings with some economy of time, effort, and finances.

## WHAT WALT DISNEY WORLD ENCOMPASSES

WALT DISNEY WORLD COMPRISES 43 square miles, an area twice as large as Manhattan. Situated strategically in this vast expanse are the **Magic Kingdom, Epcot, Disney's Hollywood Studios,** and **Disney's Animal Kingdom** theme parks; 2 swimming theme parks; a sports complex; 5 golf courses; 41 hotels and a campground; more than 100 restaurants; 4 interconnected lakes; a shopping complex; 8 convention venues; a nature preserve; and a transportation system consisting of four-lane highways, elevated monorails, and a network of canals.

Walt Disney World has around 62,000 employees, or "cast members," making it the largest single-site employer in the United States. Keeping the costumes of those cast members clean requires the equivalent of 16,000 loads of laundry a day and the dry cleaning of 30,000 garments daily. (Mickey Mouse alone has 290 different sets of duds, ranging from a scuba wet suit to a tux; Minnie boasts more than 200 outfits.) Each year, Disney restaurants serve 10 million burgers, 6 million hot dogs, 75 million Cokes, 9 million pounds of French fries, and 150 tons of popcorn. In the state of Florida, only Miami and Jacksonville have bus systems larger than Disney World's. The Disney monorail trains have logged mileage equal to more than 30 round-trips to the moon.

## DISNEY-SPEAK POCKET TRANSLATOR
## AND GUIDE TO COMMON ABBREVIATIONS

IT MAY COME AS A SURPRISE to many, but Walt Disney World has its own somewhat peculiar language. The following charts list some terms and abbreviations you're likely to bump into, both in this guide and in the larger Disney (and Universal) community.

| THE DISNEY LEXICON IN A NUTSHELL |
| --- |
| **ADVENTURE** Ride |
| **ATTRACTION** Ride or theater show |
| **ATTRACTION HOST** Ride operator |
| **AUDIENCE** Crowd |
| **BACKSTAGE** Behind the scenes, out of view of customers |
| **CAST MEMBER** Employee |
| **CHARACTER** Disney character impersonated by an employee |
| **COSTUME** Work attire or uniform |
| **DARK RIDE** Indoor ride |
| **DAY GUEST** Any customer not staying at a Disney resort |
| **FACE CHARACTER** A character who doesn't wear a head-covering costume (Snow White, Cinderella, Jasmine, and the like) |
| **GENERAL PUBLIC** Same as day guest |

| | |
|---|---|
| **GREETER** Employee positioned at an attraction entrance |
| **GUEST** Customer |
| **HIDDEN MICKEYS** Frontal silhouette of Mickey's head worked subtly into the design of buildings, railings, golf greens, attractions, and just about anything else |
| **ON STAGE** In full view of customers |
| **PRESHOW** Entertainment at an attraction before the feature presentation |
| **RESORT GUEST** A customer staying at a Disney resort |
| **ROLE** A cast member's job |
| **SOFT OPENING** Opening a park or attraction before its stated opening date |
| **TRANSITIONAL EXPERIENCE** An element of the queuing area and/or preshow that provides information essential to understanding the attraction |

| COMMON ABBREVIATIONS AND WHAT THEY STAND FOR | |
|---:|---|
| **CM** | Cast member |
| **DCL** | Disney Cruise Line |
| **DDRA** | Downtown Disney Resort Area |
| **DDV** | Disney Deluxe Villas |
| **DHS** | Disney's Hollywood Studios |
| **DTS** | Disney Transportation System |
| **DVC** | Disney Vacation Club |
| **EMH** | Extra Magic Hours |
| **FP+/FPP** | FastPass+ |
| **I-DRIVE** | International Drive (major Orlando thoroughfare) |
| **IOA** | Universal's Islands of Adventure theme park |
| **TTC** | Ticket and Transportation Center |
| **USF** | Universal Studios Florida theme park |
| **WDI** | Walt Disney Imagineering |
| **WDTC** | Walt Disney Travel Company |
| **WDW** | Walt Disney World |

## THE MAJOR THEME PARKS

### The Magic Kingdom

When people think of Walt Disney World, most think of the Magic Kingdom, opened in 1971. It consists of the adventures, rides, and shows featuring the Disney cartoon characters, and Cinderella Castle. It's only one element of Disney World, but it remains the heart.

The Magic Kingdom is divided into six "lands," with five arranged around a central hub. First you come to **Main Street, U.S.A.,** which connects the Magic Kingdom entrance with the hub. Clockwise around the hub are **Adventureland, Frontierland, Liberty Square, Fantasyland,** and **Tomorrowland.** Five hotels (**Bay Lake Tower;** the **Contemporary, Polynesian,** and **Grand Floridian** resorts; and **The Villas at the Grand Floridian**) are connected to the Magic Kingdom by monorail and boat. Three other hotels, **Shades of Green, Wilderness Lodge & Villas,** and

**Four Seasons Orlando at Walt Disney World Resort,** are nearby but aren't served by the monorail.

## Epcot

Opened in October 1982, Epcot is twice as big as the Magic Kingdom and comparable in scope. It has two major areas: **Future World** consists of pavilions concerning human creativity and technological advancement; **World Showcase,** arranged around a 40-acre lagoon, presents the architectural, social, and cultural heritages of almost a dozen nations, each country represented by replicas of famous landmarks and settings familiar to world travelers.

The Epcot resort hotels—the **BoardWalk Inn & Villas, Caribbean Beach Resort, Dolphin, Swan,** and **Yacht & Beach Club Resorts and Beach Club Villas**—are within a 5- to 15-minute walk of the International Gateway, the World Showcase entrance to the theme park. The hotels are also linked to Epcot and Disney's Hollywood Studios by canal and walkway. Epcot is connected to the Magic Kingdom and its hotels by monorail.

## Disney's Hollywood Studios

Opened in 1989 as Disney-MGM Studios and a little larger than the Magic Kingdom, Disney's Hollywood Studios has two areas. One area, occupying about 75% of the Studios, is a theme park focused on the motion picture, music, and television industries. Park highlights include a re-creation of Hollywood and Sunset Boulevards from Hollywood's Golden Age, four high-tech rides, several musical shows, and a movie stunt show.

The second area encompasses soundstages, a back lot of streets and sets, and an outdoor theater for an automobile stunt show. Public access to the soundstages is limited to a tour which takes visitors behind the scenes of Disney animation and moviemaking.

Disney's Hollywood Studios is connected to other Walt Disney World areas by highway and canal but not by monorail. Guests can park in the Studios' pay parking lot or commute by bus. Guests at Epcot resort hotels can reach the Studios by boat or on foot.

We wouldn't be surprised to hear a major expansion of the Studios announced soon.

## Disney's Animal Kingdom

About five times the size of the Magic Kingdom, Disney's Animal Kingdom combines zoological exhibits with rides, shows, and live entertainment. The park is arranged in a hub-and-spoke configuration somewhat like the Magic Kingdom. A lush tropical rainforest serves as Main Street, funneling visitors to **Discovery Island,** the park's hub. Dominated by the park's central icon, the 14-story-tall, hand-carved **Tree of Life,** Discovery Island offers services, shopping, and dining. From there, guests can access the themed areas: **Africa, Asia,** and **DinoLand U.S.A.** Discovery Island, Africa, and DinoLand U.S.A. opened in 1998, followed by Asia in 1999. Africa, the largest themed area, at 100 acres, features free-roaming herds in a re-creation of the Serengeti Plain.

**Camp Minnie-Mickey,** the park's character-greeting area, also opened in 1998 but closed in 2014 to make way for a new "land" based on James Cameron's *Avatar* films, with construction ongoing until 2017.

Disney's Animal Kingdom has its own parking lot and is connected to other Walt Disney World destinations by the Disney bus system. Although no hotels lie within Animal Kingdom proper, the All-Star Resorts, Animal Kingdom Lodge & Villas, and Coronado Springs Resort are all nearby.

## THE WATER PARKS

DISNEY WORLD HAS TWO MAJOR water parks: **Typhoon Lagoon** and **Blizzard Beach.** Opened in 1989, Typhoon Lagoon is distinguished by a wave pool capable of making 6-foot waves. Blizzard Beach is newer, having opened in 1995, and it features more slides. Both parks are beautifully landscaped, and great attention is paid to atmosphere and aesthetics. Typhoon Lagoon and Blizzard Beach have their own adjacent parking lots and can be reached by Disney bus.

## OTHER WALT DISNEY WORLD VENUES

### Downtown Disney (a.k.a. Disney Springs: Marketplace, West Side, and Pleasure Island)

Downtown Disney is a large shopping, dining, and entertainment complex encompassing **Downtown Disney Marketplace** on the east, **Downtown Disney West Side** on the west, and **Pleasure Island** in the middle. Downtown Disney Marketplace contains the world's largest Disney-character-merchandise store, upscale resort-wear and specialty shops, and several restaurants, including **Rainforest Cafe** and **T-REX.** Downtown Disney West Side combines nightlife, shopping, dining, and entertainment. The **House of Blues** serves Cajun-Creole dishes in its restaurant and electric blues in its music hall. **Bongos Cuban Café,** a nightclub and café created by Gloria Estefan and her husband, Emilio, offers Cuban rhythms and flavors. **Wolfgang Puck Grand Cafe,** sandwiched among pricey boutiques, is the West Side's prestige eatery. For entertainment, you'll find a 24-screen **AMC Theater; Splitsville,** an upscale bowling alley and restaurant; a permanent showplace for the extraordinary **Cirque du Soleil *La Nouba;*** and **DisneyQuest,** an interactive virtual reality and electronic-games venue. Access Downtown Disney via Disney buses from Disney resorts.

Since the nighttime-entertainment venues at the former Pleasure Island were shuttered in 2008, The Big Mouse has suffered great angst in trying to arrive at an overall vision for Downtown Disney. After several false starts, Disney has embarked on an expansion with a Florida-waterfront-town theme. Called **Disney Springs,** it will encompass the current three areas and add a fourth. Pleasure Island will become **Town Center** and be built out toward the parking lot. Adjacent to the waterfront will be **The Landing,** with shops, restaurants, docks, and a promenade. Construction began in April 2013 and will be completed in 2016.

### Disney's BoardWalk

Near Epcot, the BoardWalk is an idealized replication of an East Coast 1930s waterfront resort. Open all day, the BoardWalk features upscale restaurants, shops and galleries, a brewpub, and an ESPN sports bar. In the evening, a nightclub with dueling pianos and a DJ dance club join the lineup. Both are for guests age 21 and up only. There's no admission fee for the BoardWalk, but the piano bar levies a cover charge at night. This area is anchored by the BoardWalk Inn and Villas, along with its adjacent convention center. The BoardWalk is within walking distance of the Epcot resorts, Epcot's International Gateway, and Disney's Hollywood Studios. Boat transportation is available to and from Epcot and Disney's Hollywood Studios; buses serve other Disney World locations.

## ESPN Wide World of Sports Complex

The 220-acre Wide World of Sports is a state-of-the-art competition and training facility consisting of a 9,500-seat ballpark, two field houses, and venues for baseball, softball, tennis, track and field, beach volleyball, and 27 other sports. The spring-training home of the Atlanta Braves, the complex also hosts a mind-boggling calendar of professional and amateur competitions. Walt Disney World guests not participating in events may pay admission to watch any of the scheduled competitions.

## Disney Cruise Line

In 1998, the Walt Disney Company launched (literally) its own cruise line with the 2,400-passenger *Disney Magic.* Its sister ship, the *Disney Wonder,* first sailed in 1999. Most cruises depart from Port Canaveral, Florida (about a 90-minute drive from Walt Disney World) or Miami, on three-, four-, and seven-night itineraries. Caribbean and Bahamian cruises include a day at **Castaway Cay,** Disney's private island. Cruises can be packaged with a stay at Disney World. Although the cruises are family-oriented, extensive children's programs and elaborate child-care facilities allow parents plenty of opportunity for time away from the kids. In 2011 and 2012, respectively, two new ships, the **Disney Dream** and the **Disney Fantasy**, joined the fleet, enabling the Disney Cruise Line to expand sailings to the Caribbean, Alaska, the Mediterranean, and Northern Europe. For more on Disney Cruise Line, see Part Five.

## THE PEOPLE

HOW YOU'RE TREATED BY THE CAST MEMBERS you encounter at Walt Disney World can make or break a vacation. Fortunately, Disney staff often go the extra mile to make your visit special, as the following three readers report. First, from a New York City man:

*I lost my glasses during the trip and had to go 24 hours awaiting a spare pair to be sent by overnight mail. Went to Sunshine Seasons for lunch; found a cast member and explained my situation. Said I couldn't read the menu displays and asked for a printed menu. He said they didn't have those but offered to tell me what was available. I said that would be too much bother; his response: "You're why I'm here." He took me to each of the four stations and described every dish. When I had my order, he took me to the dessert station and told me every option. Then he got my drink for me along with napkins, utensils, and a straw, then escorted me to the cashier.*

A family from St. Joseph, Michigan, has this to relate:

*We had a very unexpected and wonderful surprise waiting in our stroller after the Country Bear Jamboree. Out of nearly 30 strollers, ours had been visited by Santa Mickey while we were in the show. We came out to a stroller decorated with silly bands, Christmas orna-ments, and a snowman Mickey plush toy. Our 5-year-old son was delighted, not to mention the rest of our party. Just another way that WDW goes one more step to make a magical experience.*

From a Pelham, Alabama, reader:

*I was riding Peter Pan's Flight when the ride malfunctioned and stopped unexpectedly. Within 30 seconds, a cast member with a flashlight was walking under our ride vehicles, calling up to us that they were working on the problem and we should all just sit tight. Within 5 minutes, another cast member came through and tossed free Mickey ice-cream bars up to all the stranded riders! Less than 15 minutes later, firefighters appeared with the biggest stepladder I've ever seen and rescued us, starting with small children first. Even when things go wrong, the Disney people are really on top of things!*

Finally, from a suburban Philadelphia family:

*At Expedition Everest, I witnessed expert handling of a group of teenage line-jumpers by Disney staff. Once they reached the loading area, cast members ushered them aside in a very calm and friendly fashion, causing no apparent disruption. I didn't see where they were ushered or what happened next, but I did not see them board the ride. It was as if they were never there.*

# UNIVERSAL ORLANDO

## TIME TO TAKE OFF THE BLINDERS

READERS ASK US EVERY YEAR why we cover Universal theme parks in this guide. Simply stated, Universal is a high-quality direct competitor of Walt Disney World, and we think you should have detailed informa-tion on both the Disney and Universal parks so you can make an informed decision about where to spend your time. We also get com-ments from readers who are under the impression that Universal's offer-ings are inferior to Disney's. By any objective measure, they are not. The title of this guide remains *The Unofficial Guide to Walt Disney World,* but it should probably be *The Unofficial Guide to Walt Disney World and Universal Orlando.*

In many ways, Universal Orlando will never achieve parity with Walt Disney World. It's minuscule compared with the 27,000-odd acres of Walt Disney World. The Universal property can't accommodate golf courses, marinas, campgrounds, or even additional theme parks. But in the areas where it *can* compete with Disney—namely, in theme park design and attraction quality—Universal has pulled even, if not ahead.

Universal has been technologically ascendant for several years, introducing revolutionary ride systems and special effects on both rides and in theater performances. On the other hand, the Magic Kingdom's new and enlarged Fantasyland is a point in contrast: Though visually stunning, its attractions break little new ground. Neither the sophisticated animatronics of Under the Sea—Journey of the Little Mermaid nor the multimotional ride vehicles of the Seven Dwarfs Mine Train come anywhere close to **Harry Potter and the Forbidden Journey** at Universal's Islands of Adventure or the new **Harry Potter and the Escape from Gringotts** at Universal Studios Florida. While Disney relies conservatively on a combination of highly detailed themed areas, beloved characters, and inspiration from classic animated features (that many young people under age 16 have never seen), Universal takes more technological swings for the fences.

*unofficial* **TIP**
If you visit Central Florida and limit your choices to parks, hotels, restaurants, and nightspots with Disney labels, you'll be missing a lot.

Granted, Disney parks do have their share of high-tech attractions, and not all Universal attractions approach the creative genius of Forbidden Journey or Escape from Gringotts. But while guests at both Disney and Universal report high levels of satisfaction, it's the next-gen technology manifested in Universal's headliners that delivers true "Wow!" moments. Plus, **Port of Entry** and **Jurassic Park** at Islands of Adventure—along with **The Wizarding World of Harry Potter,** now encompassing both **Hogsmeade** at IOA and **Diagon Alley** at USF—clearly demonstrate that Universal can create exquisitely detailed and totally immersive themed areas.

We see the two Universal parks and the four Disney World parks as rough equals, and every one a gem. There's more for little kids at Disney's Magic Kingdom and Hollywood Studios than at the other parks, and more for teens and young adults at the Universal parks. In keeping with that young-adult demographic, Universal offers the **CityWalk** nightclub venue, just outside the park gates, for those with the energy to make a night of it; Disney World has nothing comparable. Both Universal and Disney have splendid on-site hotels, with Universal offering more perks to its guests. Disney parks have the edge in landscaping as well as full-service dining.

# STUFF UNIVERSAL SHOULD WIZARD-IZE TO MAKE MORE MONEY:

**WATER FOUNTAINS**

**CHANGING TABLES**

**VALET PARKING**

**BUSES**

**PARK MAPS**

Chris Eliopoulos

## South Orlando & Walt Disney World Area

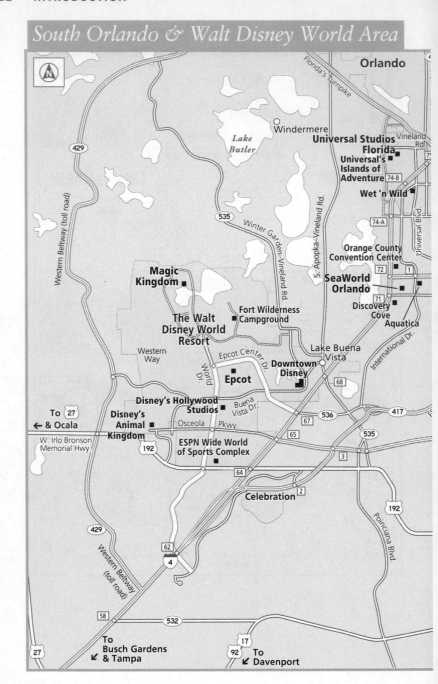

Orlando

Florida's Turnpike

Windermere

Lake Butler

Universal Studios Florida

Vineland Rd.

Universal's Islands of Adventure

74-B

Wet 'n Wild

75

74-A

Universal Blvd.

535

Winter Garden-Vineland Rd.

S. Apopka-Vineland Rd.

Orange County Convention Center

72

1

Magic Kingdom

SeaWorld Orlando

71

Fort Wilderness Campground

Discovery Cove

The Walt Disney World Resort

Aquatica

Western Way

Epcot Center Dr.

Lake Buena Vista

International Dr.

World Dr.

Epcot

Downtown Disney

68

Disney's Hollywood Studios

Buena Vista Dr.

To 27 & Ocala

Disney's Animal Kingdom

Osceola Pkwy.

536

417

67

W. Irlo Bronson Memorial Hwy.

192

65

535

ESPN Wide World of Sports Complex

64

3

Celebration

2

192

429

Western Beltway (toll road)

Poinciana Blvd.

62

4

58

532

27

To Busch Gardens & Tampa

17

92

To Davenport

429

Western Beltway (toll road)

## Walt Disney World

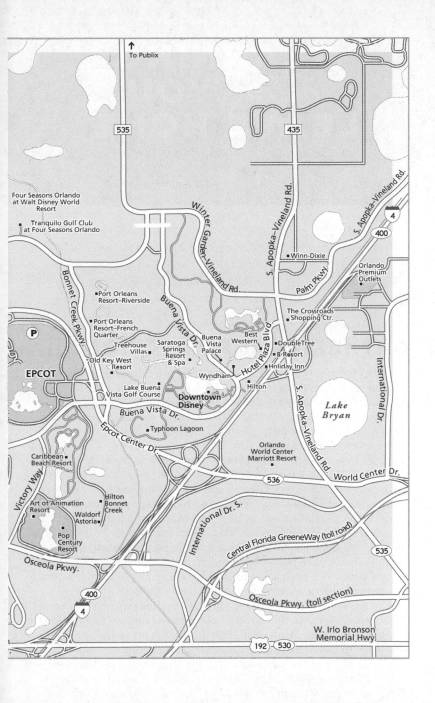

# PART ONE

# PLANNING *before* YOU LEAVE HOME

*Visiting Walt Disney World is a bit like childbirth—you never really believe what people tell you, but once you have been through it your-self, you know exactly what they were saying!*

—Hilary Wolfe, a mother and
*Unofficial Guide* reader from Swansea, Wales

# GATHERING INFORMATION

IN ADDITION TO USING THIS GUIDE, we recommend that you visit our website, **touringplans.com,** which offers essential tools for planning your trip and saving you time and money, and its companion blog, **blog.touringplans.com,** which lists breaking news for Walt Disney World, Universal Orlando, the Disney Cruise Line, and Disneyland.

We sent our photography team door-to-door at Disney's resorts for the site's newest feature—**hotel-room views,** which show the scenery you'll get at all 30,000-plus hotel rooms in Walt Disney World. Spend some time looking at these photos and videos, and you'll be surprised at how much the views can vary even within the same resort. (Case in point: Some standard-view rooms at All-Star Music look out over a quiet little pond in the woods. Other rooms face a giant green electrical box.) We show you which rooms have the best views and the exact wording to use when requesting a specific room from Disney. The photos and videos can also show you whether upgrading to a more expensive category, like a water-view room, is worth the cost.

Though the guide you're reading now contains *our best and most effective touring plans,* the site offers **computer-optimized touring plans** for Disney World and Universal. With these, you choose the attractions you want to experience, including character greetings, parades, fireworks, meals, and midday breaks, and we'll give you a step-by-step itinerary for your specific dates of travel showing you how to see everything with minimal waits in line. The touring plans can incorporate your existing FastPass+ reservations (see page 84) and suggest where to use any remaining FastPass+ opportunities.

You can update the touring plans when you're in the parks, too. Let's say your touring plan calls for riding The Haunted Mansion next but your family really needs an ice-cream break and 30 minutes out of the sun. Get the ice cream and take the break; then, when you're done, click the "Optimize" button for your plan and you'll get an update on what to do next. The ability to redo your plan lets you recover from any situation while still minimizing your waits for the rest of the day.

Another really popular part of touringplans.com is our **Crowd Calendar,** which shows crowd projections for each Disney and Universal theme park for every day of the year. Look up the dates of your visit, and the calendar will not only show the projected wait times for each day but will also indicate for each day which theme park will be the least crowded. Historical wait times are also available, so you can see how crowded the parks were last year for your upcoming trip dates.

We've also got complete **dining menus** for every food cart, stand, kiosk, counter-service restaurant, and sit-down restaurant in Walt Disney World, including wine lists—more than 20,000 items. The whole thing is searchable, too, so you can find every restaurant in Epcot that serves prime rib (and its prices) or see which snacks at Starring Rolls Cafe are eligible for the Disney Dining Plan. Updated regularly, these menus represent the most accurate collection of Disney dining information available anywhere.

The touring plans, menus, Crowd Calendar, and more are available within **Lines,** our mobile app, which provides continuous real-time updates on wait times at Walt Disney World, Universal, and Disneyland. Using in-park research and updates sent in by readers, Lines shows you the current wait and FastPass+ distribution times at every attraction in every park, as well as our estimated actual waits for these attractions for the rest of the day. For example, Lines will tell you that the posted wait time for Space Mountain is 60 minutes, and that based on what we know about how Disney manages Space Mountain's queue, the actual time you'll probably wait in line is 48 minutes. Lines is the only Disney-parks app that shows you both posted and actual wait times.

Lines' chat feature, through which you can ask questions and give travel tips, has grown into a thriving virtual community. Hundreds of "Liners" interact every day in discussions that stay remarkably on-topic for an Internet forum, and the group organizes regular in-park meets. We're thrilled with it.

Lines is available free to touringplans.com subscribers for the Apple iPhone and iPad at the iTunes Store (search for "TouringPlans"; requires iOS 4.3 or later) and for Android devices at the Google Play Store (requires Android 2.1 Eclair or later). Owners of BlackBerries, Windows Phones, and other data-enabled phones can use the web-based version at **m.touringplans.com.**

As long as you've got that smartphone handy while visiting the World, we and your fellow *Unofficial Guide* readers would love it if you'd pitch in and report on the actual wait times you get while you're there. Simply open Lines, log in to your user account, and click "+Time" in the upper right corner. Because Walt Disney World has free Wi-Fi now, you international users can help, too. We'll use your findings to update the wait times for everyone in the park.

Lines has been extremely well received—it's rated higher than Disney's official park apps—and we get lots of comments on it. A family from New York used Lines and got neighborhood bragging rights:

*We used your iPhone mobile app for our trip to WDW and barely waited for anything! We have neighbors whose vacation overlapped ours by a couple of days. They didn't have your app, and they complained about long lines and crowds.*

A mom from Monroe, North Carolina, loved the "Optimize" feature:

*The "Optimize" button was invaluable in that it empowered us to make spur-of-the-moment changes without worrying whether our plans would be negatively impacted—it's like a safety valve for impulsive tourers. We sailed through the choppy sea of congestion and knew which pitfalls to avoid.*

From a Zionsville, Indiana, mom:

*Take the nap, use the app. By using a touring plan every day as our basic guide, updating the plan with real-time park information on my phone, and leaving the park each afternoon for a nap, we managed seven days in the parks—and only one toddler meltdown!*

Much of our online content, including new research, menus, and updates and changes to this book, is completely free. Access to parts of the site, including the Crowd Calendar, hotel room views, and more touring plans, requires a small subscription fee (current-book owners get a substantial discount). This nominal charge—less than a meal at Flame Tree Barbecue in Disney's Animal Kingdom—pays the salaries of the staff who keep the site running day and night. And if you're not satisfied, we offer a 45-day money-back guarantee.

Next, we recommend that you obtain the following:

1. **THE WALT DISNEY TRAVEL COMPANY FLORIDA VACATIONS BROCHURE AND DVD** These cover Walt Disney World in its entirety, list rates for all Disney resort hotels and campgrounds, and describe Disney World package vacations. They're available from most travel agents, by calling the Walt Disney Travel Company at ☎ 407-828-8101 or 407-934-7639, or by visiting **disneyworld.com.** Be prepared to hold. When you get a representative, ask for the DVD vacation planner.

2. **THE DISNEY CRUISE LINE BROCHURE AND DVD** This brochure provides details on vacation packages that combine a cruise on the Disney Cruise Line with a stay at Disney World. Disney Cruise Line also offers a free DVD that tells you all you need to know about Disney cruises and then some. To obtain a copy, call ☎ 800-951-3532 or order at **disneycruise.com.**

3. **ORLANDO MAGICARD** If you're considering lodging outside Disney World or if you think you might patronize out-of-the-World attractions and restaurants, obtain an Orlando Magicard, a Vacation Planner, and the Orlando Official Vacation Guide (all free) from the Orlando Official Visitor Center. The Magicard entitles you to discounts for hotels, restaurants, ground transportation, shopping malls, dinner theaters, and non-Disney theme parks and attractions. The Orlando Magicard can be conveniently downloaded for printing at **orlandoinfo.com/magicard.**

## Important Walt Disney World Addresses

**GENERAL INFORMATION; COMPLIMENTS, COMPLAINTS, AND SUGGESTIONS; LETTERS TO MICKEY MOUSE**
Walt Disney World Guest Communications
P.O. Box 10040
Lake Buena Vista, FL 32830-0040
**wdw.guest.communications@disneyworld.com**
*General online help:* **disneyworld.disney.go.com/help/email**

**CONVENTION AND BANQUET INFORMATION**
Walt Disney World Resort South
P.O. Box 10000
Lake Buena Vista, FL 32830-1000

**MERCHANDISE MAIL ORDER (GUEST SERVICE MAIL ORDER)**
P.O. Box 10070
Lake Buena Vista, FL 32830-0070
**merchandise.guest.services@disneyparks.com**

**WALT DISNEY WORLD CENTRAL RESERVATIONS**
P.O. Box 10100
Lake Buena Vista, FL 32830-0100

**WALT DISNEY WORLD EDUCATIONAL PROGRAMS**
P.O. Box 10000
Lake Buena Vista, FL 32830-1000

**WALT DISNEY WORLD TICKET MAIL ORDER**
P.O. Box 10140
Lake Buena Vista, FL 32830-0140; **ticket.inquiries@disneyworld.com**

To order the accommodations guide, call ☎ 800-643-9492. For more information and materials, call ☎ 407-363-5872 weekdays during business hours and 9 a.m.–3 p.m. Eastern time weekends, or go to **visitorlando.com**.

4. *HOTELCOUPONS.COM FLORIDA GUIDE* Another good source of discounts on lodging, restaurants, and attractions statewide is the *HotelCoupons.com Florida Guide*. You can sign up at **hotelcoupons .com** to have a free monthly guide sent to you by e-mail, or you can view the guide online. If you prefer a hard copy over a digital version, you can request one by calling ☎ 800-222-3948 Monday–Friday, 8 a.m.–5 p.m. Eastern time. The guide is free, but you pay $4 for handling ($6 if it's shipped to Canada).

5. *KISSIMMEE VISITOR'S GUIDE* This full-color guide is one of the most complete resources available and is of particular interest to those who intend to lodge outside of Disney World, featuring ads for hotels, rental houses, time-shares, and condominiums, as well as a directory of attractions, restaurants, special events, and other useful info. For a copy, call the Kissimmee Convention and Visitors Bureau at ☎ 800-327-9159 or 407-742-8200, or view it online at **floridakiss.com**.

6. *GUIDEBOOK FOR GUESTS WITH DISABILITIES* Available at Guest Relations when entering the theme/water parks, at resort front desks, and wheelchair-rental areas (listed in each theme park chapter). More-limited information is available at **disneyworld.disney.go.com/plain-text**.

## DISNEY ONLINE: OFFICIAL AND OTHERWISE

THE WALT DISNEY COMPANY HAS ROLLED OUT a set of high-tech enhancements to its theme parks and hotels. This collection of

## Walt Disney World Phone Numbers

| | |
|---|---|
| General Information | ☎ 407-824-4321 or 407-824-2222 |
| General Information for the Hearing-Impaired (TTY) | ☎ 407-827-5141 |
| Accommodations/Reservations | ☎ 407-W-DISNEY (934-7639) |
| All-Star Movies Resort | ☎ 407-939-7000 |
| All-Star Music Resort | ☎ 407-939-6000 |
| All-Star Sports Resort | ☎ 407-939-5000 |
| AMC Downtown Disney 24 Theatres | ☎ 888-262-4386 |
| Animal Kingdom Lodge & Villas (*Jambo House & Kidani Village*) | ☎ 407-938-3000 |
| Art of Animation Resort | ☎ 407-938-7000 |
| Beach Club Resort | ☎ 407-934-8000 |
| Blizzard Beach Information | ☎ 407-560-3400 |
| BoardWalk Inn | ☎ 407-939-5100 |
| Caribbean Beach Resort | ☎ 407-934-3400 |
| Celebration Realty Office | ☎ 407-361-2555 |
| **Centra Care** | |
| *Kissimmee* | ☎ 407-390-1888 |
| *Lake Buena Vista* | ☎ 407-934-2273 |
| *Universal–Dr. Phillips* | ☎ 407-291-8975 |
| Cirque du Soleil | ☎ 407-939-7600 |
| Contemporary Resort–Bay Lake Tower | ☎ 407-824-1000 |
| Convention Information | ☎ 407-828-3200 |
| Coronado Springs Resort | ☎ 407-939-1000 |
| Dining Advance Reservations | ☎ 407-WDW-DINE (939-3463) |
| Disabled Guests Special Requests | ☎ 407-939-7807 |
| Disney Institute | ☎ 407-824-7997 or 321-939-4600 |
| DisneyQuest | ☎ 407-828-4600 |
| Downtown Disney Information | ☎ 407-827-2281 |
| ESPN Wide World of Sports Complex | ☎ 407-939-GAME (4263) |
| Fantasia Gardens Miniature Golf | ☎ 407-560-4753 |
| Fort Wilderness Resort & Campground | ☎ 407-824-2900 |
| Golf Reservations and Information | ☎ 407-WDW-GOLF (939-4653) |
| Grand Floridian Resort & Spa/Villas | ☎ 407-824-3000 |
| Group Camping | ☎ 407-939-7807 (press *4*) |
| Guided-Tour Information | ☎ 407-WDW-TOUR (939-8687) |

| | |
|---|---|
| Guided VIP Solo Tours | ☎ 407-560-4033 |
| House of Blues Tickets & Information | ☎ 407-934-2583 |
| **Lost and Found** (for articles lost): | |
| *Today at Disney's Animal Kingdom* | ☎ 407-938-2785 |
| *Today at Disney's Hollywood Studios* | ☎ 407-560-4668 |
| *Today at Epcot* | ☎ 407-560-7500 |
| *Today at the Magic Kingdom* | ☎ 407-824-4521 |
| *Today at Universal Orlando (Universal Studios, Islands of Adventure, and CityWalk)* | ☎ 407-224-4233 |
| *Yesterday or before (at all Disney parks)* | ☎ 407-824-4245 |
| Merchandise Guest Services | ☎ 407-363-6200 |
| Ocala/Marion County Chamber of Commerce | ☎ 352-629-8051 |
| Old Key West Resort | ☎ 407-827-7700 |
| Outdoor Recreation Reservations & Information | ☎ 407-WDW-PLAY (939-7529) |
| Polynesian Resort | ☎ 407-824-2000 |
| Pop Century Resort | ☎ 407-938-4000 |
| Port Orleans French Quarter Resort | ☎ 407-934-5000 |
| Port Orleans Riverside Resort | ☎ 407-934-6000 |
| Resort Dining | ☎ 407-WDW-DINE (939-3463) |
| Saratoga Springs Resort & Spa, Treehouse Villas | ☎ 407-827-1100 |
| **Security** | |
| *Routine* | ☎ 407-560-7959 |
| *Urgent* | ☎ 407-560-1990 |
| Shades of Green Resort | ☎ 407-824-3400 |
| Telecommunication for the Deaf Reservations | ☎ 407-939-7670 |
| Tennis Reservations & Lessons | ☎ 321-228-1146 |
| Walt Disney Travel Company | ☎ 407-939-6244 |
| Walt Disney World Dolphin | ☎ 407-934-4000 |
| Walt Disney World Speedway | ☎ 407-939-0130 |
| Walt Disney World Swan | ☎ 407-934-3000 |
| Walt Disney World Ticket Inquiries | ☎ 407-566-4985 |
| Weather Information | ☎ 407-827-4545 |
| Wilderness Lodge & Villas | ☎ 407-824-3200 |
| Winter Summerland Miniature Golf | ☎ 407-560-3000 |
| Wrecker Service (if closed, call Security, above) | ☎ 407-824-0976 |
| Yacht Club Resort | ☎ 407-934-7000 |

initiatives, officially known as **MyMagic+,** includes issuing rubber wrist-bands (**MagicBands**) with embedded computer chips that function as admission tickets and hotel keys; it also involved major changes to Disney's Fastpass ride-reservation system, restaurants, and attractions.

The changes to Fastpass—now known as **FastPass+**—require that you make reservations months in advance to ride Disney's headliner attractions, if you want any chance of avoiding long waits in line. Other features, such as MagicBands and restaurant reservations, require you to enter detailed information about your traveling party.

Disney has revamped its website (**disneyworld.com**) and mobile app to be the "glue" binding all of this together. Because you've got to plan so much more before you leave home, we're covering the basics of Disney's website and app in this section. While we provide navigational instructions here, Disney's web designers change direction faster than hypercaffeinated squirrels in traffic, so you may have to hunt around to find some features. Full coverage of MagicBands starts on page 62; details on the FastPass+ system start on page 84.

## My Disney Experience at DisneyWorld.com

A lot of work has gone into the new Disney website. You can make hotel, dining, and recreation reservations; buy admission; and get park hours, attraction information, and much more.

The most important of the site's features support the new My Disney Experience campaign. To make use of some of these, you'll need to register by providing your e-mail address and choosing a password. You'll also need to have reserved a room at a Disney-owned hotel or have in your possession a valid theme park ticket.

**GETTING STARTED** In the upper-right corner of the home page, click "My Disney Experience" to access a welcome page with links to any existing hotel and dining reservations. Click the "Create Your Family & Friends" link, then enter the names and ages of everyone traveling with you. You'll need this information when you make your FastPass+ and dining reservations.

Back on the "My Disney Experience" page, click "My Itinerary" in the top right corner of the page. A calendar will then appear—if you've got a Disney-hotel reservation, the calendar should display those dates of travel. If not, you'll need to manually enter your reservation number, then select your travel dates using the calendar.

For each day of your trip, the website will display operating hours for the theme and water parks. Select the theme park you'll be visiting on a particular day; if you're visiting more than one, select the one at which you want to make reservations now.

**MAKING FASTPASS+ RESERVATIONS** Click the "Make FastPass+ Selections" link from the menu on the right side of your screen. Next, select one of your displayed travel dates, then indicate which members of your group will be with you and which park you'll be visiting on that date. At press time, you could use FastPass+ at just one park per day—this may change, however.

Now you'll see a list of your chosen park's participating FastPass+ attractions. Select the ones you'd like to reserve; if an attraction is grayed out, all of its available FastPass+ reservations are gone.

Now the website will ask you to prioritize your list of selections by moving your most important attractions to the top of the list. (Changing priorities will give you different return times, but we can't see a pattern that explains Disney's logic for assigning them.)

At this point, the website will give you a "Best Match" set of Fast-Pass+ reservations and return times for your attractions, plus three optional sets of return times. Select the set that most closely fits the rest of your plans for the day, or, if you're using our touring plans, select the set that most closely matches the suggested FastPass+ return times on the plans. After confirming your selections, you can check for alternative return-time windows for each attraction.

You'll need to repeat these steps for every day for which you want to use FastPass+ in the theme parks. Having fun yet?

If you're unsure of the attractions or times of day for which you should use FastPass+, our touring plan software can make recommendations that will minimize your time in line. See page 84 for details.

**MAKING DINING RESERVATIONS** From the "My Itinerary" page, click the "Reserve Dining" link. (You may have to reenter your travel dates.) A list of every Disney World eatery will be displayed. Use the filtering criteria at the top of the page to narrow the list.

Once you've settled on a restaurant, click the restaurant's name to check availability for your dining time and the number of people in your party. If space is available and you want to make a reservation, you'll need to indicate which members of your party will be joining you. If you want to make other dining reservations, you'll need to repeat this process for every reservation.

Once you've made your initial set of FastPass+ and dining reservations, you'll be able to view and edit them (along with your hotel reservation) in the "My Reservation" section of My Disney Experience.

**OTHER WEBSITE CHANGES** Besides these new features, some existing functions were made much easier to use. In particular, Disney's site now displays prices for every room category available at a specific hotel in a clean, easy-to-read vertical format, and it no longer defaults you to the most expensive options for room views or tickets.

## My Disney Experience Mobile App

Along with the website, Disney offers a companion app for iOS and Android devices. It includes park hours, attraction operating hours and descriptions, restaurant hours and descriptions, the ability to make FastPass+ and dining reservations online, GPS-based directions, and more. My Disney Experience is optimized for the latest phones and tablets, so some features may not be available on all devices.

Early versions of My Disney Experience had many issues, and it was rated iTunes' second-worst app for navigating Disney World (and the very worst on the Google Play Store). But Disney's a big company with lots of money, and the most recent versions of the app are better. You still see only Disney's "official" information, including intentionally wrong attraction wait times so you'll go somewhere else in the park. Search for "My Disney Experience" on iTunes, Google Play, or the Amazon Appstore for Android to try the latest version.

## Our Recommended Websites

Searching online for Disney information is like navigating an immense maze for a very small piece of cheese: There's a lot of information available, but you may find a lot of dead-ends before getting what you want. Our picks follow.

**BEST Q&A SITE** Who knew? Walt Disney World has a **Mom's Panel** all chosen from among 10,000-plus applicants. The panelists have a website, **disneyworldmoms.com,** where they offer tips and discuss how to plan a Disney World vacation. Several moms have specialized experience in areas such as the Disney Cruise Line, runDisney, and traveling with sports groups; some speak Spanish, too. The parents are unpaid and are free to speak their minds.

**BEST GENERAL UNOFFICIAL WALT DISNEY WORLD WEBSITE** Besides touringplans.com, Deb Wills's **allears.net** is the first website we recommend to friends who want to make a trip to Disney World. Updated several times a week, the site includes breaking news, tons of photos, Disney restaurant menus, resort and ticket information, tips for guests with special needs, and more. We also check **wdwmagic.com** for news and happenings around Walt Disney World.

**BEST MONEY-SAVING SITE** MouseSavers (**mousesavers.com**) keeps an updated list of discounts and reservation codes for use at Disney resorts. Codes are separated into categories such as "For the general public" and "For residents of certain states." Anyone who calls or books online can use a current code and get the discounted rate. Savings can be considerable—up to 40% in many cases. MouseSavers also has discount codes for rental cars and non-Disney hotels in the area, along with a calendar showing when Disney sales typically launch.

**BEST WALT DISNEY WORLD PREVIEW SITE** If you want to see what a particular attraction is like, **touringplans.com** offers free videos or photos of every attraction. Videos of indoor ("dark") rides are sometimes inferior to those of outdoor rides due to poor lighting, but even the videos and photos of indoor rides generally provide a good sense of what the attraction is about. **YouTube** is also an excellent place to find videos of Disney and other Central Florida attractions.

**SOCIAL MEDIA** Facebook, Twitter, and Instagram are popular places for Disney fans to gather online and share comments, tips, and photos. Following fellow Disneyphiles as they share their in-park experiences can make you feel like you're there, even as you're stuck in a cubicle at work. For Disney World's official social-media outlets, visit **facebook.com/waltdisneyworld, twitter.com/waltdisneyworld,** and **instagram.com/waltdisneyworld.**

**BEST INTERNET RADIO STATION** MouseWorld Radio (**mouseworldradio.com**) plays everything from attraction themes and hotel background music to sound clips from old TV ads for Disney resorts. What makes MouseWorld Radio special is that the tracks match what the Disney parks are playing at the time of day you're listening. Also try the **Walt Disney World Today Podcast** on iTunes and at **wdwtoday.com,** cohosted by the *Unofficial Guide*'s Len Testa.

**BEST THEME-PARK-INSIDER SITE** It's been said that people who eat sausage should never watch it being made. If you have the stomach to learn how theme parks get built, take a look around **jimhillmedia.com.** Jim's got insider accounts of the politics, frantic project management, and pipe dreams that somehow combine to create the attractions that Disney and Universal build.

**BEST DISNEY DISCUSSION BOARDS**  There are tons of these; among the most active are **disboards.com, forums.wdfwmagic.com, micechat.com,** and, for Brits, **thedibb.co.uk** (*DIBB* stands for "Disney Information Bulletin Board").

**BEST SITE FOR GUESTS WITH FOOD ALLERGIES**  At **allergyeats.com /disney,** you put in your allergies and your park, and it shows you where and what you can eat.

**BEST SITES FOR TRAFFIC, ROADWORK, CONSTRUCTION, AND SAFETY INFORMATION**  Visit **expresswayauthority.com** for the latest information on roadwork in the Orlando and Orange County areas. The site also contains detailed maps, directions, and toll-rate information for the most popular tourist destinations. Check **flhsmv.gov/fhp/cps** to learn about state child-restraint requirements. Finally, we like **mapquest.com** for driving directions.

# WHEN *to* GO *to* WALT DISNEY WORLD

*Why do they call it tourist season if we can't shoot them?*

—Palatka, Florida, outdoorsman

## SELECTING THE TIME OF YEAR FOR YOUR VISIT

WALT DISNEY WORLD IS BUSIEST Christmas Day through the first few days of January. Next busiest is the spring-break period from mid-March through the week of Easter, then Thanksgiving week. Following those are the first few weeks of June, when summer vacation starts, and the week of Presidents Day.

*un*official **TIP**
Though crowds have grown in September and October as a result of promotions aimed at families without school-age children and the international market, these months continue to be good for touring.

The least busy time is from Labor Day in September through the beginning of October. Next slowest are the weeks in mid-January after the Martin Luther King Jr. holiday weekend up to Presidents Day in February (except when the Walk Disney World Marathon runs after MLK Day). The weeks after Thanksgiving and before Christmas are less crowded than average, as is mid-April–mid-May, after spring break and before Memorial Day.

Late February, March, and early April are dicey. Crowds ebb and flow according to spring-break schedules and the timing of Presidents Day weekend. Besides being asphalt-melting hot, July brings throngs of South American tourists on their winter holiday.

A family who vacationed during the slow period following the Thanksgiving holiday had this to say:

*My family went down when the Christmas decorations were up, and it was AMAZING! The decorations were incredible and put you in just the right mood for the holidays. It leaves you speechless, especially when you see the castle at the Magic Kingdom lit up at night.*

## The Downside of Off-Season Touring

Though we strongly recommend going to Disney World in the fall, winter, or spring, there are a few trade-offs. The parks often close early during the off-season, either because of low crowds or special events such as the Halloween and Christmas parties at the Magic Kingdom. This drastically reduces touring hours. Even when crowds are small, it's difficult to see big parks such as the Magic Kingdom between 9 a.m. and 7 p.m. Early closing also usually means no evening parades or fireworks. And because these are slow times, some rides and attractions may be closed. Finally, Central Florida temperatures fluctuate wildly during late fall, winter, and early spring; daytime highs in the 40s and 50s aren't uncommon.

*unofficial* **TIP**
In our opinion, the risk of encountering colder weather and closed attractions during an off-season visit to Walt Disney World is worth it.

Given the choice, however, smaller crowds, bargain prices, and stress-free touring are worth risking cold weather or closed attractions. Touring in fall and other "off" periods is so much easier that our research team, at the risk of being blasphemous, would advise taking children out of school for a Disney World visit.

Most readers who've tried Disney World at various times agree. A New Hampshire parent writes:

*I took my grade-school children out of school for a few days to go during a slow time and would highly recommend it. We communicated*

*with the teachers about a month before traveling to seek their prefer-
ence for whether classwork and homework should be completed
before, during, or after our trip. It's so much more enjoyable to be at
Disney when your children can experience rides and attractions and all
that is Disney rather than standing in line. And traveling at a time of
year when it's not unbearably hot makes such a difference as well. I
would be hard-pressed to go during a hot or busy time ever again.*

There's another side to this story, and we've received some well-
considered letters from parents and teachers who don't think taking
kids out of school is such a hot idea. From a father in Fairfax, Virginia:

*My wife and I are disappointed that you seem to
be encouraging families to take their children out
of school to avoid the crowds at WDW during
the summer months. My wife is an eighth-grade
teacher of chemistry and physics. She has parents
pull their children, some honor-roll students, out
of school for vacations, only to discover when they
return that the students are unable to comprehend
the material. Parents' suspicions about the quality
of their children's education should be raised when
children go to school for 6 hours a day yet supposedly can complete this same instruction with "less
than an hour of homework" each night.*

**unofficial TIP**
Instead of taking the kids
out of school, consider
scheduling your Disney
World trip immediately
following the last week of
school in the spring or
during the week before
school starting in the fall.
The crowds will be well
below summer peak.

A Martinez, California, teacher offers this compelling analogy:

*There are a precious 180 days for us as teachers to instruct our stu-
dents, and there are 185 days during the year for Disney World. I
have seen countless students during my 14 years of teaching struggle
to catch up the rest of the year due to a week of vacation during critical instructional periods. The analogy I use with my students' parents is that it's like walking out of a movie after watching the first
5 minutes, then returning for the last 5 minutes and trying to figure
out what happened.*

But a teacher from Penn Yan, New York, sees things differently:

*I've read the comments by teachers saying that they all think it's hor-
rible for a parent to take a child out for a vacation. As a teacher and
a parent, I disagree. If a parent takes the time to let us know that a
child is going to be out, we help them get ready for upcoming homework the best we can. If the child is a good student, why shouldn't
they go have a wonderful experience with their family? I also don't
understand when teachers say they can't get something together for
the time the student will be out. We all have to plan ahead, and we
know what we are teaching days, if not weeks, in advance. Take 20
minutes out of your day and set something up. Learn to be flexible!*

**BE UNCONVENTIONAL** Orlando's Orange County Convention Center
hosts some of the largest conventions and trade shows in the world.
Rooms anywhere near Walt Disney World are hard to find when there's
a big convention and, as this Toronto reader points out, expensive:

*If saving money on accommodations is an important part of your trip, be sure to check rates on the Net before you settle on a date. Trade shows at the Orange County Convention Center can host over 100,000 attendees, with most of them staying one to a room. This drives rates on even average properties to two or three times normal rates. Since all large conventions are scheduled over one year out, these spikes in room rates should be visible up to 12 months prior.*

You can check the convention schedule at the Orlando Orange County Convention Center for the next seven months at **occc.net /global/calendar.**

**DON'T FORGET AUGUST** Kids go back to school pretty early in Florida (and in a lot of other places, too). This makes mid- to late August a good time to visit Walt Disney World for families who can't vacation during the off-season. A New Jersey mother of two school-age children spells it out:

*The end of August is the PERFECT time to go (just watch out for hurricanes, it's the season). There were virtually no wait times, 20 minutes at the most.*

A mom from Rapid City, South Dakota, agrees:

*School starts very early in Florida, so our mid-August visit was great for crowds, but not for heat.*

And from a family from Roxbury, New Jersey:

*I recommend the last two weeks of August for anyone traveling there during the summer. We have visited twice during this time of year and have had great success touring the parks.*

**HIGH-LOW, HIGH-LOW, IT'S OFF TO DISNEY WE GO** Though we recommend off-season touring, we realize that it's not possible for many families. We want to make it clear, therefore, that you can have a wonderful experience regardless of when you go. Our advice, irrespective of season, is to arrive early at the parks and avoid the crowds by using one of our touring plans. If attendance is light, kick back and forget the touring plans.

**WE'VE GOT WEATHER!** Long before Walt Disney World, tourists visited Florida year-round to enjoy the temperate tropical and subtropical climates. The best weather months generally are October, November, March, and April. Fall is usually dry, whereas spring is wetter. December, January, and February vary, with average highs of 72°–73°F intermixed with highs in the 50°–65°F range. May is hot but tolerable. June, July, August, and September are the warmest months. Rain is possible anytime, usually in the form of scattered thunderstorms. An entire day of rain is unusual.

**CROWD CONDITIONS AND THE BEST AND WORST PARKS TO VISIT FOR EACH DAY OF THE YEAR** We receive thousands of e-mails and letters inquiring about crowd conditions on specific dates throughout the year.

Readers also want to know which park is best to visit on each day of their stay. To make things easier for you (and us!), we provide at **touringplans.com** a calendar covering the next year (click "Crowd Calendar" on the home page). For each date, we offer a crowd-level

## Walt Disney World Climate

| | JAN | FEB | MAR | APR | MAY | JUN | JUL | AUG | SEP | OCT | NOV | DEC |
|---|---|---|---|---|---|---|---|---|---|---|---|---|
| **AVERAGE DAILY LOW (°F)** | | | | | | | | | | | | |
| | 47 | 50 | 54 | 59 | 65 | 71 | 73 | 73 | 72 | 66 | 58 | 51 |
| **AVERAGE DAILY HIGH (°F)** | | | | | | | | | | | | |
| | 71 | 73 | 78 | 83 | 89 | 91 | 92 | 92 | 90 | 84 | 78 | 72 |
| **AVERAGE DAILY TEMPERATURE (°F)** | | | | | | | | | | | | |
| | 60 | 61 | 67 | 71 | 77 | 81 | 82 | 83 | 81 | 75 | 68 | 62 |
| **AVERAGE DAILY HUMIDITY PERCENTAGES** | | | | | | | | | | | | |
| | 62 | 73 | 71 | 70 | 68 | 70 | 74 | 76 | 76 | 75 | 74 | 73 |
| **AVERAGE RAINFALL PER MONTH (INCHES)** | | | | | | | | | | | | |
| | 2.9 | 2.7 | 4.0 | 2.3 | 3.1 | 8.3 | 7.0 | 7.7 | 5.1 | 2.5 | 2.1 | 2.9 |
| **NUMBER OF DAYS OF RAIN PER MONTH** | | | | | | | | | | | | |
| | 6 | 7 | 8 | 6 | 8 | 14 | 17 | 16 | 14 | 9 | 6 | 6 |

index based on a scale of 1–10, with 1 being least crowded and 10 being most crowded. Our calendar takes into account all holidays, special events, and more, as described below.

Because Disney is constantly testing resort discounts and tinkering with park hours, it's just not possible to include an accurate calendar in this book. Keeping the online Crowd Calendar updated requires year-round work from our statisticians. Thus, we have to charge a modest subscription fee. The same fee also provides access to additional touring plans and other features. Owners of the current edition of the guide are eligible for a substantial discount on the subscription. See the beginning of this chapter for more information about our website.

A Bristol, Tennessee, couple had good luck with the calendar:

*The UG Crowd Calendar is 100% accurate. We love it and will continue to use it every trip. We even tested it in heavy-duty crowds just to see if it worked, and you were dead-on correct!*

But a Braintree, Massachusetts, woman cautions:

*It should be emphasized that parks can still feel really crowded on a low-crowd day, especially the Magic Kingdom. But you will notice the difference when you see the wait times for the rides. Anyone expecting to have room to roam freely in certain parts of the Magic Kingdom on a low attendance day will be disappointed. The same is true for Animal Kingdom: We went there on a "low" attendance day in the afternoon, and it was extremely congested and difficult to walk through some areas of the park.*

**HOW WE DETERMINE CROWD LEVELS AND BEST DAYS** A number of factors contribute to the models we use to predict both crowd levels and the best days to visit each theme park.

Data we use to predict crowd levels:

- Historical wait times from the same time period in past years
- Historical theme park hours from the same time period in past years
- Future hotel-room bookings in the Orlando area

## TOP 10 AMERICAN THEME PARKS

| | THEME PARK | 2013 ATTENDANCE | CHANGE FROM 2012 | DAILY AVERAGE |
|---|---|---|---|---|
| 1. | The Magic Kingdom | 18.59 million | +6.0% | 50.926 |
| 2. | Disneyland | 16.20 million | +1.5% | 44,389 |
| 3. | Epcot | 11.23 million | +1.5% | 30,764 |
| 4. | Disney's Animal Kingdom | 10.20 million | +2.0% | 27,940 |
| 5. | Disney's Hollywood Studios | 10.11 million | +2.0% | 27,699 |
| 6. | Disney California Adventure | 8.51 million | +9.5% | 23.326 |
| 7. | Universal's Islands of Adventure | 8.14 million | +2.0% | 22,304 |
| 8. | Universal Studios Florida | 7.06 million | +14.0% | 19,348 |
| 9. | Universal Studios Hollywood | 6.15 million | +4.0% | 16,844 |
| 10. | SeaWorld Orlando | 5.09 million | −5.0% | 13,945 |

Source: *Themed Entertainment Association/AECOM Global Attractions Attendance Report 2013 (released June 3, 2014)*

- Disney's special-events calendar (for example, Mickey's Not-So-Scary Halloween Party)
- Legal holidays in the United States
- Public-school schedules (including spring-break schedules for the 100 largest school districts east of the Mississippi River, plus Massachusetts and Connecticut)

We collect thousands of wait times from every Disney park every day, including posted and actual times. Historical park hours include the actual operating hours for all of the theme parks over the past five years. Special events include everything from official Walt Disney World–sanctioned events to such independent events as Gay Days. Our Central Florida tourism demographics cover everything from where Orlando visitors come from and how long they stay to how many people make up each party and which theme parks they visit.

**CROWD-CALENDAR REASONING AND ACCURACY** Our online Crowd Calendar explains why we rate the parks a specific way on a specific day, including how we weigh each of the factors listed above. The site also shows you our predictions versus actual crowd levels for past days, so you can see how we fared with our predictions.

## EXTRA MAGIC HOURS

EXTRA MAGIC HOURS (EMHs) is a perk for families staying at a Walt Disney World resort, including the Swan, Dolphin, and Shades of Green, and the Hilton in the Downtown Disney Resort Area. On selected days of the week, Disney resort guests will be able to enter a Disney theme park 1 hour earlier or stay in a selected theme park about 2 hours later than the official park-operating hours. Theme park visitors not staying at a Disney resort may stay in the park for Extra Magic Hour evenings, but they can't experience any rides, attractions, or shows. In other words, they can shop and eat. The swimming theme parks, Typhoon Lagoon and Blizzard Beach, rarely offer EMHs. If they do, it's usually during the summer.

**WHAT'S REQUIRED?** A valid admission ticket or MagicBand wristband is required to enter the park, and you must show your Disney resort ID or have your MagicBand scanned when entering. For evening EMHs, you may be asked to show your Disney resort ID or MagicBand to experience rides or attractions.

**WHEN ARE EMHS OFFERED?** You can check the Crowd Calendar at **touringplans.com** for the dates of your visit, check the parks calendar at **disneyworld.com,** or call Walt Disney World Information at ☎ 407-824-4321 or 407-939-6244 (press *0* for a live representative).

| TYPICAL EXTRA MAGIC HOURS SCHEDULE *(frequently varies)* | | | | | | |
|---|---|---|---|---|---|---|
| **MORNING** | | | | | | |
| **MON** | **TUES** | **WED** | **THUR** | **FRI** | **SAT** | **SUN** |
| Animal Kingdom | Epcot | Animal Kingdom | Magic Kingdom | – | DHS | — |
| **EVENING** | | | | | | |
| **MON** | **TUES** | **WED** | **THUR** | **FRI** | **SAT** | **SUN** |
| DHS | — | — | — | Epcot | — | Magic Kingdom |

In addition to these, it's common for Epcot to have EMHs on Friday mornings and Tuesday evenings.

**WHAT DO EXTRA MAGIC HOURS MEAN TO YOU?** Disney seems to use EMHs in two ways: to provide Disney resort guests some extra park time on days when those parks are traditionally crowded, and as an incentive to visit one park on days when another park is typically more crowded.

Crowds typically range from slightly below average to average at Disney's Animal Kingdom and the Magic Kingdom on days when those parks host Extra Magic Hours. Crowds are higher than average at Disney's Hollywood Studios, and slightly higher than average at Epcot, on days when they have EMHs.

*unofficial* **TIP**
If you're going to get up early for one morning Extra Magic Hour session during your vacation, make sure that it's for the Magic Kingdom.

Not many families have the stamina to take advantage of morning and evening EMHs on consecutive days. If you have to choose between morning or evening Extra Magic Hour sessions, consider first whether your family functions better getting up early or staying up late. Also, consider the time at which the parks close to day guests. Evening EMHs are most useful when the crowds are low and the parks close relatively early to the general public, so your family doesn't have to stay up past midnight to take advantage of the perk.

## MORNING EXTRA MAGIC HOURS (A.K.A. EARLY ENTRY)

MORNING EXTRA MAGIC HOURS are offered at all four theme parks throughout the year, and rarely (during summer) at Blizzard Beach and Typhoon Lagoon water parks. Several days of the week, Disney resort guests are invited to enter a designated theme park 1 hour before the general public. During this hour, guests can enjoy selected attractions opened early just for them.

## How Early Entry Affects Attendance at the Theme Parks

Morning Extra Magic Hours strongly affect attendance at Disney's Hollywood Studios and Epcot, especially during busier times of year. Crowds at those parks are usually larger than average, as a Winston-Salem, North Carolina, mom discovered:

> *Disney Hollywood Studios was a MADHOUSE. Do NOT go on Extra Magic Hours days. After spending about 3 hours to ride three rides, I just wanted to trample the people stampeding to the exit.*

Magic Kingdom crowds are about average when it has morning EMHs (usually Thursday). Because Disney's Animal Kingdom typically has two morning EMHs but no evening EMHs, crowds are spread out, resulting in lower-than-average waits on both days. Disney's decision to drop Animal Kingdom's single evening session in favor of two morning sessions seems like it was the correct thing to do.

If you're staying at a Disney resort, remember these three things about Extra Magic Hours:

1. The Magic Kingdom has more attractions open for morning EMHs than any other park. Coupled with a good touring plan, we think the Magic Kingdom's morning session is the most worthwhile of any EMHs at any park.

2. Morning EMHs are least useful at Disney's Animal Kingdom because it has fewer rides overall. There's simply not as much benefit for the lost sleep.

3. If you think it unlikely that you'll be at the park offering morning Extra Magic Hours 30 minutes before it opens, visit another park instead.

During holiday periods and summer, when Disney hotels are full, getting in early makes a tremendous difference in crowds at the designated park. The program funnels so many people into the EMH park that it fills by about 10 a.m. and is practically gridlocked by noon. A mother of three from Lee's Summit, Missouri, writes:

> *Our first full day at WDW, we went to the Magic Kingdom on an early-entry day for resort guests. We were there at 7:30 a.m. and were able to walk onto all the rides in Fantasyland with no wait. At 8:45 a.m. we positioned ourselves at the Adventureland rope and ran toward Splash Mountain when the rope dropped. We were able to ride Splash Mountain with no wait and then Big Thunder with about a 15-minute wait. We then went straight to the Jungle Cruise and the wait was already 30 minutes, so we skipped it. The park became incredibly crowded as the day progressed, and we were all exhausted from getting up so early. We left the park around noon. After that day, I resolved to avoid early-entry days and instead be at a non-early-entry park about a half-hour before official opening time.*

Note that during holidays, the Magic Kingdom opens to regular guests at 8 a.m. Morning EMHs begin at 7 a.m., so you'll need to be at the Magic Kingdom entrance at around 6:30 a.m. You won't be alone, but relatively few people are willing to get up that early for a theme park, and your first hour in the parks will be (pardon us) magical.

This note from a North Bend, Washington, dad emphasizes the importance of arriving at the beginning of the early-entry period.

*We only used early entry once—to Disney's Hollywood Studios. We got there 20 minutes after early entry opened, and the wait for Tower of Terror was 1½ hours long without FastPass+. We skipped it.*

## Morning Extra Magic Hours and Park-Hopping

An alternative strategy for Disney resort guests is to take advantage of morning Extra Magic Hours, but only until the designated park gets crowded. At that time, move to another park.

A Dillsburg, Pennsylvania, mom has another tip:

*If you have FastPass+ opportunities [see page 84], schedule them for the park you're visiting second.*

This works particularly well at the Magic Kingdom for families with young children who love the attractions in Fantasyland. However, it will take you about an hour to commute to the second park of the day. If, for example, you depart the Magic Kingdom for Disney's Hollywood Studios at 11 a.m., you'll find the Studios pretty crowded when you arrive at about noon, as this Texas mom found:

*We made the mistake of doing a morning at the Magic Kingdom and an afternoon at the Studios. Worst idea ever. By the time we got to the Studios, all the [FastPass+ reservations] were gone for Toy Story Midway Mania!, the Tower of Terror, and Rock 'n' Roller Coaster. And all three rides had at least 90-minute waits.*

Keeping these and other considerations in mind, here are some guidelines:

**1.** Use the morning-EMH–park-hopping strategy during the less busy times of year when the parks close early. You'll get a jump on the general public and add an hour to what, in the off-season, is an already short touring day.

**2.** Use the morning-EMH–park-hopping strategy to complete touring a second park that you've already visited on a previous day, or specifically to see live entertainment in the second park.

Don't hop to Disney's Animal Kingdom if it closes before 7 p.m. Crowds generally start leaving between 3 and 4 p.m. If the park closes at 5 or 6, you'll have only 1–3 hours of touring with lower crowds.

On any day except its EMH days, hopping to Epcot is usually good. Epcot is equipped to handle large crowds better than any other Disney park, minimizing the effects of a midday arrival. Also, World Showcase has a large selection of interesting dining options, making it a good choice for evening touring.

Don't hop to the park with morning EMHs. The idea is to avoid crowds, not join them. Finally, limit your hopping to two parks per day. Hopping to a third park in one day would result in more time spent commuting than saved by avoiding crowds.

## Evening Extra Magic Hours

The evening Extra Magic Hours program lets Disney resort guests enjoy a different theme park on specified nights for about 2 hours after it closes to the general public. Guests pay no additional charge to participate but must scan their MagicBands (see page 62) at each ride or attraction they wish to experience. You can also show up at the turnstiles at any point after evening Extra Magic Hours have started. Note that if you've been in another park that day, you'll need the Park Hopper feature on your admission ticket to enter. Evening Extra Magic Hours are offered at the Magic Kingdom, Epcot, and Disney's Hollywood Studios, but not at Disney's Animal Kingdom.

Evening sessions are usually more crowded at the Magic Kingdom and the Studios than at Epcot. Those evening EMH crowds can be just as large as those throughout the day. During summer, when the Magic Kingdom's evening EMH session runs until 1 a.m., lines at headliner attractions can still be long at midnight. A mom from Fairhaven, Massachusetts, doesn't mince words:

> *I say steer clear of a park that is open late. There are only a few attractions open and tons of people trying to get on them.*

More attractions operate during evening EMHs than during morning EMHs. Certain fast-food and full-service restaurants remain open as well.

## SUMMER AND HOLIDAYS

A READER FROM COLUMBUS, OHIO, once observed, "The main thing I learned from your book is not to go during the summer or at holiday times. Once you know that, you don't need a guidebook."

While we might argue with the reader's conclusion, we agree that avoiding summer and holidays is a wise strategy. That said, we also understand that many folks have no choice concerning the time of year they visit Disney World. Much of this book, in fact, is dedicated to making sure those readers who visit during busier times enjoy their experience. Sure, off-season touring is preferable, but, armed with knowledge and some strategy, you can have a great time whenever you visit.

To put things in perspective, early summer (up to about June 15) and late summer (after August 15) aren't nearly as crowded as the intervening period. And even midsummer crowds pale in comparison to the hordes during holiday periods. If you visit in midsummer or during a holiday, the first thing you need to know is that the theme parks' guest capacity is not infinite. In fact, once a park reaches capacity, only Disney resort guests arriving via the Disney transportation system are allowed to enter. If you're not staying in the World, you may find yourself in a situation similar to this Boise, Idaho, dad's:

> *The Magic Kingdom and Hollywood Studios were so full they closed the parks. For three days we couldn't enter those parks, so we were forced to go to Epcot and use up two days of our four-day pass. We paid for another night at our hotel to see if the crowds would let up, but no luck. All we could do was drive around Orlando and sightsee.*

We hasten to point out that this reader would've had no difficulty gaining admission to the parks of his choice had he committed to being at the turnstiles 35–60 minutes before official opening time.

## Packed-Parks Compensation Plan

The thought of teeming throngs jockeying for position in endless lines under the baking Fourth of July sun is enough to wilt the will and ears of the most ardent Mouseketeer. Disney, however, feeling bad about those long lines and challenging touring conditions on packed holidays, compensates patrons with a no-less-than-incredible array of first-rate live entertainment and events.

Shows, parades, concerts, and pageantry continue throughout the day. In the evening, so much is going on that you have to make tough choices. Concerts, parades, light shows, laser shows, fireworks, and dance productions occur almost continuously. Disney also provides colorful decorations for most holidays, plus special parades and live entertainment for Christmas, New Year's, Easter, and Fourth of July, among others. (See "The Walt Disney World Calendar," next, for specific holiday advice.) No question about it: You can go to Walt Disney World on the Fourth of July or any crowded extended-hours day, never get on a ride, and still have a good time.

If you visit on a nonholiday midsummer day, arrive at the turnstile 30–40 minutes before the stated opening on a non–Extra Magic Hour morning day. If you visit during a major holiday period, arrive 1 hour before. To save time in the morning, buy your admission in advance. Also, consider bringing your own stroller or wheelchair instead of renting one of Disney's.

Hit your favorite rides early using one of our touring plans, then go back to your hotel for lunch, a swim, and perhaps a nap. If you're interested in the special parades and shows, return to the park in late afternoon or early evening. Assume that unless you use FastPass+, early morning will be the only time you can experience the attractions without long waits. Finally, don't wait until the last minute in the evening to leave the park—the exodus at closing is truly mind-boggling. Above all, bring your sense of humor, and pay attention to your group's morale.

## THE WALT DISNEY WORLD CALENDAR

DISNEY CELEBRATES SPECIAL EVENTS throughout the year. Some commemorate major holidays, while others are events designed specifically by Disney to boost attendance during otherwise-slow times of year.

**JANUARY** Usually held the second weekend after New Year's, the **Walt Disney World Marathon** pulls in more runners and their families every year. In 2014, some 50,000 runners participated in the event—enough people to affect crowd conditions and pedestrian traffic throughout Disney World. In the spirit of participatory journalism, *Unofficial Guide* coauthor Len Testa usually runs one of the 5K, 10K, half, or full marathons. (Bob ices Len's tequila.) Following the marathon by a few days is the **Castaway Cay 5K**, but you'll need passage on Disney Cruise Line to run it. Information on all Disney running events can be found at **rundisney.com.** Also check **wdwtoday.com** podcast archives for in-depth coverage and tips.

**FEBRUARY** **Black History Month** is celebrated throughout Walt Disney World with displays, artisans, storytellers, and entertainers. The Kinsey Collection at Epcot's United States Pavilion is a highlight.

**Presidents Day** is Monday, February 16, 2015, and **Mardi Gras** is February 17. These holidays will bring increases in attendance starting the weekend before. Usually held at the end of this week is the **Princess Half-Marathon** event, February 19–22 in 2015. The schedule for that weekend includes a health expo, kids' races, a family 5K, a 10K, and the big race. The 2014 event drew more than 20,000 runners, enough to increase park attendance and affect vehicular and pedestrian traffic.

**MARCH** The **Epcot International Flower & Garden Festival** runs annually from mid-March to mid-May or June. Expert horticulturists showcase exotic floral displays and share gardening tips. The 30 million blooms from some 1,200 species will make your eyes pop, and best of all, the event doesn't seem to affect crowd levels at Epcot. Disney has added food and beverage kiosks to the festival, making it more like September's Food & Wine event (see below), only with flowers.

**APRIL** Disney doesn't need much to boost attendance, what with **Easter** (April 5, 2015) and some spring-break vacations happening.

**MAY** Disney's Hollywood Studios hosts *Star Wars* **Weekends** annually beginning this month, with appearances from that franchise's actors and technicians. These events draw mainly local sci-fi fans, but some come from all over the country. While the impact on regular Disney World crowds is low, you'll find long lines if you want to meet the celebrities.

Also this month: the **Expedition Everest Challenge**, a 5K race at Disney's Animal Kingdom. Impact on crowds is low, but traffic is affected by the runners getting to and from the park.

Disney usually announces a **"free" Disney Dining Plan** promotion around the first week of May for travel dates in September. See page 213 for more details.

**JUNE** Events this month include both *Star Wars* **Weekends** and **Gay Days,** June 2–8, 2015. Since 1991, lesbian, gay, bisexual, and transgender (LGBT) people from around the world have been converging on and around the World in early June for a week of events centered around the theme parks. Today, Gay Days attracts more than 160,000 LGBT visitors and their families and friends. For additional information, visit **gaydays.com.**

**SEPTEMBER** Radio personality Tom Joyner hosts an extremely popular party at Walt Disney World. Held Labor Day weekend (around September 4–7 in 2015), the **Allstate Tom Joyner Family Reunion** typically features live musical performances, comedy acts, and family-oriented discussions. For more information, visit **familyreunion.blackamerica web.com.**

**Night of Joy,** a Christian-music festival, is staged at the Magic Kingdom the first or second weekend of the month (September 5 and 6 in 2014). About 16 nationally known acts perform concerts on Friday and Saturday evenings after the park has closed. For information or to purchase tickets, call ☎ 407-W-DISNEY (934-7639) or visit **tinyurl.com/wdwnightofjoy.** One-day tickets are $62.84 per person for adults and children, including tax; two-day tickets are $115.02. Same-day tickets cost $74.69 per person for adults and children, including tax.

Those who say Christmas is the most wonderful time of year have never been to the **Epcot International Food & Wine Festival.** Held in World Showcase from mid-September through mid-November, the celebration represents 25 nations and cuisines, including demonstrations, wine seminars, tastings, and opportunities to see some of the world's top chefs. Although many activities are included in Epcot admission, some workshops and tastings are by reservation only and cost over $100. Call ☎ 407-WDW-DINE starting around the beginning of August for more information. We think the culinary demos and the wine-and-beverage seminars (about $12–$16 each) are the best values at the festival. Because most of the food kiosks are set up around World Showcase, it can be difficult to walk through the crowds at some of the popular spots. Wait times at Epcot's attractions, however, are affected only slightly.

Held around 22 nights each year from mid-September through October 31 (and occasionally into November), **Mickey's Not-So-Scary Halloween Party** runs from 7 p.m. to midnight at the Magic Kingdom. The event includes trick-or-treating in costume, parades, live music, storytelling, and a fireworks show. Advance tickets for the 2014 events went on sale in early May and cost (including tax) $66–$71 for adults, $61–$66 for kids; same-day tickets cost $72–$82 for adults, $67–$77 for kids. Discounts are available for members of the US military, Disney Annual Pass holders, and Disney Vacation Club members. The least-crowded events are typically in September and on Tuesdays; tickets for the late-October dates usually sell out one to four days in advance. See **tinyurl.com/mickeysnotsoscary** for more information.

If you're wondering what "really crowded" looks like, here's how an Atlanta reader describes it:

*The only time the crowds were unbearable was during the Halloween party. When I say it was sold out—man, was it sold out! Just moving 20 feet took forever. My 72-year-old mom ended up renting a scooter at the end of the day because her hip was bothering her. Anytime we wanted to go somewhere, it was an ordeal. The lines for the characters were off the chain, so we skipped them entirely. We loved the parade and the people in costume, but the intense crowds made it way less fun than we expected. Candy lines stayed long until the end, and we were glad we rode The Haunted Mansion early, as the end of the line was way past the Liberty Belle boat all evening.*

Fortunately, the party isn't always jam-packed. A Maryland family of four had a great experience:

*Went to Mickey's Not-So-Scary Halloween Party. Had read a lot of mixed reviews both in your book and online, mostly complaining about crowds, and based on these reviews we almost decided to skip it but were talked out of it by a friend. The event was fantastic—plenty of trick-or-treating, a great parade, and no problems with rides. We are very glad we took our 8- and 5-year-olds.*

**OCTOBER** Disney's Hollywood Studios hosts the **Twilight Zone Tower of Terror 10-Miler** road race in October. Registration usually opens in February and sells out quickly. See **rundisney.com** for details.

**NOVEMBER** The **Wine and Dine Half-Marathon** early this month revolves around a 13.1-mile race that ends with a party amid Epcot's International Food & Wine Festival. The number of runners and their "cheer squads"—combined with the guests who descend upon Epcot for the food festival alone—blows up the crowd levels like an agitated pufferfish. Again, vehicular and pedestrian traffic is disturbed by the running courses throughout Disney property.

**DECEMBER** The **Pop Warner Super Bowl** and **Pop Warner National Cheer & Dance Championships** are held at Disney World's ESPN Wide World of Sports Complex each year in early December. The 2014 championships run December 6–13. The Value resorts, especially All-Star Sports, fill up fast with these participants. Because they're competing, the 20,000 or so participants and their families tend to spend more time at Wide World of Sports than the parks.

The annual **Disney Parks Christmas Day Parade**, televised on December 25, is usually taped at the Magic Kingdom on the weekend that falls nine days after Thanksgiving, roughly the last weekend in November or first week of December. The parade ties up pedestrian traffic on Main Street, U.S.A. all day.

## Christmas and New Year's at the Theme Parks

Don't expect to see all the attractions in a single day of touring at any park. That said, Disney's Animal Kingdom is usually the least crowded park during the winter holidays, especially on New Year's Eve, because the park doesn't have fireworks. Epcot is a good choice, too, because it typically has lower crowds and about twice the land of the Magic Kingdom. (It also has fewer attractions, but many of them are high-capacity shows and rides.)

As with summer, your best bet during winter holidays is to arrive early, take a midday break, and head back to the parks around dusk. Touring in the evening will reward you with stunning displays of holiday decorations and slightly smaller crowds than during the day. In particular, Disney's Hollywood Studios is a good choice for evening touring. Crowds will be larger than normal, but the decorations make up for it. One must-see is the **Osborne Family Spectacle of Dancing Lights,** featuring a staggering 5 million Christmas lights. They're typically turned on at 6 p.m., so you'll want to be in line by 5:30 p.m.

A Bridgewater, Massachusetts, mom loves Disney World during the holidays but warns that it's not the best time for everyone:

> *Having just completed our first holiday trip, I would never recommend a Christmas-week vacation for first-time visitors. But for anyone who's visited enough to navigate the parks without a map, the opportunity to experience the beauty and joy of the holiday season outweighs the huge crowds. You must accept that access to rides and shows will be limited and instead concentrate on the unique offerings such as the Osborne lights at the Studios and the parades and fireworks at the Magic Kingdom. Allow yourself time to visit the resorts—the gingerbread house at the Grand Floridian must be seen to be believed. And arrive early: We were in the MK by 7:10 a.m. on New Year's Eve and enjoyed all of the parades, shows, and*

*fireworks, as well as all the major rides (except Splash Mountain—
it was too cold).*

The Magic Kingdom stages the New Year's Eve fireworks on both December 30 and 31 for those who either wish to see fireworks in multiple parks or who don't wish to be caught in the largest crowds of the year on New Year's Eve.

**MICKEY'S VERY MERRY CHRISTMAS PARTY** This event is staged 7 p.m.– midnight (after regular hours) on about 20 evenings in November and December. Advance tickets for the 2014 events went on sale in early May and cost (including tax) $73 for adults, $67 for kids; same-day tickets cost $77–$80 for adults, $71–$75 for kids. Tickets for busier dates usually sell out one to four days in advance. Included in the cost is the use of all attractions during party hours, holiday-themed stage shows featuring Disney characters, cookies and hot chocolate, performances of Mickey's Once Upon a Christmastime Parade, carolers, "a magical snowfall on Main Street," white lights on Cinderella Castle, and fireworks. The least crowded dates are usually the weeks before Thanksgiving week, and the week after. Tuesday (and the rare Wednesday) parties are the slowest, too. See **tinyurl.com/mickeysverymerryxmas** for more details.

A reader from Pineville, Louisiana, tried the Very Merry Christmas Party and found the guest list too large for her liking:

> *Another thing I will not do again is go to the Very Merry Christmas Party. We went in early December to avoid crowds and were taken by surprise to find wall-to-wall people. They offered some great shows, but we could not get to them. The parade at 9 p.m. and the fireworks at 10 p.m., then fighting our way back to the parking lot, was all we could muster.*

If your schedule permits, we advise visiting in early December, when you can enjoy the decorations and festivities without the crowds.

# PART TWO

# MAKING *the* MOST *of* YOUR TIME *and* MONEY

## ■ ALLOCATING MONEY

### RAISE PRICES, RINSE, REPEAT

LONGTIME READERS KNOW that we usually begin this chapter with statistics showing how much more expensive it is to visit Walt Disney World now than in the Good Old Days. For example:

> In 1989, a family of four could take a two-night, three-day trip to Walt Disney World, staying at Disney's Caribbean Beach Resort, for $800 inflation-adjusted dollars, not counting food or transportation. In 2013, the same tickets and hotel cost almost $1,600.

We've written about these trends for years. And for years we've wondered how long these price increases could continue. For this edition of the *Unofficial Guide*, we thought we'd find out.

What follows is the spreadsheet equivalent of a back-of-the-napkin calculation about Disney's prices and who can afford them, based on various US government statistics. If you're an economist, a stock analyst, or a grad student looking for a research topic, drop us a line and we'll share the data.

Back to that long weekend at Disney World: The bad news is that it now costs more than an entire year's travel budget for 80% of US households. If you're one of the 230 million Americans in a household making less than $100,000 annually, a trip to the World probably isn't for you.

The good news—for Disney, anyway—is that the top 20% of US households, about 79 million people, spend more on travel each year than the bottom 80% combined: about $3,700, versus $3,200 in 2010. What Disney really cares about is *revenue*, not attendance, and a pool of 79 million high-spending tourists is a big enough market to fill its parks.

So how much more *can* Disney charge? After all, every price hike means fewer families can afford to go. Let's assume that a 5% price increase means the average family has to earn 5% more to pay for the trip. (Actually, it doesn't, but play along.) Are there enough Americans earning $105,000 who want to visit the World? Yes, per the US Census Bureau. Even if Disney raised prices 10% and targeted only households making $110,000 per year, its revenue would be about the same.

However, 10% is about the limit right now. If Disney marked up its vacations by 15% and targeted only those households making more than $115,000 per year—the top 16%—there aren't enough Americans with that kind of money to take enough trips to Orlando, and Disney's revenue would drop. A 20% increase would eliminate 30% of the people in the top-earning US households, and the numbers get uglier from there.

What this means is that you can expect Disney to continue raising prices 2–5% beyond the rate of inflation for the next few years. By the time that strategy runs its course, Disney should have its *Avatar*-themed land open at Animal Kingdom, which it hopes will draw in folks who've saved up for years. The only thing that could derail this plan is—just maybe—a plucky, moderately priced local competitor.

To paraphrase one of Disney's newest princesses: "Help us, Harry Potter. You're our only hope."

In any case, we get lots of comments about the cost of a Disney World vacation. This complaint from a Cincinnati reader is typical:

> *We travel to WDW frequently, and we were disgusted by the obvious trend toward "pay more, get less" that we observed in almost every area of our last Disney vacation. Unfortunately, the trend appears to be completely on the side of Disney profits rather than guest satisfaction.*

It's a different story for off-site hotels, which lack services like free shuttles and extra time in the theme parks. Very good third-party resorts, such as the Waldorf Astoria, adjacent to Disney property, offer

## WDW Theme Park Ticket Options

| | 1-DAY | 2-DAY | 3-DAY | 4-DAY | 5-DAY |
|---|---|---|---|---|---|
| **BASE TICKET AGES 3–9** | | | | | |
| MK: $99.05 EP/AK/DHS: $93.72 | $186.38 | $271.58 | $291.81 | $302.46 |
| — | ($93.19/day) | ($90.53/day) | ($72.95/day) | ($60.49/day) |
| **BASE TICKET AGE 10 AND UP** | | | | | |
| MK: $105.44 EP/AK/DHS: $100.11 | $200.22 | $291.81 | $313.11 | $323.76 |
| — | ($100.11/day) | ($97.27/day) | ($78.28/day) | ($64.75/day) |

*Base Ticket* admits guest to one theme park each day of use.

| **PARK HOPPER ADD-ON** *(1-day prices include admission)* | | | | | |
|---|---|---|---|---|---|
| Ages 3–9: $136.32 Age 10+: $142.71 | $52.19 | $52.19 | $63.90 | $63.90 |
| — | ($26.09/day) | ($17.40/day) | ($15.98/day) | ($12.78/day) |

*Park Hopper* option entitles guest to visit more than one theme park on each day of use.

| **WPFAM ADD-ON** *(1-day prices include admission)* | | | | | |
|---|---|---|---|---|---|
| Ages 3–9: $157.62 Age 10+: $164.01 | $63.90 | $63.90 | $63.90 | $63.90 |
| 2 visits | 2 visits | 3 visits | 4 visits | 5 visits |

*Water Park Fun and More* option entitles guest to a specified number of visits (between 2 and 10) to a choice of entertainment and recreation venues.

| **PARK HOPPER + WPFAM** *(1-day prices include admission)* | | | | | |
|---|---|---|---|---|---|
| Ages 3–9: $185.31 Age 10+: $191.70 | $91.59 | $91.59 | $91.59 | $91.59 |
| — | ($45.80/day) | ($30.53/day) | ($22.90/day) | ($18.32/day) |

| **NO EXPIRATION ADD-ON** | | | | | |
|---|---|---|---|---|---|
| — | $42.60 | $53.25 | $106.50 | $170.40 |
| — | ($21.30/day) | ($17.75/day) | ($26.63/day) | ($34.08/day) |

*No Expiration* makes unused admissions on a ticket valid indefinitely.

rates 30–60% less than those of comparable Disney hotels. It helps considerably if you've got a car, even if you factor in the cost of gas.

## WALT DISNEY WORLD ADMISSION OPTIONS

DISNEY OFFERS A NUMBER OF different admission options in order to accommodate various vacation needs. These range from the humble **1-Day Base Ticket,** good for a single day's entry into one Disney theme park, to the blinged-out **Premium Annual Pass,** good for 365 days of admission into every Disney theme or water park, plus DisneyQuest, Disney's Oak Trail Golf Course, and more.

| | 6-DAY | 7-DAY | 8-DAY | 9-DAY | 10-DAY |
|---|---|---|---|---|---|
| *Note:* All ticket and add-on prices include 6.5% sales tax. | | | | | |
| **BASE TICKET AGES 3–9** | | | | | |
| | $313.11 | $323.76 | $344.41 | $345.06 | $355.71 |
| | ($52.19/day) | ($46.25/day) | ($41.80/day) | ($38.34/day) | ($35.57/day) |
| **BASE TICKET AGE 10 AND UP** | | | | | |
| | $334.41 | $345.06 | $355.71 | $366.36 | $377.01 |
| | ($55.74/day) | ($49.29/day) | ($44.46/day) | ($40.71/day) | ($37.70/day) |
| Park choices are Magic Kingdom, Epcot, Disney's Hollywood Studios, or Disney's Animal Kingdom. | | | | | |
| **PARK HOPPER ADD-ON** *(1-day prices include admission)* | | | | | |
| | $63.90 | $63.90 | $63.90 | $63.90 | $63.90 |
| | ($10.65/day) | ($9.13/day) | ($7.99/day) | ($7.10/day) | ($6.39/day) |
| Park choices are any combination of Magic Kingdom, Epcot, Disney's Hollywood Studios, or Disney's Animal Kingdom on each day of use. | | | | | |
| **WPFAM ADD-ON** *(1-day prices include admission)* | | | | | |
| | $63.90 | $63.90 | $63.90 | $63.90 | $63.90 |
| | 6 visits | 7 visits | 8 visits | 9 visits | 10 visits |
| Choices are Disney's Blizzard Beach water park, Disney's Typhoon Lagoon water park, DisneyQuest, Oak Trail Golf Course, ESPN Wide World of Sports Complex, or Winter Summerland or Fantasia mini-golf. | | | | | |
| **PARK HOPPER + WPFAM** *(1-day prices include admission)* | | | | | |
| | $91.59 | $91.59 | $91.59 | $91.59 | $91.59 |
| | ($15.27/day) | ($13.08/day) | ($11.45/day) | ($10.18/day) | ($9.16/day) |
| **NO EXPIRATION ADD-ON** | | | | | |
| | $223.65 | $266.25 | $287.55 | $314.18 | $362.10 |
| | ($37.28/day) | ($38.04/day) | ($35.94/day) | ($34.91/day) | **($36.21/day)** |

*Note:* Check **touringplans.com** for the latest ticket prices, which are subject to change. All tickets expire 14 days after first use unless No Expiration is purchased.

The number of ticket options available makes it difficult to sort out which option represents the least expensive way to see and do everything you want. The average family staying for a week at an off-World hotel and planning a couple of activities outside the theme parks has about a dozen different ticket options to consider.

Adding to the complexity, Disney's reservation agents are trained to avoid answering subjective questions about which ticket option is "best." Many families, we suspect, become overwhelmed trying to sort out the different options and simply purchase an expensive ticket with more features than they'll use.

As an example, a family of two adults and two children who want to visit the theme parks for five days and a water park for one day could buy everyone a 5-Day Base Ticket plus the Water Park Fun and More option, for $1,508 total. Or they could buy separate admissions to the theme and water parks from a third-party vendor for $1,310, a savings of $198. The problem is that comparing options requires detailed knowledge of the myriad perks included with specific admissions.

## THIS IS A JOB FOR . . . A COMPUTER!

IT'S COMPLICATED ENOUGH that we wrote a computer program to solve it. Visit **touringplans.com** and try our **Park Ticket Calculator,** on the home page. It aggregates ticket prices from Disney and a number of online ticket vendors. Answer a few questions relating to the size of your party and the parks you intend to visit, and the calculator will identify your four cheapest ticket options. It'll also show you how much you'll save.

The program will also make recommendations for considerations other than price. For example, Annual Passes might cost more, but Disney often offers substantial resort discounts and other deals to Annual Pass holders. These resort discounts, especially during the off-season, can more than offset the price of the pass.

The Park Ticket Calculator has saved readers millions of dollars over the past few years, as this husband discovered:

*You just saved me from making a $408 mistake and needless expense!*

## MAGIC YOUR WAY

WALT DISNEY WORLD OFFERS AN ARRAY of theme park ticket options, grouped into a program called Magic Your Way. The simplest option, visiting one theme park for one day, is called a **1-Day Base Ticket.** Other features, such as the ability to visit more than one park per day ("park-hopping"), or the inclusion of admission to Disney's minor venues (Typhoon Lagoon, Blizzard Beach, DisneyQuest, mini-golf, and the like), are available as individual add-ons to the Base Ticket.

In 2013 Disney introduced separate pricing for a single day's admission to the Magic Kingdom versus the World's other theme parks. An adult 1-Day Base Ticket for the Magic Kingdom costs $105.44, while one day's admission to any other theme park is $100.11 (including tax).

Multiday pricing is still uniform across the parks. The more days of admission you buy, the lower the cost per day. For example, if you buy an adult 5-Day Base Ticket for $323.76 (tax included), each day costs $64.75, compared with $100.11 a day for a one-day pass to Epcot, the Studios, or Animal Kingdom and $105.44 for the Magic Kingdom. Tickets can be purchased from 1 up to 10 days and admit you to exactly one theme park per day; you can reenter your chosen park as many times as you like on that day.

Disney says its tickets expire within 14 days of the first day of use. In practice, they really mean 13 days after the first day of use. If, say, you purchase a 4-Day Base Ticket on June 1 and use it that day for admission to the Magic Kingdom, you'll be able to visit a single Disney theme park on any of your three remaining days from June 2 through June 14. After that, the ticket expires and any unused days will be lost.

Through another add-on, however, you can avoid the 14-day expiration and make your ticket valid forever. More on that later.

## TICKET ADD-ONS

NAVIGATING THE MAGIC YOUR WAY PROGRAM is like ordering dinner à la carte at an upscale restaurant: many choices, mostly expensive, virtually all of which require some thought.

Three add-on options are offered with the Magic Your Way Ticket, each at an additional cost:

**PARK HOPPER** This add-on you lets you visit more than one theme park per day. The cost is about $37–$42 (including tax) on top of the price of an adult 1-Day Base Ticket and a flat $52.19 tacked on to adult or child 2- and 3-Day Base Tickets—exorbitant for one or two days, but more affordable the longer your stay. For tickets of four or more days, the cost is a flat $63.90 with tax. As an add-on to a 7-Day Base Ticket, the flat fee works out to $9.13 per day for park-hopping privileges. If you want to visit the Magic Kingdom in the morning and eat at Epcot in the evening, this is the feature to request.

**NO EXPIRATION** Adding this option to your ticket means that unused admissions to the major theme parks and the swimming parks, as well as other minor venues, never expire. If you added this option to a 10-Day Ticket and used only 4 days this year, the remaining 6 days could be used for admission at any date in the future. No Expiration ranges from $42.60 with tax for a 2-Day Base Ticket to $362.10 for a 10-Day Base Ticket. This option is unavailable for single-day tickets, and you must buy it on-site before the ticket expires—at press time, No Expiration was unavailable for purchase at the Disney website.

**WATER PARK FUN AND MORE (WPFAM)** This option gives you a single admission to one of Disney's water parks (Blizzard Beach and Typhoon Lagoon), DisneyQuest, Oak Trail Golf Course, Fantasia Gardens or Winter Summerland mini-golf, or the ESPN Wide World of Sports Complex. The cost is a flat $63.90, including tax. Except for the single-day WPFAM ticket, which gives you two admissions, the number of admissions equals the number of days on your ticket. If you buy an 8-Day Base Ticket, for example, and add the WPFAM option, you get eight WPFAM admissions. What you *can't* do is, say, buy a 10-Day Base Ticket with only three WPFAM admissions or a 3-Day Base Ticket with four WPFAM admissions. You can, however, skip WPFAM entirely and buy an individual admission to any of these minor parks—that's almost always the best deal if you want to visit only one of the venues above.

Disney also offers a **Park Hopper-WPFAM combo** for $91.59, including tax. If you plan to spend a lot of time at the water parks and other WPFAM venues, the combo will save you $36 over buying the two options separately.

The foregoing add-ons are available for purchase in any combination, except for No Expiration, which can't be added to 1-Day Base Tickets. If you buy a ticket and then decide later on that you want one or more of the options, you can upgrade the ticket to add the feature(s) you desire. Disney doesn't prorate the cost, so you'll pay the same price regardless of when you buy the option: If you add the Park

Hopper option on the last day of your trip, you'll pay the same $63.90 as if you'd bought it before you left home.

## Annual Passes

An **Annual Pass** provides unlimited use of the major theme parks for one year; a **Premium Annual Pass** also provides unlimited use of the minor parks. Annual Pass holders also get perks, including free parking and seasonal offers such as room-rate discounts at Disney resorts. The Annual Pass is not valid for special events, such as admission to Mickey's Very Merry Christmas Party. Tax included, Annual Passes run $675.21 for both adults and kids age 3 and up. A Premium Annual Pass, at $803.01 for adults and kids age 3 and up, provides unlimited admission to Blizzard Beach, Typhoon Lagoon, DisneyQuest, and Oak Trail Golf Course, in addition to the four major theme parks, plus mini-golf discounts.

## Florida Resident Passes

Disney offers several special admission options to Florida residents. The **Florida Resident Annual Pass** ($516.53 for adults and kids age 3 and up) and the **Florida Resident Premium Annual Pass** ($644.33 for adults and kids age 3 and up) both offer unlimited admission and park-hopping privileges to the four major theme parks. The Florida Resident Premium Annual Pass also provides unlimited admission to Blizzard Beach, Typhoon Lagoon, DisneyQuest, and Oak Trail Golf Course, in addition to the four major theme parks, plus mini-golf discounts. AAA offers some nice discounts on these passes. And the **Florida Resident Seasonal Pass** ($339.74 for adults and kids age 3 and up) provides unlimited admission to the four major theme parks except on select blackout dates. In addition to Annual Passes, Florida residents are eligible for discounts on one-day theme park Base Tickets (about 10%) as well as on various add-on options.

*unofficial* **TIP**
It doesn't cost as much to renew an Annual Pass as it does to buy it in the first place. When you renew any Annual Pass, you get an 8–9% savings from the cost of the original pass.

## ANOTHER ONE BITES THE DUST

DISNEY CLOSES MONEY-SAVING LOOPHOLES each time it updates admission prices and options. Considering that most guests need only four or five days' admission, the most cost-effective strategy would seem to be to buy a 10-Day Base Ticket plus the No Expiration option so you could roll over any unused admission days to a subsequent trip. When Disney first rolled out Magic Your Way, the No Expiration option made this investment a reasonable choice.

Well, they couldn't let *that* continue, could they?

If you buy an adult 10-Day Base Ticket for $377.01 plus No Expiration for $362.10, you'll pay $738.11 including tax, or $73.91 a day— $9 more a day compared with simply buying a 5-Day Base Ticket each time you visit Walt Disney World. While it's true that admission prices might go up before you visit again, in which case No Expiration would be to your benefit, it's equally true that you might misplace the tickets you bought in the previous scenario, or that you might have some better use for the $362.10 you shelled out on top of your ticket purchase.

## HOW TO GET THE MOST FROM MAGIC YOUR WAY

FIRST, BE REALISTIC about what you want out of your vacation. A seven-day theme park ticket with seven WPFAM admissions might seem like a wonderful idea when you're snowbound in February and planning your trip. But actually trying to visit all those parks in a week in July might end up feeling more like Navy SEAL training. If you're going to visit only one water park, DisneyQuest, or ESPN Wide World of Sports, you're almost always better off purchasing that admission separately rather than in the WPFAM option. If you plan to visit two or more WPFAM venues, you're better off buying the add-on.

Next, think carefully about paying for No Expiration. An inside source reports that fewer than 1 in 10 admission tickets with unused days are ever used at a Disney theme park. The rest are misplaced, discarded, or forgotten. Unless you're absolutely certain you'll be returning to the World within the next year or two and you've identified a safe place to keep those unused tickets, we don't think the additional cost is worth the risk. (We've lost a few of these passes ourselves.)

## ANTICIPATING PRICE INCREASES

DISNEY USUALLY RAISES PRICES ONCE A YEAR, with the last couple of increases having gone into effect just before the crowds arrived: The latest hike came in February 2014, the three before came in June, and the five before that in August. Price increases have generally run about 5% a year, but specific ticket categories are frequently bumped much more. In 2014, the average increase for Base Tickets was 5%, and 4% for add-on options. (While Disney did discount the Park Hopper option for 1, 2, and 3-Day Base Tickets by 17%, it increased the No Expiration option by 5–14%.) If you're putting a budget together, assume at least a 5% increase, but know that it could be *much* higher.

*unofficial* **TIP**
Save money on tickets by planning ahead—buy them before the next price increase.

A Georgia dad puts Disney's price hikes in perspective:

> In the spring of 1983 as a working student, I purchased a [pre–Magic Your Way] 3-Day Park Hopper for $35 (including tax). Minimum wage was $3.35/hour, meaning it took less than 11 hours of work to pay for that ticket. With the latest increase, a 3-Day Base Ticket plus Park Hopper costs $344, or about **47 hours** of work at today's minimum wage of $7.25/hour.

## TICKETS, BIOMETRICS, WRISTBANDS, AND RFID

TO THIS POINT IN THE BOOK, we've used the word *ticket* to describe that thing you carry around as proof of your admission to the park. In fact, Disney admission media come in two forms—neither of which is a ticket. While we use *ticket* as shorthand for "admission medium," you'll be better prepared by knowing what you'll actually be handed when you plunk down your money.

If you're staying at a Disney resort, your admission medium is a rubber wristband about the size and shape of a small wristwatch. Called a **MagicBand** and introduced in 2013, it contains a tiny radio frequency identifier (RFID) chip, on which is stored a link to the record of your admission purchase in Disney's computers. Your MagicBand also functions as your hotel-room key, and it can (optionally) work as a credit card for most food and merchandise purchases throughout the park.

If you don't want a MagicBand, you get a **Key to the World Card,** which looks like a credit card. If you're staying off-property or you bought your admission from a third-party vendor, your ticket is a flexible, credit card–size piece of plastic-coated paper. Both alternatives also contain an RFID chip; upgrading them to a MagicBand costs $13. The inner workings of RFID are discussed in detail starting on page 62.

In addition to using RFID chips, Disney's computer systems store the dimensions of one finger from your right hand, a reference to which is also stored on your MagicBand or laminated card. Recording this biometric information requires a quick and painless measurement, taken the first time you use the ticket. When you use it again, you'll be asked to scan the same finger to validate your identity. If the scans don't match—say, you use a different finger—you may be asked to present photo identification.

If you're buying admission for your entire family and you're worried that you won't be able to keep everyone's tickets straight, Disney's computer system should have every family member's data linked to every ticket, allowing anyone in your group to enter with anyone else's ticket. We've confirmed this by having a platoon of *Unofficial Guide* researchers (including men, women, and children) swap MagicBands with each other; all were admitted.

## WHERE TO PURCHASE MAGIC YOUR WAY TICKETS

YOU CAN BUY YOUR ADMISSION PASSES on arrival at Walt Disney World or buy them in advance. Passes are available at Walt Disney World resorts and theme parks, at some non-Disney hotels and shopping centers, and through independent ticket brokers. Because Disney admissions are only marginally discounted in the Walt Disney World–Orlando area, the chief reason for you to buy from an independent broker is convenience. Offers of free or heavily discounted tickets abound, but they generally require you to attend a time-share sales presentation.

Magic Your Way tickets are available at Disney Stores and at **disney world.com** for the same prices listed in the chart on pages 52 and 53.

*unofficial* **TIP**
If you order tickets in advance, allow enough time for them to be mailed to your home.

If you're trying to keep costs to an absolute minimum, consider using an online ticket wholesaler, such as the **Official Ticket Center, Undercover Tourist, Kissimmee Guest Services,** or **Maple Leaf Tickets,** especially for trips with five or more days in the parks. All tickets sold are brand-new, and the savings can range from $3 to more than $81, depending on the ticket and options chosen. If any options don't make sense for your specific vacation plans, the representatives will tell you so.

All four companies offer discount tickets for almost all Central Florida attractions, including Disney, Universal, SeaWorld, and Cirque du Soleil. Discounts for the major theme parks range from about 6% to 12%; tickets for other attractions are more deeply discounted. The

**Official Ticket Center** (3148 Vineland Rd., Kissimmee; daily, 8 a.m.–8:30 p.m. Eastern time; ☎ 407-396-9020 or 877-406-4836; fax 407-396-9323; **officialticketcenter.com**) offers USPS Certified Mail for free or Priority Mail for $10. For the same price, they'll also deliver to area hotels; pickup at their office is free. **Undercover Tourist** (US: ☎ 800-846-1302; Monday–Friday, 9 a.m.–4 p.m. Eastern time; UK: ☎ 0800 081 1702; Monday–Friday, 2 p.m.–9 p.m. Greenwich mean time; ☎ +1 386-239-8624 worldwide; fax +1 386-252-3469; **undercovertourist.com**) offers free delivery and has a sweetheart relationship with **MouseSavers** (**mousesavers.com**). If you subscribe to the MouseSavers e-newsletter, you can access Undercover Tourist through a special "secret" link that provides additional savings on top of the normal discount. **Kissimmee Guest Services** (950 Celebration Blvd., Suite H, Celebration; ☎ 321-939-2057; Monday–Saturday, 8 a.m.–5 p.m., Sunday, 8 a.m.–noon, all Eastern time; UK: ☎ 0208 432 4024; **kgstickets.com**) offers free ticket delivery to area hotels for tickets ordered by phone, but tickets ordered online are cheaper. **Maple Leaf Tickets** (4647 W. Irlo Bronson Memorial Hwy., Kissimmee; daily, 8 a.m.–6 p.m. Eastern time; ☎ 407-396-0300 or 800-841-2837; fax 407-396-4127; **mapleleaftickets.com**) offers the same deal on pickup at their store and for $6.95 delivery to area hotels; USPS Priority Mail is a flat $6.95 per order.

### Where Not to Buy Passes

In addition to the many authorized sellers of Disney admissions, a number of unauthorized sellers exist. They buy unused days on legitimately purchased passes, then resell them as if they were newly issued. These resellers are easy to identify: They insist that you specify the exact days when you plan to use the ticket. They know, of course, how many days are left on the pass and when it expires. If you tell them you plan to use it tomorrow and the next two days, they'll sell you a ticket that has three days remaining and expires in three days. Naturally, because they don't tell you this, you assume the usual 14-day expiration period from the date of first use. In the case of your tickets, however, the original purchaser triggered the 14-day expiration period. If you decide to skip a day instead of using the pass on the next three consecutive days, you'll discover to your chagrin that it has expired.

*un*official **TIP**
Also steer clear of passes offered on eBay and Craigslist.

### FOR ADDITIONAL INFORMATION ON PASSES

IF YOU HAVE A QUESTION OR CONCERN regarding admissions that can be addressed only through a person-to-person conversation, call **Disney Ticket Inquiries** at ☎ 407-566-4985, or e-mail **ticket.inquiries@disneyworld.com**. If you call, be aware that you may spend a considerable time on hold; if you e-mail, be aware that it can take up to three days to get a response. In contrast, the ticket section of the Disney World website— **disneyworld.disney.go.com/tickets**—is surprisingly straightforward in showing how ticket prices breaks down.

*un*official **TIP**
What to do with the kid's pass you bought long before your 6-foot-tall teenager hit puberty? Go to Guest Relations and ask to have it changed into a regular-admission pass for the number of days left on the ticket.

## WHERE THE REAL DEALS ARE

BOTH GREAT THEME PARKS, **Universal Studios Florida** and **Universal's Islands of Adventure** routinely offer admission discounts and specials at **universalorlando.com**. For a family of four—say, Mom, Dad, and two kids under age 10—the total cost to visit both Universal parks for two days is around $605, including tax. For the same family to spend two days at Disney parks with park-hopping privileges during the same period, it cost a whopping $982, tax included. Even in the absence of any discounts, two days of park-hopping at Universal for our family of four cost $375 less than the same admission at Walt Disney World.

## THE BRITISH ARE COMING!

IN THE UNITED KINGDOM, Disney offers advance-purchase tickets not available in the US. The **Seven-Day Premium Ticket** (£278 for adults and £258 for children) provides unlimited admission as well as park-hopping privileges to the major theme parks, and seven admissions to the minor venues. It expires 14 days from the date of first use.

**Ultimate Tickets** are priced at £278 for adults and £258 for kids for 7-day passes, £285 for adults and £265 for kids for 14-day passes, and £305 and £285 for 21-day passes. The Ultimate Tickets provide unlimited admission to both major and minor parks along with park-hopping privileges to the major parks. The 7- and 14-day Ultimate Tickets expire 14 days after first use, and the 21-day Ultimate Ticket expires 21 days after first use. For additional information call ☎ 0870-242-4900 UK or ☎ 407-566-4985 US, or see **wdtc.disneyinternational.com/tickets** or the **Disney Information Bulletin Board** at **thedibb.co.uk**.

## MORE DISCOUNTS ON ADMISSIONS

### Discounts Available to Certain Groups and Individuals

**AAA** Members can buy passes for a discount of 3–5%.

**DISNEY VACATION CLUB** Members get a discount on Annual Passes.

**CONVENTION-GOERS** Disney World, Universal, SeaWorld, and other parks sometimes set up a link cited in convention materials to purchase discounted afternoon and evening admissions. See **tinyurl.com/disney conventiontix** and **tinyurl.com/seaworldconventiontix**.

**DISNEY CORPORATE SPONSORS** If you work for a Disney World corporate sponsor, you might be eligible for discounted admissions or preferential treatment at the parks. Ask your employee-benefits office.

**FLORIDA RESIDENTS** get substantial savings on virtually all tickets. You'll need proof of residency, such as a driver's license or state-issued photo ID, to purchase these tickets.

**MILITARY, DEPARTMENT OF DEFENSE, CIVIL SERVICE** Active-duty and retired military, Department of Defense (DOD) civilian employees, some civil-service employees, and dependents of these groups can buy Disney multiday admissions at a 9–10% discount. At most military and DOD installations, the passes are available from the Morale, Welfare, and Recreation office. Civil-service employees should contact their personnel office to see if they're eligible. Military personnel can buy a discounted admission for nonmilitary guests as long as the military member accompanies the nonmilitary member. If a group seeks the discount, at least half must be eligible for the military discount.

**DISNEY YOUTH EDUCATION SERIES** Disney runs programs for K–12 students to learn how the parks incorporate everything from performing arts to physics. The program runs every day and offers substantial ticket discounts (with substantial restrictions). Disney usually requires a 10-person minimum to attend these events, but it waives that requirement on occasion. See **disneyyouth.com** for more information.

### Special Passes

Walt Disney World offers a number of special and situational passes that are not known to the general public and are not sold at any Disney World ticket booth. The best information we've found on these passes is available on the Internet at **tinyurl.com/wdwdiscounttix**.

## HOW MUCH DOES IT COST PER DAY?

A TYPICAL DAY WOULD COST $714.18, excluding lodging and transportation, for a family of four—Mom, Dad, 12-year-old Abner, and 8-year-old Agnes—driving their own car and staying outside of Disney World. They plan to stay a week, so they buy 5-Day Base Tickets with the Park Hopper option.

*unofficial* **TIP**
Almost half the cost of a day in the parks is in food.

The biggest outlay is usually food costs, which increase at least twice a year. We think it's easier for Disney to raise food prices because most families look closely only at the cost of transportation, lodging, and tickets when budgeting for a Disney vacation.

| HOW MUCH DOES A DAY COST? | |
|---|---|
| Breakfast for four at Denny's with tax and tip | **$37.80** |
| Epcot parking fee (free for pass holders and resort guests) | **$17.00** |
| Four day admission on a 5-Day Ticket with Park Hopper | **$305.85** |
| **Dad:** *Adult 5-Day with tax is $387.66 divided by five days = $77.53* | |
| **Mom:** *Adult 5-Day with tax is $387.66 divided by five days = $77.53* | |
| **Abner:** *Adult 5-Day with tax is $387.66 divided by five days = $77.53* | |
| **Agnes:** *Child 5-Day with tax is $366.30 divided by five days = $73.26* | |
| Morning break (soda or coffee) | **$10.61** |
| Fast-food lunch (sandwich or burger, fries, soda), no tip | **$57.00** |
| Afternoon break (soda and popcorn) | **$26.63** |
| Dinner at Italy (3 appetizers, 4 entrees, 3 desserts), with tax and tip | **$210.41** |
| Souvenirs (Mickey T-shirts for Abner and Agnes) with tax* | **$48.88** |
| **One-day total (without lodging or transportation)** | $714.18 |
| **Increase over last year's total ($683.19)** | 4.3% |

*Cheer up—you won't have to buy souvenirs every day.*

**BACK TO THE SALT MINES!** Our math could be off, but it appears that the cost of a Disney vacation has increased roughly three times faster than US workers' median wages (6.2% vs. 1.9%) since 2005. To put that in perspective, it took the average worker about 3.8 hours to earn enough money for a 1-Day Base Ticket in 2005. Today it's 4.9 hours. If current trends continue, it'll be 8 hours in a decade.

### The *Unofficial* No-Frills Guide to Walt Disney World

With even a bare-bones visit to the World now out of reach of many families, being frugal is becoming ever more necessary. These tips can help:

1. Buy your admission online from one the sellers on page 59. Get tickets only for the number of days you plan to visit, and skip all add-on options.

2. Book a hotel outside of Walt Disney World. Hotels on US 192 (Irlo Bronson Memorial Highway) are usually the least expensive. Also, consider renting a vacation home (see discussion starting on page 235) if you have four or more people in your group.

3. Eat breakfast in your hotel room from a cooler; take lunch, snacks, and drinks from your cooler to the park; and eat dinner outside the World using discount coupons from local visitor guides or from the Internet.

4. Avoid parking fees by using your hotel's shuttle service or by taking Disney transportation from Downtown Disney or the water parks, where (for the moment) parking is free. Note that the second suggestion eats up a lot of time, so do it only if you're budgeting to the penny.

5. Buy discounted Disney-brand apparel and souvenirs from one of Orlando's two Disney Character Warehouse outlets (see page 763).

## RFID: IT'S ALL IN THE WRIST

WITH ITS MYMAGIC+ CAMPAIGN (see page 32), Disney introduced **MagicBands**—reusable rubber wristbands—as a sort of wearable theme park ticket. Small and reusable across trips, a MagicBand is imprinted with your first name, an ID number, and some legalese, along with a Mickey logo. A tiny radio-frequency-identification (RFID) chip embedded in the wristband holds your ticket and travel information.

Each RFID chip—not much larger than the end of a pencil—sends a unique serial number over short distances via radio waves. When you purchase theme park admission, Disney's computers will store that serial number, along with your ticket information. To enter a theme park, you'll touch your MagicBand to an RFID reader instead of going through a turnstile. The RFID reader will collect your MagicBand's serial number, compare your biometric information, and verify with Disney's computer systems that you've got the correct admission to enter the park.

RFID technology has been used for many years in the retail and transportation industries to track everything from the location of cargo containers to the receipt, stocking, and purchase of T-shirts. Many bus and subway systems have switched to RFID-enabled cards from paper tickets. The US government also puts RFID chips in all new passports to prevent forgery.

*unofficial* **TIP**
Old non-RFID tickets must be converted to the new media before you can enter the theme parks or use FastPass+. You can get this done only at Guest Relations, just outside each park.

Disney hotel guests get a MagicBand by default but may request a plastic **Key to the World (KTTW) Card** instead. If you're staying off-site or you bought your admission through a third party, you can upgrade to a MagicBand for $13; otherwise you get a credit card–sized laminated ticket. Like the MagicBand, the two card options use RFID.

Each member of your family gets his or her own MagicBand, each with a unique serial number. Along with the wristband, each family member will be asked to select a four-digit personal-identification number (PIN) for purchases—more on that below. The wristbands are resizable and waterproof, and they have ventilation holes for cooling. Eight colors are available: red, black, blue, green, pink, orange, yellow, and gray (the default). You can choose your colors and personalize your bands when you book your resort stay at the Disney World website.

Disney says using RFID at park entrances speeds admittance, because the readers are more reliable than the old magnetic-stripe kind.

## RFID for Payment, Hotel-Room Access, and Photos

Disney's hotel-room doors have RFID readers, allowing you to enter your room simply by tapping your wristband or KTTW Card against the reader. The same technology has been in use for years at upscale hotels around the world.

RFID readers are also installed at virtually every Disney cash register on-property, allowing you to pay for food, drinks, and souvenirs by tapping your MagicBand/KTTW Card against the reader. You'll be asked to verify your identity by entering your PIN on a small keypad to complete your purchase. This technology, known as "contactless payment," has been in use worldwide for many years, too.

If you're using Disney's **Memory Maker** service (see page 409), your MagicBand/KTTW Card serves as the link between your photos and your family. Each photographer carries a small RFID reader, against which you tap your MagicBand before having your photo taken. The computers running the Memory Maker system will link your photos to you, and you'll be able to view them on the Disney World website.

Disney's onboard ride-photo computers incorporate RFID technology, too. As you begin down the big drop near the finale of Splash Mountain, for example, RFID sensors read the serial number on your MagicBand and pass it to Splash Mountain's cameras. When those cameras snap your family plunging into the briar patch, they attach your MagicBands' serial number to the photo, allowing you to see your ride photos together after you've returned home. Because ride sensors may not pick up the signal from an RFID card sitting in a wallet or purse, we're fairly sure that on-board ride photos require MagicBands.

## The Future of RFID

Other innovative uses of RFID technology are rumored to be in the works. In one scenario we've heard, you'll provide Disney with some information about your child before your visit, such as his or her favorite color and pet's name. Later, when your child visits Cinderella, an RFID reader next to Cinderella will recognize your child's wristband and display the previously gathered information on a hidden prompter for Cinderella to work into conversation. And because Disney's computer systems will know from your MagicBand which rides you've been on and where you've eaten, Cinderella may mention those details, too.

But as impressive as all this sounds, many people are understandably concerned about multinational corporations tracking their movements. As noted earlier, guests who prefer not to wear MagicBands can instead obtain KTTW Cards, which are somewhat more difficult to track (inexpensive RFID-blocking wallets are available online). Disney claims that guests who opt out of MagicBands don't get the full range of ride experiences, though, so there's a trade-off to be made.

# ALLOCATING TIME

DURING DISNEY WORLD'S FIRST DECADE, a family with a week's vacation could enjoy the Magic Kingdom and the now-closed River Country and still have several days left for the beach or other area attractions. Since Epcot opened in 1982, however, Disney World has steadily been enlarging to monopolize the family's entire vacation. Today, with the addition of Blizzard Beach, Typhoon Lagoon, Disney's Hollywood Studios, Disney's Animal Kingdom, and Downtown Disney, you should allocate 6 days for a whirlwind tour (7–10 if you insist on a little relaxation during your vacation). If you don't have that much time, be prepared to make some hard choices.

The theme parks and water parks are huge and require a lot of walking and, sometimes, a lot of waiting in lines. Approach Walt Disney World the same way you would an eight-course Italian dinner: with plenty of time between courses. Don't cram too much into too little time.

### WHICH PARK TO SEE FIRST?

THIS QUESTION IS LESS ACADEMIC than it appears, especially if your party includes children or teenagers. Children who see the Magic Kingdom first expect the same type of entertainment at the other parks. At Epcot, they're often disappointed by the educational orientation and serious tone (as are many adults). Disney's Hollywood Studios offers some wild action along with family-friendly stage shows and attractions. Children may not find Animal Kingdom as exciting as the Magic Kingdom or DHS, because animals can't be programmed to entertain on cue.

First-time visitors should see Epcot first; you'll be able to enjoy it without having been preconditioned to think of Disney entertainment as solely fantasy or adventure.

See Disney's Animal Kingdom second. Like Epcot, it's educational, but its live animals provide a change of pace.

Next, see Disney's Hollywood Studios, which helps all ages transition from the educational Epcot and Animal Kingdom to the fanciful Magic Kingdom. Also, because DHS is smaller, you won't walk as much or stay as long. Save the Magic Kingdom for last—having said that, we know that most readers make a beeline for the Magic Kingdom, mostly for the reason that this North Carolina reader asserts:

> *Although you recommend sort of a reverse order for park visitation, ending up at the Magic Kingdom last, I disagree. We went to the Magic Kingdom first, which is Disney World for many of us.*

### OPERATING HOURS

THE DISNEY WORLD WEBSITE publishes preliminary park hours 180 days in advance, but schedule adjustments can happen at any time, including the day of your visit. Check **disneyworld.com** or call ☎ 407-824-4321 for the exact hours before you arrive. Off-season, parks may be open as few as 8 hours (9 a.m.–5 p.m.). At busy times (particularly holidays), they may operate 8 a.m.–2 a.m.

## OFFICIAL OPENING VERSUS REAL OPENING

WHEN YOU CALL, you're given "official hours." On many days, the parks open earlier. If the official hours are 9 a.m.–9 p.m., for instance, Main Street in the Magic Kingdom might open at 8:30 a.m. and the remainder of the park at 9 a.m.

Disney surveys local hotel reservations, estimates how many visitors to expect on a given day, and opens the theme parks early to avoid bottlenecks at parking facilities and ticket windows and to absorb crowds as they arrive.

Rides and attractions shut down at approximately the official closing time. Main Street in the Magic Kingdom remains open 30 minutes to an hour after the rest of the park has closed.

## THE VACATION THAT FIGHTS BACK

VISITING DISNEY WORLD REQUIRES levels of stamina more often associated with running a marathon. A mother from Middletown, New York, spells it out:

> *A vacation at WDW is not a vacation in the usual sense. Rather, it's a vacation that's frankly exhausting, but definitely worth doing. WDW is a magical place, where the visitor feels welcomed from the minute they arrive at their accommodations to the last second before boarding the shuttle bus back to the airport.*

A British gentleman, thinking we exaggerated about the walking required, measured his outings using a pedometer. His discovery:

> *I decided to wear a pedometer for our recent visit to WDW. Our visits to the theme parks were spread over five days, during which my wife and I (ages 51 and 55) walked a total of 68 miles for an average of 13 miles per day!*

The point is, at Walt Disney World less is more. Take the World in small doses, with plenty of swimming, napping, reading, and relaxing in between. If you don't see everything, you can always come back.

An articulate Anchorage, Alaska, teen and her family found out the hard way the importance of building in time to decompress:

> *We discovered that trying really hard to have lots of fun can actually get in the way of having fun. We crammed our schedule a little too full (seven parks—Disney, Universal, and SeaWorld—in eight full days). My older sisters would speed-walk from attraction to attraction while my parents straggled behind trying to keep up, while I was caught in the middle, both wanting to get to the next ride as fast as I could and wanting just to spend some quality time with my parents. No family should spend more than two consecutive days at the parks without a low-key day in the middle. I wish I'd known this going in.*

## Hitting the Wall

As you plan your time at Disney World, consider your physical limitations. It's exhausting to rise at dawn and run around a theme park for 8–12 hours day after day. Sooner or later (usually sooner), you hit the wall. To avoid that, use these two tips alone or in combination:

1. Take at least a morning off (preferably the entire day) after two consecutive days in the parks.

2. Return to your hotel for a 3- to 5-hour break each day you're in the theme parks.

A Suwanee, Georgia, reader discovered the first tip on his own:

*My initial plan for the family entailed a day at MK, one day each at Epcot, Animal Kingdom, Disney's Hollywood Studios, Universal Studios, and Islands of Adventure, one down day, and a leftover day for a second visit to something we hadn't finished. By day two, I became acutely aware that there was no way we would be able to keep up that pace.*

A La Grange, Illinois, mother discovered the second tip through her child:

*As I was planning, I was very sure we wouldn't be taking a swim/nap break in the middle of the day. No way! On the very first day of touring (at the Magic Kingdom), my 7-year-old said (at 9:30 a.m.—after only 2 hours at the park), "I'm hot—when can we go back to the hotel and swim?" Needless to say, we took that little break every day.*

Finally, a Boston mom underscores the importance of timing:

*The days we didn't take the break were a nightmare. Don't make the decision when the kids are doing fine at noon. Think about that tired, cranky, sweaty child in about 3 hours. Then imagine the same child at 5 p.m.!*

## THE PRACTICALITY OF RETURNING TO YOUR HOTEL FOR REST

MANY READERS WRITE ABOUT the practicality of departing the theme park for a nap and swim at the hotel. A dad from Sequim, Washington, made the following request:

*I would like to see nearness to the parks emphasized in your accommodation guide. We tried going back to the hotel for midday breaks, but it was too time-consuming. By the time you got to the car, negotiated traffic, rested, and reversed the process to get back to the park, it took 2–3 hours for a short rest and was not worth it!*

First, in response to the reader's request, we publish a chart in Part Three, Accommodations, that provides the commuting times to each of the Disney theme parks from virtually every hotel within 20 miles of Walt Disney World. But to address the larger issue, we think the reader was overly anxious about the time away from the parks. Two to three hours really won't cut it. Had he resigned himself to a 4- to 5-hour break, his family would've stayed rested and relaxed.

Here's the scoop: At Disney's Animal Kingdom, Disney's Holly-wood Studios, and Epcot, you can get to your car in the parking lot in about 15–20 minutes. From the Magic Kingdom, it will take you 30–35 minutes. Obviously, if you're at the farthest point from the park entrance when you decide to return to the hotel, or you barely miss a parking-lot tram, it will take longer. But from most places in the parks, the previous times are correct. Once in your car, you'll be able to commute to most US 192 hotels, all Disney World hotels, all Lake Buena Vista hotels, and most hotels along the Interstate 4 corridor and south International Drive ("I-Drive") in 20 minutes or less. It will take about the same time to reach hotels on I-Drive north of Sand Lake Road and in the Universal Orlando area.

So, for most people, the one-way commute will average 30 minutes. But here's what you get for your time: a less-expensive lunch at a restaurant of your choosing; a swim; and a 1½- to 2-hour nap. If you add up the times, you'll be away from the parks about 4–5 hours, counting the commute. If you want, eat dinner outside the World before returning. Clearly, this won't work during times of year when the parks close early, but these aren't times when most families go to Disney World. If you visit when the parks close early, you'll see more attractions in less time, owing to reduced attendance, and you'll be able to leave the parks earlier and take your break in the late afternoon or early evening. Not ideal, but neither are the crowds and heat of summer.

## ARRIVAL- AND DEPARTURE-DAY BLUES: WHAT TO DO WHEN YOU HAVE ONLY HALF A DAY

ON ARRIVAL AND DEPARTURE DAYS, you probably will have only part of a day for touring or other recreational pursuits. It's a common problem: You roll into the World about 1 p.m., excited and ready to go—but where?

The first question: Do you feel comfortable using a full day's admission to the parks when you have less than a full day to tour? The incremental cost to add another day of admission is small when you're visiting for three or more days, but significant if you're there for only a long weekend. Your arrival time and the parks' closing times are also considerations, but so is the touring disadvantage you suffer by not being on hand when a park opens. **FastPass+,** a reservation system for popular attractions (discussed starting on page 84), provides some relief from long afternoon lines, but it isn't available for every attraction, nor is there an unlimited supply of passes.

### Opting for a Partial Day at the Theme Parks

If you decide to use one day's admission on a half-day or less, refer to our *Unofficial Guide* Crowd Calendar at **touringplans.com** for the least-crowded park to visit.

You can make FastPass+ reservations for each park's most popular rides up to 60 days before your visit at **disneyworld.com** (it's 30 days in advance for Annual Pass holders and off-site guests with a valid ticket). You could try to obtain FastPass+ reservations when you arrive, but be aware that the daily allocation of FastPasses may be gone by then.

One option, if you can reach the park before 1 p.m. and stay until closing (5–8 p.m., depending on season), is Disney's Animal Kingdom, which requires the least time to tour. Because guests who arrive at opening frequently complete their tour by about 3 p.m., crowds thin in late afternoon. Try to make FastPass+ reservations for Kilimanjaro Safaris or Expedition Everest in advance.

Whenever you arrive at a theme park (including Universal parks) after 10 a.m., you should go to higher-capacity attractions where waiting time is relatively brief, even during the most crowded part of the day. Besides FastPass+, another time-saver at Test Track in Epcot, Expedition Everest in Disney's Animal Kingdom, Rock 'n' Roller Coaster in Disney's Hollywood Studios, and several Universal Orlando attractions is the **singles line,** a separate line for individuals who are alone or don't mind riding alone. The objective is to fill odd spaces left by groups that don't quite fill the entire ride vehicle. Because there aren't many singles and most groups are unwilling to split up, singles lines are usually much shorter than regular lines.

Disney parks are better for partial-day touring than Universal parks because Disney parks generally operate more high-capacity attractions than Universal does. We like the Universal parks and admire their cutting-edge technology, but the best way to see them is to be there at opening and follow our touring plans.

Our clip-out Touring Plan Companions in the back of the book list attractions in each Disney park that require the least waiting during the most crowded part of the day. Although the queues for these attractions may seem humongous, they move quickly. Also check out parades, stage shows, and other live entertainment. Popular attractions generally stay packed until an hour or so before closing; however, they often require little waiting during evening parades, shows, or fireworks.

## Alternatives to the Theme Parks on Arrival Day

Before you head out for fun on arrival day, you must check in, unpack, and buy admissions, and you probably will detour to the grocery or convenience store to buy snacks, drinks, and breakfast food. At all Disney resorts and many non-Disney hotels, you cannot occupy your room until after 3 p.m. (4 p.m. for DVC resorts); however, many properties will check you in, sell you tickets, and store your luggage before that hour.

The least expensive way to spend your arrival day is to check in, unpack, do your chores, and relax at your hotel swimming pool.

Other daytime options include a trip to a local water park. Because the Disney water parks are so crowded (during summer you need to be on hand for opening, just as you do at the other Disney parks), we recommend **Wet 'n Wild** (**wetnwildorlando.com**) on International Drive, which is generally less crowded than Disney's water parks but more expensive. What's great about Wet 'n Wild is that it stays open late in summer. Any water park that stays open past 5 p.m. is worth a look, because crowds at all parks clear out substantially after 4 p.m. If the park is open late and you get hungry, you'll find ample fast food. No matter which water park you choose, slather on broad-spectrum sunscreen. (For details on water parks, see Part Twenty.)

If you want something drier, we heartily recommend **Gatorland,** a quirky attraction on US 441 near Kissimmee (about 20 minutes from Walt Disney World). Gatorland, a slice of pre-Disney Florida, is exceptionally interesting and well managed. It's perfect for a half-day outing, provided you like alligators, snakes, and lizards. For information, call ☎ 800-393-JAWS or go to **gatorland.com.**

If none of the previous fires your boiler, consider miniature golf (expensive in the World; more reasonable outside it) or **DisneyQuest,** a venue at Downtown Disney West Side featuring interactive games and simulator technology. Alas, like the Disney parks, DisneyQuest is expensive and doesn't handle crowds particularly well. Late mornings and early afternoons are the best times to go.

### In the Evening

Dinner provides a great opportunity to plan the next day's activities. If you're hungry for entertainment too, take in a show at or after dinner. If you go the show route, we recommend **Cirque du Soleil** *La Nouba* at Downtown Disney West Side. Cirque is expensive, but we think it's the single best thing in all of Walt Disney World. Disney also offers some dinner shows, of which the *Hoop-Dee-Doo Musical Revue* is our pick of the litter. Both Cirque and *Hoop-Dee-Doo* are extremely popular; make reservations far in advance.

If you're not up for Cirque or a dinner show, consider **CityWalk,** Universal's nighttime-entertainment complex. Other options include **Jellyrolls,** a dueling-pianos club at the BoardWalk, and **Raglan Road,** an Irish pub with live music and good food at Downtown Disney. All are best appreciated by adults—energetic adults, at that.

### Departure Days

Departure days don't seem to cause as much consternation as arrival days. If you want to visit a theme park on your departure day, get up early and be there when it opens. If you have a lot of time, check out and store your luggage with the bell desk or in your car. Or, if you can arrange a late checkout, you might want to return to your hotel for a shower and change of clothes before departing. Some hotels are quite lenient regarding late checkouts; others assess a charge.

## THE CARDINAL RULES FOR SUCCESSFUL TOURING

MANY VISITORS DON'T HAVE SIX DAYS to devote to Disney. Some are en route to other destinations or may wish to sample additional Central Florida attractions. For these visitors, efficient touring is a must.

Even the most time-effective touring plan won't allow you to comprehensively cover two or more major theme parks in one day. Plan to allocate an entire day to each park (an exception to this is when the parks close at different times, allowing you to tour one park until closing, then proceed to another).

### One-Day Touring

A comprehensive one-day tour of the Magic Kingdom, Epcot, Disney's Animal Kingdom, or Disney's Hollywood Studios is possible but requires

*unofficial* **TIP**
If your schedule permits only one day of touring, concentrate on one theme park and save the others for another visit.

knowledge of the park, good planning, good navigation, and plenty of energy and endurance. One-day touring leaves little time for sit-down meals, prolonged browsing in shops, or lengthy breaks. One-day touring can be fun and rewarding, but allocating two days per park, especially for the Magic Kingdom and Epcot, is preferable.

Successfully touring the Magic Kingdom, Epcot, Animal Kingdom, or Disney's Hollywood Studios hinges on three rules:

### 1. Determine in Advance What You Really Want to See

Which attractions appeal to you most? Which ones would you like to experience if you have time left? What are you willing to forgo?

To help you set your touring priorities, we describe the theme parks and their attractions in detail in. In each description, we include the authors' evaluation of the attraction and the opinions of Disney World guests expressed as star ratings. Five stars is the highest rating.

Finally, because attractions range from midway-type rides and horse-drawn trolleys to high-tech extravaganzas, we have developed a hierarchy of categories to pinpoint an attraction's magnitude:

**SUPER-HEADLINERS** The best attractions the theme park has to offer. Mind-boggling in size, scope, and imagination. Represent the cutting edge of attraction technology and design.

**HEADLINERS** Multimillion-dollar, full-scale, themed adventures and theater presentations. Modern in technology and design and employing a full range of special effects.

**MAJOR ATTRACTIONS** More modestly themed adventures, but ones that incorporate state-of-the-art technologies. Or larger-scale attractions of older design.

**MINOR ATTRACTIONS** Midway-type rides, small "dark" rides (cars on a track, zigzagging through the dark), small theater presentations, transportation rides, and elaborate walk-through attractions.

**DIVERSIONS** Exhibits, both passive and interactive. Includes playgrounds, video arcades, and street theater.

Though not every attraction fits neatly into these descriptions, the categories provide a comparison of attraction size and scope. Remember that bigger and more elaborate doesn't always mean better. Peter Pan's Flight, a minor attraction in the Magic Kingdom, continues to be one of the park's most beloved rides. Likewise, for many young children, no attraction, regardless of size, surpasses Dumbo.

### 2. Arrive Early! Arrive Early! Arrive Early!

This is the single most important key to efficient touring and avoiding long lines. First thing in the morning, there are no lines and fewer people. The same four rides you experience in 1 hour in early morning can take as long as 3 hours after 10:30 a.m. Eat breakfast before you arrive; don't waste prime touring time sitting in a restaurant.

The earlier a park opens, the greater your advantage. This is because most vacationers won't rise early and get to a park before it opens. Fewer people are willing to make an 8 a.m. opening than a 9 a.m. opening. If you visit during midsummer, arrive at the turnstile 30–40 minutes before opening. During holiday periods, arrive 45–60 minutes early.

Many readers share their experiences about getting to the parks before opening. From a 13-year-old girl from Bloomington, Indiana:

*Please stress this to your readers: If you want to ride anything with a short wait, you have to get up in the morning! If this is a sacrifice you aren't willing to make, reconsider a Disney World vacation.*

A Pennsylvania mom of two found that slacking didn't pay:

*This is emphasized in the guide multiple times, but I want to say it again: Be at rope drop. I went during one of the slowest times of the year, and the morning I didn't wake up for rope drop I was able to experience less than half of what I did the other days.*

Likewise, from a Tecumseh, Ontario, reader:

*There were a couple of days that we did not want to be tied to a schedule and tried to take it easy a bit, starting out with breakfast at a restaurant. Well, we sure made a mistake on those days! It made us late for park opening and really messed up the whole day.*

A Minneapolis mother of three managed a compromise:

*Getting there early meant we could do the popular things without a long wait. That way I got my type-A "get things done" stuff out of the way in the morning and my husband got to indulge his "let's wander without a plan" personality the rest of the day.*

If getting the kids up earlier than usual makes for rough sailing, don't despair: You'll have a great time no matter when you get to the park. Many families with young children have found that it's better to accept the relative inefficiencies of arriving at the park a bit late than to jar the children out of their routine. In our guide especially for families, The Unofficial Guide to Walt Disney World with Kids, we provide a number of special touring plans (including touring plans for sleepyheads) that we don't have room for in this guide.

### 3. Avoid Bottlenecks

Helping you avoid bottlenecks is what the *Unofficial Guide* is about. This involves being able to predict where, when, and why they occur. Concentrations of hungry people create bottlenecks at restaurants during lunch and dinner; concentrations of people moving toward the exit near closing time cause gift shops en route to clog; concentrations of visitors at new and popular rides, and at rides slow to load and unload, create logjams and long lines.

Our solution for avoiding bottlenecks is touring plans for the Magic Kingdom, Epcot, Disney's Animal Kingdom, Disney's Hollywood Studios, and the two Disney water parks. We also provide detailed information on rides and performances, enabling you to estimate how long you may have to wait in line and allowing you to compare rides for their crowd capacity.

All touring plans are in the back of this book, following the indexes. Plans for Magic Kingdom begin on page 822 and for Epcot on page 828. One-day touring plans for Animal Kingdom and Disney's Hollywood Studios follow, on pages 833 and 834, respectively. Next come one-day touring plans for Universal's Islands of Adventure and Universal Studios Florida, on pages 835 and 836, respectively; a plan for both parks is on page 837. Touring plans for Blizzard Beach and Typhoon Lagoon water parks are found on pages 839 and 840, respectively.

## WHAT'S A QUEUE?

ALTHOUGH IT'S NOT COMMONLY USED in the United States, *queue* (pronounced "cue") is the universal English word for a line, such as one in which you wait to cash a check at the bank or to board a ride at a theme park. Queuing theory, a mathematical area of specialization within the field of operations research, studies and models how lines work. Because the *Unofficial Guide* draws heavily on this discipline, we use some of its terminology. In addition to the noun, the verb *to queue* means to get in line, and a *queuing area* is a waiting area that accommodates a line. When guests decline to join a queue because they perceive the wait to be too long, they're said to *balk*.

## OF UTMOST IMPORTANCE: READ THIS!

IN ANALYZING READER SURVEYS, we were astonished by the percentage of readers who *don't* use our touring plans. Scientifically tested and proven, these plans can save you **4 entire hours** or more of waiting in line in a single day—4 fewer hours of standing, 4 hours freed up to do something fun. Our groundbreaking research that created the touring plans has been the subject of front-page articles in the *Dallas Morning News* and *The New York Times* and has been cited in numerous scholarly journals. So why would you not use them?

We get a ton of reader mail—98% of it positive—commenting on our touring plans. First, from a mother who planned a last-minute trip:

> We rode all of the main attractions in Epcot, Magic Kingdom, and Hollywood Studios over a three-day period, and we didn't wait more than 10 minutes for any ride—and this was during spring break! We had a five-day pass, so we used the evenings and another day to stroll through the parks, enjoying the sights and minor attractions.

From a Ferndown, England, mother of two:

> We were stunned by how effective the touring plans were straight out of the book. We would get to the given park early, and by the time the plan suggested lunch it could be about 10:30 (and this was at Easter!). We got straight on a clamshell at The Seas with Nemo & Friends, and as we took our seats we saw a line form after us.

An Ohio family felt the wind in their sails:

> The whole time we were in the Magic Kingdom, following the touring plan, it seemed that we were traveling in front of a hurricane— we'd wait 10 minutes or so for an attraction (or less—sometimes we just walked right on), but when we got out and started moving on to the next one, we could see the line building for what we just did.

For a Glasgow, Scotland, reader, touring the *Unofficial* way contributed to family harmony:

> *Trying to decide where to go next wasn't something we had to worry about. There was none of that "Whatever you think" / "I don't mind"–type discussion that can haunt even the best of holidays.*

A 30-something mom of two from Oconomowoc, Wisconsin, found that the touring plans fanned the flames of *amour:*

> *My husband was a bit doubtful about using a touring plan, but on our first day at Magic Kingdom, after we'd done all the Fantasyland attractions and ridden Splash Mountain twice before lunch, he looked at me with amazement and said, "I've never been so attracted to you."*

Finally from an Edmonds, Washington, family who used the touring plans for Universal's Islands of Adventure:

> *This trip was the first time we were actually going to leave the property (gasp!) and go to Universal, and I was very happy that you included a touring plan for Islands of Adventure. It worked like a charm! I've always wondered how it feels to follow your plans not ever having seen the park before, and now I know—it was easy!*

## TOURING PLANS: WHAT THEY ARE AND HOW THEY WORK

### See More, Do More, Wait Less

From the first edition of the *Unofficial Guide,* minimizing our readers' waits in line has been a top priority. We know from our research and that of others that theme park patrons measure overall satisfaction based on the number of attractions they're able to experience during a visit: the more attractions, the better. Thus, we developed and offered our readers field-tested touring plans that allow them to experience as many attractions as possible with the least amount of waiting in line.

Our touring plans have always been based on theme-park-traffic flow, attraction capacity, the maximum time a guest is willing to wait (called a *balking constraint*), walking distance between attractions, and waiting-time data collected at every attraction in every park, every day of the year. The plans derived from a combinatorial model (for anyone who cares) that married the well-known assignment problem of linear programming with queuing (waiting-line) theory. The model approximated the most time-efficient sequence in which to visit the attractions of a specific park. After we created a preliminary touring plan from the model, we field-tested it in the park, using a test group (who followed our plan) and a control group (who didn't have our plan and who toured according to their own best judgment).

The two groups were compared, and the results were amazing. On days of heavy attendance, the groups touring without our plans spent an average of 4 hours more in line and experienced 37% fewer attractions than did those who did use the plans.

*unofficial* **TIP**
The facts and figures in our books come from years of data collection and analysis by expert statisticians, programmers, field researchers, and lifelong Disney enthusiasts.

Over the years, this research has been recognized by both the travel industry and academe, having been cited by such diverse sources as the *New York Times, USA Today, Travel Weekly, Bottom Line, Money, Operations Research Forum,* CBS News, Fox News Channel, the BBC, the Travel Channel, the *Dallas Morning News,* and the *Atlanta Journal-Constitution.* The methodology behind our touring plans was also used as a case study in the 2010 book *Numbers Rule Your World,* by Kaiser Fung.

### John Henry and the Nail-Driving Machine

As sophisticated as our model may sound, we recognized that it was cumbersome and slow, and that it didn't approximate the "perfect" touring plan as closely as we desired. Moreover, advances in computer technology and science, specifically in the field of genetic algorithms, demonstrated that it wouldn't be long before a model, or program, was created that would leave ours in the dust.

Do you remember the story of John Henry, the fastest nail driver on the railroad? One day a man appeared with a machine he claimed could drive spikes faster than any man. John Henry challenged the machine to a race, which he won, but which killed him in the process. We felt a bit like John Henry. We were still very good at what we did but knew with absolute certainty that sooner or later we'd have to confront the touring plan version of a nail-driving machine.

Our response was to build our own nail-driving machine. We teamed up during the mid-1990s with Len Testa, a scientist and computer programmer who was working in the field of evolutionary algorithms and who, coincidentally, was a Disney junkie. Marrying our many years of collecting Walt Disney World observations and data to Len's vision and programming expertise, we developed a state-of-the-art program for creating nearly perfect touring plans.

Several university professors, many of them leaders in their fields, have contributed research or ideas to the software program. Findings from early versions of the software have been published in peer-reviewed academic journals. The most recent versions of the program are protected through pending patent applications. Special thanks go to Albert C. Esterline, PhD, and Gerry V. Dozier, PhD, of North Carolina A&T State University. Credit is also due to Nikolaos Sahinidis, PhD, as well as his graduate students at the University of Illinois at Urbana-Champaign, who have contributed a number of exceptionally helpful studies. Chryssi Malandraki, PhD, of United Parcel Service and Robert Dial, PhD, of the Volpe National Transportation System Center have likewise provided assistance and encouragement over the years.

It has been a process of evolution and refinement, but in each year of its development, the new program came closer to beating the results of our long-lived model. In 2002 at field trials during the busy spring-break period, the new program beat the best touring plan generated by the traditional *Unofficial* model by 90 minutes at the Magic Kingdom. This was in addition to the 3 hours saved by the earlier model. Getting there, however, wasn't easy.

## The Challenge

One thing that makes creating good touring plans difficult is that there are many different ways to see the same attractions. For example, if we want to visit Space Mountain, Pirates of the Caribbean, and Splash Mountain as soon as the Magic Kingdom opens, there are six ways that we can do so:

1. First ride Space Mountain, then Pirates of the Caribbean, then Splash Mountain.

2. First ride Space Mountain, then Splash Mountain, then Pirates of the Caribbean.

3. First ride Splash Mountain, then Space Mountain, then Pirates of the Caribbean.

4. First ride Splash Mountain, then Pirates of the Caribbean, then Space Mountain.

5. First ride Pirates of the Caribbean, then Splash Mountain, then Space Mountain.

6. First ride Pirates of the Caribbean, then Space Mountain, then Splash Mountain.

Some of these combinations make better touring plans than others. Because the queue for Space Mountain increases rapidly, it's best to ride this particular attraction first thing in the morning. For similar reasons, it would be better to ride Splash Mountain before Pirates. In this example, Touring Plan 2 would probably save us the most time standing in line. Touring Plan 5 would probably result in the most waiting in line.

As we add attractions to our list, the number of possible touring plans grows rapidly. Adding a fourth attraction would result in 24 possible touring plans, since there are four possible variations for each of the 6 plans listed previously. In general, the number of possible touring plans for $n$ attractions is $n \cdot (n-1) \cdot (n-2) \ldots \cdot 1$. (Don't let the mathematical notation throw you. If we plug real numbers in, it's quite simple.) For five attractions, as an example, there are $5 \times 4 \times 3 \times 2 \times 1$ possible touring plans. If you don't have a calculator handy, that adds up to 120 potential plans. For six attractions, there are $6 \times 5 \times 4 \times 3 \times 2 \times 1$, or 720 possible plans. A list of 10 attractions has more than 3 million possible plans. The 24 attractions in the Magic Kingdom One-Day Touring Plan for Adults have a staggering 620,448,401,733,239,439,360,000 possible touring plans—more than **620 billion trillion** combinations, or roughly 90 times as many as the estimated number of grains of sand on Earth. Adding in complexities such as FastPass+, meals, and breaks further increases the combinations.

Scientists have been working on similar problems for years. Companies that deliver packages, for example, plan each driver's route to minimize the distance driven, saving time and fuel. In fact, finding ways to visit many places with minimal effort is such a common problem that it has its own nickname: the traveling-salesman problem.

For more than a few attractions, the number of possible touring plans is so large that it would take a very long time for even a powerful computer to find the single best plan. A number of proposed techniques give very good, but not necessarily exact, solutions to the traveling-salesman problem in a reasonable amount of time.

The *Unofficial Guide* touring plan program contains two algorithms that allow it to quickly analyze tens of millions of possible plans in a very short time. (An algorithm is to a computer what a recipe is to a chef. Just as a chef takes specific steps to make a cake, a computer takes specific steps to process information. Those steps, when grouped, form an algorithm.) The program can analyze FastPass+ distribution patterns at all attractions, for example, and suggest the best times and attractions to use FastPass+. The software can also schedule rest breaks throughout the day. If you're going to eat lunch in the park, the software can suggest restaurants near where you'll be at lunchtime that will minimize the time you spend looking for food. Numerous other features are available, many of which we'll discuss in the next section.

The program, however, is only part of what's needed to create a good touring plan. Good data is also important. Since 1998, we've been collecting data in the theme parks at every conceivable time of year. With the introduction of our Lines mobile app in 2010, we've been able to collect wait times from every theme park every day of the year— more than 5 million to date. We supplement this data with actual wait times submitted by Lines users, too, and use all of it to calibrate our touring plan models.

So how good *are* the touring plans in the *Unofficial Guide*? Our computer program typically gets within about 2% of the optimal touring plan and finds an optimal plan for most straightforward situations around 70% of the time. To put this in perspective, if the hypothetical "perfect" Adult One-Day Touring Plan took about 10 hours to complete, the *Unofficial* touring plan would take around 10 hours and 12 minutes. Because it would take about 30 years for a really powerful computer to find that "perfect" plan, the extra 12 minutes is a reasonable trade-off.

In the 2003 edition of this guidebook, we noted the possibility of using our software to see every attraction in the Magic Kingdom in one day. We dubbed this the Ultimate Magic Kingdom Touring Plan and offered it free to anyone up for the challenge. Dozens of otherwise-sane families have completed this plan since that time, and hundreds have come close. The current record-holders are Jordyn, Kenny, and Nathan White of Gun Barrel City, Texas, who saw 82 attractions in 24 hours and 21 minutes on February 29, 2012 (the Magic Kingdom was open for 24 consecutive hours). That works out to roughly 1 attraction every 18 minutes. Other "ultimate" plans exist for Epcot, DHS, and Disney's Animal Kingdom. Drop us a line or visit **touringplans.com/ultimate** if you're up for the challenge. Note that these plans aren't intended for families, first-time visitors, or anyone simply wanting a nice day in the parks. To the contrary, they're like running a marathon.

## Customize Your Touring Plans

The attractions included in our touring plans are the most popular as determined by almost 53,000 reader surveys. If you've never been to Walt Disney World, we suggest using the plans in this book. Besides being the best our program can produce, these plans have been field-tested by tens of thousands of families. They'll ensure that you see the best Disney attractions with as little waiting in line as possible.

If you're a return visitor, your favorite attractions may be different. One way to customize the plans is to go to **touringplans.com** to create personalized versions. Tell the software the date, time, and park you've chosen to visit, along with the attractions you want to see. The plan will tell you, for your specific travel date and time, the exact order in which to visit the attractions to minimize your waits in line. Lines also supports "switching off" (see page 341) on thrill rides. Besides attractions, you can schedule meals, breaks, character greetings, and more. You can even tell Lines how fast you plan to walk, and it'll make the necessary adjustments. Plus, the app can handle any FastPass+ reservations you've already got and tell you which attractions would benefit most from using them.

Alternatively, some changes are simple enough to make on your own. If a plan calls for an attraction you're not interested in, simply skip it and move on to the next one. You can also substitute similar attractions in the same area of the park. If a plan calls for, say, riding Dumbo and you'd rather not, but you would enjoy the Mad Tea Party (which is not on the plan), then go ahead and substitute that for Dumbo. As long as the substitution is a similar attraction—substituting a show for a ride won't work—and is pretty close by the attraction called for in the touring plan, you won't compromise the plan's overall effectiveness.

A family of four from South Slocan, British Columbia, found they could easily tailor the touring plans to meet their needs:

> We amended your touring plans by taking out the attractions we didn't want to do and just doing the remainder in order. It worked great, and by arriving before the parks opened, we got to see everything we wanted, with virtually no waits!

As did a Jacksonville, Florida, family:

> We used a combination of the Two-Day Touring Plan for Parents with Small Children and the Two-Day Touring Plan for Adults. We were able to get on almost everything with a 10-minute wait or less. Our longest wait was on our second day for the Jungle Cruise, but the wait was still only 20 minutes.

Finally, from a Magnolia, Mississippi, family of four:

> One of the things we love most about the book and the website is the ability to adjust any of the plans to our family's preferences simply by omitting a step or two. The plans work for any style of touring, from commando to laid-back.

## OVERVIEW OF THE TOURING PLANS

OUR TOURING PLANS ARE STEP-BY-STEP guides for seeing as much as possible with a minimum of standing in line. They're designed to help you avoid crowds and bottlenecks on any day of the year. The plans will save time on days when attendance is lighter (see "Selecting the Time of Year for Your Visit," page 35), but they won't be as critical to successful touring.

## What You Can Realistically Expect from the Touring Plans

Though we present one-day touring plans for each theme park, be aware that the Magic Kingdom and Epcot have more attractions than you can reasonably expect to see in one day. Because the two-day plans for the Magic Kingdom and Epcot are the most comprehensive, efficient, and relaxing, we strongly recommend them over the one-day plans. However, if you must cram your visit into a single day, the one-day plans will allow you to see as much as is humanly possible. Although Disney's Hollywood Studios has grown considerably since its 1989 debut, seeing everything in one day is still possible. Likewise, Disney's Animal Kingdom is a one-day outing.

## Variables That Affect the Success of the Touring Plans

The plans' success will be affected by how quickly you move from ride to ride; when and how many refreshment and restroom breaks you take; when, where, and how you eat meals; and your ability (or lack thereof) to find your way around. Smaller groups almost always move faster than larger groups, and parties of adults generally cover more ground than families with young children. Switching off (page 341), also known as "The Baby Swap," among other things, inhibits families with little ones from moving expeditiously among attractions. Plus, some folks simply cannot conform to the plans' "early to rise" conditions, as this reader from Cleveland Heights, Ohio, recounts:

*Our touring plans were thrown totally off by one member who could not be on time for opening. Even in October, this made a huge difference in our ability to see attractions without waiting.*

And a family from Centerville, Ohio, says:

*The toughest thing about your touring plans was getting the rest of the family to stay with them. Getting them to pass by attractions in order to hit something across the park was no easy task.*

The Disney Dining Plan's required restaurant reservations impose a rigid schedule that can derail a touring plan, as this Wichita, Kansas, mom attests:

*The [printed] touring plans were impractical if used with the dining plan. The hour-long meals wreaked havoc on the itinerary, and we never seemed to be able to get back on track, even with low crowd levels and rainy afternoons.*

Along with dining breaks, the appearance of a Disney character usually stops a touring plan in its tracks. While some characters stroll the parks, it's equally common that they assemble in a specific venue where families queue up for photos and autographs. Meeting characters, posing for photos, and getting autographs can burn hours of touring time.

If your kids collect character autographs, you need to anticipate these interruptions by including character greetings when creating your online touring plans, or else negotiate some understanding with your children about when you'll collect autographs. Note that queues for autographs, especially in the Magic Kingdom and Disney's Animal Kingdom, are sometimes as long as or longer than the queues for major attractions. The only time-efficient ways to collect autographs are to use FastPass+ where available (such as for Mickey Mouse and the Disney princesses at the Magic Kingdom) or to line up at the character-greeting areas first thing in the morning. Early morning is also the best time to experience popular attractions, so you may have some tough choices to make.

Some things are beyond your control. Chief among these are the manner and timing of bringing a particular ride to capacity. For example, Big Thunder Mountain Railroad, a roller coaster in the Magic Kingdom, has five trains. On a given morning, it may begin operation with two of the five, then add the other three when needed. If the waiting line builds rapidly before operators go to full capacity, you could have a long wait, even in early morning.

A variable that can give your touring plans a boost is the singles line (see page 68), as this English reader explains:

> We used the touring plans to the letter and found that not only did they work, but they worked even better in conjunction with single-rider queues. The only rides that we queued up for normally were ones with a 20-minute-or-less queue time and wet rides.

Another variable is your arrival time for a theater show. You'll wait from the time you arrive until the end of the presentation in progress. Thus, if a show is 15 minutes long and you arrive 1 minute after it has begun, your wait will be 14 minutes. Conversely, if you arrive as the show is wrapping up, your wait will be only a minute or two.

While we realize that following the plans isn't always easy, we nevertheless recommend continuous, expeditious touring until around noon. After that, breaks and diversions won't affect the plans significantly.

## What to Do if You Lose the Thread

If unforeseen events interrupt a plan:

1. If you're following a touring plan in our **Lines** app (**touringplans.com /lines**), just press "Optimize" when you're ready to start touring again. Lines will figure out the best possible plan for the remainder of your day.

2. If you're following a printed touring plan, skip a step on the plan for every 20 minutes' delay. For example, if you lose your wallet and spend an hour hunting for it, skip three steps and pick up from there.

3. Forget the plan and organize the remainder of the day using the standby wait times listed in Lines or the Clip-Out Touring Plan Companions in the back of the book.

## What to Expect When You Arrive at the Parks

Because most touring plans are based on being present when the theme park opens, you need to know about opening procedures. Disney transportation to the parks begins 1½–2 hours before official opening. The parking lots open at around the same time.

Each park has an entrance plaza outside the turnstiles. Usually, you're held there until 30 minutes before the official opening time, when you're admitted. What happens next depends on the season and the day's crowds:

1. **STANDARD OPENING PROCEDURES**  At Epcot, Disney's Hollywood Studios, and Animal Kingdom, all guests are permitted through the turnstiles, and you'll find that one or several specific attractions are open early. At Epcot, Spaceship Earth and sometimes Test Track or Soarin' will be operating. At Animal Kingdom, you may find it's Kilimanjaro Safaris, Expedition Everest, and TriceraTop Spin. At Hollywood Studios, look for Tower of Terror, Toy Story Midway Mania!, and/or Rock 'n' Roller Coaster.

   At the Magic Kingdom, you may be admitted past the turnstiles 15 minutes before park opening, but you'll usually be confined to a small section of the park, such as Main Street, U.S.A., until official opening time. A human wall of Disney cast members keeps you there until opening, when the wall speed-walks you back to the headliner attractions (to prevent anyone from running or getting trampled).

2. **HIGH-ATTENDANCE DAYS**  When large crowds are expected, you'll usually be admitted through the turnstiles up to 30 minutes before official opening, and most of the park will be operating.

   In the first scenario above, you gain a big advantage if you're already past the turnstiles when the park opens. While everyone else is stuck in line waiting for the people ahead to find their tickets and figure out how the biometric scans work, the lucky few already in the park will be in line for their first attraction. You'll probably be done and on your way to your second before many of them are even in the park, and the time savings accrue throughout the rest of the day.

## Clip-Out Touring Plans

For your convenience, we've prepared graphical clip-out copies of all touring plans. These pocket versions combine touring plan itineraries with maps and directions. Select the plan appropriate for your party, and get familiar with it. Then clip the pocket version from the back of this guide and carry it with you as a quick reference at the theme park.

## Will the Plans Continue to Work Once the Secret Is Out?

*Yes!* First, all the plans require that a patron be there when a park opens. Many Disney World patrons simply won't get up early while on vacation. Second, less than 2% of any day's attendance has been exposed to the plans—too few to affect results. Last, most groups tailor the plans, skipping rides or shows according to taste.

## How Frequently Are the Touring Plans Revised?

We revise them every year, and updates are always available at **touring plans.com.** Be prepared for surprises, though: Opening procedures and showtimes may change, for example, and you can't predict when an attraction might break down.

## Tour Groups on Steroids

We've discovered that tour groups of up to 200 people sometimes use our plans. A woman from Memphis, Tennessee, writes:

*When we arrived at the Land Pavilion at Epcot, a tour guide was holding your book and shouting into a bullhorn, "Step 7—proceed to Journey into Imagination!" With this, about 65 Japanese tourists in red T-shirts ran out the door.*

## "Bouncing Around"

Some readers object to crisscrossing a theme park as our touring plans sometimes require. A woman from Decatur, Georgia, told us she "got dizzy from all the bouncing around." Believe us, we empathize.

We've worked hard over the years to eliminate the need to crisscross a theme park in our touring plans. (In fact, our customized software can minimize walking instead of waiting in line, if that's important to you.) Occasionally, however, it's possible to save a lot of time in line with a few extra minutes of walking.

The reasons for this are varied. Sometimes a park is designed intentionally to require walking. In the Magic Kingdom, for example, the most popular attractions are positioned as far apart as possible—in the north, east, and west corners of the park—so that guests are more evenly distributed throughout the day. Other times, you may be visiting just after a new attraction has opened that everyone wants to try. In that case, a special trip to visit the new attraction may be required earlier in the day than normal, in order to avoid longer waits later. And live shows, especially at the Studios, sometimes have performance schedules so at odds with each other (and the rest of the park's schedule) that orderly touring is impossible.

If you want to experience headliner attractions in one day without long waits, you can see those first (requires crisscrossing the park), use FastPass+ (if available), or hope to squeeze in visits during parades and the last hour the park is open (may not work).

If you have two days to visit the Magic Kingdom or Epcot, use the Two-Day Touring Plans (see pages 825 and 826 for the Magic Kingdom and 831 and 832 for Epcot). These spread the popular attractions over two mornings and work great even when the parks close early.

## Touring Plans and the Obsessive-Compulsive Reader

We suggest sticking to the plans religiously, especially in the mornings, if you're visiting during busy times. The consequence of touring spontaneity in peak season is hours of standing in line. When using the plans, however, relax and always be prepared for surprises and setbacks.

If you find your type-A brain doing cartwheels, reflect on the advice of a woman from Trappe, Pennsylvania:

*I had planned for this trip for two years and researched it by use of guidebooks, computer programs, videotapes, and information received from WDW. On night three of our trip, I ended up taking an unscheduled trip to the emergency room. When the doctor asked what seemed to be the problem, I responded, "I don't know, but I can't stop shaking, and I can't stay here very long because I have to get up in a couple hours to go to Disney's Hollywood Studios." Diagnosis: an anxiety attack caused by my excessive itinerary.*

An Omaha, Nebraska, couple devised their own way to cope:

*We created our own 4.25 x 5.5 guidebook for our trip that included a number of pages from the* **touringplans.com** *website. This was the first page:*

---

### The Type-A Spouse's Bill of Rights

**1.** We will not see everything in one vacation, and any attempt to do so may be met with blunt trauma.

**2.** Len Testa will not be vacationing with us. His plans don't schedule time for benches. Ours may.

**3.** We may deviate from the touring plans at some point. Really.

**4.** Even if it isn't on the Disney Dining Plan, a funnel cake or other snack may be purchased without a grouchy face from the nonpurchasing spouse.

**5.** Sometimes, sitting by the pool may sound more fun than going to a park, show, or other scheduled event. On this vacation, that will be fine.

**6.** "But I thought we were going to . . ." is a phrase that must be stricken from the discussion of any plans that had not been previously discussed as a couple.

**7.** Other items may be added as circumstances dictate at the parks.

---

*It was a much happier vacation with these generally understood principles in writing.*

## Touring Plan Rejection

Some folks don't respond well to the regimentation of a touring plan. If you encounter this problem with someone in your party, roll with the punches as this Maryland couple did:

*The rest of the group was not receptive to the use of the touring plans. I think they all thought I was being a little too regimented about planning this vacation. Rather than argue, I left the touring plans behind as we ventured off for the parks. You can guess the outcome. We took our camcorder with us and watched the movies when we returned home. About every 5 minutes or so there's a shot of us all gathered around a park map trying to decide what to do next.*

A reader from Royal Oak, Michigan, ran into trouble by not getting her family on board ahead of time:

*The one thing I will suggest is if one member of the family is doing most of the research and planning (like I did), that they communicate what the book/touring plans suggest. I failed to do this and it led to some, shall we say, tense moments between my husband and me on our first day. However, once he realized how much time we were saving, he understood why I was so bent on following the plans.*

## Touring Plans for Low-Attendance Days

We receive a number of letters each year similar to the following one from Lebanon, New Jersey:

*The guide always assumed there would be large crowds. We had no lines. An alternate tour for low-traffic days would be helpful.*

There are, thankfully, still days on which crowds are low enough that a full-day touring plan isn't needed. However, some attractions in each park bottleneck even if attendance is low:

**MAGIC KINGDOM**  Space Mountain, Splash Mountain, The Many Adventures of Winnie the Pooh, Enchanted Tales with Belle, Peter Pan's Flight, and the Seven Dwarfs Mine Train

**EPCOT**  Test Track and Soarin'

**DISNEY'S ANIMAL KINGDOM**  Kilimanjaro Safaris and Expedition Everest

**DHS**  Rock 'n' Roller Coaster, The Twilight Zone Tower of Terror, and Toy Story Midway Mania!

Immense lines also build for meet-and-greets involving characters from Disney's latest films. In early 2014, for example, it was common at park opening for a 3-hour line to form to meet the princesses from Disney's *Frozen.* For this reason, we recommend following a touring plan through the first five or six steps. If you're pretty much walking onto every attraction, scrap the remainder of the plan. Alternatively, see the attractions above right after the park opens, or use FastPass+.

## EXTRA MAGIC HOURS AND THE TOURING PLANS

IF YOU'RE A DISNEY RESORT GUEST and use your morning Extra Magic Hours privileges, complete your early-entry touring before the general public is admitted, then position yourself to follow the touring plan. When the public is admitted, the park will suddenly swarm. A Wilmington, Delaware, mother advises:

*The early-entry times went like clockwork. We were finishing up the Great Movie Ride when Disney's Hollywood Studios opened to the public, and we had to wait in line quite a while for* Voyage of the Little Mermaid, *which sort of screwed up everything thereafter. Early-opening attractions should be finished up well before regular opening time so you can be at the plan's first stop as early as possible.*

In the Magic Kingdom, early-entry attractions currently operate in Fantasyland and Tomorrowland. At Epcot, they're in the Future World section. At Disney's Animal Kingdom, they're in DinoLand U.S.A., Asia, Discovery Island, and Africa. At Disney's Hollywood Studios, they're dispersed. Practically speaking, see any attractions on the plan that are open for early entry, crossing them off as you do. If you finish all early-entry attractions and have time left before the general public is admitted, sample early-entry attractions not included in the plan. Stop touring about 10 minutes before the public is admitted, and position yourself for the first attraction on the plan that wasn't open for early entry. During early entry in the Magic Kingdom, for example, you can almost always experience Seven Dwarfs Mine Train and Under the Sea: Voyage of the Little Mermaid in Fantasyland, plus Space Mountain in Tomorrowland. As official opening nears, go to the boundary between Fantasyland and Liberty Square and be ready to blitz Splash and Big Thunder mountains according to the touring plan when the rest of the park opens.

Evening Extra Magic Hours, when a designated park remains open for Disney resort guests 2 hours beyond normal closing time, have less effect on the touring plans than early entry in the morning. Parks are almost never scheduled for both early entry and evening Extra Magic Hours on the same day. Thus a park offering evening Extra Magic Hours will enjoy a fairly normal morning and early afternoon. It's not until late afternoon, when park hoppers coming from the other theme parks descend, that the late-closing park will become especially crowded. By that time, you'll be well toward the end of your touring plan.

## FASTPASS+

AS YOU SAW ON PAGE 2, we couldn't resist poking fun at the latest evolution of this 15-year-old ride-reservation system. Verily, FastPass+ is a milestone in Disney's never-ending quest to create something more complicated than the US tax code or the Affordable Care Act.

The original iteration of FastPass (also styled as "Fastpass" and "FASTPASS" over the years) was introduced in 1999 as a way to moderate high wait times at some of Disney's headliner attractions. A new version of the system, called FastPass+, completely replaced the old one in January 2014. Whereas the old system printed your reservation times on small slips of paper dispensed from ATM-like kiosks next to each attraction, the new FastPass+ system is (with one exception described later) entirely electronic: You must use a computer, mobile device, or in-park terminal to make and modify FastPass+ reservations, and you must use your RFID-enabled MagicBand, Key to the World Card, or day-guest card to redeem the reservation. As before, FastPass+ is free of charge to all Walt Disney World guests.

*unofficial* **TIP**
Disney offers FastPass+ only for select attractions—around 70 in all— and only during busy times of year for some. Specific FastPass+ information for each Disney theme park is provided in its respective chapter.

Because FastPass+ has a learning curve, understanding how to use it is important for success when using our touring plans, especially if you want to experience lots of attractions or you're unable to arrive at park opening. Somewhat like making a dinner reservation at a restaurant, FastPass+ allows you to reserve a ride on an attraction at a Disney theme park. You can request a specific time, such as 7:30 p.m., or you can let the system give you its "first available" reservation.

Although we take issue with the new system's complicated rules and procedures, we do concede that it can help you see more with less waiting, provided you know how to use it. Like the old FastPass, it reduces waits for designated attractions by distributing guests at those attractions throughout the day. FastPass+ provides an incentive—a shorter wait—for guests willing to postpone experiencing a given attraction until later in the day. The system also, in effect, imposes a penalty— standby status—on guests who don't use it. However, spreading out guest arrivals sometimes decreases waits for standby guests as well.

FastPass+ doesn't eliminate the need to arrive early at a theme park. Because each park offers a limited number of FastPass+ attractions, you still have to make an early start if you want to avoid long lines at non-FastPass+ attractions. Plus, a limited supply of FastPasses is available for each attraction on any day. If you don't reserve in advance and you arrive at your park of choice after noon, you might find no more spots available for your favorites.

## Making a FastPass+ Reservation

Anyone with an upcoming stay at a Walt Disney World hotel can make FastPass+ reservations up to 60 days in advance at **disneyworld.com** and through the My Disney Experience app; Annual Pass holders staying off-property may reserve up to 30 days in advance, as may day guests with a valid ticket.

If you buy your admission the day you arrive at the park or you want to change your previous FastPass+ selections once you're inside, you can do so using the mobile app or new in-park computer terminals.

You should set aside *at least* 30 minutes to complete the advance-booking process. Before you begin, make sure that you have the following items on hand:

- A valid admission ticket or purchase-confirmation number for everyone in your group
- Your hotel-reservation number, if you're staying on-site
- A computer, smartphone, or tablet connected to the Internet
- An e-mail account that you can access easily while traveling
- An account at **mydisneyexperience.com**
- A schedule of the parks you'll be visiting each day, including arrival and departure times, plus the times of any midday breaks

- The dates, times, and confirmation numbers of any dining or recreation reservations you've already made
- A fistful of Xanax
- The patience of Job

If you're coordinating travel plans with friends or family who live elsewhere, the following information is also good to have:

- The names and (optionally) e-mail addresses of the people you're traveling with
- A schedule of the parks these folks are visiting on each day of their trip, including their arrival, departure, and break times
- The dates and times of any dining or recreation reservations these folks have made

Again, the only way to make FastPass+ reservations before your trip is to use the My Disney Experience (MDE) website or app—you can't make them by phone, the way you would for a restaurant reservation. We think it's easier to use the website, so we'll describe that here; the steps for the app are similar.

**1. E-MAIL ACCESS** Because the MDE site uses your e-mail address to identify you and send you new login credentials should you forget your old ones (see next step), you need to make sure you'll have easy access to your account while you're in the parks. If you don't have a mobile app for your e-mail account, download and configure it before you leave home. And if you don't have an account with a web-based service such as Gmail, go ahead and set one up—it's much easier to configure for mobile devices than e-mail you get through your ISP.

**2. MY DISNEY EXPERIENCE ACCESS** Now go to the MDE site and click "Sign In or Create Account" in the upper-right corner; then click "Create Account" on the screen that follows. You'll be asked for your e-mail address, along with your name, home address, and birthdate. (Disney uses your home address to send your MagicBands and, if applicable, hotel-reservation information.) You'll also be asked to choose two security questions and answers—write these down and store them in a safe place, or save them as a text file. If you forget your MDE login information, Disney will ask you these questions to verify your identity.

**3. DISNEY HOTEL INFORMATION** Next, MDE asks whether you'll be staying at a Disney hotel. If you are, enter your reservation number. This associates your MDE account with your hotel stay in Disney's computer systems. If you've booked a travel package that includes theme park admission, Disney computers will automatically link the admission to your MDE account, allowing you to skip Step 5 below.

**4. REGISTER FRIENDS AND FAMILY** You'll now be asked for the names, ages, and e-mail addresses of everyone traveling with you. This is so you can make dining and FastPass+ reservations for your entire group at the same time later in the process. You can add family and friends at any time, but you might as well do it now.

**5. REGISTER TICKETS** If you've bought your admission from a third-party ticket reseller or you have tickets or MagicBands left over from a previous trip, you'll be asked to register those next. On each ticket is printed a unique ID code, usually a string of 12–20 numbers, printed in one corner on the back; on MagicBands, look for a 12-digit number printed inside the band. Enter the ID code for each ticket you have.

You can make FastPass+ reservations for as many days as there are on your ticket. If you decide later to extend your stay, you'll be able to make reservations for additional days. If you've got a voucher that needs to be converted to a ticket at the parks, you can still register it by calling Disney tech support at ☎ 407-939-7765.

**6. SELECT A DATE** Click on the My Disney Experience logo in the upper right corner of your screen. A menu should appear, with "FastPass+" as one of the choices. Click on "FastPass+."

The next screen should display a rolling seven-day calendar, beginning around the start of your trip's dates. Select one of these dates and click "Next."

**7. SELECT TRAVEL PARTY** On the screen that follows, you'll choose which of your friends and family will use the FastPass+ reservations you're making. Note that everyone you select during this step will get the same set of FastPass+ attractions and times: If your FastPass+ choices include, say, Space Mountain and your father-in-law doesn't do roller coasters, you'll need to tweak his selections in Step 11. For now, choose all the members of your group and click "Next."

**8. SELECT ATTRACTIONS** On this screen you choose your FastPass+ experiences from a list of eligible attractions. Because Disney has rules governing the combinations of FastPasses you can get at Epcot and Disney's Hollywood Studios (see page 90), the attractions will be grouped into the correct tiers for those parks, and you'll see how many opportunities you have in each tier. If all FastPasses for an attraction have been distributed, the message "Standby Available" will appear next to its name.

If you don't choose an attraction for every opportunity MDE gives you—for instance, if you choose only two attractions when MDE says you can choose three—you'll automatically be assigned random attractions for all remaining opportunities.

**9. PRIORITIZE ATTRACTIONS** After you've selected your attractions, MDE will ask you to rank the attractions from most important to least important. Your prioritization seems to affect how Disney assigns your initial set of FastPass+ return times (shown in the next step)—different priorities yield different times—but we're not sure how Disney determines which attractions are scheduled earlier and which later.

**10. CHOOSE INITIAL RETURN TIMES** Next, MDE will give you four different sets of FastPass+ return times, grouped as Options A, B, and C, plus Best Match. Each option contains one return time for each attraction that you selected in Step 8. Again, we're not sure how Disney assigns the return times or what Disney thinks "Best Match" means. We do know that you have to choose all of the return times in Options A–C and Best Match. For now, choose the set of return times that's closest to what you want, and you'll be able to modify them in the next step.

**11. MODIFY RETURN TIMES OR ATTRACTIONS** If the initial set of FastPass+ return times conflicts with your plans, you can check whether alternate times are available that better fit your schedule. The good news is that you can change each attraction's return times separately. Plus, if none of the return times for a particular attraction work for you, you can pick another attraction at this stage without having to start over.

OK, you've booked one set of FastPasses for one park visit—now you'll need to repeat Steps 6–11 for every park you plan to visit, on every day of your trip. Simple, no?

A reader from White Plains, New York, found it all too much work:

> It's frustrating that you have to pick three attractions, when often I wanted to choose only one or two. It was also tough to set up for a big group—we ended up just getting the same FastPasses for everyone.

You've gotta hand it to Disney. Making FastPass+ reservations online combines the efficiency of a third-world bureaucracy with all the excitement of double-entry bookkeeping.

*unofficial* **TIP**
To see how Adolf Hitler feels about FastPass+, go to **tinyurl.com/hitlerfastpass.**

### Buying Tickets and Making FastPass+ Reservations On Arrival

If (1) you buy your admission the day you arrive at the parks or (2) you have to delay making your FastPass+ selections until you're inside, Disney has placed new computer terminals throughout the parks where you can make reservations; we've listed the specific locations in each theme park's chapter. Each set of terminals—look for the FP+ KIOSK signs—is staffed by a group of cast members who can walk you through the reservation process.

If you're tech-challenged, not to worry: You can use a paper Fast-Pass+ form, sort of like a cafeteria menu, that lets you tick off checkboxes next to the rides you want to experience. A cast member will take your form and enter your selections into the kiosk for you. You'll still need to provide your MDE username and password, however.

Be aware that the number of kiosks is limited, and most locations can process reservations for no more than 150 people per hour, as a Cleveland family found out:

> On our first day, I had to wait in line for around a half-hour at a Fast-Pass+ kiosk, and by the time it was my turn they had run out of passes for two of the three selections I had wanted: Peter Pan's Flight and Enchanted Tales with Belle. I was a pro by our third day there, but I miss the old system, which was much more user-friendly.

**RETURNING TO RIDE** Each FastPass+ reservation lasts for an hour, and Disney officially enforces the ride return time. Thus, if you make a FastPass+ reservation to ride Space Mountain at 7:30 p.m., you have until 8:30 p.m. to either use it or change it to something else. Just like a restaurant reservation, your FastPass+ may be canceled if you don't show up on time. In practice, however, we've found you can usually be up to 5 minutes early or 15 minutes late to use your reservation.

*unofficial* **TIP**
You'll be notified of any issues with FastPass+ reservations through the My Disney Experience mobile app.

When you return to Space Mountain at the designated time, you'll be directed to a FAST-PASS+ RETURN line. Before you enter the line, you'll need to validate your reservation by touching your MagicBand or RFID ticket to a reader at the FastPass+ Return entrance. Then you'll proceed with minimal waiting to the attraction's preshow or boarding area.

If technical problems cause an attraction to be closed during your return time, Disney will automatically adjust your FastPass+ reservation in one of three ways:

1. If it's early in the day, Disney will offer you the chance to return to the attraction at any point in the day after it reopens.

2. Alternatively, Disney may let you choose another FastPass+ attraction in the same park, on the same day.

3. If it's late in the day, Disney will automatically give you another selection good for any FastPass+ attraction at any park the following day.

At a number of FastPass+ attractions, listed in the chart below, the time gap between getting your pass and returning to ride can range from 3 to 7 hours. To ensure that you have enough time to ride on the day of your visit, either book FastPass+ in advance for these attractions or reserve them in the parks as early in the day as possible.

| GET FASTPASS+ *BEFORE 11 A.M.* FOR THE FOLLOWING: | | | | | | |
|---|---|---|---|---|---|---|
| **MAGIC KINGDOM** | | | | | | |
| Buzz Lightyear's Space Ranger Spin | Peter Pan's Flight | Seven Dwarfs Mine Train | Space Mountain | Splash Mountain | Winnie the Pooh | *Frozen* Meet-and-Greet |
| **EPCOT** | Mission: SPACE | | Soarin' | Test Track | | |
| **ANIMAL KINGDOM** | Expedition Everest | Kilimanjaro Safaris | | | | |
| **DHS** | Rock 'n' Roller Coaster | | Toy Story Midway Mania! | | | |

## FastPass+ Rules

Disney has put rules in place to prevent guests from obtaining certain combinations of FastPass+ reservations before they get to the parks:

**RULE #1: You can obtain only one advance FastPass+ reservation per attraction, per day, but you can get more once you're in the park and you've used your first set of three.** You can't make multiple advance FastPass+ reservations for, say, Toy Story Midway Mania!—you must select three different attractions. But once you've entered Hollywood Studios for the day and your first three reservations have been used or have expired, you can obtain more for Toy Story Midway Mania! if they're available.

It's generally a bad idea to make advance FastPass+ reservations for any of the evening parades or fireworks, because you won't be able to get any more reservations while you're in the park. We suggest checking around 4 p.m. to see if any reservations are available for the fireworks and parades. If they are and you're done with the headliner attractions, go ahead and grab a FastPass+.

**RULE #2: FastPass+ reservation times can't overlap**—Disney's computer system doesn't allow it. If you've got a FastPass+ reservation for 2–3 p.m., you can't make another reservation later than 1 p.m. or earlier than 3 p.m. in the same park.

**FASTPASS+ TIERS** Disney also prohibits guests from using FastPass+ on all of a park's headliner attractions. The practice, known informally as "FastPass+ tiers," was in effect only at Epcot and Disney's Hollywood Studios at press time but will probably be extended to all four parks eventually.

At Epcot, by way of example, the FastPass+ attractions are divided into the following two tiers:

| TIER A (*Choose* 1) | TIER B (*Choose* 2) |
| --- | --- |
| • *IllumiNations* | • *Captain EO* |
| • Living with the Land | • Epcot Character Spot |
| • Soarin' | • Journey into Imagination |
| • Test Track | • Maelstrom |
| | • Mission: SPACE (Green or Orange) |
| | • Spaceship Earth |
| | • The Seas with Nemo & Friends |
| | • *Turtle Talk with Crush* |

FastPass+ lets you choose only one attraction from Tier A and two attractions from Tier B. Note that Tier A comprises the attractions with the longest lines: This ensures that most guests get to choose either Soarin' or Test Track. Also, note that few of the attractions in Tier B actually require FastPass+ for most of the year.

The system upsets quite a few guests, such as this Baltimore reader:

*We were at Epcot on the last day of the traditional Fastpass system, and we were able to ride Test Track once with a short line and then later use Fastpass for it and Soarin'. The next day, we discovered you had to pick either Soarin' OR Test Track. As for the other Tier A attractions . . . Maelstrom on the same level as Test Track and Soarin? Give me a break!*

*unofficial* **TIP**
Because an attraction's FastPass+ availability is limited by its hourly rider capacity, those who book last-minute trips or buy admission at the gate may find that reservations are no longer available at their favorite attractions.

Again, though, the tiers don't apply beyond your first three advance FastPass+ reservations—any reservations you make beyond the first three when you're in the parks are totally up to you.

Clearly, the FastPass+ rules are designed to do three things: encourage you to stay at a Disney resort, book your trip well in advance, and tell Disney exactly where you plan to be every day. These three things increase Disney's revenue. They also decrease Disney's operating expenses, because Disney can adjust its staffing levels at each park based on how many people have made FastPass+ reservations. More importantly, by promising lower wait times in advance, Disney encourages you to spend more time at its parks and discourage you from last-minute trips to Universal or other parks.

### How FastPass+ Affects Your Waits in Line

At press time, there were only about 10 Walt Disney World attractions at which FastPass+ was having a noticeable effect on standby lines.

That's according to our initial analysis of 500,000 standby wait times collected at Walt Disney World since FastPass+ went into effect in January, 2014. We compared those with 3.9 million standby wait times collected across Walt Disney World since 2009 and adjusted for higher attendance levels in 2013 and 2014.

Standby wait times are down significantly at these attractions:

- Winnie the Pooh (-11 minutes)
- Space Mountain (-11 minutes)
- Tower of Terror (-7)
- Expedition Everest (-6)

One possible reason for the decrease in wait times is that before FastPass+, guests would use legacy Fastpass much more often. Now that there are limits on the number of FastPass+ reservations that guests can obtain in advance, coupled with the byzantine process for obtaining FastPasses online, people are riding these attractions less frequently.

Wait times are *up* at these attractions:

- DINOSAUR (+12 minutes)
- Pirates of the Caribbean (+10)
- Primeval Whirl (+7)
- Jungle Cruise (+7)
- The Haunted Mansion (+6)
- Spaceship Earth (+5)
- Kilimanjaro Safaris (+5)

We think waits are up at DINOSAUR because (a) Disney requires guests to choose three FastPass+ attractions and (b) DINOSAUR appears at the top of the alphabetical list of attractions to choose from. In the past, people would have had to hike to a remote corner of the park to find DINOSAUR's Fastpass machines. Now that DINOSAUR is a more visible choice in the app, it's getting more traffic.

Pirates of the Caribbean, The Haunted Mansion, and Spaceship Earth didn't have Fastpass in the couple of years leading up to the introduction of FastPass+. Here, we think the increase in wait times here owes primarily to the preferential treatment FastPass+ guests get in boarding these rides. It's possible for cast members to load 10, 20, or 30 FastPass+ guests for every 1 standby guest in line, and enough people are selecting these attractions as their third FastPass+ choice for that policy to have an impact.

We're not sure what accounts for the small increases at Kilimanjaro Safaris or Primeval Whirl, both of which had legacy FastPass. Maybe, like DINOSAUR, Primeval Whirl is the third choice of a lot of Animal Kingdom guests, or maybe people who would have otherwise run to the Safaris standby line in the morning are sleeping in a bit more on their vacation. If you've chosen either of these two attractions for FastPass+, write or e-mail us to explain why.

## How FastPass+ Affects Your Touring Plans

We think most *Unofficial Guide* readers will probably spend a few less minutes per day walking around the parks, because they no longer need to walk to an attraction's Fastpass machines. The time saved from walking is slightly more than the overall increases in standby waits at secondary attractions, so FastPass+—when it works—is roughly a break-even proposition for folks using our touring plans.

We say "when it works" because we've heard from plenty of readers whose waits in return lines are significantly longer than expected. The issue seems to be the speed at which the attractions' RFID readers can confirm a FastPass+ reservation stored on a MagicBand.

In the old Fastpass system, a cast member usually took only a few seconds to glance at the time on the paper pass before sending you on to the return line. Plus, the cast member usually looked at just one Fastpass for an entire family, on the assumption that everyone's passes were the same.

The new computer system is taking around 15–30 seconds per person, to read the band, look up the reservation, and validate it. And every family member must submit to the validation. This isn't an issue when guests' returns are spread somewhat evenly throughout the day, but it stops the line dead when a big group arrives at once. The result has been occasional waits of up to 30 minutes to redeem a FastPass+ reservation—sometimes longer than the standby wait for the same ride.

Thankfully, Disney is putting a lot of effort into streamlining the validation process, which we expect to be smoothed out by the beginning of 2015.

## Your FastPass+ Priorities at Each Park

Including the touring plans in this book and on our website, we've updated almost 200 touring plans to use FastPass+ exclusively. Each plan now lists the suggested FastPass+ start times for the attractions that will save you the most time in line, like this:

### SUGGESTED START TIMES FOR FASTPASS+ RESERVATIONS

- Peter Pan's Flight: 10 a.m.
- Buzz Lightyear's Space Ranger Spin: 5 p.m.
- *Enchanted Tales with Belle:* 7 p.m.

When we updated the plans, we kept count of how many times each attraction was identified as needing FastPass+. It turns out that this is a prioritized list of the attractions for which you should use FastPass+ to avoid long waits in line. We've added this information to a new Fast-Pass+ section in each theme park's chapter.

## Customized Touring Plans and FastPass+

The touring plans in this guide, which have all been revised to incorporate FastPass+, are our most efficient, provided you're willing to arrive at the park 35–60 minutes before opening. Likewise, both our computer-optimized custom plans and our Lines app support FastPass+. With these, you choose the attractions you want to experience, including character greetings, parades, fireworks, meals, and midday breaks, and we'll give you a step-by-step itinerary for your specific dates of travel showing you how to see everything with minimal waits in line. The touring plans can incorporate your existing FastPass+ reservations and suggest where to use any remaining opportunities.

You can update FastPass+ reservations while you're in the park, too. If you decide to change a reservation from Splash Mountain to Big Thunder Mountain, you can tell Lines to reoptimize your plan based on your new FastPass+ times. This allows you to handle any situation while still minimizing your waits for the rest of the day.

That said, most of the Studios' and Animal Kingdom's shows, never require FastPass+. The touring plans already do a good job of getting you to the show at least 15 minutes in advance (or earlier for *Fantasmic!*), in which case you'll almost always be able to get in to see that performance. In the worst-case scenario, you'll have to wait only until the next show. Also, because you can get a FastPass+ reservation for either *Fantasmic!* or Toy Story Midway Mania! at the Studios, you'll almost always end up with a shorter wait in line if you use the Toy Story FastPass+.

The same logic applies at Disney World's parades and fireworks. We don't usually recommend using FastPass+ for the Main Street Electrical Parade or *Wishes* fireworks at the Magic Kingdom, *IllumiNations* at Epcot, or many theater shows (unless you've got extra FastPasses at the end of your second day). FastPass+ at parades, fireworks, and shows usually guarantees you only somewhere to sit or stand. Because you still have to arrive early to claim a prime viewing location, you end up not saving much time. A reader from Charleston, South Carolina, figured this out on his own:

> *FastPass+ for* IllumiNations *and shows like* Beauty and the Beast *is a waste. They give away many more reservations for* IllumiNations *than actually provide a good view, so unless you arrive early and stake out a place (which you can do without FastPass+), there really is no point. For* Beauty and the Beast, *they don't reserve any special seating—you just get a guaranteed seat, which, at least in my experience, is unnecessary if you just arrive 15–20 minutes before the show.*

## Readers React to FastPass+

FastPass+ generates more comments than anything we've seen in years. A mother from Kansas likes the ability to schedule rides in advance:

> *It was great to schedule our FastPasses ahead of time and know when and where we were going to be. If a ride was closed during our scheduled time, we got an e-mail, and we were able to go back at any time the rest of the day or switch the attraction or time.*

A Columbia, Maryland, woman, however, laments that ride reservations are yet another chore on her vacation to-do list:

> *Between the need for scheduling meals 180 days in advance and rides 60 days out, Disney World has become a vacation for those who enjoy planning every hour of their day.*

A common complaint is that FastPass+ is targeted to tech-savvy younger guests, as this 60-something from Bemidji, Minnesota, notes:

> *Many seniors, and a surprising number of others, aren't into technology. I have a laptop and an old-fashioned flip phone, and my husband has a Kindle for reading—that's it. I know a lot of people can't go anywhere without their gadgets, but there are a LOT of us, young and old,*

*who don't have them or don't want to use them on vacation. It seems that those without iPhones, etc., are at a disadvantage.*

# UNDERSTANDING WALT DISNEY WORLD ATTRACTIONS

DISNEY WORLD'S PRIMARY APPEAL IS IN ITS rides and shows. Understanding how these are engineered to accommodate guests is interesting and invaluable to developing an efficient itinerary.

All attractions, regardless of location, are affected by two elements: capacity and popularity. Capacity is how many guests the attraction can serve at one time. Popularity shows how well visitors like an attraction. Capacity can be adjusted at some attractions. It's possible, for example, to add trams at the Studio Backlot Tour at Disney's Hollywood Studios or put extra boats on the Magic Kingdom's Jungle Cruise. Generally, however, capacity remains relatively fixed.

Designers try to match capacity and popularity as closely as possible. A high-capacity ride that isn't popular is a failure. Lots of money, space, and equipment have been poured into the attraction, yet there are empty seats. Journey into Imagination at Epcot fits this profile.

It's extremely unusual for a new attraction not to measure up, but it's fairly common for an older ride to lose appeal. Some attractions, such as Space Mountain at the Magic Kingdom, have sustained great appeal years beyond their debut, while others declined in popularity after a few years. Most attractions, however, work through the honeymoon, then settle down to handle the level of demand for which they were designed. When this happens, there are enough interested guests during peak hours to fill almost every seat, but not so many that long lines develop.

Sometimes Disney correctly estimates an attraction's popularity but fouls the equation by mixing in a third variable such as location. Spaceship Earth, the ride inside the geosphere at Epcot, is a good example. Placing the ride squarely in the path of every person entering the park assures that it will be inundated during morning when the park is filling. On the flip side, *The American Adventure*, at the opposite end of Epcot, has huge capacity but plays to a partially filled theater until midafternoon, when guests finally reach that part of the park.

*unofficial* **TIP**
Generally, attractions are immensely popular when they're new, and thus have longer lines.

If demand is high and capacity is low, large lines materialize. The Studios' Toy Story Midway Mania! is the only headliner attraction without a minimum height requirement that is open during morning Extra Magic Hours. Thus, it's the only headliner many families can experience, so demand quickly outstrips the ride's capacity. The result of this mismatch is that children and parents often suffer hour-long waits for a 6½-minute ride.

Capacity design is predicated on averages: the average number of people in the park, the normal distribution of traffic to specific areas, and the average number of staff needed to operate the ride. On a holiday weekend, when the averages are exceeded, all but a few attractions operate at maximum capacity, and even then they're overwhelmed by huge crowds. On days of low attendance in the fall, capacity is often not even approximated, and guests can ride without a wait.

*unofficial* **TIP**
The Magic Kingdom offers the greatest variety in capacity and popularity, with vastly differing rides and shows.

Only the Magic Kingdom and Disney's Animal Kingdom offer low-capacity midway rides and spook-house "dark" rides. They range from state-of-the-art to antiquated. This diversity makes efficient touring of the Magic Kingdom much more challenging. If guests don't understand the capacity–popularity relationship and don't plan accordingly, they might spend most of the day in line.

Although Epcot, Animal Kingdom, and Disney's Hollywood Studios have fewer rides and shows than the Magic Kingdom, almost all their attractions are major features on par with the Magic Kingdom's Pirates of the Caribbean and The Haunted Mansion in scope, detail, imagination, and spectacle. All but one or two Epcot, Animal Kingdom, and DHS rides are fast-loading, and most have large capacities. Because Epcot, Animal Kingdom, and DHS attractions are generally well engineered and efficient, lines may appear longer than those in the Magic Kingdom but usually move more quickly. There are no midway rides at Epcot or DHS, and fewer attractions at those parks are intended for kids.

In the Magic Kingdom, crowds are more a function of the popularity and engineering of individual attractions. At Epcot and Animal Kingdom, traffic flow and crowding are more affected by park layout. For touring efficiency, it's important to understand how Magic Kingdom rides and shows operate. At Epcot and Animal Kingdom, this knowledge is less important.

To develop an efficient touring plan, it's necessary to understand how rides and shows are designed and function. We'll examine both.

## CUTTING YOUR TIME IN LINE BY UNDERSTANDING THE RIDES

WALT DISNEY WORLD HAS MANY TYPES OF RIDES. Some, such as The Great Movie Ride at Disney's Hollywood Studios, can carry more than 3,000 people an hour. At the other extreme, TriceraTop Spin at Animal Kingdom can handle only around 500 people an hour. Most rides fall somewhere in between. Many factors figure into how long you'll wait to experience a ride: its popularity; how it loads and unloads; how many persons can ride at once; how many units (cars, rockets, boats, flying elephants, and the like) are in service at a time; and how many cast members are available to operate the ride. Let's take the factors one by one.

### 1. How Popular Is the Ride?

Newer rides such as the Magic Kingdom's Seven Dwarfs Mine Train attract a lot of people, as do such longtime favorites as the same park's Big Thunder Mountain Railroad. If a ride is popular, you need to know how it operates in order to determine the best time to ride. But a ride need not be especially popular to generate long lines; in some cases, such lines are due not to a ride's popularity but to poor traffic engineering.

This is the case at the Mad Tea Party and Prince Charming Regal Carrousel (among others) in Fantasyland. Both rides serve only a small percentage of any day's attendance at the Magic Kingdom, yet because they take so long to load and unload, long lines form regardless.

### 2. How Does the Ride Load and Unload?

Some rides never stop. They're like conveyor belts that go around and around. These are "continuous loaders." The Haunted Mansion at the Magic Kingdom and Under the Sea: Journey of the Little Mermaid and Spaceship Earth at Epcot are continuous loaders. The number of people that can be moved through in an hour depends on how many cars— "doom buggies" or whatever—are on the conveyor. The Haunted Mansion and Spaceship Earth have lots of cars on the conveyor, and each consequently can move more than 2,000 people an hour.

Other rides are "interval loaders." Cars are unloaded, loaded, and dispatched at set intervals (sometimes controlled manually, sometimes by computer). Space Mountain in Tomorrowland is an interval loader. It has two tracks (the ride has been duplicated in the same facility). Each track can run as many as 14 space capsules, released at 36-, 26-, or 21-second intervals. (The bigger the crowd, the shorter the interval.)

In one kind of interval loader, empty cars, as in Space Mountain's space capsules, return to where they reload. In a second kind, such as Splash Mountain, one group of riders enters the vehicle while the previous group departs. Rides of the latter type are referred to as "in and out" interval loaders. As a boat docks, those who have just completed their ride exit to the left; at almost the same time, those waiting to ride enter the boat from the right. The reloaded boat is released to the dispatch point a few yards down the line, where it's launched according to the interval being used.

Interval loaders of both types can be very efficient people-movers if (1) the dispatch (launch) interval is relatively short and (2) the ride can accommodate many vehicles at one time. Since many boats can float through Pirates of the Caribbean at one time, and since the dispatch interval is short, almost 3,000 people can see this attraction each hour.

The least efficient rides, in terms of traffic engineering, are "cycle rides," also called "stop and go" rides. Those waiting to ride exchange places with those who have just ridden. Unlike in-and-out interval rides, cycle rides shut down during loading and unloading. While one boat is loading and unloading in It's a Small World (an interval loader), many other boats are advancing through the ride. But when Dumbo touches down, the whole ride is at a standstill until the next flight launches (ditto Prince Charming Regal Carrousel and the Mad Tea Party).

In cycle rides, the time in motion is "ride time." The time the ride idles while loading and unloading is "load time." Load time plus ride time equals "cycle time," or the time from the start of one run of the ride until the start of the next. The only cycle rides in Disney World are in the Magic Kingdom and Disney's Animal Kingdom.

### 3. How Many Persons Can Ride at One Time?

This figure expresses "system capacity," or the number of people who can ride at one time. The greater the carrying capacity of a ride (all other things being equal), the more visitors it can accommodate per hour. Some rides can add extra units (cars, boats, and such) as crowds build, to increase capacity; others, such as the Astro Orbiter in Tomorrowland, have a fixed capacity (it's impossible to add more rockets).

## 4. How Many Units Are in Service at a Given Time?

Unit is our term for the vehicle in which you ride. At the Mad Tea Party the unit is a teacup, at Peter Pan's Flight a pirate ship. On some rides (mostly cycle rides), the number of units operating at one time is fixed. There are always 32 flying elephants at Dumbo and 90 horses on Prince Charming Regal Carrousel. There's no way to increase the capacity of such rides by adding units. On a busy day, the only way to carry more people each hour on a fixed-unit cycle ride is to shorten the loading time or decrease the ride time. The bottom line: On a busy day for a cycle ride, you'll wait longer and possibly be rewarded with a shorter ride. This is why we steer you away from cycle rides unless you're willing to ride them early in the morning or late at night. These are the cycle rides:

**THE MAGIC KINGDOM** Astro Orbiter, Dumbo the Flying Elephant, Mad Tea Party, The Magic Carpets of Aladdin, Prince Charming Regal Carrousel, The Barnstormer

**DISNEY'S ANIMAL KINGDOM** TriceraTop Spin

Many other rides throughout Disney World can increase their capacity by adding units as crowds build. For example, if attendance is light, Big Thunder Mountain Railroad in Frontierland can start the day by running only one of its five mine trains from one of two available loading platforms. If lines build, the other platform is opened and more mine trains are placed into operation. At capacity, the five trains can carry about 2,400 persons an hour. Likewise, Star Tours at Disney's Hollywood Studios can increase its capacity by using all its simulators, and the Maelstrom boat ride at Epcot can add more Viking ships. Sometimes a long queue will disappear almost instantly when new units are brought online. When an interval loader places more units into operation, it usually shortens the dispatch intervals, allowing more units to be dispatched more often.

## 5. How Many Cast Members Are Available to Operate the Ride?

Adding cast members to a ride can allow more units to operate or additional loading or holding areas to open. In the Magic Kingdom, Pirates of the Caribbean and It's a Small World can run two waiting lines and loading zones. The Haunted Mansion has a 1½-minute preshow staged in a "stretch room." On busy days, a second stretch room can be activated, permitting a more continuous flow of visitors to the actual loading area.

Additional staff makes a world of difference to some cycle rides. Often, the Mad Tea Party has only one attendant. This person alone must clear visitors from the ride just completed, admit and seat visitors for the upcoming ride, check that each teacup is secured, return to the control panel, issue instructions to the riders, and finally activate the ride (whew!). A second attendant divides these responsibilities and cuts loading time by 25–50%.

## CUTTING YOUR TIME IN LINE BY UNDERSTANDING THE SHOWS

MANY FEATURED ATTRACTIONS AT DISNEY WORLD are theater presentations. While they aren't as complex as rides, understanding them from a traffic-engineering standpoint may save you touring time.

Most theater attractions operate in three phases:

1. Guests are in the theater viewing the presentation.

2. Guests who have passed through the turnstile wait in a holding area or lobby. They will be admitted to the theater as soon as the show in progress concludes. Several attractions offer a preshow in their lobby to entertain guests until they're admitted to the main show. Examples include *Enchanted Tiki Room* and *Stitch's Great Escape!* in the Magic Kingdom; *Captain EO* at Epcot; and *Muppet-Vision 3-D* at Disney's Hollywood Studios.

3. A line waits outside. Guests in line enter the lobby when there's room and will ultimately move into the theater.

Theater capacity, the presentation's popularity, and park attendance determine how long lines will be at a show. Except for holidays and other days of heavy attendance, the longest wait for a show usually doesn't exceed the length of one performance. As almost all theater attractions run continuously, stopping only long enough for the previous audience to leave and the waiting audience to enter, a performance will be in progress when you arrive. *O Canada!* at Epcot's Canada Pavilion lasts 15 minutes; your longest wait under normal circumstances is about 15 minutes if you arrive just after the show has begun.

## A WORD ABOUT DISNEY THRILL RIDES

READERS OF ALL AGES should try to be open-minded about Disney "thrill rides." In comparison with those at other theme parks, the Disney attractions are quite tame, with more emphasis on sights, atmosphere, and special effects than on the motion, speed, or feel of the ride. While we suggest you take Disney's pre-ride warnings seriously, we can tell you that guests of all ages report enjoying rides such as Tower of Terror, Big Thunder Mountain, and Splash Mountain.

That said, seniors who experience Disney thrills generally enjoy the smoother rides like Splash Mountain, Big Thunder Mountain, and Tower of Terror and tend to dislike more jerky attractions. This letter from a Gig Harbor, Washington, woman is typical:

> *I am a senior woman of small stature and good health. My experience is that all of the rides, with the exception of Star Tours, were wonderful. Star Tours is too jerky and fast, the music is too loud, and I found it to be unacceptable.*

Notwithstanding this letter, most comments we receive from seniors about Star Tours are positive. The Rock 'n' Roller Coaster and Expedition Everest, however, are a different story. Both are serious coasters that share more in common with Revenge of the Mummy at Universal Studios than they do with Space Mountain or Big Thunder Mountain.

Mission: SPACE, a high-tech simulation ride at Epcot, is a toss-up (pun intended)—it absolutely has the potential to make you sick. After many guest incidents, Disney made half of the ride a tamer, no-spin experience—one that's less likely to launch your lunch.

# CENTRAL FLORIDA ROLLER COASTERS

IF YOU EVER GO to a party where guests are discussing Immelmanns, heartline rolls, dive loops, and LIM launchers, don't mistake the guests

## The Top 16 Central Florida Roller Coasters

| COASTER | HOST PARK | CENTRAL FLORIDA RANK | INTER-NATIONAL RANK |
|---|---|---|---|
| MANTA | SeaWorld | 1 | 36 |
| EXPEDITION EVEREST | Animal Kingdom | 2 | 104 |
| CHINESE FIREBALL | Islands of Adventure | 3 | 57 |
| CHEETAH HUNT | Busch Gardens | 4 | 72 |
| MONTU | Busch Gardens | 5 | 16 |
| INCREDIBLE HULK COASTER | Islands of Adventure | 6 | 66 |
| KUMBA | Busch Gardens | 7 | 29 |
| HUNGARIAN HORNTAIL | Islands of Adventure | 8 | 71 |
| KRAKEN | SeaWorld | 9 | 59 |
| SHEIKRA | Busch Gardens | 10 | 37 |
| HOLLYWOOD RIP RIDE ROCKIT | Universal Studios FL | 11 | 125 |
| ROCK 'N' ROLLER COASTER | DHS | 12 | 155 |
| GWAZI | Busch Gardens | 13 | 121 |
| REVENGE OF THE MUMMY | Universal Studios FL | 14 | 107 |
| SPACE MOUNTAIN | Magic Kingdom | 15 | 150 |
| BIG THUNDER MOUNTAIN | Magic Kingdom | 16 | 189 |
| ESCAPE FROM GRINGOTTS | Universal Studios FL | N/A* | N/A |
| SEVEN DWARFS MINE TRAIN | Magic Kingdom | N/A | N/A |

Source: **bestrollercoasterpoll.com**    *N/A = data unavailable at press time

for fighter pilots. Incredibly, you'll be among the intelligentsia of roller-coaster aficionados. This growing population, along with millions of other not-quite-so-fanatical coaster lovers, is united in the belief that roller coasters are—or ought to be—the heart of every theme park.

Though Disney pioneered the concept of super-coasters with the **Matterhorn Bobsleds** at Disneyland in 1959, it took them 16 years to add another roller coaster, **Space Mountain** at Walt Disney World, to their repertoire. In relatively quick succession followed Space Mountain at Disneyland and **Big Thunder Mountain Railroad** at both Disneyland's and Walt Disney World's Magic Kingdoms. Irrespective of the Mountains' popularity, Disney didn't build another coaster in the United States for almost 20 years. In the interim, coasters enjoyed a technical revolution that included aircraft carrier–type launching devices and previously unimaginable loops, corkscrews, vertical drops, and train speeds. Through all this, Disney sat on the sidelines. After all, Disney parks didn't offer "rides" but, rather, "adventure experiences" in which the sensation of the ride itself was always secondary to storylines and visuals. But when archrival Universal announced plans for its Islands of Adventure theme park, featuring an entire arsenal of thrill rides, Disney—spurred by competition—went to work.

The upshot was a banner year in 1999 for Central Florida coasters, with **The Incredible Hulk Coaster, Dueling Dragons: Fire** and **Ice** (now

| TYPE | LENGTH (FEET) | HEIGHT (FEET) | INVERSIONS | SPEED (MPH) | RIDE TIME | RIDE FEEL |
|---|---|---|---|---|---|---|
| Steel/inverted | 3,359 | 140 | 4 | 56 | 2:35 | Very smooth |
| Steel/sit-down | 4,424 | 112 | 0 | 50 | 3:45 | Very smooth |
| Steel/inverted | 3,200 | 125 | 5 | 60 | 2:25 | Very smooth |
| Steel/sit-down | 4,429 | 102 | 1 | 60 | 3:30 | Smooth |
| Steel/inverted | 3,983 | 150 | 7 | 60 | 3:00 | Smooth |
| Steel/sit-down | 3,700 | 110 | 7 | 67 | 2:15 | Smooth |
| Steel/sit-down | 3,978 | 143 | 7 | 60 | 2:54 | Slightly rough |
| Steel/inverted | 3,200 | 125 | 5 | 55 | 2:25 | Very smooth |
| Steel/sit-down | 4,177 | 149 | 7 | 65 | 2:02 | Smooth |
| Steel/sit-down | 3,188 | 200 | 1 | 70 | 3:00 | Very smooth |
| Steel/sit-down | 3,800 | 167 | 2 | 65 | 2:30 | Rough |
| Steel/sit-down | 3,403 | 80 | 3 | 57 | 1:22 | Very smooth |
| Wood/sit-down | 3,508 | 91 | 0 | 51 | 2:30 | Very rough |
| Steel/sit-down | 2,200 | 45 | 0 | 40 | 3:00 | Very smooth |
| Steel/sit-down | 3,196 | 90 | 0 | 27 | 2:35 | Rough |
| Steel/sit-down | 2,780 | 45 | 0 | 36 | 3:30 | Smooth |
| Steel/sit-down | N/A | N/A | 0 | N/A | N/A | Smooth |
| Steel/sit-down | 2,000 | 41 | 0 | 34 | 2:15 | Very smooth |

**Dragon Challenge: Chinese Fireball** and **Hungarian Horntail**) opening at Universal's Islands of Adventure, the **Rock 'n' Roller Coaster** coming online at the Disney's Hollywood Studios, and **Gwazi,** a wooden coaster, premiering at Busch Gardens Tampa. Close on their heels in early 2000 was **Kraken** at SeaWorld. These six coasters made Space and Big Thunder mountains look like cupcakes and wienie buns. All except Gwazi featured inversions, corkscrews, and rollovers. Best of all for coaster lovers, none of the players were content to rest on their laurels. Universal Studios came back with **Revenge of the Mummy** in 2004, followed by **SheiKra** at Busch Gardens in 2005 and the awe-inspiring **Expedition Everest** at Disney's Animal Kingdom in 2006.

The spring and summer of 2009 marked the debut of **Manta** at SeaWorld Orlando and **Hollywood Rip Ride Rockit** at Universal Studios Florida. Manta is an inverted steel coaster on which riders are suspended under the tracks, prone and facedown; Rip Ride Rockit is also a steel coaster, only here you sit as opposed to being suspended. The first hill is a 16-second *vertical* climb, followed by a 65-mph plunge.

The spring and summer of 2014 witnessed the unveiling of two new coasters: **Seven Dwarfs Mine Train** at the Magic Kingdom and **Harry Potter and the Escape from Gringotts** at Universal Studios Florida. Seven Dwarfs is a family coaster with modest speeds and small hills; its notable feature is that the ride vehicles swing slightly from side to side. Gringotts is a 3-D steel coaster ride through the bank vaults made famous in the Harry Potter books and movies. Stunning visual effects are emphasized over raw speed or height—there are no loops or inversions.

Today there are 15 big-time coasters in Central Florida, 20 if you want to include the measurably tamer Space Mountain, Seven Dwarfs Mine Train, and Big Thunder Mountain at the Magic Kingdom, plus Flying School and Coastersaurus at Legoland. The Incredible Hulk, Cheetah Hunt, Rock 'n' Roller Coaster, and Revenge of the Mummy feature accelerated launch systems in which the train is hurled as opposed to ratcheted up the first hill; Rock 'n' Roller Coaster and Revenge of the Mummy are indoor coasters augmented by mind-blowing visuals, special effects, and soundtracks. Expedition Everest is the most fully realized attraction of the 15, with a storyline, astounding attention to detail, and a track that plunges in and out of the largest (albeit artificial) mountain in Florida. Kraken, Cheetah Hunt, and Expedition Everest are the longest of the lot, their tracks exceeding 4,000 feet long. **Montu** at Busch Gardens, along with Dragon Challenge at Universal, are inverted, meaning the track is overhead and your feet dangle.

Having ridden all the coasters until we could no longer walk straight, we rank them as follows. (For a glossary of roller-coaster terminology, see **ultimaterollercoaster.com/coasters/glossary.**)

**1. MANTA, SEAWORLD** There are coasters you barely survive and coasters you savor. Manta is clearly among the latter: a supersmooth experience that leaves you grinning from ear to ear. An inverted flying steel coaster, Manta gently lowers you into a suspended Superman position and you, well, fly. Many coaster fans consider the most memorable moments a sweeping loop in the first half of the ride and near-misses of a pond or rock wall (depending where you're sitting) in the second half. Technically, Manta has it all. After a first drop of 113 feet, it zooms through a pretzel loop, a 360-degree incline roll, and two corkscrews while reaching a height of 140 feet and speeds of 55 mph.

**2. EXPEDITION EVEREST, DISNEY'S ANIMAL KINGDOM** This coaster offers such a complete package, with something to dazzle each of the senses, that it overcomes its lack of loops and inversions. The segment on Expedition Everest where the train corkscrews downward in the dark may be the most unusual in roller-coaster annals. Though you begin the segment in reverse, you soon succumb to an almost disembodied and dreamlike state of drifting in a void, with an exhilarating sense of speed but with no certain sense of direction. When you can see, there's plenty to look at. The mountain, with its caverns, cliffs, and crags, is a work of art; then there's that pesky yeti who menaces you throughout the ride. And for those of you who hate rough coasters, Expedition Everest is oh-so-smooth.

**3. DRAGON CHALLENGE: CHINESE FIREBALL, UNIVERSAL'S ISLANDS OF ADVENTURE** Previously called Dueling Dragons, Dragon Challenge was given a new theme and incorporated into The Wizarding World of Harry Potter–Hogsmeade, which opened at Universal's Islands of Adventure in June 2010. The number-three ranking was disputed within our research group, with several of us placing Montu at Busch Gardens third. Dragon Challenge has two trains, Chinese Fireball and Hungarian Horntail (formerly Fire and Ice), that are launched in short succession, creating a sense of chase between the two. Though both trains have identical lift hills, their respective layouts are different, and Chinese Fireball offers the superior ride. The action is unrelenting yet very smooth, with a 115-foot drop, five inversions, and speeds of 60 mph. Because this is an inverted coaster, your feet dangle throughout.

**4. CHEETAH HUNT, BUSCH GARDENS** With a 4,429-foot track, Cheetah Hunt is the longest coaster in Florida. A complete experience both tactilely and visually, Cheetah Hunt hurls you through the scenic, wildlife-rich Serengeti Plain section of the park. The ride emulates the hunting style of the cheetah with sudden bursts of speed. This is accomplished with linear-synchronous-motor launches similar to the accelerated launch systems of The Incredible Hulk Coaster at Universal and Rock 'n' Roller Coaster at DHS. With Cheetah Hunt, however, you're launched three times—once at the start of the ride and twice more during the circuit. The layout includes a 130-foot drop into a shallow canyon, over-banked turns, parabolas, and a heartline-roll inversion. The linear out-and-back course allows more opportunity for viewing the animals than would the more common concentric, twisting layouts from which it's almost impossible to take in your surroundings.

**5. MONTU, BUSCH GARDENS** Montu is a little longer than Chinese Fireball and features seven inversions—including loops of 104 and 60 feet and a 0-g roll—on a layout distinguished by its very tight turns. With an initial drop of 128 feet, Montu posts top speeds of 60 mph and pulls 3.8 g's. Also inverted, Montu is intense and exhilarating but less visually interesting than and not as smooth as Chinese Fireball.

**6. THE INCREDIBLE HULK COASTER, UNIVERSAL'S ISLANDS OF ADVENTURE** Hulk doesn't have any weak points. A tire-propelled launch system takes you from 0 to 40 mph in 2 seconds up the first hill, hurling you into a twisting dive of 105 feet. From there it's two loops, two flat-spin corkscrews, a cobra roll, and a plunge through a 150-foot-long tunnel to the end. You hit speeds of 67 mph and pull as many as 4 g's. Unequivocally, the Hulk has the best start of any roller coaster in Central Florida. The ride, however, is not quite as smooth as Chinese Fireball's, and it's not inverted like Chinese Fireball and Montu, which is why we've ranked it sixth.

**7. KUMBA, BUSCH GARDENS** With a track of almost 4,000 feet, seven inversions, a 135-foot first drop, g-forces of 3.8, a top speed of 60 mph, and a very tight layout, Kumba can hold its own with any coaster. Features include a 114-foot-tall vertical loop, two rolls, and interlocking corkscrews, among others. We find Kumba a little rough, but sitting toward the back of the train mitigates the problem somewhat.

**8. DRAGON CHALLENGE: HUNGARIAN HORNTAIL, UNIVERSAL'S ISLANDS OF ADVENTURE** Hungarian Horntail is Chinese Fireball's slightly less evil twin, with speeds of 55 mph and a first drop of 95 feet, compared with Chinese Fireball's 60 mph and 115 feet. So too Hungarian Horntail's design elements are different, though both coasters hit you with five inversions bundled in a mix of rolls, corkscrews, and a loop. Like Chinese Fireball, Hungarian Horntail is an inverted coaster.

**9. KRAKEN, SEAWORLD** Based on ancient myth, the Kraken was a ferocious sea monster kept caged by Poseidon, Greek god of the sea. Much of Kraken's track is over water, and the ride takes a number of sweeping dives into subterranean caverns. A very fast coaster, Kraken hits speeds of 65 mph with one drop of 144 feet, and it boasts loops, rolls, and corkscrews for a total of seven inversions. Though not inverted, the cars are open-sided and floorless.

**10. HOLLYWOOD RIP RIDE ROCKIT, UNIVERSAL STUDIOS** "The Triple R," as some locals call it, opened in August 2009 as Universal's second roller coaster. A steel sit-down coaster, RRR trades full inversions for steep dives and tight corkscrew turns. The ride is a lot more jarring than we expected, with a fair amount of lateral shaking. The gimmick here is that you can select your own music to accompany the ride. Views from the top of the 167-foot lift hill are killer. The Triple R reaches top speeds of 65 mph.

**11. SHEIKRA, BUSCH GARDENS** While the higher-rated coasters do a lot of things well, SheiKra is pretty much one-dimensional—it drops like a rock straight down (a sheikra is an African hawk known for diving vertically on its prey). That's right: a no-slope, 90-degree free fall. After scaling the 200-foot lift hill, the coaster descends over the lip of the first drop and brakes to a stop. There you're suspended, dangling for a few anxious moments until the train is released. On the way down, you hit speeds of 70 mph—a very high speed for roller coasters—and enjoy the best airtime of any Florida coaster. (Airtime is the sensation of floating when your body is forced up from the seat bottom, creating air between the seat and your body.) Following a loop, the drill is repeated on a second, more modest drop. The cars on SheiKra are the widest we've seen, seating eight people across in each of three rows. Accordingly, the track is very wide. This width, among other things, makes for a plodding, uninspiring ride except during the two big drops. More compelling is the view of downtown Tampa from the top of the lift hill.

**12. ROCK 'N' ROLLER COASTER, DISNEY'S HOLLYWOOD STUDIOS** This wasn't a unanimous ranking either. The Rock 'n' Roller Coaster reaches a height of only 80 feet, lasts only 1 minute and 22 seconds, and incorporates just a couple of design elements, but that 0- to 57-mph launch in 2 seconds is totally sweet. Rock 'n' Roller Coaster is a dark ride (that is, it's indoors) and the story is that you're on your way to an Aerosmith concert in Hollywood in a big stretch limousine. Speakers in each car blast a soundtrack of the group's hits synchronized with the myriad visuals that erupt out of the gloom. The ride is smooth. Not the biggest or baddest coaster in the realm, but like Expedition Everest, it'll put a big grin on your face every time.

**13. GWAZI, BUSCH GARDENS** As the only traditional wooden coaster of the 16 rides ranked, Gwazi at first looked like a snore: no inversions, corkscrews, loops, barrel rolls, or any of the other stuff that had been rearranging our innards. Wrong! This coaster serves up an unbelievably wild ride that seems literally out of control most of the time. Teeth-rattlingly rough, with much side-to-side lurching, Gwazi reaches a top speed of 51 mph but feels twice that fast. In the best wooden-coaster tradition, riders attempt to hold their arms in the air, but on Gwazi it's impossible. The track is hard to read, and the way the train shifts and banks surprises you constantly. Gwazi's coaster trains were replaced in 2011, making the ride marginally smoother (*marginally* being the operative word). Gwazi is a racing coaster (a dual-track roller coaster whose trains leave the station at the same moment and race each other through the circuit) with two trains, Lion/Yellow and Tiger/Blue. Of the two, Tiger/Blue gives you the biggest bang for your buck.

**14. REVENGE OF THE MUMMY, UNIVERSAL STUDIOS** If we were ranking attractions as opposed to roller coasters, this one would rank much higher. Revenge of the Mummy is a super-headliner hybrid, of which its coaster dimension is only one aspect. A complete description of the attraction can be found starting on page 689; for the moment, however, we can tell you that Revenge of the Mummy is a dark ride full of tricks and surprises, and in roller-coaster mode only for about a third of the ride. The ride is wild enough, but the visuals and special effects are among the best you'll find.

**15. SPACE MOUNTAIN, THE MAGIC KINGDOM** When you strip away the theme of this beloved Disney favorite, you're left with a souped-up version of the Wild Mouse, a midway staple with sharp turns and small, steep drops that runs with two- or four-passenger cars instead of trains. But when you put a Wild Mouse in the dark—where you can't anticipate the turns and drops—it's like feeding the mouse steroid-laced cheese. With Space Mountain, Disney turned a dinky coaster with no inversions and a top speed of 27 mph into a fairly robust attraction that set the standard for Disney thrill rides until the debut of The Twilight Zone Tower of Terror. Space Mountain may be close to the bottom of our ranking, but in the hearts of many theme park guests, it remains number one.

**16. BIG THUNDER MOUNTAIN RAILROAD, THE MAGIC KINGDOM** With its runaway-mine-train storyline, Big Thunder is long on great visuals but ranks as a very innocuous roller coaster. Though many riders consider it jerky and rough, it's a Rolls-Royce compared with the likes of Gwazi and Kumba at Busch Gardens. Unlike on Gwazi, it's not only possible but easy to ride with your arms in the air. Though a steel coaster, Big Thunder offers no inversions and a top speed of only 36 mph. Then again, the higher-ranked coasters don't offer falling boulders, flash floods, possums, buzzards, and dinosaur bones.

**17. HARRY POTTER AND THE ESCAPE FROM GRINGOTTS, UNIVERSAL STUDIOS** This was the most anticipated new attraction in the world in 2014, but like Seven Dwarfs Mine Train (below), Escape from Gringotts is mostly eye candy. This indoor steel coaster incorporates 3-D projection, amazingly detailed sets, and a storyline of the Potter Fab Three rumbling through the underground vaults of Gringotts Wizarding Bank as they try to escape archenemy Voldemort. There's a load of action, some nifty track-switching, and a free-fall simulation, but the ride itself is much tamer than that of Harry Potter and the Forbidden Journey, assuming you can handle the visuals. As far as the track goes, there's one big drop and one big up-launch, with no change in track elevation in between.

**18. SEVEN DWARFS MINE TRAIN, THE MAGIC KINGDOM** The mildest roller coaster on this list, Seven Dwarfs is designed to be the first or second roller-coaster experience for grade-schoolers. Its unique feature is that the ride vehicles swing slightly from side to side, which amplifies the turning sensation you feel in the ride's tight curves. Like Big Thunder, Seven Dwarfs is a steel coaster with no inversions, and it has a top speed of around 34 mph. Because the track is much smoother than Big Thunder's or Space Mountain's, you may not feel as if you're moving very fast.

# PART THREE

# ACCOMMODATIONS

## ▌ *The* BASIC CONSIDERATIONS

LOCATING A SUITABLE HOTEL OR CONDO is critical to planning any Walt Disney World vacation. The basic question is whether to stay inside the World. Luxury lodging can be found both in and out of Disney World. Budget lodging is another story. In the World, room rates range from about $100 on a weeknight during what Disney calls "Value season" to more than $1,300 per night during the holidays. Outside, rooms are as low as $35 a night.

Beyond affordability is convenience. We've lodged both in and out of Disney World, and there's special magic and peace of mind associated with staying inside the World. "I feel more a part of everything and less like a visitor," one guest writes.

There's no real hardship in staying outside Disney World and driving or taking a hotel shuttle to the theme parks. Meals can be less expensive, and rooming outside the World makes you more receptive to other Orlando-area attractions and eating spots. **Universal Studios** and **Universal's Islands of Adventure, Kennedy Space Center Visitor Complex, SeaWorld,** and **Gatorland** are well worth your attention.

Because Walt Disney World is so large, some off-property hotels are closer in time and distance to many of the theme parks than are some Disney resorts. Check our Hotel Information Chart on pages 269–286, which lists commuting times from both Disney and non-Disney hotels. Lodging prices can change, but it's possible to get a hotel room comparable to one at a Disney's Moderate resort for half the cost during holidays, or a room twice the size for the same money, all within a 15-minute drive of the Magic Kingdom.

If you have young children, read Part Six, Walt Disney World with Kids, before choosing lodging. Seniors, couples on a honeymoon or romantic holiday, and disabled guests should read the applicable sections of Part Seven, Special Tips for Special People, before booking.

### THE TAX MAN COMETH

SALES AND LODGING TAXES can add a chunk of change to the cost of your hotel room. Cumulative tax in Orange County is 12.5% and in adjacent Osceola County, 13%. Lake Buena Vista, the Universal Orlando area, International Drive, and all the Disney resorts except the All-Star Resorts are in Orange County.

## ABOUT HOTEL RENOVATIONS

WE INSPECT SEVERAL HUNDRED HOTELS in the Disney World area to compile the *Unofficial Guide*'s list of lodging choices. Each year we call each hotel to verify contact information and inquire about renovations or refurbishments. If a hotel has been renovated or has refurbished its guest rooms, we reinspect it, along with any new hotels, for the next edition of the *Guide*. Hotels reporting no improvements are rechecked every two years. We inspect most Disney-owned hotels every 6–12 months, and no less than once every two years.

*unofficial* **TIP**
Request a renovated room at your hotel—these can be much nicer than the older rooms.

Many hotels more than five years old, both in and out of the World, refurbish 10–20% of their guest rooms each year. This incremental approach minimizes disruption, but it makes your room assignment a crapshoot—you might luck into a newly renovated room, or you might be assigned a threadbare one.

Disney reservationists won't guarantee you a recently refurbished room but will note your request and will try to accommodate you. On the other hand, non-Disney hotels *will* often guarantee you an updated room when you book.

*unofficial* **TIP**
Power shoppers, rejoice: If you're staying on Disney property, you can charge theme park and Downtown Disney purchases to your hotel room.

## BENEFITS OF STAYING IN THE WORLD

GUESTS WHO STAY ON DISNEY PROPERTY enjoy privileges and amenities unavailable to those staying outside the World. Though some of these perks are advertising gimmicks, others are real and potentially valuable. Here are the benefits and what they mean:

**1. CONVENIENCE** If you don't have a car, commuting to the parks is easy via the Disney transportation system. This is especially advantageous if you stay in a hotel connected by monorail or boat service. If you have a car, however, dozens of hotels outside Disney World are within 5–10 minutes of theme-park parking lots.

**2. EARLY ACCESS TO RIDE AND RESTAURANT RESERVATIONS** Disney hotel and campground guests, along with guest staying at the Swan, Dolphin, and Four Seasons resorts, can make FastPass+ ride reservations 60 days before they arrive—30 days earlier than the general public. Disney resort guests can also make dining reservations up to 190 days before their visit, 10 more than the general public.

**3. EXTRA MAGIC HOURS AT THE THEME PARKS** Disney World lodging guests (including guests at the Hilton in the Downtown Disney Resort Area) are invited to enter a designated park 1 hour earlier than the general public each day or to enjoy a designated theme park for up to 2 hours after it closes to the general public in the evening.

Extra Magic Hours can be valuable if you know how to use them. They can also land you in gridlock. (See our detailed discussion starting on page 40.)

**4. BABYSITTING AND CHILD-CARE OPTIONS** Disney hotel and campground guests have several options for babysitting, child care, and children's programs. The **Polynesian Resort** and **Animal Kingdom Lodge,** along with several other Disney hotels, offer "clubs"—themed childcare centers where potty-trained children ages 3–12 can stay while the adults go out.

Though somewhat expensive, the clubs are highly regarded by children and parents. On the negative side, they're open only in the evening, and not all Disney hotels have them. If you're staying at a Disney hotel without a club, you're better off using a private in-room babysitting service (see page 354). In-room babysitting is also available at hotels outside Disney World.

**5. DISNEY'S MAGICAL EXPRESS SERVICE** If you arrive in Orlando by air, Disney will collect your checked baggage and send it by bus directly to your Walt Disney World resort, allowing you to bypass baggage claim. The service is available daily 5 a.m.–10 p.m.; there's also a bus waiting to transport you to your hotel, but if you arrive after 10 p.m., you'll have to collect your baggage yourself and take it with you on the bus. Transportation to your resort hotel will usually include stops at other resorts. The time from deplaning to arriving at your resort will be anywhere from 45 to 90 minutes depending on your resort (35 minutes of that will be driving to Walt Disney World property).

*unofficial* **TIP**
You'll need your MagicBands (see page 62) to board Disney's Magical Express, so pack them in your carry-on luggage rather than your checked bags.

When it's time to go home, you can check your baggage and receive your boarding pass at the front desk of your Disney resort. This service is available to all guests at Disney hotels (excluding the Swan, the Dolphin, Shades of Green, and hotels of the Downtown Disney Resort Area), even those who don't use Magical Express (folks who have rental cars, for example). Resort check-in counters are open 5 a.m.–1 p.m., and you must check in no later than 3 hours before your flight (within the US and Puerto Rico) or 4 hours for international flights. Participating airlines are **AirTran, Alaska, American, Delta, JetBlue, Southwest, United,** and **US Airways.** All of the preceding airlines have restrictions on the number of bags, checking procedures, and related items; consult your carrier before leaving home for specifics. For an in-depth discussion of Disney's Magical Express, see Part Eight, Arriving.

**6. PRIORITY THEME PARK ADMISSIONS** On days of unusually heavy attendance, Disney may restrict admission into the theme parks for all customers. When deciding whom to admit into the parks, priority is given to guests staying at Disney resorts. In practice, no guest is turned away until a park's parking lot is full. When this happens, that park will be packed to gridlock.

**7. CHILDREN SHARING A ROOM WITH THEIR PARENTS** There's no extra charge per night for children younger than 18 sharing a room with their parents. Many hotels outside Disney World also offer this.

**8. FREE PARKING** Disney resort guests with cars pay nothing to park in theme park lots. This saves $17 per day.

**9. RECREATIONAL PRIVILEGES** Disney guests get preferential treatment for tee times at the golf courses.

## STAYING IN OR OUT OF THE WORLD: WEIGHING THE PROS AND CONS

**1. COST** If cost is a primary consideration, you'll lodge much less expensively outside Disney World. Our ratings of hotel quality, cost, and commuting times to the theme parks encompass hotels both in and out of the World (see "How the Hotels Compare" and the Hotel Information Chart, both later in this chapter).

**2. EASE OF ACCESS** Even if you stay in Disney World, you're dependent on some mode of transportation. It may be less stressful to use the Disney transportation system, but with the single exception of commuting to the Magic Kingdom, the fastest, most efficient, and most flexible way to get around is usually a car. If you're at Epcot, for example, and want to take the kids back to Disney's Contemporary Resort for a nap, forget the monorail. You'll get back much faster by car.

A reader from Raynham, Massachusetts, who stayed at the Caribbean Beach Resort writes:

> Even though the resort is on the Disney bus line, I recommend renting a car if it fits one's budget. The buses don't go directly to many destinations, and often you have to switch buses. Getting a bus back to the hotel after a hard day can mean a long wait in line.

Readers complain about problems with the Disney transportation system more than most topics. These comments from a Havertown, Pennsylvania, dad are typical:

> WDW bus transportation is quite inefficient. When traveling from the BoardWalk to anywhere else, we had to pick up other passengers at the Swan, Dolphin, and Yacht and Beach Clubs before heading off to the parks. Same story upon return.

Although it's only for the use and benefit of Disney guests, the Disney transportation system is nonetheless public, and users must expect inconveniences: conveyances that arrive and depart on their schedule, not yours; the occasional need to transfer; multiple stops; time lost loading and unloading passengers; and, generally, the challenge of understanding and using a large, complex transportation network.

Relatively few Americans use public transportation frequently, but guests who do—as did this Heswall, England, reader—tend to be more satisfied with Disney's bus system:

> I really feel that you are a bit hard on the Disney transport service. This may be an American thing, but we Brits are more used to buses. We were told buses were running every 20 minutes, but in practice we never waited more than 10.

If you plan to have a car, consider this: Disney World is so large that some destinations within the World can be reached more quickly from off-property hotels than from Disney hotels. For example, guests at lodgings on US 192 (near the so-called Walt Disney World Maingate) are closer to Disney's Hollywood Studios, Animal

Kingdom, and Blizzard Beach water park than guests at many hotels inside Disney World.

A Kentucky dad overruled his family about staying at a Disney resort and is glad he did:

> *My wife read in another guidebook that it can take 2 hours to commute to the parks if you stay outside Walt Disney World. I guess it could take 2 hours if you stayed in Tampa, but from our hotel on US 192 we could commute to any of the parks except the Magic Kingdom and have at least one ride under our belt in about an hour. (We found out later that the writer of the other guidebook worked for* Disney Magazine.)

For commuting times from specific non-Disney hotels, see our Hotel Information Chart on pages 269–286.

**3. YOUNG CHILDREN** Although the hassle of commuting to most non-World hotels is only slightly (if at all) greater than that of commuting to Disney hotels, a definite peace of mind results from staying in the World. Regardless of where you stay, make sure you get your young children back to the hotel for a nap each day.

**4. SPLITTING UP** If you're in a party that will probably split up to tour (as frequently happens in families with teens or children of widely varying ages), staying in the World offers more transportation options and, thus, more independence. Mom and Dad can take the car and return to the hotel for a relaxed dinner and early bedtime while the teens remain in the park for evening parades and fireworks.

**5. FEEDING THE ARMY OF THE POTOMAC** If you have a large crew that chows down like cattle on a finishing lot, you may do better staying outside the World, where food is far less expensive.

**6. VISITING OTHER ORLANDO-AREA ATTRACTIONS** If you'll be visiting SeaWorld, Kennedy Space Center Visitor Complex, Universal Orlando, or other area attractions, it may be more convenient to stay outside the World.

# *The* DISNEY RESORTS

## DISNEY RESORTS 101

BEFORE YOU MAKE ANY DECISIONS, understand these basics regarding Disney resorts.

**1. RESORT CLASSIFICATIONS** Disney loves to categorize, so it's not surprising that they've developed a hierarchy of resort classifications. **Deluxe resorts** are Disney's top-of-the-line hotels. **Disney Deluxe Villa (DDV) resorts,** also known as **Disney Vacation Club (DVC) resorts,** offer suites, some with full kitchens. These resorts equal or surpass Deluxe resorts in quality; several are attached to Deluxe resorts. (Be aware that all Disney hotels except DDV resorts levy a nightly surcharge for every additional adult over age 18 in a room beyond the standard two.) **Moderate resorts**

*unofficial* **TIP**
Understand that Disney Reservation Center and Walt Disney Travel Company representatives don't have detailed personal knowledge of resorts.

are a step down in guest-room quality, amenities, and cost. Anchoring the bottom of the list are **Value resorts,** with the smallest rooms, most limited amenities, and lowest rates of any Disney-owned hotels. Standard rooms at the these resorts are generally the smallest on-property, but two-room "family suites" are available at certain Value resorts. Finally, there's **Fort Wilderness Resort & Campground,** which offers both campsites and fully equipped cabins.

**2. MAKING RESERVATIONS**  Whether you book through Disney, a travel agent, online, with a tour operator, or through an organization like AAA, you'll frequently save by booking the room exclusive of any vacation package. This is called a *room-only reservation.* Though later in this chapter we'll scrutinize the advantages and disadvantages of buying a package, we'll tell you now that Disney World packages at list price rarely save you money (though they can certainly be convenient).

In dealing with Disney for rooms only, use **disneyworld.com** instead of calling the Disney Reservation Center (DRC) at ☎ 407-W-DISNEY (934-7639). Because of some administrative and operational consolidation, reservationists at the DRC are trained to sell only Walt Disney Travel Company packages. Even if you insist that you want just a room, they'll try to bundle it with some small extra, like a miniature-golf pass, so that your purchase can be counted as a package. Seems innocuous enough, but that little upgrade allows Disney to apply numerous restrictions and cancellation policies that you wouldn't be saddled with if you bought a room by itself—for example, Disney might add trip insurance to your package automatically.

One instance where you might find it worth upgrading to a package is if you want the Disney Dining Plan, which can usually be added to a discounted room-only reservation (see page 216 for exceptions).

Regarding cancellation, know that there are trade-offs. If you book a package and cancel 2–44 days before arrival, you lose your $200 deposit. If you cancel fewer than 2 days before arrival, you lose the entire package cost, including airfare and insurance. If you reserve only a room and cancel less than a week before arrival, you lose your deposit of one night's room charge, which can easily be more than $200 if you booked at a Moderate, Deluxe, or DDV resort. Further, Disney imposes a $65 fee for changing your package's details, including travel dates, moving to a cheaper resort, or adding a discount code.

If you call, tell the agent what you want in terms of lodging and get a room-only rate quote. Then tell the agent what you're looking for in terms of admissions. When you've pinned down your room selection and lodging costs, ask the agent if he or she can offer any packages that beat the à la carte prices. But don't be swayed by little sweeteners included in a package unless they have real value for you. If the first agent you speak to isn't accommodating, hang up and call back. There are a couple hundred agents, some more helpful than others.

When dealing with Disney reservations, a careful shopper from West Lafayette, Indiana, advises both wariness and toughness:

*unofficial* **TIP**
Booking online is *much* faster than calling DRC. If you must call, do so before 11 a.m. or after 3 p.m. Eastern.

*Making reservations through W-DISNEY is like buying a car: You need to know the sales tricks, have a firm idea of what you want, and be prepared to walk away if you don't get what you want at a price you want to pay.*

If you need specific information, call the resort directly, ask for the front desk, and pose your question before phoning the DRC. If your desired dates aren't available, keep calling back or check online. Something might open up.

**3. A MOST CONFUSING VIEW** Rates at Disney hotels vary from season to season (see the next section) and from room to room according to view. Further, each Disney resort has its own seasonal calendar. Seasons such as "Regular," "Value," "Peak," and "Holiday" vary depending on the resort instead of that tired old January–December calendar that the rest of us use. But confusing as Disney seasons are, they're logic personified compared to the panoply of guest-room views the resorts offer. Depending on the resort, you can choose standard views, water views, pool views, lagoon views, garden views, or savanna views, among others. "Standard view," the most ambiguous category, crops up at about three-fourths of Disney resorts. It's usually interpreted as a view of infrastructure or unremarkable scenery. At Animal Kingdom Lodge, for example, you have savanna views, pool views, and standard views. Savanna views overlook the replicated African savanna, pool views overlook the swimming pool, and standard views offer stunning vistas of . . . rooftops and parking lots.

With a standard view, however, you can at least pinpoint what you won't be seeing. Every resort defines views of water differently. At the Grand Floridian Resort & Spa, for example, rooms with views of Seven Seas Lagoon are sensibly called "lagoon view" rooms, while those with views of the marina or pools are enigmatically called "garden view" rooms.

*unofficial* **TIP**
If you book a king room at a Moderate resort, you can request a water-view room at no extra charge (this isn't guaranteed, though).

Zip over to the Yacht Club Resort, another Deluxe property. Like the Grand Floridian, the Yacht Club is on a lake and has a pool and a marina. Views of all three are lumped into one big "lagoon or pool view" category—anything wet counts! If somehow you can glimpse the lake or a swimming pool, you have a water view.

It's worth noting that scoring a Grand Floridian room with a view of the Magic Kingdom requires exacting verbiage, as a mom from Pontefract, England, attests:

> We stayed at the Grand Floridian, which was lovely. However, I paid extra for a Magic Kingdom view. I was soooo disappointed when all I could see from the balcony was Space Mountain (unless I hung out so far I risked falling over). I was so looking forward to sitting on the balcony with a glass of wine and watching the fireworks. I know that next time I will have to ask for a view of Cinderella Castle, not just a Magic Kingdom view.

For many readers a good view is considered essential to the enjoyment of their hotel room. Getting the view you want, however, doesn't necessarily mean that you'll have the experience you want, as a Rochester, New York, couple points out:

*We stayed in the Conch Key building at the Grand Floridian. The view was lovely, but all we heard was the boat's horn blasting every 20 minutes, 7 a.m.–midnight. It was obnoxious and kept us up.*

Our favorite water views are at the Contemporary Resort's Garden Building, which extends toward Bay Lake to the east of the giant A-frame. Rooms in this three-story structure, such as Room 6109, afford some of the best lake vistas in Disney World (see **tinyurl.com /contemporary6109** for a view from one of these rooms). Many rooms are so near the water, in fact, you could spit a prune pit into the lake from your window. And their category? Garden views.

We could go on and on, but pinning Disney down on precisely what will be outside your window is the point. In our discussion of individual resorts later in this chapter, we'll tell you which rooms have the good views.

Our website's new **Hotel Room View** project uses more than 30,000 photos to show the view you get from every hotel room in Walt Disney World, plus instructions on how to request each specific room. It uses interactive maps for every building in every resort, so you can search for rooms by cost, view, walking distance, noise, handicap accessibility, and more. As you read this chapter, visit **touring plans.com/walt-disney-world/hotels** to see photos of the rooms we recommend.

> **unofficial TIP**
> Disney will guarantee connecting rooms if your party includes more children than adults. (In Disney terms, *adjoining rooms* are next to each other and *connecting rooms* have a door between them.)

**4. HOW TO GET THE ROOM YOU WANT** Disney will not guarantee a specific room when you book but will post your request on your reservation record. Our experience indicates that making a request by room number confuses the Disney reservationists; as a result, they're unsure where to place you if the room you've asked for is unavailable. To increase your odds of getting the room you want, tell the reservationist exactly what characteristics and amenities you desire—for example: "I'd like a room with a balcony on the second or third floor of the Contemporary Resort's Garden Building with an unobstructed view of the lake." (It's unnecessary to ask for a nonsmoking room at a Disney resort, as all rooms were designated smoke-free in 2007.)

Be direct and politely assertive when speaking to the Disney agent. At Port Orleans Riverside, for example, rooms with king beds have options for standard-, garden-, pool-, preferred-, and river-view rooms. If you want to overlook the river, say so; likewise, if you want a pool view, speak up. Similarly, state clearly such preferences as a particular floor, a corner room, a room near restaurants, or a room away from elevators and ice machines. If you have a long list of preferences, type it in order of importance and e-mail, fax, or snail-mail it to the hotel. Include your contact information and reservation-confirmation number. Use abbreviations where possible—we're told Disney's reservation system may hold only around 80 characters of preference text.

> **unofficial TIP**
> Three to four days before you arrive, call the resort front desk. Call late in the evening when they're not so busy, and reconfirm the requests that by now should be appearing in their computers.

It will be someone from the resort who actually assigns your room. Call back in a few days to make sure your preferences were posted to your record.

We'll provide info needed for each resort to frame your requests, including a resort layout map and our recommendations for specific rooms or buildings. We'll use a dash (–) to indicate a range of rooms. Thus, "Rooms 2230–2260" refers to the 31 rooms within that range. Sometimes we'll specify even- or odd-numbered rooms within a range, for example, "odd-numbered rooms 631–639." In this case we're referring to Rooms 631, 633, 635, 637, and 639. Note that our Hotel Room View project (see previous page) will give you the exact wording to use when requesting a specific room.

## HOW TO GET DISCOUNTS ON LODGING

THERE ARE SO MANY GUEST ROOMS in and around Disney World that competition is brisk, and everyone, including Disney, wheels and deals to fill them. Disney, however, has its own atypical way of managing its room inventory. To uphold the brand integrity of its hotels, Disney prefers to use inducements rather than discounts per se. For example, Disney might include free dining if you reserve a certain number of nights at rack rate, or offer special deals only by e-mail to returning guests. Consequently, many of the strategies for obtaining discounted rates in most cities and destinations don't work well for Disney hotels. We'll explore these strategies in-depth when we discuss booking non-Disney hotels near Walt Disney World; for the moment, though, here are some tips for getting price breaks at Disney properties:

**1. SEASONAL SAVINGS** Save from 15–35% per night or more on a Disney hotel room by visiting during the slower times of year. However, Disney uses so many adjectives ("Regular," "Holiday," "Peak," "Value," and the like) to describe its seasonal calendar that it's hard to keep up. Plus, the dates for each "season" vary among resorts. Disney also changes the price of its hotel rooms with the day of the week, charging more for the same room on Friday and Saturday nights. The increased rates range from $23 to $90 or more per room, per night.

**2. ASK ABOUT SPECIALS** When you talk to Disney reservationists, ask specifically about specials. For example, "What special deals or discounts are available at Disney hotels during the time of our visit?" Being specific and assertive paid off for a Warren Township, New Jersey, dad:

> Your tip on asking Disney employees about discounts was invaluable. They will not volunteer this information, but by asking we saved almost $500 on our hotel room using a AAA discount.

Another New Jersey reader takes a high-calorie approach:

> My husband and I begin planning each WDW vacation the same way: Call the famous 407-W-DISNEY number and speak to someone with a ridiculous name (this time it was Flower and Buffy). I present my vacation plan to the operator, which consists of my specific date, WDW resort, and ticket choice. She quotes me a price; I thank her for her help and hang up. I call again and present my exact same plan to a new operator, who quotes me a totally different price! I repeat

*the phone process again and obtain another price for the same plan. After three years, my husband and I feel like we're playing "Spin the Wheel to Get a Price for the WDW Vacation." Now, instead of getting disgusted, we make it a night of calling with coffee and dessert.*

A family from West Springfield, Massachusetts, discovered that if you keep on shopping even after you've booked, your efforts can really pay off:

*I booked our trip online with Disney using a special-offer discount we had received in the mail. Two months before our trip, and after I had already paid in full, Disney ran a special that was actually better than the one I had booked. I gave them a call, and they politely, quickly, and efficiently credited me with the difference.*

Be aware that specials can include discounts on vacation packages in addition to discounts on rooms. Discounts on park admission or dining packages (see "Spring for 'Free Dining,'" in the "Disney Lodging for Less" box on page 213) can be substantial, depending on the number of people in your traveling party or where you're staying.

**3. "TRADE-UP" OR "UPSELL" RATES** If you request a room at a Disney Value resort and none is available, you may be offered a discounted room in the next category up (Moderate resorts, in this example). Similarly, if you ask for a room in a Moderate resort and none is available, Disney will usually offer a deal for Disney Deluxe Villa rooms or a Deluxe resort. You can angle for a trade-up rate by asking for a resort category that's more likely to be sold out.

**4. KNOW THE SECRET CODE** The folks at **MouseSavers** (**mousesavers .com**) maintain an updated list of discounts and reservation codes for Disney resorts. The codes are separated into categories such as "for anyone," "for residents of certain states," and "for Annual Pass holders." Anyone calling ☎ 407-w-DISNEY can use a current code and get the discounted rate.

Be aware that Disney targets people with PIN codes in e-mails and direct mailings. PIN-code discounts are offered to specific individuals and are correlated with a given person's name and address. When you try to make a reservation using the PIN, Disney will verify that the street or e-mail address to which the code was sent is yours.

MouseSavers has a great historical list of when discounts were released and what they encompassed at **mousesavers.com/historical wdwdiscounts.html.** You can also sign up for the MouseSavers newsletter, with discount announcements, Disney news, and exclusive offers not available to the general public.

To get your name in the Disney system for a PIN code, call ☎ 407-w-DISNEY and request written info or the free trip-planning DVD. If you've been to Walt Disney World before, your name and address will of course already be on record, but you won't be as likely to receive a PIN-code offer as you would by calling and requesting that information be mailed to you. On the web, go to **disneyworld .com** and sign up (via the trip-planning DVD) to

*unofficial* **TIP**
To enhance your chances of receiving a PIN-code offer, you need to get your name and street or e-mail address into the Disney system.

automatically be sent offers and news at your e-mail address. You might also consider getting a **Disney Rewards Visa Card,** which entitles you to around two days' advance notice when a discount is released (visit **disney.go.com/visa** for details).

**5. INTERNET SELLERS** Online travel sellers **Expedia (expedia.com), Travelocity (travelocity.com),** and **One Travel (onetravel.com)** sell Disney hotels, but usually at a price approximating the going rate obtainable from the Walt Disney Travel Company or Walt Disney World Central Reservations. Most breaks are in the 7–25% range, but they can go as deep as 40%. Disney also places its hotel rooms on **Priceline (priceline .com).** While still abstaining from the "Name Your Own Price" aspect of the site, Disney's hotel rooms are now in Priceline's inventory and available through its conventional booking engine at a discounted rate.

**6. WALT DISNEY WORLD WEBSITE** Disney still offers deals when it sees lower-than-usual future demand. Go to **disneyworld.com** and look for "Explore Our Special Offers" on the home page. In the same place, also look for seasonal discounts, usually listed as "Summertime Savings" or "Fall Savings" or something similar. You can also go to "Places to Stay" at the top of the home page, where you'll find a link to Special Offers. You must click on the particular special to get the discounts: If you fill out the information on "Price Your Vacation," you'll be charged the full rack rate. Reservations booked online are subject to a $100–$200 penalty if canceled less than 45 days before arrival. Before booking rooms on Disney's or any website, click "Terms and Conditions" and read the fine print.

**7. RENTING DISNEY VACATION CLUB POINTS** The Disney Vacation Club (DVC) is Disney's time-share-condominium program. DVC resorts (a.k.a. Disney Deluxe Villa [DDV] resorts) at Walt Disney World are **Animal Kingdom Villas, Bay Lake Tower at the Contemporary Resort,** the **Beach Club Villas, BoardWalk Villas, Old Key West Resort, Saratoga Springs Resort & Spa, Treehouse Villas at Saratoga Springs, Grand Floridian Villas,** and **Wilderness Lodge Villas;** currently under construction is a new DVC development at the **Polynesian Resort** (see page 147 for details). Each DVC resort offers studios and one- and two-bedroom villas; some resorts also offer three-bedroom villas. (Room types at the upcoming Polynesian complex weren't confirmed at press time, but we think they'll consist only of studios and two-bedroom bungalows.) Studios are equipped with kitchenettes, wet bars, and fridges; villas come with full kitchens. Most accommodations have patios or balconies.

DVC members receive a number of "points" annually that they use to pay for their Disney accommodations. Sometimes members elect to "rent" (sell) their points instead of using them in a given year. Though Disney is not involved in the transaction, it allows DVC members to make these points available to the general public. The going rental rate is usually in the range of $13–$14 per point. Renting a studio for a summer week at Animal Kingdom Lodge & Villas would run you $3,930 with tax for Regular season if you booked through the DRC. The same studio costs the DVC member 76 points for a week. If you rented her points at $14 per point, the same studio would cost you $1,120 with tax—more than $2,800 less.

You have two options when renting points: go through a company that specializes in DVC points rental, or locate and deal directly with the selling DVC member. For a fixed rate of around $14 per point, the folks at **David's Disney Vacation Club Rentals (dvcrequest.com)** will act on your behalf as a points broker, matching your request for a specific resort and dates to their available supply. They'll also take requests months in advance and notify you as soon as something becomes available. We've used these folks for huge New Year's Eve events and last-minute trips, and they're tops. Plus they accept major credit cards.

In addition to David's, some readers, like this one from St. Louis, have had good results with **The DVC Rental Store (dvcrentalstore.com)**:

> *We rented DVC points for this trip through the DVC Rental Store, and we had a wonderful experience. Unlike David's, they don't charge to check availability, and you don't have to pay the entire cost upon booking. For our stay at Wilderness Lodge Villas, we paid just over half what we were planning to pay for the Wilderness Lodge.*

When you deal directly with the selling DVC member, you pay him or her directly, such as by certified check (few members take credit cards). The DVC member makes a reservation in your name and pays Disney the requisite number of points. Arrangements vary, but the going rate seems to be around $12 per point. Trust is required from both parties. Usually your reservation is documented by a confirmation sent from Disney to the owner and then passed along to you. Though the deal you cut is strictly up to you and the owner, you should always insist on receiving the aforementioned confirmation before making more than a one-night deposit.

We suggest checking online at one of the various Disney discussion boards if you're not picky about where you stay and when you go and you're willing to put in the effort to ask around. If you're trying to book a particular resort, especially during a busy time of year, there's something to be said for the low-hassle approach of a points broker.

**8. TRAVEL AGENTS** are active players and particularly good sources of information on limited-time programs and discounts. We believe a good travel agent is the best friend a traveler can have. And though we at the *Unofficial Guide* know a thing or two about the travel industry, we always give our agent a chance to beat any deal we find. If she can't beat it, we let her book it anyway if she can get commission from it, thus nurturing the relationship.

As you might expect, there are travel agents and agencies that specialize, sometimes exclusively, in selling Walt Disney World. These agents have spent an incredible amount of time at the resort, and they have also completed extensive Disney-education programs. They're usually the most Disney-knowledgeable agents in the travel industry. Most of these specialists and their agencies display the "Earmarked" logo stating that they're Authorized Disney Vacation Planners.

These Disney specialists are so good we use them ourselves. The needs of our research team are many, and our schedules are complicated. When we work with an Authorized Disney Vacation Planner, we know we're dealing with someone who knows Disney inside and out, including where to find the deals and how to use all tricks of the trade that keep our research budget under control. Simply stated, they save us time and money, sometimes lots of both.

Each year we ask our readers to rate the travel agent who helped plan their Disney trip. We received more than 3,800 responses this year. The best of the best include **Sue Pisaturo** of **Small World Vacations,** whom we've used many times and who contributes to this guide (**sue@small worldvacations.com**); **Michelle Cunningham** (**michelle@mei-travel.com**) and **Stephanie Hudson** (**stephanie@mousefantravel.com**), both on their third appearance in this guide (Michelle for the third year in a row); and newcomers **Minnie Babb** (**minnie@smallworldvacations.com**) and **Darren Wittko** (**darren@magicalvacationstravel.com**).

Our reader-survey results indicate that for Walt Disney World, you'll be much more satisfied using a travel agent who specializes in Disney and much more likely to recommend those agents to a friend. While the agents above are among the ones most consistently recommended in our surveys, you'll find good Disney specialists throughout the country if you prefer to work with someone close to home.

**9. ORGANIZATIONS AND AUTO CLUBS** Disney has developed time-limited programs with some auto clubs and organizations. AAA, for example, can often offer discounts on hotels and packages comparable to those Disney offers its Annual Pass holders. Such deals come and go, but the market suggests there will be more. If you're a member of AARP, AAA, or any travel or auto club, ask whether the group has a program before shopping elsewhere.

**10. ROOM UPGRADES** Sometimes a room upgrade is as good as a discount. If you're visiting Disney World during a slower time, book the least expensive room your discounts will allow. Checking in, ask very politely about being upgraded to a "water view" or "pool view" room. A fair percentage of the time, you'll get one at no additional charge. Understand, however, that a room upgrade should be considered a favor. Hotels are under no obligation to upgrade you, so if your request is not met, accept the decision graciously. Also, note that suites at Deluxe resorts are exempt from discount offers.

**11. MILITARY DISCOUNTS** The **Shades of Green Armed Forces Recreation Center,** near the Grand Floridian Resort & Spa, offers luxury accommodations at rates based on a service member's rank, as well as attraction tickets to the theme parks. For rates and other information, call ☎ 888-593-2242 or see **shadesofgreen.org.**

**12. YEAR-ROUND DISCOUNTS AT THE SWAN AND DOLPHIN RESORTS** Government workers, teachers, nurses, military, and AAA and *Entertainment Coupon Book* members can save on their rooms at the Dolphin or the Swan resort (when space is available, of course). Call ☎ 888-828-8850.

## CHOOSING A WALT DISNEY WORLD HOTEL

IF YOU WANT TO STAY IN THE WORLD but don't know which hotel to choose, consider these factors:

**1. COST** Consider your budget. Hotel rooms start at about $100 a night at the **All-Star** and **Pop Century Resorts** during Value season and top out

| COSTS PER NIGHT OF DISNEY HOTEL ROOMS, LATE 2014 (rack rate) | |
| --- | --- |
| Rates are for standard rooms except where noted. | |
| All-Star Resorts | $110–$198 |
| All-Star Music Resort Family Suites | $244–$442 |
| Animal Kingdom Lodge | $319–$555 |
| Animal Kingdom Villas (studio, Jambo/Kidani) | $357–$673 |
| Art of Animation Family Suites | $299–$511 |
| Art of Animation Resort | $123–$221 |
| Bay Lake Tower at Contemporary Resort (studio) | $492–$698 |
| Beach Club Resort | $400–$671 |
| Beach Club Villas (studio) | $411–$682 |
| BoardWalk Inn | $411–$682 |
| BoardWalk Villas (studio) | $411–$682 |
| Caribbean Beach Resort | $191–$284 |
| Contemporary Resort (Garden Building) | $378–$630 |
| Coronado Springs Resort | $196–$290 |
| Dolphin (Sheraton) | $159–$299 |
| Fort Wilderness Resort & Campground (cabins) | $330–$562 |
| Grand Floridian Resort & Spa | $549–$856 |
| Grand Floridian Villas (studio) | $554–$865 |
| Old Key West Resort (studio) | $367–$531 |
| Polynesian Resort | $482–$760 |
| Pop Century Resort | $112–$209 |
| Port Orleans Resort (French Quarter, Riverside) | $191–$284 |
| Saratoga Springs Resort & Spa (studio) | $367–$531 |
| Swan (Westin) | $159–$299 |
| Treehouse Villas | $797–$1,287 |
| Wilderness Lodge | $325–$561 |
| Wilderness Lodge Villas (studio) | $420–$621 |
| Yacht Club Resort | $400–$671 |

near $1,300 at the **Grand Floridian Resort & Spa** during Holiday Season. Suites, of course, are more expensive than standard rooms.

**Animal Kingdom Villas, Bay Lake Tower, Beach Club Villas, Board-Walk Villas, Grand Floridian Villas, Old Key West Resort, Saratoga Springs Resort & Spa,** and **Wilderness Lodge Villas** offer condo-type accommodations with one-, two-, and (at Saratoga Springs, Board-Walk Villas, Old Key West, Animal Kingdom Villas, Grand Floridian Villas, and Bay Lake Tower) three-bedroom units with kitchens, living rooms, DVD players, and washers and dryers. Studios have a kitchenette (with microwave, mini-fridge, and sink) but no washer or dryer.

Prices range from $357 per night for a studio suite at Animal Kingdom Villas to more than $2,600 per night for a three-bedroom villa at Bay Lake Tower. Fully equipped cabins (minus a washer and dryer) at **Fort Wilderness Resort & Campground** cost $330–$562 per night. Family Suites at All-Star Music and Art of Animation have kitchenettes, separate bedrooms, and two bathrooms. A few suites without kitchens are available at the more expensive Disney resorts.

For any extra adults in a room (more than two), the nightly surcharge for each extra adult is $26.63 per night with tax at all resorts but DDV resorts, which levy no surcharge.

Also at Disney World are the seven hotels of the **Downtown Disney Resort Area (DDRA).** Accommodations range from fairly luxurious to motel-like. While the DDRA is technically part of Disney World, staying there is like visiting a colony rather than the motherland. Free parking at theme parks isn't offered—nor is early entry, with one exception, the Hilton—and hotels operate their own buses rather than use Disney transportation. For more information on DDRA properties, see the chart and discussion starting on page 201.

| WHAT IT COSTS TO STAY IN THE DOWNTOWN DISNEY RESORT AREA | |
| --- | --- |
| **Best Western Lake Buena Vista Resort Hotel** | $85–$145 |
| **B Resort** | $159–$216 |
| **Buena Vista Palace Hotel & Spa** | $119–$179 |
| **DoubleTree Guest Suites** | $139–$299 |
| **Hilton in the WDW Resort** | $99–$209 |
| **Holiday Inn in the WDW Resort** | $108–$190 |
| **Wyndham Lake Buena Vista Resort** | $95–$199 |

**2. LOCATION** Once you determine your budget, think about what you want to do at Disney World. Will you go to all four theme parks or concentrate on one or two?

*unofficial* **TIP**
If you plan to use Disney transportation to visit all four major parks and one or both of the water parks, book a centrally located resort that has good transportation connections. The Epcot resorts and the Polynesian, Caribbean Beach, Art of Animation, Pop Century, Coronado Springs, and Port Orleans Resorts fill the bill.

If you'll be driving a car, your Disney hotel's location isn't especially important unless you plan to spend most of your time at the Magic Kingdom. (Disney transportation is always more efficient than your car in this case because it bypasses the Transportation and Ticket Center, the World's transportation hub, and deposits you at the theme park entrance.) If you haven't decided whether you want a car for your Disney vacation, see "How to Travel Around the World" (page 386).

Most convenient to the Magic Kingdom are the three resort complexes linked by monorail: the **Grand Floridian** and its **Villas,** the **Contemporary** and **Bay Lake Tower,** and the **Polynesian.** Commuting to the Magic Kingdom by monorail is quick and simple, allowing visitors to return to their hotel for a nap, swim, or meal.

Contemporary Resort and Bay Lake Tower, in addition to being on the monorail, are only a 10- to 15-minute walk to the Magic Kingdom. Guests reach Epcot by monorail but must transfer at the Transportation and Ticket Center. Buses connect the resorts to Disney's Hollywood Studios, Disney's Animal Kingdom, the water parks, and Downtown Disney–Disney Springs. No transfer is required, but the bus makes several stops before reaching either destination.

The Polynesian is served by the Magic Kingdom monorail and is an easy walk from the transportation center. At the center, you can catch an express monorail to Epcot. This makes the Polynesian the only Disney resort with direct monorail access to both Epcot and the Magic Kingdom. To minimize your walk to the transportation center, request a standard room in the Rarotonga guest building or, once construction is complete, a DVC studio in Rapa Nui or Tahiti (see page 147).

**Wilderness Lodge & Villas,** along with **Fort Wilderness Resort & Campground,** are linked to the Magic Kingdom by boat and to everywhere else in the World by somewhat-convoluted bus service. The new **Four Seasons Resort Orlando at Walt Disney World,** behind what used to be Osprey Ridge Golf Course, has bus service to the Magic Kingdom.

The most centrally located resorts in Walt Disney World are the Epcot hotels: the **BoardWalk Inn, BoardWalk Villas, Yacht & Beach Club Resorts, Beach Club Villas, Swan,** and **Dolphin**—and **Coronado Springs,** near Disney's Animal Kingdom. The Epcot hotels are within easy walking distance of Disney's Hollywood Studios and Epcot's International Gateway. Except at Coronado Springs, boat service is also available at these resorts, with vessels connecting to DHS. Epcot hotels are best for guests planning to spend most of their time at Epcot or DHS.

**Caribbean Beach Resort, Pop Century Resort,** and **Art of Animation Resort** are just south and east of Epcot and DHS. Along Bonnet Creek, **Disney's Old Key West** and **Port Orleans Resorts** also offer quick access to those parks. Also along Bonnet Creek, pretty much surrounded by Walt Disney World, is a parcel of land that Disney was unable to acquire and that went undeveloped for decades. Now that property is home to the 70-acre **Bonnet Creek Resort,** comprising four non-Disney hotels: the **Waldorf Astoria Orlando;** the **Hilton Orlando Bonnet Creek;** and two **Wyndham** properties: the **Wyndham Bonnet Creek Resort** and its more luxurious sibling, the **Wyndham Grand Orlando Bonnet Creek Resort.** Technically, the complex isn't in Walt Disney World, but you can access it only via Disney property and roads—a real sore spot with Disney. The hotels of the Bonnet Creek Resort are as close to the theme parks as Disney's own, offer transportation to the parks and Downtown Disney, and are every bit as good as Disney's best, often at around half the price. We profile the Hilton, the Waldorf Astoria, and the Wyndham Bonnet Creek later in this chapter in "Hotels Outside of Walt Disney World."

Though not centrally located, the **All-Star Resorts** and **Animal Kingdom Lodge & Villas** have very good bus service to all Disney World destinations and are closest to Animal Kingdom.

If you plan to play golf, book **Old Key West Resort** or **Saratoga Springs Resort & Spa,** both of which are built around golf courses. The

| HOTEL | ROOM-QUALITY RATING |
|-------|:---:|
| 1. BAY LAKE TOWER | 95 |
| 2. CONTEMPORARY RESORT | 93 |
| 3. GRAND FLORIDIAN RESORT & SPA, VILLAS | 93 |
| 4. POLYNESIAN RESORT | 92 |
| 5. ANIMAL KINGDOM VILLAS | 91 |
| 6. SHADES OF GREEN | 91 |
| 7. BEACH CLUB RESORT | 90 |
| 8. BEACH CLUB VILLAS (studio) | 90 |
| 9. BOARDWALK VILLAS (studio) | 90 |
| 10. SARATOGA SPRINGS RESORT & SPA (studio) | 90 |
| 11. OLD KEY WEST RESORT ((studio) | 90 |
| 12. DOLPHIN | 90 |
| 13. SWAN | 90 |
| 14. TREEHOUSE VILLAS (studio) | 90 |
| 15. WILDERNESS LODGE VILLAS (studio) | 90 |
| 16. ANIMAL KINGDOM LODGE | 89 |
| 17. BOARDWALK INN | 89 |
| 18. YACHT CLUB RESORT | 89 |
| 19. FORT WILDERNESS CABINS | 86 |
| 20. WILDERNESS LODGE | 86 |
| 21. CORONADO SPRINGS RESORT | 85 |
| 22. PORT ORLEANS FRENCH QUARTER | 84 |
| 23. PORT ORLEANS RIVERSIDE | 83 |
| 24. CARIBBEAN BEACH RESORT | 80 |
| 25. ART OF ANIMATION RESORT | 78 |
| 26. ALL-STAR RESORTS | 73 |
| 27. POP CENTURY RESORT | 71 |

military-only **Shades of Green** resort is adjacent to two courses. Near but not on a golf course are the **Grand Floridian, Polynesian,** and **Port Orleans Resorts.**

For boating and water sports, try the **Polynesian, Contemporary,** or **Grand Floridian Resorts, Fort Wilderness Resort & Campground,** or **Wilderness Lodge & Villas.** The lodge and campground are also great for hikers, bikers, and joggers.

**3. ROOM QUALITY** Few Disney guests spend much time in their hotel rooms, though these rooms are among the best designed and most well appointed anywhere. Plus, they're meticulously maintained. At the top of the line are the luxurious rooms of the **Contemporary, Grand Floridian,** and **Polynesian Resorts;** bringing up the rear are the small rooms of the **All-Star Resorts.** But even these economy rooms are sparkling-clean and quite livable.

The chart above shows how Walt Disney World hotels (along with the **Swan** and **Dolphin,** which are Westin and Sheraton hotels) stack up for quality.

| HOTEL: THEME |
|---|
| **ALL-STAR RESORTS:** Sports, music, and movies |
| **ANIMAL KINGDOM LODGE & VILLAS:** African game preserve |
| **ART OF ANIMATION RESORT:** Disney's animated films |
| **BAY LAKE TOWER:** Upscale, ultramodern urban hotel |
| **BEACH CLUB RESORT & VILLAS:** New England beach club of the 1870s |
| **BOARDWALK INN:** East Coast boardwalk hotel of the early 1900s |
| **BOARDWALK VILLAS:** East Coast beach cottage of the early 1900s |
| **CARIBBEAN BEACH RESORT:** Caribbean islands |
| **CONTEMPORARY RESORT:** Future as perceived by past, present generations |
| **CORONADO SPRINGS RESORT:** Northern Mexico and the American Southwest |
| **DOLPHIN:** Modern Florida resort |
| **GRAND FLORIDIAN RESORT & SPA, VILLAS:** Turn-of-the-20th-century luxury hotel |
| **OLD KEY WEST RESORT:** Key West |
| **POLYNESIAN RESORT:** Hawaii–South Seas islands |
| **POP CENTURY RESORT:** Icons from various decades of the 20th century |
| **PORT ORLEANS FRENCH QUARTER RESORT:** Turn-of-the-19th-century New Orleans |
| **PORT ORLEANS RIVERSIDE RESORT:** Antebellum Louisiana plantation, bayou-side retreat |
| **SARATOGA SPRINGS RESORT & SPA:** 1880s Victorian lake |
| **SWAN:** Modern Florida resort |
| **TREEHOUSE VILLAS:** Rustic vacation homes with modern amenities |
| **WILDERNESS LODGE & VILLAS:** National-park grand lodge of the early 1900s |
| **YACHT CLUB RESORT:** New England seashore hotel of the 1880s |

**4. THE SIZE OF YOUR GROUP** Larger families and groups may be interested in how many persons a Disney resort room can accommodate, but only Lilliputians would be comfortable in a room filled to capacity. Groups requiring two or more guest rooms should consider condo or villa accommodations in or out of the World. The most cost-efficient Disney lodging for groups of five is the **Alligator Bayou** section of **Port Orleans Riverside.** The cheapest digs for six are the **All-Star Music Family Suites.** If your party includes more than six people, you'll need either two hotel rooms, a suite, or a condo. The Disney room-layout schematics on the following pages show the rooms' relative sizes and configurations, along with the maximum number of persons per room.

**5. THEME** All Disney hotels are themed. Each is designed to make you feel you're in a special place or period of history.

Some resorts carry off their themes better than others, and some themes are more exciting. **Wilderness Lodge & Villas,** for example, is extraordinary, reminiscent of a grand national-park lodge from the early 20th century. The lobby opens eight stories to a timbered ceiling supported by giant columns of bundled logs. One look eases you into the Northwest-wilderness theme. The lodge is a great choice for couples and seniors and is heaven for children.

# DISNEY DELUXE RESORTS ROOM DIAGRAMS

### Contemporary Resort

**Typical room, 394 square feet**
*Rooms accommodate 5 guests, plus 1 child under age 3 in a crib.*

### Polynesian Resort

**Typical room, 415 square feet**
*Rooms accommodate 5 guests, plus 1 child under age 3 in a crib.*

### Grand Floridian Resort & Spa

**Typical room, 440 square feet**
*Rooms accommodate 5 guests, plus 1 child under age 3 in a crib.*

### BoardWalk Inn

**Typical room, 371 square feet**
*Rooms accommodate 4 guests, plus 1 child under age 3 in a crib.*

### Beach Club Resort

**Typical room, 381 square feet**
*Rooms accommodate 5 guests, plus 1 child under age 3 in a crib.*

### Yacht Club Resort

**Typical room, 381 square feet**
*Rooms accommodate 5 guests, plus 1 child under age 3 in a crib.*

### Wilderness Lodge

**Typical room, 344 square feet**
*Rooms accommodate 4 guests, plus 1 child under age 3 in a crib.*

### Animal Kingdom Lodge

**Typical room, 344 square feet**
*Rooms accommodate 4 guests, plus 1 child under age 3 in a crib.*

**Animal Kingdom Lodge & Villas** replicates grand safari lodges of Kenya and Tanzania and overlooks its own African game preserve. By far the most exotic Disney resort, it's made to order for couples on romantic getaways and for families with children. The **Polynesian,** likewise dramatic, conveys the feeling of the Pacific Islands. It's great for romantics and families. Many waterfront rooms offer a perfect view of Cinderella Castle and the Magic Kingdom fireworks across Seven Seas Lagoon.

*Continued on page 127*

# DISNEY DELUXE VILLA RESORTS ROOM DIAGRAMS

### Old Key West Resort

*Studio (gray): 376 square feet
One-bedroom: 942 square feet
Two-bedroom: 1,333 square feet
Grand Villa: 2,202 square feet*

### Animal Kingdom Villas
### (Jambo House & Kidani Village)

*Studio (gray): 316–365 square feet (Jambo House),
366 square feet (Kidani Village)
One-bedroom: 629–710 square feet (Jambo House),
807 square feet (Kidani Village)
Two-bedroom: 945–1,075 square feet (Jambo House),
1,173 square feet (Kidani Village)
Grand Villa: 2,349 square feet (Jambo House),
2,201 square feet (Kidani Village)*

### Bay Lake Tower
### at Contemporary Resort

*Studio (gray): 339 square feet
One-bedroom: 803 square feet
Two-bedroom: 1,152 square feet
Grand Villa: 2,044 square feet*

### BoardWalk Villas

*Studio (gray): 412 square feet
One-bedroom: 814 square feet
Two-bedroom: 1,236 square feet
Grand Villa: 2,491 square feet*

### Treehouse Villas at
### Saratoga Springs Resort & Spa

*Three-bedroom:
1,074 square feet*

### The Villas at
### Grand Floridian Resort & Spa

*Studio (gray): 374 square feet
One-bedroom (white): 844 square feet
Two-bedroom lock-off (gray and white):
1,232 square feet*

**DDV guest-occupancy limits** Studios: 4 persons at all but Grand Floridian and Wilderness Lodge (5). One-bedroom villas: 4 at Beach Club, BoardWalk, Saratoga Springs, and Wilderness Lodge; 4 or 5 at Animal Kingdom Lodge (Jambo House); 5 everywhere else. Two-bedroom villas: 8 or 9 at Animal Kingdom Lodge (Jambo House); 9 at Animal Kingdom Lodge (Kidani Village), Bay Lake Tower, and Old Key West; 9 or 10 at Grand Floridian; 8 everywhere else. Three-bedroom and Grand Villas: 9 at Treehouse Villas; 12 everywhere else. *Note:* To all these limits you may add 1 child under age 3 in a crib.

## DISNEY DELUXE VILLA RESORTS ROOM DIAGRAMS *(continued)*

### Wilderness Lodge Villas

*Studio (gray): 356 square feet*
*One-bedroom: 727 square feet*
*Two-bedroom: 1,080 square feet*

### Saratoga Springs Resort & Spa

*Studio (gray): 355 square feet*
*One-bedroom: 714 square feet*
*Two-bedroom: 1,075 square feet*
*Grand Villa: 2,113 square feet*

### Beach Club Villas

*Studio (gray): 356 square feet*
*One-bedroom: 726 square feet*
*Two-bedroom: 1,083 square feet*

### Disney's Polynesian Village DVC Unit (Author's Concept)

*Studio: 454 square feet*

## DISNEY MODERATE RESORTS ROOM DIAGRAMS

### Coronado Springs Resort

**Typical room, 314 square feet**
*Rooms accommodate 4 guests,*
*plus 1 child under age 3 in a crib.*

### Port Orleans French Quarter Resort

**Typical room, 314 square feet**
*Rooms accommodate 4 guests,*
*plus 1 child under age 3 in a crib.*

### Caribbean Beach Resort

**Typical room, 314 square feet**
*Rooms accommodate 4 guests,*
*plus 1 child under age 3 in a crib.*

### Port Orleans Resort Riverside

**Typical room, 314 square feet**
*Rooms accommodate 4 guests,*
*plus 1 child under age 3 in a crib.*
*Alligator Bayou has trundle bed for*
*extra child (54" long) at no extra charge.*

## DISNEY VALUE RESORTS ROOM DIAGRAMS

**All-Star Resorts Family Suite**

**Typical suite, 520 square feet**
*Suites accommodate 6 guests,
plus 1 child under age 3 in a crib.*

**All-Star Resorts**

**Typical room, 260 square feet**
*Rooms accommodate 4 guests,
plus 1 child under age 3 in a crib.*

**Pop Century Resort**

**Typical room, 260 square feet**
*Rooms accommodate 4 guests,
plus 1 child under age 3 in a crib.*

**Art of Animation Resort,**
*Finding Nemo* **Family Suite**

**Typical room, 565 square feet**
*Rooms accommodate 6 guests,
plus 1 child under age 3 in a crib.*

**Art of Animation Resort,**
*Little Mermaid* **Standard Room**

**Typical room, 277 square feet**
*Rooms accommodate 4 guests,
plus 1 child under age 3 in a crib.*

## FORT WILDERNESS RESORT CABIN DIAGRAM

**Fort Wilderness Resort & Campground**

**Cabins, 504 square feet**
*Cabins accommodate 6 guests,
plus 1 child under age 3 in a crib.*

*Continued from page 124*

Grandeur, nostalgia, and privilege are central to the **Grand Floridian Resort & Spa, Grand Floridian Villas, Yacht & Beach Club Resorts, BoardWalk Inn,** and **BoardWalk Villas.** Though modeled after Eastern-seaboard seaside hotels of different eras, the resorts are similar. **Saratoga Springs Resort & Spa,** supposedly representative of an upstate New York country retreat, looks like what you'd get if you crossed the Beach

Club with the Wilderness Lodge. For all the resorts inspired by northeastern resorts, thematic distinctions are subtle and lost on many guests.

**Port Orleans French Quarter Resort** lacks the mystery and sultriness of the real New Orleans French Quarter but captures enough of its architectural essence to carry off the theme. **Port Orleans Riverside Resort** likewise succeeds with its plantation and bayou setting. **Old Key West Resort** gets the architecture right, but cloning its inspiration on such a large scale totally glosses over the real Key West's idiosyncratic patchwork personality. The **Caribbean Beach Resort**'s theme is much more effective at night, thanks to creative lighting. By day, it looks like a Miami condo development.

**Coronado Springs Resort** offers several styles of Mexican and southwestern American architecture. Though the lake setting is lovely and the resort is attractive and inviting, the theme (with the exception of the main swimming area) isn't especially stimulating—more like a Scottsdale, Arizona, country club than a Disney resort.

The **All-Star Resorts** comprise 30 three-story, T-shaped hotels with almost 6,000 guest rooms. There are 15 themed areas: 5 celebrate sports (surfing, basketball, tennis, football, and baseball), 5 recall Hollywood movies, and 5 have musical motifs. The resort's design, with entrances shaped like giant Dalmatians, Coke cups, footballs, and the like, is pretty adolescent, sacrificing grace and beauty for energy and novelty. Guest rooms are small, with decor reminiscent of a teenage boy's bedroom. Despite the theme, there is neither sports nor music; however, movies are shown nightly at all three resorts. **Pop Century Resort** is pretty much a clone of All-Star Resorts, only here the giant icons symbolize decades of the 20th century (Big Wheels, 45-rpm records, silhouettes of people doing period dances, and such), and period memorabilia decorates the rooms. Across the lake from Pop Century Resort is the **Art of Animation Resort,** with icons and decor based on four animated features: Cars, Finding Nemo, The Lion King, and The Little Mermaid.

Pretense aside, the **Contemporary, Swan,** and **Dolphin** are essentially themeless though architecturally interesting. The original Contemporary Resort is a 15-story A-frame building with monorails running through the middle. Views from guest rooms here and in Bay Lake Tower are among the best at Disney World. Swan and Dolphin are massive yet whimsical. Designed by Michael Graves, they're excellent examples of "entertainment architecture."

**6. DINING** The best resorts for dining quality and selection are the Epcot resorts: the **Beach Club Villas, BoardWalk Inn & Villas, Dolphin, Swan,** and **Yacht & Beach Club Resorts.** Each has good restaurants and is within easy walking distance of the others and of the 15 restaurants in Epcot's World Showcase section. If you stay at an Epcot resort, you have a total of 32 restaurants within a 5- to 12-minute walk.

The only other place in Disney World where restaurants and hotels are similarly concentrated is in the **Downtown Disney Resort Area.** In addition to restaurants in the hotels themselves, the **Hilton, Holiday Inn at Walt Disney World, Wyndham Lake Buena Vista Resort,** and **Buena Vista Palace Hotel & Spa,** as well as **Saratoga Springs Resort & Spa,** are within walking distance of restaurants in Downtown Disney.

Guests at the **Contemporary, Polynesian,** and **Grand Floridian** can eat in their hotels, or they can commute to restaurants in the Magic Kingdom (not recommended) or in other monorail-linked hotels. Riding the monorail to another hotel or to the Magic Kingdom takes about 10 minutes each way, plus waiting for the train.

All the other Disney resorts are somewhat isolated. This means you're stuck dining at your hotel unless (1) you have a car or (2) you're content to eat at the theme parks or Downtown Disney.

Here's the deal. Disney transportation works fine for commuting from hotels to theme parks and Downtown Disney, but it's useless for getting from one hotel to another. If you're staying at Port Orleans and want to dine at the Swan, forget it. It can take you up to an hour and a half each way by bus. You could take a bus to the Magic Kingdom and catch a train to one of the monorail-served hotels for dinner. That would take "only" 45 minutes each way. When all is said and done, your best strategy for commuting from hotel to hotel by road is to use your car or pony up for a cab.

Of the more-isolated resorts, **Wilderness Lodge & Villas** and **Animal Kingdom Lodge & Villas** serve the best food. **Coronado Springs, Port Orleans, Old Key West,** and **Caribbean Beach Resorts** each have a full-service restaurant, and all but Old Key West have a food court and pizza delivery. None of the isolated resorts, however, offer enough variety for the average person to be happy eating in his/her hotel every day. **Pop Century Resort, Art of Animation Resort,** and the **All-Star Resorts** (Disney's most isolated hotel complex) have nearly 10,500 guest rooms and suites, but no full-service restaurants. There are five food courts, but you have to get to them before 11 p.m. in most cases.

**7. AMENITIES AND RECREATION**  Disney resorts offer a staggering variety of amenities and recreational opportunities (see charts on the following pages). All provide elaborate swimming pools, themed shops, restaurants or food courts, bars or lounges, and access to five Disney golf courses. The more you pay for your lodging, the more amenities and opportunities are at your disposal. **Animal Kingdom Lodge & Villas, BoardWalk Inn, Wilderness Lodge,** and the **Contemporary, Grand Floridian, Polynesian,** and **Yacht & Beach Club Resorts,** for example, all offer concierge floors.

For swimming and sunning, the **Contemporary** and **Bay Lake Tower, Polynesian, Wilderness Lodge & Villas,** and **Grand Floridian & Villas** offer both pools and white-sand nonswimming beaches on Bay Lake or Seven Seas Lagoon. **Caribbean Beach Resort,** the **Dolphin,** and the **Yacht & Beach Club** also provide both pools and nonswimming beaches. Though lacking a lakefront beach, **Saratoga Springs Resort & Spa, Animal Kingdom Lodge & Villas, Port Orleans** and **Coronado Springs Resorts,** and **BoardWalk Inn & Villas** have exceptionally creative pools. See the chart on page 133 for our rankings of the swimming facilities at each Disney resort.

Bay Lake and Seven Seas Lagoon are the best venues for boating. Resorts fronting these lakes are the **Contemporary** and **Bay Lake Tower,** the **Polynesian, Wilderness Lodge & Villas,** the **Grand Floridian & Villas,** and **Fort Wilderness Resort & Campground.**

## DISNEY RESORT AMENITIES

| RESORT | SUITES | CONCIERGE FLOOR | NUMBER OF ROOMS | ROOM SERVICE (full) | FREE IN-ROOM WI-FI | FRIDGE/ MINI-FRIDGE |
|---|---|---|---|---|---|---|
| ALL-STAR RESORTS | • | — | 5,406 | — | • | • |
| ANIMAL KINGDOM LODGE | • | • | 972 | • | • | • |
| ANIMAL KINGDOM VILLAS | • | • | 458 | • | • | • |
| ART OF ANIMATION RESORT | • | — | 1,984 | — | • | • |
| BAY LAKE TOWER | • | — | 295 | • | • | • |
| BEACH CLUB VILLAS | • | — | 282 | • | • | • |
| BOARDWALK INN | • | • | 371 | • | • | • |
| BOARDWALK VILLAS | • | — | 532 | • | • | • |
| CARIBBEAN BEACH RESORT | — | — | 2,112 | — | • | • |
| CONTEMPORARY RESORT | • | • | 655 | • | • | • |
| CORONADO SPRINGS RESORT | • | • | 1,915 | • | • | • |
| DOLPHIN | • | — | 1,509 | • | — | • |
| FORT WILDERNESS CABINS | — | — | 409 | — | • | • |
| GRAND FLORIDIAN RESORT & SPA, VILLAS | • | • | 1,067 | • | • | • |
| OLD KEY WEST RESORT | • | — | 761 | — | • | • |
| POLYNESIAN RESORT | • | • | 847 | • | • | • |
| POP CENTURY RESORT | — | — | 2,880 | — | • | • |
| PORT ORLEANS RESORT | — | — | 3,056 | — | • | • |
| SARATOGA SPRINGS RESORT & SPA | • | — | 1,260 | — | • | • |
| SHADES OF GREEN | • | — | 586 | • | • | • |
| SWAN | • | — | 758 | • | — | • |
| TREEHOUSE VILLAS | • | — | 60 | — | • | • |
| WILDERNESS LODGE & VILLAS | • | • | 863 | • | • | • |
| YACHT & BEACH CLUB RESORTS | • | • | 1,197 | • | • | • |

Though on smaller bodies of water, **BoardWalk Inn & Villas, Coronado Springs,** the **Dolphin,** and the **Yacht & Beach Club** also rent watercraft.

Most convenient for golf are **Shades of Green, Saratoga Springs, Old Key West, Contemporary** and **Bay Lake Tower,** the **Polynesian,** the **Grand Floridian & Villas,** and **Port Orleans.** Tennis is available at the resorts indicated with bullets (•) in the chart on the facing page. Disney resorts with fitness and weight-training facilities are rated and ranked in the chart on page 132 (resorts not listed don't have such facilities).

While there are many places to bike or jog at Disney World (including golf-cart paths), the best biking and jogging are at **Fort Wilderness Resort & Campground** and the adjacent **Wilderness Lodge & Villas. Caribbean Beach Resort** offers a lovely hiking, biking, and jogging trail around the lake. Also good for biking and jogging is the area along Bonnet Creek extending through **Port Orleans** and **Old Key West** toward Downtown Disney. Epcot resorts offer a lakefront promenade and bike path, as well as a roadside walkway suitable for jogging.

## DISNEY RESORT RECREATION

| | FITNESS CENTER | WATER SPORTS | MARINA | BEACH | TENNIS | BIKING |
|---|---|---|---|---|---|---|
| ALL-STAR RESORTS | — | — | — | — | — | — |
| ANIMAL KINGDOM LODGE & VILLAS | • | — | — | — | •* | — |
| ART OF ANIMATION RESORT | — | — | — | — | — | — |
| BAY LAKE TOWER | • | • | • | • | — | — |
| BEACH CLUB VILLAS | • | • | • | • | • | — |
| BOARDWALK INN | • | • | • | — | • | • |
| BOARDWALK VILLAS | • | • | • | — | • | • |
| CARIBBEAN BEACH RESORT | — | — | — | • | — | • |
| CONTEMPORARY RESORT | • | • | • | • | — | • |
| CORONADO SPRINGS RESORT | • | • | — | — | • | • |
| DOLPHIN | • | • | • | • | • | • |
| FORT WILDERNESS RESORT | — | • | • | • | • | • |
| GRAND FLORIDIAN RESORT & SPA, VILLAS | • | • | • | • | • | • |
| OLD KEY WEST RESORT | • | — | • | — | • | • |
| POLYNESIAN RESORT | — | • | • | • | — | • |
| POP CENTURY RESORT | — | — | — | — | — | • |
| PORT ORLEANS RESORT | — | — | • | — | — | • |
| SARATOGA SPRINGS RESORT & SPA, TREEHOUSE VILLAS | • | — | — | — | • | • |
| SHADES OF GREEN | • | — | — | — | • | • |
| SWAN | • | — | • | • | • | — |
| WILDERNESS LODGE & VILLAS | • | • | • | • | — | • |
| YACHT & BEACH CLUB RESORTS | • | • | • | • | • | — |

*Kidani Village only

On-site child-care programs are offered at **Animal Kingdom Lodge & Villas,** the **Dolphin,** the **Hilton in the Walt Disney World Resort,** the **Polynesian,** the **Swan, Wilderness Lodge & Villas,** and the **Yacht & Beach Club Resorts.** All other resorts offer in-room babysitting (see page 354 for details).

Disney offers free public Wi-Fi at all resorts as well as at the theme parks, water parks, ESPN Wide World of Sports Complex, and several other public areas. The resort Wi-Fi, while free, is occasionally slow and unreliable. Two teens from Dallas had this to say:

> We wish the "free" Wi-Fi was better. We put free in quotes because the Wi-Fi sucks so much that it's not really free. It costs you the price of the two Advil you have to take trying to get it to work!

Thankfully, Disney continues to improve its Wi-Fi speed and reliability. If you find yourself unable to connect, try configuring your Wi-Fi adapter's wireless-mode setting to **802.11b.**

**8. NIGHTLIFE** The boardwalk at **BoardWalk Inn & Villas** has an upscale dance club (albeit one that has never lived up to its potential); a club

| HOTEL | FITNESS-CENTER RATING |
|---|---|
| **1. Saratoga Springs Resort & Spa, Treehouse Villas** | ★★★★★ |
| **2. Grand Floridian Resort & Spa, Villas** | ★★★★½ |
| **3. Animal Kingdom Lodge & Villas** | ★★★★ |
| **4. BoardWalk Inn & Villas** | ★★★★ |
| **5. Yacht & Beach Club Resorts** (shared facility) | ★★★★ |
| **6. Contemporary Resort–Bay Lake Tower** (shared facility) | ★★★½ |
| **7. Coronado Springs Resort** | ★★★½ |
| **8. Wilderness Lodge & Villas** | ★★★½ |
| **9. Dolphin** | ★★★ |
| **10. Shades of Green** | ★★★ |
| **11. Swan** | ★★★ |
| **12. Old Key West Resort** | ★½ |

featuring a live band, dueling pianos, and sing-alongs; a brewpub; and a sports bar. The BoardWalk clubs are within easy walking distance of all Epcot resorts. Most non-Disney hotels in the **Downtown Disney Resort Area,** as well as **Saratoga Springs Resort & Spa,** are within walking distance of Downtown Disney–Disney Springs nightspots. Nightlife at other Disney resorts is limited to lounges that stay open late.

*unofficial* **TIP**
The best resort lounges are the DVC-only **Top of the World** at Bay Lake Tower (make friends with an owner for access) and **Victoria Falls** at Animal Kingdom Lodge. Honorable mention goes to the **Territory Lounge** at Wilderness Lodge, where you can sometimes order from the menu of the adjacent Artist Point restaurant.

At the Contemporary Resort's **California Grill** and its adjoining lounge, you can relax over dinner or cocktails and watch the *Wishes* fireworks at the nearby Magic Kingdom.

### All the Goodies Without the Big Bucks

A Roanoke, Virginia, couple share how they enjoyed Disney's luxury resorts on the cheap:

*One thing I think you should emphasize in your guide is how lovely it is to enjoy the Deluxe resorts without having to pay to stay there. We had a rental car, so it was easy for us to drive to Animal Kingdom Lodge, the Grand Floridian, and Wilderness Lodge for dinner. We allowed enough time before our reservation to explore each resort, have a drink in the bar, and then be shown to our table. We felt very thrifty enjoying these expensive resorts and then going back to our moderately priced resort to sleep.*

## RESEARCHING WALT DISNEY WORLD HOTELS

THE UNOFFICIAL GUIDE HOTEL TEAM inspects hundreds of hotel rooms each year throughout North America and stays abreast of current trends and issues in the lodging industry. One such issue is the list of

| HOTEL | POOL RATING |
|---|---|
| **1.** YACHT & BEACH CLUB RESORTS & BEACH CLUB VILLAS *(shared complex)* | ★★★★★ |
| **2.** ANIMAL KINGDOM VILLAS *(Kidani Village)* | ★★★★½ |
| **3.** GRAND FLORIDIAN RESORT & SPA, VILLAS | ★★★★½ |
| **4.** PORT ORLEANS RESORT | ★★★★½ |
| **5.** SARATOGA SPRINGS RESORT & SPA, TREEHOUSE VILLAS | ★★★★½ |
| **6.** WILDERNESS LODGE & VILLAS | ★★★★½ |
| **7.** ANIMAL KINGDOM LODGE & VILLAS *(Jambo House)* | ★★★★ |
| **8.** BAY LAKE TOWER | ★★★★ |
| **9.** CORONADO SPRINGS RESORT | ★★★★ |
| **10.** DOLPHIN | ★★★★ |
| **11.** POLYNESIAN RESORT | ★★★★ |
| **12.** SWAN | ★★★★ |
| **13.** CARIBBEAN BEACH RESORT | ★★★★ |
| **14.** BOARDWALK INN & VILLAS | ★★★½ |
| **15.** CONTEMPORARY RESORT | ★★★½ |
| **16.** ALL-STAR RESORTS | ★★★ |
| **17.** ART OF ANIMATION RESORT | ★★★ |
| **18.** OLD KEY WEST RESORT | ★★★ |
| **19.** FORT WILDERNESS RESORT & CAMPGROUND | ★★★ |
| **20.** POP CENTURY RESORT | ★★★ |
| **21.** SHADES OF GREEN | ★★★ |

frequent complaints hotel guests make regarding their rooms. Over the years, the most common complaints have included excessive noise, uncomfortable beds, poor lighting, outdated furnishings, and substandard towels. Because these complaints are ongoing concerns, the hotel team undertook a complete reevaluation of every Walt Disney World resort (including the **Swan** and **Dolphin**) in each of these areas.

### In the Lab with Dr. Fluffy

Our tests included everything from the quality of the bed linens to the age of the mattresses to the fluffiness (loft) of the pillows. While evaluation criteria for linens and mattresses are fairly well known, we couldn't find any standard test to measure pillow fluffiness. A search of *Consumer Reports'* website failed to find anything, and fear of another restraining order kept us from making all the phone calls to the magazine that we wanted. So we had to invent our own.

The method we came up with is based on measuring how far a half-filled gallon jug of water sank into the middle of a pillow. (Two quarts of water weigh between one-third and one-half as much as a typical human head, according to most estimates. Also, a gallon jug is easy to find, and no one thinks twice if you bring one into a hotel lobby. Not so with a replica of a human head—trust us.)

Key to this experiment was determining the proper range of support a good pillow should provide. A test bottle that sank too deep

## DISNEY HOTELS: *Complaints and Comparisons*

| | SOUND | LIGHTING | PILLOWS | OVERALL |
|---|---|---|---|---|
| **ALL-STAR MOVIES** | D | C | B | C- |
| **ALL-STAR MUSIC** | A | C | C | B |
| **ALL-STAR SPORTS** | A | C | B | B |
| **ANIMAL KINGDOM LODGE & VILLAS** (Jambo House) | F | A | B | C+ |
| **ANIMAL KINGDOM VILLAS** (Kidani Village) | C | C | B | C |
| **ART OF ANIMATION** (standard rooms) | C | B | B | B- |
| **ART OF ANIMATION** (suites) | B | B+ | B | B |
| **BAY LAKE TOWER** | A | C | B | B+ |
| **BEACH CLUB RESORT & VILLAS** | B | D | B | C |
| **BOARDWALK INN** | B | C | B | B |
| **BOARDWALK VILLAS** | B | C | B | B |
| **CARIBBEAN BEACH RESORT** | B | C | B | B |
| **CONTEMPORARY RESORT** | D | A | A | B+ |
| **CORONADO SPRINGS RESORT** (studios) | B | B+ | B | B |
| **DOLPHIN** | A | D | A | B+ |
| **FORT WILDERNESS RESORT** (cabins) | C | D | D | D |
| **GRAND FLORIDIAN RESORT & SPA** | F | A | A | B- |
| **OLD KEY WEST RESORT** | A | D | A | B+ |
| **POLYNESIAN RESORT** | F | A | B | C+ |
| **POP CENTURY RESORT** | B | D | B | C |
| **PORT ORLEANS FRENCH QUARTER** | B | C | C | C |
| **PORT ORLEANS RIVERSIDE** | A | C | C | B |
| **SARATOGA SPRINGS RESORT & SPA** | B | C | C | C |
| **SWAN** | A | D | A | B+ |
| **TREEHOUSE VILLAS AT SARATOGA SPRINGS RESORT & SPA** | A | B | B | B+ |
| **WILDERNESS LODGE** | F | A | A | B- |
| **WILDERNESS LODGE VILLAS** | B | D | B | C |
| **YACHT CLUB RESORT** | D | A | A | B+ |

into a pillow would indicate not enough support; on the other hand, a bottle that sank very little might indicate an experience akin to sleeping on a brick. We therefore evaluated a wide range of pillows before the test to establish the proper range of support.

The best pillows are found at the non-Disney-owned **Swan** and **Dolphin** resorts. It's probably no coincidence that they're made with goose feathers and down; Disney's Deluxes use down, too, while the rest use polyester fiberfill. Perhaps that's why Disney's Deluxe and DVC resorts have improved their pillows by the greatest margin over the past few years. Decent pillows are found at the **Grand Floridian, Contemporary, Wilderness Lodge and Villas,** and **Old Key West.** The pillows at the Value resorts are better than they were five years ago, but nothing you'd want to buy for home.

Mattresses at all the Walt Disney World resorts come from brand-name manufacturers such as Sealy and Simmons. Value resorts typically have either two full-size mattresses or one king; Moderate and Deluxe resorts have two queen beds (each about 20% larger than a full) or one king. Exceptions are found at two Moderates: **Fort Wilderness Cabins** and **Caribbean Beach,** which use full mattresses; another notable exception is the **Swan,** which uses Westin's aptly named Heavenly Bed mattresses. Throughout the resorts, almost all the mattresses we inspected were less than 2 years old, and about half were less than a year old. The oldest mattress we found on Disney property—in service for 8 years—was at Disney's **Fort Wilderness Cabins.** (Outside Disney, we've seen 17-year-old mattresses still in use.)

Disney's Value and Moderate resorts use the same brand of 180-thread-count sheets for their bed linens. Disney's Deluxe and DDV resorts and the independent **Swan** and **Dolphin** resorts all use 250-thread-count sheets or better.

## Pipe Down Out There

Noisy rooms rank near the top of hotel guests' complaints every year. A well-designed room blocks both the noise coming from an adjacent room's television and from the swimming pool across the resort. Based on our initial tests of both interior and exterior soundproofing, and for the reasons outlined on the next page, we believe that a room's exterior door is the critical component in keeping sound out.

Chris Eliopoulos

Our test equipment consisted of a digital sound meter, a portable CD player, and a copy of The Who's greatest hits. We first calibrated the volume of the CD player until Roger Daltrey's ear-piercing wail in "Baba O'Riley" reached 70 decibels on the sound meter. Next, we took the CD player outside the room and placed the meter on top of the pillow of the bed closest to the exterior door. We replayed "Baba O'Riley" and recorded the decibel reading on the sound meter. For good measure, we also recorded the sound level in the room with and without the AC running, and around the resort in general.

Surprisingly, six of the seven worst results came from Disney Deluxe resorts, with **Animal Kingdom Lodge (Jambo House),** the **Grand Floridian,** the **Polynesian,** and **Wilderness Lodge Villas** making up the bottom four. Eight hotels earned top marks: **All-Star Music, All-Star Sports, Bay Lake Tower,** the **Dolphin, Old Key West Resort, Port Orleans Riverside Resort,** the **Swan,** and **Treehouse Villas.** In addition to the Deluxe resorts mentioned previously, the **Contemporary** and **Wilderness Lodge** were near the bottom, along with the Value **All-Star Movies Resort.**

Overall, Value and Moderate resorts did much better than Deluxe resorts when it came to blocking out exterior noise, with Disney's

All-Star Music and All-Star Sports, both Value resorts, being the overall winners (the Art of Animation Resort was not yet open). That certainly runs counter to what consumers would expect, so we set about trying to find an explanation. Like any good detective, we looked for an economic motive first.

The explanation turns out to be fairly simple, and it does come down to money—Disney's money. At most Disney Value and Moderate resorts (and, notably, Disney Vacation Club resorts), each room's exterior door opens onto the great outdoors, just as the average home's exterior door opens to the outside world. These exterior doors must have extensive weather stripping to keep out wind and rain. Also, exterior-facing walls tend to be thicker and better insulated than interior walls, as these measures reduce Disney's costs to heat and cool the rooms. Such walls also work really well at blocking noise.

In contrast, Disney's Deluxe rooms typically have doors that open onto an interior hallway that Disney is already paying to heat and cool. Thus, there's little economic incentive for Disney to put the same materials into the outward-facing doors and walls of some Deluxe resorts, since the temperature range outside the room is relatively constant and there's no need to keep rain or wind out. (In fact, many Deluxe resorts have a small gap of ¼–¾ inch at the bottom of their doors to aid in getting fresh air *into* the rooms.) Unfortunately, this permits more sound to enter. Finally, the interior hallways themselves can function as giant echo chambers, allowing sounds to bounce off the walls back and forth, up and down the hallway. Not so at the other resorts, where many sounds bounce off an exterior wall and out into space.

| QUIETEST ROOMS IN WALT DISNEY WORLD |
| --- |
| **ALL-STAR MUSIC** Buildings 5 and 6, rooms facing west |
| **ALL-STAR SPORTS** Building 3, rooms facing west; Building 2, rooms facing north |
| **BAY LAKE TOWER** Any room is good here—rooms are the quietest in WDW |
| **BEACH CLUB** Easternmost buildings, rooms facing east |
| **BEACH CLUB VILLAS** Rooms facing southeast |
| **BOARDWALK INN** All rooms facing courtyard, just east of main lobby |
| **CARIBBEAN BEACH** Trinidad South, Buildings 35 and 38, rooms facing lake; Barbados, Buildings 11 and 12, facing south |
| **PORT ORLEANS RIVERSIDE** Alligator Bayou, Buildings 26 and 28, rooms facing east; Acadian House, north wings, rooms facing west |
| **PORT ORLEANS FRENCH QUARTER** Building 1, rooms facing water; Building 7, north wing, rooms facing water; Building 6, north wing, rooms facing water |
| **TREEHOUSE VILLAS** Any room is good |
| **WILDERNESS LODGE** Middle of northernmost wing, rooms facing northwest (woods) |
| **WILDERNESS LODGE VILLAS** Southernmost part of the building, water-view rooms facing east |

Room soundproofing, however, is only half of the story. The other half, as any good real estate agent knows, is location; despite the resort's relatively good performance, a pool-view room at All-Star Sports is likely to pick up a lot more noise than an upper-floor corner room at the Grand Floridian, because the former faces a heavily used public space. So our next task was to determine the amount of external noise affecting every single room at Walt Disney World.

We assigned *Unofficial Guide* researcher Rich Vosburgh to the task. Using a combination of resort maps, aerial photography, and a whole lot of old-fashioned legwork, Rich created an External Noise Potential metric for each hotel room on Disney property, taking into account factors including the floor level, pedestrian traffic, proximity to public spaces, and number of nearby hotel rooms. Finally, the research team revisited every building in every resort to verify our rankings.

For the most part, we were spot on. But there were a couple of surprises that we're sure we would've overlooked had we not reviewed every single room. For example, the northwest-facing rooms in Buildings 4 and 5 of Disney's **All-Star Music** resort are situated well away from most public spaces in the resort and overlook the extreme end of a parking lot. There's not a lot of pedestrian traffic around, and the rooms themselves tested well for soundproofing—hey, these should be some quiet rooms, right? Well, when we visited the resort, we discovered that this particular section of parking lot, because it was away from most guest rooms, is where Disney decides to warm up its diesel buses in the morning before servicing the three All-Star Resorts. At 6 a.m., the area around these buildings sounded like Daytona International Speedway on race day.

Our research indicates that quiet rooms can be found in almost any resort. For readers who put peace and quiet at the top of their list, we've listed the 12 quietest spots among all WDW resorts in the chart on the facing page.

## Let There Be Light

As with noise, poor lighting generally ranks near the top of hotel guests' complaints. Of particular concern is the lighting in the bathroom and grooming area, the head of the bed (for reading), and the desk or table area (for working). In fact, lighting here is so important that professional associations publish standards listing the minimum amount of lighting needed for each area. Our evaluations incorporate the standards and recommendations of the Illuminating Engineering Society of North America (IESNA), a leading institution for lighting research, technology, and its applications.

Our test equipment was an industrial-grade digital light meter, able to detect a wide range of light levels. In addition to testing the lighting at the grooming, desk, and bed areas, we also tested the bath/shower area, the armchair or sitting area (if the room had one), and the overall light level in the room. The results were weighted to emphasize the quality of light in the grooming, desk, and bed areas.

The rooms with the best lighting were found at **Animal Kingdom Lodge & Villas (Jambo House),** the **Contemporary,** the **Grand Floridian,** the **Polynesian,** and **Wilderness Lodge & Villas,** all Deluxe resorts. **Coronado Springs** was the highest-scoring Moderate resort. No Value resort posted acceptable scores in lighting.

Rooms at the Polynesian exceeded the IESNA's minimum recommendations in every area, and the Contemporary's rooms exceeded the recommendations in all except the armchair reading area. Disney seems to be giving special attention to room lighting when doing its resort rehabs, and it's paying off.

Outside the Contemporary and Polynesian, the **Caribbean Beach** and **Grand Floridian** scored high with their grooming-and-bath-area lighting, while the **Wilderness Lodge Villas** and **Coronado Springs** had the best lighting in the desk/work area, with Coronado Springs using a specially designed ceiling lamp to ensure bright work surfaces; and **Wilderness Lodge** and **Port Orleans Riverside** had the best bed lighting. The worst scores were recorded at the **BoardWalk Inn,** the **Swan, Pop Century Resort,** and the **Yacht Club Resort.** How bad is the lighting? Rooms this dim are fertile ground for Barry White music as you put the moves on your sweetie.

## Check-in and Checkout

Up to 60 days before you arrive, you can log on to **mydisneyreservation .com** to complete the check-in process, make room requests, and FastPass+ reservations, choose MagicBands, and note events such as birthdays and anniversaries you're celebrating during your trip. Provide a credit card number and your arrival and departure times, and Disney will send you an e-mail confirmation that your check-in is complete. When you arrive at your resort, you'll bypass the regular check-in desk and head for another desk reserved for those who've already done so online. *Procrastinators, take note:* Online check-in should be completed at least 24 hours before you arrive; using your smartphone to check in online as you saunter up to the resort won't work.

If you're unable to check in online before your trip, don't worry. Disney has spent a lot of time and effort on reengineering the check-in process, cutting the average wait significantly. At the Value resorts, such as All-Star Sports, which get lots of tour and sports-team traffic, Disney has separate check-in areas for those groups, leaving the huge main check-in desk free for regular travelers. A cast member also roams the lobby and can issue an "all hands on deck" alert when lines develop.

The arrival of a busload of guests can sometimes overwhelm the front desk of Deluxe resorts, which have smaller front desks and fewer agents, but this is the exception rather than the rule.

If your room is unavailable when you arrive, Disney will either give you a phone number to call to check on the room or will offer to call or send a text message to your cell phone when it's ready.

A Cleveland mom shares her family's strategy for being content until their room is ready:

> My husband and I can't believe how people complain about the downtime people have while waiting for their room to be ready. We pack our swimsuits and sunscreen in our carry-ons. We arrive, check in, and leave our cell number for a text when the room is ready and head to the pool. By the time it's ready, we're rarin' to go!

Checking out is a snap. Your bill will be prepared and affixed to your doorknob or slipped under your door the night before you leave. If everything is in order, you have only to pack up and depart. If there's a problem with your bill, however, you'll have to resolve it at the front desk, where the previous order of most efficient to least efficient is a good gauge of the probable hassle you're in for.

## *UNOFFICIAL GUIDE* READERS SPEAK OUT

MANY READERS SHARE with us their experiences and criticisms regarding Disney hotels through our survey questionnaire (at **touring plans.com/walt-disney-world/survey**). Some copy us on letters of complaint sent to Disney. If you've written or copied us about a bad experience, you might be surprised that we haven't quoted your letter. Any business can have a bad day, even a Disney hotel, and a single incident might not be indicative of the hotel's general level of quality and service. In our experience, if a problem is endemic the same complaint will usually surface in a number of letters. But even with our voluminous reader mail, your comments often paint a mixed picture. For instance, for every letter we get that's critical of the Grand Floridian, it's not unusual for us to receive another letter telling us it's the best place the reader ever stayed.

We tend to hear more often from readers when things go badly than when things go well. Whether your experience was positive or negative, we encourage you to share it with us. The more comments we receive, the more accurate and complete a picture we can provide.

## READERS' 2014 DISNEY RESORT REPORT CARD

EACH YEAR, SEVERAL THOUSAND READERS send in their responses to our reader surveys. Found on the next two pages, the Resort Report Card documents their opinions of the Disney resorts as well as the Swan, the Dolphin, and Shades of Green. **Room quality** reflects readers' satisfaction with their rooms, while **Check-in efficiency** rates the speed and ease of check-in. **Quietness of room** measures how well, in the guests' perception, their rooms are insulated from external noise. **Shuttle service** rates Disney bus, boat, and/or monorail service to and from the hotels. **Pool** reflects reader satisfaction with the resorts' swimming pools. **Staff** measures the friendliness and helpfulness of the resort's employees, and **Dining** rates resorts' overall food value.

Readers have ranked Disney resorts about the same over the past four years, with most properties receiving an overall B rating. Also for a fourth consecutive year, bus transportation and dining options are the areas where Disney scores lowest. Check-in efficiency is an area where they do better than most. Off-site hotels are, on average, rated slightly lower than Disney hotels, with problems noted in food courts and transportation. Disney has also reopened its ratings lead over off-site hotels, which had dropped during the recession.

### Putting It All Together: Reader Picks for Best and Worst Resorts

Deluxe and DDV resorts generally rank higher than other Disney hotels in our annual survey, and this edition is no exception. Apparently, a woodsy theme helps: Readers rated **Wilderness Lodge, Wilderness Lodge Villas,** and **Fort Wilderness Cabins** highly across our surveys. The **Beach Club Villas** also scored well. **Treehouse Villas at Saratoga Springs** was the lowest-scoring resort in this category—its lack of on-site dining

## READERS' 2014 DISNEY RESORT REPORT CARD

| HOTEL |
| --- |
| ALL-STAR MOVIES |
| ALL-STAR MUSIC |
| ALL-STAR SPORTS |
| ANIMAL KINGDOM LODGE |
| ANIMAL KINGDOM VILLAS |
| ART OF ANIMATION RESORT |
| BAY LAKE TOWER |
| BEACH CLUB RESORT |
| BEACH CLUB VILLAS |
| BOARDWALK INN |
| BOARDWALK VILLAS |
| CARIBBEAN BEACH RESORT |
| CONTEMPORARY RESORT |
| CORONADO SPRINGS RESORT |
| DOLPHIN |
| FORT WILDERNESS CABINS |
| GRAND FLORIDIAN RESORT & SPA |
| OLD KEY WEST RESORT |
| POLYNESIAN RESORT |
| POP CENTURY RESORT |
| PORT ORLEANS FRENCH QUARTER |
| PORT ORLEANS RIVERSIDE |
| SARATOGA SPRINGS RESORT & SPA |
| SHADES OF GREEN |
| SWAN |
| TREEHOUSE VILLAS |
| WILDERNESS LODGE |
| WILDERNESS LODGE VILLAS |
| YACHT CLUB RESORT |
| AVERAGE FOR DISNEY HOTELS |
| AVERAGE FOR OFF-SITE HOTELS |

dissatisfies many readers, and it does much worse than average on our "Would you stay here again?" and "Would you recommend this hotel to a friend?" questions.

After the Fort Wilderness Cabins, **Port Orleans French Quarter** was the next highest-rated Moderate resort, with **Caribbean Beach** the lowest. Among Disney's Value resorts, **Art of Animation** scored highest and **Pop Century** scored lowest.

| ROOM QUALITY | CHECK-IN EFFICIENCY | QUIETNESS OF ROOM | SHUTTLE SERVICE | POOL | STAFF | DINING | OVERALL RATING |
|---|---|---|---|---|---|---|---|
| C | B | B- | B | B | A | C | B |
| B | B | B | B | B | B+ | C | B |
| B | B | B- | B- | B | B+ | C | B |
| B | B | B | C | A | A | C | B |
| B | A | B | B | B | A | C | B |
| B | B | B | B- | B | A | C | B |
| A | B | B | B | B | A | C | B |
| B | B | C | B | A | B | D | B |
| B | A | A | B | A- | B | C | B |
| B | A | B- | B+ | B | A | C | B |
| B | A | B | B- | C+ | A | F | B |
| C | B | B | B- | B | B | D | B- |
| B | B | B | B | B | B | C | B |
| B | B- | B | B | B | B | D | B- |
| B+ | A | A | C | A | B | D | B |
| B | B+ | A | B- | A | A | C- | B |
| B | B | B | B | B | B | C | B |
| B | B | B | B | B | B | F | B |
| A | A | B | B+ | B | A | D | B |
| C | A- | C | B | B | A- | C | B |
| B | A | B+ | B | B | A | C | B |
| B | B | B | C | B | B | C | B |
| A | B | A | C | B | A | C | B |
| A | C | A | F | C | B | D | B |
| A | B- | B | B- | C+ | B+ | C | B |
| A- | A- | B- | B | A | A- | D- | B |
| B | A | B | B | B | A | B | B |
| B | B | A | B- | A- | A | C+ | B |
| B | B | B | B- | A | A | F | B |
| **B** | **B** | **B** | **C** | **B** | **B+** | **C-** | **B** |
| B | C+ | B | F | C | B | F | B |

As in years past, readers tended to be tougher than the *Unofficial Guide* hotel inspectors when it came to ratings. (For example, we really prefer Pop Century to the All-Stars.) But remember that readers are rating one guest room during a specific visit, while our inspectors provide a comparative rating of more than 250 Disney and non-Disney hotels in and around Walt Disney World. For our ratings, see "How the Hotels Compare," on pages 263–268.

| WOULD YOU RECOMMEND THIS HOTEL TO A FRIEND? | |
|---|---|
| **RESORT NAME** | definitely recommend |
| Fort Wilderness Cabins | 100% |
| Port Orleans French Qtr. | 100% |
| Polynesian Resort | 97% |
| Dolphin | 96% |
| All-Star Movies | 95% |
| Wilderness Lodge | 95% |
| Wilderness Lodge Villas | 95% |
| Art of Animation | 94% |
| Animal Kingdom Lodge | 93% |
| Contemporary Resort | 93% |
| Beach Club Resort | 92% |
| Animal Kingdom Villas | 91% |
| Beach Club Villas | 91% |
| Old Key West | 91% |
| Yacht Club Resort | 91% |
| BoardWalk Inn | 90% |
| BoardWalk Villas | 89% |
| Port Orleans Riverside | 88% |
| Shades of Green | 88% |
| Grand Floridian Resort | 87% |
| Bay Lake Tower | 86% |
| All-Star Music | 84% |
| Pop Century Resort | 83% |
| Saratoga Springs Resort | 82% |
| Coronado Springs Resort | 76% |
| All-Star Sports | 75% |
| Swan | 75% |
| Caribbean Beach Resort | 67% |
| Treehouse Villas | 52% |
| **Average for WDW hotels** | 87% |
| **Average for off-site hotels** | 93% |

| WOULD YOU STAY AT THIS HOTEL AGAIN? | |
|---|---|
| **RESORT NAME** | would stay again |
| Beach Club Villas | 100% |
| BoardWalk Inn | 100% |
| Fort Wilderness Cabins | 100% |
| Wilderness Lodge Villas | 100% |
| Port Orleans French Qtr. | 98% |
| Wilderness Lodge | 97% |
| Beach Club Resort | 96% |
| Contemporary Resort | 96% |
| Dolphin | 96% |
| Bay Lake Tower | 95% |
| Grand Floridian Resort | 95% |
| Polynesian Resort | 94% |
| Shades of Green | 94% |
| Art of Animation | 93% |
| Animal Kingdom Villas | 91% |
| Port Orleans Riverside | 91% |
| Yacht Club Resort | 91% |
| All-Star Movies | 89% |
| All-Star Music | 89% |
| Animal Kingdom Lodge | 89% |
| BoardWalk Villas | 89% |
| Pop Century Resort | 87% |
| Swan | 86% |
| Old Key West | 82% |
| Saratoga Springs Resort | 82% |
| Coronado Springs Resort | 76% |
| All-Star Sports | 75% |
| Caribbean Beach Resort | 73% |
| Treehouse Villas | 52% |
| **Average for WDW hotels** | 88% |
| **Average for off-site hotels** | 96% |

# WALT DISNEY WORLD HOTEL PROFILES

FOR THOSE OF YOU WHO'VE PLOWED through the foregoing and remain undecided, here are our profiles of each Disney resort. For photos, video, and up-to-date information on the Walt Disney World resorts, check out our website, **touringplans.com**.

## THE MAGIC KINGDOM RESORTS

### Disney's Grand Floridian Resort & Spa *(see map on page 144)*

WALT DISNEY WORLD'S FLAGSHIP HOTEL is inspired by Florida's grand Victorian seaside resorts. A complex of four- and five-story white frame buildings, the Grand Floridian integrates verandas, intricate

| *UNOFFICIAL* PICKS FOR DISNEY ON-SITE RESORTS |
| --- |
| **ADULTS** |
| **Value: Pop Century** For the nostalgic decor. |
| **Moderate: Coronado Springs** For a bit of sophistication at reasonable rates |
| **Deluxe: Swan and Dolphin** For a great location, lots of adult-oriented restaurants nearby, and lower rates than the other Crescent Lake resorts |
| **GROUPS OF FIVE OR MORE** |
| **Value: Art of Animation** Newest suites with two baths |
| **Moderate: Port Orleans Riverside** Any two connecting rooms |
| **Deluxe: Old Key West** Two-bedroom villa (booked with DVC rental points) |
| **FAMILIES WITH YOUNG KIDS** |
| **Value: Art of Animation** Kids will delight in the architecture and themed pools. |
| **Moderate: Caribbean Beach** Like a beach vacation while you're at Disney. |
| **Deluxe: Animal Kingdom Lodge** Fantastic interactive and educational programs. *Alternate:* **Polynesian** after construction is finished. |
| **FAMILIES WITH OLDER KIDS** |
| **Value: Pop Century** A lively pool scene means meeting new friends. Very teen-friendly food court. |
| **Moderate: Fort Wilderness** There's plenty of opportunity for independent exploration of this massive resort, and having a kitchen means you don't have to take out a second mortgage to feed the bottomless pits of teen stomachs. |
| **Deluxe: Yacht & Beach Club** For Stormalong Bay and easy access to Epcot and Disney's Hollywood Studios |

latticework, dormers, and turrets beneath a red-shingle roof to capture the most memorable elements of 19th-century ocean-resort architecture. Covering 40 acres along Seven Seas Lagoon, the Grand Floridian offers lovely pools, white-sand beaches, and a multifaceted marina.

The 867 guest rooms, with wood trim and soft goods (curtains, linens, towels, and the like) in tones of peach, pink, and green, are luxurious but not stuffy or too feminine. The woodwork, marble-topped sinks, and ceiling fans amplify the Victorian theme. Large by any standard, the typical room is 440 square feet (dormer rooms are smaller) and furnished with two queen beds, a daybed, a reading chair, and a table with two side chairs. Many rooms have a balcony.

| STRENGTHS | WEAKNESSES |
| --- | --- |
| • Low guest-to-staff ratio | • Most expensive of the Walt Disney World resorts |
| • Excellent dining options for adults | |
| • Large rooms with day beds | • Self-parking is across the street |
| • Recently refurbished on-site spa | • Public areas often blocked by wedding parties |
| • Fantastic kids' *Alice in Wonderland*–themed splash area | • Only one on-site restaurant suitable for younger children |
| • Boat and monorail transportation to the Magic Kingdom | • Close to ongoing construction at the Polynesian through early 2016 |
| • Diverse recreational options | • Bus transportation to DHS, Animal Kingdom, water parks, and Downtown Disney is shared by the other monorail resorts |
| • Close to Palm, Magnolia, and Oak Trail Golf Courses | |

*Grand Floridian Resort & Spa & Grand Floridian Villas*

With a high ratio of staff to guests, service is outstanding. The resort has several full-service restaurants, and others are a short monorail ride away. The hotel is connected directly to the Magic Kingdom by monorail and to other Disney World destinations by bus. Walking time to the monorail and bus-loading areas from the most remote guest rooms is about 7–10 minutes.

The Grand Floridian's **Senses Spa,** modeled after the Disney Cruise Line's, is one of the best in the Orlando area (see our review in Part Four). Recently refurbished, the pools are among the nicest on Disney property. The Courtyard Pool, large enough that local waterfowl mistake it for a lake, added a zero-entry ramp in 2013 for small children to splash in. Cabanas are available to rent here, too. The Beach Pool was also refurbished during summer 2013. An *Alice in Wonderland*–themed splash area was added between the Grand Flo's main building and the Villas. If your kids like water and their college fund is paid up, this is the place to be.

Besides the pool refurbishments, the resort has refurbished some of its quick-service-dining options.

Most reader comments concerning the Grand Floridian are positive. First, from a Durham, North Carolina, mother of two preschoolers:

*The Grand Floridian pool with the waterslide was a big hit with our kids. They also loved taking the boat across the lagoon to return from the Magic Kingdom.*

**GOOD (AND NOT-SO-GOOD) ROOMS AT THE GRAND FLORIDIAN** The resort is spread over a peninsula jutting into Seven Seas Lagoon. In addition to the main building, there are five dispersed rectangular buildings. Most rooms have a balcony, and most balconies are enclosed by a rail that affords good visibility. Dormer rooms, just beneath the roof in each building, have smaller enclosed balconies that limit visibility when you're seated. Most dormer rooms, however, have vaulted ceilings and a coziness that compensates for the less-desirable balconies.

If you want to be near the bus and monorail, most of the restaurants, and shopping, ask for a room in the main building (all concierge rooms). The best rooms are 4321–4329 and 4421–4429, which have full balconies and overlook the lagoon in the direction of the beach and the Polynesian. (*Note:* You'll be seeing a lot of the Polynesian's construction work through 2014 and into 2015.) Other excellent main-building rooms are 4401–4409, with full balconies overlooking the marina and an unobstructed view of Cinderella Castle across the lagoon.

Of the five lodges, three—Conch Key, Boca Chica, and Big Pine Key—have one long side facing the lagoon and the other facing inner courtyards and swimming pools. At Conch Key, full-balcony rooms 7228–7231, 7328–7331, and 7425–7431 offer vistas across the lagoon to the Magic Kingdom and castle. Less-expensive rooms in the same building that offer good views are 7211, 7311, and 7411; 7413, 7415, 7417, 7419, and 7421; 7212, 7312, and 7412; and 7414. (Grand Floridian room numbers are coded. Take Room 7213: 7 is the building number, 2 is the floor, and 13 is the room number.) In Boca Chica and Big Pine Key, ask for a lagoon-view room on the first, second, or third floor. Many garden-view rooms in Big Pine Key, and a few in Boca Chica, have views obstructed by a poolside building. These are the worst views from any Grand Floridian room.

The two remaining buildings, Sugar Loaf Key (concierge only) and Sago Key, face each other across the marina. The opposite side of Sugar Loaf Key faces a courtyard, while the other side of Sago Key faces a finger of the lagoon and a forested area. These views are pleasant but not in the same league as those from the rooms listed previously. Exceptions are end rooms in Sago Key that have a view of the lagoon and Cinderella Castle (Rooms 5144, 5145, 5242–5245, 5341–5345, and 5439–5445).

**THE VILLAS AT DISNEY'S GRAND FLORIDIAN RESORT & SPA** This Disney Deluxe Villa property opened in the fall of 2013. The 200-room T-shaped building sits with the main hotel along the shore of Seven Seas Lagoon. The Villas offer studio, one-, two-, and three-bedroom accommodations that sleep 5–12 adults; among DDV resorts, the studios were among the first to accommodate a maximum of 5.

Decorated in neutral tones with mostly green accents, rooms are the nicest of any DDV property. Most have vaulted living-room ceilings and faux-wood balconies or porches. Those balconies stretch the entire length of the room, giving everyone enough space for a good view.

The studios have a kitchenette with mini-refrigerator, sink, and coffeemaker, while the larger rooms have full kitchens. Those feature a stainless-steel oven range, with the dishwasher and refrigerator tucked behind white-wood panels that match the glass door cabinets. Other amenities in the full kitchens include a full-size coffeemaker, a toaster, frying pans, and the usual set of plates, glasses, cups, and cutlery. Also in the kitchen are a banquette seat and table with room for six.

The living room has a sofa that seats three comfortably, an upholstered chair and ottoman, a coffee table, and a large, flat-panel television. The sofa converts into a bed that sleeps two; a cabinet below the TV hides a small pulldown bed. We'd use these for kids, not adults.

Studio rooms have a queen bed in addition to the folding options listed above. One-bedroom villas have a king bed plus the folding options; two-bedroom villas have a king mattress in one bedroom and two queen mattresses in the other, plus the folding options; the Grand Villa's third bedroom has an additional two queen mattresses.

The one- and two-bedroom units and the Grand Villa bedrooms include a large writing desk, a flat-panel TV with DVD player, two nightstands with convenient electric plugs, and a side chair. They've also got large walk-in closets.

Bathrooms are large, with marble tile and, yes, flat-panel TVs built into the mirrors. Studio bathrooms have a separate toilet and shower area; in the one-bedroom configuration, a tub and dressing area sit adjacent to the bedroom. The bathroom and shower are connected by a pocket door, allowing two groups of people to get dressed at the same time. The tiled shower looks as if it could comfortably hold eight people should the need arise. (We're not kidding—it's large enough that if you stand right outside and yell "Echo!," it'll echo.)

The Villas have their own parking lot next to the building, but no on-site dining. Within walking distance, however, are the restaurants of both the main Grand Floridian and the Polynesian, giving you a bit more variety than other Magic Kingdom resorts. Room service is available from the Grand Floridian's in-room dining menu. Rates are high, as you might expect, but renting Disney Vacation Club points helps in that regard.

**GOOD (AND NOT-SO-GOOD) ROOMS AT THE GRAND FLORIDIAN VILLAS**
Rooms 1X14, 1X16, and 1X18 face the Magic Kingdom and have views of Space Mountain and the castle and fireworks; 1X14 has probably the best views of any room in all of the Villas. (X indicates a floor number.)

Even-numbered rooms 1X02–1X12 face west, toward the Polynesian and Seven Seas Lagoon, and have a good view of the nightly water pageant as it floats by. Until the Polynesian refurb is done in 2015, however, construction equipment and unfinished buildings will be a part of the views from these rooms.

Rooms 1X15, 1X17, 1X19–1X22, 1X24, 1X26, and 1X28 face Disney's Wedding Pavilion, the parking lot, the monorail, and landscaping. Odd-numbered rooms 1X03–1X13 and 1X25, 1X27, and 1X29 look out onto the pool facilities and landscaping.

## Disney's Polynesian Resort (see map on next page)

| STRENGTHS | WEAKNESSES |
|---|---|
| • Most family-friendly dining on the monorail loop | • Ongoing DVC/DDV construction through at least fall 2015 |
| • Fun South Seas theme | • No spa or exercise facilities (guests must use those at the Grand Floridian) |
| • On-site child care | |
| • Boat and monorail transportation to the Magic Kingdom | • Bus transportation to DHS, Animal Kingdom, water parks, and Downtown Disney is shared with the other monorail resorts |
| • Walking distance to Epcot monorail | |
| • Among the best club levels of the Deluxe resorts | |
| • Close to Palm, Magnolia, and Oak Trail Golf Courses | |

SOUTH PACIFIC TROPICS ARE RE-CREATED at this Deluxe resort, which currently consists of two- and three-story Hawaiian "longhouses" situated around the four-story Great Ceremonial House. Buildings feature wood tones, with exposed-beam roofs and tribal-inspired geometric inlays in the cornices. The Great Ceremonial House contains restaurants, shops, and (for now) a rainforest atrium lobby with a rocky waterfall and more than 70 species of tropical plants. Spread across 39 acres along Seven Seas Lagoon, the resort has three white-sand beaches, some with volleyball courts. Its pool complex likewise captures the South Pacific theme. The Polynesian has no on-site fitness center, but its guests are welcome at the Grand Floridian's facilities, a short quarter-mile walk or 2-minute monorail ride away. Landscaping is superb—garden-view rooms are generally superior to garden- or standard-view rooms at other resorts.

The Polynesian will be undergoing major construction through at least the fall of 2015, to convert some existing rooms to DVC/DDV units and add approximately 20 new bungalows on stilts on Seven Seas Lagoon. These various projects affect the entire resort, including parking, check-in, restaurants, pools, beaches, child-care facilities, and more. When the work is completed, the resort's name will revert to the one that it opened with in 1971: **Disney's Polynesian Village Resort.**

The Polynesian's Tahiti, Tokelau, and Rapa Nui buildings are moving into Disney's time-share program. Rooms here will be remodeled, and although Disney hasn't yet provided specifics, we think they'll be studio accommodations, probably with kitchenettes.

When the remodel is finished, the Polynesian Village will have fewer than 500 standard hotel rooms. We wouldn't be surprised to see rates surpass those at the Grand Floridian.

If you're booking a stay in late 2014 or anytime during 2015 and the Poly is your first-choice resort, check with Disney regarding the specific construction activities scheduled for your dates. Another good resource for news and updates is **tikimanpages.com,** run by longtime *Unofficial Guide* friend Steve Seifert.

Although the Polynesian is one of Disney's oldest resorts, periodic refurbishments keep it well maintained. Refurbishments started in

## Polynesian Resort

2013 include new paint, carpet, headboards, soft goods, and bath-room designs for all rooms.

Rooms have light-green walls and white bed comforters with green-and-brown tropical-print coverlets. Amenities include built-in closets and dressers with flat-panel televisions. Each dresser includes two horizontal shelves above and below the TV for extra storage capacity. The closets are spacious, light, and eminently functional. A nice touch on most of the furniture and woodwork is the textured surfaces (some of them carved). Lighting throughout the rooms, including that for the desks/work areas and beds, is still among the best on Disney property.

King beds were also added to some rooms in the 2013 update and can be booked directly instead of your having to make a request. King rooms are found in the Fiji, Rarotonga, and Samoa longhouses only, and only garden views are available.

Bathrooms are well designed but kind of small. The 2013 redesign put in dual sinks for the old singles and added more open space to the whole bath. Shelves above and below sinks allow plenty of storage. Outward-curving shower rods efficiently add elbow room.

Easily accessible by monorail are full-service restaurants at the Grand Floridian and Contemporary Resorts, as well as restaurants in the Magic Kingdom. The Polynesian has a monorail station on-site and is within easy walking distance of the Transportation and Ticket Center. Bus service is available to other Disney destinations. Walking time to the bus- and monorail-loading areas from the most remote rooms is 8–11 minutes.

Some readers, like this family from Summerville, South Carolina, wouldn't stay anywhere else on Disney property but the Polynesian:

> Polynesian was WONDERFUL. We could walk to the Transporta-tion and Ticket Center to get on the buses to Disney's Hollywood Studios and Animal Kingdom without getting on the monorail. From now on, we will ONLY stay at the Polynesian. Well worth the extra $.

A Maryland family of four found the guest-room soundproofing somewhat lacking, confirming our own research:

> We took towels from the pool and stuffed them under the door to deaden the noise coming from the connecting room.

**GOOD (AND NOT-SO-GOOD) ROOMS AT THE POLYNESIAN RESORT** The Polynesian's 11 guest-room buildings, called *longhouses,* are spread over a long strip of land bordered by the monorail on one side and Seven Seas Lagoon on the other. All the buildings, except for the more recently added Tahiti, Rapa Nui, and Tokelau (now earmarked for the DVC project), opened with the Magic Kingdom in 1971. All buildings feature first-floor patios and third-floor balconies. The older buildings, com-prising more than half the resort's rooms, have fake balconies on their second floors. (The newer buildings offer full balconies on both the second and third floors, and patios on the first.) A small number of patios in the first-floor rooms have views blocked by mature vegetation, but these patios provide more room than do the balconies on the third floor. If view is important and you're staying in one of the eight older longhouses, ask for a third-floor room.

Within the Great Ceremonial House are most restaurants and shops, as well as the resort lobby, guest services, and bus and monorail stations. Longhouses most convenient to the Great Ceremonial House (Fiji, Tonga suites, Rarotonga, Niue, and Samoa) offer views of the swimming complex, a small marina, or inner gardens. There are no lagoon views except for oblique views from the upper floors of Fiji and Samoa, Aotearoa, and Tokelau, and a tunnel view from Tonga (suites only). Samoa, however, by virtue of its proximity to the main swimming complex, is a good choice for families who plan to spend time at the pool. If your children are under age 8, request a first-floor room on the Nanea Volcano Pool side of Samoa.

You can specifically request a lagoon- or Magic Kingdom–view room at the Polynesian, if you're willing to pay extra. The best of these rooms are on the second and third floors in Tahiti (which, again, will be a DVC building), the third floor in Tuvalu, and, if you're staying in a concierge room, the third floor in Hawaii.

There are some quirks in the way Disney categorizes room views at the Polynesian, and it's possible to get a view of the castle and fireworks while staying in a garden-view room. Second- and third-floor rooms in the future DVC building Tokelau (Rooms 2901–2913, 2939–2948, 3901–3913, and 3939–3948) offer the best shot at sideways views of the castle and fireworks, though readers say taller palm trees may block even these upper rooms. First-floor rooms (1901–1913 and 1939–1948) may also have landscaping blocking some of the Magic Kingdom views, but the patio provides more room to move to find a better spot, too.

In addition to second-floor rooms in the older buildings (the buildings with fake balconies), also avoid the monorail-side rooms in Rarotonga and the parking-lot side of Rapa Nui (which will also become a DVC building). Garden-view rooms in Aotearoa are especially nice, but the monorail, though quiet, runs within spitting distance.

Many of the first-floor rooms in Hawaii (1501–1518) have been downgraded from theme-park-view to garden- or lagoon-view rooms because their scenery is now blocked by the new bungalows. These rooms still offer a chance to see the evening fireworks, however, and cost a little less expensive than similar rooms on higher floors.

If you plan to spend a lot of time at Epcot, Tahiti and Rapa Nui are within easy walking distance of the Transportation and Ticket Center (TTC) and the Epcot monorail. Even if you're going to the Magic Kingdom, it's a shorter walk from Tahiti and Rapa Nui to the TTC and Magic Kingdom monorail than to the monorail station at the Great Ceremonial House. Tuvalu, Fiji, and Aotearoa are the most distant accommodations from the Polynesian's bus stop. For large strollers or wheelchair access, take the ferry to the Magic Kingdom.

**POLYNESIAN VILLAGE VILLAS?** At press time, Disney hadn't released the official name of the Polynesian's new time-share rooms. As noted on page 147, we do know that the DVC/DDV units will likely include newly refurbished studio rooms throughout the Rapa Nui, Tahiti, and Tokelau buildings, along with about 20 new two-bedroom bungalows built on stilts and sitting just offshore of Tahiti in Seven Seas Lagoon. No word on whether there'll be a separate parking lot for these rooms, but we're confident that dining, child care, and transportation will be shared with the main resort. Views from the new lagoon bungalows should be incredible . . . with breathtaking prices to match.

## Disney's Wilderness Lodge & Villas *(see map on next page)*

| STRENGTHS | WEAKNESSES |
|---|---|
| • National-park-lodge theme is a favorite of kids and adults alike | • Transportation to Magic Kingdom is by bus or boat only |
| • Along with Animal Kingdom Lodge, it's the least expensive Disney Deluxe resort | • One of two Deluxe resorts without character dining |
| • Excellent lounge for adults | • Whispering Canyon Cafe noise can spill out into lobby and rooms near it |
| • Close to recreational options at Fort Wilderness | • Villas guests must access most services through main hotel |
| • Great views from guest rooms | • Bus transportation to Magic Kingdom sometimes shared with Fort Wilderness |
| • Rooms with bunk beds available | |
| • On-site child care | |
| • Exceptionally peaceful location and public areas (Villas) | • Smallest rooms of Disney's Deluxe resorts |

THIS DELUXE RESORT IS INSPIRED by national-park lodges of the early 20th century. Situated on the shore of Bay Lake, the lodge consists of an eight-story central building augmented by two seven-story guest wings and a wing of studio and one- and two-bedroom condominiums. The hotel features exposed timber columns, log cabin–style facades, and dormer windows. The lobby boasts an 82-foot-tall stone fireplace and two 55-foot Pacific Northwest totem poles. Although the resort isn't on vast acreage, it does have a beach and a delightful pool modeled on a mountain stream.

The lodge's 727 guest rooms, refurbished in 2012, have darkly stained Mission-style furniture accented by soft goods done in blue-and-red American Indian patterns. Carved-wood headboards, rough-hewn armoires, and rustic light fixtures create a log-cabin coziness. Typical rooms have two queen-size beds; some have one queen bed and bunk beds. All rooms have a table and chairs and a vanity outside the bathroom. Most rooms have balconies.

Part of the DVC time-share program, the 136 adjoining Villas at Disney's Wilderness Lodge are studio and one- and two-bedroom units in a freestanding building to the right of the lodge. Studios offer kitchenettes; one- and two-bedroom villas come with full kitchens. The villas' rustic decor was updated in 2014, with pine furniture, leaf-motif rugs and curtains, and woodland creatures from Disney's *Bambi* decorating the pillows and bedding. The villas share restaurants, pools, and other amenities with Wilderness Lodge.

Refurbished in 2014, the villas' studios got fold-down sleeper sofas like those at the Grand Floridian Villas. All villas got new armoires and flat-panel TVs; new stainless-steel kitchen appliances (one-and two-bedroom units); new bathroom tile and fixtures; and new flooring, wallpaper, and kitchen countertops.

## Wilderness Lodge & Villas

There are two full-service restaurants on-site, with several more a boat ride away. The resort is connected to the Magic Kingdom by boat and to other Disney parks by bus. Boat service may be suspended during thunderstorms, so if it's raining or looks like it's about to, Disney will provide buses. Walking time to buses and boats from the most remote rooms is about 5–8 minutes.

Two adult couples from Fort Smith, Arkansas, think the Wilderness Lodge is great, with one reservation (pardon the pun):

> *There has been a real downturn in our opinion in the efficacy of the bus transportation. The ambience of the lodge makes up for it, though.*

A Boone County, Indiana, reader concurs about the transportation:

> *To paraphrase Mark Twain, rumors that Wilderness Lodge's transportation problems have been resolved are greatly exaggerated—it's an easy ride to the Magic Kingdom, but trips to the Studios and Animal Kingdom take nearly an hour, which is just inexcusable.*

**GOOD (AND NOT-SO-GOOD) ROOMS AT WILDERNESS LODGE & VILLAS**
The lodge is shaped like a very blocky V. The main entrance and lobby are at the closed end of the V. Next are middle wings that connect the lobby to the parallel end sections, which extend to the open part of the V. The V's open end flanks pools and gardens and overlooks Bay Lake directly or obliquely. Avoid rooms on the fourth, fifth, and sixth floors numbered 67–99; these overlook the main lobby and pick up every whoop, holler, and shout from the boisterous Whispering Canyon Cafe

downstairs. The noise makes it difficult to get to sleep before Whispering Canyon closes, usually at 10 p.m.

The better rooms are on floors 4, 5, and 6, toward the V's open end. On the very end of the V, rooms 4000–4003, 4166–4169, 5000–5003, 5166–5169, 6000–6003, and 6166–6169 offer a direct frontal view of the lake. Toward the end of the V on the parallel wings, but facing inward, odd-numbered rooms 4005–4023, 4147–4165, 5005–5023, 5147–5165, 6005–6023, and 6147–6165 face the courtyard, but with excellent oblique lake views. Even-numbered rooms 5004–5034 and 6004–6034 front a woodland northwest of the lodge, and beyond the woodland, the Magic Kingdom. Odd-numbered rooms 5035–5041, 5123–5129, 6035–6041, and 6123–6129, on the lake end of the parallel middle wings, offer a direct but distant view of the lake, with pools and gardens in the foreground. Rooms looking southeast face the Wilderness Lodge Villas, a garden area, and woods. (The map suggests that these rooms offer a lake view, but trees block the line of sight.)

A handful of rooms overlook parking lots, service areas, and such—of these, avoid fourth- and fifth-floor rooms X042–X066. The rooms listed above afford the most desirable views, but if you can't score one, you're pretty much assured of a woodland view or a room fronting the faux rocks and creek in the V's inner courtyard. Concierge rooms on the seventh floor aren't recommended: Only those facing the Magic Kingdom have nice views, and even those have a service area in the foreground. Almost all rooms at the lodge have balconies. Avoid 1538, 1540, 1542, and 1544, which face a giant green electrical transformer.

Except for a few rooms overlooking the pool, rooms at Wilderness Lodge Villas offer woodland views. The best are odd-numbered rooms 2531–2563 and 3531–3563, which open to the lake (northeast) side of the resort (you can't see the lake, though). Rooms on the opposite side of the same wing offer similar views, but with some roads and parking lots visible, and with traffic noise.

### Disney's Contemporary Resort and Bay Lake Tower
*(see map on next page)*

| STRENGTHS | WEAKNESSES |
|---|---|
| • Iconic architecture; the only hotel that the monorail goes *through* | • "Magic Kingdom view" rooms mostly look out at parking lots and are overpriced |
| • Large, very attractive guest rooms with nice views of Bay Lake | • Very small studios in Bay Lake Tower sleep no more than two people comfortably |
| • Easy walk to the Magic Kingdom | |
| • Rooms in the Garden Building can be a relatively good value | • Hordes of bugs are attracted to the Garden Building's entry lighting |
| • Convenient parking | • Hallway decor at Bay Lake Tower can feel institutional |
| • Best lounge at Walt Disney World (Top of the World, Bay Lake Tower) | • Bus transportation to DHS, Animal Kingdom, water parks, and Downtown Disney is shared with the other monorail resorts |
| • Recreation options on Bay Lake | |
| • Boat service to Fort Wilderness Resort & Campground | |
| | • No on-site child care |

## Contemporary Resort & Bay Lake Tower

THIS 655-ROOM DELUXE RESORT ON BAY LAKE is unique in that its A-frame design permits the Magic Kingdom monorail to pass through the structure's cavernous atrium. The only real source of color in the atrium is a 90-foot mosaic depicting American Indian children and nature. The off-white central tower is augmented by a three-story Garden Building fronting Bay Lake to the south and by Bay Lake Tower, a 295-room, 15-story Disney Deluxe Villa development, to the north.

Standard rooms in the A-frame afford fantastic views of Bay Lake or the Magic Kingdom, and all have balconies. At 394 square feet each, they're only slightly smaller than equivalent rooms at the Grand Floridian.

The Contemporary's rooms are, in our opinion, among the nicest of any Disney resort. Rooms were refurbished in 2013, and the decor still lives up to the resort's name. Amenities include flat-panel LCD TVs, built-in closets, stylish soft goods, and comfortable beds. Wood accents in warm tones are a welcome relief from the bland beige that dominates so many hotel palettes. Orange and yellow accent pieces add just the right splash of color. The flat-panel TV is surrounded by a modern interpretation of the traditional family hearth: Two expansive curved shelves (perfect for storing small items) serve as the hearth's mantel, while a colorful tiled display underneath simulates the fireplace. Functional, attractive, and clever, it's the furniture equivalent of George Clooney.

A lot of thought went into the bathroom design, too. You enter the bath through a sliding pocket door instead of a traditional hinged model. The pocket door provides plenty of room and makes it easy to move around inside. (It's such a great idea, Len has adopted it in his own home.) The curved shower-curtain rod is inspired. Combined with the pocket door, the curtain rod makes the bathroom feel much bigger than it is. Another thoughtful touch: A small motion sensor detects when you're up and moving at night, and turns on a dimmed bathroom light to help you find your way.

Bathroom sinks have an avant-garde flat-bottom design. If you can name a single Belgian architect or you own shoes made in Scandinavia, you'll probably love them; other folks think they look like lab equipment. When brushing your teeth, spit directly over the drain; otherwise, the toothpaste glob doesn't move. One minor gripe: You have to scoot around one of the sinks to get in the shower. (We're sure George Clooney has his quirks, too.)

The work area has ample surface space provided by an L-shaped, glass-topped desk; it looks high-tech, but rounded corners perfectly soften the piece. Lighting is superb, with top scores in the bathroom grooming, reading, and work areas. Small, stylish overhead lights are more than ample for reading in bed, assuming you're not exhausted.

The Contemporary's beds are topped with 250-thread-count sheets and down-filled pillows. The air-conditioning system is a little louder than most. If you like to sleep with a bit of white noise in the background, however, you'll be in heaven.

Dining options abound. On the first floor is The Wave . . . of American Flavors, a 220-seat "health-conscious 21st-century" restaurant. What does "health-conscious" mean in Disney-speak? You can still get bacon for breakfast, but the coffee it comes with is certified organic and bird-friendly. The Contempo Cafe, a counter-service restaurant on the fourth floor's Grand Canyon Concourse, serves upscale sandwiches, salads, and flatbread pizzas. Chef Mickey's, also on the fourth floor, hosts a popular character buffet at breakfast and dinner. On the 15th floor, the award-winning California Grill serves contemporary American cuisine.

The pool has slides for kids, and cabanas for rent. The resort has around a half-dozen shops, too. The Contemporary is within easy walking distance of the Magic Kingdom; monorail transportation is available to both the Magic Kingdom and Epcot. Other destinations can be accessed by bus or boat. Walking time to transportation loading areas from the most remote rooms is 6–9 minutes.

### GOOD (AND NOT-SO-GOOD) ROOMS AT THE CONTEMPORARY RESORT

There are two guest-room buildings at the Contemporary: the A-frame tower and the Garden Building. Rooms in the A-frame overlook either Bay Lake and the marina and swimming complex on one side, or the parking lot with Seven Seas Lagoon and the Magic Kingdom in the background on the other. Except for most second- and third-floor rooms in the Garden Wing, each guest room has a balcony with two chairs and a table. If you stay on the Magic Kingdom side of the A-frame, ask for a room on the ninth floor or higher. The parking lot and connecting roads are less distracting there. On the Bay Lake side, the view is fine from all floors, though higher floors are preferable.

In the Garden Building, all ground-floor rooms have patios. Only end rooms on the second and third floors facing Bay Lake have full balconies; all other rooms have balconies only a foot deep. Also, note that the Garden Building is a fair walk from the restaurants, shops, front desk, guest services, and monorail station in the A-frame.

On our last visit, swarms of Florida love bugs circled the Garden Building's entrances at night, apparently attracted to the yellow lighting inside—you'll need to step over thousands of bug bodies if you leave through those doors in the morning. If you're grossed out at the prospect, try the westernmost entrance nearest the main building, and avoid the north-facing doors nearest the marina. Insects aside, the Garden rooms' isolation is a plus when it comes to scenery and tranquility.

There's a lot of boat traffic in the lake and canal alongside the Garden Building. Nearest the lake and quietest are Rooms 6116–6123, 6216–6223, and 6316–6323. At the water's edge but noisier are Rooms 6107–6115, 6207–6215, and 6307–6315. Flanking the canal connecting Bay Lake and Seven Seas Lagoon are Rooms 5128–5143, 5228–5251, and 5328–5351. All these have nice canal and lake views, but they're subjected to a lot of noise from passing watercraft.

The Garden Building also has rooms facing the marina, pool, and playground; these work well for families with young children. The view isn't comparable to views from the rooms previously listed, but ground-floor rooms 5110–5125 provide easy access to the pool.

In addition to offering some of the most scenic and tranquil guest rooms in Disney World, the Garden Building likewise contains some of the most undesirable ones. Avoid rooms ending with numbers 52 through 70—almost all of these look directly onto a parking lot.

**BAY LAKE TOWER AT DISNEY'S CONTEMPORARY RESORT** Opened in 2009, Bay Lake Tower is a 15-story, 295-unit DDV resort featuring studios and one-, two-, and three-bedroom villas, as well as two-story, three-bedroom Grand Villas with spectacular views of Bay Lake and the Magic Kingdom. Laid out in a semicircle, Bay Lake Tower is connected to the Contemporary by an elevated, covered walkway and shares the main resort's monorail service.

Rooms are well appointed, with flat-panel TVs, DVD players, mini-fridges, microwaves, and coffeemakers. Brightly colored accessories, paintings, and accent walls complement an otherwise-neutral color scheme. Wood tables and granite countertops add a natural touch. Each room has a private balcony or patio. The rooms we've stayed in tested as the quietest on Disney property but average for lighting and bedding.

Studios sleep up to four people and include one queen-size bed and one double sleeper sofa. The part of the studio with the bed, sofa, and TV measures about 170 square feet and feels small with just two people; four would be an adventure. A refurbishment of all studio rooms moved the bath's sink from the kitchen to the bathroom.

One-bedroom villas sleep five and provide a formal kitchen, a second bathroom, and a living room in addition to the studio bedroom. The living room's chair and sofa fold out to sleep three more people.

Two-bedroom villas sleep nine and include all of the kitchen amenities found in a one-bedroom, plus an extra bathroom. One of the baths is attached to a second bedroom with two queen beds or a queen bed plus a sleeper-sized sofa. As with the one-bedrooms, a sofa bed and sleeper chair in the living room provide extra places to snooze, though they're best suited to small children. Bathrooms in the two-bedroom villas are laid out a bit better than those in the one-bedrooms, with more room to move about. One odd feature in these (also found at other DVC resorts) is a folding door separating the tub from the master bedroom. Nevertheless, we think the two-bedroom villas are the best of Bay Lake Tower's standard offerings.

The two-story Grand Villas sleep 12 and include four bathrooms, the same master-bedroom layout, and two bedrooms with two queen beds apiece. An upstairs seating area overlooking the main floor provides a sleeper sofa and chair. These rooms have two-story windows that offer unparalleled views of either Bay Lake or the Magic Kingdom—with unparalleled prices to match.

*Unofficial Guide* reader opinions of Bay Lake Tower have been mostly positive. A Minnesota family of four loved it:

> *We had a studio with a Magic Kingdom view. The balcony was a private oasis where my husband and I would relax and watch the fireworks together after the kids were asleep. On our second night he looked at me and said, "We're always going to stay here."*

A Tennessee family wasn't in love with Bay Lake Tower's views:

> *The Magic Kingdom view isn't as magical as Disney wants you to believe. You can see the fireworks from your room, but they're off-center over Space Mountain. During the day, your view is the Bay Lake Tower parking lot. The lake view, on the other hand, may be the most peaceful at Walt Disney World.*

Bay Lake Tower has its own check-in desk as well as its own private pool and pool bar, plus a small fire pit on the beach. Its Top of the World Lounge is the best bar on Disney property but, alas, only for DVC owners. If need be, offer to buy a round of drinks in exchange for an invite.

A 1-mile jogging path loops around Bay Lake Tower and the Contemporary's garden wing. Dining, transportation, and other recreational activities are shared with the Contemporary Resort.

If you're paying for a Magic Kingdom view, request a room on an upper level—above the seventh floor, at least—if you don't want to look out on the parking lot. Even-numbered rooms XX06–XX16 have the best viewing angle of the park. Rooms XX24–XX30 may technically be described as having Magic Kingdom views, but they're oriented toward the Contemporary, and you have to turn the other way to see the park.

## Shades of Green *(see map on page 159)*

THIS DELUXE RESORT is owned and operated by the US Armed Forces and is open to US military personnel (including members of the National Guard and reserves, retired military, and employees of the US Public Health Service and the Department of Defense) and their families, foreign military personnel attached to US units, and some civilian contractors. Shades of Green consists of one three-story and one five-story building nestled among three golf courses that are open to Disney guests.

At 455 square feet each, the 586 guest rooms at Shades of Green are larger than those at the Grand Floridian. Decor is pleasant though thoroughly unremarkable—pretty much the same as at any midpriced hotel. Most rooms have two queen-size beds, a daybed, and a table and four chairs, as well as a television in an armoire. All rooms have a patio or balcony.

**SHADES OF GREEN**

| STRENGTHS | |
|---|---|
| • Large guest rooms | • On-site car rental (Alamo) |
| • Discount tickets for military personnel with ID | **WEAKNESSES** |
| • Quiet setting | • No interesting theme |
| • Views of golf course from guest rooms | • Limited on-site dining |
| • Convenient self-parking | • Limited bus service |
| • Swimming complex, fitness center | • Daily parking fee ($5) |
| | • No free parking at theme parks |

A Minot AFB, North Dakota, father of three thinks Shades of Green is the way to go—mostly:

> As an active-duty military member, I can tell you there's no better deal on a WDW vacation than at Shades of Green. A couple of drawbacks, though, were the midlevel quality of the food at the Italian restaurant and the lack of a place to get a drink.

A mom from Winchester, Virginia, weighs in:

> Shades of Green has an AAFES [Army & Air Force Exchange Service] on-site. In addition to carrying everything one might find in a hotel gift/sundries shop, this small store carries Disney merchandise. It's also a Class Six [a military version of a package store]. We were able to purchase everything we needed there and never had to leave WDW in search of a grocery store. Plus there's no tax on purchases.

A military mom from Plainfield, Indiana, makes a case for exploring all your options:

> While it's true that SoG is often a good deal for service members and veterans, military families should still do some comparison shopping. Room rates are tiered based on rank—the higher your rank, the higher your rate. Definitely check into military rates at Disney properties; when we traveled to WDW in 2009, it was cheaper for us to stay at a Disney Moderate resort than at SoG. Also, military-connected guests should check out the **Armed Forces Vacation Club** for condos near WDW [see **afvclub.com** for participating Orlando-area properties]. This time around, we rented a two-bedroom, two-bath condo with a full kitchen and awesome pool area for seven nights, and it cost us less than two nights at a Disney hotel.

Even though the resort isn't operated by Disney, service is comparable to that at Disney Deluxe properties. Transportation to all theme parks is by bus, with a transfer required to almost all destinations. Walking time to the bus-loading area from the most remote rooms is about 5 minutes. If you're visiting during holidays or a long weekend, book as early as possible (up to seven months in advance).

You don't have to worry much about bad rooms at Shades of Green. Except for a small percentage that overlook the entrance road and parking lot, most offer views of the golf courses that surround the

## Shades of Green

| | |
|---|---|
| Ⓔ Elevator | 🚹🚺 Restroom |
| ⤴ Stairs | Ⓒ Telephone |
| Ⓥ Vending and ice | |

**To theme parks ↓**

1. AAFES Shopette
2. ATM
3. Attraction Ticket Sales
4. Bell stand & front desk
5. Bus stop
6. Evergreens Sports Bar & Grille
7. Express Café
8. Fitness Center
9. The Garden Gallery Restaurant
10. Game rooms
11. Guest laundry
12. Guest Services
13. Hot tub & Magnolia Pool Grille
14. Java Café
15. Kiddie Pool
16. Lobby
17. Made in the Shade Gift Shop
18. Magnolia Ballroom
19. Magnolia Pool Area
20. Magnolia Spa
21. Mangino's Bistro
22. Mill Pond Pool Area
23. Parking garage
24. Playground
25. Registration
26. Remember the Fun Walkway
27. Sales & Marketing
28. Tennis courts

hotel, or the swimming area. When you reserve, make your preference known. Shades of Green has its own website, **shadesofgreen.org.**

## THE EPCOT RESORTS

THE EPCOT RESORTS ARE ARRAYED around Crescent Lake between Epcot and Disney's Hollywood Studios (but closer to Epcot). Both theme parks are accessible by boat and on foot. No Epcot resort offers transportation to Epcot's main entrance. As a Greenville, South Carolina, mom reports, this can be a problem:

> *The only transportation to Epcot is by boat or foot. There's no bus available to take you to the front gates. We had to walk through the International Gateway and all the way to the front of Epcot to ride Future World attractions. And if we finished Epcot at the end of the day near the front entrance, the only way back home was a long hike through Future World and the International Gateway.*

A reader from Emporia, Kansas, overcame this obstacle:

> *We had no transportation to the front gate of Epcot for arrival before opening. So we decided to do early entry at Magic Kingdom (7 a.m.), take in one popular attraction, and then catch the monorail to Epcot. Worked like a charm. We were at Epcot by 8:20 a.m.*

### Disney's Yacht & Beach Club Resorts and Beach Club Villas

THESE ADJOINING DELUXE RESORTS are similarly themed. Both have clapboard facades with whitewashed-wood trim. The Yacht Club is painted a subdued gray, the Beach Club a brighter blue. The Yacht Club has a nautical theme with model ships and antique navigational instruments in public areas. The Beach Club is embellished with beach scenes in foam-green and white. Both have themed lobbies, with a giant globe in the Yacht Club's and sea-horse fixtures in the Beach Club's. The resorts face the 25-acre Crescent Lake and share an elaborate swimming complex.

There are 621 rooms at the Yacht Club, 576 rooms at the Beach Club, and 282 studio and one- and two-bedroom villas at the Beach Club Villas, part of the DVC time-share program. Most of the rooms

| STRENGTHS | WEAKNESSES |
|---|---|
| • Best pool complex of any WDW resort | • Lack of good quick-service dining options |
| • Walking distance to Epcot's International Gateway | • Views and balcony size are hit-or-miss |
| • Very underrated and relatively affordable full-service restaurant (Captain's Grille) | • Bus service to Magic Kingdom, Animal Kingdom, water parks, and Downtown Disney is shared with other Epcot resorts |
| • Close to many BoardWalk and Epcot dining options | |
| • Well-themed public spaces | • No three-bedroom Grand Villas at the Beach Club Villas |
| • Bright and attractive guest rooms | |
| • Boat transportation to Disney's Hollywood Studios | • Beach Club Villas have fewer baths per bedroom than newer DVC/DDV properties |

## Yacht & Beach Club Resorts & Beach Club Villas

are 381 square feet and have two queen-size beds, a daybed, and a desk and a chair. Like the Grand Floridian's, rooms have a lot of drawer space. Yacht Club rooms are decorated in blue and white; Beach Club offers light blue and burgundy tones. Some rooms have balconies.

The Beach Club Villas evoke seaside Victorian cottages. Studio accommodations offer kitchenettes; one- and two-bedroom villas have full kitchens. Subject to availability, villas are open to the public as well as to DVC (time-share) members. The villas share restaurants, pools, and other amenities with the Yacht & Beach Club Resorts. A small business center serves guests' work needs for both the Yacht and Beach Clubs and Beach Club Villas.

As Disney Deluxe resorts, the Yacht Club and Beach Club provide excellent service. They offer nine restaurants and lounges and are within walking distance of Epcot and the BoardWalk. Transportation to other destinations is by bus or boat. Walking time to the transportation loading areas from the most remote rooms is 7 minutes.

Although the Yacht & Beach Club Resorts are arrayed along Crescent Lake opposite Disney's BoardWalk, a relatively small percentage of guest rooms actually overlook the lake. Many additional rooms have an oblique view of the lake but face a courtyard or garden. To complicate matters, the resorts don't differentiate between a room with a lake view and one overlooking a swimming pool, pond, or canal. There's only one category for anything wet: "lagoon or pool view." Go to **touringplans .com** to see specific views from these rooms.

The Beach Club consists of a long main building with several wings protruding toward Crescent Lake. Looking at the resort from Crescent Lake, the Beach Club adjoins the Yacht Club on the left and spreads toward Epcot on the right. The main building and the various wings range from three to five stories. Most rooms have balconies or, on the ground floor, patios. Balconies are either big enough for a couple of chairs or about 6 inches deep (stand at the rail or sit in a chair inside the room). Top-floor rooms often have enclosed balconies inset into the roof. Unless you're standing, visibility is somewhat limited from these dormer balconies.

We receive a lot of mail about the Yacht & Beach Club Resorts, most of it positive. First, these remarks from a Wayland, Massachusetts, mother of two:

> This was the first time we stayed at the Beach Club, and for us the amazing pool complex was worth the extra money. Several nights we climbed up to the top of the waterslide as the sun was setting, and it was an incredible sight—truly a memorable experience!

This mom from Brownsville, Texas, however, has some issues with the Beach Club:

> The room doors at the Beach Club don't fit very snugly, so any noise from the hall was practically broadcast into our room. Our room was close to the elevators, so it sounded like everyone in the hotel was stampeding past our door in the morning. If we go back, I'll ask for a more remote room way at the end of the hall.

**GOOD (AND NOT-SO-GOOD) ROOMS AT THE BEACH CLUB RESORT** The Beach Club's better views are from rooms that have full balconies, and from those that overlook the lake. Other good rooms include those facing woods, with Epcot in the background. The woods-facing rooms are the resort's quietest, most peaceful accommodations, in terms of both lack of noise and attractive scenery. These rooms are also nearest to Epcot's International Gateway entrance if you're walking, but farthest from the resort's main pool area, lobby, and restaurants.

Of the remaining rooms, most face courtyards, with some of these providing oblique views of the lake, and others overlooking parking lots and the resort's front entrance.

The following are our recommendations for good rooms at the Beach

Club Resort. All room numbers are four digits, with the first digit specifying the floor and the remaining three digits specifying the room number.

**Water-view rooms with full balconies facing the lake** Odd-numbered rooms 2641–2645 and suite 2647; 3501–3507; 3683–3689 and suite 3691; 3699–3725; 5683–5691; and Club Level rooms 5699–5725. (The Beach Club will charge you for a water view if there's so much as a bird-bath in sight. If you're going to spend the money, get a real water view.)

**Standard-view rooms with full balconies facing the woods and Epcot** Even-numbered rooms 3512–3530 and 4578–4596.

**GOOD (AND NOT-SO-GOOD) ROOMS AT THE YACHT CLUB RESORT** When you look at the Yacht Club from Crescent Lake, the resort is connected to the Beach Club on the right and angles toward the Dolphin hotel on the left. All Yacht Club rooms offer full balconies or, on the ground floor, patios. Rooms with the best views are as follows (the higher the last three digits in the room number, the closer to lobby, main pool area, and restaurants):

**Fifth-floor rooms with full balconies directly facing the lake, with the BoardWalk Inn in the background** Club-level rooms 5161, 5163, and 5241.

**Fifth-floor rooms directly facing Epcot** Rooms 5171–5185.

Some other rooms face the BoardWalk or Epcot across Crescent Lake, but they're inferior to the rooms just listed.

Avoid standard-view rooms at either resort except for Rooms 3512–3536 and 4578–4598 at the Beach Club; these overlook a dense pine thicket. In addition to offering a nice vista for a standard-view rate, these are the closest rooms to Epcot available at any resort on Crescent Lake.

**BEACH CLUB VILLAS** This Disney Deluxe Villa property is supposedly inspired by the grand Atlantic seaside homes of the early 20th century. We'll bet the villas don't resemble any seaside home you ever saw. Thematically, there's little to differentiate the Beach Club Villas from the Yacht & Beach Club Resorts, or from the parts of the BoardWalk Inn & Villas that don't front the BoardWalk.

Configured roughly in the shape of a fat Y or slingshot, the Beach Club Villas are set back away from the lake adjoining the front of the Beach Club Resort. Arrayed in connected four- and five-story taffy-blue sections topped with cupolas, the villas are festooned with white wood-work and slat-railed balconies. The effect is clean, breezy, and evocative . . . though we're not certain of what. Accommodations include studios, with a kitchenette, one queen bed, and a sofa sleeper; and one- and two-bedroom villas with full kitchens. The rooms are a bit small but attractively decorated in pastels with New England–style summer-home furniture. Patterned carpets and seashore-themed art complete the package.

We don't like the Beach Club Villas as well as the Wilderness Lodge Villas (they're more visually interesting) or the villas of Old Key West Resort (they're roomier, more luxurious, and more private). The Beach Club Villas have their own modest swimming pool but otherwise share the restaurants, facilities, and transportation options of the adjoining Yacht & Beach Club Resorts. The villas' strengths and weaknesses include all of those listed for the Yacht & Beach Club Resorts.

Additional strengths include laundry and kitchen facilities in the one- and two-bedroom units, and self-parking directly adjacent to the building. The villas' one additional weakness is that they offer no lake view.

**GOOD (AND NOT-SO-GOOD) ROOMS AT THE BEACH CLUB VILLAS** Though the studios and villas are attractive and livable, the location of the Beach Club Villas, between parking lots, roads, and canals, leaves much to be desired. Rooms facing the pool offer a limited view of a small canal but are subject to traffic noise. Ditto the rooms on the northeast side, but they don't face the pool. Only southeast-facing rooms provide both a scenic landscape (woods) and relative relief from traffic noise. The nearby road is two lanes only, and traffic noise probably won't bother you if you're indoors with the balcony door closed, but for the bucks you shell out to stay at the villas, you can find nicer, quieter accommodations elsewhere on Disney property. If you elect to stay at the Beach Club Villas, go for odd-numbered rooms 225–251, 325–351, 425–451, and 525–551.

## Disney's BoardWalk Inn & Villas

| STRENGTHS | overly fussy |
|---|---|
| • Walking distance to Epcot's International Gateway and Disney's Hollywood Studios | • Limited quick-service dining options suitable for children |
| • Unique garden suites | • Not as many rooms overlook the BoardWalk as you might think |
| • Vast selection of dining options for adults | • Clown pool may freak you out |
| • Fitness center is larger than Yacht & Beach Club's | • Bus service to Magic Kingdom, Animal Kingdom, water parks, and Downtown Disney is shared with other Epcot resorts |
| • Clown pool is whimsical | |
| **WEAKNESSES** | • BoardWalk Villas have fewer baths per bedroom than newer DVC/DDV properties |
| • Long, confusing hallways | |
| • Some may find room theming | |

ON CRESCENT LAKE ACROSS from the Yacht & Beach Club Resorts, the BoardWalk Inn is another of the Walt Disney World Deluxe resorts. The complex is a detailed replica of an early-20th-century Atlantic coast boardwalk. Facades of hotels, diners, and shops create an inviting and exciting waterfront skyline. In reality, the BoardWalk Inn & Villas are a single integrated structure behind the facades. Restaurants and shops occupy the boardwalk level, while accommodations rise up to six stories above. Painted bright red and yellow along with weathered pastel greens and blues, the BoardWalk resorts are the only Disney hotels that use neon signage as architectural detail. The complex shares a pool having an old-fashioned amusement-park theme (there are also two quiet pools).

The BoardWalk Inn's 371 Deluxe rooms measure 371 square feet each. Most contain two queen-size beds with hardwood headboards, an upholstered sleeper sofa, a cherry desk and chair, an alarm clock with 30-pin iPhone dock, and ceiling fans. Decor includes yellow-and-white-striped wallpaper and striped green curtains. Closet space exceeds that in other Disney Deluxe rooms. Most rooms have balconies.

# BoardWalk Inn & Villas

1. Atlantic Dance Hall
2. Belle Vue Lounge
3. Big River Grille & Brewing Works
4. BoardWalk Bakery
5. Disney's Character Carnival
6. Dundy's Sundries
7. Bus stop
8. Community Hall
9. Conference Center
10. DVC Sales Center
11. ESPN Club
12. Flying Fish Cafe
13. Health club
14. Jellyrolls
15. Lobby
16. Luna Park Pool
17. Quiet pools
18. Screen Door General Store
19. Seabreeze Point
20. Seashore Sweets
21. Thimbles & Threads
22. Transportation dock
23. Wyland Galleries
24. Yard Arcade

The 532 BoardWalk Villas are decorated in warmer tones and primary colors, with bright tiles in the kitchens and bathrooms. Villas range from 412 to 2,491 square feet (studio through three-bedroom) and sleep 4–12 people. Many villas have full kitchens, laundry rooms, and whirlpool tubs. The villas tend to be more expensive than similar accommodations at other Disney resorts—you pay for the address.

The inn and villas are well staffed and offer excellent service. They're also home to some of Disney World's better restaurants and shops, including the BoardWalk Bakery, serving lunch sandwiches and salads along with morning pastries and coffee. The complex is within walking distance of Epcot and is connected to other destinations by bus and boat. Walking time to transportation loading areas from the most remote rooms is 5–6 minutes.

Reader comments about the BoardWalk Inn & Villas include the following. From an Iowa City, Iowa, family:

> *We were surprised that so relatively few rooms at the BoardWalk Inn have interesting views. We were in a group staying there before a Disney cruise, and the one couple who actually had a view of the boardwalk said it was noisy.*

A number of readers have complained about the bus service at the BoardWalk Inn. This comment is typical:

> *The transportation by bus (to Animal Kingdom and Magic Kingdom) was the worst. We waited at least 40 minutes every time and almost missed a dinner reservation (for which we had left 1½ hours early).*

**GOOD (AND NOT-SO-GOOD) ROOMS AT THE BOARDWALK INN & VILLAS**
The complex comprises several wings that radiate from the lobby complex, in a rough H-shape. Crescent Lake and the Promenade (pedestrian boardwalk) are to the north, the entrance is to the south, and the canal that runs to Disney's Hollywood Studios is to the west. If you book a BoardWalk room through Disney's agents or website, "water view" means Crescent Lake and the BoardWalk area only; views of the canal or pool are considered "standard view." But if you book a villa through a DVC member or the DVC site, the same pool and canal are called "garden or pool view," and the view of the BoardWalk is called "BoardWalk view." Two concierge floors cater to those wanting extra service.

Most rooms at the inn and villas have a balcony or patio, though balconies on the standard upper-floor rooms alternate between large and medium. The BoardWalk Inn & Villas each share about half the frontage on the Promenade, which overlooks Crescent Lake. The Promenade's clubs, stores, and attractions are spread about equally between the two sections, leading to similar levels of noise and commotion. However, the inn side is closer to Epcot and the nearby access road; this provides better views of Epcot fireworks and easier access to that park, but it also means more road noise.

Otherwise, the inn is actually less noisy than the more expensive villas; there's one tranquil, enclosed courtyard, and another half-enclosed area with a quiet pool (where BoardWalk's Garden Suites are). There are many rooms to avoid at the inn, starting with rooms overlooking access roads and parking lots, and rooms looking down on the roof of the adjacent conference center. And although the afore-mentioned quiet rooms face courtyards, the views are pretty ho-hum. When you get right down to it, the only rooms with decent views are those fronting the Promenade and lake, specifically odd-numbered rooms 3213–3259 and 4213–4259. We're told by Disney insiders that most of these rooms are reserved more than 10 months in advance, so snagging one requires advance planning and a lot of luck. As for the others, you're more likely to get a better view at the far less expensive Port Orleans, Caribbean Beach, or Coronado Springs Resort.

The villas are somewhat better. Most overlook a canal to the west with the Swan resort and its access road and parking lots on the far side. Worse are the rooms that front BoardWalk's entrance and car lots. As at the inn, the villas offer only a handful of rooms with good views. Odd-numbered rooms 3001–3047, 4001–4033, and 5001–5047 afford dynamic views of the Promenade and Crescent Lake, with Epcot in the background. Rooms X05, X07, X13, X15, X29, and X31 are studios. They're a little noisy if you open your balcony door but otherwise offer a glimpse of one of Disney World's more happening places. Unless you bag one of these rooms, however, you'll spend a bundle for a very average (or worse) view.

Promenade-facing villa rooms have noise issues identical to their inn counterparts. The midsection of the canal-facing villas look out on Luna Park Pool, a carnival-themed family-pool complex that gets extremely noisy during the day. Some of the quieter villas are away from the Promenade with views of the canal and a partially enclosed quiet pool. Noise is practically nonexistent; the only downside is that the rooms are relatively distant from the Promenade and Epcot. Rooms on the opposite side of this wing are almost as quiet, but they face BoardWalk's parking lot and thus are less desirable.

### The Walt Disney World Swan and Walt Disney World Dolphin
*(see map on page 169)*

ALTHOUGH THESE RESORTS ARE INSIDE THE WORLD and Disney handles their reservations, they're owned by Sheraton (Dolphin) and Westin (Swan) and can be booked directly through their parent companies, too. Both are served by Disney transportation to the theme parks and participate in Extra Magic Hours and FastPass+, but neither offers Disney's Magical Express bus service to and from the airport or participates in the Disney Dining Plan.

Opened in 1990, the resorts face each other on either side of an inlet of Crescent Lake. The Dolphin is a 27-story triangular turquoise building. On its roof are two 56-foot-tall fish balanced with their tails in the air. The Swan has a 12-story main building flanked by two seven-story towers. Two 47-foot-tall swans adorn its roof, paralleling their marine counterparts across the way.

Both the Swan and the Dolphin have been described as bizarre and stylistically disjointed ("Art Deco gone haywire" comes to mind). They're definitely architectural period pieces. The giant swans look swanlike, but the Dolphin's fish more closely resemble catfish from outer space. The effect could be described as adventurous or unsettling, depending on your point of view.

## WDW SWAN AND WDW DOLPHIN

| STRENGTHS | WEAKNESSES |
|---|---|
| • Best-priced location on Crescent Lake | • Conventioneers may be off-putting to vacationing families |
| • Both hotels participate in Starwood Preferred Guest program | • Daily resort and parking fees |
| • Good on-site and nearby dining | • No Disney's Magical Express or Disney Dining Plan |
| • Only hotels within walking distance to mini-golf (Fantasia Gardens) | • Bus service to Magic Kingdom, Animal Kingdom, water parks, and Downtown Disney is shared with other Epcot resorts |
| • Large variety of upscale restaurants; 24-hour food available at Picabu | |
| • On-site car rental through National | • Architecture that was on the cutting edge 25 years ago now seems dated |
| • Very nice pool complex | |
| • Impressive public spaces | • Self-parking is quite distant from the hotels' entrances |
| • Walking distance to both Epcot International Gateway and DHS | |

The Dolphin's lobby is the more ornate, featuring a rotunda with spokelike corridors branching off to shops, restaurants, and other public areas. At the other end of the spectrum, the Swan's lobby is so small that it seems an afterthought. Both resorts feature art of wildly different styles and eras (from Matisse to Roy Lichtenstein). The Dolphin's Grotto Pool is shaped like a seashell and has a waterfall, while the Swan's pool is a conventional rectangle.

The Dolphin's rooms underwent a complete redesign several years back; soft goods and televisions were updated in 2010. Where garish decor had characterized (some say branded) the hotel's rooms for years, the current design incorporates light-colored woods, floral earth-tone carpeting, and pastel-blue draperies. The plush Heavenly Beds are buttressed by oversize wood headboards adorned with abstract murals. A sleek, contemporary dresser–desk combo and a reading chair complete the furnishings. Some rooms have balconies.

Renovated in 2011, the Swan's guest rooms are decorated in restful earth-tone pastels and furnished with handsome Scandinavian-modern blond bedsteads and dressers. Westin's Heavenly Beds make for ultracomfy sleeping. Reading light is great in or out of bed. A huge, round mirror framed in blond wood hangs above the dresser. The bath, though small for a Disney World hotel, is elegantly appointed.

Because the Swan and the Dolphin aren't run by Disney, service is less relentlessly cheerful than at other on-property resorts. They'll also nickel-and-dime you to death. For example, both tack on a $20-per-day "resort fee" and another $16 per day for self-parking. Even more shocking is the price the Dolphin's gift shop charges for sundries: We paid almost $10 for a pint of Ben & Jerry's ice cream—roughly $3 more than Disney charges in its gift shops (and twice as much as Publix). Whatever rate you're quoted at the Swan and the Dolphin, temper your expectations by adding another $45 per day in miscellaneous costs.

The two hotels collectively house more than a dozen restaurants and lounges and are within easy walking distance of Epcot and the BoardWalk. They're also connected to other destinations by bus and boat. Walking time from the most remote rooms to the transportation loading areas is 7–9 minutes.

Reader comments about the Swan and Dolphin touch on the same several themes. The following remarks from an El Paso, Texas, reader are representative:

> We scored a great deal through MouseSavers and decided to give the Swan a try. The pool setup was super, and our room was beautiful and had a great view looking toward Epcot. Taking the two hotels together, the restaurant selection was the best I've seen in or out of the World. On the downside, both hotels are really spread out, and it was quite a hike from self-parking to the entrance of the Swan.

A couple from Nashua, New Hampshire, also touts the pools:

> We stayed at the Dolphin and found that neither the Disney nor the Swan and Dolphin websites, nor anything else, depicts how great the pool complex is. Not only are there multiple pools, a sandy beach, swan boats, whirlpools, a waterfall, a waterslide, and maybe the best poolside bar in all of Disney World, there's also a wonderfully green, restful grotto-in-tropical-forest theme.

**GOOD (AND NOT-SO-GOOD) ROOMS AT THE SWAN AND THE DOLPHIN**
These sprawling hotels are configured very differently, and their irregular shapes mean it's easier to discuss groups of rooms in relation to exterior landmarks and compass directions rather than by room numbers. When speaking with a Disney reservationist, use our tips to ask for a particular view or area.

**THE SWAN** East-facing rooms offer prime views, particularly in the upper half of the seven-story wing above Il Mulino New York Trattoria. From this vantage point, guests overlook a canal and the BoardWalk, with Epcot in the distance. *IllumiNations* fireworks enliven the view nightly. Balcony rooms are available on floors 5, 6, and 7 for an additional $30 and up per night. However, rooms in the wing nearest the hotel's main section have the southern portion of their view obscured by the building's easternmost portion, which juts east beyond the seven-story wing. There are some east-facing rooms on that portion of the main section, sans balconies. Lofty palm trees obscure the view from east-facing rooms below the fourth floor. The best rooms with an Epcot view are 626 and 726.

North-facing rooms afford views of the Dolphin and (generally) of the courtyard. Exceptions are the north-facing rooms on the easternmost portion of the main section, which look across Crescent Terrace to the BoardWalk. These afford angled views of Epcot and are buffered by palms on the lowest three floors. The few north-facing rooms at the end of the Swan's two eight-story wings directly overlook Crescent Lake. However, the bulk of north-facing rooms are in the main section and overlook the courtyard, with greenery, fountains, and an indoor café in its center. Courtyard-facing rooms are subject to noise from below, though never much.

Above the eighth floor, north-facing rooms in the main section overlook roofs of the shorter wings. In these rooms, height enhances the vista from your window, but only near the center of the hotel is the view not seriously marred by rooftops below.

North-facing main-section rooms have a more direct view of the Dolphin across the lake than the courtyard-facing rooms in either eight-story wing. However, most wing rooms can view the lake at an angle. Those on the northern edge of the western wing also view the BoardWalk at an angle.

Most courtyard-facing rooms have balconies; 224 rooms are so equipped, and these balconies offer panoramic 180-degree views. Of course, from most rooms at the Swan, part of any 180-degree view will include another section of the hotel.

The Swan's worst views are from west-facing rooms above the fourth floor, which overlook the unsightly roof of the hotel's western wing. The northernmost rooms in the wing directly above Kimonos restaurant are an exception—their balconies overlook the pool and the beach on Crescent Lake's western shore. Rooms 680–691 offer nice pool views.

Above the Swan's main entrance, south-facing rooms overlook the parking lot, with forest and the Hollywood Studios in the distance. However, the canal is also visible to the east. These rooms lack balconies.

**THE DOLPHIN** Consisting of a central A-frame with large wings jutting off each side and four smaller arms extending from the rear of the building, the Dolphin is attached to a large conference center, which means that the majority of guests are ostensibly there on business. The same amenities found at Disney Deluxe resorts are found at the Dolphin. All parks are accessible from a shuttle stop or a boat dock between the Dolphin and the Swan.

If you want a room with easy access to shopping, dining, and transportation to and from the parks, almost any Dolphin room will do. The shuttle (outside the main entrance) and the boat dock are equidistant from the main front and rear exits. Restaurants and shopping are primarily on the first and third floors.

If, however, you also want a view of something other than parking-lot asphalt, your choices narrow considerably. Rooms in the Dolphin with pleasant views are in the four arms on the rear of the building. Rooms on all the arms sport balconies from the first through fourth floors, then offer balconies or windows alternately on floors five through nine.

One of the Dolphin's best views overlooks the Grotto Pool on the far west side of the building. An artificial beach with a small waterfall is visible from rooms at the very end of the large west wing. None of these rooms has a balcony, but that might be a blessing, since the pool comes with canned tiki music and a bar. A better bet would be to ask for a room on the far west side of the first rear arm. These outer rooms have balconies and are more removed from the pool. Rooms on the inner, west part of that arm overlook a bladderwort-encrusted reflecting pool; these aren't recommended. Nor are the facing rooms on the next arm.

Between the second and third arms looms the monstrous Dolphin fountain; the better room choices here are on the top two floors. Here, from arm two you can see the BoardWalk (including any nighttime fireworks), and from arm three you can see the Grotto Pool. Otherwise, you may find you have a view of massive green-concrete fish scales. The noise from the water is loud, and the fountain gushes continuously—it's either soothing or maddening depending on your temperament.

Arms three and four are situated around a reflecting pool. A concern for rooms in this area is that the ferry toots its horn every time it approaches and departs the dock. Its path runs right by these rooms, and the horn blows just as it passes. The first time that happens, it's quaint. By the 117th, your hair will be coming out in clumps.

The Crescent Lake side of arm four, and the small jut of the large Dolphin wing perpendicular to it, offer arguably the best views. You have an unobstructed view of the lake and Epcot fireworks, a fine BoardWalk view for people-watching, and, from higher floors, a view of the beach at Beach Club. There's ferry noise, but these rooms still have the most going for them. The best of the best in this arm are Rooms 8015, 7015, 5015, 4015, and 3015. Rooms with balconies at the Dolphin generally run upwards of $30 a night more than rooms without.

## Disney's Caribbean Beach Resort *(see map on page 173)*

THE CARIBBEAN BEACH RESORT OCCUPIES 200 acres surrounding a 45-acre lake called Barefoot Bay. This midpriced resort, modeled after resorts in the Caribbean, consists of the registration area ("Custom House") and six two-story "villages" named after Caribbean islands. Each village has its own pool, laundry room, and beach. The Caribbean motif is maintained with blue metal roofs, widow's walks,

## CARIBBEAN BEACH RESORT

| STRENGTHS | WEAKNESSES |
|---|---|
| • Colorful Caribbean theme | • Check-in is far from rest of resort |
| • Rooms with *Pirates of the Caribbean* and *Finding Nemo* themes | • Sit-down dining is mediocre at best |
| | • Multiple bus stops |
| • Lakefront setting | • Some "villages" are a good distance from restaurants and shops |
| • Large food court | |

and wooden railed porches. The atmosphere is cheerful, with buildings painted blue, lime green, and sherbet orange. In addition to the six village pools, the resort's main swimming pool is themed as an old Spanish fort, complete with slides and water cannons.

Most of the 2,112 guest rooms are 314 square feet and contain two double beds and a table and two chairs. Some are decorated with bright tropical colors, while others are decorated with neutral beach tones. All are outfitted with the same light-oak furniture. Rooms don't have balconies, but the access passageways are external and have railings. Rooms in Trinidad South are themed to a *Pirates of the Caribbean* motif. These rooms cost about $50–$70 more than comparable ones elsewhere in the resort. The soft goods and headboards in all non-*Pirates*-themed rooms have a subtle *Finding Nemo* theme.

South and east of Epcot and the Studios, Caribbean Beach offers transportation to all Disney World destinations by bus. Though it has one full-service restaurant and a food court, food service is woefully inadequate for a resort of this size. Walking time to the transportation loading area from the most remote rooms is 7–9 minutes, so guests should seriously consider having a car.

Despite these limitations, many readers love the Caribbean Beach. An Edgewater, Colorado, couple comes to its defense:

*Caribbean Beach was great. The hotel was full, but we saw very few people. It's laid out so you have some privacy, even though there was a bit of walking. However, the food court didn't prepare food on-site— it was always served at the same temperature and degree of staleness.*

A Philadelphia dad with two tots in tow also had mostly positive things to say:

*The Caribbean Beach Resort was beautiful. Our island (Barbados) was very quiet and relaxing on the courtyard/garden side, but the walk to the bus stop with a child was a bit of a haul. The bus service was also slower than in my past experiences.*

From a Ridgeway, Virginia, mother of one:

*The Caribbean Beach Resort was great—especially the housekeeping staff, who creatively rearranged my daughter's toys every day. Made coming back to the room much more fun. My only complaint with CBR was the inefficiency of checkout—although express checkout was available, someone had to be present to have luggage moved from the room to the main house for transport via Magical Express. We had scheduled a late-afternoon flight on our last day so we could*

## Caribbean Beach Resort

Buena Vista Dr.
Sea Breeze Dr.
Aruba
Promenade
Registration
Custom House
Jamaica
Barbados
Martinique
Promenade
Old Port
Royale
Centertown
Trinidad
North
Trinidad
South
Victory Way

Beach 　 Playground
Bus stop 　 Pool

*all spend one last morning in the park—I missed most of it because I had to go and sit with the luggage. I was not happy AT ALL.*

A mom from Fenton, Michigan, found bus service lacking:

*We recommend renting a car and/or paying for a preferred room location—especially if you're going in the hotter months or are impatient. The buses just take way too long with all the stops, and we thought it was a long hike to the food court and pools in the heat.*

**GOOD (AND NOT-SO-GOOD) ROOMS AT THE CARIBBEAN BEACH RESORT**
The resort's grounds are quite pleasant. Landscaping—lots of ferns and palm trees—is verdant, especially in the courtyards. The six "islands," or groups of buildings clustered around Barefoot Bay, are identical. The two-story motel-style structures are arranged in various ways to face courtyards, pools, the bay, and so forth. The setup is similar to Disney's Coronado Springs Resort in nearly every way but theme.

In general, corner rooms are preferable since they have more windows. Standard-view rooms face either the parking lots or courtyards, and the usual broad interpretation of water views is in play here. Beyond that, your main choices will revolve around your preference for proximity to (or distance from) the Custom House, pools, parking lots, pirates, or beaches on Barefoot Bay. Each island has direct access to at least one beach, playground, bus stop, and parking lot.

The island of Barbados is nearest the Custom House, but its central location guarantees that it also experiences the most foot traffic and road noise. It also shares its only beach and playground with Martinique, which probably is the best area for families. Martinique has access to two beaches, is adjacent to the main pool and playground at Old Port Royale Centertown, and yet is removed enough from the Custom House to offer a little serenity for parents.

The islands of Aruba and Jamaica are similar in character to Martinique, but each has only one beach, and guests must cross a footbridge to reach Old Port Royale center. Trinidad North comprises three buildings, and its thin layout means that noise penetrates its courtyard from surrounding roads and from rambunctious kids at Old Port Royale next door. The quietest island is Trinidad South, which is most remote from resort facilities. It has its own playground and beach, and the beach has a bonus—the view across Barefoot Bay is of wild, undeveloped Florida forest, a rarity on Disney property.

After you've sorted out your convenience and location priorities, think about the view. Avoid the standard-view rooms; all look onto a parking lot, road, or tiny garden. Water views at the Caribbean overlook swimming pools or Barefoot Bay. Pool views are less than enchanting, and there's lots of noise and activity around the pools. Bay views are the pick of the litter at the Caribbean. Such rooms in Barbados, Martinique, Trinidad North, and Trinidad South catch the afternoon sun. Bay-view rooms in Aruba and Jamaica catch the morning sun. Because we like the sun at our back in the evening, we always go for Rooms 4246–4252 in Jamaica, 1246–1248 in Barbados, or 5257–5264 and 5541–5548 (but not 5545) in Aruba. If you don't mind the sun in your eyes during cocktail time, Rooms 2251–2256, 2413–2416, and 2445–2448 in Martinique are good bets, as are all lake-facing second-story rooms in buildings 35, 38, and 39 in Trinidad South. We're not crazy about any room in Trinidad North. Be aware that the aging air-conditioning units for individual buildings are pretty loud. One room with an especially nice bay view (2525 in Martinique) is nonetheless not recommended because of its proximity to a clunky AC unit. Try Room 2558 instead.

## THE BONNET CREEK RESORTS

*Not to be confused with the Disney resorts that follow, the* **Bonnet Creek Resort** *is a 70-acre hotel, golf, and convention complex along Bonnet Creek. Although adjacent to and accessible from the World, it is not owned by Disney. Two of its four hotels are reviewed in "Hotels Outside Walt Disney World."*

### Disney's Saratoga Springs Resort & Spa (see map on page 176)

### Treehouse Villas at Disney's Saratoga Springs Resort & Spa (see map on page 177)

SARATOGA SPRINGS, A DISNEY DELUXE VILLA RESORT, has a theme wordily described by Disney as recalling an "1880s, Victorian, upstate New York lakeside retreat" amid "pastoral landscapes, formal gardens, bubbling springs, and natural surroundings." Saratoga Springs comprises 1,260 studio and one-, two-, and three-bedroom villas across the lake from Downtown Disney–Disney Springs. Housed in 12 buildings, most accommodations are of recent vintage, while the fitness center and check-in building are retooled vestiges of the erstwhile Disney Institute. An adjacent 60-unit DDV complex, **Treehouse Villas at Disney's Saratoga Springs Resort & Spa,** opened in 2009.

The fitness center is by far the best at Walt Disney World. The Senses spa, like the Grand Floridian's, was refurbished in 2013 along the lines of those on Disney's cruise ships. Service and decor are very good, and

## SARATOGA SPRINGS RESORT & SPA

| STRENGTHS | WEAKNESSES |
|---|---|
| • Often available at discounted rates or as a DVC/DDV rental | • Newly refurbished spa and fitness center |
| • Attractive main pool; multiple well-themed quiet pools with snack bars | **WEAKNESSES**<br>• On-site dining is limited for a resort of this size |
| • Closest resort to Downtown Disney and Typhoon Lagoon | • Theme is dull compared with those of other Disney resorts |
| • Convenient parking | • Villas are beginning to show some wear |
| • Only WDW-owned resort with dedicated golf (Lake Buena Vista Golf Course) | • Fewer baths per bedroom than newer DVC/DDV properties |
| • Grocery options in gift shop | |

## TREEHOUSE VILLAS

| STRENGTHS | WEAKNESSES |
|---|---|
| • Spectacular stand-alone three-bedroom villas | • Long distance from Saratoga Springs services like check-in and dining |
| • Quiet location | • Kids may find all that quiet boring |
| • Historical connection to the Treehouses from the 1970s | • Lackluster pool |
| • Innovative round design feels more spacious than other villas with the same square footage | • Limited number of units makes the Treehouses among the most difficult accommodations to book at WDW |
| | • Only two baths per villa |
| | • Bus travelers connect through Saratoga Springs |

this Senses location is easier to get to than the one at the Grand Floridian if you're staying east of the World. See page 291 for a full review.

Surrounded on three sides by golf courses, Saratoga Springs is the only Disney-owned resort that affords direct access to the links (the military-only Shades of Green also provides golf on-property).

Furnishings and soft goods are less whimsical and more upscale and masculine than at other Disney resorts. Chairs, sofas, and tables are substantial—perhaps a little too substantial for the rooms they inhabit. The overall effect, however, is sophisticated and restful. A Gulf Shores, Alabama, family, however, takes a slight exception to the restful part:

> Saratoga Springs Resort was beautiful, comfortable, and exactly what we needed for our family of five. It was VERY quiet . . . except for the toilets. When you flushed, it sounded like the space shuttle launching.

A couple from Peru, Indiana, takes a more critical tack:

> Saratoga Springs is our least favorite resort. We didn't enjoy the theming, and unless you have a car, getting around by bus is a real hassle. The food court is very small and the food expensive. Also, checkout was very slow, and our room seemed smaller than comparable rooms at BoardWalk Villas and Old Key West.

## Saratoga Springs Resort & Spa

**ACCOMMODATIONS**
1. The Carousel (7101–7836)
2. Congress Park (1101–2836)
3. The Grandstand (8101–9836)
4. The Paddock (4501–6836)
5. The Springs (3101–4436)

**AMENITIES**
6. The Artist's Palette
7. Backstretch Pool Bar
8. BBQ Grill Area
9. On the Rocks Pool Bar
10. Turf Club Bar & Grill

A Cartersville, Georgia, reader echoes the previous complaint about bus service:

> No matter when we tried to leave a park for Saratoga Springs, there were no buses—45 minutes was the norm. Why pay the premium when you end up driving or taking cabs so as not to waste 2–3 hours per day?

## Treehouse Villas at Saratoga Springs Resort & Spa

**GOOD (AND NOT-SO-GOOD) ROOMS AT SARATOGA SPRINGS RESORT & SPA** This resort's sprawling size puts some of its best rooms very far away from the main lobby, restaurants, and shops. If you don't have a car, the best rooms are those in The Springs, numbered 3101–3436 and 3501–3836. Ask for a room toward the northeast side of these buildings (away from the lobby), as the southwest rooms border a well-traveled road. Avoid Rooms 4101–4436 in Building 14; a pedestrian walkway runs behind the patios of this building and gets a lot of use in the early morning from guests headed to breakfast.

If you've got a car or you don't mind a couple of extra furlongs' walk to the lobby, Rooms 1101–1436 and 2501–2836 in Congress Park offer quietness, a view of Downtown Disney, and a relatively short walk to the bus stop. Also good are Rooms 4501–4826, 6101–6436, and 6501–6836 in The Paddock. Avoid rooms on the northeast side of the

5101–5435 building of The Paddock, as well as the northwest side of the 5501–5836 building; these border a swimming pool and bus stop.

In addition to being quiet, Rooms 1101–1436 of Congress Park and Rooms 6101–6436 and 6501–6836 of The Paddock afford the closest walks to Downtown Disney shops, restaurants, and entertainment.

**TREEHOUSE VILLAS AT DISNEY'S SARATOGA SPRINGS RESORT & SPA**
Opened in 2009, this complex of 60 three-bedroom villas lies between Old Key West Resort and the Grandstand section of Saratoga Springs proper, with a separate entrance off Disney Vacation Club Way. The treehouses are bordered by Lake Buena Vista Golf Course to the northeast and a waterway to the southwest that feeds into Village Lake.

True to their name, the villas stand on stilts 10 feet off the ground (ramps provide wheelchair access) and are surrounded by a densely wooded landscape. Each villa is an eight-sided structure with three bedrooms and two full bathrooms in about 1,074 square feet.

Each villa holds nine people, about the same number as comparably sized rooms at the other DVC/DDV resorts. The master and second bedrooms have queen beds, and the third bedroom has bunk beds. A sofa bed and sleeper chair in the living room round out the mattress lineup. As with sleeper sofas and chairs in general, we think these are more appropriate for kids than adults.

The three-bedroom Treehouses cost about $100–$170 more per night than a comparably sized two-bedroom villa elsewhere at Saratoga Springs. The tradeoff, however, is that you get an extra bedroom and give up some living space elsewhere. You probably won't notice the missing space because the layout of the kitchen, dining, and living areas is so open. Beware the master-bathroom shower, which is next to the tub in an enclosed glass wall: Tilt down to shave your legs or grab a bottle of shampoo, and you could whack your head on the side of the tub.

The interior of each villa is decorated with natural materials, such as stone floors in the kitchen, granite countertops, and stained wood furniture. End tables, picture frames, and bunk beds are made from rustic logs. Bathrooms, outfitted in modern tile, have showers and tubs plus a decent amount of counter space.

Because of its location, Treehouse Villas has few amenities of its own: Each villa has a large wooden deck with grill, and all villas share a small pool with spa. A walking path connects the complex to the rest of Saratoga Springs; Treehouse guests can use all of main resort's facilities. Two dedicated bus stops serve the Treehouses.

A family from Columbus, New Jersey, thinks a stay at the Treehouse Villas is money well spent:

> I give them five stars for value. We were trying to be economical, as there were nine people in our party and it saved us about $700–$1,000 per night. Our villa had three rooms and a pullout couch that comfortably housed our group. It had a great eat-in kitchen as well, which further helped us save money on breakfast.

Treehouses 70249–7034 and 7058–7060 are closest to one of the villas' two dedicated bus stops and the walkway to Saratoga Springs; 7026–7033 also have water views. Treehouses 7008–7011, 7045–7049, and 7052–7054 are closest to the other bus stop; 7020–7023 are closest to the boat docks. Finally, Treehouses 7035–7037, 7055, 7056, and 7060 surround the pool.

## Disney's Old Key West Resort *(see map on next page)*

| STRENGTHS | • Boat service to Downtown Disney |
|---|---|
| • Largest villas of the DVC/ DDV resorts | • Grocery selection in gift shop |
| | • Convenient parking |
| • Often available at discounted rates or as DVC rental | **WEAKNESSES** |
| • Mature landscaping | • Multiple bus stops |
| • Homey, well-themed lounge (The Gurgling Suitcase) | • No elevators in many buildings |
| | • Fewer baths per bedroom than newer DVC/DDV properties |
| • Close to Lake Buena Vista Golf Course | • Mediocre on-site dining |

THIS WAS THE FIRST DVC/DDV PROPERTY. Although the resort is a time-share property, units not being used by owners are rented on a nightly basis. Old Key West Resort is a large aggregation of two- to three-story buildings modeled after Caribbean-style residences and guesthouses of the Florida Keys. Set subdivision-style around a golf course and along Bonnet Creek, the buildings are arranged in small, neighborhood-like clusters. They feature pastel facades, white trim, and shuttered windows. The registration area is in Conch Flats Community Hall, along with a full-service restaurant, modest fitness center, marina, and sundries shop. Each cluster of accommodations has a quiet pool; a larger pool is at the community hall. (A waterslide in the shape of a giant sandcastle can be found at the main pool.)

This resort offers some of the roomiest accommodations at Walt Disney World, with all rooms having been refurbished in 2010. Studios are 376 square feet; one-bedroom villas, 942; and two-bedroom villas, 1,333. Studios contain two queen-size beds, a table and two chairs, and an extra vanity outside the bathroom. One-bedroom villas have a king-size bed in the master bedroom, a queen-size sleeper sofa in the living room, a laundry room, and a full kitchen. Two-bedroom villas feature a king-size bed in the master bedroom, a queen-size sleeper sofa and fold-out chair in the living room, and two queen beds in the second bedroom. All villas have enough closet space to contain your entire wardrobe. Studios and villas are tastefully decorated with leather and upholstered furniture in neutral tan or green color schemes. The wood kitchen table and chairs are painted white. One-bedroom and larger villas have wood flooring instead of carpet. Each villa has a private balcony that opens to views of the golf course, landscape, or a waterway.

Transportation to other Disney World destinations is by bus. Walking time to transportation loading areas from the most remote rooms is about 6 minutes.

An Erie, Pennsylvania, reader thinks Old Key West is Walt Disney World's most well-kept secret:

*Old Key West has the most spacious rooms and villas and the easiest access to your car—right outside your door! It's in a great location*

## Old Key West Resort

and built around a gorgeous golf course. There are a number of small, almost private pools, so you don't have to go to the main pool to swim.

**GOOD (AND NOT-SO-GOOD) ROOMS AT OLD KEY WEST RESORT** Old Key West is huge, with 49 three-story villa buildings offering a mix of studio and multiroom villas. Views are nice from almost all villas; all multiroom villas and some studios have a large balcony furnished with a table and chairs. Though nice vistas are easy to come by, quiet is more elusive. Because the resort is bordered by busy Bonnet Creek Parkway and even busier Buena Vista Drive, the best villas are those as far from the highway noise as possible. For quiet isolation and a lovely river view, ask for Building 46 or 45, in that order. For a lake and golf-course view away from road noise but closest to restaurants, recreation, the marina, the main swimming complex, and shopping, ask for Building 13. Nearby, Buildings 12 and 11 are likewise quiet and convenient but offer primarily golf-course views. Next-best choices are Buildings 32 and 34. Building 32 looks onto a lake with the golf course in the background, while 34 faces the golf course with tennis courts to the left and a lake to the right. None of the buildings recommended is more than a 2- to 5-minute walk to the nearest bus stop or pool. Avoid Buildings 19–22, 38 and 39, 41 and 42, and 49–51, which border Bonnet Creek Parkway.

### Disney's Port Orleans Resort–French Quarter
*(see map on next page)*

| STRENGTHS | • Good place to walk or run for fitness |
|---|---|
| • Most compact of the WDW Moderate resorts | **WEAKNESSES** |
| • One bus stop | • Ho-hum pool |
| • Live entertainment in Scat Cat's Club | • Shares bus service with Port Orleans Riverside during slower times of year |
| • Beignets in food court! | |
| • Attractively themed lobby | • No full-service dining |

### Disney's Port Orleans Resort–Riverside *(see map on page 183)*

A MODERATE RESORT, Port Orleans is divided into two sections. The smaller, southern part is called the French Quarter; the larger section is labeled Riverside.

| STRENGTHS | • Close driving distance to Magic Kingdom |
|---|---|
| • Interesting narrative to theming | • Good place to walk or run for fitness |
| • Disney princess–themed rooms in Magnolia Bend | • Recreation options (bikes, boats) |
| • Live entertainment in River Roost Lounge | **WEAKNESSES** |
| • The only Moderate resort (for now) that can sleep five, in a Murphy bed at Alligator Bayou | • Multiple bus stops; shares service with Port Orleans French Quarter during slower times of year |
| • Very nice feature pool | • Mediocre full service restaurant |

**PORT ORLEANS RESORT–FRENCH QUARTER** The 1,008-room French Quarter section is a sanitized Disney version of New Orleans's Vieux Carré. Consisting of seven three-story guest-room buildings next to the Sassagoula River, the resort suggests what New Orleans would look like if its buildings were painted every year and garbage collectors never went on strike. Prim pink-and-blue guest buildings are festooned with wrought-iron filigree, shuttered windows, and old-fashioned iron lampposts. In keeping with the Crescent City theme, French Quarter is landscaped with magnolia trees and overgrown vines. The centrally located Mint contains the registration area and food court and is a reproduction of a turn-of-the-19th-century building where Mississippi Delta farmers sold their harvests. The registration desk features a vibrant Mardi Gras mural and old-fashioned bank-teller windows. Doubloon Lagoon surrounds a colorful fiberglass creation depicting Neptune riding a sea serpent.

French Quarter rooms measure 314 square feet. Most contain two queen beds, a table and two chairs, a dresser–credenza, a mini-fridge, a coffeemaker, and a vanity outside the bathroom. With their cherry headboards, Mardi Gras–purple bedspreads, cherry-wood credenzas with oak inlays, and olive carpet, the rooms are themed but tasteful. No rooms have balconies, but ornamental iron-railed accessways on each floor provide a good (though less private) substitute.

There's a food court but no full-service restaurant. The closest full-service eatery is in the adjacent Riverside section of the resort, about a 15-plus-minute walk. The commute to restaurants in other hotels may be 40–60 minutes each way. The Disney bus system links the French Quarter to all Disney World destinations. Walking time to bus-loading areas from the most remote French Quarter rooms is 5 minutes or less.

Most readers really like Port Orleans French Quarter. This comment from a Wynnewood, Pennsylvania, father of two is typical:

> I highly recommend Port Orleans French Quarter. We stayed at All-Star Movies on our last trip and didn't think it made sense to stay anywhere else. Well, we were wrong. The price difference wasn't that big, and what we got for the difference was well worth it: uncrowded pool, bellhop service, front-door greeters with great tips for touring, and a bigger, more comfortable room. Totally worth the extra money.

One Philadelphia Gen Xer wasn't flush with joy about his stay:

> The in-room toilets seem to be powered by jet thrusters. We were

## Port Orleans Riverside Resort

woken up far too many times in the night when someone in a neighboring room would flush.

An unidentified e-mailer backs him up:

*The reader comment about the toilets is 100% correct. They're air-pressure-forced rather than water-flow-and-gravity-operated—like an airplane toilet, only MUCH louder. Every morning I was woken up at 7:30 a.m. with an hour's worth of whooooshing.*

**GOOD (AND NOT-SO-GOOD) ROOMS AT PORT ORLEANS FRENCH QUARTER** Seven guest-room buildings flank the pool and Guest Relations building and bus stop. The best views are from rooms facing the river and pine forest on the opposite bank. Wings of Buildings 1, 2, 5, 6, and 7 flank the river and provide the best river views in all of Port Orleans. River-view rooms in Buildings 1, 6, and 7 are a long walk from French Quarter public facilities, but they're the most tranquil. Families with children should request river-view rooms in Buildings 2 and 5, nearest the swimming complex. Make sure the reservationist understands that you're requesting a room with a river view, not just a water view. All river-view rooms are also water-view rooms, but not vice versa. Note that standard-view rooms look onto a courtyard or a parking lot.

Following are the best river-view rooms in each building:

**BUILDING 1**   Rooms 1127–1132, 1227–1232, 1327–1332

**BUILDING 2**   Rooms 2227–2232, 2327–2332

**BUILDING 5**   Rooms 5117–5123, 5218–5224, 5318–5325

**BUILDING 6**   Rooms 6123–6126, 6223–6226, 6323–6326, 6133–6140, 6233–6240, 6333–6340, 6145–6148, 6245–6248, 6345–6348

**BUILDING 7**   Rooms 7142–7147, 7242–7247, 7342–7347

**PORT ORLEANS RESORT–RIVERSIDE** This resort draws on the lifestyle and architecture of Mississippi River communities in antebellum Louisiana. Spread along the Sassagoula River, which encircles "Ol' Man Island" (the section's main swimming area), Riverside is subdivided into two more themed areas: the "mansion" area, which features plantation-style architecture, and the "bayou" area, with tin-roofed rustic (imitation) wooden buildings. Mansions are three stories tall, while bayou guesthouses are a story shorter. Riverside's food court houses a working cotton press powered by a 32-foot waterwheel.

Each of Riverside's 2,048 rooms is 314 square feet. Most provide one king or two queen beds, a table and two chairs, a mini-fridge and coffeemaker, and two pedestal sinks outside the bathroom. Rooms in the Alligator Bayou section of Riverside feature brass bathroom fixtures, hickory-branch bedposts, Murphy beds, and quilted bedspreads. Rooms in the plantation-themed Magnolia Bend section of Riverside are more conventional, with light-green walls, chestnut-colored wood furnishings, olive carpets, and dark-blue bedspreads.

Two Riverside buildings, Parterre Place and Oak Manor, contain exclusively Disney princess–themed rooms—512 in all—similar in concept to the Disney-themed rooms at Caribbean Beach. Riverside's rooms are themed to *The Princess and the Frog*, with appearances by Tiana's other princess friends. These rooms cost around $42 more per night than other rooms.

Rooms in Alligator Bayou are unique among Disney's Moderate properties in that they sleep five people; the fifth is a fold-down, Murphy-style bed, more suitable for children than adults.

Many readers have written asking us to emphasize that, aside from the differences in guest rooms described previously, all the rooms are more or less the same regardless of the facade of your building, as a New York City reader observed:

> Although the Riverside section is modeled after mansions of the Old South, the outside of each building is simply a "shell"—there's little or no decor inside your room that corresponds to the theme outside.

A Lexington, Kentucky, mom touts Riverside's counter-service food:

> The counter service at Riverside was the most convenient, efficient, and spacious of any we've experienced at Disney. The pasta bar was one of the most enjoyable meals we experienced—and we had counter service at the Grand Floridian, the Polynesian, and the Contemporary, plus we ate at Cinderella's Royal Table, Chef Mickey's, The Crystal Palace, the Biergarten, and Akershus.

**GOOD (AND NOT-SO-GOOD) ROOMS AT PORT ORLEANS RIVERSIDE RESORT** Riverside is so large that we use bicycles whenever we work there. All told, there are 20 guest-room buildings (not counting flanking wings on two buildings). Divided into two sections, Alligator Bayou and Magnolia Bend, the resort is arrayed around two pine groves and a watercourse that Disney calls the Sassagoula River. Magnolia Bend consists of four three-story, grand plantation–style complexes named Acadian House, Magnolia Terrace, Oak Manor, and Parterre Place. Though Magnolia Bend is on the river, only about 15% of the guest rooms have an unobstructed view of the water. The vast majority of rooms overlook a courtyard or parking lot. Trees and other vegetation block the view of many rooms actually facing the river. The best views in Magnolia Bend are from the third-floor river side of Acadian House (Building 80), which overlooks the river and Ol' Man Island: Rooms 8417–8419.

To the south are Magnolia Terrace (Building 85) and Oak Manor (Building 90), each in an H shape. They're nearer the front desk, restaurant, lounge, and shopping complex than Acadian House. Continuing south, Parterre Place (Building 95) has a number of rooms facing the river, but the views are blocked by trees or extend to the parking lot on the opposite shore. In general, with the few previous exceptions, if you want a nice river view, opt for Port Orleans French Quarter downriver.

Alligator Bayou, the other part of Port Orleans Riverside, forms an arch around the resort's northern half. Sixteen smaller, two-story guest-room buildings, set among pine groves and abundant gardens, offer a cozy alternative to the more-imposing structures of the Magnolia Bend section of Riverside and Port Orleans French Quarter. If you want a river view, ask for a second-story water-view room in Building 27 or 38. Building 14 also offers some river-view rooms and is convenient to shops, the front desk, and the restaurant, but it's in a noisy, high-traffic area. A good compromise for families is Building 18. It's insulated from traffic and noise by landscaping, yet is next to a satellite swimming pool and within an easy walk of the Guest Relations building.

Disney's Port Orleans Riverside map shows two lakes north of the river bend, suggesting additional water views in Alligator Bayou. But these are dried-up lakes now forested with pine. This area, however, is richly landscaped to complement the "pine islands," and though out of sight of water, it offers the most peaceful and serene accommodations in the Port Orleans resort. In this area, we recommend Buildings 26, 25, and 39, in that order. Note that these buildings are somewhat distant from the resort's central facilities, and there's no adjacent parking. In Alligator Bayou, avoid Buildings 15, 16, 17, and 24, all of which are subject to traffic noise from nearby Bonnet Creek Parkway.

*Remember:* All Port Orleans guest buildings have exterior corridors. When you look out your window, a safety rail will be in the foreground, and other guests will periodically walk past.

## THE ANIMAL KINGDOM RESORTS

### Disney's Animal Kingdom Lodge & Villas: Jambo House
### Disney's Animal Kingdom Villas: Kidani Village
(see map of both on page 187)

IN THE FAR SOUTHWEST CORNER OF THE WORLD and adjacent to Disney's Animal Kingdom theme park, Animal Kingdom Lodge opened in 2001. Designed by Peter Dominick of Wilderness Lodge fame, the resort fuses African tribal architecture with the rugged style of grand East African national-park lodges. Five-story thatched-roof guest-room wings fan out from a vast central rotunda housing the lobby. Public areas and about half of the rooms offer panoramic views of a private

## JAMBO HOUSE

| STRENGTHS | WEAKNESSES |
|---|---|
| • Magnificent lobby | • Jambo House villas are smaller than those at Kidani Village |
| • Excellent on-site dining options | |
| • Large, beautiful feature pool | • Rooms are among the smallest of the Deluxe resorts |
| • On-site cultural and nature programs | |
| • Best theming of any Disney hotel | • No direct nonbus transportation to any theme park |

## KIDANI VILLAGE

| STRENGTHS | • Close to Jambo House amenities |
|---|---|
| • Nice pool with excellent splash area | • One of the nicest fitness rooms on-property |
| • Underground parking close to elevators | |
| • Beautiful, understated lobby | **WEAKNESSES** |
| • Sanaa restaurant is an *Unofficial Guide* favorite | • Savanna views can be hit-or-miss |
| • Beautiful Grand Villas sleep 13 | • No quick-service food other than pool bar |

43-acre wildlife preserve, punctuated with streams and elevated *kopje* (rock outcrops) and populated with some 200 free-roaming animals and 130 birds.

Most of the 972 guest rooms measure 344 square feet and boast hand-carved furnishings and richly colored soft goods. Standard amenities include a flat-panel TV, desk with two chairs, ceiling fan, mini-fridge, and coffee maker. Behind each headboard sits faux mosquito netting. (Perhaps the tan curtains are supposed to be the folds of a safari tent.) Bathrooms have animal-themed wallpaper, two sinks, and a large mirror. Almost all rooms have full balconies.

The resort is divided into Jambo House, which has both regular hotel rooms and DDV units, and the all-DDV Kidani Village.

Jambo House offers fine dining in a casual setting at Jiko—The Cooking Place. Twin wood-burning ovens are the focal point of the restaurant, which serves meals inspired by the myriad cuisines of Africa. Boma—Flavors of Africa, the family restaurant, serves a buffet with food prepared in an exhibition kitchen featuring a wood-burning grill and rotisserie. Tables are under thatched roofs. The Mara, a quick-service restaurant with extended hours, and Victoria Falls, a delightful mezzanine lounge overlooking Boma, round out the hotel's food-and-beverage service. Other amenities include an elaborate swimming area, a village marketplace, and a 1-hour nighttime safari tour exclusively for Lodge guests ages 8 and up. The tour costs $70 per person and takes place on Wednesday–Monday at 10 p.m.

Consisting of a separate building shaped like a backwards 3, Kidani Village comprises 324 units, a dedicated savanna, a well-themed pool and splash zone, and Sanaa, a sit-down restaurant combining Indian and African cuisines. Other amenities include a fitness center, an arcade, a gift shop, and tennis, shuffleboard, and basketball courts. Kidani Village is connected to Jambo House by a half-mile walking trail; DDV guests at either resort can use the facilities at both buildings.

## Animal Kingdom Lodge & Villas

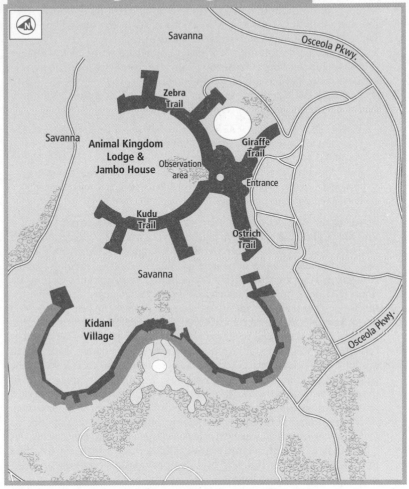

Both Jambo House and Kidani Village have studios and one-, two-, and three-bedroom villas. Most rooms at Kidani Village are larger, however, and the difference is anywhere from 50 square feet for a studio to more than 200 square feet for a two-bedroom unit. (The three-bedroom Grand Villas at Jambo House, 148 square feet larger than those in Kidani Village, are the exception.) Kidani's villas also have one more bathroom for one-, two-, and three-bedroom units. Because of the difference in area, one-bedroom units in Kidani Village can accommodate up to five people and two-bedroom units can hold up to nine via a sleeper chair in the living room. At Jambo House, one-bedroom "value" rooms sleep four; standard, savanna, and Club Level rooms sleep five.

Having stayed at Kidani Village at least half a dozen times, we think it's quiet and relaxed. The lobby and rooms have a smaller, more personal feel than Jambo House's. The exterior isn't anything special—essentially a set of green rectangles with oversize African-themed decorations attached. Kidani's distance from Jambo House makes it feel especially remote. The bus stops are a fair distance from the main building, too, and it's easy to head in the wrong direction when you're coming back from the parks at night.

Animal Kingdom Lodge & Villas is connected to the rest of Disney World by bus, but because of the resort's remote location, you should seriously consider having a car if you stay there.

A family of four from Lincoln, England, gives Animal Kingdom Lodge a mixed, though mostly positive, review:

> We had a fab holiday, but we wouldn't recommend people paying the extra money to have a savanna room. The animals are scarce, and you don't really spend much time in your room. The pool and the kids' club were fantastic and the hotel stunning. The food court was fine, although we wished they'd change the menu, as after two weeks you're fed up of the same choices.

**GOOD (AND NOT-SO-GOOD) ROOMS AT ANIMAL KINGDOM LODGE & VILLAS** A glance at the resort map tells you where the best rooms and villas are. Kudu Trail and Zebra Trail, two wings branching from the rear of Jambo House, form a semicircle around the central wildlife savanna. Along each wing are seven five-story buildings, with accommodations on floors 2–5. Five buildings on each wing form the semicircle, while the remaining two buildings jut away from the center. The best rooms—on floors 3 and 4, facing into the circle—are high enough to survey the entire savanna yet low enough to let you appreciate the ground-level detail of this amazing wildlife exhibit; plus, these rooms offer the easiest access to the lobby and restaurants. Second-floor rooms really can't take in the panorama, and fifth-floor rooms are a little too high for intimate views of the animals. Most of the fourth-floor rooms in Jambo House are reserved for concierge guests, and the fifth and sixth floors house the DDV units.

Most rooms in the outward-jutting buildings, as well as rooms facing away from the interior, also survey a savanna, but one not as compelling as that of the inner circle. On the Zebra Trail, the first two buildings plus the first jutting building provide savanna views on one side and look onto the swimming complex on the other.

Less attractive still are two smaller wings, Ostrich Trail and Giraffe Trail, branching from either side of the lodge near the main entrance. Some rooms on the left side of Ostrich Trail (see map on previous page) overlook a small savanna. Rooms on the opposite side of the same buildings overlook the front entrance. Least desirable is Giraffe Trail, extending from the right side of the lobby: Its rooms overlook either the pool (water view) or the resort entrance (standard view). A Portage, Indiana, family begs to differ with our assessment, however:

> We stayed in a pool-view room in Giraffe Trail and loved it. The view was beautiful, even without the animals (which you can see elsewhere). The proximity to the pool, lobby, and restaurants was great, and we saved about $500 over what we would've spent on a savanna view.

The best views in Kidani Village are the north-facing rooms near the bottom and middle of the backwards 3. Try rooms 7X38–7X44,

7X46–7X52, 7X06–7X11, 7X68–7X82, and 7X61–7X67 (X = numbers 0–9). These overlook the savanna next to Jambo House's Kudu Trail rooms and beyond into undeveloped woods. West- and south-facing rooms in the bottom half of Kidani Village overlook the parking lot; west-facing rooms in the top half have either pool or savanna views.

## Disney's Coronado Springs Resort *(see map on next page)*

| STRENGTHS | WEAKNESSES |
|---|---|
| • Most sophisticated room decor of the Moderate resorts | • Conventioneers may be off-putting to vacationing families |
| • Setting is beautiful at night | • Some rooms are a long distance from check-in, lobby, and restaurants |
| • Themed swimming area with waterslides | |
| • Large feature pool | • Multiple bus stops |
| • On-site business center | |
| • Best public Wi-Fi at any Disney resort | |

NEAR ANIMAL KINGDOM, Coronado Springs Resort is Disney's only midpriced convention property. Inspired by northern Mexico and the American Southwest, the resort is divided into three separately themed areas. The two- and three-story Ranchos call to mind Southwestern cattle ranches, while the two-story Cabanas are modeled after Mexican beach resorts. The multistoried Casitas embody elements of Spanish architecture found in Mexico's great cities. The lobby, part of the Casitas, features a mosaic ceiling and tiled floor.

The vast resort surrounds a 22-acre lake, and there are three small pools as well as one large swimming complex. The main pool features a reproduction of a Mayan step pyramid with a waterfall cascading down its side.

Most of the 1,915 guest rooms measure 314 square feet and contain two queen beds, a desk and chair, a mini-fridge, a coffeemaker, and a vanity outside the bathroom. Rooms are decorated with a subtle Southwestern theme, with turquoise accents. None of the rooms have their own balconies.

Perhaps because Coronado Springs is geared to conventions, getting work done here is easier than at any other Disney Moderate resort. A specially designed light fixture above the desk holds a down-pointing bulb and provides excellent illumination of the work area. Wi-Fi is available throughout the resort, and the business-center staff is friendly and knowledgeable.

Coronado Springs offers one full-service restaurant as well as Disney World's most interesting food court. Unfortunately, there's not nearly enough food service for a resort this large and remote. We suggest having a car to expand your dining options. The resort is connected to other Disney destinations by bus only. Walking time from the most remote rooms to the bus stop is 8–10 minutes.

Cabana 9B holds Coronado's Business Class rooms, with access to a private lounge for serving breakfast and snacks throughout the day.

## Coronado Springs Resort

These rooms cost around $56 per night more than standard rooms, depending on the season.

Reader opinions concerning Coronado Springs are split. A family from Cumming, Georgia, was disappointed:

> *The convention center really interferes with a family vacation—everyone we met there was working and wanted to talk about work while we were trying to get away from work!*

A Portsmouth, England, mother had a very different experience:

> *The concierge team and staff were amazingly helpful. Although there were many conferences at the time we stayed there, it never interfered with our stay or enjoyment of the resort.*

A family from Indianapolis liked the swimming pools:

*The pool at Coronado Springs was excellent—the kids loved the slide! Also utilized smaller pool close to our room—was good for kids to relax before bedtime.*

Finally, a Canvey Island, England, reader was fair and balanced:

*We stayed at Coronado Springs and were very satisfied overall. The Pepper Market food court was overly complicated (stamping tickets to pay at the end, multiple tickets per party), but the quality was good. The Maya Grill was a disappointment, overpriced for the quality of the food. The walk around the lake on a nice day is a delight.*

As convention hotels go, Coronado Springs is an odd duck. Whereas at comparable hotels everything is centrally located and guest rooms are in close proximity, rooms here are spread around a huge lake. If you're assigned a room on the opposite side of the lake from the meeting area and restaurants, plan on an 11- to 15-minute hike every time you leave your room. If your organization books Coronado Springs for a meeting, consider having your meals catered—the restaurants simply don't have the capacity during a large convention to accommodate the breakfast rush or to serve a quick lunch between sessions.

**GOOD (AND NOT-SO-GOOD) ROOMS AT CORONADO SPRINGS RESORT**
Coronado Springs encircles a large artificial lake called Lago Dorado. In addition to the main building (El Centro), which contains shopping venues, restaurants, and a conference center, there are three communities of accommodations. Moving clockwise around the lake, the Casitas are near the lobby, restaurants, shops, and convention center. Standard-view rooms face parking lots or a courtyard. Water-view rooms cover pools, the lake, and so on. For a good view of Lago Dorado, book one of these rooms:

3220–3287 (except 3224, 3227–3240, 3260–3265, 3266, 3279, and 3280)
3320–3387 (except 3324, 3330–3335, 3360–3365, and 3374–3379)
3420–3487 (except 3424, 3430–3435, 3460–3465, and 3474–3479)
4230–4266
5200–5213, 5223–5263 (except 5250)
5300–5313, 5323–5363 (except 5350)
5400–5413, 5423–5463 (except 5450)

Next come the Ranchos, set back from the lake. The desert theme translates to lots of cactus and gravel, not much water or shade, and almost no good views. The Ranchos are a hike from everything but the main swimming area. Rooms 6X00–6X04 afford the best views.

Now come the Cabanas, which offer some very nice lake views. Cabana 9B is our favorite, near restaurants and the convention center, and only a moderate walk to the main pool. Rooms with the best views are 9500–9507, 9528–9547, 9554–9557, 9600–9611, and 9650–9657, with lake views, and 9640–9647, with a view of a small lagoon. Rooms overlooking the lake are subject to some generally tolerable traffic noise.

Other lake-view rooms we recommend include the following:

8129, 8131, and 8140–8147
8500–8510, 8550–8553, and 8573
8600–8610, 8650–8653, and 8673
9150–9153, 9250–9253, and 9273

## Disney's All-Star Resorts: Movies, Music, and Sports

| STRENGTHS | WEAKNESSES |
|---|---|
| • Least expensive of the Disney resorts | • Most likely Disney resorts to host large school groups |
| • Rooms recently refurbished | • Rooms are small |
| • Family suites at All-Star Music are less expensive than those at Art of Animation | • No full-service dining; food courts often overwhelmed at mealtimes |
| • Convenient parking | • All three resorts share buses during slower times of year; bus stops often crowded |
| • Lots of pools | • Public spaces are showing wear |
| • Lovely landscaping, if you know where to look (Music) | • Perhaps *Fantasia 2000* and *The Mighty Ducks* weren't the best choices to theme two entire sections around? |
| • In-room pizza delivery | |

DISNEY'S ORIGINAL VERSION OF A BUDGET RESORT features three distinct themes executed in the same hyperbolic style. Spread over a vast expanse, the resorts comprise 30 three-story motel-style guest-room buildings. Although the three resorts are neighbors, each has its own lobby, food court, and registration area. All-Star Sports features huge sports icons: bright football helmets, tennis rackets, and baseball bats—all taller than the buildings they adorn. Similarly, All-Star Music features 40-foot guitars, maracas, and saxophones, while All-Star Movies showcases giant popcorn boxes and icons from Disney films. The food courts were recently refurbished, and all three resorts offer in-room pizza delivery. Lobbies are loud (in both decibels and brightness) and cartoonish, with checkerboard walls and photographs of famous athletes, musicians, or film stars. There's even a photo of Mickey Mouse with Alice Cooper. Each resort has two main pools; Music's are shaped like musical instruments (the Piano Pool and the guitar-shaped Calypso Pool), and one of Movies' is star-shaped. All six pools feature plastic replicas of Disney characters, some shooting water pistols.

At 260 square feet, standard rooms at the All-Star Resorts are very small—the same size as those at Pop Century Resort and slightly smaller than Art of Animation's standard rooms. All-Star rooms are so small, in fact, that a family of four attempting to stay in one room might redefine "family values" by week's end. Each room has two double beds or one king bed, mini-fridge (no coffeemaker), a separate vanity area, and a table and chairs. Bathrooms have curved shower rods, an improvement. Except for artwork and bathroom wallpaper, all three resorts' rooms are furnished identically. No rooms have balconies.

*un*official **TIP**
Movies has the best food court. Sports has the best bus service.

If you're planning to save for a Disney vacation, you may want to save enough for a bigger room at another resort if space is an important consideration. Also, the All-Stars are the noisiest Disney resorts, though guest rooms are well soundproofed and quiet.

## All-Star Resorts

Main Entrance

W. Buena Vista Dr.

Stadium Blvd.

**Sports**

Hoops Hotel

Surf's Up!

Laundry

Check-in

Bus Stop

Dugout Dr.

Surfboard Bay & Kiddie Pool

Stadium Hall

Hoops Hotel

Center Court

Surf's Up!

Touchdown!

Center Court

Playground

Grand Slam Pool

Home Run Hotel

Laundry

Hall of Fame Ln.

Home Run Hotel

Melody Ln.

W. Buena Vista Dr.

Rock Inn

Rock Inn

Calypso

**Music**

Country Fair

Jazz Inn

Calypso Pool & Kiddie Pool

Laundry

Check-in

Melody Hall

Bus Stop

Stardust Dr.

Piano Pool

Laundry

Jazz Inn

Calypso

Director's Dr.

Country Fair

Broadway Hotel

Playground

Melody Ln.

Broadway Hotel

Mighty Ducks

Duck Pond Pool

Mighty Ducks

Melody Ln.

Show Biz Ln.

Laundry

Love Bug

101 Dalmatians

101 Dalmatians

Premiere Way

Fantasia

Fantasia Pool & Kiddie Pool

Check-in

Show Biz Ln.

Love Bug

Fantasia

Laundry

Cinema Hall

Bus Stop

W. Buena Vista Dr.

Playground

Show Biz Ln.

Toy Story

Toy Story

**Movies**

Due to the low staff-to-guest ratio, service is mediocre Also, there are no full-service restaurants, and the bus ride from the remote All-Stars to a sit-down restaurant at another resort is about 45 minutes one-way (there is, however, a McDonald's about a quarter-mile away). Bus service to the theme and water parks is pretty efficient. Walking time to the bus stop from the most remote guest rooms is about 8 minutes.

We receive a lot of letters commenting on the All-Star Resorts. From a family group of 13 from East Greenbush, New York:

*The All-Star Resorts are perfectly family-oriented. Some nice touches that were not mentioned in your guide—a small amphitheater set up in the lobby to occupy the kids while you check in, and soft sidewalk material surrounding the kiddie pool. And the playground has two separate jungle gyms—one for older kids and one for younger kids.*

A Baltimore family had a similarly positive experience:

*We were pleasantly surprised by All-Star Movies. Yes, the rooms are small, but the overall magic there is amazing. The lobby played Disney movies, which is perfect if you get up early and the buses aren't running yet. Customer service was impeccable.*

A Canadian family had a not-so-positive experience:

*The guide didn't prepare us for the large groups of students who take over the resorts. They're very noisy and very pushy when it comes to getting on buses. Our scariest experience was when we tried getting on a bus and got mobbed by about 100 students.*

From a Massachusetts family of four:

*I would never recommend the All-Star for a family. It was like dormitory living. Our room was a long hike from the bus stop, and it was tiny—you needed to step into the bathroom, shut the door, then step around the toilet that blocked half the tub.*

**ALL-STAR MUSIC FAMILY SUITES** In the Jazz and Calypso Buildings, the 192 suites measure roughly 520 square feet, slightly larger than the cabins at Fort Wilderness but slightly smaller than Art of Animation's Family Suites. Each suite, formed from the combination of two formerly separate rooms, includes a kitchenette with mini-refrigerator, microwave, and coffeemaker. Sleeping accommodations include a queen bed in the bedroom, plus a pullout sleeper sofa, a chair bed, and an ottoman bed. We're not sure we'd let adult friends (ones we want to keep, anyway) on the sofa bed or the chair or ottoman beds, but they're fine for children. A hefty door separates the two rooms.

The All-Star Music Family Suites also feature flat-panel TVs plus two bathrooms—one more than the Fort Wilderness cabins. The suites cost about 25% less than the cabins and about 20% less than the Art of Animation Family Suites, but they don't have the kitchen space or appliances to prepare anything more than rudimentary meals. If you're trying to save money by eating in your room, the cabins are your best bet. If you just want a little extra space and somewhere to nuke your Pop-Tarts in the morning, the All-Star suites are just fine.

Reader comments about the family suites are generally positive, though measured. First, from a North Carolina family of five:

*It was so nice to have a place to unwind without the kids at night, along with two bathrooms and extra space for breakfast/snacks/ drinks in the kitchen area. My only issue was that we weren't comfortable leaving the kids on the foldouts because they're right next to the front door, plus my husband and I didn't want to be confined to the bedroom from the time we put the kids to bed, so we slept on a foldout. The first night was hell, but the second night we took the mattresses off the pullout chair and ottoman and put them on top of the mattress on the couch—MUCH better!*

From a Skokie, Illinois, family of five:

*We found the All-Star Music Family Suite to be very roomy for the six of us. Our teenagers and preteen were quite comfortable on the pullout sofa, chair, and ottoman. Having the two bathrooms was a must, and the kitchen area was great; lots of shelf space for the food we had delivered from GardenGrocer (they're excellent, by the way) [see page 412]. Our only complaint is that from 7:30 a.m. until midnight there's always music playing—it can get annoying to always have that beat going in the background. The rooms are soundproofed but not enough; had to use earplugs.*

**GOOD (AND NOT-SO-GOOD) ROOMS AT THE ALL-STAR RESORTS**
Though the layouts of All-Star Resorts' Movies, Music, and Sports sections are different, the buildings are identical three-story, three-winged structures. The T-shaped buildings are further grouped into pairs, generally facing each other, and share a common subtheme. For example, there's a *Toy Story* pair in the Movies section. In addition to being named by theme, such as *Fantasia*, buildings are numbered 1–10 in each section. Rooms are accessed via a motel-style outdoor walkway, but each building has an elevator.

Parking is plentiful, all of it in sprawling lots buffering the three sections. A room near a parking lot means easier loading and unloading but also unsightly views of the lot during your stay. The resort offers a luggage service, but it often takes up to an hour for your bags to arrive.

The sure way to avoid a parking-lot vista is to request a room facing a courtyard or pool. The trade-off is noise. The sound of cars starting in the parking lot is no match for shrieking children or hooting teenagers in the pool. But don't count on a good view of the pool, even if your room faces it directly. The buildings' themed facade decorations are placed on their widest face—the top of the T— which is also the side facing the pool or courtyard. In some cases, as with the surfboards in the Sports section, these significantly obstruct the view from nearby rooms. Floodlights are trained on these facades and if you step out of your room at night to view the action below, looking down may result in temporary blindness.

*unofficial* **TIP**
Music 5654 may be the best room at the All-Star Resorts. This third-floor corner room overlooks a small pond in a wooded area behind the resort.

The sort of traveler you are should dictate the room you request. If you choose an All-Star Resort because you'd rather spend time and money at the parks, book a room near the bus stop, your link to the rest of the World. Note that buses leave from the central public buildings of each section, which are near the larger, noisier pools. If you're planning to return to your room for an afternoon nap, request a room farther from the pools. Also consider an upper-story room to minimize foot traffic past your door. On the other hand, if you choose All-Star for its kid-friendly aspects, consider roosting near the action. A bottom-floor room provides easy pool access, and a room looking out on a courtyard or pool allows you to keep an eye on children playing outside.

For travelers without young children (infants excluded), the best bets for privacy and quiet are buildings that overlook the forest behind the resort, Buildings 2 and 3 in All-Star Sports and 5 and 6 in All-Star Music. Interior-facing rooms in these buildings (and their partners) also fill the bill, since they overlook courtyards farthest from the large pools. The courtyards vary with theme but are generally only mildly amusing.

If you're traveling with children, opt for a section and building with a theme that appeals to your kids. Often, that will be a film—movies are the lifeblood of the Disney empire—but it might be a sport. If you're staying in Home Run Hotel, don't forget the ball and gloves to maximize the experience (just keep games of catch away from the pool). Older elementary- and middle-school children probably will want to spend hotel time in or near the bigger pools or arcades in nearby halls. Periodically, cadres of teenagers—too cool for their younger siblings—effectively commandeer the smaller secondary pools. Playgrounds are tucked behind Building 9 in All-Star Music and behind Building 6 in All-Star Sports. Rooms facing these are ideal for families with children too young or timid for the often-chaotic larger pools. In All-Star Movies, the playground is nearer to the food court than to any rooms.

The following tip from a former All-Star Resorts cast member from Fayetteville, Georgia, illustrates just how big these resorts are:

> *Rooms at the far end of the Mighty Ducks building of All-Star Movies are closer to the All-Star Music food court, pool, and buses than to All-Star Movies' own facilities. Follow the walkway from the Ducks building north to All-Star Music's Melody Hall.*

### Disney's Pop Century Resort *(see map on page 199)*

ON VICTORY WAY near the ESPN Wide World of Sports Complex is Pop Century Resort. Originally designed to be completed in phases, the resort opened its first section in 2004. The second phase was canceled in favor of a new Value resort, Disney's Art of Animation (see page 198).

Pop Century is a near-clone of the All-Star Resorts—that is, four-story, motel-style buildings built around a central pool, food court, and registration area. Decorative touches make the difference. Where the All-Star Resorts display larger-than-life icons from sports, music, and movies and Art of Animation is inspired by Disney cartoons, Pop Century draws its icons from decades of the 20th century and their attendant popular culture: building-sized Big Wheels, hula hoops,

| STRENGTHS | • Convenient parking |
|---|---|
| • Theming is fun for anyone over 35 | **WEAKNESSES** |
| • Our favorite pool bar of the Value resorts | • Theming may be lost on kids and teens |
| • One bus stop | • Small rooms that are the same size as All-Stars' but slightly more expensive |
| • Walking trail around Hour Glass Lake and connecting bridge to Art of Animation | • Bus stops at theme parks are a long distance from park entrances |
| • In-room pizza delivery | |

and the like, punctuated by silhouettes of people doing the jitterbug and the twist.

The public areas at Pop Century are marginally more sophisticated than the ones at the All-Star Resorts, with 20th-century period furniture and decor rolled up in a saccharine, those-were-the-days theme. A food court, a bar, a playground, pools, and so on emulate the All-Star Resorts model in size and location. A Pop Century departure from the All-Star precedent has merchandise retailers thrown in with the fast-food concessions in a combination dining-and-shopping area. This apparently is what happens when a giant corporation tries to combine selling pizza with hawking Goofy hats. (You just know the word *synergy* was used like cheap cologne in those design meetings.) As at the All-Star Resorts and Art of Animation, there's no full-service restaurant. The resort is connected to the rest of Walt Disney World by bus, but because of the limited dining options, we recommend having a car.

Running $106–$209 per night, guest rooms at Pop Century are small at 260 square feet. The decor is upbeat, with white bedspreads and blue walls. Wall art depicts pop memorabilia from decades past. Cherry-finish wood-inlaid furniture and blue-and-tan-patterned carpet provide an upscale touch, but these are not rooms you'd want to spend a lot of time in. Bathrooms are tiny and counter space a scarce commodity. Worst of all, we've received many complaints from readers that the soundproofing between rooms is inadequate. A lake separating Pop Century from the Art of Animation Resort offers water views not available at the All-Star Resorts.

A reader from Dublin, Georgia, thinks we underrate Pop:

*I can't believe you don't like Pop Century. (1) It's far superior to the All-Star Resorts. (2) There's a lake at a Value resort and a view of fireworks. (3) The courtyards have Twister games and neat pools for little children. (4) The memorabilia is interesting to us of a certain age. (5) I love the gift shop, food court, and bar combo. The [dinner entrees are among] the best bargains and the best food anywhere. (6) Bus transportation is better than anywhere else, including Grand Floridian! (7) The layout is more convenient to the food court. (8) I never hear construction noise, and the noise from neighbors is not worse than anywhere else. (9) Where else do the cast members do the shag to oldies?*

Don't know what it is about Pop Century fans, but they seem to have a propensity for making lists—take this Waukee, Iowa, family:

*We loved Pop Century Resort: (1) It was cheap enough that we had plenty of money left over for other fun things at Disney. (2) The shrimp [entree] was one of the most awesome fast-food items we've had at Disney. (3) Although the rooms are a little small and the lighting isn't the best, the resort is affordable enough that without tax two rooms at the Pop Century are in the same price range as one room at other resorts. (4) It's not far from any park at Disney, nor from Downtown Disney. (5) The combo food court–shopping area really works: My grandparents can eat breakfast in the food court while my brother, sister, parents, and I shop. (6) Food is actually pretty affordable for Disney. (7) Great pools that are not too far from our rooms. (8) You can request a room on the first floor, near the parking lot. They were really accommodating when we explained that I had to have a rather heavy oxygen tank brought to our room, so it would be easier on us to stay on the first floor. (9) Check-in takes probably the least amount of time that I have ever seen at a Disney resort.*

But a Springfield, Illinois, dad gives Pop Century a mixed review:

*We wanted something different from All-Star Movies (two stays in the previous three years), so we gave Pop Century a shot. Believe the noise complaints—they're true. It's like the walls were made of papier-mâché. Although the bus service was great and the pool (and splash pools) were nice for a Value resort, we'll be back at All-Star Movies the next time around.*

**GOOD (AND NOT-SO-GOOD) ROOMS AT POP CENTURY RESORT**
The best rooms for both view and convenience are the lake-view rooms in Buildings 4 and 5, representing the 1960s. However, they're subject to noise from Victory Way and Osceola Parkway. A safer bet, though with a less compelling view, would be rooms in the same building facing east, toward the registration and food-court building. Next-best choices would be the east-facing rooms of Building 3 in the 1950s, and of Building 6 in the 1970s. Avoid south-facing rooms in 1980s Building 7 and 1990s Building 8. Both are echo chambers for noise from nearby Osceola Parkway. Finally, so-called "preferred" rooms at Pop Century, which are closer to the main pool and lobby, cost about $15–$20 more than others. They're definitely closer, but they probably save only 5–10 minutes of walking per day and subject you to more noise from guests walking past your room. We don't think these rooms are worth the extra cost. Finally, note that guest rooms don't have private patios or balconies.

### Disney's Art of Animation Resort

OPENED IN MAY 2012, Art of Animation is a Value resort across Hour Glass Lake from Pop Century. It was originally designed to be part of Pop Century and represent the years 1900–1949, but recessions and an abundance of hotel capacity prevented Disney from ever completing construction. When the time came for a new Value resort, Disney

## Pop Century Resort & Art of Animation Resort

switched the theme to its animated movies, which still fit in well with the pop-culture motif across the lake.

As at Pop Century, Art of Animation's standard rooms are housed in four-story buildings and exterior-facing walkups, with a series of themed swimming pools and a food court. However, the majority of the resort's accommodations are suites similar to those at Disney's All-Star Music Resort. All told, there are 864 standard rooms and 1,120 suites. The suites have interior hallways to the guest rooms instead of the exterior walkways found at Disney's other Value resorts.

**STRENGTHS**

- Exceptional theming, particularly *Cars* and *Lion King* areas
- Best pool of the Value resorts
- Landscape of Flavors food court is an *Unofficial Guide* favorite
- Family Suites are innovatively designed and themed
- In-room pizza delivery
- Walking trail around Hour Glass Lake and connecting bridge to Pop Century

- Just one bus stop

**WEAKNESSES**

- Most expensive Value resort
- Terrible in-room mobile reception
- The number of made-to-order meals at the food court can mean long waits in line
- The resort's Family Suites are rarely discounted
- Poor soundproofing

Art of Animation's suites are around 565 square feet, about what you'd get by combining two standard rooms into one suite. Each suite has a master bedroom, a living room, two full bathrooms, and a kitchenette with mini-fridge, microwave, and coffeemaker. Sleeping accommodations include a queen bed in the bedroom, a sleeper sofa, and a living-room table that converts into a full-size bed. The bedroom and living room have flat-panel TVs.

Slightly larger than comparable rooms at other Value resorts, standard rooms are 277 square feet and include one king or two double beds, a flat-panel TV, a mini-fridge, and a table and chairs.

Theming incorporates characters from four Disney films: *Cars, Finding Nemo, The Lion King,* and *The Little Mermaid.* All but the Mermaid-themed rooms are suites. As at Pop Century, large, colorful icons stand in the middle of each group of buildings; here, though, they represent film characters rather than pop-culture touchstones. An interesting departure from the other Value resorts is the outside paint schemes: Rather than using pastels, Disney has decorated the exteriors with giant murals stretching the length of each structure. The *Cars* buildings, for example, each display a four-story panoramic vista of the American desert, with the movie's iconic characters in the middle, while the *Lion King* buildings capture a single verdant jungle scene. It's a great idea.

Three of the four sets of themed buildings have pools; the *Lion King* complex has a playground instead. Like the other Value resorts, Art of Animation has a central building—here called Animation Hall—for check-in and bus transportation; it also holds the resort's food court, Landscape of Flavors; a gift shop; and a video-game arcade.

Speaking of check-in, the wall behind the front desk is a dazzling rainbow of colors from floor to ceiling. In sharp contrast to the faded paints and photos at, say, the All-Stars, Art of Animation's backlight displays and wall art are bright and vibrant and should stand up well to Florida's weather.

Most comments concerning Art of Animation have been positive. A mom from Blountville, Tennessee, says:

*The Art of Animation Resort was the highlight of our trip! Out daughter loves The Little Mermaid, and the rooms, while small and basic, were adorable. The courtyards, the pools, the main lobby areas, etc.— Disney is fantastic at attention to detail. Our daughter loved pointing out* Lion King, Nemo, *and* Little Mermaid *characters every day.*

Readers complain, however, about the long walk from the *Little Mermaid*–themed buildings to the food court and front desk. Mobile reception was also singled out as a problem. A woman from Houston related the following:

*There was no AT&T service inside the building where our rooms were. There was plenty of service outside the building, but the moment we stepped inside it was like a vacuum. It was very upsetting.*

Noise and soundproofing are likewise issues. A mom from Boise, Idaho, comments:

*Art of Animation was great, but I'm not sure if we would stay there again because of the noise. The suites were great, but the pool area was very noisy. I think this is just how it is at the Value resorts.*

A Guyton, Georgia, mom agrees:

*The room was very poorly soundproofed. I heard snoring and bathroom noises from other rooms that I should not have been able to hear. One afternoon my toddler and I returned to the room for a nap—I suppose housekeeping was cleaning the room above ours, but it sounded like someone was bowling up there.*

**GOOD (AND NOT-SO-GOOD) ROOMS AT ART OF ANIMATION** The quietest suites are south- and east-facing rooms in Buildings 3 (*Cars*), 4 (*Finding Nemo*), and 6 (*The Lion King*). The quietest standard rooms are east-facing rooms in Building 8 and south-facing rooms in Building 7 (both *The Little Mermaid*). Avoid northwest-facing rooms in Building 1 and southwest-facing rooms in Building 10, which face the Disney bus route and Art of Animation's bus stops.

## INDEPENDENT HOTELS OF THE DOWNTOWN DISNEY RESORT AREA

THE SEVEN HOTELS of the Downtown Disney Resort Area (DDRA) were created back when Disney had far fewer of its own resorts. The hotels—the **Best Western Lake Buena Vista Resort Hotel, B Resort,** the **Buena Vista Palace Hotel & Spa, DoubleTree Guest Suites,** the **Hilton in the Walt Disney World Resort,** the **Holiday Inn in the Walt Disney World Resort,** and **Wyndham Lake Buena Vista Resort**—are chain-style affairs with minimal or nonexistent theming, though the Buena Vista Palace especially is pretty upscale. Several of the larger properties have shifted their focus to convention and business travelers.

### AMENITIES AT DDRA HOTELS

| HOTEL | CHILDREN'S PROGRAMS | DINING | KID-FRIENDLY | POOL(S) | RECREATION |
|---|---|---|---|---|---|
| Best Western LBV Resort | None | ★★½ | ★★★ | ★★½ | ★★ |
| B Resort | None | ★★★½ | ★★½ | ★★½ | ★★★ |
| Buena Vista Palace | ★★★★ | ★★ | ★★★½ | ★★★½ | ★★★★ |
| DoubleTree Guest Suites | None | ★★ | ★★★ | ★★½ | ★★½ |
| Hilton WDW Resort | None | ★★½ | ★★½ | ★★★ | ★★½ |
| Holiday Inn WDW Resort | None | ★★ | ★★ | ★★★ | ★★ |
| Wyndham LBV Resort | ★★½ | ★★½ | ★★★ | ★★★ | ★★★ |

The main advantage to staying in the DDRA is being in Disney World and next to Downtown Disney–Disney Springs. Guests at the Hilton, Wyndham Lake Buena Vista Resort, Buena Vista Palace, and Holiday Inn are an easy 5- to 15-minute walk from the Marketplace on the east side of Downtown Disney. Guests at B Resort, the Best Western Lake Buena Vista, and DoubleTree Guest Suites are about 10 minutes farther by foot. Disney transportation can be accessed at Downtown Disney, though the buses take a notoriously long time to leave due to the number of stops throughout the complex. Although all DDRA hotels offer shuttle buses to the theme parks, the service is provided by private contractors and is somewhat inferior to Disney transportation in frequency of service, number of buses, and hours of operation. Get firm details in advance about shuttle service from any DDRA hotel you're considering. All these hotels are easily accessible by car and are only marginally farther from the Disney parks than several of the Disney resorts; DDRA hotels are also quite close to Typhoon Lagoon water park.

DDRA hotels, even the business- and convention-focused ones, try to appeal to families. Some have pool complexes rivaling those at any Disney resort, whereas others offer a food court or all-suite rooms. A few sponsor character meals and organized kids' activities; all have counters for buying Disney tickets, and most have Disney gift shops.

## A Difficult Value Proposition

With the exception of the Buena Vista Palace, the Hilton, and perhaps the Holiday Inn, we find it difficult to recommend these hotels. The rooms at many are in need of refurbishment. Further, for much of the year there's little price difference between these rooms and those at Disney's Value resorts, especially when Disney offers discounts.

Speaking of prices, all of the DDRA resorts tack on daily charges for self-parking, Internet access, or some cockamamy "resort fee." These fees add $12–$46 per night to your stay, plus tax.

| ADDITIONAL FEES AT THE DDRA RESORTS | | | | |
|---|---|---|---|---|
| **HOTEL** | **SELF-PARKING** | **RESORT FEE** | **INTERNET** | **TOTAL PER DAY** |
| **BEST WESTERN LBV RESORT** | Free | $14 | Free | $14 |
| **B RESORT** | $16 | $20 | Free | $36 |
| **BUENA VISTA PALACE** | Free | $22 | Free | $22 |
| **DOUBLETREE GUEST SUITES** | $15 | None | $10 | $25 |
| **HILTON WDW RESORT** | $14 | $22 | $10 | $46 |
| **HOLIDAY INN WDW RESORT** | $12 | None | Free | $12 |
| **WYNDHAM LBV RESORT** | $8 | $18 | Free | $26 |

A special thumbed nose to the Hilton, which was tacking on $46 per day in fees to a $169-per-night reservation in June 2014. Send napkins to Disney—they're gonna be eating your lunch.

Heaven knows Disney's Deluxe resorts are overpriced, but it's hard to see how any DDRA property can compete with the value proposition of Disney's inexpensive hotels, which offer free airport transportation, better bus service, free parking, and extra time at the theme parks. We suspect most readers who choose the DDRA resorts do so either because they've earned enough rewards points to qualify for a free stay or the Disney resorts are sold out. We'd be hard-pressed to think of another reason to stay at these hotels, especially if we had a car.

Descriptions of each DDRA resort follow. Also take a peek at the combined website for the DDRA hotels at **downtowndisneyhotels .com.** Finally, check the comparative chart above.

## B Resort  ★★★½

B RESORTS, a Florida hotel chain, relaunched the former Royal Plaza in the summer of 2014 after an extensive multiyear renovation. Located within walking distance of shops and restaurants and situated 5 miles or less from the Disney parks, the 394-room hotel targets couples, families, groups, and business travelers.

1905 Hotel Plaza Blvd.
☎ 407-828-2828 or
   800-66-BHOTELS
bresortlvb.com

Decorated in cool blues, whites, and grays, guest rooms and suites afford views of downtown Orlando, area lakes, and theme parks. Along with B Resorts–exclusive Blissful Beds, each room is outfitted with sleek modern furnishings and a large interactive flat-screen TV. Additional touches include a mini-fridge, in-room snacks, and gaming consoles (available upon request). Some rooms are also equipped with bunk beds, kitchenettes, or wet bars.

Amenities include free Wi-Fi, a spa, beauty salon, and fitness center. The main restaurant, American Q, serves a modern upscale take on classic barbecue in regional styles ranging from Carolina to Kansas City. Hungry guests can also choose from a poolside bar and grill; The Pickup, a grab-and-go shop just off the lobby that serves quick breakfasts, snacks, picnic lunches, and ice cream; and 24/7 in-room dining.

Other perks: a zero-entry pool with interactive water features; a kids' area; loaner iPads; Monscierge, a digital touchscreen concierge and destination guide in the lobby; and more than 25,000 square feet of meeting and multiuse space. Though not served by Disney transportation, B Resort provides bus service to the parks and other Disney World venues. A resort fee of $20 per day applies.

## Best Western Lake Buena Vista Resort Hotel  ★★★

THE 18-STORY, 325-ROOM Best Western Lake Buena Vista has relatively few of the extras common to most other DDRA properties. The rooms are in need of refurbishment. Parking is a hike from many rooms, and to get to them you pass through hallways and areas that could use a good scrubbing. The most surprising thing was the attitude of general indifference from several of the staff when we needed help checking in.

2000 Hotel Plaza Blvd.
☎ 407-828-2424 or
800-348-3765
lakebuenavista
resorthotel.com

A breakfast buffet and dinner service of American fare are available in the Trader's Island Grill, while the Parakeet Café offers sandwiches and snacks. The poolside Flamingo Cove Lounge provides its own menu of pub standards as well as alcoholic refreshment. The pool is small though pleasantly landscaped, and there's a kiddie pool as well. Other amenities include a fitness room and game room. Although there are no organized children's programs, the resort can arrange child care.

## Buena Vista Palace Hotel & Spa  ★★★½

THE BUENA VISTA PALACE IS upscale and convenient. Surrounded by an artificial lake and plenty of palms, the spacious pool area comprises three heated pools, the largest of which is partially covered; a whirlpool and sauna; a basketball court; and a sand volleyball court. A pool concierge will fetch your favorite

1900 E. Buena Vista Dr.
Lake Buena Vista
☎ 407-827-2727 or
866-397-6516
buenavistapalace.com

magazine or fruity drink. On Sunday, the Watercress Café hosts a character brunch ($25 for adults and $12 for children). The 897 guest rooms are posh and spacious; each comes with desk, coffeemaker, hair dryer, satellite TV with pay-per-view movies, iron and board, and mini-fridge. There are also 117 suites. In-room babysitting is available. One lighted tennis court, a European-style spa offering 60 services, a fitness center, an arcade, a playground, and a beauty salon round out amenities. Two restaurants and a mini-market are on-site. And if you aren't wiped out after time in the parks, consider dropping by the Lobby Lounge or the full-menu sports bar for a nightcap. *Note:* All these amenities and services come at a price—a $22-per-night resort fee will be added to your bill.

## DoubleTree Guest Suites ★★★½

2305 Hotel Plaza Blvd.
☎ 407-934-1000
doubletreeguestsuites.com

THIS GIANT WHITE BUNKER of a hotel is the only all-suite establishment on Disney property. What it lacks in atmosphere and creative attributes, it makes up for in convenience and comfort. Within walking distance of Downtown Disney, the 229 suites are spacious for a family, although the decor is startling, with no apparent theme. No rooms have balconies, though ground floors offer patios.

Amenities include a safe, hair dryer, refrigerator, microwave, coffeepot, fold-out bed, and two TVs (bedroom and living room).

Children will enjoy their own check-in desk, the free chocolate-chip cookie, and the small playground. The heated pool, children's pool, and whirlpool spa are moderate in size; a minus is that traffic noise from Interstate 4 can be heard faintly from the pool deck. The tiny fitness center (more like a fitness closet), pool table, four tennis courts, and outdoor bar are adjacent to the pool. High-speed Internet and a business center in the lobby are convenient for those on working holidays. The Market (open 7 a.m.–midnight) offers groceries, drinks, ice cream, and sundaes for those late-night munchies; the EverGreen Cafe serves breakfast, lunch, and dinner. Babysitting is available.

## Hilton in the Walt Disney World Resort ★★★★

1751 Hotel Plaza Blvd.
☎ 407-827-4000
hilton-wdwv.com

THE HILTON IS THE ONLY DDRA HOTEL offering Disney's Extra Magic Hours program to its guests. Although the resort fees are outrageous and the decor is dated, the rooms are comfortable and nicer than some others in the DDRA. On-site dining includes Covington Mill Restaurant, offering sandwiches and pasta; Andiamo, an Italian bistro; and Benihana, a Japanese steakhouse and sushi bar (the last two are reviewed in Part Ten). Covington Mill hosts a Disney-character breakfast on Sundays. The two pools are matched with a children's "spray pool" and a 24-hour fitness center. An exercise room and a game room are on-site, as is a 24-hour market. Babysitting is available, but there are no organized children's programs.

A Denver family of five found the Hilton's shuttle service lacking:

*The transportation, provided by a company called Mears, was unreliable. They did a better job of getting guests back to the hotel from the park than getting them to the park from the hotel.*

*Shuttles from the hotel were randomly timed and went repeatedly to the same parks—skipping others and leaving guests to wait for up to an hour.*

## Holiday Inn in the Walt Disney World Resort  ★★★½

COMPLETELY RENOVATED IN 2010, the Holiday Inn is modern and comfortable. The layout remains the same, with tower rooms grouped around an atrium and wing rooms overlooking the pool. The feel of the hotel is modern and contemporary yet relaxed and comfortable. Downtown Disney is just a short walk away.

1805 Hotel Plaza Blvd.
☎ 407-828-8888
or 888-465-4329
hiorlando.com

The totally upgraded rooms feature pillow-top beds with triple sheeting and firm or soft pillows. Each room has a 32-inch flat-panel HDTV and free high-speed Internet. The bathrooms are clean and well designed—the nicest in any DDRA resort. Amenities include granite countertops and showerheads with a choice of comfort sprays.

The Palm Breezes Restaurant and Bar serves breakfast, lunch, and dinner at reasonable prices. A breakfast buffet is available, as well as à la carte items. The Grab n Go Outlet in the lobby offers quick snacks and sandwiches. Other amenities include a large and well-kept zero-entry pool, along with a Jacuzzi in the pool area. A separate entrance brings you into the convention center, ballroom, and meeting room areas, with a business center nearby.

## Wyndham Lake Buena Vista Resort  ★★★½

ACROSS FROM DOWNTOWN DISNEY, the Wyndham Lake Buena Vista was formerly known as Regal Sun Resort. The lobby is bright and airy and check-in service friendly. Rooms are larger than most and have in-room refrigerators. Pool-facing rooms in the hotel's

1850 Hotel Plaza Blvd.
☎ 407-828-4444
or 800-624-4109
wyndhamlakebuena vista.com

wings have exterior hallways that overlook the pool and center courtyard; these hallways can be noisy during summer months. Elevators are available, but they're unusually slow—it's probably faster to walk to the second and third floors, assuming you're up for the exercise. Disney-character breakfasts take place on Tuesdays, Thursdays, and Saturdays at LakeView Restaurant.

## CAMPING AT WALT DISNEY WORLD

DISNEY'S FORT WILDERNESS RESORT & CAMPGROUND is a spacious area for tent and RV camping. Fully equipped, air-conditioned prefabricated log cabins are also available for rent.

**Tent/Pop-Up** campsites provide water, electricity, and cable TV and run $49–$105 a night depending on season. **Full Hook-Up** campsites have all the previous amenities, accommodate large RVs, and run $61–$108 per night. **Preferred Hook-Up** campsites for tents and RVs add sewer connections and run $66–$124 per night. **Premium** campsites add an extra-large concrete parking pad and run $81–$137 a night.

All sites are level and provide picnic tables, waste containers, grills, and free Wi-Fi. Fires are prohibited except in the grills. Pets are permitted in some Premium and Preferred loops.

## FORT WILDERNESS RESORT & CAMPGROUND

| STRENGTHS | WEAKNESSES |
|---|---|
| • Informality | • Isolated location |
| • Children's play areas | • Complicated bus service |
| • Best recreational options at WDW | • Confusing campground layout |
| • Special day and evening programs | • Lack of privacy |
| • Campsite amenities | • Very limited on-site dining options |
| • Shower and toilet facilities | • Crowding at beaches and pools |
| • *Hoop-Dee-Doo Musical Revue* show | • Small baths in cabins |
| • Convenient self-parking | • Extreme distance to store and |
| • Off-site dining via boat at Magic Kingdom | restaurant facilities from many campsites |

Campsites are arranged on loops accessible from one of three main roads. There are 28 loops, with Loops 100–2000 for tent and RV campers, and Loops 2100–2800 offering cabins at $294–$500 per night. RV sites are roomy by eastern-US standards, with the Premium and Full Hook-Up campsites able to accommodate RVs more than 45 feet long, but tent campers will probably feel a bit cramped. (Note that tent stakes cannot be put into the concrete at the Premium sites.) On any given day, 90% or more of campers are RVers.

Fort Wilderness Resort & Campground arguably offers the most recreational facilities and activities of any Disney resort. Among them are two video arcades; nightly campfire programs; Disney movies; a dinner theater; two swimming pools; a beach; walking paths; bike, boat, canoe, golf-cart, and water-ski rentals; a petting zoo; horseback riding; hayrides; fishing; and tennis, basketball, and volleyball courts. There are two convenience stores, a restaurant, and a tavern. Comfort stations with toilets, showers, pay phones, ice machine, and laundry facilities are within walking distance of all campsites.

Access to the Magic Kingdom is by boat from Fort Wilderness Landing and to Epcot by bus, with a transfer at the Transportation and Ticket Center (TTC) to the Epcot monorail. Boat service may be suspended during thunderstorms, in which case Disney will provide buses. An alternate route to the Magic Kingdom is by internal bus to the TTC, then by monorail or ferry to the park. Transportation to all other Disney destinations is by bus. Motor traffic within the campground is permitted only when entering or exiting. Get around within the campground by bus, golf cart, or bike, the latter two available for rent.

For tent and RV campers, there's a fairly stark trade-off between sites convenient to pools, restaurant, trading posts, and other amenities, and those that are most scenic, shady, and quiet. RVers who prefer to be near guest services, the marina, the beach, and the restaurant and tavern should go for Loops 100, 200, 700, and 400 (in that order). Loops near the campground's secondary facility area with pool, trading post, bike and golf-cart rentals, and campfire program are 1400, 1300, 600, 1000, and 1500, in order of preference. If you're looking for a tranquil, scenic setting among mature trees, we recommend Loops 1800, 1900, 1700, and 1600, in that order, and the backside sites on the 700 loop.

The best loop of all, and the only one to offer both a lovely setting and proximity to key amenities, is Loop 300. The best loops for tents and pop-up campers are 1500 and 2000, with 1500 being nearest a pool, a convenience store, and the campfire program.

With the exception of Loops 1800 and 1900, avoid sites within 40 yards of the loop entrance. These sites are almost always flanked by one of the main traffic arteries within Fort Wilderness. Further, sites on the outside of the loop are almost always preferable to those in the center of the loop. RVers should be forewarned that all sites are back-ins and that although most sites will accommodate large rigs, the loop access roads are pretty tight and narrow.

Rental cabins offer a double bed and two bunk beds in the only bedroom, augmented by a Murphy bed (pulls down from the wall) in the living room. There's one rather small bathroom with shower and tub.

The prefab log cabins (classified as Moderate resorts in the Disney hierarchy) are warm and homey, but the stem-to-stern interior wood paneling and smallish windows make for pretty dark accommodations at night. Neither the lighting fixtures provided nor the wattage of their bulbs are up to the job of lighting the cabins once the sun goes down.

All cabins offer air-conditioning, televisions with DVD players and/or VCRs, fully equipped kitchens, and dining tables. Housekeeping is provided daily. Most readers are crazy about the cabins. Some representative comments follow. A Wappingers Falls, New York, family writes:

> We stayed at Fort Wilderness in a cabin because (1) we wanted a separate bedroom area; (2) we wanted a kitchen; (3) our kids are very lively, and the cabins were apart from each other so we wouldn't disturb other guests; and (4) we thought the kids might meet other children to play with. The cabins worked out just right for us. Although the kids didn't meet any other children to play with, they had a ball chasing the little lizards and frogs, kicking around pinecones, sitting on the deck to eat ice pops, and sleeping in bunk beds.

From a Downers Grove, Illinois, family of five:

> We spent a LOT of time waiting for buses and ferries, more than we remember waiting a few years ago. They've recently made some changes to the bus routes, and while we liked having a stop at the Meadow area, there was always a long wait for a purple bus to take us back to the cabin when returning from the parks (from both depots). They need a separate bus route just for the cabins.

A Rochester, New York, dad agrees:

> If you're staying at Fort Wilderness, we highly recommend getting a golf cart. There's a lot going on at the campground, and the bus system can be cumbersome. Also, our 3-year-old wasn't always up for the walk—just getting from our cabin to the main loop was a lot for her.

This Mechanicsville, Virginia, mom concurs on the golf cart:

> Loved the cabins at Fort Wilderness. The location was perfect with the boat transportation to the Magic Kingdom. A golf cart is a must, though it drives the cost to stay there into the Deluxe price range.

Continued on page 210

Fort Wilderness Resort & Campground

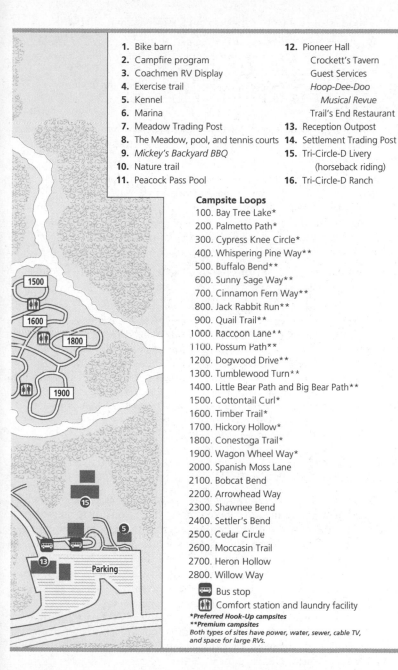

1. Bike barn
2. Campfire program
3. Coachmen RV Display
4. Exercise trail
5. Kennel
6. Marina
7. Meadow Trading Post
8. The Meadow, pool, and tennis courts
9. *Mickey's Backyard BBQ*
10. Nature trail
11. Peacock Pass Pool
12. Pioneer Hall
    Crockett's Tavern
    Guest Services
    *Hoop-Dee-Doo*
        *Musical Revue*
    Trail's End Restaurant
13. Reception Outpost
14. Settlement Trading Post
15. Tri-Circle-D Livery
    (horseback riding)
16. Tri-Circle-D Ranch

**Campsite Loops**
100. Bay Tree Lake*
200. Palmetto Path*
300. Cypress Knee Circle*
400. Whispering Pine Way**
500. Buffalo Bend**
600. Sunny Sage Way**
700. Cinnamon Fern Way**
800. Jack Rabbit Run**
900. Quail Trail**
1000. Raccoon Lane**
1100. Possum Path**
1200. Dogwood Drive**
1300. Tumblewood Turn**
1400. Little Bear Path and Big Bear Path**
1500. Cottontail Curl*
1600. Timber Trail*
1700. Hickory Hollow*
1800. Conestoga Trail*
1900. Wagon Wheel Way*
2000. Spanish Moss Lane
2100. Bobcat Bend
2200. Arrowhead Way
2300. Shawnee Bend
2400. Settler's Bend
2500. Cedar Circle
2600. Moccasin Trail
2700. Heron Hollow
2800. Willow Way

 Bus stop

Comfort station and laundry facility

*Preferred Hook-Up campsites*
**Premium campsites**
*Both types of sites have power, water, sewer, cable TV,
and space for large RVs.*

*Continued from page 207*

A mother of two from Albuquerque, New Mexico, offers this:

*We stayed in a cabin and liked having all the space and the full kitchen. However, the pool nearest our cabin (a quarter-mile away!) never even had a lifeguard. I had hoped to be able to send the kids to swim when we needed some time to ourselves, but with the distance and lack of lifeguards, there was no way to do that.*

Though the cabins are especially popular, RV and tent campers love Fort Wilderness, too. First from a Marietta, Georgia, multigenerational family:

*I do wish you'd stress more the advantages of Fort Wilderness. With sites for any size/type of camper/tent, it's FAR more affordable than any hotel inside the park. Additionally, you could theoretically (although not likely) prepare all of your own meals. We usually had breakfast, packed snacks, and returned for lunch and dinner every day.*

A mother of two from Mechanicsville, Virginia, puts Fort Wilderness on a pedestal as well:

*The most important thing—the family time. This is the only resort where you're encouraged to go outside and play! You can bike, swim, visit two arcades, hike the nature trail, ride a horse, rent a boat, play volleyball, go to the beach, attend a free character sing-along and marshmallow roast followed by a classic Disney movie that many younger families never knew existed (we were introduced to Snowball Express), enjoy multiple playgrounds, play tennis, rent a golf cart, walk around at night to see the festively decorated campsites (many Disney-themed), take a romantic carriage ride, take your first pony ride, and see a wild turkey. Don't forget the fishing or the great view of the fireworks from the beach or the up-close water light parade.*

*With all of this stuff, much of it free or very affordable, who needs the parks? We visited last June and never set foot in a park.*

Bus service at Fort Wilderness leaves a lot to be desired, so much in fact that we wouldn't stay there unless we had our own car. To go anywhere, you first have to catch an internal bus that makes many, many stops. If your destination is outside Fort Wilderness, you then have to transfer to a second bus. To complicate things, buses serving destinations outside the campground depart from two locations, the Reception Outpost and Pioneer Hall. This means you have to keep track of which destinations each transfer center serves.

Finally, if you rent a cabin or camp in a tent or RV, particularly in fall or spring, keep abreast of local weather conditions.

A number of independent campgrounds are within 30 miles of Walt Disney World. Here are the closest:

**Kissimmee-Orlando KOA** ☎ 407-396-2400; **koa.com/campgrounds /kissimmee.** 96 licensed sites; about 6 miles to Walt Disney World US 192 (Maingate) entrance

**Sherwood Forest RV Resort** ☎ 800-548-9981; **rvonthego.com.**
531 licensed sites; about 4 miles to Walt Disney World US 192
(Maingate) entrance

**Tropical Palms Resort** ☎ 407-396-4595; **tropicalpalmsrv.com.**
365 licensed sites; about 2.5 miles to WDW US 192 (Maingate) entrance

# HOW *to* EVALUATE *a* WALT DISNEY WORLD TRAVEL PACKAGE

HUNDREDS OF WALT DISNEY WORLD package vacations are offered each year. Some are created by the Walt Disney Travel Company, others by airlines, independent travel agents, and wholesalers. Almost all include lodging at or near Disney World plus theme park admissions. Packages offered by airlines include air transportation.

> *un*official **TIP**
> If you consider a non-Disney hotel, check its quality as reported in independent travel references such as the *Unofficial Guides,* AAA directories, *Forbes* guides, or *Frommer's* guides.

Prices vary seasonally; mid-March–Easter, summer, and holiday periods are the most expensive. Off-season, there are plenty of empty rooms, and you can negotiate great discounts, especially at non-Disney properties. Similarly, airfares and rental cars are cheaper off-peak.

Almost all package ads are headlined "5 Days at Walt Disney World from $645" (or such). The key word is *from:* The rock-bottom price includes the least desirable hotels; if you want better or more-convenient digs, you'll pay more—often much more.

Packages offer a wide selection of hotels. Some, like the Disney resorts, are very dependable. Others run the gamut of quality.

Checking two or three independent sources is best. Also, before you book, ask how old the hotel is and when the guest rooms were last refurbished. Locate the hotel on a map to verify its proximity to Disney World. If you won't have a car, make sure that the hotel has adequate shuttle service.

Packages with non-Disney lodging are much less expensive. But guests at Disney-owned properties get Extra Magic Hours privileges, the opportunity to make dining and FastPass+ reservation far in advance, free parking, and access to Disney transportation. These privileges (except Extra Magic Hours for Hilton guests) don't apply to guests at the Downtown Disney Resort Area hotels (see page 201).

Packages should be a win–win proposition for both buyer and seller. The buyer makes only one phone call and deals with one salesperson to set up the whole vacation (transportation, rental car, admissions, lodging, meals, and even golf and tennis). The seller, likewise, deals with the buyer only once. Some packagers also buy airfares in bulk on contract, not unlike a broker playing the commodities market. By buying a large number of airfares in advance, the packager saves significantly over posted fares. The practice is also applied to hotel

# DISNEY LODGING FOR LESS

**Mary Waring,** *former webmaster at* **MouseSavers (mousesavers.com;** *see page 34), knows more about Disney hotel packages than anyone on the planet. Here are her money-saving suggestions.*

**BOOK "ROOM-ONLY."** It's frequently a better deal to book a room-only reservation instead of buying a vacation package. Disney likes to sell vacation packages because they're easy and profitable. When you buy a package, you're typically paying a premium for convenience. You can often save money by putting together your own package. It's not hard: Just book room-only at a resort and buy passes, meals, and extras separately.

Disney now prices its standard packages at the same rates as if you had purchased individual components separately at full price. However, what Disney doesn't tell you is that components can usually be purchased separately at a discount—and those discounts are not reflected in the brochure prices of Disney's packages. (Sometimes you can get special-offer packages that do include discounts; see below.)

Keep in mind that Disney's packages often include extras you're unlikely to use. Also, packages require a $200 deposit and full payment 45 days in advance; plus, they have stringent change and cancellation policies. Generally, booking room-only requires a deposit of one night's room rate with the remainder due at check-in. Your reservation can be changed or canceled for any reason until five days before check-in.

Whether you decide to book a Disney vacation package or create your own, there are a number of ways to save:

- **USE DISCOUNT CODES TO REDUCE YOUR ROOM-ONLY OR PACKAGE RATE.** Disney uses these codes to push unsold rooms at certain times of year and occasionally offers packages that include resort discounts or value-added features. Check a website like mousesavers.com to learn about codes that may be available for your vacation dates. Some codes are available to anyone, while others are just for Florida residents, Annual Pass holders, and so on.

  Discount codes aren't always available for every hotel or every date, and they typically don't appear until two to six months in advance. The good news is that you can usually apply

rooms. Because selling packages is efficient and the packager often can buy package components in bulk at discount, the seller's savings in operating expenses are sometimes passed on to the buyer, making the package not only convenient but also an exceptional value.

In practice, however, the seller may realize all the economies and pass on no savings. Packages sometimes are loaded with extras that cost the packager almost nothing but run the package's price sky-high. Savings passed on to customers are still somewhere in Fantasyland.

a code to an existing room-only reservation. Simply call the Disney Reservation Center at ☎ 407-W-DISNEY (934-7639) (or contact a Disney-savvy travel agent) and ask whether any rooms are available at your preferred hotel for your preferred dates using the code.

- **BE FLEXIBLE.** Buying a room or package with a discount code is a little like shopping for clothes at a discount store: If you wear size XX-small or XXXX-large, or you like green when everyone else is wearing pink, you're a lot more likely to score a bargain. Likewise, resort discounts are available only when Disney has excess rooms. You're more likely to get a discount during less-popular times (such as value season) and at larger or less-popular resorts. Animal Kingdom Lodge and Old Key West Resort seem to have discounted rooms available more often than the other resorts do.

- **BE PERSISTENT.** This is the most important tip. Disney allots a certain number of rooms to each discount. Once the discounted rooms are gone, you won't get that rate unless someone cancels. Fortunately, people change and cancel reservations all the time. If you can't get your preferred dates or hotel with one discount code, try another one (if available) or keep calling back first thing in the morning to check for cancellations the system resets overnight, and any reservations with unpaid deposits are automatically released for resale.

- **SPRING FOR "FREE DINING."** One of Disney's biggest package bargains, this promotion has been offered since 2005 during less-busy times of year. When you purchase a full-price room and full-price tickets for each person in the room, you get a Disney Dining Plan for your entire stay. The trick is to choose one of Disney's cheapest rooms and enjoy all that free food: If you choose a Value resort, you get the Quick-Service Dining Plan; if you choose a Moderate resort, you get the standard Disney Dining Plan. You can also book a Value resort and pay the difference to upgrade from Quick-Service to the regular plan. Free Dining is always offered throughout September (a slow time due to heat, humidity, hurricane season, and kids going back to school); sometimes it's offered in late August or at other times during the year.

Choose a package that includes features you're sure to use. You'll pay for all of them whether you use them or not. If price is more important than convenience, call around to see what the package would cost if you booked its components on your own. If the package price is less than the à la carte cost, the package is a good deal. If costs are about equal, the package probably is worth it for the convenience. Much of the time, however, you'll find you save significantly by buying the components individually.

## CUT TO THE CHASE

IT'S MUCH FASTER TO BOOK a Disney resort room online than it is to call the Disney reservations number (☎ 407-W-DISNEY). If you call, you'll be subjected to about 5–10 minutes of recorded questions (many just fishing for nonrelevant personal information). If you actually want to make a reservation, slog on through. (When the question "Have you called us before?" pops up, answer "yes" unless you want to be corralled into an additional survey for "first-timers.") If you just want to ask a question or speak to a live person, touch 0 to bypass all the recorded stuff.

## WALT DISNEY TRAVEL COMPANY MAGIC YOUR WAY PACKAGES

DISNEY'S MAGIC YOUR WAY travel-package program mirrors the admission-ticket program of the same name. Here's how it works: You begin with a base package room and tickets. Tickets can be customized to match the number of days you intend to tour the theme parks, and range in length from 1 to 10 days. As with theme park admissions, the package program offers strong financial incentives to book a longer stay. "The longer you play, the less you pay per day," is the way Disney puts it, borrowing a page from Sam Walton's concept of the universe. An adult 1-Day Base Ticket for the Magic Kingdom (with tax) costs $100.11, whereas if you buy a 7-Day Base Ticket, the average cost per day drops to $49.29. You can purchase options to add on to your Base Tickets, such as hopping between theme parks; playing mini-golf; visiting water parks, DisneyQuest, or ESPN Wide World of Sports; and buying your way out of an expiration date for any unused ticket features.

With Magic Your Way packages, you can avoid paying for features you don't intend to use. You need not purchase a package with theme park tickets for the entire length of your stay. With Magic Your Way you can choose to purchase as many days of admission as you intend to use. On a one-week vacation, for example, you might want to spend only five days in the Disney parks, saving a day each for Universal Studios and SeaWorld. With Magic Your Way you can buy only five days of admission on a seven-day package. Likewise, if you don't normally park-hop, you can purchase multiday admissions that don't include the Park Hopper feature. If you don't use all your admissions, you can opt for the No Expiration add-on, and the unused days will be good forever. Best of all, you can buy the various add-ons at any time during your vacation.

Before we deluge you with a boxcar of options and add-ons, let's define the basic components of Disney's Magic Your Way package:

- One or more nights of accommodations at your choice of any Disney resort. Rates vary with lodging choice: The Grand Floridian is usually the most expensive, and the All-Star, Pop Century, and Art of Animation Resorts are the least expensive.
- Base Ticket for the number of days you tour the theme parks
- Unlimited use of the Disney transportation system
- Free theme park parking
- Official Walt Disney Travel Company luggage tag (one per person)

## Magic Your Way Dining Plans

Disney offers dining plans to accompany its Magic Your Way ticket system. They're available to all Disney resort guests except those staying at the Swan, the Dolphin, the hotels of the Downtown Disney Resort Area, and Shades of Green. Guests must also purchase a Magic Your Way package from Disney (not through an online reseller), have Annual Passes, or be members of the Disney Vacation Club (DVC) to participate in the plan. Except for DVC members, a three-night minimum stay is typically also required. Overall cost is determined by the number of nights you stay at a Disney resort.

As a family of five from Waldron, Michigan, learned, you must purchase a Disney package vacation to be eligible for a dining plan:

> We read through the Unofficial Guide *and noticed that it said not to book a package during slow season. We were overwhelmed with the decisions that we had to make, so we booked the resort first, then the tickets, and then we wanted the dining plan. Well, they wouldn't add the dining plan on because we had already booked everything.*

**MAGIC YOUR WAY PLUS DINING PLAN** This plan provides, for each member of your group, for each night of your stay, one counter-service meal, one full-service meal, and one snack at participating Disney dining locations and restaurants, including room service at some Disney resorts (type "Disney Dining Plan Locations" into your favorite search engine to find sites with the entire list). The plan also includes one refillable drink mug per person, per package, but it can be filled only at Disney resort counter-service restaurants. For guests age 10 and up, the price is $60.64, tax included; for guests ages 3–9, the price is $19.23 per night, tax included. Children younger than age 3 eat free from an adult's plate.

The counter-service meal includes a main course (sandwich, dinner salad, pizza, or the like), dessert, and nonalcoholic drink, or a complete combo meal (a main course and a side dish—think burger and fries), dessert, and nonalcoholic drink, including tax. The full-service sit-down meals include a main course, dessert, nonalcoholic drink, and tax. If you're dining at a buffet, the full-service meal includes the buffet, a non-alcoholic drink, and tax. The snack includes items normally sold from carts or stands throughout the parks and resorts: ice cream, popcorn, soft drinks, fruit, chips, apple juice, and the like.

For instance, if you're staying for three nights, you'll be credited with three counter-service meals, three full-service meals, and three snacks for each member of your party. All those meals will be put into a group "meal account." Meals in your account can be used by anyone in your group, on any combination of days, so you're not required to eat every meal every day. Thus, you can skip a full-service meal one day and have two on another day.

Disney's top-of-the-line restaurants (dubbed "Disney Signature" restaurants in the plan), along with Cinderella's Royal Table, all the dinner shows, regular room service, and in-room pizza delivery, count as two full-service meals. If you dine at one of these locations, two full-service meals will be deducted from your account for each person dining.

In addition to the preceding, the following rules apply:

- Everyone staying in the same resort room must participate in the Disney Dining Plan.
- Children ages 3–9 must order from the kids' menu, if available. This rule is occasionally not enforced at Disney's counter-service restaurants, enabling older kids to order from the regular menu.
- Alcoholic and some nonalcoholic drinks are not included in the plan.
- A full-service meal can be breakfast, lunch, or dinner. The greatest savings occur when you use your full-service-meal credits for dinner.
- The meal plan expires at midnight **on the day you check out** of the Disney resort. **Unused meals are nonrefundable.**
- The dining plan can usually be added to a discounted room-only reservation. You can't however, add Disney's Free Dining (see page 213). Also, in a few instances, a reservationist's computer may not be programmed to handle adding the dining plan.

**QUICK-SERVICE DINING PLAN** This plan includes meals, snacks, and nonalcoholic drinks at most counter-service eateries in Walt Disney World. The cost (including tax) is $41.99 per day for guests age 10 and up, $16.03 per day for kids ages 3–9. The plan includes two counter-service meals and one snack per day, in addition to one refillable drink mug per person, per package (eligible for refills only at counter-service locations in your Disney resort). The economics of the plan are difficult to justify unless you're drinking gallons of soda or coffee.

**MAGIC YOUR WAY DELUXE DINING PLAN** This plan offers a choice of full- or counter-service meals for three meals a day at any participating restaurant. In addition to the three meals a day, the plan also includes two snacks per day and a refillable drink mug. The Deluxe Plan costs $109.53 for adults and children age 10 and older and $29.86 for children ages 3–9 for each night of your stay (prices include tax). Cranking it up another notch, there are even more extravagant dining plans associated with Magic Your Way Premium and Platinum Packages, both described a little later.

*unofficial* **TIP**
In our survey of families who've purchased the Magic Your Way Plus Dining Plan, 57% said they'd buy it again.

Not only does the Deluxe Dining Plan cost a lot of money, it also costs a lot of time, as a dad from Hudson Falls, New York, explains:

*The Deluxe Dining Plan gave us a chance to try restaurants we normally would never go to, but it felt like most of our trip revolved around food: get to the restaurant, wait to be seated, order drinks, wait, get drinks, wait, order meals, wait, get meals, wait, order dessert, wait, get dessert, wait, get the check, wait, give the wait staff your room card, wait, figure out the tip, and wait. With three meals a day, we lost 4.5–6 hours a day just on eating, plus the travel time.*

In addition to food, all the plans include "sweeteners" such as a free round of miniature golf; discounts on spa treatments and salon services; and deals on recreational activities like fishing and watersports.

Disney ceaselessly tinkers with the dining plans' rules, meal definitions, and participating restaurants. For example, it's possible (though not documented) to exchange a sit-down-meal credit for a counter-service meal, although doing this even once can negate any savings you get from using a plan in the first place.

**THINGS TO CONSIDER WHEN EVALUATING THE PLUS DINING PLAN** The dining plan has been one of the most requested of Disney's package add-ons since its introduction; families report that their favorite aspect is the peace of mind that comes from knowing their meals are paid for ahead of time, rather than having to keep track of a budget while they're in the parks. Families also enjoy the communal aspect of sitting down together for a full meal, without having to worry about who's picking up the food or doing the dishes.

Cost-wise, however, it's difficult for many families to justify using the plan. If you prefer to always eat at counter-service restaurants, you'll be better off with the Quick-Service plan. You should also avoid the Plus plan if you've got finicky eaters, you're visiting during holidays or summer, or you can't get reservations at your first- or second-choice sit-down restaurants. In addition, if you've got children age 10 and up, be sure that they can eat an adult-sized dinner at a sit-down restaurant every night; if not, you'd probably come out ahead just paying for everyone's meals without the plan.

If you opt for the plan, skipping one full-service meal during a visit of five or fewer days can mean the difference between saving and losing money. In our experience, having a scheduled sit-down meal for every day of a weeklong vacation can be mentally exhausting, especially for kids. One option might be to schedule a meal at a Disney Signature restaurant, which requires two full-service credits, and have no scheduled sit-down meal on another night in the middle of your trip, allowing everyone to decide on the spot if they're up for something formal.

As already noted, many of the most popular restaurants are fully booked as soon as their reservation windows open. If you're still interested in the dining plan, book your restaurants as soon as possible, typically 90–180 days before you visit. Then decide whether the plan makes economic sense. For more on Advance Reservations—the term is Disney-speak (hence the capital letters) and not exactly what it implies—see Part Ten.

If you're making reservations to eat at Disney hotels other than your own, a car allows you to easily access all the participating restaurants. When you use the Disney transportation system, dining at the various resorts can be a logistical nightmare. Those without a car may want to weigh the immediate services of a taxi—typically $10–$12 each way across Disney property, versus a 50- to 75-minute trip on Disney transportation each way.

When Disney offers Free Dining discounts (typically in September), they generally charge rack rate for the hotel. You should work out the math, but Free Dining is typically a good deal for families who have two children under age 10, are staying at a Value resort, and book lots of character meals. Light eaters and childless couples, especially those staying at Deluxe resorts, may find it cheaper to take a room discount and pay for food separately.

For an in-depth discussion of the various plans, including number crunching (with algebra, even!), visit **touringplans.com** (scroll down and click "Dining" on the home page, then "Disney Dining Plan").

Readers who tried the Disney dining plan had varying experiences, but frustration seems to be a common refrain. A St. Louis family of three comments:

> We purchased the dining plan and would never do it again. Far too expensive, far too much food, and then you have to tip on top of the expense. Much easier to purchase what you want, where and when you want.

A New Hampshire family concurs:

> Dining plans are NOT for us. Keeping track of the meals, figuring out what you can and can't buy, and rushing around on the last day trying to use up what's left is just too stressful. We'd rather just buy what we want, when and where we want it.

A reader from The Woodlands, Texas, laments that the plan has altered the focus of her vacation:

> For me, the Disney Dining Plan has taken a lot of the fun out of going to Disney World. Now, dining for each day must be planned months in advance unless one is to eat just hot dogs, pizza, and other walk-up items. I want to have fun. I don't want to be locked into a tight schedule, always worrying about where we need to be when it's time to eat, and I don't want to eat when I'm not hungry just because I have a reservation somewhere.

A Tennessee mother of a 3-year-old gives the plan two thumbs up:

> We LOVED the dining plan. It was wonderful to not have to stress every day about trying to keep up with a budget for food. The plan turned out to be a fantastic deal for us, especially since we did four character meals that would have cost at least $400 otherwise.

A mom from Baltimore agrees about character meals:

> I'd recommend the Disney Dining Plan only to those who wish to use it for character dining—that's where the value is. Otherwise, save your money and pay out of pocket as you go.

And a Belmont, Massachusetts, dad is a fan of the Quick Service Dining Plan:

> If you intend to eat Disney food, the counter-service meal plan is a good option. We didn't want the full plan because the restaurants seemed overpriced, and the necessity of reservations months in advance seemed crazy and a bar to flexibility. You get two counter-service meals (entree/combo, dessert, drink) and two snacks (food item or drink) per person per day as part of the plan, and even though kids' meals are cheaper, there's no distinction when you order—kids can order [more-expensive] adult meals.

A mom from Orland Park, Illinois, comments on the difficulty of getting Advance Reservations:

> It's impossible to get table reservations anywhere good—the restaurants that are available are available for a reason. We found ourselves taking whatever was open and were unhappy with every sit-down

*meal we had, except for lunch at Liberty Tree Tavern. I don't enjoy planning my day exclusively around eating at a certain restaurant at a certain time, but that is what you must do six months in advance if you want to eat at a good sit-down restaurant in Disney.*

As this reader from San Jose, California, explains, guests who are not on the dining plan need to know how the plan has affected obtaining Advance Reservations:

*When planning 90 days out for the off-season, I was told by the Disney rep to make all my reservations then because the restaurants are booked by people on the dining plan. In fact, I was told that most of the sit-down restaurants don't even take walk-ins anymore. Sure enough, even though I was well over 90 days away from my vacation, a lot of my restaurant choices were unavailable. I had to rearrange my entire schedule to fit the open slots at the restaurants I didn't want to miss.*

A family from Wilmington, Massachusetts, shared this:

*We found the basic dining plan somewhat limiting, and it provided way too much food. Dessert came with both the counter-service and table-service meals. If you tell the server that you don't want dessert at either of these meals, he or she will try hard to convince you that you are making a life-altering mistake because you aren't getting your money's worth. I understand that the dining plan is a great value for many people, but we aren't a "strap on the feedbag" kind of group.*

Many readers report that Disney cast members are more knowledgeable about the dining plan these days. A Washington, D.C.–area couple writes:

*The kinks are worked out, and everyone at the parks we talked to seemed to get it, but we still spent $40 or more at most sit-down dinners on drinks and tips.*

A Hickory, North Carolina, reader agrees:

*Most cast members knew the plans well and were happy to explain to us what our options were.*

A mum from Sutton Coldfield, England, warns that toddlers fall through the cracks:

*We were traveling with two 6-year-olds and a 2-year-old. My youngest did not qualify for the dining plan, which worked well in the buffet-style restaurants where he could eat free. However, if you eat in a full-service restaurant and your 2-year-old is eating off the menu, there's no infant option—you have to pay for a child's meal.*

A Land O' Lakes, Florida, dad bumped into this problem:

*We had some trouble with our Deluxe Dining Plan being "invalidated" after checkout, though it was supposed to be valid until midnight of our checkout date. That was annoying, since calls to the resort were needed to verify the meals left on our passes for The Crystal Palace and for some snacks later.*

From a Midwestern reader:

*We could almost relate our dining experience to that of a person who receives food stamps—very restricted and always at the mercy of someone else for food selection.*

From a Wisconsin father of two:

*On the last day of our visit, we were still learning about acceptable substitutions. For example, at breakfast you can have two drinks (coffee and OJ). You can also do this for lunch, but you have to give up your dessert. In the 90-degree heat, I would've gladly given up my fattening dessert to have a bottle of cold water to bring along.*

The dining plan left a family of five from Nashville, Tennessee, similarly dazed and confused:

*What was annoying was the inconsistency. You can get a 16-ounce chocolate milk on the kids' plan, but only 8 ounces of white milk at many places. At Earl of Sandwich, you can get 16 ounces of either kind. A pint of milk would count as a snack (price $1.52), but they wouldn't count a quart of milk (price $1.79) because it wasn't a single serving. However, in Animal Kingdom, my husband bought a water-bottle holder (price $3.75) and used a snack credit.*

## Reader Tips for Getting the Most Out of the Plan

A mom from Radford, Virginia, shares the following tip:

*Warn people to eat lunch early if they have dinner reservations before 7 p.m. Disney doesn't skimp on food—if you eat a late lunch (where, by the way, they feed you the same ungodly amount of food), you WILL NOT be hungry for dinner.*

A mom from Brick Township, New Jersey, found that the dining plan streamlined her touring:

*We truly enjoyed our Disney trip, and this time we purchased the Dining Plan. This was great for the kids because we did a character-dining experience every day. This helped us in the parks because we didn't have to wait in line to see the characters. Instead, we got all of our autographs during our meals.*

A Saskatoon, Saskatchewan, father of three says you have to watch vendors like a hawk:

*We had a problem with a vendor who charged us meal service for each of the ice cream bars we purchased. This became evident at our final sit-down meal, when we didn't have any meal vouchers left. Check the receipts after every purchase!*

A mom from Lawrence, Kansas, offers this tip:

*The quick-service meals aren't really designated for kids or adults when they ring you up and subtract the food from your plan. I wish I'd have known early on that if they couldn't see I had a child under 9, I could have ordered a regular meal and gotten more food. We figured that out toward the end and started ordering bigger meals for our 7-year-old (we saved the desserts to share later).*

Finally, a Brooklyn family of four warns that the plan doesn't always eliminate the need to use cash:

*We ate dinner at Jiko—we each ordered a salad and a main course and skipped dessert—and while the food was good, we ended up leaving annoyed by Disney's cheapness. We were on the dining plan and were told that our meals would be two credits each. This trans-lates to about $80 apiece. Fine. But when the check came, we were not only charged the two credits each, we were charged $12 each for the salads. Plus tips. I asked why we had been charged extra, and I was told that dessert was included in the meal plan but not first courses. It's pretty annoying to pay $80 per person for a one-course dinner and STILL have to put down more cash.*

## Magic Your Way Premium Package

*unofficial* **TIP**
For all Magic Your Way plans, everyone in the room must be on the same package and ticket options. All tickets must be used within 14 days of first use, unless the No Expiration option is purchased.

With the Magic Your Way Premium Package you get lodging; Magic Your Way Base Tickets; break-fast, lunch, and dinner (including two snacks per day plus gratuities and one refillable resort drink mug per person), character meals, and dinner shows; unlimited golf, tennis, fishing excursions, and water sports; select theme park tours; Cirque du Soleil show tickets; unlimited use of child-care facilities—everything you can think of except for alcoholic beverages. The Premium Package costs $194 for adults and $144 for kids ages 3–9 (tax included) in addition to the cost of the standard Magic Your Way package. *Note:* A minimum three-night stay at Walt Disney World is required in order to book the Premium Package.

Disney, needless to say, has built a nice profit into every component of the Magic Your Way Premium Package. If you don't use all the fea-tures and didn't purchase the No Expiration option on your tickets, Disney makes out even better.

**PLATINUM PACKAGE** The favorite of high rollers who want to prepay for everything they might desire while at Walt Disney World, the Platinum Package gets you lodging; Base Tickets; breakfast, lunch, and dinner in full-service restaurants; unlimited golf, tennis, boating, and recreation; unlimited dinner shows and character breakfasts; primo Cirque du Soleil seats; private in-room child care; unlimited use of child-care facilities; personalized itinerary planning; the Richard Petty Ride-Along Experience; a ride on the Characters in Flight balloon at Disney Springs; a spa treatment; a fireworks cruise; admission to select tours; reserved seating for *Fantasmic!;* and (here's the kicker) nightly turn-down service! Everything you can think of, in other words, except alco-holic beverages. Per diem prices (including tax) for the Platinum Package are $254 for adults and $184 for kids in addition to the cost of a stan-dard Magic Your Way package—but anyone who buys this package doesn't give a Goofy fart what the prices are anyway. As with the Premium Package, a minimum three-night stay is required.

## NUMBER CRUNCHING

COMPARING A MAGIC YOUR WAY PACKAGE with purchasing the package components separately is a breeze.

1. Pick a Disney resort and decide how many nights you want to stay.

2. Next, work out a rough plan of what you want to do and see so you can determine the admission passes you'll require.

3. When you're ready, call the Disney Reservation Center (DRC) at ☎ 407-W-DISNEY and price a Magic Your Way package with tax for your selected resort and dates. The package will include both admissions and lodging. It's also a good idea to get a quote from a Disney-savvy travel agent (see page 118).

4. Now, to calculate the costs of buying your accommodations and admission passes separately, call the DRC a second time. This time, price a room-only rate for the same resort and dates. Be sure to ask about the availability of any special deals. While you're still on the line, obtain the prices, with tax, for the admissions you require. If you're not sure which of the various admission options will best serve you, consult our free Ticket Calculator at **touringplans.com.**

5. Add the room-only rates and the admission prices. Compare this sum to the DRC quote for the Magic Your Way package.

6. Check for deals and discounts for packages, room-only rates, and admission.

When you upgrade to a Premium Package, you load the plan with so many features that it's difficult to price them individually. For a rough comparison, price the plan of your choice using the previous steps. To complete the picture, work up a dining budget, excluding alcohol. Add your estimated dining costs to the room-only quote and admissions quote, and compare this to the price of the plan.

Regarding the economics of the dining plan, it's illustrative to know how the cost of one day on the plan is spent on each component. We'll spare you the math, but an approximate value for each item across every 2014 Disney Dining Plan is as follows:

- Each counter-service meal is worth **$14.75–$18.07.**
- Each table-service meal is worth **$33.50–$36.72.**
- Every snack is worth around **$4.35.**
- The refillable mug is worth **$8–$12.**

## THROW ME A LINE!

IF YOU BUY A PACKAGE FROM DISNEY, don't expect reservationists to offer suggestions or help you sort out your options. Generally, they respond only to your specific questions, ducking queries that require an opinion. A reader from North Riverside, Illinois, complains:

*My wife made two telephone calls, and the representatives from WDW were very courteous. However, they only answered the questions posed and were not eager to give advice on what might be most cost-effective. I feel a person could spend 8 hours on the phone with WDW reps and not have any more input than you get from reading the literature.*

If you can't get the information you need from Disney, contact a good travel agent. Chances are the agent can help you weigh your options.

## PACKAGES FROM A DIFFERENT PERSPECTIVE

WE'VE ALWAYS EVALUATED PACKAGES from a dollars-and-cents point of view, paying scant attention to other considerations such as time, economy, and convenience. A reader from Westchester County, New York, finally got our attention, writing:

> I fully understand your position not to recommend the Premium plans in your guide, because they're expensive. However, when one books six rooms, as I have, with guests ages 4–59, including a wife, grandchildren, children, sons- and daughters-in-law, and a nanny, the thought of trying to find out what way each family segment would like to go and then arranging for it on a daily basis is a scary scenario. With the Premium Plan, they can go where they want, eat where they want, and Gramps and his roommate don't have the hassle.

A Mobile, Alabama, couple also liked the Premium Plan, although they had some reservations (pardon the pun) about dining:

> While we had plenty of time to see and do things, had we been there for a week or less we probably would've been frustrated with how much time it took to eat three table-service meals a day, once you calculate the secondary time expense of traveling to the restaurant (which may or may not be in the park you're in at the moment). There was one time in particular where we finished eating lunch and basically had to go check in for dinner almost immediately!

### Purchasing Room-Only Plus Passes versus a Package

SUE PISATURO of **Small World Vacations** (**smallworldvacations.com**), a travel agency that specializes in Disney, also thinks there's more involved in a package-purchase decision than money.

> Should you purchase a Walt Disney World package or buy all the components of the package separately? There's no single answer to this confusing question.
>
> A Walt Disney World package is like a store-bought prepackaged kids' meal, the kind with the little compartments filled with meat, cheese, crackers, drink, and dessert: You just grab the package and go. It's easy, and if it's on sale, why bother doing it yourself? If it's not on sale, it still may be worth the extra money for convenience.
>
> Purchasing the components of your vacation separately is like buying each of the meal's ingredients, cutting them up into neat piles and packaging the lunch yourself. Is it worth the extra time and effort to do it this way? Will you save money if you do it this way?
>
> You have two budgets to balance when you plan your Disney World vacation: time and money. Satisfying both is your ultimate goal. Research and planning are paramount to realizing your Disney vacation dreams. Create your touring plans before making a final decision with regard to the number of days and options on your theme park passes. Create your dining itinerary (along with Advance Reservations, if possible) to determine if Disney's dining plan can save you some money.

# HOTELS *outside*
# WALT DISNEY WORLD

## SELECTING AND BOOKING A HOTEL
## OUTSIDE WALT DISNEY WORLD

LODGING COSTS OUTSIDE DISNEY WORLD vary incredibly. If you shop around, you can find a clean motel with a pool within 5–20 minutes of the World for as low as $40 a night. Because of hot competition, discounts abound, particularly for AAA and AARP members.

There are four primary out-of-the-World areas to consider:

**1. INTERNATIONAL DRIVE AREA** This area, about 15–25 minutes northeast of the World, parallels I-4 on its eastern side and offers a wide selection of hotels and restaurants. Prices range from $56 to $400 per night. The chief drawbacks are terribly congested roads, countless traffic signals, and inadequate access to westbound I-4. While I-Drive's biggest bottleneck is its intersection with Sand Lake Road, the mile between Kirkman and Sand Lake Roads is almost always gridlocked. We provide tips for avoiding this traffic in Part Eight (see "Sneak Routes," page 388).

Regarding traffic on International Drive (known locally as I-Drive), a convention-goer from Islip, New York, weighed in with this:

> When I visited Disney World with my family last summer, we wasted huge chunks of time in traffic on International Drive. Our hotel was in the section between the big McDonald's [at Sand Lake Road] and Wet 'n Wild [at Universal Boulevard]. There are practically no left-turn lanes in this section, so anyone turning left can hold up traffic for a long time.

Traffic aside, a man from Ottawa, Ontario, sings the praises of his I-Drive experience:

> International Drive is the place to stay when going to Disney. Your description of this location failed to point out that there are several discount stores, boutiques, restaurants, mini-putts, and other entertainment facilities, all within walking distance of remarkably inexpensive accommodations and a short drive away from WDW.

I-Drive hotels are listed in the *Official Vacation Guide,* published by the Orlando–Orange County Convention and Visitors Bureau. To obtain a copy, call ☎ 800-972-3304 or 407-363-5872, or check **visit orlando.com.**

**2. LAKE BUENA VISTA AND THE I-4 CORRIDOR** A number of hotels are along FL 535 and west of I-4 between Disney World and I-4's intersection with Florida's Turnpike. They're easily reached from the interstate and are near many restaurants, including those on International Drive. The *Official Vacation Guide* (see above) lists most of them. For some traffic-avoidance tips, see "The I-4 Blues" (page 376) in Part Eight, Arriving and Getting Around.

**3. US 192 (IRLO BRONSON MEMORIAL HIGHWAY)** This is the highway to Kissimmee, to the southeast of Disney World. In addition to large full-service hotels, there are many small, privately owned motels that are often a good value. Several dozen properties on US 192 are nearer

Disney parks than are more expensive hotels inside the World. The number and variety of restaurants on US 192 has increased markedly, compensating for the area's primary shortcoming. Locally, US 192 is called Irlo Bronson Memorial Highway. The section to the west of I-4 and the Disney "Maingate" is designated Irlo Bronson Memorial Highway West, while the section from I-4 running southeast toward Kissimmee is Irlo Bronson Memorial Highway East.

The combined east and west sections have numbered mile markers that simplify navigation if you know which marker is closest to your destination. Though traffic is heavy on Irlo Bronson west of the Maingate, it doesn't compare to the congestion east of the Maingate and I-4 between Mile Markers 8 and 13. This section can—and should—be avoided by using **Osceola Parkway,** a toll road that parallels Irlo Bronson to the north and terminates in Walt Disney World at the entrance to Animal Kingdom.

A senior citizen from Brookfield, Connecticut, was pleased with lodging in the US 192–Kissimmee area:

> We were amazed to find that from our cheaper and superior accommodations in Kissimmee it took only 5 minutes longer to reach the park turnstiles than it did from the Disney accommodations.

Hotels on US 192 and in Kissimmee are listed in the *Kissimmee Visitor's Guide.* Order a copy by calling ☎ 800-327-9159, or view it online at **floridakiss.com.**

**4. UNIVERSAL STUDIOS AREA** In the triangular area bordered by I-4 on the southeast, Vineland Road on the north, and Turkey Lake Road on the west are Universal Orlando and the hotels most convenient to it. Running north–south through the middle of the triangle is Kirkman Road, which connects to I-4. On the east side of Kirkman are a number of independent hotels and restaurants. Universal hotels, theme parks, and CityWalk are west of Kirkman. Traffic in this area is not nearly as congested as on nearby International Drive, and there are good interstate connections in both directions.

## DRIVING TIME TO THE PARKS FOR VISITORS LODGING OUTSIDE WALT DISNEY WORLD

OUR HOTEL INFORMATION CHART on pages 269–286 shows the commuting time to the Disney theme parks from each hotel listed. Those commuting times represent an average of several test runs. Your actual time may be shorter or longer depending on traffic, road construction (if any), and delays at traffic signals.

The commuting times in our Hotel Information Chart show conclusively that distance from the theme parks is not necessarily the dominant factor in determining commuting times. Among those we list, the hotels on Major Boulevard opposite the Kirkman Road entrance to Universal Orlando, for example, are the most distant (in miles) from the Disney parks. But because they're only one traffic signal from easy access to I-4, commuting time to the parks is significantly less than for many closer hotels.

*Continued on page 230*

## Hotel Concentrations Around Walt Disney World

**Orlando**

1. International Drive Area
2. Lake Buena Vista Resort Area and the I-4 Corridor
3. US 192–Kissimmee Resort Area
4. Universal Orlando Area

# International Drive & Universal Areas

**Interstate 4 Exits**

| | |
|---|---|
| 77 | Florida's Turnpike |
| 75A | Universal Studios/ International Drive |
| 75B | Kirkman Road |
| 74B | Universal Studios |
| 74A | Sand Lake Road |
| 72 | FL 528 (Beachline Expressway) |
| 71 | Central Florida GreeneWay |

## Lake Buena Vista Resort Area & the I-4 Corridor

# US 192–Kissimmee Resort Area

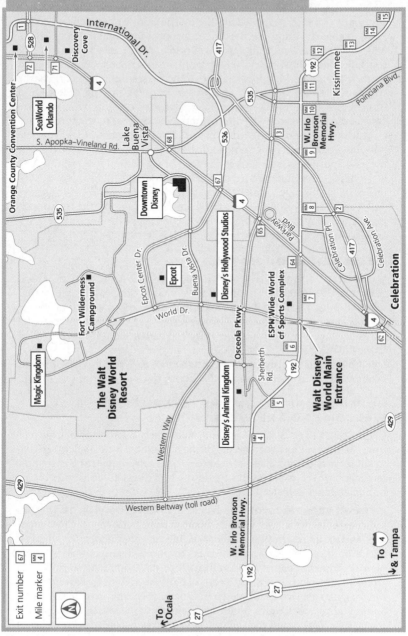

*Continued from page 225*

Note that times in the chart differ from those in the Door-to-Door Commuting Times chart in Part Eight. The door-to-door chart in Part Eight compares using the Disney transportation system and driving your own car *inside* Walt Disney World. These times include actual transportation time plus tram, monorail, or other connections required to get from the parking lots to the entrance turnstiles. The hotel chart's commuting times, by contrast, represent only the driving time to and from the entrance of the respective parking lot of each park, with no consideration for getting to and from the parking lot to the turnstiles.

Add to the commuting times in the Hotel Information Chart a few minutes for paying your parking fee and parking. Once you park at the Transportation and Ticket Center (Magic Kingdom parking lot), it takes 20–30 minutes more to reach the Magic Kingdom via monorail or ferry. To reach Epcot from its parking lot, add 7–10 minutes. At Disney's Hollywood Studios and Animal Kingdom, the lot-to-gate transit is 5–12 minutes. If you haven't purchased your theme park admission in advance, tack on another 10–20 minutes.

## GOOD NEIGHBOR HOTELS

SOME HOTELS PAY DISNEY a marketing fee to display a "Good Neighbor" designation. Usually there is a ticket shop in the lobby that sells full-price Disney tickets. Other than that, the designation means nothing for the consumer. It doesn't guarantee quality—some Good Neighbor hotels are very nice, others not so much. Some are close to Walt Disney World, while others are quite far away. Disney requires Good Neighbor hotels to provide free shuttle service to Walt Disney World but prohibits them from offering shuttle service to Universal or SeaWorld.

## HOTEL SHOPPING ON THE INTERNET: WELCOME TO THE WILD WEST

UNMATCHED AS AN EFFICIENT and timely distributor of information, the Internet has become the primary resource for travelers seeking to shop for and book their own air travel, hotels, rental cars, entertainment, and travel packages. It's by far the best direct-to-consumer distribution channel in history.

**INTERNET ECONOMICS 101** The evolution of selling travel on the web has radically altered the way airlines, hotels, cruise lines, rental-car companies, and the like do business. Before the Internet, they depended on travel agents or direct contact with customers by phone. Transaction costs were high because companies were obligated to pay commissions and fund labor-intensive in-house reservations departments. With the advent of the Internet, inexpensive e-commerce transactions became possible: Airlines and rental-car companies began using their own websites to effectively cut travel agents out of the sales process. Hotels also developed websites but continued to depend on wholesalers and travel agents as well.

It didn't take long before independent websites sprang up that sold travel products from a wide assortment of suppliers, often at deep discounts. These sites, called **online travel agencies (OTAs),** include such familiar names as Travelocity, Orbitz, Priceline, Expedia, Hotels.com, and Hotwire. Those mentioned and others like them attract huge numbers of customers shopping for hotels.

**OTAS AND THE MERCHANT MODEL** In the beginning, hotels paid OTAs about the same commission that they paid travel agents, but then the OTAs began applying the thumbscrews, forcing hotels to make the transition from a simple commission model to what's called a merchant model. Under this model, hotels provide an OTA with a deeply discounted room rate that the OTA then marks up and sells. The difference between the marked-up price and the discounted rate paid to the hotel is the OTA's gross profit. If, for example, a hotel makes $120 rooms available to an OTA at a 33% discount, or $80, and the OTA sells the room at $110, the OTA's gross profit is $30 ($110 – $80).

The merchant model, originally devised for wholesalers and tour operators, has been around since long before the Internet. Wholesalers and tour operators, then and now, must commit to a certain volume of business, commit to guaranteed room allotments, pay deposits, and bundle the discounted rates with other travel services so that the actual hotel rate remains hidden within the bundle. This is known as *opaque pricing*. The merchant model costs the hotel two to three times the normal travel-agent commission—considered justifiable because the wholesalers and tour operators also promote the hotel through brochures, websites, trade shows, print ads, and events.

OTAs now demand the equivalent of a wholesale commission or higher but are subject to none of the requirements imposed on wholesalers and tour operators. For instance, they don't have to commit to a specified volume of sales or keep discounted room rates opaque. In return, hotels give up 20–50% of gross profit and are rewarded by having their rock-bottom rates plastered all over the Internet, with corresponding damage to their image and brand. (This last is why it's very rare to see a Disney hotel advertised on an OTA site at a price lower than what you can obtain from Disney itself.)

What's more, doing business with OTAs is very expensive for hotels. The cost for a hotel to sell a multiday booking on its own website is $10–$12, including site hosting and analytics, marketing costs, and management fees. This is 10–20 times cheaper than the cost of the same booking through an OTA. Let's say a hotel sells a $100 room for six nights on its own website. Again, the booking would cost the hotel around $12, or $2 per night. If an OTA books the same room having secured it from the hotel at a 30% discount, the hotel receives $70 per night from the OTA. Thus the hotel's cost for the OTA booking is $30 per night, or $180 for six nights—15 times as costly as selling the room online with no middleman.

In the hotel industry, occupancy rates are important, but simply getting bodies into beds doesn't guarantee a profit. A more critical metric is *revenue per available room* (RevPAR). For a hotel full of guests booked through an OTA, RevPAR will be 20–50% lower than for the same number of guests who booked the hotel directly, either through the hotel's website or by phone.

It's no wonder, then, that hotels and OTAs have a love–hate relationship. Likewise, it's perfectly understandable that hotels want to maximize direct bookings through their own websites and minimize OTA bookings. Problem is, the better-known OTAs draw a lot more web traffic than a given hotel's (or even hotel chain's) website. So the challenge for the hotel becomes how to shift room-shoppers away from the OTAs and channel them to its website. A number of hotel corporations, including Choice, Hilton, Hyatt, InterContinental, Marriott, and Wyndham, have risen to that challenge by forming their own OTA called **Room Key** (**roomkey.com**). The participating chains hope that working together will generate enough visitor traffic to make Room Key competitive with the Expedias and Travelocities of the world.

**MORE POWER TO THE SHOPPER** Understanding the market dynamics we've described gives you a powerful tool for obtaining the best rates for the hotel of your choice. It's why we tell you to shop the web for the lowest price available and then call your travel agent or the hotel itself to ask if they can beat it. Any savvy reservationist knows that selling you the room directly will both cut the hotel's cost and improve gross margin. If the reservationist can't help you, ask to speak to his or her supervisor. (We've actually had to explain hotel economics to more than a few clueless reservation agents.)

As for travel agents, they have clout based on the volume of business they send to a particular hotel or chain and can usually negotiate a rate even lower than what you've found on the Internet. Even if the agent can't beat the price, he or she can often obtain upgrades, preferred views, free breakfasts, and other deal sweeteners. When we bump into a great deal on the web, we call our agent. Often she can beat the deal or improve on it, perhaps with an upgrade. *Reminder:* Except for special arrangements agreed to by you, the fee or commission due to your travel agent will be paid by the hotel.

**THE SECRET** The key to shopping on the Internet is, well, shopping. When we're really hungry for a deal, there are a number of sites that we always check out:

| OUR FAVORITE ONLINE HOTEL RESOURCES |
| --- |
| **mousesavers.com** Best site for hotels in Disney World |
| **hotelcoupons.com** Self-explanatory |
| **floridakiss.com** Primarily US 192–Kissimmee area hotels |
| **orlandovacation.com** Great rates for condos and home rentals |
| **visitorlando.com** Good info; not user-friendly for booking |

We scour these sites for unusually juicy hotel deals that meet our criteria (location, quality, price, amenities). If we find a hotel that fills the bill, we check it out at other websites and comparative travel search engines such as **Kayak** (**kayak.com**) and **Mobissimo** (**mobissimo.com**) to see who has the best rate. (As an aside, Kayak used to be purely a search engine but now sells travel products, raising the issue of whether products not sold by Kayak are equally likely to come up in a search. Mobissimo, on the other hand, only links potential buyers to provider websites.) Your initial shopping effort should take about 15–20 minutes, faster if you can zero in quickly on a particular hotel.

Next, armed with your insider knowledge of hotel economics, call the hotel or have your travel agent call. Start by asking about specials. If there are none, or if the hotel can't beat the best price you've found on the Internet, share your findings and ask if the hotel can do better. Sometimes you'll be asked for proof of the rate you've discovered online—to be prepared for this, go to the site and enter the dates of your stay, plus the rate you've found to make sure it's available. If it is, print the page with this information and have it handy for your travel agent or for when you call the hotel. (*Note:* Always call the hotel's local number, not its national reservations number.)

**INDEPENDENT AND BOUTIQUE HOTEL DEALS** While chain hotels worry about sales costs and profit margins, independent and so-called boutique hotels are concerned about discoverability—making themselves known to the traveling public. The market is huge and it's increasingly hard for these hotels to get noticed, especially when they're competing with major chains. Independent and boutique hotels work on the premise that if they can get you through the front door, you'll become a loyal customer. For these hotels, substantially discounting rates is part of their marketing plan to build a client base. Because such hotels get lost on the big OTA sites and on search engines like Kayak and Google, they've jumped on the flash-sale bandwagon. Offering almost irresistible rates on daily-coupon sites like **Groupon** and **LivingSocial,** the independents can get their product in front of thousands of potential guests.

These offers are very generous but also time-limited. If you're in the market, though, you'll be hard-pressed to find better deals. While an OTA such as Expedia generally obtains rooms at a 20–35% discount off the hotel's published rate, flash sites cut deals at an extra-deep discount. This allows their subscribers to bid on or secure coupons for rooms that are often as much as 50% lower than the hotel's standard rate, and that frequently include perks such as meals, free parking, waived resort fees, shopping vouchers, spa services, and entertainment. On Groupon's home page, click "Getaways" or just wait for Getaway coupons by e-mail as part of your free subscription. On LivingSocial you have to specifically subscribe to "Adventures" and "Escapes"; otherwise, you'll receive only non-travel-related offers.

**ANOTHER WRINKLE** Finally, a quick word about a recent trend: bidding sites. On these sites you enter the type of accommodation you desire and your travel dates, and hotels will bid for your reservation. Some sites require that you already have a confirmed booking from a hotel before you can bid. A variation is that you reserve a room at a particular hotel (including Disney hotels) for a set rate. If the rate drops subsequently, you get money back; if the rate goes up, your original rate is locked in.

Late 2011 and early 2012 saw the launch of TripAdvisor's **Tingo** (**tingo.com**), Silicon Valley–based **Guestmob** (**guestmob.com**), and Montreal-based **BackBid** (**backbid.com**), all claiming to be able to beat rates offered by hotel websites and OTAs.

Simply put, bidding sites work best when hotels are dumping inventory—something that almost never happens with Disney resorts and is rare among the better non-Disney properties. Two-star hotels can always be booked for two-star prices, so nobody bids on the hotels with fewer than three stars.

**IS IT WORTH IT?** You might be asking yourself if it's worth all this effort to save a few bucks. Saving $10 on a room doesn't sound like a big deal, but if you're staying six nights that adds up to $60. Earlier we referred to unusually juicy deals, deep discounts predicated by who-knows-what circumstances that add up to big money. They're available every day, and with a little perseverance you'll find them—not often for Disney hotels, but for hotels that are just as good. Good hunting!

## New Is Better and Sometimes Cheaper

New hotels rarely burst on the scene at 100% occupancy. During a hotel's first year, when it strives to generate buzz and attract clientele, it often offers deeply discounted rooms. This is true even of prestigious brands. One thing's for sure: A new hotel will charge less the first few months it's open than subsequently, and a hotel that opens during low season will discount more than hotels that come on line during high season.

## Two Other Discount Sources Worth Mentioning

**1. ORLANDO MAGICARD** This discount program is sponsored by Visit Orlando. Cardholders are eligible for discounts of 12–50% at about 50 hotels. The Magicard is also good for discounts at some area attractions, three dinner theaters, museums, performing-arts venues, restaurants, shops, and more. Valid for up to six persons, the card isn't available for larger groups or conventions.

To obtain a free Magicard and a list of participating hotels and attractions, call ☎ 800-643-9492 or 407-363-5872. On the web, go to **visitorlando.com/magicard;** the Magicard and accompanying brochure can be printed from a personal computer. If you miss getting one before you leave home, obtain one at the Convention and Visitors Bureau Information Center at 8723 International Dr. When you call for your Magicard, also request the *Official Vacation Guide.*

**2. HOTELCOUPONS.COM** *FLORIDA GUIDE* This book of coupons for lodging statewide is free in many restaurants and motels on main highways leading to Florida. Because most travelers make reservations before leaving home, picking up the book en route doesn't help much. To view it online or sign up for a free monthly guide sent by e-mail, visit **hotelcoupons.com.** For a hard copy ($3 for handling, $5 if shipped to Canada), call ☎ 800-222-3948 Monday–Friday, 8 a.m.–5 p.m. Eastern time.

## Scratch That Itch . . . for Information

Granted, it won't help you find good deals on hotels, but **The Bedbug Registry** (**bedbugregistry.com**), is nonetheless a useful resource, allowing you to peruse reports of bedbug and other insect infestations at any hotel in the US. Simply enter the name, city, and state of the property in question; you can also submit a report of your own. Understand that bedbug outbreaks are usually confined to particular rooms and that the creepy-crawlies were usually brought in by previous guests. If you suspect an infestation, report it to management immediately.

## CONDOMINIUMS AND VACATION HOMES

VACATION HOMES ARE FREESTANDING, while condominiums are essentially one- to three-bedroom accommodations in a larger building housing a number of similar units. Because condos tend to be part of large developments (frequently time-shares), amenities such as swimming pools, playgrounds, game arcades, and fitness centers often rival those found in the best hotels. Generally speaking, condo developments don't have restaurants, lounges, or spas.

With a condo, if something goes wrong, there will be someone on hand to fix the problem. Vacation homes rented from a property-management company likewise will have someone to come to the rescue, though responsiveness tends to vary vastly from company to company. If you rent directly from an owner, correcting problems is often more difficult, particularly when the owner doesn't live in the same area as the rental home.

In a vacation home, all the amenities are contained in the home (though in planned developments there may be community amenities available as well). Depending on the specific home, you might find a small swimming pool, hot tub, two-car garage, family room, game room, and even a home theater. Features found in both condos and vacation homes include full kitchens, laundry rooms, TVs, DVD players/VCRs, and frequently stereos. Interestingly, though almost all freestanding vacation homes have private pools, very few have backyards. This means that, except for swimming, the kids are pretty much relegated to playing in the house.

Time-share condos are clones when it comes to furniture and decor, but single-owner condos and vacation homes are furnished and decorated in a style that reflects the taste of the owner. Vacation homes, usually one- to two-story houses in a subdivision, very rarely afford interesting views (though some overlook lakes or natural areas), while condos, especially the high-rise variety, sometimes offer exceptional ones.

### The Price Is Nice

The best deals in lodging in the Walt Disney World area are vacation homes and single-owner condos. Prices range from about $65 a night for two-bedroom condos and town homes to $200–$500 a night for three- to seven-bedroom vacation homes. Forgetting about taxes to keep the comparison simple, let's compare renting a vacation home to staying at one of Disney's Value resorts. A family of two parents, two teens, and two grandparents would need three hotel rooms at Disney's All-Star Resorts. At the lowest rate obtainable, that would run you $110 per night, per room, or $330 total. Rooms are 260 square feet each, so you'd have a total of 780 square feet. Each room has a private bath and a television.

Renting at the same time of year from **All Star Vacation Homes** (no relation to Disney's All-Star Resorts), you can stay at a 2,053-square-foot, four-bedroom, three-bath vacation home with a private pool 3 miles from Walt Disney World for $289—not quite as economical as Disney's Value resorts, but plenty of value all the same: With four

*Continued on page 238*

# Rental-Home Developments Near WDW

Abbey/West Haven 7
Acadia Estates 10
Ashley Manor 7
Aviana 7
Aylesbury 8
Bahama Bay 9
Bass Lake Estates 5
Bass Lake US 27 9
BellaVida 5
Bentley Oaks 7
Blue Heron Beach 1
Briargrove 7
Bridgewater
    Crossing 7
Bridgewater Town Ctr. 7
Buenaventura Lakes 4
Calabay Parc 9
Calabay Tower Lake 8
Calabria 7
Cane Island 5

ChampionsGate 7, 8
Chatham Park 5
Clear Creek 9
Club Cortile 5
Country Creek 9
Countryside Manor 6
Creekside 5
Crescent Lakes 6
Crystal Cove 5
Cumbrian Lakes 5
Cypress Lakes 3
Davenport Lakes 9
Doral Woods 6
Eagle Pointe 5
Emerald Island 10
Esprit/Fairways 9
Fiesta Key 5
Flamingo Lakes 3
Florida Pines 9
Floridays 2
Formosa Gardens 10
Four Corners 9
Glenbrook 9
Grand Palms 9
Grand Reserve 7
Greater Groves 9
Hamilton Reserve 5

Hamlet at West Haven 7
Hampton Lakes 9
Highgate Park 9
High Grove 9
Highlands Reserve 9
Hillcrest Estates 9
Indian Creek 10
Indian Point 5
Indian Ridge 10
Indian Ridge Oaks 10
Indian Wells 1
Island Club West 9
Laguna Bay 5
Lake Berkley 5
Lake Davenport 9
Lake Wilson
    Preserve 7
Lakeside 4
Legacy Park 9
Liberty Village 5
Lighthouse Key Resort 9
Lindfields 9
Loma Linda 7
Loma Vista 4
Lucaya Village Resort 5
Magic Landings 4
Manors at Westridge 9

Marbella 8
Meadow Woods 4
Millbrook Manor 9
Mission Park 9
Montego Bay 5
Oak Island Cove 10
Oak Island Harbor 10
Oakpoint 7
Orange Lake 10
Orange Tree 9
The Palms 9
Paradise Woods 7
Pines West 8
Pinewood 7
Regal Palms 9
Remington Golf Club 4
Remington Point 4
Retreat at West Haven 7
Reunion 7

Ridgewood Lakes 8
Robbins Rest 7
Rolling Hills 10
Royal Oaks 5
Royal Palm Bay 5
Royal Palms 8
Runaway Beach Club 5
Sanctuary at
    West Haven 7
Sandy Ridge 10
Santa Cruz 7
Seasons 5

**Walt Disney World**

○ **Lake Buena Vista** ⑤③⑤

㉗

⑤④⑤

Western Way

①⑨②

○ Citrus Ridge

▲ Bunker Hill

④②⑨ (toll road)

①⑨②

④①⑦

④ **Celebration**

## Zone 9

## Zone 10

㉗

⑰ Intercession City ◇

Loughman ◇

## Zone 8

㉗

④

## Zone 7

## Zone 6

0 ————————— 3 mi
0 ————————— 3 km

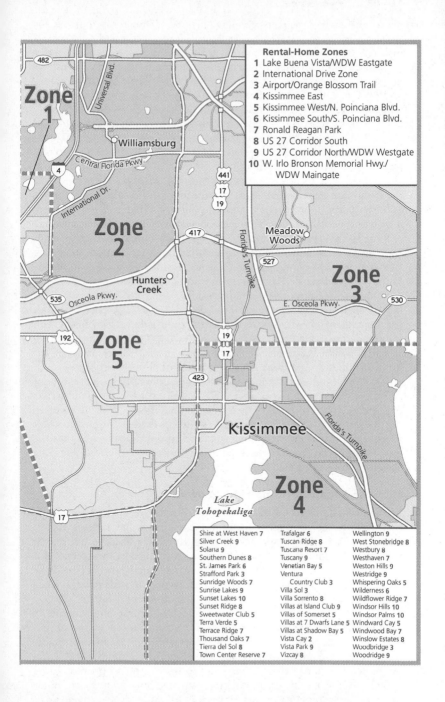

**Rental-Home Zones**
1 Lake Buena Vista/WDW Eastgate
2 International Drive Zone
3 Airport/Orange Blossom Trail
4 Kissimmee East
5 Kissimmee West/N. Poinciana Blvd.
6 Kissimmee South/S. Poinciana Blvd.
7 Ronald Reagan Park
8 US 27 Corridor South
9 US 27 Corridor North/WDW Westgate
10 W. Irlo Bronson Memorial Hwy./
   WDW Maingate

Zone 1

Zone 2

Zone 3

Zone 5

Zone 4

482
Universal Blvd.
Williamsburg
Central Florida Pkwy.
4
International Dr.
441
17
19
417
Meadow Woods
Florida's Turnpike
527
Hunters Creek
535 Osceola Pkwy.
E. Osceola Pkwy.
530
192
19
17
423
Kissimmee
Florida's Turnpike
17
Lake Tohopekaliga

| | | |
|---|---|---|
| Shire at West Haven 7 | Trafalgar 6 | Wellington 9 |
| Silver Creek 9 | Tuscan Ridge 8 | West Stonebridge 8 |
| Solana 9 | Tuscana Resort 7 | Westbury 8 |
| Southern Dunes 8 | Tuscany 9 | Westhaven 7 |
| St. James Park 6 | Venetian Bay 5 | Weston Hills 9 |
| Strafford Park 3 | Ventura | Westridge 9 |
| Sunridge Woods 7 | Country Club 3 | Whispering Oaks 5 |
| Sunrise Lakes 9 | Villa Sol 3 | Wilderness 6 |
| Sunset Lakes 10 | Villa Sorrento 8 | Wildflower Ridge 7 |
| Sunset Ridge 8 | Villas at Island Club 9 | Windsor Hills 10 |
| Sweetwater Club 5 | Villas of Somerset 5 | Windsor Palms 10 |
| Terra Verde 5 | Villas at 7 Dwarfs Lane 5 | Windward Cay 5 |
| Terrace Ridge 7 | Villas at Shadow Bay 5 | Windwood Bay 7 |
| Thousand Oaks 7 | Vista Cay 2 | Winslow Estates 8 |
| Tierra del Sol 8 | Vista Park 9 | Woodbridge 3 |
| Town Center Reserve 7 | Vizcay 8 | Woodridge 9 |

*Continued from page 235*

bedrooms, each of the teens can have his or her own room. Further, for the dates we checked, All Star Vacation Homes was running a special in which they threw in a free rental car with a one-week home rental.

But that's not all—the home comes with the following features and amenities: a flat-screen LED TV with a DVD player (assorted games and DVDs available for complimentary checkout at the rental office); a heatable private pool; five additional flat-screen TVs and DVD players (one in each bedroom and one in the game room); a fully equipped kitchen; a game room with an air-hockey table and video-game console; a hot tub; a full-size washer and dryer; a fully furnished private patio; and a child-safety fence.

The home is in a community with a 24-hour gated entrance. At the community center are a large swimming pool; a whirlpool; tennis, volleyball, and half-court basketball courts; a children's playground; a gym and exercise room; a convenience store; and a 58-seat cinema.

One thing we like about All Star Vacation Homes is that its website, (**allstarvacationhomes.com,** offers detailed information, including a dozen or more photos of each specific home. When you book, the home you've been looking at is the actual one you're reserving. If you want to see how the home previously described is furnished, for instance, go to the home page, scroll down to "Select Code" and look for a small search window in the upper-right side of the photograph that reads "Search a Property Code." Enter **2-8137 SP-WP** in the search window. You'll be taken to another page with a description of the home, a slide show, a floor plan, and additional information.

On the other hand, some vacation-home companies, like rental-car agencies, don't assign you a specific home until the day you arrive. These companies provide photos of a "typical home" instead of making information available on each of the individual homes in their inventory. In this case, you have to take the company's word that the typical home pictured is representative and that the home you'll be assigned will be just as nice.

## How the Vacation-Home Market Works

In the Orlando–Walt Disney World area, there are more than 26,000 rental homes, including stand-alone homes, single-owner condos (that is, not time-shares), and town homes. The same area has about 116,000 hotel rooms. Almost all the rental homes are occupied by their owners for at least a week or two each year; the rest of the year, the owners make the homes available for rent. Some owners deal directly with renters, while others enlist the assistance of a property-management company.

Incredibly, about 700 property-management companies operate in the Orlando–Walt Disney World market. Most of these are mom-and-pop outfits that manage an inventory of 10 homes or less (probably fewer than 70 companies oversee more than 100 rental homes).

Homeowners pay these companies to maintain and promote their properties and handle all rental transactions. Some homes are made available to wholesalers, vacation packagers, and travel agents in deals negotiated either directly by the owners or by property-management

companies on the owners' behalf. A wholesaler or vacation packager will occasionally drop its rates to sell slow-moving inventory,
but more commonly the cost to renters is higher than when dealing
directly with owners or management companies: Because most wholesalers and packagers sell their inventory through travel agents, both
the wholesaler/packager's markup and the travel agent's commission
are passed along to the renter. These costs are in addition to the owner's cut and/or the fee for the property manager.

Along similar lines, logic may suggest that the lowest rate of all can
be obtained by dealing directly with owners, thus eliminating middle-
men. Although this is sometimes true, it's more often the case that
property-management companies offer the best rates. With their marketing expertise and larger customer base, these companies can produce a higher occupancy rate than can the owners themselves. What's
more, management companies, or at least the larger ones, can achieve
economies of scale not available to owners regarding maintenance,
cleaning, linens, even acquiring furniture and appliances (if a house
is not already furnished). The combination of higher occupancy rates
and economies of scale adds up to a win–win situation for owners,
management companies, and renters alike.

## Location, Location, Location

The best vacation home is one that is within easy commuting distance
of the theme parks. If you plan to spend some time at SeaWorld and the
Universal parks, you'll want something just to the northeast of Walt
Disney World (between the World and Orlando). If you plan to spend
most of your time in the World, the best selection of vacation homes is
along US 192 to the south of the park.

Walt Disney World is mostly in Orange County but has a small
southern tip that dips into Osceola County, which, along with Polk
County to the west of the World, is where most vacation homes and
single-owner condos and town houses are. Zoning laws in Orange
County (which also includes most of Orlando, Universal Studios, Sea
World, Lake Buena Vista, and the International Drive area) used to
prohibit short-term rentals of homes and single-owner condos, but in
recent years the county has loosened its zoning restrictions in a few
predominantly tourist-oriented areas.

By our reckoning, about half the rental homes in Osceola County
and all the rental homes in Polk County are too far away from Walt
Disney World for commuting to be practical. That said, an entrance to
Walt Disney World off the FL 429 four-lane toll road halves the commute from many of the vacation-home developments arrayed around
the intersection of US 192 and US 27. FL 429 runs north–south from
I-4 south of Walt Disney World to Florida's Turnpike. You might be
able to save a few bucks by staying farther out, but the most desirable
homes to be found are in Vista Cay and in developments no more than
4 miles from Disney World's main entrance on US 192 (Irlo Bronson
Memorial Highway), in Osceola County.

To get the most from a vacation home, you need to be close enough
to commute in 20 minutes or less to your Walt Disney World destination. This will allow for naps, quiet time, swimming, and dollar-saving

meals you prepare yourself. Though traffic and road conditions are as important as the distance from a vacation home to your Disney destination, we recommend a home no farther than 5 miles away in areas northeast of Walt Disney World and no farther than 4.5 miles away in areas south of the park. Bear in mind that rental companies calculate distance from the vacation home to the absolute nearest square inch of Disney property, so in most instances you can expect to commute another 3 or more miles within Walt Disney World to reach your ultimate destination.

### Shopping for a Vacation Home

The only practical way to shop for a rental home is on the web. This makes it relatively easy to compare different properties and rental companies; on the downside, there are so many owners, rental companies, and individual homes to choose from that you could research yourself into a stupor. There are three main types of websites in the home-rental game: those for property-management companies, which showcase a given company's homes and are set up for direct bookings; individual owner sites; and third-party listings sites, which advertise properties available through different owners and sometimes management companies as well. Sites in the last category will usually refer prospective renters to an owner's or management company's site for reservations.

We've found that most property-management sites are not very well designed and will test your patience to the max. You can practically click yourself into old age trying to see all the homes available or figure out where on earth they are. Nearly all claim to be "just minutes from Disney." (By that reasoning, we should list our homes; they're also just minutes from Disney . . . 570 minutes, to be exact!)

Many websites list homes according to towns (such as Auburndale, Clermont, Davenport, Haines City, and Winter Garden) or real estate developments (including Eagle Pointe, Formosa Gardens, Indian Ridge, and Windsor Palms) in the general Disney area, none of which you're likely to be familiar with. The information that counts is the distance of a vacation home or condo from Walt Disney World; for that you often must look for something like "4 miles from Disney" embedded in the home's description. If you visit a site that lists homes by towns or real estate developments, begin by looking at our map on pages 236 and 237, which shows where all these places are in relation to Walt Disney World. If the map is unhelpful in determining distance, we suggest that you find another location for your stay.

The best websites provide the following:

- Numerous photos and in-depth descriptions of individual homes to make comparisons quick and easy
- Overview maps or text descriptions that reflect how far specific homes or developments are from Walt Disney World
- The ability to book the rental home of your choice on the site
- An easy-to-find phone number for bookings and questions

The best sites are also easy to navigate, let you see what you're interested in without your having to log in or divulge any personal information, and list memberships in such organizations as the Better

Business Bureau and the Central Florida Vacation Rental Managers Association (visit **cfvrma.com** for the association's code of ethics).

## Recommended Websites

After checking out dozens upon dozens of sites, here are the ones we recommend. All of them meet the criteria listed at the bottom of the preceding page. If you're stunned that there are so few of them, well, so were we. (For the record, we elected not to list some sites that met our criteria but whose homes are too far away from Walt Disney World.)

**All Star Vacation Homes (allstarvacationhomes.com)** is easily the best of the management-company sites, with easily accessible photos and plenty of details about featured homes. All the company's rental properties are within either 4 miles of Walt Disney World or 3 miles of Universal Studios.

**#1 Dream Homes (floridadreamhomes.com)** has a good reputation for customer service and now has photos of and information about the homes in its online inventory.

**Orlando's Finest Vacation Homes (orlandosfinest.com)** represents both homeowners and property-management companies. Offering a broad inventory, the Orlando's Finest website features photos and information on individual homes. Although the info is not as detailed as that offered by the All Star Vacation Homes site, friendly sales agents can fill in the blanks.

**Vacation Rentals by Owner (vrbo.com)** is a nationwide vacation-homes listings service that puts prospective renters in direct contact with owners. The site is straightforward and always lists a large number of rental properties in Celebration, Disney's planned community situated about 8–10 minutes from the theme parks. Two similar listings services with good websites are **Vacation Rentals 411 (vacationrentals411.com)** and **Last Minute Villas (lastminutevillas.net)**.

The website for **Visit Orlando (visitorlando.com)** is the place to go if you're interested in renting a condominium at one of the many timeshare developments (click on "Places to Stay" at the site's home page). You can call the developments directly, but going through this website allows you to bypass sales departments and escape their high-pressure invitations to sit through sales presentations. The site also lists hotels and vacation homes. For all types of accommodations, you can sort by distance from where you'll spend your touring time. Distance-sorting categories include Walt Disney World, Universal, the Orange County Convention Center, and downtown Orlando, among others. If you select Universal, for example, the list of accommodations will be ordered from the closest to the most distant.

## Making Contact

Once you've found a vacation home you like, check around the website for a Frequently Asked Questions (FAQ) page. If there's not a FAQ page, here are some of the things you'll want to check out on the phone with the owner or rental company.

1. How close is the property to Walt Disney World?
2. Is the home or condominium that I see on the Internet the one I'll get?

3. Is the property part of a time-share development?

4. Are there any specials or discounts available?

5. Is everything included in the rental price, or are there additional charges? What about taxes?

6. How old is the home or condo I'm interested in? Has it been refurbished recently?

7. What is the view from the property?

8. Is the property near any noisy roads?

9. What is your smoking policy?

10. Are pets allowed? This consideration is as important to those who want to avoid pets as to those who want to bring them.

11. Is the pool heated?

12. Is there a fenced backyard where children can play?

13. How many people can be seated at the main dining table?

14. Is there a separate dedicated telephone at the property?

15. Is high-speed Internet access available?

16. Are linens and towels provided?

17. How far are the nearest supermarket and drugstore?

18. Are child-care services available?

19. Are there restaurants nearby?

20. Is transportation to the parks provided?

21. Will we need a car?

22. What is required to make a reservation?

23. What is your change/cancellation policy?

24. When is checkout time?

25. What will we be responsible for when we check out?

26. How will we receive our confirmation and arrival instructions?

27. What are your office hours?

28. What are the directions to your office?

29. What if we arrive after your office has closed?

30. Whom do we contact if something goes wrong during our stay?

31. How long have you been in business?

32. Are you licensed by the state of Florida?

33. Do you belong to the Better Business Bureau and/or the Central Florida Vacation Rental Managers Association?

We frequently receive letters from readers extolling the virtues of renting a condo or vacation home. This endorsement by a family from Ellington, Connecticut, is typical:

> Our choice to stay outside Disney was based on cost and sanity. We've found over the last couple of years that our children can't share the same bed. We have also gotten tired of having to turn off the lights at 8 p.m. and lie quietly in the dark waiting for our children to fall asleep. With this in mind, we needed a condo/suite layout.

*Anything in Disney offering this option [BoardWalk Villas, Beach Club Villas, Old Key West, and the like] was going to cost $400–$500 a night. This was not built into our Disney budget. We decided on the Sheraton Vistana Resort. We had a two-bedroom villa with full kitchen, living room, three TVs, and washer/dryer. I packed for half the trip and did laundry almost every night. The facilities offered a daily children's program and several pools, kiddie pools, and play-scapes. Located on FL 535, we had a 5- to 10-minute drive to most attractions, including SeaWorld, Disney, and Universal.*

A St. Joe, Indiana, family had a good experience renting a vacation home, writing:

*We rented a home in Kissimmee this time, and we'll never stay in a hotel at WDW again. It was by far the nicest, most relaxing time we've ever had down there. Our rental home was within 10–15 min-utes of all the Disney parks, and 25 minutes from SeaWorld. We had three bedrooms, two baths, and an in-ground pool in a screened enclosure out back. We paid $90 per night for the whole shootin' match. We did spring for the pool heating, $25 per night extra in Feb-ruary. We used AAA Dream Homes Rental Company and they did a great job by us. They provided us with detailed info before we went down so we'd know what we needed to bring.*

A New Jersey family of five echoes the above:

*I cannot stress enough how important it is if you have a large fam-ily (more than two kids) to rent a house for your stay! We had vis-ited WDW several times in the past by ourselves when we were newly-weds. Fast-forward 10 years later, when we took our three kids, ages 6 years, 4 years, and 20 months. We stayed at Windsor Hills Resort, which I booked through* **globalresorthomes.com.** *I was able to see all the homes and check availability when I was reserving the house. This development is 1.5 miles from the Disney Maingate. It took us about 10 minutes to drive there in the a.m., and we had no traffic issues at all.*

## THE BEST HOTELS FOR FAMILIES OUTSIDE WALT DISNEY WORLD

WHAT MAKES A SUPER FAMILY HOTEL? Roomy accommoda-tions, in-room fridge, great pool, complimentary breakfast, child-care options, and programs for kids are a few of the things the *Unofficial Guide* hotel team researched in selecting the top hotels for families from among hundreds of properties in the Disney World area. Some of our picks are expensive, others are more reasonable, and some are a bargain. Regardless of price, be assured that these hotels understand a family's needs.

Though all of the following hotels offer some type of shuttle to the theme parks, some offer very limited service. Call the hotel before you book and ask what the shuttle schedule will be when you visit. Since families, like individuals, have different wants and needs, we haven't ranked these properties; they're listed by zone and alphabetically.

# INTERNATIONAL DRIVE & UNIVERSAL AREAS

## Castle Hotel ★★★½

**Rate per night** $149–$219. **Pool** ★★★. **Fridge in room** Yes ($15/day). **Shuttle to parks** Yes (Universal, SeaWorld, and Wet 'n Wild). **Maximum number of occupants per room** 4. **Special comments** For an additional fee ($11.95 for adults, children age 12 and under free with paying adult), up to 4 people receive a full breakfast. Pets up to 50 pounds welcome ($150 nonrefundable fee).

8629 International Dr.
Orlando
☎ 407-345-1511 or
877-317-5753
castlehotelorlando.com

YOU CAN'T MISS THIS ONE: It's the only castle on I-Drive. Previously a Holiday Inn and before that a DoubleTree, the Castle is now part of Marriott's Autograph Collection. A recent $6.5 million renovation left the hotel's over-the-top ambience refreshed but largely unchanged: Inside you'll find the same royal colors (purple predominates), opulent fixtures (antlers are a recurring motif), European art, and Renaissance music.

The 216 rooms and suites also retain the royal treatment, but the decor is a bit more tasteful and streamlined after the renovation. All rooms are fairly large and well equipped with flat-screen TV, minibar (fridge is available at an extra charge), free Wi-Fi, coffeemaker, iron and board, hair dryer, and safe. The Garden Bistro & Bar off the lobby serves full or Continental breakfast. For lunch or dinner, you might walk next door to Vito's Chop House (dinner only) or Café Tu Tu Tango (an *Unofficial* favorite). The heated circular pool is 5 feet deep and features a fountain in the center, a poolside bar, and a whirlpool. There's no separate kiddie pool. Other amenities include the Poseidon Spa, a fitness center, gift shop, lounge, valet laundry service and facilities, and guest-services desk with park passes for sale and babysitting recommendations. Security feature: Elevators require an electronic key card.

## CoCo Key Hotel and Water Resort–Orlando ★★★★½

**Rate per night** $75–$108. **Pools** ★★★★. **Fridge in room** Yes. **Shuttle to parks** Yes (Aquatica, SeaWorld, Universal, Wet 'n Wild). **Maximum number of occupants per room** 4. **Special comments** Daily $22 resort fee for use of the water park; day guests may use the water park for $22.95/person Monday–Friday ($24.95 on weekends and $19.95 for Florida residents).

7400 International Dr.
Orlando
☎ 407-351-2626 or
877-875-4681
cocokeyorlando.com

NOT FAR FROM THE UNIVERSAL ORLANDO theme parks, CoCo Key combines a tropical-themed hotel with a canopied water park featuring 3 pools and 14 waterslides, as well as poolside food and arcade entertainment. A full-service restaurant serves breakfast and dinner; a food court offers family favorites such as burgers, chicken fingers, and pizza.

A unique feature of the resort is its cashless payment system, much like that on a cruise ship. At check-in, families receive bar-coded wristbands that allow purchased items to be easily charged to their room.

The unusually spacious guest rooms include 37-inch flat-panel TVs, free Wi-Fi, granite showers and countertops, and plenty of accessible outlets for guests' electronics.

## DoubleTree by Hilton Orlando at SeaWorld   ★★★★½

**Rate per night** $129–$179. **Pools** ★★★½. **Fridge in room** Standard in some rooms; available in others for $10/day. **Shuttle to parks** Yes. **Maximum number of occupants per room** 4. **Special comments** Good option if you're visiting SeaWorld or Aquatica. Pets welcome (1 per room, 25-pound limit, $75).

ON 28 LUSH, TROPICAL ACRES with a Balinese feel, the DoubleTree is adjacent to SeaWorld and Aquatica water park. The 1,094 rooms and suites—classified as "resort" or "tower"—are suitable for business travelers or families. We recommend the tower rooms for good views and the resort rooms for maximum convenience. The Bamboo Grille serves steak and seafood, along with breakfast; you can also get a quick bite at Bangli Lounge, the deli, or the pool bar. Relax and cool off at one of the three pools (there are two more just for kids), or indulge in a special spa treatment. A fitness center, mini-golf course and putting green, children's day camp, and game area afford even more diversions. The resort is about a 15-minute drive to Walt Disney World, a 12-minute drive to Universal, or a short walk to SeaWorld.

10100 International Dr. Orlando
☎ 407-352-1100 or 800-327-0363
doubletreeorlando idrive.com

## Nickelodeon Suites Resort   ★★★½

**Rate per night** $149–$209. **Pools** ★★★★. **Fridge in room** Yes. **Shuttle to parks** Yes. **Maximum number of occupants per room** 8. **Special comments** Daily character breakfast; resort fee of $30/night.

SPONGEBOB SQUAREPANTS, eat your heart out. This resort is as kid-friendly as they come. Decked out in all themes Nickelodeon, the hotel is sure to please any fan of TV shows the likes of *SpongeBob, Dora the Explorer,* and *Avatar: The Last Airbender,* to name a few. Nickelodeon characters from the channel's many shows hang out in the resort's lobby and mall area, greeting kids while parents check in.

14500 Continental Gateway Orlando
☎ 407-387-5437 or 877-NICK-111
nickhotel.com

   Guests can choose from among 777 suites—one-bedroom Family Suites and two- and three-bedroom KidSuites—executed in a number of different themes—all very brightly and creatively decorated. All suites include kitchenettes or full kitchens; also standard are microwave, fridge, coffeemaker, TV, iron and board, hair dryer, and safe. KidSuites feature a semiprivate kids' bedroom with bunk or twin beds, pull-out sleeper bed, 32-inch TV, CD player, and activity table. The master bedroom offers ample storage space that the kids' bedroom lacks.

   Additional amenities include a video arcade, Studio Nick—a game-show studio that hosts several game shows a night for the entertainment of a live studio audience, a buffet (kids age 3 and younger eat free with a paying adult), a food court offering Subway and other choices, the full-service Nicktoons Cafe (offers character breakfasts), a convenience store, a lounge, a gift shop, a fitness center, a washer and dryer in each courtyard, and a guest-activities desk (buy Disney tickets and get recommendations on babysitting). Not to be missed—don't worry, your kids won't let you—are the resort's two pools, Oasis and Lagoon.

Oasis features a water park complete with water cannons, rope ladders, geysers, and dump buckets, as well as a hot tub for adults (with a view of the rest of the pool so you can keep an eye on little ones) and a smaller play area for younger kids. Kids will love the huge, zero-entry Lagoon Pool with 400-gallon dump bucket, plus a nearby basketball court and nine-hole mini-golf course. Pool activities for kids are scheduled several times a day, seasonally; some games feature the infamous green slime. Whatever you do, avoid letting your kids catch you saying the phrase "I don't know" while you're here—trust us.

## Rosen Shingle Creek ★★★★

**Rate per night** $179–$190. **Pools** ★★★★. **Fridge in room** Yes. **Shuttle to parks** Yes (Universal, Wet 'n Wild, Discovery Cove, Aquatica, and SeaWorld only). **Maximum number of occupants per room** 4.

9939 Universal Blvd.
Orlando
☎ 407-996-9939 or
866-996-6338
rosenshinglecreek.com

BEAUTIFUL ROOMS (east-facing ones have great views) and excellent restaurants distinguish this mostly meeting- and convention-oriented resort. The pools are large and lovely and include a lap pool, a family pool, and a kiddie wading pool. There's an 18-hole golf course on-site as well as a superior spa and an adequate fitness center. Child care is provided as well. Though a state-of-the-art video arcade will gobble up your kids' pocket change, the real kicker, especially for the 8-years-and-up crowd, is a natural area encompassing lily ponds, grassy wetlands, Shingle Creek, and an adjacent cypress swamp. Running through the area is a nature trail complete with signs to help you identify wildlife. Great blue herons, wood storks, coots, egrets, mallard ducks, anhingas, and ospreys are common, as are sliders (turtles), chameleons, and skinks (lizards). Oh yeah, there are alligators and snakes, too—real ones, but that's part of the fun. If you stay at Shingle Creek and plan to visit the theme parks, you'll want a car. Shuttle service is limited, departing and picking up at rather inconvenient times and stopping at three other hotels before delivering you to your destination.

## Universal's Cabana Bay Beach Resort ★★★½

**Rate per night** $119–$194 standard rooms, $174–$294 suites. **Pools** ★★★★. **Fridge in room** Suites only. **Shuttle to parks** Yes (bus). **Maximum number of occupants per room** 4 for standard rooms, 6 for suites.

6550 Adventure Way
Orlando
☎ 407-503-4000 or
888-464-3617
tinyurl.com/cabanabay

OPENED IN THE SPRING OF 2014, Cabana Bay is Universal's first on-site hotel aimed at the value and moderate markets. The theme is midcentury modern, with lots of windows, bright colors, and period-appropriate lighting and furniture. We think the resort would be right at home in the deserts of Palm Springs or Las Vegas, while our British friends say the decor reminds them of Butlin's Bognor Regis resort circa 1985.

Whatever Cabana Bay reminds you of, we think you'll like it. Kids will love the two large and well-themed pools (one with a lazy river), the amount of space they have to run around in, and the vintage cars parked outside the hotel lobby. Adults will appreciate the sophisticated kitsch of the decor, the multiple lounges, and the on-site Starbucks. We think Cabana Bay is an excellent choice for price- and/or space-conscious families visiting Universal.

The hotel's closest competitor in the Orlando area is Disney's Art of Animation Resort, and the two share many similarities. Both have standard rooms and family suites. At 430 square feet per suite, Cabana Bay suites are about 135 square feet smaller than comparable suites at AofA and have only one bathroom. We found them well appointed for two to four people per room (though not for the six Loews claims as its capacity). Rack rates for the suites are around $175–$210 per night depending on the season—about $140–$300 per night less than Art of Animation's ($317–$511).

Each family suite has a small bedroom with two queen beds, divided from the living area and kitchenette by a sliding screen; a foldout sofa in the living area offers additional sleeping space. (Standard rooms also have two queen beds.) The bath is divided into three sections: toilet, sink area, and shower room with additional sink. The kitchenette has a microwave, coffeemaker with pods, and mini-fridge. A bar area allows extra seating for quick meals, and a large closet has enough space to store everyone's luggage. Built-in USB charging outlets for your devices are a thoughtful touch.

Recreational options include the 10-lane Galaxy Bowl (about $20 per person with shoe rental), poolside table tennis and billiards, and a large Jack LaLanne fitness center. (Fitness centers aren't found at any Disney Value or Moderate resort except Coronado Springs.) Outdoor movies are shown nightly near the pool. We're also told that Cabana Bay guests can use the pools at the other three Universal hotels.

In addition to the Starbucks, a food court with seating area shows 1950s TV clips. Swizzle Lounge in the lobby, two pool bars, in-room pizza delivery, and the Galaxy Bowl round out the on-site dining options. You'll find more restaurants and clubs nearby at the Royal Pacific Resort and Universal CityWalk.

Unlike the other Universal resorts, Cabana Bay offers no watercraft service to the parks—it's either take the bus or walk. Due to the amount of traffic around Universal, we recommend the former. Cabana Bay guests are eligible for early entry at Universal but do not get a complimentary Universal Express pass.

At the time of this review, signage guiding guests to the resort from the Universal area was nearly nonexistent. In the meantime, use your GPS or follow the signs for the Pacifica Ballroom at the Royal Pacific until you see the one sign leading you to the drive into the resort.

## Universal's Hard Rock Hotel  ★★★★

**Rate per night** $249–$404. **Pool ★★★★**. **Fridge in room** $15/day. **Shuttle to parks** Yes (Universal, SeaWorld, Discovery Cove, Aquatica, and Wet 'n Wild). **Maximum number of occupants per room** 5 (double-queen) or 3 (king).
**Special comments** Microwaves available for $15/day. Pets welcome ($50).

5800 Universal Blvd.
Orlando
☎ 407-503-2000 or
888-464-3617
hardrockhotel
orlando.com

OPENED IN 2001, the Hard Rock Hotel is both Universal Orlando's least expensive on-site resort and the closest resort to Universal's theme parks. The exterior has a California Mission theme, with white stucco walls, arched entryways, and rust-colored roof tiles. Inside, the lobby is a tribute to rock-and-roll style, all marble, chrome, and stage lighting.

The eight floors hold 650 rooms and 29 suites, with the rooms categorized into standard, deluxe, and club-level tiers. Standard rooms are 375 square feet, slightly larger than rooms at Disney's Moderate resorts and a bit smaller than most Disney Deluxe rooms. Standard rooms are furnished with two queen beds, with smooth, plush, comfortable linens and more pillows than you'll know what to do with. Rooms also include a flat-panel LCD television, refrigerator, coffeemaker, and an alarm clock with a 30-pin iPhone docking port.

A six-drawer dresser and separate closet with sliding doors ensure plenty of storage space. In addition, most rooms have a reading chair and a small desk with two chairs. An optional rollaway bed, available at an extra charge, allows standard rooms to sleep up to five people.

Each room's dressing area features a sink and hair dryer. The bathroom is probably large enough for most adults to get ready in the morning while another person gets ready in the dressing area.

Guests staying in standard rooms can choose from one of three views: "standard," which can include anything from walkways and parking lots to lawns and trees; "garden view," which includes the lawn, trees, and (in some rooms) the waterway around the resort; and "pool view," which includes the Hard Rock's expansive pool.

That pool is an attraction unto itself, and the place to see and be seen. Situated in the middle of the resort's C-shaped main building, the 12,000-square-foot pool includes a 250-foot waterslide, a sand beach, and underwater speakers so you can hear the music while you swim. Adjacent to the pool are a fountain play area for small children, a sand-volleyball court, hot tubs and a poolside bar. The Hard Rock also has a small, functional fitness center.

On-site dining includes The Kitchen, a casual full-service restaurant open for breakfast, lunch, and dinner, featuring American food such as burgers, steaks, and salads. The Palm Restaurant is an upscale steakhouse available for dinner only. And, of course, the Hard Rock Café is just a short distance away at Universal CityWalk.

In 2014, rack rates for standard rooms at the Hard Rock ranged from a low of $200 per night to a high of $404 per night, plus tax. It's difficult to justify those costs based on the guest rooms or the hallways leading to them—both need new paint, carpet, and lighting. Further, the Hard Rock charges a $20 daily fee for self-parking and $15 for in-room Internet, which is out of line with most comparable hotels and also the hotel's biggest competitor—Disney—down the road. What you're paying for at the Hard Rock is a short walk to the theme parks and unlimited Universal Express first, and the room second.

## Universal's Portofino Bay Hotel ★★★★½

5601 Universal Blvd.
Orlando
☎ 407-503-1000 or
888-464-3617
tinyurl.com
/portofinobay

**Rate per night** $285–$445. **Pools** ★★★★. **Fridge in room** Minibar; fridge available for $15/day. **Shuttle to parks** Yes (Universal, SeaWorld, Discovery Cove, Aquatica, and Wet 'n Wild). **Maximum number of occupants per room** 4. **Special comments** Character dinner on Friday.

UNIVERSAL'S TOP-OF-THE-LINE HOTEL evokes the Italian sea-side city of Portofino, complete with a man-made Portofino Bay past the lobby. To Universal's credit, the layout, color, and theming of the guest-room buildings are a good approximation of the architecture around the harbor in the real Portofino (Universal's version has fewer yachts, however).

Inside, the lobby is decorated with pink marble floors, white-wood columns, and arches. The space is both airy and comfortable, with side rooms featuring seats and couches done in bold reds and deep blues.

Portofino Bay was refurbished in 2013. Most guest rooms are 450 square feet, larger than most at Disney's Deluxe resorts, and have either one king bed or two queen beds. King rooms sleep up to three people with an optional rollaway bed; the same option allows queen rooms to sleep up to five. Two room-view options are available: "Garden" rooms look out over the landscaping and trees—many of these are the east-facing rooms in the resort's east wing, others face one of the three pools; "bay view" rooms face either west or south and over-look Portofino Bay, with a view of the piazza behind the lobby, too.

Rooms come furnished with a 32-inch LCD flat-panel TV, a refrigera-tor, a coffeemaker, and an alarm clock with a 30-pin iPhone docking port. Other amenities include a small desk with two chairs, a comfort-able reading chair with lamp, a chest of drawers, and a standing closet. Wi-Fi is $15 per day in guest rooms, free in the lobby. Beds are large, plush, and comfortable.

Guest bathrooms at Portofino Bay the best on Universal property. We've seen smaller New York apartments! The best thing is the shower, which has enough water pressure to strip paint from old furniture, not to mention an adjustable spray nozzle that varies the water pulses to simulate everything from monsoon season in the tropics to the rhyth-mic thumps of wildebeest hooves during migrating season. We love it.

Portofino Bay has three pools, the largest of which is the Beach Pool, on the west side of the resort. Two smaller quiet pools sit at the far end of the east wing and to the west of the main lobby. The Beach Pool has a zero-entry design and a waterslide themed after a Roman aqueduct, plus a children's play area, hot tubs, and a poolside bar and grill. The Villa Pool has private cabana rentals for that Italian Riviera feeling. Rounding out the luxuries are a full-service Mandara Spa and a complete fitness center with weight machines, treadmills, and more.

On-site dining includes three sit-down restaurants serving Italian cuisine; a deli; a pizzeria; and a café serving coffee and gelato. Some of the food prices go well beyond what we'd consider reasonable, even for a theme park hotel.

In 2014, rack rates ranged from a low of $210 per night to a high of $445 per night. While we think Portofino Bay has Universal's best rooms, the prices put it on par with the Ritz-Carlton—something its good points can't quite justify. On the other hand, the Ritz isn't a short walk from The Wizarding World of Harry Potter.

## Universal's Royal Pacific Resort  ★★★★

**Rate per night** $229–$374. **Pools** ★★★★. **Fridge in room** Minibar; fridge available for $15/day. **Shuttle to parks** Yes (Universal, SeaWorld, Discovery

Cove, Aquatica, and Wet 'n Wild). **Maximum number of occupants per room** 5 (double queen) or 3 (king). **Special comments** Microwaves available for $15/day.

6300 Hollywood Way
Orlando
☎ 407-503-1000 or
888-464-3617
tinyurl.com
/royalpacific

YOU MAY BE TEMPTED, as we were initially, to write off the Royal Pacific, which opened in 2002, as a knock-off of Disney's Polynesian Resort. There are indeed similarities, but the Royal Pacific is attractive enough, and has enough strengths of its own, for us to recommend that you try a stay there to compare for yourself.

The South Seas–inspired theming is both relaxing and structured. Guests enter the lobby from a walkway two stories above an artificial stream that surrounds the resort. Once you're inside, the lobby's dark teak-wood accents contrast nicely with the enormous amount of light coming in from the windows and three-story A-frame roof. Palms line the walkway through the lobby, and through these you see that the whole lobby surrounds an enormous outdoor fountain.

The 1,000 guest rooms are spread among three Y-shaped wings attached to the main building. Standard rooms are 335 square feet—about the size of a room at Disney's Moderate resorts—and feature one king or two queen beds. King rooms sleep up to three people with an optional rollaway bed; queen rooms sleep five with that rollaway bed. The beds, fitted with 300-thread-count sheets, are very comfortable.

Rooms are decorated in neutral beige tones, with dark wood and paint accents and forest-colored carpet, and include a 32-inch flat-panel LCD TV, a refrigerator, a coffeemaker, and an alarm clock with a 30-pin iPhone docking port. Other amenities include a small desk with two chairs, a comfortable reading chair, a chest of drawers, and a large closet. Wi-Fi is $15 per day in guest rooms, free in the lobby.

A dressing area with sink is separated from the rest of the room by a wall. Next to the dressing area is the bathroom, with a tub, shower, and toilet. While they're acceptable, the bathroom and dressing areas at the Royal Pacific are our least favorite in the Universal resorts.

Guests in north- and west-facing rooms in Tower 1 are closest to the attractions at Islands of Adventure and can hear the roar from IOA's Incredible Hulk Coaster throughout the day and night. East-facing rooms in Towers 1 and 2 are exposed to traffic noise from Universal Boulevard and, more distantly, Interstate 4. Quietest are south-facing pool-view rooms in Tower 1 and south-facing rooms in Tower 3.

As at the Hard Rock, the Royal Pacific's zero-entry pool includes a sand beach, volleyball court, play area for kids, hot tub, and cabanas for rent, plus a poolside bar and grill.

Amenities include a 5,000-square-foot fitness facility ($10 per day, free with club-level rooms), two full-service restaurants, three bars, and a luau. Of the table-service restaurants, only the Islands Dining Room is open for breakfast. Emeril Lagasse's Tchoup Chop, the other table-service option, is open for lunch and dinner (reservations recommended).

# LAKE BUENA VISTA & I-4 CORRIDOR

## B Resort ★★★½

**Rate per night** $135–$172. **Pools** ★★★½. **Fridge in room** Yes. **Shuttle to parks** Yes (Disney only). **Maximum number of occupants per room** 4 plus child in crib. **Special comments** $20/night resort fee. *See full profile on page 203.*

## Buena Vista Palace Hotel & Spa ★★★½

**Rate per night** $121–$226. **Pools** ★★★½. **Fridge in room** Yes. **Shuttle to parks** Yes (Disney only). **Maximum number of occupants per room** 4. **Special comments** Sunday character brunch available; $22/night resort fee. *See full profile on page 203.*

## Four Seasons Resort Orlando at Walt Disney World Resort *(opens summer 2014)*

**Rate per night** $545-$845. **Pools** Not open at press time. **Fridge in room** Yes. **Shuttle to parks** Yes (Disney only). **Maximum number of occupants per room** 4 (3 adults or 2 adults and 2 children). **Special comments** Resort opens July 2014; some restaurants open September 2014.

SET BEHIND WHAT USED TO BE Disney's Osprey Ridge Golf Course, the Four Seasons and its relatively small 434 guest rooms should redefine the words *deluxe resort* on Disney property. The resort opened in early August 2014—a little too late for us to inspect it for this edition—so look for a full review with photos on **blog.touringplans.com** by the time you read this.

10100 Dream Tree Blvd. Orlando
☎ 407-313-7777 or 800-267-3046
fourseasons.com /orlando

Standard rooms measure around 500 square feet and include one king bed or two double beds with down-filled pillows. King rooms contain a queen-size fold-out sofa bed, while double rooms can accommodate a crib. No rollaway beds are available. Amenities include a flat-panel television, coffeemaker, small refrigerator, electronic safe, work desk with two chairs, iPod/iPhone-enabled docking station, and digital clock. Most rooms have an 80-square-foot balcony with table and chairs—perfect for a morning coffee or evening nightcap.

Bathrooms have glass-walled showers, a separate tub, marble vanities with two sinks, mosaic-tile floors, hair dryers, lighted mirrors, and a TV in the mirror above the sink so you can keep an eye on your portfolio via the Bloomberg crawl.

Standard-view rooms look out onto the resort's lawns, gardens, and nearby homes in Golden Oak. Lake-view rooms, which overlook the lake, the Tom Fazio–designed Tranquilo Golf Club (formerly Osprey Ridge), or the pool, cost about $100 more per night than standard-view rooms. "Park view" rooms, on floors 6–16, cost about $200 more per night than standard-view rooms and offer views of the Magic Kingdom's nightly fireworks. (Suites are available with views of Epcot, too.)

The resort has two adult outdoor pools (with cabanas for rent); a separate kids' pool with lazy river and island play area; a full-service spa; and a fitness center. Other services include everything from babysitting to shoe shines.

Capa, a Spanish-themed rooftop restaurant, serves seafood and steaks (open nightly 6–10 p.m.; dress is resort casual, and reservations are recommended). Ravello, on the first floor, serves American breakfasts (6:30–11 a.m.) and Italian dinners (5:30–10 p.m.; reservations are recommended, and dress is smart casual). PB&G (Pool Bar and Grill) serves barbecued meats and salads by the main pool (11 a.m.–6 p.m.).

Finally, Plancha serves Cuban-inspired cuisine at the golf course's clubhouse. If you're looking for grab-and-go coffee and food, try Lickety-Split in the lobby. Both Capa and Ravello have separate bars for drinks, light appetizers, and desserts (usually open until midnight).

## Hilton in the Walt Disney World Resort ★★★★

**Rate per night** $161–$241. **Pools** ★★★½. **Fridge in room** Minibar; mini-fridge available free on request. **Shuttle to parks** Yes (Disney theme and water parks only). **Maximum number of occupants per room** 4. **Special comments** Sunday character breakfast and Disney Extra Magic Hours program; $22/night resort fee. *See full profile on page 204.*

## Hilton Orlando Bonnet Creek ★★★★

**Rate per night** $119–$249. **Pool** ★★★★½. **Fridge in room** Yes. **Shuttle to parks** Yes. **Maximum number of occupants per room** 4. **Special comments** $22/night resort fee.

14100 Bonnet Creek
Resort Lane
Orlando
☎ 407-597-3600
hiltonbonnetcreek.com

THE HILTON BONNET CREEK is one of our favorite non-Disney hotels in Lake Buena Vista, and the value for the money beats anything in Disney's Deluxe category. Behind Disney's Caribbean Beach and Pop Century Resorts, this Hilton is much nicer than the one in the Downtown Disney Resort Area.

Standard rooms measure around 414 square feet—comparable to Disney's Deluxe resorts—and have either one king bed or two queen beds. The beds' mattresses and linens are very comfortable. Other features include a 37-inch flat-panel TV, a spacious work desk, an armoire, a small reading chair with floor lamp, a nightstand, and a digital clock. A coffeemaker, small refrigerator, ironing board, and iron are all standard, along with free wired and wireless Internet.

Bathrooms include tile floors with glass showers and a hairdryer. Unfortunately, the layout isn't as up-to-date as other hotels'—where many upscale hotel bathrooms have two sinks (so two people can primp at once), the Hilton's has only one. And where modern bathroom configurations often include a dressing area separate from the bath and a separate water closet for the commode, everything is in the bathroom here. That makes it harder for four-person families to get ready in the morning.

The Hilton's public areas are stylish and spacious. Families will enjoy the huge zero-entry pool, complete with waterslide, as well as the 3-acre lazy river. Even better, the Hilton staff run art and craft activities poolside during the day, allowing parents to grab a quick swim and a cocktail. Pool-facing cabanas are also available for rent at around $300 per day or $150 per half-day. If you're trying to get in swimsuit shape, a nice fitness center sits on the ground floor.

The Hilton participates in the Waldorf Astoria's Kids Club next door, for children ages 5–12. A daytime program is available 10:30 a.m.–2:30 p.m., and an evening program is available 6–10 p.m. on Friday and Saturday. Price is $75 for the first child, $25 for each additional child.

There are more than a dozen restaurants and lounges between the Hilton and the Waldorf Astoria, with cuisine including an upscale steakhouse, Italian, sushi, tapas, a coffee bar, an American bistro, and breakfast buffet choices. Breakfast hours usually run 7–11:30 a.m., lunch 11:30 a.m.–5 p.m, and dinner 5–10 p.m. Reservations are recommended for the fancy places.

## Holiday Inn Resort Lake Buena Vista ★★★½

**Rate per night** $80–$164 **Pool** ★★★. **Fridge in room** Yes. **Shuttle to parks** Yes (Disney only). **Maximum number of occupants per room** 4–6. **Special comments** The first hotel in the world to offer KidSuites; resort fee of $13/night entitles guests to numerous perks, including use of fitness center and daily fountain drinks for kids.

13351 FL 535
Orlando
☎ 407-239-4500
or 866-808-8833
hiresortlbv.com

THE BIG LURE HERE IS KIDSUITES—405-square-foot rooms, each with a separate children's area. Themes include a tree house, jail, space capsule, and fort, among others. The kids' area sleeps two to four children in one or two sets of bunk beds. The separate adult area has its own TV, safe, hair dryer, and mini-kitchenette with fridge, microwave, sink, and coffeemaker. Standard guest rooms offer these adult amenities. Other kid-friendly amenities include the tiny Castle Movie Theater, which shows movies all day, every day; a playground; an arcade with video games and air hockey, among its many games; and a basketball court. Other amenities include a fitness center for the grown-ups and a large free-form pool complete with kiddie pool and two whirlpools. Applebee's serves breakfast and dinner and offers an à la carte menu for dinner. There's also a minimart. More perks: Kids age 12 and younger eat free from a special menu when dining with one paying adult (maximum four kids per adult), and "Dive-Inn" poolside movies are shown on Saturday nights. Finally, pets weighing 30 pounds or less are welcome for an additional $40 nonrefundable fee.

## Hyatt Regency Grand Cypress ★★★★½

**Rate per night** $169–$334. **Pool** ★★★★★. **Fridge in room** Yes, plus minibar. **Shuttle to parks** Yes (Disney, Universal, SeaWorld). **Maximum number of occupants per room** 4. **Special comments** $25/night resort fee.

1 Grand Cypress Blvd.
Orlando
☎ 407-239-1234
grandcypress.hyatt.com

THERE ARE MYRIAD REASONS to stay at the 1,500-acre Grand Cypress, but the pool ranks as reason number one. The 800,000-gallon tropical paradise has two 45-foot waterslides, waterfalls, caves and grottoes, and a suspension bridge. New in 2013 were a waterslide tower, a splash zone, a pool bar, and children's rock-climbing facilities.

The Hyatt also is a golfer's paradise. With 45 holes of Jack Nicklaus–designed championship golf, a 9-hole pitch-and-putt course, and a golf academy, there's something for golfers of all abilities. Other recreational perks include a racquet facility with hard and clay courts, a private lake with beach, a refurbished fitness center, and miles of trails for biking, walking, and jogging. (*Note:* A daily $25 resort fee applies.) The 769 standard guest rooms are 360 square feet and have a Florida ambience, with green and reddish hues, touches of rattan, and private balconies. Amenities include minibar, iron and board, safe, hair dryer, ceiling fan, and cable/satellite TV with pay-per-view movies and video games. Suite and villa accommodations offer even more amenities.

A business lounge is available. Camp Hyatt provides supervised programs for kids ages 3–12; in-room babysitting is available. Six restaurants offer dining options. Four lounges provide nighttime entertainment. If outdoor recreation is high on your family's list, Hyatt is an excellent high-end choice.

## Marriott Village at Lake Buena Vista ★★★

**Rate per night** $74–$189. **Pools** ★★★. **Fridge in room** Yes. **Shuttle to parks** Disney only, $7. **Maximum number of occupants per room** 4 (Courtyard and Fairfield) or 5 (SpringHill). **Special comments** Free Continental breakfast at Fairfield and SpringHill.

8623 Vineland Ave.
Orlando
☎ 407-938-9001
or 800-761-7829
marriottvillage.com

THIS GATED HOTEL COMMUNITY INCLUDES a 388-room Fairfield Inn (★★★½), a 400-suite SpringHill Suites (★★★), and a 312-room Courtyard (★★★½). Whatever your budget, you'll find a room here to fit it. If you need a bit more space, book SpringHill Suites; if you're looking for value, try the Fairfield Inn; if you need limited business amenities, reserve at the Courtyard. Amenities at all three properties include fridge, cable TV, iron and board, hair dryer, and microwave. Cribs and roll-away beds are available at no extra charge at all locations. Swimming pools at all three hotels are attractive and medium-sized, featuring children's interactive splash zones and whirlpools; in addition, each property has its own fitness center. The incredibly convenient Village Marketplace food court includes Pizza Hut, Village Grill, Village Coffee House, and a 24-hour convenience store. Bahama Breeze and Golden Corral full-service restaurants are within walking distance. Other services and amenities include a Disney planning station and ticket sales, an arcade, and a Hertz car-rental desk. Shoppers will find the Orlando Premium Outlets adjacent. You'll get plenty of bang for your buck at Marriott Village.

## Sheraton Lake Buena Vista Resort ★★★★

**Rate per night** $163–$200. **Pool** ★★★★. **Fridge in room** Yes. **Shuttle to parks** Yes (Disney only). **Maximum number of occupants per room** 4–6. **Special comments** Dogs 80 pounds and under allowed; $19.95/night resort fee.

12205 S. Apopka–
Vineland Rd.
Orlando
☎ 407-239-0444
or 800-325-3535
sheratonlakebuena
vistaresort.com

COMPRISING 400 GUEST ROOMS and 90 family junior suites, this resort has a sleek, modern feel. Amenities in each room include Sheraton Sweet Sleeper beds, free Wi-Fi, 42-inch HDTV, refrigerator, coffeemaker, hair dryer, safe, clock-radio, and iron and board. The family junior suites provide bunk beds for children in addition. Microwaves are available at an extra charge. The relaxing pool area features cabanas with food service (for a fee), and youngsters can enjoy the cascading waterfall and waterslide.

The Top of the Palms Spa offers massages, facials, manicures, and pedicures. Also on-site are two restaurants, a business center, a fitness center, an arcade, and a gift shop.

## Sheraton Vistana Resort Villas ★★★★½

**Rate per night** $127–$254. **Pools** ★★★½. **Fridge in room** Yes. **Shuttle to parks** Yes (Disney free; other parks for a fee). **Maximum number of**

**occupants per room** 4–8. **Special comments** Though time-shares, the villas are rented nightly as well.

THE SHERATON VISTANA is deceptively large, stretching across both sides of Vistana Centre Drive. Because Sheraton's emphasis is on selling the time-shares, the rental angle is little known. But families should consider it; the Vistana is one of Orlando's

8800 Vistana Centre Dr.
Orlando
☎ 407-239-3100 or
866-208-0003
tinyurl.com/vistanaresort

best off-Disney properties. If you want a serene retreat from your days in the theme parks, this is an excellent base. The spacious villas come in one-bedroom, two-bedroom, and two-bedroom-with-lock-off models (which can be reconfigured as one studio room and a one-bedroom suite). All are decorated in beachy pastels, but the emphasis is on the profusion of amenities. Each villa has a full kitchen (including fridge/freezer, microwave, oven/range, dishwasher, toaster, and coffeemaker, with an option to prestock with groceries and laundry products), clothes washer and dryer, TVs in the living room and each bedroom (one with DVD player), stereo with CD player in some villas, separate dining area, and private patio or balcony in most. Grounds offer seven swimming pools (three with bars), four playgrounds, two restaurants, game rooms, fitness centers, a mini-golf course, sports equipment rental (including bikes), and courts for basketball, volleyball, tennis, and shuffleboard. A mind-boggling array of activities for kids (and adults) ranges from crafts to games and sports tournaments. Of special note: Vistana is highly secure, with locked gates bordering all guest areas, so children can have the run of the place without parents worrying about them wandering off.

## Waldorf Astoria Orlando ★★★★½

**Rate per night** $234–$424. **Pool** ★★★★. **Fridge in room** Yes. **Shuttle to parks** Yes (Disney only) **Maximum number of occupants per room** 4, plus child in crib. **Special comments** Good alternative to Disney Deluxe resorts; $25/night resort fee.

14200 Bonnet Creek
Resort Lane
Orlando
☎ 407-597-5500
waldorfastoria
orlando.com

THE WALDORF ASTORIA is between I-4 and Disney's Pop Century Resort, near the Hilton Orlando at the back of the Bonnet Creek Resort property. Getting here requires a GPS or good directions, so be prepared with those before you travel. Once you arrive, however, you'll know the trip was worth it. Beautifully decorated and well manicured, the Waldorf is more elegant than any Disney resort. Service is excellent, and the staff-to-guest ratio is far lower than at Disney properties.

At just under 450 square feet, standard rooms feature either two queen beds or one king. A full-size desk allows you to get work done if it's absolutely necessary, and rooms also have flat-panel televisions, high-speed Internet, and Wi-Fi. The bathrooms are spacious and gorgeous, with cool marble floors, glass-walled showers, separate tubs, and enough counter space for a Broadway makeup artist. This space is so nice that we've debated whether we'd rather stay at Pop Century with three others or sleep in a Waldorf bathroom by ourselves.

Amenities include a fitness center, a spa, a golf course, six restaurants, and two pools (including one zero-entry pool for kids). Poolside cabanas are available for rent. The resort offers shuttle service to the Disney parks about every half-hour, but check with the front desk for the exact schedule when you arrive. Runners will enjoy the relative solitude—it's about a 1-mile round-trip to the nearest busy road.

## Wyndham Bonnet Creek Resort  ★★★★½

**Rate per night** $229–$359. **Pool** ★★★★. **Fridge in room** Yes. **Shuttle to parks** Yes (Disney only). **Maximum number of occupants per room** 4–12 depending on room/suite. **Special comments** A non-Disney suite hotel within Walt Disney World.

9560 Via Encinas
Lake Buena Vista
☎ 407-238-3500
or 888-743-2687
wyndhambonnet
creek.com

THIS CONDO HOTEL lies on the south side of Buena Vista Drive, about a quarter-mile east of Disney's Caribbean Beach Resort. The property has an interesting history: When Walt Disney began secretly buying up real estate in the 1960s under the names of numerous front companies, the land on which this resort stands was the last holdout and was never sold to Disney, though the company tried repeatedly to acquire it through the years. (The owners reportedly took issue with the way Disney went about acquiring land and preferred to see the site languish undeveloped.)

The 482-acre site was ultimately bought by Marriott, which put up a Fairfield Inn time-share development in 2004. The Wyndham is part of a luxury-hotel complex on the same site that includes a 500-room Waldorf Astoria (see page previous profile), a 400-room Wyndham Grand, and a 1,000-room Hilton (see page 252). The development is surrounded on three sides by Disney property and on one side by I-4.

One- and two-bedroom condos have fully equipped kitchens, washers and dryers, jetted tubs, and balconies. Activities and amenities include two outdoor swimming pools, a "lazy river" float stream, a children's activities program, a game room, a playground, and miniature golf. Free scheduled transportation serves all the Disney parks. One-bedroom units are furnished with a king bed in the bedroom and a sleeper sofa in the living area; two-bedroom condos have two double beds in the second bedroom, a sleeper sofa in the living area, and an additional bath.

# US 192 AREA

## Clarion Suites Maingate  ★★★½

**Rate per night** $99–$169. **Pool** ★★★. **Fridge in room** Yes. **Shuttle to parks** Yes (Disney, Universal, and SeaWorld). **Maximum number of occupants per room** 6 for most suites. **Special comments** Free Continental breakfast is served daily.

7888 W. Irlo Bronson
Memorial Hwy.
Kissimmee
☎ 407-390-9888 or
888-390-9888
clarionsuites
kissimmee.com

THIS PROPERTY HAS 150 SPACIOUS one-room suites, each with double sofa bed, microwave, fridge, coffeemaker, TV, hair dryer, and safe. The suites aren't lavish, but they're clean and contemporary, with muted deep-purple and beige tones. Extra bathroom counter space is especially convenient for larger families. The heated pool is large and has plenty of lounge chairs and moderate landscaping. A kiddie pool, whirlpool, and poolside bar complete the courtyard. Other amenities include an arcade and a gift shop. But Maingate's big plus is its location next door to a shopping center with about everything a family could need. There, you'll find 10 dining options, including Outback Steakhouse, Red Lobster, Subway, T.G.I. Friday's, and Chinese, Italian, and Japanese eateries; a Winn-Dixie Marketplace; a liquor store; a bank; a dry cleaner; and a tourist-information center with park passes for sale, among other services. All this is a short walk from your room.

## Gaylord Palms Resort & Convention Center

★★★★½

6000 W. Osceola Pkwy.
Kissimmee
☎ 407-586-2000
gaylordpalms.com

**Rate per night** $257–$283. **Pool** ★★★★. **Fridge in room** Yes. **Shuttle to parks** Yes (Disney only). **Maximum number of occupants per room** 4. **Special comments** Probably the closest you'll get off-World to Disney-level extravagance. Resort fee of $20/day.

THIS DECIDEDLY UPSCALE RESORT has a colossal convention facility and caters strongly to business clientele, but it's still a nice (if pricey) family resort. Hotel wings are defined by the three themed, glass-roofed atriums they overlook. Key West's design is reminiscent of island life in the Florida Keys; Everglades is an overgrown spectacle of shabby swamp chic, complete with piped-in cricket noise and a robotic alligator; and the immense, central St. Augustine harks back to Spanish Colonial Florida. Lagoons, streams, and waterfalls cut through and connect all three, and walkways and bridges abound. A fourth wing, Emerald Bay Tower, overlooks the Emerald Plaza shopping and dining area of the St. Augustine atrium. These rooms are the nicest and the most expensive, and they're mostly used by convention-goers. Though rooms have fridges and alarm clocks with CD players (as well as other perks such as high-speed Internet access), the rooms themselves really work better as retreats for adults than for kids. However, children will enjoy wandering the themed areas, playing in the family pool (with water-squirting octopus). In-room child care is provided by Kid's Nite Out (see page 355).

## Orange Lake Resort  ★★★★½

**Rate per night** $107–$159. **Pools** ★★★★. **Fridge in room** Yes. **Shuttle to parks** Yes (fee varies depending on destination). **Maximum number of occupants per room** Varies. **Special comments** This is a time-share property, but if you rent directly through the resort as opposed to the sales office, you can avoid time-share sales pitches; $8/night resort fee.

YOU COULD SPEND YOUR ENTIRE VACATION never leaving this property, about 6–10 minutes from the Disney theme parks. From its 10 pools and two mini–water parks to its golfing opportunities (36 holes of championship greens plus two 9-hole executive courses), Orange Lake offers an extensive menu of

8505 W. Irlo Bronson
Memorial Hwy.
Kissimmee
☎ 407-239-0000 or
800-877-6522
orangelake.com

amenities and recreational opportunities. If you tire of lazing by the pool, try waterskiing, wakeboarding, tubing, fishing, or other activities on the 80-acre lake. There's also a live alligator show, exercise programs, organized competitive sports and games, arts-and-crafts sessions, and miniature golf. Activities don't end when the sun goes down. Karaoke, live music, a Hawaiian luau, and movies at the resort cinema are some of the evening options.

The 2,412 units are tastefully decorated and comfortably furnished, ranging from suites and studios to three-bedroom villas, all with fully equipped kitchens. If you'd rather not cook on vacation, try one of the seven restaurants scattered across the resort: two cafés, three grills, one pizzeria, and a fast-food eatery. If you need help with (or a break from) the kids, babysitters are available to come to your villa, accompany your family on excursions, or take your children to attractions for you.

### Radisson Resort Orlando-Celebration ★★★★

**Rate per night** $99–$155. **Pool** ★★★★½. **Fridge in room** Yes. **Shuttle to parks** Yes (Disney only). **Maximum number of occupants per room** 5. **Special comments** $20/day resort fee; kids age 10 and younger eat free with a paying adult at Mandolin's restaurant.

2900 Parkway Blvd. Kissimmee
☎ 407-396-7000 or 800-634-4774
radissonorlandoresort.com

THE POOL ALONE IS WORTH A STAY HERE, but the Radisson Resort gets high marks in all areas. The free-form pool is huge, with a waterfall and waterslide surrounded by palms and flowering plants, plus a smaller heated pool, two whirlpools, and a kiddie pool. Other outdoor amenities include two lighted tennis courts, sand volleyball, a playground, and jogging areas. Kids can also blow off steam at the arcade, while adults might visit the fitness center. Rooms are elegant, featuring Italian furnishings and marble baths. They're of ample size and include minibar (some rooms), coffeemaker, TV, iron and board, hair dryer, and safe. Dining options include Mandolin's for breakfast (buffet) and dinner, and a 1950s-style diner serving burgers, sandwiches, shakes, and Pizza Hut pizza, among other fare. A sports lounge with a 6 x 11–foot TV offers nighttime entertainment. Guest services can help with tours, park passes, car rental, and babysitting. While there are no children's programs per se, there are plenty of activities such as face painting by a clown, juggling classes, bingo, and arts and crafts at the pool.

# HOTELS *and* MOTELS:
## *Rated and Ranked*

IN THIS SECTION, WE COMPARE HOTELS in four main areas outside Walt Disney World (see page 224) with those inside the World.

In addition to Disney properties, we rate hotels in the four lodging areas defined earlier in this chapter. Additional hotels can be found at the intersection of US 27 and I-4, on US 441 (Orange Blossom Trail), and in downtown Orlando. Most of these require more than 30 minutes of commuting to Disney World and thus are not rated. We also haven't rated lodging east of Siesta Lago Drive on US 192.

## WHAT'S IN A ROOM?

EXCEPT FOR CLEANLINESS, state of repair, and decor, travelers pay little attention to hotel rooms. There is, of course, a clear standard of quality that differentiates Motel 6 from Holiday Inn, Holiday Inn from Marriott, and so on. Many guests, however, fail to appreciate that some rooms are better engineered than others. Making the room usable to its occupants is an art that combines both form and function.

Decor and taste are important. No one wants to stay in a room that's dated, garish, or ugly. But beyond decor, how "livable" is the room? In Orlando, for example, we've seen some beautifully appointed rooms that aren't well designed for human habitation. Even more than decor, your room's details and design elements are the things that will make you feel comfortable and at home.

## ROOM RATINGS

TO EVALUATE PROPERTIES FOR THEIR QUALITY, tastefulness, state of repair, cleanliness, and size of their standard rooms, we have grouped the hotels and motels into classifications denoted by stars—the overall star rating. Star ratings in this guide apply only to Orlando-area properties and don't necessarily correspond to ratings awarded by *Frommer's*, Mobil, AAA, or other travel critics. Because stars have little relevance when awarded in the absence of recognized standards of comparison, we have tied our ratings to expected levels of quality established by specific American hotel corporations.

Overall star ratings apply only to room quality and describe the property's standard accommodations. For most hotels, a standard accommodation is a room with one king bed or two queen beds. In an all-suite property, the standard accommodation is either a studio or a one-bedroom suite. In addition to standard accommodations, many hotels offer luxury rooms and special suites, which aren't rated in this guide. Star ratings for rooms are assigned without regard to whether a property has restaurant(s), recreational facilities, entertainment, or other extras.

In addition to stars (which delineate broad categories), we use a numerical rating system—the room-quality rating. Our scale is 0–100, with 100 being the best possible rating and zero (0) the worst. Numerical ratings show the difference we perceive between one property and another. For instance, rooms at both the Stay Sky Suites I-Drive Orlando and the Clarion Suites Maingate are rated 3½ stars (★★★½). In the supplemental numerical ratings, the former is an 82 and the latter a 76. This means that within the 3½-star category, Stay Sky Suites has slightly nicer rooms than Clarion Suites.

The location column identifies the area around Walt Disney World where you'll find a particular property. The designation **WDW** means the property is inside Walt Disney World. A **1** means it's on or near International Drive. Properties on or near US 192 (a.k.a. Irlo Bronson Memorial Highway, Vine Street, and Space Coast Parkway) are indicated by a **3**, and those in the vicinity of Universal Orlando as **4**. All others are marked with **2** and for the most part are along FL 535 and the I-4 corridor, though some are in nearby locations that don't meet any other criteria.

| **LODGING AREAS** *(see map on page 226)* | |
|---|---|
| **WDW** Walt Disney World | |
| **1** International Drive | **2** Lake Buena Vista and I-4 Corridor |
| **3** US 192 (Irlo Bronson Memorial Highway) | **4** Universal Orlando Area |

Names of properties along US 192 also designate location (for example, Holiday Inn Maingate West). The consensus in Orlando seems to be that the main entrance to Disney World is the broad interstate-type road that runs off US 192. This is called the **Maingate**. Properties along US 192 call themselves Maingate East or West to differentiate their positions along the highway. So, driving southeast from Clermont or Florida's Turnpike, the properties before you reach the Maingate turnoff are called Maingate West, while the properties after you pass the Maingate turnoff are called Maingate East.

Cost estimates are based on the hotel's published rack rates for standard rooms. Each **$** represents $50. Thus a cost symbol of **$$$** means that a room (or suite) at that hotel will be about $150 a night; amounts over $200 are indicated by **$ x 5** and so on.

| **OVERALL STAR RATINGS** | | |
|---|---|---|
| ★★★★★ | Superior rooms | Tasteful and luxurious by any standard |
| ★★★★ | Extremely nice rooms | What you'd expect at a Hyatt Regency or Marriott |
| ★★★ | Nice rooms | Holiday Inn or comparable quality |
| ★★ | Adequate rooms | Clean, comfortable, and functional without frills—like a Motel 6 |
| ★ | Super-budget | These exist but are not included in our coverage |

We've focused on room quality and excluded consideration of location, services, recreation, or amenities. In some instances, a one- or two-room suite is available for the same price or less than that of a single standard hotel room.

If you've used an earlier edition of this guide, you'll notice that new properties have been added and many ratings and rankings have changed, some because of room renovation or improved maintenance or housekeeping. Lax housekeeping or failure to maintain rooms can bring down ratings.

*unofficial* **TIP**
The key to avoiding disappointment is to snoop in advance. Ask how old the hotel is and when its guest rooms were last renovated.

Before you shop for a hotel, consider this letter from a man in Hot Springs, Arkansas:

*We canceled our room reservations to follow the advice in your book and reserved a hotel highly ranked by the* Unofficial Guide. *We wanted inexpensive, but clean and cheerful. We got inexpensive, but also dirty, grim, and depressing. The room spoiled the holiday for me aside from our touring.*

This letter was as unsettling to us as the bad room was to the reader—our integrity as travel journalists is based on the quality of the information we provide. When rechecking the hotel, we found our rating was representative, but the reader had been assigned one of a small number of threadbare rooms scheduled for renovation.

Be aware that some chains use the same guest-room photo in promotional literature for all their hotels and that the rooms at a specific property may bear no resemblance to the photo in question. When you or your travel agent calls, ask how old the property is and when the guest room you're being assigned was last renovated. If you're assigned a room that is inferior to your expectations, demand to be moved.

## A WORD ABOUT TOLL-FREE TELEPHONE NUMBERS

AS WE'VE REPEATED SEVERAL TIMES in this chapter, it's essential to communicate with the hotel directly when shopping for deals and stating your room preferences. Most toll-free numbers are routed directly to a hotel chain's central reservations office, and the customer-service agents there typically have little or no knowledge of the individual hotels in the chain or of any specials those hotels may be offering. In our Hotel Information Chart (pages 269–286), therefore, we list the toll-free number only if it connects directly to the hotel in question; otherwise, we provide the hotel's local phone number. We also provide local numbers for the Disney resorts in the Hotel Information Chart and in the Walt Disney World Phone Numbers chart on pages 30 and 31, but note that these hotels must be booked through the Disney Reservation Center (☎ 407-w-DISNEY). After you've reserved your room, you can check online to make sure the reservation is in order.

## THE 30 BEST HOTEL VALUES

IN THE CHART ON THE NEXT PAGE, we look at the best combinations of quality and value in a room. Rankings are calculated without consideration for location or the availability of restaurant(s), recreational facilities, entertainment, and/or amenities.

A reader wrote to complain that he had booked one of our top-ranked rooms in terms of value and had been very disappointed in the room. We noticed that the room the reader occupied had a quality rating of ★★½. Remember that the list of top deals is intended to give you some sense of value received for dollars spent. A ★★½ room at $40 may have the same *value* as a ★★★★ room at $115, but that doesn't mean the rooms will be of comparable *quality*. Regardless of whether it's a good deal, a ★★½ room is still a ★★½ room.

For example, the Magic Castle Inn and Suites is a clean, reasonably comfortable motel with an exceptionally friendly staff, within 15 minutes of every Disney theme park. During one Christmas season they had available basic rooms for around $54 per night when every other hotel within 20 miles of Walt Disney World was charging $150. The catch? They're right next door to a place that gives helicopter tours of Orlando . . . all day long. You won't notice a thing if you don't plan on midday breaks, but our midafternoon naps were filled with visions of *M\*A\*S\*H* and *Apocalypse Now*. We'd still stay there again, but our significant others have different opinions.

## THE TOP 30 BEST DEALS

| HOTEL | LODGING AREA | OVERALL QUALITY | ROOM QUALITY | ($ = $50) |
|---|---|---|---|---|
| 1. Rodeway Inn Maingate | 3 | ★★½ | 59 | $− |
| 2. Vacation Village at Parkway | 3 | ★★★★½ | 91 | $$− |
| 3. Monumental Hotel | 1 | ★★★★½ | 94 | $$ |
| 4. Barefoot'n Resort | 3 | ★★★★ | 85 | $$− |
| 5. Seralago Hotel & Suites Main Gate East | 3 | ★★★ | 71 | $ |
| 6. Super 8 Kissimmee/Maingate | 3 | ★★★ | 70 | $ |
| 7. Claremont Hotel Kissimmee | 3 | ★★½ | 59 | $− |
| 8. Monumental MovieLand Hotel | 1 | ★★★ | 68 | $ |
| 9. Radisson Resort Orlando-Celebration | 3 | ★★★★ | 86 | $$ |
| 10. Holiday Inn Main Gate East | 3 | ★★★★½ | 90 | $$+ |
| 11. Extended Stay America Universal | 4 | ★★★½ | 75 | $$− |
| 12. Hawthorn Suites Orlando Convention Center | 1 | ★★★½ | 80 | $$− |
| 13. Extended Stay Deluxe Orlando Lake Buena Vista | 2 | ★★★★ | 83 | $$ |
| 14. Maingate Lakeside Resort | 3 | ★★★ | 67 | $+ |
| 15. Extended Stay America Convention Center/Westwood | 1 | ★★★★ | 84 | $$ |
| 16. Shades of Green | WDW | ★★★★½ | 91 | $$+ |
| 17. Hilton Grand Vacations Club at SeaWorld | 1 | ★★★★½ | 95 | $$$− |
| 18. Extended Stay Deluxe Orlando Universal | 4 | ★★★½ | 75 | $$− |
| 19. Howard Johnson Inn Orlando I-Drive | 1 | ★★½ | 59 | $ |
| 20. Champions World Resort | 3 | ★★★ | 66 | $+ |
| 21. Super 8 Kissimmee | 3 | ★★½ | 60 | $ |
| 22. La Quinta Inn Orlando I-Drive | 1 | ★★★ | 73 | $+ |
| 23. Ramada Gateway Kissimmee (tower) | 3 | ★★★ | 71 | $+ |
| 24. Grand Lake Resort | 1 | ★★★½ | 76 | $$− |
| 25. Days Inn Orlando/I-Drive | 1 | ★★½ | 61 | $ |
| 26. Destiny Palms Maingate West | 3 | ★★½ | 60 | $ |
| 27. DoubleTree Universal | 4 | ★★★★ | 89 | $$+ |
| 28. Motel 6 Orlando–I-Drive | 1 | ★★½ | 61 | $ |
| 29. Hampton Inn & Suites Orlando–South Lake Buena Vista | 3 | ★★★½ | 80 | $$ |
| 30. Galleria Palms Kissimmee Hotel | 3 | ★★★ | 74 | $$− |

# How the Hotels Compare

| HOTEL | LODGING AREA | OVERALL QUALITY | ROOM QUALITY | ($ = $50) |
|---|---|---|---|---|
| Omni Orlando Resort at ChampionsGate | 2 | ★★★★★ | 96 | $- x 5 |
| Bay Lake Tower at Disney's Contemporary Resort | WDW | ★★★★½ | 95 | $- x 11 |
| Disney's Animal Kingdom Villas (Kidani Village) | WDW | ★★★★½ | 95 | $- x 9 |
| Hilton Grand Vacations Club at SeaWorld | 1 | ★★★★½ | 95 | $$$- |
| Rosen Centre Hotel | 1 | ★★★★½ | 95 | $$$$+ |
| Sheraton Vistana Resort Villas | 2 | ★★★★½ | 95 | $ x 5 |
| Gaylord Palms Resort & Convention Center | 3 | ★★★★½ | 94 | $- x 6 |
| Monumental Hotel | 1 | ★★★★½ | 94 | $$ |
| The Ritz-Carlton Orlando, Grande Lakes | 1 | ★★★★½ | 94 | $+ x 6 |
| Disney's Contemporary Resort | WDW | ★★★★½ | 93 | $+ x 8 |
| Disney's Grand Floridian Resort & Spa | WDW | ★★★★½ | 93 | $- x 12 |
| JW Marriott Orlando Grande Lakes | 1 | ★★★★½ | 93 | $- x 6 |
| Orange Lake Resort | 3 | ★★★★½ | 93 | $$$+ |
| Renaissance Orlando at SeaWorld | 1 | ★★★★½ | 93 | $$$ |
| Universal's Hard Rock Hotel | 4 | ★★★★½ | 93 | $+ x 7 |
| The Villas at Disney's Grand Floridian Resort & Spa | WDW | ★★★★½ | 93 | $- x 12 |
| Waldorf Astoria Orlando | 2 | ★★★★½ | 93 | $- x 6 |
| Westgate Town Center | 2 | ★★★★½ | 93 | $$$$- |
| Disney's Polynesian Resort | WDW | ★★★★½ | 92 | $- x 11 |
| DoubleTree by Hilton Orlando at SeaWorld (resort) | 1 | ★★★★½ | 92 | $$$+ |
| DoubleTree by Hilton Orlando at SeaWorld (tower) | 1 | ★★★★½ | 92 | $$$+ |
| Hilton Orlando | 1 | ★★★★½ | 92 | $$$$+ |
| Hyatt Regency Grand Cypress | 2 | ★★★★½ | 92 | $- x 5 |
| Marriott's Grande Vista | 1 | ★★★★½ | 92 | $$$+ |
| Marriott's Sabal Palms | 2 | ★★★★½ | 92 | $+ x 5 |
| Universal's Portofino Bay Hotel | 4 | ★★★★½ | 92 | $+ x 8 |
| Villas of Grand Cypress | 2 | ★★★★½ | 92 | $+ x 5 |
| Westgate Lakes Resort & Spa | 2 | ★★★★½ | 92 | $$$ |
| Disney's Animal Kingdom Villas (Jambo House) | WDW | ★★★★½ | 91 | $+ x 6 |
| Shades of Green | WDW | ★★★★½ | 91 | $$+ |
| Vacation Village at Parkway | 3 | ★★★★½ | 91 | $$- |
| Bohemian Celebration Hotel | 2 | ★★★★½ | 90 | $$$$- |
| CoCo Key Water Resort–Orlando | 1 | ★★★★½ | 90 | $$$- |
| Disney's Beach Club Resort | WDW | ★★★★½ | 90 | $+ x 9 |
| Disney's Beach Club Villas | WDW | ★★★★½ | 90 | $- x 9 |
| Disney's BoardWalk Villas | WDW | ★★★★½ | 90 | $- x 12 |
| Disney's Old Key West Resort | WDW | ★★★★½ | 90 | $- x 8 |
| Disney's Saratoga Springs Resort & Spa | WDW | ★★★★½ | 90 | $- x 8 |

# How the Hotels Compare (continued)

| HOTEL | LODGING AREA | OVERALL QUALITY | ROOM QUALITY | ($ = $50) |
|---|---|---|---|---|
| Four Points by Sheraton Orlando Studio City | 1 | ★★★★½ | 90 | $$$- |
| Grand Beach | 1 | ★★★★½ | 90 | $ x 6 |
| Holiday Inn Main Gate East | 3 | ★★★★½ | 90 | $$+ |
| Hyatt Regency Orlando | 1 | ★★★★½ | 90 | $- x 6 |
| Lighthouse Key Resort & Spa | 3 | ★★★★½ | 90 | $- x 5 |
| Liki Tiki Village | 3 | ★★★★½ | 90 | $$$$- |
| Marriott's Harbour Lake | 2 | ★★★★½ | 90 | $$$$- |
| Polynesian Isles Resort (Diamond Resorts) | 3 | ★★★★½ | 90 | $$$$ |
| Rosen Plaza Hotel | 1 | ★★★★½ | 90 | $$$$- |
| Treehouse Villas at Disney's Saratoga Springs Resort & Spa | WDW | ★★★★½ | 90 | $ x 16 |
| Universal's Royal Pacific Resort | 4 | ★★★★½ | 90 | $ x 6 |
| The Villas at Disney's Wilderness Lodge | WDW | ★★★★½ | 90 | $+ x 9 |
| Walt Disney World Dolphin | WDW | ★★★★½ | 90 | $- x 5 |
| Walt Disney World Swan | WDW | ★★★★½ | 90 | $- x 5 |
| Westgate Vacation Villas | 2 | ★★★★½ | 90 | $ x 5 |
| Wyndham Bonnet Creek Resort | 2 | ★★★★½ | 90 | $+ x 5 |
| Courtyard Orlando Lake Buena Vista at Vista Centre | 2 | ★★★★ | 89 | $$$- |
| Disney's Animal Kingdom Lodge | WDW | ★★★★ | 89 | $- x 9 |
| Disney's BoardWalk Inn | WDW | ★★★★ | 89 | $+ x 9 |
| Disney's Yacht Club Resort | WDW | ★★★★ | 89 | $+ x 9 |
| DoubleTree Universal | 4 | ★★★★ | 89 | $$+ |
| Orlando World Center Marriott Resort | 2 | ★★★★ | 89 | $- x 5 |
| Caribe Royale All-Suite Hotel & Convention Center | 1 | ★★★★ | 88 | $$$$- |
| Hilton Garden Inn Lake Buena Vista/Orlando | 2 | ★★★★ | 88 | $$$- |
| Hilton Grand Vacations Club on I-Drive | 1 | ★★★★ | 88 | $- x 6 |
| Hilton Orlando Bonnet Creek | 1 | ★★★★ | 88 | $$$- |
| Rosen Shingle Creek | 1 | ★★★★ | 88 | $- x 5 |
| Sheraton Lake Buena Vista Resort | 2 | ★★★★ | 88 | $- x 5 |
| WorldQuest Orlando Resort | 1 | ★★★★ | 88 | $$$$ |
| Hawthorn Suites Lake Buena Vista | 2 | ★★★★ | 87 | $$+ |
| Hilton in the Walt Disney World Resort | WDW | ★★★★ | 87 | $$$+ |
| Mystic Dunes Resort & Golf Club | 3 | ★★★★ | 87 | $$$$- |
| Westin Imagine Orlando | 1 | ★★★★ | 87 | $- x 5 |
| Wyndham Cypress Palms | 3 | ★★★★ | 87 | $$$- |
| Disney's Fort Wilderness Resort (cabins) | WDW | ★★★★ | 86 | $- x 8 |
| Disney's Wilderness Lodge | WDW | ★★★★ | 86 | $- x 8 |
| Floridays Resort Orlando | 1 | ★★★★ | 86 | $- x 7 |
| Marriott's Cypress Harbour | 1 | ★★★★ | 86 | $- x 6 |
| Marriott's Imperial Palms | 1 | ★★★★ | 86 | $- x 9 |

## How the Hotels Compare (continued)

| HOTEL | LODGING AREA | OVERALL QUALITY | ROOM QUALITY | ($ = $50) |
|---|---|---|---|---|
| Radisson Resort Orlando-Celebration | 3 | ★★★★ | 86 | $$ |
| Barefoot'n Resort | 3 | ★★★★ | 85 | $$- |
| Best Western Lake Buena Vista Resort Hotel | WDW | ★★★★ | 85 | $$$- |
| Caribe Cove Resort Orlando | 3 | ★★★★ | 85 | $$+ |
| Homewood Suites by Hilton LBV-Orlando | 2 | ★★★★ | 85 | $$$+ |
| Legacy Vacation Club Lake Buena Vista | 2 | ★★★★ | 85 | $$$$- |
| Marriott's Royal Palms | 1 | ★★★★ | 85 | $+ x 5 |
| Residence Inn Orlando at SeaWorld | 2 | ★★★★ | 85 | $$$$- |
| Disney's Port Orleans Resort–French Quarter | WDW | ★★★★ | 84 | $$$$+ |
| Extended Stay America Convention Center/Westwood | 1 | ★★★★ | 84 | $$ |
| Hyatt Place Orlando/Universal | 4 | ★★★★ | 84 | $$$+ |
| Star Island Resort & Club | 3 | ★★★★ | 84 | $$$$+ |
| Buena Vista Suites | 1 | ★★★★ | 83 | $$$+ |
| Disney's Coronado Springs Resort | WDW | ★★★★ | 83 | $$$$+ |
| Disney's Port Orleans Resort–Riverside | WDW | ★★★★ | 83 | $$$$+ |
| Extended Stay Deluxe Orlando Lake Buena Vista | 2 | ★★★★ | 83 | $$ |
| Wyndham Orlando Resort I-Drive | 1 | ★★★★ | 83 | $$$$ |
| B Resort | WDW | ★★★½ | 82 | $$$$- |
| Castle Hotel | 1 | ★★★½ | 82 | $$$ |
| Courtyard Orlando LBV in Marriott Village | 2 | ★★★½ | 82 | $$$- |
| Crowne Plaza Orlando–Lake Buena Vista | 2 | ★★★½ | 82 | $$$$- |
| Universal's Cabana Bay Beach Resort | 4 | ★★★½ | 82 | $$$ |
| Holiday Inn Resort Lake Buena Vista | 2 | ★★★½ | 82 | $$$ |
| Inn at Calypso | 3 | ★★★½ | 82 | $$+ |
| Nickelodeon Suites Resort | 1 | ★★★½ | 82 | $$$- |
| Parkway International Resort | 3 | ★★★½ | 82 | $$$$- |
| The Point Orlando Resort | 1 | ★★★½ | 82 | $$$- |
| Radisson Hotel Orlando Lake Buena Vista | 2 | ★★★½ | 82 | $$$$+ |
| Stay Sky Suites I-Drive Orlando | 1 | ★★★½ | 82 | $$ |
| Embassy Suites Orlando–Lake Buena Vista | 2 | ★★★½ | 81 | $$$- |
| Homewood Suites by Hilton I-Drive | 1 | ★★★½ | 81 | $$$+ |
| Westgate Towers | 2 | ★★★½ | 81 | $$$- |
| Buena Vista Palace Hotel & Spa | WDW | ★★★½ | 80 | $$$- |
| Comfort Inn Orlando–Lake Buena Vista | 2 | ★★★½ | 80 | $$ |
| Disney's Art of Animation Resort | WDW | ★★★½ | 80 | $$$ |
| Disney's Caribbean Beach Resort | WDW | ★★★½ | 80 | $$$$+ |
| Embassy Suites Orlando I-Drive/Jamaican Court | 1 | ★★★½ | 80 | $$+ |
| Fairfield Inn & Suites Near Universal Orlando Resort | 4 | ★★★½ | 80 | $$$+ |
| Hampton Inn & Suites Orlando–South Lake Buena Vista | 3 | ★★★½ | 80 | $$ |

## How the Hotels Compare (continued)

| HOTEL | LODGING AREA | OVERALL QUALITY | ROOM QUALITY | ($ = $50) |
|---|---|---|---|---|
| Hawthorn Suites Orlando Convention Center | 1 | ★★★½ | 80 | $$- |
| Hilton Garden Inn Orlando at SeaWorld | 1 | ★★★½ | 80 | $$$ |
| Hilton Garden Inn Orlando I-Drive North | 1 | ★★★½ | 80 | $$ |
| Legacy Vacation Club Orlando | 3 | ★★★½ | 80 | $$$+ |
| Orbit One Vacation Villas | 3 | ★★★½ | 80 | $$$+ |
| Residence Inn Orlando Convention Center | 1 | ★★★½ | 80 | $$+ |
| SpringHill Suites Orlando Convention Center | 1 | ★★★½ | 80 | $- x 5 |
| Holiday Inn in the Walt Disney World Resort | WDW | ★★★½ | 79 | $$$- |
| Courtyard Orlando I-Drive | 1 | ★★★½ | 78 | $$$$- |
| Fairfield Inn & Suites Orlando Lake Buena Vista (rooms) | 2 | ★★★½ | 78 | $$$+ |
| Fairfield Inn & Suites Orlando Lake Buena Vista (suites) | 2 | ★★★½ | 78 | $$$+ |
| Park Inn by Radisson Resort and Conference Center | 3 | ★★★½ | 77 | $$ |
| Clarion Suites Maingate | 3 | ★★★½ | 76 | $$ |
| Grand Lake Resort | 1 | ★★★½ | 76 | $$- |
| Hampton Inn Orlando/Lake Buena Vista | 2 | ★★★½ | 76 | $$ |
| Palms Hotel & Villas | 3 | ★★★½ | 76 | $$$$- |
| Best Western Plus Universal Inn | 4 | ★★★½ | 75 | $$ |
| Best Western Premier Saratoga Resort Villas | 3 | ★★★½ | 75 | $$$$ |
| Embassy Suites Orlando I-Drive | 1 | ★★★½ | 75 | $$+ |
| Extended Stay America Universal | 4 | ★★★½ | 75 | $$- |
| Extended Stay Deluxe Orlando Universal | 4 | ★★★½ | 75 | $$- |
| Fairfield Inn & Suites Orlando LBV in Marriott Village | 2 | ★★★½ | 75 | $$$ |
| Hawthorn Suites Orlando I-Drive | 1 | ★★★½ | 75 | $$+ |
| Holiday Inn & Suites Orlando Universal | 4 | ★★★½ | 75 | $$$ |
| Quality Suites Royale Parc Suites | 3 | ★★★½ | 75 | $$$- |
| Residence Inn Orlando Lake Buena Vista | 2 | ★★★½ | 75 | $$$$- |
| Rosen Inn at Pointe Orlando | 1 | ★★★½ | 75 | $$+ |
| Sonesta ES Suites Orlando | 1 | ★★★½ | 75 | $$$- |
| Wyndham Lake Buena Vista Resort | WDW | ★★★½ | 75 | $$$+ |
| Fairfield Inn & Suites Orlando I-Drive/ Convention Center | 1 | ★★★ | 74 | $$$$ |
| Galleria Palms Kissimmee Hotel | 3 | ★★★ | 74 | $$- |
| Quality Suites Lake Buena Vista | 2 | ★★★ | 74 | $$$- |
| Quality Suites Turkey Lake | 2 | ★★★ | 74 | $$- |
| Disney's All-Star Movies Resort | WDW | ★★★ | 73 | $$$- |
| Disney's All-Star Music Resort | WDW | ★★★ | 73 | $$$- |
| Disney's All-Star Sports Resort | WDW | ★★★ | 73 | $$$- |
| International Palms Resort & Conference Center | 1 | ★★★ | 73 | $$ |
| La Quinta Inn Orlando I-Drive | 1 | ★★★ | 73 | $+ |

# How the Hotels Compare (continued)

| HOTEL | LODGING AREA | OVERALL QUALITY | ROOM QUALITY | ($ = $50) |
|---|---|---|---|---|
| Baymont Inn & Suites Celebration | 3 | ★★★ | 72 | $$- |
| Extended Stay America Orlando Convention Center | 1 | ★★★ | 72 | $$- |
| Ramada Plaza Resort and Suites Orlando I-Drive | 1 | ★★★ | 72 | $$+ |
| Staybridge Suites Lake Buena Vista | 2 | ★★★ | 72 | $$$$- |
| Disney's Pop Century Resort | WDW | ★★★ | 71 | $$$- |
| DoubleTree Guest Suites | WDW | ★★★ | 71 | $$$$- |
| Ramada Gateway Kissimmee (tower) | 3 | ★★★ | 71 | $+ |
| Seralago Hotel & Suites Main Gate East | 3 | ★★★ | 71 | $ |
| SpringHill Suites Orlando LBV in Marriott Village | 2 | ★★★ | 71 | $$$- |
| Comfort Suites Universal | 4 | ★★★ | 70 | $$ |
| Crown Club Inn | 3 | ★★★ | 70 | $$ |
| Hampton Inn I-Drive/Convention Center | 1 | ★★★ | 70 | $$$ |
| Super 8 Kissimmee/Maingate | 3 | ★★★ | 70 | $ |
| Monumental MovieLand Hotel | 1 | ★★★ | 68 | $ |
| Westgate Palace | 1 | ★★★ | 68 | $+ x 5 |
| The Enclave Hotel & Suites | 1 | ★★★ | 67 | $$$- |
| Hampton Inn Universal | 4 | ★★★ | 67 | $$$- |
| Maingate Lakeside Resort | 3 | ★★★ | 67 | $+ |
| Champions World Resort | 3 | ★★★ | 66 | $+ |
| Quality Inn Universal Studios I-Drive Area | 1 | ★★★ | 66 | $+ |
| Best Western I-Drive | 1 | ★★★ | 65 | $$+ |
| Ramada Convention Center I-Drive | 1 | ★★★ | 65 | $$- |
| Ramada Maingate West Kissimmee | 3 | ★★★ | 65 | $$ |
| Rosen Inn International Hotel | 1 | ★★★ | 65 | $$- |
| Clarion Inn & Suites at I-Drive | 1 | ★★½ | 64 | $$+ |
| Clarion Inn Lake Buena Vista | 2 | ★★½ | 64 | $$ |
| Hampton Inn South of Universal | 1 | ★★½ | 64 | $$+ |
| Ramada Gateway Kissimmee (garden) | 3 | ★★½ | 64 | $+ |
| Silver Lake Resort | 3 | ★★½ | 64 | $$$$+ |
| Country Inn & Suites Orlando Universal | 1 | ★★½ | 63 | $$+ |
| The Floridian Hotel & Suites | 1 | ★★½ | 63 | $+ |
| La Quinta Inn Orlando–Universal Studios | 4 | ★★½ | 63 | $$- |
| Orlando Metropolitan Express | 1 | ★★½ | 63 | $+ |
| Avanti Resort Orlando | 1 | ★★½ | 62 | $$$+ |
| Celebration Suites | 3 | ★★½ | 61 | $+ |
| Days Inn Orlando/I-Drive | 1 | ★★½ | 61 | $ |
| Motel 6 Orlando–I-Drive | 1 | ★★½ | 61 | $ |
| Comfort Inn I-Drive | 1 | ★★½ | 60 | $$- |
| Comfort Inn Maingate | 3 | ★★½ | 60 | $$$- |

## How the Hotels Compare *(continued)*

| HOTEL | LODGING AREA | OVERALL QUALITY | ROOM QUALITY | ($ = $50) |
|---|---|---|---|---|
| Continental Plaza Hotel Kissimmee | 3 | ★★½ | 60 | $+ |
| Days Inn Orlando/Convention Center | 1 | ★★½ | 60 | $+ |
| Days Inn Orlando/Universal Maingate | 4 | ★★½ | 60 | $+ |
| Destiny Palms Maingate West | 3 | ★★½ | 60 | $ |
| Royal Celebration Inn | 3 | ★★½ | 60 | $ |
| Super 8 Kissimmee | 3 | ★★½ | 60 | $ |
| Claremont Hotel Kissimmee | 3 | ★★½ | 59 | $– |
| Howard Johnson Inn Orlando I-Drive | 1 | ★★½ | 59 | $ |
| Rodeway Inn Maingate | 3 | ★★½ | 59 | $– |
| Extended Stay Deluxe Pointe Orlando | 1 | ★★½ | 58 | $$– |
| Red Roof Inn Orlando Convention Center | 1 | ★★½ | 58 | $ |
| Knights Inn Maingate Kissimmee/Orlando | 3 | ★★ | 55 | $– |
| Quality Inn & Suites Eastgate | 3 | ★★ | 55 | $ |
| Travelodge Suites East Gate Orange | 3 | ★★ | 55 | $+ |

# Hotel Information Chart

**Avanti Resort Orlando** ★★½
8738 International Dr.
Orlando, FL 32819
☎ 407-313-0100
**avantiresort.com**

| | |
|---|---|
| LOCATION | 1 |
| ROOM RATING | 62 |
| COST ($ = $50) | $$$+ |

Commuting times to parks (*in minutes*):
| | |
|---|---|
| MAGIC KINGDOM | 22:00 |
| EPCOT | 17:15 |
| ANIMAL KINGDOM | 20:15 |
| DHS | 19:45 |

**B Resort** ★★★½
1905 Hotel Plaza Blvd.
Lake Buena Vista, FL 32830
☎ 407-828-2828
**bresortlbv.com**

| | |
|---|---|
| LOCATION | WDW |
| ROOM RATING | 82 |
| COST ($ = $50) | $$$$– |

Commuting times to parks (*in minutes*):
| | |
|---|---|
| MAGIC KINGDOM | 15:45 |
| EPCOT | 11:00 |
| ANIMAL KINGDOM | 15:00 |
| DHS | 12:45 |

**Barefoot'n Resort** ★★★★
2754 Florida Plaza Blvd.
Kissimmee, FL 34746
☎ 407-589-2127
**barefootn.com**

| | |
|---|---|
| LOCATION | 3 |
| ROOM RATING | 85 |
| COST ($ = $50) | $$– |

Commuting times to parks (*in minutes*):
| | |
|---|---|
| MAGIC KINGDOM | 17:00 |
| EPCOT | 14:00 |
| ANIMAL KINGDOM | 14:00 |
| DHS | 12:00 |

**Bay Lake Tower at Disney's Contemporary Resort** ★★★★½
4600 N. World Dr.
Lake Buena Vista, FL 32830
☎ 407-824-1000
**tinyurl.com/baylaketower**

| | |
|---|---|
| LOCATION | WDW |
| ROOM RATING | 95 |
| COST ($ = $50) | $– X 11 |

Commuting times to parks (*in minutes*):
| | |
|---|---|
| MAGIC KINGDOM | ON MONORAIL |
| EPCOT | 11:00 |
| ANIMAL KINGDOM | 17:15 |
| DHS | 14:15 |

**Baymont Inn & Suites Celebration** ★★★
7601 Black Lake Rd.
Kissimmee, FL 34747
☎ 407-396-1100
**tinyurl.com/baymontcelebration**

| | |
|---|---|
| LOCATION | 3 |
| ROOM RATING | 82 |
| COST ($ = $50) | $$– |

Commuting times to parks (*in minutes*):
| | |
|---|---|
| MAGIC KINGDOM | 8:30 |
| EPCOT | 8:15 |
| ANIMAL KINGDOM | 5:30 |
| DHS | 7:45 |

**Best Western I-Drive** ★★★
8222 Jamaican Ct.
Orlando, FL 32819
☎ 407-345-1172
**tinyurl.com/bwidrive**

| | |
|---|---|
| LOCATION | 1 |
| ROOM RATING | 65 |
| COST ($ = $50) | $$+ |

Commuting times to parks (*in minutes*):
| | |
|---|---|
| MAGIC KINGDOM | 8:30 |
| EPCOT | 8:15 |
| ANIMAL KINGDOM | 11:15 |
| DHS | 10:45 |

**Best Western Lake Buena Vista Resort Hotel** ★★★★
2000 Hotel Plaza Blvd.
Lake Buena Vista, FL 32830
☎ 407-828-2424
**lakebuenavistaresorthotel.com**

| | |
|---|---|
| LOCATION | WDW |
| ROOM RATING | 85 |
| COST ($ = $50) | $$$– |

Commuting times to parks (*in minutes*):
| | |
|---|---|
| MAGIC KINGDOM | 16:00 |
| EPCOT | 11:15 |
| ANIMAL KINGDOM | 15:15 |
| DHS | 13:00 |

**Best Western Plus Universal Inn** ★★★½
5618 Vineland Rd.
Orlando, FL 32819
☎ 407-226-9119
**tinyurl.com/bwuniversal**

| | |
|---|---|
| LOCATION | 4 |
| ROOM RATING | 75 |
| COST ($ = $50) | $$ |

Commuting times to parks (*in minutes*):
| | |
|---|---|
| MAGIC KINGDOM | 17:30 |
| EPCOT | 13:00 |
| ANIMAL KINGDOM | 16:00 |
| DHS | 15:30 |

**Best Western Premier Saratoga Resort Villas** ★★★½
4787 W. US 192*
Kissimmee, FL 34746
☎ 407-997-3300
**bestwesternpremier
kissimmee.com**

| | |
|---|---|
| LOCATION | 3 |
| ROOM RATING | 75 |
| COST ($ = $50) | $$$$ |

Commuting times to parks (*in minutes*):
| | |
|---|---|
| MAGIC KINGDOM | 20:00 |
| EPCOT | 15:00 |
| ANIMAL KINGDOM | 16:00 |
| DHS | 12:00 |

**Bohemian Celebration Hotel** ★★★★½
700 Bloom St.
Celebration, FL 34747
☎ 407-566-6000
**celebrationhotel.com**

| | |
|---|---|
| LOCATION | 2 |
| ROOM RATING | 90 |
| COST ($ = $50) | $$$$– |

Commuting times to parks (*in minutes*):
| | |
|---|---|
| MAGIC KINGDOM | 13:30 |
| EPCOT | 13:00 |
| ANIMAL KINGDOM | 13:00 |
| DHS | 12:30 |

**Buena Vista Palace Hotel & Spa** ★★★½
1900 E. Buena Vista Dr.
Lake Buena Vista, FL 32830
☎ 407-827-2727
**buenavistapalace.com**

| | |
|---|---|
| LOCATION | WDW |
| ROOM RATING | 80 |
| COST ($ = $50) | $$$– |

Commuting times to parks (*in minutes*):
| | |
|---|---|
| MAGIC KINGDOM | 16:00 |
| EPCOT | 11:15 |
| ANIMAL KINGDOM | 15:15 |
| DHS | 13:00 |

**Buena Vista Suites** ★★★★
8203 World Center Dr.
Orlando, FL 32821
☎ 407-239-8588
**bvsuites.com**

| | |
|---|---|
| LOCATION | 1 |
| ROOM RATING | 83 |
| COST ($ = $50) | $$$+ |

Commuting times to parks (*in minutes*):
| | |
|---|---|
| MAGIC KINGDOM | 9:15 |
| EPCOT | 4:30 |
| ANIMAL KINGDOM | 7:30 |
| DHS | 8:15 |

*US 192 in Kissimmee is also known locally as Irlo Bronson Memorial Highway.

# Hotel Information Chart *(continued)*

**Caribe Cove Resort Orlando**
★★★★
9000 Treasure Trove Ln.
Kissimmee, FL 34747
☎ 407-997-4444
caribecove.com

| | |
|---|---|
| **LOCATION** | 3 |
| **ROOM RATING** | 85 |
| **COST ($ = $50)** | $$+ |

Commuting times to parks (*in minutes*):

| | |
|---|---|
| **MAGIC KINGDOM** | 23:00 |
| **EPCOT** | 22:00 |
| **ANIMAL KINGDOM** | 13:00 |
| **DHS** | 17:00 |

**Caribe Royale All-Suite Hotel & Convention Center** ★★★★
8101 World Center Dr.
Orlando, FL 32821
☎ 407-238-8000
cariberesorts.com

| | |
|---|---|
| **LOCATION** | 1 |
| **ROOM RATING** | 88 |
| **COST ($ = $50)** | $$$$– |

Commuting times to parks (*in minutes*):

| | |
|---|---|
| **MAGIC KINGDOM** | 9:15 |
| **EPCOT** | 4:45 |
| **ANIMAL KINGDOM** | 7:45 |
| **DHS** | 8:15 |

**Castle Hotel** ★★★½
8629 International Dr.
Orlando, FL 32819
☎ 407-345-1511
castlehotelorlando.com

| | |
|---|---|
| **LOCATION** | 1 |
| **ROOM RATING** | 82 |
| **COST ($ = $50)** | $$$ |

Commuting times to parks (*in minutes*):

| | |
|---|---|
| **MAGIC KINGDOM** | 22:30 |
| **EPCOT** | 17:45 |
| **ANIMAL KINGDOM** | 20:45 |
| **DHS** | 20:15 |

**Clarion Inn & Suites at I-Drive**
★★½
9956 Hawaiian Ct.
Orlando, FL 32819
☎ 407-351-5100
tinyurl.com/clarionidrive

| | |
|---|---|
| **LOCATION** | 1 |
| **ROOM RATING** | 64 |
| **COST ($ = $50)** | $$+ |

Commuting times to parks (*in minutes*):

| | |
|---|---|
| **MAGIC KINGDOM** | 19:30 |
| **EPCOT** | 14:15 |
| **ANIMAL KINGDOM** | 17:15 |
| **DHS** | 16:45 |

**Clarion Inn Lake Buena Vista**
★★½
8442 Palm Pkwy.
Lake Buena Vista, FL 32836
☎ 407-996-7300
clarionlbv.com

| | |
|---|---|
| **LOCATION** | 2 |
| **ROOM RATING** | 64 |
| **COST ($ = $50)** | $$ |

Commuting times to parks (*in minutes*):

| | |
|---|---|
| **MAGIC KINGDOM** | 13:15 |
| **EPCOT** | 8:30 |
| **ANIMAL KINGDOM** | 11:30 |
| **DHS** | 11:00 |

**Clarion Suites Maingate** ★★★½
7888 W. US 192*
Kissimmee, FL 34747
☎ 407-390-9888
clarionsuiteskissimmee.com

| | |
|---|---|
| **LOCATION** | 3 |
| **ROOM RATING** | 76 |
| **COST ($ = $50)** | $$ |

Commuting times to parks (*in minutes*):

| | |
|---|---|
| **MAGIC KINGDOM** | 10:00 |
| **EPCOT** | 9:15 |
| **ANIMAL KINGDOM** | 7:00 |
| **DHS** | 9:00 |

**Comfort Inn Orlando– Lake Buena Vista** ★★★½
8686 Palm Pkwy.
Orlando, FL 32836
☎ 407-239-8400
tinyurl.com/comfortinnlbv

| | |
|---|---|
| **LOCATION** | 2 |
| **ROOM RATING** | 80 |
| **COST ($ = $50)** | $$ |

Commuting times to parks (*in minutes*):

| | |
|---|---|
| **MAGIC KINGDOM** | 14:15 |
| **EPCOT** | 9:45 |
| **ANIMAL KINGDOM** | 12:45 |
| **DHS** | 12:15 |

**Comfort Suites Universal** ★★★
5617 Major Blvd.
Orlando, FL 32819
☎ 407-363-1967
tinyurl.com/csuniversal

| | |
|---|---|
| **LOCATION** | 4 |
| **ROOM RATING** | 70 |
| **COST ($ = $50)** | $$ |

Commuting times to parks (*in minutes*):

| | |
|---|---|
| **MAGIC KINGDOM** | 17:45 |
| **EPCOT** | 13:15 |
| **ANIMAL KINGDOM** | 16:15 |
| **DHS** | 15:15 |

**Continental Plaza Hotel Kissimmee**
★★½
7785 W. US 192*
Kissimmee, FL 34747
☎ 407-396-1828
continentalplazahotels.com

| | |
|---|---|
| **LOCATION** | 3 |
| **ROOM RATING** | 60 |
| **COST ($ = $50)** | $+ |

Commuting times to parks (*in minutes*):

| | |
|---|---|
| **MAGIC KINGDOM** | 9:15 |
| **EPCOT** | 8:45 |
| **ANIMAL KINGDOM** | 6:30 |
| **DHS** | 8:30 |

**Courtyard Orlando LBV in Marriott Village** ★★★½
8623 Vineland Ave.
Orlando, FL 32821
☎ 407-938-9001
tinyurl.com/courtyardlbv
marriottvillage

| | |
|---|---|
| **LOCATION** | 2 |
| **ROOM RATING** | 82 |
| **COST ($ = $50)** | $$$– |

Commuting times to parks (*in minutes*):

| | |
|---|---|
| **MAGIC KINGDOM** | 12:00 |
| **EPCOT** | 7:15 |
| **ANIMAL KINGDOM** | 10:15 |
| **DHS** | 9:45 |

**Crown Club Inn** ★★★
105 Summer Bay Blvd.
Clermont, FL 34711
☎ 407-239-8315
crownclubinn.com

| | |
|---|---|
| **LOCATION** | 3 |
| **ROOM RATING** | 70 |
| **COST ($ = $50)** | $$ |

Commuting times to parks (*in minutes*):

| | |
|---|---|
| **MAGIC KINGDOM** | 14:00 |
| **EPCOT** | 9:15 |
| **ANIMAL KINGDOM** | 11:30 |
| **DHS** | 13:15 |

**Crowne Plaza Orlando– Lake Buena Vista** ★★★½
12490 S. Apopka–Vineland Rd.
Orlando, FL 32836
☎ 407-239-4646
tinyurl.com/crowneplazalbv

| | |
|---|---|
| **LOCATION** | 2 |
| **ROOM RATING** | 82 |
| **COST ($ = $50)** | $$$$– |

Commuting times to parks (*in minutes*):

| | |
|---|---|
| **MAGIC KINGDOM** | 13:00 |
| **EPCOT** | 8:30 |
| **ANIMAL KINGDOM** | 11:30 |
| **DHS** | 11:00 |

*US 192 in Kissimmee is also known locally as Irlo Bronson Memorial Highway.

### Celebration Suites ★★½
5820 W. US 192*
Kissimmee, FL 34746
☎ 407-396-7900
suitesatoldtown.com

| | |
|---|---|
| LOCATION | 3 |
| ROOM RATING | 61 |
| COST ($ = $50) | $+ |

Commuting times to parks (*in minutes*):
| | |
|---|---|
| MAGIC KINGDOM | 11:15 |
| EPCOT | 11:00 |
| ANIMAL KINGDOM | 9:15 |
| DHS | 10:30 |

### Champions World Resort ★★★
8660 W. US 192*
Kissimmee, FL 34747
☎ 407-396-4500
championsworldresort.com

| | |
|---|---|
| LOCATION | 3 |
| ROOM RATING | 66 |
| COST ($ = $50) | $+ |

Commuting times to parks (*in minutes*):
| | |
|---|---|
| MAGIC KINGDOM | 13:45 |
| EPCOT | 13:45 |
| ANIMAL KINGDOM | 10:45 |
| DHS | 13:00 |

### Claremont Hotel Kissimmee ★★½
6051 W. US 192*
Kissimmee, FL 34747
☎ 407-396-1748
claremontkissimmee.com

| | |
|---|---|
| LOCATION | 3 |
| ROOM RATING | 59 |
| COST ($ = $50) | $-N |

Commuting times to parks (*in minutes*):
| | |
|---|---|
| MAGIC KINGDOM | 11:15 |
| EPCOT | 11:00 |
| ANIMAL KINGDOM | 8:15 |
| DHS | 10:30 |

### CoCo Key Water Resort–Orlando ★★★★½
7400 International Dr.
Orlando, FL 32819
☎ 407-351-2626
cocokeywaterresort.com

| | |
|---|---|
| LOCATION | 1 |
| ROOM RATING | 90 |
| COST ($ = $50) | $$$– |

Commuting times to parks (*in minutes*):
| | |
|---|---|
| MAGIC KINGDOM | 21:00 |
| EPCOT | 16:30 |
| ANIMAL KINGDOM | 19:00 |
| DHS | 19:30 |

### Comfort Inn I-Drive ★★½
8134 International Dr.
Orlando, FL 32819
☎ 407-313-4000
tinyurl.com/comfortidrive

| | |
|---|---|
| LOCATION | 1 |
| ROOM RATING | 60 |
| COST ($ = $50) | $$– |

Commuting times to parks (*in minutes*):
| | |
|---|---|
| MAGIC KINGDOM | 20:00 |
| EPCOT | 15:30 |
| ANIMAL KINGDOM | 18:30 |
| DHS | 18:00 |

### Comfort Inn Maingate ★★½
7675 W. US 192*
Kissimmee, FL 34747
☎ 407-396-4000
comfortinnkissimmee.com

| | |
|---|---|
| LOCATION | 3 |
| ROOM RATING | 60 |
| COST ($ = $50) | $$$– |

Commuting times to parks (*in minutes*):
| | |
|---|---|
| MAGIC KINGDOM | 8:30 |
| EPCOT | 8:00 |
| ANIMAL KINGDOM | 5:30 |
| DHS | 7:30 |

### Country Inn & Suites Orlando Universal ★★½
7701 Universal Blvd.
Orlando, FL 32819
☎ 407-313-4200
countryinns.com/orlandofl_universal

| | |
|---|---|
| LOCATION | 1 |
| ROOM RATING | 63 |
| COST ($ = $50) | $$+ |

Commuting times to parks (*in minutes*):
| | |
|---|---|
| MAGIC KINGDOM | 21:00 |
| EPCOT | 16:15 |
| ANIMAL KINGDOM | 19:15 |
| DHS | 18:45 |

### Courtyard Orlando I-Drive ★★★½
8600 Austrian Ct.
Orlando, FL 32819
☎ 407-351-2244
tinyurl.com/courtyardidrive

| | |
|---|---|
| LOCATION | 1 |
| ROOM RATING | 78 |
| COST ($ = $50) | $$$$– |

Commuting times to parks (*in minutes*):
| | |
|---|---|
| MAGIC KINGDOM | 21:45 |
| EPCOT | 17:00 |
| ANIMAL KINGDOM | 20:00 |
| DHS | 19:30 |

### Courtyard Orlando Lake Buena Vista at Vista Centre ★★★★
8501 Palm Pkwy.
Lake Buena Vista, FL 32836
☎ 407-239-6900
tinyurl.com/courtyardlbv

| | |
|---|---|
| LOCATION | 2 |
| ROOM RATING | 89 |
| COST ($ = $50) | $$$– |

Commuting times to parks (*in minutes*):
| | |
|---|---|
| MAGIC KINGDOM | 13:15 |
| EPCOT | 8:30 |
| ANIMAL KINGDOM | 11:30 |
| DHS | 11:00 |

### Days Inn Orlando/Convention Center ★★½
9990 International Dr.
Orlando, FL 32819
☎ 407-352-8700
daysinnorlandohotel.com

| | |
|---|---|
| LOCATION | 1 |
| ROOM RATING | 60 |
| COST ($ = $50) | $+ |

Commuting times to parks (*in minutes*):
| | |
|---|---|
| MAGIC KINGDOM | 18:45 |
| EPCOT | 14:00 |
| ANIMAL KINGDOM | 17:00 |
| DHS | 16:30 |

### Days Inn Orlando/I-Drive ★★½
5858 International Dr.
Orlando, FL 32819
☎ 407-351-4410
tinyurl.com/daysinnidrive

| | |
|---|---|
| LOCATION | 1 |
| ROOM RATING | 61 |
| COST ($ = $50) | $ |

Commuting times to parks (*in minutes*):
| | |
|---|---|
| MAGIC KINGDOM | 20:30 |
| EPCOT | 16:00 |
| ANIMAL KINGDOM | 19:00 |
| DHS | 18:30 |

### Days Inn Orlando/Universal Maingate ★★½
5827 Caravan Ct.
Orlando, FL 32819
☎ 407-351-3800
tinyurl.com/daysinnuniversal

| | |
|---|---|
| LOCATION | 4 |
| ROOM RATING | 60 |
| COST ($ = $50) | $+ |

Commuting times to parks (*in minutes*):
| | |
|---|---|
| MAGIC KINGDOM | 18:45 |
| EPCOT | 14:00 |
| ANIMAL KINGDOM | 17:00 |
| DHS | 16:30 |

# Hotel Information Chart (*continued*)

### Destiny Palms Maingate West
★★½
8536 W. US 192*
Kissimmee, FL 34747
☎ 407-396-1600
destinypalmshotel.com

| LOCATION | 3 |
| ROOM RATING | 60 |
| COST ($ = $50) | $ |

Commuting times to parks (*in minutes*):
| MAGIC KINGDOM | 13:45 |
| EPCOT | 13:15 |
| ANIMAL KINGDOM | 11:00 |
| DHS | 13:00 |

### Disney's All-Star Movies Resort
★★★
1701–1901 W. Buena Vista Dr.
Lake Buena Vista, FL 32830
☎ 407-934-7639
tinyurl.com/allstarmovies

| LOCATION | WDW |
| ROOM RATING | 73 |
| COST ($ = $50) | $$$– |

Commuting times to parks (*in minutes*):
| MAGIC KINGDOM | 6:15 |
| EPCOT | 5:45 |
| ANIMAL KINGDOM | 4:15 |
| DHS | 5:15 |

### Disney's All-Star Music Resort
★★★
1701–1901 W. Buena Vista Dr.
Lake Buena Vista, FL 32830
☎ 407-934-7639
tinyurl.com/allstarmusicresort

| LOCATION | WDW |
| ROOM RATING | 73 |
| COST ($ = $50) | $$$– |

Commuting times to parks (*in minutes*):
| MAGIC KINGDOM | 6:15 |
| EPCOT | 5:45 |
| ANIMAL KINGDOM | 4:15 |
| DHS | 5:15 |

### Disney's Animal Kingdom Villas (Kidani Village) ★★★★½
2901 Osceola Pkwy.
Lake Buena Vista, FL 32830
☎ 407-938-3000
tinyurl.com/akkidani

| LOCATION | WDW |
| ROOM RATING | 95 |
| COST ($ = $50) | $– X 9 |

Commuting times to parks (*in minutes*):
| MAGIC KINGDOM | 8:15 |
| EPCOT | 6:15 |
| ANIMAL KINGDOM | 2:15 |
| DHS | 6:00 |

### Disney's Art of Animation Resort
★★★½
1850 Animation Way
Lake Buena Vista, FL 32830
☎ 407-938-7000
tinyurl.com/artofanimationresort

| LOCATION | WDW |
| ROOM RATING | 80 |
| COST ($ = $50) | $$$ |

Commuting times to parks (*in minutes*):
| MAGIC KINGDOM | 12:00 |
| EPCOT | 10:00 |
| ANIMAL KINGDOM | 12:00 |
| DHS | 3:00 |

### Disney's Beach Club Resort
★★★★½
1800 Epcot Resorts Blvd.
Lake Buena Vista, FL 32830
☎ 407-934-8000
tinyurl.com/beachclubresort

| LOCATION | WDW |
| ROOM RATING | 90 |
| COST ($ = $50) | $+ X 9 |

Commuting times to parks (*in minutes*):
| MAGIC KINGDOM | 7:15 |
| EPCOT | 5:15 |
| ANIMAL KINGDOM | 6:45 |
| DHS | 4:00 |

### Disney's Caribbean Beach Resort
★★★½
900 Cayman Way
Lake Buena Vista, FL 32830
☎ 407-934-3400
tinyurl.com/caribbeanbeachresort

| LOCATION | WDW |
| ROOM RATING | 80 |
| COST ($ = $50) | $$$$+ |

Commuting times to parks (*in minutes*):
| MAGIC KINGDOM | 8:00 |
| EPCOT | 6:00 |
| ANIMAL KINGDOM | 7:15 |
| DHS | 4:15 |

### Disney's Contemporary Resort
★★★★½
4600 N. World Dr.
Lake Buena Vista, FL 32830
☎ 407-824-1000
tinyurl.com/contemporarywdw

| LOCATION | WDW |
| ROOM RATING | 93 |
| COST ($ = $50) | $+ X 8 |

Commuting times to parks (*in minutes*):
| MAGIC KINGDOM | ON MONORAIL |
| EPCOT | 11:00 |
| ANIMAL KINGDOM | 17:15 |
| DHS | 14:15 |

### Disney's Coronado Springs Resort
★★★★
1000 W. Buena Vista Dr.
Orlando, FL 32830
☎ 407-939-1000
tinyurl.com/coronadosprings

| LOCATION | WDW |
| ROOM RATING | 83 |
| COST ($ = $50) | $$$$+ |

Commuting times to parks (*in minutes*):
| MAGIC KINGDOM | 5:30 |
| EPCOT | 4:00 |
| ANIMAL KINGDOM | 4:45 |
| DHS | 4:45 |

### Disney's Polynesian Resort
★★★★½
1600 Seven Seas Dr.
Lake Buena Vista, FL 32830
☎ 407-824-2000
tinyurl.com/polynesianresort

| LOCATION | WDW |
| ROOM RATING | 92 |
| COST ($ = $50) | $– X 11 |

Commuting times to parks (*in minutes*):
| MAGIC KINGDOM | 12:00 |
| EPCOT | 8:00 |
| ANIMAL KINGDOM | 16:15 |
| DHS | 12:30 |

### Disney's Pop Century Resort
★★★
1050 Century Dr.
Lake Buena Vista, FL 32830
☎ 407-938-4000
tinyurl.com/popcenturywdw

| LOCATION | WDW |
| ROOM RATING | 71 |
| COST ($ = $50) | $$$– |

Commuting times to parks (*in minutes*):
| MAGIC KINGDOM | 8:30 |
| EPCOT | 6:30 |
| ANIMAL KINGDOM | 6:15 |
| DHS | 5:00 |

### Disney's Port Orleans Resort–French Quarter ★★★★
2201 Orleans Dr.
Lake Buena Vista, FL 32830
☎ 407-934-5000
tinyurl.com/portorleansfq

| LOCATION | WDW |
| ROOM RATING | 84 |
| COST ($ = $50) | $$$$+ |

Commuting times to parks (*in minutes*):
| MAGIC KINGDOM | 12:00 |
| EPCOT | 8:00 |
| ANIMAL KINGDOM | 16:15 |
| DHS | 12:30 |

*US 192 in Kissimmee is also known locally as Irlo Bronson Memorial Highway.

## Disney's All-Star Sports Resort
★★★
1701–1901 W. Buena Vista Dr.
Lake Buena Vista, FL 32830
☎ 407-934-7639
tinyurl.com/allstarsports

| | |
|---|---|
| **LOCATION** | WDW |
| **ROOM RATING** | 73 |
| **COST ($ = $50)** | $$$– |

Commuting times to parks (*in minutes*):

| | |
|---|---|
| **MAGIC KINGDOM** | 6:15 |
| **EPCOT** | 5:45 |
| **ANIMAL KINGDOM** | 4:15 |
| **DHS** | 5:15 |

## Disney's Animal Kingdom Lodge
★★★★
2901 Osceola Pkwy.
Lake Buena Vista, FL 32830
☎ 407-938-3000
tinyurl.com/aklodge

| | |
|---|---|
| **LOCATION** | WDW |
| **ROOM RATING** | 89 |
| **COST ($ = $50)** | $– X 9 |

Commuting times to parks (*in minutes*):

| | |
|---|---|
| **MAGIC KINGDOM** | 8:15 |
| **EPCOT** | 6:15 |
| **ANIMAL KINGDOM** | 2:15 |
| **DHS** | 6:00 |

## Disney's Animal Kingdom Villas
(Jambo House)  ★★★★½
2901 Osceola Pkwy.
Lake Buena Vista, FL 32830
☎ 407-938-3000
tinyurl.com/akjambo

| | |
|---|---|
| **LOCATION** | WDW |
| **ROOM RATING** | 91 |
| **COST ($ = $50)** | $+ X 6 |

Commuting times to parks (*in minutes*):

| | |
|---|---|
| **MAGIC KINGDOM** | 8:15 |
| **EPCOT** | 6:15 |
| **ANIMAL KINGDOM** | 2:15 |
| **DHS** | 6:00 |

## Disney's Beach Club Villas
★★★★½
1900 Epcot Resorts Blvd.
Lake Buena Vista, FL 32830
☎ 407-934-2175
tinyurl.com/beachclubvillas

| | |
|---|---|
| **LOCATION** | WDW |
| **ROOM RATING** | 90 |
| **COST ($ = $50)** | $– X 9 |

Commuting times to parks (*in minutes*):

| | |
|---|---|
| **MAGIC KINGDOM** | 7:15 |
| **EPCOT** | 5:15 |
| **ANIMAL KINGDOM** | 6:45 |
| **DHS** | 4:00 |

## Disney's BoardWalk Inn  ★★★★
2101 N. Epcot Resorts Blvd.
Lake Buena Vista, FL 32830
☎ 407-939-5100
tinyurl.com/boardwalkinn

| | |
|---|---|
| **LOCATION** | WDW |
| **ROOM RATING** | 89 |
| **COST ($ = $50)** | $+ X 9 |

Commuting times to parks (*in minutes*):

| | |
|---|---|
| **MAGIC KINGDOM** | 7:15 |
| **EPCOT** | 5:30 |
| **ANIMAL KINGDOM** | 7:00 |
| **DHS** | 3:00 |

## Disney's BoardWalk Villas
★★★★½
2101 N. Epcot Resorts Blvd.
Lake Buena Vista, FL 32830
☎ 407-939-5100
tinyurl.com/boardwalkvillas

| | |
|---|---|
| **LOCATION** | WDW |
| **ROOM RATING** | 90 |
| **COST ($ = $50)** | $– X 12 |

Commuting times to parks (*in minutes*):

| | |
|---|---|
| **MAGIC KINGDOM** | 7:15 |
| **EPCOT** | 5:30 |
| **ANIMAL KINGDOM** | 7:00 |
| **DHS** | 3:00 |

## Disney's Fort Wilderness Resort
(cabins)  ★★★★
4510 N. Fort Wilderness Trail
Lake Buena Vista, FL 32830
☎ 407-824-2837
tinyurl.com/ftwilderness

| | |
|---|---|
| **LOCATION** | WDW |
| **ROOM RATING** | 86 |
| **COST ($ = $50)** | $– X 8 |

Commuting times to parks (*in minutes*):

| | |
|---|---|
| **MAGIC KINGDOM** | 13:15 |
| **EPCOT** | 8:30 |
| **ANIMAL KINGDOM** | 20:00 |
| **DHS** | 14:00 |

## Disney's Grand Floridian
Resort & Spa  ★★★★½
4401 Floridian Way
Lake Buena Vista, FL 32830
☎ 407-824-3000
tinyurl.com/grandflresort

| | |
|---|---|
| **LOCATION** | WDW |
| **ROOM RATING** | 93 |
| **COST ($ = $50)** | $– X 12 |

Commuting times to parks (*in minutes*):

| | |
|---|---|
| **MAGIC KINGDOM** | ON MONORAIL |
| **EPCOT** | 4:45 |
| **ANIMAL KINGDOM** | 11:45 |
| **DHS** | 6:45 |

## Disney's Old Key West Resort
★★★★½
1510 North Cove Rd.
Lake Buena Vista, FL 32830
☎ 407-827-7700
tinyurl.com/oldkeywest

| | |
|---|---|
| **LOCATION** | WDW |
| **ROOM RATING** | 90 |
| **COST ($ = $50)** | $– X 8 |

Commuting times to parks (*in minutes*):

| | |
|---|---|
| **MAGIC KINGDOM** | 10:45 |
| **EPCOT** | 6:00 |
| **ANIMAL KINGDOM** | 14:30 |
| **DHS** | 10:30 |

## Disney's Port Orleans Resort–
Riverside  ★★★★
1251 Riverside Dr.
Lake Buena Vista, FL 32830
☎ 407-934-6000
tinyurl.com/portorleansriverside

| | |
|---|---|
| **LOCATION** | WDW |
| **ROOM RATING** | 83 |
| **COST ($ = $50)** | $– X 5 |

Commuting times to parks (*in minutes*):

| | |
|---|---|
| **MAGIC KINGDOM** | 12:00 |
| **EPCOT** | 8:00 |
| **ANIMAL KINGDOM** | 16:15 |
| **DHS** | 12:30 |

## Disney's Saratoga Springs
Resort & Spa  ★★★★½
1960 Broadway
Lake Buena Vista, FL 32830
☎ 407-827-1100
tinyurl.com/saratogawdw

| | |
|---|---|
| **LOCATION** | WDW |
| **ROOM RATING** | 90 |
| **COST ($ = $50)** | $– X 8 |

Commuting times to parks (*in minutes*):

| | |
|---|---|
| **MAGIC KINGDOM** | 14:45 |
| **EPCOT** | 8:45 |
| **ANIMAL KINGDOM** | 18:15 |
| **DHS** | 14:30 |

## Disney's Wilderness Lodge**
★★★★
901 Timberline Dr.
Lake Buena Vista, FL 32830
☎ 407-824-3200
tinyurl.com/wildernesslodge

| | |
|---|---|
| **LOCATION** | WDW |
| **ROOM RATING** | 86 |
| **COST ($ = $50)** | $– X 8 |

Commuting times to parks (*in minutes*):

| | |
|---|---|
| **MAGIC KINGDOM** | N/A |
| **EPCOT** | 10:00 |
| **ANIMAL KINGDOM** | 15:15 |
| **DHS** | 13:30 |

**Primary transportation to Wilderness Lodge and Wilderness Lodge Villas is by ferry rather than by car.

## Hotel Information Chart (*continued*)

**Disney's Yacht Club Resort**
★★★★
1700 Epcot Resorts Blvd.
Lake Buena Vista, FL 32830
☎ 407-934-7000
tinyurl.com/yachtclubwdw

| | |
|---|---|
| LOCATION | WDW |
| ROOM RATING | 89 |
| COST ($ = $50) | $+ X 9 |

Commuting times to parks (*in minutes*):

| | |
|---|---|
| MAGIC KINGDOM | 7:15 |
| EPCOT | 5:15 |
| ANIMAL KINGDOM | 6:45 |
| DHS | 4:00 |

**DoubleTree by Hilton Orlando at SeaWorld (resort)** ★★★★½
10100 International Dr.
Orlando, FL 32821
☎ 407-352-1100
doubletreeorlandoidrive.com

| | |
|---|---|
| LOCATION | 1 |
| ROOM RATING | 92 |
| COST ($ = $50) | $$$+ |

Commuting times to parks (*in minutes*):

| | |
|---|---|
| MAGIC KINGDOM | 17:45 |
| EPCOT | 13:00 |
| ANIMAL KINGDOM | 16:00 |
| DHS | 15:30 |

**DoubleTree by Hilton Orlando at SeaWorld (tower)** ★★★★½
10100 International Dr.
Orlando, FL 32821
☎ 407-352-1100
doubletreeorlandoidrive.com

| | |
|---|---|
| LOCATION | 1 |
| ROOM RATING | 92 |
| COST ($ = $50) | $$$+ |

Commuting times to parks (*in minutes*):

| | |
|---|---|
| MAGIC KINGDOM | 17:45 |
| EPCOT | 13:00 |
| ANIMAL KINGDOM | 16:00 |
| DHS | 15:30 |

**Embassy Suites Orlando I-Drive/ Jamaican Court** ★★★½
8250 Jamaican Ct.
Orlando, FL 32819
☎ 407-345-8250
orlandoembassysuites.com

| | |
|---|---|
| LOCATION | 1 |
| ROOM RATING | 80 |
| COST ($ = $50) | $$+ |

Commuting times to parks (*in minutes*):

| | |
|---|---|
| MAGIC KINGDOM | 20:15 |
| EPCOT | 15:30 |
| ANIMAL KINGDOM | 18:30 |
| DHS | 18:00 |

**Embassy Suites Orlando– Lake Buena Vista** ★★★½
8100 Lake Ave.
Orlando, FL 32836
☎ 407-239-1144
embassysuiteslbv.com

| | |
|---|---|
| LOCATION | 2 |
| ROOM RATING | 81 |
| COST ($ = $50) | $$$– |

Commuting times to parks (*in minutes*):

| | |
|---|---|
| MAGIC KINGDOM | 12:45 |
| EPCOT | 8:00 |
| ANIMAL KINGDOM | 11:00 |
| DHS | 10:30 |

**The Enclave Hotel & Suites** ★★★
6165 Carrier Dr.
Orlando, FL 32819
☎ 407-351-1155
enclavesuites.com

| | |
|---|---|
| LOCATION | 1 |
| ROOM RATING | 67 |
| COST ($ = $50) | $$$– |

Commuting times to parks (*in minutes*):

| | |
|---|---|
| MAGIC KINGDOM | 20:45 |
| EPCOT | 16:15 |
| ANIMAL KINGDOM | 19:15 |
| DHS | 18:45 |

**Extended Stay Deluxe Orlando Lake Buena Vista** ★★★★
8100 Palm Pkwy.
Orlando 32836
☎ 407-239-4300
tinyurl.com/esdlbv

| | |
|---|---|
| LOCATION | 2 |
| ROOM RATING | 83 |
| COST ($ = $50) | $$ |

Commuting times to parks (*in minutes*):

| | |
|---|---|
| MAGIC KINGDOM | 13:45 |
| EPCOT | 9:00 |
| ANIMAL KINGDOM | 12:00 |
| DHS | 11:30 |

**Extended Stay Deluxe Orlando Universal** ★★★½
5610 Vineland Rd.
Orlando, FL 32819
☎ 407-370-4428
tinyurl.com/esduniversal

| | |
|---|---|
| LOCATION | 4 |
| ROOM RATING | 75 |
| COST ($ = $50) | $$– |

Commuting times to parks (*in minutes*):

| | |
|---|---|
| MAGIC KINGDOM | 18:00 |
| EPCOT | 14:15 |
| ANIMAL KINGDOM | 18:00 |
| DHS | 16:00 |

**Extended Stay Deluxe Pointe Orlando** ★★½
8750 Universal Blvd.
Orlando, FL 32819
☎ 407-903-1500
tinyurl.com/esdpointe

| | |
|---|---|
| LOCATION | 1 |
| ROOM RATING | 58 |
| COST ($ = $50) | $$– |

Commuting times to parks (*in minutes*):

| | |
|---|---|
| MAGIC KINGDOM | 17:45 |
| EPCOT | 13:00 |
| ANIMAL KINGDOM | 17:00 |
| DHS | 15:30 |

**Fairfield Inn & Suites Orlando Lake Buena Vista (suites)** ★★★½
12191 S. Apopka–Vineland Rd.
Lake Buena Vista, FL 32836
☎ 407-239-1115
tinyurl.com/fairfieldlbv

| | |
|---|---|
| LOCATION | 2 |
| ROOM RATING | 78 |
| COST ($ = $50) | $$$+ |

Commuting times to parks (*in minutes*):

| | |
|---|---|
| MAGIC KINGDOM | 14:00 |
| EPCOT | 9:15 |
| ANIMAL KINGDOM | 12:15 |
| DHS | 11:45 |

**Fairfield Inn & Suites Orlando LBV in Marriott Village** ★★★½
8615 Vineland Ave.
Orlando, FL 32821
☎ 407-938-9001
tinyurl.com/fairfieldlbv
marriottvillage

| | |
|---|---|
| LOCATION | 2 |
| ROOM RATING | 75 |
| COST ($ = $50) | $$$ |

Commuting times to parks (*in minutes*):

| | |
|---|---|
| MAGIC KINGDOM | 12:00 |
| EPCOT | 7:15 |
| ANIMAL KINGDOM | 10:15 |
| DHS | 9:45 |

**Floridays Resort Orlando**
★★★★
12562 International Dr.
Orlando, FL 32821
☎ 407-238-7700
floridaysresortorlando.com

| | |
|---|---|
| LOCATION | 1 |
| ROOM RATING | 86 |
| COST ($ = $50) | $– X 7 |

Commuting times to parks (*in minutes*):

| | |
|---|---|
| MAGIC KINGDOM | 14:30 |
| EPCOT | 9:45 |
| ANIMAL KINGDOM | 12:45 |
| DHS | 12:15 |

### DoubleTree Guest Suites ★★★
2305 Hotel Plaza Blvd.
Lake Buena Vista, FL 32830
☎ 407-934-1000
doubletreeguestsuites.com

| | |
|---|---|
| **LOCATION** | WDW |
| **ROOM RATING** | 71 |
| **COST ($ = $50)** | $$$$- |

Commuting times to parks (*in minutes*):

| | |
|---|---|
| **MAGIC KINGDOM** | 13:00 |
| **EPCOT** | 8:30 |
| **ANIMAL KINGDOM** | 12:30 |
| **DHS** | 10:00 |

### DoubleTree Universal ★★★★
5780 Major Blvd.
Orlando, FL 32819
☎ 407-351-1000
doubletreeorlando.com

| | |
|---|---|
| **LOCATION** | 4 |
| **ROOM RATING** | 89 |
| **COST ($ = $50)** | $$+ |

Commuting times to parks (*in minutes*):

| | |
|---|---|
| **MAGIC KINGDOM** | 19:00 |
| **EPCOT** | 14:15 |
| **ANIMAL KINGDOM** | 17:15 |
| **DHS** | 16:45 |

### Embassy Suites Orlando I-Drive
★★★½
8978 International Dr.
Orlando, FL 32819
☎ 407-352-1400
embassysuitesorlando.com

| | |
|---|---|
| **LOCATION** | 1 |
| **ROOM RATING** | 75 |
| **COST ($ = $50)** | $$+ |

Commuting times to parks (*in minutes*):

| | |
|---|---|
| **MAGIC KINGDOM** | 22:00 |
| **EPCOT** | 17:15 |
| **ANIMAL KINGDOM** | 20:15 |
| **DHS** | 19:45 |

### Extended Stay America Convention Center/Westwood ★★★★
6443 Westwood Blvd.
Orlando, FL 32821
☎ 407-351-1982
tinyurl.com/extendedstay
westwood

| | |
|---|---|
| **LOCATION** | 1 |
| **ROOM RATING** | 84 |
| **COST ($ = $50)** | $$ |

Commuting times to parks (*in minutes*):

| | |
|---|---|
| **MAGIC KINGDOM** | 17:30 |
| **EPCOT** | 12:45 |
| **ANIMAL KINGDOM** | 15:45 |
| **DHS** | 15:30 |

### Extended Stay America Orlando Convention Center ★★★
6451 Westwood Blvd.
Orlando, FL 32821
☎ 407-352-3454
tinyurl.com/extendedstayorlando

| | |
|---|---|
| **LOCATION** | 1 |
| **ROOM RATING** | 72 |
| **COST ($ = $50)** | $$- |

Commuting times to parks (*in minutes*):

| | |
|---|---|
| **MAGIC KINGDOM** | 17:30 |
| **EPCOT** | 12:45 |
| **ANIMAL KINGDOM** | 15:45 |
| **DHS** | 15:30 |

### Extended Stay America Universal ★★★½
5620 Major Blvd.
Orlando, FL 32819
☎ 407-351-1788
tinyurl.com/esuniversal

| | |
|---|---|
| **LOCATION** | 4 |
| **ROOM RATING** | 75 |
| **COST ($ = $50)** | $$- |

Commuting times to parks (*in minutes*):

| | |
|---|---|
| **MAGIC KINGDOM** | 18:00 |
| **EPCOT** | 14:15 |
| **ANIMAL KINGDOM** | 18:00 |
| **DHS** | 16:00 |

### Fairfield Inn & Suites Near Universal Orlando Resort ★★★½
5614 Vineland Rd.
Orlando, FL 32819
☎ 407-581-5600
tinyurl.com/fairfielduniversal

| | |
|---|---|
| **LOCATION** | 4 |
| **ROOM RATING** | 80 |
| **COST ($ = $50)** | $$$+ |

Commuting times to parks (*in minutes*):

| | |
|---|---|
| **MAGIC KINGDOM** | 17:30 |
| **EPCOT** | 12:45 |
| **ANIMAL KINGDOM** | 15:45 |
| **DHS** | 15:15 |

### Fairfield Inn & Suites Orlando I-Drive/Convention Center ★★★
8214 Universal Blvd.
Orlando, FL 32819
☎ 407-581-9001
tinyurl.com/fairfieldocc

| | |
|---|---|
| **LOCATION** | 1 |
| **ROOM RATING** | 74 |
| **COST ($ = $50)** | $$$$ |

Commuting times to parks (*in minutes*):

| | |
|---|---|
| **MAGIC KINGDOM** | 23:00 |
| **EPCOT** | 18:15 |
| **ANIMAL KINGDOM** | 21:15 |
| **DHS** | 20:45 |

### Fairfield Inn & Suites Orlando Lake Buena Vista (rooms) ★★★½
12191 S. Apopka-Vineland Rd.
Lake Buena Vista, FL 32836
☎ 407-239-1115
tinyurl.com/fairfieldlbv

| | |
|---|---|
| **LOCATION** | 2 |
| **ROOM RATING** | 78 |
| **COST ($ = $50)** | $$$+ |

Commuting times to parks (*in minutes*):

| | |
|---|---|
| **MAGIC KINGDOM** | 14:00 |
| **EPCOT** | 9:15 |
| **ANIMAL KINGDOM** | 12:15 |
| **DHS** | 11:45 |

### The Floridian Hotel & Suites
★★½
7531 Canada Ave.
Orlando, FL 32819
☎ 407-202-3021
thefloridianhotel.com

| | |
|---|---|
| **LOCATION** | 1 |
| **ROOM RATING** | 63 |
| **COST ($ = $50)** | $+ |

Commuting times to parks (*in minutes*):

| | |
|---|---|
| **MAGIC KINGDOM** | 20:15 |
| **EPCOT** | 15:45 |
| **ANIMAL KINGDOM** | 18:45 |
| **DHS** | 18:15 |

### Four Points by Sheraton Orlando Studio City ★★★★½
5905 International Dr.
Orlando, FL 32819
☎ 407-351-2100
fourpointsorlandostudiocity.com

| | |
|---|---|
| **LOCATION** | 1 |
| **ROOM RATING** | 90 |
| **COST ($ = $50)** | $$$- |

Commuting times to parks (*in minutes*):

| | |
|---|---|
| **MAGIC KINGDOM** | 20:30 |
| **EPCOT** | 15:45 |
| **ANIMAL KINGDOM** | 18:45 |
| **DHS** | 18:15 |

### Galleria Palms Kissimmee Hotel
★★★
3000 Maingate Ln.
Kissimmee, FL 34747
☎ 407-396-6300
galleriapalmsorlando.com

| | |
|---|---|
| **LOCATION** | 3 |
| **ROOM RATING** | 74 |
| **COST ($ = $50)** | $$- |

Commuting times to parks (*in minutes*):

| | |
|---|---|
| **MAGIC KINGDOM** | 8:15 |
| **EPCOT** | 7:30 |
| **ANIMAL KINGDOM** | 5:15 |
| **DHS** | 7:15 |

## Hotel Information Chart (*continued*)

**Gaylord Palms Resort & Convention Center** ★★★★½
6000 W. Osceola Pkwy.
Kissimmee, FL 34746
☎ 407-586-0000
gaylordpalms.com

| | |
|---|---|
| LOCATION | 3 |
| ROOM RATING | 94 |
| COST ($ = $50) | $– × 6 |

Commuting times to parks (*in minutes*):

| | |
|---|---|
| MAGIC KINGDOM | 9:00 |
| EPCOT | 8:45 |
| ANIMAL KINGDOM | 7:00 |
| DHS | 8:15 |

**Grand Beach** ★★★★½
8317 Lake Bryan Beach Blvd.
Orlando, FL 32821
☎ 407-238-2500
diamondresorts.com /grand-beach

| | |
|---|---|
| LOCATION | 1 |
| ROOM RATING | 90 |
| COST ($ = $50) | $ × 6 |

Commuting times to parks (*in minutes*):

| | |
|---|---|
| MAGIC KINGDOM | 17:00 |
| EPCOT | 11:00 |
| ANIMAL KINGDOM | 18:00 |
| DHS | 12:00 |

**Grand Lake Resort** ★★★½
7770 W. US 192*
Kissimmee, FL 34747
☎ 407-396-3000
dailymanagementresorts.com

| | |
|---|---|
| LOCATION | 1 |
| ROOM RATING | 76 |
| COST ($ = $50) | $$– |

Commuting times to parks (*in minutes*):

| | |
|---|---|
| MAGIC KINGDOM | 9:15 |
| EPCOT | 8:30 |
| ANIMAL KINGDOM | 6:15 |
| DHS | 8:30 |

**Hampton Inn South of Universal** ★★½
7110 S. Kirkman Rd.
Orlando, FL 32819
☎ 407-345-1112
tinyurl.com/hamptonkirkman

| | |
|---|---|
| LOCATION | 1 |
| ROOM RATING | 64 |
| COST ($ = $50) | $$+ |

Commuting times to parks (*in minutes*):

| | |
|---|---|
| MAGIC KINGDOM | 21:15 |
| EPCOT | 16:45 |
| ANIMAL KINGDOM | 19:45 |
| DHS | 19:15 |

**Hampton Inn Universal** ★★★
5621 Windhover Dr.
Orlando, FL 32819
☎ 407-351-6716
tinyurl.com/hamptonuniversal

| | |
|---|---|
| LOCATION | 4 |
| ROOM RATING | 67 |
| COST ($ = $50) | $$$– |

Commuting times to parks (*in minutes*):

| | |
|---|---|
| MAGIC KINGDOM | 19:00 |
| EPCOT | 14:15 |
| ANIMAL KINGDOM | 17:15 |
| DHS | 16:45 |

**Hawthorn Suites Lake Buena Vista** ★★★★
8303 Palm Pkwy.
Orlando, FL 32836
☎ 407-597-5000
hawthornlakebuenavista.com

| | |
|---|---|
| LOCATION | 2 |
| ROOM RATING | 87 |
| COST ($ = $50) | $$+ |

Commuting times to parks (*in minutes*):

| | |
|---|---|
| MAGIC KINGDOM | 20:15 |
| EPCOT | 15:30 |
| ANIMAL KINGDOM | 18:30 |
| DHS | 18:00 |

**Hilton Garden Inn Orlando at SeaWorld** ★★★½
6850 Westwood Blvd.
Orlando, FL 32821
☎ 407-354-1500
tinyurl.com/hgiseaworld

| | |
|---|---|
| LOCATION | 1 |
| ROOM RATING | 80 |
| COST ($ = $50) | $$$ |

Commuting times to parks (*in minutes*):

| | |
|---|---|
| MAGIC KINGDOM | 15:30 |
| EPCOT | 11:00 |
| ANIMAL KINGDOM | 14:00 |
| DHS | 13:30 |

**Hilton Garden Inn Orlando I-Drive North** ★★★½
5877 American Way
Orlando, FL 32819
☎ 407-363-9332
hiltongardenorlando.com

| | |
|---|---|
| LOCATION | 1 |
| ROOM RATING | 80 |
| COST ($ = $50) | $$ |

Commuting times to parks (*in minutes*):

| | |
|---|---|
| MAGIC KINGDOM | 21:15 |
| EPCOT | 16:30 |
| ANIMAL KINGDOM | 19:30 |
| DHS | 19:00 |

**Hilton Grand Vacations Club at SeaWorld** ★★★★½
6924 Grand Vacations Way
Orlando, FL 32821
☎ 407-239-0100
tinyurl.com/hgvseaworld

| | |
|---|---|
| LOCATION | 1 |
| ROOM RATING | 95 |
| COST ($ = $50) | $$$– |

Commuting times to parks (*in minutes*):

| | |
|---|---|
| MAGIC KINGDOM | 17:00 |
| EPCOT | 12:30 |
| ANIMAL KINGDOM | 16:30 |
| DHS | 15:30 |

**Hilton Orlando Bonnet Creek** ★★★★
14100 Bonnet Creek Resort Ln.
Orlando, FL 32821
☎ 407-597-3600
hiltonbonnetcreek.com

| | |
|---|---|
| LOCATION | 1 |
| ROOM RATING | 88 |
| COST ($ = $50) | $$$– |

Commuting times to parks (*in minutes*):

| | |
|---|---|
| MAGIC KINGDOM | 8:00 |
| EPCOT | 6:00 |
| ANIMAL KINGDOM | 7:15 |
| DHS | 4:15 |

**Holiday Inn & Suites Orlando Universal** ★★★½
5905 Kirkman Rd.
Orlando, FL 32819
☎ 407-351-3333
hiuniversal.com

| | |
|---|---|
| LOCATION | 4 |
| ROOM RATING | 75 |
| COST ($ = $50) | $$$ |

Commuting times to parks (*in minutes*):

| | |
|---|---|
| MAGIC KINGDOM | 19:00 |
| EPCOT | 14:15 |
| ANIMAL KINGDOM | 17:15 |
| DHS | 16:45 |

**Holiday Inn in the Walt Disney World Resort** ★★★½
1805 Hotel Plaza Blvd.
Lake Buena Vista, FL 32830
☎ 407-828-8888
hiorlando.com

| | |
|---|---|
| LOCATION | WDW |
| ROOM RATING | 79 |
| COST ($ = $50) | $$$– |

Commuting times to parks (*in minutes*):

| | |
|---|---|
| MAGIC KINGDOM | 15:30 |
| EPCOT | 10:45 |
| ANIMAL KINGDOM | 12:30 |
| DHS | 14:45 |

*US 192 in Kissimmee is also known locally as Irlo Bronson Memorial Highway.

## Hampton Inn & Suites Orlando–South Lake Buena Vista ★★★½
4971 Calypso Cay Way
Kissimmee, FL 34746
☎ 407-452-3126
tinyurl.com/hamptonsouthlbv

| | |
|---|---|
| LOCATION | 3 |
| ROOM RATING | 80 |
| COST ($ = $50) | $$ |

Commuting times to parks (in minutes):
| | |
|---|---|
| MAGIC KINGDOM | 21:00 |
| EPCOT | 15:00 |
| ANIMAL KINGDOM | 17:00 |
| DHS | 15:00 |

## Hampton Inn I-Drive/Convention Center ★★★
8900 Universal Blvd.
Orlando, FL 32819
☎ 407-354-4447
tinyurl.com/hamptonocc

| | |
|---|---|
| LOCATION | 1 |
| ROOM RATING | 70 |
| COST ($ = $50) | $$$ |

Commuting times to parks (in minutes):
| | |
|---|---|
| MAGIC KINGDOM | 21:30 |
| EPCOT | 17:00 |
| ANIMAL KINGDOM | 20:00 |
| DHS | 19:30 |

## Hampton Inn Orlando/Lake Buena Vista ★★★½
8150 Palm Pkwy.
Orlando, FL 32836
☎ 407-465-8150
tinyurl.com/hamptonlbv

| | |
|---|---|
| LOCATION | 2 |
| ROOM RATING | 76 |
| COST ($ = $50) | $$ |

Commuting times to parks (in minutes):
| | |
|---|---|
| MAGIC KINGDOM | 12:45 |
| EPCOT | 8:00 |
| ANIMAL KINGDOM | 11:00 |
| DHS | 10:30 |

## Hawthorn Suites Orlando Convention Center ★★★½
6435 Westwood Blvd.
Orlando, FL 32821
☎ 407-351-6600
hawthornsuitesorlando.com

| | |
|---|---|
| LOCATION | 1 |
| ROOM RATING | 80 |
| COST ($ = $50) | $$– |

Commuting times to parks (in minutes):
| | |
|---|---|
| MAGIC KINGDOM | 17:30 |
| EPCOT | 12:45 |
| ANIMAL KINGDOM | 15:45 |
| DHS | 15:30 |

## Hawthorn Suites Orlando I-Drive ★★★½
7975 Canada Ave.
Orlando, FL 32819
☎ 407-345-0117
tinyurl.com/hawthornidrive

| | |
|---|---|
| LOCATION | 1 |
| ROOM RATING | 75 |
| COST ($ = $50) | $$+ |

Commuting times to parks (in minutes):
| | |
|---|---|
| MAGIC KINGDOM | 20:00 |
| EPCOT | 15:15 |
| ANIMAL KINGDOM | 18:15 |
| DHS | 17:45 |

## Hilton Garden Inn Lake Buena Vista/Orlando ★★★★
11400 Marbella Palm Ct.
Orlando, FL 32836
☎ 407-239-9550
tinyurl.com/hgilakebuenavista

| | |
|---|---|
| LOCATION | 2 |
| ROOM RATING | 88 |
| COST ($ = $50) | $$$– |

Commuting times to parks (in minutes):
| | |
|---|---|
| MAGIC KINGDOM | 18:00 |
| EPCOT | 12:00 |
| ANIMAL KINGDOM | 18:00 |
| DHS | 14:00 |

## Hilton Grand Vacations Club on I-Drive ★★★★
8122 Arrezzo Way
Orlando, FL 32821
☎ 407-465-2600
tinyurl.com/hgvidrive

| | |
|---|---|
| LOCATION | 1 |
| ROOM RATING | 88 |
| COST ($ = $50) | $– X 6 |

Commuting times to parks (in minutes):
| | |
|---|---|
| MAGIC KINGDOM | 16:15 |
| EPCOT | 14:00 |
| ANIMAL KINGDOM | 17:00 |
| DHS | 16:30 |

## Hilton in the Walt Disney World Resort ★★★★
1751 Hotel Plaza Blvd.
Lake Buena Vista, FL 32830
☎ 407-827-4000
hilton-wdwv.com

| | |
|---|---|
| LOCATION | WDW |
| ROOM RATING | 87 |
| COST ($ = $50) | $$$+ |

Commuting times to parks (in minutes):
| | |
|---|---|
| MAGIC KINGDOM | 15:15 |
| EPCOT | 10:30 |
| ANIMAL KINGDOM | 14:30 |
| DHS | 12:15 |

## Hilton Orlando ★★★★½
6001 Destination Pkwy.
Orlando, FL 32819
☎ 407-313-4300
thehiltonorlando.com

| | |
|---|---|
| LOCATION | 1 |
| ROOM RATING | 92 |
| COST ($ = $50) | $$$$+ |

Commuting times to parks (in minutes):
| | |
|---|---|
| MAGIC KINGDOM | 20:00 |
| EPCOT | 14:00 |
| ANIMAL KINGDOM | 20:00 |
| DHS | 16:00 |

## Holiday Inn Main Gate East ★★★★½
5711 W. US 192*
Kissimmee, FL 34746
☎ 407-396-4222
holidayinnmge.com

| | |
|---|---|
| LOCATION | 3 |
| ROOM RATING | 90 |
| COST ($ = $50) | $$+ |

Commuting times to parks (in minutes):
| | |
|---|---|
| MAGIC KINGDOM | 12:15 |
| EPCOT | 12:00 |
| ANIMAL KINGDOM | 10:15 |
| DHS | 11:30 |

## Holiday Inn Resort Lake Buena Vista ★★★½
13351 FL 535
Orlando, FL 32821
☎ 407-239-4500
hiresortlbv.com

| | |
|---|---|
| LOCATION | 2 |
| ROOM RATING | 82 |
| COST ($ = $50) | $$$ |

Commuting times to parks (in minutes):
| | |
|---|---|
| MAGIC KINGDOM | 10:45 |
| EPCOT | 6:00 |
| ANIMAL KINGDOM | 9:00 |
| DHS | 8:30 |

## Homewood Suites by Hilton I-Drive ★★★½
8745 International Dr.
Orlando, FL 32819
☎ 407-248-2232
homewoodsuitesorlando.com

| | |
|---|---|
| LOCATION | 1 |
| ROOM RATING | 81 |
| COST ($ = $50) | $$$+ |

Commuting times to parks (in minutes):
| | |
|---|---|
| MAGIC KINGDOM | 21:45 |
| EPCOT | 17:00 |
| ANIMAL KINGDOM | 20:00 |
| DHS | 19:30 |

# Hotel Information Chart (*continued*)

**Homewood Suites by Hilton LBV-Orlando** ★★★★
11428 Marbella Palm Ct.
Orlando, FL 32836
☎ 407-239-4540
tinyurl.com/homewoodsuiteslbv

| LOCATION | 2 |
| ROOM RATING | 85 |
| COST ($ = $50) | $$$+ |

Commuting times to parks (*in minutes*):
| MAGIC KINGDOM | 18:00 |
| EPCOT | 12:00 |
| ANIMAL KINGDOM | 18:00 |
| DHS | 14:00 |

**Howard Johnson Inn Orlando I-Drive** ★★½
6603 International Dr.
Orlando, FL 32819
☎ 407-351-2900
tinyurl.com/hojoidrive

| LOCATION | 1 |
| ROOM RATING | 59 |
| COST ($ = $50) | $ |

Commuting times to parks (*in minutes*):
| MAGIC KINGDOM | 21:00 |
| EPCOT | 16:30 |
| ANIMAL KINGDOM | 19:30 |
| DHS | 19:00 |

**Hyatt Place Orlando/Universal** ★★★★
5895 Caravan Ct.
Orlando, FL 32819
☎ 407-351-0627
orlandouniversal.place.hyatt.com

| LOCATION | 4 |
| ROOM RATING | 84 |
| COST ($ = $50) | $$$+ |

Commuting times to parks (*in minutes*):
| MAGIC KINGDOM | 19:00 |
| EPCOT | 14:15 |
| ANIMAL KINGDOM | 17:45 |
| DHS | 16:45 |

**International Palms Resort & Conference Center** ★★★
6515 International Dr.
Orlando, FL 32819
☎ 407-351-3500
internationalpalms.com

| LOCATION | 1 |
| ROOM RATING | 73 |
| COST ($ = $50) | $$ |

Commuting times to parks (*in minutes*):
| MAGIC KINGDOM | 21:15 |
| EPCOT | 16:45 |
| ANIMAL KINGDOM | 19:45 |
| DHS | 19:15 |

**JW Marriott Orlando Grande Lakes** ★★★★½
4040 Central Florida Pkwy.
Orlando, FL 32837
☎ 407-206-2300
jw-marriott.grandelakes.com

| LOCATION | 1 |
| ROOM RATING | 93 |
| COST ($ = $50) | $- X 6 |

Commuting times to parks (*in minutes*):
| MAGIC KINGDOM | 23:00 |
| EPCOT | 18:15 |
| ANIMAL KINGDOM | 21:30 |
| DHS | 20:45 |

**Knights Inn Maingate Kissimmee/Orlando** ★★
7475 W. US 192*
Kissimmee, FL 34747
☎ 407-396-4200
tinyurl.com/knightsinnmgk

| LOCATION | 3 |
| ROOM RATING | 55 |
| COST ($ = $50) | $- |

Commuting times to parks (*in minutes*):
| MAGIC KINGDOM | 8:15 |
| EPCOT | 7:45 |
| ANIMAL KINGDOM | 5:45 |
| DHS | 7:30 |

**Legacy Vacation Club Orlando** ★★★½
2800 N. Poinciana Blvd.
Kissimmee, FL 34746
☎ 407-997-5000
legacyvacationresorts.com

| LOCATION | 3 |
| ROOM RATING | 80 |
| COST ($ = $50) | $$$+ |

Commuting times to parks (*in minutes*):
| MAGIC KINGDOM | 16:30 |
| EPCOT | 16:15 |
| ANIMAL KINGDOM | 14:30 |
| DHS | 15:30 |

**Lighthouse Key Resort & Spa** ★★★★½
8545 W. US 192*
Kissimmee, FL 34747
☎ 321-329-7000
lighthousekeyresort.com

| LOCATION | 3 |
| ROOM RATING | 90 |
| COST ($ = $50) | $- X 5 |

Commuting times to parks (*in minutes*):
| MAGIC KINGDOM | 20:00 |
| EPCOT | 21:00 |
| ANIMAL KINGDOM | 16:00 |
| DHS | 16:00 |

**Liki Tiki Village** ★★★★½
17777 Bali Blvd.
Winter Garden, FL 34787
☎ 407-239-5000
likitiki.com

| LOCATION | 3 |
| ROOM RATING | 90 |
| COST ($ = $50) | $$$$- |

Commuting times to parks (*in minutes*):
| MAGIC KINGDOM | 9:00 |
| EPCOT | 8:45 |
| ANIMAL KINGDOM | 5:15 |
| DHS | 8:15 |

**Marriott's Harbour Lake** ★★★★½
7102 Grand Horizons Blvd.
Orlando, FL 32821
☎ 407-465-6100
tinyurl.com/harbourlake

| LOCATION | 2 |
| ROOM RATING | 90 |
| COST ($ = $50) | $$$$- |

Commuting times to parks (*in minutes*):
| MAGIC KINGDOM | 18:00 |
| EPCOT | 13:30 |
| ANIMAL KINGDOM | 18:00 |
| DHS | 16:30 |

**Marriott's Imperial Palms** ★★★★
8404 Vacation Way
Orlando, FL 32821
☎ 407-238-6200
tinyurl.com/imperialpalmvillas

| LOCATION | 1 |
| ROOM RATING | 86 |
| COST ($ = $50) | $- X 9 |

Commuting times to parks (*in minutes*):
| MAGIC KINGDOM | 9:45 |
| EPCOT | 5:00 |
| ANIMAL KINGDOM | 8:00 |
| DHS | 7:30 |

**Marriott's Royal Palms** ★★★★
8404 Vacation Way
Orlando, FL 32821
☎ 407-238-6200
tinyurl.com/marriottsroyalpalms

| LOCATION | 1 |
| ROOM RATING | 85 |
| COST ($ = $50) | $+ X 5 |

Commuting times to parks (*in minutes*):
| MAGIC KINGDOM | 9:45 |
| EPCOT | 5:00 |
| ANIMAL KINGDOM | 8:00 |
| DHS | 7:30 |

*US 192 in Kissimmee is also known locally as Irlo Bronson Memorial Highway.

**Hyatt Regency Grand Cypress**
★★★★½
1 Grand Cypress Blvd.
Orlando, FL 32836
☎ 407-239-1234
grandcypress.hyatt.com

| LOCATION | 2 |
| ROOM RATING | 92 |
| COST ($ = $50) | $- X 5 |

Commuting times to parks (in minutes):
| MAGIC KINGDOM | 13:30 |
| EPCOT | 8:45 |
| ANIMAL KINGDOM | 11:45 |
| DHS | 11:15 |

---

**Hyatt Regency Orlando**
★★★★½
9801 International Dr.
Orlando, FL 32819
☎ 407-284-1234
orlando.regency.hyatt.com

| LOCATION | 1 |
| ROOM RATING | 90 |
| COST ($ = $50) | $- X 6 |

Commuting times to parks (in minutes):
| MAGIC KINGDOM | 19:30 |
| EPCOT | 15:15 |
| ANIMAL KINGDOM | 18:15 |
| DHS | 17:45 |

---

**Inn at Calypso** ★★★½
5001 Calypso Cay Way
Kissimmee, FL 34746
☎ 407-997-1400
calypsocay.com/the-inn.php

| LOCATION | 3 |
| ROOM RATING | 82 |
| COST ($ = $50) | $$+ |

Commuting times to parks (in minutes):
| MAGIC KINGDOM | 13:30 |
| EPCOT | 13:00 |
| ANIMAL KINGDOM | 11:30 |
| DHS | 12:30 |

---

**La Quinta Inn Orlando I-Drive**
★★★
8300 Jamaican Ct.
Orlando, FL 32819
☎ 407-351-1660
tinyurl.com/lqidrive

| LOCATION | 1 |
| ROOM RATING | 73 |
| COST ($ = $50) | $+ |

Commuting times to parks (in minutes):
| MAGIC KINGDOM | 21:45 |
| EPCOT | 17:15 |
| ANIMAL KINGDOM | 20:15 |
| DHS | 19:45 |

---

**La Quinta Inn Orlando–**
**Universal Studios** ★★½
5621 Major Blvd.
Orlando, FL 32819
☎ 407-313-3100
tinyurl.com/lquniversal

| LOCATION | 4 |
| ROOM RATING | 63 |
| COST ($ = $50) | $$- |

Commuting times to parks (in minutes):
| MAGIC KINGDOM | 18:00 |
| EPCOT | 13:15 |
| ANIMAL KINGDOM | 16:15 |
| DHS | 16:00 |

---

**Legacy Vacation Club**
**Lake Buena Vista** ★★★★
8451 Palm Pkwy.
Lake Buena Vista, FL 32836
☎ 407-238-1700
legacyvacationresorts.com

| LOCATION | 2 |
| ROOM RATING | 85 |
| COST ($ = $50) | $$$$- |

Commuting times to parks (in minutes):
| MAGIC KINGDOM | 13:15 |
| EPCOT | 8:30 |
| ANIMAL KINGDOM | 11:30 |
| DHS | 11:00 |

---

**Maingate Lakeside Resort** ★★★
7769 W. US 192*
Kissimmee, FL 34747
☎ 407-396-2222
maingatelakesideresort.com

| LOCATION | 3 |
| ROOM RATING | 67 |
| COST ($ = $50) | $+ |

Commuting times to parks (in minutes):
| MAGIC KINGDOM | 9:15 |
| EPCOT | 8:30 |
| ANIMAL KINGDOM | 6:30 |
| DHS | 8:30 |

---

**Marriott's Cypress Harbour**
★★★★
11251 Harbour Villa Rd.
Orlando, FL 32821
☎ 407-238-1300
tinyurl.com/cypressharbourvillas

| LOCATION | 1 |
| ROOM RATING | 86 |
| COST ($ = $50) | $- X 6 |

Commuting times to parks (in minutes):
| MAGIC KINGDOM | 17:45 |
| EPCOT | 13:15 |
| ANIMAL KINGDOM | 17:45 |
| DHS | 16:15 |

---

**Marriott's Grande Vista**
★★★★½
5925 Avenida Vista
Orlando, FL 32821
☎ 407-238-7676
tinyurl.com/marriottsgrandevista

| LOCATION | 1 |
| ROOM RATING | 92 |
| COST ($ = $50) | $$$+ |

Commuting times to parks (in minutes):
| MAGIC KINGDOM | 15:00 |
| EPCOT | 12:45 |
| ANIMAL KINGDOM | 15:45 |
| DHS | 15:15 |

---

**Marriott's Sabal Palms** ★★★★½
8805 World Center Dr.
Orlando, FL 32821
☎ 407-238-6200
tinyurl.com/marriottssabalpalms

| LOCATION | 2 |
| ROOM RATING | 92 |
| COST ($ = $50) | $+ X 5 |

Commuting times to parks (in minutes):
| MAGIC KINGDOM | 15:00 |
| EPCOT | 9:00 |
| ANIMAL KINGDOM | 16:00 |
| DHS | 10:00 |

---

**Monumental Hotel** ★★★★½
12120 International Dr.
Orlando, FL 32821
☎ 407-239-1222
monumentalhotelorlandofl.com

| LOCATION | 1 |
| ROOM RATING | 94 |
| COST ($ = $50) | $$ |

Commuting times to parks (in minutes):
| MAGIC KINGDOM | 14:45 |
| EPCOT | 10:00 |
| ANIMAL KINGDOM | 13:00 |
| DHS | 12:30 |

---

**Monumental MovieLand Hotel**
★★★
6233 International Dr.
Orlando, FL 32819
☎ 407-351-3900
monumentalmovielandhotel.com

| LOCATION | 1 |
| ROOM RATING | 68 |
| COST ($ = $50) | $ |

Commuting times to parks (in minutes):
| MAGIC KINGDOM | 20:30 |
| EPCOT | 15:45 |
| ANIMAL KINGDOM | 18:45 |
| DHS | 18:15 |

# Hotel Information Chart (*continued*)

**Motel 6 Orlando–I-Drive** ★★½
5909 American Way
Orlando, FL 32819
☎ 407-351-6500
tinyurl.com/motel6idrive

| LOCATION | 1 |
| ROOM RATING | 61 |
| COST ($ = $50) | $ |

Commuting times to parks (*in minutes*):
| MAGIC KINGDOM | 20:15 |
| EPCOT | 16:00 |
| ANIMAL KINGDOM | 19:00 |
| DHS | 18:30 |

**Mystic Dunes Resort & Golf Club**
★★★★
7600 Mystic Dunes Ln.
Kissimmee, FL 34747
☎ 407-396-1311
mystic-dunes-resort.com

| LOCATION | 3 |
| ROOM RATING | 87 |
| COST ($ = $50) | $$$$– |

Commuting times to parks (*in minutes*):
| MAGIC KINGDOM | 10:45 |
| EPCOT | 10:30 |
| ANIMAL KINGDOM | 7:45 |
| DHS | 10:00 |

**Nickelodeon Suites Resort**
★★★½
14500 Continental Gateway
Orlando, FL 32821
☎ 407-387-5437
nickhotel.com

| LOCATION | 1 |
| ROOM RATING | 82 |
| COST ($ = $50) | $$$– |

Commuting times to parks (*in minutes*):
| MAGIC KINGDOM | 9:45 |
| EPCOT | 5:00 |
| ANIMAL KINGDOM | 8:00 |
| DHS | 7:30 |

**Orlando Metropolitan Express**
★★½
6323 International Dr.
Orlando, FL 32819
☎ 407-351-4430
orlandometropolitanexpress.com

| LOCATION | 1 |
| ROOM RATING | 63 |
| COST ($ = $50) | $+ |

Commuting times to parks (*in minutes*):
| MAGIC KINGDOM | 20:45 |
| EPCOT | 16:00 |
| ANIMAL KINGDOM | 19:00 |
| DHS | 18:30 |

**Orlando World Center**
**Marriott Resort** ★★★★
8701 World Center Dr.
Orlando, FL 32821
☎ 407-239-4200
marriottworldcenter.com

| LOCATION | 2 |
| ROOM RATING | 89 |
| COST ($ = $50) | $– X 5 |

Commuting times to parks (*in minutes*):
| MAGIC KINGDOM | 9:45 |
| EPCOT | 5:00 |
| ANIMAL KINGDOM | 8:00 |
| DHS | 7:30 |

**Palms Hotel & Villas** ★★★½
3100 Parkway Blvd.
Kissimmee, FL 34747
☎ 407-396-2229
thepalmshotelandvillas.com

| LOCATION | 3 |
| ROOM RATING | 76 |
| COST ($ = $50) | $$$$– |

Commuting times to parks (*in minutes*):
| MAGIC KINGDOM | 8:30 |
| EPCOT | 8:15 |
| ANIMAL KINGDOM | 6:30 |
| DHS | 7:45 |

**Polynesian Isles Resort**
**(Diamond Resorts)** ★★★★½
3045 Polynesian Isles Blvd.
Kissimmee, FL 34746
☎ 407-396-1622
polynesianisle.com

| LOCATION | 3 |
| ROOM RATING | 90 |
| COST ($ = $50) | $$$$ |

Commuting times to parks (*in minutes*):
| MAGIC KINGDOM | 14:30 |
| EPCOT | 14:15 |
| ANIMAL KINGDOM | 12:30 |
| DHS | 14:00 |

**Quality Inn & Suites Eastgate** ★★
4960 W. US 192*
Kissimmee, FL 34746
☎ 407-396-1376
tinyurl.com/qieastgate

| LOCATION | 3 |
| ROOM RATING | 55 |
| COST ($ = $50) | $ |

Commuting times to parks (*in minutes*):
| MAGIC KINGDOM | 15:45 |
| EPCOT | 15:30 |
| ANIMAL KINGDOM | 13:45 |
| DHS | 14:45 |

**Quality Inn Universal Studios**
**I-Drive Area** ★★★
6101 Sand Lake Rd.
Orlando, FL 32919
☎ 407-363-7886
tinyurl.com/qualityuniversal

| LOCATION | 1 |
| ROOM RATING | 66 |
| COST ($ = $50) | $+ |

Commuting times to parks (*in minutes*):
| MAGIC KINGDOM | 22:15 |
| EPCOT | 17:30 |
| ANIMAL KINGDOM | 20:30 |
| DHS | 20:00 |

**Radisson Hotel Orlando**
**Lake Buena Vista** ★★★½
12799 Apopka-Vineland Rd.
Orlando, FL 32836
☎ 407-597-3400
tinyurl.com/radissonlbv

| LOCATION | 2 |
| ROOM RATING | 82 |
| COST ($ = $50) | $$$$+ |

Commuting times to parks (*in minutes*):
| MAGIC KINGDOM | 13:45 |
| EPCOT | 9:00 |
| ANIMAL KINGDOM | 12:00 |
| DHS | 11:30 |

**Radisson Resort Orlando–**
**Celebration** ★★★★
2900 Parkway Blvd.
Kissimmee, FL 34747
☎ 407-396-7000
tinyurl.com/radissonoc

| LOCATION | 3 |
| ROOM RATING | 86 |
| COST ($ = $50) | $$ |

Commuting times to parks (*in minutes*):
| MAGIC KINGDOM | 8:30 |
| EPCOT | 8:00 |
| ANIMAL KINGDOM | 6:30 |
| DHS | 7:45 |

**Ramada Convention Center I-Drive**
★★★
8342 Jamaican Ct.
Orlando, FL 32819
☎ 407-363-1944
tinyurl.com/ramadaidrive

| LOCATION | 1 |
| ROOM RATING | 65 |
| COST ($ = $50) | $$– |

Commuting times to parks (*in minutes*):
| MAGIC KINGDOM | 20:15 |
| EPCOT | 15:30 |
| ANIMAL KINGDOM | 18:30 |
| DHS | 18:00 |

*US 192 in Kissimmee is also known locally as Irlo Bronson Memorial Highway.

## Omni Orlando Resort at ChampionsGate ★★★★★
1500 Masters Blvd.
ChampionsGate, FL 33896
☎ 407-390-6664
tinyurl.com/omnichampionsgate

| | |
|---|---|
| LOCATION | 2 |
| ROOM RATING | 96 |
| COST ($ = $50) | $- X 5 |

Commuting times to parks (*in minutes*):
| | |
|---|---|
| MAGIC KINGDOM | 15:30 |
| EPCOT | 15:00 |
| ANIMAL KINGDOM | 15:00 |
| DHS | 14:30 |

## Orange Lake Resort ★★★★½
8505 W. US 192*
Kissimmee, FL 34747
☎ 407-239-0000
tinyurl.com/orangelakeresort orlando

| | |
|---|---|
| LOCATION | 3 |
| ROOM RATING | 93 |
| COST ($ = $50) | $$$+ |

Commuting times to parks (*in minutes*):
| | |
|---|---|
| MAGIC KINGDOM | 8:45 |
| EPCOT | 8:30 |
| ANIMAL KINGDOM | 5:30 |
| DHS | 8:00 |

## Orbit One Vacation Villas ★★★½
2950 Entry Point Blvd.
Kissimmee, FL 34741
☎ 407-396-1300
tinyurl.com/orbitonevillas

| | |
|---|---|
| LOCATION | 3 |
| ROOM RATING | 80 |
| COST ($ = $50) | $$$+ |

Commuting times to parks (*in minutes*):
| | |
|---|---|
| MAGIC KINGDOM | 15:00 |
| EPCOT | 14:00 |
| ANIMAL KINGDOM | 7:00 |
| DHS | 9:00 |

## Park Inn by Radisson Resort and Conference Center ★★★½
3011 Maingate Ln.
Kissimmee, FL 34747
☎ 407-396-1400
parkinn.com/hotel-orlando

| | |
|---|---|
| LOCATION | 3 |
| ROOM RATING | 77 |
| COST ($ = $50) | $$ |

Commuting times to parks (*in minutes*):
| | |
|---|---|
| MAGIC KINGDOM | 8:15 |
| EPCOT | 7:45 |
| ANIMAL KINGDOM | 5:45 |
| DHS | 7:45 |

## Parkway International Resort ★★★½
6200 Safari Trail
Kissimmee, FL 34746
☎ 407-396-6600
parkwayresort.com

| | |
|---|---|
| LOCATION | 3 |
| ROOM RATING | 82 |
| COST ($ = $50) | $$$$- |

Commuting times to parks (*in minutes*):
| | |
|---|---|
| MAGIC KINGDOM | 8:30 |
| EPCOT | 8:15 |
| ANIMAL KINGDOM | 6:15 |
| DHS | 7:45 |

## The Point Orlando Resort ★★★½
7389 Universal Blvd.
Orlando, FL 32819
☎ 407-956-2000
thepointorlando.com

| | |
|---|---|
| LOCATION | 1 |
| ROOM RATING | 82 |
| COST ($ = $50) | $$$- |

Commuting times to parks (*in minutes*):
| | |
|---|---|
| MAGIC KINGDOM | 23:00 |
| EPCOT | 17:00 |
| ANIMAL KINGDOM | 23:00 |
| DHS | 19:00 |

## Quality Suites Lake Buena Vista ★★★
8200 Palm Pkwy.
Orlando, FL 32836
☎ 407-465-8200
qualitysuiteslbv.com

| | |
|---|---|
| LOCATION | 2 |
| ROOM RATING | 74 |
| COST ($ = $50) | $$$- |

Commuting times to parks (*in minutes*):
| | |
|---|---|
| MAGIC KINGDOM | 13:45 |
| EPCOT | 9:15 |
| ANIMAL KINGDOM | 12:15 |
| DHS | 11:45 |

## Quality Suites Royale Parc Suites ★★★½
5876 W. US 192*
Kissimmee, FL 34746
☎ 407-396-8040
royaleparcsuitesorlando.com

| | |
|---|---|
| LOCATION | 3 |
| ROOM RATING | 75 |
| COST ($ = $50) | $$$- |

Commuting times to parks (*in minutes*):
| | |
|---|---|
| MAGIC KINGDOM | 11:15 |
| EPCOT | 11:00 |
| ANIMAL KINGDOM | 9:15 |
| DHS | 10:30 |

## Quality Suites Turkey Lake ★★★
9350 Turkey Lake Rd.
Orlando, FL 32819
☎ 407-351-5050
qualitysuites-lbv.com

| | |
|---|---|
| LOCATION | 2 |
| ROOM RATING | 74 |
| COST ($ = $50) | $$- |

Commuting times to parks (*in minutes*):
| | |
|---|---|
| MAGIC KINGDOM | 20:45 |
| EPCOT | 16:00 |
| ANIMAL KINGDOM | 19:00 |
| DHS | 18:30 |

## Ramada Gateway Kissimmee (garden) ★★½
7470 W. US 192*
Kissimmee, FL 34747
☎ 407-396-4400
tinyurl.com/ramadakiss

| | |
|---|---|
| LOCATION | 3 |
| ROOM RATING | 64 |
| COST ($ = $50) | $+ |

Commuting times to parks (*in minutes*):
| | |
|---|---|
| MAGIC KINGDOM | 8:15 |
| EPCOT | 8:00 |
| ANIMAL KINGDOM | 6:00 |
| DHS | 7:45 |

## Ramada Gateway Kissimmee (tower) ★★★
7470 W. US 192*
Kissimmee, FL 34747
☎ 407-396-4400
tinyurl.com/ramadakiss

| | |
|---|---|
| LOCATION | 3 |
| ROOM RATING | 71 |
| COST ($ = $50) | $+ |

Commuting times to parks (*in minutes*):
| | |
|---|---|
| MAGIC KINGDOM | 8:15 |
| EPCOT | 8:00 |
| ANIMAL KINGDOM | 6:00 |
| DHS | 7:45 |

## Ramada Maingate West Kissimmee ★★★
7491 W. US 192*
Kissimmee, FL 34747
☎ 407-396-6000
tinyurl.com/ramadamgw

| | |
|---|---|
| LOCATION | 3 |
| ROOM RATING | 65 |
| COST ($ = $50) | $$ |

Commuting times to parks (*in minutes*):
| | |
|---|---|
| MAGIC KINGDOM | 8:15 |
| EPCOT | 7:30 |
| ANIMAL KINGDOM | 5:00 |
| DHS | 7:15 |

# Hotel Information Chart (*continued*)

## Ramada Plaza Resort and Suites Orlando I-Drive ★★★
6500 International Dr.
Orlando, FL 32819
☎ 407-345-5340
tinyurl.com/ramadaplazaidrive

| LOCATION | 1 |
| ROOM RATING | 72 |
| COST ($ = $50) | $$+ |

Commuting times to parks (*in minutes*):

| MAGIC KINGDOM | 21:30 |
| EPCOT | 16:45 |
| ANIMAL KINGDOM | 19:45 |
| DHS | 19:15 |

## Red Roof Inn Orlando Convention Center ★★½
9922 Hawaiian Ct.
Orlando, FL 32819
☎ 407-352-1507
tinyurl.com/redroofkiss

| LOCATION | 1 |
| ROOM RATING | 58 |
| COST ($ = $50) | $ |

Commuting times to parks (*in minutes*):

| MAGIC KINGDOM | 19:00 |
| EPCOT | 14:15 |
| ANIMAL KINGDOM | 17:15 |
| DHS | 16:45 |

## Renaissance Orlando at SeaWorld ★★★★½
6677 Sea Harbor Dr.
Orlando, FL 32821
☎ 407-351-5555
tinyurl.com/renorlandoseaworld

| LOCATION | 1 |
| ROOM RATING | 93 |
| COST ($ = $50) | $$$ |

Commuting times to parks (*in minutes*):

| MAGIC KINGDOM | 16:45 |
| EPCOT | 12:15 |
| ANIMAL KINGDOM | 15:15 |
| DHS | 14:45 |

## The Ritz-Carlton Orlando, Grande Lakes ★★★★½
4012 Central Florida Pkwy.
Orlando, FL 32837
☎ 407-206-2400
grandelakes.com

| LOCATION | 1 |
| ROOM RATING | 94 |
| COST ($ = $50) | $+ X 6 |

Commuting times to parks (*in minutes*):

| MAGIC KINGDOM | 23:00 |
| EPCOT | 18:15 |
| ANIMAL KINGDOM | 21:30 |
| DHS | 20:45 |

## Rodeway Inn Maingate ★★½
5995 W. US 192*
Kissimmee, FL 34747
☎ 407-396-4300
tinyurl.com/rodewaymaingate

| LOCATION | 3 |
| ROOM RATING | 59 |
| COST ($ = $50) | $- |

Commuting times to parks (*in minutes*):

| MAGIC KINGDOM | 11:15 |
| EPCOT | 11:00 |
| ANIMAL KINGDOM | 9:15 |
| DHS | 10:30 |

## Rosen Centre Hotel ★★★★½
9840 International Dr.
Orlando, FL 32819
☎ 407-996-9840
rosencentre.com

| LOCATION | 1 |
| ROOM RATING | 95 |
| COST ($ = $50) | $$$$+ |

Commuting times to parks (*in minutes*):

| MAGIC KINGDOM | 19:45 |
| EPCOT | 15:15 |
| ANIMAL KINGDOM | 18:15 |
| DHS | 17:45 |

## Rosen Shingle Creek ★★★★
9939 Universal Blvd.
Orlando, FL 32819
☎ 407-996-9939
rosenshinglecreek.com

| LOCATION | 1 |
| ROOM RATING | 88 |
| COST ($ = $50) | $- X 5 |

Commuting times to parks (*in minutes*):

| MAGIC KINGDOM | 21:00 |
| EPCOT | 16:15 |
| ANIMAL KINGDOM | 19:30 |
| DHS | 18:45 |

## Royal Celebration Inn ★★½
4944 W. US 192*
Kissimmee, FL 34746
☎ 407-396-4455
royalcelebrationorlando.com

| LOCATION | 3 |
| ROOM RATING | 60 |
| COST ($ = $50) | $ |

Commuting times to parks (*in minutes*):

| MAGIC KINGDOM | 15:45 |
| EPCOT | 15:30 |
| ANIMAL KINGDOM | 13:45 |
| DHS | 15:00 |

## Seralago Hotel & Suites Main Gate East ★★★
5678 W. US 192*
Kissimmee, FL 34746
☎ 407-396-4488
seralagohotel.com

| LOCATION | 3 |
| ROOM RATING | 71 |
| COST ($ = $50) | $ |

Commuting times to parks (*in minutes*):

| MAGIC KINGDOM | 12:15 |
| EPCOT | 12:00 |
| ANIMAL KINGDOM | 10:15 |
| DHS | 11:30 |

## Silver Lake Resort ★★½
7751 Black Lake Rd.
Kissimmee, FL 34747
☎ 407-397-2828
silverlakeresort.com

| LOCATION | 3 |
| ROOM RATING | 64 |
| COST ($ = $50) | $$$$+ |

Commuting times to parks (*in minutes*):

| MAGIC KINGDOM | 8:15 |
| EPCOT | 8:00 |
| ANIMAL KINGDOM | 4:30 |
| DHS | 7:30 |

## Sonesta ES Suites Orlando ★★★½
8480 International Dr.
Orlando, FL 32819
☎ 407-352-2400
sonesta.com/orlando

| LOCATION | 1 |
| ROOM RATING | 75 |
| COST ($ = $50) | $$$- |

Commuting times to parks (*in minutes*):

| MAGIC KINGDOM | 21:15 |
| EPCOT | 16:30 |
| ANIMAL KINGDOM | 19:30 |
| DHS | 19:00 |

## SpringHill Suites Orlando Convention Center ★★★½
8840 Universal Blvd.
Orlando, FL 32819
☎ 407-345-9073
tinyurl.com/shsconventioncenter

| LOCATION | 1 |
| ROOM RATING | 80 |
| COST ($ = $50) | $- X 5 |

Commuting times to parks (*in minutes*):

| MAGIC KINGDOM | 22:30 |
| EPCOT | 17:50 |
| ANIMAL KINGDOM | 20:45 |
| DHS | 20:20 |

*US 192 in Kissimmee is also known locally as Irlo Bronson Memorial Highway.

### Residence Inn Orlando at SeaWorld ★★★★
11000 Westwood Blvd.
Orlando, FL 32821
☎ 407-313-3600
tinyurl.com/residenceinnseaworld

| | |
|---|---|
| LOCATION | 2 |
| ROOM RATING | 85 |
| COST ($ = $50) | $$$$– |

Commuting times to parks (in minutes):
| | |
|---|---|
| MAGIC KINGDOM | 15:45 |
| EPCOT | 11:15 |
| ANIMAL KINGDOM | 14:15 |
| DHS | 13:45 |

### Residence Inn Orlando Convention Center ★★★½
8800 Universal Blvd.
Orlando, FL 32819
☎ 407-226-0288
tinyurl.com/resinn
conventioncenter

| | |
|---|---|
| LOCATION | 1 |
| ROOM RATING | 80 |
| COST ($ = $50) | $$+ |

Commuting times to parks (in minutes):
| | |
|---|---|
| MAGIC KINGDOM | 22:00 |
| EPCOT | 17:30 |
| ANIMAL KINGDOM | 20:30 |
| DHS | 20:00 |

### Residence Inn Orlando Lake Buena Vista ★★★½
11450 Marbella Palm Ct.
Orlando, FL 32836
☎ 407-465-0075
tinyurl.com/residenceinnlbv

| | |
|---|---|
| LOCATION | 2 |
| ROOM RATING | 75 |
| COST ($ = $50) | $$$$– |

Commuting times to parks (in minutes):
| | |
|---|---|
| MAGIC KINGDOM | 15:40 |
| EPCOT | 11:00 |
| ANIMAL KINGDOM | 14:00 |
| DHS | 13:30 |

### Rosen Inn at Pointe Orlando ★★★½
9000 International Dr.
Orlando, FL 32819
☎ 407-996-8585
roseninn9000.com

| | |
|---|---|
| LOCATION | 1 |
| ROOM RATING | 75 |
| COST ($ = $50) | $$+ |

Commuting times to parks (in minutes):
| | |
|---|---|
| MAGIC KINGDOM | 22:15 |
| EPCOT | 17:30 |
| ANIMAL KINGDOM | 20:30 |
| DHS | 20:00 |

### Rosen Inn International Hotel ★★★
7600 International Dr.
Orlando, FL 32819
☎ 407-996-1600
roseninn7600.com

| | |
|---|---|
| LOCATION | 1 |
| ROOM RATING | 65 |
| COST ($ = $50) | $$– |

Commuting times to parks (in minutes):
| | |
|---|---|
| MAGIC KINGDOM | 19:45 |
| EPCOT | 15:00 |
| ANIMAL KINGDOM | 18:00 |
| DHS | 17:30 |

### Rosen Plaza Hotel ★★★★½
9700 International Dr.
Orlando, FL 32819
☎ 407-996-9700
rosenplaza.com

| | |
|---|---|
| LOCATION | 1 |
| ROOM RATING | 90 |
| COST ($ = $50) | $$$$– |

Commuting times to parks (in minutes):
| | |
|---|---|
| MAGIC KINGDOM | 20:45 |
| EPCOT | 16:15 |
| ANIMAL KINGDOM | 19:15 |
| DHS | 18:45 |

### Shades of Green ★★★★½
1950 W. Magnolia Palm Dr.
Lake Buena Vista, FL 32830
☎ 407-824-3400
shadesofgreen.org

| | |
|---|---|
| LOCATION | WDW |
| ROOM RATING | 91 |
| COST ($ = $50) | $$+ |

Commuting times to parks (in minutes):
| | |
|---|---|
| MAGIC KINGDOM | 3:30 |
| EPCOT | 4:45 |
| ANIMAL KINGDOM | 9:30 |
| DHS | 6:15 |

### Sheraton Lake Buena Vista Resort ★★★★
12205 S. Apopka-Vineland Rd.
Orlando, FL 32836
☎ 407-239-0444
sheratonlakebuenavistaresort.com

| | |
|---|---|
| LOCATION | 2 |
| ROOM RATING | 88 |
| COST ($ = $50) | $– X 5 |

Commuting times to parks (in minutes):
| | |
|---|---|
| MAGIC KINGDOM | 13:45 |
| EPCOT | 9:00 |
| ANIMAL KINGDOM | 12:00 |
| DHS | 11:30 |

### Sheraton Vistana Resort Villas ★★★★½
8800 Vistana Centre Dr.
Orlando, FL 32821
☎ 407-239-3100
tinyurl.com/vistanavillas

| | |
|---|---|
| LOCATION | 2 |
| ROOM RATING | 95 |
| COST ($ = $50) | $ X 5 |

Commuting times to parks (in minutes):
| | |
|---|---|
| MAGIC KINGDOM | 11:15 |
| EPCOT | 6:30 |
| ANIMAL KINGDOM | 9:30 |
| DHS | 9:00 |

### SpringHill Suites Orlando LBV in Marriott Village ★★★
8601 Vineland Ave.
Orlando, FL 32821
☎ 407-938-9001
tinyurl.com/springhillmarriott
village

| | |
|---|---|
| LOCATION | 2 |
| ROOM RATING | 71 |
| COST ($ = $50) | $$$– |

Commuting times to parks (in minutes):
| | |
|---|---|
| MAGIC KINGDOM | 12:00 |
| EPCOT | 7:15 |
| ANIMAL KINGDOM | 10:15 |
| DHS | 9:45 |

### Star Island Resort & Club ★★★★
5000 Avenue of the Stars
Kissimmee, FL 34746
☎ 407-997-8000
star-island.com

| | |
|---|---|
| LOCATION | 3 |
| ROOM RATING | 84 |
| COST ($ = $50) | $$$$+ |

Commuting times to parks (in minutes):
| | |
|---|---|
| MAGIC KINGDOM | 15:45 |
| EPCOT | 15:15 |
| ANIMAL KINGDOM | 14:15 |
| DHS | 13:30 |

### Stay Sky Suites I-Drive Orlando ★★★½
7601 Canada Ave.
Orlando, FL 32819
☎ 407-581-2151
stayskysuitesidriveorlando.com

| | |
|---|---|
| LOCATION | 1 |
| ROOM RATING | 82 |
| COST ($ = $50) | $$ |

Commuting times to parks (in minutes):
| | |
|---|---|
| MAGIC KINGDOM | 20:15 |
| EPCOT | 15:45 |
| ANIMAL KINGDOM | 18:45 |
| DHS | 19:15 |

## Hotel Information Chart (*continued*)

| Staybridge Suites Lake Buena Vista ★★★ | |
|---|---|
| 8751 Suiteside Dr. | |
| Orlando, FL 32836 | |
| ☎ 407-238-0777 | |
| tinyurl.com/staybridgelbv | |
| LOCATION | 2 |
| ROOM RATING | 72 |
| COST ($ = $50) | $$$$– |
| Commuting times to parks (*in minutes*): | |
| MAGIC KINGDOM | 14:15 |
| EPCOT | 9:30 |
| ANIMAL KINGDOM | 12:30 |
| DHS | 12:00 |

| Super 8 Kissimmee ★★½ | |
|---|---|
| 1815 W. Vine St. | |
| Kissimmee, FL 34741 | |
| ☎ 407-847-6121 | |
| tinyurl.com/super8kiss | |
| LOCATION | 3 |
| ROOM RATING | 60 |
| COST ($ = $50) | $ |
| Commuting times to parks (*in minutes*): | |
| MAGIC KINGDOM | 11:45 |
| EPCOT | 11:15 |
| ANIMAL KINGDOM | 11:00 |
| DHS | 9:45 |

| Super 8 Kissimmee/Maingate ★★★ | |
|---|---|
| 5875 W. US 192* | |
| Kissimmee, FL 34746 | |
| ☎ 407-396-8883 | |
| tinyurl.com/super8maingate | |
| LOCATION | 3 |
| ROOM RATING | 70 |
| COST ($ = $50) | $ |
| Commuting times to parks (*in minutes*): | |
| MAGIC KINGDOM | 8:30 |
| EPCOT | 8:00 |
| ANIMAL KINGDOM | 7:45 |
| DHS | 5:45 |

| Universal's Hard Rock Hotel ★★★★½ | |
|---|---|
| 5800 Universal Blvd. | |
| Orlando, FL 32819 | |
| ☎ 407-503-2000 | |
| hardrockhotelorlando.com | |
| LOCATION | 4 |
| ROOM RATING | 93 |
| COST ($ = $50) | $+ X 7 |
| Commuting times to parks (*in minutes*): | |
| MAGIC KINGDOM | 21:45 |
| EPCOT | 17:00 |
| ANIMAL KINGDOM | 20:00 |
| DHS | 19:30 |

| Universal's Portofino Bay Hotel ★★★★½ | |
|---|---|
| 5601 Universal Blvd. | |
| Orlando, FL 32819 | |
| ☎ 407-503-1000 | |
| tinyurl.com/portofinobay | |
| LOCATION | 4 |
| ROOM RATING | 92 |
| COST ($ = $50) | $+ X 8 |
| Commuting times to parks (*in minutes*): | |
| MAGIC KINGDOM | 21:45 |
| EPCOT | 17:15 |
| ANIMAL KINGDOM | 20:15 |
| DHS | 19:45 |

| Universal's Royal Pacific Resort ★★★★½ | |
|---|---|
| 6300 Hollywood Way | |
| Orlando, FL 32819 | |
| ☎ 407-503-3000 | |
| tinyurl.com/royalpacific | |
| LOCATION | 4 |
| ROOM RATING | 90 |
| COST ($ = $50) | $ X 6 |
| Commuting times to parks (*in minutes*): | |
| MAGIC KINGDOM | 20:00 |
| EPCOT | 15:15 |
| ANIMAL KINGDOM | 18:15 |
| DHS | 17:45 |

| Villas of Grand Cypress ★★★★½ | |
|---|---|
| 1 N. Jacaranda | |
| Orlando, FL 32836 | |
| ☎ 407-239-4700 | |
| grandcypress.com | |
| LOCATION | 2 |
| ROOM RATING | 92 |
| COST ($ = $50) | $+ X 5 |
| Commuting times to parks (*in minutes*): | |
| MAGIC KINGDOM | 14:00 |
| EPCOT | 12:00 |
| ANIMAL KINGDOM | 19:00 |
| DHS | 15:00 |

| Waldorf Astoria Orlando ★★★★½ | |
|---|---|
| 14200 Bonnet Creek Resort Ln. | |
| Lake Buena Vista, FL 32830 | |
| ☎ 407-597-5500 | |
| waldorfastoriaorlando.com | |
| LOCATION | 2 |
| ROOM RATING | 93 |
| COST ($ = $50) | $– X 6 |
| Commuting times to parks (*in minutes*): | |
| MAGIC KINGDOM | 8:00 |
| EPCOT | 6:00 |
| ANIMAL KINGDOM | 7:15 |
| DHS | 4:15 |

| Walt Disney World Dolphin ★★★★½ | |
|---|---|
| 1500 Epcot Resorts Blvd. | |
| Lake Buena Vista, FL 32830 | |
| ☎ 407-934-4000 | |
| swandolphin.com | |
| LOCATION | WDW |
| ROOM RATING | 90 |
| COST ($ = $50) | $– X 5 |
| Commuting times to parks (*in minutes*): | |
| MAGIC KINGDOM | 6:45 |
| EPCOT | 5:00 |
| ANIMAL KINGDOM | 6:15 |
| DHS | 4:00 |

| Westgate Towers ★★★½ | |
|---|---|
| 7600 West US 192* | |
| Kissimmee, FL 34747 | |
| ☎ 407-396-2500 | |
| westgateresorts.com/towers | |
| LOCATION | 2 |
| ROOM RATING | 81 |
| COST ($ = $50) | $$$– |
| Commuting times to parks (*in minutes*): | |
| MAGIC KINGDOM | 8:45 |
| EPCOT | 8:30 |
| ANIMAL KINGDOM | 5:45 |
| DHS | 8:00 |

| Westgate Town Center ★★★★½ | |
|---|---|
| 7700 Westgate Blvd. | |
| Kissimmee, FL 34747 | |
| ☎ 407-396-2500 | |
| westgateresorts.com /town-center | |
| LOCATION | 2 |
| ROOM RATING | 93 |
| COST ($ = $50) | $$$$– |
| Commuting times to parks (*in minutes*): | |
| MAGIC KINGDOM | 8:45 |
| EPCOT | 8:30 |
| ANIMAL KINGDOM | 5:45 |
| DHS | 8:00 |

| Westgate Vacation Villas ★★★★½ | |
|---|---|
| 7700 Westgate Blvd. | |
| Kissimmee, FL 34747 | |
| ☎ 407-239-0510 | |
| westgateresorts.com /vacation-villas | |
| LOCATION | 2 |
| ROOM RATING | 90 |
| COST ($ = $50) | $ X 5 |
| Commuting times to parks (*in minutes*): | |
| MAGIC KINGDOM | 8:45 |
| EPCOT | 8:30 |
| ANIMAL KINGDOM | 5:45 |
| DHS | 8:00 |

*US 192 in Kissimmee is also known locally as Irlo Bronson Memorial Highway.

**Travelodge Suites**
**East Gate Orange** ★★
5399 W. US 192*
Kissimmee, FL 34746
☎ 407-396-7666
tinyurl.com/travelodgeego

| | |
|---|---|
| LOCATION | 3 |
| ROOM RATING | 55 |
| COST ($ = $50) | $+ |

Commuting times to parks (*in minutes*):
| | |
|---|---|
| MAGIC KINGDOM | 13:30 |
| EPCOT | 13:15 |
| ANIMAL KINGDOM | 11:45 |
| DHS | 12:45 |

**Treehouse Villas at Disney's**
**Saratoga Springs Resort & Spa**
★★★★½
1960 Broadway
Lake Buena Vista, FL 32830
☎ 407-827-1100
tinyurl.com/saratogawdw

| | |
|---|---|
| LOCATION | WDW |
| ROOM RATING | 90 |
| COST ($ = $50) | $ X 16 |

Commuting times to parks (*in minutes*):
| | |
|---|---|
| MAGIC KINGDOM | 12:45 |
| EPCOT | 7:15 |
| ANIMAL KINGDOM | 16:45 |
| DHS | 12:30 |

**Universal's Cabana Bay**
**Beach Resort** ★★★★
6550 Adventure Way
Orlando, FL 32819
☎ 407-503-2000
tinyurl.com/cabanabay

| | |
|---|---|
| LOCATION | 3.5 |
| ROOM RATING | 82 |
| COST ($ = $50) | $$$ |

Commuting times to parks (*in minutes*):
| | |
|---|---|
| MAGIC KINGDOM | 20:00 |
| EPCOT | 17:00 |
| ANIMAL KINGDOM | 18:00 |
| DHS | 14:00 |

**Vacation Village at Parkway**
★★★★½
2949 Arabian Nights Blvd.
Kissimmee, FL 34747
☎ 407-396-9086
dailymanagementresorts.com

| | |
|---|---|
| LOCATION | 3 |
| ROOM RATING | 91 |
| COST ($ = $50) | $$- |

Commuting times to parks (*in minutes*):
| | |
|---|---|
| MAGIC KINGDOM | 8:30 |
| EPCOT | 8:15 |
| ANIMAL KINGDOM | 6:45 |
| DHS | 7:45 |

**The Villas at Disney's Grand**
**Floridian Resort & Spa** ★★★★½
4401 Floridian Way
Lake Buena Vista, FL 32830
☎ 407-824-3000
tinyurl.com/grandfloridianvillas

| | |
|---|---|
| LOCATION | WDW |
| ROOM RATING | 93 |
| COST ($ = $50) | $- X 12 |

Commuting times to parks (*in minutes*):
| | |
|---|---|
| MAGIC KINGDOM | ON MONORAIL |
| EPCOT | 4:45 |
| ANIMAL KINGDOM | 11:45 |
| DHS | 6:45 |

**The Villas at Disney's**
**Wilderness Lodge**** ★★★★½
901 Timberline Dr.
Lake Buena Vista, FL 32830
☎ 407-824-3200
tinyurl.com/wlvillas

| | |
|---|---|
| LOCATION | WDW |
| ROOM RATING | 90 |
| COST ($ = $50) | $+ X 9 |

Commuting times to parks (*in minutes*):
| | |
|---|---|
| MAGIC KINGDOM | N/A |
| EPCOT | 10:00 |
| ANIMAL KINGDOM | 15:15 |
| DHS | 13:30 |

**Walt Disney World Swan**
★★★★½
1200 Epcot Resorts Blvd.
Lake Buena Vista, FL 32830
☎ 407-934-3000
swandolphin.com

| | |
|---|---|
| LOCATION | WDW |
| ROOM RATING | 90 |
| COST ($ = $50) | $- X 5 |

Commuting times to parks (*in minutes*):
| | |
|---|---|
| MAGIC KINGDOM | 6:30 |
| EPCOT | 4:45 |
| ANIMAL KINGDOM | 6:15 |
| DHS | 4:00 |

**Westgate Lakes Resort & Spa**
★★★★½
10000 Turkey Lake Rd.
Orlando, FL 32819
☎ 407-345-0000
westgateresorts.com/lakes

| | |
|---|---|
| LOCATION | 2 |
| ROOM RATING | 92 |
| COST ($ = $50) | $$$ |

Commuting times to parks (*in minutes*):
| | |
|---|---|
| MAGIC KINGDOM | 17:30 |
| EPCOT | 14:30 |
| ANIMAL KINGDOM | 19:15 |
| DHS | 18:00 |

**Westgate Palace** ★★★
6145 Carrier Dr.
Orlando, FL 32819
☎ 407-996-6000
westgateresorts.com/palace

| | |
|---|---|
| LOCATION | 1 |
| ROOM RATING | 68 |
| COST ($ = $50) | $+ X 5 |

Commuting times to parks (*in minutes*):
| | |
|---|---|
| MAGIC KINGDOM | 20:45 |
| EPCOT | 16:15 |
| ANIMAL KINGDOM | 19:15 |
| DHS | 18:45 |

**Westin Imagine Orlando** ★★★★
9501 Universal Blvd.
Orlando, FL 32819
☎ 407-233-2200
westinimagineorlando.com

| | |
|---|---|
| LOCATION | 1 |
| ROOM RATING | 87 |
| COST ($ = $50) | $- X 5 |

Commuting times to parks (*in minutes*):
| | |
|---|---|
| MAGIC KINGDOM | 19:45 |
| EPCOT | 15:00 |
| ANIMAL KINGDOM | 18:15 |
| DHS | 17:30 |

**WorldQuest Orlando Resort**
★★★★
8849 Worldquest Blvd.
Orlando, FL 32821
☎ 407-387-3800
worldquestorlando.com

| | |
|---|---|
| LOCATION | 1 |
| ROOM RATING | 88 |
| COST ($ = $50) | $$$$ |

Commuting times to parks (*in minutes*):
| | |
|---|---|
| MAGIC KINGDOM | 17:00 |
| EPCOT | 11:00 |
| ANIMAL KINGDOM | 17:00 |
| DHS | 13:00 |

**Wyndham Bonnet Creek Resort**
★★★★½
9560 Via Encinas
Lake Buena Vista, FL 32830
☎ 407-238-3500
wyndhambonnetcreek.com

| | |
|---|---|
| LOCATION | 2 |
| ROOM RATING | 90 |
| COST ($ = $50) | $+ X 5 |

Commuting times to parks (*in minutes*):
| | |
|---|---|
| MAGIC KINGDOM | 8:00 |
| EPCOT | 6:00 |
| ANIMAL KINGDOM | 7:15 |
| DHS | 4:15 |

**Primary transportation to Wilderness Lodge and Wilderness Lodge Villas is by ferry rather than by car.

# Hotel Information Chart (continued)

### Wyndham Cypress Palms
★★★★
5324 Fairfield Lake Dr.
Kissimmee, FL 34746
☎ 407-397-1600
cypresspalms.com

| | |
|---|---|
| LOCATION | 3 |
| ROOM RATING | 87 |
| COST ($ = $50) | $$$– |

Commuting times to parks (*in minutes*):

| | |
|---|---|
| MAGIC KINGDOM | 15:15 |
| EPCOT | 15:00 |
| ANIMAL KINGDOM | 14:45 |
| DHS | 14:45 |

### Wyndham Lake Buena Vista
Resort ★★★½
1850 Hotel Plaza Blvd.
Lake Buena Vista, FL 32830
☎ 407-828-4444
wyndhamlakebuenavista.com

| | |
|---|---|
| LOCATION | WDW |
| ROOM RATING | 75 |
| COST ($ = $50) | $$$+ |

Commuting times to parks (*in minutes*):

| | |
|---|---|
| MAGIC KINGDOM | 15:15 |
| EPCOT | 10:45 |
| ANIMAL KINGDOM | 14:45 |
| DHS | 12:15 |

### Wyndham Orlando Resort I-Drive
★★★★
8001 International Dr.
Orlando, FL 32819
☎ 407-351-2420
wyndham.com/hotels/MCOWD

| | |
|---|---|
| LOCATION | 1 |
| ROOM RATING | 83 |
| COST ($ = $50) | $$$$ |

Commuting times to parks (*in minutes*):

| | |
|---|---|
| MAGIC KINGDOM | 19:45 |
| EPCOT | 15:00 |
| ANIMAL KINGDOM | 18:15 |
| DHS | 17:30 |

# PART FOUR

# SERENITY NOW!
## A Look at Disney-Area Spas

YOU'VE JUST SUGGESTED another theme park mini-marathon to your spouse, and from her barely audible murmur you realize she's debating which relative should get the kids when she stands trial for your homicide. Fortunately for you, Orlando is awash in spas ready to rub, wrap, and restore your loved one to domestic tranquility.

Note that the cost of a basic 1-hour massage is well over $100 before tip at most of these places. In an effort to get you the most inner peace for your money, we sent the *Unofficial Guide* research team to evaluate nine Walt Disney World–area spas.

At each resort, our team got a standard massage, a basic facial, and a manicure–pedicure combination. Each service was scheduled during a different week to ensure that one person's bad day didn't mar the whole evaluation. Also, we used the same researchers throughout the tests to ensure consistent comparisons of what is admittedly a somewhat subjective experience.

We rated each spa on a scale of one star (poor) to five stars (excellent) in three areas. **Customer service** includes our interactions with the spa staff on everything from scheduling appointments to the actual treatments to follow-up questions after the visit. **Facilities** rates the amenities, functionality, and decor of the locker rooms, waiting areas, and equipment used before and after the services. **Amenities** rates secondary spa offerings such as food, pools, fitness centers, and the like. In addition, **sales pressure** (rated from low to high) indicates how hard the spa staff pushes you to buy its products after your treatment. (Underlying our star system is a numerical quality scale of 0–100, so spas with the same overall star rating may have different numerical ratings.)

**Senses Spa at Disney's Grand Floridian Resort** has been getting rave reviews since its 2013 refurbishment, including everything from the new heated-stone lounge chairs in the post-treatment rooms to the pre-treatment snacks. It remains the top spa in our rankings.

**The Waldorf Astoria Spa,** in the Bonnet Creek Resort, surrounded by Disney property, is a close second. Besides offering luxurious service, it's slightly larger than Senses, and its four-year-old facilities are

*unofficial* **TIP**
Check whether a gratuity has already been added to your bill before you pay. Most spas, including Disney's, tack on a tip of 18–20%.

still up-to-date. Dropping from first to third is **The Ritz-Carlton Spa, Orlando.** The service is still fantastic, but the facilities are now nearly a decade old and, in our opinion, in need of freshening up. So for now, you can enjoy the best spa services in Orlando without having to venture off Disney property.

In addition to the Grand Floridian, Disney revamped its other spa at **Saratoga Springs Resort.** Also called **Senses,** it offers services and amenities similar to those at the Grand Floridian's Senses; see page 291 for a full review. And opening in August 2014 is **The Spa at Four Seasons,** in the new **Four Seasons Resort Orlando** (see page 251 for a sneak peek).

A fabulous money-saving idea is to find out if the spa you're interested in offers a day pass. These inexpensive tickets ($8–$35 among the spas we reviewed) typically allow use of the spa's fitness center, pool, sauna, steam room, and showers for an entire day. Senses at the Grand Floridian offers passes only to hotel guests, but the other spas we checked—except the one at Orlando World Center Marriott Resort, which doesn't offer passes at all—will accommodate anyone regardless of whether they're staying at that resort.

| ORLANDO SPAS RATED & RANKED | |
| --- | --- |
| **SPA** | **OVERALL RATING** |
| **1.** SENSES SPA AT DISNEY'S GRAND FLORIDIAN RESORT | ★★★★½ |
| **2.** THE WALDORF ASTORIA SPA | ★★★★½ |
| **3.** THE RITZ-CARLTON SPA, ORLANDO | ★★★★ |
| **4.** SENSES SPA AT DISNEY'S SARATOGA SPRINGS RESORT | ★★★★ |
| **5.** MANDARA SPA AT UNIVERSAL'S PORTOFINO BAY HOTEL | ★★★★ |
| **6.** RELÂCHE SPA AT GAYLORD PALMS | ★★★★ |
| **7.** KAY CASPERSON LIFESTYLE SPA AT THE BUENA VISTA PALACE | ★★★½ |
| **8.** MANDARA SPA AT THE DOLPHIN | ★★★½ |
| **9.** THE SPA AT ORLANDO WORLD CENTER MARRIOTT RESORT | ★★½ |

# SPA PROFILES

## Kay Casperson Lifestyle Spa at the Buena Vista Palace
★★★½

1900 E. Buena Vista Dr., Lake Buena Vista; ☎ 407-827-3200; **buenavistapalace.com/things-to-do/spa-salon**

**Customer service** ★★★★★. **Facilities** ★★★½. **Amenities** ★★★★. **Sales pressure** Low. **Price range** $80–$408 spa services; $20–$75 nail services; $25–$65 kids' services (ages 6–12); $25–$150 teens' services (ages 13–19); 15% discount for Florida residents Monday–Friday; 20% service charge (does not include gratuity).

**COMMENTS** Plush, swallow-you-whole robes are the first of the pleasures awaiting guests at Buena Vista Palace's spa, part of a chain run by beauty maven Kay Casperson. Locker rooms offer two small, private changing rooms and a posh vanity area. Treatment rooms are small and nondescript but clean. Separate waiting rooms are provided for men and women. On the downside, the facilities are older and in need of updating. Treatments were top-notch; staff encouraged the use of the sauna, steam room, and other facilities, and took time to explain the benefits of each. All of our services were administered with care and professionalism.

Water was from a cooler, and no fruit or other snacks were offered during our visits. On the upside, sales pressure after our visits was low, with no attempt to sell any of the oils, lotions, or robes applied to our bodies. A tip was included in the service, so read the receipt before adding a gratuity. Children's treatments are available, but the money's better spent on you and your sanity.

## Mandara Spa at Universal's Portofino Bay Hotel  ★★★★

Universal Studios, 5601 Universal Blvd., Orlando;
☎ 407-503-1244; **mandaraspa.com**

**Customer service** ★★★★★. **Facilities** ★★★★½. **Amenities** ★★★. **Sales pressure** Medium. **Price range** $65–$585 spa services; $25–$155 hair and nail services; $75–$210 kids' services (ages 13–17); fitness pass, $10 hotel guests, $25 nonguests. 10–20% discount for Universal Annual Pass holders; 20% service charge.

**COMMENTS** The Universal Orlando Mandara was renovated in 2013, retaining its Asian ambience despite its location in an Italy-themed resort. We like the contrast, though, and find it slightly exotic. Waiting areas are decorated in comforting earth tones; treatment rooms feature silk-draped ceilings. Changing and bathroom areas are spacious and clean, but they also include less-than-subtle advertisements for products sold on premises. The remodeled treatment rooms feature additional decorative lighting and accessories.

The emphasis on tranquility extends to the stellar spa services, which included free self-heating oil for our massages. Men and women enjoy separate steam and sauna facilities; the whirlpool is unisex. The Portofino's sand-bottom pool is conveniently located near the entrance to the spa, as are nail services. The fitness center is still on the other side of the glass wall, however, so you may feel a bit like that doggy in the window.

## Mandara Spa at the Dolphin  ★★★½

Walt Disney World Dolphin, 1500 Epcot Resorts Blvd.,
Lake Buena Vista; ☎ 407-934-4772; **mandaraspa.com**

**Customer service** ★★★★★. **Facilities** ★★★. **Amenities** ★★★. **Sales pressure** High. **Price range** $65–$585 spa services; $25–$155 hair and nail services; $75–$210 kids' services (ages 13–17); Disney Vacation Club members get 10–20% off; Disney Annual Pass holders get 10% off; 20% service charge.

**COMMENTS** Although the Mandaras at the Dolphin and the Portofino Bay Hotel share an Asian theme, everything is dialed down a notch at the Dolphin spa, starting with the waiting areas, of which there are two: the Meditation room, stocked with teas, water, and fruit; and the Consultation room, which is so close to the treatment rooms that voices occasionally disrupt the clients' treatment experience.

Missing are the comfy sofas and chairs found at the Portofino Bay Mandara: At the Dolphin, it's standing-room-only. And we were surprised that both of this spa's two waiting rooms are unisex.

The treatment rooms, though pleasant, are also not on par with the Portofino Mandara's. Instead of silk-draped ceilings, an Asian-inspired wall hanging decorates one wall. Trappings aside, the Dolphin's spa also lacks a sauna, offering patrons only a coed steam room.

The one important asset that both Mandara Spas have in common is exceptional treatments delivered by skilled staff. The Dolphin's employees seemed to be the most talkative of any we encountered.

## Relâche Spa at Gaylord Palms ★★★★

Gaylord Palms Hotel & Convention Center, 6000 W. Osceola Parkway, Kissimmee; ☎ 407-586-4772; **gaylordpalms.com/spa**

**Customer service** ★★★★. **Facilities** ★★★★½. **Amenities** ★★★★. **Sales pressure** Low. **Price range** Price range $75–$400 spa services; $25–$100 nail services; $25–$50+ kids' services (ages 4–10); 10% discount for Florida residents Monday–Friday.

COMMENTS  *Relâche* means "relax" in French, and the name is no exaggeration. The staff's courtesy and professionalism were apparent from our initial phone call to our reception upon arrival to the technicians and assistants who worked on us. A complete tour of the facilities is given when you arrive, and you're encouraged to show up early to enjoy everything.

After changing into a comfy robe and slippers in a spacious and clean locker room, you're ushered into either the men's or women's waiting room, where lemon water, delicious teas, and fresh and dried fruits and nuts are provided. From there you move into the coed Tea Room, with more refreshments, very comfortable seating, and soft lights and music.

The soft lights and music continue in the immaculate treatment rooms. A facial includes neck, décolleté, hand, and foot massages. Luscious, fruity creams and serums are applied and are available for purchase afterward, but sales pressure is kept low.

Our manicure was just as enjoyable, with the same refreshments available. The nail salon is clean and comfortable. As with our facial, the products used during our treatments were waiting on a tray as we checked out, but there was no sales pressure.

## The Ritz-Carlton Spa, Orlando ★★★★

4012 Central Florida Parkway, Orlando; ☎ 407-393-4200; **ritzcarlton.com/en/properties/orlando/spa**

**Customer service** ★★★★★. **Facilities** ★★★★★. **Amenities** ★★★★★. **Sales pressure** Low-medium. **Price range** $145–$415 spa services; $25–$105 nail services; $49–$130 kids'/teens' services; 15% discount for Florida residents Sunday–Friday; 20% service charge.

COMMENTS  The Ritz-Carlton Spa was so far ahead of anything else in Orlando when it opened almost a decade ago that it was in a class by itself. The facilities were much larger than anything in the area, and our interactions with the staff were the very definition of exemplary customer service. But while the service is still as fabulous as ever, the facilities are starting to look dated.

The spa is housed in a separate three-story building behind the main hotel. Every level is tastefully and elegantly decorated, including locker rooms, treatment rooms, and waiting rooms. Both single-sex and coed waiting areas are available. The waiting rooms and treatment rooms, while clean and functional, are showing their age, and our reviewer noted that they don't have niceties such as fresh flowers, mood lighting, or prewarmed robes—all of which the Senses Spas at the Grand Floridian and Saratoga Springs offer.

Spa-goers also have the use of a separate whirlpool tub, sauna and steam rooms, and an outside lap pool where an attendant supplies complimentary towels, water, and sunscreen. All the equipment we used and observed was in working order during our visits.

## Senses Spa at Disney's Grand Floridian Resort ★★★★½

Grand Floridian Resort, 4401 N. Floridian Way, Lake Buena Vista; ☎ 407-939-7727; **disneyworld.com/spas**

**Customer service** ★★★★. **Facilities** ★★★★★. **Amenities** ★★★★. **Sales pressure** None. **Price range** $135–$495 spa services; $55–$90 nail services; $30–$45 kids' services (ages 4–12); 15% off for Disney Annual Pass holders and 10% off for Disney Vacation Club members.

**COMMENTS** Reopened in 2013 after a much-needed total renovation, Senses at the Grand Floridian is modeled—and named—after the spas on the *Disney Dream* and *Disney Fantasy* cruise ships. The decor features cool greens and whites, with dark furniture and marble counters. Wallpaper in the lobby depicts an unspoiled Florida-as–Garden of Eden.

Treatment rooms have glass tile, marble countertops, and mosaic-tile walls. Facials include a paraffin treatment for your hands as well as a neck, shoulder, and décolleté massage. Our reviewer says, "The treatment bed was very comfortable, and the silky-feeling sheets are divine."

The Hand and Foot Spa was created by walling off part of the entrance lobby. Treatments here are sumptuous and include hand–arm and foot–leg massages. At the end of your treatment, you also receive a goodie bag that contains all the implements used, plus bottles of nail polish.

Massage beds are heated, and the treatments are likewise soothing and invigorating. You'll even get a prewarmed robe to relax in when you're done.

Sales pressure during our visits was nonexistent—no one asked us to buy anything, ever. The one downside to Senses is the waiting area: It gets a lot of foot traffic, so it's not as relaxing as it could be.

## Senses Spa at Disney's Saratoga Springs Resort ★★★★

1490-A Disney Vacation Club Way, Lake Buena Vista; ☎ 407-827-4455; **disneyworld.com/spas**

**Customer service** ★★★★. **Facilities** ★★★★★. **Amenities** ★★★★. **Sales pressure** None. **Price range** $135–$495 spa services; $55–$90 nail services; $30–$45 kids' services (ages 4–12); 15% off for Disney Annual Pass holders and 10% off for Disney Vacation Club members.

**COMMENTS** Saratoga Springs' spa was completely remodeled in 2013 to match the Senses Spa theming found on Disney's cruise ships and at its Grand Floridian Resort. Services, amenities, and prices at the Saratoga Springs Senses are in line with those at its Grand Floridian sibling, although the setting at Saratoga Springs is perhaps a little less formal. If you're staying at Saratoga Springs, Old Key West, or the Downtown Disney resorts, or you're coming from an off-site hotel east of Disney World, we'd recommend the shorter drive and easier commute of the Senses at Saratoga Springs.

Our reviewer enjoyed the custom-made pedicure chairs at Saratoga Springs, as well as the heated massage tables. As with many spas' mani-pedi services, you'll get to keep a bottle of the nail polish you choose, for later touch-ups. It's a nice extra.

## The Spa at Orlando World Center Marriott Resort ★★½

8701 World Center Dr., Orlando; ☎ 407-238-8705; **marriottworldcenter.com/spa**

**Customer service ★★★★. Facilities ★★. Amenities ★★★. Sales pressure** High. **Price range** $100–$450 spa services; $35–$115 nail services.

**COMMENTS** In a small, separate building at the back of a sprawling hotel complex, The Spa at Orlando World Center Marriott Resort requires a hike from your room, or a really good set of directions if you're coming by car.

The women's locker room has no private changing areas; however, the bathroom stalls are big enough to make do. Spa-goers have the use of steam rooms and fitness facilities. Women should know that once they're in their spa robes, they're directed to a coed quiet room to await treatments. (On our visit, the spa was rife with male bonding.)

A staffer pressured us insistently to buy expensive oils and lotions after our treatments. Worse yet, the nail-drying equipment was either broken or nonexistent when we visited for our manicure: After shelling out $35 (plus tip), we were told to sit in the quiet room and blow on our nails to dry them.

## Waldorf Astoria Spa ★★★★½

Waldorf Astoria Orlando, 14200 Bonnet Creek Resort Lane, Orlando; ☎ 407-597-5360; **waldorfastoriaorlando.com/spaandfitness/spa**

**Customer service ★★★★★. Facilities ★★★½. Amenities ★★★★★. Sales pressure** None. **Price range** $149–$350 facials; $149–$450 massages; $20–$90 nail services; $20 day pass; 10% discount for Florida residents; complimentary valet parking (no self-parking); 20% service charge.

**COMMENTS** The Waldorf Astoria Spa is just a short walk from the lobby, and our first impressions are very positive. Upon your arrival, an attendant takes you on a tour of the facilities. Once you are given your key, locker, robe, and slippers, you are free to wander the rooms before settling in the Tea Lounge. It's comfortable, but we like the lounge chairs at the Senses spas better.

The locker room and bathrooms are clean and modern. The showers are spacious and very clean, with small iridescent tiles. Beyond these is the Tea Lounge, where your treatment person meets you—which is fortunate, because the place is big enough to get lost in.

Our massage, facial, and mani–pedi were all excellent. The pedicure came with a glass of Champagne. Clearly, these are people who know what we need.

A couple of quirks: Our reviewer was not offered nail-drying machines for either her manicure or pedicure. Also, because you walk through the spa's waiting room between some services, you may wish to get dressed between treatments. Still, we give the Waldorf very high marks, and it compares well with Senses at the Grand Floridian and Saratoga Springs.

# PART FIVE

# The DISNEY CRUISE LINE

## ■ The MOUSE at SEA

DISNEY CRUISE LINE (DCL) has been in business since 1998, when it launched the *Disney Magic.* An almost identical ship, the *Disney Wonder,* entered service in 1999. Two new, larger ships, the *Disney Dream* and *Disney Fantasy,* entered service in 2011 and 2012, respectively.

In starting a cruise line, Disney put together a team of respected industry veterans, dozens of the world's best-known ship designers, and its own unrivaled creative talent. Together, they created the Disney ships, recognizing that every detail is critical to the line's success.

The result? They succeeded, starting with the ships' appearance: classic yet forward-thinking. Exteriors are traditional, reminiscent of great

## Disney Cruise Line Standard Features

**OFFICERS**  American and international

**STAFF**  American and international

**DINING**  Three themed family restaurants with "rotational dining"; alternative adults-only restaurants; indoor/outdoor cafe for buffet breakfast and lunch, snacks, and buffet dinner; pool bar/grill; ice-cream bar

**SPECIAL DIETS**  On request at the time of booking; healthy-cuisine program

**ROOM SERVICE**  24 hours

**DRESS CODE**  Casual by day; casual–semiformal in the evenings

**ELECTRICAL OUTLETS**  110 AC

**WHEELCHAIR ACCESS**  Yes

**SMOKING**  Only in designated areas

**TIPPING**  DCL automatically charges tips for servers and cabin stewards to guests' onboard accounts (see **tinyurl.com/dcltipping** for details). If you didn't prepay these gratuities when you booked or made your final payment, you'll receive a letter upon check-in explaining the charges. You may change the amounts or pay in cash at your ship's Guest Services desk. Tips for dining managers and room service are at your discretion. A 15% service charge is added automatically to bar, lounge, and cafe bills.

**CREDIT CARDS**  All major cards for cruise payment and onboard charges ocean liners of the past, but even there you'll find a Disney twist or two. Inside, the ships are up-to-the-minute technologically and full of novel ideas for dining, entertainment, and cabin design. Even Disney's exclusive cruise terminal at Port Canaveral, Florida, is part of the overall strategy, aiming to make even embarking and disembarking enjoyable.

For Port Canaveral and Miami cruises, Disney's private island, **Castaway Cay,** avoids the hassle of tendering. As for dining, Disney practically reinvented the concept for cruises when it introduced "rotational dining," where each evening you eat in a different restaurant with a different motif but your waiters and dinner companions move with you.

The foundation of DCL's business is built on Bahamian and Caribbean cruises out of Port Canaveral, about 90 minutes from Walt Disney World, and Miami. Disney also offers Alaskan, Californian, Canadian, and European cruises as well as repositioning cruises. Other departure ports include Galveston, Texas; San Diego, California; San Juan, Puerto Rico; Barcelona, Spain; Vancouver, British Columbia; and Venice, Italy.

All Bahamian cruises originating in Port Canaveral and Miami make at least one port call at Castaway Cay. DCL's Alaskan and European itineraries are well conceived and interesting, its Bahamian and Caribbean itineraries unimaginative and prosaic.

DCL's target audience is families with children or grandchildren. But like the parks, the cruise line is a Disney product for kids of all ages. Because the ships' decor and entertainment are based almost entirely on Disney films and characters, we don't recommend DCL for anyone not already enraptured by Mickey and the gang.

To cater to varied constituencies, some facilities, services, and programs were designed specifically for seniors, honeymooners, and adults without kids. Each ship has at least one alternative restaurant, swimming pool, and nightclub for use by adults only, as well as entertainment for the entire family. Disney continues trying to enhance the grown-up experience with such facilities as an adults-only cafe, an adult-oriented sports bar, and an area for teens.

Initially, cruise experts questioned whether Disney could fill its ships when kids are in school, but Disney estimated that if 1–2% of the estimated 40 million annual visitors to its resorts and parks bought a cruise vacation, the ships would sell out. Today, after more than 15 years of success, no one is questioning them.

DCL offers a "seamless vacation package" to those who want to combine a stay at Walt Disney World with a cruise departing from Florida. Passengers are met at the airport by Disney staff and transported to the terminal in easily identifiable buses. During the ride, they watch a cruise video.

## COMPETITION AND PRICES

D C L' S T A R G E T A U D I E N C E is first-time cruisers. Disney uses its reputation for quality, service, and entertainment to dispel novices' doubts about cruise vacations. Its main competitor, **Royal Caribbean International,** offers Caribbean, Mediterranean, and Alaskan cruises similar to Disney's, with most of the same departure and destination ports.

While the itineraries may be similar, remember when comparing prices that Disney's cabins are larger than Royal Caribbean's. An inside cabin for an Alaska voyage on *Disney Magic,* for example, is about 11% larger than a similar cabin on Royal Caribbean's *Radiance of the Seas:* 184 square feet versus 165. Ocean-view staterooms on both ships arc 214 and 170 square feet, respectively, or about 25% larger on the *Magic.*

In addition, Disney's fares include unlimited fountain soda, plain coffee, tea, and water (bottled costs extra), while Royal Caribbean charges around $6 per person, per day, just for soda. For a family of four on a seven-night cruise, that comes out to $168.

Nevertheless, the fact remains that DCL charges a premium for its product. For example, on seven-night Eastern Caribbean cruises out of Port Canaveral during the second half of 2014, Disney's prices were $4,250–$8,650 for one inside cabin depending on the specific date; Royal Caribbean's prices were $2,450–$5,100, or 40% less than Disney for very similar cruises. (Fares assume a family of four.)

## CRUISING WITH KIDS

LET US START BY SAYING that your kids will have a great time on a Disney cruise.

As parents, we know that one of the most difficult parts of planning a vacation with kids is making sure they'll be entertained. This usually means ensuring that every travel day has at least a couple of things designed specifically to appeal to our kids and their friends, and which we'd prefer doesn't involve sitting in front of a video screen.

The stress of planning this way is a prime reason that a trip to Disney World is so appealing to parents: The theme parks provide a nearly constant and wide-ranging stream of entertainment options for kids and adults alike. Disney cruises work the same way—family activities are scheduled throughout the day, on virtually every day of every sailing: trivia contests, scavenger hunts, shuffleboard, you name it.

If you think your kids would benefit from spending some time with their peers, Disney provides organized activities throughout the day for children ages 3–17. Some activities for younger children get started as early as 7 a.m., while activities for older teens can run until 2 a.m. Off the ships, Castaway Cay offers dedicated beach and recreation spots for families, teens, and tweens, plus a splash area for little ones. There are shore excursions just for families, too.

DCL sets aside plenty of space on its ships for kids' clubs, though on the newer *Dream* and *Fantasy* and the newly refurbished *Magic,* they take up substantially more space than on the older *Wonder.* Also, concurrent, age-appropriate activities frequently take place within the same club: For example, the Oceaneer Club accepts children ages 3–12, but counselors may have the younger kids play a game with marshmallows in one area of the club while the older kids sing karaoke in another.

*un*official **TIP** From September to May, all four Disney ships are based out of Florida and sail the Caribbean. The *Magic* summers in Europe, and the *Wonder* heads to the West Coast and Alaska when it's not in Florida.

Our own kids have found Disney's kids' activities more fun than hanging around with us on the ship—in fact, we saw them only during meals, at bedtime, or when we specifically scheduled things to do as a family. Thanks to the web, our kids are still in contact with the friends they've made on their cruises, even though some are an ocean away.

## 2015 DCL Cruise Areas and Ports of Call

### ALASKA

- **7-NIGHT ALASKAN CRUISE** Vancouver, Tracy Arm Fjord, Skagway, Juneau, Ketchikan

### BAHAMAS

- **3-NIGHT BAHAMIAN CRUISE** (1) Port Canaveral, Nassau, Castaway Cay; (2) Miami, Castaway Cay

- **4-NIGHT BAHAMIAN CRUISE** (1) Port Canaveral, Nassau, Castaway Cay (one or two stops); 2) Miami, Nassau, Castaway Cay, Key West

- **5-NIGHT BAHAMIAN CRUISE** (1) Port Canaveral, Castaway Cay (two stops), Nassau; (2) Port Canaveral, Key West, Nassau, Castaway Cay

- **6-NIGHT BAHAMIAN CRUISE** Galveston, Key West, Castaway Cay

- **7-NIGHT BAHAMIAN CRUISE** Galveston, Nassau, Castaway Cay, Key West

### CALIFORNIA COAST (INCLUDING CANADA AND MEXICO)

- **2-NIGHT WEEKEND GETAWAY CRUISE** San Diego (at sea; no ports)

- **3-NIGHT GETAWAY CRUISE** San Diego, Ensenada

- **5-NIGHT BAJA CRUISE** San Diego, Ensenada, Cabo San Lucas

- **4-NIGHT VANCOUVER–SAN DIEGO** Vancouver, Victoria, San Diego

- **5-NIGHT SAN DIEGO–VANCOUVER** San Diego, San Francisco, Vancouver

### CARIBBEAN

- **4-NIGHT WESTERN CARIBBEAN CRUISE** Galveston, Cozumel

- **5-NIGHT WESTERN CARIBBEAN CRUISE** (1) Miami, Cozumel, Castaway Cay; (2) Miami, Grand Cayman, Cozumel; (3) Miami, Grand Cayman, Castaway Cay

- **7-NIGHT WESTERN CARIBBEAN CRUISE** (1) Port Canaveral, Key West, Grand Cayman, Cozumel, Castaway Cay; (2) Port Canaveral, Cozumel, Grand Cayman, Falmouth (Jamaica), Castaway Cay; (3) Galveston, Cozumel, Grand Cayman, Falmouth

- **7-NIGHT EASTERN CARIBBEAN CRUISE** (1) Port Canaveral, St. Maarten, St. Thomas, Castaway Cay; (2) Port Canaveral, St. Thomas, San Juan, Castaway Cay; (3) Port Canaveral, St. Maarten, San Juan, Castaway Cay

### HAWAII

- **10-NIGHT HAWAIIAN CRUISE** (1) Vancouver, Hilo, Nawiliwili, Kahului, Honolulu; (2) Honolulu, Kahului, Nawiliwili, Vancouver

## CRUISE DESTINATIONS

DCL OFFERS AROUND 60 separate itineraries, ranging from 2-night weekend getaways to 15-night voyages between two oceans using the Panama Canal. The cruise you select is likely to be determined by how much vacation time you have, the ship you want to sail on, the cost, and the ports that interest you.

We're fans of the *Dream* and *Fantasy*, Disney's larger, newer ships. They sail only in the Bahamas and the Caribbean. If either of those destinations is acceptable to you, you can skip to the next section now.

If you're trying to decide between Caribbean and Bahamian cruises, you've only got two questions to answer: First, are you interested in

## MEDITERRANEAN

- **4-NIGHT DOVER–BARCELONA CRUISE**  Dover, Vigo (Spain), Lisbon, Gibraltar, Barcelona
- **4-NIGHT MEDITERRANEAN CRUISE**  Barcelona, Palma de Mallorca, Ibiza
- **5-NIGHT MEDITERRANEAN CRUISE**  Barcelona, Villefranche, La Spezia, Rome
- **7-NIGHT MEDITERRANEAN CRUISE**  Barcelona, Villefranche, La Spezia, Rome, Naples
- **9-NIGHT MEDITERRANEAN CRUISE**  Venice, Olympia, Athens, Ephesus, Rhodes, Mykonos
- **12-NIGHT MEDITERRANEAN CRUISE**  (1) Barcelona, Villefranche, La Spezia, Rome, Athens, Ephesus, Mykonos, Malta; (2) Barcelona, Villefranche, La Spezia, Rome, Naples, Sicily, Corfu, Dubrovnik, Venice; (3) Venice, Athens, Ephesus, Rhodes, Crete, Mykonos, Santorini, Malta, Barcelona

## NORTHERN EUROPE

- **7-NIGHT NORTHERN EUROPE CRUISE**  Copenhagen, Tallinn (Estonia), St. Petersburg, Helsinki, Stockholm
- **12-NIGHT NORTHERN EUROPE CRUISE**  Dover, Copenhagen (one or two days), Warnemünde (Germany), Stockholm, Helsinki, St. Petersburg, Tallinn
- **7-NIGHT NORWEGIAN FJORDS CRUISE**  Copenhagen, Stavanger, Alasund, Geiranger, Bergen
- **9-NIGHT NORWEGIAN FJORDS CRUISE**  Copenhagen, Stavanger, Alasund, Geiranger, Molde, Olden, Bergen
- **11-NIGHT NORWEGIAN FJORDS AND ICELAND CRUISE**  Copenhagen, Oslo, Kristiansand, Stavanger, Akureyri (Iceland), Reykjavík, Kirkwall (Scotland), Dover

## REPOSITIONING

- **11-NIGHT WESTBOUND TRANSATLANTIC CRUISE**  Barcelona, Funchal, Castaway Cay, Miami
- **15-NIGHT EASTBOUND TRANSATLANTIC CRUISE**  Port Canaveral, New York City, St. John's (Newfoundland), Reykjavík, Oslo, Copenhagen
- **14-NIGHT WESTBOUND PANAMA CANAL CRUISE**  Miami, Cozumel, Cartagena, Panama Canal, Puerto Vallarta, Cabo San Lucas, San Diego
- **14-NIGHT EASTBOUND PANAMA CANAL CRUISE**  San Diego, Cabo San Lucas, Puerto Vallarta, Panama Canal, Cartagena, Cozumel, Galveston

exploring the culture of the ports you're visiting? Second, if so, are you more interested in Caribbean towns or Mayan history?

If the answer to the first question is no—if your perfect vacation involves lying on a beach, taking the kids snorkeling, scuba diving, or swimming with dolphins—you can do that in every port from Barbados to Cozumel. Pick any itinerary that includes Castaway Cay and that also fits your schedule and budget, and you're set.

If you're interested in local color, choose between the **Eastern** and **Western Caribbean itineraries.** The Eastern itineraries offer the best ports to explore. **St. John** and **St. Thomas** are great stops, but Disney gives you only 5 or 6 hours there. **St. Maarten** is fun because it's Dutch.

On Western Caribbean cruises, **Costa Maya** and **Cozumel** are notable only for their inland tours of Mayan ruins. If those interest you more than Caribbean towns, pick a Western itinerary.

Now, lest you think we're making an "all those people look the same" argument in advising you how to choose between Bahamas and Caribbean itineraries, rest assured we're not. Rather, we think the cruise industry's overbooking of the same Caribbean ports has led to a certain sameness of experience virtually everywhere.

### Itinerary Recommendations for First-Time Cruisers

We think the ideal itinerary for first-time cruisers is four or five nights on the *Dream* or seven nights on the *Fantasy.* Why? They're newer ships, with better restaurants, bars, and spas; more space for kids' activities (including the Midship Detective Agency interactive game); and more space on deck for pools and lounging.

In addition, an ideal cruise for first-timers includes two stops at **Castaway Cay** (see page 308), Disney's private island. You'll need one visit to become familiar with the island and its features; by the second day, you'll be more knowledgeable and relaxed.

Sailings for the *Dream* that meet the previous criteria in 2015 are the **4-Night** and **5-Night Bahamian Cruises.** You could also choose a **7-Night Eastern Caribbean** cruise aboard the *Fantasy* with three days at sea, plus stops at St. Maarten; San Juan, Puerto Rico; and Castaway Cay.

# THE SHIPS

LAUNCHED IN 1998, the *Magic* holds roughly 2,700 passengers and 950 crew members. The *Wonder* has the same capacity and was launched in 1999. The *Dream* and *Fantasy,* which took their maiden voyages in 2011 and 2012, respectively, hold up to 4,000 passengers and 1,450 crew.

All four share sleek lines, twin smokestacks, and nautical styling that calls to mind classic ocean liners, but with instantly recognizable Disney signatures. The colors—black, white, red, and yellow—and the famous face-and-ears silhouette on the stacks are clearly those of Mickey Mouse. Look closely at the *Magic*'s stern ornamentation, for example, and you'll see a 15-foot Goofy hanging by his overalls. (It's Donald on the *Wonder*'s stern, Mickey on the *Dream*'s, and Dumbo on the *Fantasy*'s.)

Interiors combine nautical themes with Art Nouveau and Art Deco inspiration. (Art Nouveau incorporates natural shapes, such as from plants and animals, into its geometric designs; Art Deco has the geometry without the nature.) Disney images are everywhere, from Mickey's profile in the wrought-iron balustrades to the bronze statue of Admiral Donald at the center of the *Dream*'s atrium. A grand staircase on each ship sweeps from the atrium lobby to shops peddling Disney Cruise Line–themed clothing, collectibles, jewelry, sundries, and more.

Ships have two lower decks with cabins, three decks with dining rooms and showrooms, then three or five upper decks of cabins. Two sports and sun decks offer separate pools and facilities for families and for adults without children. Signs point toward lounges and facilities, and all elevators are clearly marked as forward, aft, or midships.

Each ship has a few unique features, too. The *Fantasy* has **Satellite Falls,** an adults-only splash pool and sun deck, on Deck 13; and **Bibbidi Bobbidi Boutique,** a salon specializing in Disney-princess makeovers for little girls, on Deck 5. The *Magic* has **AquaDunk,** a vertical-start waterslide, while the *Wonder* does not; on the *Dream* and

*Fantasy,* the waterslide is called **AquaDuck**—and it's very popular, as this Campbellton, New Brunswick, reader found out:

> *AquaDuck is extremely fun but very difficult to ride without baking in the Caribbean sun 45–60 minutes while you wait. Happily, on our second day, my stepbrother and I figured out the secret: Go at night in the hour before it closes (usually between 10 and 11 p.m.). No sunburn, and best of all, NO LINES!*

The *Wonder,* however, is the only ship with **Outlook Café,** an indoor, windowed coffee bar–lounge on Deck 10 that's perfect for keeping warm while enjoying the views on Alaskan cruises.

### The "Reimagined" *Disney Magic*

DCL promoted the six-week dry dock of the *Magic* from late September to the end of October 2013 as a reimagining of its oldest ship in the fleet. We cruised the *Magic* before and after and felt that Disney oversold the extent of the rehab. The major changes were to the kids' areas, with new Marvel- and Pixar-inspired additions, and the pool deck, with the AquaDunk waterslide and a new splash area and slide for the kids' pool.

The adult lounges were rethemed with new decor and lighting. Two restaurants got renovations: The buffet got a much-needed overhaul which improved traffic flow, and the dismal Parrot Cay (our least favorite of the DCL eateries) was rethemed (with a new paint job and props) and an updated Brazilian menu. Animator's Palate is now up-to-date with the same technology that the *Dream* and *Fantasy* have.

*Not* added were additional adult dining, "virtual portholes" for inside staterooms, interactive art in the public areas, or the Midship Detective Agency game.

**RANKING THE SHIPS** If your cruise destination is the Bahamas or Caribbean, you can choose which ship you'll sail on. Ignoring the different itineraries each ship serves, we rank the *Fantasy* first, followed by the *Dream, Magic,* and *Wonder.* The *Fantasy* and *Dream* have better restaurants, bars, and pools than the other two, plus more on-deck activities, more space for children's activities, more deck space for tanning, better spas, and more interactive games. All this makes up for the slightly smaller cabin sizes on the two newer ships, whose nonconcierge staterooms are 2–9% (5–22 square feet) smaller than corresponding cabins on the *Magic* and *Wonder.* Another, minor downside: Because the newer ships carry more passengers, Castaway Cay is more crowded when they're in port.

### STATEROOMS

DCL SHIPS BOAST some of the largest cabins in the cruise industry, which helps explain why their fares are correspondingly high, too. An inside cabin, generally the least expensive on any ship, is 169–184 square feet, compared with 114–165 square feet on Royal Caribbean's and 160–185 on Carnival's. Disney's ocean-view and verandah (balcony) cabins are larger than Royal Caribbean's and Carnival's, too.

In addition to space, Disney's bathroom layout is an improvement over that of other cruise lines. Most Disney staterooms—those in Categories 10–4—feature a split-bath design, in which the shower and toilet are in separate compartments, each with its own door and sink. This lets two people get ready at the same time. (Staterooms in Categories 11 and 12 have the shower and toilet in the same compartment.)

Disney's clever incorporation of storage space is one of the things we were most impressed with on our first few cruises. Most cabins have two sliding-door closets, each big enough for one large or two small suitcases; under-bed storage for carry-on or soft-sided luggage; and several drawers built in to the cabin's desk area. In addition, some cabins on the *Wonder* offer a steamer trunk for storage. (For a list of these cabins, see **tinyurl.com/steamertrunklist.**)

While Disney's staterooms are well designed and large for the cruise industry, most are smaller than a typical hotel room. A room at a Disney Value resort, such as Pop Century, is about 260 square feet—about 40% larger than a DCL inside cabin. Even a well-appointed "family" ocean-view stateroom with verandah is 304 square feet, a little smaller than a room at a Moderate hotel such as Caribbean Beach Resort.

## Cabin Appointments

Every Disney Cruise Line stateroom is outfitted with the following:
- Private bath with sink and toilet
- Desk with chair and dedicated lighting
- Sleeper sofa
- Satellite television with remote
- Closet with two sliding doors
- Hooks (for towels) and hangars (for clothes)
- Electronic safe—for passports, wallets, and other small valuables
- Coffee table—some open for storage.
- Privacy curtain—at the foot of the bed, separating the sleeping area from the sofa
- Beverage cooler—keeps drinks cool, not necessarily cold. No freezer.
- In-room phone with voice mail
- Wave phone—a mobile phone you can use aboard the ship
- Digital alarm clock—typically an iHome. (Bring a Lightning-to-30-pin converter if you have a newer iPhone.)
- H2O Plus soap, shampoo, conditioner, and body lotion
- Life jackets
- Room-service menus
- Bedside lamps
- Ice bucket and glasses
- Digital thermostat—can be set to Fahrenheit or Celsius
- Custom artwork

Cabins with exterior windows also have blackout curtains, which do an amazing job of blocking the sun. If you need light to wake up in the morning, don't shut them unless you want to sleep until noon.

**WHAT YOU *WON'T* FIND** Cabins don't have minibars, coffeemakers, microwaves, teakettles, steam irons, or ironing boards. An iron and board are available in each deck's laundry room.

## Our Stateroom Recommendations

A **Standard Inside Stateroom** is 169–184 square feet, enough room for two adults with or without one small child. It's not luxury cruising—remember, they give you 60 square feet in prison—but a group of this size shouldn't have much contention for bathrooms when getting ready.

If you're a family of three or four and you have two tweens or teens, you'll appreciate the extra space of a **Deluxe Oceanview with Verandah** stateroom (246 or 268 square feet) or **Deluxe Family Oceanview with Verandah** stateroom (about 300 square feet). Alternatively, you could book two cabins: two inside connecting rooms or an inside and outside cabin across the hall from each other. Along with the advantage of extra space, the kids can sleep late if they want.

## Which Deck to Choose

We don't have a preference regarding the deck on which our cabin is located, as both the lower and upper decks have their advantages.

Cabins on lower decks tend to be less expensive and smaller than higher cabins on all DCL ships. And while lower cabins involve shorter walks to most restaurants, bars, theaters, and children's clubs, they're farther from the spa, fitness center, pools, and buffet. To get to those from the lower decks, you'll either spend quite a bit of time waiting for an elevator or expend quite a lot of effort climbing stairs. A compromise: Book a cabin on Decks 5–8, giving you relatively short climbs almost everywhere throughout the ship.

For us, cabin size and price are always more important concerns than the deck location. Besides, being on a lower deck is a good excuse to eat dessert (hey, gotta keep your energy up).

## A Word About Seasickness

If you're prone to getting seasick, select a cabin on a lower deck, as close to the middle of the ship as possible. These cabins are much less affected by rough seas than cabins toward the bow or stern or on higher decks. If, like us, you enjoy feeling the motion of the ocean, select a cabin on a higher deck toward either end of the ship. Be forewarned that cruises from Florida's east coast to the Bahamas cross the Gulf Stream at a right angle; on such an itinerary, under otherwise-calm weather conditions, this will usually be the roughest going you'll encounter.

# ■ SERVICES *and* AMENITIES

PASSENGERS LAVISHLY PRAISE DISNEY CAST MEMBERS. They're among the most accommodating you'll ever encounter in travel, and they try hard to smooth your way from boarding to departure. Cruise writer Kay Showker reports, "More than once when I stopped to get my bearings, a Disney cast member was there within seconds to help me."

You'll receive a *Disney Magic Passport,* a purse-sized booklet covering about everything you need to know for your cruise. Daily in your cabin, you'll receive a "Personal Navigator," a newsletter listing entertainment and activities, with options for teens, children, adults, and families, as well as information on shore excursions.

## DINING

YOU'LL NEVER GO HUNGRY ON A DISNEY CRUISE. The variety of dining options is staggering—everything from coffee shops and pizza stands to Vegas-size buffets to ritzy French and Italian restaurants. Even with all these choices available, we've learned how to increase our chances of enjoying memorable meals while on board. This section describes your dining options and advises you on how to make the most of them.

### Rotational Dining

One of the innovations that DCL brought to the cruise industry is the concept of rotational dining, in which you visit one of three standard restaurants on a different night of your cruise. As you change from restaurant to restaurant, your server team—your waiter, beverage person, head waiter, and maître d'—all move with you. Your team will quickly learn your dining proclivities, including preferred drinks and favorite desserts, and make menu suggestions.

The rotational restaurants have two dinner seatings, typically 5:45 p.m. and 8:15 p.m. Because Disney sets the schedule, there's no need to make reservations each night. You can request either the earlier or later seating when booking your trip or once aboard the ship. You can also request changes to your rotation once aboard, specifying which restaurants you visit each night.

You'll repeat at least one of the three standard restaurants on cruises of four nights and longer. Rather than visit the same restaurant twice on a four-night cruise, we recommend using one of those nights to visit **Palo** (on any ship) or **Remy** (on the *Dream* and *Fantasy*). You must pay an additional charge to dine at these restaurants, but the food is stellar, the crowds are small, and the service is impeccable.

### The Food

In general, food offerings on the Disney Cruise Line are differentiated by freshness, quality, and service:

**COUNTER SERVICE** Fast food, available on each ship's pool decks, includes staples such as burgers, chicken fingers, pizza, and sandwiches.

In Part Ten, Dining, we equate the quality of Disney's counter-service restaurants in the theme parks with that of McDonald's and Taco Bell. With a few exceptions, the food quality at DCL's counter-service restaurants is more like what you'd find in your local supermarket's frozen-food aisle. The best items on board are the fresh sandwiches and wraps and, if your timing is right, pizza straight from the oven.

**BUFFETS** Each ship has at least one large buffet, usually open for breakfast and lunch. Buffets tend to serve a bit of everything at each meal and are the easiest way to satisfy disparate appetites. The buffets at **Cabanas** on the *Magic, Dream,* and *Fantasy* are as large and diverse as those at many Las Vegas hotels. Besides offering variety, buffets let picky kids see exactly what food they're getting. They also offer plenty of seating with ocean views, indoors and out.

**SIT-DOWN RESTAURANTS** Each Disney ship has four or five full-service restaurants. Three of these are part of the standard rotational-dinner schedule. Another is the upscale Italian restaurant **Palo,** found on each ship and for which Disney charges a $25 additional fee. The *Dream* and *Fantasy* have a fifth restaurant, **Remy,** which serves high-end French cuisine and levies a $75 surcharge. Both Palo and Remy are difficult to get into. Book a table at **disneycruise.com** at least 75 days before your sail date. If you forget, make reservations as soon as you board.

Along with dinner, one sit-down restaurant is usually open for breakfast and lunch each day, even when the ship is in port. Both breakfast and lunch may include both a mini-buffet and the option to order from a menu.

Virtually all of the food served at the rotational restaurants will be familiar to American palates. Most dishes, especially at dinner, feature cuts of steak, chicken, and fish no different from those you'd find at a chain eatery. DCL's chefs will add some sort of flavor twist to these, such as soy and sesame if it's an Asian-themed restaurant, but the basic ingredients will be recognizable to almost everyone.

Although fresher and of higher quality than the counter-service restaurants, most of the food served at the sit-down restaurants is prepared well ahead of time. You get your order faster this way, but it's also well-nigh impossible to customize that order. We've been told, for instance, that we couldn't order a roast-beef-and-mayo sandwich without the mayo.

**CAFES AND LOUNGES**   Each ship has a dedicated coffee bar called **Cove Café,** which serves espresso, cappuccino, teas, and smoothies, plus wine and cocktails. A small selection of complementary cold appetizers is also available at meal times. Besides Cove Café, a few of the ships' bars and lounges serve appetizers, too.

## The Restaurants

Each Disney ship has a restaurant called **Animator's Palate,** and all four pay tribute to Disney's (and Pixar's) animation processes. Disney characterizes the cuisine as "Pacific Rim/American," but again, it's really just standard chain-restaurant fare. There are probably as many Italian selections—pasta, risotto, focaccia—as Asian. A handful of dishes, such as the vegetable stir-fry, have origins in the East; others are American dishes enrobed in a culinary kimono of sesame, ginger, or teriyaki sauce to make them "Pacific Rim." The food isn't *bad* . . . but neither is it Asian.

The breakfast and lunch buffets at **Cabanas** (*Dream, Fantasy,* and *Magic*) serve about as wide a variety of items as you're likely to find. Breakfast includes everything from fruit, yogurt, and oatmeal to doughnuts, lox, and custom-made omelets. Even cold cereal has options: Besides the usual cornflakes and granola, there's a "build your own" muesli bar where you can add ingredients ranging from brown sugar to exotic dried fruits. Don't worry if you skipped dessert last night—you can get several at breakfast here. We haven't asked, but we'd bet hard cash that the staff would make you filet mignon if you requested nicely. Lunch is a similarly lavish spread, with everything from chicken tenders, sandwiches, and burgers to salmon steaks and pasta. Cabanas switches from buffet to sit-down service for dinner.

Most ships also have a French-inspired restaurant. It's **Lumiere's** on the *Magic*, **Royal Court** on the *Fantasy*, **Royal Palace** on the *Dream*, and

**Triton's** on the *Wonder*. Just as Animator's Palate is more Applebee's than Asian, the menus here are more American bistro than Parisian brasserie. Aside from the substitution of brioche for bread, the most French thing on the menu is usually the use of *julienne* to describe the cut of the vegetables and *consommé* to describe the soup.

There's usually at least one pork dish (such as roast pork tenderloin), one chicken dish (baked or roasted), and steak or prime rib available, along with several seafood and vegetarian options. You could pick up these menus and plunk them down at any other rotational-dining restaurant without anyone noticing.

Each ship has **Palo,** an upscale Italian restaurant serving dinner nightly and brunch on days at sea. For dinner appetizers, try the fish-and-seafood soup, which comes with a large portion of mussels, clams, and lobster. The antipasto *freddo,* with a selection of familiar cheeses and cured meats, could be a little more adventurous. Our favorite entrees are the lobster ravioli in truffle-butter sauce; the spicy penne *arrabbiata;* and the rack of lamb, roasted with garlic and shallots. The chocolate soufflé, by far the most popular dessert, comes with both dark- and white-chocolate sauces.

If you're a lobster junkie, a mother of two from Benson, Arizona, offers this advice:

> *If you book Palo the same night as lobster-tail night in the main dining rooms, you can no longer order lobster tail in Palo, and you miss out completely. If I had known this, I would have adjusted my dates.*

Palo's brunch menu is the best on board. One large table is dedicated to breads, muffins, and pastries, along with sliced fruits and fresh vegetables (the roasted asparagus is tasty). An entire aquarium's worth of fish is available in another section, including shrimp cocktail, cured salmon, smoked-trout mousse, seared tuna, scallops, crab legs, crawfish, and mussels. Eggs cooked in every conceivable way, including Benedict, Florentine, Julia, and customized omelets, are on the menu, too. Not enough? Try the selection of made-to-order pizzas.

What makes a great restaurant, such as *Dream's* and *Fantasy's* **Remy,** different from restaurants that are simply very good is that while the latter usually have a few signature dishes that they do very well, virtually everything at Remy is nothing short of exceptional. An appetizer of carrots—yes, the root vegetable—will be the most extraordinary carrots you've ever had, probably in varieties and colors you didn't know existed, and with a flavor that is the pure essence of carrot-ness. Now imagine a meal of three to eight courses, all equally as good, ranging from soups, seafood, and beef to sides, cheese courses, and desserts. That's an average evening at Remy.

Remy offers both a standard dinner menu and a chef's tasting menu. If you've got the time or the inclination, order the latter—it allows you to savor every bit of creativity and technical mastery the kitchen can muster. The tasting menu also offers a wine pairing for most courses. Note that while the selections are excellent, it's a *lot* of wine that could easily be split between two people.

Remy serves a luxurious brunch on days when the ship is at sea. As with the brunch at Palo, the selection is extensive and includes fruit, pastries, seafood, beef, pork, pasta, and fish. A Champagne pairing is available for an additional $25 per person. We prefer the dinner experience, but spending the morning at Remy is a lovely way to start a day at sea.

DCL's newest restaurant, **Carioca's** on the *Magic,* is named for José Carioca, one of the three birds in Disney's animated 1944 film *The Three Caballeros.* The word *carioca* is slang for a native of Rio de Janeiro, Brazil, and so Carioca's theme is "Brazilian festival." The signature dish is the José Cariocas: three grilled skewers of Brazilian sausage, chili-crusted lamb, and beef tenderloin, with a side of tomato-flavored rice and a delicious *chimichurri* sauce (think a South American pesto). At least one person at your table should try this.

The other entree we really like—in small bites—is the slow-roasted pork belly, with sides of mashed sweet potatoes, grits, and collard greens. The pork belly's skin is incredibly crispy, almost to the point where you'd think it was fried, yet the meat underneath is tender and juicy. It's almost *too* rich, which is why we suggest ordering this as an entree for the table to share.

Finally, if you subscribe to the "Everything tastes better on a stick" philosophy and you're also in the mood for seafood, try the lobster, shrimp, and mahimahi skewers, served on a salad of quinoa with dried-mango, pineapple, and toasted-coconut salsa.

On the flip side, there's the *Wonder's* **Parrot Cay**—the most expendable restaurant on the entire ship, if not of the entire cruise line. It's also the least attractive: Done up in blue, green, and teal, it's supposed to evoke images of Caribbean island architecture; unfortunately, the low ceiling and poor lighting make it feel more like a "Jamaica Me Crazy" party at a college frat house.

## ENTERTAINMENT AND NIGHTLIFE

LIVE ENTERTAINMENT IS PRESENTED at the **Walt Disney Theatre** most nights, on most itineraries. Shows are typically either Disney-themed theatrical productions (typically musicals) or variety acts such as comedians, magicians, or ventriloquists. The theatrical shows are usually of two types: retellings of familiar stories and "jukebox" musicals.

*Disney's Aladdin: A Musical Spectacular,* on the *Fantasy,* is an example of the retelling genre. The cruise version features live actors and multiple Arabian-themed sets reprising key scenes from the animated film, including the most popular songs, in about half the time of the original movie. The *Magic's* **Twice Charmed,** a twist on the original Cinderella story, is probably the best show in this category; The *Fantasy's* *Aladdin* is a distant second, and the *Wonder's* **Toy Story: The Musical** is third.

Examples of jukebox musicals include **Disney Dreams, Disney Wishes, Disney's Believe, Villains Tonight!, Walt Disney: The Dream Goes On,** and **The Golden Mickeys.** Each features songs and characters from many different Disney films, the numbers linked by an original story. We're generally not fans of these shows, especially *Villains Tonight!* The storylines are threadbare, serving to string together the musical numbers rather than provide interesting narrative. Lack of plot, however, isn't our primary objection to these shows—we realize it's a Disney cruise. Rather, they recycle the same handful of characters and songs played in every entertainment venue throughout the ship. If you haven't heard "Be Our Guest" from *Beauty* and *the Beast* performed a dozen times on board, have your hearing checked when you get home.

Finally, most cruises put on a welcome-aboard show on the first night and a farewell show on the last. The welcome show commingles a few musical numbers with a review of the ship's major features and schedule. The farewell show is a recap of the same, with guest photos from throughout the cruise thrown in. These are good times to go to the spa.

Besides stage shows, recent Disney movies (including new releases), are shown at the **Buena Vista Theatre** on each DCL ship. Disney classics are also shown on a giant 24 x 14–foot LED screen perched high above each ship's family pool (**Goofy's Pool** on Deck 9 on the *Magic* and *Wonder*; **Donald's Pool** on Deck 11 on the *Fantasy* and *Dream*.)

**Studio Sea,** modeled after a television- or film-production set, is a family-oriented nightclub offering dance music, cabaret acts, passenger game shows, karaoke, and multimedia entertainment. The Art Deco **Promenade Lounge** offers a haven for reading and relaxing by day and enjoying cocktails and piano music by night. *Magic* features After Hours, an adult-oriented evening-entertainment district with shops and three themed nightclubs: **Fathoms,** with live bands playing rock and roll, Top 40, and country music; **O'Gills,** an Irish pub featuring televised sports events; and **Keys,** a casual place to enjoy easy-listening music and jazz.

*unofficial* **TIP**
Disney ships have no casinos or libraries.

On *Wonder*, After Hours is replaced with the **Route 66** club complex: **WaveBands** features live bands playing pop and oldies; **Cadillac Lounge** is the place for quiet music. The *Wonder*'s **Outlook Café**, with a small bar, plenty of seating, and floor-to-ceiling windows, affords incredible views. Adults-only venues on the *Dream* include four lounges: **Skyline,** one of our favorite bars on any Disney ship, where virtual cityscapes change minute-by-minute; **Meridian,** specializing in martinis; **687,** a sports bar; and **Pink,** designed to look like the inside of a Champagne bottle. **Evolution** dance club completes the after-dark roster. The *Fantasy* also features a version of **Skyline** along with **The Tube,** a club inspired by the London subway system, hosting dancing and live shows; **O'Gills,** the aforementioned pub and sports bar; **Ooh La La,** a Parisian boudoir–themed space specializing in Champagne and fancy (that is, expensive) drinks; and **La Piazza,** modeled after an Italian plaza, serving wine, beer, cocktails, and bar food.

## CHILDREN'S PROGRAMS

PLAYROOMS AND OTHER KIDS' FACILITIES occupy more than 15,000 square feet of each ship. Age-specific programs are among the most extensive in cruising. They include challenging interactive activities and play areas supervised by trained counselors. Age groups are 3–13 and teens. Babysitting (ages 12 weeks–3 years) is provided in the nursery; hours vary according to itinerary. Cost is $9 per hour for the first child, $8 per hour for each additional child. Book at **disneycruise.com** at least 75 days before your sail date (see page 310). If you forget, make reservations as soon as you board. On the *Wonder*, the nursery is called **Flounder's Reef;** on the *Magic*, *Dream*, and *Fantasy*, it's called **It's a Small World Nursery.**

The **Oceaneer Club** (ages 3–12), themed to resemble such settings as Captain Hook's pirate ship and Andy's Room from *Toy Story*, offers plenty of activity space; **Oceaneer Lab** (ages 3–12), has video games, computers, lab equipment, and an area for listening to music. New to the Oceaneer Club on the *Magic* is **Marvel Avengers Academy,** a high-tech interactive-play area. Kids wear ID bracelets, and parents receive pagers for staying in touch with them. As with babysitting, you can register your children in advance for the programs described at the Disney Cruise Line website.

**Vibe** is the teen (ages 14–17) club on all four ships. On the *Magic* and *Wonder* it has a college-coffeehouse feel, while on the *Dream* and *Fantasy* it looks like a sleek urban ultralounge, complete with not only a dance floor and DJ booth but an outdoor sun deck with splash pools.

A Canadian Maritimes teen notes:

> *The private sunbathing deck and splash pools at Vibe are very cool, and you feel like a celebrity getting exclusive use of them. The problem is it's almost never open to use! Usually they're only supervised for 2 hours a day at really strange times.*

In addition to the teen haunts, the ships offer **Edge,** an exclusive space for the tween (11–14) crowd. Finally, the *Magic, Dream,* and *Fantasy* have the teens-only **Chill Spa,** a spa-within-a-spa at the otherwise-grown-up Senses Spa (see next section).

## SPORTS, FITNESS, AND BEAUTY

ALL DCL SHIPS OFFER a comprehensive **fitness center** with modern, well-maintained weight machines, free weights, treadmills, stair-climbers, elliptical machines, stationary bikes, and more. The gyms are also outfitted with yoga mats, large plastic step-aerobics benches, exercise balls, and elastic bands for resistance training. Men's and women's locker rooms (no use fees) have showers, saunas, sinks, robes, towels, toiletries, and lockers with electric locks. We've spent a lot of time in the gyms on every ship and are happy with the variety of equipment available.

Runners and walkers will appreciate the 0.3-mile **jogging track** on Deck 4 of the *Magic* and *Wonder* and the 0.4-mile track on Deck 4 of the *Dream* and *Fantasy.* One of the great things about running on the ship is the amazing scenery, which (almost) makes you forget you're exercising while you're seeing it. If your itinerary includes a trip to Castaway Cay, Disney usually hosts a free 5K run around the island starting around 9 a.m.

If running's not your thing, every DCL ship has an outdoor **basketball court,** surrounded by woven-rope fencing to keep errant balls from flying overboard. The court can be converted to a miniature soccer field or volleyball court, too, if you can find enough people to play.

Ships also have **shuffleboard courts** and outdoor **tennis tables.** (Readers report that the windy conditions on deck make it difficult to play table tennis, but perhaps your game will benefit from a bit of unpredictability.) The *Dream* and *Fantasy* each have an outdoor Disney-themed **miniature-golf course** on Deck 13, and these are a lot of fun for the entire family. The *Dream* and *Fantasy* also have **Foosball tables** outdoors.

Some of the most relaxing times we've spent on Disney's ships have been in their **spas.** Whether you're looking for a massage, manicure, new hairstyle, or just some time to unwind in a hot sauna, you'll find it here. We recommend visiting the spa on your first afternoon aboard the ship to sign up for any last-minute treatments and see if any specials are available.

The *Wonder*'s **Vista Spa & Salon** has treatment rooms for individuals and couples, men's and women's locker rooms, and a thermal-baths room with saunas and heated-stone chairs. Women can get a head-to-toe makeover, starting with hairstyling. Manicures and pedicures come with a heated-stone massage of your various digits. Additional services include facials and massages.

**Senses Spa and Salon,** on the *Magic, Dream,* and *Fantasy,* is better-themed and includes a hair salon, treatment rooms for individuals and couples, men's and women's locker rooms, and a Rainforest Room with steam baths and showers. Our favorite spa experience is the **Rainforest Thermal Suite,** which costs around $25 per person, per day. This gets you access to three saunas with varying levels of heat and humidity: the Laconium, a dry sauna with mild heat and low humidity; the Caldarium, with medium heat and humidity; and the Hamam, a full-on *shvitz* with hot temperatures and lots and lots of steam. In addition to different levels of steam, each sauna has its own scent and music. We enjoy hopping between these saunas and the nearby Rainforest showers. The best thing about the Rainforest package is that Disney sells only a limited number of them per cruise.

# CASTAWAY CAY

EACH CARIBBEAN AND BAHAMIAN CRUISE includes a day at Castaway Cay, Disney's 1,000-acre private island. The island's environment and beauty have been preserved, with white-sand beaches surrounded by emerald water. A pier allows access without tendering. An open tram (like those at Disney parks) links the ship to **Scuttle's Cove** family beach. The tram runs every 5 minutes; you could walk the quarter-mile to the beach, but it's inadvisable in the blistering heat. (Bring sunblock and wear a hat.) Strollers are available, as are rental floats, bikes, kayaks, and snorkel gear. Lounge chairs shaded by umbrellas are plentiful, and hammocks swing under the palms, but there's very little shade otherwise.

Disney Imagineers have created shops, restrooms, and pavilions that give the impression they've been there for years. A supervised children's area includes a "dig" at a half-buried whale skeleton. Water sports are offered in a protected lagoon.

One snorkeling course is near shore; the other, farther out, requires more endurance. On the distant course, snorkelers see fish they identify from a waterproof card provided with rental equipment; lifeguards watch all snorkelers. A Campbellton, New Brunswick, reader describes the experience:

*We really enjoyed snorkeling on Castaway Cay, and while $30 a person is a bit much for the equipment, you can use it all day and even just while swimming in the bay. But be warned! The advanced snorkeling trail is not for wussies—it's easily a mile-long round-trip of swimming.*

A shore excursion provides guests with the opportunity to pet and feed stingrays in a private lagoon. A teen beach area features swimming, snorkeling, kayaking, volleyball, tetherball, basketball, pool, and more. In addition, there are restaurants, private cabanas, and **Pelican Plunge,** a 2,400-square-foot floating platform with an enclosed corkscrew slide, a 140-foot open slide, and a supersized bucket that douses swimmers below. An aqua-play area for toddlers boasts a 1,200-square-foot soft, wet deck with fountains and water jets.

The cruise line has planted several "shipwrecks." On one, in about 10 feet of water, snorkelers see Mickey Mouse riding the ship's bow. Rental equipment costs $25 for adults and $10 for children ages 5–9. Nature trails and bike paths are available. The main beach offers kids' activities, live Bahamian music, and shops. A free 5K fun run is held each morning, weather permitting. Three restaurants serve a buffet lunch of burgers, steaks, ribs, hot dogs, baked beans, slaw, corn on the cob, fruit, and potato chips.

A second tram connects to **Serenity Bay,** the adult beach on the island's opposite side. A bar serves drinks, and passengers can enjoy a massage in one of the private cabanas opening on the sea. Passengers must be back aboard by 4:30 p.m. Many cruisers say they would've liked more time on the island.

# DISNEY CRUISE LINE DEALS

MAKE NO MISTAKE: A Disney cruise is expensive. We initially thought that was because DCL had a built-in audience for Port Canaveral sailing—the port is, after all, within 90 minutes of Walt Disney World. But Disney is also expensive for ports far away from its theme parks: We spot-checked DCL's seven-night Alaska cruises out of Vancouver, British Columbia, for 2014 and found they were priced 60–70% higher than Royal Caribbean's—a difference of $2,800–$3,200 per cruise. That kind of money buys a lot of ice.

One area where Disney is price-competitive with Royal Caribbean is on seven-night Mediterranean cruises out of Barcelona, Spain. When we compared fares for random dates in 2014, Disney was only about 15–40% higher, on average, than Royal Caribbean.

DCL tends to offer deep discounts on less-popular ports (such as Galveston, Texas) or itineraries. If you're within driving distance of Florida, the best deals are often found on cruises leaving Miami.

Check websites such as **cruisecritic.com, cruisemates.com,** and **last minutetravel.com** for the latest discounts. If you prefer to buy directly from Disney, call ☎ 800-951-6499 or 800-951-3532, fax 407-566-7739, or go to **disneycruise.disney.go.com/special-offers.**

DCL offers a free planning DVD that tells all you need to know about Disney cruises and then some. To obtain a copy, call ☎ 888-DCL-2500 or watch it online at **disneycruise.com.**

## CRUISE-WDW PACKAGES

DISNEY OFFERS VACATION PACKAGES that combine Florida cruises with any length of stay at Walt Disney World. Regarding the latter part of the package, an Ithaca, New York, mom complains:

*If you're cruising also, you don't get to use the last day of your ticket in the World due to the 11 a.m. bus departure to the terminal.*

## ADVANCE RESERVATIONS FOR SHORE EXCURSIONS, SPA, PALO, REMY, AND CHILDREN'S PROGRAMS

DISNEY CRUISE LINE OFFERS SHORE EXCURSIONS at each port of call on all of its itineraries. These excursions can be previewed and booked at the Disney Cruise Line website. On the home page, mouse over "Cruises & Destinations," then choose "Port Adventures" from the pop-up menu.

When you can reserve depends on the accommodations you book and whether you've cruised before. Here's the deal:

**Concierge and Platinum Castaway Club guests** (Categories V, T, S, and R; Platinum Castaway Club guests have sailed with DCL at least 10 times previously) *paid in full* can book shore excursions, spa treatments, children's programs, and meals at Palo and Remy 120 days before their sail date.

**Gold Castaway Club guests** (five to nine previous cruises) paid in full can reserve the previous 105 days before their sail date.

**Silver Castaway Club guests** (one to four previous cruises) paid in full can reserve the previous 90 days before their sail date.

First-time cruisers paid in full can reserve the previous 75 days before their sail date.

*unofficial* **TIP**
Disney releases bookable activities on a rolling basis, with only a limited number for Concierge and Castaway Club guests in the beginning; they release more as the 75-day mark approaches. So if you can't get an excursion at the 120-, 105, or 90-day mark, try again 75 days before you sail.

# *A* FEW TIPS

1. First, check out our *Unofficial Guide to Disney Cruise Line,* which covers all four DCL ships in detail.

2. If you opt for a week that includes a cruise and a Walt Disney World stay, go first to Disney World. Cruising at the end of your vacation will ensure you arrive home rested.

3. At least 75 days before you sail and as soon as your booking is paid in full, reserve meals at Palo and Remy, spa treatments, kids' programs, babysitting, and any shore excursions you can't do without at **disneycruise.com**.

4. Board the ship as early as possible. Check your dining rotation, and change it if desired. If you haven't reserved Palo or Remy, spa treatments, children's programs, or babysitting, do it now.

5. Disney requests that gentlemen wear jackets (no ties required) in the evening at Palo and Remy.

6. All cabins have a mini-fridge or cooling box; bring your own snacks and drinks.

7. The best lounges are the **Cadillac Lounge** on the *Wonder,* **Skyline** on the *Fantasy,* **Pink** on the *Dream,* and **Fathoms** on the *Magic.* Make a before- or after-dinner drink there part of your routine.

8. Don't miss the kids' programs.

# PART SIX

# WALL DISNEY WORLD *with* KIDS

## The **ECSTASY** *and the* **AGONY**

SO OVERWHELMING IS THE DISNEY MEDIA and advertising presence that any child who watches TV or shops with Mom is likely to get revved up about going to Walt Disney World. Parents, if anything, are even more susceptible. Almost all parents brighten at the prospect of guiding their children through this special place. But the reality of taking a young child (particularly during the summer) can be closer to the agony than to the ecstasy.

A Dayton, Ohio, mother who took her 5-year-old to Disney World one summer recalls:

> I felt so happy and excited before we went. I guess it was all worth it, but when I look back I think I should have had my head examined. The first day we went to the Magic Kingdom, it was packed. By 11 in the morning, we had walked so far and stood in so many lines that we were all exhausted. Kristy cried about going on anything that looked or even sounded scary and was frightened by all of the Disney characters (they're so big!) except Minnie and Snow White.
>
> We got hungry about the same time as everyone else, but the lines for food were too long and my husband said we'd have to wait. By 1 in the afternoon we were just plugging along, not seeing anything we were really interested in, but picking rides because the lines were short, or because whatever it was, was air-conditioned. At around 2:30, we finally got something to eat, but by then we were so hot and tired that it felt like we had worked in the yard all day. At the end, we were so P.O.'d and uncomfortable that we weren't having any fun.

Before you stiffen in denial, let us assure you that this family's experience is not unusual. Most young children are as picky about rides as they are about what they eat, and many preschoolers are intimidated by the Disney characters. Few humans (of any age) are mentally or physically equipped to march all day in a throng of 50,000 people in the hot Florida sun. And would you be surprised to learn that almost 60% of preschoolers said the thing they liked best about their Disney vacation was the hotel swimming pool?

But even somewhat older kids will surprise you, as this Windsor, Ontario, mom relates:

> On day three, as we pursued our "Around the World in 80 Minutes" through the World Showcase, our two girls suddenly stopped in their tracks between Italy and Germany. They looked around for a minute, and we asked what was wrong. Turns out they'd finally seen something other than characters that appealed to them. "Could we just run around on that grass over there for a few minutes?" they wanted to know. "We won't take too long." So away they went to chase each other on the grass for 10 minutes, and now, 10 years later, that is what they remember about the trip. Ever since, we've tried to include time in each trip plan to "run around on that grass over there," wherever "there" might be.

*un*official **TIP**
When considering a trip to Walt Disney World, think about whether your kids are old enough to enjoy what can be a very fun, but taxing, trip.

With realistic objectives, a good plan, and a sense of humor, you'll be e-mailing us messages like this one from a Harrisburg, Pennsylvania, mom:

> I knew it would be fun for my daughter, but what I didn't expect was just how much fun it would be for me.

## REALITY TESTING: WHOSE DREAM IS IT?

REMEMBER WHEN YOU WERE LITTLE and you got that nifty remote control car for Christmas, the one Dad wouldn't let you play with? Did you wonder who the car was really for? Ask yourself a similar question about your vacation to Walt Disney World. Whose dream are you trying to make come true: yours or your child's?

Young children read their parents' emotions. When you ask, "Honey, how would you like to go to Disney World?" your child will respond more to your smile and enthusiasm than to any notion of what Disney World is all about. The younger the child, the more this holds true. From many preschoolers, you could elicit the same excitement by asking, "Sweetie, how would you like to go to Cambodia on a dogsled?"

So, is your happy fantasy of introducing your child to Disney magic a pipe dream? Not necessarily, but you have to be practical and open to reality testing. For example, would you increase the probability of a successful visit by waiting a year or two? Is your child adventuresome enough to sample the variety of Disney World? Will your child have sufficient endurance and patience to cope with long lines and large crowds?

## RECOMMENDATIONS FOR MAKING THE DREAM COME TRUE

WHEN YOU'RE PLANNING A DISNEY WORLD VACATION with young children, consider the following:

**AGE** Although Walt Disney World's color and festivity excite all children and specific attractions delight toddlers and preschoolers, Disney entertainment is generally oriented to older children and adults. Children should be a fairly mature 7 years old to *appreciate* the Magic Kingdom and Disney's Animal Kingdom, a year or two older to get much out of Epcot or Disney's Hollywood Studios.

Readers continually debate how old a child should be or the ideal age to go to Disney World. A Rockaway, New Jersey, mom writes:

> You were absolutely right about young kids; I found myself rereading your section "The Ecstasy and the Agony." Unfortunately, our experience was pure agony, with the exception of our hotel pool. It was the one and only thing our kids wanted to do. I planned this trip and saved for over a year and cried all week at the disappointment that our kids just wanted to swim.

A dad from Columbus, Ohio, felt like he was in a maternity ward:

> We were shocked to see so many newborns as well. I could have sworn that one woman gave birth at the bus stop, her baby was so small.

An overly ambitious mother of a toddler received a reality check:

> It took me a day to realize that I had to LET some things GO. We were traveling with a 3-year-old, and it wasn't fun for anyone when I was seeing Disney as one big to-do list. I still made sure that we hit the highlights for her—Pooh, Little Mermaid, characters, princesses, and so on, but we didn't make it to many things on my list. I had to accept that and be OK with it. I was getting too stressed out trying to mark things off of my list!

An Iowa City, Iowa, mother of three administers some tough love:

> Get over it! In my opinion, people think too much about the age thing. If taking your 3-year-old to Disney World would make you happy, that's all that counts. End of story. It doesn't matter if the trip is really for you or your child—it's all good. You shouldn't have to jump through a bunch of hoops to give yourself permission to go.

A Lawrenceville, Georgia, mother of two toddlers advises maintaining the children's normal schedule:

> The first day, we tried your suggestion about an early start; so we woke the children (ages 4 and 2) and hurried them to get going. BAD IDEA with toddlers. This put them off schedule for naps and meals the rest of the day. It's best to let young ones stay on their schedule and see Disney at their own pace.

*unofficial* **TIP**
Coupled with a sense of humor and a little preparedness on your part, our touring plans and tips for families ensure a super experience at any time of year.

**WHEN TO VISIT** Avoid the hot, crowded summer months, especially if you have preschoolers. Go in October, November (except Thanksgiving), early December, January, February, or May. If you have children of varied ages and they're good students, take the older ones out of school and visit during the cooler and less congested off-season. Arrange special assignments relating to educational aspects of Disney World. If your children can't afford to miss school, take your vacation as soon as the school year ends. Alternatively, try late August before school starts. Please understand that you don't have to visit during one of the more ideal times of year to have a great vacation.

A Peterborough, England, woman agrees:

*We visited WDW at the end of August, and we expected that the crowds would be almost unbearable. However, we were surprised to find that since most local schools were back in session, we could walk on most headliner rides up until late afternoon, and even then there was only a short wait—some rides at Universal Studios didn't even open until 11 a.m. because we were visiting on a low-attendance day! We'd recommend that more people go this time of year, especially those people whose children don't return to school until later.*

**BUILD NAPS AND REST INTO YOUR ITINERARY** The parks are huge: Don't try to see everything in one day. Tour in the early morning and return to your hotel around 11:30 a.m. for lunch, a swim, and a nap. Even during off-season, when crowds are smaller and the temperature is more pleasant, the major parks' size will exhaust most children younger than age 8 by lunchtime. Return to the park in late afternoon or early evening and continue touring. A family from Texas underlines the importance of naps and rest:

*Probably the most important tip your guide gave us was going to the hotel to swim and regroup during the day. The parks became unbearable by noon—and so did my husband and boys. The hotel was an oasis that calmed our nerves! After about 3 hours of playtime, we headed out to a different park for dinner and a cool evening of fun.*

Regarding naps, this mom doesn't mince words:

*For parents of small kids: Take the book's advice and get out of the park and take the nap, take the nap, TAKE THE NAP! Never in my life have I seen so many parents screaming at, ridiculing, or slapping their kids. (What a vacation!) WDW is overwhelming for kids and adults.*

A Matthews, North Carolina, family pooped out in two days:

*This was our first trip to Disney, and we learned the hard way why it's important to rest and get out of the parks awhile. Our first two days were packed with touring, followed by a princess makeover and dining with the princesses in Cinderella Castle. Needless to say, by day three we were exhausted, grumpy, and beginning to see no magic in Disney. We ended our third day by noon at Epcot and headed back to the resort to rest and relax for the rest of the night. After that, I rearranged all of our touring plans for rest and relaxing time, which allowed us to finish our vacations with happy (most of the time) children and parents.*

If you plan to return to your hotel at midday and want your room made up, let housekeeping know.

**WHERE TO STAY** The time and hassle involved in commuting to and from the theme parks will be less if your hotel is close by. This doesn't necessarily mean you have to lodge inside Disney World. Because the World is so geographically dispersed, many off-property hotels are closer to the parks than some Disney resorts (see our Hotel Information Chart in Part Three, showing commuting times

*unofficial* **TIP**
If you must rent a car to make returning to your hotel practicable, do it.

from Disney and non-Disney hotels). Regardless of where you stay, it's imperative that you take young children out of the parks each day for a few hours of rest. Neglecting to relax can ruin the day—or the vacation—for everyone.

If you have young children, book a hotel that is within a 20-minute driving distance from the theme parks. It's true that you can revive somewhat by retreating to a Disney hotel for lunch or by finding a quiet restaurant in the parks, but there's no substitute for returning to the comfort of your hotel. Regardless of what you've heard, children too large to sleep in a stroller won't relax unless you take them back to your hotel.

*unofficial* **TIP**
The way to protect your considerable investment in your Disney vacation is to stay happy and have a good time. You don't have to meet a quota for experiencing attractions. *Do what you want.*

If you're traveling with children 12 years old and younger and you want to stay in the World, we recommend the Polynesian, Grand Floridian & Villas, or Wilderness Lodge & Villas (in that order), if they fit your budget. For less expensive rooms, try Port Orleans French Quarter. The least expensive on-site rooms are available at the All-Star Resorts. In addition to standard hotel rooms, the All-Star Music and Art of Animation Resorts offer two-room family suites that can sleep as many as six and provide kitchenettes. Log cabins at Fort Wilderness and the DDV resorts are also an option for families who need a little more space. Outside the World, check our top hotels for families (see page 243), but know that many more good options exist.

**BE IN TOUCH WITH YOUR FEELINGS** When you or your kids get tired and irritable, call time-out. Trust your instincts. What would feel best? Another ride, an ice cream break, or going back to the room for a nap?

**LEAST COMMON DENOMINATORS** Somebody is going to run out of steam first, and when he or she does, the whole family will be affected. Sometimes a snack break will revive the flagging member. Sometimes, however, it's better to return to your hotel. Pushing the tired or discontented beyond their capacity will spoil the day for them—and you. Energy levels vary. Be prepared to respond to members of your group who poop out. *Hint:* "We've driven a thousand miles to take you to Disney World and now you're ruining everything!" is not an appropriate response.

**BUILDING ENDURANCE** Though most children are active, their normal play usually doesn't condition them for the exertion required to tour a Disney park. Start family walks four to six weeks before your trip to get in shape. A mother from Wescosville, Pennsylvania, reports:

> We had our 6-year-old begin walking with us a bit every day one month before leaving—when we arrived at Disney World, her little legs could carry her, and she had a lot of stamina.

From a Middletown, Delaware, mom::

> You recommended walking for six weeks prior to the trip, but we began months in advance, just because. My husband lost 10 pounds, my daughter never once complained, and we met a lot of neighbors! We wouldn't have made it without you—thanks!

**SETTING LIMITS AND MAKING PLANS** In order to avoid arguments and disappointment, establish guidelines for each day and get everybody committed. Include the following:

1. Wake-up time and breakfast plans
2. When to depart for the park
3. What to take with you
4. A policy for splitting the group or for staying together
5. What to do if the group gets separated or someone is lost
6. What you want to see, including plans in the event an attraction is closed or too crowded
7. A policy on what you can afford for snacks
8. How long you plan to tour in the morning and what time you'll return to your hotel to rest
9. When you'll return to the park and how late you'll stay
10. Dinner plans
11. A policy for buying souvenirs, including who pays: Mom and Dad or the kids
12. Bedtimes

**BE FLEXIBLE** Any day at Disney World includes surprises; be prepared to adjust your plan. Listen to your intuition.

**WHAT KIDS WANT** According to the travel-research firm Yesawich, Pepperdine, Brown, and Russell, 71% of children between the ages of 6 and 17 say they need a vacation because school and homework get them down. The chart below shows what kids want and don't want when taking a vacation. Kids surveyed have a lot in common about what they do want, not as much concerning what they don't.

| WHAT DO KIDS WANT? | WHAT DO KIDS NOT WANT? |
|---|---|
| To go swimming/have pool time 80% | To get up early 52% |
| To eat in restaurants 78% | To ride in a car 36% |
| To stay at a hotel or resort 76% | To play golf 34% |
| To visit a theme park 76% | To go to a museum 31% |
| To stay up late 73% | |

**MAINTAINING SOME SEMBLANCE OF ORDER AND DISCIPLINE** OK, OK, wipe that smirk off your face. Order and discipline on the road may seem like an oxymoron to you, but you won't be hooting when your 5-year-old launches a tantrum in the middle of Fantasyland. Your willingness to give this subject serious consideration before you leave home may well be the most important element of your pre-trip preparation.

Discipline and maintaining order are more difficult when traveling than at home because everyone is, as a Boston mom put it, "in and out"—in strange surroundings and out of the normal routine. For children, it's hard to contain excitement and anticipation that pop to the surface in the form of fidgety hyperactivity, nervous energy, and sometimes, acting out. Confinement in a car, plane, or hotel room only exacerbates the situation, and kids often tend to be louder than normal, more aggressive with siblings, and much more inclined to push the envelope of parental patience. Once you're in the theme parks, it doesn't get much better. There's more elbow room, but there are also overstimulation, crowds, heat, and miles of walking. All this, coupled with marginal or inadequate rest, can lead to a meltdown in the most harmonious of families.

Sound parenting and standards of discipline practiced at home, applied consistently, will suffice to handle most situations on vacation. Still, it's instructive to study the hand you're dealt when traveling. For starters, aside from being jazzed and ablaze with adrenaline, your kids may believe that rules followed at home are somehow suspended when traveling. Parents reinforce this misguided intuition by being inordinately lenient in the interest of maintaining peace in the family. While some of your home protocols (like cleaning your plate and going to bed at a set time) might be relaxed to good effect on vacation, differing from your normal approach to discipline can precipitate major misunderstanding and possibly disaster.

*un*official **TIP**
Just because the kids are on vacation doesn't mean you should let them monopolize your trip—maintain some of your everyday rules, and you'll all have a better time together.

Children, not unexpectedly, are likely to believe that a vacation (especially a vacation to Walt Disney World) is intended just for them. This reinforces their focus on their own needs and largely erases any consideration of yours. Such a mind-set dramatically increases their sense of hurt and disappointment when you correct them or deny them something they want. An incident that would hardly elicit a pouty lip at home could well escalate to tears or defiance when traveling. It's important before you depart on your trip, therefore, to discuss your vacation needs with your children, and to explore their wants and expectations as well.

The stakes are high for everyone on a vacation—for you because of the cost in time and dollars, but also because your vacation represents a rare opportunity for rejuvenation and renewal. The stakes are high for your children, too. Children tend to romanticize travel, building anticipation to an almost unbearable level. Discussing the trip in advance can ground expectations to a certain extent, but a child's imagination will, in the end, trump reality every time. The good news is that you can take advantage of your children's emotional state to establish preset rules and conditions for their conduct while on vacation. Because your children want what's being offered *sooooo* badly, they will be unusually accepting and conscientious regarding whatever rules are agreed upon.

According to *Unofficial Guide* child psychologist Karen Turnbow, PhD, successful response to (or avoidance of) behavioral problems on the road begins with a clear-cut disciplinary policy at home. Both at home and on vacation the approach should be the same, and should be based on the following key concepts:

**1. LET EXPECTATIONS BE KNOWN** Discuss what you expect from your children, but don't try to cover every imaginable situation (that's what lawyers are for—just kidding). Cover expectations regarding compliance with parental directives, treatment of siblings, resolution of disputes, schedules (including morning wake-up and bedtimes), courtesy and manners, staying together, and who pays for what.

**2. EXPLAIN THE CONSEQUENCES OF NONCOMPLIANCE** Detail very clearly and firmly the consequence of not meeting expectations. This should be very straightforward and unambiguous: "If you do X (or don't do X), this is what will happen."

**3. WARNING** You're dealing with excited, expectant children, not machines, so it's important to issue a warning before meting out discipline. It's critical to understand that we're talking about one unequivocal warning rather than multiple warnings or nagging. These last undermine your credibility and make your expectations appear relative or less than serious. Multiple warnings or nagging also effectively pass control of the situation from you to your child (who sometimes may continue acting out as an attention-getting strategy).

**4. FOLLOW THROUGH** If you say you're going to do something, do it. Period. Children must understand that you mean business.

**5. CONSISTENCY** Inconsistency makes discipline a random event in the eyes of your children. Random discipline encourages random behavior, which translates to a nearly total loss of parental control. Long term, both at home and on the road, your response to a given situation or transgression must be perfectly predictable. Structure and repetition, essential for a child to learn, cannot be achieved in the absence of consistency.

Although the previous methods are the five biggies, there are several corollary concepts and techniques worthy of consideration.

Understand that whining, tantrums, defiance, sibling friction, and even holding up the group are ways in which children communicate with parents. Frequently the object or precipitant of a situation has little or no relation to the unacceptable behavior. A fit may on the surface appear to be about the ice cream you refused to buy little Robby, but there's almost always something deeper, a subtext that is closer to the truth (this is why ill behavior often persists after you give in to a child's demands). As often as not, the real cause is a need for attention. This need is so powerful in some children that they will subject themselves to certain punishment and parental displeasure to garner the attention they crave, even if it's negative.

*unofficial* **TIP**
Teaching your kids to tell you clearly what they want or need will help make the trip more enjoyable for everyone.

To get at the root cause of the behavior in question requires both active listening and empowering your child with a "feeling vocabulary." Active listening is a concept that's been around a long time. It involves being alert not only to what a child says, but also to the context in which it's said, to the words used and possible subtext, to the child's emotional state and body language, and even to what's not said. Sounds complicated, but it's basically being attentive to the larger picture and, more to the point, being aware that there *is* a larger picture.

Helping your child develop a feeling vocabulary consists of teaching your child to use words to describe what's going on. The idea is to teach the child to articulate what's really troubling him, to be able to identify and express emotions and mood states in language. Of course, learning to express feelings is a lifelong learning experience, but it's much less dependent on innate sensitivity than on being provided the tools for expression and being encouraged to use them.

It all begins with convincing your child that you're willing to listen attentively and take what he's saying seriously. By listening to your child, you help him transcend the topical by reframing the conversation to address the underlying emotional state(s). That his brother hit him may have precipitated the mood state, but the act is topical and of secondary importance. What you want is for your child to be able to communicate how that makes him feel, and to get in touch with those emotions. When you reduce an incident (hitting) to the emotions triggered (anger, hurt, rejection), you have the foundation for helping him develop constructive coping strategies. Being in touch with one's feelings and developing constructive coping strategies are essential to emotional well-being, and they also have a positive effect on behavior. A child who can tell his mother why he is distressed is a child who has discovered a coping strategy far more effective (not to mention easier for all concerned) than a tantrum.

Children are almost never too young to begin learning a feeling vocabulary. And helping your child to be in touch with—and to communicate—his or her emotions will stimulate you to focus on your feelings and mood states in a similar way. In the end, with persistence and effort, the whole family will achieve a vastly improved ability to communicate.

Until you get the active listening and feeling vocabulary going, be careful not to become part of the problem. There's a laundry list of adult responses to bad behavior that only make things worse. Hitting, swatting, yelling, name-calling, insulting, belittling, using sarcasm, pleading, nagging, and inducing guilt figure prominently on the list.

Responding to a child appropriately in a disciplinary situation requires thought and preparation. Following are things to keep in mind and techniques to try when your world blows up while waiting in line for Dumbo.

**1. BE THE ADULT** It's well understood that children can push their parents' buttons faster and more skillfully than just about anyone or anything else. They've got your number, know precisely how to elicit a response, and are not reluctant to go for the jugular. Fortunately (or unfortunately), you're the adult, and to deal with a situation effectively, you've got to act like one. If your kids get you ranting and caterwauling, you effectively abdicate your adult status. Worse, you suggest by way of example that being out of control is an acceptable expression of hurt or anger. No matter what happens, repeat the mantra, "I am the adult in this relationship."

**2. FREEZE THE ACTION** Being the adult and maintaining control almost always translates to freezing the action, to borrow a sports term. Instead of responding in knee-jerk fashion (that is, at a maturity level closer to your child's than yours), freeze the action by disengaging. Wherever you are or whatever the family is doing, stop in place and concentrate on one thing, and one thing only: getting all involved calmed down. Practically speaking this usually means initiating a time-out. It's essential that you take this action immediately. Grabbing your child by the arm or collar and dragging him toward the car or hotel room only escalates the turmoil by prolonging the confrontation and by adding a coercive physical dimension to an already volatile emotional event. For the sake of everyone involved, including the people around you (as when a toddler throws a tantrum in church), it's essential to retreat to a more private place. Choose the first place available. Firmly sit the child down and refrain from talking to him until you've both cooled off. This might take a little time, but the investment is worthwhile. Truncating the process is like trying to get on your feet too soon after surgery.

**3. ISOLATE THE CHILD** You'll be able to deal with the situation more effectively and expeditiously if the child is isolated with one parent. Dispatch the uninvolved members of your party for a snack break or have them go on with the activity or itinerary without you (if possible) and arrange to rendezvous later at an agreed time and place. In addition to letting the others get on with their day, isolating the offending child with one parent relieves him of the pressure of being the group's focus of attention and object of anger. Equally important, isolation frees you from the scrutiny and expectations of the others in regard to how to handle the situation.

**4. REVIEW THE SITUATION WITH THE CHILD** If, as discussed a few pages back, you've made your expectations clear, stated the consequences of failing to meet those expectations, and administered a warning, review the situation with the child and follow through with the discipline warranted. If, as often occurs, things are not so black-and-white, encourage the child to communicate his feelings. Try to uncover what occasioned the acting out. Lectures and accusatory language don't work well here, nor do threats. Dr. Turnbow suggests that a better approach (after the child is calm) is to ask, "What can we do to make this a better day for you?"

**5. FREQUENT TANTRUMS OR ACTING OUT** The preceding four points relate to dealing with an incident as opposed to a chronic condition. If a child frequently acts out or throws tantrums, you'll need to employ a somewhat different strategy.

Tantrums are cyclical events evolved from learned behavior. A child learns that he can get your undivided attention by acting out. When you respond, whether by scolding, admonishing, threatening, or negotiating, your response further draws you into the cycle and prolongs the behavior. When you accede to the child's demands, you reinforce the effectiveness of the tantrum and raise the cost of capitulation next time around. When a child thus succeeds in monopolizing your attention, he effectively becomes the person in charge.

To break this cycle, you must disengage from the child. The object is to demonstrate that the cause-and-effect relationship (that is, tantrum elicits parental attention) is no longer operative. This can be accomplished by refusing to interact with the child as long as the untoward behavior continues. Tell the child that you're unwilling to discuss his problem until he calms down. You can ignore the behavior, remove yourself from the child's presence (or vice versa), or isolate the child with a time-out. It's important to disengage quickly and decisively with no discussion or negotiation.

Most children don't pick the family vacation as the time to start throwing tantrums. The behavior will be evident before you leave home, and home is the best place to deal with it. Be forewarned, however, that bad habits die hard, and that a child accustomed to getting attention by throwing tantrums will not simply give up after a single instance of disengagement. More likely, the child will at first escalate the intensity and length of his tantrums. By your consistent refusal over several weeks (or even months) to respond to his behavior, however, he will finally adjust to the new paradigm.

Children are cunning as well as observant. Many understand that a tantrum in public is embarrassing to you and that you're more likely to cave in than you would at home. Once again, consistency is the key, along with a bit of anticipation. When traveling, it's not necessary to retreat to the privacy of a hotel room to isolate your child. You can carve out space for a time-out almost anywhere: on a theme park bench, in a park, in your car, in a restroom, even on a sidewalk.

You can often spot the warning signs of an impending tantrum and head it off by talking to the child before he reaches an explosive emotional pitch. And don't forget that tantrums are about getting attention. Giving your child attention when things are on an even keel often preempts acting out.

**6. SALVAGE OPERATIONS** Who knows what evil lurks in the hearts of children? What's for sure is that they're full of surprises, and sometimes the surprises are not good. If your sweet child manages to pull a stunt of mammoth proportions, what do you do? This happened to an Ohio couple, resulting in the offending kid pretty much being grounded for life. Fortunately there were no injuries or lives lost, but the parents had to determine what to do for the remainder of the vacation. For starters, they split up the group. One parent escorted the offending child back to the hotel, where he was effectively confined to his guest room for the duration. That evening, the parents arranged for in-room sitters for the rest of the stay. Expensive? You bet, but better than watching your whole vacation go down the tubes.

A family at Walt Disney World's Magic Kingdom theme park had a similar experience, although the offense was of a more modest order of magnitude. Because it was their last day of vacation, they elected to place the misbehaver in time-out, in the theme park, for the rest of the day. One parent monitored the culprit while the other parent and the siblings enjoyed the attractions. At agreed times the parents would switch places. Once again, not ideal, but preferable to stopping the vacation.

### Parenting Advice: Readers Weigh In

Though the foregoing section was developed by top child psychologists, it rubs some readers the wrong way. Take this teacher from Corryton, Tennessee:

> *The one thing I don't like is the section on how to make your kids behave. As a preschool teacher, I can honestly say that people who need this advice won't take it anyway—so why bother?*

But a North Carolina psychiatrist disagrees:

> *The section of the* Unofficial Guide *dealing with child behavioral issues while traveling is one of the most concise and well-articulated presentations on this subject that I have encountered anywhere. I recommend it to many of my patients who are contemplating traveling with their children.*

A New Hampshire father of two had this to say:

*Your advice on touring with children was fabulous. Your book gave us confidence to do the parks without being deer caught in the headlights.*

## ABOUT THE *UNOFFICIAL GUIDE* TOURING PLANS

PARENTS WHO USE OUR TOURING PLANS are often frustrated by interruptions and delays caused by their young children. Here's what to expect:

**1. CHARACTER ENCOUNTERS CAN WREAK HAVOC WITH THE TOURING PLANS.** Many children will stop in their tracks whenever they see a Disney character. Attempting to haul your child away before he has satisfied his curiosity is likely to cause anything from whining to full-scale revolt. Either go with the flow or specify a morning or afternoon for photos and autographs. Be aware that queues for autographs can be as long as the queues for major attractions; our touring plans use FastPass+ (see page 84) to minimize waits in line.

**2. OUR TOURING PLANS CALL FOR VISITING ATTRACTIONS IN A SEQUENCE, OFTEN SKIPPING ATTRACTIONS ALONG THE WAY.** Children don't like to skip anything! If something catches their eye, they want to see it that moment. Some can be persuaded to skip attractions if parents explain their plans in advance. Other kids flip out at skipping something, particularly in Fantasyland. A mom from Charleston, South Carolina, writes:

*We didn't have too much trouble following the touring plans at Disney's Hollywood Studios and at Epcot. The Magic Kingdom plan, on the other hand, turned out to be a train wreck. When we were on Dumbo, my 5-year-old saw eight dozen other things in Fantasyland she wanted to see. The long and the short is that after Dumbo, there was no getting her out of there.*

A mother of two from Burlington, Vermont, adds:

*I found out that my kids were very curious about the castle because we had read Cinderella at home. Whenever I wanted to leave Fantasyland, I would just say, "Let's go to the castle and see if Cinderella is there." Once we got as far as the front door to the castle, it was no problem going out to the Central Plaza and then to another land.*

**3. IF YOU'RE USING A STROLLER, YOU WON'T BE ABLE TO TAKE IT INTO ATTRACTIONS OR ONTO RIDES.** This includes rides such as the Walt Disney World Railroad that are included in the touring plans as in-park transportation. (An exception: Folding strollers are permitted on the railroad.) Well-marked stroller parking is available throughout the theme parks.

**4. YOU PROBABLY WON'T FINISH THE TOURING PLAN.** Varying hours of operation, crowds, your group's size, your children's ages, and your stamina will all affect how much of the plan you'll complete. Tailor your expectations to this reality, or you'll be frustrated.

While our touring plans allow you to make the most of your time at the parks, it's impossible to define what "most" will be. It differs from family to family. If you have two young children, you probably won't see as much as two adults will. If you have four children, you probably won't see as much as a couple with only two children.

## STUFF TO THINK ABOUT

**OVERHEATING, SUNBURN, AND DEHYDRATION**  These are the most common problems of younger children at Disney World. Carry and use sunscreen. Apply it on children in strollers, even if the stroller has a canopy. To avoid overheating, stop for rest regularly—say, in the shade, or in a restaurant or at a show with air-conditioning.

> *unofficial* **TIP**
> Keep little ones well covered in sunscreen and hydrated with fluids. Don't count on hydrating young children with soft drinks and stops at water fountains. Carry plastic bottles of water. Bottles with screw caps are sold in all major parks for about $3. *Remember:* Excited kids may not tell you when they're thirsty or hot.

**BLISTERS AND SORE FEET**  In addition to wearing comfortable shoes, bring along some blister bandages if you or your children are susceptible to blisters. These bandages (which are also available at First Aid, if you didn't heed our warnings) offer excellent protection, stick well, and won't sweat off. Remember, a preschooler may not say anything about a blister until it's already formed, so keep an eye on things during the day. For an expanded discussion, see pages 406 and 407.

**FIRST AID**  Each major theme park has a first-aid center. In the Magic Kingdom, it's at the end of Main Street to your left, between Casey's Corner and The Crystal Palace. At Epcot, it's on the World Showcase side of Odyssey Center. At Disney's Hollywood Studios, it's in the Guest Relations Building inside the main entrance. At Disney's Animal Kingdom, it's in Discovery Island, on your left just before you cross the bridge to Africa, behind Creature Comforts. And in all four parks, First Aid and the Baby Care Center are right next to each other. If you or your children have a medical problem, go to a first-aid center. They're friendlier than most doctor's offices and are accustomed to treating everything from paper cuts to allergic reactions.

**CHILDREN ON MEDICATION**  Some parents of hyperactive children on medication discontinue or decrease the child's dosage at the end of the school year. If you have such a child, be aware that Disney World might overstimulate him or her. Consult your physician before altering your child's medication regimen.

**GLASSES AND SUNGLASSES**  If your kids (or you) wear them, attach a strap or string to the frames so the glasses will stay on during rides and can hang from the child's neck while indoors.

**THINGS YOU FORGOT OR RAN OUT OF**  Rain gear, diapers, baby formula, sunburn treatments, memory cards, and other sundries are sold at all major theme parks and at Typhoon Lagoon, Blizzard Beach, and Downtown Disney. If you don't see something you need, ask if it's in stock. Basic over-the-counter meds are often available free in small quantities at the First Aid Centers in the parks.

**INFANTS AND TODDLERS AT THE THEME PARKS**  The major parks have centralized facilities for infant and toddler care. Everything necessary for changing diapers, preparing formulas, and warming bottles and food is available. Supplies are for sale, and rockers and special chairs for nursing mothers are provided. At the Magic Kingdom, the Baby Care Center is next to The Crystal Palace at the end of Main Street. At Epcot, the Baby Care Center is in the Odyssey Center, between Test Track in Future World and Mexico in World Showcase. At Disney's Hollywood Studios, the Baby Care Center is in the Guest Relations Building left of the main entrance. At Disney's Animal Kingdom, the Baby Care Center is behind Creature Comforts. Dads are welcome at the centers and can use most services. In addition, many men's restrooms in the major parks have changing tables.

A mom from New Berlin, Wisconsin, offers this tip for families with babies on formula:

> *A note to families with infants: We got hot water from the food vendors at WDW and mixed the formula as we went. It eliminated keeping bottles cold and then warming them up.*

Infants and toddlers are allowed in any attraction that doesn't have minimum height or age restrictions. But as a Minneapolis mother reports, some attractions are better for babies than others:

> *Theater and boat rides are easier for babies (ours was almost a year old, not yet walking). Rides where there's a bar that comes down are doable, but harder. Peter Pan was our first encounter with this type of ride, and we had barely gotten situated when I realized he might fall out of my grasp. The standing auditorium films are too intense; the noise level is deafening and the images inescapable.*

The same mom also advises:

> *We used a baby sling on our trip and thought it was great when standing in lines—much better than a stroller, which you have to park before getting in line (and navigate through crowds).*

If you think you might try nursing during a theater attraction, be advised that most shows run about 17–20 minutes. Exceptions are *The Hall of Presidents* at the Magic Kingdom and *The American Adventure* at Epcot, which run 23 and 29 minutes, respectively.

**RUNNING OUT OF GAS** When Bob was preparing to hike from the Colorado River to the rim of the Grand Canyon—a 5,000-foot ascent— a park ranger told him to mix an electrolyte-replacement powder in his water and eat an energy-boosting snack at least twice every hour. While there's not much ascending to do at Walt Disney World, battling the heat, humidity, and crowds contributes to poop-out, especially where kids are concerned. Limiting calorie consumption to mealtimes just won't get it, as an experienced and wise grandma points out:

> *Children who get cranky during a visit often do so from all that time and energy expended without food. Feed them! A snack at any price goes a long way to keeping the little ones happy and parents sane. Oh, and the security people are very nice about you taking snacks or drinks in, but DO NOT bring glass containers!*

## STROLLERS

STROLLERS ARE AVAILABLE for rent at all four theme parks and the Downtown Disney area (single stroller, $15 per day with no deposit,

$13 per day for the entire stay; double stroller, $31 per day with no deposit, $27 per day for the entire stay; stroller rentals at Downtown Disney require a $100 credit card deposit; double strollers not available at Downtown Disney). Strollers are welcome at Blizzard Beach and Typhoon Lagoon, but no rentals are available. With multiday rentals, you can skip the rental line entirely after your first visit—just head over to the stroller-handout area, show your receipt, and you'll be wheeling out of there in no time. If you rent a stroller at the Magic Kingdom and you decide to go to Epcot, Disney's Animal Kingdom, or Disney's Hollywood Studios, turn in your Magic Kingdom stroller and present your receipt at the next park. You'll be issued another stroller at no additional charge.

You can pay in advance for stroller rentals—this allows you to bypass the "paying" line and head straight for the "pickup" line. Disney resort guests can pay in advance at their resort's gift shop. Save receipts! Obtain strollers at the Magic Kingdom entrance, to the left of Epcot's Entrance Plaza and at Epcot's International Gateway, and at Oscar's Super Service just inside the entrance of Disney's Hollywood Studios. At Disney's Animal Kingdom, they're at Garden Gate Gifts, to the right just inside the entrance. Returning the stroller is a breeze. You can ditch your rental stroller anywhere in the park when you're ready to leave. To see what the rental strollers look like, Google "rental strollers at Walt Disney World."

Strollers are a must for infants and toddlers, but we've seen many sharp parents rent strollers for somewhat older children—the stroller spares parents from having to carry kids when they sag, and it provides a convenient place to tote water and snacks.

A family from Tulsa, Oklahoma, recommends springing for a double stroller:

> We rent a double for baggage room or in case the older child gets tired of walking.

But a New Lenox, Illinois, family advocates not leaving anyone out:

> If your kids are 8 or under, RENT STROLLERS for all of them! An 8-year-old will fit in a stroller, and you can fit up to four kids in two doubles. My husband suggested getting a stroller for our 6-year-old and the two "babies" (ages 4 and 3). We plowed through crowds, and the kids didn't get nearly as tired since they could be seated whenever they wanted.

We've always advocated using strollers for any child who will fit; however, a McKean, Pennsylvania, reader thinks the situation has gotten out of hand:

*Please tell parents their children don't have to be in strollers if (a) they're old enough to vote, (b) they've served in the armed services, (c) they smoke, and/or (d) they have kids of their own. It's gotten really ridiculous—this last visit we saw more 10+-year-olds in strollers than sub-10-year-olds. Strollers add congestion, especially with dingbat parents using them to blast through crowds like child-first battering rams. I never knew walking was bad for you.*

A Charleston, West Virginia, mom recommends a backup plan:

*Strollers are not allowed in lines for rides, so if you have a small child (ours was 4) who needs to be held, you might end up holding him a long time. If I had it to do over, I'd bring along some kind of child carrier for when he was out of the stroller.*

If you go to your hotel for a break and intend to return to the park, leave your rental stroller in stroller parking near the park entrance, marking it with something personal like a bandanna. When you return, your stroller will be waiting.

Rental strollers are too large for all infants and many toddlers. If you plan to rent a stroller for your infant or toddler, bring pillows, cushions, or rolled towels to buttress him in.

Bringing your own stroller is permitted. However, only collapsible strollers are allowed on monorails, parking-lot trams, and buses. Your stroller is unlikely to be stolen, but mark it with your name.

Having her own stroller was indispensable to a Mechanicsville, Virginia, mother of two toddlers:

*How I was going to manage to get the kids from the parking lot to the park was a big worry for me before I made the trip. I didn't read anywhere that it was possible to walk to the entrance of the parks instead of taking the tram, so I wasn't sure I could do it.*

*Since I have two kids ages 1 and 2, it was easier to walk to the entrance of the park from the parking lot with the kids in my own stroller than to take the kids out of the stroller, fold the stroller (while trying to control the two kids and associated gear), load the stroller and the kids onto the tram, etc. No matter where I was parked, I could always just walk to the entrance. It sometimes took a while, but it was easier for me.*

A Secaucus, New Jersey, mom weighed all the considerations in exemplary type-A fashion:

*If your child is under age 2, bring your own stroller. Three reasons to bring your own: First, you have all the way from your car to the Transportation and Ticket Center to the monorail (or ferry) to the stroller rental without a stroller, but with your child, diaper bag, and own self and stuff in tow. Not half as bad as doing it in reverse when leaving, when you're exhausted and have added to your luggage with purchases and the toddler who might have walked in wants to be carried out. Second, the WDW stroller is simply too large for most children under age 2 to be comfortable without significant padding. The seat is so low that the child is forced to keep their legs straight out in front of them. Third, despite being sooo big, there's NO PLACE to store anything.*

*Now, if your child is past needing a diaper bag, the WDW strollers seem like a pretty good deal. You won't need the storage space, and they do maneuver very well. They seem especially good for children who no longer need a stroller at home (ages 4–6) but who won't make it walking all day.*

*If your child is 2 or 3, it's a toss-up. If you're a type-A mom, like me, who carries extra clothes, snacks, toys, enough diapers for three days, along with a pocketbook and extra-jackets-for-everyone-just-in-case, you've probably found a stroller that suits your needs and will be miserable with the WDW kind. If you're a type-B "we can get everything else we need at the park; I'll just throw a diaper in my back pocket" mom, you'll probably be tickled with the WDW strollers.*

An Oklahoma mom, however, reports a bad experience with bringing her own stroller:

*It's much easier to rent a stroller in the park. The stroller we brought was nearly impossible to get on the buses and was a hassle at the airport. I remember feeling dread when a bus pulled up—people look at you like you have a cage full of chickens when you drag a heavy stroller onto the bus.*

**PARKING YOUR STROLLER** Well-marked stroller parking is available in all the "lands" of every park. If you leave your stroller in front of an attraction instead of a designated parking area, it will be moved.

**STROLLER-RENTAL OPTIONS** With Disney pricing its own stroller rentals so high, several Orlando companies have sprung up, able to undercut Disney's prices, provide more comfortable strollers, and deliver them to your hotel. Most of the larger companies offer the same stroller models (the Baby Jogger City Mini Single, for example), so the primary differences between the companies are price and service.

*unofficial* **TIP**
When you enter a show or board a ride, you must park your stroller, usually in an open area. Bring a cloth or towel to dry it if it rains before you return.

To rate stroller companies, we had mom and *Unofficial Guide* researcher Scarlett Litton, along with **touringplans.com** blogger Shelley Caran, rent the same strollers from each company, use the strollers in the parks, and return them. Our evaluation covers the overall experience, from the ease with which the stroller was rented to the delivery of the stroller, its condition upon arrival, and the return process.

**Baby Wheels Orlando** (☎ 800-510-2480; **babywheelsorlando .com**) had the best combination of price and service. Upon request, Baby Wheels will include a rain cover and beverage cooler free—both of which are useful during Florida's summer months. A one-day rental is $30, three nights are $40, and five nights are $48. Thus, the break-even point for using Baby Wheels Orlando instead of Disney is four nights. Drop-off and pickup went without incident, and customer service is excellent.

We also recommend **Orlando Stroller Rentals, LLC** (☎ 800-281-0884; **orlandostrollerrentals.com**), which has slightly higher prices and whose strollers have a few more miles on them. The service is excellent, though.

**STROLLER WARS** Sometimes strollers disappear while you're enjoying a ride or show. Disney staff will often rearrange strollers parked outside an attraction. This may be done to tidy up or to clear a walkway. Don't assume that your stroller is stolen because it isn't where you left it. It may be neatly arranged a few feet away—or perhaps more than a few feet away, as this Skokie, Illinois, dad reports:

> *The stroller reorganizations while you're on rides are a bit unnerving. More than once, our stroller was moved out of visible distance from the original spot. On one occasion, it was moved to a completely different stroller-parking area near another ride, and no sign or cast member was around to advise where. We had to track a cast member down, and she had to call in to find out where it had been moved. Be prepared for this.*

Sometimes, however, strollers are taken by mistake or ripped off by people not wanting to spend time replacing one that's missing. Don't be alarmed if yours disappears. You won't have to buy it, and you'll be issued a new one.

While replacing a stroller is no big deal, it's inconvenient. A Minnesota family complained that their stroller was taken six times in one day at Epcot and five times in a day at Disney's Hollywood Studios. Even with free replacements, larceny on this scale represents a lot of wasted time. Through our own experiments and readers' suggestions, we've developed a technique for hanging on to a rented stroller: Affix something personal (but expendable) to the handle. Evidently, most strollers are pirated by mistake (they all look alike) or because it's easier to swipe someone else's than to replace one that has disappeared. Because most stroller "theft" results from confusion or laziness, the average pram-pincher will hesitate to haul off a stroller containing another person's property. We tried several items and concluded that a bright, inexpensive scarf or bandanna tied to the handle works well as identification. A sock partially stuffed with rags or paper works even better (the weirder and more personal the object, the greater the deterrent). A multigenerational family from Utah went a step further and made their stroller difficult to move:

*unofficial* **TIP**
Don't try to lock your stroller to a fence, post, or anything else at WDW. You'll get in big trouble.

> *We decorated our stroller with electrical tape to make it stand out, and my son added a small cowbell to make it clang if moved.*

**STROLLERS AS LETHAL WEAPONS** A middle-aged couple from Brunswick, Maine, lobbies for a temporary stroller ban:

> *As an over-45 couple, we couldn't believe the number and sizes of strollers and those ubiquitous scooters. You had to be constantly vigilant or you would have your foot run over or path slowed down by them. We've decided that one day a week, in one theme park, there should be a "no wheels" day. (Ah, but we live in Fantasyland!)*

You'd be surprised at how many people are injured by strollers pushed by parents who are driving aggressively or in a hurry. Given the number of strollers, pedestrians, and tight spaces, mishaps are inevitable on both sides. A simple apology and a smile are usually the best remediation.

# LOST CHILDREN

ALTHOUGH IT'S AMAZINGLY EASY TO LOSE a child (or two) in the theme parks, it usually isn't a serious problem: Disney employees are schooled in handling the situation. If you lose a child in the Magic Kingdom, report it to a Disney employee, and then check at the Baby Care Center and at City Hall, where lost-children logs are kept. At Epcot, report the loss, then check at the Baby Care Center in the Odyssey Center. At Disney's Hollywood Studios, report the loss at the Guest Service Building, at the entrance end of Hollywood Boulevard. At Disney's Animal Kingdom, go to the Baby Care Center in Discovery Island. Paging isn't used, but in an emergency, an "all-points bulletin" can be issued throughout the park(s) via internal communications. If a Disney employee encounters a lost child, he or she will take the child immediately to the park's Baby Care Center.

Sew a label into each child's shirt that states his or her name, your name, the name of your hotel, and if you have one, your cell phone number. Accomplish the same thing by writing the information on a strip of masking tape.

An easier and trendier option is a temporary tattoo with your child's name and your phone number. Unlike labels, ID bracelets, or wristbands, the tattoos cannot fall off or be lost. Temporary tattoos last about two weeks, won't wash or sweat off, and are not irritating to the skin. They can be purchased online from SafetyTat at **safety tat.com,** or from Tattoos With A Purpose at **tattooswithapurpose .com.** Special tattoos are available for children with food allergies or cognitive impairment such as autism.

A Kingston, Washington, reader recommends recording vital info for each child on a plastic key tag or luggage tag and affixing it to the child's shoe. This reader also snaps a photo of the kids each morning to document what they're wearing. A mother from Rockville, Maryland, reported a strategy one step short of a cattle brand:

> *Traveling with a 3-year-old, I was very anxious about losing him. I wrote my cell phone number on his leg with a permanent marker, and felt much more confident that he'd get back to me quickly if he became lost.*

*unofficial* **TIP**
We suggest that kids younger than 8 be color-coded by dressing them in purple T-shirts or equally distinctive clothes.

One way to better keep track of your family is to buy each person a "Disney uniform"—in this case, the same brightly and distinctively colored T-shirt. A Yuma, Arizona, family tried this with great success:

> *We all got the same shirts (bright red) so that we could easily spot each other in case of separation (VERY easy to do). It was a lifesaver when our 18-month-old decided to get out of the stroller and wander off. As I've heard before, Dumbo seems to draw them in, and lo and behold, guess where we found him (still dragging his leash but with*

*a nice cast member following him). No matter what precautions you may try, it seems there are always those opportunities to lose a child, but the recognizable shirts helped tremendously.*

## HOW KIDS GET LOST

CHILDREN GET SEPARATED FROM THEIR PARENTS every day at Disney theme parks under remarkably similar (and predictable) circumstances:

**1. PREOCCUPIED SOLO PARENT** The party's only adult is preoccupied with something like buying refreshments, reading a map, or using the restroom. Junior is there one second and gone the next.

**2. THE HIDDEN EXIT** Sometimes parents wait on the sidelines while two or more young children experience a ride together. Parents expect the kids to exit in one place and the youngsters pop out elsewhere. Exits from some attractions are distant from entrances. Know exactly where your children will emerge before letting them ride by themselves.

**3. AFTER THE SHOW** At the end of many shows and rides, a Disney staffer announces, "Check for personal belongings and take small children by the hand." When dozens, if not hundreds, of people leave an attraction simultaneously, it's easy for parents to lose their children unless they have direct contact.

*unofficial* **TIP**
Children under age 14 must be accompanied by someone age 14 or older when entering Disney World's theme parks and water parks, as well as DisneyQuest.

**4. RESTROOM PROBLEMS** Mom tells 6-year-old Tommy, "I'll be sitting on this bench when you come out of the restroom." Three possibilities: One, Tommy exits through a different door and becomes disoriented (Mom may not know there's another door). Two, Mom decides she also will use the restroom, and Tommy emerges to find her gone. Three, Mom pokes around in a shop while keeping an eye on the bench but misses Tommy when he comes out.

If you can't find a companion- or family-accessible restroom, make sure there's only one exit. The restroom on a passageway between Frontierland and Adventureland in the Magic Kingdom is the all-time worst for disorienting visitors. Children and adults alike have walked in from the Adventureland side and walked out on the Frontierland side (and vice versa). Adults realize quickly that something is wrong. Children, however, sometimes fail to recognize the problem.

Designate a distinctive meeting spot and give clear instructions: "I'll meet you by this flagpole. If you get out first, stay right here." Have your child repeat the directions back to you. When children are too young to leave alone, sometimes you have to think outside the box, as our Rockville, Maryland, mom (quoted on the previous page) did:

*It was very scary for me at times, being alone with children who had just turned 1 and 2. I'm reminded of the time on the trip when I couldn't fit the double stroller into the bathroom. I was at Epcot inside one of the buildings and I had to leave my kids with a WDW employee outside of the restroom because the stroller just wouldn't fit inside with me. Thinking about the incident now makes me laugh. The good news is that I found that most WDW bathrooms*

*can accommodate a front-and-back double stroller inside the handi-
capped stall with you.*

**5. PARADES** There are many parades and shows at which the audience
stands. Children tend to jockey for a better view. By moving a little this
way and that, the child quickly puts distance between you and him
before either of you notices.

**6. MASS MOVEMENTS** Be on guard when huge crowds disperse after fireworks or a parade, or at park closing. With 20,000–40,000 people at once
in an area, it's very easy to get separated from a child or others in your
party. Use extra caution after the evening parade and fireworks in the
Magic Kingdom, *Fantasmic!* at Disney's Hollywood Studios, and *Illumi
Nations* at Epcot. Plan where to meet in the event you get separated.

**7. CHARACTER GREETINGS** When the Disney characters appear, children
can slip out of sight. (See "Then Some Confusion Happened," page 347.)

**8. GETTING LOST AT DISNEY'S ANIMAL KINGDOM** It's especially easy to
lose a child in Animal Kingdom, particularly at the Oasis entryway, on
the Maharajah Jungle Trek, and on the Pangani Forest Exploration
Trail. Mom and Dad will stop to observe an animal. Junior stays close
for a minute or so, and then, losing patience, wanders to the exhibit's
other side or to a different exhibit.

Especially in the multipath Oasis, finding a lost child can be maddening, as a Safety Harbor, Florida, mother describes:

> *Manny wandered off in the paths that lead to the jungle village while
> we were looking at a bird. It reminded me of losing somebody in the
> supermarket when you run back and forth looking down each aisle
> but can't find the person you're looking for because they're running
> around too. I was nutso before we even got to the first ride.*

A mother from Flint, Michigan, came up with yet another way to
lose a kid: abandonment.

> *From the minute we hit the park it was gripe, whine, pout, cry, beg,
> scream, pick, pester, and aggravate. When he went to the restroom for
> the ninth time before 11 a.m., I thought, "I'm outta here! Let the lit-
> tle snothead walk back to Flint." Unfortunately, I was brought up
> Catholic with lots of guilt, so I didn't follow through.*

# DISNEY, KIDS, *and* SCARY STUFF

**unofficial TIP**
Monsters and special
effects at Disney's Hollywood Studios are more
real and sinister than
those in the other parks.

DISNEY RIDES AND SHOWS ARE ADVEN-
TURES, and they focus on themes of all adventures:
good and evil, death, beauty and ugliness, fellow-
ship and enmity. As you sample the attractions at Walt Disney World,
you'll transcend the spinning and bouncing of midway rides to thought-
provoking and emotionally powerful entertainment. All the endings are
happy, but the adventures' impact, given Disney's gift for special effects,
often intimidates and occasionally frightens young children.

*Continued on page 335*

# Small-Child Fright-Potential Chart

This is a quick reference to identify attractions to be wary of, and why. The chart represents a generalization, and all kids are different. It relates specifically to kids ages 3–7. On average, children at the younger end of the range are more likely to be frightened than children in their sixth or seventh year.

## THE MAGIC KINGDOM

### MAIN STREET, U.S.A.

**MAIN STREET VEHICLES** Not frightening in any respect.

**WALT DISNEY WORLD RAILROAD** Not frightening in any respect.

### ADVENTURELAND

**JUNGLE CRUISE** Some macabre sights. A good test attraction for little ones.

**PIRATES OF THE CARIBBEAN** Slightly intimidating queuing area; intense boat ride with gruesome (though humorously presented) sights and a short, unexpected slide down a flume.

**THE MAGIC CARPETS OF ALADDIN** Much like Dumbo. A favorite of young children.

**SWISS FAMILY TREEHOUSE** Kids who are afraid of heights may want to skip it.

**WALT DISNEY'S ENCHANTED TIKI ROOM** A thunderstorm, loud volume level, and simulated explosions frighten some preschoolers.

### FRONTIERLAND

**BIG THUNDER MOUNTAIN RAILROAD** Visually intimidating from outside, with moderately intense visual effects. The roller coaster is wild enough to frighten many adults, particularly seniors. Switching-off option provided (see page 341).

**COUNTRY BEAR *JAMBOREE*** Not frightening in any respect.

**FRONTIERLAND SHOOTIN' ARCADE** May be frightening to children who are scared of guns.

**SPLASH MOUNTAIN** Visually intimidating from outside, with moderately intense visual effects. The ride culminates in a 52-foot plunge down a steep chute. Switching-off option provided (see page 341).

**TOM SAWYER ISLAND AND FORT LANGHORN** Some very young children are intimidated by dark walk-through tunnels that can be easily avoided.

### LIBERTY SQUARE

**THE HALL OF PRESIDENTS** Not frightening, but boring for young ones.

**THE HAUNTED MANSION** Name raises anxiety, as do sounds and sights of waiting area. Intense attraction with humorously presented macabre sights. The ride itself is gentle.

**LIBERTY BELLE RIVERBOAT** Not frightening in any respect.

### FANTASYLAND

**ARIEL'S GROTTO** Not frightening in any respect.

**DUMBO THE FLYING ELEPHANT** A tame midway ride; a great favorite of most young children.

**THE BARNSTORMER** May frighten some preschoolers.

**ENCHANTED TALES WITH BELLE** Not frightening in any respect.

**IT'S A SMALL WORLD** Not frightening in any respect.

**MAD TEA PARTY** Midway-type ride can induce motion sickness in all ages.

**THE MANY ADVENTURES OF WINNIE THE POOH** Frightens a small percentage of preschoolers.

**PETER PAN'S FLIGHT** Not frightening in any respect.

**PETE'S SILLY SIDESHOW** Not frightening in any respect.

**PRINCE CHARMING REGAL CARROUSEL** Not frightening in any respect.

**PRINCESS FAIRYTALE HALL** Only the length of the line is frightening.

**SEVEN DWARFS MINE TRAIN** May frighten some preschoolers.

**UNDER THE SEA: JOURNEY OF THE LITTLE MERMAID** Animatronic octopus character frightens some preschoolers.

## TOMORROWLAND

**ASTRO ORBITER** Visually intimidating from the waiting area, but the ride is relatively tame.

**BUZZ LIGHTYEAR'S SPACE RANGER SPIN** Dark ride with cartoonlike aliens. May frighten some preschoolers.

**MONSTERS, INC. LAUGH FLOOR** May frighten a small percentage of preschoolers.

**SPACE MOUNTAIN** Very intense roller coaster in the dark; the Magic Kingdom's wildest ride and a scary roller coaster by any standard. Switching-off option provided (see page 341).

**STITCH'S GREAT ESCAPE!** Very intense. May frighten children age 9 and younger. Switching-off option provided (see page 341).

**TOMORROWLAND SPEEDWAY** Noise of waiting area slightly intimidates preschoolers; otherwise, not frightening.

**TOMORROWLAND TRANSIT AUTHORITY PEOPLEMOVER** Not frightening in any respect.

**WALT DISNEY'S CAROUSEL OF PROGRESS** Not frightening in any respect.

## EPCOT

### FUTURE WORLD

**SUM OF ALL THRILLS** Intense roller-coaster simulator may frighten some kids.

**IMAGINATION!: CAPTAIN EO** Extremely intense visual effects and loudness frighten many young children.

**JOURNEY INTO IMAGINATION WITH FIGMENT** Loud noises and unexpected flashing lights startle younger children.

**THE LAND: THE CIRCLE OF LIFE** Not frightening in any respect.

**THE LAND: LIVING WITH THE LAND** Not frightening in any respect.

**THE LAND: SOARIN'** May frighten kids age 7 and younger, or anyone with a fear of heights. Otherwise a very mellow ride.

**MISSION: SPACE** Extremely intense space-simulation ride that has been known to frighten guests of all ages. Preshow may also frighten some children. Switching-off option provided (see page 341).

**THE SEAS—THE SEAS WITH NEMO & FRIENDS** Very sweet but may frighten some toddlers.

**THE SEAS: MAIN TANK AND EXHIBITS** Not frightening in any respect.

**THE SEAS: TURTLE TALK WITH CRUSH** Not frightening in any respect.

**SPACESHIP EARTH** Dark, imposing presentation intimidates a few preschoolers.

**TEST TRACK** Intense thrill ride may frighten guests of any age. Switching-off option provided (see page 341).

**UNIVERSE OF ENERGY: ELLEN'S ENERGY ADVENTURE** Dinosaur segment frightens some preschoolers; visually intense, with some intimidating effects.

## Small-Child Fright-Potential Chart *(continued)*

### EPCOT

#### WORLD SHOWCASE

**CANADA:** *O CANADA!* Not frightening, but audience must stand.

**CHINA:** *REFLECTIONS OF CHINA* Not frightening in any respect.

**FRANCE:** *IMPRESSIONS DE FRANCE* Not frightening in any respect.

**GERMANY** Not frightening in any respect.

**ITALY** Not frightening in any respect.

**JAPAN** Not frightening in any respect.

**MEXICO: GRAN FIESTA TOUR** Not frightening in any respect.

**MOROCCO** Not frightening in any respect.

**NORWAY: MAELSTROM** Visually intense in parts. Ride ends with a plunge down a 20-foot flume. A few preschoolers are frightened.

**UNITED KINGDOM** Not frightening in any respect.

**UNITED STATES:** *THE AMERICAN ADVENTURE* Not frightening in any respect.

### DISNEY'S ANIMAL KINGDOM

**THE OASIS** Not frightening in any respect.

**RAFIKI'S PLANET WATCH** Not frightening in any respect.

#### DISCOVERY ISLAND

**THE TREE OF LIFE /** *IT'S TOUGH TO BE A BUG!* Very intense and loud, with special effects that startle viewers of all ages and potentially terrify little kids.

#### AFRICA

*FESTIVAL OF THE LION KING* A bit loud, but otherwise not frightening.

**KILIMANJARO SAFARIS** A "collapsing" bridge and the proximity of real animals make a few young children anxious.

**PANGANI FOREST EXPLORATION TRAIL** Not frightening in any respect.

**WILDLIFE EXPRESS TRAIN** Not frightening in any respect.

#### ASIA

**EXPEDITION EVEREST** Can frighten guests of all ages. Switching-off option provided (see page 341).

*FLIGHTS OF WONDER* Swooping birds alarm a few small children.

**KALI RIVER RAPIDS** Potentially frightening and certainly wet for guests of all ages. Switching-off option provided (see page 341).

**MAHARAJAH JUNGLE TREK** Some children may balk at the bat exhibit.

#### DINOLAND U.S.A.

**THE BONEYARD** Not frightening in any respect.

**DINOSAUR** High-tech thrill ride rattles riders of all ages. Switching-off option provided (see page 341).

**PRIMEVAL WHIRL** A beginner roller coaster. Most children age 7 and older will take it in stride. Switching-off option provided (see page 341).

**THEATER IN THE WILD /** *FINDING NEMO—THE MUSICAL* Not frightening in any respect, but loud.

**TRICERATOP SPIN** A midway-type ride that will frighten only a small percentage of younger children.

## DISNEY'S HOLLYWOOD STUDIOS

### HOLLYWOOD BOULEVARD

**THE GREAT MOVIE RIDE** Intense in parts, with very realistic special effects and some visually intimidating sights. Frightens many preschoolers.

### SUNSET BOULEVARD

*FANTASMIC!* Terrifies some preschoolers.

**ROCK 'N' ROLLER COASTER** The wildest coaster at Walt Disney World. May frighten guests of any age. Switching-off option provided (see page 341).

**THEATER OF THE STARS /** *BEAUTY AND THE BEAST—LIVE ON STAGE* Not frightening in any respect.

**THE TWILIGHT ZONE TOWER OF TERROR** Visually intimidating to young children; contains intense and realistic special effects. The plummeting elevator at the ride's end frightens many adults as well as kids. Switching-off option provided (see page 341).

### ECHO LAKE

*THE AMERICAN IDOL EXPERIENCE* **(CLOSES JANUARY 2015)** At times, the singing may frighten anyone.

*INDIANA JONES EPIC STUNT SPECTACULAR!* An intense show with powerful special effects, including explosions, but young kids generally handle it well.

**STAR TOURS—THE ADVENTURES CONTINUE** Extremely intense visually for all ages; too intense for children under age 8. Switching-off option provided (see page 341).

### STREETS OF AMERICA

*HONEY, I SHRUNK THE KIDS* **MOVIE SET ADVENTURE** Not scary (though oversized)

*JIM HENSON'S MUPPET-VISION 3-D* Intense and loud, but not frightening.

*LIGHTS, MOTORS, ACTION! EXTREME STUNT SHOW* Super stunt spectacular; intense with loud noises and explosions, but not threatening in any way.

**STUDIO BACKLOT TOUR** Sedate and nonintimidating except for Catastrophe Canyon, where an earthquake and a flash flood are simulated. Prepare younger children for this part of the tour.

### PIXAR PLACE

**TOY STORY MIDWAY MANIA!** Dark ride may frighten some preschoolers.

### MICKEY AVENUE

*THE LEGEND OF CAPTAIN JACK SPARROW* Skeletons, monsters, and shooting can frighten small children.

*WALT DISNEY: ONE MAN'S DREAM* Not frightening in any respect.

### ANIMATION COURTYARD

*DISNEY JUNIOR—LIVE ON STAGE!* Not frightening in any respect.

**THE MAGIC OF DISNEY ANIMATION** Not frightening in any respect.

*VOYAGE OF THE LITTLE MERMAID* Some children are creeped out by Ursula.

*Continued from page 331*

There are attractions with menacing witches, burning towns, skeletons, and ghouls popping out of their graves, all done with humor, provided you're old enough to understand the joke.

If your child has difficulty coping with the ghouls of The Haunted Mansion, then you should think twice about exposing him at the

Studios to earthquakes in the Backlot Tour or machine-gun battles and the creature from *Alien* in The Great Movie Ride.

You can reliably predict that Walt Disney World will, at one time or another, send a young child into system overload. Be sensitive, alert, and prepared for almost anything, even behavior that is out of character for your child. Most children take Disney's macabre trappings in stride, and others are easily comforted by an arm around the shoulder or a squeeze of the hand. Parents who know that their children tend to become upset should take it slow and easy, sampling benign adventures like the Jungle Cruise, gauging reactions, and discussing with the children how they felt about what they saw.

Sometimes young children will rise above their anxiety in an effort to please their parents or siblings. This doesn't necessarily indicate a mastery of fear, much less enjoyment. If children leave a ride in apparently good shape, ask if they would like to go on it again (not necessarily now, but sometime). The response usually will indicate how much they actually enjoyed the experience.

Evaluating a child's capacity to handle the visual and tactile effects of Disney World requires patience, understanding, and experimentation. Each of us has our own demons. If a child balks at or is frightened by a ride, respond constructively. Let your children know that lots of people, adults and children, are scared by what they see and feel. Help them understand that it's OK if they get frightened and that their fear doesn't lessen your love or respect. Take pains not to compound the discomfort by making a child feel inadequate; try not to undermine self-esteem, impugn courage, or ridicule. Most of all, don't induce guilt by suggesting the child's trepidation might be ruining the family's fun. It's also sometimes necessary to restrain older siblings' taunting.

A reader from New York City expresses strong feelings about pressuring children:

*As a psychologist who works with children, I felt ethically torn (and nearly filed a report!) watching parents force their children to go on rides they didn't want to ride (especially the Tower of Terror and DINOSAUR). The Disney staff were more than willing to organize a parental swap to save these children from such abuse!*

A visit to Disney World is more than an outing or an adventure for a young child. It's a testing experience, a sort of controlled rite of passage. If you help your little one work through the challenges, the time can be immeasurably rewarding and a bonding experience for you both.

## THE FRIGHT FACTOR

WHILE EACH YOUNGSTER IS DIFFERENT, following are seven attraction elements that alone or combined could push a child's buttons and indicate that a certain attraction isn't age appropriate for that child:

**1. NAME OF THE ATTRACTION** Young children will naturally be apprehensive about something called, say, The Haunted Mansion or Tower of Terror.

**2. VISUAL IMPACT OF THE ATTRACTION FROM OUTSIDE** Splash Mountain, the Tower of Terror, and Big Thunder Mountain Railroad look scary enough to give adults second thoughts, and they terrify many young children. A Utah family of six reports the following:

> At 5 years old, my granddaughter was big enough and willing to go on almost everything. The problem was with the preliminary introductions to Haunted Mansion and Tower of Terror. Walking through and learning the stories before the actual rides were what frightened her and made her opt out without going in. The rides themselves would not have been bad; she loved Splash Mountain [and] Big Thunder Mountain, but she could SEE those rides before entering.

**3. VISUAL IMPACT OF THE INDOOR-QUEUING AREA** The caves at Pirates of the Caribbean and the dungeons and "stretch rooms" of The Haunted Mansion can frighten children.

**4. INTENSITY OF THE ATTRACTION** Some attractions inundate the senses with sights, sounds, movement, and even smell. Animal Kingdom's *It's Tough to be a Bug!*, for example, combines loud sounds, lights, smoke, and animatronic insects with 3-D cinematography to create a total sensory experience.

A Johnston, Iowa, mom describes the situation well:

> The 3-D and 4-D experiences are way too scary for even a very brave 5-year-old girl. The shows that blew things on her, shot smells in the air, had bugs flying, etc. scared the bejesus out of her. We escorted her crying from It's Tough to Be a Bug!, Mickey's PhilharMagic, and Stitch's Great Escape!

**5. VISUAL IMPACT OF THE ATTRACTION** Sights in various attractions range from falling boulders to lurking buzzards, from grazing dinosaurs to waltzing ghosts. What one child calmly absorbs may scare the bejeebers out of another the same age.

**6. DARK** Many Disney World attractions operate indoors in the dark. For some children, this triggers fear. A child who gets frightened on one dark ride (The Haunted Mansion, for example) may be unwilling to try other indoor rides.

**7. THE TACTILE EXPERIENCE** Some rides are wild enough to cause motion sickness, wrench backs, and discombobulate guests of any age.

As a footnote to the preceding, be aware that gaining the courage and confidence in regard to the attractions is not necessarily an upwardly linear process. A dad from Maryland explains:

> As a 4-year-old, my daughter absolutely adored The Haunted Mansion. At 5 she was scared to death on it! At 6 she was fine again. Just because a child loves a ride at one age doesn't mean that he or she will love it on the next trip.

## A BIT OF PREPARATION

WE RECEIVE MANY TIPS FROM PARENTS telling how they prepared their young children for the Disney experience. A common strategy is to acquaint children with the characters and stories behind the attractions by reading Disney books and watching Disney videos at home. A more direct approach is to watch videos that show the attractions. Of the latter, a Lexington, Kentucky, mom reports:

*My timid 7-year-old daughter and I watched rides and shows on YouTube, and we cut out all the ones that looked too scary. At the parks, she still didn't like, and cried at, It's Tough to Be a Bug! Ellen's Energy Adventure made her tense up, but she loved, loved, loved Kali River Rapids.*

A Gloucester, Massachusetts, mom solved the problem on the spot:

*My 3½-year-old was afraid of The Haunted Mansion. We just pulled his hat over his face and quietly talked to him while we rode.*

You can order a free **Walt Disney World Vacation Planning DVD** by clicking on "Free Planning DVD" at the **disneyworld.com** home page or by calling ☎ 407-w-disney (934-7639). As a YouTube supplement, it gives your kids an adequate sense of what they'll see. Allow at least one month for delivery. For more immediate gratification, you can also watch the **Travel Channel**'s Walt Disney World specials on iTunes or Netflix streaming.

## ATTRACTIONS THAT EAT ADULTS

YOU MAY SPEND SO MUCH ENERGY worrying about Junior that you forget to take care of yourself. The attractions below can cause motion sickness or other problems for older kids and adults:

| POTENTIALLY PROBLEMATIC ATTRACTIONS FOR GROWN-UPS |
| --- |
| **THE MAGIC KINGDOM** |
| **FANTASYLAND** Mad Tea Party |
| **FRONTIERLAND** Big Thunder Mountain Railroad, Splash Mountain |
| **TOMORROWLAND** Space Mountain |
| **EPCOT** |
| **FUTURE WORLD** Mission: SPACE, Sum of All Thrills, Test Track |
| **DISNEY'S ANIMAL KINGDOM** |
| **ASIA** Expedition Everest, Kali River Rapids |
| **DINOLAND, U.S.A.** DINOSAUR |
| **DISNEY'S HOLLYWOOD STUDIOS** |
| **ECHO LAKE** Star Tours—The Adventures Continue |
| **SUNSET BOULEVARD** Rock 'n' Roller Coaster, The Twilight Zone Tower of Terror |

## A WORD ABOUT HEIGHT REQUIREMENTS

A NUMBER OF ATTRACTIONS REQUIRE children to meet minimum height and age requirements. If you have children too short or too young to ride, you have several options, including switching off (see page 341). Although the alternatives may resolve some practical and logistical issues, your smaller children may nonetheless be resentful of their older (or taller) siblings who qualify to ride. A mom from Virginia writes of such a situation:

*You mention height requirements for rides but not the intense sibling jealousy this can generate. Frontierland was a real problem in that respect. Our very petite 5-year-old, to her outrage, was stuck*

# Attraction and Ride Restrictions

## THE MAGIC KINGDOM

| | |
|---|---|
| The Barnstormer | 35" minimum height |
| Big Thunder Mountain Railroad | 40" minimum height |
| Seven Dwarfs Mine Train | 38" minimum height |
| Space Mountain | 44" minimum height |
| Splash Mountain | 40" minimum height |
| *Stitch's Great Escape!* | 40" minimum height |
| Tomorrowland Speedway | 32" to ride, 54" to drive unassisted |

## EPCOT

| | |
|---|---|
| Mission: SPACE | 44" minimum height |
| Soarin' | 40" minimum height |
| Sum of All Thrills | 48" minimum height, 54" for inversions |
| Test Track | 40" minimum height |

## DISNEY'S ANIMAL KINGDOM

| | |
|---|---|
| DINOSAUR | 40" minimum height |
| Expedition Everest | 44" minimum height |
| Kali River Rapids | 38" minimum height |
| Primeval Whirl | 48" minimum height |

## DISNEY'S HOLLYWOOD STUDIOS

| | |
|---|---|
| Honey, I Shrunk the Kids Movie Set Adventure | 10 yrs. maximum recommended age |
| Rock 'n' Roller Coaster | 48" minimum height |
| Star Tours—The Adventures Continue | 40" minimum height |
| The Twilight Zone Tower of Terror | 40" minimum height |

## BLIZZARD BEACH WATER PARK

| | |
|---|---|
| Chair Lift | 32" minimum height |
| Downhill Double Dipper slide | 48" minimum height |
| Slush Gusher slide | 48" minimum height |
| Summit Plummet slide | 48" minimum height |
| T-Bar (in Ski Patrol Training Camp) | 60" maximum height |
| Tike's Peak children's area | 48" maximum height |

## TYPHOON LAGOON WATER PARK

| | |
|---|---|
| Bay Slides | 60" minimum height |
| Crush 'n' Gusher | 48" minimum height |
| Humunga Kowabunga slide | 48" minimum height |
| Ketchakiddee Creek children's area | 48" maximum height |
| Shark Reef saltwater reef swim: | 10 yrs. minimum age unless accompanied by adult |
| Wave Pool | *Adult supervision required* |

## DISNEYQUEST

| | |
|---|---|
| Buzz Lightyear's AstroBlasters | 51" minimum height |
| CyberSpace Mountain | 51" minimum height |
| Mighty Ducks Pinball Slam | 48" minimum height |
| Pirates of the Caribbean—Battle for Buccaneer Gold | 35" minimum height |

*hanging around while our 8-year-old went on Splash Mountain and Big Thunder Mountain with her grandma and granddad, and the nearby alternatives weren't helpful (too long a line for rafts to Tom Sawyer Island, etc.). The best areas had a playground or other quick attractions for short people near the rides with height requirements, like The Boneyard near the DINOSAUR ride at Animal Kingdom.*

The reader makes a point, though splitting the group and meeting later can be more complicated than she imagines. If you split up, ask the Disney attendant (called a greeter) at the entrance to the attraction(s) with height requirements how long the wait is. If you tack 5 minutes for riding on to the anticipated wait and add 5 or so minutes to exit and reach the meeting point, you'll have a sense of how long the younger kids (and their supervising adult) will have to do other stuff. Our guess is that even with a long line for the rafts, the reader would've had sufficient time to take her daughter to Tom Sawyer Island while the sibs rode Splash Mountain and Big Thunder Mountain with the grandparents. For sure, she had time to tour the Swiss Family Treehouse in adjacent Adventureland.

For more information, see the chart on the previous page.

# WAITING-LINE STRATEGIES *for* ADULTS *with* YOUNG CHILDREN

CHILDREN HOLD UP BETTER through the day if you limit the time they spend in lines. Arriving early and using our touring plans greatly reduce waiting. Here are other ways to reduce stress for children:

**1. LINE GAMES** Anticipate that children will get restless in line, and plan activities to reduce the stress and boredom. In the morning, have waiting children discuss what they want to see and do during the day. Later, watch for and count Disney characters or play simple games such as 20 Questions. Lines move continuously; games requiring pen and paper are impractical. Waiting in the holding area of a theater attraction is a different story. Here, tic-tac-toe, hangman, drawing, and coloring make the time fly.

A Springfield, Ohio, mom reports on an unexpected but welcome assist from her brother:

*I have a bachelor brother who joined my 5-, 7-, and 9-year-olds and me for vacation. Pat surprised all of us with a bunch of plastic animal noses he had in his hip pack. When the kids got restless or cranky in line, he'd turn away and pull out a pig nose or a parrot nose or something. When he turned back around with the nose on, the kids would majorly crack up.*

A Waco, Texas, dad broke out the bubbly:

*I took bubbles along with us. My boys loved them and so did the other children waiting in line. (I bought wedding-size bottles that would fit into everyone's fanny pack.)*

**2. SWITCHING OFF** Several attractions have minimum height and/or age requirements. Some couples with children too small or too young forgo these attractions, while others take turns riding. Missing some of Disney's best rides is an unnecessary sacrifice, and waiting in line twice for the same ride is a tremendous waste of time.

| ATTRACTIONS WHERE SWITCHING OFF IS COMMON | |
| --- | --- |
| **THE MAGIC KINGDOM** | **DISNEY'S ANIMAL KINGDOM** |
| Big Thunder Mountain Railroad | DINOSAUR |
| Seven Dwarfs Mine Train | Expedition Everest |
| Space Mountain | Kali River Rapids |
| Splash Mountain | Primeval Whirl |
| *Stitch's* Great Escape! | |
| **EPCOT** | **DISNEY'S HOLLYWOOD STUDIOS** |
| Mission: SPACE | Rock 'n' Roller Coaster |
| Test Track | Star Tours—The Adventures Continue |
| | The Twilight Zone Tower of Terror |

Instead, take advantage of "switching off," also known as "The Baby Swap" or "The Rider Swap" (or "The Baby/Rider Switch"). To switch off, there must be at least two adults. Adults and children wait in line together. When you reach a cast member, say you want to switch off. The cast member will allow everyone, including young children, to enter the attraction. When you reach the loading area, one adult rides while the other exits with the kids. Then the riding adult disembarks and takes charge of the children while the other adult rides. A third member of the party, either an adult or an older child, can ride twice, once with each switching-off adult, so that the switching-off adults don't have to ride alone.

On most FastPass+ attractions, Disney handles switching off somewhat differently. When you tell the cast member that you want to switch off, you'll get a special "rider exchange" FastPass good for three people. One parent and the nonriding child (or children) will at that point be asked to leave the line. When those riding reunite with those waiting, the waiting adult and two others from the party can ride using the special FastPass. This eliminates confusion at the boarding area while sparing the nonriding adult and child the tedium of waiting in line.

**3. COMBINING THE FASTPASS+ SYSTEM WITH SWITCHING OFF** You can incorporate FastPass+ into switching off in order to secure passes for multiple attractions at the same time.

**4. LAST-MINUTE COLD FEET** If your young child gets cold feet just before boarding a ride where there's no age or height requirement, you usually can arrange a switch-off with the loading attendant. (This happens frequently in Pirates of the Caribbean's dungeon waiting area.)

No law says you have to ride. If you reach the boarding area and someone is unhappy, tell an attendant you've changed your mind and you'll be shown the way out.

**5. THROW YOURSELF ON THE GRENADE, MILDRED!** For long-suffering parents who are determined to sacrifice themselves on behalf of their children, we provide a Magic Kingdom One-Day Touring Plan called the Dumbo-or-Die-in-a-Day Touring Plan for Parents with Small Children. This plan (see page 827) will ensure that you run yourself ragged. Designed to help you forfeit everything of personal interest for your children's pleasure, the plan guarantees you'll go home battered and exhausted, with extraordinary stories of devotion and perseverance. By the way, it really works. Anyone under age 8 will love it.

# The **DISNEY CHARACTERS**

THE LARGE AND FRIENDLY COSTUMED versions of Mickey, Minnie, Donald, Goofy, and others—known as Disney characters—provide a link between Disney animated films and the theme parks. To people emotionally invested, the characters in Disney films are as real as next-door neighbors, never mind that they're drawings on plastic. In recent years, theme park personifications of the characters also have become real to us. It's not a person in a mouse costume; it's Mickey himself. Similarly, meeting Belle or Snow White is an encounter with a celebrity, a memory to be treasured.

*unofficial* **TIP**
Don't underestimate your child's excitement at meeting the Disney characters—but also be aware that very small children may find the large costumed characters a little frightening.

While Disney animated-film characters number in the hundreds, only about 250 have been brought to life in costume. Of these, fewer than a fifth mix with guests; the others perform in shows or parades. Originally confined to the Magic Kingdom, characters are now found in all major theme parks and at Disney Deluxe resorts that host character meals.

We receive hundreds of comments from readers telling us how much the Disney characters enhanced their theme park experience. This e-mail from a Wisconsin mom is representative:

> *I can't say enough about the characters and how they react to the children and just people in general. They are obviously highly trained in people skills and just add an extra dimension to the park.*

**CHARACTER WATCHING** Watching characters has become a pastime. Families once were content to meet a character occasionally. They now pursue them relentlessly, armed with autograph books and cameras. Because some characters are only rarely seen, character watching has become character collecting. (To cash in on character collecting, Disney sells autograph books throughout the World.) Mickey, Minnie, and Goofy are a snap to bag; they seem to be everywhere. But some characters, like the Queen of Hearts and Friar Tuck, seldom come out, and quite a few appear only in parades or stage shows. Other characters appear only in a location consistent with their starring role. The Fairy Godmother is often near Cinderella Castle in Fantasyland, while Buzz Lightyear appears close to his eponymous attraction in Tomorrowland.

A Brooklyn dad complains that character collecting has gotten out of hand:

> *This year, when we took our youngest child (who is now 8 years old), he had already seen his siblings' collection and was determined to outdo them. However, rather than random meetings, the characters are now available practically all day long at different locations, according to a printed schedule, which our son was old enough to read. We spent more time standing in line for autographs than we did for the most popular rides!*

*unofficial* **TIP**
Many kids take special delight in meeting the "face characters," such as Tiana, Jasmine, Aladdin, and Cinderella, who can speak to them and engage them in a way that the mute animal characters can't.

## WDW Character-Greeting Venues

### THE MAGIC KINGDOM

#### MICKEY AND HIS POSSE

**Chip 'n' Dale**  Town Square, Tomorrowland
**Daisy, Donald, Goofy, Minnie**  Pete's Silly Sideshow (FastPass+)
**Mickey**  Town Square Theater (FastPass+)
**Pluto**  Town Square

#### DISNEY ROYALTY (*Princesses, Princes, Suitors, and Such*)

**Aladdin, Jasmine**  Adventureland
**Anna and Elsa**  Princess Fairytale Hall (FastPass+)
**Ariel**  Ariel's Grotto (FastPass+)
**Aurora, Cinderella, Rapunzel, Snow White**  Princess Fairytale Hall (FastPass+)
**Belle**  *Enchanted Tales with Belle* (FastPass+)
**The Fairy Godmother, the Tremaines**  Near Cinderella Castle
**Gaston**  Fountain outside Gaston's Tavern
**Merida**  Fairytale Garden
**Naveen, Tiana**  Liberty Square

#### FAIRIES

**Tinker Bell and Friends**  Town Square Theater (FastPass+)

#### MISCELLANEOUS

*ALICE IN WONDERLAND*
  **Alice, the White Rabbit, Tweedledum and Tweedledee**  Mad Tea Party
  **The Queen of Hearts**  Mad Tea Party, Town Square
*THE ARISTOCATS*  **Marie**  Town Square
*LILO AND STITCH*  **Stitch**  Tomorrowland
*PETER PAN*  **Hook, Smee**  Adventureland
  **Peter, Wendy**  Near Peter Pan's Flight in Fantasyland
*TOY STORY*  **Bullseye, Jessie, Woody**  Frontierland
  **Buzz Lightyear**  Tomorrowland

### EPCOT

#### MICKEY AND HIS POSSE

**Chip 'n' Dale**  Outside on the Land side of the Epcot Character Connection
**Daisy**  On the right as you enter Epcot through the main turnstiles
**Donald, Goofy, Minnie, Mickey, Pluto**  Epcot Character Spot (FastPass+)

#### DISNEY ROYALTY

**Aladdin, Jasmine**  Morocco   **Aurora, The Beast, Belle**  France
**Mulan**  China   **Snow White**  Germany

A family from Birmingham, Alabama, found some benefit in their children's pursuit of characters:

> We had no idea we'd be caught up in this madness, but after my daughters grabbed your guidebook to get Pocahontas to sign it (we had no blank paper), we quickly bought a Disney autograph book and gave in. It was actually the highlight of their trip, and my son even got into the act by helping get places in line for his sisters. It was an amazing, totally unexpected part of our visit.

**PREPARING YOUR CHILDREN TO MEET THE CHARACTERS** Almost all characters are quite large, and several, like Baloo, are huge! Small children don't expect this, and preschoolers especially can be intimidated.

**EPCOT** (*continued*)

**FAIRIES**

**Tinker Bell and Friends:** Future World between Mouse Gear and the Agent P World Showcase Adventure sign-up booth

**MISCELLANEOUS**

**Alice, Pooh, Mary Poppins and Bert** United Kingdom  **Geppetto, Pinocchio** Italy

**Marie (*The Aristocats*)** France  **The Three Caballeros** Mexico

## DISNEY'S ANIMAL KINGDOM

**MICKEY AND HIS POSSE**

**Chip 'n' Dale** Rafiki's Planet Watch at Conservation Station

**Daisy** Character Landing on Discovery Island

**Donald** DinoLand, U.S.A., to the left of the DINOSAUR exit on Cretaceous Trail

**Mickey, Minnie** Adventurers Outpost on Discovery Island (FastPass+)

**DISNEY ROYALTY**

**Pocahontas** Discovery Island trails that run behind the Tree of Life

**MISCELLANEOUS**

*THE JUNGLE BOOK* **King Louie and Baloo** On the walkway between Asia and Africa

*UP* **Dug, Russell** By *It's Tough to Be a Bug!*

## DISNEY'S HOLLYWOOD STUDIOS

**MICKEY AND HIS POSSE**

**Chip 'n' Dale** Sorcerer's Hat, The Magic of Disney Animation

**Goofy, Minnie, Pluto, Sorcerer Mickey** The Magic of Disney Animation

**CURRENT-MOVIE PALS**

**(Characters vary)** Animation Courtyard

**DISNEY CHANNEL STARS**

**Phineas and Ferb** Streets of America

**Sofia the First** Animation Courtyard near *Disney Junior—Live on Stage!*

**PIRATES**

**Jack Sparrow** Near *The Legend of Captain Jack Sparrow*

**MISCELLANEOUS**

*THE INCREDIBLES* **Frozone, Mr. and Mrs. Incredible** The Magic of Disney Animation

*MONSTERS, INC.* **Mike, Sully** Backlot

*STAR WARS* **Darth Maul, Darth Vader, Stormtroopers** Near Star Tours

*TOY STORY* **Buzz, Jessie, Woody** Pixar Place

Discuss the characters with your children before you go. On first encounter, don't thrust your child at the character. Allow the little one to deal with this big thing from whatever distance feels safe. If two adults are present, one should stay near the youngster while the other approaches the character and demonstrates that it's safe and friendly. Some kids warm to the characters immediately; some never do. Most take a little time and several encounters.

There are two kinds of characters: "furs," or those whose costumes include face-covering headpieces (including animal characters and

*un*official **TIP**
If you're using our Lines app in the parks, don't worry about losing time for meet-and-greets. Just tap "Optimize" after getting your autograph, and we'll tell you where to go next.

such humanlike characters as Captain Hook), and "face characters," those for whom no mask or headpiece is necessary. These include Tiana, Mary Poppins, Ariel, Jasmine, Aladdin, Cinderella, Belle, Snow White, Merida, and Prince Charming, among others.

Only face characters speak. Because cast members couldn't possibly imitate the furs' distinctive cinema voices, Disney has determined that it's more effective to keep such characters silent. Lack of speech notwithstanding, headpiece characters are warm and responsive, and they communicate effectively with gestures. Tell children in advance that these characters don't talk. As an aside, Disney has been implementing technology for making some of the furs, most notably Mickey and Minnie, talk.

Some character costumes are cumbersome and give cast members very poor visibility. (Eyeholes frequently are in the mouth of the costume or even on the neck or chest.) Children who approach the character from the back or side may not be noticed, even if the child touches the character. It's possible in this situation for the character to accidentally step on the child or knock him down. A child should approach a character from the front, but occasionally not even this works. Duck characters (Donald and Daisy), for example, have to peer around their bills. If a character appears to be ignoring your child, the character's handler will get its attention. Finally, some characters, such as Buzz Lightyear, can't sign autographs because of their costumes.

It's OK for your child to touch, pat, or hug the character. Understanding the unpredictability of children, the character will keep his feet still, particularly refraining from moving backward or sideways. Most characters will pose for pictures or sign autographs. Costumes make it difficult for characters to wield a normal pen. If your child collects autographs, carry a pen the width of a Magic Marker.

**"THEN SOME CONFUSION HAPPENED"** Kids sometimes become lost at character encounters. Usually, there's a lot of activity around a character, with both adults and children touching it or posing for pictures. Most commonly, Mom and Dad stay in the crowd while Junior approaches the character. In the excitement and with the character moving around, Junior heads in the wrong direction to look for Mom and Dad. In the words of a Salt Lake City mom: "Milo was shaking hands with Dopey one minute, then some confusion happened and Milo was gone."

We recommend that parents with preschoolers stay with them when they meet characters, stepping back only to take a quick picture.

**CHARACTER HOGS** While we're on the subject of cameras, give other families a chance. Especially if you're shooting video, consider the perspective of this Houston mom:

*One of the worst things to deal with is people who shoot about 3 minutes of their child with Mickey, asking everyone else to move. A photo takes about 2 seconds.*

## MEETING CHARACTERS FOR FREE

DISNEY HAS CREATED many permanent greeting locations intended to satisfy its guests' inexhaustible desire to meet characters. The chart on pages 344 and 345 lists them by park and character.

Meeting characters at the greeting locations may be free, but it can eat up of hours of time. A reader from Panama City, Florida, offers this advice:

*Use FastPass+ for character greetings whenever you can. We did this for Ariel in Fantasyland and with Rapunzel at Princess Fairytale Hall, and we got in superfast!*

# CHARACTER DINING

BECAUSE OF THE INCREDIBLE POPULARITY of character dining, reservations can be hard to come by if you wait until a couple of months before your vacation to book your choices. What's more, if you want to book a character meal, you must provide Disney with a credit card number. Your card will be charged $10 *per person* if you no-show or cancel your reservation less than 24 hours in advance; you may, however, reschedule with no penalty. See "Getting Advance Reservations at Popular Restaurants" (page 423) for the full story.

At very popular character meals like the breakfast at Cinderella's Royal Table, you're required to make a for-real reservation and guarantee it with a for-real deposit.

## WHAT TO EXPECT

CHARACTER MEALS ARE BUSTLING AFFAIRS held in the largest full-service restaurants at the theme parks and on-property resorts, plus the Walt Disney World Swan and select hotels in the Downtown Disney Resort Area and the Bonnet Creek Resort (including the just-about-to-open Four Seasons).

## Character-Meal Hit Parade

### 1. CINDERELLA'S ROYAL TABLE MAGIC KINGDOM

**MEALS SERVED DAILY** Breakfast, lunch, and dinner

**SETTING** ★★★★

**CHARACTERS** Cinderella, Fairy Godmother, Aurora, Belle, Jasmine, Snow White

**TYPE OF SERVICE** Fixed menu **FOOD VARIETY & QUALITY** ★★★

**NOISE LEVEL** Quiet **CHARACTER-GUEST RATIO** 1:26

### 2. AKERSHUS ROYAL BANQUET HALL EPCOT

**MEALS SERVED** Breakfast, lunch, and dinner **SETTING** ★★★★

**CHARACTERS** 4–6 characters chosen from Alice, Ariel, Belle, Jasmine, Mary Poppins, Mulan, Sleeping Beauty, Snow White

**TYPE OF SERVICE** Family-style and menu (all you care to eat)

**FOOD VARIETY & QUALITY** ★★★½ **NOISE LEVEL** Quiet

**CHARACTER-GUEST RATIO** 1:54

### 3. CHEF MICKEY'S CONTEMPORARY

**MEALS SERVED** Breakfast, dinner **SETTING** ★★★

**CHARACTERS** *Breakfast:* Mickey, Minnie, Donald, Goofy, Pluto (sometimes Chip 'n' Dale) *Dinner:* Mickey, Minnie, Donald, Goofy, Pluto (sometimes Chip 'n' Dale)

**TYPE OF SERVICE** Buffet

**FOOD VARIETY & QUALITY** Breakfast ★★★ Dinner ★★★½

**NOISE LEVEL** Loud **CHARACTER-GUEST RATIO** 1:56

### 4. THE CRYSTAL PALACE MAGIC KINGDOM

**MEALS SERVED** Breakfast, lunch, and dinner **SETTING** ★★★

**CHARACTERS** Pooh, Eeyore, Piglet, Tigger **TYPE OF SERVICE** Buffet

**FOOD VARIETY & QUALITY** Breakfast ★★½ Lunch and dinner ★★★

**NOISE LEVEL** Very loud

**CHARACTER-GUEST RATIO** Breakfast 1:67 Lunch and dinner 1:89

### 5. 1900 PARK FARE GRAND FLORIDIAN

**MEALS SERVED** Breakfast, dinner **SETTING** ★★★

**CHARACTERS** *Breakfast:* Mary Poppins, Alice, Mad Hatter, Pooh *Dinner:* Cinderella, Prince Charming, Lady Tremaine, the two stepsisters

**TYPE OF SERVICE** Buffet

**FOOD VARIETY & QUALITY** Breakfast ★★★ Dinner ★★★½

**NOISE LEVEL** Moderate **CHARACTER-GUEST RATIO** Breakfast 1:54 Dinner 1:44

Character breakfasts offer a fixed menu served individually, family-style, or on a buffet. The typical breakfast includes scrambled eggs; bacon, sausage, and ham; hash browns; waffles or French toast; biscuits, rolls, or pastries; and fruit. With family-style service, the meal is served in large skillets or platters at your table. The character breakfast at Akershus Royal Banquet Hall, for example, is served family-style and consists of typical breakfast fare such as eggs, bacon and sausage, and Danish pastries. Seconds (or thirds) are free. Buffets offer much the same fare, but you fetch it yourself.

### 6. GARDEN GRILL RESTAURANT   EPCOT

**MEAL SERVED** Dinner   **SETTING** ★★★★½

**CHARACTERS** Mickey, Pluto, Chip 'n' Dale   **TYPE OF SERVICE** Family-style

**FOOD VARIETY & QUALITY** ★★★½   **NOISE LEVEL** Very quiet

**CHARACTER–GUEST RATIO** 1:46

### 7. TUSKER HOUSE RESTAURANT   DISNEY'S ANIMAL KINGDOM

**MEALS SERVED** Breakfast, lunch   **SETTING** ★★★

**CHARACTERS** Donald, Daisy, Mickey, Goofy   **TYPE OF SERVICE** Buffet

**FOOD VARIETY & QUALITY** ★★★   **NOISE LEVEL** Very loud

**CHARACTER–GUEST RATIO** 1:112

### 8. CAPE MAY CAFE   BEACH CLUB

**MEAL SERVED** Breakfast   **SETTING** ★★★   **CHARACTERS** Goofy, Donald, Minnie

**TYPE OF SERVICE** Buffet   **FOOD VARIETY & QUALITY** ★★½

**NOISE LEVEL** Moderate   **CHARACTER–GUEST RATIO** 1:67

### 9. 'OHANA   POLYNESIAN

**MEAL SERVED** Breakfast   **SETTING** ★★

**CHARACTERS** Lilo and Stitch, Mickey, Pluto   **TYPE OF SERVICE** Family-style

**FOOD VARIETY & QUALITY** ★★½   **NOISE LEVEL** Moderate

**CHARACTER–GUEST RATIO** 1:57

### 10. HOLLYWOOD & VINE   DISNEY'S HOLLYWOOD STUDIOS

**MEALS SERVED** Breakfast, lunch   **SETTING** ★★½

**CHARACTERS** Handy Manny, Sofia the First, Doc McStuffins, Jake (*Jake and the Never Land Pirates*)

**TYPE OF SERVICE** Buffet   **FOOD VARIETY & QUALITY** ★★★

**NOISE LEVEL** Moderate   **CHARACTER–GUEST RATIO** 1:71

### 11. GARDEN GROVE   SWAN

**MEALS SERVED** Breakfast (Sat & Sun only), dinner   **SETTING** ★★★

**CHARACTERS** Rafiki, Timon, Goofy, Pluto   **TYPE OF SERVICE** Buffet

**FOOD VARIETY & QUALITY** ★★★½   **NOISE LEVEL** Moderate

**CHARACTER–GUEST RATIO** 1:198, but often much better

Character dinners range from a set menu to buffets to ordering off the menu. Character-dinner buffets, such as those at 1900 Park Fare at the Grand Floridian and Chef Mickey's at the Contemporary Resort, separate the kids' fare from the grown-ups', though everyone is free to eat from both lines. Typically, the children's buffet includes hamburgers, hot dogs, pizza, fish sticks, chicken nuggets, macaroni and cheese, and peanut-butter-and-jelly sandwiches. Selections at the adult buffet usually include prime rib or other carved meat, baked or broiled Florida seafood, pasta, chicken, an ethnic dish or two, vegetables, potatoes, and salad.

At all meals, characters circulate around the room while you eat. During your meal, each of the three to five characters present will visit your table, arriving one at a time to cuddle the kids (and sometimes the adults), pose for photos, and sign autographs. Keep autograph books (with pens) handy and cameras or mobile phones at the ready. For the best photos, adults should sit across the table from their children. Seat the children where characters can easily reach them. If a table is against a wall, for example, adults should sit with their backs to the wall and children on the aisle.

Theresa Brown posted this great tip for getting the best photos at the independent Disney website **allears.net:**

> We did several character meals. At first, we would only use our cameras to take pictures of our children with the characters after they had signed the autograph books and were posing with them. But after the second meal, we started snapping away as soon as the characters approached our table. We're so glad we did this, because we captured a very funny sequence of events while at 1900 Park Fare at the Grand Floridian. These candid shots tell a funny story showing the playful interaction between my sons and the characters. After that, we started snapping away at all of the character meals, and now that we're back, we see that the candid shots usually gave us better pictures than the posed ones! Of course, you want the posed pictures, but the candid ones just might end up being your favorite memories of the meals!

At some larger restaurants, including 'Ohana at the Polynesian Resort and Chef Mickey's at the Contemporary, character meals involve impromptu parades of characters and children around the room, group singing, napkin waving, and other organized madness.

Even without parades and such, character meals are pretty frenetic, as this mother of a 3-year-old attests:

> The character meals are NOT relaxing. I wish I had known how frantic and rushed I would be. I was literally sprinting to the buffet to throw food on my plate, so I wouldn't miss a character at our table. I still HIGHLY recommend them, as the food was actually pretty good, and the meals were the BEST part of our daughter's trip. But just be prepared for it to be a semi-hectic affair.

## WHEN TO GO

ATTENDING A CHARACTER BREAKFAST usually prevents you from arriving at the theme parks in time for opening. Because early morning is best for touring and you don't want to burn daylight lingering over breakfast, we suggest:

1. Schedule your in-park character breakfast for the first seating if the park opens at 9 a.m. or later. You'll be admitted to the park before other guests (admission is still required) through a special line at the turnstiles. Arrive early to be among the first parties seated.

2. Go to a character dinner or lunch instead of breakfast. It'll be a nice break.

3. Schedule the last seating for breakfast. Have a light snack such as cereal or bagels before you head to the parks for opening, hit the most popular attractions until 10:15 or so, and then head for brunch. The buffet should keep you fueled until dinner, especially if you eat another light snack in the afternoon.

4. Go on arrival or departure day. The day you arrive and check in is usually good for a character dinner. Settle at your hotel, swim, then dine with the characters. This strategy has the added benefit of exposing your children

to the characters before chance encounters at the parks. Some children, moreover, won't settle down to enjoy the parks until they have seen Mickey. Departure day also is good for a character meal. Schedule a character breakfast on your check-out day before you head for the airport or begin your drive home.

5. Go on a rest day. If you plan to stay five or more days, you'll probably take a day or half-day from touring to rest or do something else. These are perfect days for a character meal.

## HOW TO CHOOSE A CHARACTER MEAL

MANY READERS ASK FOR ADVICE about character meals. This question from a Waterloo, Iowa, mom is typical:

*Are all character breakfasts pretty much the same or are some better than others? How should I go about choosing one?*

In fact, some *are* better, sometimes much better. When we evaluate character meals, we look for:

**1. THE CHARACTERS**  The meals offer a diverse assortment of characters. Pick a meal that features your kids' favorites. Check out our Character-Meal Hit Parade chart (see pages 348 and 349) to see which characters are assigned to each meal. Most restaurants stick with the same characters. Even so, check the lineup when you call to make your Advance Reservations.

**2. ATTENTION FROM THE CHARACTERS**  At all character meals, characters circulate among guests, hugging children, posing for pictures, and signing autographs. How much time a character spends with you and your children depends primarily on the ratio of characters to guests. The more characters and fewer guests, the better. Because many character-meal venues never fill to capacity, the character-to-guest ratios in our Character-Meal Hit Parade chart have been adjusted to reflect an average attendance. Even so, there's quite a range. The best ratio is at Cinderella's Royal Table, where there's about 1 character to every 26 guests.

The worst ratio is theoretically at the Swan resort's Garden Grove, where there could be as few as 1 character for every 198 guests. We say "theoretically," however, because in practice there are far fewer guests at the Garden Grove than at character meals in Disney-owned resorts, and often more characters. During one recent meal, friends of ours were literally the only guests in the restaurant for breakfast and had to ask the characters to leave them alone to eat.

A Jerseyville, Illinois, mom gives the face characters high marks:

*Our 7-year-old daughter wanted to have dinner with Sleeping Beauty, so we scheduled a character dinner with the princesses in the Norway Pavilion. The princesses were so accessible and took their time with our child, answering questions and smiling for pictures. In fact, our daughter told us she "had the best day of her life," and parents want to hear that from their child.*

An Indiana mother of two relates the importance of keeping tabs on the characters:

*For character meals, take note of which characters are there when you arrive, and mentally check them off as they visit your table. If*

*the last one or two seem slow to arrive, seek out the "character man-*
*ager" and let him or her know ASAP.*

**3. THE SETTING** Some character meals are in exotic settings. For others, moving the event to an elementary-school cafeteria would be an improvement. Our chart rates each meal's setting with the familiar scale of zero (worst) to five (best) stars. Two restaurants, Cinderella's Royal Table in the Magic Kingdom and Garden Grill Restaurant in the Land Pavilion at Epcot, deserve special mention. Cinderella's Royal Table is on the first and second floors of Cinderella Castle in Fantasyland, offering guests a look inside the castle. Garden Grill is a revolving restaurant overlooking several scenes from the Living with the Land boat ride. Also at Epcot, the popular Princess Storybook Meals are held in the castlelike Akershus Royal Banquet Hall. Though Chef Mickey's at the Contemporary Resort is rather sterile in appearance, it affords a great view of the monorail running through the hotel. Themes and settings of the remaining character-meal venues, while apparent to adults, will be lost on most children.

**4. THE FOOD** Although some food served at character meals is quite good, most is average (palatable but nothing to get excited about). In variety, consistency, and quality, restaurants generally do a better job with breakfast than with lunch or dinner (if served).

Some restaurants offer a buffet, while others opt for "one-skillet" family-style service, in which all hot items are served from the same pot or skillet. Regarding the latter, a Texas mom notes:

> *The family-style meals are much better for character dining. At the buffet, you're scared to leave your table in case you miss a character or other action.*

To help you sort everything out, we rate the food at each character meal in our chart using the five-star scale.

**5. THE PROGRAM** Some larger restaurants stage modest performances where the characters dance, head a parade around the room, or lead songs and cheers. For some guests, these activities give the meal a celebratory air; for others, they turn what was already mayhem into absolute chaos. Either way, the antics consume time the characters could spend with families at their table.

**6. NOISE** If you want to eat in peace, character meals are a bad choice. That said, some are much noisier than others. Our chart gives you an idea of what to expect.

**7. WHICH MEAL?** Although breakfasts seem to be most popular, character lunches and dinners are usually more practical because they don't interfere with early-morning touring. During hot weather, a character lunch can be heavenly.

**8. COST** Dinners cost more than lunches and lunches more than breakfasts. Prices for meals (except at Cinderella Castle) vary only about $10 from the least expensive to the most expensive restaurant. Breakfasts run $21–$53 for adults and $11–$34 for kids ages 3–9. For character lunches, expect to pay $26–$57 for adults and $15–$36 for kids. Dinners are $36–$67 for adults and $14–$41 for children. Little ones ages 2 years and younger eat free. The meals at the high end of the price range are at Cinderella's Royal Table in the Magic Kingdom and Akershus Royal Banquet Hall at Epcot. The reasons for the sky-high prices: (1) Cinderella's Royal Table is small but in great demand and (2) the prices at Cinderella's and Akershus include a set of photos of your group taken by a Disney photographer. Whereas photos at other venues are optional, at Cindy's and Akershus you don't have a say in the matter.

**BOOSTING SALES OF MEMENTOS AND SOUVENIRS** Usually when Disney sees a horse carrying moneybags, it rides the beast until it drops. Disney's latest scheme of bundling photos in the price of character meals at Cinderella's Royal Table extends to Akershus Royal Banquet Hall at Epcot. Adding photos of your group taken by a Disney photographer is Disney's justification for raising the price of the character meals by about 60%. Disney insists that you're getting the photos at a bargain price. This is well and good if you're in the market, but if buying photos was not in your plans, well, they gotcha. It's a matter of some conjecture how far Disney will run with this idea. Maybe next year the price will be $200 and include fanciful medieval costumes for your entire party (charges for the changing room and locker to store your street clothes not included).

**9. ADVANCE RESERVATIONS** Disney makes Advance Reservations for character meals 180 days before you wish to dine (Disney resort guests can reserve 190 days out, or 10 additional days in advance); moreover, Disney resort guests can make Advance Reservations for all meals during their stay. Advance Reservations for most character meals are easy to obtain even if you call only a couple of weeks before you leave home. Meals at Cinderella's Royal Table and Be Our Guest are another story. For these two, you'll need our strategy (see Part Ten), as well as help from Congress and the Pope.

**10. CHECKING IT TWICE** Disney occasionally shuffles the characters and theme of a character meal. If your little one's heart is set on Pooh and Piglet, getting Hook and Mr. Smee is just a waste of time and money. Reconfirm all character-meal Advance Reservations three weeks or so before you leave home by calling ☎ 407-WDW-DINE.

**11. "FRIENDS"** For some venues, Disney has stopped specifying characters scheduled for a particular meal. Instead, they say it's a given character "and friends"—for example, "Pooh and friends," meaning Eeyore, Piglet, and Tigger, or some combination thereof, or "Mickey and friends" with some assortment chosen among Minnie, Goofy, Pluto, Donald, Daisy, Chip, and Dale.

**12. THE BUM'S RUSH** Most character meals are leisurely affairs, and you can usually stay as long as you want. An exception is Cinderella's Royal Table at the Magic Kingdom. Because Cindy's is in such high demand, the restaurant does everything short of pre-chewing your food to move you through, as this European mother of a 5-year-old can attest:

*We dined a lot, did three character meals and a few signature restaurants, and every meal was awesome except for lunch with Cinderella in the castle. While I'd often read it wouldn't be a rushed affair, it was exactly that. We had barely sat down when the appetizers were thrown on our table, the princesses each spent just a few seconds with our daughter—almost no interaction—and the side dishes were cold. We were out of there within 40 minutes and felt very stressed. Considering the price for the meal, I cannot recommend it.*

## GETTING AN ADVANCE RESERVATION AT CINDERELLA'S ROYAL TABLE

ONCE UPON A TIME, breakfast was the only character meal at Cinderella Castle in the Magic Kingdom. Reservations for every table were gone within minutes of becoming available each morning. Disney responded to this popularity by adding character lunches and dinners— and jacking up the price to almost $60–$70 per adult. As a result, it's now much easier to get into Cinderella's Royal Table for some meals during your stay. Also, the opening of the wildly popular **Be Our Guest** restaurant in Fantasyland has taken a lot of pressure off Cindy's. If you're visiting during peak periods or you've got to have a reservation at a specific, popular time, see our Advance Reservation tips starting on page 423.

**DISNEY'S ROYAL ALTERNATIVES** If you're unwilling to fund Cinderella's shoe habit or you simply weren't able to get an Advance Reservation before young Ariel graduates from college, rest assured there are other venues that will feed you in the company of princesses.

**Akershus Royal Banquet Hall,** in the Norway Pavilion of Epcot's World Showcase, serves family-style breakfast, lunch, and dinner. Disney tends to define *princess* quite loosely, so you may see any character who's ever donned a dress (with the exception of Cinderella) at this meal. Entrees are a combination of traditional buffet fare and the occasional Scandinavian dish.

Dinner at the Grand Floridian's **1900 Park Fare** features the whole crew from *Cinderella,* including Lady Tremaine and the stepsisters (breakfast is a character buffet with Winnie the Pooh and friends). At $40 per adult and $22 for children age 9 and under, this is a far more economical option for diners wishing to get their princess on, and the stepsisters are an absolute hoot. This meal is also a little more boy-friendly if you're entertaining a mixed crowd. Finally, remember that your princess may be feeding off your own excitement over eating in the Castle—she might be just as happy with a plastic crown purchased in the gift shop and a burger from Cosmic Ray's.

## OTHER CHARACTER EVENTS

A CAMPFIRE AND SING-ALONG are held nightly (times vary with the season) near the Meadow Trading Post and Bike Barn at Fort Wilderness Resort & Campground. Chip 'n' Dale lead the songs, and a Disney film is shown. The program is free and open to resort guests (☎ 407-824-2900). Another character encounter at Fort Wilderness is *Mickey's Backyard BBQ,* held seasonally on Thursday and Saturday. See page 771 for details.

# BABYSITTING

**CHILD-CARE CENTERS** Child care isn't available inside the theme parks, but two Magic Kingdom resorts connected by monorail or boat

## CHILD-CARE CLUBS*

| HOTEL | NAME OF PROGRAM | AGES | PHONE |
|---|---|---|---|
| **ANIMAL KINGDOM LODGE** | | | |
| Simba's Cubhouse | | 3–12 | ☎ 407-938-4785 |
| **DOLPHIN AND SWAN** | | | |
| Camp Dolphin | | 4–12 | ☎ 407-934-4241 |
| **POLYNESIAN RESORT** | | | |
| Club Disney | | 3–12 | ☎ 407-824-1639 |
| **YACHT & BEACH CLUB RESORTS** | | | |
| Sandcastle Club | | 3–12 | ☎ 407-934-3750 |
| **WILDERNESS LODGE & VILLAS** | | | |
| Cub's Den | | 3–12 | ☎ 407-824-1083 |

*Child-care clubs operate afternoons and evenings. Before 4 p.m., call the hotels rather than the numbers listed above. All programs require reservations; call ☎ 407-WDW-DINE (939-3463).

## Babysitting Services

| KID'S NITE OUT | FAIRY GODMOTHERS |
|---|---|
| ☎ 407-828-0920 or 800-696-8105 **kidsniteout.com** | ☎ 407-277-3724 |
| **HOTELS SERVED** All WDW and Orlando-area hotels | **HOTELS SERVED** All WDW hotels and those in the general WDW area |
| **SITTERS** Men and women | **SITTERS** Mothers and grandmothers, female college students |
| **MINIMUM CHARGES** 4 hours | **MINIMUM CHARGES** 4 hours |
| **BASE HOURLY RATES** 1 child, $16; 2 children, $18.50; 3 children, $21; 4 children, $23.50 | **BASE HOURLY RATES** 1 child, $16; 2 children, $16; 3 children, $16; 4 children, $18 |
| **EXTRA CHARGES** Transportation fee, $10; starting before 6:30 a.m. or after 9 p.m., +$2 per hour; additional fee for holidays | **EXTRA CHARGES** Transportation fee, $14; starting after 10 p.m., +$2 per hour |
| **CANCELLATION DEADLINE** 24 hours before service | **CANCELLATION DEADLINE** 3 hours before service |
| **FORM OF PAYMENT** AE, D, MC, V; tips in cash | **FORM OF PAYMENT** Cash or traveler's checks for actual payment; tips in cash |
| **THINGS SITTERS WON'T DO** Transport children in private vehicle, take children swimming, give baths | **THINGS SITTERS WON'T DO** Transport children, give baths. Swimming is at sitter's discretion. |

(Polynesian and Wilderness Lodge & Villas), four Epcot resorts (the Yacht & Beach Club Resorts, the Swan, and the Dolphin), and Animal Kingdom Lodge, along with the Hilton at Walt Disney World, have child-care centers for potty-trained children age 3 and older (see top chart above). Services vary, but children generally can be left between 4:30 p.m. and midnight. Milk and cookies and blankets and pillows are provided at all centers, and dinner is provided at most. Play is

*unofficial* **TIP**
Child-care clubs close at or before midnight. If you intend to stay out late, in-room babysitting is your best bet.

supervised but not organized, and toys, videos, and games are plentiful. Guests at any Disney resort or campground may use the services.

The most elaborate of the child-care centers (variously called "clubs" or "camps") is **Club Disney** at the Polynesian Resort. The rate for ages 3–12 is $11.50 per hour, per child (2-hour minimum).

All the clubs accept reservations (some six months in advance!) with a credit card guarantee. Call the club directly, or reserve through Disney at ☎ 407-WDW-DINE. Most clubs require a 24-hour cancellation notice and levy a hefty penalty of 2 hours' time or $23 per call for no-shows. A limited number of walk-ins are usually accepted on a first-come, first-served basis.

If you're staying in a Disney resort that doesn't offer a child-care club and you *don't* have a car, then you're better off using in-room babysitting. Trying to take your child to a club in another hotel by Disney bus requires a 50- to 90-minute trip each way. By the time you've deposited your little one, it will almost be time to pick him or her up again.

**IN-ROOM BABYSITTING** Two companies provide in-room sitting in Walt Disney World and surrounding areas: **Kid's Nite Out** and **Fairy Godmothers** (no kidding). Kid's Nite Out also serves hotels in the greater Orlando area, including downtown. All three provide sitters older than age 18 who are insured, bonded, screened, reference-checked, police-checked, and trained in CPR. In addition to caring for your kids in your room, the sitters will, if you direct (and pay), take your children to the theme parks or other venues. Both services offer bilingual sitters. (See the bottom chart on page 355 for details.)

# SPECIAL PROGRAMS
## *for* CHILDREN

SEVERAL CHILDREN'S PROGRAMS ARE AVAILABLE at Walt Disney World parks and resorts. While all are undoubtedly fun, we find them somewhat lacking in educational focus.

**DISNEY'S FAMILY MAGIC TOUR** This is a 1 1/2- to 2-hour guided tour of the Magic Kingdom for the entire family. Even children in strollers (no younger than age 3) are welcome. The tour combines information about the Magic Kingdom with the gathering of clues that ultimately solve "diabolical" problems. There's usually a marginal plot such as saving Wendy from Captain Hook, in which case the character at the end of the tour is Wendy. The tour departs daily at 10 a.m. The cost is about $36 per person with tax, plus a valid Magic Kingdom admission. The maximum group size is 20 persons. Reservations can be made up to one year in advance by calling ☎ 407-WDW-TOUR (939-8687).

**DISNEY'S PIRATE ADVENTURE** Children ages 4–12 get to don bandannas, hoist the Jolly Roger, and set out on a boat trip to search for buried treasure by following a map. At the final port of call, the kids find the treasure (doubloons, beads, and rubber bugs!) and wolf down PB&J sandwiches. The treasure is split among the kids. The adventure costs about $36 per child with tax and is offered at Port Orleans Riverside (Bayou Pirate Adventure), the Grand Floridian (Pirate Adventure), the Yacht Club (Albatross Treasure Cruise), and the Caribbean Beach Resort (Islands of the Caribbean). All programs are offered daily, weather permitting; call ☎ 407-WDW-PLAY (939-7529) for days offered and other information. Boys and girls alike really love this outing—many report it as the highlight of their vacation. *Note:* No parents allowed.

**DISNEY'S THE MAGIC BEHIND OUR STEAM TRAINS**  Kids must be age 10 or older for this 3-hour tour, presented Monday–Saturday. At the 7:30 a.m. start time, join the crew of the Walt Disney World Railroad as they prepare their steam locomotives for the day. Cost is about $58 per person with tax, plus a valid Magic Kingdom admission. Call ☎ 407-WDW-TOUR for information and reservations.

**MY DISNEY GIRL'S PERFECTLY PRINCESS TEA PARTY**  It certainly takes a princely sum to cover the tab on this Grand Floridian gathering, hosted by Rose Petal, an enchanted storytelling rose. Your little princess gets dressed up in her favorite regal attire and sips tea with Princess Aurora. Girls receive an 18-inch My Disney Girl doll dressed in a matching Princess Aurora gown plus accessories. Other loot includes a ribbon tiara, silver link bracelet, fresh rose, scrapbook set, and "Best Friend" certificate. A luncheon is served as well. The cost is about $250 with tax and tip for one adult and one child ages 3–11; add an additional adult for $85 or an additional child for $165. *Note:* **This event is not covered by the Disney Dining Plan.** The tea party is held every Sunday, Monday, and Wednesday–Friday, 10:30 a.m.–noon. Call ☎ 407-939-6397 for reservations and information.

**WONDERLAND TEA PARTY**  Held at 1900 Park Fare restaurant in the Grand Floridian Monday–Friday afternoons at 2 p.m. for $43 per child (ages 4–12, with tax), the program consists of decorating (and eating) cupcakes and having lunch and tea with characters from Alice in Wonderland. Reservations can be made by calling ☎ 407-WDW-DINE 90 days in advance.

An Illinois mom ponied up for two of the programs:

*We splurged on the Perfectly Princess Tea Party. It was nice but a bit too long with all the singing and stories. Not easy for a 4-year-old to sit that long. I'm not sure it was worth it, and I would not do it again. We also booked the Wonderland Tea Party. That was a much better cost, and I thought my daughter would love decorating a cupcake. She was so freaked out by the Mad Hatter that the nice workers there called me and asked me to come get her. They said many kids are scared of him, so I'm not sure why they don't have Alice and another character.*

# BIRTHDAYS *and*
# SPECIAL OCCASIONS

IF SOMEONE IN YOUR FAMILY CELEBRATES A BIRTHDAY while you're at Disney World, don't keep it a secret. A Lombard, Illinois, mom put the word out and was glad she did:

My daughter was turning 5 while we were there; our hotel asked me who her favorite character was and did the rest. We came back to our room on her birthday and there were helium balloons, a card, and a Cinderella photo autographed in ink! When we entered the Magic Kingdom, we received an "It's My Birthday Today" pin (FREE!), and at the restaurant she got a huge cupcake with whipped cream, sprinkles, and a candle. IT PAYS TO ASK!

# PART SEVEN

# SPECIAL TIPS *for* SPECIAL PEOPLE

## WALT DISNEY WORLD *for* PEOPLE *with* BAD ATTITUDES

YOU'D BE AMAZED at how many people are dragged unwillingly to Walt Disney World by their friends and families. If someone doesn't care for Disney World based on past experience, it's best to leave him or her at home. But for skeptics and cynics who've never visited, there's hope, as described by a 25-year-old woman from Williamstown, Massachusetts:

> My boyfriend is sort of anti-Disney, so to save our relationship and vacation, I steered us clear of some traditional must-sees. (It's a Small World, for example, might have sent him over the edge.) I made sure that Soarin' was one of the first rides we went on. He absolutely loved it, and it opened his mind to the rest of the Disney experience.

A mom from Fort Knox, Kentucky, offers this:

> I made a deal with my husband that if he went to Disney World this year, we'd all go camping in Yellowstone National Park next year, something he's been trying to get me to do for ages.

## WALT DISNEY WORLD *for* SINGLES

DISNEY WORLD IS GREAT FOR SINGLES. It's safe, clean, and low-pressure. Safety and comfort are unsurpassed, especially for women traveling alone. Parking lots are well lit and constantly patrolled.

If you're looking for a place to relax without being hit on, Disney World is perfect. The bars, lounges, and nightclubs are among the most laid-back and friendly you're likely to find. Between the BoardWalk and Downtown Disney, nightlife abounds; virtually every type of entertainment is available at a reasonable price. If you overimbibe and you're a Disney resort guest, Disney buses will return you safely to your hotel.

See "Tips for Going Solo" on the following pages for more ways to enjoy Disney World on your own.

## TIPS FOR GOING SOLO

*Single* can mean traveling alone as well as unmarried, and being by yourself doesn't mean that you can't have a great time at Disney World. Deb Wills, creator of the all-things-Disney website **allears.net**, offers this advice:

- Keep your schedule as open as you can. One of the best parts about traveling solo is that you can be your own boss. Sleep in, have leisurely morning coffee on the balcony, relax by the pool . . . or not. If you'd rather get up and go early, who's to stop you?

- Put some spontaneity into your day. If you're taking Disney transportation, get on the first park bus that arrives.

- Get on the resort monorail (not the Express!) at the Magic Kingdom, and visit each of the resorts it stops at. Each resort has its own theme and character, with lots to see and explore.

- Did you know that you can walk through the queues and view the preshows of the thrill rides even if you don't want to ride? Wander through at your own pace, then tell the cast member before boarding that you don't wish to ride, and you'll be shown to a nearby exit.

- If you *do* want to experience the thrill rides, take advantage of the single-rider lines for the Rock 'n' Roller Coaster, Expedition Everest, and Test Track. They can cut your wait time significantly.

- If you encounter folks taking photos of each other, ask if they would like to be in one photo, and then offer to snap the picture. This is a great way to make friends.

- Get your favorite Disney snack, find a bench, and people-watch. You'll be amazed at what you see: the honeymooning

# WALT DISNEY WORLD *for* COUPLES

MANY COUPLES THINK Walt Disney World is strictly for kids. Not so, an Evans City, Pennsylvania, woman attests:

> *I have many friends who think I was crazy to travel to Walt Disney World without my children (ages 9 and 12). I absolutely loved it! Instead of rushing from thrill ride to thrill ride with all the other hordes of people, we were able to slow down and enjoy all of the amazing details that make WDW the incredibly special place that it is. It is an entirely different, but equally magical, experience.*

So many couples tie the knot or honeymoon in the World that Disney has a dedicated department to help arrange the day of your dreams. **Disney's Fairy Tale Weddings & Honeymoons** (☎ 321-939-4610;

couple wearing bride-and-groom mouse ears, toddlers giving Mickey and the characters their first hugs, grandparents smiling indulgently as their grandchildren smear ice cream all over their faces. If you're missing the smiles of your own children, buy a couple of balloons and give them away. You'll help make the kids near you very, very happy.

- Learn how some of the magic is created. Take a behind-the-scenes tour (see Part Nineteen) or one of the Deluxe hotel tours.

- Visit Animal Kingdom Lodge and relax at an animal-viewing area. Find an animal keeper; they'll gladly discuss care of the wild animals at the resort.

- Don't hesitate to strike up conversations with cast members or guests in line with you. Foreign cast members in Epcot's World Showcase are happy to share stories about their homelands.

- Enjoy a leisurely shopping adventure around the World. Some stores (Arribas Brothers in Downtown Disney, and Mitsukoshi Department Store in the Japan section of World Showcase) have really neat displays and exhibits.

- Go to that restaurant you've always wanted to try but your picky eater has always declined. You don't have to order a full meal; try several appetizers or, better yet, just dessert.

- Use common sense about your personal security. I feel very comfortable and safe traveling alone at Disney World and have done so many times, but I still don't do things that I wouldn't do at home (like announce to anyone listening that I'm traveling solo). If you aren't comfortable walking to your room alone, ask at the front desk for a security escort. Use extra caution in the parking lots at night, just as you would at home.

disneyweddings.com) offers a range of ceremony venues and services, plus honeymoon planning and registries.

## WEDDINGS, COMMITMENT CEREMONIES, AND VOWS RENEWALS

FOR COUPLES WISHING TO GET HITCHED, all packages include a bouquet, a two-tier cake and Champagne toast (not part of the Memories Collection), live music (an organist or violinist, depending on the venue), photo package, limousine service, wedding-planning website, a wedding coordinator, and Annual Passes to Disney World for the happy couple (not part of the Memories Collection). The officiant and marriage certificate are not included with any package. Disney has a list of local officiants from which to choose, or the couple can bring their own.

Many couples make a special trip to Walt Disney World to plan their weddings in person, though it's entirely possible to make all arrangements by phone and e-mail. While it may seem that a Disney wedding is the ultimate cookie-cutter event, many options exist for making your

*unofficial* **TIP**
Contact Disney as soon as you have a date in mind for your event— popular dates may not be available with short notice. If you wish to have your ceremony inside a theme park, you're restricted to very early in the morning or late at night, when the park is closed to guests.

day personal and special. The best resource for planning a Disney wedding is ***Passporter's Disney Weddings & Honeymoons,*** by Carrie Hayward (available in print at Amazon or as an e-book at **passporter.com/weddings.asp**).

## LEGALITIES

WHILE ONLY MALE–FEMALE COUPLES may legally marry in Florida, Walt Disney World offers same-sex commitment ceremonies with the same options as weddings; planning and booking are handled identically as well. To marry in the World, you need a marriage license, issued at any Florida courthouse. There is no waiting period; your license is issued when you apply. Florida residents must complete a 4-hour premarital counseling session to marry sooner than three days after obtaining their license; all weddings must occur within 60 days of getting the license. Blood tests aren't required, but both parties must present ID. If you were widowed or divorced within 300 days of the wedding, you must present a certified copy of the deceased spouse's death certificate or your divorce decree.

## HONEYMOONS AND HONEYMOON REGISTRIES

HONEYMOON PACKAGES are adaptations of regular Walt Disney World travel packages, though you may purchase add-ons such as flowers and in-room gifts to make your trip more special. Some couples who honeymoon at Walt Disney World create a registry that allows friends and family to bestow gifts of tours, spa packages, special dinners, and the like. (Couples receive gift funds by bank transfer or check.) For more information on honeymoon registries, visit **disney.honeymoonwishes.com**.

## ROMANTIC GETAWAYS

DISNEY WORLD IS A FAVORITE GETAWAY FOR COUPLES, but not all Disney hotels are equally romantic. Some are too family-oriented; others swarm with convention-goers. For romantic (though expensive) lodging, we recommend **Animal Kingdom Lodge & Villas; Bay Lake Tower** at the Contemporary; the **Polynesian Resort; Wilderness Lodge & Villas;** the **Grand Floridian Resort, Spa, & Villas; BoardWalk Inn & Villas;** and the **Yacht & Beach Club Resorts.** The Alligator Bayou section at **Port Orleans Riverside,** a Moderate Disney resort, also has secluded rooms. In Part Three, we provide recommendations for the best rooms in each Disney resort, taking into consideration view, quiet, and convenience.

## CELEBRATING

WALT DISNEY WORLD IS ALL ABOUT CELEBRATING—marriages, birthdays, anniversaries, the works—and can add a special touch to your big day, but only if you let somebody know. A St. Louis newlywed offers this advice:

*If you're celebrating, WEAR YOUR BUTTONS! Cast members regularly congratulated my new husband and me, and I'm relatively certain we were seated at better tables for dinner (for example, right next to the tank at Coral Reef Restaurant) based solely on our buttons.*

# WALT DISNEY WORLD
## *"At Large"*

YOU'VE JUST SPENT A SMALL FORTUNE for your vacation. If you're a person of size, you don't want to worry about whether you'll have trouble fitting in the ride vehicles. Fortunately, Disney World realizes that its guests come in all shapes and sizes and is quite accommodating. Deb Wills and Debra Martin Koma, authors of *PassPorter's Open Mouse for Walt Disney World and the Disney Cruise Line: Easy Access Vacations for Travelers with Extra Challenges*, offer these suggestions.

- Remember that you'll be on your feet for hours at a time. Be sure to wear comfortable, broken-in shoes. Pay attention to your feet: If you feel a blister starting, take care of it quickly. (Note that each park has a first-aid station where you can find bandages and other necessities. For more on blister prevention, see page 406.)

- If you're prone to chafing, consider bringing a commercial antifriction product (such as Bodyglide) that is designed to control or eliminate rubbing. You can find this and similar products at most pharmacies and sporting-goods stores.

- Know before you go! Not all attractions have the same types of vehicles or seating. Some have bench seats, while others have individual seats; some have overhead harnesses, while others have seat belts or lap bars. Learn what type of seating or vehicle each attraction has before you go so you know what to expect. Check out **allears.net** for the details. If the attraction has a seat belt, pull it all the way out before you sit down to make it easier to strap yourself in. Note that some attractions even have seat-belt extenders—ask a cast member about these.

- Several attractions (Expedition Everest, for example) offer a sample ride vehicle for you to try out before you get in line. These are usually discreetly out of view of the general public; ask a cast member for the location.

- Front seats (such as those in the Rock 'n' Roller Coaster and Test Track) often have more legroom.

- In restaurants, look for chairs without arms. If you don't see any, the host or hostess should be able to provide one for you.

- Request a resort hotel room with a king-size bed. Everyone needs a good night's sleep, especially after touring the parks all day. It may cost a bit more, but it will be more than worth it!

# WALT DISNEY WORLD
## *for* EXPECTANT MOTHERS

IT'S SAID THAT A GOOD SHEPHERD will lay down his life for his sheep. Heaven knows we've tried to be good shepherds for you. While researching this guide, we have spun in teacups and been jostled in simulators until we turned green. We have baked in the sun, flapped in the wind, and been drenched in the rain.

But we have failed expectant mothers. Try as they might, the authors have never become pregnant. Consequently, the *Unofficial Guide* has never included firsthand information for mothers-to-be. Then to the rescue came Debbie Grubbs, a Colorado reader in her fifth month of pregnancy. She fearlessly waddled all over Disney World, compiling observations and tips for expectant moms. Here are her conclusions.

## Magic Kingdom

*Splash Mountain is restricted obviously due to the drop, or so I thought. It turns out that the seat configuration in the "logs" has more to do with it than the drop. The seats are made so that your knees are higher than your rear, causing compression on the abdomen (when it's this large). This is potentially harmful to the baby. As always, better safe than sorry.*

*Big Thunder Mountain Railroad is also restricted for obvious reasons. It's just not a good idea to ride roller coasters when pregnant.*

*Mad Tea Party may be OK if you don't spin the cups. We didn't ride this one because my doctor advised me not to ride things with centrifugal [or centripetal] force. Dumbo in Fantasyland and the Astro Orbiter in Tomorrowland are OK, though.*

*Space Mountain is one of my favorite rides, but a roller coaster nonetheless.*

*Tomorrowland Speedway is not recommended due to the amount of rear-ending that always occurs from overzealous younger drivers.*

We think Debbie would've passed on Seven Dwarfs Mine Train's swinging cars.

**Disney's Animal Kingdom:** *Both DINOSAUR and Primeval Whirl are very jerky and should be avoided.*

We think Debbie would've avoided Expedition Everest, too.

**Epcot:** *Mission: SPACE and Test Track are restricted, as are all simulator rides. They're too rough and jerky, much like a roller coaster. [Non-moving seats are available in some simulation attractions—ask a cast member.] Soarin' is fine.*

**Disney's Hollywood Studios:** *Tower of Terror is restricted for the drop alone, and Star Tours is restricted because it's a simulator. The Rock 'n' Roller Coaster is clearly off-limits.*

**Water Parks:** *Slides are off-limits. Pregnant women can, however, do Shark Reef at Typhoon Lagoon with an extra-large wet-suit vest. The wave pools and floating creeks are great for getting the weight off your feet.*

A mother of three from Bethesda, Maryland, adds:

*First, anyone who is pregnant should go to a golf shop and buy one of those canes that has a seat attached to it. They're lightweight and easy to carry. Without a seat, I would've been a goner. Second, a pregnant woman must come with some type of support or a BellyBra.*

## MORE TIPS FOR MOMS-TO-BE

IN ADDITION TO DEBBIE'S TIPS, here are a few of ours:

1. Discuss your Disney World plans with your obstetrician before your trip.
2. Be prepared for a lot of walking. Get in shape by walking at home, gradually building endurance and distance.
3. Get as much rest as you need, even if you have to sacrifice some time at the theme parks. Try to nap each afternoon.
4. Eat properly. Drink plenty of water throughout the day, especially in warmer months.
5. Use in-park transportation whenever available to cut down on walking.
6. Stay in the World if possible. This will make it easier to return to your hotel for rest.

# WALT DISNEY WORLD
## *for* SENIORS

> *unofficial* **TIP**
> Because seniors are varied and willing, there are few attractions we suggest that they avoid.

SENIOR CITIZENS have much the same problems and concerns as all Disney visitors. Older guests do, however, get into predicaments caused by touring with younger people. Pressured by their grandchildren to endure a frantic pace, many seniors concentrate on surviving Disney World rather than enjoying it. Seniors must either set the pace or dispatch the young folks to tour on their own.

An older reader in Alabaster, Alabama, writes:

> *Being a senior is not for wussies. At Disney World particularly, it requires courage and pluck. Things that used to be easy take a lot of effort, and sometimes your brain has to wait for your body to catch up. Half the time, your grandchildren treat you like a crumbling ruin and then turn around and trick you into getting on a roller coaster in the dark. What you need to tell seniors is that they have to be alert and not trust anyone. Not their children or even the Disney people, and especially not their grandchildren. When your grandchildren want you to go on a ride, don't follow along blindly like a lamb to the slaughter. Make sure you know what the ride is all about. Stand your ground and don't waffle. He who hesitates is launched!*

Most seniors we interview enjoy Disney World much more when they tour with folks their own age. If, however, you're considering visiting Disney World with your grandchildren, we recommend making an orientation visit without them first. If you know firsthand what to expect, the easier it'll be to establish limits, maintain control, and set a comfortable pace later on.

If you're *determined* to take the grandkids, read carefully the sections of this book that discuss family touring. (*Hint:* The Dumbo-or-Die-in-a-Day Touring Plan has been known to bring grown-ups of all ages to their knees.)

Personal taste is more important than age. We hate to see mature visitors pass an exceptional attraction like Splash Mountain because it's a so-called thrill ride. Splash Mountain is a full-blown adventure that gets its appeal more from music and visual effects than from the thrill of the ride. Because you must choose among attractions that might interest you, we provide facts to help you make informed decisions.

## GETTING AROUND

MANY SENIORS LIKE TO WALK, but a 7-hour visit to a theme park includes 4–10 miles on foot. If you're not up to that, let someone push you in a rented wheelchair (theme parks: $12 per day with no deposit, $10 per day for multiday rentals; Downtown Disney: $100 rental deposit required); free at your Disney resort with a $315 refundable deposit. The theme parks also offer fun-to-drive electric carts (electric convenience vehicles, or ECVs) for $50 per day, with a $20 refundable deposit; Downtown Disney: $50 per day with a $100 refundable deposit. Don't let your pride keep you from having a good time. Sure, you could march 10 miles if you had to—*but you don't have to!*

Your wheelchair-rental deposit slip is good for a replacement wheelchair in any park during the same day. You can rent a chair at the Magic Kingdom in the morning, return it, go to Epcot, present your deposit slip, and get another chair at no additional charge.

## TIMING YOUR VISIT

RETIREES SHOULD MAKE THE MOST of their flexible schedules and go to Disney World in fall or spring (excluding holiday weeks), when the weather is nicest and crowds are thinnest. Crowds are also sparse from late January through early February, but the weather can be unpredictable. If you visit in winter, take coats and sweaters, plus warm-weather clothing. Be prepared for anything from near-freezing rain to afternoons in the 80s.

## LODGING

IF YOU CAN AFFORD IT, STAY IN DISNEY WORLD. Rooms are among the Orlando-Kissimmee area's nicest, and transportation is always available to any Disney destination at no additional cost.

Disney hotels reserve rooms close to restaurants and transportation for guests of any age who can't tolerate much walking. They also provide golf carts to pick up and deliver guests at their rooms. Service can vary dramatically depending on the time of day and the number of guests requesting carts. At check-in time (around 3 p.m.), for example, the wait for a ride can be as long as 40 minutes.

Here are four reasons to consider staying in Disney World:

1. The quality of the properties is consistently above average.
2. Buses run only hourly or so for "outside" hotels. Disney buses run about every 20 minutes. Staying in the World guarantees transportation when you need it. On the flip side, the buses that serve out-of-the-World areas usually operate on a fixed schedule so you know exactly what time to be at the loading point.
3. You get free parking in major theme parks' lots.
4. You get preferential tee times on resort golf courses.

Disney hotels are spread out. It's easy to avoid most stairs, but it's often a long hike to your room from parking lots or bus stops. Seniors intending to spend more time at Epcot and Hollywood Studios than at the Magic Kingdom or Animal Kingdom should consider the **Yacht & Beach Club Resorts,** the **Swan,** the **Dolphin,** or **BoardWalk Inn & Villas.**

The **Contemporary Resort** and **Bay Lake Tower** are good choices for seniors who want to be on the monorail system. So are the **Grand Floridian** and the **Polynesian,** though they cover many acres, necessitating a lot of walking. For a restful, rustic feeling, choose **Wilderness Lodge & Villas.** If you want a kitchen and the comforts of home, book **Old Key West Resort, Animal Kingdom Villas, Beach Club Villas, Grand Floridian Villas,** or **BoardWalk Villas.** If you enjoy watching birds and animals, try **Animal Kingdom Lodge & Villas.** Try **Saratoga Springs** for golf.

RVers will find pleasant surroundings at **Disney's Fort Wilderness Resort & Campground.** Several independent campgrounds are within 30 minutes of Disney World (see pages 210 and 211). None offers the wilderness setting or amenities that Disney does, but they cost less.

## TRANSPORTATION

ROADS IN DISNEY WORLD CAN BE DAUNTING. Armed with a decent sense of direction and a great sense of humor, however, even the most timid driver can get around.

If you drive, parking isn't a problem. Lots are served by trams linking the parking area and the theme park's entrance. Parking for the disabled is available adjacent to each park's entrance. Pay-booth attendants will provide a dashboard ticket and direct you to the reserved spaces. Disney requires that you be recognized officially as disabled to use this parking, but temporarily disabled or injured persons also are permitted access.

## SENIOR DINING

EAT BREAKFAST AT YOUR HOTEL RESTAURANT or save money by having juice and rolls in your room. Carry snacks in a fanny pack supplemented by fruit, fruit juice, and soft drinks purchased from vendors. Make Advance Reservations for lunch before noon to avoid the crowds. Follow with an early dinner and be out of the restaurants, ready for evening touring and fireworks, long before the main crowd even thinks about dinner.

We recommend that seniors fit dining and rest into each day. Plan lunch as a break. Sit back, relax, and enjoy. Then return to your hotel for a nap or swim during the hot, crowded hours of the day.

# WALT DISNEY WORLD *for* GUESTS *with* SPECIAL NEEDS

DISNEY WORLD IS SO ATTUNED TO GUESTS with physical challenges that unscrupulous people have been known to fake a disability in order to take unfair advantage. If you have a disability, Disney World is prepared to meet your needs.

Each theme park offers a free booklet describing disabled services and facilities at **disneyworld.disney.go.com/guest-services/guests-with-disabilities.** Or get it when you enter the parks, at resort front desks, and at wheelchair-rental locations inside the parks. More-limited information is available online at **disneyworld.disney.go.com/plain-text.**

For specific requests, such as those for special accommodations at hotels or on the Disney transportation system, call ☎ 407-939-7807 (voice) or 407-939-7670 (TTY). When the recorded menu comes up, press 1. Limit your questions and requests to those regarding disabled services and accommodations (address other questions to ☎ 407-824-4321 or 407-827-5141 [TTY]). If you'll be staying at a Disney resort, let the reservation agent know of any special needs you have when you book your room.

The following equipment, services, and facilities are available at Disney hotels, though not all hotels offer all items:

| | |
|---|---|
| • Accessible vanities | • Refrigerators |
| • Bed and bathroom rails | • Rubber bed padding |
| • Braille on signs and elevators | • Shower benches |
| • Closed-captioned televisions | • Strobe-light smoke detectors |
| • Double peepholes in doors | • Roll-in showers |
| • Handheld showerheads | • TTYs |
| • Knock and phone alerts | • Wheelchairs |
| • Lowered beds | • Wider bathroom doors |
| • Portable commodes | |

Service animals are welcome in all Disney resorts.

Much of the Disney transportation system is disabled-accessible. Monorails can be accessed by ramp or elevator, and all bus routes are served by vehicles with wheelchair lifts, though unusually wide or long wheelchairs (or motorized chairs) may not fit the lift. Watercraft accommodations for wheelchairs are iffier. If you plan to stay at Wilderness Lodge & Villas, Fort Wilderness Campground, or an Epcot resort, call ☎ 407-939-7807 (voice) or 407-939-7670 (TTY) for the latest information on watercraft accessibility.

Food and merchandise locations at theme parks, Downtown Disney, and hotels are generally accessible, but some fast-food queues and shop aisles are too narrow for wheelchairs. At these locations, ask a cast member or member of your party for assistance.

Disabled guests and their families give Disney high marks for accessibility and sensitivity. An Arlington, Virginia, woman writes:

*Disney is dynamite in its treatment of handicapped vacationers. My mom has mobility problems that got a lot worse between the time my dad made reservations and the time we arrived, and she was worried about getting around. Disney supplied a free wheelchair, every bus had kneeling steps for wheelchair users, and the hosts sprang into action when they saw us coming.*

## VISITORS WITH DISABILITIES

WHOLLY OR PARTIALLY NONAMBULATORY guests may rent wheelchairs. Most rides, shows, attractions, restrooms, and restaurants accommodate the nonambulatory disabled. If you're in a park and need assistance, go to Guest Relations.

A limited number of electric carts, ECVs (electric convenience vehicles), and ESVs (electric standing vehicles) are available for rent.

Easy to drive, they give nonambulatory guests tremendous freedom and mobility.

All Disney lots have close-in parking for disabled visitors. Request directions when you pay your parking fee. All monorails and most rides, shows, restrooms, and restaurants accommodate wheelchairs.

Wheelchairs rent for $12 with no deposit required, $10 per day for multiday rentals; free at your Disney resort ($315 deposit). ECVs and ESVs are $50 per day, plus a $20 refundable deposit (prices do not include tax). Rentals are available at all Disney World theme parks (see Parts Eleven through Fourteen for specific locations) and Downtown Disney; to reserve an ESV, call ☎ 407-824-5217. Wheelchairs are welcome at Blizzard Beach and Typhoon Lagoon water parks but are not available for rent; the rental deposit at Downtown Disney is $100. If you're looking to save money on an ECV, **Buena Vista Scooters** rents them for $30 per day with delivery and pick up at your Disney resort. See **buenavistascooters.com** for details.

*un*official **TIP**
Park maps issued to each guest on admission are coded to show which attractions accommodate wheelchairs.

Even if an attraction doesn't accommodate wheelchairs, ECVs, or ESVs, nonambulatory guests may ride if they can transfer from their wheelchair to the ride's vehicle. Disney staff, however, aren't trained or permitted to assist with transfers—guests must be able to board the ride unassisted or have a member of their party assist them. Either way, members of the nonambulatory guest's party will be permitted to ride with him or her.

Because the waiting areas of most attractions won't accommodate wheelchairs, nonambulatory guests and their parties should request boarding instructions as soon as they arrive at an attraction. Almost always, the entire group will be allowed to board without a lengthy wait.

A reader from New Orleans who traveled to Disney World with a nonambulatory friend writes:

> I went with a very dear friend of mine who is paraplegic. It was his first trip to WDW, and we were a little apprehensive about how much we'd be able to do. The official brochure is helpful but implies limits to accessibility. The reality is that nonambulatory visitors are able to do much more; one only has to ask the cast members what is really allowed. Brian is a very active person who is able to transfer from his wheelchair without too much difficulty, so we were able to ride almost everything we wanted.

**DIETARY RESTRICTIONS** Walt Disney World restaurants work very hard to accommodate guests' special dietary needs. When you make a dining reservation online or by phone, you'll be asked about food allergies and the like. The host or hostess and your server will also ask about this and send the chef out to discuss the menu; if you're not asked, just talk to your server when you're seated. For counter-service restaurants or kiosks, ask at Guest Relations or at the venue itself. For more information, e-mail **special.diets@disneyworld.com** or visit **tinyurl.com/wdwspecialdiets**.

An Idaho mom and her teenage daughter found Disney restaurants very responsive to their dietary needs:

*My daughter and I both have a gluten allergy. I have never felt so well cared for and safe eating anywhere else in the world. From our resort (both the food court and Boatwright's) to every single quick-service or sit-down restaurant, we had several choices, and we never waited longer than 8 minutes for our "special" orders.*

To request kosher meals at table-service restaurants, call ☎ 407-WDW-DINE 24 hours in advance. All Disney menus have vegetarian options; vegans may have to talk to the chef. Vegetarians, vegans, and pescetarians should speak up when making dining reservations.

Folks with special diets *and* a sweet tooth should try **BabyCakes NYC**'s vegan, gluten-free, and kosher treats, available at many Disney hotel food courts and Animal Kingdom's Garden Kiosk. You can also order custom cakes and baked goods from BabyCakes by phone or online (☎ 407-938-9044; **babycakesnyc.com**).

**SIGHT- AND/OR HEARING-IMPAIRED GUESTS** Guest Relations at the parks provides free assistive-technology devices to visually and hearing-impaired guests ($25 refundable deposit, depending on the device). Sight-impaired guests can customize the given information (such architectural details, restroom locations, and descriptions of attractions and restaurants) through an interactive audio menu that is guided by a GPS in the device. Hearing-impaired guests can benefit from amplified audio and closed-captioning for attractions loaded into the same device.

Braille guidebooks are available from Guest Relations at all parks ($25 refundable deposit), and Braille menus are available at some theme park restaurants. Some rides provide closed-captioning; many theater attractions provide reflective captioning.

Disney provides sign-language interpretations of live shows at the theme parks on certain designated days of the week:

**THE MAGIC KINGDOM: Mondays and Thursdays**
**EPCOT: Tuesdays and Fridays**
**DISNEY'S ANIMAL KINGDOM: Saturdays**
**DISNEY'S HOLLYWOOD STUDIOS: Sundays and Wednesdays**

Get confirmation of the interpreted-performance schedule a minimum of one week in advance by calling Disney World information at ☎ 407-824-4321 (voice) or 407-827-5141 (TTY). You'll be contacted before your visit with a show schedule that lists the names, dates, and times of the interpreted performances.

**NONAPPARENT DISABILITIES** We receive many letters from readers whose traveling companion or child requires special assistance but who, unlike a person in a wheelchair, is not visibly disabled. Autism, for example, makes it very difficult or impossible for someone with the disorder to wait in line for more than a few minutes or in queues surrounded by a crowd.

A trip to Disney World can be nonetheless positive and rewarding for guests with autism and similar conditions. And while any Disney vacation requires planning, a little extra effort to accommodate the affected person will pay large dividends.

Disney's PDF **Guide for Guests with Cognitive Disabilities** is available for download at **tinyurl.com/cognitivedisabilitiesguide**.

## Disney's Disability Access Service (DAS)

*un**official** TIP

Disney revised its procedures for assisting disabled guests in late 2013, in response to reports from the national media that its then-current Guest Assistance Card (GAC) program was being abused rampantly.

You can have only one active return time on your DAS card. If you choose to return to ride after your specified time, you may not ride any other attraction on your card has been ridden or a cast member has crossed it off because you've decided not to ride.

The new program, called Disability Access Service (DAS), is still designed to accommodate guests who can't wait in regular standby lines, and, as with the old GAC program, you must still obtain a DAS card at the Guest Relations window of the first theme park you visit. The same card works in every subsequent park you visit.

When you get to Guest Relations, you'll need to present identification and describe your or your family member's limitations. You don't need to disclose a disease or medical condition— what Disney's looking for is a description of how the condition affects you in the parks. Rather than an attempt to have you "prove" your condition, the goal here is to get you the right level of assistance.

Be as detailed as possible in describing limitations. For instance, if your child is on the autism spectrum, has trouble waiting in long lines, and has sensory issues that make it difficult for him or her to stand or be subjected to loud noises, you need to let the cast member know each of these things. "He doesn't wait in lines" isn't enough to go on.

The new DAS card requires a photograph. Pictures are taken with an iPad; the cast member will come to you if you can't make it up to the counter. If the DAS card is for a child, you may either use the child's photo or substitute your own if you'd rather not use the child's. Finally, you must sign the card and agree to be bound by its rules.

DAS cards can be used at any attraction or meet-and-greet with a FastPass+ line. Present the card to a cast member at the attraction you want to ride. If the ride's standby wait time is less than 10 minutes, you'll usually be escorted through the standby entrance or FastPass+ entrance. If the standby time is higher, the cast member will enter on the back of the DAS card the attraction name, time of day, wait time, and a return time for you to come back to ride. The return time will be the current wait time minus 10 minutes. So if you get to Splash Mountain at 12:20 p.m. and the standby time is 40 minutes, your return time will be 30 minutes later, at 12:50 p.m.

You may return at the specified time or at any time thereafter. When you return, you'll be given access to the FastPass+ line. The cardholder need not be present to obtain a return time but must be present with his or her party for anyone to gain admission.

DAS cards are good for parties of up to six people. For parties of more than six, all members of the party must be present when the card is used. DAS cards are good (1) for the duration of your vacation, (2) for 14 days, or (3) until the back of the card is full, whichever of these times is shortest. If you fill your card, you must return to Guest Relations and get another.

Finally, note that you can use FastPass+ while you're using the DAS. In fact, cast members will suggest that you do so. It may take some extra planning on the front end, but using FastPass+ helps your DAS access.

## FRIENDS OF BILL W.

ALCOHOLICS ANONYMOUS MEETINGS convenient to Walt Disney World take place at 3 p.m. Monday–Saturday; visit **friendsofbillw orlando.org** for additional information. For information on other meetings in the surrounding area (including Celebration, Four Corners, Kissimmee, and St. Cloud), visit **osceolaintergroup.org**. For information on **Al-Anon/Ala-Teen** meetings in the area, visit **alanon-orlando.com**.

## INTERNATIONAL VISITORS

DISNEY HAS DEVELOPED A WIRELESS DEVICE called **Ears to the World** that provides synchronized narration in French, German, Japanese, Portuguese, or Spanish for more than 30 attractions in the theme parks. The wireless, lightweight headsets provide real-time translation and are available for a $100 refundable deposit at Guest Relations in all parks.

A mom from Minorca, Spain, offers advice to readers who are making the long haul to Walt Disney World:

> *You cannot predict how the time difference is going to affect you or the little people. Coming from Spain, we were looking at a 9-hour flight (from the UK) and a 6-hour time difference and spent our first few days in a haze of tiredness after trying to do too much too soon. We tried to fight it—don't!*

*Unofficial* friend Andrew Dakoutros of London sent us this grab bag of tips and warnings for other Disney-bound Brits:

> *(1) Magical Express doesn't automatically take your bags from the carousel; (2) Jellyrolls [the piano bar at Disney's BoardWalk] doesn't accept UK drivers' licences as ID for entry; (3) MagicBands are not [mailed] to addresses in the UK; (4) many MouseSavers codes [see page 115] can't be used from the UK; (5) the Twinings tea at The Tea Caddy [at Epcot] doesn't taste as good as in London.*
>
> *Additionally, you need to emphasise how hot Florida is and the importance of sunscreen. Most Britons holiday in Spain or Greece, where the sun is nowhere near as strong.*
>
> *Brits also like to go shopping, to two stores in particular: Abercrombie and Hollister. We consider these luxury brands—prices in Florida are about 30% less than in the UK—so every holiday to the US tends to involve a visit to one of those two stores.*

# PART EIGHT

# ARRIVING *and* GETTING AROUND

## GETTING THERE

### DIRECTIONS

**unofficial TIP**
*Warning!* I-4 is an east–west highway but takes a north–south drop through the Orlando–Kissimmee area. This change in direction complicates getting oriented in and around Disney World. Logic suggests that highways branching off I-4 should run north and south, but most run east and west here.

YOU CAN DRIVE TO ANY Walt Disney World destination via World Drive off US 192; via Epcot Center Drive off Interstate 4, which connects Daytona and Tampa; via FL 536 and West Osceola Parkway from FL 417/Central Florida GreeneWay; or from the Hartzog Road/Walt Disney World interchange off FL 429, a.k.a. the Western Beltway (see all maps in this chapter).

**FROM INTERSTATE 10** Take I-10 east across Florida to I-75 southbound at Exit 296A/Tampa; then take Florida's Turnpike (toll road) southbound at Exit 328 (on the left) toward Orlando. Take FL 429 (another toll road) to Exit 267A/Tampa southbound off the turnpike. Leave FL 429 at Exit 8, the Hartzog Road/Walt Disney World interchange, in the direction of Walt Disney World, and follow the signs to your Disney destination. Also use these directions to reach hotels along US 192, the Irlo Bronson Memorial Highway.

**FROM INTERSTATE 75 SOUTHBOUND** Take I-75 south onto Florida's Turnpike via Exit 328 (on the left) toward Orlando. Take FL 429 (toll) southbound off the turnpike. Leave FL 429 at Exit 8, the Hartzog Road/Walt Disney World interchange, in the direction of Walt Disney World, and follow the signs to your Disney destination. Also use these directions to reach hotels along US 192.

**FROM INTERSTATE 95 SOUTHBOUND** Take Exit 67/FL 536, marked Epcot/Downtown Disney, and follow the signs. During rush hour, take FL 417/Central Florida GreeneWay; take Exit 6 to FL 536 West or Exit 3 to Osceola Parkway, and follow the signs. Take Exit 67/FL 536, marked Epcot/Downtown Disney (or take other appropriate exit—see pages 375 and 376 for the full list of I-4 exits), and follow the signs.

**FROM DAYTONA, SANFORD INTERNATIONAL AIRPORT (SFB), OR ORLANDO** Head west on I-4 through Orlando. Take Exit 67/FL 536,

## I-4 & Walt Disney World Area

Orlando

Florida's Turnpike

Winter Garden-Vineland Rd.

429

Windermere

Lake Butler

Universal Studios Florida

Universal's Islands of Adventure

Vineland Rd.

439

75B

74B

S. Apopka-Vineland Rd.

Wet 'n Wild

75A

74A

535

Kilgore Rd.

Darlene Dr.

Facet Ct.

Universal Blvd.

1

72

Turkey Lake Rd.

Magic Kingdom

Fort Wilderness Campground

Lake Buena Vista

Smith Bennett Rd.

71

**The Walt Disney World Resort**

Fenton St.

Lake St.

(toll road)

Western Beltway

Western Way

Epcot Center Dr.

Downtown Disney

Palm Pkwy.

68

**↑ To Ocala**

27

World Dr.

Epcot

Buena Vista Dr.

Disney's Hollywood Studios

Disney's Animal Kingdom

Osceola Pkwy.

67

536

417

65

3

535

International Dr.

W. Irlo Bronson Memorial Hwy.

192

**ESPN Wide World of Sports Complex**

64

429

62

417

2

192

Celebration Pl.

**Celebration**

Celebration Ave.

Poinciana Blvd.

4

27

58

532

Intercession City

55

**↙ To Busch Gardens & Tampa**

17

92

4

**↙ To Davenport**

marked Epcot/Downtown Disney (or take other appropriate exit—see the facing page for the full list of I-4 exits), and follow the signs.

**FROM THE ORLANDO INTERNATIONAL AIRPORT (MCO)** There are two routes from the airport to Walt Disney World (see the South Orlando and Walt Disney World Area map on pages 22 and 23). Both routes take almost exactly the same time to drive, except during rush-hour traffic when Route One via FL 417 is far less congested than Route Two via the Beachline Expressway. Also, Route One eliminates the need to drive on I-4, which is always very congested.

**Route One:** Drive southwest on FL 417/Central Florida GreeneWay, a toll road. Take Exit 6/International Drive toward FL 535. FL 536 will cross I-4 and become Epcot Center Drive. From here, follow the signs to your Walt Disney World destination. If you're going to a hotel on US 192 (Irlo Bronson Memorial Highway), follow the same route until you reach I-4. Take I-4 west toward Tampa. Take the first US 192 exit if your hotel is on West Irlo Bronson, the second exit if your hotel is on East Irlo Bronson. If your hotel is in Lake Buena Vista, take Exit 6 onto FL 536 as described previously, and then turn right on FL 535 to the Lake Buena Vista area. If you're headed to Animal Kingdom, Animal Kingdom Lodge, Pop Century, Art of Animation, All-Star Resorts, or ESPN Wide World of Sports, the quickest route is to take Exit 3/Osceola Parkway and follow the signs to your destination.

> *unofficial* **TIP**
> If you take either of these two routes from the airport, you'll need money for tolls. Some exits are unmanned and require exact change, so be sure you have at least $2 in quarters. Also, note that while the manned toll booths take bills up to $20, they don't accept credit cards. For details, see **sunpass.com**.

**Route Two:** Take FL 528/Beachline Expressway, a toll road, west for about 12 miles to the intersection with I-4. Go west on I-4 to Exit 67/FL 536, marked Epcot/Downtown Disney, and then follow the signs to your Walt Disney World destination. This is also the route to take if your hotel is on International Drive or Universal Boulevard, near Universal Studios, near SeaWorld, or near the Orange County Convention Center. For these destinations, take I-4 east toward Orlando.

**FROM MIAMI, FORT LAUDERDALE, AND SOUTHEASTERN FLORIDA** Head north on Florida's Turnpike to I-4 westbound. Take Exit 67/FL 536, marked Epcot/Downtown Disney, and follow the signs.

**FROM TAMPA AND SOUTHWESTERN FLORIDA** Take I-75 northbound to I-4. Go east on I-4, take Exit 64 onto US 192 West, and follow the signs.

## Walt Disney World Exits off I-4

East to west (in the direction of Orlando to Tampa), five I-4 exits serve Walt Disney World.

**EXIT 68 (FL 535/LAKE BUENA VISTA)** primarily serves the Downtown Disney Resort Area and Downtown Disney, including Downtown Disney Marketplace and Downtown Disney West Side. It also serves non-Disney hotels with a Lake Buena Vista address. This exit puts you on a road with lots of traffic signals. Avoid it unless you're headed to one of the preceding destinations.

**EXIT 67 (FL 536/EPCOT/DOWNTOWN DISNEY)** delivers you to a four-lane expressway into the heart of Disney World. It's the fastest and most convenient way for westbound travelers to access almost all Disney destinations except Disney's Animal Kingdom and ESPN Wide World of Sports Complex.

**EXIT 65 (OSCEOLA PARKWAY)** is the best exit for westbound travelers to access Animal Kingdom, Animal Kingdom Lodge, Pop Century Resort, Art of Animation Resort, All-Star Resorts, and ESPN Wide World of Sports Complex.

**EXIT 64 (US 192/MAGIC KINGDOM)** is the best route for eastbound travelers to all Disney destinations.

**EXIT 62 (DISNEY WORLD/CELEBRATION)** is the first Disney exit you'll encounter heading east. This four-lane, controlled-access highway connects to the Walt Disney World Maingate. Accessing Disney World via the next exit, Exit 64, also routes you through the main entrance.

## THE I-4 BLUES

OVER MANY YEARS of covering Walt Disney World, we've watched I-4 turn from a modern interstate highway into a parking lot. The greatest congestion used to be between the Universal Orlando–International Drive area and downtown Orlando, but the section to the southwest serving the Disney World exits has become the new choke point, seemingly irrespective of the time of day. If you're going from Walt Disney World toward Orlando (east), the jam usually breaks up after you've passed the FL 535 exit. As you head west toward Tampa, traffic calms down after the US 192 interchange.

Ameliorating (or complicating) the situation, the good news is that the state of Florida is renovating a 21-mile stretch of I-4, from FL 434 in the northeast to Kirkman Road in the southwest to improve traffic flow and capacity in these areas. The construction project will renovate 15 of the busiest interchanges, build 56 new bridges, and replace more than 70 overpasses, plus add four variable-charge toll lanes to help pay for the $2 billion estimated cost. The bad news is that construction is likely to last through 2019, assuming everything goes according to schedule.

On long road trips, we always use a GPS device that's smart enough to accept traffic updates and route us around delays. Our TomTom GPS unit, for example, has a $5 accessory cable that picks up traffic signals from HD radio broadcasts. If you've got a newer smartphone, the free mobile app **Waze** (**waze.com;** iOS, Android, and Windows Phone), also does this trick.

If you're considering a hotel on or near International Drive, try to find one toward the southern end of I-Drive. If the I-4 traffic becomes intolerable, it's pretty easy to commute from the Universal Florida–International Drive area to Walt Disney World via Turkey Lake Road, connecting to Palm Parkway and FL 535 on the northwest side of I-4, or on the southernmost section of I-Drive, connecting to FL 536 on the southeast side of the interstate.

## ALTERNATIVE AIRPORTS

A SHORT DISTANCE northeast of Orlando is **Sanford International Airport (SFB; orlandosanfordairport.com).** Small, convenient, and easily accessible, it's low-hassle compared with the huge Orlando International Airport (MCO) and its block-long security-checkpoint lines.

The primary domestic carrier serving Sanford International is **Allegiant Air** (☎ 702-505-8888; **allegiantair.com**), with service from large and small airports throughout the Eastern and Midwestern United

States. European carriers include **ArkeFly** (Netherlands; ☎ 855-808-4015; arkefly.nl), **Icelandair** (☎ 800-223-5500; icelandair.com), **Monarch** (UK: ☎ 0871 940 5040; flymonarch.com), and **Thomson Airways** (UK: ☎ 0871 231 4787; thomson.co.uk). Finally, **SST Air** (☎ 407-288-8820; sstair.com) offers seasonal charter flights between Sanford and various cities in Brazil.

A reader from Roanoke, Virginia, uses Sanford frequently, writing:

*The 45-minute drive to WDW is more than made up for by avoiding the chaos at Orlando International, and it's stress-free.*

Other readers, like this couple from White Township, New Jersey, prefer flying into Tampa instead:

*We've found that flying from Newark to Tampa instead of Orlando saves us money and our sanity. It means significantly lower fares, fewer children on the plane, and shorter security lines.*

(Note that it's an 80-mile drive from Tampa International Airport to the Magic Kingdom—about an hour and 15 minutes.)

## SECURITY AT ORLANDO INTERNATIONAL AIRPORT

THIS AIRPORT HANDLES about 35 million passengers a year. It's not unusual to see lines from the checkpoints snaking out of the terminal and into the main shopping corridor and food court. Airport officials sometimes actually shut down moving sidewalks to use them for more queuing space.

*un*official **TIP** We recommend arriving at MCO 90 minutes–2 hours before your scheduled departure.

A number of passengers have reported missing their flights even when they arrived at the airport 90 minutes before departure. System improvements have alleviated some, but by no means all, of the congestion. Most waits to clear security are 25 minutes on average, compared with as many as 55 minutes before the improvements. Even so, there are substantial fluctuations, with peak waits nearing an hour.

## GETTING TO DISNEY WORLD FROM THE AIRPORT

YOU HAVE FOUR OPTIONS for getting from Orlando International to Walt Disney World:

**1. TAXI** Taxis carry four to eight passengers (depending on vehicle type). Rates vary according to distance. If your hotel is in the World, your fare will be about $48–$65, plus tip. For the US 192 Maingate area, it will cost about $50. To International Drive or downtown Orlando, expect to pay in the neighborhood of $33–$40.

**2. SHUTTLE SERVICE** Mears Transportation Group (☎ 888-983-3346; mearstransportation.com) provides your transportation if your vacation package includes airport transfers. Nonpackage travelers can also use the service. The shuttles collect passengers until they fill a van (or bus). They're then dispatched. Mears charges *per-person* rates (children under age 3 ride free). One-way and round-trip services are available. See the next page for a fare breakdown.

You might have to wait at the airport until a vehicle fills. Once under way, the shuttle will probably stop several times to discharge passengers before reaching your hotel. Obviously, it takes less time to fill a van than a bus, and less time to deliver and unload those passengers.

From your hotel to the airport, you're likely to ride in a van (unless you're part of a tour group, for which Mears might send a bus). Because shuttles make several pickups, they ask you to leave much earlier than you'd depart if you were taking a cab or returning a rental car.

| FROM THE AIRPORT TO: | ONE-WAY ADULT/CHILD | ROUND-TRIP ADULT/CHILD |
|---|---|---|
| INTERNATIONAL DRIVE | $20/$15 | $32/$24 |
| DOWNTOWN ORLANDO | $19/$15 | $31/$23 |
| WALT DISNEY WORLD–LAKE BUENA VISTA | $22/$17 | $36/$27 |
| US 192 MAINGATE AREA | $22/$17 | $36/$27 |

**3. TOWN-CAR SERVICE** Like a taxi, town-car service will transport you directly from the airport to your hotel. The driver will usually be waiting for you in your airline's baggage-claim area. If saving time and hassle is worth the money, book a town car.

Each town-car service we surveyed offers large, well-appointed late-model sedans, such as the Lincoln Town Car series, or limousines. These hold four persons. To reserve a child's car seat, call ahead. Trunks easily hold golf bags.

**Tiffany Towncar Service** (☎ 888-838-2161 or 407-370-2196; **tiffany towncars.com**) provides a prompt, clean ride. The round-trip fee to a Disney or non-Disney resort in a town car is $115–$150 plus tip; one-way is about $65–$80. Tiffany offers a free 30-minute stop at a Publix supermarket en route to your hotel. Also, check Tiffany's website for a coupon worth $5 off a round-trip (valid with online reservations only).

**Quicksilver Tours & Transportation** (☎ 888-GO-TO-WDW [468-6939] or 407-299-1434; **quicksilver-tours.com**) offers eight-person limos and ten-person vans in addition to four-person town cars. Round-trip rates in a town car range from $125 to $130 depending on location; round-trip rates in a van range from $140 to $145; round-trip limo rate is $240.

**Mears Transportation Group** (☎ 407-423-5566; **mearstranspor tation.com**) also offers a town-car service for around $170 round-trip.

**4. RENTAL CARS** Short- and long-term rentals are available. Most companies allow drop-off at certain hotels or subsidiary locations in the Disney area if you don't want the vehicle for your entire stay. Likewise, any time during your stay, you can pick up a car at those hotels and locations. Check **mousesavers.com** for rental-car discount codes.

The preferred routes to Walt Disney World, Universal Orlando, SeaWorld, International Drive, and US 192 all involve toll roads. Some roads require exact change to enter or exit via automated gates, and manned toll booths will not accept any denomination bill higher than a $20 bill. So before you leave the airport, make sure you're armed with at least a couple of dollars in quarters and some lower-denomination currency.

## Dollars and Sense

Which option is the best deal depends on how many people are in your party and how much you value your time. If you're traveling solo or have only two in your party and you're pretty sure you won't need a rental car, the shuttle is your least expensive bet. A cab for two makes sense if you want to get to your hotel faster than the shuttle can arrange. The cab will cost about $53–$70, including tip. That's $27–$35 per person. The shuttle will cost $53 each (one-way), saving $5–$13 per person. You must decide whether the cab's timeliness and convenience are worth the extra bucks. A one-day car rental costs $40–$70, plus you have to take time to complete the paperwork, get the vehicle, and fill the tank before you return it. The more people in your group, the more economical the cab becomes over the shuttle. Likewise with the rental car, though the cab will get you there faster.

## DISNEY'S MAGICAL EXPRESS

THIS FREE BUS SERVICE is available to guests of Disney-owned and -operated resorts for transportation between Orlando International Airport and Walt Disney World. (Nonparticipating resorts are the Swan, the Dolphin, Shades of Green, and the hotels of Bonnet Creek Resort and the Downtown Disney Resort Area.) Magical Express even provides free luggage delivery to your resort (unless your flight arrives between 10 p.m. and 5 a.m.—then you need to pick up your stuff from baggage claim before boarding the bus).

First, register your flight information with your resort reservation, either at the time of booking or as soon as you've booked your flights, by calling ☎ 866-599-0951 or using **mydisneyexperience.com.**

US and Canadian travelers will receive their Magical Express paperwork in the mail 20–40 days before they arrive. The packet contains detailed instructions for getting around the airport, bus vouchers, and tags for checked luggage (two per traveler). Just check your bags as you normally would and plan to see them again in your hotel room. If you know how a cruise line's luggage-valet service works, the procedure is very similar.

Except for Canadians, travelers from other countries will not receive vouchers or tags and will need to go through Customs with bags in hand. Disney will take the bags for transport at the Magical Express Welcome Center, where international guests will also get their bus vouchers.

The Magical Express Welcome Center is on the B side of the airport's lower level. Cast members are stationed throughout the area to help you find your way. You can pick them out by their nautical costumes, the signs they're holding, and the big white Mickey gloves they wear.

If you already have your bus vouchers, just head straight to the bus check-in. A cast member will scan your vouchers and direct you to a holding area for your resort's bus line. If you've lost or accidentally packed your vouchers or you need other assistance, you'll be directed to the Welcome Center desk.

There's no seating inside the holding area, so if a member of your party will have trouble standing for an extended period, let a cast member know. Lines generally move quickly, with waits to board rarely exceeding 20 minutes. Once on the bus, try to get a seat up front, since you'll be among the first to get off (and get in line at your hotel).

*unofficial* **TIP**
This is a good place to remind you of Disney's online check-in (see page 138), which will save you time registering at your hotel.

Buses are shared among resorts—for example, a bus to Old Key West may also stop at Saratoga Springs or Port Orleans. Most of the time, Disney will try to fill a bus before sending it on its way. Each bus has 55 seats, and five buses may load at once. On more than one occasion, particularly for flights arriving very early in the morning or late at night, we've been the only passengers on our bus.

We've usually arrived at our resorts within 90 minutes of stepping off our plane. When you consider that you don't have to wait for your bags and that the trip takes 30 minutes regardless of who's driving, Magical Express is about as efficient an operation as you could hope for.

Your checked bags are picked up at the airport, sorted by destination, and sent directly on to your room—if it's ready. If not, bell services will hold your bags until you're able to get into your room. Because you may be separated from your checked bags for a few hours, remember the following:

- Don't check valuables such as cameras, laptops, or jewelry. This is good advice whether you use Magical Express or not.

- Keep anything you might need upon arrival with you—travel documents, phone chargers, glasses, medications, and such.

- Pack swimsuits and sunscreen in your carry-on bag and enjoy the pool before your bags arrive.

- Strollers and wheelchairs can be stored under your bus for use when you're dropped off at your resort. There's no need to check them.

If you booked your trip too late to receive luggage tags, you can still use the delivery service. Just give the luggage-claim numbers your airline gave you to the cast members at the Magical Express check-in desk, and they'll pick up and deliver your bags. We've done this before and it worked without any issues.

**THE TRIP HOME** The day before you check out of your resort, you'll get a notification from Disney with your return information on it. This will include a time for you to board your bus back to MCO.

If you're checking bags, you'll need to pick up luggage tags separately at your resort lobby's Airline Check-in Desk. As of this edition, seven airlines participate in advance check-in: **Alaska, American, Delta, JetBlue, Southwest, United,** and **US Airways;** guests using these airlines for international flights may use the service as well. As this is also your airline check-in, you'll need to show ID just as you would at the airport. (You'll also get your boarding passes when you drop off your bags.) The major downside to using Magical Express for your return trip is that you'll board your bus around 3 hours before your flight is scheduled to depart (4 hours for international flights).

## Magical Express Considered

What's our take on Magical Express? Normally, when we see the word *free* attached to a travel package, our first question is, "What's the catch?" Disney is nothing if not crafty, and the goal of getting folks on their bus service is to keep people and their wallets inside Walt Disney World. If seeing other Orlando-area sights, such as Universal, or eating off-site is a priority for you, think about renting a car either from the airport or at one of the Disney on-site rental desks (see our next section on renting a car).

A Provo, Utah, mom loved the Express:

*Magical Express was heavenly. Not worrying about lugging six suitcases around and arriving and departing quickly and comfortably was the cherry on top of the vacation.*

But a dad from Monroe, Washington, is rethinking the whole deal:

*One thing I think you need to stress is planning around the Magical Express. It took over 2 hours to get from the airport to Animal Kingdom Lodge as we were waiting for the bus to fill up, and AKL is the last stop for the drop-off. Luckily, we were able to push our dinner reservations out, but next time I think I'll take a shuttle or a cab.*

A Bloomington, Illinois, couple narrowly made their flight:

*Magical Express? Well, that's a misnomer if I've ever heard one. On the way to our resort, we stopped at three other resorts first, which had us beginning our vacation 30–40 minutes later than we'd hoped. I thought, "Fine, we'll be able to sleep in a little on the last day." Wrong! We stopped at the same three resorts AFTER we were picked up, arriving at the last resort 50 minutes after we had departed. We were on the bus on departure day for a total of 1 hour and 40 minutes, and our flight began boarding less than 15 minutes after we reached the gate. That's cutting it a little close in my opinion—and we were picked up 3 hours before our departure time!*

A dad from Ontario, Canada, warns:

*On the return trip to the airport, your bags do not automatically go on the Magical Express—you must get them using claim tickets and put them on the bus yourself. Had it not been for the bus driver, I would have left the resort without my baggage and arrived at the airport thinking that all I had to do was show the driver my claim ticket.*

Finally, a California reader strikes a frustrated note:

*Magical Express is quick and efficient to drop off but iffy when it picks up. I've seen it full on several departure trips and had to wait another 30–45 minutes while another is dispatched. It ticks everyone off because we're asked to be there 3 hours ahead of time, but they don't follow through, and then what? It's a bad way to end a vacation.*

## RENTING A CAR

READERS PLANNING TO STAY in Walt Disney World ask frequently if they'll need a car. If your plans don't include restaurants, attractions, or destinations outside Disney World, then the answer is a very qualified no. But take into account the thoughts of this reader from Snohomish, Washington:

*We rented a car and were glad we did. With a car we could drive to the grocery store to restock our snack supply. It also came in handy for our night out. I shudder at how long it might have taken us to get from the Caribbean Beach to the Polynesian to leave our kids at the child-care facility, then back to the Polynesian to get the kids, and then back to the Caribbean Beach.*

A dad from Avon Lake, Ohio, adds:

*Although we stayed at the Grand Floridian, we found the monorail convenient only for the Magic Kingdom. Of the six nights we stayed, we used our car five days.*

From an Ann Arbor, Michigan, mother of three:

*During our stay it was almost impossible to get into any of the Disney restaurants. Purely out of desperation, we rented a car so we could eat outside WDW. We had no problem finding good places to eat at a fraction of what you'd pay inside.*

A dad from Vancouver, British Columbia, implores readers to get their act together before they reach the rental counter:

*When I arrived at the Dollar counter at Orlando Airport, there were 20 customers waiting in line and 5 agents. Everyone in front of me took at least 10 minutes with an agent; one guy spent most of his time talking to someone on his phone, trying to decide what to get! When it was my turn—45 minutes later—it took me 2 minutes because I knew what I wanted and I had already filled out my rental info online.*

**PLAN TO RENT A CAR**

**1.** If your hotel is outside Walt Disney World.

**2.** If your hotel is in the World and you want to dine someplace other than the theme parks and your hotel.

**3.** If you plan to return to your hotel for naps or swimming during the day.

**4.** If you plan to visit other area theme parks or water parks (including Disney's).

## Renting a Car at Orlando International Airport

The airport has two terminals: A and B. Airlines serving Orlando are assigned to one or the other. Each terminal has three levels and a parking garage. Ticket counters are on Level Three. Baggage claim is on Level Two. Level One is where car-rental counters are or where you'll catch a courtesy vehicle to an off-site rental company location.

Orlando is the world's largest rental-car market. At last count, 31 companies competed for your business. Ten—**Alamo, Avis, Budget, Dollar, Enterprise, E-Z Rent-A-Car, Firefly Car Rental, Hertz, L&M, National,** and **Thrifty**—have counters on Level One of both terminals. **Payless** and 19 other companies have locations near the airport and provide courtesy shuttles outside Level One at both terminals. Most shuttles run continuously; you don't have to call for pickup. We prefer using one of the companies inside the airport because (1) you can complete your paperwork while you wait for your checked luggage to arrive at baggage claim and (2) it's a short walk to the garage to pick up your car (no shuttle needed).

If you rent from an on-site company, you'll return your car to the garage adjacent to the terminal where your airline is located. If you

## Rental-Car Discount-Code Whac-A-Mole

In past editions of this book, we've published the best car-rental discount codes we could find. Then, within a few weeks of the book's release, rental companies discontinue the best of the ones we've printed.

Enter the website **Zalyn** (**zalyn.com**). It starts off like any other car-rental site, asking for your travel destination, dates, and car preferences. Here's where the genius comes in: Zalyn knows of virtually every discount and coupon available for every car-rental agency, and it will apply all of them to see which gives you the lowest overall cost.

It's a little tricky to navigate Zalyn's results, and once you find a rate you like, you usually have to book it through another service such as Orbitz. But the savings are substantial, and it beats spending half an hour entering obscure discount codes on a bunch of different sites.

return your car to the wrong garage, you'll have to haul your luggage from one side of the airport to the other to reach your check-in.

Most rental companies charge about $5–$8 a gallon to fill the gas tank. If you plan to drive a lot, prepay for a fill-up so you can return the car empty, or fill up near your hotel on your way back to the airport. If you're taking FL 417, turn right at the Airport/Boggy Creek Road exit and drive about a mile to find the closest gas station to MCO.

### How the Orlando Rental-Car Companies Stack Up

When it comes to Orlando car-rental companies, most *Unofficial Guide* readers are looking for the following, as reflected in the table below:

**1.** Quick, courteous, and efficient processing on pickup.
**2.** A nice, well-maintained, late-model automobile.
**3.** A car that is clean and odor-free.
**4.** Quick, courteous, and efficient processing on return.
**5.** If applicable, an efficient shuttle between the rental agency and airport.

| COMPANY | PICKUP EFFICIENCY | CONDITION OF CAR | CLEANNESS OF CAR | RETURN EFFICIENCY | SHUTTLE EFFICIENCY | OVERALL RATING |
|---|---|---|---|---|---|---|
| ADVANTAGE | C | B | B | B | — | B |
| ALAMO | B | A | A | A | — | A |
| AVIS | B | B | A | A | — | B+ |
| BUDGET | B | B | A | A | — | B+ |
| DOLLAR | B | B | B | B | — | B |
| ENTERPRISE | B | A | A | A | — | A |
| E-Z RENT-A-CAR | B | A | A | B | — | B+ |
| HERTZ | B | B | A | A | — | A |
| NATIONAL | A | A | A | A | — | A |
| PAYLESS | D | A | B | C | C | C |
| SIXT | B | A | A | B | B | B |
| THRIFTY | C | B | B | B | — | B |

On a scale from A (best) to F (worst), the table shows how readers rate the Orlando operations of each company based on the columns

*unofficial* **TIP**
Orlando is the least expensive US car-rental city, with an average rate of $25/day for the most affordable car (New York City is the most expensive at $76/day).

shown. If you'd like to participate in our survey, go to **touringplans.com/walt-disney-world /survey.**

**National Car Rental** is once again ranked highest in this year's survey, and **Enterprise** maintains its position near the top, where it's been for the last few editions. With the exception of **Payless** and **Thrifty,** all of the major rental-car companies in Orlando seem to be delivering consistently good customer experiences.

If you're looking to rent something distinctive yet remain within a budget, consider **Sixt** (**sixt.com**) or **Fox** (**foxrentacar.com**). Sixt has affordable vehicles from Mercedes and VW (including the Eos convertible), while Fox has the *adorable* Fiat 500 at bargain prices.

If you rent a car, a 6–7% sales tax, $2.80-per-day state surcharge, and 45¢- to $2.02-per-day vehicle-license-recovery fee will be heaped onto your final bill. If you rent from an agency with airport facilities or shuttles, a 10% airport tax will be added. Luckily, you can rent a car at your hotel on the day you actually need it.

## The Insurance Thing

Anyone who rents a car should know what his or her auto insurance does and doesn't cover. If you have the slightest question about your coverage, call your agent. A corollary discussion pertains to added coverage from your credit card company if the rental fee is charged on the card. Usually, credit card coverage picks up deductibles and some ancillary charges that your auto-insurance policy doesn't cover. The tune is the same, however: Make sure you understand what is and isn't covered.

## The Public-Transportation Alternative

Some hotel shuttles outside of Walt Disney World don't operate early enough to get you to the parks before opening. An alternative is the **LYNX** public bus system. If you're staying in downtown Orlando, on International Drive south of the Beachline Expressway, or along Palm Parkway in Lake Buena Vista, you can take the LYNX **#50 bus** to the Walt Disney World Transportation and Ticket Center (TTC). The bus runs outbound daily from 5:15 a.m. to 11:48 p.m. and inbound from 5:23 a.m. to 1:05 a.m. Precise hours of service vary depending on where along the route you are. Use the online trip planner at **golynx.com** or call ☎ 407-841-LYNX for travel information. A Slaughter, Louisiana, woman gives the service high marks:

> We stayed at a hotel that was on the LYNX #50 bus line. It was perfect for getting to and from the park without having to wait for the hotel shuttles to start, which would have had us arriving after park opening. For 8 bucks, we couldn't beat it!

The downside is that the trip on the #50 bus takes almost 2 hours terminal-to-terminal; figure about 50 minutes or so if you board south of the Beachline Expressway. The **#56 bus** runs from Kissimmee to the TTC along Irlo Bronson Memorial Highway (US 192), a trip of 1½ hours one-way. The closer you are to Disney World and the farther from downtown Kissimmee, the shorter the trip.

# GETTING ORIENTED

## A GOOD MAP

READERS FREQUENTLY COMPLAIN about signs and maps provided by Disney. While it's easy to find the major theme parks, locating other Disney destinations can be challenging: Disney-supplied maps are often hard to read or lacking in detail. Your best bet, in addition to the maps in this guide, is a Walt Disney World road map created by **Alamo Rent A Car.** Get it from the front desk or concierge at the resorts.

A very good map of the Orlando–Kissimmee–Disney World area is free at the **AAA Car Care Center** operated by Goodyear near the Magic Kingdom parking lot.

## GPS COORDINATES FOR THE THEME PARKS

CHECK WHETHER YOUR GPS already includes Disney's theme parks as points of interest. If not, use these GPS coordinates for driving directions. Supplement them with Disney's road signs, which will direct you to parking lots as you get close.

| DESTINATION PARKING LOT | GPS ADDRESS | LATITUDE AND LONGITUDE |
| --- | --- | --- |
| THE MAGIC KINGDOM | 3111 World Dr. Lake Buena Vista, FL 32830 | N28° 25.124' W81° 34.871' |
| EPCOT | 200 Epcot Center Dr. Lake Buena Vista, FL 32830 | N28° 22.869' W81° 32.964' |
| ANIMAL KINGDOM | 551 N. Rainforest Rd. Lake Buena Vista, FL 32380 | N28° 21.480' W81° 35.426' |
| HOLLYWOOD STUDIOS | 351 S. Studio Dr. Lake Buena Vista, FL 32830 | N28° 21.425' W81° 33.618' |
| BLIZZARD BEACH | 1534 Blizzard Beach Dr. Lake Buena Vista, FL 32830 | N28° 21.338' W81° 34.384' |
| TYPHOON LAGOON | 1145 Buena Vista Dr. Lake Buena Vista, FL 32830 | N28° 22.162' W81° 31.576' |
| DOWNTOWN DISNEY– DISNEY SPRINGS | 1490 E. Buena Vista Dr. Lake Buena Vista, FL 32830 | N28° 22.064' W81° 31.167' |

## FINDING YOUR WAY AROUND

WALT DISNEY WORLD IS LIKE ANY BIG CITY: It's easy to get lost. Signs for the theme parks are excellent, but finding a restaurant or hotel is often confusing. The easiest way to orient yourself is to think in terms of five major areas, or clusters:

1. The first encompasses all hotels and theme parks around Seven Seas Lagoon. This includes the Magic Kingdom, hotels connected by the monorail, Shades of Green Resort, and the Palm, Magnolia, and Oak Trail Golf Courses.

2. The second includes developments on and around Bay Lake: Wilderness Lodge & Villas, Fort Wilderness Campground, and the new Four Seasons Resort Orlando and Tranquilo Golf Club.

3. Cluster three contains Epcot, Disney's Hollywood Studios, the BoardWalk, ESPN Wide World of Sports, Epcot resort hotels, Pop Century Resort, Art of Animation Resort, and Caribbean Beach Resort.

4. The fourth cluster encompasses Downtown Disney (including Downtown Disney Marketplace and Downtown Disney West Side); Typhoon Lagoon water park; Lake Buena Vista Golf Course; the Downtown Disney Resort Area; and the Port Orleans, Saratoga Springs, and Old Key West resorts.

5. The fifth cluster contains Disney's Animal Kingdom; Blizzard Beach water park; and Animal Kingdom Lodge & Villas, the All-Star Resorts, and Coronado Springs Resort.

# HOW *to* TRAVEL *around the* WORLD *(or, The Real Mr. Toad's Wild Ride)*

TRYING TO COMMUTE around Walt Disney World can be frustrating. A Magic Kingdom street vendor, telling us how to get to Epcot, proposed, "You can take the ferry or the monorail to the Transportation and Ticket Center. Then you can get another monorail, or you can catch the bus, or you can take a tram out to your car and drive over there yourself." What he didn't say was that it would be easier to ride a mule than to take any conceivable combination from this transportation smorgasbord.

## TRANSPORTATION TRADE-OFFS FOR GUESTS LODGING OUTSIDE WALT DISNEY WORLD

DAY GUESTS (those staying outside the World) can use the monorail, bus, and boat systems. Our most important advice for these guests is to park in the lot of the theme park (or other Disney destination) where they plan to finish their day. This is critical if you stay at a park until closing.

### Moving Your Car from Lot to Lot on the Same Day

Once you've paid to park in any major theme park lot ($15 per day), show your receipt and you'll be admitted into another park's lot on the same day without further charge. Annual Pass holders and Disney resort guests park free in any theme park lot.

## ALL YOU NEED TO KNOW ABOUT DRIVING TO THE THEME PARKS

**1. POSITIONING OF THE PARKING LOTS** Disney's Animal Kingdom, Disney's Hollywood Studios, and Epcot parking lots are adjacent to each park's entrance. The Magic Kingdom lot is adjacent to the Transportation and Ticket Center (TTC). From the TTC, take a ferry or monorail to the park's entrance.

**2. PAYING TO PARK** Disney resort guests and Annual Pass holders park free. All others pay. If you pay to park and you move your car during that day, show your receipt and you won't have to pay at the new lot.

**3. FINDING YOUR CAR WHEN IT'S TIME TO DEPART** Jot down, text, or take a phone picture of the section and row where you park. If you're driving a rental car, note the license-plate number.

**4. GETTING FROM YOUR CAR TO THE PARK ENTRANCE** Each lot provides trams to the park entrance or, at the Magic Kingdom, to the TTC.

If you arrive early in the morning, it may be faster to walk to the entrance (or TTC) than to take the tram. At the TTC, Disney has added digital wait-time boards, showing you how long the wait is to board the express monorail to the Magic Kingdom or board the ferry. Choose the shorter of the two lines.

**5. GETTING TO DISNEY'S ANIMAL KINGDOM FOR PARK OPENING** If you're staying on-property and are planning to be at this theme park when it opens, take a Disney bus from your resort instead of driving. For some reason, Animal Kingdom's parking lot frequently opens 15 minutes before the park itself—which doesn't leave you enough time to park, hop on a tram, and pass through security before park opening.

**6. HOW MUCH TIME TO ALLOT FOR PARKING AND GETTING TO THE PARK ENTRANCE** At Epcot and Disney's Animal Kingdom, figure about 10–15 minutes to pay, park, and walk or ride to the entrance. At Disney's Hollywood Studios, allow 8–12 minutes; at the Magic Kingdom, 10–15 minutes to the TTC and another 20–30 to reach the park entrance via the monorail (most of which is waiting to board) or ferry (slower but usually less in demand). If you haven't purchased your theme park admission in advance, tack on another 10–20 minutes before you actually enter the park.

**7. COMMUTING FROM PARK TO PARK** You can commute among the theme parks via Disney bus, to and from the Magic Kingdom and Epcot by monorail, or to and from Epcot and Disney's Hollywood Studios by boat. You also, of course, can commute in your own car. Using Disney transportation or your car, allow 45–60 minutes entrance to entrance one-way. If you plan to park-hop, leave your car in the lot of the park where you'll finish the day.

**8. LEAVING THE PARK AT THE END OF THE DAY** If you stay at a park until closing, expect the parking-lot trams, monorails, and ferries to be mobbed. (The Magic Kingdom has wait-time displays showing the lines for the monorail and ferry.) If the wait for the tram is unacceptable, walk to your car, or walk to the first stop on the tram route and wait there for a tram. When someone gets off, you can get on.

**9. DINNER AND A QUICK EXIT** One way to beat closing crowds at the Magic Kingdom is to arrange reservations for dinner at a restaurant in the Contemporary Resort. When you leave the Magic Kingdom for dinner, move your car from the TTC lot to the Contemporary lot. After dinner, walk (8–10 minutes) or take the monorail back to the Magic Kingdom. When the park closes and everyone else is fighting to board the monorail or ferry, you can stroll back to the Contemporary, claim your car, and get on your way. Use the same strategy at Epcot by arranging a reservation at an Epcot resort. When the park closes after *IllumiNations,* exit via the International Gateway and walk to the resort where you parked.

**10. CAR TROUBLE** All parking lots have security patrols. If you have a dead battery or minor automotive problem, the patrols will help you.

For more serious trouble, the **AAA Car Care Center** (☎ 407-824-0976), operated by Goodyear near the Magic Kingdom parking lot, will help. Prices for most services are comparable to those at home. The facility stays busy; expect to leave your car unless the fix is simple. Hours are Monday–Friday, 7 a.m.–7 p.m., and Saturday, 7 a.m.–4 p.m.

**11. SCORING A GREAT PARKING PLACE** If you arrive at a park after noon or move your car from park to park, there will be empty parking spaces near the entrance vacated by early guests who have left. Instead of following Disney signage or being directed by staff to a distant space, drive to the front and hunt a space, or use the approach of a Coopersburg, Pennsylvania, couple:

> After leaving Epcot on our first day for a lunch break, we returned to find a fullish parking lot. We were unhappy because we had left a third-row parking spot. My husband told the attendant that we had left just an hour ago and that there were lots of spaces up front. Without a word of protest, he waved us to the front, and we got the same spot we had left!

**12. AAA PARKING** If you purchase certain Walt Disney World vacation packages from AAA, you may receive a special Diamond parking card. Show it at the parking-fee booth and you'll be directed to a reserved parking area (if capacity allows). Each park's AAA area is handled differently. Parking-lot cast members will instruct you as required.

## GOOD FUZZ, BAD FUZZ

FOR AS LONG AS ANYONE CAN REMEMBER, Disney World security imposed little to no restraint on speeding drivers. In more than 20 years, we've received not one letter or e-mail from readers about being pulled over. However, we've been alerted to the increasing presence of Orange County law enforcement busting speeders on Disney World property. So for the lead-footed among you, there will be no more Fairy Godmother treatment, and the character with the flashing blue lights isn't Goofy.

## SNEAK ROUTES

SNEAK ROUTE IS A WHITEWATER-PADDLING TERM for an easy way through tough rapids. Unfortunately, not all difficult rapids have a sneak route. For those that don't, there's only one way through: the hard way. As we research this guide, we're constantly looking for ways to avoid traffic snarls. For some roads and areas, there are no alternative routes. For others, we've discovered sneak routes.

**THE LIGHTS OF DOWNTOWN DISNEY** Although dozens of searchlights blaze at Downtown Disney after dark, what we're talking about here are the many multifunction traffic signals on Buena Vista Drive in front of Downtown Disney. Buena Vista Drive near Downtown Disney is a traffic bottleneck of the first order. Heaven help you if you're traveling from Coronado Springs Resort to Downtown Disney—you'll encounter up to 15 traffic signals in the 5-mile drive, or roughly one every third of a mile. In the evening especially, this commute can take up to 30 minutes. It wouldn't be so bad if only traffic to Downtown Disney was affected, but because Buena Vista Drive is one of Walt Disney World's most important traffic arteries, the traffic jam is on the order of a blocked coronary ventricle.

Most traffic entering and exiting Walt Disney World from the FL 535 entrance must run this traffic-signal gauntlet, and so too must guests staying at the seven hotels of the Downtown Disney Resort Area and Saratoga Springs Resort when traveling to Epcot, Disney's Hollywood Studios, the Magic Kingdom, Disney's Animal Kingdom, and Typhoon Lagoon. To avoid the bottlenecked area requires long but nearly traffic-free circumnavigation. Coming from the theme parks, you can bypass the mess by taking I-4 or alternatively by looping around on Bonnet Creek Parkway and Disney Vacation Club Way. If you're going back to an Epcot or Magic Kingdom resort from Downtown Disney, it may be faster to take I-4 West and follow the signs back to Disney property. Any way you look at it, though, it's a small (congested) world.

**INTERNATIONAL DRIVE (I-DRIVE)** This is by far the most difficult area to navigate without long traffic delays Most hotels on I-Drive are between Kirkman Road to the north and FL 417/Central Florida GreeneWay to the south. Between Kirkman Road and FL 417, three major roads cross I-Drive. From north to south on I-Drive (in the direction of Disney World), the first major crossroad is Universal Boulevard. Next south is Sand Lake Road (FL 482), pretty squarely in the middle of the hotel district. Then farther south, the Beachline Expressway (FL 528) connects I-4 and the airport.

*unofficial* **TIP**
To locate your I-Drive hotel, check **iridetrolley.com** or call ☎ 866-243-7483 and request the I-Ride Trolley Route Map. It will help you pinpoint your hotel within about 200 yards.

I-Drive is a mess for a number of reasons: scarcity of left-turn lanes, long multidirectional traffic signals, and, most critically, limited access to westbound I-4 (toward Disney). From the Orange County Convention Center south to the Beachline Expressway and FL 417/Central Florida GreeneWay, getting on westbound I-4 is straightforward and easy, but in the stretch where the hotels are concentrated (from Kirkman to about a mile south of Sand Lake), the only way most visitors know to access I-4 westbound is to fight through the gridlock of the I-Drive–Sand Lake Road intersection en route to the I-4–Sand Lake Road interchange. A long, long traffic signal, a sea of motorists, and insufficient turn lanes make this absolutely grueling.

The object, therefore, is to access I-4 westbound without getting on Sand Lake Road. If your hotel is north of Sand Lake, access Kirkman Road by going north on I-Drive (in the opposite direction of the heaviest traffic) to the Kirkman Road intersection and turning left, or by cutting over to Kirkman via eastbound Carrier Drive. In either case, take Kirkman north over I-4, and at the first traffic signal (at the entrance to Universal Orlando), make a U-turn. This will put you directly onto an I-4 westbound ramp. A second way to access I-4 westbound from this section of I-Drive is to take Universal Boulevard (parallels I-Drive to the east) north. After you cross I-4 onto Universal property, stay left and follow the signs through two left turns to I-4. The signs are small, so stay alert.

If your hotel is south of Sand Lake Road but north of Austrian Court, cut over to Universal Boulevard, which parallels I-Drive to the east. Do this via Austrian Row. Turn right (south) on Universal Boulevard. Continue until you intersect the Beachline Expressway, and then take the Beachline west to I-4 (no toll).

*Continued on page 394*

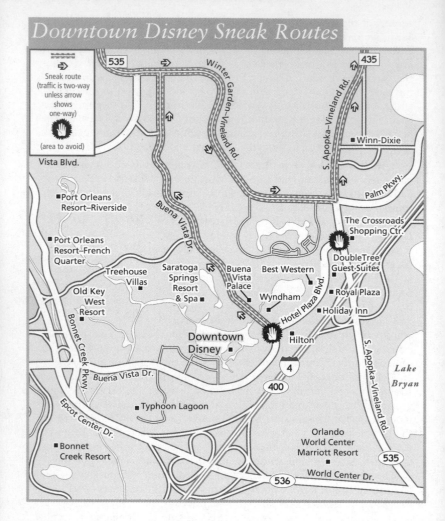

*Downtown Disney Sneak Routes*

## International Drive Area Sneak Routes

Windover Dr.

Florida's Turnpike

↗ **East to Downtown Orlando**

Vineland Rd.

435

77

Major Blvd.

Caravan Ct.

75B

Oak Ridge Rd.

W. Oak Ridge Rd.

**Universal Orlando**

Hollywood Way

**Prime Outlets Orlando**

Adventure Way

74B

75A

American Way

**Wet 'n Wild**

Carrier Dr.

Kirkman Rd.

Grand National Dr.

International Dr.

Del Verde Way

Turkey Lake Rd.

International Dr.

Canada Ave.

74A

482

Sand Lake Rd.

Jamaican Ct.

Universal Blvd.

Austrian Ct.

**Official Visitor Center**

Austrian Row

**International Dr.**

Samoan Ct.

Universal Blvd. W.

**Universal Blvd.**

4

**Orange County Convention Center**

Destination Pkwy.

**To Orlando International Airport →**

Hawaiian Ct.

72

(no toll)

**Aquatica**

528

Beachline Expy. (toll road)

Turkey Lake Rd.

**West to Walt Disney World Resort & Tampa** ↙

71

Westwood Blvd.

Sea Harbor Dr.

International Dr.

**SeaWorld Orlando**

**Discovery Cove**

Central Florida GreeneWay

**Legend:**

━━━ Sneak route (two-way traffic)

━━━ International Drive (area to avoid)

━━━ Bridge or overpass

**Interstate 4 Exits**

| 77 | Florida's Turnpike |
| 75A | Universal Studios/ International Drive |
| 75B | Kirkman Road |
| 74B | Universal Studios |
| 74A | Sand Lake Road |
| 72 | FL 528 (Beachline Expressway) |
| 71 | Central Florida GreeneWay |

# US 192–Kissimmee Resort Area Sneak Routes

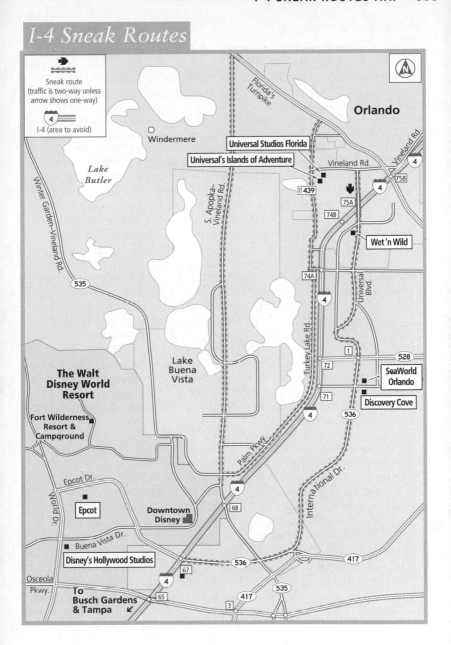

*Continued from page 389*

**US 192 (IRLO BRONSON MEMORIAL HIGHWAY)** This road runs east–west along the southern border of Walt Disney World. From the Disney World entrance west on US 192/Irlo Bronson toward Clermont and east toward Kissimmee is a concentration of hotels. The highway was widened in 2001–02, and, though heavily used, it has ample turn lanes. The problem is the many long, poorly timed multidirectional traffic signals. Even so, driving US 192 is easy compared with International Drive. Best of all, there are no godawful intersections like that of I-Drive and Sand Lake Road.

Conspicuous mile markers are posted along US 192. If you know which marker is closest to your hotel, navigation is a snap. The main entrance (Maingate) to Disney World is between Mile Markers 6 and 7, and almost all US 192 hotels and restaurants are between Mile Markers 4 and 15. If your hotel is between Markers 5 and 8, no sneak routes are necessary. If it's between Markers 1 and 5, save time by entering Disney property via Sherberth Road, which runs into Disney's Animal Kingdom and the west end of Osceola Parkway. This road existed before Animal Kingdom or Osceola Parkway, but there are few signs on US 192 indicating that Sherberth Road affords a shortcut into and out of Disney property. When you turn onto Sherberth from US 192, bear right almost immediately at the fork. Continue until you reach a major intersection with Disney signage. Turn right and then continue straight to Osceola Parkway and most of Disney World, or go left to Animal Kingdom Lodge. To get to Animal Kingdom, turn right and look immediately for the turn lane that will take you into the theme park's parking lot. Osceola Parkway, a toll road, doesn't levy tolls until it crosses I-4 and leaves Disney property.

If your hotel is between Markers 8 and 15, save time (but pay modest tolls) by taking Osceola Parkway west to Disney World. If your hotel is between Markers 8 and 11, go north on Poinciana Boulevard to access Osceola Parkway. If your hotel is between Markers 11 and 15, go north on FL 535. Turn west onto Osceola Parkway to reach Disney's Animal Kingdom and Disney's Hollywood Studios. For Epcot, the Magic Kingdom, and Downtown Disney, continue on FL 535 past the Osceola Parkway to the intersection with FL 536. Turn left on FL 536 and follow the signs to your Disney destination.

**FL 535 (APOPKA–VINELAND ROAD)** There are a number of hotels northeast and southwest of I-4 on FL 535 and on streets connecting to it. Though many guests commute to the parks through Disney property via Hotel Plaza Drive to Downtown Disney and then via Buena Vista Drive, it's much easier to take I-4 west from FL 535 and enter Disney property on Epcot Center Drive for Epcot and the Magic Kingdom, and on Osceola Parkway for Disney's Hollywood Studios and Disney's Animal Kingdom.

**I-4** Expect heavy traffic and possible delays westbound on I-4 from 7 to about 9:30 a.m. Eastbound toward Orlando, expect heavy traffic from 4 to 7 p.m. If you want to avoid I-4 altogether, check out our I-4 sneak routes, detailed in the map on the previous page.

## TAKING A SHUTTLE BUS FROM
## YOUR OUT-OF-THE-WORLD HOTEL

MANY INDEPENDENT HOTELS and motels near Disney World provide trams and buses. They're fairly carefree, depositing you near theme park entrances and saving you parking fees. The rub is that they might not get you there as early as you desire (a critical point if you take our touring advice) or be available when you wish to return to your lodging. Each service is different; check details before you make reservations.

Some shuttles go directly to Disney World, while others stop at other hotels en route. This can be a problem if your hotel is the second or third stop on the route. During periods of high demand, buses frequently fill up at the first stop, leaving little or no room for passengers at subsequent stops. Before booking, inquire how many hotels are on the route and the sequence of the stops. The different hotels are often so close together that you can easily walk to the first hotel on the route and board there. Similarly, if there's a large hotel nearby, it might have its own dedicated bus service that is more efficient. Use it instead of the service provided by your hotel. The majority of out-of-the-World shuttles work on a fixed schedule instead of arriving and departing somewhat randomly like the Disney buses. Knowing exactly when a bus will depart makes it easier to plan your day.

*unofficial* **TIP**
*Warning:* Most shuttles don't add vehicles at park-opening or -closing times. In the mornings, you may not get a seat.

A multigenerational family from Seattle shares their experience:

> We stayed at a hotel off-site and it was fine, but I think next time we'll stay in the World. The shuttles weren't all that convenient or frequent, so we ended up taking taxis more than we thought we would.

At closing or during a hard rain, more people will be waiting for the shuttle than it can hold, and some will be left behind. Most shuttles return for stranded guests, but guests may wait 20 minutes to more than an hour.

If you're depending on shuttles, leave the park at least 45 minutes before closing. If you stay until closing and don't want the hassle of the shuttle, take a cab. Cab stands are near the Bus Information buildings at Disney's Animal Kingdom, Epcot, Disney's Hollywood Studios, and the TTC. If no cabs are on hand, a cast member will call one for you. If you're leaving the Magic Kingdom at closing, it's easier to take the monorail to a hotel and hail a cab from there rather than at the TTC.

*unofficial* **TIP**
If you want to go from resort to resort or almost anywhere else, you'll have to transfer at a hub.

## THE DISNEY TRANSPORTATION SYSTEM

THE DISNEY TRANSPORTATION SYSTEM (DTS) is large, diversified, and generally efficient, but it sometimes is overwhelmed, particularly at park-opening and -closing times. If you could be assured of getting on a bus, boat, or monorail at these critical times, we would advise you to leave your car at home. However, when huge crowds want to go somewhere at the same time, delays are unavoidable. In addition, some destinations are served directly, while many others require one or more transfers. Finally, it's sometimes difficult to figure how the buses, boats, and monorails interconnect.

Basically, Disney has a "hub and spoke" system. Hubs include the TTC, Downtown Disney, and all four major theme parks (from 2 hours before official opening time to 1 hour after closing). Although there are exceptions, there's direct service from Disney resorts to the major theme parks and Downtown Disney, and between parks.

If a hotel offers boat or monorail service, its bus service will be limited; you'll have to transfer at a hub for many destinations. If you're staying at a Magic Kingdom resort that's served by the monorail (Polynesian, Contemporary–Bay Lake Tower, Grand Floridian and Villas), you'll be able to commute efficiently to the Magic Kingdom. If you want to visit Epcot, you must take the monorail to the TTC and transfer to the Epcot monorail. (Guests at the Polynesian can eliminate the transfer by walking 5–10 minutes to the TTC and catching the direct monorail to Epcot.)

If you're staying at an Epcot resort (Swan, Dolphin, Yacht & Beach Club Resorts, BoardWalk Inn & Villas), you can walk or commute via boat to Epcot's International Gateway (backdoor) entrance. Although direct buses link Epcot resorts to the Magic Kingdom and Disney's Animal Kingdom, there's no direct bus to Epcot's main entrance or Disney's Hollywood Studios. To reach the Studios from Epcot resorts, you must take a boat or walk.

The Caribbean Beach, Pop Century, Art of Animation, Saratoga Springs, Port Orleans, Coronado Springs, Old Key West, Animal Kingdom Lodge & Villas, and All-Star resorts offer direct buses to all theme parks. The rub is that guests sometimes must walk a long way to bus stops or endure more than a half-dozen additional pickups before actually heading for the park(s). Commuting in the morning from these resorts is generally easy, though you may have to ride standing. Returning in the evening, however, can be a different story. Shades of Green runs continuous shuttles from the resort to the TTC, where guests can transfer to their final destinations.

Hotels of the Downtown Disney Resort Area (DDRA) (except the Hilton) terminated their guest-transportation contract with Disney some years ago and provide service through another carrier. The substitute, which we feel doesn't measure up, constitutes a real problem for guests at these hotels. Before booking a hotel in the DDRA, check the nature and frequency of shuttles.

Fort Wilderness guests must use campground buses to reach boat landings or the Settlement Depot and Reception Outpost bus stops. From these points, guests can travel directly by boat to the Magic Kingdom or by bus to other destinations. Except for going to the Magic Kingdom, the best way for Fort Wilderness guests to commute is in their car.

## The Disney Transportation System
## Versus Driving Your Own Car

To help you assess your transportation options, we've developed a chart (see pages 398 and 399) comparing the approximate commuting times from Disney resorts to various Walt Disney World destinations, using Disney transportation or your own car.

**DISNEY TRANSPORTATION** Times on the chart in the DTS columns represent an average-case and worst-case scenario. For example, if you want to go from the Caribbean Beach Resort to Epcot, the chart indicates the times as 35 (49). The first number, 35, indicates how many minutes your commute will take on an average day. It assumes that buses run every 17 minutes, there are no major delays, and everything else is as usual. It represents the average time we observed during our research of the transportation system. For the pessimists, the number in parentheses (49) indicates the worst-case scenario. (*Example:* The bus is pulling away as you arrive at the stop, and you must wait 17 minutes for the next one. When you finally board, the bus makes a number of additional stops before heading for Epcot. Once en route, the bus hits every red light.) When planning your transportation time, you'll do best to assume that your trip will take about the same time as the average in the chart (the first number). If you're running on a rigid schedule and you need to be sure of your arrival time, you can use the maximum time (the second number) to plan conservatively.

By far the biggest influence on your travel time between two points on the DTS is the amount of time you have to wait for your bus to arrive. Once you hop on your bus, the travel time is pretty consistent barring any unusual traffic problems; but your time waiting for the bus can vary greatly. Most cast members will tell you that buses run every 20 minutes. Our data indicates they run slightly more often—about every 16 minutes, an improvement of 1 minute over last year's numbers. Service at Old Key West and Saratoga Springs has improved the most: On average a bus arrives every 17 minutes now, down from 25 minutes last year.

Bus schedules are also adjusted based on demand and fuel costs. We observed and timed almost 560 bus routes for this edition of the book: The intervals between buses arriving at a resort and those headed for the same destination ranged from 1 minute to 56 minutes, although the average wait is, as noted, around 17 minutes. Still, if you've ever waited for an Epcot bus while three empty Downtown Disney buses drive past, you know that Disney still has a lot of opportunity to optimize its bus-routing system.

The first number in the chart expresses the average transportation time, but our data shows that about 20% of the time your actual travel time will be less than half the average. So don't be surprised if your trip from Caribbean Beach Resort to Epcot takes only 15 minutes instead of the 35 (49) listed. Consider yourself lucky and enjoy the extra 20 minutes, doing something fun.

**DRIVING YOUR OWN CAR** The chart's "Your Car" column indicates the average-case and worst-case scenario for driving. To make these times directly comparable to DTS times, we added the time needed to get from your parked car to the park's entrance. While buses and monorails deposit guests at the park's entrance, those who drive must take a tram from their car to the gate or walk. At the Magic Kingdom, you must take a tram from the parking lot to the TTC, then catch a monorail or ferry to the entrance.

*Continued on page 399*

## Door-to-Door Commuting Times to and from the Disney Resorts and Parks

| AVERAGE TIME (maximum time) IN MINUTES FROM | TO MAGIC KINGDOM | | TO EPCOT | | TO DHS | | |
|---|---|---|---|---|---|---|---|
| | YOUR CAR | DISNEY SYSTEM | YOUR CAR | DISNEY SYSTEM | YOUR CAR | DISNEY SYSTEM | |
| ALL-STAR RESORTS | 37 (47) | 20 (26) | 18 (23) | 25 (32) | 16 (20) | 17 (24) | |
| ANIMAL KINGDOM | 37 (48) | 50 (68) | 16 (17) | 27 (38) | 16 (17) | 24 (34) | |
| ANIMAL KINGDOM LODGE & VILLAS | 39 (50) | 19 (37) | 19 (21) | 27 (41) | 18 (19) | 22 (32) | |
| ART OF ANIMATION RESORT | 40 (51) | 20 (30) | 23 (28) | 19 (30) | 20 (24) | 18 (28) | |
| BEACH CLUB | 36 (46) | 23 (33) | 16 (21) | 18 (29*) | 14 (18) | 26 (37) | |
| BLIZZARD BEACH | 36 (46) | 28 (39) | 18 (23) | 51 (70) | 18 (22) | 39 (54) | |
| BOARDWALK INN & VILLAS | 36 (46) | 19 (31) | 16 (21) | 11 (22*) | 14 (18) | 26 (37) | |
| CARIBBEAN BEACH | 37 (47) | 31 (43) | 18 (23) | 35 (49) | 15 (19) | 23 (33) | |
| CONTEMPORARY-BAY LAKE | — | 12 (17) | 21 (26) | 21 (29) | 23 (27) | 29 (39) | |
| CORONADO SPRINGS | 37 (47) | 23 (32) | 18 (23) | 20 (28) | 16 (20) | 18 (26) | |
| DHS | 36 (46) | 25 (35) | 19 (24) | 25 (35) | — | — | |
| DOLPHIN | 35 (45) | 20 (30) | 15 (20) | 24 (36*) | 15 (19) | 22 (32) | |
| DOWNTOWN DISNEY | Bus service only back to your Disney resort | | | | | | |
| DOWNTOWN DISNEY RESORT AREA | 41 (51) | 69 (91) | 21 (26) | 47 (62) | 20 (24) | 45 (60) | |
| EPCOT | 36 (46) | 26 (37) | — | — | 19 (23) | 21 (30) | |
| FORT WILDERNESS | 37 (47) | 17 (27) | 18 (23) | 49 (67) | 19 (23) | 39 (54) | |
| GRAND FLORIDIAN & VILLAS | — | 7 (8) | 18 (23) | 33 (45) | 20 (24) | 23 (33) | |
| MAGIC KINGDOM | — | — | 26 (39) | 33 (45) | 22 (29) | 24 (34) | |
| OLD KEY WEST | 36 (46) | 24 (40) | 18 (23) | 24 (36) | 18 (22) | 25 (44) | |
| POLYNESIAN | — | 11 (14) | 17 (22) | 38 (53**) | 19 (23) | 19 (29) | |
| POP CENTURY RESORT | 40 (51) | 26 (32) | 23 (28) | 23 (30) | 20 (24) | 18 (30) | |
| PORT ORLEANS FRENCH QUARTER | 37 (47) | 25 (43) | 19 (24) | 24 (41) | 19 (23) | 25 (44) | |
| PORT ORLEANS RIVERSIDE | 38 (48) | 24 (46) | 20 (25) | 20 (34) | 20 (24) | 25 (47) | |
| SARATOGA SPRINGS | 38 (48) | 25 (41) | 18 (23) | 29 (43) | 20 (24) | 31 (45) | |
| SHADES OF GREEN | 28 (36) | 35 (49) | 18 (23) | 33 (45) | 20 (24) | 20 (28) | |
| SWAN | 35 (45) | 19 (43) | 15 (20) | 24 (36*) | 15 (19) | 22 (32) | |
| TREEHOUSE VILLAS | 37 (47) | 27 (38) | 18 (23) | 27 (38) | 19 (23) | 25 (36) | |
| TYPHOON LAGOON | 37 (47) | 41 (56) | 18 (23) | 51 (70) | 15 (19) | 62 (85) | |
| WILDERNESS LODGE | — | 20 (35) | 20 (25) | 22 (35) | 22 (26) | 27 (45) | |
| YACHT CLUB | 36 (46) | 25 (40) | 16 (21) | 26 (57*) | 14 (18) | 34 (45) | |

\# Transportation between Downtown Disney and the parks requires transfers at a nearby resort.

\* This hotel is within walking distance of Epcot; time given is for boat transportation to the International Gateway (Epcot's rear entrance).

\*\* By foot to Transportation and Ticket Center and then by Epcot monorail

† Driving time vs. time on DTS. Driving times include time in your car, stops to pay tolls, time to park, and transfers on Disney trams and monorails where applicable.

| in Your Car Versus the Disney Transportation System[†] | | | | | | | |
|---|---|---|---|---|---|---|---|
| TO ANIMAL KINGDOM | | TO TYPHOON LAGOON | | TO DOWNTOWN DISNEY | | TO BLIZZARD BEACH | |
| YOUR CAR | DISNEY SYSTEM | YOUR CAR | DISNEY SYSTEM | YOUR CAR | DISNEY SYSTEM | YOUR CAR | DISNEY SYSTEM |
| 11 (12) | 19 (35) | 12 (13) | 28 (50) | 13 (14) | 29 (51) | 6 (7) | 29 (39) |
| — | — | 17 (19) | 45 (63) | 19 (21) | — | 10 (13) | 21 (30) |
| 9 (10) | 17 (31) | 19 (21) | 44 (62) | 22 (24) | 32 (54) | 11 (14) | 27 (39) |
| 14 (16) | 18 (27) | 12 (14) | 26 (42) | 15 (16) | 29 (44) | 10 (12) | 22 (31) |
| 17 (18) | 24 (36) | 9 (10) | 29 (41) | 10 (11) | 22 (33) | 12 (13) | 28 (40) |
| 10 (13) | 26 (38) | 13 (14) | 60 (83) | 14 (15) | — | — | — |
| 17 (18) | 20 (32) | 9 (10) | 24 (51) | 10 (11) | 25 (52) | 12 (13) | 20 (32) |
| 17 (18) | 31 (45) | 6 (7) | 26 (38) | 7 (8) | 30 (42) | 12 (13) | 40 (56) |
| 20 (21) | 25 (37) | 17 (18) | 27 (39) | 16 (17) | 37 (52) | 15 (16) | 42 (58) |
| 11 (12) | 18 (27) | 12 (13) | 17 (25) | 13 (14) | 27 (39) | 6 (7) | 24 (35) |
| 16 (17) | 20 (30) | 8 (9) | 57 (79) | 9 (10) | — | 11 (12) | 36 (51) |
| 16 (17) | 23 (35) | 10 (11) | 33 (47) | 11 (12) | 27 (39) | 11 (12) | 19 (28) |
| Bus service only back to your Disney resort | | | | | | | |
| 21 (22) | 48 (64) | 9 (10) | 6 (9) | 6 (7) | — | 16 (17) | 46 (61) |
| 16 (17) | 33 (48) | 12 (13) | 30 (42) | 13 (14) | — | 11 (12) | 31 (45) |
| 24 (25) | 41 (57) | 10 (11) | 37 (52) | 11 (12) | 45 (63) | 19 (20) | 42 (58) |
| 18 (19) | 23 (35) | 15 (16) | 39 (55) | 16 (17) | 49 (68) | 13 (14) | 30 (44) |
| 17 (18) | 45 (63) | 23 (31) | 39 (55) | 27 (36) | — | 12 (13) | 41 (57) |
| 19 (20) | 31 (57) | 8 (9) | 22 (33) | 9 (10) | 27 (40) | 14 (15) | 35 (50) |
| 17 (18) | 19 (31) | 14 (15) | 44 (62) | 15 (16) | 54 (75) | 12 (13) | 32 (46) |
| 14 (16) | 23 (29) | 12 (14) | 28 (48) | 15 (16) | 31 (50) | 10 (12) | 41 (51) |
| 19 (20) | 29 (42) | 9 (10) | 26 (52) | 10 (11) | 27 (53) | 14 (15) | 24 (37) |
| 20 (21) | 33 (54) | 10 (11) | 24 (41) | 11 (12) | 26 (53) | 15 (16) | 20 (28) |
| 21 (22) | 36 (49) | 9 (10) | 24 (35) | 6 (7) | 29 (44) | 16 (17) | 34 (49) |
| 18 (19) | 22 (33) | 15 (16) | 39 (55) | 18 (20) | 49 (68) | 13 (14) | 30 (44) |
| 16 (17) | 19 (44) | 10 (11) | 33 (47) | 11 (12) | 35 (46) | 11 (12) | 19 (28) |
| 17 (19) | 41 (59) | — | — | 6 (7) | 16 (24) | 13 (14) | 42 (60) |
| 20 (21) | 28 (40) | 9 (10) | 23 (34) | 8 (9) | — | 15 (16) | 35 (50) |
| 20 (21) | 30 (47) | 17 (18) | 33 (51) | 18 (19) | 30 (48) | 15 (16) | 25 (42) |
| 17 (18) | 22 (38) | 8 (10) | 37 (49) | 10 (12) | 29 (59) | 12 (13) | 36 (48) |

*Continued from page 397*

## The Disney Transportation System for Teenagers

If you're staying at Disney World and have teens in your party, familiarize yourself with the Disney bus system. Safe, clean, and operating until 1 hour after the parks close (later from Downtown Disney), buses are a great way for teens to get around. Note that children under age 14 must be accompanied by someone age 14 or older to be admitted to the theme parks, water parks, and DisneyQuest.

## Walt Disney World Bus Service

Disney buses have an illuminated panel above the windshield that flashes the bus's destination. Also, theme parks have designated waiting areas for each Disney destination. To catch the bus to the Caribbean Beach Resort from Disney's Hollywood Studios, for example, go to the bus stop and wait in the area marked TO THE CARIBBEAN BEACH RESORT. At the resorts, go to any bus stop and wait for the bus displaying your destination on the illuminated panel. Directions to Disney destinations are available when you check in or at your hotel's Guest Relations desk. Guest Relations can also answer questions about the transportation system.

Service from resorts to major theme parks is fairly direct. You may have intermediate stops, but you won't have to transfer. Service to the water parks and other Disney resorts sometimes requires transfers.

The fastest way to commute among resorts by bus is to take a bus from your resort to one of the major theme parks and transfer there for your resort destination. This works, of course, only when the parks are open (actually, from 2 hours before opening until 1 hour after closing). If you're attempting to commute to another resort for a late dinner during the off-season, when parks close early, you'll have to transfer at Downtown Disney. Disney, in its transportation instructions, somewhat disingenuously lists Downtown Disney as the transfer point for all resort-to-resort commuting, hoping that you'll stop and do a little shopping en route. If the theme park buses are running, however, proceed to the theme park closest to your resort and transfer to the bus going to the resort where you'll be dining.

Bus service to the theme parks begins about 7 a.m. on days when the parks' official opening is 9 a.m. Generally, the buses run every 20 minutes. Buses to all four parks deliver you to the park entrance.

To be on hand for opening time (when official opening is 9 a.m.), catch direct buses to Epcot, Disney's Animal Kingdom, and Disney's Hollywood Studios between 7:30 and 8 a.m. Catch direct buses to the Magic Kingdom between 8 and 8:15 a.m. If you must transfer to reach your park, leave 15–20 minutes earlier. On days when official opening is 7 or 8 a.m., move up your departure time accordingly.

For your return bus trip in the evening, leave the park 40 minutes to an hour before closing to avoid the rush. If you're caught in the exodus, you may be inconvenienced, but you won't be stranded. Buses, boats, and monorails continue to operate for 1 hour after the parks close.

A woman from Charlotte, North Carolina, thinks Disney bus service needs some work:

> The bus service to the parks from Animal Kingdom Lodge was poor in the evenings. We had to wait an hour two times because there were so many people waiting. I think Animal Kingdom Lodge should use the chain system [i.e., create an organized queuing area] like the Value resorts do to maintain the queue. Guests pushed their way to the front when others had clearly been waiting longer.

From a Decatur, Georgia, reader:

> I was really gung-ho about staying on-site and using the buses, but having done it, I would probably not do it again. The buses were

*just too crowded and unpleasant. Even staying at one of the closest resorts (by bus), we found it took about an hour each way by the time we walked to the bus stations, waited, and walked back to our rooms.*

A reader who stayed at Port Orleans reports:

*The Disney transportation system was wildly erratic, but we ended up with more luck than not. For every time we had to wait a half-hour at the bus stop, there were two or three times with no wait at all.*

If you're planning on riding a bus from Port Orleans Riverside to a park around opening time, going to the West or North bus stop may be your best option. These are the first stops on the route, and the bus is sometimes full or standing-room-only before it gets to all the stops.

From a Huntsville, Alabama, mother of three:

*Best advice given was driving to the park instead of relying on buses.*

## Not All Hubs Are Created Equal

All major theme parks, Downtown Disney, and the TTC are hubs on the bus system. If your route requires you to transfer at a hub, transfer at the closest park or the TTC, except at theme park closing time. Avoid Downtown Disney as a transfer point. Because each bus makes multiple stops within Downtown Disney, it takes 16–25 minutes just to get out of the complex!

> *unofficial* **TIP**
> There are multiple stops at Downtown Disney, so never use it as a transfer point except as a last resort.

As elsewhere in Walt Disney World, bus service at Downtown Disney is kind of a crapshoot. A Lindenhurst, New York, mom who stayed at the All-Star Resorts recounts her experience:

*The one big problem we had was the bus coming back from Downtown Disney. We waited for an hour, and during that time six buses came for Pop Century and five for Art of Animation. Only two buses came to service the All-Star hotels, but because they were already full from picking up people at the other stops, they didn't take any passengers! We called to try to get more buses sent, but they just kept telling us that another bus would come in 15–20 minutes.*

*I use a wheelchair in the parks because of illness, so finally we gave up and took a taxi back to the hotel. As I was leaving, two workers told me to please stay in the walkway—I had to step onto the road to get around the line that was now at least 75–100 people long. Really? You do nothing about the line, don't walk up and talk to us, or try to get another bus, but that you do? Once I finally got back to the hotel, though, the person I spoke to was very understanding and reimbursed me for the cab.*

Note that with the exception of Fort Wilderness Resort & Campground, buses do not run between the TTC and the Disney resort hotels. If you're commuting from resort to resort, you must transfer at Downtown Disney or one of the major theme parks during park operating hours. If you're parked at the TTC and you want to travel to a Disney resort, go to the right of the Magic Kingdom entrance to catch a bus to your destination.

## Downtown Disney Resort Area Bus Service

Although inside Disney World, the independent hotels of the Downtown Disney Resort Area (DDRA) provide their own bus service—one that many guests, including a Prospect, Connecticut, family, find lacking:

> We were disappointed in the shuttle bus for the DDRA hotels. They don't run often enough, and there's no schedule. The bus at the parks picks up in the middle of busy parking lots. Treats you as second-class compared to Disney resort guests. Take a cab instead of waiting late at night to get back to your hotel. Costs only $9.

## Walt Disney World Monorail Service

*unofficial* **TIP**
Monorails run for 1 hour after the Magic Kingdom and Epcot close. If a train is too crowded or you need transportation after the monorails have stopped (for example, during Evening Extra Magic Hours), catch a bus or boat. *Note:* As a safety measure, Disney no longer permits guests to ride in the front of a train.

Picture the monorail system as three loops. Loop A is an express route that runs counterclockwise connecting the Magic Kingdom with the TTC. Loop B runs clockwise alongside Loop A, making all stops, with service (in order) to the TTC, Polynesian Resort, Grand Floridian & Villas, Magic Kingdom, Contemporary Resort and Bay Lake Tower, and back to the TTC. The long Loop C dips southeast, connecting the TTC with Epcot. The hub for all loops is the TTC (where you usually park to visit the Magic Kingdom).

The monorail serving the Magic Kingdom resorts usually starts an hour and a half before official opening. If you're staying at a Magic Kingdom resort and wish to be among the first in the Magic Kingdom when official opening is 9 a.m., board the monorail at these times:

| | |
|---|---|
| From the Contemporary Resort and Bay Lake Tower | 7:45–8 a.m. |
| From the Polynesian Resort | 7:50–8:05 a.m. |
| From the Grand Floridian Resort & Villas | 8–8:10 a.m. |

If you're a day guest, you'll be allowed on the monorail at the TTC between 8:15 and 8:30 a.m. when official opening is 9 a.m. If you want to board earlier, walk from the TTC to the Polynesian Resort and board there.

The monorail connecting Epcot and the TTC begins operating at 7:30 a.m. when Epcot's official opening is 9 a.m. To be at Epcot when it opens, catch the Epcot monorail at the TTC by 8:05 a.m.

While your Park Hopper pass suggests you can flit among parks, getting there is more complicated. For example, you can't go directly from the Magic Kingdom to Epcot. You must catch the express monorail (Loop A) to the TTC and transfer to the Loop C monorail to Epcot. If lines to board either monorail are short, you can usually reach Epcot in 30–40 minutes. But should you want to go to Epcot for dinner (as many do) and you're departing the Magic Kingdom in late afternoon, you may have to wait 30 minutes or longer to board the Loop A monorail. Adding this delay boosts your commute to 50–60 minutes.

# PART NINE

# BARE NECESSITIES

# MONEY, ETC.

### CREDIT CARDS

AMERICAN EXPRESS, DINERS CLUB, Discover, Japan Credit Bureau, MasterCard, and Visa are accepted throughout Disney World.

### BANKING SERVICES

AT THE THEME PARKS, banking is limited to ATMs, which are marked on the park maps and are plentiful throughout Walt Disney World; most MasterCard and Visa cards are accepted.

To use an American Express card, you must sign an agreement with Amex before your trip. If your credit card doesn't work in the ATMs, a teller at any **SunTrust Bank** full-service location will process your transaction. The SunTrust closest to Disney World is at 1675 E. Buena Vista Dr., across from Downtown Disney Marketplace; for other Orlando-area branches, visit **suntrust.com**.

### CURRENCY EXCHANGE

IN THE MAGIC KINGDOM, it's at Guest Relations in City Hall, on Main Street, U.S.A. In Epcot, it's at Guest Relations on the west side of the Epcot Entrance Plaza. In the Studios or Animal Kingdom, exchange your euros, krones, or zloty at Guest Relations to the left of the entrance turnstiles.

### A LICENSE TO PRINT MONEY

ONE OF DISNEY'S MORE SUBLIME PLOYS for separating you from your money is the printing and issuing of **Disney Dollars.** Available throughout Disney World or in advance by phone (☎ 407-934-7639) in denominations of $1, $5, and $10, each emblazoned with a Disney character or ride, the colorful cash can be used for purchases in Disney World, Disneyland, and Disney stores nationwide. Disney Dollars can also be exchanged one-for-one with US currency, but only while you're in Disney World.

*unofficial* **TIP**
Disney gift cards are available online in denominations up to $1,500, have no service fee or expiration date, and can be replaced if lost or stolen.

Also, you need your sales receipt to exchange for US dollars. Some guests keep the money as souvenirs. Others forget to spend or exchange it before they leave the World, then fail to go to a Disney Store or to exchange it by mail. A Michigan family, however, found a way to make their Disney Dollars useful:

> *Since we had planned on going to Disney a year ahead of time, we asked people giving our children money for birthdays, Christmas, Tooth Fairy, etc., to give Disney Dollars instead. This forced both of our children (ages 5 and 7) to save the money for the trip.*

### VISITING MORE THAN ONE PARK IN A SINGLE DAY

IF YOUR ADMISSION ALLOWS YOU to visit all four theme parks in the same day, it will be validated with the date when you enter your first park. To enter another park, present your pass or MagicBand and have the fingertip of your index finger scanned by a biometric reader.

# PROBLEMS *and*
# UNUSUAL SITUATIONS

### ATTRACTIONS CLOSED FOR REPAIRS

FIND OUT IN ADVANCE what rides and attractions may be closed during your visit. For complete refurbishment schedules, check online at **touringplans.com** or use our mobile app, **Lines.**

### CAR TROUBLE

SECURITY PATROLS WILL HELP if you lock the keys in your parked car or find the battery dead. For more serious problems, the closest repair facility is the **AAA Car Care Center** near the Magic Kingdom parking lot (☎ 407-824-0976).

The nearest off-World repair center is **Maingate Citgo** (US 192 west of I-4; ☎ 407-396-2721). Disney security can help you find it. Farther away but highly recommended by one of our Orlando-area researchers is **Riker's Automotive & Tire** (5700 Central Florida Parkway, near SeaWorld; ☎ 407-238-9800; **rikersauto.com**).

### CELL PHONE SNAFUS

THIS WOMAN from Leawood, Kansas, tells it like it is:

> *In our group, we were using three different carriers, and we all had problems sending and receiving texts and calls.*

The problem of signal strength is compounded by crowd noise and the ambient music played throughout the parks. Even if you have a decent signal, it's an exasperating challenge to find someplace quiet enough to have a conversation. When possible, opt for texting.

### GASOLINE

THERE ARE THREE **Hess** gas stations on Disney property. One station is adjacent to the AAA Car Care Center on the exit road from the Transportation and Ticket Center (Magic Kingdom) parking lot. It's also convenient to the Shades of Green, Grand Floridian, and Polynesian resorts. Most centrally located is the station at the corner of Buena Vista Drive and Epcot Resorts Boulevard, near the BoardWalk Inn. A third station, also on Buena Vista Drive, is across from Downtown Disney.

## LOST AND FOUND

IF YOU LOSE (OR FIND) SOMETHING in the Magic Kingdom, go to **City Hall.** At Epcot, Lost and Found is in the **Entrance Plaza.** At Disney's Hollywood Studios, it's at **Hollywood Boulevard Guest Relations,** and at Disney's Animal Kingdom, it's at **Guest Relations** at the main entrance. If you discover your loss after you've left the park(s), call ☎ 407-824-4245 (for all parks). See page 31 for the number(s) to call if you're at the park(s) and discover your loss.

It's unusual for readers to send us tips about Lost and Found, but a mom from Indianapolis sent two!

> Hold on to your things on Space Mountain! My daughter lost her bag going over the first turn, and on an 80-minute-wait-time day they had to shut the ride down to retrieve the bag! If you lose something on a ride and it has medication in it, Disney cast members will shut down a ride for 45 seconds to try and retrieve it. If they can't find it or it didn't contain meds, you have to come back to Lost and Found for it at the end of the day.
>
> Also, don't forget to write down the serial numbers on your Park Hopper passes. With the serial number, a cast member can look up when it was last used, giving you an idea of where it was lost.

**LOST MAGICBANDS** Duplicates can be made at Guest Relations at any of the theme parks or resort hotels.

**LOST CARS** Don't forget where you parked—write down your section and row, send yourself a text, or snap a picture with your phone or digital camera.

## MEDICAL MATTERS

**HEADACHE RELIEF** Aspirin and other sundries are sold at the **Emporium** on Main Street, U.S.A. in the Magic Kingdom (behind the counter; you must ask); at most retail shops in Epcot's Future World and World Showcase, Disney's Hollywood Studios, and Disney's Animal Kingdom; and at each Disney resort's gift shop.

**ILLNESSES REQUIRING MEDICAL ATTENTION** For the locations of the **First Aid** centers in the theme parks, see the respective park chapters. Guests who use the service are generally very positive about it. This Hickory, North Carolina, reader's experience is representative:

> We visited First Aid a time or two in the parks (my wife needed her blood pressure checked because she was worried about the heat and her pregnancy). We found trained medical staff, no wait, and all the friendliness and knowledge you would expect from Disney.

Off-property, a **Centra Care** walk-in clinic is at 12500 S. Apopka–Vineland Rd. (☎ 407-934-CARE). It's open 8 a.m.–midnight weekdays and 8 a.m.–8 p.m. weekends. Centra Care operates a 24-hour physician-house-call service and runs a free shuttle (☎ 407-938-0650).

A North Carolina family of four had a good experience at **Buena Vista Urgent Care** (8216 World Center Dr., Suite D; ☎ 407-465-1110):

> *We started day one needing medical care for our son, who has asthma and had developed croup. We found great care 2 miles down FL 535 at Buena Vista Urgent Care. We waited 20 minutes, and then we were off to the parks.*

**The Medical Concierge** (☎ 855-326-5252; **themedicalconcierge** **.com**) has board-certified physicians available 24-7 for house calls to your hotel room. They offer in-room X-rays and IV therapy service as well as same-day dental and specialist appointments. They also rent medical equipment. Insurance receipts, insurance billing, and foreign-language interpretation are provided. Walk-in clinics are also available. You can also inquire about transportation arrangements.

**DOCS** (Doctors on Call Service; ☎ 407-399-DOCS; **doctorsoncall** **service.com**) offers 24-hour house-call service. All physicians are certified by the American Board of Medical Specialties. A father of two from O'Fallon, Illinois, gives them a thumbs-up:

> *My wife's cold developed into an ear infection that required medical attention, and DOCS was able to respond in 40 minutes. The doctor had medicine with him and was very professional and friendly.*

**Physician Room Service** (☎ 407-238-2000; **physicianroomservice** **.com**) provides board-certified doctor house calls to Disney World–area guest rooms for adults and children.

**DENTAL NEEDS** Call **Celebration Dental Group** (☎ 407-566-2431).

**PRESCRIPTION MEDICINE** Two nearby pharmacies are **Walgreens Lake Buena Vista** (☎ 407-238-0600) and **Winn-Dixie Pharmacy Lake Buena Vista** (☎ 407-465-8606). **Turner Drugs** (☎ 407-828-8125) charges $7.50 to deliver a filled prescription to your Disney hotel's front desk, $10–$15 for non-Disney hotels. The fee is charged to your hotel account.

## SERGEANT BLISTERBLASTER'S GUIDE TO HAPPY FEET

**1. ON YOUR FEET!** Get up, La-Z-Boy rider: When you go to Walt Disney World, you'll have to walk a lot farther than to the refrigerator. You can log 5–12 miles a day at the parks, so now's the time to shape up them dogs. Start with short walks around the neighborhood. Increase your distance gradually until you can do 6 miles without CPR.

**2. A-TEN-SHUN!** During your training program, pay attention when those puppies growl. They'll give you a lot of information about your feet and the appropriateness of your shoes. Listen up! No walking in flip-flops, loafers, or sandals. Wear well-constructed, broken-in running or hiking shoes. If you feel a "hot spot," that means a blister is developing. The most common sites for blisters are heels, toes, and balls of the feet. If you develop a hot spot in the same place every time you walk (a clue!), cover it with a Johnson & Johnson blister bandage (in drugstores without a prescription) before you set out.

**3. SOCK IT UP, TRAINEE!** Good socks are as important as good shoes. When you walk, your feet sweat like a mule in a peat bog, and the moisture only increases friction. To minimize friction, wear a pair of socks, such as SmartWool or CoolMax, that wick perspiration away from your feet (SmartWool makes socks of varying thicknesses). To further combat moisture, dust your dogs with antifungal talcum powder.

**4. WHO DO YOU THINK YOU ARE, JOHN WAYNE?** Don't be a hero. Take care of a foot problem the minute you notice it. Carry a small foot-emergency kit for your platoon. Include gauze, Betadine antibiotic ointment, moleskin or Johnson & Johnson blister bandages, scissors, a sewing needle or such (to drain blisters), and matches to sterilize the needle. Extra socks and talcum powder are optional.

**5. BITE THE BULLET!** If you develop a hot spot, cover it ASAP with a blister bandage. Cut the material large enough to cover the skin surrounding the spot. If you develop a blister, air out and dry your foot. Next, drain the fluid, but don't remove the top skin. Clean the area with Betadine and place a blister bandage over the blister. The bandages come in several sizes, including specially shaped ones for fingers and toes; they're also good for covering hot spots. If you don't have blister bandages, don't cover the hot spot or blister with Band-Aids; they'll slip and wad up.

**6. TAKE CARE OF YOUR PLATOON.** If you have young, green troops in your outfit, they might not sound off when a hot spot develops. Stop several times a day and check their feet. If you forgot your emergency kit and a problem arises, call the Disney medics. They have all the stuff you need to keep your command in action.

## RAIN

WEATHER BAD? Go to the parks anyway. The crowds are lighter, and most attractions and waiting areas are under cover. Showers, especially during warmer months, are short.

*unofficial* **TIP**
Raingear isn't always displayed in shops, so you have to ask for it.

Ponchos are about $7, umbrellas about $12. All ponchos sold at Disney World are made of clear plastic, so picking out somebody in your party on a rainy day can be tricky. Walmart sells an inexpensive green poncho that will make your family emerald beacons in a plastic-covered sea of humanity.

A Wilmington, North Carolina, mom thinks high-quality raingear is worth the investment:

> We're outdoor-sports people, and so we have very good raincoats. It rained every day on this trip, driving many people out of the parks and leaving others looking miserable in their ponchos. Meanwhile, we hardly noticed the rain from inside our high-end jackets as we walked right onto many of the attractions.

Some unusually heavy rain precipitated (no pun intended) dozens of reader suggestions for dealing with soggy days. The best came from this Memphis, Tennessee, mom:

1. Rain gear should include ponchos *and* umbrellas. When rain isn't beating down on your ponchoed head, it's easier to ignore.
2. Buy blue ponchos at Walgreens. We could keep track of each other much easier because we had blue ponchos instead of clear ones.

**3.** If you're using a stroller, bring a plastic sheet or extra poncho to protect it from rain. (Ponchos cover only Disney's single strollers.) Carry a towel in a plastic bag to wipe off your stroller after experiencing an attraction during a rainfall.

*Unofficial Guide* researcher Connie Wolosyk adds, "It helps to wear a baseball cap under the poncho hood—without it, the hood never covers your head properly, and your face always gets wet."

## HOW TO LODGE A COMPLAINT WITH DISNEY

COMPLAINING ABOUT A LEAKY FAUCET or not having enough towels is pretty straightforward, and you usually will find Disney folks highly responsive. However, a more global gripe, or one beyond an on-site manager's ability to resolve, is likely to founder in the labyrinth of Disney bureaucracy.

One of our readers' foremost gripes relates to Disney's unresponsiveness in fielding complaints. A Providence, Rhode Island, dad's remarks are typical:

*It's all warm fuzzies and big smiles until you have a problem. Then everybody plays hide-and-seek. The only thing you know for sure is it's never the responsibility of the Disney person you're talking to.*

A Mobile, Alabama, mother echoes his comment:

*I made call after call, with one Disney person passing me on to the next, until finally I ran out of steam. Basically, I had to choose between getting my problem addressed, which was pretty much a full-time job, or going ahead with my vacation.*

A Portland, Maine, reader summed it up in quintessential New England style:

*Lodging a complaint with Disney is like shouting at a brick.*

Like most companies, Disney would rather hear from you when the message is good. Regarding complaints, Disney prefers to receive them in writing, but by the time you get home and draft a letter, it's often too late to correct the problem. And though Disney would have you believe that it's a touchy-feely outfit, it generally isn't a company that will make things right for you after the fact. You may receive a letter thanking you for writing and expressing regret without acknowledging responsibility (for example, "We're sorry you felt inconvenienced"—as if the perception somehow arose from your imagination). It's unlikely, though, that they'll offer to do anything remedial. That said, if you want to lodge a complaint, write to **Walt Disney World Guest Communications, P.O. Box 10040, Lake Buena Vista, FL 32830-0040.** If you're really steamed, try writing the following higher-ups:

| **Robert Iger, CEO** | **Thomas Staggs, Chairman** | **Meg Crofton** |
|---|---|---|
| The Walt Disney Company | Walt Disney Parks & Resorts | Walt Disney Parks & Resorts Operations, US/France |
| 500 S. Buena Vista St. | 500 S. Buena Vista St. | P.O. Box 10040 |
| Burbank, CA 91521 | Burbank, CA 91521 | Lake Buena Vista, FL 32830 |

If Disney doesn't respond, you can always go public:
**Letters to the Editor,** *Orlando Sentinel*
633 N. Orange Ave., MP-218
Orlando, FL 32801-1349
☎ 407-420-5000; fax 407-420-5286; **insight@orlandosentinel.com**

# SERVICES

## MESSAGES

MESSAGES LEFT AT CITY HALL in the Magic Kingdom, Guest Relations at Epcot, Hollywood Boulevard Guest Relations at Disney's Hollywood Studios, or Guest Relations at Disney's Animal Kingdom can be retrieved at any of the four.

## PET CARE

ACROSS FROM THE PORT ORLEANS RESORTS, the plush **Best Friends Pet Resort** accommodates up to 270 dogs in a variety of standard and luxury suites, some with private outdoor patios and play yards; the Kitty City pavilion houses up to 30 felines in two- and four-story cat condos. There's also a separate area just for birds and "pocket pets" such as hamsters. Encompassing more than 17,000 square feet of air-conditioned indoor space plus 10,000 square feet of covered outdoor runs and play areas, the resort is open to both Walt Disney World resort guests and visitors staying off-property. For more information, call ☎ 877-4-WDW-PETS (877-493-9738) or visit **bestfriendspetcare.com**. (*Note:* Pet parents must provide written proof of current vaccination from a veterinarian, either at check-in or by fax at 203-840-5266.)

## PHOTOS

FOR YEARS NOW, Disney has employed roving bands of photographers to take digital photos of families who don't use their own cameras. And, of course, Disney sells those pictures back to you through a website, where you can choose the images you want to keep, customize them with text and colorful borders, order CDs, and so on.

The latest version of the photo program, called **Memory Maker** (**disneyworld.disney.go.com/memory-maker**), costs $149 if you buy it in advance, $199 if you buy it in the parks. Memory Maker replaces Disney's PhotoPass system and adds to your package photos taken of your family on rides, such as Splash Mountain and Tower of Terror. Because Memory Maker is linked to your My Disney Experience (MDE) account (see page 32), you're also able to see photos of friends and family you've linked to there. Here's how it works:

1. Find a Memory Maker photographer to take your first picture. Photographers roam throughout the theme parks and water parks, including near park entrances, in restaurants (and during character meals), and around iconic attractions such as Splash Mountain.

2. The photographer will scan your RFID ticket or MagicBand. This links your pictures to your MDE account. Onboard ride-photo systems should automatically detect your MagicBand and link the photos to your account.

**3.** Visit the MDE website within 45 days of your trip and enter your ID number to view your photos. You can add decorative borders and short captions to your pictures, too, as well as share photos online.

*unofficial* **TIP**
You must have a My Disney Experience account to buy a Memory Maker package.

You have a couple of options when buying photo packages. If you're already signed in to My Disney Experience, your purchase will be automatically linked to your account. If you're not logged in, you'll be asked to do so (or sign up for MDE) to complete the purchase.

You can download Memory Maker photos as many times as you want, subject to a few restrictions: First, if you prepurchase, you must do so at least three days before your trip in order to have all of your photos included. If you prepurchase fewer than three days before you arrive, you'll have to buy separately any photos taken during that three-day window. Next, Disney will store your photos for 45 days, so you'll need to download them promptly once you return home (you can also pay for extra time). Finally, once you've downloaded the first photo, you've got 30 days to download the rest.

You're granted a limited license to reproduce the photos for personal use. Disney retains ownership of and copyright to all of the photos taken by their photographers.

## EXCUSE ME, BUT WHERE CAN I FIND . . .

**RELIGIOUS SERVICES IN THE WALT DISNEY WORLD AREA?** See **allears .net/btp/church.htm** for a complete list.

**SOMEPLACE TO CHARGE MY CELL PHONE?** You can drop your phone off to be charged at any **Guest Relations** desk in any park. While they have cords and plugs for most phones, it helps to bring yours along. You'll be issued a claim check to pick up your phone; phones are usually done charging in 1–2 hours. Charging stations are also available near the *Tangled*-themed bathrooms in Fantasyland in the Magic Kingdom. They're built into the faux-wood posts near the seating area.

*unofficial* **TIP**
Be aware that Package Pick-Up closes 2 hours before the park. Disney resort guests can have their purchases delivered to their hotel's gift shop.

If you prefer to charge on the go, we use **Mophie** and **New Trent** external batteries for our devices. Both are available on **Amazon.com.**

**SOMEPLACE TO PUT ALL THESE PACKAGES?** Lockers are available on the ground floor of the Main Street railroad station in the Magic Kingdom, to the right of Spaceship Earth in Epcot, and on the Transportation and Ticket Center's east and west ends. At Disney's Hollywood Studios, lockers are to the right of the entrance at Oscar's Classical Car Souvenirs. Disney's Animal Kingdom lockers are to the left inside the entrance. Cost is $7 a day for small lockers and $9 a day for large lockers; prices include a $5 refundable deposit. Lockers at Blizzard Beach and Typhoon Lagoon water parks cost $13 (small) and $15 (large), also with a $5 refundable deposit.

Package Pick-Up is available at each of the major parks. Ask the salesperson to send your purchases to Package Pick-Up. When you leave the park, they'll be waiting for you. Epcot has two exits, thus two Package Pick-Ups; specify the main entrance or the International Gateway. If you're staying at a Disney resort, you can also have the packages delivered to your resort's gift shop for pickup the following day. If you're leaving within 24 hours, however, take them with you or use the in-park pickup location.

**AN OLD-FASHIONED CAMERA?** **Camera Centers** at the parks sell disposable point-and-shooters with flash for $16.95 plus tax. Developing is available at Camera Centers and most Disney resort gift shops.

**A GROCERY STORE?** Our first piece of advice is to avoid the **Gooding's Supermarket** in the Crossroads Shopping Center, across FL 535 from the Disney World entrance. While its location makes it undeniably convenient, its selection is poor and you'll find the prices higher and more frightening than the Tower of Terror. For down-to-earth prices, try **Publix** at either the intersection of International Drive and US 192 or just north of the intersection of Reams Road and FL 535, or **Winn-Dixie** on Apopka–Vineland Road, about a mile north of Crossroads Shopping Center.

A new **Winn-Dixie Marketplace,** at US 192 on the west side of I-4 (7840 W. Irlo Bronson Memorial Hwy.; ☎ 407-397-2210), is the closest and largest supermarket for anyone staying near the Western Way, Sherberth Road, or World Drive (Maingate) entrances to Disney World.

We compiled a list of common vacation grocery items and went shopping. No item we bought was on sale. The chart below shows how prices at GardenGrocer, Publix, Super Target, and Winn-Dixie compare.

| ITEM | GARDEN GROCER | PUBLIX | SUPER TARGET | WINN-DIXIE |
|---|---|---|---|---|
| **12 DOUGHNUTS** (store brand) | $4.19 | $7.38 | $4.99 | $3.99 |
| **MAXWELL HOUSE COFFEE** (11.5 oz.) | $6.79 | $4.59 | $3.59 | $3.89 |
| **COFFEE FILTERS** (store brand, 200 count) | $2.49 | $1.39 | $2.58 | $2.29 |
| **1 GALLON MILK** (store brand) | $5.39 | $4.09 | $3.99 | $4.19 |
| **TROPICANA ORANGE JUICE** (59 oz.) | $5.99 | $3.99 | $3.29 | $4.29 |
| **CHEERIOS** (8.9 oz.)* | $4.49 | $3.59 | $2.79 | $3.79 |
| **COCA-COLA** (12-pack, 12-oz. cans) | $6.59 | $4.99 | $3.99 | $5.29 |
| **LAY'S POTATO CHIPS** (10.5 oz.) | $5.39 | $4.29 | $3.79 | $4.29 |
| **SUGAR** (2 lbs., store brand)** | $4.19 | $1.75 | $2.24 | $1.79 |
| **JIF PEANUT BUTTER** (12 oz.) | $3.69 | $3.19 | $2.59 | $3.09 |
| **CHIPS AHOY COOKIES** (13.72 oz.) | $4.49 | $3.59 | $2.54 | $3.59 |
| **BANANAS** (4 lbs.)*** | 49¢ | $2.76 | $2.28 | $2.76 |
| **WONDER BREAD** (1 loaf) | N/A | $2.59 | $2.49 | $2.59 |
| **BUDWEISER** (12-pack, 12-oz. cans) | $13.99 | $10.00 | $11.79 | $11.59 |
| **WELCH'S GRAPE JELLY** (18 oz.)**** | $3.36 | $2.59 | $1.94 | $2.59 |
| **COLGATE TOOTHBRUSH** | $2.49 | $2.79 | $1.97 | $3.09 |
| **BANANA BOAT SPORT SPF 30 SUNSCREEN** (8 oz.) | $10.99 | $7.99 | $6.49 | $7.99 |
| **TOTAL** | **$85.01** | **$71.56** | **$63.34** | **$71.10** |

*\* Smallest box of Cheerios that Target carries is 14 ounces.*

*\*\* Target and GardenGrocer sell only 4-pound bags of sugar.*

*\*\* GardenGrocer prices by the banana rather than by the pound.*

*\*\*\*\*\* GardenGrocer carries only Smucker's jelly in the 32-ounce jar.*

**GROCERY MARKETS THAT DELIVER?** If you don't have a car or you don't want to take the time to go to the supermarket, **GardenGrocer (garden grocer.com)** will shop for you and deliver your groceries. The best way to compile your order is on GardenGrocer's website before you leave home. It's simple, and the selection is huge. If there's something you want that's not on their list of available items, they'll try to find it for you (including alcohol). Delivery arrangements are per your instructions. If you're staying at a hotel, you can arrange for your groceries to be left with bell services. For the sake of order-fulfillment accuracy and customer service, GardenGrocer is primarily set up for online ordering. If you can't get online, though, you can order by phone (☎ 866-855-4350). For orders of $200 or more, there's a $2 delivery fee; for orders less than $200, the delivery charge is $14; a minimum order of $40 is required. As of this writing, GardenGrocer doesn't deliver to the Swan or Dolphin. Also note that Garden Grocer's delivery schedule may fill completely around holidays, at which point they'll stop accepting orders for delivery on those dates.

We get lots of positive reader feedback about GardenGrocer. The following review from an Eagan, Minnesota, family is representative:

*GardenGrocer was fabulous. I ordered our groceries online about one week before our arrival. I had a few questions, so I called and actually spoke with a human who was very helpful! Our flight got in about 7 p.m., and I called to let them know we were on our way. They arrived about 20 minutes after we did with everything we ordered.*

**WINE, BEER, AND LIQUOR?** Wine and beer are sold in grocery stores. The best range of adult beverages is sold at the **ABC Fine Wine & Spirits** store less than a mile north of the Crossroads shopping center (11951 S. Apopka–Vineland Rd.; ☎ 407-239-0775).

# PART TEN

# DINING *in* AND *around* WALT DISNEY WORLD

# DINING *outside* WALT DISNEY WORLD

UNOFFICIAL GUIDE RESEARCHERS love good food and invest a fair amount of time scouting new places to eat. And because food at Walt Disney World is so expensive, we (like you) have an economic incentive for finding palatable meals outside the World. Alas, the area surrounding Disney World is not exactly a culinary nirvana. If you thrive on fast food and the fare at chain restaurants (Denny's, T.G.I. Friday's, The Olive Garden, and the like), you'll be as happy as an alligator at a chicken farm. But if you're in the market for a superlative dining experience, you'll find the pickings outside the World of about the same quality as those inside, only less expensive. Plus, some ethnic cuisines aren't represented in Walt Disney World restaurants.

Among specialty restaurants both in and out of the World, location and price will determine your choice. For instance, both Walt Disney World and adjoining tourist areas have some decent Italian restaurants—which one you select depends on how much money you want to spend and how convenient the place is to reach. Our recommendations for specialty and ethnic fare served outside of Disney World are summarized in the table that starts on page 416.

Better restaurants outside Walt Disney World cater primarily to adults. That's a plus, however, if you're looking to escape children or you want to eat in peace and quiet.

## DINING AT UNIVERSAL CITYWALK

DINING AND SHOPPING are the focus at CityWalk, whose restaurants tends to cater more to adult tastes than do the theme park restaurants. Probably the best of the bunch is **Emeril's Orlando,** but each restaurant has a couple of decent options if you know what to look for. One thing all of them have in common is noise: Your fussy toddler will have to fight to be heard in some of these places. On the upside, many of the restaurants use **OpenTable** (**opentable.com**) for online reservations, making it easy to get seats before you go park-hopping.

## In or Out of the World for These Cuisines?

**American** Good selections both in and out of the World.

**Barbecue** Better out of the World.

**Buffets** A toss-up—Disney buffets are expensive but offer excellent quality and variety. Out-of-World buffets aren't as upscale but are inexpensive.

**Chinese** Better out of the World.

**French** Toss-up; good but expensive both in and out of the World.

**German** Passable but not great, in or out of the World.

**Italian** Tie on quality; better value out of the World.

**Japanese/sushi** **Teppan Edo** in the Japan Pavilion at Epcot is tops for teppanyaki (table grilling). For sushi and sashimi, try **Tokyo Dining,** also in Japan, or visit **Kimonos** at the Swan resort.

**Mexican** **La Hacienda de San Angel** at Epcot is good but expensive, with more-affordable food right next door at the quick-service **La Cantina de San Angel.** For decent Tex-Mex, try **El Patron** outside the World.

**Middle Eastern** More choice and better value out of the World.

**Seafood** Toss-up.

**Steak/prime rib** Try **Shula's Steak House** at the Dolphin or **The Capital Grille** on International Drive out of the World. For more-affordable but nevertheless-delicious wads o' meat, try one of the **Black Angus** steakhouses on International Drive, Lake Buena Vista, or US 192.

**ANTOJITOS** ☎ 407-224-3663; tinyurl.com/antojitoscitywalk. The name means "little cravings," the Mexican equivalent of Spain's small-plate *tapas,* so it's only natural that the best dishes are the appetizers. Try the empanada trio (beef, chicken, and mushroom) and the *esquites asados,* roasted corn-off-the-cob with queso fresco and mayo. Free custom-painted luchador masks are handed out Wednesday–Sunday. Antojitos carries more than 200 tequila brands, too, and makes a tasty margarita.

**BOB MARLEY—A TRIBUTE TO FREEDOM** ☎ 407-224-3663; tinyurl .com/bobmarleytribute. Set in a replica of the reggae singer's Jamaica home, the building is filled with memorabilia and photos showcasing his career and life. The Caribbean-inspired dishes—beef patties, yucca fries, oxtail stew, and such—aren't particularly memorable, but the laid-back atmosphere makes it worth a visit.

**BREAD BOX (NOT OPEN AT PRESS TIME)** An upscale custom-sandwich shop promising bread baked daily, plus soups and salads.

**BUBBA GUMP SHRIMP CO.** ☎ 407-903-0044; bubbagump.com/locations /orlando. This seafood eatery is part of an international chain inspired by *Forrest Gump.* Take a wild guess what the specialty here is.

**THE COWFISH (NOT OPEN AT PRESS TIME)** "Burger joint–sushi bar" is pretty far down our list of fusion-cuisine concepts to try, but that's what you get: cheeseburgers and tuna *futomaki* in one place.

**EMERIL'S ORLANDO** ☎ 407-224-2424; emerilsrestaurants.com/emerils -orlando. Not to be confused with Emeril Lagasse's fancier and more expensive Asian-inspired Tchoup Chop at the nearby Royal Pacific Resort, this is the Florida outpost of Emeril's original restaurant in New

Orleans. The cuisine—CityWalk's best—is Louisiana-style with creative flair. The smoked-mushroom appetizer is outstanding, and the banana cream pie will renew your faith in humanity.

**HARD ROCK CAFE** ☎ 407-351-7625; **hardrock.com/orlando**. The best meals we've had here have consisted of drinks and appetizers or desserts. You'd be hard-pressed to differentiate the entrees—burgers, sandwiches, steaks, and such—from anything you'd get at, say, NASCAR Sports Grille or NBA City. More remarkable is the collection of music memorabilia, including a pink 1959 Cadillac revolving over the bar. It's the biggest such collection on display anywhere in the Hard Rock chain.

**HOT DOG HALL OF FAME (NOT OPEN AT PRESS TIME)** The menu is inspired by the food served at baseball stadiums around the US, complete with bleacher seating and broadcasts of live and classic baseball games.

**JIMMY BUFFETT'S MARGARITAVILLE** ☎ 407-224-2155; **margaritaville orlando.com**. A boisterous tribute to the head Parrothead. The focal point is a volcano that spews margarita mix instead of lava. The food is Floridian-Caribbean, so expect lots of seafood and jerk seasoning and Key lime pie. If you're not a Buffett fan, it isn't worth a special trip.

**NASCAR SPORTS GRILLE** ☎ 407-224-7223; **nascarsportsgrille orlando.com**. A large and noisy tribute to all things motorized. You may find yourself sitting under a full-size race car that from time to time starts up and roars at a too-realistic sound level. The food is generic (see Hard Rock Cafe)—if you want to watch the race, stick to drinks and order the nachos with pulled pork.

**NBA CITY** ☎ 407-363-5919; **tinyurl.com/nbacity**. Serves decent theme-restaurant eats. The dining area looks like a miniature basketball arena, and TVs throughout play videos of famous basketball players and key moments in roundball history.

**PAT O'BRIEN'S** ☎ 407-224-2106; **patobriens.com/orlando**. This and **CityWalk's Rising Star** are mostly music venues that serve some food. Pat O'Brien's, behind a facade that looks remarkably similar to the New Orleans original, has the best bites (try the jambalaya).

**RED OVEN PIZZA BAKERY** ☎ 407-224-3663; **tinyurl.com/redoven pizza**. Artisan pizza baked in a 900°F oven. Choose from five white and five red Neapolitan-style pies, made with San Marzano tomatoes, organic extra-virgin olive oil, buffalo mozzarella, fine-ground "00" flour, and filtered water. Pizzas run $9–$14 and serve two people.

**VIVO ITALIAN KITCHEN** ☎ 407-224-2253; **tinyurl.com/vivocitywalk**. Upscale Italian restaurant with pasta made on-site nightly. Try the Nonna Cake for dessert.

## BUFFETS AND MEAL DEALS OUTSIDE WALT DISNEY WORLD

BUFFETS, RESTAURANT SPECIALS, and discount dining abound in the area surrounding Walt Disney World, especially on US 192 (a.k.a. Irlo Bronson Memorial Highway) and along International Drive. The local visitor magazines, distributed free at non-Disney hotels, among other places, are packed with advertisements and discount coupons for

*Continued on page 418*

## Where to Eat Outside Walt Disney World

**AMERICAN**

**JOHNNIE'S HIDEAWAY** 12551 FL 535, Orlando; ☎ 407-827-1111; **talkofthe townrestaurants.com/johnnies.html;** moderate to expensive. Seafood and steaks, with an emphasis on Florida cuisine.

**THE RAVENOUS PIG\*** 1234 N. Orange Ave., Winter Park; ☎ 407-628-2333; **theravenouspig.com;** moderate–expensive. New American cuisine with an award-winning menu that changes frequently depending on seasonal ingredients.

**SEASONS 52** 7700 W. Sand Lake Rd., Orlando; ☎ 407-354-5212; **seasons 52.com;** moderate–expensive. Delicious, creative New American food that's low in fat and calories. Extensive wine list.

**BARBECUE**

**BUBBALOU'S BODACIOUS BAR-B-QUE** 5818 Conroy Rd., Orlando (near Universal Orlando); ☎ 407-295-1212; **bubbalous.com;** inexpensive. Tender, smoky barbecue; tomato-based Killer Sauce.

**4 RIVERS SMOKEHOUSE** 11764 University Blvd., Orlando; ☎ 855-368-7748; **4rsmokehouse.com;** inexpensive. Award-winning beef brisket; fried pickles, cheese grits, fried okra, and collard greens.

**CARIBBEAN**

**BAHAMA BREEZE** 8849 International Dr., Orlando; ☎ 407-248-2499; **bahamabreeze.com;** moderate. A creative and tasty version of Caribbean cuisine from the owners of the Olive Garden and Red Lobster chains.

**CHINESE**

**MING'S BISTRO\*** 1212 Woodward St., Orlando; ☎ 407-898-9672; inexpensive. Authentic Chinese, including dim sum, crispy roast pork, and roast duck.

**CUBAN/SPANISH**

**COLUMBIA** 649 Front St., Celebration; ☎ 407-566-1505; **columbiarestau rant.com;** moderate. Authentic Cuban and Spanish creations, including paella and the famous 1905 Salad.

**ETHIOPIAN**

**NILE ETHIOPIAN RESTAURANT** 7040 International Dr., Orlando; ☎ 407-354-0026; **nile07.com;** inexpensive–moderate. Authentic stews and delicious vegetarian dishes. Bob's favorite Orlando/WDW-area restaurant.

**FRENCH**

**LE COQ AU VIN\*** 4800 S. Orange Ave., Orlando; ☎ 407-851-6980; **lecoq auvinrestaurant.com;** moderate–expensive. Country French cuisine in a relaxed atmosphere. Reservations suggested.

**INDIAN**

**MEMORIES OF INDIA** 7625 Turkey Lake Rd., Orlando; ☎ 407-370-3277; **memoriesofindiacuisine.com;** inexpensive–moderate. Classic tandoori dishes, samosas, tikka masala, Sunday Champagne brunch with buffet.

**ITALIAN**

**BICE ORLANDO RISTORANTE** Loews Portofino Bay Hotel, Universal Orlando Resort, 5601 Universal Blvd., Orlando; ☎ 407-503-1415; **orlando .bicegroup.com;** expensive. Authentic Italian; great wines.

*\*20 minutes or more from Walt Disney World*

**ANTHONY'S COAL-FIRED PIZZA** 8031 Turkey Lake Rd., Orlando; ☎ 407-363-9466; **anthonyscoalfiredpizza.com;** inexpensive. Pizzas, eggplant, pastas, beer and wine.

### JAPANESE/SUSHI

**AMURA** 7786 W. Sand Lake Rd., Orlando; ☎ 407-370-0007; **amura.com;** moderate. A favorite sushi bar for locals. The tempura is popular, too.

**HANAMIZUKI** 8255 International Dr., Orlando; ☎ 407-363-7200; **hana mizuki.us;** moderate–expensive. Pricey but very authentic.

**NAGOYA SUSHI** 7600 Dr. Phillips Blvd., Suite 66, in the very rear of The Marketplace at Dr. Phillips; ☎ 407-248-8558; **nagoyasushi.com;** moderate. A small, intimate restaurant with great sushi and an extensive menu.

### MEXICAN

**CANTINA LAREDO** 8000 Via Dellagio Way, Orlando; ☎ 407-345-0186; **cantinalaredo.com;** moderate–expensive. Authentic Mexican in an upscale atmosphere.

**CHEVYS FRESH MEX** 12547 FL 535, Lake Buena Vista; ☎ 407-827-1052 or 407-827-1119; **chevys.com;** inexpensive-moderate. Conveniently located across from the FL 535 entrance to WDW.

**EL PATRON** 12167 S. Apopka–Vineland Rd., Orlando; ☎ 407-238-5300; **el patronorlando.com;** inexpensive. Family-owned restaurant serving freshly prepared Mexican dishes. Full bar.

**MOE'S SOUTHWEST GRILL** 7541-D W. Sand Lake Rd., Orlando; ☎ 407-264-9903; **moes.com;** inexpensive. Dependable southwestern fare.

**TAQUITOS JALISCO** 1041 S. Dillard St., Winter Garden; ☎ 407-654-0363; inexpensive. Low-key atmosphere; flautas, chicken mole, fajitas, hearty burritos, good vegetarian.

### NEW WORLD

**NORMAN'S** 4012 Central Florida Parkway, in the Ritz-Carlton Orlando; ☎ 407-393-4333; **normans.com;** expensive. Norman Van Aken, dean of New World cuisine, offers a menu that changes often—but you'll always find his sinfully delicious conch chowder. World-class wine menu.

### SEAFOOD

**BONEFISH GRILL** 7830 W. Sand Lake Rd., Orlando; ☎ 407-355-7707; **bonefishgrill.com;** moderate. Casual setting along busy Restaurant Row on Sand Lake Road. Choose your fish, and then choose a favorite sauce to accompany. Also steaks and chicken.

**CELEBRATION TOWN TAVERN** 721 Front St., Celebration; ☎ 407-566-2526; **thecelebrationtowntavern.com;** moderate. Popular hangout for locals, with New England–style seafood. Clam chowder is a big hit.

**OCEAN PRIME** 7339 W. Sand Lake Rd., Orlando; ☎ 407-781-4880; **ocean -prime.com;** expensive. Elegant supper-club ambience; classic fare focusing on fresh seafood, perfectly cooked meats. Outdoor dining and piano bar.

### STEAK/PRIME RIB

**BULL & BEAR** Waldorf Astoria Orlando, 14200 Bonnet Creek Resort Ln., Orlando; ☎ 407-597-5500; **waldorfastoriaorlando.com/dining/bulland bear;** expensive. Classic steakhouse with a clubby ambience. Steaks, seafood, lamb chops, and more.

**THE CAPITAL GRILLE** Pointe Orlando, 9101 International Dr., Orlando; ☎ 407-370-4392; **thecapitalgrille.com;** expensive. Dry-aged steaks, good wine list, and classic decor.

## Where to Eat Outside Walt Disney World (continued)

**STEAK/PRIME RIB** (continued)

**TEXAS DE BRAZIL** 5259 International Dr., Orlando; ☎ 407-355-0355; **texas debrazil.com;** expensive. All-you-care-to-eat in an upscale Brazilian-style *churrascaria.* Filet mignon, sausage, pork ribs, chicken, lamb, and more. Kids age 6 and under free, ages 7–12 half-price. Salad bar with 40+ options.

**VITO'S CHOP HOUSE** 8633 International Dr., Orlando; ☎ 407-354-2467; **tinyurl.com/vitosorlando;** moderate. Surprisingly upscale meat house with a taste of Tuscany.

**THAI**

**THAI SILK** 6803 S. Kirkman Rd. at International Drive, Orlando; ☎ 407-226-8997; **thaisilkorlando.com;** moderate. Housed in an unassuming strip-mall location and acclaimed by Orlando dining critics for its authentic Thai dishes. Delicious vegetarian options; impressive wine list. Try the distinctly non-Thai fried cheesecake for dessert.

**THAI THANI** 11025 International Dr., Orlando; ☎ 407-239-9733; 600 Market St., Celebration, ☎ 407-239-9733; **thaithani.net;** moderate. Specializes in Thai duck preparations. Some Chinese stir-fry.

*Continued from page 415*

seafood feasts, Chinese buffets, Indian buffets, breakfast buffets, and a host of combination specials for everything from lobster to barbecue. For a family trying to economize, some of the come-ons are mighty sweet. But are these places any good? Is the food fresh, tasty, and appealing? Are the restaurants clean and inviting? Armed with little more than a roll of Tums, the *Unofficial* research team tried all the eateries that advertise heavily in the tourist magazines. Here's what we discovered.

**CHINESE SUPER BUFFETS** *Whoa!* Talk about an oxymoron. If you've ever tried preparing Chinese food, especially a stir-fry, you know that split-second timing is required to avoid overcooking. So it should come as no big surprise that Chinese dishes languishing on a buffet lose their freshness, texture, and flavor in a hurry.

For the past few editions of this guide, we were able to find several Chinese buffets that were better than the rest and that we felt comfortable recommending. Unfortunately, however, our endorsements seem to be the kiss of death: We return the next year to discover that quality has slipped precipitously. We tried to find a new buffet to replace the ones we deleted from the book, and we can tell you that wasn't fun work. At the end of the day, **Dragon Court Chinese Buffet & Sushi Bar** (12384 S. Apopka–Vineland Road, just after FL 535 turns 90 degrees to the west; ☎ 407-238-9996; **dragoncourtchinese.com**); and **Ace Plus Chinese Buffet** (8701 W. Irlo Bronson Memorial Hwy.; ☎ 407-390-7588; **acepluschinesebuffet.com**) are the only Asian buffets we've elected to list. Dragon Court is friendly and low-key, with a faithful local clientele and a good selection of mainly Chinese dishes. Ace Plus is a good choice if you're staying near where West Irlo Bronson intersects the FL 429 toll road.

**INDIAN BUFFETS** Indian food works better on a buffet than Chinese food; in fact, it actually improves as the flavors marry. In the Disney World area, most Indian restaurants offer a buffet at lunch only—not too convenient if you're spending your day at the theme parks. If you're out shopping or taking a day off, these Indian buffets are worth trying:

**AASHIRWAD INDIAN CUISINE** 5748 International Dr., at the corner of International Drive and Kirkman Road; ☎ 407-370-9830

**PUNJAB INDIAN RESTAURANT** 7451 International Dr.; ☎ 407-352-7887

**SOUTH AMERICAN BUFFETS** A number of these have sprung up along International Drive. The best of these is **Café Mineiro** (6432 International Dr.; ☎ 407-248-2932; **cafemineiroorlando.com**), a Brazilian steakhouse north of Sand Lake Road. The Argentinean churrasco specialties at **The Knife** (12501 FL 535; ☎ 786-866-3999; **thekniferestaurant.com**) are worth a try as well.

**SEAFOOD AND LOBSTER BUFFETS** These affairs don't exactly fall under the category of inexpensive dining. The main draw (no pun intended) is all the lobster you can eat. The problem is that lobsters, like Chinese food, don't wear well on a steam table. After a few minutes on the buffet line, they make better tennis balls than dinner. If, however, there's someone in the kitchen who knows how to steam a lobster, and if you grab your lobster immediately after a fresh batch has been brought out, it'll probably be fine. Two lobster buffets are on International Drive, and another is on US 192. Although all three do a reasonable job, we prefer **Boston Lobster Feast** (6071 W. Irlo Bronson Memorial Hwy.; ☎ 407-396-2606; and 8731 International Dr., five blocks north of the Convention Center; ☎ 407-248-8606; **bostonlobsterfeast.com**). Both locations are distinguished by a vast variety of seafood in addition to the lobster. The International Drive location is cavernous and noisy, which is why we prefer the Irlo Bronson location, where you can actually have a conversation over dinner. The International Drive location has ample parking, while the Irlo Bronson restaurant does not. At about $38 for early birds (4–6 p.m.) and $43 after 6 p.m., dining is expensive at both locations.

**SALAD BUFFETS** The most popular of these in the Walt Disney World area is **Sweet Tomatoes** (6877 S. Kirkman Rd., ☎ 407-363-1616; 12561 S. Apopka–Vineland Rd., ☎ 407-938-9461; 3236 Rolling Oaks Blvd., off US 192 near the FL 429 western entrance to Disney World, ☎ 407-966-4664; **sweettomatoes.com**). During lunch and dinner, you can expect a line out the door, but fortunately one that moves fast. The buffet features prepared salads and an extensive array of ingredients for building your own. In addition to the rabbit food, Sweet Tomatoes offers a variety of soups, a modest pasta bar, a baked-potato bar, an assortment of fresh fruit, and ice-cream sundaes. Dinner runs $10.49 for adults, $5 for children ages 6–12, and $3.49 for children ages 3–5. Lunch is $8.89 for adults and the same prices as dinner for children.

**BREAKFAST AND ENTREE BUFFETS** Most chain steakhouses in the area, including **Ponderosa, Sizzler,** and **Golden Corral,** offer entree buffets. Among them, they have 18 locations in the Walt Disney World area. All serve breakfast, lunch, and dinner. At lunch and dinner, you get the buffet when you buy an entree, usually a steak; breakfast service is a straightforward buffet (that is, you don't have to buy an entree). As for the food, it's chain-restaurant quality but decent all the same. Prices are a bargain, and you can get in and out at lightning speed—important at breakfast when you're trying to get to the parks early. Some locations offer lunch and dinner buffets at a set price without your having to buy an entree.

Though you can argue about which chain serves the best steak, **Golden Corral** wins the buffet contest hands-down, with at least twice as many offerings as its three competitors. While buffets at Golden Corral and Ponderosa are pretty consistent from location to location, the buffets at the different Sizzlers vary a good deal. Our pick of the Sizzlers is the one at 7602 W. Irlo Bronson Memorial Hwy. (☎ 407-397-0997). In addition to the steakhouses, WDW-area **Shoney's** also offer breakfast, lunch, and dinner buffets. Local freebie visitor magazines are full of discount coupons for all of the previous restaurants.

**MEAL DEALS** Discount coupons are available for a wide range of restaurants, including some wonderful upscale-ethnic places such as **Ming Court** (Chinese; 9188 International Dr., Orlando; ☎ 407-351-9988; **ming-court.com**).

A meat eater's delight is the Feast for Four at **Sonny's Real Pit Bar-B-Q.** For $40 per family of four, you get sliced pork and beef plus chicken, ribs, your choice of three sides (choose from beans, slaw, fries, among others), garlic bread or corn bread, and soft drinks or tea, all served family-style. The closest Sonny's location to Walt Disney World and Universal is at 7423 S. Orange Blossom Trail in Orlando (☎ 407-859-7197; **sonnysbbq.com.**) No coupons are available (or needed) for Sonny's, but they're available for the other "meateries."

A meatery to approach with caution is **Western Sizzlin's Wood Grill Buffet** (11701 International Dr.; ☎ 407-778-4844), whose ubiquitous ads tantalizingly depict steak, ribs, and the like. In point of fact, none of these items are available for lunch, and we advise calling ahead to see what's available for dinner.

**COUPONS** Find discounts and two-for-one coupons for many of the restaurants mentioned in freebie visitor guides available at most hotels outside of Walt Disney World. The **Orlando–Orange County Official Visitors Center** (8723 International Dr.; ☎ 407-363-5872; open daily, 8:30 a.m.–6:30 p.m., except Christmas) offers a treasure trove of coupons and free visitor magazines. On the Internet, check out **coupons alacarte.com** and **orlandocoupons.com** for printable coupons.

# DINING *in* WALT DISNEY WORLD

THIS SECTION AIMS TO HELP YOU find good food without going broke or tripping over a culinary land mine. More than 135 restaurants operate within the World, including about 70 full-service establishments, more than 30 of which are inside the theme parks. Disney restaurants offer exceptional variety, serving everything from Moroccan lamb to Texas barbecue. Most restaurants are expensive, and many serve less-than-distinguished fare, but there are good choices in every area of Walt Disney World.

## GETTING IT RIGHT

ALTHOUGH WE WORK HARD to be fair, objective, and accurate, many readers, like this woman from Charleston, West Virginia, think we're too critical of Walt Disney World restaurants:

> Get a life! It's crazy and unrealistic to be so snobbish about restaurants at a theme park. Considering the number of people Disney feeds each day, I think they do a darn good job. Also, you act so surprised that the food is expensive. Have you ever eaten at an airport? HELLO IN THERE? . . . Surprise, you're a captive! It's a theme park!

And a mom from Erie, Pennsylvania, struck a practical note:

> Most of the food at Walt Disney World is OK. If you pay attention to what other visitors say and what's in the guidebooks, you can avoid the yucky places. It's true that you pay more than you should, but it's more convenient to eat in Walt Disney World than to run around trying to find cheaper restaurants somewhere else.

As you may infer from these reader comments, researching and reviewing restaurants is no straightforward endeavor—to the contrary, it's fraught with peril. We have read dining reviews by writers who turn up their noses at anything except four-star French restaurants. We've read reviews absolutely devoid of criticism, written by "experts" unwilling to risk offending the source of their free meals. Finally, we've seen reviews in dining guides that are wholly based on surveys submitted by diners whose credentials for evaluating fine dining are mysterious at best and questionable at least.

*un*official **TIP**
Our research team has eaten at every restaurant, kiosk, bar, cart, and food stand in Walt Disney World many times.

How, then, do we go about presenting the best possible dining coverage? At the *Unofficial Guide,* we begin with highly qualified culinary experts and then balance their opinions with those of our readers— which, by the way, don't always coincide. (Likewise, the coauthors' assessments don't always agree with those of our dining experts.)

In the spirit of democracy, we encourage you to fill out our online reader survey at **touringplans.com/walt-disney-world/survey.** If you'd like to share your dining experience in greater depth, we also invite you to write us at the address on page 13 or send us an e-mail: **unofficialguides@menasharidge.com.**

# DISNEY DINING 101

## DISNEY DINING PLANS

DISNEY OFFERS SEVERAL DINING PLANS. If you choose to sign up for a plan, you must do so when you book your Disney resort room or package vacation; for this reason, we explore the topic in-depth in Part Three, Accommodations.

## WAITER, THESE PRICES ARE GIVING ME HEARTBURN!

INCREASES IN DISNEY'S TICKET COSTS are always sure to grab headlines, but most people haven't noticed that Disney's restaurant prices rise about as fast. For example, while the cost of a one-day theme park ticket has increased about 20% since 2010, the average entree price at Le Cellier has gone from around $30 to $40—an increase of 38%. Plus, Disney levies a "dining surcharge" during the summer and other busy times of year. Factoring in the surcharge, an adult breakfast at The Crystal Palace has increased almost 43% during the same time.

You might need a stiff drink after seeing those menu prices, but booze is no bargain either. While the average bottle of wine in WDW costs three times as much as retail, some wines have much higher markups. For example, a $6 bottle of Placido Pinot Grigio costs $39 in Epcot and various Disney resort lounges—six-and-a-half times as much as the retail price. If you rent a car and eat dinner each day at non-Disney restaurants, you'll save enough to more than pay for the rental cost.

This comment from a New Orleans mom spells it out:

*Disney keeps pushing prices up and up. For us, the sky is NOT the limit. We won't be back.*

## BEHIND THE SCENES AT ADVANCE RESERVATIONS

THOUGH THEY'RE CALLED Advance Reservations, most reservations at Disney World don't guarantee you a table at a specific time as they would at your typical hometown restaurant. Disney restaurants operate on what they call a "template system." Instead of scheduling Advance Reservations for actual tables, reservations fill time slots. The number of slots available is based on the average length of time that guests occupy a table at a particular restaurant, adjusted for seasonality.

Here's a rough example of how it works: Let's say Coral Reef Restaurant at Epcot has 40 tables for four and 8 tables for six, and that the average length of time for a family to be seated, order, eat, pay, and depart is 40 minutes. Add 5 minutes to bus the table and set it up for the next guests, and the table is turning every 45 minutes. The restaurant provides Disney's central dining-reservations system **(CDRS)** with a computer template of its capacity, along with the average time the table is occupied. When you use Disney World's dining website (**disney world.disney.go.com/dining**) or call its dining hotline (at ☎ 407-WDW-DINE, 939-3463), both access CDRS for your requests.

Thus, when you use the website to make Advance Reservations for four people at 6:15 p.m., CDRS removes one table for four from overall capacity for 45 minutes. The template on the system indicates that the table will be unavailable for reassignment until 7 p.m. (45 minutes later). So it goes for all tables in the restaurant, each being subtracted from overall capacity for 45 minutes, then listed as available again, then assigned to other guests and subtracted again, and so on, throughout the meal period. CDRS tries to fill every time slot for every seat in the restaurant, or come as close to filling every slot as possible. No seats—repeat, none—are reserved for walk-ins.

Templates are filled differently depending on the season and restaurant. All Disney restaurants now charge a no-show fee; this has reduced the no-show rate to as little as 2%, and these restaurants are booked every day according to their actual capacity.

A couple of tips: Only one person needs to dine at the restaurant for Disney to consider your reservation fulfilled, even if you've got a reservation for more people. Also, while Disney says it requires 24 hours' notice, you can cancel up until midnight of the day before your meal. The upside to the no-show fee is that it's easier to book most restaurants closer to the date of your visit, as the fee discourages tentative plans.

With Advance Reservations, your wait will usually be less than 20 minutes during peak hours, and often less than 10 minutes. If you're a walk-in, especially during busier seasons, expect to either wait 40–75 minutes or be told that no tables are available.

## GETTING ADVANCE RESERVATIONS AT POPULAR RESTAURANTS

DINNER AT THE MAGIC KINGDOM'S **Be Our Guest** restaurant, in Fantasyland, and the 8 a.m. breakfast slots at **Cinderella's Royal Table,** in Cinderella Castle, are the two hardest-to-get reservations in Walt Disney World. Why? Be Our Guest has arguably the best food in the park, awesome special effects, and good word of mouth; Cinderella's Royal Table is Disney's tiniest character-meal restaurant, accommodating only about 130 diners at a time. You'll have to put in some effort to secure an Advance Reservation at these places.

*unofficial* **TIP** Disney charges a $10-to-$25-per-person penalty for missing an Advance Reservation, or if you cancel on the day of the meal.

The easiest and fastest way to get a reservation is go to **disneyworld.disney.go.com/dining** starting at 6 a.m. Eastern time, a full hour before phone reservations open. To familiarize yourself with how the site works, try it out a couple of days before you actually make reservations. You'll also save time by setting up an account online before your 180-day booking window, making sure to enter any credit card information needed to guarantee your reservations.

If you live in California and have to get up at 3 a.m. Pacific time to make a reservation, Disney couldn't care less: There's no limit to the number of hoops they can make patrons jump through if demand exceeds supply.

Disney's website is usually within a few seconds of the official time as determined by the US Naval Observatory or the National Institute of Standards and Technology, accessible online at **time.gov.** Using this site, synchronize your computer to the second the night before your 180-day window opens.

Early on the morning you want to make reservations, take a few minutes to type the date of your visit into a word processor in MM/DD/YYYY format (for example, 11/16/2015 for November 16, 2015). Select the date and copy it to your computer's clipboard by pressing the **Ctrl** and **C** keys simultaneously (**Command-C** on Mac) or right-clicking your mouse and selecting "Copy"). This will save you from having to type in the date when the site comes online.

Next, start trying Disney's website about 3 minutes before 6 a.m. You'll see a text box where you can specify the date of your visit. Click the text box and press **Ctrl-A,** then **Ctrl-V** (substitute **Command** for **Ctrl** on Mac) to paste the date; then press the tab key on your keyboard. (You can also click on the blue calendar icon to flip through

## Advance Reservations: The Official Line

YOU CAN RESERVE THE FOLLOWING up to 180 days in advance:

**AFTERNOON TEA AND CHILDREN'S PROGRAMS** at the Grand Floridian Resort & Spa

**ALL DISNEY TABLE-SERVICE RESTAURANTS** and character-dining venues

***FANTASMIC!* DINING PACKAGE** at Disney's Hollywood Studios

***HOOP-DEE-DOO MUSICAL REVUE*** at Fort Wilderness Resort & Campground

***MICKEY'S BACKYARD BBQ*** at Fort Wilderness Resort & Campground

***SPIRIT OF ALOHA DINNER SHOW*** at the Polynesian Resort

Guests staying at Walt Disney World resorts—these do not include the Swan, the Dolphin, Shades of Green, or the hotels of the Downtown Disney Resort Area—can book their dining 180 days before their arrival date and can book dining reservations for their entire length of stay (up to 10 days).

a month-by-month calendar, or you can select the entire date in the text box, right-click your mouse, and select "Paste," but these are slower.) You'll also see a place to specify the time of your meal and your party size; you can fill these in ahead of time, too.

Above the "Party Size" widget is a text box with the words "Search Within Dining." Start typing your restaurant name in that text box. As soon as you start typing, the website will start guessing which restaurant you want and offer a list of suggestions. It's faster if you just type a few letters—*bog* or *cin* is enough for the site to know you mean Be Our Guest or Cinderella's Royal Table, respectively. Click on the desired restaurant in the list of suggestions. Finally, click "Find a Table" or hit the Enter key on your keyboard—both submit your request to CDRS.

If your date isn't yet available, a message will appear saying "There is a problem searching for reservations at this time" or something similar. If this happens, refresh the browser page and start over. If you don't see an error message, however, the results returned will tell you whether your restaurant has a table available.

Note that while you're typing, other guests are trying to make Advance Reservations, too, so you want the transaction to go down as quickly as possible. Flexibility on your part counts—it's much harder to get a seating for a large group, so give some thought to breaking your group into numbers that can be accommodated at tables for four. Also make sure that you have your credit card out where you can read it.

All Advance Reservations for Cinderella's Royal Table character meals, the *Fantasmic!* Dining Package, the *Hoop-Dee-Doo Musical Revue,* the *Spirit of Aloha Dinner Show,* and *Mickey's Backyard BBQ* require complete prepayment with a credit card at the time of the booking. The name on the booking can't be changed after the Advance Reservation is made. Reservations may be canceled, with the deposit refunded in full, by calling ☎ 407-WDW-DINE at least 24 hours (Cindy's) or 48 hours (*Fantasmic!* and the dinner shows) before seating time.

While many readers have been successful using our strategies, some have not:

## Advance Reservations: The *Unofficial* Scoop

BECAUSE DISNEY CHARGES a $10-to-$25-per-person no-show penalty at its restaurants, no-show rates have dropped almost to zero. The penalty ensures that serious diners have some chance to get into Disney's better restaurants.

These days you'll need to reserve only a few breakfast venues in advance most times of the year. The most popular of these is **Cinderella's Royal Table** at the Magic Kingdom. If you don't care what time you eat, you'll need to call about 10 weeks out to get in for breakfast. If you're visiting during a holiday or peak season, or you want a specific time such as 8 a.m., you'll need to call a full 180 days in advance. If Cindy's is unavailable, we recommend **'Ohana** at the Polynesian Resort, which can be booked as little as a week before your trip.

Likewise, only a handful of restaurants require lunch reservations. The most popular is Epcot's **Le Cellier Steakhouse,** in the Canada Pavilion, which fills up about three months in advance; Cinderella's Royal Table, which fills up during about the same time frame; and **Akershus Royal Banquet Hall** in the Norway Pavilion, which fills up about 7-10 weeks out.

Except for **Be Our Guest Restaurant** at the Magic Kingdom, for which reservations are snapped up as soon as they're available, dinner reservations are generally easy to get within 60 days at most locations, as long as you're not particular about the time you eat. (If that's critical to your family's happiness, click or call 180 days in advance.)

*I got up extra-early 180 days before our trip to get Thanksgiving reservations at Le Cellier for my husband's birthday. Even though I logged on to Disney's website right at 6 a.m., by the time I got done typing and clicking the only table that was available was for 8:40 p.m.—too late for our children, and we would have missed IllumiNations.*

On most days, a couple hundred users slam Disney's computer system within milliseconds of one another. With this volume, a 20th of a second or less can make the difference between getting a table and not getting one. As it happens, there are variables beyond your control. One is the number of computers through which your request passes before it reaches Disney's reservation system. The explanation is somewhat technical, but the same principle applies whether you're trying to get dining reservations online with Disney or concert seats through Ticketmaster.

When you enter a URL into your browser, the request for that page gets passed through a series of intermediate computers spread throughout the Internet. The specific route is chosen based on network speed and traffic volume, and preference is given to faster routes. For example, from Len Testa's house in Greensboro, North Carolina, the request for Disney's dining page usually goes from his computer to a small Time Warner Cable facility in Greensboro. From there it's routed through Raleigh, North Carolina, to Washington, D.C. From Washington it goes through Chicago, then Denver, and then Las Vegas before finally making it to Disney's computers. (This also tells us that Disney's computers may be hosted somewhere out west—nowhere near Orlando.)

Distance counts too, though we're talking milliseconds. Thus, it takes just a bit longer for a request to reach Disney's computers from Chicago than from Atlanta, longer yet if you're trying from New York.

If you don't have access to a computer at 6 a.m. on the morning you need to make reservations, be ready to call ☎ 407-WDW-DINE at 7 a.m. Eastern time and follow the prompts to speak to a live person. You may still get placed on hold if call volume is higher than usual, and you'll be an hour behind the early birds with computers. Still, you'll be well ahead of those who couldn't make it up before sunrise.

Also, if you're on the Disney Dining Plan and you want to book the *Fantasmic!* package, Cinderella's Royal Table, or one the dinner shows, you may be better off reserving by phone. The online system may not recognize your table-service credits, but you can book and pay with a credit card and then call ☎ 407-WDW-DINE after 7 a.m. and have them credit the charge for the meal back to your card (a potential hassle if you get an uncooperative cast member). When you get to Walt Disney World, you'll use credits from your dining plan to "pay" for the meal. (Sometimes the online system has glitches and shows no availability; in this case, call after 7 a.m. to confirm if the online system is correct.)

**NEVER, NEVER, NEVER, NEVER GIVE UP** Not getting what you want the first time you try doesn't mean the end of the story. A mom from Cincinnati advises persistence in securing Advance Reservations:

> *I was crushed when I called and tried to reserve Chef Mickey's and couldn't. I decided not to give up and would go online once or twice a day to check reservations for Chef Mickey's and the other restaurants I wanted. It took me about a week, but sooner or later I ended up booking every single reservation I wanted except 'Ohana.*

**LAST-MINUTE ADVANCE RESERVATIONS** Because Advance Reservations require a credit card, and because a fee is charged for failing to cancel in time, you can often score a last-minute reservation. This is attributable to reservation-holders who are tired or have last-minute conflicts calling in at the last moment to avoid paying the $10-per-head penalty. As long as the reservation-holder calls to cancel before midnight the day before, he or she won't be charged. So your best shot at picking up a canceled reservation is to repeatedly call or ping **disneyworld.disney.go.com/dining** as often as possible between 10 and 11 p.m.

***STILL* CAN'T GET AN ADVANCE RESERVATION?** Go to the restaurant on the day you wish to dine and try for a table as a walk-in (most full-service restaurants take walk-ins between 2:30 and 4:30 p.m.). This is a long shot, though you may be able to swing it during the least busy times of year or on cold or rainy days during busier seasons, when there's a greater chance of no-shows. If you try to walk in then, your chances are best during the last hour of serving.

*un*official **TIP**
Smoking is banned at all restaurants and lounges at Walt Disney World.

Landing an Advance Reservation for Cinderella's Royal Table at dinner is somewhat easier than for breakfast or lunch, but the price is a whopping $73 for adults and $43 for children ages 3–9. As at the other two meals, five photos of your group, a photo of Cinderella Castle, and a Cinderella-themed photo holder are included in the price—like it or not. If you're unable to lock up a table for breakfast or lunch, a dinner reservation will at least get your children inside the castle.

**NO-SHOW FEES**  As noted earlier, Disney charges a per-person penalty if you fail to show up for an Advance Reservation the day of the meal. A $10 no-show fee is enforced at all Disney sit-down restaurants; at **Victoria & Albert's,** it's $25 for the main dining room, $50 for Queen Victoria's Room and Chef's Table (the latter two also require 48 hours' notice to cancel an Advance Reservation).

## DRESS

DRESS IS INFORMAL at most theme park restaurants, but Disney has a "business casual" dress code for some of its resort restaurants: khakis, dress slacks, jeans, or dress shorts with a collared shirt for men and capris, skirts, dresses, jeans, and dress shorts for women. Restaurants with this dress code are **Jiko—The Cooking Place** at Animal Kingdom Lodge & Villas, the **Flying Fish Cafe** at the BoardWalk, the **California Grill** at the Contemporary Resort, **Monsieur Paul** at Epcot's France Pavilion, **Cítricos** and **Narcoossee's** at the Grand Floridian Resort & Spa, **Artist Point** at Wilderness Lodge & Villas, **Yachtsman Steakhouse** at the Yacht Club Resort, **Todd English's bluezoo** and **Shula's Steak House** at the Dolphin, and **Il Mulino New York Trattoria** at the Swan. **Victoria & Albert's** at the Grand Floridian is the only Disney restaurant that requires men to wear a jacket to dinner.

## FOOD ALLERGIES AND SPECIAL REQUESTS

IF YOU HAVE SPECIAL DIETARY NEEDS, make them known when you make your Advance Reservations. For more information, see Part Seven, Special Tips for Special People.

A Phillipsburg, New Jersey, mom reports her family's experience:

*My 6-year-old has many food allergies. When making my Advance Reservations, I indicated these to the clerk. When we arrived at the restaurants, the staff was already aware of my child's allergies and assigned our table a chef who double-checked the list of allergies with us. The chefs were very nice and made my son feel very special.*

## A FEW CAVEATS

BEFORE YOU BEGIN EATING your way through the World, you need to know a few things:

1. Theme park restaurants rush their customers in order to make room for the next group of diners. Dining at high speed may appeal to a family with young, restless children, but for people wanting to relax, it's more like eating in a pressure chamber than fine dining.

2. Disney restaurants have comparatively few tables for parties of two, and servers are generally disinclined to seat two guests at larger tables. If you're a duo, you might have to wait longer—sometimes much longer— to be seated.

3. At full-service Disney restaurants, an automatic gratuity of 18% is added to your tab for parties of six or more—even at buffets where you serve yourself.

4. If you're dining in a theme park and cost is an issue, make lunch your main meal. Lunch entrees are similar to dinner entrees, but they're significantly cheaper.

**5.** Disney frequently adds a surcharge of $4 per adult and $2 per child to certain popular restaurants during weeks of peak attendance, including Presidents Day, Spring Break, Easter, mid-December–New Year's Eve, and every day from early June to early August. The following restaurants participate in the gouging: **Akershus Royal Banquet Hall** (Princess Storybook Dining), **Biergarten, Boma—Flavors of Africa** (breakfast and dinner), **Cape May Cafe** (breakfast and dinner buffet), **Chef Mickey's** (breakfast and dinner), **Cinderella's Royal Table, The Crystal Palace, Garden Grill Restaurant, Hollywood & Vine** (Play 'n Dine character buffets), *Liberty Tree Tavern* (dinner), **1900 Park Fare** (Supercalifragilistic Breakfast and Cinderella's Happily Ever After Dinner), **'Ohana** (breakfast and dinner), the *Spirit of Aloha Dinner Show,* **Trail's End Restaurant** at Fort Wilderness (an exception: $2 extra for adults and $1 for kids), and **Tusker House Restaurant.**

# WALT DISNEY WORLD RESTAURANT CATEGORIES

IN GENERAL, food and beverage offerings at Walt Disney World are defined by service, price, and convenience:

**FULL-SERVICE RESTAURANTS** Full-service restaurants are in all Disney resorts (except the All-Star Resorts, Art of Animation, Port Orleans French Quarter, and Pop Century) and all major theme parks, Downtown Disney Marketplace, and Downtown Disney West Side. Disney operates most of the restaurants in the theme parks and its hotels, while contractors or franchisees operate the restaurants in hotels of the Downtown Disney Resort Area (DDRA), the Swan and Dolphin resorts, and some in Disney's Animal Kingdom, Epcot, the BoardWalk, and Downtown Disney Marketplace–West Side. Advance Reservations (see pages 422–426) are recommended for most full-service restaurants except those in the DDRA. The restaurants accept American Express, Carte Blanche, Diners Club, Japan Credit Bureau, MasterCard, and Visa.

**BUFFETS AND FAMILY-STYLE RESTAURANTS** Many of these have Disney characters in attendance, and most have a separate children's menu featuring dishes such as hot dogs, burgers, chicken nuggets, pizza, macaroni and cheese, and spaghetti and meatballs. In addition to the buffets, several restaurants serve a family-style, all-you-can-eat, fixed-price meal.

Advance Reservations are required for character buffets and recommended for all other buffets and family-style restaurants. Most credit cards are accepted. As noted earlier, an automatic 18% gratuity is added to the bill for parties of six or more, but when the tipping is at your discretion, a North Carolina reader urges generosity with the waitstaff:

> I've seen diners leave a dollar or two per person at buffets. I've also heard of people protesting Disney's prices by leaving a small tip or none at all. This is unacceptable—these servers keep your drinks full, keep your plates clean, and check on you constantly. They deserve at least 15–18%. If you can't afford to tip, you shouldn't eat there.

If you want to eat a lot but don't feel like standing in yet another line, then consider one of the all-you-can-eat family-style restaurants. These feature platters of food brought to your table in courses by a server. You can eat as much as you like—even go back to a favorite

## Walt Disney World Buffets and Family-Style Restaurants

| LOCATION | RESTAURANT | CUISINE | MEALS SERVED | CHAR-ACTERS |
|---|---|---|---|---|
| ANIMAL KINGDOM LODGE | Boma— Flavors of Africa | African (D), American (B) | B, D | No |
| BEACH CLUB RESORT | Cape May Cafe | American | B, D | Yes (B) |
| CONTEMPORARY RESORT | Chef Mickey's | American | B, D | Yes |
| DISNEY'S ANIMAL KINGDOM | Tusker House | African (L, D), American (B) | B, L, D | Yes (B, L) |
| DISNEY'S HOLLYWOOD STUDIOS | Hollywood & Vine | American | B, L, D | Yes (B, L) |
| EPCOT | Akershus Royal Banquet Hall | American (B), Norwegian (L, D) | B, L, D | Yes |
| EPCOT | Biergarten | German | L, D | No |
| EPCOT | The Garden Grill | American | D | Yes |
| FORT WILDERNESS | Hoop-Dee-Doo Musical Revue | American | D | No |
| FORT WILDERNESS | Mickey's Backyard BBQ | American | D | Yes |
| FORT WILDERNESS | Trail's End Restaurant | American | B***, L, D*** | No |
| GRAND FLORIDIAN | 1900 Park Fare | American | B, D | Yes |
| THE MAGIC KINGDOM | Cinderella's Royal Table | American | B*, L, D | Yes |
| THE MAGIC KINGDOM | The Crystal Palace | American | B, L, D | Yes |
| THE MAGIC KINGDOM | Liberty Tree Tavern | American | L, D† | No |
| POLYNESIAN RESORT | 'Ohana | Polynesian | B, D | Yes (B) |
| POLYNESIAN RESORT | Spirit of Aloha Dinner Show | American | D | No |
| SWAN | Garden Grove | American | B‡, L‡, D | Yes (B**) |
| WILDERNESS LODGE | Whispering Canyon Cafe | American | B, L, D | No |
| WYNDHAM LAKE BUENA VISTA RESORT | LakeView Restaurant | American | B****, D | Yes (B§) |
| YACHT CLUB RESORT | Captain's Grille | American | B*, L, D | No |

| | |
|---|---|
| * | Serves family-style meals only at breakfast. |
| ** | Character-breakfast buffet served only on weekends. |
| *** | Serves buffet-style meals only at breakfast and dinner. |
| **** | Serves buffet-style meals only at breakfast. |
| § | Character-breakfast buffet served three times a week. |
| † | Serves family-style meals only at dinner. |
| ‡ | Serves family-style meals only at breakfast and lunch. |

appetizer after you finish the main course. The food tends to be a little better than what you'll find on a buffet line.

The table above lists buffets and family-style restaurants (where you can belly up for bulk loading) at Walt Disney World.

**FOOD COURTS** Featuring a collection of counter-service eateries under one roof, food courts can be found at the Moderate resorts (Coronado

Springs, Caribbean Beach, Port Orleans) and Value resorts (All-Star, Art of Animation, and Pop Century). (The closest thing to a food court at the theme parks is **Sunshine Seasons** at Epcot; see below and page 453.) Advance Reservations are neither required nor available at these restaurants.

**COUNTER SERVICE** Counter-service fast food is available in all theme parks and at Downtown Disney Marketplace, the BoardWalk, and Downtown Disney West Side. The food compares in quality with Captain D's, McDonald's, or Taco Bell but is more expensive, though often served in larger portions.

**FAST CASUAL** Somewhere between burgers and formal dining are the establishments in Disney's "fast casual" category, including three in the theme parks: **Be Our Guest** in the Magic Kingdom (lunch service), **Sunshine Seasons** in Epcot, and **Studio Catering Co.** in Disney's Hollywood Studios. Fast-casual restaurants feature menu choices a cut above what you'd normally see at a typical counter-service location. At Sunshine Seasons, for example, chefs will prepare grilled salmon on an open cooking surface while you watch, or you can choose from rotisserie chicken or pork, tasty noodle bowls, or large sandwiches made with artisanal breads. Entrees cost about $2 more on average than traditional counter service, but the variety and food quality more than make up for the difference.

**VENDOR FOOD** Vendors abound at the theme parks, Downtown Disney Marketplace, Downtown Disney West Side, and the BoardWalk. Offerings include popcorn, ice-cream bars, churros (Mexican pastries), soft drinks, bottled water, and (in theme parks) fresh fruit. Prices include tax; many vendors are set up to accept credit cards, charges to your room at a Disney resort, and the Disney Dining Plan. Others take only cash (look for a sign near the cash register).

## HARD CHOICES

DINING DECISIONS WILL DEFINITELY affect your Walt Disney World experience. If you're short on time and you want to see the theme parks, avoid full service. Ditto if you're short on funds. If you do want full service, arrange Advance Reservations—again, they won't actually reserve you a table, but they can minimize your wait.

### Integrating Meals into the *Unofficial Guide* Touring Plans

Arrive before the park of your choice opens. Tour expeditiously, using your chosen plan (taking as few breaks as possible), until about 11 or 11:30 a.m. Once the park becomes crowded around midday, meals and other breaks won't affect the plan's efficiency. If you intend to stay in the park for evening parades, fireworks, or other events, eat dinner early enough to be finished in time for the festivities.

### Character Dining

A number of restaurants, primarily those that serve all-you-can-eat buffets and family-style meals, offer character dining. At character meals, you pay a fixed price and dine in the presence of one to five Disney characters who circulate throughout the restaurant, hugging children (and sometimes adults), posing for photos, and signing autographs. Character breakfasts, lunches, and dinners are served at restaurants in and out of the theme parks. For an extensive discussion of character dining, see the section starting on page 347 in Part Six, Walt Disney World with Kids.

## FULL-SERVICE DINING FOR FAMILIES WITH YOUNG CHILDREN

*unofficial* TIP
Disney Kids' Meals are for kids ages 3–9.

DISNEY RESTAURANTS OFFER an excellent (though expensive) opportunity to introduce young children to the variety and excitement of ethnic food. No matter how formal a restaurant appears, the staff is accustomed to fidgety, impatient, and often boisterous children. **Les Chefs de France** at Epcot, for instance, may be the nation's only French restaurant where most patrons wear shorts and T-shirts and at least two dozen young diners are attired in basic black . . . mouse ears.

Almost all Disney restaurants offer kids' menus, and all have booster seats and high chairs. Servers understand how tough it may be for children to sit still for an extended period of time, and they'll supply little ones with crackers and rolls and serve your dinner much faster than in comparable restaurants elsewhere. Reader letters suggest that being served too quickly is much more common than having a long wait.

### Good Walt Disney World Theme Park Restaurants for Children

In Epcot, preschoolers most enjoy the **Biergarten** in Germany, **San Angel Inn** in Mexico, and **Coral Reef Restaurant** at the Seas with Nemo & Friends Pavilion in Future World. The Biergarten combines a rollicking and noisy atmosphere with good basic food, including roast chicken; a German oompah band entertains, and kids can often participate in Bavarian dancing. San Angel Inn is in the Mexico village marketplace. From the table, children can watch boats on the Gran Fiesta Tour drift beneath a smoking volcano. With a choice of chips, tacos, and other familiar items, picky kids usually have no difficulty finding something to eat. (Be aware, though, that the service here is sometimes glacially slow.) Coral Reef, with tables beside windows looking into The Seas' aquarium, offers a satisfying mealtime diversion for all ages. If your children don't eat fish, Coral Reef also serves beef and chicken.

The Biergarten offers reasonable value, plus good food. The Coral Reef Restaurant and San Angel Inn are overpriced, though the food is palatable.

**Be Our Guest Restaurant** and **Cinderella's Royal Table,** both in Fantasyland, are the hot tickets in the Magic Kingdom, but reservations are often unobtainable. (At present, there are no characters at Be Our Guest.) We think the best kids' fare is at the **Liberty Tree Tavern,** and it's easy to book, too.

At Disney's Hollywood Studios, all ages enjoy the atmosphere and entertainment at **Hollywood & Vine,** the **Sci-Fi Dine-In Theater Restaurant,** and the **50's Prime Time Cafe.** Unfortunately, the Sci-Fi's food is close to dismal except for dessert, and the Prime Time's is uneven.

The three full-service restaurants at Disney's Animal Kingdom are **Tusker House Restaurant** (actually a buffet); **Rainforest Cafe,** a great favorite of children; and **Yak & Yeti Restaurant.**

## QUIET, ROMANTIC PLACES TO EAT

RESTAURANTS WITH GOOD FOOD and a couple-friendly ambience are rare in the theme parks. Only a handful of dining locales satisfy both requirements: **Coral Reef Restaurant,** an alfresco table at **Tutto Italia Ristorante,** the terrace at the **Rose & Crown Dining Room,** and the upstairs tables at the France Pavilion's **Monsieur Paul,** all in Epcot; and the corner booths at **The Hollywood Brown Derby** in Disney's Hollywood Studios. Waterfront dining (though not necessarily quiet or romantic) is available at **Fulton's Crab House, Paradiso 37,** and **Portobello** at Downtown Disney and **Narcoossee's** at the Grand Floridian.

**Victoria & Albert's** at the Grand Floridian is the World's showcase gourmet restaurant; expect to pay big bucks. Other good choices for couples include **Artist Point** at Wilderness Lodge, **Yachtsman Steakhouse** at the Yacht Club, **Shula's Steak House** at the Dolphin, **Jiko—The Cooking Place** at Animal Kingdom Lodge, and **Flying Fish Cafe** at the BoardWalk.

*unofficial* **TIP**
The **California Grill** atop the Contemporary Resort has the best view at Walt Disney World.

Eating later in the evening and choosing a restaurant we've mentioned will improve your chances for intimate dining; nevertheless, children—well behaved or otherwise—are everywhere at Walt Disney World, and there's no way to escape them. These honeymooners from Slidell, Louisiana, write:

> We made dinner reservations at some of the nicer Disney restaurants. We made sure to reserve past dinner hours, and we tried to stress that we were on our honeymoon. In every restaurant we went to, we were seated next to large families. The kids were usually tired and cranky. It's very difficult to enjoy a romantic dinner when there are small children crawling around under your table. Our suggestion: Seat couples without children together and families with kids elsewhere.

## FAST FOOD IN THE THEME PARKS

BECAUSE MOST MEALS DURING a Disney World vacation are consumed on the run while touring, we'll tackle counter-service and vendor foods first. Plentiful in all theme parks are hot dogs, hamburgers, chicken sandwiches, salads, and pizza. They're augmented by special items that relate to the park's theme or the part of the park you're touring. In Epcot's Germany, for example, counter-service bratwurst and beer are sold. In Frontierland in the Magic Kingdom, vendors sell smoked turkey legs. Counter-service prices are fairly consistent from park to park. Expect to pay the same for your coffee or hot dog at Disney's Animal Kingdom as at Disney's Hollywood Studios.

Getting your act together in regard to counter-service restaurants in the parks is more a matter of courtesy than necessity. Rude guests rank fifth among reader complaints. A mother from Fort Wayne, Indiana, points out that indecision can be as maddening as outright discourtesy, especially when you're hungry:

> Every fast-food restaurant has menu signs the size of billboards, but do you think anybody reads them? People waiting in line spend enough time in front of these signs to memorize them and still don't have a clue what they want when they finally get to the counter. If by some miracle they've managed to choose between the hot dog and the hamburger, they then fiddle around another 10 minutes deciding what size Coke to order. Folks, PULEEEZ get your orders together ahead of time!

## THE COST OF COUNTER-SERVICE FOOD

| | |
|---|---|
| BAGEL OR MUFFIN | $2.99 |
| BROWNIE | $3.99 |
| BURRITO | $7.79–$8.99 |
| CAKE OR PIE | $3.19–$3.99 |
| CEREAL WITH MILK | $3.69 |
| CHEESEBURGER WITH FRIES | $10.19–$10.79 |
| CHICKEN-BREAST SANDWICH *(grilled)* | $9.19–$9.99 |
| CHICKEN NUGGETS WITH FRIES | $8.69–$9.29 |
| CHILDREN'S MEAL | $5.99 |
| CHIPS | $2.79–$3.00 |
| COOKIES | $2.50 |
| FISH *(fried)* BASKET WITH FRIES | $7.99–$9.29 |
| FRENCH FRIES | $2.99 |
| FRUIT *(whole)* | $1.49 |
| FRUIT CUP / FRUIT SALAD | $3.59 |
| HOT DOG | $6.99 *(basket)*, $8.59 *(gourmet)* |
| ICE CREAM / FROZEN NOVELTIES | $3.75 |
| NACHOS WITH CHEESE | $3.99–$7.69 |
| PB&J SANDWICH | $2.49 *(à la carte)*, $6.99 *(kids' meal)* |
| PIZZA *(personal)* | $7.29–$9.69 |
| POPCORN | $3.50–$5.25 |
| PRETZEL | $2.95–$4.75 |
| SALAD (ENTREE) | $7.99–$14.00 |
| SALAD (SIDE) | $3.29 |
| SMOKED TURKEY LEG | $9.79 |
| SOUP / CHILI | $3.29–$7.99 |
| SUB / DELI SANDWICH | $5.99–$11.99 |
| TACO SALAD | $7.89–$8.79 |
| VEGGIE BURGER | $8.99 |

## THE COST OF COUNTER-SERVICE DRINKS

| DRINKS | SMALL | LARGE |
|---|---|---|
| BEER | $6.00–$8.00 | $7.99–$12.00 |
| BOTTLED WATER | $1.50 | $2.50 |
| LATTE *(one size)* | $3.99 | $3.99 |
| COFFEE *(one size)* | $2.29 | $2.29 |
| FLOAT, MILKSHAKE, OR SUNDAE *(one size)* | $4.75–$6.25 | $4.75–$6.25 |
| FRUIT JUICE | $2.99 | $3.29 |
| HOT TEA AND COCOA *(one size)* | $2.29 | $2.29 |
| MILK | $1.69 | $2.39 |
| SOFT DRINKS, ICED TEA, AND LEMONADE | $2.69 | $3.19 |

*Refillable souvenir mugs cost $9–$18 (free refills) at Disney resorts and $10 at water parks. Each person on a Disney Dining Plan gets a free mug, refillable at any Disney resort.*

A North Carolina reader offers a tip for helping things along:

*Many counter-service registers serve two queues each, one to the left and one to the right of each register. People are not used to this and will instinctively line up in one queue per register, typically on the right side, leaving the left vacant. We had register operators wave us up to the front several times to start a left queue instead of waiting behind others on the right.*

### Healthful Food at Walt Disney World

*unofficial* **TIP**
Look for the **Mickey Check** icon on healthy menu items such as fresh fruit and low-fat milk.

One of the most commendable developments in food service at Walt Disney World has been the introduction of healthier foods and snacks. People who have diabetes, vegetarians, dieters, those requiring kosher meals, and the like should have no trouble finding something to eat. The same goes for anyone seeking wholesome, nutritious food. Health-conscious choices such as fresh fruit are available at most fast-food counters and even from vendors.

### News for Java Junkies

**Starbucks** are on the Magic Kingdom's Main Street, in Epcot's Future World, and in Downtown Disney (with likely additions in the other parks soon). Also, Disney has replaced its widely panned Nescafé swill with **Joffrey's,** a huge improvement in coffee quality.

### Beyond Counter Service: Tips for Saving Time and Money

Even if you confine your meals to quick-service fare, you lose a lot of time getting food in the theme parks. Here are some ways to minimize the time you spend hunting and gathering:

1. Eat breakfast before you arrive. Restaurants outside the World offer some outstanding breakfast specials. Plus, some hotels furnish small refrigerators in their guest rooms, or you can rent a fridge or bring a cooler. If you can get by on cold cereal, rolls, fruit, and juice, this will save a ton of time.

2. After a good breakfast, buy snacks from vendors in the parks as you tour, or stuff some snacks in a fanny pack.

3. All theme park restaurants are busiest between 11:30 a.m. and 2:15 p.m. for lunch and 6 and 9 p.m. for dinner. For shorter lines and faster service, don't eat during these hours, especially 12:30–1:30 p.m.

4. Many counter-service restaurants sell cold sandwiches. Buy a cold lunch minus drinks before 11:30 a.m., and carry it in small plastic bags until you're ready to eat (within an hour or so of purchase). Ditto for dinner. Buy drinks at the appropriate time from any convenient vendor.

5. Most fast-food eateries have more than one service window. Regardless of the time of day, check the lines at all windows before queuing. Sometimes a window that's staffed but out of the way will have a much shorter line or none at all. Note, however, that some windows may offer only certain items.

6. If you're short on time and the park closes early, stay until closing and eat dinner outside Disney World before returning to your hotel. If the

park stays open late, eat dinner about 4 or 4:30 p.m. at the restaurant of your choice. You should sneak in just ahead of the dinner crowd.

Our readers use variations on these tips with great success. A Missouri mom writes:

*We arrived at WDW after some days on the beach south of Sarasota. We shopped there and arrived with our steel Coleman cooler well stocked with milk and sandwich fixings. I froze a block of ice in a milk bottle, and we replenished it daily with ice from the resort ice machine. I also froze small packages of deli-type meats for later in the week. We ate cereal, milk, and fruit each morning, with boxed juices. I also had a hot pot to boil water for instant coffee, oatmeal, and soup.*

*Each child had a belt bag of his own, which he filled from a special box of "goodies" each day with things like packages of crackers and cheese, packets of peanuts and raisins. Each child also had a small, rectangular plastic water bottle that could hang on the belt. We filled these at water fountains before getting into lines.*

*We left the park before noon, ate sandwiches, chips, and soda in the room, and napped. We purchased our evening meal in the park, at a counter-service eatery. We budgeted for both morning and evening snacks from a vendor but often didn't need them.*

A Whiteland, Indiana, mom suggests:

*If you're traveling with younger kids, take a supply of small paper or plastic cups to split drinks, which are both huge and expensive.*

Finally, from an Acworth, Georgia, mom of two:

*I can't stress the importance of bringing in your own food and drinks— it was a lifesaver. My husband carried a backpack with ice packs for cold food, and I carried the noncold items like chips and candy.*

# DISNEY DINING SUGGESTIONS

FOLLOWING ARE SUGGESTIONS for dining at each of the major theme parks. If you want to try a full-service restaurant at one of the parks, be aware that the restaurants continue to serve after the park's official closing time. We once showed up at The Hollywood Brown Derby just as Disney's Hollywood Studios closed at 8 p.m. We were seated almost immediately and enjoyed a leisurely dinner while the crowds cleared out.

*unofficial* **TIP**
Don't worry about dining late if you're depending on Disney transportation: Buses, boats, and monorails run 1–2 hours after the parks close.

## THE MAGIC KINGDOM

OF THE PARK'S SIX full-service restaurants, **Be Our Guest** (dinner) in Fantasyland is the best, followed by **Liberty Tree Tavern** in Liberty Square and **The Plaza Restaurant** on Main Street. **Cinderella's Royal Table** in the castle and **The Crystal Palace** on Main Street serve a decent-but-expensive character buffet. Avoid **Tony's Town Square Restaurant** on Main Street.

### AUTHORS' FAVORITE COUNTER-SERVICE RESTAURANTS

Be Our Guest (lunch)   *Fantasyland*
Columbia Harbour House   *Liberty Square*

These two restaurants' menus have the most variety within the Magic Kingdom. Be Our Guest serves a tasty tuna niçoise salad (with seared tuna), a grilled-ham-and-cheese sandwich that's better than you'd expect, and a juicy braised-pork entree. Columbia Harbour House's offerings include lobster rolls, grilled salmon, and a delicious hummus sandwich on multigrain bread. Beyond these, the Magic Kingdom's fast-food eateries are undistinguished, not to mention about twice as expensive as McDonald's, for about the same quality. On the positive side, portions are large, sometimes large enough for children to share. Check our mini-profiles of the park's counter-service restaurants before you queue up.

Our dining recommendations for a day at the Magic Kingdom:

1. Obtain a FastPass+ reservation for lunch at Be Our Guest. See **beourguestlunch.disney.go.com.**

2. Take the monorail to one of the hotels for lunch. The trip takes very little time, and because most guests have left the hotels for the parks, the resorts' restaurants are often uncrowded. The food is better than the Magic Kingdom's, the service is faster, the atmosphere is more relaxed, and mixed drinks are available.

3. Full-service restaurants that accept Advance Reservations fill quickly in the summer and during holidays. To obtain Advance Reservations, visit **disneyworld.disney.go.com/reservations/dining,** call ☎ 407-939-3463, or hotfoot it to your chosen restaurant as soon as you enter the park. Advance Reservations are explained starting on page 422, and Magic Kingdom full-service and counter-service restaurants are profiled later in this chapter.

4. A good rule at any full-service restaurant is to keep it simple. Order sandwiches or basic dishes (such as roast turkey and mashed potatoes).

Here are some comments from readers about Magic Kingdom full-service and counter-service restaurants. First, regarding Cinderella's Royal Table, two perspectives from two different readers:

*Reader 1: Our whole family did Cinderella's Royal Table for lunch. Our two little boys (ages 3 and 4) loved it even more than their 6-year-old sister. They loved all the princesses paying special attention to them since they were the only guys in the whole place. My 3-year-old left with his face covered in lipstick and even managed to propose to Cinderella—who, sadly, mentioned she was already married.*

*Reader 2: The food was OK. The place wasn't that big, but the characters spent a lot of time at each table—so much time that we only got to meet Snow White and Belle. Wasn't worth the trouble of getting the seating.*

A mom from Glen Burnie, Maryland, says she was given plenty of time to eat her (mediocre) food:

*The many comments I read about Cinderella's Royal Table rushing guests out the door aren't consistent with our experience. It's a character meal—it's not like guests are eating a leisurely 3-hour multicourse feast at a French restaurant. The food wasn't particularly good, but we never felt rushed. Our server was attentive, and the princesses all spent quite a bit of time making our princess feel like an honored guest.*

There are two things everyone agrees on concerning Be Our Guest: The food is good and it's hard to get into. First, from a Burlington, Ontario, dad:

*The best thing about the vacation: eating lunch at Be Our Guest. The atmosphere and quality of food were unlike any quick-service I'd ever had at Disney.*

From a Kansas City, Missouri, mom:

*Be Our Guest must be the new Cinderella's Royal Table. I tried to get a dinner reservation when we first planned our vacation four months ahead, and I couldn't get one. Fortunately, you can line up for lunch to see the inside of the castle.*

And finally, from a Belgium, Wisconsin, reader:

*I thought the appetizers and desserts at Be Our Guest were far superior to the actual entrees. Also Disney artificially inflates the exclusivity of this restaurant by not utilizing one of the dining rooms at less-than-peak periods and by having, at best, minimal staff, causing my table to have to wait 40 minutes for dessert.*

The Crystal Palace gets mixed reviews. A sampling:

*The food quality and selection were the worst I've seen in 10 years of going there, and the characters were stretched way too thin—only two came to our table in an hour and a half. No longer worth the price, even if it's been a tradition for my family.*

*Of all the restaurants we visited, I can't rave enough about The Crystal Palace. or Liberty Tree Tavern. The food was great (you just can't beat The Crystal Palace's breakfast buffet!), the service was wonderful, and the characters were awesome.*

Like the previous reader, the following reader really liked the Liberty Tree Tavern:

*Didn't expect much here but made a reservation based on your book. What a surprise! The food was great as well as the atmosphere.*

So did this Broussard, Louisiana, couple—though their enthusiasm isn't exactly unqualified:

*We booked a reservation for dinner at Liberty Tree Tavern. What we didn't realize is that it was a set menu. The food was excellent—like Thanksgiving dinner—but the price was crazy! Dinner for two with drinks and tip ran us $90. Not what we were expecting.*

A mom of four from Charleston, South Carolina, enjoyed Columbia Harbour House:

*The lobster roll was yummy. My teen daughter said the shrimp was the best she had ever had, and my teen son loved his salmon. We all left full and happy.*

## EPCOT

SINCE THE BEGINNING, dining has been an integral component of Epcot's entertainment product. The importance of dining is reflected in the number of restaurants and their ability to serve consistently interesting and well-prepared meals. World Showcase has many more restaurants than attractions, and Epcot has added bars, tapas-style eateries, and full-service restaurants faster than any park in memory.

For the most part, Epcot's restaurants have always served decent food, though the World Showcase restaurants have occasionally been timid about delivering honest representations of their host nations' cuisine. That seems to be changing faster in some areas (Mexico) than others (Morocco), but we're hopeful that we see a trend. It's still true that the less adventuresome diner can find steak and potatoes on virtually every menu, but the same kitchens will serve up the real thing for anyone willing to ask.

Many Epcot restaurants are overpriced, most conspicuously **Monsieur Paul** (France) and **Coral Reef Restaurant** (The Seas). Combining attractive ambience and well-prepared food with good value are **Via Napoli** (Italy), **Biergarten** (Germany), and **La Hacienda de San Angel** (Mexico). Biergarten (along with **Restaurant Marrakesh** in Morocco) also features live entertainment.

*un**official* **TIP**
Epcot has 17 full-service restaurants: 2 in Future World and 15 in World Showcase. With a couple of exceptions, these are among the best restaurants at Walt Disney World, in or out of the theme parks.

While eating at Epcot can be a consummate hassle, an afternoon without Advance Reservations for dinner in World Showcase is like not having a date on the day of the prom. Each pavilion (except United States) has a beautifully seductive ethnic restaurant or two, offering the gastronomic delights of the world. To tour these exotic settings and not partake is almost beyond the limits of willpower. And while the fare in some World Showcase restaurants isn't always compelling, the overall experience is exhilarating. If you fail to dine in World Showcase, you'll miss one of Epcot's most delightful features.

| FULL-SERVICE RESTAURANTS IN EPCOT | |
| --- | --- |
| **FUTURE WORLD** | |
| Coral Reef Restaurant  The Seas | Garden Grill Restaurant  The Land |
| **WORLD SHOWCASE** | |
| Akershus Royal Banquet Hall  Norway | Rose & Crown Dining Room  United Kingdom |
| Biergarten  Germany | San Angel Inn  Mexico |
| Le Cellier Steakhouse  Canada | Spice Road Table  Morocco |
| Les Chefs de France  France | Teppan Edo  Japan |
| La Hacienda de San Angel  Mexico | Tokyo Dining  Japan |
| Monsieur Paul  France | Tutto Italia Ristorante  Italy |
| Nine Dragons Restaurant  China | Via Napoli  Italy |
| Restaurant Marrakesh  Morocco | |

**AUTHORS' FAVORITE COUNTER-SERVICE RESTAURANTS**

Les Halles Boulangerie Patisserie  *France*        Sunshine Seasons  *The Land*
Sommerfest  *Germany*                              Tangierine Cafe  *Morocco*

**Les Halles Boulangerie Patisserie** sells pastries, sandwiches, and quiches. The pastries are made on-site, and the sandwiches are as close to actual French street food—in taste, size, and price—as you'll get anywhere in Epcot. (We had one of those *Ratatouille* flashback scenes while eating one, only ours was in the Marais.) Another favorite is the chicken-and-lamb *shawarma* platter at Morocco's **Tangierine Cafe.** Besides juicy lamb, it comes with some of the best tabbouleh we've tasted in Florida.

In addition to these, we recommend the following ethnic counter-service specialties:

| | |
|---|---|
| GERMANY | **Sommerfest** for bratwurst and Beck's beer |
| JAPAN | **Katsura Grill** for noodle dishes, teriyaki, and tempura |
| NORWAY | **Kringla Bakeri og Kafe** for pastries, open-face sandwiches, wand Carlsberg beer (our favorite) |
| UNITED KINGDOM | **Rose & Crown Pub** for Guinness, Harp, and Bass beers |

*Unofficial Guide* readers have diverse opinions of Epcot's full-service restaurants. Concerning the much-hyped Les Chefs de France:

*What a joke! Premade food that anyone can get where they live, served by snotty little princesses.*

*We were very disappointed by Les Chefs de France. We were served cold food—it might as well have been a defrosted frozen dinner. The mashed potatoes tasted like a powdered mix. The service was rushed, the food pedestrian—only the manner was* haute.

Coral Reef Restaurant in The Seas with Nemo & Friends fared a bit better—but just a bit:

*You were dead-on; we went and it was fairly disastrous. I think my dinner was prepared under water.*

*Tried Coral Reef for the first time, despite reviews. Waited 40 minutes beyond our reserved time, and the food was mediocre and pricey. Next time I'll cook a burger next to my daughter's goldfish bowl.*

*We were surprised by how much everyone loved Coral Reef. We had great service, and the food was awesome. We had a booth directly in front of the tank and didn't even request it!*

Restaurant Marrakesh likewise garnered mixed reviews:

*Restaurant Marrakesh is overrated. It may be a walk on the wild side for someone from, say, Wichita, but I can find better and more exotic food at a dozen places in my neighborhood.*

(For all you folks in Wichita who are wondering where this reader is from: Arlington, Virginia.) More comments from a Royal Oak, Michigan, woman:

*We'd been to Morocco and wanted to see how the Disney version compared. Of course, they're not the same, but the food was excellent and the setting was nearly as exotic as the real thing. The big* *shock came when the bill arrived and there was a $6.99-per-person charge for the musical entertainment and belly dancing. They played for maybe 30 minutes, and after the expensive meal, the music charge was off-putting. I had to laugh, though, because that unexpected charge made me feel like I really was back in Morocco.*

Le Cellier has risen from obscurity to become a Signature Dining experience on the Disney Dining Plan, and one of the most coveted reservations in Epcot:

*Le Cellier is one of the hardest restaurants for which to get Advance Reservations [see page 422]. It wasn't available any of the 10 days of my trip, and I called more than 90 days in advance.*

*The filet mignon I got at Le Cellier may indeed have been the best steak I've ever had—and it had better have been for that price.*

A couple of pointed comments about Nine Dragons in China:

*The food was horrible, and the noise level was extremely high. I've had better Chinese at our local strip mall. Luckily, Nine Dragons isn't one of the more expensive restaurants, so we didn't waste too much money.*

*I think they should rename it Nine Tums.*

Akershus Royal Banquet Hall in the Norway Pavilion has become quite the favorite of character-dining enthusiasts:

*I took my 4-year-old daughter and 4-year-old niece, who were of course obsessed with seeing the princesses. The girls got to see Belle, Ariel, Cinderella, Aurora, and Jasmine. Each princess came to the table one at a time, the food was great, the dessert was to die for, and the waitstaff was extremely friendly and outgoing. The princesses were really engaged with the girls, and the best thing was that Ariel saw my daughter outside while she was leaving the restaurant. Ariel swooped down and planted a kiss on her cheek—my daughter wouldn't wash her cheek for the rest of the day!*

And, finally, about the San Angel Inn:

*Expensive, but where else can you drink Corona beer and dine under a moonlit sky at the base of a vaulted pyramid while boats drift by?*

But a Bristol, Tennessee, reader complained of cramped conditions:

*At San Angel Inn, the tables are so close together you could easily swipe food off a plate at the next table and they might never notice.*

## Drinking Around the World (Showcase)

A popular adult pastime at Epcot is to make a complete circuit of the World Showcase, sampling the exceptional alcoholic drinks native to each nation represented. Perhaps knowing this, Disney has added stand-alone bars to five pavilions.

**LA CAVA DEL TEQUILA, MEXICO** Inside the pyramid, La Cava stocks more than 100 kinds of tequila and mezcal (similar to tequila, with a smoky flavor), almost a dozen kinds of margaritas, and various light appetizers. La Cava seats just over 50 people but is far more popular than that. On weekends and on special events such as the Food & Wine Festival or Cinco de Mayo, expect a wait to get a table.

La Cava is Len's favorite bar in Walt Disney World. Two things set it apart: First, a dedicated tequila expert is on hand most days to explain the different types of tequila and provide tasting notes. (Her name is Hilda, and she's from the town of Tequila in Jalisco, Mexico—tell her Len sent you.) Second, the team that runs La Cava is very engaged with the Disney community on social media, which makes it easy to ask questions about the drinks and menus. As of this writing, folks who follow @**cavadeltequila** on Twitter get free chips and salsa.

**TUTTO GUSTO WINE CELLAR, ITALY** Tutto Gusto serves wine, spirits, and light appetizers in a setting reminiscent of an underground wine cellar. Perhaps learning from La Cava, which opened first, Tutto Gusto has seating for 113. Our favorite spot is a small room just inside the entrance, to the right, with a fireplace, a couple of comfy chairs, and tables big enough to hold your food and drinks.

The menu is divided into three sections. The "small plates" section offers four choices that each serve two people: combinations of cured meats and salamis, cheeses, olives, veggies, and seafood. Prices start at $24 each. Besides these, there's a selection of sandwichlike panini available, but the bread isn't as good as you'd expect. The best, and most reasonably priced, thing on the menu is the pasta. Try the hand-rolled *pici* (like spaghetti, only fatter) with lamb. When it comes to dessert, the cannoli are some of the best we've ever had. The wine list is extensive. Service is good.

Tutto Gusto is a poster child for how Disney's restaurant management can ruin a good thing. We loved it when it first opened—the menu had lots of à la carte options and was (for Epcot) reasonably priced. Within a year, however, Disney jacked up the prices and condensed the menu, removing the charcuterie (meat and cheese) options. Now it's just another restaurant.

**SAKE BAR, JAPAN** Not much more than a small circular table at the far end of the retail space on the first floor of the Japan Pavilion. It's common to see customers lined up two deep to sip and discuss their favorite rice wines. A decent and affordable selection of sakes can be purchased from a shelf right next to the bar-table. Frankly, we're amazed that this hasn't been expanded into a proper dedicated room.

**WEINKELLER, GERMANY** Decorated in stone, dark woods, heavy chandeliers, and thick wood tables, Weinkeller serves wines by the glass (around $5) and in flights of three 2-ounce pours (about $10). If you like sweet white wines, this is the place to be. Selections usually include a couple of Rieslings, a Liebfraumilch, dessert wines, and ice wines. The bar has no seating and serves no food, but the wine pours are generous—and that counts for something.

**SPICE ROAD TABLE, MOROCCO** Offering waterside food and drinks, Spice Road Table is a surprisingly crowded spot for *IllumiNations* dining. Unique cast-member costuming, a highly detailed interior, and an open-air patio are the highlights of the setting and atmosphere. Choose from beer, wine, cocktails, and tapas-style small plates, including mussels, lamb sausage, and salted-cod croquettes. For dessert, the almond ice cream is made on-site. Most of the food gets mixed reviews, and at $7–$16, the prices are on the high side for what you get.

In addition to the preceding, the UK Pavilion has had the **Rose & Crown Pub** for years. But with the growing popularity of watering holes in World Showcase, we wouldn't be surprised if Disney added a few more.

Along with the spirits and wine, the beer is great (Carlsberg beer in Norway is our favorite), but the price per brew makes the circumnavigation only slightly less expensive than an actual around-the-world tour, as this reader laments:

> As a beer lover, I was looking forward to tasting beers from around the world. That was quickly put to a stop by the $7.50-per-cup cost.

## DISNEY'S ANIMAL KINGDOM

BECAUSE TOURING ANIMAL KINGDOM takes less than a day, crowds are heaviest from 9:30 a.m. until about 3:30 p.m. Expect a mob at lunch and thinner crowds at dinner. We recommend you tour early after a good breakfast, then eat a very late lunch or graze on vendor food. If you tour later in the day, eat lunch before you arrive, then enjoy dinner in or out of the theme park. Animal Kingdom full-service and counter-service restaurants are profiled later in this chapter.

Animal Kingdom isn't particularly exotic. You'll find a lot of counter-service fast food, along with **Tusker House,** a buffet-style restaurant, and **Yak & Yeti,** a table-service restaurant, in Asia. You'll also find plenty of traditional theme park food—hot dogs, burgers, and the like—but even the fast food is superior to typical Disney fare. Our two counter-service favorites: **Flame Tree Barbecue** in Discovery Island, with its waterfront dining pavilions, and **Yak & Yeti Local Food Cafes** (just outside the full-service Yak & Yeti) for casual Asian dishes from egg rolls to crispy honey chicken.

A Whitestone, New York, dad thinks we sell Tusker House short:

> You really underestimate Tusker House. It was easily the best buffet, and the characters at lunch ended up making it a great meal.

A Cambridge, England, reader loved the full-service Yak & Yeti:

> Our meal was the best we had in the World—in fact, some of the best Asian cuisine we had tried since our travels in Southeast Asia—yet we were dismayed to see tables of Americans next to us ordering burgers with so many Asian specialties to choose from.

### AUTHORS' FAVORITE COUNTER-SERVICE RESTAURANT
Flame Tree Barbecue *Discovery Island*

The third full-service restaurant in Animal Kingdom, **Rainforest Cafe,** has entrances both inside and outside the park, meaning you don't have to buy park admission to eat there. Both Rainforest Cafes (the other is at Downtown Disney Marketplace) accept Advance Reservations.

## DISNEY'S HOLLYWOOD STUDIOS

DINING AT DHS is more interesting than at the Magic Kingdom but less ethnic than at Epcot. The park has five restaurants where Advance Reservations are recommended or required: **The Hollywood Brown Derby, 50's Prime Time Cafe, Sci-Fi Dine-In Theater Restaurant, Mama Melrose's Ristorante Italiano,** and the **Hollywood & Vine** buffet. The upscale Brown Derby is by far the best restaurant at the Studios. For simple Italian food, including pizza, Mama Melrose's is fine; just don't expect anything fancy. At the Sci-Fi Dine-In, you eat in little cars at a simulated drive-in movie from the 1950s. Though you won't find a more entertaining restaurant in Walt Disney World, the food is quite disappointing. Somewhat better is the 50's Prime Time Cafe, where you sit in Mom's time-warp kitchen and scarf down meat loaf while watching clips of classic sitcoms. It's fun and the food is a step up. The best way to experience either restaurant is to stop in for dessert or a drink between 2:30 and 4:30 p.m. Hollywood & Vine features singing and dancing characters from the Disney Channel during breakfast and lunch. DHS full-service and counter-service restaurants are profiled later in this chapter.

### AUTHORS' FAVORITE COUNTER-SERVICE RESTAURANTS

| | |
|---|---|
| ABC Commissary *Echo Lake* | Min and Bill's Dockside Diner *Echo Lake* |
| Backlot Express *Echo Lake* | Toluca Legs Turkey Company *Sunset Boulevard* |

We receive considerable mail from readers recounting their DHS dining experiences. A reader from Sumter, South Carolina, writes:

> We had lunch at the Sci-Fi Dine-In. In the guide you gave it a terrible review, but I've always felt you guys are too hard on the Disney restaurants, so we went ahead and ate there. Well, on this one you were right on target! While the atmosphere was fun and the clips were a hoot, the food was lousy . . . and expensive!

A Mechanicsville, Virginia, family agrees:

> You tried to warn us about the Sci-Fi Dine-In, but my 4-year-old was dying to eat there. The food was even worse than you said, and the cost—$9.50 for basic food!

From an East Lansing, Michigan, woman who'd had it to here with togetherness:

> I disagree with your review of the Sci-Fi Dine-In. After a busy and hot day of touring, it's heaven to be in a dark, air-conditioned room, with no pressure to keep up conversation with the other members of your party, who you could no doubt use a break from after much time spent in line or waiting for the bus together.

The 50's Prime Time Cafe is always a hot topic. First, from a Maryland reader:

> 50's Prime Time Cafe was a fun experience, but the food was mediocre at best. If my mom cooked that way, I would've run away from home. The poor food quality pushed us quickly into the car and out of WDW. I never thought I would get down on my knees and kiss the sidewalk outside of a Perkins Pancake House.

But a West Newton, Massachusetts, family loved the Prime Time:

*50's Prime Time Cafe: We know you guys didn't rate it very well, but we decided to go against your recommendation and give it a shot. We're so glad we did! For the five of us (ages 16–20), this dining experience was a blast. Our waiter (and big brother for the meal), "Leroy," came and sat at our table and helped us set our places so we wouldn't get in trouble with "Mom." When one member of our party cursed, "Mom" arrived to punish him, making him clear the table onto her tray, which he did shamefully. Overall, the experience was a total kick that we talked about for the rest of the trip.*

Ditto from this Wisconsin gentleman:

*I can't say enough about how much I enjoyed the food at 50's Prime Time. Big props to the dish with the combination of fried chicken, pot roast, and meat loaf.*

The Brown Derby was a favorite of a San Diego reader:

*Delicious food, great selections, and an excellent end to an evening at the Studios.*

While yet another reader made a culinary find at Mama Melrose's Ristorante Italiano:

*Great flatbread pizza, although our waiter was as slow as a snail.*

Other readers agreed about the slow-service part, not so much about the food:

*At Mama Melrose's, we had reservations at 4:20 p.m. for dinner and a show package to see Fantasmic! The food was TERRIBLE and the service was even worse. A person in our party ordered the grilled salmon—it was burned to a crisp. We got no refills on our drinks, and at 5:50 we still had not gotten our dessert (and never did).*

If you arrive at DHS without having arranged Advance Reservations for meals, you can make them at the Advance Reservations kiosk at the corner of Hollywood and Sunset Boulevards or at the restaurants. **The Hollywood Brown Derby,** expensive but tasty, is usually among the last to fill.

If you have no Advance Reservations and you get hungry, try **Studio Catering Co.** or **Min & Bill's Dockside Diner.** Min & Bill's sometimes flies under the radar of the teeming hordes.

## MORE READER COMMENTS ABOUT WALT DISNEY WORLD DINING

EATING IS A POPULAR TOPIC among *Unofficial Guide* readers. In addition to participating in our annual restaurant survey, many readers share their thoughts. The following comments are representative.

Here's a 13-year-old girl from Omaha, Nebraska, who doesn't get bent out of shape over one bad meal:

*Honestly, when was the last time you came home from Disney World and said, "Gosh, my vacation really sucked because I ate at a bad restaurant"? Disney World is Disney World, no matter what.*

A reader from Carbondale, Illinois, exhorts other readers to be adventuresome in their choice of restaurants:

*Please advise your readers to try "different" restaurants at Epcot! We had a blast dining at Akershus and Marrakesh! The service was great; food was different but not weird. My husband is a picky eater, but even he was able to say that he tried Norwegian and Moroccan food at the end of our vacation!*

A Kelso, Washington, mom has a warning for those staying in resorts with food courts:

*Nearly all food courts close at 11 p.m. Plan accordingly for those late-night hunger pangs!*

A big thumbs-up from a Troup, Texas, reader for the California Grill:

*You recommended the California Grill for the view of the Magic Kingdom fireworks show, but you didn't mention being able to see IllumiNations. We scheduled a 9:15 dinner and arrived early. The staff was extremely helpful and allowed us to have a drink in the lounge area and watch the fireworks at the Magic Kingdom. When we were seated at 8:20, the hostess told us that we had a great view of Epcot and we should watch for the fireworks at 9 o'clock. The food was exceptional, the service was outstanding, and the view was amazing.*

*Note:* Much of *IllumiNations* takes place below tree line, so only the higher aerial fireworks can be seen from the California Grill. Still, it's a treat. A Canadian mom raises a caution, however:

*We ate dinner on our last night at the California Grill. It was beautiful and delicious, but it took 3 hours. This is not a great place to take your kids. We were there from 7 to 10 p.m., and it was just too much for them.*

And from a Columbia, Maryland, woman:

*We found the renovated California Grill excellent. The menu is improved and the new decor much more pleasant and relaxing.*

A family of five loved Whispering Canyon Cafe at Wilderness Lodge:

*Our best experience for dining was at the Whispering Canyon. My girls (ages 6, 10, and 11) thought the servers were great. They joked with each other, shouted, and laughed with the kids. Our waiter even sat down with our kids and helped my oldest "finish" her salad and showed my youngest how to eat whipped cream off her nose. Out of all the places we ate, this was my kids' (and Mom's and Dad's) favorite. Oh, and the food was pretty good, too.*

An Albuquerque, New Mexico, couple is very enthusiastic about Artist Point, also at Wilderness Lodge:

*Our meal at Artist Point was one of the best we've ever experienced. My husband got the cheese platter for an appetizer and couldn't even finish it because of the size. Our steaks were so good we're still talking about them months later.*

We've received consistent raves for Boma—Flavors of Africa at Animal Kingdom Lodge:

*Please stop telling everyone how wonderful Boma—Flavors of Africa is, because I love it so much there and I don't want everyone to know the secret as it's already difficult to get a table! Prime rib and Zebra Domes—yum!*

Sanaa, in the Kidani Village section of Animal Kingdom Lodge, really impressed an Ellicott City, Maryland, family:

*Sanaa is one of the best-kept secrets on Disney property. It's a beautiful restaurant with delicious and inexpensive (for Disney) food that you can't find anywhere else in Walt Disney World. We had a fabulous adults-only evening here, but I would bring children too for an early dinner overlooking the savanna. Disney hit a home run with this place!*

A Baltimore reader thinks we sell Wolfgang Puck short:

*Bob, you greatly underestimated the Wolfgang Puck Express Cafe in Marketplace. It's not five-star, but it's a great fast-food alternative. We got yummy gourmet pizzas and rotisserie chicken . . . but the best part was the beer barrels. We ended up eating there on two occasions.*

But a mom from New Richmond, Wisconsin, points out that service is important too:

*The service at Wolfgang Puck Cafe was terrible. They had no booster seats for smaller children, and it took 30 minutes to get a high chair.*

A woman from Verona, Wisconsin, praises character dining:

*We think the character meals are underrated. These meals are in pleasant settings and provide an easy, efficient way for little kids to interact with characters while providing adults with an opportunity to relax. Yes, they're a little pricey, but you get more than food.*

A Tallahassee, Florida, reader thinks we underrate Cítricos at the Grand Floridian:

*How come you gave Cítricos only 3½ stars? We had the most amazing meal ever there! The service was outstanding, and so was the food. My grandmother had some dietary restrictions; the chef came to our table to talk with her about what she could eat, then sent her out a side dish free of charge. They even let her order from the kids' menu even though she's way over the 9-year-old limit.*

(For the record, Cítricos is one our favorite eateries. The food is indeed excellent.)

A couple from Oxford, England, had a discount coupon and still didn't like Planet Hollywood:

*We got $15 off at Planet Hollywood, but it was so noisy with loud music that children were covering their ears—it ruined the meal.*

A Pennsylvania Gen Y guy likes PH—and clearly knows how to deal with the LM (loud music, that is):

*Planet Hollywood had the best (strongest) mixed drinks, and great ribs and ravioli.*

A mother of three from Jamaica, New York, waited 2 hours and 40 minutes for a table at the Rainforest Cafe and still had a good time:

*The Rainforest Cafe was an absolute delight. Our 6-year-old sat right next to a gorilla that ranted every few minutes, our 10-month-old loved the huge fish tanks, and they loved the food. Our wait for a table was 2 hours, so we went back to the hotel and returned 2 hours later. We still had to wait 40 minutes, but it was worth it.*

But a Richardson, Texas, family had this to say:

*It was wild, wet, and loud, and the service was the worst in WDW.*

(Most negative reader comments concerning Rainforest Cafe pertain to the Downtown Disney location, not the one at Animal Kingdom.)

We get lots of comments about the dinosaur-themed T-REX restaurant at Downtown Disney. From a Charlotte, North Carolina, mom:

*This was a surprise for our dinosaur-loving grandson—I thought he would come out of his skin! No matter how many times the thunderstorm happened, he was just as excited. We had to make complete tours of the restaurant to check out each creature. Well worth the trip.*

On the other hand, from a Dartmouth, Nova Scotia, mom . . .

*Terrible experience! Overpriced, bad food, VERY LOUD—we couldn't even hear each other. They put us in the ice-cave room, which has no dinosaur; it felt like I was taking my toddlers to a mini-rave with all the flashing lights. Wouldn't recommend unless you had a die-hard dinosaur fan . . . or request a table outside the ice cave.*

But what was a negative for the previous parent was a blessing for a Beaverton, Oregon, mother of two:

*I learned that the best place for your kids to have a tantrum is T-REX. No one can hear them screaming!*

And finally, Raglan Road at Downtown Disney was a big hit with another mom of two, this one from Los Angeles:

*Cannot say enough about this amazing Irish pub. The ambience, the food, the entertainment were all absolutely top-notch. I feel like its presence could be overshadowed by other more flashy restaurants at Downtown Disney, but it was a HUGE highlight of our trip.*

# COUNTER-SERVICE
## *Mini-Profiles*

TO HELP YOU FIND palatable fast food that suits your tastes, we provide thumbnail profiles of the theme park counter-service restaurants, listed alphabetically by park. They're rated for quality, portion size, and value. (The average thumbs-up rating for all Disney counter-service restaurants is 84%, with a standard deviation of 3.6%.) Value ratings range from A to F, as follows:

| A Exceptional value; a real bargain | D Somewhat overpriced |
|---|---|
| B Good value | F Extremely overpriced |
| C Fair value; you get exactly what you pay for | |

## THE MAGIC KINGDOM
### Aloha Isle

**QUALITY** Excellent **VALUE** B+ **PORTION** Medium **LOCATION** Adventureland
**READER-SURVEY RESPONSES** 95% 👍 5% 👎 **DISNEY DINING PLAN?** No

**Selections** Soft-serve ice cream; ice-cream floats; fresh pineapple spears; chips; juice, bottled water, coffee, tea.

**Comments** The pineapple Dole Whip soft-serve is a must-try.

### Be Our Guest Restaurant

**QUALITY** Excellent **VALUE** B+ **PORTION** Medium **LOCATION** Fantasyland
**READER-SURVEY RESPONSES** 91% 👍 9% 👎 **DISNEY DINING PLAN?** Yes

**Selections** Tuna niçoise salad; *croque monsieur;* carved-turkey and roast-beef sandwiches; braised pork with bacon mashed potatoes; veggie quiche; quinoa salad. Kids' meals include carved turkey sandwich, pulled pork, a tasty meat loaf, or pasta with marinara sauce.

**Comments** The best counter-service restaurant in the Magic Kingdom, and one of the best in all of Disney World. Our favorite lunch selections are the seared-tuna niçoise salad and the *croque monsieur* sandwich. The tuna, slightly peppery, is served on a bed of greens with chilled green beans, potatoes, olives, peppers, and tomatoes and topped with a hard-poached egg. The croque monsieur is a grown-up version of grilled ham and cheese, with carved ham, Gruyère cheese, and béchamel sauce and pommes frites on the side.

*Note:* Lines for lunch start forming as early as 9:30 a.m. Expect at least a 30-minute wait if you go between 11 a.m. and 1 p.m. FastPass+ reservations for lunch are available online at **beourguestlunch.disney.go.com.** Disney is also rolling out advance ordering for lunch via its My Disney Experience mobile app. See page 463 for a review of Be Our Guest's sit-down dinner service.

### Casey's Corner

**QUALITY** Fair **VALUE** B **PORTION** Medium **LOCATION** Main Street, U.S.A.
**READER-SURVEY RESPONSES** 85% 👍 .15% 👎 **DISNEY DINING PLAN?** Yes

**Selections** Hot dogs, corn-dog nuggets, fries, and brownies.

**Comments** The hot dogs are frequently lukewarm and the buns stale, so ask for an extra-hot dog and a toasted bun. Len recommends the barbecue slaw dog; our dining insider favors the chili-cheese dog. Indoor and outdoor seating areas were expanded in 2014.

### Columbia Harbour House

**QUALITY** Good **VALUE** B **PORTION** Medium **LOCATION** Liberty Square
**READER-SURVEY RESPONSES** 93% 👍 7% 👎 **DISNEY DINING PLAN?** Yes

**Selections** Healthful options such as grilled salmon with couscous and broccoli and the Lighthouse Sandwich with hummus and broccoli slaw. Other choices: fried fish and shrimp; lobster rolls; chicken nuggets; child's plate with macaroni and cheese, PB&J sandwich, chicken nuggets, or tuna sandwich with grapes; New England clam chowder; vegetarian chili; coleslaw; garden salad; chocolate cake, seasonal cobbler, strawberry yogurt.

**Comments** No trans fats in the fried items, and the soups and sandwiches are a cut above most fast-food fare.

## Cosmic Ray's Starlight Cafe

| QUALITY | Good | VALUE | B | PORTION | Large | LOCATION | Tomorrowland |
|---------|------|-------|---|---------|-------|----------|--------------|
| READER-SURVEY RESPONSES | 85% 👍 | 15% 💬 | | DISNEY DINING PLAN? | Yes | | |

**Selections** Rotisserie chicken and ribs; burgers (and vegetarian burgers); hot dogs; Greek salad; chicken, turkey and vegetable sandwiches; chicken-noodle soup; chili-cheese fries; strawberry yogurt for dessert. Kosher choices available by request.

**Comments** Plenty of options. Generous toppings bar. Ray's old outside seating area, which wasn't used often during the summer, was enclosed and air-conditioned in 2014, with nice views of the center of the park.

## Friar's Nook

| QUALITY | Good | VALUE | B | PORTION | Medium-large | LOCATION | Fantasyland |
|---------|------|-------|---|---------|--------------|----------|-------------|
| READER-SURVEY RESPONSES | 87% 👍 | 13% 💬 | | DISNEY DINING PLAN? | Yes | | |

**Selections** Hot dogs, specialty macaroni and cheese (bacon cheeseburger, blue cheese with balsamic vinegar), veggies and chips with hummus, freshly made potato chips, lemonade slush.

**Comments** Stir the blue-cheese mac and cheese before you eat it, so the balsamic vinegar coats everything.

## Gaston's Tavern

| QUALITY | Good | VALUE | C | PORTION | Medium | LOCATION | Fantasyland |
|---------|------|-------|---|---------|--------|----------|-------------|
| READER-SURVEY RESPONSES | 88% 👍 | 12% 💬 | | DISNEY DINING PLAN? | Yes | | |

**Selections** Roast pork shank (the porcine equivalent of the giant turkey leg), hummus with chips, cinnamon rolls, chocolate croissants, LeFou's Brew (frozen apple juice flavored with toasted marshmallow).

**Comments** Clever setting, limited menu. Most everyone is here for the ginormous pork shank or a cinnamon roll.

## Golden Oak Outpost

| QUALITY | Good | VALUE | B+ | PORTION | Medium-large | LOCATION | Frontierland |
|---------|------|-------|----|---------|--------------|----------|--------------|
| READER-SURVEY RESPONSES | 76% 👍 | 24% 💬 | | DISNEY DINING PLAN? | Yes | | |

**Selections** Chicken nuggets; fried-chicken-breast sandwiches; fries; chocolate cake, carrot cake, and cookies.

**Comments** Entrees are served with apple slices or French fries.

## The Lunching Pad

| QUALITY | Good | VALUE | B- | PORTION | Medium | LOCATION | Tomorrowland |
|---------|------|-------|----|---------|--------|----------|--------------|
| READER-SURVEY RESPONSES | 74% 👍 | 26% 💬 | | DISNEY DINING PLAN? | Yes | | |

**Selections** Sweet cream-cheese pretzel, frozen sodas, hot dogs.

**Comments** The frozen carbonated drinks—cola, cherry, blue raspberry—are a treat in summer's heat.

## Pecos Bill Tall Tale Inn & Cafe

| QUALITY | Good | VALUE | B | PORTION | Medium–large | LOCATION | Frontierland |
|---------|------|-------|---|---------|--------------|----------|--------------|
| READER-SURVEY RESPONSES | 86% 👍 | 14% 💬 | | DISNEY DINING PLAN? | Yes | | |

**Selections** One-third-pound Angus cheeseburgers; barbecue-pork sandwiches; veggie burgers; steak-and-chicken platter; Southwest chicken salad; taco salad; chili; child's plate with burger or salad with grilled chicken and child's beverage; fries and chili-cheese fries; strawberry yogurt and carrot cake.

**Comments** Garnish your burger at the fixin's station.

## The Pinocchio Village Haus

| QUALITY Fair | VALUE C | PORTION Medium | LOCATION Fantasyland |
| --- | --- | --- | --- |
| READER-SURVEY RESPONSES 77% 👍 23% 👎 | DISNEY DINING PLAN? Yes | | |

**Selections** Personal pizzas; chicken nuggets; fries; Caesar salad with chicken; meatball sub sandwiches; Mediterranean salad; kids' meals of pizza, mac and cheese, or PB&J.

**Comments** An easy stop for families in Fantasyland, but it's usually crowded. Consider Columbia Harbour House and Pecos Bill Tall Tale Inn & Cafe, both only a few minutes' walk away (and tastier, too).

## Tomorrowland Terrace Restaurant *(open seasonally)*

| QUALITY Fair | VALUE C | PORTION Medium-large | LOCATION Tomorrowland |
| --- | --- | --- | --- |
| READER-SURVEY RESPONSES 82% 👍 18% 👎 | DISNEY DINING PLAN? Yes | | |

**Selections** One-third-pound Angus bacon cheeseburger; fried-chicken sandwich; chicken nuggets; pasta alone or with shrimp or chicken; lobster roll; beef-and-blue-cheese salad; citrus shrimp salad; chocolate cake, carrot cake, or yogurt for dessert.

**Comments** The ancient kitchen wasn't designed for much more than keeping food warm, making the fare a snooze. That's a shame, because we like the setting better than Cosmic Ray's. Stick to nuggets or salads and avoid the pasta.

## Tortuga Tavern *(open seasonally)*

| QUALITY Fair | VALUE B | PORTION Medium-large | LOCATION Adventureland |
| --- | --- | --- | --- |
| READER-SURVEY RESPONSES 81% 👍 19% 👎 | DISNEY DINING PLAN? Yes | | |

**Selections** Beef taco salad; chicken Caesar salad; beef nachos; chicken, beef, or vegetarian burritos; quesadillas and PB&J sandwiches for kids.

**Comments** Large, shaded eating area. Generous toppings bar with tomatoes, lettuce, cheese, and salsa.

# EPCOT

## L'Artisan des Glaces

| QUALITY Excellent | VALUE C | PORTION Large | LOCATION France |
| --- | --- | --- | --- |
| READER-SURVEY RESPONSES 95% 👍 5% 👎 | DISNEY DINING PLAN? Yes | | |

**Selections** Flavors change but can include vanilla, chocolate, mint chocolate, pistachio, hazelnut, profiterole, caramel with salt, cherry, white chocolate with coconut, and coffee ice creams. Sorbet flavors can include strawberry, mango, melon, lemon, pomegranate, and mixed berry. Over-21s can enjoy two scoops in a martini glass, topped with a shot of Grand Marnier, rum, or whipped cream–flavored vodka.

**Comments** The ice cream is freshly made on the spot. Our profiterole sample had chunks of chocolate-covered cookie pieces, and our white chocolate–coconut had fresh shaved coconut in it. And the chocolate macaron ice-cream sandwich is worth every calorie.

## La Cantina de San Angel

| QUALITY Good | VALUE B | PORTION Medium-large | LOCATION Mexico |
| --- | --- | --- | --- |
| READER-SURVEY RESPONSES 85% 👍 15% 👎 | DISNEY DINING PLAN? Yes | | |

**Selections** Chicken or beef tacos, nachos, cheese empanadas, guacamole and chips, churros and frozen fruit pops, margaritas.

**Comments** The Cantina is a popular spot for a quick meal, with 150 covered outdoor seats.

### Crêpes des Chefs de France

| QUALITY Excellent | VALUE B+ | PORTION Medium | LOCATION France |
|---|---|---|---|
| READER-SURVEY RESPONSES | 87% 👍 | 13% 👎 | DISNEY DINING PLAN? No |

**Selections** Crepes filled with chocolate, strawberry preserves, ice cream, or sugar; ice cream; specialty beer (Kronenbourg 1664); espresso.
**Comments** These crepes rate high—even with French guests.

### Electric Umbrella Restaurant

| QUALITY Fair–good | VALUE B– | PORTION Medium | LOCATION Innoventions East |
|---|---|---|---|
| READER-SURVEY RESPONSES | 72% 👍 | 28% 👎 | DISNEY DINING PLAN? Yes |

**Selections** Meatball subs, burgers (Angus bacon cheese, mac and cheese); veggie flatbread; Caesar salad; child's plate with cheeseburger, mac and cheese, or chicken wrap; cheesecake, no-sugar-added brownies.
**Comments** World Showcase has more-interesting fast food.

### Fife & Drum Tavern

| QUALITY Fair | VALUE C | PORTION Large | LOCATION United States |
|---|---|---|---|
| READER-SURVEY RESPONSES | 90% 👍 | 10% 👎 | DISNEY DINING PLAN? Yes |

**Selections** Turkey legs, popcorn, pretzels, ice cream, frozen slushes, beer.
**Comments** Better for a drink or a quick snack than an actual meal. Seating is available in and around the Liberty Inn, behind the Fife & Drum.

### Fountain View

| QUALITY Fair | VALUE C | PORTION Small | LOCATION Future World Plaza |
|---|---|---|---|
| READER-SURVEY RESPONSES | 94% 👍 | 6% 👎 | DISNEY DINING PLAN? Yes |

**Selections** Coffee drinks and teas; breakfast sandwiches and pastries.
**Comments** Former ice-cream shop turned Disney-themed Starbucks, with the same food and drinks you'd find in any other.

### Katsura Grill

| QUALITY Good | VALUE B | PORTION Small–medium | LOCATION Japan |
|---|---|---|---|
| READER-SURVEY RESPONSES | 88% 👍 | 12% 👎 | DISNEY DINING PLAN? Yes |

**Selections** Udon noodles with beef and tempura shrimp; chicken, beef, or salmon teriyaki; edamame; sushi; miso soup; green tea; green-tea ice cream and cheesecake; Kirin beer, sake, and plum wine.
**Comments** Pleasant gardens and outdoor seating a little off the World Showcase promenade offer a nice respite, but seating is limited.

### Kringla Bakeri og Kafe

| QUALITY Good-excellent | VALUE B | PORTION Small–medium | LOCATION Norway |
|---|---|---|---|
| READER-SURVEY RESPONSES | 92% 👍 | 8% 👎 | DISNEY DINING PLAN? Yes |

**Selections** Pastries and cakes; rice cream; sandwiches (club, ham and apple, roast beef, salmon and egg); vegetable torte; espresso, cappuccino, and imported beers (Carlsberg for $8).
**Comments** Delicious and different, but pricey. Try the rice cream (not a typo, by the way). Shaded outdoor seating.

### Les Halles Boulangerie Patisserie

| QUALITY Good | VALUE A | PORTION Small–medium | LOCATION France |
|---|---|---|---|
| READER-SURVEY RESPONSES | 92% 👍 | 8% 👎 | DISNEY DINING PLAN? Yes |

**Selections** Niçoise salad, sandwiches (ham and cheese; turkey BLT; chicken breast; grilled eggplant; brie, cranberry, and apple); imported-cheese plate; quiches; soups; pastries.
**Comments** The pastries are fine, but the sandwiches are excellent. For an authentic Parisian experience, grab a baguette or baguette sandwich

and eat it while walking around the France Pavilion. Open for breakfast. Usually crowded starting at lunch and throughout the day.

## Liberty Inn

| QUALITY | Fair | VALUE | C | PORTION | Medium | LOCATION | United States |
|---|---|---|---|---|---|---|---|
| READER-SURVEY RESPONSES | 73% | 27% | | DISNEY DINING PLAN? | Yes | | |

**Selections** California burger topped with bacon and guacamole; barbecue-pork sandwich; 6-ounce New York strip with red-wine butter, fries, and steamed broccoli; chili-cheese hot dog; veggie "chicken" sandwich; chicken nuggets; Caesar salad; chili; child's plate of grilled chicken, pasta with marinara, cheeseburger, or mac and cheese. For dessert, apple pie, brownies, and mixed fruit.

**Comments** Try the New York strip, a relative bargain at $10.69. Kosher items also available.

## Lotus Blossom Cafe

| QUALITY | Fair | VALUE | C | PORTION | Medium | LOCATION | China |
|---|---|---|---|---|---|---|---|
| READER-SURVEY RESPONSES | 67% | 33% | | DISNEY DINING PLAN? | Yes | | |

**Selections** Pork and vegetable egg rolls, pot stickers, Hong Kong–style vegetable curry (chicken optional), sesame chicken salad, shrimp fried rice, orange chicken, beef-noodle soup bowl, caramel-ginger or lychee ice cream, plum wine, Tsingtao beer.

**Comments** The worst-rated counter service in Epcot.

## Promenade Refreshments

| QUALITY | Fair | VALUE | C | PORTION | Large | LOCATION | World Showcase Promenade |
|---|---|---|---|---|---|---|---|
| READER-SURVEY RESPONSES | 79% | 21% | | DISNEY DINING PLAN? | Yes | | |

**Selections** Meatball subs, popcorn, pretzels, ice cream, beer.

**Comments** Best for a quick snack. Seating is limited to nonexistent—be prepared to walk and chew.

## Refreshment Cool Post

| QUALITY | Good | VALUE | B– | PORTION | Small | LOCATION | Between Germany and China |
|---|---|---|---|---|---|---|---|
| READER-SURVEY RESPONSES | 82% | 18% | | DISNEY DINING PLAN? | Yes | | |

**Selections** Hot dogs, soft-serve in a waffle cone, floats and sundaes, coffee or tea, draft Safari Amber beer ($6.75).

**Comments** The root beer float or a cold beer is a treat on a hot day.

## Refreshment Port

| QUALITY | Good | VALUE | B– | PORTION | Medium | LOCATION | Near Canada |
|---|---|---|---|---|---|---|---|
| READER-SURVEY RESPONSES | 71% | 29% | | DISNEY DINING PLAN? | Yes | | |

**Selections** The croissant doughnut shares this little spot with chicken nuggets and fries, flavored coffees, hot chocolate, and soft-serve ice cream.

**Comments** The trendy and calorie-laden croissant doughnut is the star here.

## Rose & Crown Pub

| QUALITY | Good | VALUE | C+ | PORTION | Medium | LOCATION | United Kingdom |
|---|---|---|---|---|---|---|---|
| READER-SURVEY RESPONSES | 94% | 6% | | DISNEY DINING PLAN? | No | | |

**Selections** Fish and chips; Scotch egg (hard-boiled, wrapped in sausage, and deep-fried); corned-beef sandwiches; English Bulldog (split sausage stuffed with mashed potatoes, bacon, and Irish Cheddar); British cheese plate; Guinness, Harp, and Bass beers, as well as other spirits.

**Comments** The attractions here are the pub atmosphere and the draft beer. Outside the pub is Yorkshire County Fish Shop (see next page), which serves food to go.

## Sommerfest

| QUALITY Good | VALUE B– | PORTION Medium | LOCATION Germany |
| --- | --- | --- | --- |
| READER-SURVEY RESPONSES 84% 👍 16% 👎 | | DISNEY DINING PLAN? Yes | |

**Selections** Bratwurst and frankfurter sandwiches with kraut; *nudelgratin* (baked macaroni with Cheddar and Swiss); curried bratwurst with paprika chips; Reuben sandwich; soft pretzels; apple strudel; Black Forest cake; cheesecake; German wine and beer.

**Comments** Tucked in the entrance to the Biergarten restaurant, Sommerfest is hard to find from the street. Very limited seating.

## Sunshine Seasons

| QUALITY Excellent | VALUE A | PORTION Medium | LOCATION The Land |
| --- | --- | --- | --- |
| READER-SURVEY RESPONSES 92% 👍 8% 👎 | | DISNEY DINING PLAN? Yes | |

**Selections** Comprises the following four areas: (1) wood-fired grills and rotisseries, with rotisserie half-chicken or slow-roasted pork chop and wood-grilled fish with seasonal vegetables; (2) sandwich shop with made-to-order sandwiches such as oak-grilled veggie flatbread, steak and blue cheese, and turkey-and-cheese on ciabatta; (3) Asian shop, with noodle bowls and various stir-fry combos; (4) soup-and-salad shop, with soups made daily and unusual creations such as seared tuna-noodle salad and roasted-beet-and-goat-cheese salad. Breakfast includes the usual suspects: pastries, bacon, eggs, and the like.

**Comments** One of the best counter-service spots in Epcot. The breakfast panini (eggs, bacon, roast pork, and cheese) is an Unofficial favorite.

## Tangierine Cafe

| QUALITY Good | VALUE B | PORTION Medium | LOCATION Morocco |
| --- | --- | --- | --- |
| READER-SURVEY RESPONSES 94% 👍 4% 👎 | | DISNEY DINING PLAN? Yes | |

**Selections** Chicken and lamb *shawarma;* hummus; tabbouleh; lentil salad; couscous salad; chicken, lamb, and falafel wraps; marinated olives; child's burger or chicken tenders with carrot sticks and apple slices; Moroccan wine and beer; baklava.

**Comments** No belly dancers as at Restaurant Marrakesh, but the food is authentic. The best seating is at the outdoor tables.

## Yorkshire County Fish Shop

| QUALITY Good | VALUE B+ | PORTION Medium | LOCATION United Kingdom |
| --- | --- | --- | --- |
| READER-SURVEY RESPONSES 92% 👍 8% 👎 | | DISNEY DINING PLAN? Yes | |

**Selections** Fish and chips, shortbread, Bass Ale draft and Harp Lager.

**Comments** There's usually a line for the crisp, hot fish and chips at this convenient fast-food window attached to the Rose & Crown Pub (see full-service profile on page 489). Outdoor seating overlooks the lagoon.

# DISNEY'S ANIMAL KINGDOM

## Flame Tree Barbecue

| QUALITY Excellent | VALUE B– | PORTION Large | LOCATION Discovery Island |
| --- | --- | --- | --- |
| READER-SURVEY RESPONSES 92% 👍 8% 👎 | | DISNEY DINING PLAN? Yes | |

**Selections** Half-slab St. Louis–style ribs; smoked half-chicken; smoked-pork sandwiches; smoked-chicken salad; jumbo turkey leg; fruit plate with honey yogurt; child's plate of baked chicken drumstick, chicken sandwich, hot dog, or PB&J sandwich; French fries, coleslaw, and onion rings; Key lime or chocolate mousse; Safari Amber beer, Bud Light, and wine.

**Comments** One of our favorites for lunch. Try the covered gazebo overlooking the water.

### Kusafiri Coffee Shop and Bakery

| QUALITY Good | VALUE B | PORTION Medium | LOCATION Africa |
|---|---|---|---|
| READER-SURVEY RESPONSES 94% 👍 6% 👎 | | DISNEY DINING PLAN? Yes | |

**Selections** Fruit turnovers, Danish and other pastries, muffins, croissants, bagels with cream cheese, cookies, brownies, cake, fruit cups, yogurt, coffee, cocoa, and juice.

**Comments** Get your morning sugar rush on the way to Kilimanjaro Safaris.

### Pizzafari

| QUALITY Fair | VALUE B | PORTION Medium | LOCATION Discovery Island |
|---|---|---|---|
| READER-SURVEY RESPONSES 69% 👍 31% 👎 | | DISNEY DINING PLAN? Yes | |

**Selections** Cheese, pepperoni, or veggie personal pizzas with Caesar salad; Italian sandwich; Caesar salad with chicken; chicken-and-veggie pasta salad. Kids' choices: mac and cheese, turkey sandwich, cheese pizza, or PB&J. Chocolate mousse or cheesecake for dessert. Beer and wine available.

**Comments** Kids love it. Hectic at peak mealtimes. The pizza is unimpressive. Kosher menu is available.

### Restaurantosaurus

| QUALITY Good | VALUE B+ | PORTION Medium-large | LOCATION DinoLand U.S.A. |
|---|---|---|---|
| READER-SURVEY RESPONSES 89% 👍 11% 👎 | | DISNEY DINING PLAN? Yes | |

**Selections** Angus bacon cheeseburger; chicken nuggets; black-bean burger; mac-and-cheese hot dog; chicken BLT salad; grilled-chicken sandwich; kids' turkey wrap, cheeseburger, or PB&J.

**Comments** Good burger-toppings bar.

### Royal Anandapur Tea Company

| QUALITY Good | VALUE B | PORTION Medium | LOCATION Asia |
|---|---|---|---|
| READER-SURVEY RESPONSES 94% 👍 6% 👎 | | DISNEY DINING PLAN? No | |

**Selections** Wide variety of hot and iced teas (fantastic frozen chai); lattes; coffee, espresso, and cappuccino; pastries.

**Comments** Halfway between Expedition Everest and Kali River Rapids, this is the kind of small, eclectic, Animal Kingdom–specific food stand that you wish other parks had. Offers nine loose-leaf teas from Asia and Africa, some organic, and many of which can be made either hot or iced. Pastries violate the "never eat anything larger than your head" rule, but everyone knows that doesn't apply when you're on vacation.

### Tamu Tamu Eats & Refreshments

| QUALITY Good | VALUE C | PORTION Large | LOCATION Africa |
|---|---|---|---|
| READER-SURVEY RESPONSES 85% 👍 15% 👎 | | DISNEY DINING PLAN? Yes | |

**Selections** Quinoa or roasted-chicken salad; chicken or vegetarian curry.

**Comments** Seating is behind the building and could easily be overlooked.

### Yak & Yeti Local Food Cafes

| QUALITY Fair | VALUE B | PORTION Large | LOCATION Asia |
|---|---|---|---|
| READER-SURVEY RESPONSES 94% 👍 6% 👎 | | DISNEY DINING PLAN? Yes | |

**Selections** Crispy honey chicken with steamed rice, sweet-and-sour chicken, beef lo mein, Mandarin chicken salad, Asian chicken sandwiches, egg rolls, chicken fried rice. Kids' menu includes chicken tenders or a cheeseburger with applesauce and carrots.

**Comments** The crispy honey chicken is the best choice.

## DISNEY'S HOLLYWOOD STUDIOS
### ABC Commissary

| QUALITY Fair | VALUE B– | PORTION Medium–large | LOCATION Echo Lake |
|---|---|---|---|
| READER-SURVEY RESPONSES | 69% 👍 31% 👎 | DISNEY DINING PLAN? Yes | |

**Selections** Asian salad (chicken or salmon); chicken club sandwich; Angus cheeseburger with fried shrimp; shrimp platter; seafood platter; couscous, quinoa, and arugula salad; child's chicken nuggets, cheeseburger, or turkey sandwich; chocolate mousse; lemon-meringue cupcake; no-sugar-added strawberry parfait; wine and beer.

**Comments** Indoors, centrally located, but hard to find. Offers kosher meals. One of the lowest-rated counter-service places in the theme parks.

### Backlot Express

| QUALITY Fair | VALUE C | PORTION Medium–large | LOCATION Echo Lake |
|---|---|---|---|
| READER-SURVEY RESPONSES | 80% 👍 20% 👎 | DISNEY DINING PLAN? Yes | |

**Selections** Cheeseburgers with fries or carrot sticks, Southwest salad with chicken, grilled turkey and cheese, chicken nuggets, hot dogs, grilled-vegetable sandwiches, salads, desserts. For kids, chicken nuggets, PB&J, or grilled-veggie sandwich. Soft drinks and beer.

**Comments** A big dining space that's often overlooked. Great burger-fixin's bar. Indoor and outdoor seating.

### Catalina Eddie's

| QUALITY Fair | VALUE B | PORTION Medium–large | LOCATION Sunset Boulevard |
|---|---|---|---|
| READER-SURVEY RESPONSES | 60% 👍 40% 👎 | DISNEY DINING PLAN? Yes | |

**Selections** Cheese and pepperoni pizzas, hot Italian deli sandwiches, salads, banana parfait, and vanilla cake with chocolate custard.

**Comments** The lowest-rated counter-service restaurant in the park. Seldom crowded. Go figure.

### Fairfax Fare

| QUALITY Fair | VALUE B | PORTION Medium–large | LOCATION Sunset Boulevard |
|---|---|---|---|
| READER-SURVEY RESPONSES | 83% 👍 17% 👎 | DISNEY DINING PLAN? Yes | |

**Selections** Breakfast: egg-and-cheese English muffins, pastries, cereal, yogurt, and fruit cup. Lunch: barbecue chicken and ribs; pulled-pork sandwiches; "designer" hot dogs (barbecue pork and coleslaw, macaroni and cheese with truffle oil); salad with tomato, roasted corn, peppers, cheese, and tortillas; chocolate cake and carrot cake for dessert.

**Comments** Like Charo on *The Love Boat,* the mac-and-cheese–truffle-oil hot dog is a standout in a sea of forgettable supporting players. Ask to have your bun warmed before your dog is served.

### Min and Bill's Dockside Diner

| QUALITY Fair | VALUE C | PORTION Small–medium | LOCATION Echo Lake |
|---|---|---|---|
| READER-SURVEY RESPONSES | 80% 👍 20% 👎 | DISNEY DINING PLAN? Yes | |

**Selections** Italian sausage, jumbo turkey legs or pork shanks, frankfurter on a pretzel roll, shakes and soft drinks, chips and cookies, beer.

**Comments** The hot dog in a pretzel roll is genius, and although the menu is very limited, all of the sandwiches are good.

### Pizza Planet

| QUALITY Good | VALUE B+ | PORTION Medium | LOCATION Streets of America |
|---|---|---|---|
| READER-SURVEY RESPONSES | 77% 👍 23% 👎 | DISNEY DINING PLAN? Yes | |

**Selections** Cheese, pepperoni, and vegetarian pizzas; meatball subs;

salads; child's meatball sub and cheese pizza; cookies and cupcakes.
**Comments** *The* pizza place at the Studios.

### Rosie's All-American Cafe

| QUALITY Fair | VALUE C | PORTION Medium | LOCATION Sunset Boulevard |
|---|---|---|---|
| READER-SURVEY RESPONSES 83% 👍 17% 👎 | | DISNEY DINING PLAN? Yes | |

**Selections** Cheeseburgers; black-bean burgers; chicken nuggets; soups;
child's turkey sandwich or chicken nuggets with carrot sticks or applesauce; banana parfait or vanilla cake with chocolate custard.
**Comments** Backlot Express is a better option for similar fare.

### Starring Rolls Cafe

| QUALITY Good | VALUE B | PORTION Small–medium | LOCATION Sunset Boulevard |
|---|---|---|---|
| READER-SURVEY RESPONSES 91% 👍 9% 👎 | | DISNEY DINING PLAN? Yes | |

**Selections** Deli sandwiches, sushi, pastries and desserts, coffee.
**Comments** Slowest—but highest-rated—counter service in the Studios.

### Studio Catering Co.

| QUALITY Good | VALUE B | PORTION Small–medium | LOCATION Streets of America |
|---|---|---|---|
| READER-SURVEY RESPONSES 85% 👍 15% 👎 | | DISNEY DINING PLAN? Yes | |

**Selections** Grilled-veggie sandwiches, pressed turkey clubs, buffalo chicken
sandwiches, toasted Tuscan deli sandwiches, sloppy joes, Greek salad.
PB&J, veggie sandwich, or chicken nuggets for kids. The adjacent High
Octane Refreshments serves margaritas and other cocktails.
**Comments** Good place for a break while your kids enjoy the Honey, I Shrunk
the Kids Movie Set Adventure. Shady outside seating.

### Toluca Legs Turkey Company

| QUALITY Good | VALUE B | PORTION Medium–large | LOCATION Sunset Boulevard |
|---|---|---|---|
| READER-SURVEY RESPONSES 83% 👍 17% 👎 | | DISNEY DINING PLAN? Yes | |

**Selections** Smoked turkey legs and pork shanks; bottled soda and beer.
**Comments** For fans of giant meat.

# FULL-SERVICE RESTAURANTS:
## *Rated and Ranked*

THE PROFILES IN THIS SECTION allow you to quickly check the
cuisine, location, star rating, cost range, quality rating, and value rating
of every full-service restaurant at Walt Disney World. Profiles are listed
alphabetically by restaurant.

**OVERALL RATING** This encompasses the entire dining experience: style,
service, ambience, and food quality. Five stars is the highest rating
attainable. Four-star restaurants are above average; three-star restaurants serve good, though not necessarily memorable, meals. Two-star
restaurants are mediocre, and one-star restaurants are below average.
Our star ratings don't correspond to those awarded by AAA, Mobil,
Zagat, or other restaurant reviewers.

**COST RANGE** This tells you how much you'll spend on a full-service
entree. Appetizers, sides, soups/salads, desserts, drinks, and tips aren't
included. Costs are categorized as *inexpensive* (less than $13), *moderate*
($13–$23), or *expensive* ($24 and up).

To give you a clearer idea of your options, we've also compiled the number of sit-down entrees available in each price range, as follows:

**Inexpensive:** 600    **Moderate:** 1,300    **Expensive:** 600

**QUALITY RATING** Food quality is rated from one to five stars, five being the best. The criteria are taste, freshness of ingredients, preparation, presentation, and creativity of food served. Price is not a consideration.

**VALUE RATING** If, on the other hand, you're looking for both quality *and* value, then you should check this rating, also expressed as stars.

**PAYMENT** All Disney restaurants take American Express, Carte Blanche, Diners Club, Discover, Japan Credit Bureau, MasterCard, and Visa.

## Readers' Restaurant-Survey Responses

For each Disney World restaurant profiled, we include the results of last year's Reader-Survey Responses. Results are expressed as a percentage of readers who liked the restaurant well enough to eat there again (thumbs-up 👍) versus the percentage who didn't (thumbs-down 👎). (Readers tend to be less critical than we are, for what it's worth.) The average thumbs-up rating for all Disney restaurants is 85%, with a standard deviation of 7%. If you'd like to participate in the ratings, go to **touringplans.com/walt-disney-world/survey.**

This edition, with more than 20 restaurants achieving scores of at least 90%, we decided that only those with ratings of 93% or above could be deemed substantially better than average. Tied at the top, at 94%, are the BoardWalk's **Flying Fish Cafe,** a seafood restaurant with a James Beard Award–nominated chef, and the Beach Club Resort's **Beaches & Cream Soda Shop,** serving made-to-order burgers and shakes in a 1950s-style diner. Also in this elite group are the Contemporary Resort's refurbished **California Grill,** Epcot's **Via Napoli** pizzeria, and Animal Kingdom's **Yak & Yeti,** all at 93%. Just missing the cut, at 92% each, were **Boma—Flavors of Africa** at Animal Kingdom Lodge, **Le Cellier Steakhouse** at Epcot, and—tumbling from 100% last edition—the tony **Victoria & Albert's** at the Grand Floridian.

Remember that our survey results report overall reader satisfaction, not just food quality. Also, the star ratings represent the opinions of our research team and our dining insider—your experience may vary.

## FULL-SERVICE RESTAURANT PROFILES
### Akershus Royal Banquet Hall  ★★★

| NORWEGIAN/BUFFET | EXPENSIVE | QUALITY ★★★ | VALUE ★★★★ |
|---|---|---|---|
| READER-SURVEY RESPONSES | 84% 👍  16% 👎 | DISNEY DINING PLAN? | Yes |

Norway, World Showcase, Epcot; ☎ 407-939-3463

**Reservations** Required for breakfast; recommended for lunch and dinner, with credit card required to reserve at breakfast and lunch. **Dining Plan credits** 1 per person, per meal. **When to go** Anytime. **Cost range** Breakfast $42 (child $25), lunch $43 (child $25), dinner $48 (child $26). *Note:* Prices may increase during peak periods (see page 428). **Service** ★★★★. **Friendliness** ★★★★. **Parking** Epcot lot. **Bar** Full service. **Wine selection** Good. **Dress** Casual. **Disabled access** Yes. **Customers** Theme park guests. **Character breakfast** Daily, 8–11:10 a.m. **Character lunch** Daily, 11:55 a.m.–3:30 p.m. **Character dinner** Daily, 4:55–8:35 p.m.

*Continued on page 461*

## Walt Disney World Restaurants by Cuisine

| CUISINE | LOCATION | OVERALL RATING | COST | QUALITY RATING | VALUE RATING |
|---|---|---|---|---|---|
| **AFRICAN** | | | | | |
| JIKO—THE COOKING PLACE | Animal Kingdom Lodge | ★★★★½ | Exp | ★★★★½ | ★★★½ |
| BOMA—FLAVORS OF AFRICA | Animal Kingdom Lodge | ★★★★ | Exp | ★★★★ | ★★★★½ |
| TUSKER HOUSE RESTAURANT | Animal Kingdom | ★★★ | Mod | ★★★ | ★★★ |
| **AMERICAN** | | | | | |
| CALIFORNIA GRILL | Contemporary | ★★★★★ | Exp | ★★★★★ | ★★★ |
| THE HOLLYWOOD BROWN DERBY | DHS | ★★★★ | Exp | ★★★★ | ★★★ |
| ARTIST POINT | Wilderness Lodge | ★★★½ | Exp | ★★★★ | ★★★ |
| CAPE MAY CAFE | Beach Club | ★★★½ | Mod | ★★★½ | ★★★★ |
| WHISPERING CANYON CAFE | Wilderness Lodge | ★★★ | Mod | ★★★½ | ★★★★ |
| CAPTAIN'S GRILLE | Yacht Club | ★★★ | Mod | ★★★½ | ★★★ |
| THE CRYSTAL PALACE | Magic Kingdom | ★★★ | Mod | ★★★½ | ★★★ |
| HOUSE OF BLUES | Downtown Disney | ★★★ | Mod | ★★★½ | ★★★ |
| 50'S PRIME TIME CAFE | DHS | ★★★ | Mod | ★★★ | ★★★ |
| LIBERTY TREE TAVERN | Magic Kingdom | ★★★ | Mod | ★★★ | ★★★ |
| TUSKER HOUSE RESTAURANT | Animal Kingdom | ★★★ | Mod | ★★★ | ★★★ |
| CINDERELLA'S ROYAL TABLE | Magic Kingdom | ★★★ | Exp | ★★★ | ★★ |
| OLIVIA'S CAFE | Old Key West | ★★★ | Mod | ★★★ | ★★ |
| T-REX | Downtown Disney | ★★★ | Mod | ★★ | ★★ |
| THE WAVE . . . OF AMERICAN FLAVORS | Contemporary | ★★★ | Mod | ★★ | ★★ |
| CHEF MICKEY'S | Contemporary | ★★½ | Exp | ★★★ | ★★★ |
| ESPN CLUB | BoardWalk | ★★½ | Mod | ★★★ | ★★★ |
| ESPN WIDE WORLD OF SPORTS CAFE | ESPN Wide World of Sports Complex | ★★½ | Mod | ★★★ | ★★★ |
| HOLLYWOOD & VINE | DHS | ★★½ | Mod | ★★★ | ★★★ |
| 1900 PARK FARE | Grand Floridian | ★★½ | Mod | ★★★ | ★★★ |
| BOATWRIGHT'S DINING HALL | Port Orleans | ★★½ | Mod | ★★★ | ★★ |
| GRAND FLORIDIAN CAFE | Grand Floridian | ★★½ | Mod | ★★★ | ★★ |
| BEACHES & CREAM SODA SHOP | Beach Club | ★★½ | Inexp | ★★½ | ★★½ |
| SPLITSVILLE | Downtown Disney | ★★½ | Mod | ★★½ | ★★ |
| PLANET HOLLYWOOD | Downtown Disney | ★★½ | Mod | ★★ | ★★ |
| RAINFOREST CAFE | Animal Kingdom and Downtown Disney | ★★½ | Mod | ★★ | ★★ |
| GARDEN GROVE | Swan | ★★ | Mod | ★★★ | ★★ |

## Walt Disney World Restaurants by Cuisine (continued)

| CUISINE | LOCATION | OVERALL RATING | COST | QUALITY RATING | VALUE RATING |
|---|---|---|---|---|---|
| **AMERICAN** (continued) | | | | | |
| WOLFGANG PUCK GRAND CAFE | Downtown Disney | ★★ | Exp | ★½ | ★½ |
| SCI-FI DINE-IN THEATER RESTAURANT | DHS | ★★ | Mod | ★★½ | ★★ |
| GARDEN GRILL RESTAURANT | Epcot | ★★ | Exp | ★★ | ★★★ |
| ONE80 SPORTGRILL & BAR | Buena Vista Palace | ★★ | Mod | ★★ | ★★★ |
| BIG RIVER GRILLE & BREWING WORKS | BoardWalk | ★★ | Mod | ★★ | ★★ |
| THE FOUNTAIN | Dolphin | ★★ | Mod | ★★ | ★★ |
| THE PLAZA RESTAURANT | Magic Kingdom | ★★ | Mod | ★★ | ★★ |
| TURF CLUB BAR & GRILL | Saratoga Springs | ★★ | Mod | ★★★ | ★★ |
| TRAIL'S END RESTAURANT | Fort Wilderness Resort | ★★ | Mod | ★★ | ★★ |
| LAKEVIEW RESTAURANT | Wyndham LBV | ★★ | Mod | ★ | ★★★ |
| MAYA GRILL | Coronado Springs | ★ | Mod | ★ | ★ |
| **BUFFET** | | | | | |
| BOMA— FLAVORS OF AFRICA | Animal Kingdom Lodge | ★★★★ | Exp | ★★★★ | ★★★★½ |
| CAPE MAY CAFE | Beach Club | ★★★½ | Mod | ★★★½ | ★★★★ |
| BIERGARTEN | Epcot | ★★★½ | Exp | ★★★ | ★★★★ |
| THE CRYSTAL PALACE | Magic Kingdom | ★★★ | Mod | ★★★½ | ★★★ |
| AKERSHUS ROYAL BANQUET HALL | Epcot | ★★★ | Exp | ★★★ | ★★★★ |
| TUSKER HOUSE RESTAURANT | Animal Kingdom | ★★★ | Mod | ★★★ | ★★★ |
| CHEF MICKEY'S | Contemporary | ★★½ | Exp | ★★★ | ★★★ |
| HOLLYWOOD & VINE | DHS | ★★½ | Mod | ★★★ | ★★★ |
| 1900 PARK FARE | Grand Floridian | ★★½ | Mod | ★★★ | ★★★ |
| GARDEN GROVE | Swan | ★★ | Mod | ★★★ | ★★ |
| TRAIL'S END RESTAURANT | Fort Wilderness Resort | ★★ | Mod | ★★ | ★★ |
| **CHINESE** | | | | | |
| NINE DRAGONS RESTAURANT | Epcot | ★★★ | Mod | ★★★ | ★★ |
| **CUBAN** | | | | | |
| BONGOS CUBAN CAFÉ | Downtown Disney | ★★ | Mod | ★★ | ★★ |
| **ENGLISH** | | | | | |
| ROSE & CROWN DINING ROOM | Epcot | ★★★ | Mod | ★★★½ | ★★ |
| **FRENCH** | | | | | |
| MONSIEUR PAUL | Epcot | ★★★★ | Exp | ★★★★½ | ★★★ |

## Walt Disney World Restaurants by Cuisine *(continued)*

| CUISINE | LOCATION | OVERALL RATING | COST | QUALITY RATING | VALUE RATING |
|---------|----------|----------------|------|----------------|--------------|
| **FRENCH** *(continued)* | | | | | |
| **BE OUR GUEST RESTAURANT** | Magic Kingdom | ★★★★ | Exp | ★★★★ | ★★★★ |
| **LES CHEFS DE FRANCE** | Epcot | ★★★ | Exp | ★★★ | ★★★ |
| **GERMAN** | | | | | |
| **BIERGARTEN** | Epcot | ★★ | Exp | ★★ | ★★★★ |
| **GLOBAL** | | | | | |
| **PARADISO 37** | Downtown Disney | ★★½ | Inexp | ★★★ | ★★★ |
| **GOURMET** | | | | | |
| **VICTORIA & ALBERT'S** | Grand Floridian | ★★★★★ | Exp | ★★★★★ | ★★★★ |
| **INDIAN/AFRICAN** | | | | | |
| **SANAA** | Animal Kingdom Villas–Kidani Village | ★★★★ | Exp | ★★★★ | ★★★★ |
| **IRISH** | | | | | |
| **RAGLAN ROAD IRISH PUB & RESTAURANT** | Downtown Disney | ★★★★ | Mod | ★★★½ | ★★★ |
| **ITALIAN** | | | | | |
| **TUTTO ITALIA RISTORANTE** | Epcot | ★★★★ | Exp | ★★★★ | ★★★ |
| **VIA NAPOLI** | Epcot | ★★★★ | Mod | ★★★½ | ★★★ |
| **ANDIAMO ITALIAN BISTRO & GRILLE** | Hilton | ★★★ | Exp | ★★★ | ★★★ |
| **IL MULINO NEW YORK TRATTORIA** | Swan | ★★★ | Exp | ★★★ | ★★ |
| **MAMA MELROSE'S RISTORANTE ITALIANO** | DHS | ★★½ | Mod | ★★★ | ★★ |
| **PORTOBELLO** | Downtown Disney | ★★½ | Exp | ★★★ | ★★ |
| **TONY'S TOWN SQUARE RESTAURANT** | Magic Kingdom | ★★½ | Mod | ★★★ | ★★ |
| **JAPANESE/SUSHI** | | | | | |
| **KIMONOS** | Swan | ★★★★ | Mod | ★★★★½ | ★★★ |
| **TEPPAN EDO** | Epcot | ★★★½ | Exp | ★★★★ | ★★★ |
| **TOKYO DINING** | Epcot | ★★★ | Mod | ★★★★ | ★★★ |
| **BENIHANA** | Hilton | ★★★ | Exp | ★★★½ | ★★★ |
| **MEDITERRANEAN** | | | | | |
| **CÍTRICOS** | Grand Floridian | ★★★½ | Exp | ★★★★½ | ★★★ |
| **FRESH MEDITERRANEAN MARKET** | Dolphin | ★★½ | Mod | ★★½ | ★★ |
| **MEXICAN** | | | | | |
| **LA HACIENDA DE SAN ANGEL** | Epcot | ★★★ | Exp | ★★★½ | ★★½ |
| **SAN ANGEL INN** | Epcot | ★★★ | Exp | ★★★ | ★★ |
| **MAYA GRILL** | Coronado Springs | ★ | Exp | ★ | ★ |

## Walt Disney World Restaurants by Cuisine *(continued)*

| CUISINE | LOCATION | OVERALL RATING | COST | QUALITY RATING | VALUE RATING |
|---|---|---|---|---|---|
| **MOROCCAN** | | | | | |
| SPICE ROAD TABLE | Epcot | ★★★½ | Mod | ★★★★ | ★★★ |
| RESTAURANT MARRAKESH | Epcot | ★★ | Mod | ★★½ | ★★ |
| **NORWEGIAN** | | | | | |
| AKERSHUS ROYAL BANQUET HALL | Epcot | ★★★ | Exp | ★★★ | ★★★★ |
| **POLYNESIAN/PAN-ASIAN** | | | | | |
| 'OHANA | Polynesian | ★★★ | Mod | ★★★½ | ★★★ |
| KONA CAFE | Polynesian | ★★★ | Mod | ★★★ | ★★★★ |
| YAK & YETI RESTAURANT | Animal Kingdom | ★★ | Exp | ★★½ | ★★ |
| **SEAFOOD** | | | | | |
| NARCOOSSEE'S | Grand Floridian | ★★★★½ | Exp | ★★★½ | ★★ |
| FLYING FISH CAFE | BoardWalk | ★★★★ | Exp | ★★★★ | ★★★ |
| ARTIST POINT | Wilderness Lodge | ★★★½ | Exp | ★★★★ | ★★★ |
| TODD ENGLISH'S BLUEZOO | Dolphin | ★★★ | Exp | ★★★★ | ★★ |
| FULTON'S CRAB HOUSE | Downtown Disney | ★★½ | Exp | ★★★½ | ★★ |
| CORAL REEF RESTAURANT | Epcot | ★★½ | Exp | ★★ | ★★ |
| SHUTTERS AT OLD PORT ROYALE | Caribbean Beach | ★★ | Mod | ★★½ | ★★ |
| **STEAK** | | | | | |
| SHULA'S STEAK HOUSE | Dolphin | ★★★★ | Exp | ★★★★ | ★★ |
| LE CELLIER STEAKHOUSE | Epcot | ★★★½ | Exp | ★★★½ | ★★★ |
| YACHTSMAN STEAKHOUSE | Yacht Club | ★★★ | Exp | ★★★½ | ★★ |
| SHUTTERS AT OLD PORT ROYALE | Caribbean Beach | ★★ | Mod | ★★½ | ★★ |

*Continued from page 457*

**SETTING AND ATMOSPHERE** Home to Princess Storybook Dining for breakfast, lunch, and dinner, the dining room is always full of antsy kids hoping for an audience with the princesses. But there are cocktails for grown-ups (even a shot of Linie Aquavit). Modeled on a 14th-century fortress, Akershus entertains its guests in a great banquet hall under A-framed ceilings and massive iron chandeliers.

**HOUSE SPECIALTIES** Dinner: *koldtbord* (cold buffet), grilled beef-tenderloin tips, catch of the day, grilled pork tenderloin, pan-seared salmon, traditional *kjottkake* (ground-beef-and-pork dumplings served with mashed potatoes, seasonal vegetables, and lingonberry sauce).

**OTHER RECOMMENDATIONS** Cold Carlsberg beer on tap.

**SUMMARY AND COMMENTS** Though the theme is Scandinavian, breakfast is all-American save for a handful of Norwegian tastes such as mackerel, herring, and *gjetost* (goat cheese). Lunch and dinner start at the *koldtbord,* where you'll find an array of cheeses, meats, seafood, and salads; entrées include roast turkey with stuffing, gravy, and cranberry sauce; pan-seared salmon; braised beef ribs; mushroom-stuffed pasta; and *kjottkake.* Picky kids will like the pasta with grilled chicken, cheese pizza, and meatballs with mashed potatoes. You can order more than one entree—just ask. Service can sometimes be slow, but the cuisine is above average. As for the prices? You're paying for the privilege of princess face time.

## Andiamo Italian Bistro & Grille ★★★

| ITALIAN | EXPENSIVE | QUALITY ★★★ | VALUE ★★★ |
|---|---|---|---|
| READER-SURVEY RESPONSES | Not enough to rate | DISNEY DINING PLAN? | No |

Hilton in the Walt Disney World Resort, Downtown Disney Resort Area; ☎ 407-827-3838

---

**Reservations** Accepted. **When to go** Early evening. **Cost range** $17–$38. **Service** ★★★. **Friendliness** ★★★★. **Parking** Valet (free) or hotel lot. **Bar** Full bar. **Wine selection** Good. **Dress** Casual. **Disabled access** Yes. **Customers** Hotel guests. **Dinner** Daily, 5:30–11 p.m.

**SETTING AND ATMOSPHERE** Casual Italian bistro and wine bar that's suitable for families (kids under age 5 eat free on weekdays).

**HOUSE SPECIALTIES** Bruschetta, shrimp scampi, pork Marsala, pastas from traditional spaghetti and meatballs to pappardelle, angel hair, rigatoni, and lasagna Bolognese.

**OTHER RECOMMENDATIONS** Broiled salmon with fresh vegetables, filet mignon.

**SUMMARY AND COMMENTS** Better-than-average Italian. Not destination dining, but vacationers at the Downtown Disney resorts can head here for a satisfying meal.

## Artist Point ★★★½

| AMERICAN | EXPENSIVE | QUALITY ★★★★ | VALUE ★★★ |
|---|---|---|---|
| READER-SURVEY RESPONSES | 88% 👍 12% 👎 | DISNEY DINING PLAN? | Yes |

Wilderness Lodge & Villas; ☎ 407-824-3200

---

**Reservations** Required. **Dining Plan credits** 2 per person, per meal. **When to go** Anytime. **Cost range** $28–$49 (child $7–$11). **Service** ★★★★★. **Friendliness** ★★★★★. **Parking** Hotel lot. **Bar** Full service. **Wine selection** All wines from Pacific Northwest. **Dress** Dressy casual. **Disabled access** Yes. **Customers** Hotel guests, locals. **Dinner** Daily, 5:30–9:30 p.m.

**SETTING AND ATMOSPHERE** Two-story-high paintings depict the landscape of the Pacific Northwest, and out the tall windows you'll see Disney's version of the Pacific Northwest: wildflowers, the lake, a waterfall off high rocks, even an erupting geyser. Cast-iron chandeliers hold 12 lanterns with milk-glass panes; tables are made of heavy wood and engraved with animals native to the Northwest.

**HOUSE SPECIALTIES** Roasted cedar-plank salmon, kettle-steamed Penn Cove mussels, smoky portobello soup, and berry cobbler.

**OTHER RECOMMENDATIONS** All-natural Kurobuta pork, pan-seared Alaskan halibut, and truffle pasta.

**SUMMARY AND COMMENTS** The cavernous dining room can feel a little sterile, but the food and friendly service warm up the place. The cedar-plank salmon is a must-try, but the slow-roasted buffalo strip steak runs a close second in today's fat- and carb-conscious world. The restaurant offers a terrific all–Pacific Northwest wine list.

## Beaches & Cream Soda Shop  ★★½

| AMERICAN | INEXPENSIVE | | QUALITY ★★½ | VALUE ★★½ |
|---|---|---|---|---|
| READER-SURVEY RESPONSES | 94% 👍 | 6% 👎 | DISNEY DINING PLAN? | Yes |

Beach Club Resort; ☎ 407-934-8000

**Reservations** Recommended. **Dining Plan credits** 1 per person, per meal. **When to go** Anytime. **Cost range** $8–$15. **Service** ★★★. **Friendliness** ★★★★. **Parking** Hotel lot. **Bar** Beer only. **Wine selection** None. **Dress** Casual. **Disabled access** Yes. **Customers** Resort guests. **Lunch and dinner** Daily, 11 a.m.–11 p.m.

SETTING AND ATMOSPHERE Casual eats with a retro soda-fountain decor. There's often a line as guests in bathing suits and flip-flops queue up for the hearty burgers (or a vegetarian falafel) and piles of hot fries.

HOUSE SPECIALTIES Burgers (singles and doubles) and fries; giant hot dogs; hand-scooped ice cream including the gargantuan $29 Kitchen Sink dessert, with five flavors of ice cream smothered in toppings.

OTHER RECOMMENDATIONS Pot roast sandwich, Milky Way sundae.

SUMMARY AND COMMENTS Grab your burger and sit at a nearby poolside table.

## Benihana  ★★★

| JAPANESE | EXPENSIVE | QUALITY ★★★½ | VALUE ★★★ |
|---|---|---|---|
| READER-SURVEY RESPONSES | Not enough to rate | DISNEY DINING PLAN? | No |

Hilton in the Walt Disney World Resort, Downtown Disney Resort Area; ☎ 407-827-4865

**Reservations** Recommended. **When to go** Anytime. **Cost range** $19–$45 (child $8.50–$10.50). **Service** ★★★★★. **Friendliness** ★★★★★. **Parking** Hotel lot. **Bar** Full service. **Wine selection** Good. **Dress** Casual. **Disabled access** Yes. **Customers** Hotel guests, some locals. **Dinner** Monday–Thursday, 4–10 p.m.; Friday–Sunday, 2–10 p.m.

SETTING AND ATMOSPHERE Large tables with built-in grills are crammed into small rooms decorated with rice-paper panels and Japanese lanterns. Lighting is low and focused on the stage—the chef's grill.

HOUSE SPECIALTIES Teppanyaki service at large tables (where the chef cooks dinner in front of you). Specialties include tenderloin, ocean scallops, lobster tail, and hibachi vegetables.

OTHER RECOMMENDATIONS Japanese onion soup.

ENTERTAINMENT AND AMENITIES Dinner is the show at this teppanyaki restaurant, where the chef does a lot of noisy chopping and grilling.

SUMMARY AND COMMENTS If you're looking for a nice, quiet dinner, be aware that diners sit at tables of eight, making private conversation almost impossible.

## Be Our Guest Restaurant  ★★★★

| FRENCH/AMERICAN | EXPENSIVE | | QUALITY ★★★★ | VALUE ★★★★ |
|---|---|---|---|---|
| READER-SURVEY RESPONSES | 91% 👍 | 9% 👎 | DISNEY DINING PLAN? | Yes |

Fantasyland, Magic Kingdom; ☎ 407-939-3463

**Reservations** Accepted. **Dining Plan credits** 1 per person, per meal (Quick-Service credit for lunch, Table-Service credit for dinner). **When to go** Lunch or dinner. **Cost range** Lunch $9–$13.50 (child $6.99–$8.50), dinner $24–$33 (child $9–$11). **Service** ★★★★. **Friendliness** ★★★★. **Parking** Magic Kingdom lot. **Bar** Wine and beer only. **Wine selection** Solid wine list that's mostly French to match the restaurant's theming—from sparkling starters to a sweet Sauternes. A handful of popular California vintages are on the list. **Dress** Casual. **Disabled access** Yes. **Customers** Magic Kingdom guests. **Lunch** Daily, 10:30 a.m.–2:30 p.m. **Dinner** Daily, 4–9:30 p.m.

**SETTING AND ATMOSPHERE** Cross the stone gargoyle bridge into the cavernous Beast's Castle to dine in one of three themed rooms inspired by *Beauty and the Beast:* the Grand Ballroom, the mysterious West Wing, and the pretty Rose Gallery. Lunch is quick-service (see page 448), and the rooms fill up fast, with a noise level to match the hordes (550 seats). The lights are dimmed at dinner, which offers table service and a tad more serenity. And—drum roll, please—for the first time, wine and beer are now served during the dinner hour in the Magic Kingdom.

**HOUSE SPECIALTIES** Pan-seared salmon on leek fondue; New York strip.

**OTHER RECOMMENDATIONS** Shrimp and scallops in puff pastry, mussels Provençal. For dessert, cupcakes and a no-sugar-added lemon-raspberry fruit puff.

**SUMMARY AND COMMENTS** The best seats in the ballroom are beneath the tall arched windows with "snow" falling outside, in an exact replica of the film. For a slightly less hectic experience, opt for the West Wing, which is smaller, darker, and a little quieter.

## Biergarten ★★

| GERMAN | EXPENSIVE | QUALITY ★★ | VALUE ★★★★ |
|---|---|---|---|
| READER-SURVEY RESPONSES | 91% 👍 9% 👎 | DISNEY DINING PLAN? | Yes |

Germany, World Showcase, Epcot; ☎ 407-939-3463

**Reservations** Accepted. **Dining Plan credits** 1 per person, per meal. **When to go** Lunch or dinner. **Cost range** Lunch $23 (child $12), dinner $35 (child $17). *Note:* Prices may increase during peak periods (see page 428). **Service ★★★★. Friendliness ★★★★. Parking** Epcot lot. **Bar** Full service. **Wine selection** German. **Dress** Casual. **Disabled access** Yes. **Customers** Theme park guests. **Lunch** Daily, noon–3:45 p.m. **Dinner** Daily, 4 p.m.–park closing.

**SETTING AND ATMOSPHERE** A hefty German buffet includes schnitzel, a variety of wursts, spaetzle, roast chicken, and sauerbraten (dinner only). Salads, breads, and desserts round out the offerings. The light level is low, and decor is inspired by a German village town square, with seating at long tables in a tiered dining room that surrounds a stage and dance floor. A lederhosen-clad oompah band plays on the stage and encourages diners to sing along and dance.

**HOUSE SPECIALTIES** Warm German potato salad, beet salad, various sausages, homemade spaetzle with gravy, *nudelgratin* (baked macaroni with cheese custard), and sauerbraten. There's also carved-to-order pork roast with German mustard and breaded pork schnitzel. The buffet is set up on wooden barrels.

**OTHER RECOMMENDATIONS** Beef *rouladen,* braised red cabbage, potato dumplings (dinner only), and beer.

**ENTERTAINMENT AND AMENITIES** Oompah band and German dancers perform after 1:15 p.m.

**SUMMARY AND COMMENTS** Unless you have a very big party, you'll be seated with other guests—great fun if you love to socialize. But the lively 25-minute dinner show (one every hour) and noisy dining room are part of the fun, especially for families. As our survey responses show, *Unofficial Guide* readers love Biergarten.

## Big River Grille & Brewing Works ★★

| AMERICAN | MODERATE | QUALITY ★★ | VALUE ★★ |
|---|---|---|---|
| READER-SURVEY RESPONSES | 71% 👍 29% 👎 | DISNEY DINING PLAN? | Yes |

BoardWalk; ☎ 407-560-0253

**Reservations** Not accepted. **Dining Plan credits** 1 per person, per meal. **When to go** Anytime. **Cost range** $10.50–$26. **Service** ★★★. **Friendliness** ★★★★. **Parking** BoardWalk lot. **Bar** Full service. **Wine selection** Minimal. **Dress** Casual. **Disabled access** Yes. **Customers** Tourists. **Lunch and dinner** Sunday–Thursday, 11 a.m.–11 p.m., Friday and Saturday until midnight.

**SETTING AND ATMOSPHERE** Industrial cubist murals of factories, machinist-metal and wood chairs and tables, and a midnight-blue neon river that flows along the ceiling of the restaurant set a working-class atmosphere. The place is small—it seems like the huge copper brewing tanks take up more room than that allotted to the diners. Outside seating and service, weather permitting.

**HOUSE SPECIALTIES** Big Brew cheeseburger, flame-grilled meat loaf.

**SUMMARY AND COMMENTS** Run by a Tennessee company, Big River Grille seems like an afterthought along the BoardWalk and competes with the nearby ESPN Club (see page 471) for the burger-and-brew crowd. But if you're looking for handcrafted beers, this is the place—they serve five beers, including a light lager, a robust ale, and seasonal choices. A good late-night-dining choice.

## Boatwright's Dining Hall ★★½

| AMERICAN/CAJUN | MODERATE | QUALITY ★★★ | VALUE ★★ |
|---|---|---|---|
| READER-SURVEY RESPONSES 83% 👍 | 17% 👎 | DISNEY DINING PLAN? Yes | |

Port Orleans Resort Riverside; ☎ 407-939-3463

**Reservations** Accepted. **Dining Plan credits** 1 per person, per meal. **When to go** Early evening. **Cost range** Dinner $18–$31 (child $8.59). **Service** ★★★. **Friendliness** ★★★★★. **Parking** Hotel lot. **Bar** Full service. **Wine selection** Fair. **Dress** Casual. **Disabled access** Yes. **Customers** Hotel guests. **Dinner** Daily, 5–10 p.m.

**SETTING AND ATMOSPHERE** Cavernous, casual dining room with wood floors and wooden tables set with a boatwright's tool kit that contains condiments. The giant skeleton of a riverboat completes the theme.

**HOUSE SPECIALTIES** Andouille-crusted catfish; jambalaya with chicken and andouille sausage.

**OTHER RECOMMENDATIONS** Prime rib, bananas Foster angel-food cake.

**SUMMARY AND COMMENTS** With seating for 200, Boatwright's serves the masses, and the cuisine—basic fare with a Cajun flair)—is pretty homogenized. It's the only table-service restaurant in Port Orleans Resort, so it gets busy and there can be waits. Order a Southern Hurricane (Southern Comfort and Myers's Rum with tropical fruit juices)—and relax.

## Boma—Flavors of Africa ★★★★

| AFRICAN | EXPENSIVE | QUALITY ★★★★ | VALUE ★★★★½ |
|---|---|---|---|
| READER-SURVEY RESPONSES 92% 👍 | 8% 👎 | DISNEY DINING PLAN? Yes | |

Animal Kingdom Lodge & Villas–Jambo House; ☎ 407-938-3000

**Reservations** Recommended for dinner. **Dining Plan credits** 1 per person, per meal. **When to go** Anytime. **Cost range** Breakfast $20 (child $12), dinner $38 (child $18). *Note:* Prices may increase during peak periods (see page 428). **Service** ★★★★. **Friendliness** ★★★★. **Parking** Valet ($20) or hotel lot. **Bar** Full service. **Wine selection** All South African. **Dress** Casual. **Disabled access** Yes. **Customers** Hotel guests. **Breakfast** Daily, 7:30–11 a.m. **Dinner** Daily, 4:30–10 p.m.

**SETTING AND ATMOSPHERE** Big dining room with side-by-side food stations that encourage diners to roam about and graze, just like the animals that wander about outside the lodge.

**HOUSE SPECIALTIES** Watermelon-rind salad, Moroccan seafood salad, roasted meats, Durban spiced roasted chicken, and vegetable skewers.

**OTHER RECOMMENDATIONS** Sweet-potato pancakes, Zebra Dome dessert, soups and stews.

**SUMMARY AND COMMENTS** The menu rarely changes, as Boma is a favorite of locals and visitors who return time and again for the salads, roasted meats, and interesting sauces. While Disney calls this a buffet, it's very different from what you'd typically expect (there are no steam tables, for starters). If you like a major bang for your buck, try Boma.

## Bongos Cuban Café ★★

| CUBAN | MODERATE | QUALITY ★★ | VALUE ★★ |
|---|---|---|---|
| READER-SURVEY RESPONSES 85% 👍 | 15% 👎 | DISNEY DINING PLAN? Yes | |

Downtown Disney West Side; ☎ 407-828-0999

**Reservations** Recommended. **Dining Plan credits** 1 per person, per meal. **When to go** Anytime. **Cost range** $10–$40 (child $6–$8). **Service** ★★★★. **Friendliness** ★★★★. **Parking** Downtown Disney lot. **Bar** Full service. **Wine selection** Moderate. **Dress** Casual. **Disabled access** Elevator to second level. **Customers** Fans of Cuban culture and cuisine; Disney guests. **Lunch and dinner** Sunday–Thursday, 11 a.m.–11 p.m., Friday and Saturday until midnight.

**SETTING AND ATMOSPHERE** This multilevel restaurant features an airy environment with a tropical theme built around a three-story pineapple. Other touches include a banana-leaf roof, banana-leaf ceiling fans, and palm tree–shaped columns. Hand-painted murals and mosaics lend an artistic air, and an open wraparound porch provides pleasant outdoor dining.

**HOUSE SPECIALTIES** *Arroz con pollo* (chicken with rice), *camarones al ajillo* (shrimp in garlic sauce), *ropa vieja* (shredded beef in tomato sauce), and *churrasco* (grilled skirt steak).

**ENTERTAINMENT AND AMENITIES** Latin music.

**SUMMARY AND COMMENTS** Gloria Estefan and her husband-producer, Emilio, created this large restaurant that marries salsa music with Cuban cuisine. Any number of mom-and-pop Cuban restaurants in the area do a better and more consistent job with this wonderful cuisine, so if you've never had Cuban food, try it somewhere else. Come here to have a drink with an umbrella in it and listen to music. Upbeat but noisy.

## California Grill ★★★★★

| AMERICAN | EXPENSIVE | QUALITY ★★★★★ | VALUE ★★★ |
|---|---|---|---|
| READER-SURVEY RESPONSES 93% 👍 | 7% 👎 | DISNEY DINING PLAN? Yes | |

Contemporary Resort; ☎ 407-939-3463

**Reservations** Required. **Dining Plan credits** 2 per person, per meal. **When to go** During evening fireworks. **Cost range** $32–$50 (child $9–$18). **Service** ★★★★★. **Friendliness** ★★★★★. **Parking** Valet ($20) or hotel lot. **Bar** Full service. **Wine selection** Fantastic. **Dress** Dressy casual. **Disabled access** Yes. **Customers** Hotel guests and locals. **Dinner** Daily, 5–10 p.m.

**SETTING AND ATMOSPHERE** California Grill turns 20 this year, and while the sweeping views of the Magic Kingdom and Seven Seas Lagoon haven't changed, a new midcentury-modern design in warm oranges and yellows gives one of Disney's top restaurants a big-city vibe. A show-stopping wine display comprises 1,600 bottles in a climate-controlled case just off the elevator. The on-stage kitchen is all new, and the popular sushi bar has been expanded. Two new communal tables are positioned for optimal Magic Kingdom fireworks viewing.

**HOUSE SPECIALTIES** Pork Two Ways (grilled tenderloin and lacquered pork belly); oak-fired filet of beef; Sonoma goat-cheese ravioli; Cape Canaveral prawns with oven-roasted tomatoes, charred lemon, and baby arugula; three-meat signature meatballs. Outstanding wine list.

**ENTERTAINMENT AND AMENITIES** Magic Kingdom fireworks are the star of the dinner show—but only diners with reservations may watch from the 15th floor.

**SUMMARY AND COMMENTS** California Grill remains one of Walt Disney World's top dining experiences.

## Cape May Cafe ★★★½

| AMERICAN/BUFFET | MODERATE | QUALITY ★★★½ | VALUE ★★★★ |
|---|---|---|---|
| READER-SURVEY RESPONSES 83% 👍 | 17% 👎 | DISNEY DINING PLAN? | Yes |

Beach Club Resort; ☎ 407-934-3358

**Reservations** Recommended. **Dining Plan credits** 1 per person, per meal. **When to go** Anytime. **Cost range** Breakfast $27 (child $14), dinner $38 (child $18). *Note:* Prices may increase during peak periods (see page 428). **Service** ★★★★★. **Friendliness** ★★★★★. **Parking** Hotel lot. **Bar** Full service. **Wine selection** Limited. **Dress** Casual. **Disabled access** Yes. **Customers** Theme park and hotel guests. **Breakfast** Daily, 7:30–11 a.m. **Dinner** Daily, 5–10 p.m.

**SETTING AND ATMOSPHERE** The natural-finish wood furniture and padded booths are executed in a clean, nautical New England style.

**HOUSE SPECIALTIES** The buffet features peel-and-eat shrimp, tasty (albeit chewy) clams, mussels, snow-crab legs, fish of the day, flank steak, roast pork, barbecue ribs, chicken, corn on the cob, lots of salads, and a good dessert bar. The kids' bar includes chicken nuggets and mac and cheese.

**OTHER RECOMMENDATIONS** The tart Key lime pie from the dessert bar.

**ENTERTAINMENT AND AMENITIES** Character breakfast with Goofy, Minnie, and Chip 'n' Dale.

**SUMMARY AND COMMENTS** Cape May has been a favorite for years because of its consistently good food and efficient service. Advance Reservations are recommended. Because Cape May is within easy walking distance of the World Showcase entrance to Epcot, it's a convenient and affordable place to dine before *IllumiNations*.

## Captain's Grille ★★★

| AMERICAN | MODERATE | QUALITY ★★★½ | VALUE ★★★ |
|---|---|---|---|
| READER-SURVEY RESPONSES 91% 👍 | 9% 👎 | DISNEY DINING PLAN? | Yes |

Yacht Club Resort; ☎ 407-939-3463

**Reservations** Accepted. **Dining Plan credits** 1 per person, per meal. **When to go** Breakfast or lunch. **Cost range** Breakfast buffet $18.99, lunch $13.50–$20 (child $8.59), dinner $15–$30. **Service** ★★★★★. **Friendliness** ★★★★★. **Parking** Hotel lot. **Bar** Full service. **Wine selection** Good. **Dress** Casual. **Disabled access** Yes. **Customers** Hotel guests. **Breakfast** Daily, 7:30–11:25 a.m. **Lunch** Daily, 11:30 a.m.–2 p.m. **Dinner** Daily, 5–9 p.m.

**SETTING AND ATMOSPHERE** This large dining room was recently spiffed up with new tables and chairs, wallpaper, and paint—along with a redesigned menu featuring more than three dozen new dishes.

**HOUSE SPECIALTIES** Breakfast features a buffet or an à la carte menu, with such selections as a butter-poached lobster omelet and citrus-scented French toast. Lunch is coffee-shop fare including New England lobster sliders, burgers, fish and chips, and crab cakes. Dinner features grilled New York strip, Cabernet-braised short ribs, rosemary-brined pork tenderloin, seasonal fish, and snow crab legs.

**SUMMARY AND COMMENTS** Not a dining destination, but it's a favorite of Disney cast members, who like it because it's quiet, the service is quick, and the food is dependable. The new menu raises the bar a bit—we've heard a local food critic rave about the lobster omelet, and the Cabernet-braised short ribs get great reviews.

## Le Cellier Steakhouse ★★★½

| STEAK | EXPENSIVE | QUALITY ★★★½ | VALUE ★★★ |
|---|---|---|---|
| READER-SURVEY RESPONSES | 92% 👍 | 8% 👎 | DISNEY DINING PLAN? Yes |

Canada, World Showcase, Epcot; ☎ 407-939-3463

**Reservations** Required. **Dining Plan credits** 2 per person, per meal. **When to go** Before 6 p.m. **Cost range** Lunch and dinner, $27–$64 (child $8–$12). **Service** ★★★★. **Friendliness** ★★★★★. **Parking** Epcot lot. **Bar** Full bar. **Wine selection** Canadian wines are featured. **Dress** Casual. **Disabled access** Yes. **Customers** Theme park guests. **Lunch** Daily, 11:30 a.m.–3 p.m. **Dinner** Daily, 4–8:50 p.m.

**SETTING AND ATMOSPHERE** Designed to look like a wine cellar, Le Cellier is kind of gloomy considering how expensive it is, but its many devoted fans make this one tough reservation to snag. Chef Al Youngman's cuisine is superb, featuring Canadian beef.

**HOUSE SPECIALTIES** Mushroom filet mignon, Canadian Cheddar cheese soup, *poutine* fries.

**OTHER RECOMMENDATIONS** Dry-aged rib eye, venison rack, five-spiced duck, jumbo-lump-crab pasta. Great selection of dessert wines at dinner.

**SUMMARY AND COMMENTS** The high-dollar menu ($64 for the rib eye!) is the same for lunch and dinner. You could make a meal of the rich Cheddar cheese soup and a salad, but if you're one of the lucky ones who's managed a reservation, you might as well splurge.

## Chef Mickey's ★★½

| AMERICAN/BUFFET | EXPENSIVE | QUALITY ★★★ | VALUE ★★★ |
|---|---|---|---|
| READER-SURVEY RESPONSES | 84% 👍 | 16% 👎 | DISNEY DINING PLAN? Yes |

Contemporary Resort; ☎ 407-939-3463

**Reservations** Required. **Dining Plan credits** 1 per person, per meal. **When to go** Early evening. **Cost range** Breakfast $33 (child $18), dinner $41 (child $20). *Note:* Prices may increase during peak periods (see page 428). **Service** ★★★★. **Friendliness** ★★★★★. **Parking** Valet ($20) or hotel lot. **Bar** Full service. **Wine selection** Fair. **Dress** Casual. **Disabled access** Yes. **Customers** Theme park guests. **Character breakfast** Daily, 7–11:30 a.m. **Character dinner** Daily, 5–9:30 p.m.

**SETTING AND ATMOSPHERE** A colorful, open dining room with the monorail running overhead, this is one of the most popular Disney-character restaurants—mostly because you're guaranteed an audience with Mickey Mouse, who dons a chef's toque and visits every single table for photos. (Goofy, Minnie, Donald, and Pluto are on hand, too.) The buffet circles the center of the room. It's loud, crowded, busy, and fun for families. We rarely see anyone here without kids in tow.

**HOUSE SPECIALTIES** Breakfast: Cheese blintzes, biscuits and gravy. Dinner: carved meats.

**OTHER RECOMMENDATIONS** Fresh greens and mixed salads, pasta selections, Parmesan mashed potatoes and gravy. Sundae bar.

**ENTERTAINMENT AND AMENITIES** Character visits.

**SUMMARY AND COMMENTS** If you go hungry, this all-you-can-eat buffet is a good value for families; there's plenty for picky eaters, and you can start or end the day with a full tummy and photos of the top Disney characters already checked off your to-do list. Selections at both breakfast and dinner are freshly prepared and served in casseroles and platters on special heated countertops—a small step up from chafing dishes. And no one cares if the kids are loud.

## Les Chefs de France  ★★★

| FRENCH | EXPENSIVE | QUALITY ★★★ | VALUE ★★★ |
| --- | --- | --- | --- |
| READER-SURVEY RESPONSES | 82% 👍 18% 👎 | DISNEY DINING PLAN? | Yes |

France, World Showcase, Epcot; ☎ 407-939-3463

**Reservations** Recommended. **Dining Plan credits** 1 per person, per meal. **When to go** Anytime. **Cost range** Lunch $13–$29 (child $7–$8), dinner $19–$40 (child $7–$8). **Service** ★★★★★. **Friendliness** ★★★★★. **Parking** Epcot lot. **Bar** Beer. **Wine selection** Very good. **Dress** Casual. **Disabled access** Yes. **Customers** Theme park guests. **Lunch** Daily, noon–3 p.m. **Dinner** Daily, 5–9 p.m.

**SETTING AND ATMOSPHERE** This bustling World Showcase dining room is usually packed and infused with the aroma of buttery croissants—as much a part of the atmosphere here as the carefully placed copies of *Le Monde* and the huge, mottled mirrors. White tablecloths and padded banquettes accentuate the classic bistro decor of the main dining room. Another room off to the side is more casual, with a better view of what's going on outside.

**HOUSE SPECIALTIES** Dishes inspired by three great French chefs, for whom the restaurant is named: Paul Bocuse, the late Gaston Lenôtre, and Roger Vergé. Sample sautéed scallops and shrimp, braised beef short ribs in Cabernet, duck à l'orange, or a silky crème brûlée.

**OTHER RECOMMENDATIONS** Onion soup topped with Gruyère; smoked-ham crêpes (lunch only); tomato-and-goat-cheese tart.

**SUMMARY AND COMMENTS** Here's your chance to eat at a restaurant created by three of France's best chefs. Jerome Bocuse, the son of Paul Bocuse, runs the restaurant, and his father still visits from time to time. Executive chef Bruno Vrignon, who trained in Lyon with Bocuse, heads the kitchen team, and the French servers make it an immersion experience. If you're on a budget, go at lunch: Many dinner entrees are available midday at reduced prices. The best deal is the three-course lunch ($26) that starts with French onion soup with Gruyère or lobster bisque and continues with the classic *croque monsieur* (toasted ham-and-cheese sandwich), quiche, or baked macaroni with Gruyère, followed by your choice of dessert.

## Cinderella's Royal Table  ★★★

| AMERICAN | EXPENSIVE | QUALITY ★★★ | VALUE ★★ |
| --- | --- | --- | --- |
| READER-SURVEY RESPONSES | 84% 👍 16% 👎 | DISNEY DINING PLAN? | Yes |

Cinderella Castle, Fantasyland, Magic Kingdom; ☎ 407-939-3463

**Reservations** Required; credit card required to reserve; must prepay in full. **Dining Plan credits** 2 per person, per meal. **When to go** Early. **Cost range** Character breakfast, $53 adults, $34 children; character lunch, $57 adults, $36 children; character dinner, $67 adults, $41 children. *Note:* Prices may increase during peak periods (see page 428). **Service** ★★★★. **Friendliness** ★★★★. **Parking** Magic Kingdom lot. **Bar** None. **Wine selection** None. **Dress** Casual. **Disabled access**

Limited. **Customers** Theme park guests. **Character breakfast** Daily, 8:05–10:40 a.m. **Character lunch** Daily, 11:45 a.m.–2:40 p.m. **Character dinner** Daily, 3:50–10 p.m.

**SETTING AND ATMOSPHERE** A medieval banquet hall, appointed with the requisite banners and Round Table–like regalia, on the second floor of Cinderella Castle. Stained-glass windows overlook Fantasyland, but the view is limited.

**HOUSE SPECIALTIES** All meals are fixed-price character affairs, with the menus changing periodically. Breakfast is standard-issue. Lunch dishes may include pan-seared cod, pork on ciabatta bread, and the signature Major Domo's Short Rib (beef in Pinot Noir sauce with potato-and-parsnip puree). Dinner fare may include bone-in pork, fish of the day, and roasted beef tenderloin; kids can choose from beef tenderloin, turkey pot pie, or a roast chicken leg with whole-grain pilaf.

**ENTERTAINMENT AND AMENITIES** Assorted princesses attend all three pricey meals. They're expensive not so much because the food is good but because Disney forces you to purchase photos of your group that are bundled into the cost of each meal. No matter—families can't seem to get enough of this "Disney magic." For more on reserving a spot here (and the travails thereof), see page 354.

## Cítricos ★★★½

| MEDITERRANEAN | EXPENSIVE | QUALITY ★★★★½ | VALUE ★★★ |
|---|---|---|---|
| READER-SURVEY RESPONSES 86% 👍 | 14% 👎 | DISNEY DINING PLAN? Yes | |

Grand Floridian Resort & Spa; ☎ 407-939-7429

**Reservations** Required; credit card required to reserve the Chef's Domain. **Dining Plan credits** 2 per person, per meal. **When to go** Anytime. **Cost range** $29–$46 (child $9–$17). Chef's Domain: $650 minimum, minus tax and tips. **Service** ★★★★★. **Friendliness** ★★★★★. **Parking** Valet ($20); self-parking is deceptively far away. **Bar** Full service. **Wine selection** Very good. **Dress** Dressy casual. **Disabled access** Yes. **Customers** Hotel guests and locals. **Dinner** Daily, 5:30–10 p.m.

**SETTING AND ATMOSPHERE** The golds and yellows of the Mediterranean color this stylish dining room on the second floor of the Grand Floridian. Diners often find Chef Phillip Ponticelli working his culinary magic in the full-view show kitchen.

**HOUSE SPECIALTIES** Sautéed shrimp with lemon, Feta cheese, tomatoes, and white wine; oak-grilled filet of beef; braised veal shank.

**OTHER RECOMMENDATIONS** Pan-seared Florida black grouper, braised short ribs, *arancini,* and Berkshire pork.

**SUMMARY AND COMMENTS** This is one of the best-kept dining secrets at Disney World. Chef Ponticelli is very hands-on, and his TLC shows. The menu changes with the seasons, so there are always delicious surprises. If you're flush with cash (OK, plastic), reserve the Chef's Domain, a private room for up to 12 guests where the chef creates a special menu.

## Coral Reef Restaurant ★★½

| SEAFOOD | EXPENSIVE | QUALITY ★★ | VALUE ★★ |
|---|---|---|---|
| READER-SURVEY RESPONSES 80% 👍 | 20% 👎 | DISNEY DINING PLAN? Yes | |

The Seas with Nemo & Friends, Future World, Epcot; ☎ 407-939-3463

**Reservations** Required. **Dining Plan credits** 1 per person, per meal. **When to go** Lunch. **Cost range** Lunch $12.50–$33 (child $9), dinner $19.50–$33 (child

$9). **Service** ★★★★. **Friendliness** ★★★★. **Parking** Epcot lot. **Bar** Full service. **Wine selection** Good. **Dress** Casual. **Disabled access** Yes. **Customers** Theme park guests. **Lunch** Daily, 11:30 a.m.–3:20 p.m. **Dinner** Daily, 4 p.m.–park closing.

**SETTING AND ATMOSPHERE** Coral Reef offers one of the best theme park views anywhere: below the water level of the humongous saltwater tank in the Seas with Nemo & Friends. Sharks, rays, and even humans swim by, and every table has a great view. Tiered seating affords perfect views; special lighting fixtures throw ripple patterns on the ceiling, creating an underwater feel.

**HOUSE SPECIALTIES** Creamy lobster soup, on the menu since the restaurant opened; seared Scottish salmon; grilled New York strip steak; Chocolate Wave dessert. For kids: fish of the day, fried shrimp, cheesy pasta, and grilled chicken breast.

**SUMMARY AND COMMENTS** The quality of the food was better in years past, but Coral Reef is the only table-service restaurant in Future World where you can sip a glass of wine and enjoy a decent meal in a quiet, informal setting.

## The Crystal Palace ★★★

| AMERICAN/BUFFET | MODERATE | QUALITY ★★★½ | VALUE ★★★ |
|---|---|---|---|
| READER-SURVEY RESPONSES | 87% 👍 | 13% 👎 | DISNEY DINING PLAN? Yes |

Main Street, U.S.A., Magic Kingdom; ☎ 407-939-3463

**Reservations** Required. **Dining Plan credits** 1 per person, per meal. **When to go** Anytime. **Cost range** Breakfast $25 (child $14), lunch $26 (child $15), dinner $40 (child $20). *Note:* Prices may increase during peak periods (see page 428). **Service** ★★★. **Friendliness** ★★★★. **Parking** Magic Kingdom lot. **Bar** None. **Wine selection** None. **Dress** Casual. **Disabled access** Yes. **Customers** Magic Kingdom guests. **Character breakfast** Daily, 8–10:30 a.m. **Character lunch** Daily, 11:30 a.m.–2:45 p.m. **Character dinner** Daily, 3:15 p.m.–park closing.

**SETTING AND ATMOSPHERE** A turn-of-the-20th-century glass pavilion awash in sunlight and decorated with plenty of summer greenery. Seating is comfortable, and buffet lines are open and accessible. A low buffet area lets kids help themselves.

**HOUSE SPECIALTIES** Menu items change often but may include waffles and pancakes layered with fresh fruit for breakfast; prime rib, roast pork, and peel-and-eat shrimp for dinner; Thai curry mussels; grilled vegetables with balsamic glaze; pasta with wild mushrooms and chicken; shrimp; and a sundae bar. We love the salads—more than a dozen—from a simple green salad to one with papaya, frisée, and arugula.

**ENTERTAINMENT AND AMENITIES** Winnie the Pooh and friends dance about and pose with the kids.

**SUMMARY AND COMMENTS** The best dining value in the Magic Kingdom—go hungry and fill up. The food is consistently fine on the state-of-the-art buffet, which, instead of steam tables, has casserole dishes and pans that sit on special heated countertops. Picky kids get their own buffet with mac and cheese and chicken fingers.

## ESPN Club ★★½

| AMERICAN/SANDWICHES | MODERATE | QUALITY ★★★ | VALUE ★★★ |
|---|---|---|---|
| READER-SURVEY RESPONSES | 71% 👍 | 29% 👎 | DISNEY DINING PLAN? Yes |

BoardWalk; ☎ 407-939-1177

**Reservations** Not accepted. **Dining Plan credits** 1 per person, per meal. **When to go** Anytime. **Cost range** $7–$21 (child $8.59). **Service** ★★★.

**Friendliness** ★★★★. **Parking** Valet ($20) or BoardWalk lot. **Bar** Full service. **Wine selection** Minimal. **Dress** Casual. **Disabled access** Yes. **Customers** Tourists. **Hours** Daily, 11:30 a.m.–1 a.m.

**SETTING AND ATMOSPHERE** A sports bar to the $n$th degree, with basketball-court flooring, sports memorabilia, and more television monitors than a network affiliate. The bar area features satellite sports-trivia video games. A large octagonal space with a wall of TVs serves as the main dining room.

**HOUSE SPECIALTIES** Red wings, panini-press Reuben, the Veggie Jackson (grilled-vegetable sandwich with goat cheese and roasted red pepper).

**SUMMARY AND COMMENTS** Family-friendly and affordable. Service is a little more brusque than at other Disney restaurants. Portions are large, and the quality is in line with the price. A good choice for late-night dining or when you have to choose between going out for a bite and staying in the room to catch the big game.

## ESPN Wide World of Sports Grill  ★★½

| AMERICAN | MODERATE | QUALITY ★★★ | | VALUE ★★★ |
|---|---|---|---|---|
| READER-SURVEY RESPONSES | Not enough to rate | DISNEY DINING PLAN? | Yes | |

ESPN Wide World of Sports Complex; ☎ 407-939-2196

**Reservations** Not necessary. **Dining Plan credits** 1 per person, per meal. **When to go** When an event is going on. *Note:* You must pay admission to the sports complex to dine. **Cost range** $8–$10 (child $8.59). **Service** ★★★. **Friendliness** ★★½. **Parking** ESPN Wide World of Sports lot. **Bar** Full service. **Wine selection** Minimal. **Dress** Jerseys if you've got 'em. **Disabled access** Yes. **Customers** Sports fans. **Hours** Open only on event days.

**SETTING AND ATMOSPHERE** Think the Hard Rock Cafe with sports memorabilia instead of musical instruments. More than 20 big-screen TVs play whatever games are on.

**HOUSE SPECIALTIES** Burgers and sandwiches.

**ENTERTAINMENT AND AMENITIES** Televised sporting events.

**SUMMARY AND COMMENTS** The food is unpretentious American cuisine—giant burgers and piles of chicken wings. The menu works for hungry fans at the ESPN Wide World of Sports Complex.

## 50's Prime Time Cafe  ★★★

| AMERICAN | MODERATE | QUALITY ★★★ | | VALUE ★★★ |
|---|---|---|---|---|
| READER-SURVEY RESPONSES | 86% 👍 14% 👎 | DISNEY DINING PLAN? | Yes | |

Echo Lake, Disney's Hollywood Studios; ☎ 407-939-3463

**Reservations** Recommended. **Dining Plan credits** 1 per person, per meal. **When to go** Lunch or dinner. **Cost range** Lunch and dinner, $13.50–$22 (child $8.59). **Service** ★★★★★. **Friendliness** ★★★★★. **Parking** DHS lot. **Bar** Full service. **Wine selection** Limited. **Dress** Casual. **Disabled access** Yes. **Customers** Theme park guests. **Lunch** Daily, 11 a.m.–3:55 p.m.; opens at 10:30 a.m. on Sunday and Wednesday. **Dinner** Daily, 4 p.m.–park closing.

**SETTING AND ATMOSPHERE** Like eating a meal in your own kitchen, 1950s-style: Pastel laminate, goosenecked lamps, and black-and-white televisions that play vintage sitcoms are the rule.

**HOUSE SPECIALTIES** Meat loaf, pot roast, fried chicken, and other homey fare. It's easy to find something that kids will like.

**ENTERTAINMENT AND AMENITIES** Fifties sitcom clips on television.

**SUMMARY AND COMMENTS** Though the restaurant is usually packed and rather noisy, the waitstaff makes it worthwhile, nagging you just like Mom did to "take your elbows off the table" and "finish every last bite." Diners really get a kick out of the roleplay as well as the classic comedies playing on black-and-white TVs. Skip the appetizers and stick with filling fare like the pot roast or golden fried chicken. Don't miss the PB&J milkshake.

## Flying Fish Cafe ★★★★

| SEAFOOD | EXPENSIVE | QUALITY ★★★★ | VALUE ★★★ |
|---|---|---|---|
| READER-SURVEY RESPONSES 94% | 6% | DISNEY DINING PLAN? Yes | |

BoardWalk; ☎ 407-939-3463

**Reservations** Required. **Dining Plan credits** 2 per person, per meal. **When to go** Anytime. **Cost range** $28–$47 (child $8–$15). **Service** ★★★★★. **Friendliness** ★★★★★. **Parking** Valet ($20) or BoardWalk lot. **Bar** Full service. **Wine selection** Excellent but pricey. **Dress** Dressy casual. **Disabled access** Good. **Customers** Tourists and locals. **Dinner** Sunday–Thursday, 5:30–10 p.m.; Friday and Saturday, 5:30–10:30 p.m.

**SETTING AND ATMOSPHERE** A contemporary setting inspired by a 1930s Coney Island roller coaster. (The coaster was actually called the Flying Turns, and one of the cars on the ride was dubbed the Flying Fish.) Booth backs resemble the climbs and swoops of a coaster. On the far wall is a stylized depiction of a Ferris wheel, and whimsical fish fly overhead on a parachute ride. Diners may choose to sit at the counter that overlooks the bar or the open kitchen.

**HOUSE SPECIALTIES** Chef Tim Keating, a repeat James Beard Foundation finalist, is a big proponent of Florida products. The fare here changes frequently, but you'll always find the potato-wrapped red snapper, the restaurant's signature dish, with creamy leek fondue and a red wine-butter sauce; char-crusted New York strip steak; and lump crab cakes. Desserts are seasonal, but the house-made sorbets and caramelized-banana Napoleon are divine. A good way to sample two of the most popular dishes is the three-course prix fixe tasting menu, which includes both the New York strip and the potato-wrapped snapper.

**OTHER RECOMMENDATIONS** For a special experience, book the Chef's Tasting Wine Dinner, where you sit at the "Chef's Counter" and watch the chef create the six courses for your meal. Each course is paired with a wine selected by the manager. This experience is designed for ages 14 and up, and you must make reservations at least one day in advance.

**SUMMARY AND COMMENTS** Locals love the Flying Fish, and for good reason. Though this is food for grown-ups, you'll often see children in the noisy dining room because of the BoardWalk location. If you can't get a table, check on seating availability at the counter.

## The Fountain ★★

| AMERICAN | MODERATE | QUALITY ★★ | VALUE ★★ |
|---|---|---|---|
| READER-SURVEY RESPONSES 88% | 12% | DISNEY DINING PLAN? No | |

Dolphin Resort; ☎ 407-934-1609

**Reservations** Not taken. **When to go** Anytime. **Cost range** $7.50–$16 (child $9). **Service** ★★★★. **Friendliness** ★★★★. **Bar** Beer and wine only. **Wine selection** Limited. **Parking** Hotel lot ($17). **Dress** Casual. **Disabled access** Yes. **Customers** Hotel guests. **Lunch and dinner** Daily, 11 a.m.–11 p.m.

**SETTING AND ATMOSPHERE** Informal soda-shop ambience.

**HOUSE SPECIALTIES** Build-your-own burgers and hot dogs, BLTs, shakes, and ice-cream cones. The PB&J milkshake is worth every calorie.

**OTHER RECOMMENDATIONS** Seared-salmon salad, ahi-tuna burger.

**SUMMARY AND COMMENTS** This is the place for Dolphin guests to get a quick bite. Create your own sundae at The Fountain Sweet Treats.

## Fresh Mediterranean Market ★★½

| MEDITERRANEAN/AMERICAN | MODERATE | QUALITY ★★½ | VALUE ★★ |
|---|---|---|---|
| READER-SURVEY RESPONSES | 57% 👍 43% 👎 | DISNEY DINING PLAN? | No |

Dolphin Resort; ☎ 407-934-1609

**Reservations** Available but not necessary. **When to go** Breakfast or lunch. **Cost range** Breakfast (buffet or à la carte) $6–$23 (child $14); lunch $14–$18 (child $12). **Service** ★★★★. **Friendliness** ★★★★. **Parking** Hotel lot ($17). **Bar** Beer, wine, and limited cocktails. **Wine selection** Limited. **Dress** Casual. **Disabled access** Yes. **Customers** Hotel guests. **Breakfast** Daily, 6:30–11 a.m. **Lunch** Monday–Friday, 11:30 a.m.–1 p.m.; Saturday and Sunday, noon–2 p.m. Days of operation may vary according to hotel occupancy.

**SETTING AND ATMOSPHERE** Brightly colored tiles, light woods, and big windows set the scene. Ask for a veranda table if you want to have a quiet conversation away from the action in the open kitchen.

**HOUSE SPECIALTIES** Breakfast: fresh fruit and vegetable juices, made-to-order omelets. Lunch: pasta, fish, burgers, and generous salads.

**OTHER RECOMMENDATIONS** Pulled-pork sandwich, lobster roll.

**SUMMARY AND COMMENTS** A pleasant, quiet spot for breakfast or lunch, with a breakfast buffet that's more healthful than many.

## Fulton's Crab House ★★½

| SEAFOOD | EXPENSIVE | QUALITY ★★★½ | VALUE ★★ |
|---|---|---|---|
| READER-SURVEY RESPONSES | 84% 👍 16% 👎 | DISNEY DINING PLAN? | Yes |

Downtown Disney Marketplace; ☎ 407-939-3463

**Reservations** Accepted. **Dining Plan credits** 2 per person, per meal. **When to go** Early evening. **Cost range** Lunch $9–$24 (child $8–$12), dinner $28–$49 (child $8–$12). **Service** ★★★★. **Friendliness** ★★★★. **Parking** Lot near the old Pleasure Island complex. **Bar** Full service. **Wine selection** Good; mostly American. **Dress** Casual. **Disabled access** Yes. **Customers** Locals and Disney guests. **Lunch** Daily, 11:30 a.m.–3:30 p.m. **Dinner** Daily, 4–11 p.m.

**SETTING AND ATMOSPHERE** Separate dining areas include the Market Room, a tribute to New York City's Fulton Fish Market (for which the restaurant is named); the Constellation Room, a semicircular room with a starlit night sky; and the Industry Room, a tribute to the commercial-fishing industry.

**HOUSE SPECIALTIES** Stone crab; fresh fish flown in daily; fresh oysters; Fulton's crab-and-lobster bisque; cioppino with crab, shrimp, scallops, clams, mussels, and fish in a tomato broth; Alaskan king and Dungeness crab.

**OTHER RECOMMENDATIONS** Prince Edward Island mussels, Florida littleneck clams, crab and lobster for two, filet mignon, grilled shrimp.

**SUMMARY AND COMMENTS** Fulton's is a great (but pricey) place to enjoy a beautiful Florida day on the back deck while slurping oysters or digging in to other fresh seafood. You can pretty much get whatever seafood you want, from raw oysters to crab, shrimp, Alaska salmon, and whole Maine lobster. In busy times of year, waits can be long—more than an hour, even on weeknights. But if you don't get fresh seafood back home, go early, request a table on the deck, order a Seafood Tower, and enjoy.

## Garden Grill Restaurant ★★

| AMERICAN | EXPENSIVE | QUALITY ★★ | VALUE ★★★ |
|---|---|---|---|
| READER-SURVEY RESPONSES | 90% 👍 10% 👎 | DISNEY DINING PLAN? | Yes |

The Land, Future World, Epcot; ☎ 407-939-3463

**Reservations** Required. **Dining Plan credits** 1 per person, per meal. **When to go** Dinner. **Cost range** $38 (child $18). *Note:* Prices may increase during peak periods (see page 428). **Service** ★★★★. **Friendliness** ★★★★★. **Parking** Epcot lot. **Bar** Wine, beer, and some mixed drinks. **Wine selection** Fair. **Dress** Casual. **Disabled access** Yes. **Customers** Theme park guests. **Character dinner** Daily, 4:30–8 p.m.

**SETTING AND ATMOSPHERE** With the popular Soarin' attraction nearby, The Garden Grill stays busy, even though the concept and the dining room are getting a little frayed around the edges. You step on a slowly revolving floor to make your way to tables that revolve above scenes from Living with the Land, the pavilion's ride-through attraction (see page 566). If service is prompt, about the time you finish a meal you've revolved around once, past scenes of a desert, a rainforest, and a farm, along with a few mural-painted walls in between. It's a great place to get photos with the Disney characters—Mickey, Chip 'n' Dale, and others make stops at tables for photo ops and greetings.

**HOUSE SPECIALTIES** Beef filet, turkey with lemon-caper sauce, and sustainable fish of the day. Dessert is a skillet cake with vanilla-bean whipped cream. The kids' menu includes mac and cheese, chicken drumsticks, sweet potatoes, and broccoli.

**ENTERTAINMENT AND AMENITIES** The view. Character dining. Complimentary nonalcoholic beverages included with meals.

**SUMMARY AND COMMENTS** Salads are made with produce grown right in The Land's garden downstairs. More of a low-key destination for filling up and taking photos with the Disney characters than a spot for delicious dining.

## Garden Grove    ★★

| AMERICAN | MODERATE | QUALITY ★★★ | VALUE ★★ |
|---|---|---|---|
| READER-SURVEY RESPONSES | 71% 👍 | 29% 👎 | DISNEY DINING PLAN? No |

Swan Resort; ☎ 407-934-1609

**Reservations** Recommended. **When to go** Anytime. **Cost range** Breakfast $12–$15 (child $7 or $8), weekday buffet $23 (child $14), weekend Disney-character breakfast buffet $24 (child $16); lunch $13–$16 (child $9–$12); dinner $30–$37 (child $18), Disney-character seafood buffet (Friday night only) $36 (child $17). **Service** ★★★. **Friendliness** ★★★. **Parking** Valet ($20) or hotel lot ($17). **Bar** Full service. **Wine selection** Good. **Dress** Casual. **Disabled access** Yes. **Customers** Hotel guests, some locals, tourists. **Breakfast, lunch, and dinner** Daily, 6:30 a.m.–9:30 p.m.; character breakfast, Saturday and Sunday, 8–11 a.m.

**SETTING AND ATMOSPHERE** The spacious dining room has a 25-foot faux oak tree as its centerpiece, and sunlight streams in from the tall windows. At night, the lights are dimmed, the oak tree is full of lanterns and twinkling lights, and street lamps create the pleasant ambience of a nighttime garden.

**HOUSE SPECIALTIES** For lunch, prime-rib melt, Reuben, fresh pasta, fish tacos. For dinner, prime rib, organic salmon, blackened chicken. Friday night features a seafood buffet (raw bar, jumbo scallops, fried-seafood basket, paella, and salmon).

**SUMMARY AND COMMENTS** It's probably not worth a special trip if you aren't already staying at the Swan, but Garden Grove serves good food, its prices are holding steady, and its character meals are a bargain compared with, say, Chef Mickey's. Based on this edition's lower reader-survey scores, though, we think diners may be missing the nightly themed buffets, which have been scaled back to once a week.

## Grand Floridian Cafe ★★½

| AMERICAN | MODERATE | | QUALITY ★★★ | | VALUE ★★ |
|---|---|---|---|---|---|
| READER-SURVEY RESPONSES | 85% 👍 | 15% 👎 | DISNEY DINING PLAN? Yes | | |

Grand Floridian Resort & Spa; ☎ 407-824-2496

**Reservations** Accepted. **Dining Plan credits** 1 per person, per meal. **When to go** Anytime. **Cost range** Breakfast $9–$19 (child $6), lunch $12.50–$27 (child $8.59), dinner $18.50–$30 (child $8.50). **Service** ★★★. **Friendliness** ★★★★. **Parking** Valet ($20); self-parking is far away. **Bar** Full service. **Wine selection** Good. **Dress** Casual. **Disabled access** Yes. **Customers** Hotel guests. **Breakfast** Daily, 7–11:30 a.m. **Lunch** Daily, 11:30 a.m.–2 p.m. **Dinner** Daily, 5–9 p.m.

SETTING AND ATMOSPHERE Basically an upscale coffee shop, the large dining room—with high ceilings and decorative windows—looks out on the Grand Floridian's pool and center courtyard.

HOUSE SPECIALTIES Breakfast includes eggs prepared virtually every way known to mankind, waffles, French toast, and lobster eggs Benedict. For lunch, there's tuna niçoise salad and the Grand sandwich with ham, turkey, and an herbed-cheese sauce. For dinner, choose from a generous burger, shrimp and grits, or the grilled pork chop.

OTHER RECOMMENDATIONS A hefty Reuben for lunch and a simple New York strip with mashed potatoes for dinner.

SUMMARY AND COMMENTS A quick place to grab a commendable bite. Scrumptious desserts by the same team that makes sweets for all of the Grand Floridian's dining rooms.

## La Hacienda de San Angel ★★★

| MEXICAN | EXPENSIVE | | QUALITY ★★★½ | | VALUE ★★½ |
|---|---|---|---|---|---|
| READER-SURVEY RESPONSES | 79% 👍 | 21% 👎 | DISNEY DINING PLAN? Yes | | |

Mexico, World Showcase, Epcot; ☎ 407-939-3463

**Reservations** Required. **Dining Plan credits** 1 per person, per meal. **When to go** Dinner. **Cost range** $24–$50 (child $8.50–$9.50). **Service** ★★★★. **Friendliness** ★★★★★. **Parking** Epcot lot. **Bar** Full. **Wine selection** All Mexican. **Dress** Casual. **Disabled access** Yes. **Customers** Theme park guests. **Dinner** 4–8:35 p.m.

SETTING AND ATMOSPHERE Traditional Mexican adobe ranch decor. Back tables have choice views of World Showcase Lagoon and IllumiNations.

HOUSE SPECIALTIES If you've ever bought soft tacos off the streets of Mexico, the upscale *taquiza* appetizer will bring back fond memories . . . at roughly 10 times the price. They take their margaritas seriously here: Don't complain that yours isn't strong enough, or they'll remake it for you and you'll wake up at Betty Ford.

SUMMARY AND COMMENTS Not what you'd typically find at your local Tex-Mex place. Our favorites are the shrimp tacos and the grilled tilapia with roasted corn and cactus leaves. You can make a meal of appetizers and a margarita—order the gooey *queso fundido* with chorizo, share some tacos, and call it happy. If you're so inclined, ask for the vegetarian menu.

## Hollywood & Vine ★★½

| AMERICAN | MODERATE | | QUALITY ★★★ | | VALUE ★★★ |
|---|---|---|---|---|---|
| READER-SURVEY RESPONSES | 84% 👍 | 16% 👎 | DISNEY DINING PLAN? Yes | | |

Echo Lake, Disney's Hollywood Studios; ☎ 407-939-3463

**Reservations** Recommended; credit card required to reserve *Fantasmic!* Dining Package (see page 623). **Dining Plan credits** 1 per person, per meal. **When to**

**go** Anytime. **Cost range** Breakfast buffet $26 (child $15), lunch buffet $26 (child $15), dinner buffet $31–$35 (child $16–$19), depending on *Fantasmic!* seating. *Note:* Prices for character meals may increase during peak periods (see page 428). **Service** ★★★★. **Friendliness** ★★★★★. **Parking** DHS lot. **Bar** Full service. **Wine selection** Limited. **Dress** Casual. **Disabled access** Yes. **Customers** Theme park guests. **Character breakfast** Daily, 8–11:20 a.m.; **Character lunch** Daily, 11:40 a.m.–2:25 p.m. **Dinner** Daily, 5–9 p.m.

**SETTING AND ATMOSPHERE** Large Art Deco–style cafeteria with tile floors, lots of chrome, and huge wall murals with vintage scenes of old Hollywood and other California landmarks. But breakfast and lunch are known as Disney Junior Play 'n Dine—featuring Sofia the First, Doc McStuffins, Handy Manny, and Jake from *Jake and the Never Land Pirates*—and that means lots of small children and parents dining at breakfast and lunch. Dinner is subdued.

**HOUSE SPECIALTIES** Chilled salads, fish of the day, carved and grilled meats, create-your-own pasta, fresh fruits and breads, dessert station with chocolate fountain. (Menu changes often.)

**SUMMARY AND COMMENTS** With all the glass, tile, and chrome, the noise echoes for days.

## The Hollywood Brown Derby    ★★★★

| AMERICAN | EXPENSIVE | QUALITY ★★★★ | VALUE ★★★ |
|---|---|---|---|
| READER-SURVEY RESPONSES | 86% 👍 | 14% 👎 DISNEY DINING PLAN? | Yes |

Hollywood Boulevard, Disney's Hollywood Studios; ☎ 407-939-3463

**Reservations** Accepted; credit card required to reserve *Fantasmic!* Dining Package (see page 623). **Dining Plan credits** 2 per person, per meal. **When to go** Early evening. **Cost range** Lunch and dinner $16–$43 (child $6–$14). **Service** ★★★★★. **Friendliness** ★★★★★. **Parking** DHS lot. **Bar** Full service. **Wine selection** Very good. **Dress** Casual. **Disabled access** Yes. **Customers** Theme park guests. **Lunch** Daily, 11:30 a.m.–3 p.m. **Dinner** Daily, 3:30 p.m.–park closing.

**SETTING AND ATMOSPHERE** A replica of the original Brown Derby restaurant (not the one shaped like a derby) in California, the elegant sunken dining room has curved booths, tables draped with yards of white linen, and romantic shaded faux candles. Tall palm trees in huge pots stand in the center of the room and reach for the high ceiling.

**HOUSE SPECIALTIES** Cobb salad (named for Bob Cobb, the original restaurant's owner), crispy spiced duck breast, and grapefruit cake.

**OTHER RECOMMENDATIONS** All-natural herb-roasted rack of lamb, Thai noodle bowl with wok-fried coconut tofu, and blue-lump-crab spring-roll appetizer.

**SUMMARY AND COMMENTS** The Brown Derby is one of the top theme park–dining experiences at Disney. The same menu is in place for both lunch and dinner, so it's pricey for midday dining, but a wonderful way to take a break and regenerate. The decor is so perfect you'll feel as if you're in 1930s Hollywood; everyone really should dress in white ties and long chiffon gowns. Service is outstanding, and the kitchen turns out stellar creations. The kids' menu includes grilled black grouper, whole-grain penne pasta, and grilled chicken breast.

New and of note: **The Hollywood Brown Derby Lounge** takes advantage of the main restaurant's heretofore-little-used patio with attractive indoor and outdoor seating. Shaded by big umbrellas, the outdoor tables are great spots for people-watching. The menu ($14–$19) is all small plates: artisanal cheeses; charcuterie; Wagyu-beef sliders with Cognac-mustard aioli and Gouda cheese; duck-confit tacos; steamed Prince Edward Island mussels; and the Derby Cocktail with jumbo lump blue crab, black tiger shrimp, avocado, and a horseradish-tomato juice. Try the strawberry-Champagne cheesecake for dessert. (You can also order from the regular menu—just ask.) Drink choices include various flights—martinis, margaritas, Champagnes, white and red wines, Scotches, and Grand Marnier vintages—along with wines by the glass or half-bottle and classic cocktails. Open daily, noon–park closing; they don't take reservations, so snag a table early when it's nice outside.

## House of Blues ★★★

| REGIONAL AMERICAN | | MODERATE | | QUALITY ★★★½ | | VALUE ★★★ |
|---|---|---|---|---|---|---|
| READER-SURVEY RESPONSES | | Not enough to rate | | DISNEY DINING PLAN? | | Yes |

Downtown Disney West Side; ☎ 407-934-2623

**Reservations** Recommended. **Dining Plan credits** 1 per person, per meal. **When to go** Lunch or early dinner; Sunday gospel brunch. **Cost range** $12–$29 (child $7–$10); brunch $40 (child $22). **Service** ★★★★. **Friendliness** ★★★. **Parking** Downtown Disney lot. **Bar** Full service. **Wine selection** Modest. **Dress** Casual. **Disabled access** Good. **Customers** Blues lovers. **Brunch** 2 seatings on Sunday, 10:30 a.m. and 1 p.m. **Lunch and dinner** Sunday–Tuesday, 11:30 a.m.–11 p.m.; Wednesday and Thursday, 11:30 a.m.–midnight; Friday and Saturday, 11:30 a.m.–1 a.m.

SETTING AND ATMOSPHERE You'd think it was a ramshackle hut in the bayou if the place weren't bigger than all of Louisiana. Nearly every available inch of wall space displays some type of voodoo-tinged folk art. The dining room, called Crossroads, is separated from the performance hall, where the main musical acts perform. A live band often performs in Crossroad on weekends as well.

HOUSE SPECIALTIES Flatbreads, buttermilk fried chicken, Juicy Lucy burger. The Smokehouse, a new walk-up window in front of the restaurant, serves barbecue sandwiches (pulled pork, brisket, and chicken), ribs, and smoked turkey legs.

OTHER RECOMMENDATIONS Jambalaya, Tennessee-style baby back ribs, shrimp and grits, lobster mac and cheese, Bourbon bread pudding.

SUMMARY AND COMMENTS For a themed restaurant, House of Blues does a good job with its food. If you're planning on taking in one of the rock or blues acts next door, we recommend seeing the show first so you can get a good seat, then coming back to eat afterward.

## Il Mulino New York Trattoria ★★★

| ITALIAN | | EXPENSIVE | | QUALITY ★★★ | | VALUE ★★ |
|---|---|---|---|---|---|---|
| READER-SURVEY RESPONSES | 64% 👍 | 36% 👎 | | DISNEY DINING PLAN? | | No |

Swan Resort; ☎ 407-934-1609

**Reservations** Accepted. **When to go** Dinner. **Cost range** $16–$45 (child $12–$16). **Service** ★★. **Friendliness** ★★. **Parking** Valet (free with validation) or hotel lot ($17). **Bar** Full service. **Wine selection** Good. **Dress** Dressy casual. **Disabled access** Yes. **Customers** Mostly hotel guests and conventioneers. **Dinner** 5–11 p.m. nightly.

SETTING AND ATMOSPHERE A spin-off of the New York City restaurant, Il Mulino takes an upscale-casual approach to Italian cuisine, with family-style platters for sharing. Tables are dark wood; an open kitchen creates a bustle. You can request private dining in one of the smaller rooms.

**HOUSE SPECIALTIES** The cuisine focuses on Italy's Abruzzi region, with hearty pastas and big cuts of meat. Try the linguine with clam sauce or the seared red snapper.

**OTHER RECOMMENDATIONS** Tuna carpaccio, pizza with fresh mozzarella, spaghetti carbonara.

**SUMMARY AND COMMENTS** The tried-and-true menu never changes. Unfortunately, with many of Il Mulino's competitors at Disney World switching things up frequently, that dependability—coupled with the high prices—seems to be a minus where *Unofficial Guide* readers are concerned, judging by the dip in this year's survey scores. (The noisy dining room probably doesn't help matters either.)

## Jiko—The Cooking Place ★★★★½

| AFRICAN/FUSION | EXPENSIVE | QUALITY ★★★★½ | VALUE ★★★½ |
|---|---|---|---|
| READER-SURVEY RESPONSES | 89% 👍 | 11% 👎 | DISNEY DINING PLAN? Yes |

Animal Kingdom Lodge & Villas–Jambo House; ☎ 407-938-3000

**Reservations** Required. **Dining Plan credits** 2 per person, per meal. **When to go** Dinner. **Cost range** $28–$46 (child $7–$12). **Service** ★★★★★. **Friendliness** ★★★★★. **Parking** Valet ($20) or hotel lot. **Bar** Full bar. **Wine selection** All South African. **Dress** Dressy casual. **Disabled access** Good. **Customers** Hotel guests and locals. **Dinner** Daily, 5:30–10 p.m.

**SETTING AND ATMOSPHERE** Jiko has a special ambience, from the young African exchange students who greet guests as they enter to a menu of unusual tastes. Jiko's spacious dining room is inspired by the opening scenes of *The Lion King*. A pair of large wood-burning ovens dominates the center of the room.

**HOUSE SPECIALTIES** Wood-fired flatbreads; African-inspired dips with house-made naan (Indian flatbread); oak-grilled filet mignon with South African red-wine sauce; maize-crusted monkfish.

**OTHER RECOMMENDATIONS** Pan-roasted local whole fish, West African jerk scallops, spice-crusted pork loin, spicy beef short rib, and a selection of artisanal cheeses. Kids' menu includes fish, steak, and mac and cheese.

**SUMMARY AND COMMENTS** Jiko has been winning awards and accolades (including AAA's Four Diamond Award) for its interesting fare and stellar wine list—one of the largest collections of South African wines in any North American restaurant, with more than 1,800 bottles. Dishes are beautifully spiced and full of flavor. Start with some flatbread and wrap up with banana-filled vanilla cake with banana-nut crunch, or a cup of Kenyan press-pot coffee or a specialty tea. Special menus for the glucose- and lactose-intolerant, vegans, and vegetarians.

## Kimonos ★★★★

| JAPANESE | MODERATE | QUALITY ★★★★½ | VALUE ★★★ |
|---|---|---|---|
| READER-SURVEY RESPONSES | 80% 👍 | 20% 👎 | DISNEY DINING PLAN? No |

Swan Resort; ☎ 407-934-1609

**Reservations** Accepted for parties of 6 or more. **When to go** Dinner. **Cost range** Sushi and rolls à la carte, $5.50–$16. **Service** ★★★★★. **Friendliness** ★★★★★. **Parking** Valet ($20) or hotel lot ($17). **Bar** Full service. **Wine selection** Very good. **Dress** Casual. **Disabled access** Yes. **Customers** Hotel guests and locals. **Dinner** Daily, 5:30 p.m.–midnight; bar opens at 5 p.m.

**SETTING AND ATMOSPHERE** The decor consists of black-lacquered tabletops and counters, tall pillars rising to bamboo rafters with rice-paper lanterns, and elegant kimonos that hang outstretched on the walls and between the dining sections. The chefs will greet you with a friendly welcome, and you'll be offered a hot towel to clean your hands.

**HOUSE SPECIALTIES** Although sushi and sashimi are the focus, Kimonos also serves hot appetizers, including tempura shrimp and vegetables, beef satay, kimchi salad with octopus, and miso soup.

**SUMMARY AND COMMENTS** The skill of the sushi artists is as much a joy to watch as is eating the wonderfully fresh creations. There are no full entrees here—just good sushi and appetizers.

## Kona Cafe ★★★

| POLYNESIAN/PAN-ASIAN | MODERATE | QUALITY ★★★ | VALUE ★★★★ |
| --- | --- | --- | --- |
| READER-SURVEY RESPONSES | 90% 👍 10% 👎 | DISNEY DINING PLAN? | Yes |

Polynesian Resort; ☎ 407-939-3463

**Reservations** Accepted. **Dining Plan credits** 1 per person, per meal. **When to go** Anytime. **Cost range** Breakfast $9–$14.50 (child $6.50), lunch $9–$18 (child $8.59), dinner $9–$30 (child $8.59). **Service** ★★★★. **Friendliness** ★★★★★. **Parking** Valet ($20) or hotel lot. **Bar** Full service. **Wine selection** OK. **Dress** Casual. **Disabled access** Yes. **Customers** Mostly hotel guests; some locals. **Breakfast** Daily, 7:30–11:45 a.m. **Lunch** Daily, noon–2:45 p.m. **Dinner** Daily, 5–9:45 p.m.

**SETTING AND ATMOSPHERE** The casual Kona Cafe has a postmodern decor, with arched railings and grillwork on the ceiling. If you want to escape the Magic Kingdom for a quiet lunch, hop on the monorail or take the resort launch to the Polynesian.

**HOUSE SPECIALTIES** Breakfast: Tonga toast (a decadent French toast layered with bananas). Lunch: sushi, stir-fried Asian noodles, barbecue-pork taco, and sticky wings. Dinner: sushi, Kona coffee–rubbed pork chop, teriyaki-style New York strip steak, and sustainable fish.

**OTHER RECOMMENDATIONS** Crab cakes, Kilauea torte (chocolate cake with a warm chocolate center), and Kona coffee served in a press pot.

**SUMMARY AND COMMENTS** This isn't a fancy dining room, but the food is on a higher plane than your average java joint's. The popular sushi selections at the adjacent Kona Island coffee bar are now also available at the main restaurant, and the full Kona Cafe menu is now available at Kona Island for dinner (they serve just coffee and pastries during breakfast and lunch hours).

## LakeView Restaurant ★★

| AMERICAN | MODERATE | QUALITY ★ | VALUE ★★★ |
| --- | --- | --- | --- |
| READER-SURVEY RESPONSES | Not enough to rate | DISNEY DINING PLAN? | No |

Wyndham Lake Buena Vista Resort, Downtown Disney; ☎ 407-828-4444

**Reservations** Accepted. **When to go** Breakfast or dinner. **Cost range** Character breakfast $25 ($13 kids ages 3–11), dinner $18–$35 ($6 kids ages 3–11). **Service** ★★★. **Friendliness** ★★★. **Parking** Hotel lot. **Bar** Limited service. **Wine selection** Good. **Dress** Casual. **Disabled access** Yes. **Customers** Hotel guests. **Breakfast** Daily, 7–11 a.m.; character breakfast Tuesday, Thursday, and Saturday, 7:30–10:30 a.m. **Dinner** Monday–Saturday, 6–10:30 p.m.

**SETTING AND ATMOSPHERE** Lakefront views.

**ENTERTAINMENT AND AMENITIES** Disney-character breakfast (usually Goofy and Pluto) three days a week.

**SUMMARY AND COMMENTS** There's nothing special about the cuisine, but the best reason to dine here is the Disney-character breakfast, with an all-you-can-eat buffet and a kid-sized buffet just for little ones. Dinner is standard hotel fare—burgers, steaks, and salads.

## Liberty Tree Tavern ★★★

| AMERICAN | MODERATE | QUALITY ★★★ | VALUE ★★★ |
|---|---|---|---|
| READER-SURVEY RESPONSES | 92% 👍 8% 👎 | DISNEY DINING PLAN? Yes | |

Liberty Square, Magic Kingdom; ☎ 407-939-3463

**Reservations** Accepted. **Dining Plan credits** 1 per person, per meal. **When to go** Lunch or dinner. **Cost range** Lunch $15–$20 (child $8.59), dinner $34 (child $17). *Note:* Dinner prices may increase during peak periods (see page 428). **Service** ★★★★★. **Friendliness** ★★★★★. **Parking** Magic Kingdom lot. **Bar** None. **Wine selection** None. **Dress** Casual. **Disabled access** Yes. **Customers** Theme park guests. **Lunch** Daily, 11:30 a.m.–3 p.m. **Character dinner** Daily, 4–9 p.m.

**SETTING AND ATMOSPHERE** Low, exposed-beam ceilings crown rooms framed by pastel-gray chair rails. Colonial-period wall art, much with a nautical theme, accents simple dark-wood tables and chairs with woven seats.

**HOUSE SPECIALTIES** For lunch: New England–style pot roast, roast turkey, and sandwiches. Family-style character dining at dinner, with all-you-can-eat turkey, carved beef, and smoked pork loin.

**OTHER RECOMMENDATIONS** Sandwiches and salads are good here, too.

**SUMMARY AND COMMENTS** Though nothing much changes at Liberty Tree (the servers still wear those Colonial-style getups), it's still among the best of the Magic Kingdom's full-service restaurants. Make Advance Reservations here for about an hour or so before parade time—after you eat, you can walk right out and watch the parade. And you can enjoy Thanksgiving turkey and stuffing any day of the year.

## Mama Melrose's Ristorante Italiano ★★½

| ITALIAN | MODERATE | QUALITY ★★★ | VALUE ★★ |
|---|---|---|---|
| READER-SURVEY RESPONSES | 81% 👍 19% 👎 | DISNEY DINING PLAN? Yes | |

Streets of America, Disney's Hollywood Studios; ☎ 407-939-3463

**Reservations** Required; credit card required to reserve *Fantasmic!* Dining Package (see page 623). **Dining Plan credits** 1 per person, per meal. **When to go** Lunch or dinner. **Cost range** $13–$30 (child $8.59). **Service** ★★★. **Friendliness** ★★★★★. **Parking** DHS lot. **Bar** Full service. **Wine selection** Limited. **Dress** Casual. **Disabled access** Yes. **Customers** Theme park guests. **Lunch** Daily, noon–3:30 p.m. **Dinner** Daily, 3:30 p.m.–park closing.

**SETTING AND ATMOSPHERE** Mama Melrose's is inspired by a big-city "red-sauce italian" restaurant of the 1930s, with red-and-white checkered tablecloths, red vinyl booths, and grapevines hanging from the rafters. By far the most relaxing restaurant at Disney's Hollywood Studios, Mama Melrose's sports a look as comfortable as an old sweatshirt.

**HOUSE SPECIALTIES** Caesar salad, crispy calamari, penne alla vodka, charred strip steak, and pork osso buco. Whole-wheat pasta available.

**OTHER RECOMMENDATIONS** Grilled tuna or four-cheese flatbread.

**SUMMARY AND COMMENTS** Because of Mama Melrose's out-of-the-way location, you can sometimes just walk in, especially in the evening. Portions here are fairly large; it's possible to dine cheaply on just an appetizer or two. The food won't win any awards—the red sauce is a little heavy, for instance—but for family-style Italian, it's fine.

## Maya Grill ★

| MEXICAN/AMERICAN | EXPENSIVE | QUALITY ★ | VALUE ★ |
|---|---|---|---|
| READER-SURVEY RESPONSES 71% 👍 29% 👎 | | DISNEY DINING PLAN? Yes | |

Coronado Springs Resort; ☎ 407-939-3463

**Reservations** Accepted. **Dining Plan credits** 1 per person, per meal. **When to go** Dinner. **Cost range** $17–$43 (child $7–$9.50). **Service** ★★★. **Friendliness** ★★★. **Parking** Hotel lot. **Bar** Full service. **Wine selection** Fair. **Dress** Casual. **Disabled access** Yes. **Customers** Hotel guests. **Breakfast** Daily, 7–11 a.m. **Dinner** Daily, 5–10 p.m.

**SETTING AND ATMOSPHERE** The dining room was designed to evoke the ancient world of the Maya, achieving "a harmony of fire, sun, and water." But the idea falls short. The kitchen is open to view—but so is the barren and starkly lit walkway outside. We keep waiting for the rumored renovation to materialize.

**HOUSE SPECIALTIES** To suit Coronado Springs' convention crowd, the kitchen leans toward overpriced Tex-Mex and Nuevo Latino dinner fare, such as sirloin or shrimp tacos, beef or pork-belly enchiladas, or the skillet platter for two with beef, chicken, and shrimp.

**SUMMARY AND COMMENTS** Utterly ordinary. Eat somewhere else.

## Monsieur Paul ★★★★

| FRENCH | EXPENSIVE | QUALITY ★★★★½ | VALUE ★★★ |
|---|---|---|---|
| READER-SURVEY RESPONSES 64% 👍 36% 👎 | | DISNEY DINING PLAN? YES | |

France, World Showcase, Epcot; ☎ 407-939-3463

**Reservations** Required. **Dining Plan credits** 2 per person, per meal on Plus and Deluxe Plans, 1 per person, per meal on Premium and Platinum Plans. **When to go** Late dinner. **Cost range** $38–$43 (child $13–$16). **Service** ★★★★. **Friendliness** ★★★★★. **Parking** Epcot or BoardWalk lot; enter through back gate. **Bar** Full service. **Wine selection** Good but pricey. **Dress** Casual. **Disabled access** Elevator to second level. **Customers** Theme park guests. **Dinner** Daily, 5:30–8:35 p.m.

**SETTING AND ATMOSPHERE** Tucked away upstairs at the France Pavilion, Monsieur Paul is an ode to legendary French chef Paul Bocuse (his son, Jerôme, also a chef, runs the pavilion's dining operations). The interiors, ornate and opulent when the restaurant was Bistro de Paris, are now light and modern, with many photos of Bocuse throughout his storied career displayed throughout. Though the white-linen tablecloths remain, the waiters' tuxes are gone, as are the heavy curtains. But despite its relaxed ambience, this is the more upscale of France's two full-service restaurants. Open only for dinner; request a table at the windows to watch the world go by on World Showcase Lagoon. Seats just 120.

**HOUSE SPECIALTIES** Black-truffle soup, available only on the fixed-price menu; red snapper in potato "scales"; roasted duck breast à l'orange.

**SUMMARY AND COMMENTS** Monsieur Paul may be a bit stuffy and high-priced for many park guests—and we suspect *les prix outrageux* sent reader-survey scores south this edition—but if you can get past the sticker shock, this is *the* spot for a quiet dinner and conversation. Young chef Francesco Santin, who worked at Bocuse's restaurant in Lyon, France, is wowing diners with his authentic, creative French cuisine. The classic tastes include mussels with a light fennel cream, seared scallops with ginger-lobster consommé, and classic Grand Marnier soufflé. There's also a fixed-price menu ($89 per person), and the wine list is solid. A rather grown-up kids' menu includes roasted chicken breast and filet mignon.

## Narcoossee's ★★★★½

| SEAFOOD | EXPENSIVE | QUALITY ★★★½ | VALUE ★★ |
|---|---|---|---|
| READER-SURVEY RESPONSES 91% 👍 | 9% 👎 | DISNEY DINING PLAN? Yes | |

Grand Floridian Resort & Spa; ☎ 407-939-3463

**Reservations** Required. **Dining Plan credits** 2 per person, per meal. **When to go** Early evening. **Cost range** $31–$72 (child $7–$15). **Service** ★★★★★. **Friendliness** ★★★★★. **Parking** Valet ($20); self-parking is deceptively far away. **Bar** Full service. **Wine selection** Good. **Dress** Dressy casual. **Disabled access** Yes. **Customers** Hotel guests and locals. **Dinner** Daily, 5:30–10 p.m.

**SETTING AND ATMOSPHERE** Stroll through the grounds of the Grand Floridian and toward the waterfront to this freestanding octagonal building at the edge of Seven Seas Lagoon. The atmosphere is upscale casual, though hardwood floors make it noisy. Diners have great views of the Magic Kingdom and the boats that dock nearby to pick up and drop off guests after a day at the park.

**HOUSE SPECIALTIES** Two-pound steamed Maine lobster, sustainable seared ahi tuna, and grilled filet mignon. Kids' menu includes grilled steak and oven-baked fish.

**OTHER RECOMMENDATIONS** Prince Edward Island mussels, jumbo lump crab cakes, and artisanal cheeses.

**SUMMARY AND COMMENTS** Narcoossee's offers excellent service, a very good wine list—and steep prices. But it is one of the few places at Disney with a seafood-centric menu, and one of the few places where you can get fresh steamed lobster. A splurge for grown-ups. Fun to sit at the bar if you don't have a reservation, and you step out on the porch to watch the nightly Electrical Water Pageant on Seven Seas Lagoon.

## Nine Dragons Restaurant ★★★

| CHINESE | MODERATE | QUALITY ★★★ | VALUE ★★ |
|---|---|---|---|
| READER-SURVEY RESPONSES 69% 👍 | 31% 👎 | DISNEY DINING PLAN? Yes | |

China, World Showcase, Epcot; ☎ 407-939-3463

**Reservations** Recommended. **Dining Plan credits** 1 per person, per meal. **When to go** Lunch or dinner. **Cost range** Lunch $13–$19 (child $8–$10), dinner $13–$27 (child $8–$10). **Service** ★★★. **Friendliness** ★★★★. **Parking** Epcot lot. **Bar** Full service. **Wine selection** Minimal. **Dress** Casual. **Disabled access** Yes. **Customers** Theme park guests. **Lunch** Daily, 11:30 a.m.–4 p.m. **Dinner** Daily, 4:30 p.m.–park closing.

**SETTING AND ATMOSPHERE** Nine Dragons' attractive interior—subdued wood tones, colorful lanterns, and beautiful backlit glass sculptures from China—and efficient service create a respite from the bustle of World Showcase.

**HOUSE SPECIALTIES** Roasted Beijing chicken, shrimp and steak, and five-spiced fish.

**OTHER RECOMMENDATIONS** Vegetarian stir-fry; noodle sampler with fresh vegetables and pork and chicken dipping sauces.

**SUMMARY AND COMMENTS** Some dishes have a light, contemporary touch, and service is friendly. Though it's pricey for Chinese, the menu is diverse and the food is well prepared.

## 1900 Park Fare ★★½

| AMERICAN/BUFFET | MODERATE | QUALITY ★★★ | VALUE ★★★ |
|---|---|---|---|
| READER-SURVEY RESPONSES 78% 👍 | 22% 👎 | DISNEY DINING PLAN? Yes | |

Grand Floridian Resort & Spa; ☎ 407-824-3000

**Reservations** Recommended. **Dining Plan credits** 1 per person, per meal. **When to go** Breakfast or dinner. **Cost range** Breakfast $22 (child $13), dinner $38 (child $19). *Note:* Prices may increase during peak periods (see page 428). **Service** ★★★★. **Friendliness** ★★★★. **Parking** Valet ($20); self-parking is deceptively far away. **Bar** Full service. **Wine selection** Limited. **Dress** Casual. **Disabled access** Yes. **Customers** Hotel and resort guests. **Character breakfast** Daily, 8–11 a.m. **Character dinner** Daily, 4:30–8:30 p.m.

**SETTING AND ATMOSPHERE** This bright, cavernous, high-ceilinged room is warmly appointed in pastels. Tables are set with linen. An antique band organ periodically provides musical accompaniment to dining.

**HOUSE SPECIALTIES** The buffet includes prime rib, salmon, and chicken Marsala.

**OTHER RECOMMENDATIONS** Separate buffet for kids includes pasta marinara, mini–corn dogs, chicken nuggets, and mac and cheese.

**ENTERTAINMENT AND AMENITIES** Character dining with Mary Poppins, Winnie the Pooh, Tigger, and Alice at breakfast, Cinderella, Prince Charming, and others at dinner.

**SUMMARY AND COMMENTS** An OK choice for character dining, but too bright and loud for adults without children. The prime rib is 1900 Park Fare's major draw at dinner, but go someplace else if you prefer your beef on the rare side of medium.

## 'Ohana ★★★

| POLYNESIAN | MODERATE | QUALITY ★★★½ | VALUE ★★★ |
|---|---|---|---|
| READER-SURVEY RESPONSES | 91% 👍 | 9% 👎 | DISNEY DINING PLAN? Yes |

Polynesian Resort; ☎ 407-939-3463

**Reservations** Recommended. **Dining Plan credits** 1 per person, per meal. **When to go** Breakfast or dinner. **Cost range** Character breakfast $22 (child $13), dinner $36 (child $18). *Note:* Prices may increase during peak periods (see page 428). **Service** ★★★★. **Friendliness** ★★★★★. **Parking** Hotel lot. **Bar** Full service. **Wine selection** Limited. **Dress** Casual. **Disabled access** Yes. **Customers** Resort guests. **Character breakfast** Daily, 7:30–11 a.m. **Dinner** Daily, 5–10 p.m.

**SETTING AND ATMOSPHERE** A large open pit is the centerpiece of the room. Here the grilled foods are prepared with flair, as well as a flare: From time to time the chef will pour some liquid on the fire, causing huge flames to shoot up. This is usually in response to something one of the strolling entertainers has said, evoking a sign from the fire gods. At any given moment, there may be a hula-hoop contest or a coconut race, where kids are invited to push coconuts around the dining room with broomsticks.

**HOUSE SPECIALTIES** Skewer service is the specialty here—there's no menu. As soon as you're seated, your server will begin to deliver food. Starters include honey-glazed chicken wings, pork fried dumplings, pineapple-coconut bread, and salad. The main course is steak, pork loin, chicken, and grilled peel-and-eat shrimp, accompanied by stir-fried vegetables and egg noodles with pineapple in peanut sauce placed on a lazy Susan in the center of the table.

**ENTERTAINMENT AND AMENITIES** Strolling singers, games, and Mickey, Pluto, Lilo, and Stitch at breakfast.

**SUMMARY AND COMMENTS** Our readers love 'Ohana, which means "family." The food is good but not superior, but if you love meat and you come hungry, it's a great place to fill up. The method of service and the fact that it just keeps coming make it all taste a little better. Request a seat in the main dining room, where the fire pit is.

## Olivia's Cafe ★★★

| AMERICAN | MODERATE | QUALITY ★★★ | VALUE ★★ |
|---|---|---|---|
| READER-SURVEY RESPONSES 75% 👍 | 25% 👎 | DISNEY DINING PLAN? Yes | |

Old Key West Resort; ☎ 407-939-3463

**Reservations** Accepted. **Dining Plan credits** 1 per person, per meal. **When to go** Lunch. **Cost range** Breakfast $9.50–$14 (child $6.50), lunch and dinner $11.50–$30 (child $8.59). **Service** ★★★★. **Friendliness** ★★★★. **Parking** Hotel lot. **Bar** Full service. **Wine selection** Limited. **Dress** Casual. **Disabled access** Yes. **Customers** Resort guests. **Breakfast** Daily, 7:30–10:30 a.m. **Lunch** Daily, 11:30 a.m.–5 p.m. **Dinner** Daily, 5–10 p.m.

SETTING AND ATMOSPHERE Disneyfied Key West: lots of pastels, mosaic-tile floors, potted palms, tropical trees in the center of the room. There is some outside seating, which looks out over the waterway. Tile, wood siding, and no tablecloths add up to a very noisy dining room that's getting a little worn around the edges. Disney Vacation Club member photos decorate the walls—Old Key West Resort was one of the first DVC resorts, so members consider Olivia's their home kitchen.

HOUSE SPECIALTIES At breakfast, traditional omelets; banana-bread French toast; and breakfast Cuban with scrambled eggs, ham, Swiss cheese, and pork loin on Cuban bread. At lunch and dinner, conch fritters; Duval Street burger topped with grilled shrimp, pepper-Jack cheese, and pico de gallo; pan-seared scallops; seafood pasta; slow-cooked prime rib; shrimp and grits; pork ribs.

OTHER RECOMMENDATIONS Crab cakes; Key lime tart; banana bread pudding sundae.

SUMMARY AND COMMENTS A fun out-of-the-way spot if you have a little extra time to navigate out to Old Key West Resort. The food has a Southern–Key West spin and is well prepared. Service is excellent.

## One80 SportGrill & Bar ★★

| AMERICAN | MODERATE | QUALITY ★★ | VALUE ★★★ |
|---|---|---|---|
| READER-SURVEY RESPONSES Too new to rate | | DISNEY DINING PLAN? No | |

Buena Vista Palace, Downtown Disney Resort Area; ☎ 407-827-2727

**Reservations** Recommended. **When to go** Lunch on weekends, dinner nightly. **Cost range** $11–$29. **Service** ★★★. **Friendliness** ★★★. **Parking** Valet (free) at rear of hotel. **Bar** Full service. **Wine selection** Limited. **Dress** Casual. **Disabled access** Yes. **Customers** Hotel guests. **Lunch** Saturday and Sunday, noon–5 p.m. **Dinner** Daily, 5:30–11 p.m.; "night owl" menu served midnight–1 a.m.

SETTING AND ATMOSPHERE Yet another new concept in this space—from Polynesian to sports bar—but it's food that vacationers love, served in a casual setting: wings, burgers, barbecue pork, ribs, New York strip.

HOUSE SPECIALTIES Sam Adams burger (beer-braised onions, bacon, Cheddar, and mustard sauce); fish tacos with mango salsa and cilantro *crema;* barbecued spare ribs with honey-Bourbon sauce.

OTHER RECOMMENDATIONS Southern-fried calamari, peanut butter pie.

SUMMARY AND COMMENTS A good place for families to fill up; not too expensive.

## Paradiso 37 ★★½

| GLOBAL | INEXPENSIVE | QUALITY ★★★ | VALUE ★★★ |
|---|---|---|---|
| READER-SURVEY RESPONSES 76% 👍 | 24% 👎 | DISNEY DINING PLAN? Yes | |

Downtown Disney; ☎ 407-934-3700

**Reservations** Accepted. **When to go** Lunch or dinner. **Dining Plan credits** 1 per person, per meal. **Cost range** $10–$27 (child $8). **Service** ★★★. **Friendliness** ★★★★. **Parking** Downtown Disney lot. **Bar** Full service. **Wine selection** Limited. **Dress** Casual. **Disabled access** Yes. **Customers** Theme park guests, locals. **Lunch and dinner** Sunday–Wednesday, 11:30 a.m.–midnight; Thursday–Saturday, 11:30 a.m.–1 a.m.

**SETTING AND ATMOSPHERE** Prime location on the waterfront at Downtown Disney. The bar is the centerpiece of a dining room that's deceptively large, with seating for 200-plus on two levels and the best seats outside. Booths, tables, and tall tables. Ambience is festive and casual, with an open kitchen. Food is inspired by street foods of Central, South, and North America, from mac-and-cheese bites to enchiladas and barbecue pork.

**HOUSE SPECIALTIES** Central American "crazy corn" (roasted on the cob with pepper sauce and cheese), Argentinean skirt steak with chimichurri sauce, bottomless homemade salsa and chips, Paradiso 37 cheeseburger, and the "mangled margarita," a combo of a margarita and sangria. (The 37 in the name refers to the number of varieties of tequila.)

**OTHER RECOMMENDATIONS** Macaroni-and-cheese bites, shrimp ceviche, and citrus barbecue pork ribs.

**SUMMARY AND COMMENTS** All the construction going on at Downtown Disney right now makes it a bit of a challenge to get here, and the drinks outshine the food. But it's one of the few Disney spots that cooks burgers medium-rare. And the joint boasts "the coldest beer in the world," served at a crisp 29°F–32°F.

## Planet Hollywood  ★★½

| AMERICAN | MODERATE | QUALITY  ★★ | VALUE  ★★ |
|---|---|---|---|
| READER-SURVEY RESPONSES  73% 👍 | 27% 👎 | DISNEY DINING PLAN?  Yes | |

Downtown Disney West Side; ☎ 407-827-7827

**Reservations** Recommended. **Dining Plan credits** 1 per person, per meal. **When to go** Late lunch. **Cost range** $11–$31 (child $8). **Service** ★★. **Friendliness** ★★. **Parking** Lot near the old Pleasure Island complex. **Bar** Full service. **Wine selection** Limited. **Dress** Casual. **Disabled access** Yes. **Customers** Tourists, locals. **Lunch and dinner** Daily, 11 a.m.–1 a.m.

**SETTING AND ATMOSPHERE** A large planet-shaped structure "floating" in the lagoon next to the redeveloping Pleasure Island. Planet Hollywood's decor is something of a movie museum, with memorabilia from famous films. Check out artifacts like the bus from the movie *Speed,* Marilyn Monroe's gloves, and the life-size likeness of Robin Williams.

**HOUSE SPECIALTIES** Pasta, fajitas, huge burgers, dinner salads, and pizzas; for dessert, try the old-fashioned chocolate cake with vanilla ice cream.

**OTHER RECOMMENDATIONS** Barbecue ribs, World Famous Chicken Crunch; mushroom, onion, and Swiss burger; shrimp Alfredo.

**SUMMARY AND COMMENTS** The home base for the PH chain has been resting on its laurels for quite a while—nothing exciting, including the food. But with the Disney Springs project under way (see page 735), look for this iconic spot to be spruced up.

## The Plaza Restaurant  ★★

| AMERICAN | MODERATE | QUALITY  ★★ | VALUE  ★★ |
|---|---|---|---|
| READER-SURVEY RESPONSES  83% 👍 | 17% 👎 | DISNEY DINING PLAN?  Yes | |

Main Street, U.S.A., Magic Kingdom; ☎ 407-939-3463

**Reservations** Required. **Dining Plan credits** 1 per person, per meal. **When to go** Lunch or dinner. **Cost range** $12–$18 (child $8.59). **Service** ★★★★.

**Friendliness** ★★★★. **Parking** Magic Kingdom lot. **Bar** None. **Wine selection** None. **Dress** Casual. **Disabled access** Yes. **Customers** Theme park guests. **Lunch and dinner** 11 a.m.–15 minutes before park closing.

**SETTING AND ATMOSPHERE** Tucked away on a side street at the end of Main Street as you head to Tomorrowland, the Plaza evokes small-town diners across America. You'll pay top dollar for a tuna-salad sandwich or a burger, but on a hot Florida day it's air-conditioned heaven.

**HOUSE SPECIALTIES** Veggie sandwich, club sandwich, chicken-strawberry salad, and ice-cream desserts such as the Plaza banana split or sundae.

**OTHER RECOMMENDATIONS** Grilled Reuben, cheeseburger, meat loaf with mashed potatoes. For kids, grilled cheese, cheeseburger, PB&J.

**SUMMARY AND COMMENTS** The Victorian-inspired Plaza is a Main Street icon, best known as a spot to escape the Florida heat and enjoy a generous hot-fudge sundae or banana split. You wouldn't head here expecting haute cuisine, but the pricey sandwiches taste just fine.

## Portobello  ★★½

| ITALIAN | EXPENSIVE | QUALITY ★★★ | VALUE ★★ |
|---|---|---|---|
| READER-SURVEY RESPONSES | 63% 👍  37% 👎 | DISNEY DINING PLAN? Yes | |

Downtown Disney; ☎ 407-934-8888

**Reservations** Recommended. **Dining Plan credits** 1 per person, per meal. **When to go** Anytime. **Cost range** Lunch $9–$15 (child $7–$11), dinner $10–$29 (child $7–$13). **Service** ★★★. **Friendliness** ★★★★. **Parking** Lot near the old Pleasure Island complex. **Bar** Full service. **Wine selection** Very good; heavily Italian. **Dress** Casual. **Disabled access** Yes. **Customers** Tourists, locals. **Lunch** Daily, 11:30 a.m.–4 p.m. **Dinner** Daily, 4–11 p.m.

**SETTING AND ATMOSPHERE** Portobello has a faux Tuscan interior designed to look like a "country Italian trattoria." A very *large* trattoria.

**HOUSE SPECIALTIES** Wood-burning-oven pizzas; farfalle pasta with roasted chicken, snow peas, asparagus, and Parmesan cream sauce.

**OTHER RECOMMENDATIONS** Filet mignon, local fish, gelatos and sorbets.

**SUMMARY AND COMMENTS** Wonderful outdoor waterfront seating on the shaded porch. Service is spotty, food is ordinary.

## Raglan Road Irish Pub & Restaurant  ★★★★

| IRISH | MODERATE | QUALITY ★★★½ | VALUE ★★★ |
|---|---|---|---|
| READER-SURVEY RESPONSES | 89% 👍  11% 👎 | DISNEY DINING PLAN? Yes | |

Downtown Disney; ☎ 407-938-0300

**Reservations** Recommended. **Dining Plan credits** 1 per person, per meal. **When to go** Monday–Saturday after 8 p.m. **Cost range** Sunday brunch, $8–$19, Lunch $15–$27 (child $7–$14), dinner $15–$29 (child $7–$14); family-style roasts (6+ people) $35–$55. **Service** ★★★½. **Friendliness** ★★★★★. **Parking** Marketplace lot or lot near the old Pleasure Island complex. **Bar** Full service specializing in Irish whiskeys and beers. **Wine selection** Better than a pub's but not extensive. **Dress** Casual. **Disabled access** Yes. **Customers** Tourists and locals. **Sunday brunch, lunch, and dinner** 11 a.m.–11 p.m., with pub food available until closing (1 a.m.–ish).

**SETTING AND ATMOSPHERE** Many elements of this pub, including the bar, were hand-crafted from hardwoods in Ireland and sent to the United States for reassembly. The venue is huge by Irish-pub standards, but the dark polished-wood paneling, as well as the snugs (small, private cubbyholes), preserves the feel of the traditional pub. The pentagonal main room sits beneath an impressive but very unpublike dome. In the middle of the room is a tall, tablelike platform accessible to Celtic dancers via a permanently attached short staircase. A modest bandstand is situated along the wall in front of a large pseudo-hearth. Branching from the cavernous domed center room are cozy dining areas and snugs.

**HOUSE SPECIALTIES** For brunch, Kevin's ham schnitzel; for lunch and dinner, roast loin of ham with cabbage and mashed potatoes, beer-battered fish and chips, a froufrou but yummy Shepherd's Pie, chicken-and-wild-mushroom pie. The must-have appetizer is the Dalkey Duo: batter-fried cocktail sausages with a mustard dipping sauce.

"Host the Roast" family-style lunches—including sides and dessert—serve six or more and must be ordered 48 hours in advance. Choose from lemon-thyme chicken, stuffed leg of lamb, pork loin, or beef rib roast.

**ENTERTAINMENT AND AMENITIES** Though you could consider a great selection of Irish lagers and stouts an amenity, the real draw here is the knockout Celtic music. A talented band plays daily. Starting in the early evening with a couple of superb acoustic sets, the band sets up as the diners filter out and the pub crawlers settle in. A Celtic dancer wanders in and dances on the aforementioned table to some of the numbers. (Think *Riverdance,* not rump shaking.)

**SUMMARY AND COMMENTS** The great thing about Irish pubs is that folks of all ages can have a wonderful time together. The traditional feel-good drinking songs, reels, and sentimental ballads transcend age. A night in a good pub, Raglan Road included, is a joyous and uplifting experience, and as the Irish say, it'll set you right up.

## Rainforest Cafe ★★½

| AMERICAN | MODERATE | QUALITY ★★ | VALUE ★★ |
|---|---|---|---|
| READER-SURVEY RESPONSES† | 78% 👍 | 22% 👎 | DISNEY DINING PLAN? Yes |

†*Average of Animal Kingdom (77% 👍) and Downtown Disney (79% 👍)*

Disney's Animal Kingdom; ☎ 407-938-9100
Downtown Disney Marketplace; ☎ 407-827-8500

**Reservations** Recommended. **Dining Plan credits** 1 per person, per meal. **When to go** After the lunch crunch, in late afternoon, and before dinner hour. **Cost range** $13–$26 (child $6–$7). **Service ★★★. Friendliness ★★★★. Parking** Marketplace lot. **Bar** Full bar. **Wine selection** Limited. **Dress.** Casual. **Disabled access** Yes. **Customers** Tourists, locals. **Hours** *Disney's Animal Kingdom:* Daily, 8:30 a.m.–park closing; *Downtown Disney Marketplace:* Sunday–Thursday, 11 a.m.–11 p.m.; Friday and Saturday, 11 a.m.–midnight. (Animal Kingdom location serves breakfast; Downtown Disney location does not.)

**SETTING AND ATMOSPHERE** There's usually a crowd at the Downtown Disney location of this national chain. It sits beneath a giant volcano that can be seen, and heard, erupting all over the Marketplace; the smoke coming from the volcano is nonpolluting, in accordance with the restaurant's conservation theme. Inside is a huge dining room designed to look like a jungle—imagine all the silk plants in the world tacked to the ceiling—complete with animatronic elephants, bats, and monkeys (not the most realistic we've seen). There's occasional thunder and even some rainfall. Large aquariums connected with glass "swimways" serve as one of several waiting areas.

**HOUSE SPECIALTIES** Rasta Pasta with grilled chicken and walnut pesto; turkey wrap; coconut shrimp; slow-roasted pork ribs; brownie cake with ice cream, caramel, and chocolate sauce.

**ENTERTAINMENT AND AMENITIES** After the wait you endure, a chair and some sustenance are all the entertainment you'll need. If you're willing to pay to avoid the long wait, stop by the day before and buy a Landry's Select Club membership for $25. By presenting your card on the day you want to dine, you'll be seated much faster (and get 10% off retail and other benefits).

**SUMMARY AND COMMENTS** While we've never been impressed by the Rainforest Cafes, a lot of our readers rave about them. The shopping and the kid appeal must be the attractions, because it certainly isn't the food: Preparations are spotty, and waits can be horrendous.

## Restaurant Marrakesh ★★

| MOROCCAN | MODERATE | QUALITY ★★½ | VALUE ★★ |
|---|---|---|---|
| READER-SURVEY RESPONSES | 74% 👍 26% 👎 | DISNEY DINING PLAN? Yes | |

Morocco, World Showcase, Epcot; ☎ 407-939-3463

**Reservations** Accepted. **Dining Plan credits** 1 per person, per meal. **When to go** Lunch or dinner. **Cost range** Lunch $15–$22 (child $8), dinner $21–$45 (child $8). **Service** ★★★★. **Friendliness** ★★★★. **Parking** Epcot lot. **Bar** Full service. **Wine selection** Limited. **Dress** Casual. **Disabled access** Yes. **Customers** Theme park guests. **Lunch** Daily, noon–3:15 p.m. **Dinner** Daily, 3:30 p.m.–park closing.

**SETTING AND ATMOSPHERE** At the very back of the Morocco Pavilion, Marrakesh re-creates a Moroccan palace with tile mosaics, inlaid-wood ceilings, brass chandeliers, subdued lighting, and red Bukhara carpets.

**HOUSE SPECIALTIES** The appetizer combo is a good way to sample the beef *brewat* (pastry filled with beef, deep-fried, and sprinkled with cinnamon sugar), *bastilla* (a minced-chicken pie sprinkled with cinnamon sugar), and *jasmina* salad. Follow with lemon chicken or roast lamb shank, and split an order of vegetable couscous.

**OTHER RECOMMENDATIONS** If you're hungry, curious, or both, try the Royal Feast or Marrakesh Feast with tastes of several courses. The creations are authentic but not too spicy.

**ENTERTAINMENT AND AMENITIES** Moroccan band and belly dancing.

**SUMMARY AND COMMENTS** This is one of the least busy World Showcase restaurants, so it's usually easy to get a table in the spacious dining room. Unlike diners at most Moroccan restaurants, those at Marrakesh sit at tables instead of on the floor, and eat with knives and forks instead of with their hands. Picky kids can choose from chicken tenders, pasta, and burgers.

## Rose & Crown Dining Room ★★★

| ENGLISH | MODERATE | QUALITY ★★★½ | VALUE ★★ |
|---|---|---|---|
| READER-SURVEY RESPONSES | 87% 👍 13% 👎 | DISNEY DINING PLAN? Yes | |

United Kingdom, World Showcase, Epcot; ☎ 407-939-3463

**Reservations** Accepted. **Dining Plan credits** 1 per person, per meal. **When to go** Lunch or dinner. **Cost range** Lunch $15–$27 (child $8.59), dinner $15–$31 (child $8.50). **Service** ★★★★★. **Friendliness** ★★★★★. **Parking** Epcot lot. **Bar** Full bar with Bass, Guinness, and Harp beers on tap. **Wine selection** Limited. **Dress** Casual. **Disabled access** Yes. **Customers** Theme park guests. **Lunch** Daily, noon–3:20 p.m. **Dinner** Daily, 4:30 p.m.–park closing.

**SETTING AND ATMOSPHERE** The Rose & Crown is both a pub and a dining establishment. The traditional English pub has a large, cozy bar with rich wood appointments, beamed ceilings, and a hardwood floor. The adjoining dining room is rustic and simple.

**HOUSE SPECIALTIES** Fish and chips, bangers and mash (sausage and mashed potatoes), and cottage pie (the vegetarian version is delicious, too), washed down with Bass ale.

**OTHER RECOMMENDATIONS** Trio of UK cheeses, Scotch egg (a hard-boiled egg with a deep-fried sausage coating), chicken masala (an Indian-style curry that's beloved in Britain), sticky toffee pudding.

**SUMMARY AND COMMENTS** This is a prime spot for viewing *IllumiNations,* so try to get a table on the patio for late evening, order fish and chips, and sit back in your front-row seat for the show.

## Sanaa ★★★★

| INDIAN/AFRICAN | EXPENSIVE | QUALITY ★★★★ | VALUE ★★★★ |
|---|---|---|---|
| READER-SURVEY RESPONSES 91% 👍 | 9% 👎 | DISNEY DINING PLAN? Yes | |

Animal Kingdom Villas–Kidani Village; ☎ 407-939-3463

**Reservations** Accepted. **Dining Plan credits** 1 per person, per meal. **When to go** Lunch or dinner. **Cost range** Lunch $12–$23 (child $8.59), dinner $17–$30 (child $8.59). **Service** ★★★★. **Friendliness** ★★★★. **Parking** Valet ($20) or garage. **Bar** Full service. **Wine selection** Good. **Dress** Casual. **Disabled access** Yes. **Customers** Theme park guests, locals, Disney Vacation Club guests. **Lunch** Daily, 11:30 a.m.–4 p.m. **Dinner** Daily, 4:30 p.m.–park closing.

**SETTING AND ATMOSPHERE** One floor down from the Kidani Village lobby, Sanaa's dining room is inspired by Africa's outdoor markets, with baskets, beads, and art on the walls. It's a cozy space, with 9-foot-tall windows that look out on the resort's savanna—giraffes, water buffalo, and other animals wander within yards of you as you dine.

**HOUSE SPECIALTIES** Indian-style breads (naan, onion *kulcha,* and *paneer paratha*) with red-chile sambal, spicy jalapeno-lime pickle, coriander chutney, and cucumber raita; tandoori chicken; sustainable fish with shrimp and scallops.

**OTHER RECOMMENDATIONS** New York strip with seasonal vegetables; lunch burger on naan with minted greens, tomato, and cucumber raita.

**SUMMARY AND COMMENTS** Sanaa (sah-**NAH**) isn't as upscale as Jiko, the resort's African restaurant (page 479), but the kitchen offers diners a chance to sample and share a variety of Indian-African creations. Diverse Old and New World wines match the cuisine.

## San Angel Inn ★★★

| MEXICAN | EXPENSIVE | QUALITY ★★★ | VALUE ★★ |
|---|---|---|---|
| READER-SURVEY RESPONSES 79% 👍 | 21% 👎 | DISNEY DINING PLAN? Yes | |

Mexico, World Showcase, Epcot; ☎ 407-939-3463

**Reservations** Accepted. **Dining Plan credits** 1 per person, per meal. **When to go** Lunch or dinner. **Cost range** Lunch $18–$24.50 (child $8.50–$9.50), dinner $23.50–$28.50 (child $8.50–$9.50). **Service** ★★★. **Friendliness** ★★★. **Parking** Epcot lot. **Bar** Full service. **Wine selection** Limited. **Dress** Casual. **Disabled access** Yes. **Customers** Theme park guests. **Lunch** Daily, 11:30 a.m.–4 p.m. **Dinner** Daily, 4:30 p.m.–park closing.

**SETTING AND ATMOSPHERE** Busy San Angel Inn is inside the great Aztec pyramid of the Mexico Pavilion. A romantically crafted open-air cantina, the restaurant overlooks both the Gran Fiesta Tour attraction and the bustling plaza of a small Mexican "village." The decor is inspired by the original San Angel Inn in Mexico City.

**HOUSE SPECIALTIES** Appetizers include *tlacoyos de chilorio,* corn cakes topped with refried beans, pork, *queso fresco,* sour cream, and green-tomatillo sauce; and quesadillas *repozadas,* battered corn quesadillas stuffed with corn, huitlacoche (Mexican truffle), mushrooms, and queso fresco. Still on the menu is the classic mole poblano—chicken in a sauce made from several kinds of chiles and unsweetened Mexican chocolate.

**OTHER RECOMMENDATIONS** Margaritas; taco and tostada appetizers.

**ENTERTAINMENT AND AMENITIES** Mariachi or marimba bands in the courtyard.

**SUMMARY AND COMMENTS** The prices are ridiculous, but the menu goes beyond typical Mexican, offering special and regional dishes that are difficult to find in the United States. We like the appetizers better than the main courses—unusual tacos and tostadas that are good for sharing.

## Sci-Fi Dine-In Theater Restaurant  ★★

| AMERICAN | MODERATE | QUALITY ★★½ | VALUE ★★ |
|---|---|---|---|
| READER-SURVEY RESPONSES | 85% 👍 | 15% 👎 | DISNEY DINING PLAN? Yes |

Commissary Lane, Disney's Hollywood Studios; ☎ 407-939-3463

**Reservations** Recommended. **Dining Plan credits** 1 per person, per meal. **When to go** Anytime. **Cost range** $13.50–$30 (child $9). **Service** ★★★★★. **Friendliness** ★★★★★. **Parking** DHS lot. **Bar** Full service. **Wine selection** Limited. **Dress** Casual. **Disabled access** Yes. **Customers** Theme park guests. **Lunch** Sunday and Wednesday, 10:30 a.m.–4 p.m.; Monday and Tuesday and Thursday–Saturday, 11 a.m.–4 p.m. **Dinner** Daily, 4 p.m.–park closing.

**SETTING AND ATMOSPHERE** Everyone gets a kick out of this unusual dining room—a facsimile of a drive-in from the 1950s, with faux classic cars instead of tables. Hop in, order, and watch campy black-and-white clips. Servers, some on roller skates, take your order from the driver's seat.

**HOUSE SPECIALTIES** Same menu at lunch and dinner, with everything from burgers to pasta and New York strip. Even with reader scores way up this year, our opinion still stands that the Sci-Fi is an attraction, not a dining destination: The concept is fun, but the prices are too high for what you get. Stick with simple fare (the Reuben is delicious and the ribs are pretty good), fill up on appetizers, or just order a shake or hot-fudge sundae.

**ENTERTAINMENT AND AMENITIES** Cartoons and clips of vintage horror and sci-fi movies, such as *Attack of the 50 Foot Woman, Robot Monster,* and *The Blob.*

**SUMMARY AND COMMENTS** If you must try Sci-Fi, we recommend making late-afternoon or late-evening Advance Reservations. Otherwise, try walking in around 11 a.m. or 3 p.m.

## Shula's Steak House  ★★★★

| STEAK | EXPENSIVE | QUALITY ★★★★ | VALUE ★★ |
|---|---|---|---|
| READER-SURVEY RESPONSES | 70% 👍 | 30% 👎 | DISNEY DINING PLAN? No |

Dolphin Resort; ☎ 407-934-1362

**Reservations** Required. **When to go** Dinner. **Cost range** $26–$130 (for the Australian lobster tail). Sides not included in entree cost. **Service** ★★★★. **Friendliness** ★★★★. **Parking** Valet (free with validation) or hotel lot ($17). **Bar** Full service. **Wine selection** Good; expensive. **Dress** Dressy. **Disabled access** Yes. **Customers** Hotel guests and locals. **Dinner** Daily, 5–11 p.m.

**SETTING AND ATMOSPHERE** Clubby and masculine, with dark woods and even darker lighting. Large gilt-framed black-and-white photographs of football players in action offer the only decoration. Shula's is a favorite of conventioneers on expense accounts (although, based on this edition's lower reader-survey scores, we think some guests are balking at the platinum-card prices and the uninspired service).

**HOUSE SPECIALTIES** In a word, meat—really expensive but very high-quality meat. Only certified Angus beef is served: filet mignon, porterhouse (including a 48-ounce cut), and prime rib.

**OTHER RECOMMENDATIONS** The steak tartare appetizer is special, and there are oysters and stone crab in season, as well as a colossal shrimp cocktail and lobster-tail appetizer.

**SUMMARY AND COMMENTS** This is part of a chain owned by former Miami Dolphins football coach Don Shula. It's classier than it is kitschy, though printing the menu on the side of a football and placing it on a kickoff tee in the center of the table is a bit much. We could also do without the rehearsed spiel from the waiters and the pretentious displaying of raw beef and live lobster at each table. But if you've got deep pockets and you're in the mood for red meat, Shula's fills the bill.

## Shutters at Old Port Royale  ★★

| STEAK AND SEAFOOD | MODERATE | QUALITY ★★½ | VALUE ★★ |
|---|---|---|---|
| READER-SURVEY RESPONSES | 60% 👍 40% 👎 | DISNEY DINING PLAN? | Yes |

Caribbean Beach Resort; ☎ 407-939-3463

**Reservations** Accepted. **Dining Plan credits** 1 per person, per meal. **When to go** Dinner. **Cost range** $17–$31.50 (child $8.59). **Service** ★★★. **Friendliness** ★★★★★. **Parking** Hotel lot. **Bar** Full service. **Wine selection** Moderate. **Dress** Casual. **Disabled access** Yes. **Customers** Hotel guests. **Dinner** Daily, 5–10 p.m.

**SETTING AND ATMOSPHERE** Basic table-service restaurant for Caribbean Beach guests. The small dining areas are claustrophobia-inducing. Nothing about the decor will make you wish you had brought a camera.

**HOUSE SPECIALTIES** New York strip steak, barbecue pork brisket, chicken wings with habanero sauce, and sustainable fish.

**OTHER RECOMMENDATIONS** Chorizo–black bean soup; pasta with shrimp, chorizo, and goat cheese.

**SUMMARY AND COMMENTS** You wouldn't come here for dinner if you weren't already staying at the hotel, but if you need to sit down and be waited on, this will meet your needs.

## Spice Road Table  ★★★½

| MOROCCAN | MODERATE | QUALITY ★★★★ | VALUE ★★★ |
|---|---|---|---|
| READER-SURVEY RESPONSES | Too new to rate | DISNEY DINING PLAN? | No |

Morocco, World Showcase, Epcot; ☎ 407-939-3463

**Reservations** Not accepted. **When to go** Anytime, but primo spot for nightly fireworks. **Cost range** $7–$16 (child $6–$8). **Service** ★★★★★. **Friendliness** ★★★★★. **Parking** Epcot lot. **Bar** Full service. **Wine selection** Limited. **Dress** Casual. **Disabled access** Yes. **Customers** Epcot guests. **Hours** Daily, 11 a.m.–park closing.

**SETTING AND ATMOSPHERE** A gorgeous, well-stocked bar is the centerpiece as you walk through the front door. Ice-blue walls and beautiful Moroccan light fixtures, tilework, and tapestries create a warm, intimate ambience. The best seats, 120 in all, are on the covered terrace, but inside seats also have great views of World Showcase Lagoon—indoors or out, this is *the* place at Epcot to watch *IllumiNations.* Friendly servers are happy to explain the menu.

**HOUSE SPECIALTIES** Tapas, Mediterranean-style: hummus and olives, mussels tagine, fried calamari, lamb sliders, rice-stuffed grape leaves.

**OTHER RECOMMENDATIONS** Spicy garlic shrimp, Mediterranean omelet.

**SUMMARY AND COMMENTS** The small plates are fun to share. Pair them with organic sangria, a Mediterranean beer, or a signature cocktail. If you aren't ready to sit and just want something cold on a hot afternoon, the adjacent Spice Road Juice Bar is the spot for a Moroccarita, Habibi

Daiquiri, Sultan's Colada, or nonalcoholic Royal Blue Oasis Slushie; beer, sangria, and wine; and house-made ice cream in unusual flavors such as toasted almond and rosewater.

## Splitsville  ★★½

| AMERICAN | MODERATE | QUALITY ★★½ | VALUE ★★ |
|---|---|---|---|
| READER-SURVEY RESPONSES | 88% 👍 12% 👎 | DISNEY DINING PLAN? Yes | |

Downtown Disney West Side; ☎ 407-938-PINS (7467)

**Reservations** Accepted. **Dining Plan credits** 1 per person, per meal. **Cost range** $7–$16 (child $7). **Service** ★★½. **Friendliness** ★★★. **Parking** Downtown Disney lot. **Bar** Full service. **Wine selection** Don't expect Lafite Rothschild. **Dress** Casual. **Disabled access** Yes. **Customers** Tourists. **Hours** Monday–Friday, 10:30 a.m.–late, opens Saturday and Sunday at 10 a.m.

**SETTING AND ATMOSPHERE** Splitsville is part of a multistate chain of "luxury lanes"—hybrid bowling alleys–restaurants. The decor is vaguely mid-century modern, with Sputnik lamps and other Space Age touches. It's loud, obviously, but there's plenty to see and also room for rambunctious kids to roam while you wait for your food.

**HOUSE SPECIALTIES** The sushi—salmon, shrimp, tuna, crab, and various combinations thereof—is the best thing on the menu. They also have decent gluten-free pizzas and rice bowls.

**OTHER RECOMMENDATIONS** Meat eaters will like the steak chimichurri or pulled-pork sandwich. The Birthday Cake Martini, garnished with sprinkles, is like having Betty Crocker as your bartender.

**SUMMARY AND COMMENTS** The menu is more spread-out than a 7/10 split: Burgers, sushi, pizza, seafood, barbecue, Mexican, and Italian are represented, plus nachos and other bar food. It would be a stretch for any kitchen to make half of these things well, let alone a kitchen in a bowling alley. We've tried almost everything on the menu, and while all of it was OK, the only thing we'd order again is the sushi. For kids, the basic pizzas are better than the burgers, which tend to be overdone.

## Teppan Edo  ★★★½

| JAPANESE | EXPENSIVE | QUALITY ★★★★ | VALUE ★★★ |
|---|---|---|---|
| READER-SURVEY RESPONSES | 89% 👍 11% 👎 | DISNEY DINING PLAN? Yes | |

Japan, World Showcase, Epcot; ☎ 407-939-3463

**Reservations** Recommended. **Dining Plan credits** 1 per person, per meal. **When to go** Lunch or dinner. **Cost range** $18–$31 (child $9.50–$13.50). **Service** ★★★★★. **Friendliness** ★★★★★. **Parking** Epcot lot. **Bar** Full service. **Wine selection** Limited. **Dress** Casual. **Disabled access** Via elevator. **Customers** Theme park guests. **Lunch** Daily, noon–3:45 p.m. **Dinner** Daily, 4 p.m.–park closing.

**SETTING AND ATMOSPHERE** Six upscale Japanese dining rooms with grills on tables and entertaining chefs chopping, slicing, and dicing.

**HOUSE SPECIALTIES** Chicken, shrimp, beef, scallops, and Asian vegetables stir-fried on a teppanyaki grill by a knife-juggling chef.

**ENTERTAINMENT AND AMENITIES** Watching the teppanyaki chefs.

**SUMMARY AND COMMENTS** The menu includes sushi and appetizers such as edamame and a sushi sampler, but most guests stick to the teppanyaki offerings. Note that diners at the teppanyaki tables are seated with other parties. Still one of the most popular family restaurants at Epcot.

## Todd English's bluezoo ★★★

| SEAFOOD | EXPENSIVE | | QUALITY ★★★★ | VALUE ★★ |
|---------|-----------|---|--------------|----------|
| READER-SURVEY RESPONSES 71% 👍 | | 29% 👎 | DISNEY DINING PLAN? No | |

Dolphin Resort; ☎ 407-934-1111

**Reservations** Recommended. **When to go** Dinner. **Cost range** $28–$60 (child $10–$16). **Service** ★★★★. **Friendliness** ★★★. **Parking** Valet (free with validation) or hotel lot ($17). **Bar** Full service. **Wine selection** Excellent. **Dress** Dressy casual. **Disabled access** Yes. **Customers** Hotel guests, locals. **Dinner** Daily, 5–11 p.m.

**SETTING AND ATMOSPHERE** The dreamy dining room is swathed in blues with iridescent bubbles suspended from the lights. The name is courtesy of celebrity chef Todd English's son, who as a young boy saw an under-the-sea movie and said it looked like a "blue zoo." Open kitchen, raw bar, and "dancing fish" on a circular rotisserie.

**HOUSE SPECIALTIES** Clam chowder, grilled fish, 2-pound Maine lobster, and dry-aged beef.

**OTHER RECOMMENDATIONS** Soft-shell crab, shake-and-bake fries.

**SUMMARY AND COMMENTS** English's stylish Florida outpost is frequented by conventioneers who don't mind the high prices ($2.75 for a single oyster, $60 for the 2-pound lobster) or the expensive wine list. Although blue-zoo is primarily a seafood place (and although readers are lukewarm about it), friends of *Unofficial* researchers say the beef tenderloin here is the best in the area.

## Tokyo Dining ★★★

| JAPANESE | MODERATE | | QUALITY ★★★★ | VALUE ★★★ |
|----------|----------|---|--------------|-----------|
| READER-SURVEY RESPONSES 82% 👍 | | 18% 👎 | DISNEY DINING PLAN? Yes | |

Japan, World Showcase, Epcot; ☎ 407-939-3463

**Reservations** Accepted. **Dining Plan credits** 1 per person, per meal. **When to go** Lunch. **Cost range** $9–$30 (child $10.50–$11.50). **Service** ★★★★. **Friendliness** ★★★. **Parking** Epcot lot. **Bar** Full service. **Wine selection** Limited. **Dress** Casual. **Disabled access** Yes. **Customers** Theme park guests. **Lunch** Daily, noon–3:45 p.m. **Dinner** Daily, 4 p.m.–park close.

**SETTING AND ATMOSPHERE** Modern Asian decor, a beautifully lighted sushi bar, and well-orchestrated service distinguish this restaurant. There are no seats at the sushi bar, but the sushi chefs are great entertainment for the entire dining room. Tables near the windows have a wonderful second-floor view of World Showcase.

**HOUSE SPECIALTIES** Grilled meats and seafood; tempura-battered deep-fried foods, featuring chicken, shrimp, scallops, and vegetables; sushi and sashimi; six kinds of sake.

**SUMMARY AND COMMENTS** The dining room is sleek, the overfriendly servers wear stylish costumes, and the overall experience is relaxing and congenial. If you're new to sushi, try one of the rolls that feature cooked fish, like the grilled salmon with mayo, cucumber, and sesame seed—it's under $10 and delicious.

## Tony's Town Square Restaurant ★★½

| ITALIAN | MODERATE | | QUALITY ★★★ | VALUE ★★ |
|---------|----------|---|-------------|----------|
| READER-SURVEY RESPONSES 74% 👍 | | 26% 👎 | DISNEY DINING PLAN? Yes | |

Main Street, U.S.A., Magic Kingdom; ☎ 407-939-3463

**Reservations** Recommended. **Dining Plan credits** 1 per person, per meal. **When to go** Late lunch or early dinner. **Cost range** Lunch $13.50–$20 (child

$8.59), dinner $17–$30 (child $8.59). **Service** ★★★★. **Friendliness** ★★★★★.
**Parking** Magic Kingdom lot. **Bar** None. **Wine selection** None. **Dress** Casual.
**Disabled access** Yes. **Customers** Magic Kingdom guests. **Lunch** Daily, 11:30
a.m.–2:45 p.m. **Dinner** Daily, 5 p.m.–park closing.

**SETTING AND ATMOSPHERE** Tony's is conveniently located just inside the park
on Main Street, with a glass-windowed porch that's wonderful for watching the action outside. The restaurant is a bit worn at the edges, with tile
floors, dark woods, and memorabilia from *Lady and the Tramp* on the
walls. Ask for a seat on the porch when you book.

**HOUSE SPECIALTIES** For lunch: sausage-and-pepperoni flatbread and spaghetti
with meatballs. For dinner: cioppino, braised short rib, and New York strip.

**SUMMARY AND COMMENTS** Tony's does a decent job with pasta. And the chef
offers multigrain pasta and keeps gluten-free pasta on hand for diners on
special diets. Go at lunch, when the prices aren't so steep.

## Trail's End Restaurant   ★★

| AMERICAN/BUFFET | MODERATE | QUALITY ★★ | VALUE ★★ |
|---|---|---|---|
| READER-SURVEY RESPONSES 82% 👍 | 18% 👎 | DISNEY DINING PLAN? | Yes |

Fort Wilderness Resort & Campground; ☎ 407-939-3463

**Reservations** Recommended. **Dining Plan credits** 1 per person, per meal.
**When to go** Breakfast or dinner. **Cost range** Breakfast $18 (child $11), lunch
$12–$17 (child $8.59), dinner $25 (child $14). *Note:* Prices may increase during
peak periods (see page 428). **Service** ★★★. **Friendliness** ★★★. **Parking** Fort
Wilderness lot. **Bar** Full-service bar next door. **Wine selection** Limited. **Dress**
Casual. **Disabled access** Yes. **Customers** Fort Wilderness campers, theme park
guests. **Breakfast** 7:30–11:30 a.m. **Lunch** 11:30 a.m.–2 p.m. **Dinner** 4:30–9:30
p.m. Sunday–Thursday, 4:30–10 p.m. Friday and Saturday.

**SETTING AND ATMOSPHERE** At Fort Wilderness, next to the *Hoop-Dee-Doo
Musical Revue,* Trail's End is what a restaurant would've looked like had
America's settlers built one out of a log cabin. The interior features
exposed log beams, oak tabletops, and walls hung with enough old-
timey kitchen equipment to start a flea market.

**HOUSE SPECIALTIES** Breakfast and dinner are served buffet-style; lunch transitions to an à la carte menu. Breakfast features eggs, sausage, bacon, waffles, and biscuits along with fruit and pastries. Lunch includes shrimp and
grits, panfried catfish, BLT flatbread, and a pulled-pork sandwich, as well
as s'mores and warm sticky-bun sundaes. The dinner lineup includes
pasta, fish, various meats, pizza, and fruit cobbler.

**OTHER RECOMMENDATIONS** Barbecue ribs and fried chicken at dinner.

**SUMMARY AND COMMENTS** The fare isn't much different from what you'd find
elsewhere around the parks, and during slow times the food sits quite a
while on the steam tables.

## T-REX   ★★★

| AMERICAN | MODERATE | QUALITY ★★ | VALUE ★★ |
|---|---|---|---|
| READER-SURVEY RESPONSES 79% 👍 | 21% 👎 | DISNEY DINING PLAN? | Yes |

Downtown Disney Marketplace; ☎ 407-828-8739

**Reservations** Recommended. **Dining Plan credits** 1 per person, per meal.
**When to go** Lunch or dinner. **Cost range** $13–$32 (child $7–$8). **Service** ★★★.
**Friendliness** ★★★. **Parking** Downtown Disney lot. **Bar** Full service. **Wine
selection** Minimal. **Dress** Casual. **Disabled access** Yes. **Customers** Families.
**Lunch and dinner** Daily, 11 a.m.–11 p.m.; open until midnight Friday and Saturday.

**SETTING AND ATMOSPHERE** Sensory overload in a cavernous dining room with
life-size robotic dinosaurs, giant fish tanks, bubbling geysers, waterfalls,

fossils in the bathrooms, and crystals in the walls. Volume: loud and louder, with meteor showers and growling dinos.

**HOUSE SPECIALTIES** Triassic Tortellini, New York strip, fried or blackened fish tacos.

**OTHER RECOMMENDATIONS** Slow-roasted ribs, Chocolate Extinction fudge cake.

**SUMMARY AND COMMENTS** Expect a wait unless there's an empty seat at the bar. But nobody's here just for the ordinary, overpriced food—it's non-stop "eatertainment," with kid-friendly food served in huge portions. The coolest spot for dining is the Ice Cave at the back of the restaurant, with glowing blue walls.

## Turf Club Bar & Grill ★★

| AMERICAN | MODERATE | QUALITY ★★★ | VALUE ★★ |
|---|---|---|---|
| READER-SURVEY RESPONSES 92% 👍 | 8% 👎 | DISNEY DINING PLAN? | Yes |

Saratoga Springs Resort & Spa; ☎ 407-939-3463

**Reservations** Accepted. **Dining Plan credits** 1 per person, per meal. **When to go** Dinner. **Cost range** Dinner $17–$31.50 (child $8.59). **Service** ★★★. **Friendliness** ★★★★. **Parking** Lot. **Bar** Full service. **Wine selection** Good. **Dress** Casual. **Disabled access** Good. **Customers** Hotel guests. **Dinner** Daily, 5–9 p.m.

**SETTING AND ATMOSPHERE** When the weather's nice, ask for an outdoor table; you can spot golfers on the adjacent Lake Buena Vista Golf Course and look across the way to Downtown Disney. Tucked off the lobby of the Saratoga Springs Resort, the dining room is equestrian-themed.

**HOUSE SPECIALTIES** Turf Club pasta with shrimp, grilled Caesar salad.

**OTHER RECOMMENDATIONS** Prime rib with mashed potatoes, grilled salmon with mustard glaze, root beer–brined pork chop.

**SUMMARY AND COMMENTS** Because this tucked-away spot caters mainly to the Disney Vacation Club crowd, it's rarely crowded. Ask for an outdoor table and enjoy a drink and appetizers on the terrace. The cuisine isn't cutting-edge and the decor is nothing special, but the Turf Club Signature Salad—grilled hearts of romaine with roasted cherry tomatoes, Caesar dressing, and balsamic reduction—goes great with a bowl of steamed mussels.

## Tusker House Restaurant ★★★

| AMERICAN/AFRICAN/BUFFET | MODERATE | QUALITY ★★★ | VALUE ★★★ |
|---|---|---|---|
| READER-SURVEY RESPONSES 92% 👍 | 8% 👎 | DISNEY DINING PLAN? | Yes |

Africa, Disney's Animal Kingdom; ☎ 407-939-3463

**Reservations** Required for character breakfast and lunch. **Dining Plan credits** 1 per person, per meal. **When to go** Anytime. **Cost range** Breakfast $29 (child $16), lunch $30 (child $17), dinner $30 (child $16). **Service** ★★★. **Friendliness** ★★★. **Parking** Animal Kingdom lot. **Bar** Full-service bar next door. **Dress** Casual. **Disabled access** Yes. **Customers** Theme park guests. **Character breakfast** Daily, 8–10:30 a.m. **Character lunch** Daily, 11:30 a.m.–3:30 p.m. **Dinner** Daily, 4 p.m.–park closing.

**SETTING AND ATMOSPHERE** Donald's Safari Breakfast features Donald, Daisy, Mickey, and Goofy. The Harambe Village setting is a bit austere, and the food is good, though not as interesting as the surroundings would lead you to expect. Still, it's fine for filling up families and a visit with the Disney characters.

**HOUSE SPECIALTIES** Carved sirloin, rotisserie pork and chicken, chicken curry, seafood stew, spiced tofu.

**OTHER RECOMMENDATIONS** African- and Indian-influenced dishes such as chutney, couscous, and curry.

**SUMMARY AND COMMENTS** The menu mixes comfort food with more-adventurous selections for lunch and dinner. The usual bacon, eggs, fruit, and pastries are served for breakfast, with a few African-inspired touches such as beef bobotie quiche and yam casserole.

## Tutto Italia Ristorante ★★★★

| ITALIAN | EXPENSIVE | QUALITY ★★★★ | VALUE ★★★ |
|---|---|---|---|
| READER-SURVEY RESPONSES | 83% 👍 17% 👎 | DISNEY DINING PLAN? Yes | |

Italy, World Showcase, Epcot; ☎ 407-939-3463

**Reservations** Recommended. **Dining Plan credits** 1 per person, per meal. **When to go** Midafternoon. **Cost range** Lunch $17–$30 (child $10), dinner $23–$30 (child $10). **Service** ★★★★. **Friendliness** ★★★★. **Parking** Epcot lot. **Bar** Beer and wine only. **Wine selection** All Italian. **Dress** Casual. **Disabled access** Yes. **Customers** Theme park guests. **Lunch** Daily, 11:30 a.m.–3:30 p.m. **Dinner** Daily, 4:30–park closing.

**SETTING AND ATMOSPHERE** The Roman decor features huge murals of an Italian piazza along the wall behind the upholstered banquettes. The atmosphere is elegant, but the dining room is noisy—nearly always full. If the weather is pleasant, request a table on the piazza. Well-run dining room with excellent service from a mostly young Italian waitstaff.

**HOUSE SPECIALTIES** Lasagna with meat *ragù*, béchamel, and Parmesan; creamy polenta with melted fontina, served with braised short ribs and meatballs; grilled butcher's steak with rosemary potatoes; cannoli.

**OTHER RECOMMENDATIONS** Any of the pastas (fettuccine, gnochetti, ravioli, spaghetti).

**SUMMARY AND COMMENTS** Tutto Italia is pricey, but the service is professional and friendly, the cuisine is authentic, and the servings are ample.

## Via Napoli ★★★★

| ITALIAN | MODERATE | QUALITY ★★★½ | VALUE ★★★ |
|---|---|---|---|
| READER-SURVEY RESPONSES | 93% 👍 7% 👎 | DISNEY DINING PLAN? Yes | |

Italy, World Showcase, Epcot; ☎ 407-939-3463

**Reservations** Recommended. **Dining Plan credits** 1 per person, per meal. **When to go** Lunch or dinner. **Cost range** Entrees $18–$24, pizzas $19 (individual)–$41 (serves 3–5). **Service** ★★★★. **Friendliness** ★★★★. **Parking** Epcot lot. **Bar** Beer and wine only. **Dress** Casual. **Disabled access** Yes. **Customers** Theme park guests. **Lunch** Daily, 11:30 a.m.–3:15 p.m. **Dinner** Daily, 4:30–9 p.m.

**SETTING AND ATMOSPHERE** The main dining room is cavernous and loud, with tile floors and stucco walls, but there are enough staff and guests moving around that it feels like a bustling Italian market. Shaded outdoor seating is available; pizza by the slice is sometimes sold outside.

**HOUSE SPECIALTIES** The best pizza in Walt Disney World. The rest of the menu is average, with the possible exception of the salads.

**SUMMARY AND COMMENTS** Because the pies are cooked at inferno-like temperatures, they don't stay in the oven for long and vegetable toppings stay crunchy. The Capriciossa (eggplant, artichokes, prosciutto, and mushrooms) and four-cheese pies are our favorites.

## Victoria & Albert's ★★★★★

| GOURMET | EXPENSIVE | QUALITY ★★★★★ | VALUE ★★★★ |
|---|---|---|---|
| READER-SURVEY RESPONSES | 93% 👍 7% 👎 | DISNEY DINING PLAN? No | |

Grand Floridian Resort & Spa; ☎ 407-939-3862

**Reservations** Mandatory; must confirm by noon the day of your seating; credit card required to reserve; call at least 180 days in advance to reserve. **When to go** Anytime. **Cost range** Fixed price, $135 per person or $200 with wine pairings; Chef's Table and Queen Victoria's Room, $210 or $315 with wine pairings. **Service** ★★★★★. **Friendliness** ★★★★. **Parking** Valet (free); self-parking is deceptively far away. **Wine selection** 700 on the menu, 4,200 more in the cellar. **Dress** Jacket required for men, evening attire for women. **Disabled access** Yes. **Customers** Hotel guests, locals. **Dinner** 2 seatings nightly at 5:45–6:30 p.m. and 9–9:45 p.m., plus 1 seating at 6 p.m. for the Chef's Table. *Note:* No children under age 10 admitted except at Chef's Table.

**SETTING AND ATMOSPHERE** Frette linens, Riedel crystal, Christofle silver—with only 18 tables in the main dining room and Queen Victoria's Room, a new private space with seating for eight, this is the top dining experience at Disney World. A winner of AAA's Five Diamond Award—the only restaurant in Central Florida so honored—Victoria & Albert's is civilized, lavish, and expensive. Waitstaff in Queen Victoria's Room expertly revive the European art of tableside finishes for each dish.

**HOUSE SPECIALTIES** The menu changes daily, but Chef Scott Hunnel's favorites include Niman Ranch lamb, Florida seafood, and coveted Japanese Iwate beef. Pastry chef Erich Herbitschek's desserts are divine.

**ENTERTAINMENT AND AMENITIES** A harpist or violinist entertains from the foyer. But the best show is in the kitchen when you book the Chef's Table, where Chef Hunnel starts the evening with a Champagne toast and crafts a personal menu.

**SUMMARY AND COMMENTS** Hunnel and his team prepare modern American cuisine with the best of the best from around the world. While the main dining room and Queen Victoria's Room are whisper-quiet, the convivial Chef's Table is a different experience altogether. For epicures, it's a bargain.

## The Wave . . . of American Flavors  ★★★

| NEW AMERICAN | MODERATE | QUALITY ★★ | VALUE ★★ |
|---|---|---|---|
| READER-SURVEY RESPONSES | 89% 👍 11% 👎 | DISNEY DINING PLAN? | Yes |

Contemporary Resort; ☎ 407-939-3463

**Reservations** Accepted. **Dining Plan credits** 1 per person, per meal. **When to go** Anytime. **Cost range** Breakfast $9–$12.50 à la carte, $18.50 buffet (child $6.50), lunch $12–$19.50 (child $9), dinner $16.50–$33 (child $9). **Service** ★★★. **Friendliness** ★★★. **Parking** Valet ($20) or hotel lot. **Bar** Full service. **Wine selection** All New World screw-caps. **Dress** Casual. **Disabled access** Yes. **Customers** Hotel guests, locals. **Breakfast** Daily, 7:30–11 a.m. **Lunch** Daily, noon–2 p.m. **Dinner** Daily, 5:30–10 p.m.

**SETTING AND ATMOSPHERE** On the first floor of the Contemporary just past the front desk, The Wave has one of the coolest lounges at Disney World, adjoining a dining room with the feel of an upscale coffee shop—wooden tables and white-linen napkins.

**HOUSE SPECIALTIES** Unusual drinks like the Antioxidant Cocktail and the strawberry-lychee margarita. For breakfast: a generous buffet, megaberry smoothie, multigrain French toast, and make-your-own muesli. For lunch: curry vegetable stew, Reuben, Mediterranean tuna salad. For dinner: sustainable fish, grilled beef tenderloin, naturally raised chicken breast.

**OTHER RECOMMENDATIONS** Grilled lamb chops with macaroni and cheese; naturally raised pork tenderloin; pan-seared sea scallops.

**SUMMARY AND COMMENTS** The kitchen continues to create healthful dining options and source local products, setting a good example for other

Disney restaurants. Organic beers, organic coffees, hip cocktails, and all-screw-cap wines—focusing on New World wines from Argentina, Australia, Chile, New Zealand, and South Africa—are part of the forward-thinking menu.

## Whispering Canyon Cafe  ★★★

| AMERICAN | MODERATE | QUALITY ★★★½ | VALUE ★★★★ |
|---|---|---|---|
| READER-SURVEY RESPONSES | 80% 👍 | 20% 👎 | DISNEY DINING PLAN? Yes |

Wilderness Lodge & Villas; ☎ 407-939-3463

**Reservations** Accepted. **Dining Plan credits** 1 per person, per meal. **When to go** Anytime. **Cost range** Breakfast $10.50–$16.50 (child $7–$8.50), lunch $14–$22 (child $9), dinner $17.50–$34 (child $9). **Service** ★★★★. **Friendliness** ★★★★. **Parking** Hotel lot. **Bar** Full service. **Wine selection** Limited. **Dress** Casual. **Disabled access** Yes. **Customers** Hotel guests. **Breakfast** Daily, 7:30–11:30 a.m. **Lunch** Daily, 11:30 a.m.–2:30 p.m. **Dinner** Daily, 5–10 p.m.

**SETTING AND ATMOSPHERE** Just off the hotel's atrium lobby, the restaurant looks out on the lobby on one side and a mountain prairie, created by Disney landscapers, on the other. Tables have a barrel-top lazy Susan where food is placed.

**HOUSE SPECIALTIES** All-you-can-eat skillets with corn bread, pulled pork, smoked pork ribs, beef brisket, citrus-crusted fish, sausage, mashed potatoes, baked beans, seasonal vegetables, and corn on the cob.

**OTHER RECOMMENDATIONS** New York strip steak, citrus-glaze rainbow trout, s'mores with marshmallow gelato.

**SUMMARY AND COMMENTS** If you're hungry, the real value here is in the family-style service, with all-you-can-eat servings brought to you on platters and in crocks to pass around to your family. You can always order off the regular menu if you don't feel like sharing, but you may end up paying more for the privilege. Lively dining room with servers who encourage kids to be rowdy—all in good fun.

## Wolfgang Puck Grand Cafe  ★★

| CREATIVE CALIFORNIAN | EXPENSIVE | QUALITY ★½ | VALUE ★½ |
|---|---|---|---|
| READER-SURVEY RESPONSES | 75% 👍 | 25% 👎 | DISNEY DINING PLAN? Yes |

Downtown Disney West Side; ☎ 407-938-9653

**Reservations** Recommended. **Dining Plan credits** 1 per person, per meal (downstairs only). **When to go** Early evening. **Cost range** Cafe $12–$29 (child $6–$9), upstairs $25–$45 (child $10–$18). **Service** ★★★. **Friendliness** ★★★. **Parking** Downtown Disney lot. **Bar** Full service. **Wine selection** Very good. **Dress** Casual in the cafe; collared and sleeved shirts for men and no jeans upstairs. **Disabled access** Yes. **Customers** Tourists, locals. **Hours** *Cafe:* Lunch and dinner daily, 11:30 a.m.–11 p.m. *Upstairs:* Dinner Sunday–Wednesday, 6–9 p.m.; Thursday–Saturday, 6–10 p.m.

**SETTING AND ATMOSPHERE** This is actually two restaurants in one—four if you count the attached Wolfgang Puck Express and the sushi bar that flows into the restaurant's lounge area. Downstairs is the actual cafe, with several open kitchen areas, colorful tile, and plenty of pictures of Wolfgang Puck hanging around (though you won't find him in the kitchen). The upstairs is a more formal dining room, but in name only. Both spaces are inordinately loud, making conversation difficult.

**HOUSE SPECIALTIES** Puck's wood-fired pizzas, including barbecue chicken and spicy shrimp. Sushi is also a good bet. Upstairs, the menu features fresh fish, chicken, and beef.

**SUMMARY AND COMMENTS** Quality has really dipped in recent years, but in spite of less-than-stellar food, there's usually a crowd. We can always recommend dining at the sushi bar. Or you can skip the entree and go straight for dessert.

## Yachtsman Steakhouse  ★★★

| STEAK | EXPENSIVE | | QUALITY | ★★★½ | | VALUE | ★★ |
|---|---|---|---|---|---|---|---|
| READER-SURVEY RESPONSES | | 74% 👍 | 26% 👎 | DISNEY DINING PLAN? | | Yes | |

Yacht Club Resort; ☎ 407-939-3463

**Reservations** Required. **Dining Plan credits** 2 per person, per meal. **When to go** Dinner. **Cost range** Dinner $30–$65 (child $8–$12). **Service** ★★★★. **Friendliness** ★★★★. **Parking** Hotel lot. **Bar** Full service. **Wine selection** Very good. **Dress** Dressy casual. **Disabled access** Yes. **Customers** Hotel guests and locals. **Dinner** Daily, 5:30–10:30 p.m.

**SETTING AND ATMOSPHERE** Wood beams, white linens, and a view of the sandy lagoon at the resort make this steakhouse appealing. The menu features seafood, lamb, fowl, and vegetarian creations. The adjacent Crew's Cup Lounge, with dozens of beers and fine wine by the glass, is a fun place to start the evening.

**HOUSE SPECIALTIES** Start with lobster bisque or a classic Caesar salad. All steaks are cut and trimmed on the premises. The filet mignon and New York strip are just some of the cuts.

**OTHER RECOMMENDATIONS** Ahi tuna; wild king salmon; carrot agnolotti pasta; truffle macaroni and cheese; chocolate-peanut cake; seasonal sorbets. All entrees except the rib eye come with a vegetable, so you can skip the ordinary sides.

**SUMMARY AND COMMENTS** The menu could probably stand a refresh (truffle mac and cheese, for instance, has become kind of a culinary cliché). Nevertheless, Yachtsman Steakhouse has a loyal following of locals—diehard meat lovers who don't mind paying for a good steak. Vintages from every major wine-producing region of the world complement the menu.

## Yak & Yeti Restaurant  ★★

| PAN-ASIAN | | EXPENSIVE | | QUALITY | ★★½ | VALUE | ★★ |
|---|---|---|---|---|---|---|---|
| READER-SURVEY RESPONSES | | 93% 👍 | 7% 👎 | DISNEY DINING PLAN? | | Yes | |

Asia, Disney's Animal Kingdom; ☎ 407-939-3463

**Reservations** Recommended. **Dining Plan credits** 1 per person, per meal. **When to go** Dinner. **Cost range** $17–$26 (child $8.50). **Service** ★★★★. **Friendliness** ★★★★. **Parking** Animal Kingdom lot. **Bar** Full service. **Wine selection** Limited. **Dress** Casual. **Disabled access** Yes. **Customers** Theme park guests. **Lunch** Daily, 11 a.m.–3:30 p.m. **Dinner** Daily, 4 p.m.–park closing.

**SETTING AND ATMOSPHERE** A rustic two-story Nepalese inn . . . with seating for hundreds. Windows on the second floor overlook the Asia section of the park.

**HOUSE SPECIALTIES** Seared miso salmon, tempura shrimp, and glazed duck; fried wontons with pineapple and cream cheese for dessert.

**SUMMARY AND COMMENTS** Though this isn't fine dining, much of the food, including the seafood and duck, stands out from the usual theme park fare. The steak-and-shrimp combo is also good, but the chicken dishes are just average.

# PART ELEVEN

# The
# MAGIC KINGDOM

OPENED IN 1971, THE MAGIC KINGDOM was the first built of Walt Disney World's four theme parks. Many of the attractions found here are originals from that park opening, and a few—including Cinderella Castle, Pirates of the Caribbean, and Splash Mountain—have helped define the basic elements of theme park attractions the world over. Indeed, the Magic Kingdom is undoubtedly what most people think of when they think of Walt Disney World.

Much of the Magic Kingdom was built by the same Disney staff who had built Disneyland almost two decades earlier. The remarkable achievement that Disney wrought in Orlando isn't that they could build a second, equally compelling theme park; rather, it's that they could do so on a much larger scale while keeping many of the fine details that make visiting a Disney park such a completely immersive experience.

| NOT TO BE MISSED AT THE MAGIC KINGDOM | |
|---|---|
| **ADVENTURELAND** • A Pirate's Adventure • Pirates of the Caribbean | |
| **FANTASYLAND** • Peter Pan's Flight • *Mickey's PhilharMagic* • Seven Dwarfs Mine Train | |
| **FRONTIERLAND** • Big Thunder Mountain Railroad • Splash Mountain | |
| **LIBERTY SQUARE** • The Haunted Mansion | |
| **SPECIAL EVENTS** • *Celebrate the Magic* • Evening Parade • *Wishes* | |
| **TOMORROWLAND** • Space Mountain | |

## ARRIVING

IF YOU DRIVE, the Magic Kingdom **Transportation and Ticket Center (TTC)** parking lot opens about 2 hours before the park's official opening. For driving directions, see page 373. After paying a fee, you're directed to a parking space, then transported by tram to the TTC, where you catch either a monorail or a ferry to the park's entrance.

If you bring a stroller, a Ridgewood, New Jersey, family recommends the ferry (which starts operating 30–60 minutes before park opening):

*The ferry from the TTC to the Magic Kingdom dock is a must if you're using a stroller. You can drive the stroller right onto the ferry and then just head to the back of the ferry to be the first ones off when it docks.*

Continued on page 504

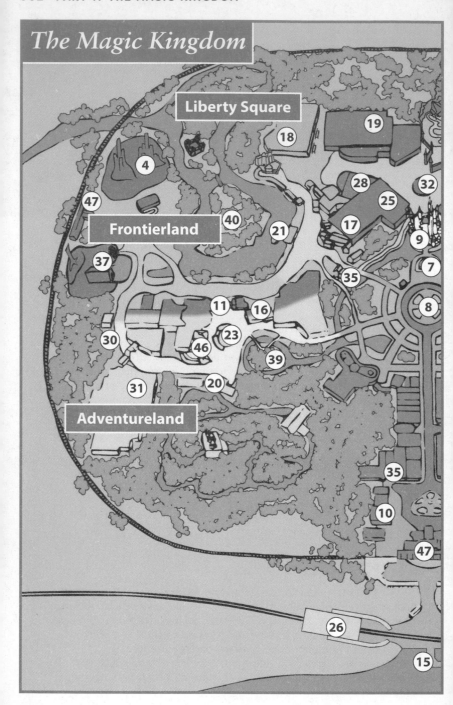

The Magic Kingdom

Liberty Square

Frontierland

Adventureland

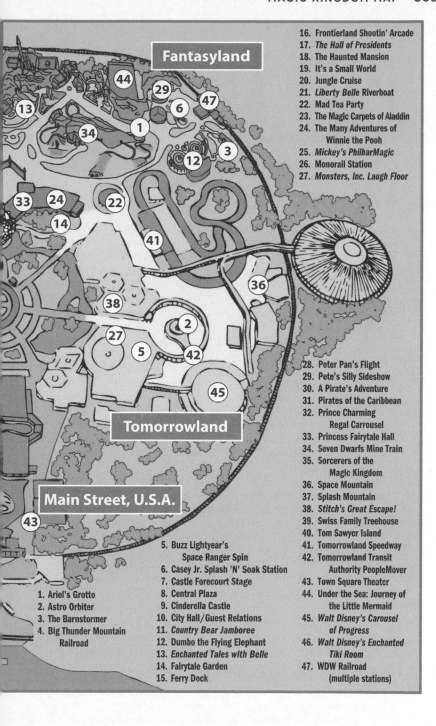

Fantasyland

Tomorrowland

Main Street, U.S.A.

16. Frontierland Shootin' Arcade
17. *The Hall of Presidents*
18. The Haunted Mansion
19. It's a Small World
20. Jungle Cruise
21. *Liberty Belle* Riverboat
22. Mad Tea Party
23. The Magic Carpets of Aladdin
24. The Many Adventures of
    Winnie the Pooh
25. *Mickey's PhilharMagic*
26. *Monorail Station*
27. *Monsters, Inc. Laugh Floor*

28. Peter Pan's Flight
29. Pete's Silly Sideshow
30. A Pirate's Adventure
31. Pirates of the Caribbean
32. Prince Charming
    Regal Carousel
33. Princess Fairytale Hall
34. Seven Dwarfs Mine Train
35. Sorcerers of the
    Magic Kingdom
36. Space Mountain
37. Splash Mountain
38. *Stitch's Great Escape!*
39. Swiss Family Treehouse
40. Tom Sawyer Island
41. Tomorrowland Speedway
42. Tomorrowland Transit
    Authority PeopleMover
43. Town Square Theater
44. Under the Sea: Journey of
    the Little Mermaid
45. *Walt Disney's Carousel
    of Progress*
46. *Walt Disney's Enchanted
    Tiki Room*
47. WDW Railroad
    (multiple stations)

1. Ariel's Grotto
2. Astro Orbiter
3. The Barnstormer
4. Big Thunder Mountain
   Railroad

5. Buzz Lightyear's
   Space Ranger Spin
6. Casey Jr. Splash 'N' Soak Station
7. Castle Forecourt Stage
8. Central Plaza
9. Cinderella Castle
10. City Hall/Guest Relations
11. *Country Bear Jamboree*
12. Dumbo the Flying Elephant
13. *Enchanted Tales with Belle*
14. Fairytale Garden
15. Ferry Dock

*Continued from page 501*

If you're staying at the Contemporary, Bay Lake Tower, Polynesian, or Grand Floridian resorts, you can commute to the Magic Kingdom by monorail (guests at the Contemporary and Bay Lake Tower can walk to the park more quickly). If you're staying at Wilderness Lodge & Villas or Fort Wilderness Resort & Campground, you can take a boat or bus. Guests at other Walt Disney World resorts can reach the park by bus. All Disney lodging guests, whether they arrive by monorail, boat, or bus, are deposited at the park's entrance, bypassing the TTC.

# GETTING ORIENTED

AT THE MAGIC KINGDOM, stroller, wheelchair, and ECV/ESV rentals are in the train station; lockers are on the right, just inside the entrance. On your left as you enter **Main Street, U.S.A.** is **City Hall,** the center for information, lost and found, guided tours, and entertainment schedules.

*unofficial* **TIP**
If you don't already have a park map, get one at City Hall or the entrance turnstiles.

The guide map found there lists all attractions, shops, and eating places; provides information about first aid, baby care, and assistance for the disabled; and gives tips for good photos. It lists times for the day's special events, live entertainment, Disney-character parades, and concerts, and it also tells when and where to find Disney characters. The guide map is supplemented by a daily entertainment schedule known as the *Times Guide.* In addition to listing performance times, the *Times Guide* provides info on Disney-character appearances and what Disney calls Special Hours. This term usually refers to attractions that open late or close early and to the operating hours of park restaurants. The My Disney Experience app (see page 32) has this same information.

Main Street, U.S.A. ends at the **Central Plaza,** a hub from which branch the entrances to five other sections of the Magic Kingdom:

*unofficial* **TIP**
Because Cinderella Castle is so large, designate a very specific meeting spot, such as the entrance to Cinderella's Royal Table restaurant at the rear of the castle.

**Adventureland, Frontierland, Liberty Square, Fantasyland,** and **Tomorrowland.**

**Cinderella Castle,** at the entrance to Fantasyland, is the Magic Kingdom's architectural icon and visual center. If you start in Adventureland and go clockwise around the Magic Kingdom, the castle spires will always be roughly on your right; if you start in Tomorrowland and go counterclockwise through the park, the spires will always be roughly on your left. The castle is an excellent meeting place if your group decides to split up during the day or is separated accidentally.

## FANTASYLAND EXPANSION

WITH THE OPENING OF **Seven Dwarfs Mine Train,** the Magic Kingdom has completed the expansion of Fantasyland begun in 2010. The first phase of "New Fantasyland" opened in 2012, with attractions and restaurants that quickly joined the Magic Kingdom's must-do list. Parents with small children now race each morning to **Princess Fairytale Hall**—a character-greeting experience—for the chance to meet *Frozen*'s Anna and Elsa the way teens head for Space Mountain. Families line up for an hour or more to eat lunch at **Be Our Guest,** which serves the best food in the Magic Kingdom (dinner requires Advance Reservations 180 days before your visit). And now Seven Dwarfs Mine Train draws Disney roller-coaster fans to Fantasyland for the first time.

We've updated our Magic Kingdom touring plans to reflect the latest developments. Check **touringplans.com** for updates.

## FASTPASS+ ATTRACTIONS IN THE MAGIC KINGDOM

**ADVENTURELAND**
- Jungle Cruise
- The Magic Carpets of Aladdin
- Pirates of the Caribbean

**FANTASYLAND**
- Ariel's Grotto
- The Barnstormer
- Dumbo the Flying Elephant
- *Enchanted Tales with Belle*
- It's a Small World
- Mad Tea Party
- The Many Adventures of Winnie the Pooh
- *Mickey's PhilharMagic*
- Peter Pan's Flight
- Princess Fairytale Hall
- Seven Dwarfs Mine Train
- Under the Sea: Journey of the Little Mermaid

**FRONTIERLAND**
- Big Thunder Mountain Railroad
- Splash Mountain

**LIBERTY SQUARE**
- The Haunted Mansion

**MAIN STREET, U.S.A.**
- Town Square Theater Meet-and-Greets

**TOMORROWLAND**
- Buzz Lightyear's Space Ranger Spin
- *Monsters, Inc. Laugh Floor*
- Space Mountain
- Tomorrowland Speedway

**ENTERTAINMENT & PARADES**
- *Celebrate the Magic*
- Festival of Fantasy Parade
- Main Street Electrical Parade
- Festival of Fantasy Parade
- *Wishes* Fireworks

WHILE THE MAGIC KINGDOM offers FastPass+ for more than two dozen attractions, as listed above, our touring plan software identifies only five as frequently needing FastPass+: **(1) Peter Pan's Flight, (2)** *Enchanted Tales with Belle,* **(3) Big Thunder Mountain Railroad, (4) Splash Mountain,** and **(5) Space Mountain.**

Why is Peter Pan's Flight listed first? First of all, it's really nobody's choice as the first attraction to visit. If you've got small children, you're probably headed to *Enchanted Tales with Belle* or Seven Dwarfs Mine Train; if you've got older kids, you're probably headed to Space Mountain or Seven Dwarfs. And no matter where you go first, you'll probably visit at least one other attraction nearby next. That means you're not getting to Peter Pan within the first 30 minutes the park is open.

Second, Peter Pan appears on virtually every Magic Kingdom touring plan. It's a classic, if simple, Disney ride with universal appeal.

Third, although it's not a headliner attraction, Peter Pan develops long lines throughout the day. Wait times during Christmas, for example, can exceed 150–180 minutes fairly often. The ride's hourly capacity is around 1,100 guests—a little more than half of Buzz Lightyear's and far less than half of Pirates of the Caribbean's.

## MAIN STREET Services

MOST PARK SERVICES are centered on Main Street, U.S.A., including:

**Baby Care Center** Next to The Crystal Palace, left around the Central Plaza (toward Adventureland)

**Banking Services** ATMs underneath the Main Street railroad station

**First Aid** Next to The Crystal Palace, left around the Central Plaza (toward Adventureland)

**Live Entertainment and Parade Information** City Hall, at the railroad-station end of Main Street

**Lost and Found** City Hall

**Lost Persons** City Hall

**Storage Lockers** Underneath the Main Street railroad station

**Walt Disney World and Local Attraction Information** City Hall

**Wheelchair, ECV/ESV, and Stroller Rentals** Ground floor of the railroad station at the end of Main Street

We think *Enchanted Tales with Belle* came in second because seeing it first thing in the morning usually doesn't make sense. Counting walking time and the elaborate preshow, you'd probably be committing about 30 minutes to that one attraction—you could probably visit two or three other attractions in Fantasyland in the same amount of time.

Big Thunder and Splash Mountain don't normally get a huge influx of guests immediately at park opening, but lines of 20–40 minutes can develop around midmorning at both as crowds make their way from Tomorrowland and Fantasyland.

Space Mountain probably made the list because of Seven Dwarfs Mine Train. The latter is not only the hot new attraction in the Magic Kingdom, it has a less stringent height requirement than Space Mountain. Plus, it's listed as the first attraction to visit in a lot of our touring plans, and it's usually followed by other Fantasyland attractions to minimize walking. All this is to say, if you're going to Seven Dwarfs first, you'll need FastPass+ for Space Mountain when you visit it later.

Note that we haven't included the popular **Anna and Elsa meet-and-greet** at Princess Fairytale Hall among our FastPass+ musts. Lines do get incredibly long—approaching 6 hours in some cases!—but hourly capacity is only around 45–50 families, or roughly 500–600 people per day. You definitely need FastPass+, but your chances of scoring reservations are very low. If by some miracle you do snag them, our touring plan software can incorporate the *Frozen* princesses into your day.

On the other hand, six Magic Kingdom attractions *never* seem to need FastPass+, either because our touring plans get you to them before long lines develop or because the attractions rarely see long waits: **The Barnstormer, It's a Small World, Mad Tea Party, The Magic Carpets of Aladdin, *Mickey's PhilharMagic*,** and ***Monsters, Inc. Laugh Floor.*** You can almost always get in to the next seating for the two shows—and if the park is so crowded that you can't, the headliner attractions will be mobbed and remain your best use of FastPass+. As for the other four, their lines never get as long as those for more-popular rides.

FastPass+ kiosk locations in the Magic Kingdom are as follows:

- At Guest Relations at City Hall on Main Street
- In Town Square Theater on Main Street

- In Heritage House, outside the *Hall of Presidents* exit in Liberty Square
- In the walkway between Adventureland and Liberty Square, near the Diamond Horseshoe Saloon and Swiss Family Treehouse
- At the entrance to Jungle Cruise in Adventureland
- Outside Mickey's PhilharMagic in Fantasyland
- At Storybook Circus, across from The Barnstormer in Fantasyland
- Near *Stitch's Great Escape!* in Tomorrowland
- Near Buzz Lightyear's Space Ranger Spin in Tomorrowland

## DINING IN THE MAGIC KINGDOM

COUNTER-SERVICE RESTAURANTS in the Magic Kingdom are profiled in Part Ten, starting on page 448. For full-service profiles, see the section starting on page 457.

# STARTING *the* TOUR

VISITORS SOON FIND THEIR FAVORITE and not-so-favorite attractions in the Magic Kingdom. Our personal experience and research indicate that each visitor differs on which attraction is most enjoyable. Don't dismiss a ride or show until *after* you've tried it.

Take advantage of what Disney does best: the fantasy adventures of Splash Mountain and The Haunted Mansion and the various animatronic (talking robot) attractions, including *The Hall of Presidents* and Pirates of the Caribbean, and the elaborate character-greeting venues in Fantasyland. Don't burn daylight browsing the shops unless you plan to spend at least two and a half days at the Magic Kingdom, and even then, wait until midday or later. Minimize the time you spend on midway-type rides; you probably have something similar back home. (Don't, however, mistake Space Mountain and Big Thunder Mountain Railroad for amusement park rides. They may be roller coasters, but they're pure Disney genius.) Eat a good breakfast early, and avoid lines at eateries by snacking during the day on food from vendors or, better yet, from your fanny pack. Except for Be Our Guest, fare at most Magic Kingdom eateries is on par with McDonald's.

# MAIN STREET, U.S.A.

BEGIN AND END YOUR VISIT ON MAIN STREET, which may open 30 minutes before and closes 30 minutes–1 hour after the rest of the park. The Walt Disney World Railroad stops at Main Street Station; get on to tour the park or ride to Frontierland or Fantasyland.

Main Street is a Disneyfied turn-of-the-19th-century small-town American street. Its buildings are real, not elaborate props. Attention to detail is exceptional: Furnishings and fixtures are true to the period. Along the street are shops, eating places, City Hall, and a fire station. Occasionally, horse-drawn trolleys, fire engines, and horseless carriages transport visitors along Main Street to the Central Plaza.

The area around the Central Plaza will be undergoing construction through 2015 to make more space for viewing parades and fireworks. If you're looking for a good place to photograph Cinderella Castle without the construction mess, try along the bridge to Liberty Square. See **tinyurl.com/magickingdomhub** for video of the proposed changes.

## Sorcerers of the Magic Kingdom ★★★

**APPEAL BY AGE** PRESCHOOL ★★★½ GRADE SCHOOL ★★★★½ TEENS ★★★★
YOUNG ADULTS ★★★★ OVER 30 ★★★★ SENIORS ★★★

**What it is** Interactive video game. **Scope and scale** Minor attraction. **When to go** Before 11 a.m. or after 8 p.m. **Special comments** Long lines to play. **Authors' rating** Great idea; ★★★. **Duration of presentation** About 2 minutes per step, 4 or 5 steps per game. **Probable waiting time per step** 10–15 minutes.

**DESCRIPTION AND COMMENTS** Sorcerers of the Magic Kingdom combines aspects of role-playing games such as Dungeons and Dragons with Disney characters and theme park attractions. Your objective: to help the wizard Merlin keep evildoers from taking over the Magic Kingdom. Merlin sends you on adventures in different parts of the park to fight these villains. Each land hosts a different adventure within the game.

The game is played with a set of trading cards—similar to baseball cards or Magic: The Gathering cards—with a different Disney character on each card. Each character possesses special properties that help it fight certain villains. Pick up the cards (free), plus a map showing where in the park you can play the game, at either the Fire Station on Main Street, U.S.A., or across from Sleepy Hollow Refreshments in Liberty Square.

You'll need your park ticket to pick up your first set of cards and start the game. One card, known as your "key," is special because it links you to your game. You'll need to present your key card when you pick up a set of cards to start your next adventure.

When you pick up your first set of cards, you'll view an instructional video explaining how to use them and the object of the game. Then you'll be sent to another location to start your first adventure. Each location in the park is associated with a unique symbol: an eye, a feather, a dragonfly, or something along those lines. Look for these symbols on the map to find the best route to your starting point.

Each adventure consists of four or five stops in a particular land. At each stop, another story will play on a video screen, outlining what your villain is trying to do. Merlin will ask you to cast a spell to stop the villain—to do so, hold one or more of your cards up to the video display. Cameras in the display read your card, deploy the spell, and show you the results.

The game has three levels: easy, medium, and hard. The easy version is the default and is appropriate for small children; holding up any one of your character cards is enough to defeat any villain. In more-advanced levels of the game, you need to display two or more character cards in specific combinations to defeat a particular villain. Different card combinations produce different spells, and only some spells work on certain characters in those advanced levels.

The audio at each step holds clues to which cards you should use against advanced villains. For example, if a villain says something like "Don't toy with me!" then you should look for cards with characters that are toys, such as the *Toy Story* characters; references to "being spotted" suggest using cards with characters from *101 Dalmatians;* and so on.

The game launched with an initial series of around 70 unique cards; you can obtain 5 new ones per day. Don't worry if you play more than once and end up with duplicate cards—a brisk trading market exists within the park. Disney plans to issue new card series over time.

An Anchorage, Alaska, couple offers these tips for playing the game:

*(1) Unless you plan to stick with every member of your group every single minute, make sure they all get their own portal keys. (2) Every card has a "rarity," located above the card number. If you want to trade cards, only trade for similar rarities. The symbol designates its rarity: planet (looks like a circle) is common, moon is uncommon, star is rare, lightning bolt is super-rare. You can only obtain lightning-bolt cards by buying card packs at the Emporium when they're in stock. They usually sell out by lunchtime, and the days they have them are random (to help increase scarcity). (4) When you're playing, be prepared for a LOT of people to come up to you and ask what you're doing. (5) Also, be prepared for people to walk in front of you when you're playing. This can cause the card reader to time out. (6) You can buy T-shirts with special designs on them that increase your power when you play at medium and hard levels.*

**TOURING TIPS** You'll probably encounter a line of 5–10 people ahead of you at each portal, especially if you play during the afternoon. One complete adventure should take about 30–60 minutes to play, depending on how crowded the park is. If the line to pick up cards is too long at the Main Street Fire Station, try the Liberty Square distribution point. If the game sounds too confusing, A Pirate's Adventure in Adventureland (see page 511) is easier.

## Town Square Theater Meet-and-Greets: Mickey Mouse, Tinker Bell and Friends *(FastPass+)* ★★★★

| APPEAL BY AGE | PRESCHOOL ★★★★½ | GRADE SCHOOL ★★★★½ | TEENS ★★★★½ |
|---|---|---|---|
| YOUNG ADULTS ★★★★ | OVER 30 ★★★★½ | | SENIORS ★★★★½ |

**What it is** Character-greeting venue. **Scope and scale** Minor attraction. **When to go** Before 10 a.m. or after 4 p.m., or use FastPass+. **Special comments** Mickey and the fairies have 2 separate queues, requiring 2 separate waits in line. **Authors' rating** It all started with this mouse; ★★★★. **Duration of experience** 2 minutes per character. **Probable waiting time** 15–25 minutes. **Queue speed** Slow.

**DESCRIPTION AND COMMENTS** Meet Mickey, along with Tinker Bell and her Pixie Hollow friends, throughout the day at the Town Square Theater on Main Street, to your right as you enter the park.

**TOURING TIPS** Lines usually drop off after the afternoon parade. Oddly enough, meeting Mickey rarely requires FastPass+.

## Transportation Rides

**DESCRIPTION AND COMMENTS** Trolleys, buses, and the like.

**TOURING TIPS** Will save you a walk to the Central Plaza. Not worth a wait.

## Walt Disney World Railroad ★★★

| APPEAL BY AGE | PRESCHOOL ★★★★½ | GRADE SCHOOL ★★★★ | TEENS ★★★½ |
|---|---|---|---|
| YOUNG ADULTS ★★★★ | OVER 30 ★★★★ | | SENIORS ★★★★½ |

**What it is** Scenic railroad ride around the perimeter of the Magic Kingdom; provides transportation to Frontierland and Fantasyland. **Scope and scale** Minor attraction. **When to go** Anytime. **Special comments** Main Street is usually the least congested station. **Authors' rating** Plenty to see; ★★★. **Duration of ride** About 20 minutes for a complete circuit. **Average wait in line per 100 people ahead of you** 8 minutes; assumes 2 or more trains operating. **Loading speed** Moderate.

**DESCRIPTION AND COMMENTS** A transportation ride blending an unusual variety of sights with an energy-saving way to get around the park. The train provides a glimpse of all "lands" except Adventureland, with most of the interesting stuff (American Indian village, animatronic animals, frontier structures) on the leg between Frontierland and Fantasyland.

**TOURING TIPS** Save the train until after you've seen the featured attractions, or use it when you need transportation. On busy days, lines form at the Frontierland Station but rarely at the Main Street Station. Wheelchair access is available at the Frontierland and Fantasyland Stations.

Only folded strollers are permitted on the train, so you can't board with your rented Disney stroller. You can, however, obtain a replacement at your destination (keep your stroller name card and rental receipt with you).

Finally, note that the railroad shuts down immediately before and during parades; check your park guide map or *Times Guide* for parade times. Needless to say, this is not the time to queue up for the train.

# ADVENTURELAND

ADVENTURELAND IS THE FIRST LAND to the left of Main Street. It combines an African-safari theme with a tropical-island atmosphere.

## Captain Jack Sparrow's Pirate Tutorial   ★★★½

| APPEAL BY AGE | PRESCHOOL ★★★★ | GRADE SCHOOL ★★★★ | TEENS ★★★½ |
|---|---|---|---|
| YOUNG  ADULTS  ★★★½ | | OVER  30  ★★★½ | SENIORS  ★★★ |

**What it is** Outdoor stage show with guest participation. **Scope and scale** Diversion. **When to go** See *Times Guide* for show schedule. **Authors' rating** Sign us up; ★★★½. **Duration of presentation** About 20 minutes.

**DESCRIPTION AND COMMENTS** Outside Pirates of the Caribbean, Cap'n Jack and a crew member teach would-be knaves the skills needed for a career in piracy. Some kids go on stage to train in the finer points of dueling, similar to *Jedi Training Academy* at Hollywood Studios (see page 628). The show finishes with everyone taking the probably-not-legally-binding pirate's oath and singing a rousing round of "A Pirate's Life for Me." If you or your kids are fans of the Pirates ride or the movie series, this show is worth a look as well.

**TOURING TIPS** The shows attract decent crowds, but the first and last show seem to be the least popular. Standing-room-only outdoors.

## Jungle Cruise *(FastPass+)*   ★★★½

| APPEAL BY AGE | PRESCHOOL ★★★★ | GRADE SCHOOL ★★★★ | TEENS ★★★½ |
|---|---|---|---|
| YOUNG  ADULTS  ★★★★ | | OVER  30  ★★★★ | SENIORS  ★★★★ |

**What it is** Outdoor safari-themed boat ride. **Scope and scale** Major attraction. **When to go** Before 10:30 a.m., during the last 2 hours before closing, or use FastPass+. **Special comments** Fun to ride at night! **Authors' rating** A classic, but kinda long in the tooth; ★★★½. **Duration of ride** 8–9 minutes. **Average wait in line per 100 people ahead of you** 3½ minutes; assumes 10 boats operating. **Loading speed** Moderate.

**DESCRIPTION AND COMMENTS** An outdoor excursion through jungle waterways. Passengers encounter animatronic elephants, lions, hostile natives, and a menacing hippo. The boatman's spiel adds to the fun. Once one of the most elaborate attractions at the Magic Kingdom, the Jungle Cruise now seems dated. Since the advent of Disney's Animal Kingdom, the attraction's appeal has diminished, but in its defense, you can always depend on the robotic critters being present as you motor past. A Pelham, Alabama, woman agrees that it's past its prime:

*Jungle Cruise severely needs an update. Our tour guide indulged in annoying comedy to make up for the lack of excitement. I would rather have been eaten by the animatronic hippos.*

**TOURING TIPS** A convoluted queuing area makes it difficult to estimate wait times. A mother from The Bronx complains:

*We got in line toward early evening; the line was deceptively long, but we really wanted to ride. Every time the winding line brought us near the loading dock and we thought we were going to get on, we'd discover a whole new section of winding lines to go through. We must have waited 20–30 minutes before we finally gave up and got out.*

Fortunately, Jungle Cruise is a FastPass+ attraction. Before you make a same-day reservation, however, ask a cast member what the estimated wait in the standby line is.

## The Magic Carpets of Aladdin *(FastPass+)*  ★★½

**APPEAL BY AGE   PRESCHOOL ★★★★½   GRADE SCHOOL ★★★★   TEENS ★★★**
**YOUNG  ADULTS  ★★★        OVER 30  ★★★        SENIORS  ★★★½**

**What it is** Elaborate midway ride. **Scope and scale** Minor attraction. **When to go** Before 11 a.m. or after 7 p.m. **Authors' rating** A visually appealing children's ride; ★★½. **Duration of ride** 1½ minutes. **Average wait in line per 100 people ahead of you** 16 minutes. **Loading speed** Slow.

**DESCRIPTION AND COMMENTS**  The Magic Carpets of Aladdin is a midway ride like Dumbo, except with magic carpets instead of elephants. A spitting camel sprays jets of water on carpet riders. Riders can maneuver their carpets up and down and side to side to avoid the water. The front seat controls vehicle height, while the backseat controls tilt—if you let the kids sit up front, prepare to get wet!

**TOURING TIPS** Like Dumbo, this ride has great eye appeal but extremely limited capacity (that is, it loads slowly). Try to get younger kids on during the first 30 minutes the park is open, or try just before park closing. FastPass+ is almost never needed.

## A Pirate's Adventure: Treasure of the Seven Seas  ★★★½

**APPEAL BY AGE   PRESCHOOL ★★★½   GRADE SCHOOL ★★★★½   TEENS ★★★★**
**YOUNG  ADULTS  ★★★½        OVER 30  ★★★½        SENIORS  ★★★★**

**What it is** Interactive game. **Scope and scale** Diversion. **When to go** Anytime. **Authors' rating** Simple, fast, and fun—especially at night; not to be missed; ★★★½. **Duration of experience** About 20 minutes to play the entire game.

**DESCRIPTION AND COMMENTS** Similar to Agent P's World Showcase Adventure at Epcot, A Pirate's Adventure features interactive areas with physical props and narrations that lead guests through a quest to find lost treasure, all within Adventureland.

Guests begin their journey at an old Cartography Shop near Golden Oak Outpost—this is the central hub for adventurers helping locate missing treasure. Groups of up to six people are given a talisman (a RFID card) that will help them on their journey. The talisman activates a video screen that assigns your group to one of five different missions. Your group is then given a map and sent off to find your first location.

Once at the location, one member of the party touches the talisman to the symbol at the station, and the animation begins. Each adventure has four or five stops throughout Adventureland, and each stop contains 30–45 seconds of activity. No strategy or action is required: Watch what unfolds on the screen, get your next destination, and head off.

We like how well each station integrates into its surroundings, and how the stations' artifacts and props tie together the attraction and movie storylines. A Pirate's Adventure also serves as a good introduction to other interactive games, such as Sorcerers of the Magic Kingdom (see page 508).

**TOURING TIPS** The effects are better at night. While we think everyone should try A Pirate's Adventure, it isn't a must if time is tight.

## Pirates of the Caribbean *(FastPass+)* ★★★★

**APPEAL BY AGE** PRESCHOOL ★★★½ GRADE SCHOOL ★★★★ TEENS ★★★★½
YOUNG ADULTS ★★★★½ OVER 30 ★★★★½ SENIORS ★★★★½

**What it is** Indoor pirate-themed boat ride. **Scope and scale** Headliner. **When to go** Before 11 a.m., after 7 p.m., or use FastPass+. **Special comments** Frightens some kids. **Authors' rating** Disney Audio-Animatronics at their best; not to be missed; ★★★★. **Duration of ride** About 7½ minutes. **Average wait in line per 100 people ahead of you** 1½ minutes; assumes both waiting lines operating. **Loading speed** Fast.

**DESCRIPTION AND COMMENTS** An indoor cruise through a series of sets that depict a pirate raid on an island settlement, from bombardment of the fortress to debauchery after the victory. Arguably one of the most influential theme park attractions ever created, the Magic Kingdom's version retains the elaborate queuing area, grand scale, and detailed scenes that have awed audiences since its debut in Disneyland in 1967. The successful *Pirates of the Caribbean* movies have boosted the ride's popularity, and guests' demands led to the addition of animatronic figures of the film's Captain Jack Sparrow and Captain Barbossa in scenes.

Regarding debauchery, Pirates of the Caribbean has been administered a strong dose of political correctness. Even so, a Rockville, Maryland, mother was not prepared for what she saw:

*I had not understood that it would be as visually violent and historically accurate as it was. I really didn't look forward to explaining to my son why those women had ropes around their necks and such. I wish I'd been better warned that this isn't the Captain Hook view of piracy, but a much more realistic one.*

**TOURING TIPS** Undoubtedly one of the park's most timeless attractions. Engineered to move large crowds in a hurry, Pirates is a good attraction to see in the late afternoon.

### DISNEY DISH WITH JIM HILL

**SAILING INTO THE SUNSET** According to Johnny Depp, *Pirates of the Caribbean: Dead Men Tell No Tales* (in theaters summer 2016) will be the final chapter of this seagoing saga. To ensure that Cap'n Jack and his scurvy crew get a proper sendoff, the Imagineers are planning all sorts of enhancements to the Pirates ride so that it'll have tributes to all five films in the series.

## Swiss Family Treehouse ★★★

**APPEAL BY AGE** PRESCHOOL ★★★½ GRADE SCHOOL ★★★ TEENS ★★★
YOUNG ADULTS ★★★½ OVER 30 ★★★ SENIORS ★★★

**What it is** Outdoor walk-through treehouse. **Scope and scale** Minor attraction.
**When to go** Anytime. **Special comments** Requires climbing a lot of stairs. **Authors'
rating** Incredible detail and execution; ★★★. **Duration of tour** 10–15 minutes. **Average wait in line per 100 people ahead of you** 7 minutes.

**DESCRIPTION AND COMMENTS** An immense replica of the shipwrecked Swiss
  Family Robinson's arboreal abode. With its multiple stories and mechanical wizardry, it's the queen of all treehouses.

**TOURING TIPS** A self-guided walk-through tour involves a lot of stairs up and
  down, but no ropes, ladders, or anything fancy. People who stop for
  extra-long looks or to rest sometimes create bottlenecks that slow the
  crowd flow. Visit in late afternoon or early evening if you're on a one-day
  tour, or in the morning of your second day.

## *Walt Disney's Enchanted Tiki Room* ★★★

**APPEAL BY AGE** PRESCHOOL ★★★½ GRADE SCHOOL ★★★½ TEENS ★★★
YOUNG ADULTS ★★★ OVER 30 ★★★½ SENIORS ★★★★

**What it is** Audio-animatronic Pacific-island musical-theater show. **Scope and scale**
Minor attraction. **When to go** Before 11 a.m. or after 3:30 p.m. **Special comments**
Frightens some preschoolers. **Authors' rating** Very, very . . . unusual; ★★★½. **Duration of presentation** 15½ minutes. **Preshow entertainment** Talking birds. **Probable
waiting time** 15 minutes.

**DESCRIPTION AND COMMENTS** The current show here is a shortened version
  of the original attraction, which premiered at Disneyland in 1963. Starring
  four singing, wisecracking parrots—José, Fritz, Michael, and Pierre—
  *Enchanted Tiki Room* remains a favorite of many, including us.
      Although most readers like the show, they caution that it may be frightening to younger children. Concerning the scary parts, a mother of three
  from Coleman, Michigan, is outspoken:

  *The* Tiki Room *show was very scary, with a thunder-and-lightning storm and
  a loud volcano. Can't Disney do anything without scaring young children?* It's
  a bird show!

**TOURING TIPS** Usually not too crowded. We go in the late afternoon, when
  we appreciate sitting in air-conditioned comfort with our brains in park.

# ▌ FRONTIERLAND

THIS "LAND" ADJOINS ADVENTURELAND as you move clockwise
around the Magic Kingdom. Frontierland's focus is on the Old West,
with stockade-type structures and pioneer trappings.

## Big Thunder Mountain Railroad *(FastPass+)* ★★★★

**APPEAL BY AGE** PRESCHOOL ★★★★ GRADE SCHOOL ★★★★½ TEENS ★★★★½
YOUNG ADULTS ★★★★½ OVER 30 ★★★★½ SENIORS ★★★★

**What it is** Tame Western mining–themed roller coaster. **Scope and scale** Headliner.
**When to go** Before 10 a.m., in the hour before closing, or use FastPass+. **Special**

**comments** 40" minimum height requirement; children younger than age 7 must ride with an adult. Switching-off option provided (see page 341). **Authors' rating** Great effects; relatively tame ride; not to be missed; ★★★★. **Duration of ride** About 3½ minutes. **Average wait in line per 100 people ahead of you** 2½ minutes; assumes 5 trains operating. **Loading speed** Moderate–fast.

**DESCRIPTION AND COMMENTS** Roller coaster through and around a Disney "mountain." The idea is that you're on a runaway mine train during the Gold Rush. We put this coaster at about a 5 on a "scary scale" of 10. Big Thunder contains first-rate examples of Disney creativity: a realistic mining town, falling rocks, and an earthquake, all humorously animated with swinging possums, petulant buzzards, and the like. Ride it after dark if you can. Seats in the back offer the best experience.

We love the interactive props in the queue. Spin a metal wheel and push on a dynamite plunger to trigger an "explosion" (of water, steam, or noise) near a passing train; watch "home movies" of the workers in the mines; see (and smell!) what some proverbial canaries experience underground; and more. Best of all, these toys are spaced just far apart for little kids to have something to do the entire time in line. Great thinking.

**TOURING TIPS** A superb Disney experience, but not too wild a roller coaster. Emphasis is more on the sights than on the thrill of the ride.

Nearby Splash Mountain affects traffic flow to Big Thunder Mountain Railroad—adventuresome guests ride Splash Mountain first, then go next door to ride Big Thunder. All this means large crowds in Frontierland all day and long waits for Big Thunder. The best way to experience the Magic Kingdom's "mountains" is to ride Seven Dwarfs Mine Train and Space Mountain one morning as soon as the park opens, then Splash Mountain and Big Thunder Mountain the next morning. If you have only one day, the order should be (1) Seven Dwarfs, (2) Splash Mountain, (3) Big Thunder, and (4) Space Mountain.

A Midwestern mom offers this tip to families with kids too short to ride:

*If you're switching off on Thunder Mountain or Splash Mountain and have young kids to entertain, there's a fantastic little playground nearby where you can pass the time. It's completely covered and near the restrooms too! It's next to Splash Mountain, under the train tracks.*

Guests experience Disney attractions differently. Consider this letter from a lady in Brookline, Massachusetts:

*Being senior citizens and having limited time, my friend and I confined our activities to attractions rated as four or five stars for seniors. Because of your recommendation, we waited an hour to board Big Thunder Mountain Railroad, which you rated a 5 on a scary scale of 10. After living through 3½ minutes of pure terror, I will rate it a 15. We were so busy holding on and screaming and even praying for our safety that we didn't see any falling rocks, a mining town, or an earthquake. The Big Thunder Mountain Railroad should not be recommended for seniors or preschool children.*

A woman from Vermont discovered that there's more to consider about Big Thunder than being scared:

*Big Thunder Mountain Railroad was rated a 5 on the scary scale, but it was much higher on the lose-your-lunch meter. One more sharp turn and the kids in front of me would've needed a dip in Splash Mountain!*

However, a reader from West Newton, Massachusetts, dubbed the ride "a roller coaster for people who don't like roller coasters."

## Country Bear Jamboree  ★★★½

**APPEAL BY AGE**   PRESCHOOL ★★★½   GRADE SCHOOL ★★★½   TEENS ★★★
YOUNG ADULTS ★★★       OVER 30 ★★★       SENIORS ★★★★

**What it is** Audio-animatronic country hoedown. **Scope and scale** Major attraction.
**When to go** Anytime. **Authors' rating** Old and worn but pure Disney; ★★★½. **Duration of presentation** 11 minutes. **Preshow entertainment** None. **Probable waiting time** It's not terribly popular but has a comparatively small capacity. Waiting time between noon and 5:30 p.m. on a busy day will average 11–22 minutes.

**DESCRIPTION AND COMMENTS** A charming cast of animatronic bears sings and stomps in a Western-style revue. Editing has cut a few minutes from the original show, quickening its pace somewhat, and it remains an air-conditioned refuge on hot days. However, most songs remain the same, and the *Jamboree* has run for so long that the geriatric bears are a step away from assisted living. Reader comments tend to echo the need for something new. From a Sandy Hook, Connecticut, mom:

*I know they consider it a classic, and kids always seem to love it, but could they PLEASE update it after half a century?*

A woman from Carmel, Indiana, put her experience in perspective:

*Here is a half-hour of my life that I can never get back.*

But a Mississippi dad defends the show:

*I find it interesting how my reactions and those of my family change to certain attractions. Take* Country Bear Jamboree, *for instance: In my 30s I enjoyed it mildly but considered it somewhat hokey and lame, yet I thoroughly enjoyed my daughter's intense love of it at ages 3 and 8 on two previous trips. This time, at age 54, I sat up fairly close with my wife and loved it—we even sang along! Of course, this was partly to embarrass my now-16-year-old daughter, who sat hunched down in the very last row. She says we have creeping senility, but I told her, "Just wait till you bring YOUR kids!"*

**TOURING TIPS** On hot and rainy days and during peak seasons, the *Jamboree* draws large crowds from midmorning on.

## Frontierland Shootin' Arcade  ★½

**APPEAL BY AGE**   PRESCHOOL ★★★   GRADE SCHOOL ★★★★   TEENS ★★★★
YOUNG ADULTS ★★★½       OVER 30 ★★★       SENIORS ★★★½

**What it is** Electronic shooting gallery. **Scope and scale** Diversion. **When to go** Anytime. **Special comments** Costs $1 per play. **Authors' rating** Absolutely not a must; ★½.

**DESCRIPTION AND COMMENTS** One of a few attractions not included in Magic Kingdom admission. Would-be gunslingers get around 30 shots per $1 play. Each shot is followed by a short delay before the next shot can be taken—this prevents small children from accidentally using all 30 shots in 5 seconds. It's barely noticeable for adults.

**TOURING TIPS** Not a place to blow your time if you're on a tight schedule. The fun is entirely in the target practice—no prizes can be won.

## Splash Mountain *(FastPass+)*  ★★★★★

**APPEAL BY AGE**   PRESCHOOL ★★★★†   GRADE SCHOOL ★★★★½   TEENS ★★★★½
YOUNG ADULTS ★★★★½       OVER 30 ★★★★½       SENIORS ★★★★½

*†Many preschoolers are too short to ride, and others are intimidated when they see the attraction from the waiting line. Among preschoolers who actually ride, most give it high marks.*

**What it is** Indoor/outdoor water-flume adventure ride. **Scope and scale** Super-headliner. **When to go** As soon as the park opens, during afternoon or evening parades, just before closing, or use FastPass+. **Special comments** 40″ minimum height requirement; children younger than age 7 must ride with an adult. Switching-off option provided (see page 341). **Authors' rating** A soggy delight, and not to be missed; ★★★★★. **Duration of ride** About 10 minutes. **Average wait in line per 100 people ahead of you** 3½ minutes; assumes ride is operating at full capacity. **Loading speed** Moderate.

**DESCRIPTION AND COMMENTS** Splash Mountain combines steep chutes and animatronics with at least one special effect for each of the senses. The ride covers more than half a mile, splashing through swamps, caves, and backwoods bayous before climaxing in a five-story plunge and Br'er Rabbit's triumphant return home. More than 100 audio-animatronic characters, including Br'er Rabbit (also known as Br'er Hare), Br'er Bear, and Br'er Fox, regale riders with songs, including "Zip-a-Dee-Doo-Dah."

**TOURING TIPS** This happy, adventuresome ride vies with Space Mountain in Tomorrowland, and now Seven Dwarfs Mine Train in Fantasyland, as one of the park's most popular attractions. Crowds build fast in the morning, and waits of more than 2 hours can be expected once the park fills on busy days. Get in line first thing, certainly no later than 45 minutes after the park opens during warmer months. Long lines will persist all day.

If you have only a day to see the Magic Kingdom, make FastPass+ reservations in advance for around 9:30 a.m. at Big Thunder Mountain Railroad and around 3:30 p.m. at Space Mountain. On the day of your visit, ride Seven Dwarfs Mine Train as soon as the park opens, then hotfoot it to Splash Mountain to ride immediately. Your FastPass+ reservation for Big Thunder will be valid by the time you're done, and you'll have experienced three of the park's four headliners in about an hour.

If you have two mornings, do the Fantasyland and Frontierland attractions—Seven Dwarfs Mine Train, Splash Mountain, and Big Thunder Mountain—on one day and Space Mountain the next. Spreading your visits over two mornings eliminates a lot of walking.

Other FastPass+ strategies combining the park's "mountains" with other headliners have been incorporated into our Magic Kingdom touring plans (see pages 822–827).

As with Space Mountain, hundreds are poised to dash to Splash Mountain when the park opens. The best strategy is to go to the end of Main Street and turn left at The Crystal Palace restaurant. In front of the restaurant is a bridge that provides a shortcut to Adventureland. Stake out a position at the barrier rope. When the park opens, move as fast as you comfortably can and cross the bridge to Adventureland.

Another shortcut: Just past the first group of buildings on your right, roughly across from the Swiss Family Treehouse, is a small passageway containing restrooms and phones. Easy to overlook, it connects Adventureland to Frontierland. Go through here into Frontierland, and take a hard left. As you emerge along the waterfront, Splash Mountain is straight ahead. If you miss the passageway, don't fool around looking for it. Continue straight through Adventureland to Splash Mountain.

Less exhausting in the morning is commuting to Splash Mountain via the Walt Disney World Railroad. Board at Main Street Station and wait for the park to open. The train will pull out of the station a few minutes after the rope drops at the Central Plaza end of Main Street. Ride to Frontierland Station and disembark. As you come down the stairs at the station, the entrance to Splash Mountain will be on your left. Because of the time required to unload at the station, train passengers will arrive at Splash Mountain a little after the lead element from the Central Plaza.

At Splash Mountain, if you ride in the front seat, you almost certainly will get wet. Riders elsewhere get splashed but usually not doused. Since you don't know which seat you'll be assigned, go prepared. On a cool day, carry a plastic garbage bag and tear holes in the bottom and sides to make a water-resistant (not waterproof) sack dress (be sure to tuck the bag under your bottom). Or store a change of clothes, including footwear, in one of the park's rental lockers. Leave your camera with a nonriding member of your group or wrap it in plastic. For any attraction where there's a distinct possibility of getting soaked, wear Tevas or some other type of waterproof sandal, and change back to regular shoes after the ride.

The scariest part of this adventure ride is the steep chute you see when standing in line, but the drop looks worse than it is. Despite reassurances, however, many children wig out when they see it. A mom from Grand Rapids, Michigan, recalls her kids' rather unique reaction:

*We discovered after the fact that our children thought they would go under water after the five-story drop and tried to hold their breath throughout the ride in preparation. They were really too preoccupied to enjoy the clever story.*

## Tom Sawyer Island and Fort Langhorn ★★★

**APPEAL BY AGE**   PRESCHOOL ★★★★  GRADE SCHOOL ★★★★  TEENS ★★★½
YOUNG ADULTS ★★★          OVER 30 ★★★½          SENIORS ★★★½

**What it is** Outdoor walk-through exhibit and rustic playground. **Scope and scale** Minor attraction. **When to go** Midmorning–late afternoon. **Special comments** Closes at dusk. **Authors' rating** The place for rambunctious kids; ★★★.

**DESCRIPTION AND COMMENTS** Tom Sawyer Island is a getaway within the park. It has hills to climb; a cave, windmill, and pioneer stockade (Fort Langhorn) to explore; a tipsy barrel bridge to cross; and paths to follow. You can watch riverboats chug past. It's a delight for adults and a godsend for children who have been in tow and closely supervised all day.

**TOURING TIPS** Tom Sawyer Island isn't one of the Magic Kingdom's more celebrated attractions, but it's one of the park's better-conceived ones. Attention to detail is excellent, and kids revel in its frontier atmosphere. It's a must for families with children ages 5–15. If your group is made up of adults, visit on your second day or on your first day after you've seen the attractions you most wanted to see.

Although children could spend a whole day on the island, plan on at least 20 minutes. Access is by raft from Frontierland; two operate simultaneously, and the trip is pretty efficient, although you may have to stand in line to board both ways. For a mother from Duncan, South Carolina, Tom Sawyer Island is as much a refuge as an attraction:

*In the afternoon when the crowds were at their peak and the weather at its hottest, our organization began to suffer. We retreated over to Tom Sawyer Island, which proved to be a true haven. My husband and I found a secluded bench and regrouped while sipping iced tea and eating delicious soft-serve ice cream. Meanwhile, the kids were able to run freely in the shade.*

## Walt Disney World Railroad

**DESCRIPTION AND COMMENTS** Stops in Frontierland on its circle tour of the park. See the description under Main Street, U.S.A. (page 509), for additional details.

**TOURING TIPS** Pleasant, feet-saving link to Main Street and Fantasyland, but the Frontierland station is more congested than those stations.

# LIBERTY SQUARE

LIBERTY SQUARE re-creates America at the time of the American Revolution. The architecture is Federal or Colonial. The Liberty Tree, a live oak more than 130 years old, lends dignity and grace to the setting.

## *The Hall of Presidents* ★★★½

| APPEAL BY AGE | PRESCHOOL ★★ | GRADE SCHOOL ★★★½ | TEENS ★★★½ |
|---|---|---|---|
| YOUNG ADULTS ★★★★ | | OVER 30 ★★★★ | SENIORS ★★★★½ |

**What it is** Audio-animatronic historical theater presentation. **Scope and scale** Major attraction. **When to go** Anytime. **Authors' rating** Impressive and moving; ★★★½. **Duration of presentation** Almost 23 minutes. **Preshow entertainment** None. **Probable waiting time** The lines for this attraction look intimidating once you're inside the lobby, but they're swallowed up as the theater exchanges audiences. It would be exceptionally unusual not to be admitted to the next show.

**DESCRIPTION AND COMMENTS** The last update was in 2009, when Barack Obama was added and the entire presentation revamped, including a new narration by Morgan Freeman and a new speech by George Washington. The father of our country joins Presidents Lincoln and Obama as the only chief executives with speaking parts. Although the show is updated roughly every decade, the presentation remains strongly inspirational and patriotic, highlighting milestones in American history. It's also one of Disney's best and most ambitious audio-animatronic efforts.

Throughout its periodic refurbishments, we've had a high opinion of *The Hall of Presidents.* That said, we receive a lot of mail from readers who get more than entertainment from it. A woman in St. Louis writes:

*We always go when my husband gets cranky, so he can take a nice nap.*

A young mother in Marion, Ohio, adds:

The Hall of Presidents *is a great place to breast-feed.*

Finally, from a New Jersey teen:

*Mom and Dad both fell asleep during* The Hall of Presidents. *Only I, a 15-year-old high school freshman, actually paid attention. It's not the most exciting thing in Disney World, but I find it very difficult to fall asleep when Morgan Freeman is speaking. His voice is way too awesome.*

**TOURING TIPS** Detail and costumes are masterful. This attraction is one of the park's most popular among older visitors. Don't be put off by long lines. The theater holds more than 700 people, thus swallowing large lines at a single gulp when visitors are admitted.

## The Haunted Mansion *(FastPass+)* ★★★★½

| APPEAL BY AGE | PRESCHOOL ★★★ | GRADE SCHOOL ★★★★ | TEENS ★★★★½ |
|---|---|---|---|
| YOUNG ADULTS ★★★★½ | | OVER 30 ★★★★½ | SENIORS ★★★★½ |

**What it is** Haunted-house dark ride. **Scope and scale** Major attraction. **When to go** Before 11 a.m. or during the last 2 hours before closing. **Special comments** Frightens some very young children. **Authors' rating** A masterpiece of detail and not to be missed; ★★★★½. **Duration of ride** 7-minute ride plus a 1½-minute preshow. **Average wait in line per 100 people ahead of you** 2½ minutes; assumes both "stretch rooms" operating. **Loading speed** Fast.

**DESCRIPTION AND COMMENTS** Only slightly scarier than a whoopee cushion, The Haunted Mansion serves up some of the Magic Kingdom's best visual effects. "Doom Buggies" on a conveyor belt transport you through the house from parlor to attic, then through a graveyard. The effects change tone with the setting: Those found in the house are generally spooky, while the graveyard effects, such as a ghostly opera singer wearing a Viking helmet, are there for laughs. Some kids become anxious about what they think they'll see; almost nobody actually gets scared.

*Unofficial Guide* writer Eve Zibart, a Haunted Mansion fan, says:

*This is one of the best attractions in the Magic Kingdom. It's jam-packed with visual puns, special effects, hidden Mickeys, and really lovely Victorian-spooky sets. It's not scary, except in the sweetest of ways, but it will remind you of the days before ghost stories gave way to slasher flicks.*

A Temple, Texas, mom isn't convinced when we say it isn't scary:

*You say the actual sights aren't really frightening. What* isn't *frightening about a hanging corpse, a coffin escapee, and an axe-wielding skeleton bride?*

Interactive elements in the left side of the outdoor queue ensure that guests have something to occupy them when lines are long. Features include a music-playing monument, an old-fashioned pipe organ, and a ship captain's tomb that squirts water.

**TOURING TIPS** Lines here ebb and flow more than those at most other Magic Kingdom hot spots because the Mansion is near *The Hall of Presidents* and the *Liberty Belle* Riverboat. These two attractions disgorge 700 and 450 people, respectively, when each show or ride ends, and many of these folks head straight for the Mansion. If you can't go before 11:30 a.m. or after 8 p.m., try to slip in between crowds.

If you're touring the Magic Kingdom in a single day, you'll find that Fast-Pass+ saves more time at other attractions than it does here. On the other hand, you may find it useful if you're touring over two or more days.

## *Liberty Belle* Riverboat  ★★½

| APPEAL BY AGE | PRESCHOOL ★★★ | GRADE SCHOOL ★★★ | TEENS ★★★ |
|---|---|---|---|
| YOUNG ADULTS ★★★½ | OVER 30 ★★★½ | | SENIORS ★★★★ |

**What it is** Outdoor scenic boat ride. **Scope and scale** Major attraction. **When to go** Anytime. **Authors' rating** Slow, relaxing, and scenic; ★★½. **Duration of ride** About 16 minutes. **Average wait to board** 10–14 minutes.

**DESCRIPTION AND COMMENTS** Large-capacity paddle-wheel riverboat navigates the waters around Tom Sawyer Island and Fort Langhorn, passing settler cabins, old mining paraphernalia, an Indian village, and a small menagerie of animatronic wildlife. A beautiful craft, the *Liberty Belle* provides a lofty perspective of Frontierland and Liberty Square.

**TOURING TIPS** The riverboat, which departs roughly every half-hour, is a good attraction for the busy middle of the day. If you encounter huge crowds, chances are that the attraction has been inundated by a wave of guests coming from a just-concluded performance of *The Hall of Presidents*.

# ∎ FANTASYLAND

FANTASYLAND IS THE HEART OF THE MAGIC KINGDOM— a truly enchanting place spread gracefully like a miniature Alpine village beneath the steepled towers of Cinderella Castle.

Fantasyland is divided into three distinct sections. Directly behind Cinderella Castle and set upon a snowcapped mountain is **Beast's Castle,** part of a *Beauty and the Beast*–themed area. Most of this section holds dining and shopping, such as the **Be Our Guest** restaurant (see reviews in Part Ten); **Gaston's Tavern,** a small quick-service restaurant; and a gift shop. The far-right corner of Fantasyland—including **Dumbo, The Barnstormer** kiddie coaster, and the Fantasyland train station—is called **Storybook Circus** as a homage to Disney's Dumbo film. These are low-capacity amusement-park rides appropriate for younger children. The middle of the new Fantasyland territory holds the headliners, including **Under the Sea** and **Seven Dwarfs Mine Train.** The placement of these two attractions allows good traffic flow either to the left (toward Beast's Castle) for dining, to the right for attractions geared to smaller children, or back to the original part of Fantasyland for classic attractions such as **Peter Pan's Flight** and **The Many Adventures of Winnie the Pooh.**

The original part of Fantasyland also hosts the incredibly popular **Princess Fairytale Hall** meet-and-greet attraction, with waits of 5 hours or more to meet *Frozen*'s Anna and Elsa. Even so, Len's daughter, Hannah, thinks it's the best character-greeting venue in Walt Disney World. (Lines for the other princesses are shorter.)

Finally, when nature (or technology) calls, don't miss the new *Tangled*-**themed restrooms and outdoor seating** (with phone-charging stations), near Peter Pan's Flight and It's a Small World.

## Ariel's Grotto *(FastPass+)*  ★★★

**APPEAL BY AGE**  PRESCHOOL ★★★★½  GRADE SCHOOL ★★★★½  TEENS ★★★★
YOUNG ADULTS  ★★★★  OVER 30  ★★★★  SENIORS  ★★★★

**What it is** Character-greeting venue. **Scope and scale** Minor attraction. **When to go** Before 10:30 a.m., during the last 2 hours before closing, or use FastPass+. **Authors' rating** Not as themed as other character greetings; ★★★. **Duration of experience** About 30–90 seconds. **Probable waiting time** 45 minutes. **Queue speed** Slow.

**DESCRIPTION AND COMMENTS** This is Ariel's home base, next to the Under the Sea: Journey of the Little Mermaid ride. In the base of the seaside cliffs under Prince Eric's Castle, Ariel (in mermaid form) greets guests from a seashell throne. The queue isn't as detailed as other character-greeting venues in the park.

**TOURING TIPS** The Grotto may close an hour before the rest of the park. The greeting area is set up almost as if to encourage guests to linger with Ariel, which keeps the line long. The queue isn't air-conditioned, which is surprising for a venue that's supposed to store fish.

## The Barnstormer *(FastPass+)*  ★★

**APPEAL BY AGE**  PRESCHOOL ★★★★  GRADE SCHOOL ★★★★  TEENS ★★★
YOUNG ADULTS  ★★★  OVER 30  ★★★  SENIORS  ★★★

**What it is** Small roller coaster. **Scope and scale** Minor attraction. **When to go** Before 11 a.m., during parades, during the last 2 hours before closing, or use FastPass+. **Special comments** 35″ minimum height requirement. **Authors' rating** Great for little ones, but not worth the wait for adults; ★★. **Duration of ride** About 53 seconds. **Average wait in line per 100 people ahead of you** 7 minutes. **Loading speed** Slow.

**DESCRIPTION AND COMMENTS** The Barnstormer is a very small roller coaster. The ride is zippy but supershort. In fact, of the 53 seconds the ride is in motion, 32 seconds are consumed in leaving the loading area, being ratcheted up the first hill, and braking into the off-loading area. The actual time you spend careering around the track is 21 seconds.

A 42-year-old woman from Westport, Connecticut, warns adults that the ride may not be as tame as it looks:

*A nightmare that should have gone in your "Eats Adults" section. It looked so innocent—nothing hidden in the dark, over quickly—but my 8-year-old son and I were terrified, and it took me hours to stop feeling nauseated.*

Though the reader's point is well taken, The Barnstormer is a fairly benign introduction to the roller-coaster genre and a predictably positive way to help your children step up to more-adventuresome rides. Simply put, a few circuits will increase your little one's confidence and improve his or her chances for enjoying Disney's more adult attractions.

**TOURING TIPS** The cars of this dinky coaster are too small for most adults and tend to whiplash taller people. Parties without children should skip this one. If you're touring with children, you have a problem: The ride is visually and aurally appealing, and most kids want to ride, subjecting the whole family to slow-moving lines. If The Barnstormer is high on your children's hit parade, try to ride within the first 2 hours that Fantasyland is open. This attraction is rarely a good use of FastPass+.

A Cary, North Carolina, mother of preschoolers offers a heads up for solo parents:

*There are some fussy rules for riding The Barnstormer. Each of the ride cars holds only two people, and every child under 7 must be accompanied by an adult. That means a single parent can't take two small children on the ride alone; you either need to rustle up another adult to help or skip it entirely.*

## Casey Jr. Splash 'N' Soak Station ★★★

| APPEAL BY AGE | PRESCHOOL ★★★★½ | GRADE SCHOOL ★★★★ | TEENS ★★★½ |
|---|---|---|---|
| YOUNG ADULTS ★★★ | OVER 30 ★★★ | | SENIORS ★★★★½ |

**What it is** Opportunity to get wet. **Scope and scale** Diversion. **When to go** When it's hot. **Authors' rating** Great way to cool off; ★★★.

**DESCRIPTION AND COMMENTS** Casey Jr., the circus train from Dumbo, plays host to an absolutely drenching experience outside the Fantasyland Train Station in the Storybook Circus area. Expect a cadre of captive circus beasts to spray water on you in this elaborate water-play area. It's a marvel to watch.

**TOURING TIPS** Puts all other theme park splash areas to soaking shame. Bring a change of clothes and a big towel.

## Dumbo the Flying Elephant *(FastPass+)* ★★★½

| APPEAL BY AGE | PRESCHOOL ★★★★½ | GRADE SCHOOL ★★★★ | TEENS ★★★ |
|---|---|---|---|
| YOUNG ADULTS ★★★½ | OVER 30 ★★★½ | | SENIORS ★★★½ |

**What it is** Disneyfied midway ride. **Scope and scale** Minor attraction. **When to go** Before 10:30 a.m., after 3 p.m., or use FastPass+. **Authors' rating** Disney's signature ride for children; ★★★½. **Duration of ride** 1½ minutes. **Average wait in line per 100 people ahead of you** 10 minutes. **Loading speed** Slow.

**DESCRIPTION AND COMMENTS** A tame, happy children's ride based on the lovable flying pachyderm. Parents and children sit inside small fiberglass "elephants" mounted on long metal arms, which spin around a central axis. Controls inside each vehicle allow you to raise the arm, making you spin higher off the ground. Despite being little different from rides at state fairs and amusement parks, Dumbo is the favorite Magic Kingdom attraction of many younger children.

As part of the Fantasyland expansion, Dumbo moved to the upper-right corner of the land. The attraction's capacity has doubled with the addition of a second ride—a clone of the first. These two changes, along with the addition of the newer Fantasyland attractions, have drastically reduced waits to ride. If you do find yourself with a wait, Dumbo also includes a covered queue featuring interactive elements (read: things your kids can play with to pass the time in line).

From a Glenelg, Maryland, mother of two preschoolers:

*One thing I didn't see described in the* Unofficial Guide *(or the companion* With Kids *title) was how fantastic the Dumbo waiting area is for young kids. That's right—what my kids look forward to most is not the actual Dumbo ride but the playground that Disney created as the waiting area.*

**TOURING TIPS** If Dumbo is essential to your child's happiness, ride within the first 2 hours the park is open. Or try Dumbo following the afternoon parade. Not only are crowds smaller, but the lighting and effects make the ride much prettier at night.

If you want to ride Dumbo twice with a minimal wait, have both adults get in line on the same side of Dumbo, and allow between 32 and 64 people to get between the first adult and child and the second adult. Pass the child to the second adult when the first ride is over.

Finally, with increased capacity and a remote location moderating its lines, Dumbo is almost never a good choice for FastPass+.

## Enchanted Tales with Belle (FastPass+)   ★★★★

| APPEAL BY AGE | PRESCHOOL ★★★★½ | GRADE SCHOOL ★★★★½ | TEENS ★★★½ |
|---|---|---|---|
| YOUNG ADULTS ★★★½ | OVER 30 ★★★★ | | SENIORS ★★★★½ |

**What it is** Interactive character show. **Scope and scale** Minor attraction. **When to go** As soon as the park opens, during the last 2 hours before closing, or use Fast-Pass+. **Authors' rating** The prettiest meet-and-greet in the park; ★★★★. **Duration of presentation** About 20 minutes. **Preshow entertainment** As described below. **Probable waiting time** 10 minutes. **Queue speed** Slow.

**DESCRIPTION AND COMMENTS** A multiscene *Beauty and the Beast* experience that takes guests into Maurice's workshop, through a magic mirror, and into Beast's library, where the audience shares a story with Belle.

You enter the attraction by walking through Maurice's cottage, where you see mementos tracing Belle's childhood, including her favorite books, and lines drawn on one wall showing how fast Belle grew every year.

From there you'll enter Maurice's workshop at the back of the cottage. An assortment of Maurice's odd wood gadgets covers every inch of the floor, walls, and ceiling. Take a moment to peruse the gadgets, then focus your attention on the mirror on the wall to the left of the entry door.

Soon enough, the room gets dark and the mirror begins to sparkle. With magic and some really good carpentry skills, the mirror turns into a full-size doorway, through which guests enter into a wardrobe room. Once in the wardrobe room, the attraction's premise is explained: You're supposed to re-enact the story of *Beauty and the Beast* for Belle on her birthday, and guests are chosen to act out key parts in the play.

Once the parts are cast, everyone walks into the castle's library and takes a seat. Cast members explain how the play will take place and introduce Belle, who gives a short speech about how thrilled she is for everyone to be there. The play is acted out within a few minutes, and all of the actors get a chance to take photos with Belle and receive a small bookmark as a memento.

During our visits, only those who were chosen to act in the play got to take photos with Belle. Also, those who took photos with Belle received a separate Memory Maker card for those photos.

*Enchanted Tales with Belle* is surely the prettiest and most elaborate meet-and-greet station in Walt Disney World. For the relative few who get to act in the play, it's also a chance to interact with Belle in a way that isn't possible in other character encounters. We also like how Disney "stages" guests in the cottage, workshop, and wardrobe rooms—it's an efficient way to handle the wait in line, and it keeps guests from getting bored. Sure, it can still be a 30-minute wait for a 3-minute play, but it's the best of its kind in Orlando, and your kids will love it.

An enthusiastic review from an Austin, Texas, mom:

*Enchanted Tales with Belle surprised us with how well it was done. In the skit, my husband was a knight, my daughter was Mrs. Potts, and my son was silverware. It was so much fun, and the kids were so proud. Of course, my teenage daughters ran up to get in the picture line, which was efficient and beautiful.*

**TOURING TIPS** *Enchanted Tales* has long lines from the time the park opens. In fact, its popularity has made it one of the hardest tickets at the Magic Kingdom, as a Lansing, Michigan, mom explains:

*We found the wait for Enchanted Tales with Belle was never below 40 minutes. It was very popular, and for good reason. Our girls completely loved it, and so did I. Parents of shy children should tell their kids that the cast member will be asking for volunteers and they should raise their hand when they're handing out parts for the play. Also, kids who are especially fond of Belle should note that the child who plays the Beast gets to dance with her for about a minute, and Belle talks to the child while they dance. It was very sweet.*

Since it's slow-loading, make *Enchanted Tales* the first thing on your touring plan if you want to see it. Alternatively, try to visit during the last 2 hours the park is open, or use FastPass+.

## It's a Small World *(FastPass+)*  ★★★½

**APPEAL BY AGE** PRESCHOOL ★★★★½  GRADE SCHOOL ★★★★  TEENS ★★★  YOUNG ADULTS ★★★  OVER 30 ★★★½  SENIORS ★★★★

**What it is** World brotherhood–themed indoor boat ride. **Scope and scale** Major attraction. **When to go** Before 11 a.m., during parades, after 7 p.m., or use FastPass+ **Authors' rating** Exponentially "cute"; ★★★½. **Duration of ride** About 11 minutes. **Average wait in line per 100 people ahead of you** 3½ minutes; assumes busy conditions with 30 or more boats operating. **Loading speed** Fast.

**DESCRIPTION AND COMMENTS** It's a Small World is a happy, upbeat indoor attraction with a mind-numbing tune that only a backhoe can remove from your brain. Small boats carry visitors on a tour around the world, with singing and dancing dolls showcasing the dress and culture of each nation. One of Disney's oldest entertainment offerings, Small World first unleashed its brainwashing song and lethally cute ethnic dolls on the real world at the 1964 New York World's Fair—the original exhibit was moved to Disneyland after the fair, and a duplicate was created for Walt Disney World when it opened in 1971.

---

### DISNEY DISH WITH JIM HILL

**SMALL WORLD'S CRAWFORD CONNECTION**  Most people credit Walt Disney with the creation of It's a Small World. But we also have screen legend Joan Crawford to thank for bringing the original idea to fruition. Back in the early 1960s, Pepsi-Cola was struggling to come up with a concept for its 1964 World's Fair pavilion. Crawford—the widow of Pepsi chairman Al Steele and a member of the company's board of directors at the time—suggested that her colleagues call up her old friend Walt. When the board later balked at funding what the Imagineers had dreamed up, Crawford stood up and declared, in inimitable *Mommie Dearest* fashion, "We are going to do this!" And so they did.

---

Though it bludgeons you with its sappy redundancy, almost everyone enjoys It's a Small World (the first time, anyway). It stands, however, with *Enchanted Tiki Room* in the "What were they smokin'?" category.

A reader from Campbellton, New Brunswick, has developed a unique mechanism for coping with the annoying repetition of the theme song:

*If, like me, you can't stand It's a Small World but get dragged on anyway, (1) ask to sit at the back of the boat, then (2) once you're in the building, pull out your iPod and headphones and blast some heavy metal. You'd be amazed at how different and deceptively funny the ride becomes!*

**TOURING TIPS**  Cool off here when it's hot. Lines are usually 30 minutes or less, so you don't need FastPass+. If you wear a hearing aid, *turn it off.*

## Mad Tea Party *(FastPass+)*  ★★

**APPEAL BY AGE  PRESCHOOL** ★★★★½ **GRADE SCHOOL** ★★★★ **TEENS** ★★★★
**YOUNG ADULTS** ★★★½ **OVER 30** ★★★½ **SENIORS** ★★★

Motion Sickness

**What it is** Midway-type spinning ride. **Scope and scale** Minor attraction. **When to go** Before 11 a.m., after 5 p.m., or use FastPass+. **Special comments** You can make the teacups spin faster by turning the wheel in the center of the cup. **Authors' rating** Fun but not worth the wait; ★★. **Duration of ride** 1½ minutes. **Average wait in line per 100 people ahead of you** 7½ minutes. **Loading speed** Slow.

**DESCRIPTION AND COMMENTS**  Riders whirl feverishly in big teacups. *Alice in Wonderland*'s Mad Hatter provides the theme. Teenagers like to lure adults onto the teacups, then turn the wheel in the middle (making the cup spin faster), until the adults are plastered against the sides and on the verge of throwing up. Unless you aspire to be a living physics experiment, don't even *consider* getting on this one with anybody younger than 21.

A reader we've dubbed Melba the Human Centrifuge advises:

*If you want to spin your teacup, don't put more than three people in one cup.*

**TOURING TIPS**  This ride, well done but not unique, is notoriously slow-loading. Ride the morning of your second day if your schedule is more relaxed. Not a good choice for FastPass+.

## The Many Adventures of Winnie the Pooh
## *(FastPass+)*  ★★★½

**APPEAL BY AGE  PRESCHOOL** ★★★★½ **GRADE SCHOOL** ★★★★ **TEENS** ★★★½
**YOUNG ADULTS** ★★★½ **OVER 30** ★★★½ **SENIORS** ★★★★

**What it is** Indoor track ride. **Scope and scale** Minor attraction. **When to go** Before 10 a.m., in last hour park is open, or use FastPass+. **Authors' rating** As cute as the Pooh Bear himself; ★★★½. **Duration of ride** About 4 minutes. **Average wait in line per 100 people ahead of you** 4 minutes. **Loading speed** Moderate.

**DESCRIPTION AND COMMENTS** Pooh is sunny, upbeat, and fun. You ride a Hunny Pot through the pages of a huge picture book into the Hundred Acre Wood, where you encounter Pooh, Piglet, Eeyore, Owl, Rabbit, Tigger, Kanga, and Roo as they contend with a blustery day. There's even a dream sequence with Heffalumps and Woozles.

A 30-something couple from Lexington, Massachusetts, thinks Pooh has plenty to offer adults:

*The attention to detail and special effects make it worth seeing even if you don't have children in your party. The Pooh dream sequence was great!*

**TOURING TIPS** Pooh is a good choice for FastPass+ if you have small children and you're touring over two or more days.

## Meet Merida at Fairytale Gardens ★★★½

**APPEAL BY AGE** PRESCHOOL ★★★★★ GRADE SCHOOL ★★★★½ TEENS ★★★½
YOUNG ADULTS ★★★½ OVER 30 ★★★½ SENIORS ★★★

**What it is** Storytelling session and character meet-and-greet. **Scope and scale** Diversion. **When to go** See *Times Guide* for schedule. **Authors' rating** Lovely lass, lovely locale; ★★★½. **Duration of presentation** About 10 minutes. **Probable waiting time** 1 hour or more. **Queue speed** Slow.

**DESCRIPTION AND COMMENTS** Merida, the flame-haired Scottish princess from *Brave,* greets guests in Fairytale Gardens, in front of Cinderella Castle on the Tomorrowland side, between the castle and Cosmic Ray's Starlight Cafe.

**TOURING TIPS** Princess meet-and-greets tend to be quite popular, especially those involving princesses from recent movies, so expect long lines. If meeting Merida is a must-do for your family, get in line early in the morning.

## *Mickey's PhilharMagic* (FastPass+) ★★★★

**APPEAL BY AGE** PRESCHOOL ★★★★ GRADE SCHOOL ★★★★½ TEENS ★★★★
YOUNG ADULTS ★★★★½ OVER 30 ★★★★½ SENIORS ★★★★½

**What it is** 3-D movie. **Scope and scale** Major attraction. **When to go** Before 11 a.m., during parades, or use FastPass+. **Authors' rating** A zany masterpiece, not to be missed; ★★★★. **Duration of presentation** About 12 minutes. **Probable waiting time** 12–30 minutes.

**DESCRIPTION AND COMMENTS** The Magic Kingdom's 3-D movie, *Mickey's PhilharMagic* features an odd collection of Disney characters, mixing Mickey and Donald with Simba and Ariel as well as Jasmine and Aladdin. Presented in a theater large enough to accommodate a 150-foot-wide screen—huge by 3-D standards—the movie is augmented by an arsenal of special effects built into the theater. The plot involves Mickey, as the conductor of the *PhilharMagic,* leaving the theater to solve a mystery. In his absence, Donald attempts to take charge, with disastrous results.

Brilliantly conceived, furiously paced, and laugh-out-loud funny, *Mickey's PhilharMagic* will leave you grinning. And where other Disney 3-D movies are loud, in-your-face affairs, this one is softer and cuddlier. Things pop out of the screen, but they're really not scary. It's the rare child who is frightened—but there are always exceptions, as was the case with the 3-year-old child of this North Carolina mom:

*Our family found PhilharMagic way too violent (what seemed like minutes on end of Donald getting the crap kicked out of him by various musical instruments). I had to haul my screaming child out of the theater and submit to a therapeutic carousel ride afterwards.*

Happily, an Oregon mom has an easy way to nip the willies in the bud:

*My advice to parents is simply to have their kids not wear the 3-D glasses. We took my daughter's off right away, and then she began giggling and having a good time watching the movie.*

**TOURING TIPS** The theater is large, so don't be alarmed to see a gaggle of people in the lobby. *PhilharMagic* never needs FastPass+.

## Peter Pan's Flight *(FastPass+)* ★★★★

| APPEAL BY AGE | PRESCHOOL ★★★★½ | GRADE SCHOOL ★★★★ | TEENS ★★★½ |
| --- | --- | --- | --- |
| YOUNG ADULTS ★★★★ | | OVER 30 ★★★★ | SENIORS ★★★★ |

**What it is** Indoor track ride. **Scope and scale** Minor attraction. **When to go** First or last 30 minutes the park is open, or use FastPass+. **Authors' rating** Nostalgic, mellow, and well done; not to be missed; ★★★★. **Duration of ride** A little over 3 minutes. **Average wait in line per 100 people ahead of you** 5½ minutes. **Loading speed** Moderate–slow.

**DESCRIPTION AND COMMENTS** Peter Pan's Flight is superbly designed and absolutely delightful, with a happy theme uniting some favorite Disney characters, beautiful effects, and charming music. This dark (indoor) ride takes you on a relaxing trip in a "flying pirate ship" over old London and thence to Never-Never Land, where Peter saves Wendy from walking the plank and Captain Hook rehearses for *Dancing with the Stars* on the snout of the ubiquitous crocodile. There's nothing here that will jump out at you or frighten young children.

**TOURING TIPS** Because Peter Pan's Flight is very popular, count on long lines all day. Fortunately, much of the queue runs under the roof of the building, out of direct sun and rain. Ride in the first 30 minutes the park is open, during a parade, just before the park closes, or use FastPass+.

Our touring plan software suggests using FastPass+ for Peter Pan's Flight more than any other Walt Disney World attraction (see page 505).

### DISNEY DISH WITH JIM HILL

**WILL IT PAN OUT?** By now many of you have experienced the fun new interactive queuing elements at The Many Adventures of Winnie the Pooh, The Haunted Mansion, and Big Thunder Mountain Railroad. Peter Pan's Flight was supposed to get something, too—that's why the restrooms once right next door were ripped out in 2012. But because Disney's MagicBands project went way over budget, any additional theming or games for kids waiting in line were put on hold.

## Pete's Silly Sideshow *(FastPass+)* ★★★½

| APPEAL BY AGE | PRESCHOOL ★★★★½ | GRADE SCHOOL ★★★★½ | TEENS ★★★½ |
| --- | --- | --- | --- |
| YOUNG ADULTS ★★★★ | | OVER 30 ★★★★ | SENIORS ★★★½ |

**What it is** Character-greeting venue. **Scope and scale** Minor attraction. **When to go** Before 11 a.m., during the last 2 hours before closing, or use FastPass+. **Authors'**

**rating** Well themed with unique character costumes; ★★★½. **Duration of experience** 7 minutes per character. **Probable waiting time** 25 minutes. **Queue speed** Slow.

**DESCRIPTION AND COMMENTS** Pete's Silly Sideshow is a circus-themed character-greeting area in the Storybook Circus part of Fantasyland. The characters' costumes are distinct from the ones normally used around the parks. Characters include Goofy as The Great Goofini, Donald Duck as The Astounding Donaldo, Daisy Duck as Madame Daisy Fortuna, and Minnie Mouse as Minnie Magnifique.

**TOURING TIPS** On non–Extra Magic Hour days, Pete's opens 45 minutes later than the rest of the park and usually closes at the same time as the first *Wishes* fireworks show. The queue is indoors and air-conditioned. There's one queue for Goofy and Donald and a second queue for Minnie and Daisy; you can meet two characters at once, but you have to line up twice to meet all four. Rarely a good use of FastPass+.

## Prince Charming Regal Carrousel ★★★

| APPEAL BY AGE | PRESCHOOL ★★★★½ | GRADE SCHOOL ★★★★ | TEENS ★★★ |
|---|---|---|---|
| YOUNG ADULTS ★★★ | OVER 30 ★★★½ | | SENIORS ★★★★ |

**What it is** Merry-go-round. **Scope and scale** Minor attraction. **When to go** Anytime. **Authors' rating** A beautiful ride for children; ★★★. **Duration of ride** About 2 minutes. **Average wait in line per 100 people ahead of you** 5 minutes. **Loading speed** Slow.

**DESCRIPTION AND COMMENTS** One of the most elaborate and beautiful merry-go-rounds you'll ever have the pleasure of seeing, especially when its lights are on.

A shy and retiring 9-year-old girl from Rockaway, New Jersey, thinks our rating of the carousel for grade-schoolers should be higher:

*I want to complain. I went on the Prince Charming Regal Carrousel four times and I loved it! Raise those stars right now!*

**TOURING TIPS** Unless young children in your party insist on riding, appreciate this attraction from the sidelines. While lovely to look at, the carousel loads and unloads very slowly.

## Princess Fairytale Hall (FastPass+) ★★★

| APPEAL BY AGE | PRESCHOOL ★★★★★ | GRADE SCHOOL ★★★★½ | TEENS ★★★★ |
|---|---|---|---|
| YOUNG ADULTS ★★★½ | OVER 30 ★★★½ | | SENIORS ★★★½ |

**What it is** Character-greeting venue. **Scope and scale** Minor attraction. **When to go** Before 10:30 a.m., after 4 p.m., or use FastPass+. **Authors' rating** You want princesses? We got 'em! ★★★. **Duration of ride** 7–10 minutes (estimated). **Average wait in line per 100 people ahead of you** 35 minutes (estimated). **Loading speed** Slow.

**DESCRIPTION AND COMMENTS** Princess Fairytale Hall is Disney-princess central in the Magic Kingdom. Inside are two greeting venues, with each holding a small reception area for two princesses. Thus, there are four princesses meeting and greeting at any time, and you can see two of them at once. Signs outside the entrance tell you which line leads to which princess pair and how long the wait will be. Rapunzel usually leads one side, typically paired with Snow White, Cinderella, or another princess, while Anna and Elsa from *Frozen* hold forth on the other side.

Around 5–10 guests at a time are admitted to each greeting area, where there's plenty of time for small talk, a photo, and a hug from each princess. Enough time is given to each family, in fact, that we ran out of things to say to Rapunzel and shuffled quietly over to Snow White.

Fairytale Hall first opened with Cinderella headlining one of the attraction's two rooms, but Cindy was drawing roughly half the crowds Rapunzel did. When Anna and Elsa debuted to 5-hour lines at Epcot's Norway Pavilion, Cinderella was demoted to backup and the Scandinavians moved to the Magic Kingdom.

**TOURING TIPS** Anna and Elsa are the hottest character-greeting ticket in all of Walt Disney World. If your child absolutely must meet them, use Fast-Pass+ (good luck with that!) or head to Fairytale Hall first thing in the morning. Understand, though, that even if you're on hand at park opening, waits can easily top 2 hours—and often much, much more than that, as this frustrated Richmond, Virginia, mom found out:

*My 8-year-old daughter wanted meet Anna and Elsa, so we rushed there at rope drop. We had a 2-hour wait, but others waited as long as 5.5 hours. Please tell your readers that the only way to see the* Frozen *princesses is to get a FastPass+ at least 60 days in advance or spend several hours in line, forgoing food, water, and bathroom breaks, and losing all sanity!*

## Seven Dwarfs Mine Train *(FastPass+)* ★★★★

| APPEAL BY AGE | PRESCHOOL –† | GRADE SCHOOL ★★★★½ | TEENS ★★★★ |
|---|---|---|---|
| YOUNG ADULTS ★★★★ | | OVER 30 ★★★★ | SENIORS ★★★★ |

†*Not enough data was available this edition to determine a rating for preschoolers.*

**What it is** Indoor/outdoor roller coaster. **Scope and scale** Major attraction. **When to go** As soon as the park opens, or use FastPass+. **Special comments** 40″ minimum height requirement. **Authors' rating** Great family coaster; not to be missed; ★★★★. **Duration of ride** About 2 minutes. **Average wait in line per 100 people ahead of you** About 4½ minutes. **Loading speed** Fast.

**DESCRIPTION AND COMMENTS** In the pantheon of Disney coasters, Seven Dwarfs Mine Train fits somewhere between The Barnstormer and Big Thunder Mountain Railroad—that is, it's geared to older grade-school kids who've been on amusement park rides before. There are no loops, inversions, or rolls in the track, and no massive hills or steep drops; rather, the Mine Train's trick is that your ride vehicle's seats swing side-to-side as you go through turns. And—what a coincidence!—Disney has designed a curvy track with steep turns. There's also an elaborate indoor section showing the Seven Dwarfs' underground operation.

The exterior design includes waterfalls, forests, and landscaping and is meant to join together all of the surrounding Fantasyland's various locations, including France and Germany. The swinging effect is more noticeable the farther back you're seated in the train.

**TOURING TIPS** If you have only a day to see the Magic Kingdom, make Fast-Pass+ reservations in advance for around 9:30 a.m. at Big Thunder

---

### DISNEY DISH WITH JIM HILL

**CARRION SOME THINGS OVER** See those two vultures perched high atop the jib crane near the entrance to Seven Dwarfs Mine Train? They spent decades frightening tourists inside Snow White's Scary Adventures. When Disney's Imagineers were looking for ways to connect that dark ride—an original Magic Kingdom attraction—with the new coaster, they decided to give the Dwarfs the bird (or birds, in this case).

Mountain Railroad and around 3:30 p.m. at Space Mountain. On the day of your visit, ride Seven Dwarfs Mine Train as soon as the park opens, then hotfoot it to Splash Mountain to ride immediately. Your FastPass+ reservation for Big Thunder Mountain will be valid by the time you're done, and you'll have experienced three of the park's four headliners in about an hour.

If you have two mornings, do the Fantasyland and Frontierland attractions—Seven Dwarfs Mine Train, Splash Mountain, and Big Thunder Mountain—on one day and Space Mountain the next. Spreading your visits over two mornings eliminates a lot of walking.

Other FastPass+ strategies combining the park's "mountains" with other headliners have been incorporated into our Magic Kingdom touring plans (see pages 822–827).

## Under the Sea: Journey of the Little Mermaid
*(FastPass+)* ★★★½

**APPEAL BY AGE** PRESCHOOL ★★★★½ GRADE SCHOOL ★★★★ TEENS ★★★½ YOUNG ADULTS ★★★★ OVER 30 ★★★★ SENIORS ★★★★

**What it is** Dark ride retelling the film's story. **Scope and scale** Major attraction. **When to go** Before 10:30 a.m., during the last 2 hours before closing, or use Fast-Pass+. **Authors' rating** Colorful, but most effects are too simple for an attraction this big; ★★★½. **Duration of ride** About 5½ minutes. **Average wait in line per 100 people ahead of you** 3 minutes. **Loading speed** Fast.

**DESCRIPTION AND COMMENTS** Under the Sea takes riders through almost a dozen scenes retelling the story of *The Little Mermaid,* this time with Audio-Animatronics, video effects, and a vibrant 3-D set the size of a small theater.

Guests board a clamshell-shaped ride vehicle running along a continuously moving track (similar to The Haunted Mansion's). Then the ride "descends" under water, past Ariel's grotto and on to King Triton's undersea kingdom. The most detailed animatronic is of Ursula, the octopus, and she's a beauty. Other scenes hit the film's highlights, including Ariel meeting Prince Eric, her deal with Ursula to become human, and, of course, the couple's happy ending.

The attraction's exterior is attractive, with detailed rock work, water, and story elements. (Our favorite effect is a "hidden Mickey"—the shape of Mickey's head and ears—that is created through a special alignment of the sun's shadow and the rock work, and only at noon on November 18, Mickey's birthday.) Our problems with the attraction are: (1) Most of the effects throughout the ride are simple and unimaginative, such as starfish that do nothing but spin on a central axis or lobsters that simply turn left and right; and (2) Virtually the entire second half of the story is condensed into a handful of small scenes crammed together at the end of the ride.

**TOURING TIPS** Expect long waits most of the day. If you can, ride early in the morning or late at night. Rarely a good choice for FastPass+.

## Walt Disney World Railroad

**DESCRIPTION AND COMMENTS** The railroad stops in Fantasyland on its circle tour of the park. See the description under Main Street, U.S.A. (page 509), for additional details.

**TOURING TIPS** Pleasant, feet-saving link to Main Street and Frontierland . . . but so crowded in the afternoon during times of peak attendance that you'll almost certainly find it faster to walk anywhere in the park.

# TOMORROWLAND

TOMORROWLAND is a mix of rides and experiences relating to technological development and what life will be like in the future. If this sounds like Epcot's theme, it's because Tomorrowland was a breeding ground for ideas that spawned Epcot. Yet Epcot and Tomorrowland are very different in more than scale. Epcot is more educational. Tomorrowland is more for fun, depicting the future as envisioned in science fiction.

Tomorrowland's design is meant to be ageless, presenting the future as imagined by dreamers and scientists in the 1920s and '30s. Entry to Tomorrowland from Main Street evokes visions of Buck Rogers, fanciful mechanical rockets, and metallic cities spread beneath towering obelisks. *Newsweek* dubbed it "retro-future" when the look debuted. If you have teens, you can mess with their heads by saying casually, "Oh, that? Yeah . . . Disney invented steampunk."

## Astro Orbiter ★★

| APPEAL BY AGE | PRESCHOOL ★★★★ | GRADE SCHOOL ★★★½ | TEENS ★★★ |
|---|---|---|---|
| YOUNG ADULTS ★★★ | | OVER 30 ★★★ | SENIORS ★★ |

**What it is** Buck Rogers–style rockets revolving around a central axis. **Scope and scale** Minor attraction. **When to go** Before 11 a.m. or during the last hour before closing. **Special comments** Not as innocuous as it appears. **Authors' rating** Not worth the wait; ★★. **Duration of ride** 1½ minutes. **Average wait in line per 100 people ahead of you** 13½ minutes. **Loading speed** Slow.

**DESCRIPTION AND COMMENTS** Though visually appealing, the Astro Orbiter is still a slow-loading carnival ride. The fat little rocket ships simply fly in circles. The best thing about the Astro Orbiter is the nice view when you're aloft.

**TOURING TIPS** Expendable on any schedule. If you ride with preschoolers, seat them first, then board. The Astro Orbiter flies higher and faster than Dumbo and frightens some young children. It also apparently messes with some adults. A mother from Lev HaSharon, Israel, writes:

*It was a nightmare—people should be forewarned. I was able to sit through all the "Mountains," the "Tours," and the like without my stomach reacting even a little, but after Astro Orbiter I thought I would be finished for the rest of the day. Very quickly I realized that my only chance for survival was to pick a point on the toe of my shoe and stare at it (and certainly not lift my eyes out of the "jet") until the ride was over. My 4-year-old was my copilot; she loved it (go figure), and she had us up high the whole time.*

## Buzz Lightyear's Space Ranger Spin *(FastPass+)* ★★★★

| APPEAL BY AGE | PRESCHOOL ★★★★½ | GRADE SCHOOL ★★★★½ | TEENS ★★★★ |
|---|---|---|---|
| YOUNG ADULTS ★★★★ | | OVER 30 ★★★★ | SENIORS ★★★★½ |

**What it is** Whimsical space travel–themed indoor ride. **Scope and scale** Minor attraction. **When to go** First or last hour the park is open, or use FastPass+. **Authors' rating** Surreal shooting gallery; ★★★★. **Duration of ride** About 4½ minutes. **Average wait in line per 100 people ahead of you** 3 minutes. **Loading speed** Fast.

**DESCRIPTION AND COMMENTS** This attraction is based on the space-commando character Buzz Lightyear from the film *Toy Story*. The marginal storyline has you and Buzz Lightyear trying to save the universe from the evil Emperor Zurg. The indoor ride is interactive to the extent that you can spin your car and shoot simulated laser cannons at Zurg and his minions. The first room's mechanical claw and red robot contain high-value targets, so aim for these.

**TOURING TIPS** Each car is equipped with two laser cannons and two score-keeping displays, enabling you to compete with your riding partner. A joystick allows you to spin the car to line up the various targets. Each time you pull the trigger, you release a red laser beam that you can see hitting or missing the target.

Most folks spend their first ride learning how to use the equipment (fire off individual shots as opposed to keeping the trigger depressed) and figuring out how the targets work. On the next ride, you'll be surprised by how much better you do.

*Unofficial* readers are unanimous in their praise of Buzz Lightyear. Some, in fact, spend several hours on it, riding again and again. The following comment from a Snow Hill, Maryland, dad is representative:

*Buzz Lightyear was so much fun it can't be legal! We hit it first on early-entry day and rode it 10 times without stopping. The kids had fun, but it was Dad who spun himself silly trying to shoot the Z's.*

Experience Buzz Lightyear after riding Space Mountain first thing in the morning, or use FastPass+.

## Monsters, Inc. Laugh Floor *(FastPass+)* ★★★½

**APPEAL BY AGE** PRESCHOOL ★★★★ GRADE SCHOOL ★★★★½ TEENS ★★★★
YOUNG ADULTS ★★★★ OVER 30 ★★★★ SENIORS ★★★★

**What it is** Interactive animated comedy show. **Scope and scale** Major attraction. **When to go** Before 11 a.m., after 4 p.m., or use FastPass+. **Special comments** Audience members may be asked to participate in skits. **Authors' rating** Good concept, although the jokes are hit-and-miss; ★★★½. **Duration of presentation** About 15 minutes.

**DESCRIPTION AND COMMENTS** We learned in Disney-Pixar's *Monsters, Inc.* that children's screams could be converted to electricity, which was used to power a town inhabited by monsters. During the film, the monsters discovered that kids' laughter worked even better as an energy source, so in this attraction the monsters have set up a comedy club to capture as many laughs as possible. Mike Wazowski, the one-eyed green monster, emcees the club's three comedy acts. Each act consists of an animated monster (most not seen in the film) trying out various bad puns, knock-knock jokes, and Abbott and Costello–like routines. Using the same cutting-edge technology as Epcot's popular *Turtle Talk with Crush,* behind-the-scenes Disney employees voice the characters and often interact with audience members during the skits. As with any comedy set, some performers are funny and some are not, but Disney has shown a willingness to experiment with new routines and jokes.

### DISNEY DISH WITH JIM HILL

*MONSTERS* OUT, *INSIDE OUT* IN Theme park purists insist that *Monsters, Inc. Laugh Floor* just doesn't belong in Tomorrowland. And if the Imagineers get their way, this unfuturistic attraction will be replaced with a new Pixar-themed show that draws its inspiration from Pixar's June 2015 release *Inside Out,* based on what really goes on inside the head of an 11-year-old girl named Riley.

A Sioux Falls, South Dakota, mom is a big fan:

*Laugh Floor was great. It's amazing how the characters interact with the audience—I got picked on twice without trying. Plus, kids can text jokes to Roz.*

**TOURING TIPS** The theater holds several hundred people, so there's no need to rush here first thing in the morning. Try to arrive late in the morning after you've visited other Tomorrowland attractions, or after the afternoon parade when guests start leaving the park. *Laugh Floor* is never a good choice for FastPass+.

## Space Mountain *(FastPass+)* ★★★★

| APPEAL BY AGE | PRESCHOOL ★★½† | GRADE SCHOOL ★★★★½ | TEENS ★★★★½ |
|---|---|---|---|
| YOUNG ADULTS ★★★★½ | | OVER 30 ★★★★½ | SENIORS ★★★½ |

*†Some preschoolers love Space Mountain; others are frightened by it.*

**What it is** Roller coaster in the dark. **Scope and scale** Super-headliner. **When to go** When the park opens or use FastPass+. **Special comments** Great fun and action; much wilder than Big Thunder Mountain Railroad. 44" minimum height requirement; children younger than age 7 must be accompanied by an adult. Switching-off option provided (see page 341). **Authors' rating** An unusual roller coaster with excellent special effects; not to be missed; ★★★★. **Duration of ride** Almost 3 minutes. **Average wait in line per 100 people ahead of you** 3 minutes; assumes 2 tracks, with 1 dedicated to FastPass+ riders, dispatching at 21-second intervals. **Loading speed** Moderate–fast.

Motion Sickness

**DESCRIPTION AND COMMENTS** Totally enclosed in a mammoth futuristic structure, Space Mountain has always been the Magic Kingdom's most popular attraction. The theme is a space flight through dark recesses of the galaxy. Effects are superb, and the ride is the fastest and wildest in the Magic Kingdom. As a roller coaster, Space Mountain is much zippier than Big Thunder Mountain Railroad, but much tamer than the Rock 'n' Roller Coaster at Hollywood Studios or Expedition Everest at Animal Kingdom.

As a headliner, Space Mountain goes through periodic refurbishments to add effects and maintain ride quality. Past improvements include new lighting and effects, an improved sound system and soundtrack, and interactive games in the queue to help pass the time in line. Roller-coaster aficionados will tell you (correctly) that Space Mountain is a designer version of the Wild Mouse, a midway ride that's been around for almost 60 years. There are no long drops or swooping hills as there are on a traditional roller coaster—only quick, unexpected turns and small drops. Disney's contribution essentially was to add a space theme to the Wild Mouse and put it in the dark. And this does indeed make the Mouse seem wilder.

An Elburn, Illinois, reader recommends bracing yourself—literally:

*They should require you to wear a neck brace on Space Mountain. That ride is painful.*

**TOURING TIPS** People who can handle a fairly wild roller-coaster ride will take Space Mountain in stride. What sets Space Mountain apart is that cars plummet through darkness, with only occasional lighting. Half the fun of Space Mountain is not knowing where the car will go next.

Space Mountain is a favorite of many Magic Kingdom visitors ages 7–60. Each morning before opening, particularly during summer and holiday periods, several hundred Space Mountain junkies await the signal to head to the ride's entrance. To get ahead of the competition, be one of the first in the park. Proceed to the end of Main Street and wait at the entrance to Tomorrowland.

Couples touring with children too small to ride Space Mountain can both ride without waiting twice in line by taking advantage of "switching off." Here's how it works: When you enter the Space Mountain line, tell the first Disney attendant (Greeter One) that you want to switch off. The attendant will allow you, your spouse, and your small child (or children) to continue together, phoning ahead to tell Greeter Two to expect you. When you reach Greeter Two (at the turnstile near the boarding area), you'll be given specific directions. One of you will proceed to ride, while the other stays with the kids. Whoever rides will be admitted by the unloading attendant to stairs leading back up to the boarding area. Here you switch off. The second parent rides, and the first parent takes the kids down the stairs to the unloading area where everybody is reunited and exits together. Switching off is also available at Big Thunder Mountain Railroad and Splash Mountain, and for FastPass+ users.

Seats are one behind another, as opposed to side by side—meaning parents can't sit next to their kids if they meet the height requirement.

If you don't catch Space Mountain first in the morning, use FastPass+ or try again during the 30 minutes before closing. To avoid overwhelming Space Mountain's air-conditioning system on hot days, would-be riders are sometimes held in line outside the entrance until the lines have subsided. The appearance from the outside is that the line is enormous when, in fact, most of the people waiting are those visible. This crowd-control technique, known as "stacking," discourages visitors from getting in line. (Stacking is also used at several Disney attractions during the hour before closing to ensure that the ride will be able to close on schedule.) Despite the apparently long line, the wait is usually no longer than if you had been allowed to queue inside.

## Stitch's Great Escape!   ★★

**APPEAL BY AGE** PRESCHOOL ★★½   GRADE SCHOOL ★★½   TEENS ★★½
YOUNG ADULTS ★★½   OVER 30 ★★   SENIORS ★★½

**What it is** Theater-in-the-round sci-fi adventure show. **Scope and scale** Minor attraction. **When to go** Before 11 a.m. or after 6 p.m.; try during parades. **Special comments** Frightens children of all ages; 40" minimum height requirement. Switching-off option provided (see page 341). **Authors' rating** P.U.; ★★. **Duration of presentation** About 12 minutes. **Preshow entertainment** About 6 minutes. **Probable waiting time** 12–35 minutes.

**DESCRIPTION AND COMMENTS** *Stitch's Great Escape!* stars the havoc-wreaking little alien from the Disney animated feature *Lilo & Stitch*. In this show, Stitch is a prisoner of the galactic authorities and is being transferred to a processing facility en route to his final place of incarceration. He manages to escape by employing an efficient though gross trick, knocking out power to the facility in the process. (One wonders why an alien civilization smart enough to master teleportation hasn't yet invented a backup power source.) The rest of the attraction consists of Stitch lumbering around in the dark while cheap sound and odor effects are unleashed on the audience.

Guest response to *Stitch's Great Escape!* is so negative that Disney has stopped trying to improve it. Our readers likewise think it stinks, although this Norton Shores, Michigan, mom at least gave it a chance going in:

*I love* Lilo and Stitch *and am a huge fan of Stitch in particular. I got on the ride just knowing it would be great—I thought the Stitch animatronic was adorable (and my husband got spit at right in the eye, so naturally this was going to be the best ride ever). Then the lights went out. From that point on, it was just a big miserable fail. My 13-year-old actually heaved from the smell of Stitch's breath, and the bouncing [overhead restraints] jabbed us all painfully and repeatedly in the shoulders. The movie is still awesome, but the ride is a giant zit on the face of Disney that needs to be popped out of existence.*

*Stitch*'s height requirement is 40 inches (the same as Big Thunder Mountain Railroad) in an attempt to keep out easily frightened younger children. The fact that Big Thunder is a roller coaster and that this ride doesn't move should be a warning to parents about its fright potential.

**TOURING TIPS** *Stitch* is more than enough to scare the pants off many kids ages 6 and younger. *Parents, note:* You're held in your seat by overhead restraints that will prevent you from getting up to comfort your child if the need arises.

## Tomorrowland Speedway *(FastPass+)* ★★

**APPEAL BY AGE** PRESCHOOL ★★★★½ GRADE SCHOOL ★★★★ TEENS ★★★½
YOUNG ADULTS ★★★ OVER 30 ★★★ SENIORS ★★★

**What it is** Drive-'em-yourself miniature cars. **Scope and scale** Major attraction. **When to go** Before 10 a.m., during the last 2 hours before closing, or use FastPass+. **Special comments** Kids must be 54" tall to drive unassisted. **Authors' rating** Boring for adults (★★); great for preschoolers. **Duration of ride** About 4¼ minutes. **Average wait in line per 100 people ahead of you** 4½ minutes; assumes 285-car turnover every 20 minutes. **Loading speed** Slow.

Motion Sickness

**DESCRIPTION AND COMMENTS** An elaborate miniature raceway with gasoline-powered cars that travel up to 7 mph. The raceway, with its sleek cars and racing noises, is quite alluring. The cars poke along on a guide rail, leaving the driver little to do, but teens and many adults still enjoy it.

**TOURING TIPS** This ride is visually appealing, and the 9-and-under crowd loves it (adults, not so much). If your child is too short to drive, ride along and allow him or her to steer the car while you work the foot pedal.

A mom from North Billerica, Massachusetts, writes:

*I was truly amazed by the number of adults in line—the only reason I could think of for that would be an insane desire to go on absolutely every ride at Disney World. The cars aren't a whole lot of fun, and they tend to pile up at the end, so it takes almost as long to get off as it did to get on. Parents riding with kids should keep the car going as slow as possible without stalling. This prolongs the child's joy and decreases the time you'll have to wait at the end.*

The line for the speedway snakes across a pedestrian bridge to the ride's loading areas. For a shorter wait, turn right off the bridge and head to the first loading area rather than continuing to the second one.

## Tomorrowland Transit Authority PeopleMover ★★★½

**APPEAL BY AGE** PRESCHOOL ★★★★ GRADE SCHOOL ★★★★ TEENS ★★★½
YOUNG ADULTS ★★★★ OVER 30 ★★★★ SENIORS ★★★★

**What it is** Scenic tour of Tomorrowland. **Scope and scale** Minor attraction. **When to go** Anytime, but especially during hot, crowded times of day (11:30 a.m.–4:30 p.m.). **Special comments** A good way to check out the line at Space Mountain and the Speedway. **Authors' rating** Scenic and relaxing; ★★★½. **Duration of ride** 10 minutes. **Average wait in line per 100 people ahead of you** 1½ minutes; assumes 39 trains operating. **Loading speed** Fast.

**DESCRIPTION AND COMMENTS** A once-unique prototype of a linear induction-powered mass-transit system, the PeopleMover has tramlike cars that carry riders on a leisurely tour of Tomorrowland, including a peek inside Space Mountain. In ancient times, the attraction was called the WEDway PeopleMover ("WED" = Walter Elias Disney).

**TOURING TIPS** A relaxing ride where lines move quickly. It's a good choice during busier times of day.

### Walt Disney's Carousel of Progress ★★★

**APPEAL BY AGE** PRESCHOOL ★★★ GRADE SCHOOL ★★★½ TEENS ★★★
YOUNG ADULTS ★★★★ OVER 30 ★★★★ SENIORS ★★★★

**What it is** Audio-animatronic theater production. **Scope and scale** Major attraction. **When to go** Anytime. **Authors' rating** Nostalgic, warm, and happy; ★★★. **Duration of presentation** 21 minutes. **Preshow entertainment** Documentary on the attraction's long history. **Probable waiting time** Less than 10 minutes.

**DESCRIPTION AND COMMENTS** *Walt Disney's Carousel of Progress* offers a nostalgic look at how technology and electricity have changed the lives of an animatronic family over several generations. The family is easy to identify with, and a cheerful, sentimental tune bridges the generations.

**TOURING TIPS** The *Carousel* handles big crowds effectively and is a good choice during busier times of day. Because of its age, Carousel seems to have more minor operational glitches than most attractions, so you may be subjected to the same dialog and songs several times. Look at it as extra air-conditioning.

# LIVE ENTERTAINMENT *in* the MAGIC KINGDOM

BANDS, DISNEY-CHARACTER APPEARANCES, parades, ceremonies, and singing and dancing further enliven the Magic Kingdom. For specific events the day you visit, check the live-entertainment schedule in your guide map (free as you enter the park or at City Hall) or in the *Times Guide* available along with the guide map. WDW live-entertainment guru Steve Soares usually posts the Magic Kingdom's performance schedule about a week in advance at **wdwent.com.**

Our one-day touring plans exclude live performances in favor of seeing as much of the park as time permits; parades and shows siphon crowds away from popular rides, thus shortening lines. Nonetheless, the color and pageantry of live events are integral to the Magic Kingdom—and a persuasive argument for a second day of touring. Here's a list of some regular performances and events that don't require reservations:

*unofficial* **TIP**
*Be aware:* If you're short on time, it's impossible to see Magic Kingdom feature attractions and the live performances.

**BAY LAKE AND SEVEN SEAS LAGOON FLOATING ELECTRICAL PAGEANT (★★★★)** Usually performed at nightfall (9 p.m. at the Polynesian Resort, 9:15 at the Grand Floridian Resort & Spa, and 10:15 at the Contemporary Resort) on Seven Seas Lagoon and Bay Lake, this is one of our favorites among the Disney extras, but it's necessary to leave the Magic Kingdom to view it.

The pageant is a stunning electric-light show aboard small barges and set to nifty electronic music. Leave the Magic Kingdom and take the monorail to the Polynesian, Grand Floridian, or Contemporary.

**CASTLE FORECOURT STAGE (★★★½)** The 20-minute *Dream-Along with Mickey* live show features Mickey, Minnie, Donald, Goofy, and a peck of princesses and other secondary characters, plus human backup dancers, in a show built around the premise that—*quelle horreur!*—Donald doesn't believe in the power of dreams. Crisis is averted through a frenetic whirlwind of song and dance.

The show is performed several times a day according to the season, with showtimes listed in the daily *Times Guide*. The Castle Forecourt Stage is elevated well above ground level, so good viewing spots are available all around Main Street's Central Plaza.

**CELEBRATE THE MAGIC (★★★★½)** In one of the most imaginative shows yet, videos and special effects are set to music and projected nightly on Cinderella Castle. The effects are tremendous: In one vignette, the entire castle becomes a kaleidoscope of brightly colored Mickeys and Donalds; in another, flames appear throughout the castle's windows to emulate a scene from the Pirates of the Caribbean ride. Best of all, Disney regularly updates the show's content to keep it fresh. While the show's soundtrack is invariably excessively sentimental, the visuals more than make up for it. We rate this as not to be missed.

**DISNEY-CHARACTER SHOWS AND APPEARANCES** A number of characters are usually on hand to greet guests when the park opens. Because they snarl pedestrian traffic and stop most children dead in their tracks, this is sort of a mixed blessing. Most days, a character is on duty for photos and autographs 9 a.m.–10 p.m. next to City Hall. Mickey, Tinker Bell, and miscellaneous fairies can be found in Main Street's Town Square Theater, to the right as you enter the park; Disney princesses are found in Fairytale Hall in Fantasyland. Check the daily *Times Guide* for character-greeting locations and times.

**FLAG RETREAT** At 5 p.m. daily at Town Square (Walt Disney World Railroad end of Main Street). Sometimes performed with large college marching bands, sometimes with a smaller Disney band.

**MAGIC KINGDOM BANDS** Banjo, Dixieland, steel drum, marching, and fife-and-drum bands play daily throughout the park.

**MOVE IT! SHAKE IT! CELEBRATE IT! PARADE (★★★½)** Starting at the Walt Disney World Railroad end of Main Street, U.S.A., and working toward the Central Plaza, this short walk incorporates about a dozen guests with a handful of floats, Disney characters, and entertainers. Music is provided by one of Disney's artists (Miley Cyrus currently), and there's a good amount of interaction between the entertainers and the crowd. Unless you're already on Main Street, however, or too pooped for anything else, we don't recommend making a special trip to view this parade.

**TINKER BELL'S FLIGHT** This nice special effect in the sky above Cinderella Castle heralds the beginning of the *Wishes* fireworks show (when the park is open late).

**TOMORROWLAND FORECOURT STAGE** This two-story space behind the Astro Orbiter occasionally hosts DJ-led dance parties. We wouldn't make a special trip to see these, but they're a nice 2-minute stop if you're passing by.

***WISHES* FIREWORKS SHOW (★★★★★)** Memorable vignettes and music from beloved Disney films combine with a stellar fireworks display while Jiminy Cricket narrates a lump-in-your-throat story about making wishes come true. For an uncluttered view and lighter crowds, watch from the end of Main Street between The Plaza Restaurant and Tomorrowland Terrace. Another good fireworks-viewing area is the second story of the Main Street railroad station.

The spot we'd previously recommended, in the Tomorrowland Terrace area, was apparently so good that Disney decided to start charging for it. To view *Wishes* from this location now costs around $24 per adult and around $13 per child. The viewing comes with a dessert buffet and nonalcoholic beverages. Reservations can be made 60 days in advance by calling ☎ 407-WDW-DINE (939-3463).

A St. Louis reader tried the dessert buffet:

> *We did the* Wishes *Dessert Party against my better judgment. While the vantage point was pretty good and the desserts were tasty, it was definitely not worth the price. We also were able to witness firsthand how we have become a nation of morbidly obese people.*

FastPass+ is also available for *Wishes,* giving you access to a special viewing area near the Central Plaza in front of Cinderella Castle. We don't recommend FastPass+, however, since (1) you still need to show up well in advance to claim a good spot and (2) you're going to wait in a very long line for one of the park's headliner attractions. You're better off staking out a decent viewing spot around 20 minutes before the show.

***WISHES* FIREWORKS CRUISE** For a different view, you can watch the fireworks from Seven Seas Lagoon aboard a chartered pontoon boat. The charter costs $293 for up to 8 people and just under $350 for 10 (tax included). Chips, soda, and water are provided; sandwiches and more-substantial food items may be arranged through reservations. Your Disney captain will take you for a little cruise and then position the boat in a perfect place to watch the fireworks. (A major indirect benefit of the charter is that you can enjoy the fireworks without fighting the mob afterward.) Because this is a private charter rather than a tour, only your group will be aboard. Life jackets are provided, but wearing them is at your discretion. To reserve a charter, call ☎ 407-WDW-PLAY (939-7529) at exactly 7 a.m. Eastern time about 180 days before the day you want to cruise. Because the Disney reservations system counts days in a somewhat atypical manner, we recommend phoning about 185 days out to have a Disney agent specify the exact morning to call for reservations.

# MICKEY'S HALLOWEEN *and* CHRISTMAS PARTIES

THE MAGIC KINGDOM HOSTS special after-hours, holiday-themed events in September, October, November, and December, celebrating

Halloween and Christmas. These events require separate admission (see "The Walt Disney World Calendar" on page 45 in Part One for details) and can sell out. Space doesn't permit us to cover these events in the book, but we provide full details, including photos, best days to go, touring advice, and more, at **blog.touringplans.com.** Search for "Halloween Party" or "Christmas Party" to see the coverage.

# PARADES

PARADES AT THE MAGIC KINGDOM ARE FULL-FLEDGED spectaculars with dozens of Disney characters and amazing special effects. We rate the afternoon parade as outstanding and the evening parade as not to be missed.

In addition to providing great entertainment, parades lure guests away from the attractions. If getting on rides appeals to you more than watching a parade, you'll find substantially shorter lines just before and during parades. Because the parade route doesn't pass through Adventureland, Tomorrowland, or Fantasyland, attractions in these lands are particularly good bets. Be forewarned: Parades disrupt traffic in the Magic Kingdom. It's nearly impossible, for example, to get to Adventureland from Tomorrowland, or vice versa, during one. Also be advised that the Walt Disney World Railroad shuts down during parades, thus making it impossible to access other lands by train.

### AFTERNOON PARADE

USUALLY STAGED AT 3 P.M., the afternoon parade features bands, floats, and marching Disney characters. A new production, **Festival of Fantasy** (★★★★), debuted in 2014, with an original score and new floats paying tribute to *The Little Mermaid, Brave,* and *Frozen,* among other Disney films. Many of the floats' pieces spin and swing to extremes not normally found in Disney parades: The *Tangled* platform has characters riding swinging wood hammers from one side of the street to the other. The most talked-about float is Maleficent (the villain from *Sleeping Beauty,* now the star of her own feature film) in dragon form—she spits actual fire at a couple of points along the route.

---

**DISNEY DISH WITH JIM HILL**

*BEAUTY* GETS THE BOOT  The Festival of Fantasy parade has Maleficent-as-dragon, Prince Phillip, and Flora, Fauna, and Merryweather from *Sleeping Beauty*—but no Aurora. She was supposed to be featured on this parade's lead float, the Princess Garden. But then *Frozen* became a monstrous hit at the box office, and Aurora found herself out in the cold as that float was reworked to make room for Anna, Elsa, and Olaf.

---

### EVENING PARADE

THIS HIGH-TECH AFFAIR employs electroluminescent and fiber-optic technologies, light-spreading thermoplastics (don't try this at home!), and clouds of underlit liquid-nitrogen smoke. Don't worry, you won't need a gas mask or lead underwear to watch. For those who

## Magic Kingdom Parade Route

flunked chemistry and physics, the parade also offers music, Mickey Mouse, and twinkling lights.

Evening-parade performances vary by season, happening as often as twice a night during the busy times of year, to two or three times a week during less busy seasons. We rate it as not to be missed.

*unofficial* **TIP**
Call ☎ 407-824-4321 before you go to be sure the evening parade is on.

The **Main Street Electrical Parade** (**MSEP;** ★ ★ ★ ★) is the current nightly cavalcade at the Magic Kingdom. Its soundtrack—*Baroque Hoedown*—is a synthesizer-heavy testament to what prog rock might have been

*unofficial* **TIP**
FastPass+ is available for premium areas to view the afternoon and evening parades. You still need to show up early for a good spot, though.

with access to modern technology and antidepressants. In our opinion, the Magic Kingdom's nighttime parade is always the best in Walt Disney World, and the Electrical Parade is the standard against which everything else is judged. Disney is known to swap out parades (MSEP replaced SpectroMagic in 2010), and may do so at any time. If you're at Disney World while MSEP is running, make a special trip to see it.

## PARADE ROUTE AND VANTAGE POINTS

MAGIC KINGDOM PARADES circle Town Square, head down Main Street, go around the Central Plaza, and cross the bridge to Liberty Square. In Liberty Square, they follow the waterfront and end in Frontierland. Sometimes they begin in Frontierland and run the route in the opposite direction. Most guests watch from the Central Plaza or from Main Street. One of the best and most popular vantage points is the upper platform of the Walt Disney World Railroad station at the Town Square end of Main Street. This is also a good place for watching the *Wishes* fireworks show, as well as for ducking out of the park ahead of the crowd when the fireworks end. The problem is, you have to stake out your position 30–45 minutes before the events begin.

Because most spectators pack Main Street and the Central Plaza, we recommend watching the parade from Liberty Square or Frontierland. Great vantage points frequently overlooked are as follows:

**1.** Sleepy Hollow snack-and-beverage shop, immediately to your right as you cross the bridge into Liberty Square. If you arrive early, buy refreshments and claim a table closest to the rail. You'll have a perfect view of the parade as it crosses Liberty Square Bridge, but only when the parade begins on Main Street.

**2.** The pathway on the Liberty Square side of the moat from Sleepy Hollow snack-and-beverage shop to Cinderella Castle. Any point along this path offers a clear and unobstructed view as the parade crosses Liberty Square Bridge. Once again, this spot works only for parades coming from Main Street.

**3.** The covered walkway between Liberty Tree Tavern and The Diamond Horseshoe Saloon. This elevated vantage point is perfect (particularly on rainy days) and usually goes unnoticed until just before the parade starts.

**4.** Elevated platforms in front of the Frontierland Shootin' Arcade, Frontier Trading Post, and the building with the sign reading FRONTIER MERCANTILE. These spots usually get picked off 10–12 minutes before parade time.

**5.** Benches on the perimeter of the Central Plaza, between the entrances to Liberty Square and Adventureland. Usually unoccupied until after the parade begins, they offer a comfortable resting place and unobstructed (though somewhat distant) view of the parade as it crosses Liberty Square Bridge.

**6.** Liberty Square and Frontierland dockside areas; spots here usually go early.

**7.** The porch of Tony's Town Square Restaurant on Main Street provides an elevated viewing platform and an easy exit path when the fireworks are over.

Assuming it starts on Main Street (evening parades normally do), the parade takes 16–20 minutes to reach Liberty Square or Frontierland.

On evenings when the parade runs twice, the first parade draws a huge crowd, siphoning guests from attractions. Many folks leave the park after the early parade, with many more departing following the fireworks (which are scheduled on the hour between the two parades). Continue to tour after the fireworks. This is a particularly good time to ride Splash Mountain and enjoy attractions in Adventureland. If you're touring Adventureland and the parade begins on Main Street, you won't have to assume your viewing position in Frontierland until 15 minutes after the parade kicks off (the time it takes the parade to reach Frontierland). If you watch from the Splash Mountain side of the street and head for the attraction as the last float passes, you'll be able to ride with only a couple minutes' wait. You might even have time to work in a last-minute ride on Big Thunder Mountain Railroad.

## VANTAGE POINTS FOR FIREWORKS

ANYWHERE ALONG MAIN STREET is fine for the fireworks. If you plan to leave the park immediately afterward, watch from the train-station end to facilitate a quick departure. Our favorite spot if we intend to remain in the park is between The Plaza Restaurant on Main Street and the Tomorrowland Terrace area to its right (if you're facing the castle).

## LEAVING THE PARK AFTER EVENING PARADES AND FIREWORKS

ARMIES OF GUESTS leave the Magic Kingdom after evening parades and fireworks. The Disney transportation system (buses, ferries, and monorail) is overwhelmed, causing long waits in boarding areas.

A mother from Kresgeville, Pennsylvania, recounts:

*unofficial* **TIP**
Digital displays at the Magic Kingdom exit show the wait to board the monorails and ferry—take the one with the shorter line.

> Our family of five made the mistake of going to the Magic Kingdom the Saturday night before Columbus Day to watch the parade and fireworks. Afterwards, we lingered at The Crystal Palace to wait for the crowds to lessen, but it was no use. We started walking toward the gates and soon became trapped by the throng, not able to go forward or back. There was no way to get to the ferry to our hotel. Our group became separated, and it became a nightmare. We left the park at 10:30 p.m. and didn't get back to the Polynesian (less than a mile away) until after midnight. Even if they were to raise Walt Disney himself from cryogenic sleep and parade him down Main Street, I would never go to the Magic Kingdom on a Saturday night again!

An Oklahoma City dad offers this advice:

> Never, never leave the Magic Kingdom just after the 10 p.m. fireworks. Go for another ride—no lines because everyone else is trying to get out!

*unofficial* **TIP**
For optimum touring and less congestion, enjoy attractions during the early parade, then break to watch the fireworks.

Congestion persists from the end of the early evening parade until closing time. Most folks watch the early parade and then the fireworks a few minutes later. If you're parked at the Transportation and Ticket Center (TTC) and are intent on beating the crowd, view the early parade from the Town Square end of Main Street, leaving the park as soon as the parade ends.

If you're staying at a Disney hotel not served by the monorail and must depend on Disney transportation, watch the early parade and fireworks, then enjoy the attractions until about 20–25 minutes before the late parade is scheduled to begin. Then leave the park and catch the Disney bus or boat back to your hotel. Don't cut it too close: Main Street will be so congested that you won't be able to reach the exit.

Here's what happened to a family from Cape Coral, Florida:

> We tried to leave the park before the parade began, but Main Street was already packed and we didn't see any way to get out of the park—we were stuck. In addition, it was impossible to move across the street, and even the shops were so crowded it was virtually impossible to maneuver a stroller through them to get close to the entrance.

If you don't have a stroller (or are willing to forgo the $1 return refund for rental strollers), catch the Walt Disney World Railroad in Frontierland and ride to the park exit at Main Street. Again, don't cut it too close—the train stops running after the parade.

If you're on the Tomorrowland side of the park, it's actually possible for you to exit during a parade. Leaving Tomorrowland, cut through Tomorrowland Terrace. Before you reach Main Street, bear left into the side door of the corner shop. Once inside, you'll see that Main Street shops have interior doors allowing you to pass from one shop to the next without having to get on Main Street. Work your way from shop to shop until you reach Town Square (easy, because people will be outside watching the parade). At Town Square, bear left and move to the train station and the park exit.

This strategy won't work if you're on the Adventureland side of the park. You can make your way through Casey's Corner restaurant to Main Street and then work your way through the interior of the Main Street shops, but when you pop out of the Emporium at Town Square, you'll be trapped by the parade. As soon as the last float passes, however, you can bolt for the exit.

*unofficial* **TIP**
Be aware that the railroad shuts down during parades because the floats must cross the tracks when entering or exiting the parade route in Frontierland.

Another strategy for beating the masses out of the park (if your car is at the TTC lot) is to watch the early parade and then leave before the fireworks begin. Line up for the ferry. One will depart about every 8–10 minutes. Try to catch the ferry that will be crossing Seven Seas Lagoon while the fireworks are in progress. The best vantage point is on the top deck to the right of the pilothouse as you face the Magic Kingdom; the sight of fireworks silhouetting the castle and reflecting off Seven Seas Lagoon is unforgettable. While there's no guarantee that a ferry will load and depart within 3 or 4 minutes of the fireworks, your chances are about 50–50 of catching it just right. If you're in the front of the line for the ferry and don't want to board the boat that's loading, stop at the gate and let people pass you. You'll be the first to board the next boat.

# TRAFFIC PATTERNS *in* *the* MAGIC KINGDOM

WHEN WE RESEARCH THE MAGIC KINGDOM, we study its traffic patterns, asking:

**1. WHICH SECTIONS OF THE PARK AND WHICH ATTRACTIONS DO GUESTS VISIT FIRST?** When the park opens, guest traffic to Fantasyland and Tomorrowland is heaviest, followed by Frontierland. Seven Dwarfs Mine Train is pulling more people than ever into the back reaches of the park, and because the *Frozen* meet-and-greet at Princess Fairytale Hall is such a low-capacity attraction, it's a race to get there early. The girls (and parents) dressed up like Anna and Elsa, rushing through the park, look like an episode of *Toddlers and Tiaras* meets *The Amazing Race.*

| ATTRACTIONS THAT GET CROWDED EARLY | |
|---|---|
| **FANTASYLAND** | *Enchanted Tales with Belle* |
| | Peter Pan's Flight |
| | Princess Fairytale Hall (Anna and Elsa) |
| | Seven Dwarfs Mine Train |
| **FRONTIERLAND** | Big Thunder Mountain Railroad |
| | Splash Mountain |
| **TOMORROWLAND** | Buzz Lightyear's Space Ranger Spin |
| | Space Mountain |
| | Tomorrowland Speedway |

Our researchers tested the frequent claim that most people turn right into Tomorrowland and tour the Magic Kingdom in a counterclockwise sequence. We found the claim to be baseless.

**2. HOW LONG DOES IT TAKE FOR THE PARK TO FILL UP? HOW ARE THE VISITORS DISPERSED IN THE PARK?** A surge of early birds arrives before or around opening time but is quickly dispersed throughout the empty park. After the initial wave is absorbed, there's a lull lasting about an hour after opening. Then the park is inundated for about 2 hours, peaking between 10 a.m. and noon. Arrivals continue in a steady but diminishing stream until around 2 p.m. The lines we sampled were longest between 1 and 2 p.m., indicating more arrivals than departures into the early afternoon. For touring purposes, most attractions develop long lines between 10 and 11:30 a.m.

*unofficial* **TIP**
As the park fills up, visitors head for the top attractions before lines get long. This, more than anything else, determines morning traffic patterns.

From late morning until early afternoon, guests are equally distributed through all the lands. However, guests concentrate in Fantasyland, Liberty Square, and Frontierland in late afternoon, with a decrease of visitors in Adventureland and Tomorrowland. Adventureland's Jungle Cruise and Tomorrowland's Buzz Lightyear and Space Mountain continue to be crowded, but most other attractions in those lands are readily accessible.

**3. HOW DO MOST VISITORS TOUR THE PARK?** Do first-time visitors tour differently from repeat guests? Many first-time visitors are guided by friends or relatives familiar with the Magic Kingdom. These tours may or may not follow an orderly sequence. First-time visitors without personal guides tend to be more orderly in their touring. Many first-time visitors, however, are drawn to Cinderella Castle upon entering the park and thus begin their rotation from Fantasyland. Repeat visitors usually go directly to their favorite attractions.

**4. HOW DOES FASTPASS+ AFFECT CROWD DISTRIBUTIONS?** In general, you won't notice much difference in crowd concentrations because of FastPass+, but empirically speaking, it increases crowds within proximity of the two anchor attractions—Space Mountain and Splash Mountain—throughout the day.

**5. HOW DO SPECIAL EVENTS, SUCH AS PARADES AND LIVE SHOWS, AFFECT TRAFFIC PATTERNS?** Parades pull huge numbers of guests away from attractions and provide a window of opportunity for experiencing the more popular attractions with less of a wait. Castle Forecourt Stage shows also attract crowds but only slightly affect lines.

**6. WHAT ARE THE TRAFFIC PATTERNS NEAR AND AT CLOSING TIME?** On our sample days, in busy times and off-season at the park, departures outnumbered arrivals beginning in midafternoon. Many visitors left in late afternoon as the dinner hour approached. When the park closed early, guests departed steadily during the 2 hours before closing, with a huge exodus at closing time. When the park closed late, a huge exodus began immediately after the early-evening parade and fireworks, with a second mass departure after the late parade, continuing until closing. Because Main Street and the transportation services remain open after the other five lands close, crowds leaving at closing mainly affect conditions on Main Street and at the monorail-, ferry-, and bus-boarding areas. In the hour before closing, the other five lands are normally uncrowded.

To get a complete view of the actual traffic patterns while you're in the park, use our mobile app, **Lines** (**touringplans.com/lines**). The app gives you current wait times and future estimates in half-hour increments for today and tomorrow. A quick glance shows how traffic patterns affect wait times throughout the day.

# MAGIC KINGDOM TOURING PLANS

*unofficial* **TIP**
Don't worry that other people will be following the plans and render them useless. Fewer than 2 in every 100 people in the park will have been exposed to this info.

STARTING ON PAGE 822, our step-by-step touring plans are field-tested for seeing *as much as possible* in one day with a minimum of time wasted in lines. They're designed to help you avoid crowds and bottlenecks on days of moderate-to-heavy attendance. Understand, however, that there's more to see in the Magic Kingdom than can be experienced in one day. Since we first began covering the Magic Kingdom, four headliner attractions have been added and an entire land created and destroyed.

On days of lighter attendance (see "Selecting the Time of Year for Your Visit," page 35), our plans will save you time but won't be as critical to successful touring as on busier days.

In response to the introduction of FastPass+, we've listed the approximate return times for which you should try to make reservations. (The plans should work with anything close to the times shown.) Because Disney limits how many FastPass+ reservations you can get, we've listed which attractions are most likely to need FastPass+, too. Check **touringplans.com** for the latest information.

## CHOOSING THE APPROPRIATE TOURING PLAN

WE PRESENT FIVE MAGIC KINGDOM TOURING PLANS:

- Magic Kingdom One-Day Touring Plan for Adults
- Magic Kingdom Authors' Selective One-Day Touring Plan for Adults
- Magic Kingdom One-Day Touring Plan for Parents with Small Children
- Magic Kingdom Two-Day Touring Plan
- Magic Kingdom Dumbo-or-Die-in-a-Day Touring Plan for Parents with Small Children

If you have two days (or two mornings) at the Magic Kingdom, the Two-Day Touring Plan is *by far* the most relaxed and efficient. The two-day plan takes advantage of early morning, when lines are short and the park hasn't filled with guests. This plan works well year-round and eliminates much of the extra walking required by the one-day plans. No matter when the park closes, our two-day plan guarantees the most efficient touring and the least time in lines. The plan is perfect for guests who wish to sample both the attractions and the atmosphere of the Magic Kingdom.

If you have only one day to visit but you wish to see as much as possible, then use the One-Day Touring Plan for Adults. It's exhausting, but it packs in the maximum. If you prefer a more relaxed visit, use the Authors' Selective One-Day Touring Plan. It includes the best the park has to offer (in the authors' opinion), eliminating the less-impressive attractions.

If you have children younger than age 8, adopt the One-Day Touring Plan for Parents with Small Children. It's a compromise, blending the preferences of younger children with those of older siblings and adults. The plan includes many children's rides in Fantasyland but omits roller-coaster rides and other attractions that frighten young children

*unofficial* **TIP**
Switching off allows adults to enjoy the more adventuresome attractions while keeping the group together.

or are off-limits because of height requirements. Or use the One-Day Touring Plan for Adults or the Authors' Selective One-Day Touring Plan for Adults, and take advantage of switching off, a technique whereby children accompany adults to the loading area of a ride with age and height requirements but don't board (see page 341).

The Dumbo-or-Die-in-a-Day Touring Plan for Parents with Small Children is designed for parents who will withhold no sacrifice for their kids. On the Dumbo-or-Die Plan, adults generally stand around, sweat, wipe noses, pay for stuff, and watch the children enjoy themselves. It's great!

### "Not a Touring Plan" Touring Plans

For the type-B reader, these touring plans (see page 820) avoid detailed step-by-step strategies for saving every last minute in line. To paraphrase one of our favorite movies, they're more guidelines than actual rules. Use these to avoid the longest waits in line while having maximum flexibility to see whatever interests you in a particular part of the park.

For the Magic Kingdom, these "not" touring plans include advice for adults and parents with one day in the park, for anyone with two days, and for anyone with an afternoon and a full day to tour.

### Two-Day Touring Plan for Families with Small Children

If you have young children and are looking for a two-day itinerary, combine the Magic Kingdom One-Day Touring Plan for Parents with Small Children with the second day of the Magic Kingdom Two-Day Touring Plan.

### Two-Day Touring Plan for Early-Morning Touring on Day One and Afternoon–Evening Touring on Day Two

Many of you enjoy an early start at the Magic Kingdom on one day, followed by a second day with a lazy, sleep-in morning, resuming your touring in the afternoon and/or evening. If this appeals to you, use the Magic Kingdom One-Day Touring Plan for Adults or the Magic Kingdom One-Day Touring Plan for Parents with Small Children on your early day. Adhere to the touring plan for as long as it feels comfortable (many folks leave after the afternoon parade). On the second day, pick up where you left off. If you intend to use FastPass+ on your second day, make reservations well in advance, before they're all gone. Customize the remaining part of the touring plan to incorporate parades, fireworks, and other live performances according to your preferences.

## MAGIC KINGDOM TOURING PLAN COMPANION

WE'VE CONSOLIDATED A GREAT DEAL OF INFORMATION about the Magic Kingdom in its Touring Plan Companion, at the back of the guide just after the touring plans. Like the plans, the companions are designed to clip out and take with you to the park. The Magic Kingdom Touring Plan Companion includes the best days to go, the best times to visit each attraction, the authors' rating, height requirements, small-child fright potential, and info on dining and cool places to take a break.

## THE SINGLE-DAY TOURING CONUNDRUM

TOURING THE MAGIC KINGDOM IN A DAY is complicated by the fact that the premier attractions are at almost opposite ends of the park: Splash Mountain and Big Thunder Mountain Railroad in Frontierland, Space Mountain and Buzz Lightyear in Tomorrowland, and Under the Sea: Journey of the Little Mermaid and Seven Dwarfs Mine Train in the top center. It's virtually impossible to ride all six without encountering lines at one or another. If you ride Space Mountain and see Buzz Lightyear immediately after the park opens, for example, you won't have much of a wait, if any. By the time you leave Tomorrowland and hurry to Fantasyland, however, the line for Seven Dwarfs will be substantial. The same situation prevails if you ride the Fantasyland duo first: Seven Dwarfs Mine Train and Under the Sea, no problem; Space Mountain and Buzz Lightyear, however, have fair-sized lines. From 10 minutes after opening until just before closing, lines are long at these headliners.

The best way to ride all six without long waits is to use FastPass+ and tour over two mornings. Make midmorning FastPass+ reservations at Big Thunder for your first day. When you arrive, ride Seven Dwarfs Mine Train as soon as the park opens, then head directly for Splash Mountain. By the time you're done riding, your FastPass+ reservation should be ready for Big Thunder. On your second day, ride Space Mountain immediately after the park opens, then ride Buzz Lightyear.

If you have only a day to see the Magic Kingdom, make FastPass+ reservations in advance for around 9:30 a.m. at Big Thunder Mountain, and around 3:30 p.m. at Space Mountain. Then, on the day of your visit, ride Seven Dwarfs Mine Train as soon as the park opens, then ride Under the Sea, then hotfoot it to Splash Mountain. Your FastPass+ reservation for Big Thunder will be valid by the time you're done, and you'll have completed three of the park's four headliners in about an hour. Save Buzz Lightyear for around 3 p.m., when everyone is watching the parade, and hop on Space Mountain afterwards.

## PRELIMINARY INSTRUCTIONS FOR ALL MAGIC KINGDOM TOURING PLANS

BECOME FAMILIAR WITH THE Magic Kingdom's park-opening procedures, as described on page 79 of Part Two. Move quickly once you're admitted into the park. On days of moderate-to-heavy attendance, follow your chosen touring plan exactly, deviating only:

1. When you're not interested in an attraction it lists. Simply skip that attraction and proceed to the next.

2. When you encounter a very long line at an attraction the touring plan calls for. If this is the case, skip the attraction in question and go to the next step, returning later to retry.

### BEFORE YOU GO

1. Call ☎ 407-824-4321 or check **disneyworld.com** the day before you go to verify official opening time.

2. Purchase admission and make FastPass+ reservations before you arrive.

3. Get familiar with park-opening procedures (see previous section) and reread the plan you've chosen so you know what you're likely to encounter.

## MAGIC KINGDOM ONE-DAY TOURING PLAN FOR ADULTS *(page 822)*

FOR Adults without young children.

ASSUMES Willingness to experience all major rides (including roller coasters) and shows.

This plan requires a lot of walking and some backtracking to avoid lines. Extra walking and morning hustling will spare you 4 or more hours of standing in line. How far you get depends on how quickly you move from ride to ride, how many times you rest or eat, how quickly the park fills, and what time the park closes.

## MAGIC KINGDOM AUTHORS' SELECTIVE ONE-DAY TOURING PLAN FOR ADULTS *(page 823)*

**FOR** Adults touring without young children.

**ASSUMES** Willingness to experience all major rides (including roller coasters) and shows.

This plan includes only the attractions we think are best. It requires a lot of walking and some backtracking to avoid lines. How far you get depends on how quickly you move from ride to ride, how many times you rest or eat, how quickly the park fills, and what time the park closes.

## MAGIC KINGDOM ONE-DAY TOURING PLAN FOR PARENTS WITH SMALL CHILDREN *(page 824)*

**FOR** Parents with children younger than age 8.

**ASSUMES** Periodic stops for rest, restrooms, and refreshments.

This plan represents a compromise between the observed tastes of adults and those of younger children. Included are many amusement-park rides that children may have the opportunity to experience at fairs and amusement parks back home. Although these rides are included in the plan, omit them if possible. These cycle-loading rides often have long lines, consuming valuable touring time:

The Barnstormer      Mad Tea Party

Dumbo the Flying Elephant      The Magic Carpets of Aladdin

This time could be better spent experiencing the many attractions that better demonstrate the Disney creative genius and are found only in the Magic Kingdom. Try instead either of the one-day plans for adults and take advantage of switching off (see page 341). This allows parents and young children to enter the ride together; at the boarding area, one parent watches the children while the other rides. Families using this plan should review Magic Kingdom attractions in our Small-Child Fright-Potential Chart in Part Six (see pages 332–335).

We recommend taking a break and returning to your hotel for a swim and a nap (even if you're not staying in the World). You won't see as much, but everyone will be more relaxed and happy.

This touring plan requires a lot of walking and some backtracking to avoid long lines. A little extra walking and some morning hustle will spare you 2–3 hours of standing in line. You may not complete the tour. How far you get depends on how quickly you move from ride to ride, how many times you rest or eat, how quickly the park fills, and what time the park closes.

### To Convert This One-Day Touring Plan into a Two-Day Touring Plan

For Day 1, make FastPass+ reservations well in advance for Peter Pan's Flight around 11 a.m., The Many Adventures of Winnie the Pooh around 6:15 p.m., and *Enchanted Tales with Belle* around 7:15 pm. When the park opens, ride Seven Dwarfs Mine Train immediately, followed by Under the Sea. See the Storybook Circus attractions next, then Splash Mountain and The Haunted Mansion, before riding Peter Pan and leaving the park for lunch. Return to the park and work in the Frontierland and Liberty Square attractions around your FastPass+ reservations.

For Day 2, ride Buzz Lightyear, Astro Orbiter, and the Tomorrowland Speedway as soon as the park opens, then visit the Adventureland attractions, starting with the Magic Carpets of Aladdin. End your day with the PeopleMover and Monsters, Inc. show in Tomorrowland, followed by the evening parade and fireworks.

## MAGIC KINGDOM TWO-DAY TOURING PLAN
*(pages 825 and 826)*

**FOR** Those wishing to spread their Magic Kingdom visit over two days.

**ASSUMES** Willingness to experience all major rides (including roller coasters) and shows.

This two-day touring plan takes advantage of early-morning touring. Each day, you should complete the structured part of the plan by about 4 p.m. This leaves plenty of time for live entertainment. If the park is open late (after 8 p.m.), consider returning to your hotel at midday for a swim and a nap. Eat an early dinner outside Walt Disney World, and return refreshed to enjoy the park's nighttime festivities.

## MAGIC KINGDOM DUMBO-OR-DIE-IN-A-DAY TOURING PLAN FOR PARENTS WITH SMALL CHILDREN
*(page 827)*

**FOR** Adults compelled to devote every waking moment to the pleasure and entertainment of their young children, or rich people who are paying someone else to take their children to the theme park.

**PREREQUISITE** This plan is designed for days when the Magic Kingdom doesn't close until 9 p.m. or later.

**ASSUMES** Frequent stops for rest, restrooms, and refreshments.

*Note:* Name aside, this plan is no joke. Whether you're loving, guilty, masochistic, selfless, or insane, this itinerary will provide a youngster with about as perfect a day as is possible at the Magic Kingdom. Families using this plan should review Magic Kingdom attractions in our Small-Child Fright-Potential Chart in Part Six (see pages 332–335).

*un*official **TIP**
Before entering the park, decide whether you'll return to your hotel for a midday rest.

This plan is a concession to adults determined to give their young children the ultimate Magic Kingdom experience. If you left the kids with a sitter yesterday or wouldn't let little Marvin eat frosting for breakfast, the plan will expiate your guilt.

### To Convert This One-Day Touring Plan into a Day-and-a-Half Touring Plan

The idea is to split the park in half so that Tomorrowland, Storybook Circus, and a few of the other Fantasyland attractions are on the second day. Here's how:

For the day of your afternoon visit, make FastPass+ reservations well in advance for Splash Mountain around 4 p.m., Pirates of the Caribbean around 5 p.m., and Jungle Cruise around 6:30 p.m. Work in the other rides, shows, and dinner around these, and end the day with the evening parade.

For your full-day visit, make FastPass+ reservations well in advance for Peter Pan's Flight around 10:30 a.m., *Enchanted Tales with Belle* around 6:30 p.m., and Buzz Lightyear around 8 p.m. Ride Seven Dwarfs Mine Train as soon as the park opens, then Winnie the Pooh on the way to Astro Orbiter and Tomorrowland Speedway. Visit Storybook Circus as you loop back to Under the Sea, then continue clockwise through Fantasyland before leaving the park for a midday break. Return to the park for dinner before your *Enchanted Tales* reservation, then see *Mickey's PhilharMagic,* the *Monsters, Inc.,* show in Tomorrowland, and Buzz Lightyear. See the parade and fireworks if you've not already done so.

# PART TWELVE

# EPCOT

EDUCATION, INSPIRATION, AND CORPORATE IMAGERY are the focus at Epcot, the most adult of the Disney theme parks. What it gains in taking a futuristic, visionary, and technological look at the world, it loses just a bit in warmth, happiness, and charm.

Some people find the attempts at education to be superficial, while others want more entertainment and less education. Most visitors, however, are in between, finding plenty of entertainment *and* education.

Epcot is more than twice as big as the Magic Kingdom or Disney's Hollywood Studios and, though smaller than Disney's Animal Kingdom, has more territory to be covered on foot. Epcot rarely sees the congestion so common in the Magic Kingdom, but it has lines every bit as long as those at the Jungle Cruise or Space Mountain.

Epcot's size means that you can't see it all in one day without skipping an attraction or two and giving others a cursory glance. A major difference between Epcot and the other parks, however, is that some Epcot attractions can be savored slowly or skimmed, depending on personal interests. For example, the first section of Chevrolet's Test Track is a thrill ride, the second a collection of walk-through exhibits. Nearly all visitors take the ride, but many people, lacking time or interest, bypass the exhibits.

*unofficial* **TIP**
Epcot visitors must be prepared to do considerable walking between attractions and a comparable amount of standing in line.

We rate several Epcot attractions as not to be missed. But part of the enjoyment of the park is that there's something for everyone.

## THE EPCOT ACRONYM

IN THE BEGINNING, Epcot was EPCOT. When envisioned by Walt Disney as a utopian working city of the future, EPCOT was the acronym for **E**xperimental **P**rototype **C**ommunity **o**f **T**omorrow. Corporate Disney ultimately altered Walt's vision, and the city became a theme park, but the name remained. And because EPCOT was clearly nothing of the sort, the acronym EPCOT became the name *Epcot*.

*Continued on page 554*

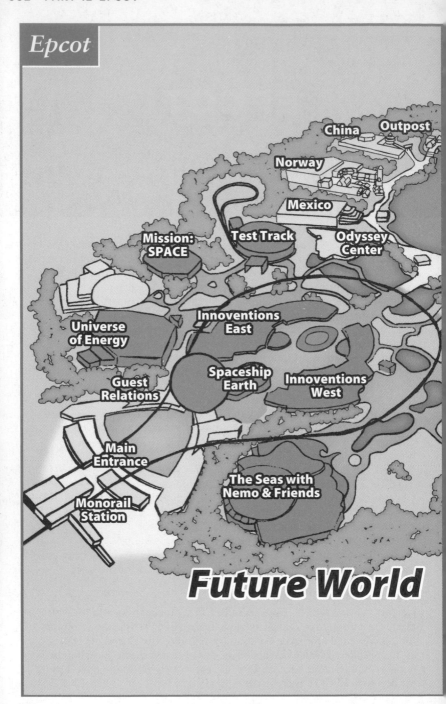

Epcot

China
Outpost
Norway
Mexico
Test Track
Mission: SPACE
Odyssey Center
Innoventions East
Universe of Energy
Spaceship Earth
Innoventions West
Guest Relations
Main Entrance
The Seas with Nemo & Friends
Monorail Station

*Future World*

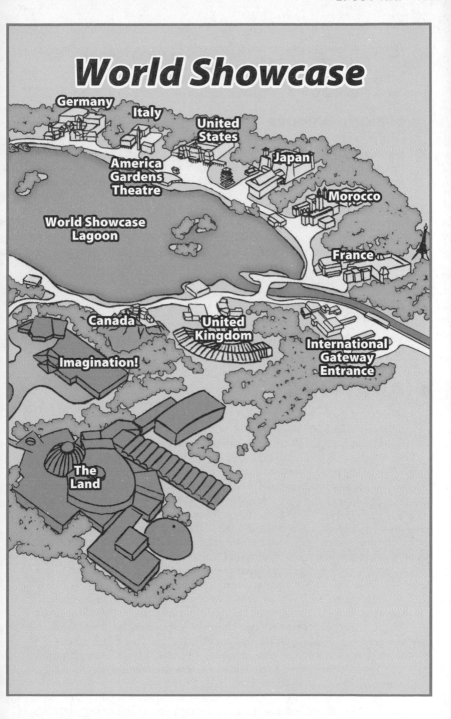

*Continued from page 551*

---

**NOT TO BE MISSED AT EPCOT**

**FUTURE WORLD**   • Living with the Land   • Mission: SPACE   • Soarin'
• Spaceship Earth   • Sum of All Thrills   • Test Track   • *Turtle Talk with Crush*

**WORLD SHOWCASE**   • *The American Adventure*   • *IllumiNations*

---

## OPERATING HOURS

EPCOT HAS TWO THEMED AREAS: **Future World** and **World Showcase.** Each has its own operating hours. Though schedules change throughout the year, Future World always opens before World Showcase in the morning. While most of Future World's attractions stay open until the entire park closes, a few close around 7 p.m. most of the year. World Showcase generally opens 2 hours later than Future World; moreover, some attractions open late or close early.

For park hours during your visit, call ☎ 407-824-4321 or visit **disneyworld.com.** For the operating schedules of specific attractions, check the park handout map or the supplemental *Times Guide,* available free throughout the park.

## DINING IN EPCOT

COUNTER-SERVICE RESTAURANTS in Epcot are profiled in Part Ten, starting on page 450. For full-service profiles, see the section starting on page 457.

# ▌▌ ARRIVING

IF YOU'RE A GUEST AT ONE OF THE EPCOT RESORTS, it will take you about 20–30 minutes to walk from your hotel to the International Gateway (back entrance of Epcot) and from there to the Future World section of the park. Instead of walking, you can catch a boat from your Epcot resort hotel to the International Gateway and then walk about 8 minutes to the Future World section. To reach the front (Future World) entrance of Epcot from the Epcot resorts, either take a boat from your hotel to Disney's Hollywood Studios and transfer to an Epcot bus, take a bus to Downtown Disney and transfer to an Epcot bus, or, best of all, take a cab.

*un*official **TIP**
Plan to arrive at the turnstiles 30–40 minutes before official opening time. Give yourself an extra 10 minutes or so to park and make your way to the entrance.

Arriving at the park by car is easy and direct. For driving directions, see page 373. Epcot has its own parking lot, and, unlike at the Magic Kingdom, there's no need to take a monorail or ferry to reach the entrance. Trams service the parking lot, or you can walk to the front gate. Monorail service connects Epcot with the Transportation and Ticket Center, the Magic Kingdom (transfer required), and Magic Kingdom resorts (transfer required).

For unknown reasons, getting through entrance security at Epcot is more cumbersome and time-consuming than at the other parks. In fact, it's a royal pain, as this unidentified reader relates:

*My biggest complaint was the amount of time it took to actually get into Epcot: 35 minutes at 10:30 a.m. to get bags checked (park had opened at 9) and another 10 minutes to get in. It took nowhere near as long at the other parks, even with the same crowd size.*

A Florida mother of a 3-year-old agrees:

*Lines were crazy first thing in the morning. Some cast members just glanced in a bag, and others opened every zipper and looked in every crevice of our bags and stroller. One time we got an overzealous employee whose line took 15 minutes—the longest line of the day.*

Take these delays into consideration if you're using one of the Epcot touring plans. A second, often overlooked, security checkpoint is on the other (east) side of the main checkpoint. If the main lines look too long, have one member of your group peek around to see if the east lines are shorter.

This reader from Sacramento, California, suggests using the International Gateway (World Showcase) entrance instead:

*With the advent of MagicBands and FastPass+, the International Gateway entrance is not inconvenient for getting into the park first thing in the morning. We entered there by boat from the Dolphin hotel and were met inside the gate by cast members who set up our FastPass+ reservations for the day. We didn't have to kill ourselves to race down to Soarin' to get a FastPass—we were able to enjoy a nice stroll with FastPasses in hand (in our MagicBands, that is).*

# GETTING ORIENTED

EPCOT'S THEMED AREAS are distinctly different: **Future World** examines where mankind has come from and where it's going; **World Showcase** features the landmarks, cuisine, and culture of almost a dozen nations and is meant to be a sort of permanent World's Fair.

Navigating Epcot is unlike getting around at the Magic Kingdom. The Magic Kingdom is designed so that nearly every location is part of a specific environment—Liberty Square or Main Street, U.S.A., for example. All environments are visually separated to preserve the integrity of the theme.

Epcot, by contrast, is visually open. And while it seems strange to see a Japanese pagoda and the Eiffel Tower on the same horizon, getting around is fairly simple. An exception is Future World, where the enormous **Innoventions East and West** buildings hide everything on their opposite sides.

At Epcot, the architectural symbol is **Spaceship Earth**. This shiny, 180-foot geosphere is visible from almost everywhere in the park. Like Cinderella Castle at the Magic Kingdom, Spaceship Earth can help you keep track of where you are in Epcot. But it's in a high-traffic area and isn't centrally located, so it isn't a good meeting place.

Any of the distinctive national pavilions in World Showcase make a good meeting place, but be specific. "Hey, let's meet in Japan!" sounds fun, but each pavilion is a mini-town with buildings, monuments, gardens, and plazas. Pick a specific place in Japan—the sidewalk side of the pagoda, for example.

## FASTPASS+ ATTRACTIONS IN EPCOT

EPCOT OFFERS FASTPASS+ for 12 attractions in two tiers:

| TIER A (*Choose one per day*) | |
|---|---|
| • *IllumiNations* | • Epcot Character Spot |
| • Living with the Land | • Journey into Imagination |
| • Soarin' | • Maelstrom |
| • Test Track | • Mission: SPACE (Green or Orange) |
| **TIER B (*Choose two per day*)** | • Spaceship Earth |
| • *Captain EO* | • The Seas with Nemo & Friends |
| | • *Turtle Talk with Crush* |

Because the tiers limit the number and combinations of FastPass+ attractions you can experience, much of our Epcot touring strategy is now dictated by the attractions in Tier A, which includes **Soarin'** and **Test Track.** Since you can't use FastPass+ for both, your best bet is to visit one as the first step in a touring plan, then use FastPass+ for the other. (*Exception:* **Living with the Land** just doesn't get comparable crowds to the others, so it's rarely a good use of FastPass+.)

Our most frequent FastPass+ recommendation is for **Spaceship Earth** in Future World, usually around lunch. Longer lines develop at Soarin' and Test Track than at Spaceship Earth, so it's important to get one of those done first thing in the morning. But because Spaceship Earth's wait times can reach 30–40 minutes, it's one of the best choices in Tier B.

Another attraction that affects Epcot touring is **Sum of All Thrills,** in which you design and then ride in your own virtual roller coaster. Though it's not to be missed, it's also not a FastPass+ attraction—that's probably because it can handle only a few hundred guests per hour and thus doesn't have enough rider capacity to allocate to reservations.

As an example, our Epcot One-Day Touring Plan for Adults minimizes the capacity constraints at Sum of All Thrills by sandwiching it between FastPass+ reservations for Test Track and Mission: SPACE, its neighbors in Future World:

1. **Soarin'**
2. **Living with the Land**
3. **Test Track:** FastPass+ for 9:15–10:15 a.m.
4. **Sum of All Thrills**
5. **Mission: SPACE (Orange):** FastPass+ for 10:15–11:15 a.m.

Get to Test Track in the second half of your 1-hour FastPass+ time window. By the time you've experienced Test Track and Sum of All Thrills, your FastPass+ window for Mission: SPACE will have started, plus it's a short walk there from Innoventions East. This strategy saves you both time in line and time walking from attraction to attraction.

In general, our touring plan software recommends FastPass+ for Soarin' more than twice as often as Test Track. Both have 40-inch height requirements, but Test Track is a harsher ride, with sudden stops, turns, and acceleration. For that reason, Test Track doesn't appear on many of our touring plans for parents with small children or those for seniors.

A second reason to use FastPass+ at Soarin' is **Test Track's single-rider line,** a feature Soarin' doesn't have. Test Track's single-rider wait times are typically less than half those of its standby (non-FastPass+) wait times. If you're willing to split up your group, the single-rider line is a good way to mitigate Test Track's standby waits.

On the other hand, we've identified four attractions for which Fast-Pass+ is *never* necessary. First, waits for **Captain EO** and **Journey into Imagination with Figment** are almost always under 10 minutes; similarly, waits for the nonspinning **Mission: SPACE (Green)** are almost always lower than those for the spinning (Orange) version.

**Epcot Character Spot** doesn't require FastPass+ in our Epcot touring plans for parents with small children. Because you can get a Fast-Pass+ for Soarin' (if your kids are old enough to ride), and because Test Track and Mission: SPACE aren't in our plans because of their intensity and height requirements, our software usually puts the Character Spot as one of the first steps in your plan.

In addition to these four, **IllumiNations** is a must-see, and FastPass+ gets you into a special viewing area for the show, but you still have to arrive a good 30–40 minutes in advance to get a good spot. What's more, there are so many other good viewing spots around World Showcase Lagoon that it's difficult to recommend FastPass+ for *Illumi Nations*—the consequence is an hour-long wait at either Soarin' or Test Track. The one exception is if you're visiting World Showcase for an evening, as there are no other Tier A attractions in World Showcase.

Look for Epcot FastPass+ kiosks in the following locations:

- In front of Mission: SPACE
- At the Soarin' entrance, downstairs in The Land
- At Guest Relations in Future World
- At the digital "tip board" in the middle of Future World Plaza (behind Spaceship Earth and the Future World fountain)
- At the International Gateway entrance to the park
- In the Future World West walkway, on the way to The Land

# FUTURE WORLD

GLEAMING FUTURISTIC STRUCTURES of immense proportions define the first themed area beyond the main entrance. Broad thoroughfares are punctuated with billowing fountains—all reflected in shiny space-age facades. Front and center is **Spaceship Earth,** flanked by **Innoventions East and West.** Pavilions dedicated to mankind's past, present, and future technological achievements ring the perimeter of Future World.

## Spaceship Earth *(FastPass+)*  ★★★★

| APPEAL BY AGE | PRESCHOOL ★★★½ | GRADE SCHOOL ★★★★ | TEENS ★★★★ |
| YOUNG ADULTS ★★★★ | OVER 30 ★★★★ | | SENIORS ★★★★½ |

**What it is** Educational dark ride through past, present, and future. **Scope and scale** Headliner. **When to go** Before 10 a.m., after 4 p.m., or use FastPass+. **Special comments** If lines are long when you arrive, try again after 4 p.m. **Authors' rating** One of Epcot's best; not to be missed; ★★★★. **Duration of ride** About 16 minutes. **Average wait in line per 100 people ahead of you** 3 minutes. **Loading speed** Fast.

## FUTURE WORLD Services

EPCOT'S SERVICE FACILITIES in Future World include the following:

**Baby Care Center** On the World Showcase side of the Odyssey Center

**Banking Services** ATMs outside the main entrance, on the Future World bridge, and in World Showcase at the US Pavilion and International Gateway entrance

**Dining Reservations** At Guest Relations, to the left of Spaceship Earth

**First Aid** Next to the Baby Care Center

**Live Entertainment Information** At Guest Relations

**Lost and Found** At the main entrance at the gift shop

**Lost Persons** At Guest Relations and the Baby Care Center

**Walt Disney World and Local Attraction Information**
At Guest Relations

**Wheelchair, ECV, ESV, and Stroller Rentals** Inside the main entrance and to the left, toward the rear of the Entrance Plaza

**DESCRIPTION AND COMMENTS** This ride spirals through the 18-story interior of Epcot's premier landmark, taking visitors past animatronic scenes depicting mankind's developments in communications, from cave painting to printing to television to space communications and computer networks. The ride shows an amazing use of the geosphere's interior.

Spaceship Earth's scenes are periodically redone to keep things fresh. The most recent include a 1970s-era computer room and a home garage showing what looks suspiciously like the invention of the Apple personal computer (perhaps a homage to Steve Jobs, who before his death was Disney's largest individual shareholder). Interactive video screens on the ride vehicles allow you to customize the ride's ending animated video. A postshow area with games and interactive exhibits rounds out the attraction.

**TOURING TIPS** Because it's near Epcot's main entrance, Spaceship Earth attracts arriving guests throughout the morning. If you want to ride Soarin' and Test Track, try to get a FastPass+ reservation for around 1 p.m. You should be almost done with Future World's attractions by then and ready to head to World Showcase. Or, if you plan on spending the afternoon in Future World and don't want to use FastPass+, try Spaceship Earth after 3 p.m.

## Innoventions East and West ★★★½

**APPEAL BY AGE** PRESCHOOL ★★★ GRADE SCHOOL ★★★★ TEENS ★★★½
YOUNG ADULTS ★★★½ OVER 30 ★★★½ SENIORS ★★★½

**What it is** Static and hands-on exhibits relating to products and technologies of the near future. **Scope and scale** Major diversion. **When to go** On your second day at Epcot or after you've seen all the major attractions. **Special comments** Most exhibits demand time and participation to be rewarding—there's not much gained here by a quick walk-through. **Authors' rating** Something for everyone; ★★★½.

**DESCRIPTION AND COMMENTS** Innoventions—a huge, busy collection of hands-on walk-through exhibits sponsored by corporations—consists of two huge, crescent-shaped, glass-walled structures separated by a central plaza. Dynamic, interactive, and forward-looking, the area resembles a high-tech trade show. Electronics and entertainment technology exhibits play a prominent role, as do ecology and "how things work" displays.

Each major exhibit is sponsored by a different manufacturer or research lab, and most emphasize the effect of the product(s) or technology on daily living. Exhibits change periodically, and there's a definite trend toward larger, more elaborate affairs—almost mini-attractions. The newer exhibits are more compelling, but they require waiting in line to be admitted. For example, a current exhibit on saving for retirement includes a short game show–type activity complete with a computerized piggy bank you carry around. Other hands-on interactive exhibits cover IBM's latest technology, fire safety, and healthy lifestyles. Our favorite attraction is Raytheon's **Sum of All Thrills,** a roller-coaster simulator in which you design the coaster track on a computer, and then climb aboard a giant robotic arm to experience your creation.

TOURING TIPS Spend time at Innoventions on your second day at Epcot. If you have only one day, visit late if you have the time and endurance. (The one exception to this is Sum of All Thrills, which you should visit in the morning after Soarin', Test Track, and Mission: SPACE.)

Although many of these productions are worthwhile, the guest capacity of each theater is so small that long lines form. A couple of exhibits, such as Where's the Fire?—an interactive program about fire safety—are worth 15 minutes of waiting in line, but they're the exception. We suggest skipping exhibits with waits of more than 10 minutes or experiencing them first thing in the morning on your second day, when there are no lines.

## CLUB COOL

DESCRIPTION AND COMMENTS Attached to the fountain side of Innoventions West is a retail space–soda fountain called Club Cool. This Coca-Cola–sponsored exhibit provides free unlimited samples of soft drinks from around the world—some selections will taste strange to Americans, but others will please. Perhaps because it's free and indoors, readers rate Club Cool higher than eight Epcot attractions and three World Showcase pavilions.

## Sum of All Thrills ★★★★

| APPEAL BY AGE | PRESCHOOL ★★ | GRADE SCHOOL ★★★★½ | TEENS ★★★★½ |
| --- | --- | --- | --- |
| YOUNG ADULTS ★★★★½ | | OVER 30 ★★★★½ | SENIORS ★★★★ |

**What it is** Hands-on exhibit and ride simulator. **Scope and scale** Minor attraction. **When to go** Before 10:30 a.m. or after 5 p.m. **Special comments** 48″ minimum height requirement, 54″ for track designs with inversions. **Authors' rating** Not to be missed; ★★★★. **Duration of attraction** 15 minutes. **Average wait in line per 100 people ahead of you** 40 minutes; assumes all simulators operating. **Loading speed** Slow.

DESCRIPTION AND COMMENTS Sum of All Thrills is a design-your-own-roller-coaster simulator in which you use a computer program to specify the drops, curves, and loops of a coaster track before boarding an industrial robotic arm to experience your creation. Three vehicle options are available: bobsled, roller coaster, and jet aircraft. It's possible to program actual loops into both the coaster and jet courses, and the robot arm will swing you upside down.

In addition to the vehicle, you select the kinds of turns, loops, and hills in your track design. Choices range from mild, broad curves to extreme multiple-loop inversions. Using computer-design tools, you can further customize these components by changing the height and width of each piece as you go. This customization makes it easy to ride Sum of All Thrills many times without experiencing the same track twice.

A New Jersey couple thinks Sum of All Thrills is simply awesome:

*Sum of All Thrills has to be the most unheralded attraction anywhere in the World. With the chance to design your own attraction and waits usually under 20 minutes, it's one of the best things to do in Future World.*

**TOURING TIPS** Not a high-capacity attraction, but also not on most guests' radar. Ride as early in the morning as possible.

## Epcot Character Spot *(FastPass+)* ★★★

| APPEAL BY AGE | PRESCHOOL ★★★★½ | GRADE SCHOOL ★★★★½ | TEENS ★★★★ |
|---|---|---|---|
| YOUNG ADULTS ★★★★ | | OVER 30 ★★★★ | SENIORS ★★★ |

**What it is** Character-greeting venue. **Scope and scale** Diversion. **When to go** Before 11 a.m., or use FastPass+. **Authors' rating** Indoors and air-conditioned; ★★★. **Duration of experience** 8 minutes. **Probable waiting time** 20–40 minutes. **Queue speed** Slow.

**DESCRIPTION AND COMMENTS** In Future World West, to the right of The Fountain restaurant, Epcot Character Spot offers the chance to meet Disney characters indoors, in air-conditioned comfort. Characters on hand typically include Mickey Mouse, Minnie Mouse, and Pluto. You may also find Chip 'n' Dale nearby outside.

**TOURING TIPS** The Character Spot should be your first stop if you have small children. Make FastPass+ reservations for Soarin' for around 9:30 a.m. so you can proceed there directly after getting autographs. The venue typically stays open until 9 p.m., even when other Future World attractions close at 7 p.m., and usually until around 10:45 p.m. during evening Extra Magic Hours, when Epcot is open until midnight.

## Universe of Energy: *Ellen's Energy Adventure* ★★★½

| APPEAL BY AGE | PRESCHOOL ★★★ | GRADE SCHOOL ★★★½ | TEENS ★★★½ |
|---|---|---|---|
| YOUNG ADULTS ★★★ | | OVER 30 ★★★½ | SENIORS ★★★★ |

**What it is** Combination dark ride–theater presentation. **Scope and scale** Major attraction. **When to go** Anytime. **Special comments** Don't be dismayed by long lines—580 people enter the pavilion each time the theater changes audiences. **Authors' rating** Fun and informative, but showing its age; ★★★½. **Duration of presentation** About 26½ minutes. **Preshow entertainment** 8 minutes. **Probable waiting time** 14 minutes.

**DESCRIPTION AND COMMENTS** This attraction begins with a preshow film starring Ellen DeGeneres. While watching TV, Ellen dozes off and dreams that she's competing on *Jeopardy!* against her know-it-all former college roommate Judy (Jamie Lee Curtis). All of the categories deal with energy, and unfortunately for Ellen, Judy has a PhD in the subject.

Luckily, Ellen's next-door neighbor happens to be Bill Nye the Science Guy, who convinces Ellen—along with everyone else in the audience—to take a time-traveling crash course in the history of energy.

You move from the preshow hall to what appears to be an ordinary theater to watch another film, this one about energy sources. Then the seats divide into six 97-passenger traveling cars that carry you from the Big Bang (the beginning of Ellen's energy lessons) to the swamps and animatronic dinosaurs of a prehistoric forest. Special effects include the feel of warm, moist swamp air and the smell of sulfur from an erupting volcano.

The dialogue between DeGeneres and Nye is humorous and upbeat, but the script was written almost 20 years ago, when ExxonMobil was sponsoring the attraction. Don't expect to hear calls to action on climate change or carbon footprints, or much more than a passing reference to alternative energy sources.

For children, it's a toss-up. The dinosaurs frighten some preschoolers, and kids of all ages lose the thread during the educational segments.

A Zionsville, Indiana, reader agrees with us that *Ellen's Energy Adventure* is more than a little dated:

*I knew that the point of the ride was to go back in time, but I didn't realize the destination was 1993. [Authors' note: It's actually 1996, but we won't split hairs.] Ellen is genuinely funny, but this attraction is so old that the video quality is only slightly better than the Zapruder film's.*

**TOURING TIPS** Because the theater has a ride component, the line doesn't move while the show is in progress. When the theater empties, however, a large chunk of the line disappears as people are admitted for the next show. Because of this, waits are generally tolerable.

## Mission: SPACE *(FastPass+)* ★★★★

**APPEAL BY AGE** PRESCHOOL ★★★½ GRADE SCHOOL ★★★★½ TEENS ★★★★ YOUNG ADULTS ★★★★ OVER 30 ★★★★ SENIORS ★★★★

Motion Sickness

**What it is** Space-flight-simulator ride. **Scope and scale** Super-headliner. **When to go** First or last hour the park is open, or use FastPass+. **Special comments** Not recommended for pregnant women or people prone to motion sickness or claustrophobia; 44" minimum height requirement; a gentler nonspinning version is also available. **Authors' rating** Impressive; not to be missed; ★★★★. **Duration of ride** About 5 minutes plus preshow. **Average wait in line per 100 people ahead of you** 4 minutes.

**DESCRIPTION AND COMMENTS** Mission: SPACE was one of the most popular rides at Disney World until two guests died after riding it in 2005 and 2006. While neither death was linked directly to the attraction, the negative publicity caused many guests to skip it entirely. In response, Disney added a tamer nonspinning version of Mission: SPACE in 2006.

Disney's lawyers probably clocked as much time as the ride engineers in designing the "lite" version. Even before you walk into the building, you're asked whether you want your ride with or without spin. Choose the spinning version and you're on the Orange team; the Green team trains on the no-spin side. Either way, you're immediately handed the appropriate "launch ticket" containing the first of myriad warnings about the attraction, as this *Unofficial Guide* reader discovered:

*I chose the more intense version and was handed the Orange launch ticket to read. Basically, it explained that if I had ever had a tonsillectomy or even a mild case of pattern baldness, I should take the less intense ride.*

Guests for both versions of the attraction enter the International Space Training Center, where they're introduced to the deep-space exploration program and then divided into groups for flight training. After orientation, they're strapped into space capsules for a simulated flight, where, of course, the unexpected happens. Each capsule accommodates a crew consisting of a group commander, pilot, navigator, and engineer, with a guest functioning in each role. The crew's skill and finesse (or, more often, lack thereof) in handling their respective responsibilities have no effect on the outcome of the flight.

The capsules are small, and both ride versions are amazingly realistic. The nonspinning version doesn't subject your body to g-forces, but it does bounce and toss you around in a manner roughly comparable to other

Disney motion simulators. A Bradenton, Florida, mom found motion sickness to be the least of her problems:

*I'd like to see warnings here about claustrophobia—I had no clue until the capsule closed that it would be so tight in there. I went into full panic mode.*

**TOURING TIPS** Disney can reconfigure the ride's four centrifuges to either version based on guest demand. In general, the kinder, gentler version has a wait time of about half that of its more harrowing counterpart.

Having experienced the industrial-strength version of Mission: SPACE under a variety of circumstances, we've always felt icky when riding it on an empty stomach, especially first thing in the morning, so we looked around for an expert to tell us why. Entities who are knowledgeable in the effects of high-g (high-gravity) forces on humans are limited to a select few: NASA, the Air Force, and Mad Tea Party cast members were the first to come to mind. As NASA is a codeveloper of Mission: SPACE, we called them. Amazingly, a spokesman told us that NASA no longer does much high-g training these days. And the agency was reluctant to pass along anything resembling medical advice to the general public.

Fortunately, a longtime friend put us in touch with a real NASA astronaut who was willing to share (anonymously) some ideas on what causes the nausea, as well as some tips for preventing it. Our expert guesses, as we do, that low blood sugar is the culprit behind the queasiness and suggests eating a normal meal 1–2 hours before experiencing the ride. Avoid milk and tomatoes; they're difficult to keep down and, as our contact noted with the voice of experience, particularly unpleasant if they come back up. A banana, we hear, is a good choice for your preflight meal.

Another trick astronauts use to avoid nausea mid-simulation is to keep a piece of hard candy or a mint in their mouths; it's not clear, though, whether the candy helps keep blood-sugar levels high or is just a placebo. If all else fails, there are airsickness bags in each simulator.

Hit the restroom before you get in line; you'll think your bladder really has been to Mars and back before you get out of this attraction. We recommend securing a midmorning FastPass+ reservation for Mission: SPACE Orange.

Few things delight our readers more than kibitzing about rides that can make you puke, and Mission: SPACE is at the top of this particular heap. From a Yakima, Washington, reader:

*Mission: SPACE is awesome. A number of people we spoke to didn't ride because they were intimidated by the warnings about motion sickness.*

A Centreville, Maryland, mom got back on the horse that threw her:

*My husband and I rode this [on a previous visit] and we both felt ill afterward. So this time we rode Mission: SPACE Green. News flash: It is BORING. Not "less intense," but genuinely dull. I didn't realize how little motion there is when the spinning is removed. So we got right back in line (still a short wait—lucky us!) and rode the Orange version. It's been toned down since the original incarnation of the ride, and it's really good. Yes, it's intense, but it's a thrill ride—it should be intense. You can still feel the g's, but they're not as intrusive.*

A woman from Lisbon, Connecticut, used Mission: SPACE as her own personal relationship lab:

*We now understand why husbands and wives will probably never go to space together after I (the "navigator") pushed his (the "pilot's") button during the flight. I couldn't help being a backseat driver—we could have crashed!*

## TEST TRACK PAVILION

**DESCRIPTION AND COMMENTS** Sponsored by Chevrolet, this pavilion consists of the Test Track attraction and Inside Track, a collection of transportation-themed exhibits and multimedia presentations. The pavilion is the last on the left before the World Showcase. Many readers tell us that Test Track "is one big commercial" for Chevrolet. We agree that promotional hype is more heavy-handed here than in most other business-sponsored attractions. But Test Track is nonetheless one of the most creatively conceived attractions in Disney World.

### Test Track *(FastPass+)*  ★★★★

**APPEAL BY AGE  PRESCHOOL** ★★★★  **GRADE SCHOOL** ★★★★★  **TEENS** ★★★★½
**YOUNG ADULTS** ★★★★½     **OVER 30** ★★★★½     **SENIORS** ★★★★

**What it is** Automobile test-track simulator ride. **Scope and scale** Super-headliner. **When to go** The first 30 minutes the park is open or just before closing, or use FastPass+. **Special comments** 40" minimum height requirement. **Authors' rating** Not to be missed; ★★★★. **Duration of ride** About 4 minutes. **Average wait in line per 100 people ahead of you** 4½ minutes. **Loading speed** Moderate–fast.

**DESCRIPTION AND COMMENTS** Test Track takes guests through the process of designing a new vehicle and then "testing" their car in a high-speed drive through and around the pavilion.

Guests entering the pavilion walk past displays of sleek, futuristic concept cars. Throughout the queue's walls are glossy video screens where engineers discuss the work of car design and consumers explain the characteristics of their perfect car.

After hearing about auto design, guests are admitted into the Chevrolet Design Studio to create their own concept car. Using a large touchscreen interface (like a giant iPad), groups of up to three guests drag their fingers to design their car's body, engine, wheels, trim, and color. The computer screen reflects each design decision's impact on four performance characteristics: capability, efficiency, responsiveness, and power. For example, designing a large truck with a huge V-8 engine increases the car's capability and power but drastically reduces its efficiency. A clock on the computer screen indicates how much time remains to finish each step in the design process, and the entire creative experience takes 5–8 minutes.

Next, guests board a six-seat ride vehicle, attached to a track on the ground, for an actual drive through Chevrolet's test track. The idea here is that guests are taking part in a computer simulation designed to test their vehicle's performance characteristics. The vehicle's tests include braking maneuvers, cornering, and acceleration, culminating in a spin around the outside of the pavilion at speeds of up to 65 miles per hour.

The ride visuals are sleek and eye-catching, but trying to understand them as a coherent narrative is pointless—like fuzzy dice and reality-TV contestants, they're there to look good, not to be useful. At various points during the ride, video screens show the virtual cars designed by the guests in your vehicle and a status update on how the vehicle's tests are progressing. Most guests figure out quickly that absolutely nothing in their car's design has any effect whatsoever on their ride experience: Designing a fuel-sipping electric hybrid results in the exact same sensations as a monster truck with huge tires.

Test Track's post-show area continues the design process by allowing guests to create commercials for their concept cars. Farther into the pavilion are displays of actual Chevrolet cars, many of which you can sit in. We've never heard of anyone attempting to buy a car from Test Track, but let us know if you have.

**TOURING TIPS** It's always been a challenge to keep Test Track running, especially in humid or wet conditions. When it's working properly, it's one of the park's better attractions—but for this London, Ontario, mom, such instances never materialized:

*Test Track breaks down more than any other ride I've ever seen. We went back there over and over again, got in line, and then had to get out. FastPass+ lines would have a 40-minute wait because no one got to ride at the proper time. What's wrong with that ride?*

A repeat visitor from East Aurora, New York, suggests that all is not lost when the ride breaks down:

*If the ride breaks down or doesn't run normally, tell a cast member. They will most likely give you a slip that allows you to skip the line and ride again. This happened to us twice during the busiest time of the year, and we were able to ride again with no problem.*

Be aware that FastPass+ reservations often run out by afternoon. In that case, try the single-rider line. Because most groups are unwilling to split up, this line is usually much shorter than the regular (standby) line.

## IMAGINATION! PAVILION

**DESCRIPTION AND COMMENTS** Multiattraction pavilion on the west side of Innoventions West and down the walk from The Land. Outside is an "upside-down" waterfall and one of our favorite Future World landmarks, the "jumping" water, a fountain that hops over the heads of unsuspecting passersby.

**TOURING TIPS** We recommend late-morning touring. See individual attractions for specifics.

### Captain EO *(FastPass+)*  ★★★

| APPEAL BY AGE | PRESCHOOL ★★½ | GRADE SCHOOL ★★½ | TEENS ★★½ |
|---|---|---|---|
| YOUNG ADULTS ★★½ | | OVER 30 ★★★ | SENIORS ★★★ |

**What they are** 3-D films with special effects. **Scope and scale** Headliner. **When to go** Anytime—FastPass+ is unnecessary. **Special comments** Adults shouldn't be put off by the sci-fi theme or rock music. The high decibels frighten some young children. **Authors' rating** ★★★. **Duration of presentation** About 17 minutes. **Preshow entertainment** 8 minutes. **Probable waiting time** 15 minutes.

**DESCRIPTION AND COMMENTS** In response to Michael Jackson's death in 2009, Disney brought back his 3-D space-themed musical film presentation *Captain EO* for a "limited" engagement in its theme parks; at Epcot, that engagement is still ongoing, having supplanted *Honey, I Shrunk the Audience. Captain EO* originally ran here from 1986 to 1994.

*Captain EO* is the ultimate 1980s-era music video. Starring the late Michael Jackson and directed by Francis Ford Coppola, this 3-D space fantasy is more than a film; it's a happening. Action on the screen is augmented by lasers, fiber optics, cannons, and a host of other special effects in the theater, as well as by some audience participation. There's not much of a story, but there's plenty of music and dancing performed by some of the most unlikely creatures ever to shake a tail feather.

All that said, *Unofficial Guide* readers rank *Captain EO* as the worst attraction in Epcot. We still think it's worth seeing, though, if only for the nostalgia of Jackson's long-form video work.

**TOURING TIPS** Shows usually begin on the hour and half-hour. The sound level is earsplitting, frightening some young children. Avoid seats in the first several rows—If you sit too close to the screen, the 3-D images don't focus properly. FastPass+ isn't needed because the theater rarely fills.

## Journey into Imagination with Figment *(FastPass+)*  ★★½

| APPEAL BY AGE | PRESCHOOL ★★★★ | GRADE SCHOOL ★★★★ | TEENS ★★★ |
| YOUNG ADULTS ★★½ | | OVER 30 ★★★ | SENIORS ★★★½ |

**What it is** Dark fantasy-adventure ride. **Scope and scale** Major attraction wannabe. **When to go** Anytime. **Authors' rating** ★★½. **Duration of ride** About 6 minutes. **Average wait in line per 100 people ahead of you** 2 minutes. **Loading speed** Fast.

**DESCRIPTION AND COMMENTS** Journey into Imagination takes you on a tour of the zany Imagination Institute. Sometimes you're a passive observer and sometimes you're a test subject as the ride provides a glimpse of the fictitious lab's inner workings. Stimulating all your senses and then some, it hits you with optical illusions, an experiment in which noise generates colors, a room that defies gravity, and other brain teasers. All along the way, Figment (a purple dragon) makes surprise appearances. After the ride, you can adjourn to an interactive exhibit area offering the latest in unique, hands-on imagery technology.

Reader responses to Figment and company are pretty consistent. First, from a Brooklyn, New York, family:

*Figment was just plain weird—talking about five senses, then only introducing three, then the dragon singing . . . huh?*

And from a Franklin, Tennessee, family of three:

*You should put a bold notation next to the Figment attraction stating it should be experienced only if you are a HUGE Figment fan. We didn't even know who Figment was, and we all hated this attraction. After the Figment disaster, I had to hide from my husband the fact that I was selecting the next attraction based on your touring plan. He was convinced after the plan sent us to Figment that all touring plans were a waste of time.*

The ride falls short of the promise suggested by its name. Will you go to sleep? No. Will you find it amusing? Probably. Will you remember it tomorrow? Only Figment knows.

**TOURING TIPS** The standby wait for this attraction rarely exceeds 15 minutes, so no need for FastPass+ here. You can enjoy the interactive exhibit without taking the ride, so save it for later in the day.

## THE LAND PAVILION

**DESCRIPTION AND COMMENTS** The Land is a huge themed area containing three attractions and two restaurants. When the pavilion was built, its emphasis was on farming, but it now focuses on the environment. Finally, be forewarned that strollers aren't allowed inside The Land. Those with babes in arms might want to bring an infant carrier.

**TOURING TIPS** This is a good place to grab a fast-food lunch. If you're coming here to see the attractions, however, stay away during mealtimes.

## *The Circle of Life*  ★★★½

| APPEAL BY AGE | PRESCHOOL ★★★½ | GRADE SCHOOL ★★★½ | TEENS ★★★ |
| YOUNG ADULTS ★★★ | | OVER 30 ★★★ | SENIORS ★★★ |

**What it is** Film exploring humans' relationship with the environment. **Scope and scale** Minor attraction. **When to go** Anytime. **Authors' rating** Inspiring and enlightening;

★★★½. **Duration of presentation** About 20 minutes. **Preshow entertainment** Ecological slide show and trivia. **Probable waiting time** 10–15 minutes.

**DESCRIPTION AND COMMENTS** This playful yet educational film, starring Pumbaa, Simba, and Timon from Disney's animated feature *The Lion King*, spotlights the environmental interdependency of all creatures, demonstrating how easily the ecological balance can be upset. The message is sobering, but one that enlightens.

A reader e-mailed us this comment:

*The Circle of Life is somewhat hypocritical. Simba berates Timon and Pumbaa because they don't understand the ecological impact of putting up a resort. Hello—am I missing something, or didn't Disney do just that?*

**TOURING TIPS** Every visitor should see this film.

## Living with the Land *(FastPass+)*  ★★★★

**APPEAL BY AGE**  PRESCHOOL ★★★½  GRADE SCHOOL ★★★½  TEENS ★★★½
YOUNG  ADULTS ★★★★  OVER 30 ★★★★  SENIORS ★★★★½

**What it is** Indoor boat ride chronicling the past, present, and future of farming and agriculture in the United States. **Scope and scale** Major attraction. **When to go** Before 11 a.m., after 1 p.m., or use FastPass+. **Special comments** Go early in the morning and save other Land attractions (except for Soarin') for later in the day. The ride is on the pavilion's lower level. **Authors' rating** Informative without being dull; not to be missed; ★★★★. **Duration of ride** About 14 minutes. **Average wait in line per 100 people ahead of you** 3 minutes; assumes 15 boats operating. **Loading speed** Moderate.

**DESCRIPTION AND COMMENTS** The boat ride takes visitors through swamps, past inhospitable farm environments, and through a futuristic greenhouse where real crops such as giant pumpkins are grown using the latest agricultural technologies.

Many Epcot guests assume that Living with the Land will be too dry and educational for their tastes. A woman from Houston writes:

*I had a bad attitude about Living with the Land—I just didn't think I was up for a movie about wheat farming. Wow, was I surprised!*

**TOURING TIPS** See this attraction before the lunch crowd hits The Land's restaurants. Living with the Land is rarely a good use of FastPass+. If you have a special interest in the agricultural techniques being demonstrated, take the **Behind the Seeds at Epcot** tour (see page 714).

## Soarin' *(FastPass+)*  ★★★★½

**APPEAL BY AGE**  PRESCHOOL ★★★★½  GRADE SCHOOL ★★★★★  TEENS ★★★★½
YOUNG  ADULTS ★★★★½  OVER 30 ★★★★½  SENIORS ★★★★★

**What it is** Flight simulator ride. **Scope and scale** Super-headliner. **When to go** First 30 minutes the park is open, or use FastPass+. **Special comments** Entrance on the lower level of the Land Pavilion. May induce motion sickness; 40″ minimum height requirement. Switching-off option provided (see page 341). **Authors' rating** Exciting and mellow at the same time; not to be missed; ★★★★½. **Duration of ride** 5½ minutes. **Average wait in line per 100 people ahead of you** 4 minutes; assumes 2 concourses operating. **Loading speed** Moderate.

Motion Sickness

**DESCRIPTION AND COMMENTS** Soarin' is a thrill ride for all ages, as exhilarating as a hawk on the wing and as mellow as swinging in a hammock. If you've ever experienced flying dreams, you'll have a sense of how Soarin' feels.

Once you enter the main theater, you're secured in a seat not unlike those on inverted roller coasters. When everyone is in place, the rows

DISNEY DISH WITH JIM HILL

**THREE TO GET READY** With a new ride film for Soarin' set to debut in 2016, thus luring even more people to The Land, the Imagineers feel they need to clear up the crowded conditions on this side of the park. So while the original two Soarin' theaters are shut down to install new projectors, they'll also be adding a third venue. The 50% increase in ride capacity should be worth the behind-the-scenes hassle of getting the extra land cleared.

of seats swing into position, making you feel as if the floor has dropped away, and you're suspended with your legs dangling. Thus hung out to dry, you embark on a simulated hang glider tour, with IMAX-quality images projected all around you and with the flight simulator moving in sync with the movie. The images are well chosen and drop-dead beautiful. Special effects include wind, sound, and even smell. The ride itself is thrilling but perfectly smooth. We think Soarin' is a must-experience for guests of any age who meet the height requirement. And yes, we've interviewed senior citizens who tried it and were crazy about it.

But a North Carolina mom says, "Wait a minute!

*Soarin' was VERY cool but definitely on the scary side for people afraid of heights or who don't like that unsteady feeling. While we were "soaring" up, I was fine, but when we were going down, I had to continually say to myself, "This is only an illusion. I cannot fall out. This is only an illusion. . . . "*

**TOURING TIPS** Having Soarin' opposite Test Track and Mission: SPACE in Future World takes some crowd pressure off both sides of the park. Keep in mind, however, that Test Track and Mission: SPACE serve up a little too much thrill for some guests. Soarin', conversely, is an almost platonic ride for any age. For that reason, it's at the top of the hit parade. See it before 9:30 a.m. or book FastPass+ reservations up to 60 days in advance; expect all reservations to be gone by 2 p.m. on days of moderate attendance or as early as noon on busier days.

## THE SEAS WITH NEMO & FRIENDS PAVILION

FEATURING CHARACTERS FROM DISNEY-PIXAR'S *FINDING NEMO*, this area encompasses one of America's top marine aquariums, a ride that tunnels through the aquarium, an interactive animated film, and a number of first-class educational walk-through exhibits. Altogether it's a stunning package, and not to be missed.

### The Seas Main Tank and Exhibits  ★★★½

**APPEAL BY AGE**  PRESCHOOL ★★★★½  GRADE SCHOOL ★★★★½  TEENS ★★★★
YOUNG  ADULTS  ★★★★        OVER 30  ★★★★        SENIORS  ★★★★

**What it is** A huge saltwater aquarium, plus exhibits on oceanography, ocean ecology, and sea life. **Scope and scale** Major attraction. **When to go** Before 11:30 a.m. or after 5 p.m. **Authors' rating** An excellent marine exhibit; ★★★½. **Average wait in line per 100 people ahead of you** 3½ minutes. **Loading speed** Fast.

**DESCRIPTION AND COMMENTS** The Seas is among Future World's most ambitious offerings. Scientists and divers conduct actual marine experiments in a 200-foot-diameter, 27-foot-deep main tank containing fish, mammals, and crustaceans in a simulation of an ocean ecosystem. Visitors can watch the activity through 8-inch-thick windows below the surface (including some in the Coral Reef restaurant). On entering The Seas, you're directed to the loading area for The Seas with Nemo & Friends (see next profile), an attraction that conveys you via a Plexiglas tunnel through The Seas' main tank. You disembark at Sea Base Alpha, where you can enjoy the other attractions. (If the wait for Nemo & Friends is too long, head straight for the exhibits by going through the pavilion's exit, around back, and to the left of the main entrance.)

The Seas' fish population is substantial, but the strength of this attraction lies in the dozen or so exhibits offered after the ride. Visitors can view fish-breeding experiments, watch short films about sea life, and more. A delightful exhibit showcases clown fish (Nemo), regal blue tang (Dory), and other species featured in *Finding Nemo*. Other highlights include a haunting, hypnotic jellyfish tank; a sea horse aquarium; a stingray exhibit; and a manatee tank.

About two-thirds of the main aquarium is home to reef species, including sharks, rays, and a number of fish that you've seen in quiet repose on your dinner plate. The other third, separated by an inconspicuous divider, houses bottle-nosed dolphins and sea turtles. As you face the main aquarium, the most glare-free viewing windows for the dolphins are on the ground floor to the left by the escalators. For the reef species, it's the same floor on the right by the escalators. Stay as long as you wish.

**TOURING TIPS** With The Seas with Nemo & Friends and *Turtle Talk with Crush*, The Seas is one of Epcot's more popular venues. We recommend experiencing the ride and *Turtle Talk* in the morning before the park gets crowded, saving the excellent exhibits for later.

## The Seas with Nemo & Friends *(FastPass+)* ★★★

| APPEAL BY AGE | PRESCHOOL ★★★★½ | GRADE SCHOOL ★★★★ | TEENS ★★★½ |
|---|---|---|---|
| YOUNG ADULTS ★★★½ | OVER 30 ★★★½ | SENIORS ★★★★ | |

**What it is** Ride through a tunnel in The Seas' main tank. **Scope and scale** Major attraction. **When to go** Before 10:30 a.m., after 3 p.m., or use FastPass+. **Authors' rating** ★★★. **Duration of ride** 4 minutes. **Average wait in line per 100 people ahead of you** 3½ minutes. **Loading speed** Fast.

**DESCRIPTION AND COMMENTS** The Seas with Nemo & Friends is a high-tech ride featuring characters from the animated hit *Finding Nemo*. The ride likewise deposits you at the heart of The Seas, where the exhibits, *Turtle Talk with Crush,* and viewing platforms for the main aquarium are.

Upon entering The Seas, you're given the option of experiencing the ride or proceeding directly to the exhibit area. If you choose the ride, you'll be ushered to its loading area, where you'll be made comfortable in a "clamobile" for your journey through the aquarium. The attraction features technology that makes it seem as if the animated characters are swimming with live fish. Very cool. Almost immediately you meet Mr. Ray and his class and learn that Nemo is missing. The remainder of the odyssey consists of finding Nemo with the help of Dory, Bruce, Marlin, Squirt, and Crush, all characters from the animated feature. Unlike the film, however, the ride ends with a musical finale.

A mom from Asheville, North Carolina, thinks we underestimate the fright factor:

*The Seas with Nemo & Friends is scary—sharks, jellyfish, and anglerfish, along with growling, and so on. My 8-year-old hated it!*

**TOURING TIPS** The earlier you experience the ride, the better (ditto for *Turtle*

*Talk with Crush*). If waits are too much, come back after 3 p.m. or so, or use FastPass+.

## Turtle Talk with Crush *(FastPass+)* ★★★★

**APPEAL BY AGE** PRESCHOOL ★★★★½ GRADE SCHOOL ★★★★½ TEENS ★★★★
YOUNG ADULTS ★★★★      OVER 30 ★★★★      SENIORS ★★★★½

**What it is** Interactive animated film. **Scope and scale** Minor attraction. **When to go** Before 11 a.m., after 3 p.m., or use FastPass+. **Authors' rating** A real spirit-lifter; not to be missed; ★★★★. **Duration of presentation** 17 minutes. **Preshow entertainment** None. **Probable waiting time** 10–20 minutes.

**DESCRIPTION AND COMMENTS** *Turtle Talk with Crush* is an interactive theater show starring the 153-year-old surfer-dude turtle from *Finding Nemo*. Although it starts like a typical Disney-theme-park movie, *Turtle Talk* quickly turns into a surprise interactive encounter as the on-screen Crush begins to have actual conversations with guests in the audience. Real-time computer graphics are used to accurately move Crush's mouth when forming words, and he's voiced by a guy who went to the *Fast Times at Ridgemont High* school of diction.

A mom from Henderson, Colorado, has a crush on Crush:

> Turtle Talk with Crush *is a must-see. Our 4-year-old was picked out of the crowd by Crush, and we were just amazed by the technology that allowed one-on-one conversation. It was adorable and enjoyed by everyone from Grammy and Papa to the 4-year-old!*

**TOURING TIPS** It's unusual to wait more than one or two shows to get in. If you find long lines in the morning, try back after 3 p.m. when more of the crowd has moved on to World Showcase, or use FastPass+.

## The "Mom, I Can't Believe It's Disney!" Fountains ★★★★

**APPEAL BY AGE** PRESCHOOL ★★★★★ GRADE SCHOOL ★★★★★ TEENS ★★★★
YOUNG ADULTS ★★★★      OVER 30 ★★★★      SENIORS ★★★★★

**What it is** Combination fountains and showers. **Scope and scale** Diversion. **When to go** When it's hot. **Special comments** Secretly installed by Martians during *Illumi-Nations*. **Authors' rating** Yes! ★★★★. **Duration of experience** As long as you like. **Probable waiting time** None.

**DESCRIPTION AND COMMENTS** These simple fountains—one on the walkway linking Future World to World Showcase, the other in Future World East, on the way to Test Track—aren't much to look at, but they offers a truly spontaneous experience: a rarity in Walt Disney World, where everything is controlled, from the snow peas in your stir-fry to how frequently the crocodile yawns in the Jungle Cruise.

Spouts of water erupt randomly from the sidewalk. You can frolic in the water or let it cascade down on you, or blow up your britches. On a broiling Florida day, when you think you might spontaneously combust, fling yourself into the fountain and cut loose. Dance, skip, sing, jump, splash, cavort, roll around, stick your toes down the spouts, or catch the water in your mouth as it descends. You can do all of this with your clothes on or, depending on your age, with your clothes off.

**TOURING TIPS** We don't know if the fountains' creator has been drummed out of the corps by the Disney Tribunal of People Who Sit on Sticks (probably), but we're grateful for his courage in introducing one thing that's not super-controlled. We do know that your kids will be right in the middle of the fun before your brain sounds the alert. Our advice: Pack a few pairs of dry shorts and turn the kids loose. You might even want to bring a spare pair for yourself. Or maybe not.

# WORLD SHOWCASE

EPCOT'S OTHER THEMED AREA, World Showcase is an ongoing World's Fair encircling a picturesque 40-acre lagoon. The cuisine, culture, history, and architecture of almost a dozen countries are permanently displayed in individual national pavilions spaced along a 1.2-mile promenade. Pavilions replicate familiar landmarks and present representative street scenes from the host countries.

---

### DISNEY DISH WITH JIM HILL

**ROOMS WITH A WORLD SHOWCASE VIEW** The next round of Disney's time-share resorts won't just be built near the theme parks, but *inside* them, giving Disney Vacation Club members the sort of access they've only dreamed about. The first of these next-generation resorts is supposedly slated for World Showcase, reportedly stretching from behind The American Adventure all the way over to Morocco.

---

World Showcase features some of the loveliest gardens in the United States. In Germany, France, United Kingdom, Canada, and, to a lesser extent, China, they're sometimes tucked away and out of sight of pedestrian traffic on the World Showcase promenade. They're best appreciated during the day, as a Clio, Michigan, woman explains:

> *Visit World Showcase in the daylight in order to view the beautiful gardens. We were sorry we didn't do this because we were following the guide and riding rides that we could have done later in the dark.*

*unofficial* **TIP**
If you don't want to spring for the Passport Kit, the Disney folks will be happy to stamp an autograph book or just about anything else—even your forehead.

Most adults enjoy World Showcase, but many children find it boring. To make it more interesting to children, most Epcot retail shops sell **Passport Kits** for about $10. Each kit contains a blank passport and stamps for every World Showcase country. As kids accompany their folks to each country, they tear out the appropriate stamp and stick it in the passport. Disney has built a lot of profit into this little product, but guests—namely, parents—don't seem to mind the cost. As this dad from Birmingham, Alabama, relates, the Passport Kit helps get the kids through World Showcase with a minimum of impatience, whining, and tantrums:

> *Adding stamps from the Epcot countries was the only way I was able to see all the displays with cheerful children.*

Children also enjoy **Kidcot Fun Stops** (see page 579), designed to make World Showcase more interesting for the 5- to 12-year-old set. The stops are usually nothing more than a large table set up somewhere in each pavilion. Tables are staffed by Disney cast members who stamp passports and lead modest craft projects relating to the host countries.

A mom from Billerica, Massachusetts, is a fan of the Fun Stops:

> *The Kidcot project at Epcot was amazing! Our 2- and 5-year-olds loved making masks and collecting stamps.*

An adult version of passport-stamp collecting is known as **Drinking Around the World** (see page 440), an activity enthusiastically endorsed by a woman from party-hearty New Orleans:

> *We drank a beer in each country at Epcot—Dad was the designated driver—and posed for photos in each, and it quickly became hilarious, as were the progression-of-drunkenness photos that followed.*

World Showcase offers some of the most diverse and interesting shopping in Walt Disney World. See Part Twenty-Two for details.

## Agent P's World Showcase Adventure ★★★★

**APPEAL BY AGE** **PRESCHOOL** ★★½ **GRADE SCHOOL** ★★★★½ **TEENS** ★★★½
**YOUNG ADULTS** ★★½ **OVER 30** ★★★½ **SENIORS** ★★½

**What it is** Interactive scavenger hunt in select World Showcase pavilions. **Scope and scale** Minor attraction. **When to go** Anytime. **Authors' rating** One of our favorite additions to the parks; ★★★★. **Duration of presentation** Allow 30 minutes per adventure. **Preshow entertainment** None. **Probable waiting time** None.

**DESCRIPTION AND COMMENTS** In their eponymous Disney Channel show, Phineas and Ferb have a pet platypus named Perry. In the presence of humans, Perry doesn't do a whole lot. (To be fair, we're not experts on typical platypus behavior, but read on.) When the kids aren't looking, though, Perry takes on the role of Agent P—a fedora-wearing, James Bond–esque secret agent who battles the evil Dr. Doofenshmirtz to prevent world domination (or at least domination of the tristate area in which the show is based).

In Agent P's World Showcase Adventure, you're a secret agent helping Perry, and you receive a cell phone–like device before you're dispatched on a mission to your choice of seven World Showcase pavilions. Once you arrive at the pavilion, the device's video screen and audio provide various clues to help you solve a set of simple puzzles necessary for defeating Doofenshmirtz's plan. As you discover each clue, you'll find special effects such as talking statues and flaming lanterns, plus live "secret agents" stationed in the pavilions just for this attraction. For example, in a prior version of the game you were instructed to utter the phrase "Danger is my cup of tea" to someone working behind the counter at the United Kingdom's tea shop; he or she would respond by handing you a Twinings tea packet on which was printed a clue to solve a puzzle.

Agent P makes static World Showcase pavilions more interactive and kid-friendly. The adventures have simple clues, fast pacing, and neat rewards for solving the puzzles. Len's teenage daughter, Hannah, will happily spend an entire afternoon in World Showcase playing this game and drinking Japanese sodas. Don't be surprised if, having completed one pavilion's adventure, your child wants to do the same.

**TOURING TIPS** Playing the game is free, and no deposit is required for the device. You'll need proof of park admission to sign up before you play, and you can choose both the time and location of your adventure.

Register and pick up your devices at the Italy or Norway Pavilion, the International Gateway (near the UK Pavilion), or the east side of the main walkway from Future World to World Showcase.

Each group can have up to three devices for the same adventure. Because you're working with a device about the size of a cell phone, it's best to have one device for every two people in your group.

A Tucker, Georgia, mother of a 7-year-old is a fan:

*My daughter and I thoroughly enjoyed Agent P's World Showcase Adventure. The interactivity was clever and exciting, the clues were challenging yet simple enough for a child to figure out, plus NO LINES!*

A Granger, Indiana, mom discovered a practical dimension to Agent P:

*A great activity if it's raining: Do the adventure in Mexico. It's all inside, and by the time you're done, the rain usually is, too.*

A Massillon, Ohio, mom was surprised at how long it took to play:

*At Epcot, our 9- and 6-year-olds really enjoyed the Agent P mission, but·it took way longer than the 25 minutes we were told (at least for the UK, the country we chose). It ended up being fine, but people should be aware.*

NOW, MOVING CLOCKWISE around the World Showcase promenade, here are the nations represented and their attractions:

## MEXICO PAVILION

**DESCRIPTION AND COMMENTS** Pre-Columbian pyramids dominate the architecture of this exhibit. One forms the pavilion's facade, and the other overlooks the restaurant and plaza alongside the boat ride—**Gran Fiesta Tour**—inside the pavilion.

**TOURING TIPS** The pyramids contain many authentic and valuable artifacts. Guests tend to zip past these treasures without stopping to look. The village scene inside the pavilion is beautiful and exquisitely detailed. A retail shop occupies most of the left half of the inner pavilion, while Mexico's Kidcot Fun Stop is in the first entryway inside the pyramid. On the opposite side of the main floor is **La Cava del Tequila,** a bar serving more than 100 varieties of tequila as well as margaritas and mezcal.

## Gran Fiesta Tour Starring the Three Caballeros ★★½

| APPEAL BY AGE | PRESCHOOL ★★★★ | GRADE SCHOOL ★★★½ | TEENS ★★★ |
|---|---|---|---|
| YOUNG ADULTS ★★★ | OVER 30 ★★★½ | | SENIORS ★★★½ |

**What it is** Indoor scenic boat ride. **Scope and scale** Minor attraction. **When to go** Before noon or after 5 p.m. **Authors' rating** Visually appealing, light, and relaxing; ★★½. **Duration of ride** About 7 minutes (plus 1½-minute wait to disembark). **Average wait in line per 100 people ahead of you** 4½ minutes; assumes 16 boats in operation. **Loading speed** Moderate.

**DESCRIPTION AND COMMENTS** The Gran Fiesta Tour incorporates animated versions of Donald Duck, José Carioca, and Panchito—an avian singing group called The Three Caballeros, from Disney's 1944 film of the same name—to spice up what has been characterized as a slower-paced Mexican-style It's a Small World.

The ride's premise is that the Caballeros are scheduled to perform at a fiesta, but Donald has gone missing. Large video screens show Donald enjoying Mexico's pyramids, monuments, and water sports while José and Panchito search other Mexican points of interest. Everyone is reunited in time for a rousing concert near the end of the ride.

At the risk of sounding like the Disney geeks we are, we must point out that Panchito is technically the only Mexican Caballero; José Carioca is from Brazil and Donald is from Burbank. In any case, more of the ride's visuals seem to be on the left side of the boat; have small children sit nearer the left to keep their attention, and listen for Donald's humorous monologue as you wait to disembark at the end of the ride.

A family of three from Fanwood, New Jersey, thinks Disney blew it with the Gran Fiesta Tour:

*The Gran Fiesta Tour was dreadful. If the idea was to rid the ride of derogatory Mexican stereotypes, the designers woefully missed the mark.*

A Wilmington, Delaware, woman blames the attraction's lack of appeal on . . . who else?

*Donald Duck has ruined even the minimal value of the Mexico ride.*

**TOURING TIPS** If the line looks longer than 5 minutes, grab a margarita (or several) at La Cava del Tequila and come back in 15.

## NORWAY PAVILION

**DESCRIPTION AND COMMENTS** The Norway Pavilion is complex, beautiful, and architecturally diverse. Surrounding a courtyard is an assortment of traditional Scandinavian buildings, including a replica of the 14th-century Akershus Castle, a wooden stave church (go inside—the doors open!), red-tiled cottages, and replicas of historic buildings representing the traditional designs of Bergen, Alesund, and Oslo. Attractions include an adventure boat ride in the mold of Pirates of the Caribbean, a movie about Norway, and a gallery of art and artifacts. The pavilion houses the **Akershus Royal Banquet Hall,** a sit-down eatery that hosts Disney-princess character meals for breakfast, lunch, and dinner; breakfast here is one of the most popular character meals in all of Walt Disney World. **Kringla Bakeri og Kafe,** an open-air café attached to a bakery, caters to those on the run. Shoppers will find native handicrafts in abundance.

### DISNEY DISH WITH JIM HILL

***FROZEN* ICED IN NORWAY** This time last year, the Imagineers were giving some semiserious thought to overhauling Maelstrom into a *Frozen*-themed attraction. But after 5-hour lines developed to see Anna and Elsa in Norway, Epcot managers saw how all that humanity gummed up the entire pavilion and made it difficult for everyone else to get around World Showcase Lagoon. Worried about traffic flow, Disney put this idea in cold storage while it searches for a way to put a really long queue into the existing Norway buildings.

### Maelstrom (*FastPass+*) ★★★

| APPEAL BY AGE | PRESCHOOL ★★★ | GRADE SCHOOL ★★★½ | TEENS ★★★½ |
|---|---|---|---|
| YOUNG ADULTS ★★★½ | OVER 30 ★★★½ | | SENIORS ★★★★ |

**What it is** Indoor adventure boat ride. **Scope and scale** Major attraction. **When to go** Before 1 p.m., after 7 p.m., or use FastPass+. **Special comments** Animatronic polar bears may frighten a few small children. **Authors' rating** Too short but has its moments; ★★★. **Duration of ride** 4½ minutes, followed by a 5-minute film with a short wait in between; about 14 minutes for all. **Average wait in line per 100 people ahead of you** 4 minutes; assumes 12 or 13 boats operating. **Loading speed** Fast.

**DESCRIPTION AND COMMENTS** In one of Disney World's shorter water rides, guests board dragon-headed ships for a voyage through the fabled rivers and seas of Viking history and legend. They brave trolls, fjords, waterfalls, and a very tame storm at sea. A second-generation Disney water ride, the Viking voyage assembles an impressive array of special effects, combining visual, tactile, and auditory stimuli in a fast-paced and often humorous odyssey. Afterward, guests see a 5-minute film on Norway. We don't have any major problems with Maelstrom, but a vocal minority of our readers consider the ride too brief.

**TOURING TIPS** Sometimes, several hundred guests from a recently concluded screening of *Reflections of China* arrive at Maelstrom en masse. Should you encounter this horde, postpone Maelstrom. If you don't want to see the Norway film, not to worry; you'll be given the opportunity to exit before the film begins. If you're spending the day at Epcot, try to get a FastPass+ reservation at Maelstrom around 2 p.m.

## CHINA PAVILION

**DESCRIPTION AND COMMENTS** A half-sized replica of the Temple of Heaven in Beijing identifies this pavilion. Gardens and reflecting ponds simulate those found in Suzhou, and an art gallery features a lotus-blossom gate and formal saddle roofline. The China Pavilion offers two restaurants: the **Lotus Blossom Cafe,** a fast-food eatery, and **Nine Dragons Restaurant,** a full-service establishment (Advance Reservations recommended) that serves lamentably lackluster Chinese food in a lovely setting. **The Joy of Tea,** a tea stand and specialty-drink vendor, will feed your caffeine addiction until you can make it to Morocco's espresso bar.

The pavilion also hosts regularly updated exhibits on Chinese history, culture, or trendsetting developments. Past exhibits have covered everything from China's indigenous peoples to the layout of Hong Kong Disneyland. The current exhibit features a look at Chinese funeral sculptures, including miniature clay warriors who protect the tombs' occupants.

### Reflections of China   ★★★½

| APPEAL BY AGE | PRESCHOOL ★★★ | GRADE SCHOOL ★★★½ | TEENS ★★★ |
|---|---|---|---|
| YOUNG ADULTS ★★★★ | OVER 30 ★★★½ | | SENIORS ★★★★½ |

**What it is** Film about the Chinese people and culture. **Scope and scale** Major attraction. **When to go** Anytime. **Special comments** Audience stands throughout performance. **Authors' rating** ★★★½. **Duration of presentation** About 14 minutes. **Preshow entertainment** None. **Probable waiting time** 10 minutes.

**DESCRIPTION AND COMMENTS** Pass through the Hall of Prayer for Good Harvest to view the Circle-Vision 360 film *Reflections of China.* Warm and appealing, it's a brilliant (albeit politically sanitized) introduction to the people and natural beauty of China.

**TOURING TIPS** The pavilion is truly beautiful—serene yet exciting. *Reflections of China* plays in a theater where guests must stand, but the film can usually be enjoyed anytime without much waiting. If you're touring World Showcase in a counterclockwise rotation and plan next to go to Norway and ride Maelstrom, position yourself on the far left of the theater (as you face the attendant's podium). After the show, be one of the first to exit. Hurry to Maelstrom as fast as you can to arrive ahead of the several hundred other *Reflections of China* patrons who will be right behind you.

## GERMANY PAVILION

**DESCRIPTION AND COMMENTS** A clock tower, adorned with boy and girl figures, rises above the *platz* (plaza) marking the Germany Pavilion. Dominated by a fountain depicting St. George's victory over the dragon, the platz is encircled by buildings in the style of traditional German architecture. The main attraction is the **Biergarten,** a buffet restaurant that serves traditional German food and beer (Advance Reservations are required; see full profile on page 464 of Part Ten). Yodeling, folk dancing, and oompah-band music are part of the mealtime festivities.

The biggest draw in Germany may be **Karamell-Küche** ("Caramel Kitchen"), offering small caramel-covered sweets including apples, fudge, and cupcakes. We love coming here for a midday snack to tide us over before dinner. Also be sure to check out the large and elaborate model railroad just beyond the restrooms as you walk from Germany toward Italy.

**TOURING TIPS** The pavilion is pleasant and festive. Tour anytime.

## ITALY PAVILION

**DESCRIPTION AND COMMENTS** The entrance to Italy is marked by an 83-foot-tall campanile (bell tower) said to mirror the tower in St. Mark's Square in Venice. Left of the campanile is a replica of the 14th-century Doge's Palace, also in the famous square. The pavilion has a waterfront on the lagoon where gondolas are tied to striped moorings.

**TOURING TIPS** Streets and courtyards in the Italy Pavilion are among the most realistic in World Showcase. For a quick lunch, **Via Napoli** occasionally offers pizza by the slice, and **Tutto Gusto Wine Cellar** serves appetizer plates along with libations. Because there's no film or ride, you can tour the rest of the pavilion at any hour.

## UNITED STATES PAVILION

### The American Adventure ★★★★

| APPEAL BY AGE | PRESCHOOL ★★½ | GRADE SCHOOL ★★★½ | TEENS ★★★½ |
|---|---|---|---|
| YOUNG ADULTS ★★★★ | OVER 30 ★★★★ | | SENIORS ★★★★½ |

**What it is** Patriotic mixed-media and audio-animatronic theater presentation on US history. **Scope and scale** Headliner. **When to go** Anytime. **Authors' rating** Disney's best historic/patriotic attraction; not to be missed; ★★★★. **Duration of presentation** About 29 minutes. **Preshow entertainment** Voices of Liberty choral singing. **Probable waiting time** 25 minutes.

**DESCRIPTION AND COMMENTS** The United States Pavilion consists (not surprisingly) of a fast-food restaurant and a patriotic show.

*The American Adventure* production is a composite of everything Disney does best. Housed in an imposing brick structure reminiscent of Colonial Philadelphia, the 29-minute show is a stirring, but sanitized, rendition of American history narrated by an animatronic Mark Twain (who carries a smoking cigar) and Ben Franklin (who climbs a set of stairs to visit Thomas Jefferson). Behind a stage (almost half the size of a football field) is a 28-by-155–foot rear-projection screen (the largest ever used) on which motion picture images are interwoven with action on stage.

Though the production rouses patriotic emotion in some viewers, others find it deadly dull. A man from Fort Lauderdale, Florida, writes:

*I've always disagreed with you about* The American Adventure. *I saw it about 10 years ago and snoozed through it. We tried it again since you said it was updated. It was still ponderous. Casey used the time for a nap, and I was checking my watch, waiting for it to be over. I'll try it again in 10 years.*

An Erie, Pennsylvania, couple resented Disney's squeaky-clean version of American history:

*Our biggest gripe was with* The American Adventure. *What was that supposed to be? My husband and I were actually embarrassed by that show. They glossed over the dark points of American history and neatly cut out the audio about who bombed Pearl Harbor (after all, Japan is right next door and everyone is happy at WDW). Why do they not focus on the natural beauty of America, the ethnic diversity, immigration, and contributions to the world society?*

But an Iowa City, Iowa, father of three thinks a lot of people are missing the point:

*Cramming all of American history into a 20-minute flick is no easy task, and face it, a theme park is hardly the place for a wholly objective, serious critique of the United States. I think that it's perfectly appropriate for the film, as an attraction in Epcot, to emphasize what's good about the United States.*

**TOURING TIPS** Architecturally, the US Pavilion isn't as interesting as most others in World Showcase. But the presentation, our researchers believe, is the very best patriotic attraction in the Disney repertoire. It usually plays to capacity audiences from around 1:30 to 3:30 p.m., but it isn't hard to get into. Because of the theater's large capacity, it is highly unusual not to be admitted into the next performance.

The adjacent **Liberty Inn** serves a quick, nonethnic fast-food meal.

## JAPAN PAVILION

**DESCRIPTION AND COMMENTS** The five-story, blue-roofed pagoda, inspired by a 17th-century shrine in Nara, sets this pavilion apart. A hill garden behind it features waterfalls, rocks, flowers, lanterns, paths, and rustic bridges. The building on the right (as one faces the entrance) was inspired by the ceremonial and coronation hall at the Imperial Palace at Kyoto. It contains restaurants and a large retail store. Through the center entrance and to the left is the **Bijutsu-kan Gallery,** exhibiting colorful displays from Japanese pop culture. Recent subjects have included everything from postwar tin toys to comics devoted to heroes with "animal spirits."

**TOURING TIPS** Tasteful and elaborate, the pavilion creatively blends simplicity, architectural grandeur, and natural beauty. Tour anytime.

## MOROCCO PAVILION

**DESCRIPTION AND COMMENTS** The bustling market, winding streets, lofty minarets, and stuccoed archways re-create the romance and intrigue of Marrakesh and Casablanca. Attention to detail makes Morocco one of the most exciting World Showcase pavilions. It also has a museum of Moorish art and **Restaurant Marrakesh,** which serves some exotic North African specialties. **Spice Road Table** serves up tasty tapas-style Mediterranean dishes and excellent views of *IllumiNations.*

**TOURING TIPS** Morocco has neither a ride nor a theater. Tour anytime.

## FRANCE PAVILION

**DESCRIPTION AND COMMENTS** *Naturellement,* a replica of the Eiffel Tower is this pavilion's centerpiece. The streets recall La Belle Époque, France's "beautiful time" between 1870 and 1910. The restaurants, along with the bakery and ice-cream shop, are very popular—perhaps explaining why readers rank France as the best World Showcase pavilion.

## *Impressions de France* ★★★½

APPEAL BY AGE   PRESCHOOL ★★½   GRADE SCHOOL ★★★½   TEENS ★★★
YOUNG ADULTS ★★★½        OVER 30 ★★★½          SENIORS ★★★★

**What it is** Film essay on the French people and country. **Scope and scale** Major attraction. **When to go** Anytime. **Authors' rating** Exceedingly beautiful film; ★★★½. **Duration of presentation** About 18 minutes. **Preshow entertainment** None. **Probable waiting time** 15 minutes (at suggested times).

**DESCRIPTION AND COMMENTS** *Impressions de France* is an 18-minute movie projected over 200 degrees onto five screens. Unlike at China and Canada, the audience sits to view this well-made film introducing France's people, cities, and natural wonders.

**TOURING TIPS** The film usually begins on the hour and half-hour. The pavilion's streets are small and become quite congested when visitors queue for the film.

## UNITED KINGDOM PAVILION

**DESCRIPTION AND COMMENTS** A variety of period architecture attempts to capture Britain's city, town, and rural atmospheres. One street alone has a thatched-roof cottage, a four-story timber-and-plaster building, a pre-Georgian plaster building, a formal Palladian exterior of dressed stone, and a city square with a Hyde Park bandstand (whew!).

The pavilion is composed mostly of shops. **The Rose & Crown Pub and Dining Room** feature dining on the water side of the promenade. For fast food, try **Yorkshire County Fish Shop.**

**TOURING TIPS** There are no attractions here, hence minimal congestion, so tour anytime. Mary Poppins, Alice in Wonderland, and/or Pooh can occasionally be found in the character-greeting area; check the *Times Guide* for a schedule. Advance Reservations aren't required for the pub section of the Rose & Crown, making it a nice place to stop for a beer.

## CANADA PAVILION

**DESCRIPTION AND COMMENTS** Canada's cultural, natural, and architectural diversity are reflected in this large and impressive pavilion. Thirty-foot-tall totem poles embellish a Canadian Indian village at the foot of a magnificent château-style hotel. Nearby is a rugged stone building said to be modeled after a famous landmark near Niagara Falls and reflecting Britain's influence on Canada. **Le Cellier,** a steakhouse on the pavilion's lower level, is one of Disney World's highest-rated restaurants. Dinner almost always requires Advance Reservations; you'd have to be incredibly lucky to get a walk-in spot, but it doesn't hurt to ask.

## *O Canada!* ★★★½

APPEAL BY AGE   PRESCHOOL ★★★   GRADE SCHOOL ★★★½   TEENS ★★★½
YOUNG ADULTS ★★★★        OVER 30 ★★★★          SENIORS ★★★★½

**What it is** Film essay on the Canadian people and their country. **Scope and scale** Major attraction. **When to go** Anytime. **Special comments** Audience stands during performance. **Authors' rating** Makes you want to catch the first plane to Canada; ★★★½. **Duration of presentation** About 15 minutes. **Preshow entertainment** None. **Probable waiting time** 9 minutes.

**DESCRIPTION AND COMMENTS** *O Canada!* showcases Canada's natural beauty and population diversity and demonstrates the immense pride that

Canadians have in their country. A film starring Martin Short features clips of Canada's stunning landscape, all the way from Swift Current to Moose Jaw. (Just kidding, eh? From Prince Edward Island to Vancouver.) Visitors leave the theater through **Victoria Gardens,** which was inspired by the famed Butchart Gardens of British Columbia.

Readers like Canada's film. This comment from a Texas mom is typical:

*O Canada!* was entertaining enough to keep our 8-year-old from being bored, and the scenery was amazing.

Speaking of Canada's immense pride, cast members often run a pre-show quiz on Canadian trivia outside the theater before the show. Helpful tips for Americans: Canada's capital is Ottawa; its $1 coin is nicknamed the Loonie, after the bird engraved on it; and the $2 coin is the Toonie—not, unfortunately, the Doubloonie.

**TOURING TIPS** This large-capacity attraction (guests must stand) gets fairly heavy late-morning attendance, as Canada is the first pavilion encountered as one travels counterclockwise around World Showcase Lagoon.

# LIVE ENTERTAINMENT
# *in* EPCOT

LIVE ENTERTAINMENT IN EPCOT is more diverse than in the Magic Kingdom. In World Showcase, it reflects the nations represented. Future World provides a perfect setting for new and experimental offerings. Information about live entertainment on the day you visit is contained in the Epcot guide map, often supplemented by a *Times Guide.* WDW live-entertainment guru Steve Soares usually posts the Epcot performance schedule about a week in advance at **wdwent.com.**

Following are some of the venues, performers, and performances you'll encounter:

**AMERICA GARDENS THEATRE** This large amphitheater, near the US Pavilion, faces World Showcase Lagoon. It hosts pop (and oldies pop) musical acts throughout much of the year, as well as Epcot's popular Candlelight Processional for the Christmas holidays.

**AROUND WORLD SHOWCASE** Impromptu performances take place in and around the pavilions. They include a strolling mariachi group in Mexico; street actors in Italy; a fife-and-drum corps or singing group (**Voices of Liberty**) at the US Pavilion; traditional songs, drums, and dances in Japan; white-faced mimes in France; street comedy and a rock band in the United Kingdom; and bagpipe rock in Canada, among other offerings. Street entertainment occurs about every half-hour.

Live entertainment in World Showcase exceeded the expectations of a mother from Rhode Island and led her son to develop a new talent:

*You should stress that Epcot's World Showcase is really quite lively. Street performances are scheduled throughout the day in the different pavilions. My 2-year-old was taken with the Chinese acrobats and variety performers. We must have watched their shows four times each! As I write this, he's balancing an empty trash can on his feet.*

An Ayden, North Carolina, woman offers this:

*I don't feel that you emphasize the street shows at Epcot enough. My husband and I loved the Japanese drumming, the Chinese and Moroccan acrobats, and the street players in Great Britain. These activities were much more indicative of foreign cultures than the rides.*

Finally, a Vero Beach, Florida, couple puts in a plug for Voices of Liberty at the US Pavilion:

*Voices of Liberty is one of our favorite attractions. The singers' period costuming, rousing songs, incredible a cappella sound, and heartwarming spirit bring forth a huge, sincere response from the audience. Some people go to several of their 15-minute performances each visit, because the singers have a different repertoire each time. American folk and patriotic songs are a delight to hear. There is a short narration for many of the songs, so the folk tradition is being passed on. We encourage you to give them much more press in your guide.*

Done!

**DINNER AND LUNCH SHOWS** Restaurants in World Showcase serve healthy portions of live entertainment to accompany the victuals. Find folk dancing and an oompah band in Germany, singing waiters in Italy, and belly dancers in Morocco. Shows are performed only at dinner in Italy and Morocco, but at both lunch and dinner in Germany. Advance Reservations are required.

**DISNEY CHARACTERS** Characters appear at the Epcot Character Spot (see profile on page 560), elsewhere throughout the park (see pages 344 and 345), and in live shows at America Gardens Theatre and the Showcase Plaza between Mexico and Canada. Times are listed in the *Times Guide*. Finally, **Garden Grill Restaurant** in The Land and **Akershus Royal Banquet Hall** in Norway offer character meals.

**IN FUTURE WORLD** A musical crew of drumming janitors work near the front entrance and at Innoventions Plaza (between the two Innoventions buildings and by the fountain) according to the daily entertainment schedule. They're occasionally complemented by an electric-keyboard band playing what today's kids would call oldies.

**INNOVENTIONS FOUNTAIN SHOW** Numerous times each day, the fountain between the two Innoventions buildings comes alive with pulsating, arching plumes of water synchronized to a musical score. Because no schedule of performances is posted, the fountain show comes as a surprise to many readers, such as this man from Berwickshire, England:

*The musical fountain came as a real surprise and treat. I sat down and listened to it from start to finish on two different occasions. The music is catchy and played through the stereo speakers; the soaring effects of both music and water are really beautiful.*

**KIDCOT FUN STOPS** World Showcase pavilions have areas called Kidcot Fun Stops, where younger children can hear a story or make some small craft representative of the host nation. The Fun Stops are informal, usually set up right on the walkway. During busy times of the year, you'll find Fun Stops at each country in World Showcase. Parents from Nanticoke, Pennsylvania, who thought Epcot would be a drag for their kids, were surprised by their experience:

> Unfortunately we saved Epcot for the last day, thinking the children (ages 5 and 6) would be bored—this was a mistake. The best part was the Kidcot Fun Stops in each pavilion. Imagine, something free at Disney World! [The kids] had a ball.

## ILLUMINATIONS: REFLECTIONS OF EARTH
### (FastPass+)

EPCOT'S GREAT OUTDOOR SPECTACLE (★★★★½) integrates fireworks, laser lights, neon, and music in a stirring tribute to the nations of the world. It's the climax of every Epcot day, and not to be missed.

*IllumiNations* has a plot and a theme, both fairly loaded with symbolism. We'll provide the CliffsNotes version here, because it all sort of runs together in the show itself. The show kicks off with colliding stars that suggest the Big Bang, following which "chaos reigns in the universe." This display is soon replaced by twittering songbirds and various other manifestations signaling the nativity of the Earth. Next comes a brief history of time, from the dinosaurs to ancient Rome, all projected in images on a huge, floating globe. Man's art and inspiration then flash across the globe "in a collage of creativity." All this stimulates the globe to unfold "like a massive flower," bringing on the fireworks crescendo heralding the dawn of a new age. Although only the artistically sensitive will be able to differentiate all this from, say, the last 5 minutes of any *Transformers* movie, we thought you'd like to know what Disney says is happening.

### Getting Out of Epcot After *IllumiNations*
### (Read This Before Selecting a Viewing Spot)

Decide how quickly you want to leave the park after the show, and then pick your vantage point. *IllumiNations* ends the day at Epcot. When it's over, only a couple of gift shops remain open. Because there's nothing to do, everyone leaves at once. This creates a great snarl at Package Pick-Up, the Epcot monorail station, and the Disney bus stop. It also pushes to the limit the tram system hauling guests to their cars in the parking lot. Stroller return, however, is extraordinarily efficient and doesn't cause any delay.

If you're staying at an Epcot resort (Swan, Dolphin, Yacht & Beach Club Resorts, and BoardWalk Inn & Villas), watch the show from somewhere on the southern (US Pavilion) half of World Showcase Lagoon and then leave through the International Gateway between France and the United Kingdom. You can walk or take a boat back to your hotel from the International Gateway. If you have a car and are visiting Epcot in the evening for dinner and *IllumiNations,* park at the Yacht Club or Beach Club. After the show, duck out the International Gateway and be on the road to your hotel in 15 minutes. We should warn you that there's a manned security gate at the entrances to most of the Epcot resorts, including the Yacht and Beach Clubs. You will, of course, be admitted if you have legitimate business, such as dining at one of the hotel restaurants, or, if you park at the BoardWalk Inn & Villas or its overflow lot across the street (requiring a slightly longer walk to Epcot), going to the clubs and restaurants at the BoardWalk. If you're staying at any other Disney hotel and you don't have a car, the fastest way home is to join the mass exodus through the main gate after *IllumiNations* and catch a bus or the monorail.

Those who have a car in the Epcot lot have a more problematic situation. To beat the crowd, find a viewing spot at the end of World Showcase Lagoon nearest Future World (and the exits). Leave as soon as *IllumiNations* concludes, trying to exit ahead of the crowd (note that thousands of people will be doing exactly the same thing). To get a good vantage point between Mexico and Canada on the northern end of the lagoon, stake out your spot 60–100 minutes before the show (45–90 minutes during less-busy periods), or use FastPass+. Otherwise, you may squander more time holding your spot before *IllumiNations* than you would if you watched from the less-congested southern end of the lagoon and took your chances with the crowd upon departure.

More groups get separated and more children get lost following *Illumi Nations* than at any other time. In summer, you'll be walking in a throng of up to 30,000 people. If you're heading for the parking lot, anticipate this congestion and preselect a point in the Epcot entrance area where you can meet if someone gets separated from the group. We recommend the fountain just inside the main entrance. Everyone in your party should be told not to exit through the turnstiles until all noses have been counted. It can be a nightmare if the group gets split up and you don't know whether the others are inside or outside the park.

For those with a car, the main problem is reaching the parking lot. Once you're there, traffic leaves the parking lot pretty well. If you paid close attention to where you parked, consider skipping the tram and walking. If you walk, watch your children closely and hang on to them for all they're worth. The parking lot is pretty wild at this time of night, with hundreds of moving cars.

## Good Locations for Viewing IllumiNations and Other World Showcase Lagoon Performances

The best place to be for any presentation on World Showcase Lagoon is in a seat on the lakeside veranda of **La Cantina de San Angel** in Mexico. Come early (at least 90 minutes before *IllumiNations*) and relax with a cold drink or snack while you wait for the show.

A woman from Pasadena, California, nailed down the seat but missed the relaxation. She writes:

> *Stake out a prime site for* IllumiNations *at least 2 hours ahead, and be prepared to defend it. We got a lakeside table at the Cantina de San Angel at 6:30 p.m. and had a great view of* IllumiNations. *Unfortunately, we had to put up with troops of people asking us to share our table and trying to wedge themselves between our table and the fence.*

**La Hacienda de San Angel** in Mexico, the **Rose & Crown Pub** in the United Kingdom, and **Spice Road Table** in Morocco also have lagoon-side seating. Because of a small wall at the Rose & Crown, however, the

## Where to View IllumiNations

view isn't quite as good as from the Cantina. If you want to combine dinner at these sit-down locations with *IllumiNations,* make a dinner reservation for about 1 hour and 15 minutes before showtime. Report a few minutes early for your seating and tell the host that you want a table outside where you can view *IllumiNations* during or after dinner. Our experience is that the staff will bend over backward to accommodate you. If you aren't able to obtain a table outside, eat inside, and then hang out until showtime. When the lights dim, indicating the start of *IllumiNations,* you'll be allowed to join the diners to watch the show.

Because most guests run for the exits after a presentation, and islands in the southern (US Pavilion) half of the lagoon block the view from some places, the most popular spectator positions are along the northern waterfront from Norway and Mexico to Canada and the United Kingdom. Although the northern half of the lagoon unquestionably offers excellent viewing, it's usually necessary to claim a spot 60–100 minutes before *IllumiNations* begins.

For those who are late finishing dinner, don't want to use FastPass+, or don't want to spend an hour or more standing by a rail, here are some good viewing spots along the southern perimeter (moving counterclockwise from the United Kingdom to Germany) that often go unnoticed until 10–30 minutes before showtime:

1. **International Gateway Island** The pedestrian bridge across the canal near International Gateway spans an island that offers great viewing. This island normally fills 30 minutes or more before showtime.

2. **Second-Floor (Restaurant-Level) Deck of the Mitsukoshi Building in Japan** An Asian arch slightly blocks your sight line, but this covered deck offers a great vantage point, especially if the weather is iffy. Only the Hacienda de San Angel in Mexico is more protected. If you take up a position on the Mitsukoshi deck and find the wind blowing directly at

you, you can be reasonably sure that the smoke from the fireworks won't be far behind.

3. **Gondola Landing at Italy**  An elaborate waterfront promenade offers excellent viewing. Claim a spot at least 30 minutes before showtime.

4. **The Boat Dock Opposite Germany**  Another good vantage point, the dock generally fills 30 minutes before *IllumiNations*. Note that this area may be exposed to more smoke from the fireworks because of Epcot's prevailing winds.

5. **Waterfront Promenade by Germany**  Views are good from the 90-foot-long lagoonside walkway between Germany and China.

Do these suggestions work every time? No. A dad from San Ramon, California, writes:

> *Your recommendations for* IllumiNations *didn't work out in the time frame you mentioned. People had the area staked out 2 hours ahead.*

None of the viewing locations are reservable, and good spots go early on busier nights. But speaking personally, we refuse to hold down a slab of concrete for 2 hours before *IllumiNations* as some people do. Most nights, you can find an acceptable vantage point 15–30 minutes before the show.

It's important not to position yourself under a tree, awning, or anything that blocks your overhead view. If *IllumiNations* is a top priority for you and you want to be certain of getting a good viewing position, claim your place an hour or more before showtime.

A New Yorker who staked out his turf well in advance made this suggestion for staying comfortable until showtime:

> *Your excellent guide also served as a seat cushion while I waited seated on the ground. Make future editions thicker for greater comfort.*

## *ILLUMINATIONS* CRUISE

FOR A REALLY GOOD VIEW, you can charter a pontoon boat for $346 with tax. Captained by a Disney cast member, the boat holds up to 10 guests. Your captain will take you for a little cruise and then position the boat in a perfect place to watch *IllumiNations*. Chips, soda, and water are provided; sandwiches and more-substantial food items may be arranged through Disney reservations or Yacht Club Private Dining at ☎ 407-934-3160. Cruises depart from Bayside Marina. A major indirect benefit of the charter is that you can enjoy *IllumiNations* without fighting the mob afterward. Because this is a private charter rather than a tour, only your group will be aboard. Life jackets are provided, but you can wear them at your discretion. Because there are few boats, charters sell out fast. To reserve, call ☎ 407-WDW-PLAY (939-7529) at exactly 7 a.m. Eastern time 180 days before the day you want to charter. Because the Disney reservations system counts days in a somewhat atypical manner, we recommend phoning about 185 days out to have a Disney agent specify the exact morning to call for reservations. Similar charters are available on the Seven Seas Lagoon to watch the Magic Kingdom fireworks.

# TRAFFIC PATTERNS
## *in* EPCOT

IN THE MAGIC KINGDOM, Main Street, U.S.A., with its shops and eateries, serves as a huge gathering place when the park opens and funnels visitors to the Central Plaza, where entrances branch off to the lands. Thus, crowds are first welcomed and entertained (on Main Street), and then distributed almost equally to the lands.

At Epcot, by contrast, Spaceship Earth, the park's premier landmark and one of its headliner attractions, is just inside the main entrance. When visitors enter the park, they almost irresistibly head for it. Hence, a bottleneck forms less than 75 yards from the turnstiles as soon as the park opens.

Early-morning crowds form in Future World because most of the park's rides and shows are there. Except at Mission: SPACE, Soarin', and Test Track, visitors are fairly equally distributed among Future World attractions. Mission: SPACE, Soarin', and Test Track are the major early-morning magnets. These three biggies will draw so many guests that the other attractions in Future World don't develop long waits until 11 a.m. or later.

Between 9 and 11 a.m., crowds build in Future World. Even when World Showcase opens (usually 11 a.m.), more people are entering Future World than are leaving for the Showcase. Attendance continues building in Future World between noon and 2 p.m. World Showcase attendance builds rapidly as lunchtime approaches. Exhibits at the far end of World Showcase Lagoon report large audiences from about noon through 6:30 or 7:30 p.m.

The Magic Kingdom's premier attractions are situated on the far perimeters of its lands to distribute crowds evenly. Epcot's cluster of attractions in Future World holds the greater part of the throng in the smaller part of the park. World Showcase has only two major draws—

*unofficial* **TIP**
Visitors aware of the congestion at Spaceship Earth can take advantage of the excellent opportunities it provides for escaping waits at other Future World attractions.

Maelstrom in Norway and The American Adventure—but these are not in the same league as the three super-headliners in Future World, and consequently you have no compelling reason to rush to see them. The bottom line: Crowds build all morning and into early afternoon in Future World. Not until the evening meal approaches do crowds equalize in Future World and World Showcase. Evening crowds in World Showcase, however, don't compare in size with morning and midday crowds in Future World. Attendance throughout Epcot is normally lighter in the evening.

Some guests leave Epcot in the early evening, but most of them exit en masse after *IllumiNations*. Upward of 30,000 people head for the parking lot and monorail station at once. Still, this congestion doesn't compare with the post-fireworks gridlock at the Magic Kingdom. One primary reason for the easier departure from Epcot is that its parking lot is adjacent to the park, not separated from it by a lake as at the Magic Kingdom. At the Magic Kingdom, departing visitors form bottlenecks at the monorail to the Transportation and Ticket Center and main parking lot. At Epcot, they proceed directly to their cars.

To get a complete view of the actual traffic patterns while you're in the park, use our mobile app, **Lines** (**touringplans.com/lines**). The app gives you current wait times and future estimates in half-hour increments for today and tomorrow. A quick glance shows how traffic patterns affect wait times throughout the day.

# EPCOT TOURING PLANS

TOURING EPCOT IS MUCH MORE STRENUOUS and demanding than touring the other theme parks. Epcot requires about twice as much walking. And, unlike the Magic Kingdom, Epcot has no effective in-park transportation; wherever you want to go, it's always quicker to walk. Our plans will help you avoid crowds and bottlenecks on days of moderate-to-heavy attendance, but they can't shorten the distance you have to walk. (Wear comfortable shoes.) On days of lighter attendance, when crowd conditions aren't a critical factor, the plans will help you organize your tour. We offer four touring plans:

- Epcot One-Day Touring Plan
- Epcot Authors' Selective One-Day Touring Plan
- Epcot One-Day Touring Plan for Parents with Small Children
- Epcot Two-Day Early-Riser Touring Plan

The One-Day Touring Plan packs as much as possible into one long day and requires a lot of hustle and stamina. The Authors' Selective One-Day Touring Plan eliminates some lesser (in the authors' opinion) attractions and offers a somewhat more relaxed tour if you have only one day. The One-Day Touring Plan for Parents with Small Children gives little ones the best of Epcot while also building in needed rest time. Finally, the Two-Day Early-Riser Touring Plan is the most efficient, eliminating 90% of the backtracking and extra walking required by the other plans while still providing a comprehensive tour.

In response to Disney introducing FastPass+, we've listed the approximate+ return times for which you should attempt to make reservations. (The touring plan should work with anything close to the times shown.) Check **touringplans.com** for the latest developments and information.

### "Not a Touring Plan" Touring Plans

For the type-B reader, these touring plans (see page 820) avoid detailed step-by-step strategies for saving every last minute in line. For Epcot, these "not" touring plans include advice for adults and parents with one day in the park, for anyone with two days, and for anyone with an afternoon and a full day to tour.

### BEFORE YOU GO

**1.** Call ☎ 407-824-4321 or check the day before you go to verify official opening time.

**2.** Make reservations at the Epcot full-service restaurant(s) of your choice 180 days before your visit.

**3.** Make FastPass+ reservations 60 or 30 days in advance.

## EPCOT ONE-DAY TOURING PLAN FOR ADULTS
*(page 828)*

**FOR** Adults and children age 8 or older.

**ASSUMES** Willingness to experience all major rides and shows.

This plan requires a lot of walking and a small amount of backtracking in order to avoid long waits in line. A little extra walking and some early-morning hustle will spare you 2–3 hours of standing in line. You might not complete the tour. How far you get depends on how quickly you move from attraction to attraction, how many times you rest and eat, how quickly the park fills, and what time it closes.

This plan is not recommended for families with very young children. If you're touring with young children and have only one day, use the Epcot Authors' Selective One-Day Touring Plan or the Epcot One-Day Touring Plan for Parents with Small Children. Break after lunch and relax at your hotel, returning to the park in late afternoon. If you can allocate two days to Epcot, use the Epcot Two-Day Early-Riser Touring Plan.

## EPCOT AUTHORS' SELECTIVE ONE-DAY TOURING PLAN FOR ADULTS *(page 829)*

**FOR** All parties.

**ASSUMES** Willingness to experience major rides and shows.

This touring plan includes only what the authors believe is the best that Epcot has to offer. Families with children younger than age 8 should review Epcot attractions in our Small-Child Fright-Potential Chart in Part Six (see pages 332–335). Rent a stroller for any child small enough to fit in one, and take your young children back to the hotel for a nap after lunch. If you can allocate two days to Epcot, use the Epcot Two-Day Early-Riser Touring Plan (see next page).

## EPCOT ONE-DAY TOURING PLAN FOR PARENTS WITH SMALL CHILDREN *(page 830)*

**FOR** Parents with children younger than age 8.

This touring plan is for parents and kids who want to experience Epcot's best attractions in a single day. It's the most popular Epcot touring plan at **touringplans.com.**

The plan includes a midday break of 3–4 hours. Make time for this break by skipping intense attractions such as Test Track and Mission: SPACE and by forgoing many World Showcase exhibits. Regarding World Showcase, we encourage families to sign up for a free interactive game called Agent P's World Showcase Adventure (see page 571), which most kids find endlessly entertaining.

Families with children younger than age 8 should review Epcot attractions in our Small-Child Fright-Potential Chart in Part Six (see pages 332–335). Rent a stroller for any child small enough to fit in one.

## EPCOT TWO-DAY EARLY-RISER TOURING PLAN
*(pages 831 and 832)*

FOR All parties.

This is the most efficient of the Epcot touring plans. It takes advantage of easy touring made possible by morning's light crowds. Most folks will complete each day of the plan by midafternoon. While the plan doesn't include *IllumiNations* or other evening festivities, these activities, along with dinner at an Epcot restaurant, can be added at your discretion.

Families with children younger than age 8 should review Epcot attractions in our Small-Child Fright-Potential Chart in Part Six (see pages 332–335). Rent a stroller for any child small enough to fit in one.

# PART THIRTEEN

# DISNEY'S ANIMAL KINGDOM

WITH ITS LUSH FLORA, WINDING STREAMS, meandering paths, and exotic setting, Disney's Animal Kingdom is a stunningly beautiful theme park. The landscaping alone conjures images of rainforest, veldt, and formal gardens. Soothing, mysterious, and exciting, every vista is a feast for the eye. Add to this loveliness a population of more than 1,000 animals, replicas of Africa's and Asia's most intriguing architecture, and a diverse array of singularly original attractions, and you have the most distinctive of all the Disney theme parks. In Animal Kingdom, Disney has created an environment to savor.

At 500 acres, Animal Kingdom is five times the size of the Magic Kingdom and almost twice the size of Epcot. But as is the case with Disney's Hollywood Studios, most of Animal Kingdom's vast geography is accessible only on guided tours or as part of attractions. Animal Kingdom consists of five sections, or "lands": **The Oasis, Discovery Island, DinoLand U.S.A., Africa,** and **Asia.**

Its size notwithstanding, Animal Kingdom features a limited number of attractions. To be exact, there are seven rides, several walk-through exhibits, an indoor theater, three amphitheaters, a conservation exhibit, and a children's playground.

Animal Kingdom's opening was seen as Disney taking dead aim at Busch Gardens in Tampa, a theme park known for its exceptional zoological exhibits, and one that had seen a marked increase in attendance in the 1990s with the addition of numerous thrill rides. Up to that time, Disney had preferred the neatly controlled movements of audio-animatronic animals to the unpredictable behaviors of real critters.

*unofficial* **TIP**
Three attractions—**DINOSAUR, Expedition Everest,** and **Kilimanjaro Safaris**—are among the best in the Disney repertoire.

Unfortunately for Disney, however, the combination of creative natural-habitat zoological exhibits and coasters developed by Busch Gardens became immensely popular, and as any student of the Walt Disney Company can attest, there's nothing like a successful competitor to make the Disney folks change their tune. So, all the press releases aside, Disney's Animal Kingdom was designed as a combination of natural-habitat zoological exhibits and thrill rides. Big surprise!

Even if the recipe was copied, the Disney version serves up more than its share of innovations. For starters, there's lots of space, thus allowing for the sweeping vistas that Discovery Channel viewers would expect in, say, an African veldt setting. Then there are the enclosures, natural in appearance, with few or no apparent barriers between you and the animals. The operative word, of course, is *apparent*. That flimsy stand of bamboo separating you from a gorilla is actually a neatly disguised set of steel rods embedded in concrete. The Imagineers even take a crack at certain animals' stubborn unwillingness to be on display: A lion that would rather sleep out of sight under a bush, for example, is lured to center stage with nice, cool, climate-controlled artificial rocks.

Animal Kingdom has received mixed reviews since it opened in 1998. Guests complain loudly about the park layout and the necessity of backtracking through Discovery Island in order to access the various themed areas. Congested walkways and lack of shade also rank high on the gripe list. However, most of the attractions have been well received. Also praised are the animal exhibits as well as the park architecture and landscaping. We marvel at the fact that readers of similar backgrounds come away with such vastly differing opinions.

In truth, Animal Kingdom is a park to linger over and savor—two things that Disney, with its crowds, lines, and regimentation, has conditioned us not to do. But many people intuit that Animal Kingdom must be approached in a different way, including this mother of three (ages 5, 7, and 9) from Hampton Bay, New York:

> Despite the crowds, we really enjoyed Animal Kingdom. In order to enjoy it, you really must have the right attitude. It's an educational experience, not a thrill park. We spoke to a cast member who played games with the kids—my daughter found a drawer full of butterflies, and the boys located a hidden ostrich egg and lion skull.

A family from the Southwest agrees, writing:

> Animal Kingdom with kids should be approached as you would bird-watching, fossil hunting, or nature walks. To enjoy it, you need to slow down, stop and look, and, especially, engage the cast members. Encourage your children to ask questions; the answers are educational, enlightening, and a wonderful alternative to standing in a hot queue.

And though we offer one-day touring plans for Animal Kingdom, a Cleveland reader argues for more time:

> I can't see how Animal Kingdom takes less than a day. There is so much to look at, animal-wise, architecturally, street performances— we kept going back at different times, and each time we saw the place literally in a new light or with different animals active.

These readers are right: Animal Kingdom's best features are its animals, nature trails, and cast members. We think the **Wilderness Explorers** scavenger hunt (see page 598) ties together all of the park's best elements, so we've added it to our Animal Kingdom touring plan. It's a lot of fun to play, and you just might learn something along the way.

*Continued on page 592*

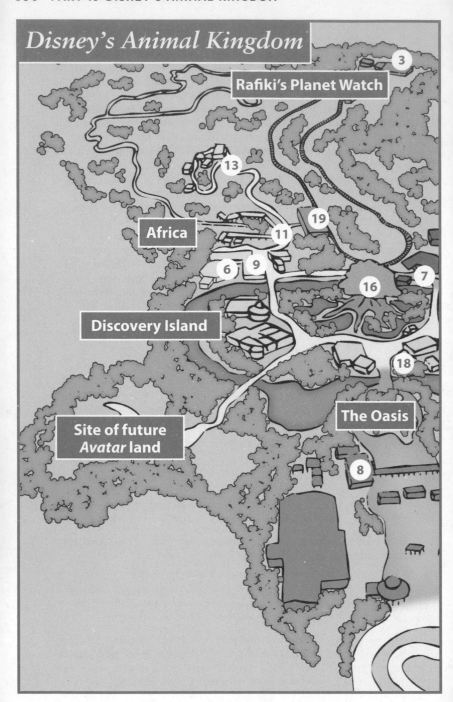

Disney's Animal Kingdom

Rafiki's Planet Watch

3

13

19

Africa

11

6   9

7

16

Discovery Island

18

The Oasis

Site of future
*Avatar* land

8

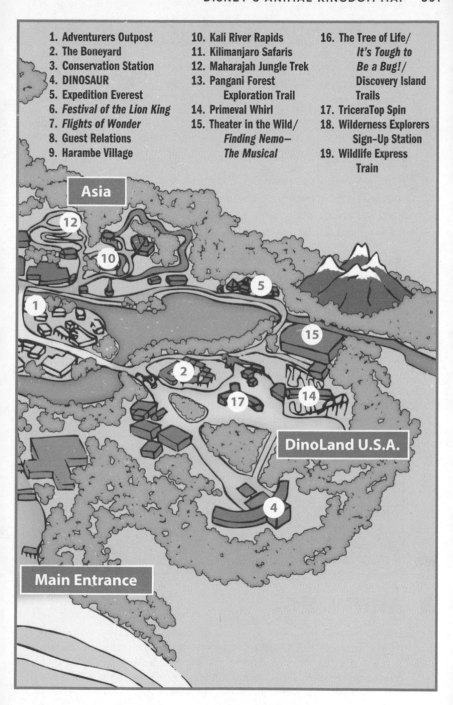

1. Adventurers Outpost
2. The Boneyard
3. Conservation Station
4. DINOSAUR
5. Expedition Everest
6. *Festival of the Lion King*
7. *Flights of Wonder*
8. Guest Relations
9. Harambe Village
10. Kali River Rapids
11. Kilimanjaro Safaris
12. Maharajah Jungle Trek
13. Pangani Forest
    Exploration Trail
14. Primeval Whirl
15. Theater in the Wild/
    *Finding Nemo—*
    *The Musical*
16. The Tree of Life/
    *It's Tough to*
    *Be a Bug!/*
    Discovery Island
    Trails
17. TriceraTop Spin
18. Wilderness Explorers
    Sign-Up Station
19. Wildlife Express
    Train

Asia

DinoLand U.S.A.

Main Entrance

## Disney's ANIMAL KINGDOM Services

MOST OF THE PARK'S SERVICE FACILITIES are inside the main entrance and on Discovery Island as follows:

**Baby Care Center** On Discovery Island, behind the MyMagic+ Service Center

**Banking Services** ATMs at the main entrance, by the turnstiles, and near DINOSAUR in DinoLand U.S.A.

**Camera Supplies** Just inside the main entrance at Garden Gate Gifts, in Africa at Mombasa Marketplace, and at other retail shops throughout the park

**Entertainment Information** In the *Times Guide,* available at Guest Relations

**First Aid** On Discovery Island, next to the MyMagic+ Service Center

**Guest Relations/Information** Inside the main entrance to the left

**Lost and Found** Inside the main entrance to the left

**Lost Persons** Can be reported at Guest Relations and at the Baby Care Center

**Storage Lockers** Inside the main entrance to the left

**Wheelchair, ECV/ESV, and Stroller Rentals** Inside the main entrance, to the right

*Continued from page 589*

Finally, a major construction project currently under way will bring the flora and fauna of James Cameron's *Avatar* to the park sometime in 2017. The area formerly known as Camp Minnie-Mickey has been demolished and its attractions relocated to other areas of the park to make way for the *Avatar* land. Most of the construction will be in backstage areas, so impact to in-park guests should be limited.

### DISNEY DISH WITH JIM HILL

**WANTED: TALL BLUE FOLKS** Disney is trying to find performers to portray the Na'vi, those tall, blue-skinned, catlike people from *Avatar*. According to the preliminary job description, applicants must have experience working on stilts, be unafraid of heights, have no allergies or skin conditions that would preclude the wearing of body paint, and be able to wear colored contact lenses. Look for auditions to get under way in late 2016, out ahead of *Avatar* land's spring 2017 opening.

# ARRIVING

DISNEY'S ANIMAL KINGDOM is off Osceola Parkway in the southwest corner of Walt Disney World and is not too far from Blizzard Beach, Coronado Springs Resort, and the All-Star Resorts. For driving directions, see page 373. Animal Kingdom Lodge is about a mile away from the park on its west side. From Interstate 4, take Exit 64B, US 192, to the so-called Walt Disney World main entrance (World Drive) and follow the signs to Animal Kingdom. Animal Kingdom has its own vast pay parking lot with close-in parking for the disabled. Once parked, you can walk to the entrance or catch a ride on one of Disney's trams.

The park is connected to other Walt Disney World destinations by the Disney bus system. If you're staying at a Disney resort and plan to arrive at Animal Kingdom before park opening, use Disney transportation rather than taking your own car.

## OPERATING HOURS

ANIMAL KINGDOM'S OPENING TIME corresponds to that of the other parks. Thus, you can expect a 9 a.m. opening during less busy times of the year and an 8 a.m. opening during holidays and high season. This park usually closes well before the others in Disney World, however—as early as 5 p.m., in fact, during off-season. More common is a 6 or 7 p.m. closing.

Animal Kingdom's standard park-opening procedure lets all guests through the turnstiles about 15–30 minutes before official park opening. When this happens, you'll usually find Kilimanjaro Safaris, Expedition Everest, and TriceraTop Spin already open.

During slower or colder times of year, Disney may delay the daily opening of Kali River Rapids in Asia, as well as the Boneyard playground, the Wildlife Express Train, and Conservation Station. These procedures may change, so check the *Times Guide* or our mobile app, **Lines,** for the exact schedule when you arrive. The rest of the attractions come online at official park opening time.

On holidays and other days of projected heavy attendance, Disney will open the park 30–60 minutes early.

Many guests wrap up their tour and leave by 3:30 or 4 p.m. Lines for the major rides and the 3-D movie in The Tree of Life will usually thin appreciably between 4 p.m. and closing time. If you arrive at 2 p.m. and take in a couple of stage shows, waits should be tolerable by the time you hit The Tree of Life and the rides.

Animal Kingdom currently holds two morning Extra Magic Hours sessions per week, although we don't think they save you all that much time in line. Our advice is to get an extra hour of sleep and visit when early entry is not in effect.

Kilimanjaro Safaris and the Pangani Forest Exploration Trail close around 30–60 minutes before sunset. Thus, as days get shorter with the change of seasons, the attractions close earlier in the day. In the fall, Disney closes all animal exhibits as early as 4:45 p.m.

# GETTING ORIENTED

AT THE ENTRANCE PLAZA ARE TICKET KIOSKS fronting the main entrance. To your right, before the turnstiles, is an ATM. After you pass through the turnstiles, wheelchair and stroller rentals are to your right. Guest Relations—the park headquarters for information, handout park maps, entertainment schedules (*Times Guides),* missing persons, and lost and found—is to the left. Nearby are restrooms, public phones, and rental lockers. Beyond the entrance plaza, you enter **The Oasis,** a lushly vegetated network of converging pathways winding through a landscape punctuated with streams, waterfalls, and misty glades and inhabited by what Disney calls "colorful and unusual animals."

The park is arranged somewhat like the Magic Kingdom, in a hub-and-spoke configuration. The lush, tropical Oasis serves as Main Street, funneling visitors to **Discovery Island** at the center of the park. Dominated by the park's central icon, the 14-story hand-carved **Tree of Life,** Discovery Island is the park's retail and dining center. From Discovery Island, guests can access the respective themed areas of **Africa, Asia,** and **DinoLand U.S.A.** Discovery Island additionally hosts a theater attraction in The Tree of Life, and a number of short nature trails.

Even if you dawdle in the shops and linger over the wildlife exhibits, you should easily be able to take in Animal Kingdom in one day.

## FASTPASS+ ATTRACTIONS IN DISNEY'S ANIMAL KINGDOM

FASTPASS+ IS OFFERED at eight attractions in the park:

| AFRICA | DINOLAND U.S.A. |
|---|---|
| • *Festival of the Lion King* | • DINOSAUR |
| • Kilimanjaro Safaris | • *Finding Nemo—The Musical* |
| | • Primeval Whirl |
| **ASIA** | |
| • Expedition Everest | **DISCOVERY ISLAND** |
| • Kali River Rapids | • *It's Tough to Be a Bug!* |
| | • Meet Favorite Disney Pals at Adventurers Outpost |

Our print and online touring plans most frequently suggest Fast-Pass+ reservations for **Kali River Rapids.** Why? Similarly to Peter Pan's Flight at the Magic Kingdom, people go elsewhere first thing in the morning and come back to Kali after they've seen a few other attractions. In Animal Kingdom, adults and teens head to Expedition Everest in Asia first, while parents with children too small for Everest head for Kilimanjaro Safaris in Africa. Using FastPass+ at Kali River Rapids allows you to experience other important attractions early in the morning, when lines are short, while still giving you a relatively short line at Kali to contend with when you arrive. Another advantage to using Fast-Pass+ for this attraction is that you can schedule your ride for either right before you leave the park (to avoid sloshing around all day) or during the warmer part of an otherwise cool day.

Our second most frequent recommendation for FastPass+ is Africa's **Kilimanjaro Safaris.** Most of our touring plans for tweens, teens, and adults start off at Expedition Everest and try to get through DINO-SAUR and Primeval Whirl in DinoLand U.S.A. before the crowds arrive. This also keeps backtracking to a minimum. Those plans generally visit the Safaris around either lunchtime or late afternoon, and using FastPass+ then will save you a lot of time in line.

**DINOSAUR** and the **Adventurers Outpost** character meet-and-greet show up on our Animal Kingdom touring plans for parents with small children. Like Kali River Rapids, these aren't going to be the first stop of your day, and using FastPass+ at these attractions will generally save more time in line than using FastPass+ at any other child-friendly attraction in our plans.

**Expedition Everest** is our least frequently suggested FastPass+ attraction. This is because our software generally puts it as the first step in any Animal Kingdom touring plan. While posted wait times at Expedition Everest can average 60–80 minutes during summer and more during holidays, getting to Everest first thing in the morning lets you avoid those lines and save FastPass+ for something else. What's more, Expedition Everest has a single-rider line—if you can't get a FastPass+ reservation and you don't mind splitting up your group for one ride, the single-rider line is a great option.

FastPass+ kiosk locations in Animal Kingdom are as follows:

- To the left of Expedition Everest's entrance in Asia
- At Kali River Rapids in Asia
- At Primeval Whirl in DinoLand U.S.A.
- In front of the Disney Outfitters store on Discovery Island
- In front of the MyMagic+ Service Center, near Island Mercantile on Discovery Island

## SPECIAL EVENTS IN DISNEY'S ANIMAL KINGDOM

THE MAGIC KINGDOM regularly hosts after-hours special events such as Mickey's Not So Scary Halloween Party and Very Merry Christmas Party. These are big moneymakers for Disney, because the park closes early to regular guests (who've paid full price for admission) and a separate entrance fee is charged for attending the party. At press time, Disney was trying the same idea at Animal Kingdom.

Called **Harambe Nights,** and running (for now) from 7 p.m. to 10:30 p.m. on Saturday nights during summer, the event includes a retelling of the *Lion King* story, including a live orchestra and digital special effects, at the *Festival of the Lion King* theater in Africa; African-themed appetizers, desserts, wine, and beer; and a post-show "street party" with live music, Disney characters, and a buffet (the Indian-African fusion menu was designed by chefs from Boma, Jiko, and Sanaa, the three acclaimed restaurants at Animal Kingdom Lodge).

Tickets start at around $84 for children ages 3–9 and $127 for adults (including tax); that gets you regular seats in the theater. Tickets including premium theater seats are $100 per child and $143 per adult.

## DINING IN DISNEY'S ANIMAL KINGDOM

COUNTER-SERVICE RESTAURANTS in Animal Kingdom are profiled in Part Ten, starting on page 453. For full-service profiles, see the section starting on page 457.

# *The* OASIS

**DESCRIPTION AND COMMENTS** Though the functional purpose of The Oasis is the same as that of Main Street in the Magic Kingdom—that is, to funnel guests to the center of the park—it also serves as what Disney calls a "transitional experience." In plain English, this means that it sets the stage and gets you into the right mood to enjoy Disney's Animal Kingdom.

You'll know the minute you pass through the turnstiles that this is not just another Main Street. Where Main Street, Hollywood Boulevard, and the Epcot entrance plaza direct you like an arrow straight into the heart of the respective parks, The Oasis immediately envelops you in an environment that is replete with choices. There's no one broad thoroughfare, but rather multiple paths. Each delivers you to Discovery Island at the center of the park, but the path you choose and what you see along the way are up to you. Nothing obvious clues you in about where you're going—there's no Cinderella Castle or giant golf ball to beckon you. Instead you'll find a lush, green, canopied landscape with streams, grottoes, and waterfalls, an environment that promises adventure without revealing its nature.

The natural-habitat zoological exhibits in The Oasis are representative of those throughout the park. Although extraordinarily lush and beautiful, the exhibits are primarily designed for the comfort and well-being of the animals.

A sign identifies the animal(s) in each exhibit, but there's no guarantee that the animals will be immediately visible. Because most habitats are large and provide ample terrain for the occupants to hide, you must linger and concentrate, looking for small movements in the vegetation. When you do spot the animal, you may make out only a shadowy figure, or perhaps only a leg or a tail.

**TOURING TIPS** The Oasis is a place to savor and appreciate, and although this is exactly what the designers intended, it will be largely lost on Disney-conditioned guests who blitz through at warp speed to queue up for the big attractions. If you're a blitzer in the morning, plan to spend some time in The Oasis on your way out of the park. The Oasis usually closes 30–60 minutes after the rest of the park.

# DISCOVERY ISLAND

DISCOVERY ISLAND COMBINES A PROFUSION of tropical greenery with whimsical equatorial African architecture. Connected to the other lands by bridges, the island is the hub from which guests can access the park's various themed areas. A village is arrayed in a crescent around the base of Animal Kingdom's signature landmark, **The Tree of Life.** Towering 14 stories above the village, it's this park's version of Cinderella Castle or Spaceship Earth. Flanked by pools, meadows, and exotic gardens populated by a diversity of birds and animals, The Tree of Life houses a theater attraction inspired by the Disney-Pixar film *A Bug's Life*.

As you enter Discovery Island over the bridge from The Oasis and the park entrance, you'll see The Tree of Life directly ahead, at 12 o'clock. The bridge to Asia is to the right of the tree at 2 o'clock, with the bridge to DinoLand U.S.A. at roughly 4 o'clock. The bridge connecting The Oasis to Discovery Island is at 6 o'clock, the bridge to the future *Avatar* land is at 8 o'clock, and the bridge to Africa is at 11 o'clock.

Discovery Island is the park's central headquarters for shopping, dining, and services. Here you'll find **First Aid** and the **Baby Care Center.** For the best selection of Disney merchandise, try **Island Mercantile.** Counter-service food and snacks are available, but there are no sit-down eateries—the three full-service restaurants in the park are the **Rainforest Cafe,** to the left of the main entrance; **Tusker House Restaurant,** in Africa; and **Yak & Yeti Restaurant,** in Asia.

## Meet Favorite Disney Pals at Adventurers Outpost
### (FastPass+) ★★★½

| APPEAL BY AGE | PRESCHOOL ★★★★ | GRADE SCHOOL ★★★★ | TEENS ★★★★ |
|---|---|---|---|
| YOUNG ADULTS ★★★½ | OVER 30 ★★★ | | SENIORS ★★★½ |

**What it is** Character-greeting venue. **Scope and scale** Minor attraction. **When to go** First thing in the morning, after 5 p.m., or use FastPass+. **Authors' rating** Nicely themed (and air-conditioned); ★★★½. **Duration of experience** About 2 minutes. **Probable waiting time** About 20 minutes. **Queue speed** Fast.

**DESCRIPTION AND COMMENTS** An indoor, air-conditioned character-greeting location for Mickey and Minnie Mouse, Adventurers Outpost is decorated with photos, memorabilia, and souvenirs from the Mouses' world travels.

**TOURING TIPS** The Outpost features two greeting rooms with two identical sets of characters, so lines move fairly quickly. Good use of FastPass+ if you have kids too small to ride Expedition Everest or DINOSAUR.

## The Tree of Life / *It's Tough to Be a Bug!* (FastPass+) ★★★★

| APPEAL BY AGE | PRESCHOOL ★★★ | GRADE SCHOOL ★★★★ | TEENS ★★★★ |
|---|---|---|---|
| YOUNG ADULTS ★★★★ | OVER 30 ★★★★ | | SENIORS ★★★★ |

**What it is** 3-D theater show. **Scope and scale** Major attraction. **When to go** Anytime. **Special comments** The theater is inside the tree. **Authors' rating** Zany and frenetic and not to be missed; ★★★★. **Duration of presentation** About 8 minutes. **Probable waiting time** 12–20 minutes.

**DESCRIPTION AND COMMENTS** The Tree of Life, apart from its size, is quite a work of art—we think it's the most visually compelling structure in any Disney park. Although from afar it's certainly magnificent and imposing, it's not until you examine the tree at close range that you truly appreciate its rich detail. What appears to be ancient gnarled bark is, in fact, hundreds of carvings depicting all manner of wildlife, each integrated seamlessly into the trunk, roots, and limbs of the tree.

In sharp contrast to the grandeur of the tree is the subject of the attraction housed within its trunk. Called *It's Tough to Be a Bug!,* this humorous 3-D presentation is about the difficulties of being a very small creature. Lighthearted and whimsical, the show is similar to *Mickey's PhilharMagic* at the Magic Kingdom in that it combines a 3-D film with an arsenal of tactile and visual special effects. We rate *Bug* as not to be missed.

**TOURING TIPS** *It's Tough to Be a Bug!* is rarely crowded even on the busiest days. Go in the morning after Kilimanjaro Safaris, Kali River Rapids, Expedition Everest, and DINOSAUR. If you miss the *Bug* in the morning, try again in the late afternoon.

Note that *It's Tough to Be a Bug!* is very intense and the special effects will do a number on guests of all ages who are squeamish about insects. A mother of two from Williamsville, New York, shared this experience:

*It's Tough to Be a Bug! was my girls' first Disney experience, and almost their last. The storyline was nebulous and difficult to follow—all they were aware of was the torture of sitting in a darkened theater being overrun with bugs. A constant stream of parents headed to the exits with terrorized children. Those that were left behind were screaming and crying as well. The 11-year-old refused to talk for 20 minutes after the fiasco, and the 3½-year-old wanted to go home— not back to the hotel, but home.*

Most readers, however, loved the bugs, including this mom from Brentwood, Tennessee:

*Comments from your readers make It's Tough to Be a Bug! sound worse than Stitch's Great Escape! It's not. It's intense, but mostly funny. The bugs are cartoonlike instead of realistic and icky, so I can't understand what all the fuss is about. Kids think nothing of walking up to a mouse the size of a portajohn but go nuts over some cartoon bugs. Get a grip!*

## Wilderness Explorers ★★★★

**APPEAL BY AGE** PRESCHOOL ★★★★ GRADE SCHOOL ★★★★½ TEENS ★★★★
YOUNG ADULTS ★★½ OVER 30 ★★★★ SENIORS ★★★

**What it is** Park-wide scavenger hunt and puzzle-solving adventure game. **Scope and scale** Diversion. **When to go** Sign up first thing in the morning and complete activities throughout the day. **Special comments** Collecting all 32 badges takes 3–5 hours, which can be done over several days. **Authors' rating** One of the best attractions in any Disney park; not to be missed; ★★★★.

**DESCRIPTION AND COMMENTS** Walt Disney World offers several interactive games in its theme parks, and Wilderness Explorers is the best of the bunch—a scavenger hunt based on Russell's Boy Scout–esque troop from the movie *Up*. Players earn "badges" (stickers given out by cast members) for completing predefined activities throughout the park. For example, to earn the Gorilla Badge, you walk the Pangani Forest Exploration Trail to observe how the primates behave, then mimic that behavior back to a cast member to show what you've seen.

Register for the game near the bridge from The Oasis to Discovery Island. You'll be given an instruction book and a map showing the park location for each badge to be earned.

Cast members have been specially trained for this game and can tailor the activities based on the age of the child playing: Small children might get an explanation about what deforestation means, for example, while older kids may have to figure out why tigers have stripes. It's tons of fun for kids and adults, and we play it every time we're in the park.

**TOURING TIPS** Activities are spread throughout the park, including areas to which many guests never venture. You have to ride specific attractions to earn certain badges, so using FastPass+ for those will save time.

# AFRICA

THE LARGEST OF ANIMAL KINGDOM'S LANDS, Africa is entered through Harambe, a Disneyfied version of a modern rural African town. A market is equipped with modern cash registers; dining options consist of a sit-down buffet, limited counter service, and snack stands. What distinguishes Harambe is its understatement: Far from the stereotypical great-white-hunter image of an African town, Harambe is definitely (and realistically) not exotic. The buildings, while interesting, are architecturally simple. Though better maintained and more idealized than the real McCoy, Disney's Harambe would be a lot more at home in Kenya than the Magic Kingdom's Main Street would be in Missouri.

Harambe serves as the gateway to the African veldt habitat, Animal Kingdom's largest and most ambitious zoological exhibit. Access to the veldt is via the **Kilimanjaro Safaris** attraction, at the end of Harambe's main drag near the fat-trunked baobab tree. Harambe is also the departure point for the train to **Rafiki's Planet Watch** and **Conservation Station** (the park's veterinary headquarters), as well as the new home of a long-running live theatrical show.

## Festival of the Lion King *(FastPass+)*  ★★★★

**APPEAL BY AGE** PRESCHOOL ★★★★½ GRADE SCHOOL ★★★★½ TEENS ★★★★½
YOUNG ADULTS ★★★★½     OVER 30 ★★★★½     SENIORS ★★★★½

**What it is** Theater-in-the-round stage show. **Scope and scale** Major attraction. **When to go** Before 11 a.m., after 4 p.m., or use FastPass+. Specific performance times are listed in the handout park map or *Times Guide*. **Authors' rating** Upbeat and spectacular; not to be missed; ★★★★. **Duration of presentation** 30 minutes. **Preshow entertainment** None. **When to arrive** 20–30 minutes before showtime.

**DESCRIPTION AND COMMENTS** This energetic production, inspired by Disney's *Lion King* feature, is part stage show, part parade, part circus; in 2014, it relocated from Camp Minnie-Mickey to Africa, behind and to the left of Tusker House. Guests sit in four sets of bleachers surrounding the stage and organized into separate cheering sections, which are called on to make elephant, warthog, giraffe, and lion noises (you won't be alone if you don't know how to make a giraffe or warthog noise). There's a great deal of parading around, some acrobatics, and a lot of singing and dancing. By our count, every tune from *The Lion King* is belted out and reprised several times. No joke—if you don't know the words to all the songs by the end of the show, you must have been asleep.

   *Unofficial Guide* readers are almost unanimous in their praise of *Festival of the Lion King.* This letter from a Naples, Florida, mom is typical:

   *Festival of the Lion King is a spectacular show with singers, dancers, fire twirlers, acrobats, robotics, and great set design. My whole family agreed this was the best thing we experienced at Animal Kingdom.*

**TOURING TIPS** This show is both popular and difficult to see. Your best bet is to go to the first show in the morning or to one of the last two performances in the evening. To see the show during the more crowded midday, you'll need to queue up at least 35–45 minutes before showtime. To minimize standing in the hot sun, refrain from hopping in line until cast members begin directing guests to the queue. If you have small children or short adults in your party, sit higher up. Rarely a good use of FastPass+.

## Kilimanjaro Safaris *(FastPass+)*  ★★★★★

**APPEAL BY AGE** PRESCHOOL ★★★★½  GRADE SCHOOL ★★★★½  TEENS ★★★★½
YOUNG ADULTS ★★★★½     OVER 30 ★★★★½     SENIORS ★★★★½

**What it is** Ride through an African wildlife reservation. **Scope and scale** Super-headliner. **When to go** As soon as the park opens or in the 2 hours before closing, or use FastPass+. **Authors' rating** Truly exceptional; not to be missed; ★★★★★. **Duration of ride** About 20 minutes. **Average wait in line per 100 people ahead of**

you 4 minutes; assumes full-capacity operation with 18-second dispatch interval. **Loading speed** Fast.

**DESCRIPTION AND COMMENTS** The park's premier zoological attraction, Kilimanjaro Safaris offers an exceptionally realistic, albeit brief, imitation of an actual African photo safari. Thirty-two guests at a time board tall, open safari vehicles and are dispatched into a simulated African veldt habitat. Animals such as zebras, wildebeests, impalas, Thomson's gazelles, giraffes, and even rhinos roam apparently free, while predators such as lions, as well as potentially dangerous large animals like hippos, are separated from both prey and guests by all-but-invisible, natural-appearing barriers. Although the animals have more than 100 acres of savanna, woodland, streams, and rocky hills to call home, careful placement of water holes, forage, and salt licks ensures that the critters are hanging out by the road when safari vehicles roll by.

Having traveled in Kenya and Tanzania, I (Bob) will tell you that Disney has done an amazing job of replicating the sub-Saharan east-African landscape. The main difference that an east African would notice is that Disney's version is greener and, generally speaking, less barren. As on a real African safari, what animals you see, and how many, is pretty much a matter of luck. We've experienced Kilimanjaro Safaris more than 100 times and had a different experience on each trip.

Winding through the Safaris is Disney's **Wild Africa Trek,** a behind-the-scenes tour of the Animal Kingdom that takes you into several of the Kilimanjaro Safaris' animal enclosures. As you drive past the hippo pool or over the crocodile pool, look up for a series of rope bridges towering far above the ground. You may see Trekkers on tour. See page 715 of Part Nineteen for a complete description.

**TOURING TIPS** Kilimanjaro Safaris is Animal Kingdom's number-two draw behind Expedition Everest. From a touring standpoint, this is good news: By distributing guests more evenly throughout the park, Expedition Everest makes it unnecessary to run to Kilimanjaro Safaris first thing in the morning. Our Animal Kingdom touring plan has you obtain FastPass+ reservations for the safaris in the afternoon. While your FastPass+ return window approaches, you'll have plenty of time to eat and tour the rest of Africa. Before Expedition Everest, seeing the Safaris early meant backtracking to Africa later in the day to see exhibits and attractions that were not open first thing in the morning; our touring plan eliminates all of that extra walking, too.

Waits for Kilimanjaro Safaris diminish in late afternoon, sometimes as early as 3:30 p.m. but more commonly somewhat later.

If you want to take photos, be advised that the vehicle isn't guaranteed to stop at any location, although the drivers try their best to do so when big animals are sighted. Be prepared to snap at any time. Also, don't worry about the ride itself: It really isn't very rough. Finally, the only thing that a young child might find intimidating is crossing an "old bridge" that seems to collapse under your truck.

## Pangani Forest Exploration Trail ★★★★

| APPEAL BY AGE | PRESCHOOL ★★★★ | GRADE SCHOOL ★★★★ | TEENS ★★★★ |
|---|---|---|---|
| YOUNG ADULTS ★★★★ | | OVER 30 ★★★★½ | SENIORS ★★★★ |

**What it is** Walk-through zoological exhibit. **Scope and scale** Major attraction. **When to go** Anytime. **Authors' rating** ★★★★. **Duration of tour** About 20–25 minutes.

**DESCRIPTION AND COMMENTS** As the trail winds between the domain of two troops of lowland gorillas, it's hard to see what, if anything, separates you from the primates. Also on the trail are a hippo pool with an underwater viewing area, and a naked-mole-rat exhibit. A highlight of the trail is an exotic-bird aviary so craftily designed that you can barely tell you're in an enclosure.

**TOURING TIPS** The Pangani Forest Exploration Trail is lush, beautiful, and jammed to the gills with people much of the time. Guests exiting Kilimanjaro Safaris can choose between returning to Harambe or walking the Pangani Forest Exploration Trail. Many opt for the trail. Thus, when the safari is operating at full tilt, it spews hundreds of guests every couple of minutes onto the Exploration Trail. The one-way trail in turn becomes so clogged that nobody can move or see much of anything. After a minute or two, however, you catch the feel of the mob moving forward in small lurches. From then on you shift, elbow, grunt, and wriggle your way along, every so often coming to an animal exhibit. Here you endeavor to work your way close to the rail but are opposed by people trapped against the rail who are trying to rejoin the surging crowd. The animals, as well as their natural-habitat enclosures, are pretty nifty if you can fight your way close enough to see them.

Clearly this attraction is either badly designed, misplaced, or both. Your only real chance for enjoying it is to walk through before 10 a.m.—that is, before the safaris hit full stride—or after 2:30 p.m.

Another strategy, especially if you're more into the wildlife than the thrill rides, is to schedule a FastPass+ reservation for the safaris 60–90 minutes after the park opens. That's long enough for an uncrowded, leisurely tour of the Pangani Forest Exploration Trail and a quick snack before you go on safari.

# RAFIKI'S PLANET WATCH

THIS AREA ISN'T REALLY a "land" and not really an attraction either. Our best guess is that Disney uses the name as an umbrella for Conservation Station, the petting zoo, and the environmental exhibits accessible from Harambe via the Wildlife Express Train. Presumably, Disney hopes that invoking Rafiki (a beloved character from *The Lion King*) will stimulate guests to make the effort to check out things in this far-flung outpost of the park.

## Conservation Station and Affection Section    ★★★½

**APPEAL BY AGE**   PRESCHOOL ★★★½   GRADE SCHOOL ★★★½   TEENS ★★★½
YOUNG  ADULTS  ★★★½       OVER 30  ★★★½          SENIORS  ★★★★

**What it is** Behind-the-scenes educational exhibit and petting zoo. **Scope and scale** Minor attraction. **When to go** Anytime. **Special comments** Opens 30 minutes after the rest of the park. **Authors' rating** Not bad; ★★★½. **Probable waiting time** None.

**DESCRIPTION AND COMMENTS** Conservation Station is Animal Kingdom's veterinary and conservation headquarters. On the perimeter of the African section of the park, Conservation Station is, strictly speaking, a backstage, working facility. Here guests can meet wildlife experts, observe some of the Station's ongoing projects, and learn about the behind-the-scenes operations of the park. The Station includes a rehabilitation area for injured animals and a nursery for recently born (or hatched) critters. Vets and other experts are on hand to answer questions.

While there are several permanent exhibits, including Affection Section (an animal-petting area), what you see at Conservation Station will largely depend on what's going on when you arrive. On most days when we visit, there isn't enough happening to warrant waiting in line twice (coming and going) for the train. Most of our readers tell us that Conservation Station is not worth the hassle. A Tinley Park, Illinois, mom writes:

*Skip Conservation Station at Animal Kingdom. Between the train ride to get to it and being there, we wasted a precious 1½ hours!*

A Denver family had a better experience:

*We really enjoyed Conservation Station. We saw a 13-foot python eating a rat!*

And a reader from Kent in the United Kingdom was amused by both the goings-on and the other guests:

*The most memorable part of Animal Kingdom for me was watching a veterinary surgeon and his team at Conservation Station perform an operation on a rat snake that had inadvertently swallowed a golf ball, presumably believing it to be an egg! This operation caused at least one onlooker to pass out.*

You can access Conservation Station by taking the Wildlife Express Train directly from Harambe. To return to the center of the park, continue the loop from Conservation Station back to Harambe.

**TOURING TIPS**  To enjoy Conservation Station, you have to invest a little effort and be inquisitive. Because it's so removed from the rest of the park, you'll never bump into it unless you take the train.

## Habitat Habit!

**DESCRIPTION AND COMMENTS**  Listed on park maps as an attraction is Habitat Habit!, on the pedestrian path between the train station and Conservation Station. It consists of a tiny collection of signs about wildlife and a few cotton-top tamarins. To call it an attraction is absurd.

## Wildlife Express Train  ★★

| APPEAL BY AGE | PRESCHOOL ★★★★ | GRADE SCHOOL ★★★½ | TEENS ★★★½ |
|---|---|---|---|
| YOUNG ADULTS ★★★ | | OVER 30 ★★★½ | SENIORS ★★★½ |

**What it is** Scenic railroad ride to Rafiki's Planet Watch and Conservation Station. **Scope and scale** Minor attraction. **When to go** Anytime. **Special comments** Opens 30 minutes after the rest of the park. **Authors' rating** Ho-hum; ★★. **Duration of ride** About 5–7 minutes one-way. **Average wait in line per 100 people ahead of you** 9 minutes. **Loading speed** Moderate.

**DESCRIPTION AND COMMENTS**  This ride snakes behind the African wildlife reserve as it makes its loop connecting Harambe to Rafiki's Planet Watch and Conservation Station. En route, you see the nighttime enclosures for the animals that populate Kilimanjaro Safaris. Similarly, returning to Harambe, you see the backstage areas of Asia. Regardless of which direction you're heading, the sights aren't especially interesting.

**TOURING TIPS**  Most guests will embark for Rafiki's Planet Watch and Conservation Station after experiencing Kilimanjaro Safaris and the Pangani Forest Exploration Trail. Thus, the train begins to get crowded between 10 and 11 a.m.

# ASIA

CROSSING THE ASIA BRIDGE from Discovery Island, you enter Asia through the village of Anandapur, a veritable collage of Asian themes inspired by the architecture and ruins of India, Thailand, Indonesia, and Nepal. Situated near the bank of the Chakranadi River (translation: "the river that runs in circles") and surrounded by lush vegetation, Anandapur provides access to a gibbon exhibit and to Asia's two feature attractions, the **Kali River Rapids** whitewater-raft ride and **Expedition Everest.** Also in Asia is *Flights of Wonder,* an educational production about birds.

Expedition Everest—yep, another mountain, and at 200 feet, the tallest in Florida—is a super-headliner roller coaster. You board an old mountain railway destined for the foot of Mount Everest and end up racing both forward and backward through caverns and frigid canyons en route to paying a social call on the Abominable Snowman. Expedition Everest is billed as a "family thrill ride," which means simply that it's more like Big Thunder Mountain Railroad than Rock 'n' Roller Coaster.

## Expedition Everest *(FastPass+)*  ★★★★½

| APPEAL BY AGE | PRESCHOOL ★★ | GRADE SCHOOL ★★★★½ | TEENS ★★★★★ |
| --- | --- | --- | --- |
| YOUNG ADULTS ★★★★★ | | OVER 30 ★★★★★ | SENIORS ★★★★ |

**What it is** High-speed outdoor roller coaster through Nepalese mountain village. **Scope and scale** Super-headliner. **When to go** Before 9:30 a.m. or after 3 p.m., or use FastPass+. **Special comments** 44" minimum height requirement. Switching-off option provided (see page 341). **Authors' rating** Contains some of the park's most stunning visual elements; not to be missed; ★★★★½. **Duration of ride** 3½ minutes. **Average wait in line per 100 people ahead of you** Just under 4 minutes; assumes 2 tracks operating. **Loading speed** Moderate–fast.

DESCRIPTION AND COMMENTS The first true roller coaster in Animal Kingdom, Expedition Everest earned the park's longest waits in line from the moment it opened—and for good reason. Your journey begins in an elaborate waiting area modeled after a Nepalese village; then you board an old train headed for the top of Mount Everest. Throughout the waiting area are posted notes from previous expeditions, some with cryptic observations regarding a mysterious creature said to guard the mountain. These ominous signs are ignored (as if you have a choice!), resulting in a high-speed encounter with the Abominable Snowman himself.

The ride consists of tight turns (some while traveling backward), hills, and dips, but no loops or inversions. From your departure at the loading station through your first high-speed descent, you'll see some of the most spectacular panoramas available in Walt Disney World. On a clear day, you'll be able to view the arrangement of the buildings at Coronado Springs, Epcot's Spaceship Earth, and possibly downtown Orlando. But look quickly, because you'll immediately be propelled, projectile-like, through the inner and outer reaches of the mountain. The final drop and last few turns are among the best-designed coaster effects Disney has ever made. A few minor criticisms: At a couple of points, your vehicle is stopped while the ride's track is reconfigured, affecting the attraction's continuity. And while the audio-animatronic Yeti is undoubtedly impressive, he breaks down more than a 30-year-old Fiat. Most days Disney just simulates the Yeti moving by flashing a strobe light on his motionless body. But don't let these small shortcomings stop you from riding.

The coaster reaches a top speed of around 50 mph, just about twice that of Space Mountain, so expect to see the usual warnings for health and safety. The first few seats of these vehicles offer the best front-seat experience of any Disney coaster, indoor or out. If at all possible, ask to sit up front. Also, look for the animal poop on display in the FastPass+ return line—a deliberate attempt at verisimilitude, or did Disney run out of money for ride props and use whatever they could find? You decide.

As you might expect of a super-headliner attraction, Expedition Everest is the subject of much reader mail. A Seattle family rated Expedition Everest four thumbs up:

*Expedition Everest is tremendous. It has enough surprises and runaway speed to make it one of the more enjoyable thrill rides in the whole Orlando area.*

A Macon, Georgia, teen recruited the aged:

*Expedition Everest was so smooooth! I went right out and brought my granny back to ride it. She didn't throw up or anything!*

Beating the morning crowds to Expedition Everest is also a hot topic. From a Yonkers, New York, man:

*When the park opened, we went right toward DinoLand U.S.A. and followed the path around the lake to Everest. We arrived about 90 seconds ahead of the crowd being walked in and were the first to ride. Upon exiting we noticed the line was already enormous, and, to our delight, the wait at the other major rides was negligible.*

A multigenerational family from Brookfield, Connecticut, had great luck with the singles line, writing:

*The single-rider line at Expedition Everest is amazing! I went there without my mother and daughter and rode seven times in a row. I think my longest wait was 3–5 minutes, but often I just walked on!*

**TOURING TIPS** Our advice is to ride Everest as soon as the park opens instead of using FastPass+. This allows you to save your reservations for other attractions or a reride of Everest later in the day. In the latter case, try riding during the last hour the park is open.

## Flights of Wonder ★★★★

| APPEAL BY AGE | PRESCHOOL ★★★★ | GRADE SCHOOL ★★★★½ | TEENS ★★★★ |
|---|---|---|---|
| YOUNG ADULTS ★★★★½ | | OVER 30 ★★★★½ | SENIORS ★★★★½ |

**What it is** Stadium show about birds. **Scope and scale** Major attraction. **When to go** Anytime. **Special comments** Performance times listed in handout park map or *Times Guide*. **Authors' rating** Unique; ★★★★. **Duration of presentation** 30 minutes. **Preshow entertainment** None. **When to arrive** 20–30 minutes before showtime.

**DESCRIPTION AND COMMENTS** *Flights of Wonder* is well paced and showcases a surprising number of bird species. The focus is on the natural talents and characteristics of the various species, so don't expect to see any parrots riding bicycles—the birds' natural behaviors far surpass any tricks learned from humans. A Brattleboro, Vermont, reader found *Flights of Wonder* especially compelling, writing:

*The ornithologist guide is not only a wealth of information but a talented, comedic entertainer. The birds are thrilling, and we especially appreciated the fact that their antics were not the results of training against the grain but actual survival techniques the birds use in the wild.*

*Flights of Wonder* exceeded the expectations of a Colorado Springs family with two elementary-school-age kids:

*A coworker with kids the same age as ours said her kids loved* Flights of Wonder. *Midway through the show I stopped taking pictures of the birds and began taking pictures of the expressions of amazement and joy on the faces of my kids and husband.*

**TOURING TIPS** *Flights of Wonder* plays at the stadium near the Asia Bridge on the walkway into Asia. Though the stadium is covered, it's not air-conditioned; thus, early-morning and late-afternoon performances are more comfortable. To play it safe, get to the stadium about 10–15 minutes before showtime.

## Kali River Rapids *(FastPass+)* ★★★½

| APPEAL BY AGE | PRESCHOOL ★★★★ | GRADE SCHOOL ★★★★½ | TEENS ★★★★½ |
|---|---|---|---|
| YOUNG ADULTS ★★★★ | | OVER 30 ★★★★ | SENIORS ★★★★ |

**What it is** Whitewater-raft ride. **Scope and scale** Headliner. **When to go** First or last hour the park is open, or use FastPass+. **Special comments** You're guaranteed to get wet. Opens 30 minutes after the rest of the park. 38" minimum height requirement. Switching-off option available (see page 341). **Authors' rating** Short but scenic; ★★★½. **Duration of ride** About 5 minutes. **Average wait in line per 100 people ahead of you** 5 minutes. **Loading speed** Moderate.

**DESCRIPTION AND COMMENTS** Whitewater-raft rides have been a hot-weather favorite of theme park patrons for more than 20 years. The ride itself consists of an unguided trip down an artificial river in a circular rubber raft with a top-mounted platform seating 12 people. The raft essentially floats free in the current and is washed downstream through rapids and waves. Because the river is fairly wide, with numerous currents, eddies, and obstacles, there's no telling exactly where the raft will drift. Thus, each trip is different and exciting.

What distinguishes Kali River Rapids from other theme park raft rides is Disney's trademark attention to visual detail. Where many raft rides essentially plunge down a concrete ditch, Kali River Rapids flows through a dense rainforest and past waterfalls, temple ruins, and bamboo thickets, emerging into a cleared area where greedy loggers have ravaged the forest, and finally drifting back under the tropical canopy as the river cycles back to Anandapur. Along the way, your raft runs a gauntlet of raging cataracts, logjams, and other dangers.

The queuing area, which winds through an ancient Southeast Asian temple, is one of the most striking and visually interesting settings of any Disney attraction. And though the sights on the raft trip itself are also first-class, the attraction is marginal in two important respects. First, it's only about 3½ minutes on the water, and second, well . . . it's a weenie ride. Sure, you get wet, but otherwise the drops and rapids aren't all that exciting, as this Kansas family points out:

*It was boiling hot, so we were happy about the prospect of being drenched. We couldn't believe how short and dull the ride was. At the end, we all looked at each other and said, "Is that IT?" We couldn't believe we'd stood in line, sweating half to death, for 75 minutes just for that.*

How wet do you get? A Plymouth, Michigan, reader has the answer:

*Beware! Rather than just getting a little wet like on Splash Mountain, you get soaked to the skin—beyond the fun kind of wet. Poncho sales were brisk the day we were there.*

You can use FastPass+ to ride later in the day when it's a little warmer. A family from Humble, Texas, who rode early in the morning on a cool day, shares this:

*Our plan hit a definite wall upon experiencing Kali River Rapids as number two on the schedule. We didn't read about the precautions for this ride in your book until after riding. The 6-year-old and mom were COMPLETELY drenched—so much so that we actually had to leave the park and go back to our room at Port Orleans to change clothes. Since the temperature was around 60 degrees that morning, we were pretty miserable by the time we got back to our room. Needless to say, our schedule was shot by that time. We wouldn't recommend Kali River Rapids so early in the morning when the weather is chilly.*

**TOURING TIPS** This attraction is hugely popular on hot summer days. Ride Kali River Rapids during the first or last hour the park is open or use Fast-Pass+. Again, you'll probably get drenched on this ride—we recommend wearing shorts to the park and bringing along a jumbo-sized trash bag or bin liner, as well as a smaller plastic bag. Before boarding the raft, take off your socks and punch a hole in your jumbo bag for your head. Though you can also cut holes for your arms, you'll probably stay drier with your arms inside the bag. Use the smaller plastic bag to wrap around your shoes. If you're worried about mussing your 'do, bring a third bag for your head.

A Shaker Heights, Ohio, family who donned our garbage-bag couture discovered that staying dry on Kali River Rapids is not without its social consequences:

*I must tell you that the Disney cast members and the other people in our raft looked at us like we had just beamed down from Mars. Plus, we didn't cut arm holes in our trash bags because we thought we'd stay drier that way. Only problem was once we sat down we couldn't fasten our seat belts. One cast member asked sarcastically whether we needed wet suits and snorkels. After a lot of wiggling and adjusting and helping each other, we finally got belted in, and off we went looking like sacks of fertilizer with little heads perched on top. Very embarrassing, but we stayed nice and dry.*

Kali River Rapids offers free 2-hour locker rental (to the left of the attraction entrance, near the restrooms). Store a change of clothes in these to keep dry. Alternatively, wear as little as the law and Disney allow. If you're wearing closed shoes, try to prop your feet up above the bottom of the raft. Slogging around in wet shoes and socks is a surefire recipe for blisters.

## Maharajah Jungle Trek ★★★★

| APPEAL BY AGE | PRESCHOOL ★★★★ | GRADE SCHOOL ★★★★ | TEENS ★★★★ |
| --- | --- | --- | --- |
| YOUNG ADULTS ★★★★½ | | OVER 30 ★★★★½ | SENIORS ★★★★½ |

**What it is** Walk-through zoological exhibit. **Scope and scale** Headliner. **When to go** Anytime. **Special comments** Opens 30 minutes after the rest of the park. **Authors' rating** A standard-setter for natural habitat design; ★★★★. **Duration of tour** About 20–30 minutes.

**DESCRIPTION AND COMMENTS** The Maharajah Jungle Trek is a zoological nature walk similar to the Pangani Forest Exploration Trail, but with an Asian setting and Asian animals. You start with Komodo dragons and then work up to Malayan tapirs. Next is a cave with fruit bats. Ruins of the maharaja's palace provide the setting for Bengal tigers. From the top of a parapet in the palace you can view a herd of blackbuck antelope and Asian deer. The trek concludes with an aviary.

Labyrinthine, overgrown, and elaborately detailed, the temple ruin would be a compelling attraction even without the animals. Throw in a few bats, bucks, and Bengals and you're in for a treat.

Most readers agree. A Washington, D.C., couple chimed in with this:

*The Maharajah Jungle Trek was absolutely amazing. We were able to see all the animals, which were awake by that time (9:30 a.m.), including the elusive tigers. The part of the trek with the birds was fabulous. If you looked, you could spot hundreds of birds, some of which were eating on the ground a mere 3 feet away from us. Take your time walking through, since most of the animals are not obvious to the breezing eye and you must look for them.*

**TOURING TIPS**  The Jungle Trek doesn't get as jammed up as the Pangani Forest Exploration Trail and is a good choice for midday touring when most other attractions are crowded. The downside, of course, is that the exhibit showcases tigers, tapirs, and other creatures that might not be as active in the heat of the day as mad dogs and Englishmen.

# DINOLAND U.S.A.

THIS MOST TYPICALLY DISNEY of Animal Kingdom's lands is a cross between an anthropological dig and a quirky roadside attraction. Accessible via the bridge from Discovery Island, DinoLand U.S.A. is home to a children's play area, a nature trail, a 1,500-seat amphitheater, and **DINOSAUR,** one of Animal Kingdom's three thrill rides.

Also in DinoLand are a couple of natural-history exhibits, including **Dino-Sue,** an exact replica of the largest, most complete *Tyrannosaurus rex* discovered to date. Named after the fossil hunter Sue Hendrickson, the replica (like the original) is 40 feet long and 13 feet tall. And no, it doesn't dance, sing, or whistle, but it will get your attention nonetheless.

## The Boneyard  ★★★

| APPEAL BY AGE | PRESCHOOL ★★★★★ | GRADE SCHOOL ★★★★½ | TEENS ★★½ |
|---|---|---|---|
| YOUNG  ADULTS  ★★½ | OVER  30  ★★★ | | SENIORS  ★★½ |

**What it is** Elaborate playground. **Scope and scale** Diversion. **When to go** Anytime. **Special comments** Opens 30 minutes after the rest of the park. **Authors' rating** Stimulating fun for children; ★★★. **Duration of visit** Varies. **Probable waiting time** None.

**DESCRIPTION AND COMMENTS**  This attraction is an elaborate playground, particularly appealing to kids age 12 and younger, but visually appealing to all ages. Arranged in the form of a rambling open-air dig site, The Boneyard offers plenty of opportunity for exploration and letting off steam. Playground equipment consists of the skeletons of *Triceratops, Tyrannosaurus rex, Brachiosaurus,* and the like, on which children can swing, slide, and climb. In addition, there are sandpits where little ones can scrounge around for bones and fossils.

**TOURING TIPS**  Not the most pristine of Disney attractions, but certainly one where younger children will want to spend some time. And aside from being dirty, or at least sandy, The Boneyard gets mighty hot in the

Florida sun. Keep your kids well hydrated, and drag them into the shade from time to time. Try to save the playground until after you've experienced the main attractions. Because The Boneyard is so close to the center of the park, it's easy to drop in whenever your kids get antsy. While the little ones clamber around on giant femurs and ribs, you can sip a tall cool one in the shade (still keeping an eye on them, of course).

As a Michigan family attests, kids love The Boneyard:

*The highlight for our kids was The Boneyard, especially the dig site. They just kept digging and digging to uncover the bones of the woolly mammoth. It was also in the shade, and there were places for parents to sit, making it a wonderful resting place.*

And so do parents. From the father of a 4-year-old:

*You should give playgrounds like The Boneyard higher ratings. After having our 4-year-old wait in lines for two days straight, she was thrilled to run around for 2 hours in The Boneyard without waiting for anything. Perhaps calling it a diversion is accurate, but it was a priceless diversion for us.*

Be aware that The Boneyard rambles over about a half acre and is multistoried. It's pretty easy to lose sight of a small child in the playground. Fortunately, there's only one entrance and exit. A mother of two from Stillwater, Minnesota, found the playground too large for her liking:

*If you're a parent who likes to have your eyes on your kids at all times, you won't like The Boneyard. Kids climb to the top of the slides, then you can't see them and you don't know what chute they'll be exiting from.*

## DINOSAUR *(FastPass+)* ★★★★

| APPEAL BY AGE | PRESCHOOL ★★½ | GRADE SCHOOL ★★★½ | TEENS ★★★★½ |
| YOUNG ADULTS ★★★★ | | OVER 30 ★★★★ | SENIORS ★★★½ |

**What it is** Motion-simulator dark ride. **Scope and scale** Super-headliner. **When to go** Before 10:30 a.m., after 4:30 p.m., or use FastPass+. **Special comments** 40" minimum height requirement. Switching-off option provided (see page 341). **Authors' rating** Not to be missed; ★★★★. **Duration of ride** 3½ minutes. **Average wait in line per 100 people ahead of you** 3 minutes; assumes full-capacity operation with 18-second dispatch interval. **Loading speed** Fast.

**DESCRIPTION AND COMMENTS** DINOSAUR is a combination track ride and motion simulator. In addition to moving along a cleverly hidden track, the ride vehicle also bucks and pitches (the simulator part) in sync with the visuals and special effects. The plot has you traveling back in time on a mission of rescue and conservation. Your objective: to haul back a living dinosaur before the species becomes extinct. Whoever is operating the clock, however, cuts it a little close, and you arrive on the prehistoric scene just as a giant asteroid is hurtling toward Earth. General mayhem ensues as you evade carnivorous predators, catch Barney, and get the heck out of Dodge before the asteroid hits.

DINOSAUR is a technological clone of the *Indiana Jones* ride at Disneyland. A good effort, although not quite as visually interesting as *Indiana Jones,* DINOSAUR serves up nonstop action from beginning to end with brilliant visual effects. Elaborate even by Disney standards, the attraction provides a tense, frenetic ride that's embellished by the entire Imagineering arsenal of high-tech gimmickry. The ride *is* jerky, but it's not too rough for seniors. The menacing dinosaurs, however, along with the intensity of the experience, make DINOSAUR a no-go for younger kids.

To its credit, Disney is unafraid to keep DINOSAUR a dark, fast ride. A mother from Kansasville, Wisconsin, liked it a lot, commenting:

*DINOSAUR is the best ride at WDW. Our group of 10, ranging in age from 65 (grandma) to 8 (grandson), immediately—and unanimously!—got back in line immediately after finishing.*

But this Illinois family of four got back in line for the bus to their hotel:

*We saw young kids in tears as they were coming off this ride, and it got mixed reviews within our own family. They snap the souvenir picture as the dinosaur is jumping out at you. We have the most awesome family picture: two of us laughing, two of us recoiling in terror!*

And from a Michigan family:

*Our 7-year-old son withstood every ride Disney threw at him, from Space Mountain to Tower of Terror. DINOSAUR, however, did him in. By the end, he was riding with his head down, scared to look around.*

**TOURING TIPS** Disney situated DINOSAUR in such a remote corner of the park that guests have to poke around to find it. This, in conjunction with the overwhelming popularity of Kilimanjaro Safaris and Expedition Everest, makes DINOSAUR the easiest super-headliner attraction at Disney World to get on. We recommend, nonetheless, that you ride early in the day, after Expedition Everest.

## Primeval Whirl *(FastPass+)*   ★★★

| APPEAL BY AGE | PRESCHOOL ★★½ | GRADE SCHOOL ★★★★ | TEENS ★★★★ |
|---|---|---|---|
| YOUNG ADULTS ★★★½ | OVER 30 ★★★½ | | SENIORS ★★★ |

**What it is** Small coaster. **Scope and scale** Minor attraction. **When to go** First or last hour the park is open or use FastPass+. **Special comments** 48″ minimum height requirement. Switching-off option provided (see page 341). **Authors' rating** "Wild mouse" on steroids; ★★★. **Duration of ride** Almost 2½ minutes. **Average wait in line per 100 people ahead of you** 4½ minutes. **Loading speed** Slow.

**DESCRIPTION AND COMMENTS** Primeval Whirl is a small coaster with short drops and curves, and it runs through the jaws of a dinosaur, among other things. What makes this coaster different is that the cars also spin. You can't control the spinning—it starts and stops according to how the ride is programmed. Sometimes the spin is braked to a jarring halt after half a revolution, and sometimes it's allowed to make one or two complete turns. The complete spins are fun, but the screeching-stop half-spins are almost painful. If you subtract the time it takes to ratchet up the first hill, the actual ride time is about 90 seconds.

**TOURING TIPS** As for Space Mountain, the ride is duplicated side-by-side, but with only one queue. When it runs smoothly, about 700 people per side can whirl in an hour—a goodly number for this type of attraction, but not enough to preclude long waits on busy-to-moderate days. If you want to ride, try to get on before 10 a.m.

## Theater in the Wild / *Finding Nemo—The Musical* *(FastPass+)*   ★★★★

| APPEAL BY AGE | PRESCHOOL ★★★★½ | GRADE SCHOOL ★★★★½ | TEENS ★★★★ |
|---|---|---|---|
| YOUNG ADULTS ★★★★½ | OVER 30 ★★★★½ | | SENIORS ★★★★½ |

**What it is** Enclosed venue for live stage shows. **Scope and scale** Major attraction. **When to go** Anytime. **Special comments** Performance times are listed in the handout park map or *Times Guide*. **Authors' rating** Not to be missed; ★★★★. **Duration of presentation** About 35 minutes. **When to arrive** 30 minutes before showtime.

**DESCRIPTION AND COMMENTS** Another chapter in the Pixar-ization of Disney theme parks, *Finding Nemo* is arguably the most elaborate live show in any Disney World theme park. Incorporating dancing, special effects, and sophisticated digital backdrops of the undersea world, it features on-stage human performers retelling Nemo's story with colorful, larger-than-life puppets. To be fair, "puppets" doesn't adequately convey the size or detail of these props, many of which are as big as a car and require two people to manipulate. An original musical score was written for the show, which is a must-see for most Animal Kingdom guests. A few scenes, such as one in which Nemo's mom is eaten, may be too intense for some very small children. Some of the midshow musical numbers slow the pace, so the main concern for parents is whether the kids can sit still for an entire show. With that in mind, we advise parents to catch an afternoon performance—around 3 p.m. would be great—after seeing most of the rest of Animal Kingdom. If the kids get restless, you can either leave the show and catch the afternoon parade, or end your day at the park.

New Jersey drama critics have their own way with words, as this family of five demonstrates:

*The* Finding Nemo *musical is da bomb! The musical was amazing! It's a flawless package of puppetry, effects, music, and lots of Disney magic! Even if you don't have kids in your party, go see it!*

**TOURING TIPS** To get a seat, show up 20–25 minutes in advance for morning and late-afternoon shows, and 30–35 minutes in advance for shows scheduled between noon and 4:30 p.m. Access to the theater is via a relatively narrow pedestrian path—if you arrive as the previous show is letting out, you'll feel like a salmon swimming upstream. *Finding Nemo* is rarely a good use of FastPass+.

## TriceraTop Spin  ★★

| APPEAL BY AGE | PRESCHOOL ★★★★½ | GRADE SCHOOL ★★★★ | TEENS ★★★ |
|---|---|---|---|
| YOUNG ADULTS ★★★ | OVER 30 ★★★ | | SENIORS ★★★½ |

**What it is** Hub-and-spoke midway ride. **Scope and scale** Minor attraction. **When to go** Before noon or after 3 p.m. **Authors' rating** Dumbo's prehistoric forebear; ★★. **Duration of ride** 1½ minutes. **Average wait in line per 100 people ahead of you** 10 minutes. **Loading speed** Slow.

**DESCRIPTION AND COMMENTS** Another Dumbo-like ride for little kids. Here you spin around a central hub until a dinosaur pops out of the top of the hub. You'd think with the collective imagination of the Walt Disney Company, they'd come up with something a little more creative.

**TOURING TIPS** Come back later if the wait exceeds 20 minutes.

# LIVE ENTERTAINMENT
# *in* DISNEY'S ANIMAL KINGDOM

WDW LIVE-ENTERTAINMENT GURU Steve Soares usually posts the Animal Kingdom performance schedule about a week in advance at **wdwent.com.**

**AFTERNOON PARADE** Disney cancelled the park's afternoon parade in mid-2014. A replacement had not been announced as we went to press.

**ANIMAL ENCOUNTERS** Throughout the day, Disney staff conduct impromptu short lectures on specific animals at the park. Look for a cast member in safari garb holding a bird, reptile, or small mammal.

At press time, Disney was about to launch a small, interactive event **Winged Encounters—The Kingdom Takes Flight,** featuring macaws and their handlers, on Discovery Island. Guests will be able to talk to the animal's trainers and see the birds fly around the middle of the park. The concept sounds a lot like *Flights of Wonder* (see page 604) on a much smaller scale. Check the *Times Guide* for performances and the exact location.

**GOODWILL AMBASSADORS** A number of Asian and African cast members are on hand throughout the park. Gracious and knowledgeable, they're delighted to discuss their native countries and the wildlife in them. Look for these ambassadors in Harambe and along the Pangani Forest Exploration Trail in Africa, and in Anandapur and along the Maharajah Jungle Trek in Asia. They can also be found near the main entrance and at The Oasis.

**KIDS' DISCOVERY CLUB** Activity stations offer kids ages 4–8 a structured learning experience as they tour Animal Kingdom. Set up along walkways in six themed areas, Discovery Club stations are manned by cast members who supervise a different activity at each station. A souvenir logbook, available free, is stamped at each station when the child completes a craft or exercise. Kids enjoy collecting the stamps and noodling puzzles in the logbook while in attraction lines.

**STREET PERFORMERS** Can be found most of the time at Harambe in Africa and at Anandapur in Asia.

Far and away the most intriguing of these performers is the one you can't see—at least not at first. Totally bedecked in foliage and luxuriant vines is a stilt walker named **DiVine** (★★★★), who blends so completely with Animal Kingdom's dense flora that you never notice her until she moves. We've seen guests standing less than a foot away gasp in amazement as DiVine brushes them with a leafy tendril. Usually found on the path between Asia and Africa, DiVine is a must-see. If you don't encounter her, ask a cast member when and where she can be found. Video of her is available at **YouTube** (go to **youtube.com** and search for "DiVine Disney's Animal Kingdom").

# TRAFFIC PATTERNS *in*
# DISNEY'S ANIMAL KINGDOM

THE FOUR CROWD MAGNETS ARE Kilimanjaro Safaris in Africa, DINOSAUR in DinoLand U.S.A., and Kali River Rapids and Expedition Everest in Asia.

Because the park hosts large crowds with only a relative handful of attractions, expect for all attractions to be extremely busy, and for Expedition Everest and Kilimanjaro Safaris to be mobbed. Most guests

*unofficial* **TIP**
If you visit during late afternoon, you'll almost certainly have to return another afternoon to finish seeing everything.

arrive in the morning, with a sizable number on hand before opening and a larger wave arriving before 10 a.m. Guests continue to stream in through the late morning and into the early afternoon, with crowds peaking at around 2 p.m. From about 2:30 p.m. on, departing guests outnumber arriving guests by a wide margin, as guests who arrived early complete their tour and leave. Crowds thin appreciably by late afternoon and continue to decline into the early evening.

Because the number of attractions, including theater presentations, is limited, most guests complete a fairly comprehensive tour in two-thirds of a day if they arrive early. Thus, generally speaking, your best bet for easy touring is either to be on hand when the park opens or to arrive at about 3 p.m. (if the park stays open until 7 or 8 p.m.), when the early birds are heading for the exits.

How guests tour Animal Kingdom depends on their prior knowledge of the park and its attractions. Newbies make their way to Discovery Island and depend on their park map to decide what to do next. Animal Kingdom experts make straight for Kilimanjaro Safaris in Africa and Expedition Everest in Asia. Kali River Rapids in Asia is also an early-morning favorite.

With so many guests heading first thing for either Kilimanjaro Safaris in Africa or Expedition Everest in Asia, DinoLand and Discovery Island are lightly trafficked backwaters until late morning. As the day wears on, the masses who have experienced Kilimanjaro Safaris and Expedition Everest turn their attention to other shows and attractions, and the crowds become more equally distributed. Less-popular attractions don't experience high traffic until 11:30.

To get a complete view of the actual traffic patterns while you're in the park, use our mobile app, **Lines** (**touringplans.com/lines**). It gives you current wait times and future estimates in half-hour increments for today and tomorrow. A quick glance shows how traffic patterns affect wait times throughout the day.

# DISNEY'S ANIMAL KINGDOM TOURING PLAN

TOURING ANIMAL KINGDOM is not as complicated as touring the other parks because it has fewer attractions. Also, most rides, shows, and exhibits are oriented to the entire family, eliminating differences of opinion regarding how to spend the day. Here, the whole family can pretty much see and enjoy everything together.

*unofficial* **TIP**
Until *Avatar* land opens in 2017, the limited number of attractions in Animal Kingdom can work to your advantage.

Because there are fewer attractions than at the other parks, expect the crowds at Animal Kingdom to be more concentrated. If a line seems unusually long, ask a cast member what the estimated wait is. If the wait exceeds your tolerance, try the same attraction again after

3 p.m., while a show is in progress at the Theater in the Wild in Dino-Land U.S.A., or while some special event is going on.

We've listed the approximate FastPass+ return times for which you should attempt to make reservations. (The touring plan should work with anything close to the times shown.) Because Disney limits how many FastPass+ reservations you can get, we've listed in the plans the attractions most likely to need FastPass+ too. Check **touringplans.com** for the latest information.

### "Not a Touring Plan" Touring Plans

For the type-B reader, these touring plans (see page 820) avoid detailed step-by-step strategies for saving every last minute in line. For Animal Kingdom, these "not" touring plans include advice for adults and parents with one day in the park, for anyone with two days, and for anyone with an afternoon and a full day to tour.

### BEFORE YOU GO

1. Call ☎ 407-824-4321 or check **disneyworld.com** the day before you go to verify official opening time.
2. Purchase your admission and make FastPass+ reservations before you arrive.

### DISNEY'S ANIMAL KINGDOM ONE-DAY TOURING PLAN *(page 833)*

THIS TOURING PLAN ASSUMES a willingness to experience all major rides and shows. If you have children under age 8, see the Small-Child Fright-Potential Chart on pages 332–335. When you're following the touring plan, simply skip any attraction you don't wish to experience.

Many readers have asked us whether fewer animals are visible from Kilimanjaro Safaris around lunchtime than at park opening, out of concern that the animals might be less active in the midday heat. Our research indicates that you'll probably see the same number of animals regardless of when you visit.

# PART FOURTEEN

# DISNEY'S HOLLYWOOD STUDIOS

FORMERLY KNOWN AS DISNEY-MGM STUDIOS, Disney's Hollywood Studios was hatched from a corporate rivalry and a wild, twisted plot. At a time when The Walt Disney Company was weak and fighting off "greenmail"—hostile-takeover bids—Universal's parent company at the time, MCA, announced it was going to build an Orlando clone of its wildly successful Universal Studios Hollywood theme park. Behind the scenes, MCA was courting the real estate–rich Bass brothers of Texas, hoping to secure their investment in the project. The Basses, however, defected to the Disney camp and were front and center when Michael Eisner suddenly announced that Disney, too, would build a movie theme park in Florida. A construction race ensued, but Universal, in the middle of developing new attraction technologies, was no match for Disney, which could import proven concepts and attractions from its other parks. In the end, Disney's Hollywood Studios opened May 1, 1989, more than a year before Universal Studios Florida.

## THE END OF THE MGM CONNECTION

SO WHAT HAPPENED TO "DISNEY-MGM STUDIOS"? Disney purchased Pixar Animation Studios after partnering with the company on a series of highly successful films, including *Toy Story; A Bug's Life; Monsters, Inc.; Finding Nemo;* and *The Incredibles.* The cost of continuing an association with MGM, coupled with Pixar's arguably greater popularity, probably convinced Disney to rename the theme park. But rather than replace *MGM* with *Pixar,* Disney decided that *Hollywood* represented a more generic reference to moviemaking. In practice, however, many folks drop the *Hollywood* entirely, referring to the park simply as "Disney Studios" or "The Studios."

## WHAT'S OFFERED AT THE STUDIOS TODAY

DHS'S SOUNDSTAGES and facilities produced many television shows and films, both live-action and animated, in the park's early years. The 2003 Disney film *Brother Bear* was largely drawn—by hand!—in the Magic of Disney Animation attraction, and cinema nerds will recognize DHS's landscape in the background of Jim Varney's magnum opus, *Ernest Saves Christmas.* TV series filmed here span everything from the

ABC hit *Who Wants to Be a Millionaire?* to the Hulk Hogan fiasco *Thunder in Paradise.*

In addition, DHS once hosted a variety of attractions that explained how TV shows and movies are made. The *Monster Sound Show,* which ran during the Studios' first decade, used audience volunteers to show how sound effects were added to films; the contemporaneous *SuperStar Television* reenacted famous TV scenes using "green screen" technology and theme park guests as actors.

Today, the *Studios* in "Disney's Hollywood Studios" is of little significance. Movie production left here long ago; it's been more than a decade since any television production of note has taken place; and only a handful of attractions remain that offer a peek behind the scenes, such as the Studio Backlot Tour and the *Indiana Jones Epic Stunt Spectacular!* Unfortunately—for those who loved its creative aspects, that is—DHS is now simply an amusement park whose theme is movies and TV.

While many of the current attractions are entertaining, Disney's self-promotion is often blatant, inescapable, and distracting. The primary goal of any new DHS development, it seems, is to market an upcoming Disney film, TV franchise, or musical act. Most visitors are willing to forgive Disney its excesses, but hardcore devotees lament these changes and remember how good the Studios was when education was the goal instead of the medium.

## HOW MUCH TIME TO ALLOCATE

WHEREAS IT'S IMPOSSIBLE to see all of Epcot or the Magic Kingdom in one day, DHS is doable: There's far less ground to cover by foot, trams carry guests through much of the back lot, and attractions are concentrated in an area about the size of Main Street, Tomorrowland, and Frontierland combined.

One fly in the ointment, however, is the park's perverse way of scheduling live shows. A West Chester, Pennsylvania, mom explains:

> *If I had it to do over, I'd skip the Studios. The shows were good, but we kept missing showtimes because either all the shows started at the same time or the walk between them was too long with little ones.*

Because DHS is smaller, it's more affected by large crowds. Our touring plan will help you stay a step ahead of the mob and minimize waiting in line. It'll also help with the show-schedule problem, but even when the park is crowded, you can see almost everything in a day.

## DISNEY'S HOLLYWOOD STUDIOS IN THE EVENING

BECAUSE DHS CAN BE SEEN in as few as 8 hours, many guests who arrive early in the morning run out of things to do by 5 p.m. or so and leave. Their departure greatly thins crowds and makes the Studios ideal for evening touring. Lines for most attractions are bearable, and the park

*Continued on page 618*

# Disney's Hollywood Studios

**Backlot**

**Echo Lake**

**Main Entrance**

1. *The American Idol Experience* (closes January 2015)
2. *Disney Junior— Live on Stage!*
3. *Fantasmic!*
4. The Great Movie Ride
5. Guest Relations
6. Honey, I Shrunk the Kids Movie Set Adventure
7. *Indiana Jones Epic Stunt Spectacular!*
8. Jedi Training Academy
9. *Jim Henson's Muppet-Vision 3-D*
10. *The Legend of Captain Jack Sparrow*
11. *Lights, Motors, Action! Extreme Stunt Show*
12. *The Magic of Disney Animation*
13. Rock 'n' Roller Coaster
14. Star Tours—The Adventures Continue
15. Studio Backlot Tour
16. *Theater of the Stars/Beauty and the Beast—Live on Stage*
17. Toy Story Midway Mania!
18. *The Twilight Zone Tower of Terror*
19. *Voyage of the Little Mermaid*
20. *Walt Disney: One Man's Dream*

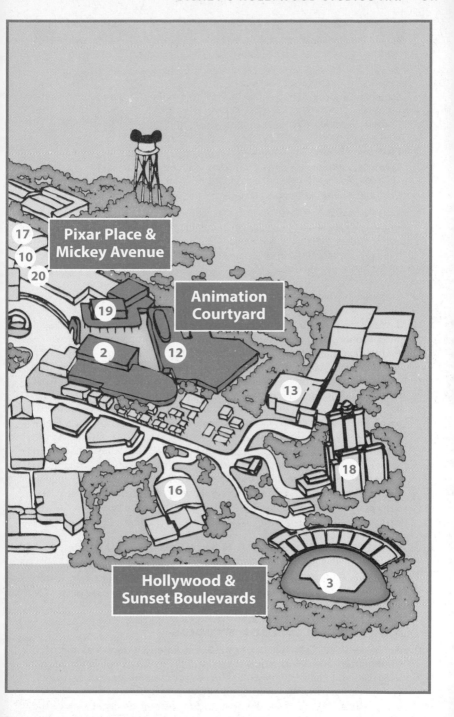

Pixar Place &
Mickey Avenue

Animation
Courtyard

Hollywood &
Sunset Boulevards

## HOLLYWOOD BOULEVARD Services

MOST OF DHS'S SERVICES are on Hollywood Boulevard, including:

**Baby Care Center** At Guest Relations; baby food and other necessities available at Oscar's Super Service

**Banking Services** ATM outside the park to the right of the turnstiles and on Streets of America near Pizza Planet restaurant

**Camera Supplies** At The Darkroom on the right side of Hollywood Boulevard as you enter the park, just past Oscar's Super Service

**First Aid** At Guest Relations

**Live Entertainment and Character Information** Available free at Guest Relations and elsewhere in the park

**Lost and Found** At Package Pick-Up, to the right of the entrance

**Lost Persons** Report lost persons at Guest Relations

**Storage Lockers** Rental lockers to the right of the main entrance, on the left of Oscar's Classic Car Souvenirs

**Wheelchair, ECV/ESV, and Stroller Rentals** To the right of the entrance, at Oscar's Super Service

*Continued from page 615*

is cooler and more comfortable. The *Indiana Jones Epic Stunt Spectacular!* and productions at other outdoor theaters are infinitely more enjoyable during the evening than in the sweltering heat of the day.

DHS is the home of *Fantasmic!* (see page 622), the most dazzling nighttime-entertainment event in the Disney repertoire. Staged at least twice weekly, weather permitting, in its own theater behind The Twilight Zone Tower of Terror, *Fantasmic!* is not to be missed. Unfortunately, *Fantasmic!* draws crowds; some guests stay longer at DHS, and others arrive after dinner from other parks expressly to see the show. Although the crowds thin in the late afternoon, they build again as performance time approaches, making *Fantasmic!* a challenge to get into. Also adversely affected are Rock 'n' Roller Coaster and, to a lesser extent, The Twilight Zone Tower of Terror, both near the entrance to *Fantasmic!* Crowd levels throughout the remainder of the park, excluding at Toy Story Midway Mania!, remain generally light.

### ARRIVING AT DISNEY'S HOLLYWOOD STUDIOS

DHS HAS ITS OWN PARKING LOT and is served by the Disney transportation system. If you drive, Disney's ubiquitous trams will convey you to the ticketing area and entrance gate. For driving directions, see page 373.

### GETTING ORIENTED AT DISNEY'S HOLLYWOOD STUDIOS

ON YOUR LEFT AS YOU ENTER, **Guest Relations** serves as the park headquarters and information center, similar to City Hall in the Magic Kingdom and Guest Relations at Epcot and Disney's Animal Kingdom. Go there for a park map, a schedule of live performances (*Times Guide*), lost persons, Package Pick-Up, lost and found (on the right side of the entrance), baby-care facilities, and general information. To the right of the entrance are locker, stroller, and wheelchair rentals.

As at the Magic Kingdom, you enter the park and pass down a main street. In this case, it's the **Hollywood Boulevard** of the 1930s and '40s. At the end of Hollywood Boulevard is a replica of the famed **Chinese Theater.** Lording over the plaza in front of the theater is a 122-foot-tall replica of the sorcerer hat Mickey Mouse wore in the animated classic *Fantasia.* Besides providing photo ops, the hat is the park's central landmark, making it a good meeting place if your group gets separated.

Though modest in size, the open-access areas of the Studios are confusingly arranged. As you face the hat, two guest areas—**Sunset Boulevard** and **Animation Courtyard**—branch off Hollywood Boulevard to the right. Branching left off Hollywood Boulevard is the **Echo Lake** area. **Streets of America** wraps around the back of **Echo Lake,** while **Pixar Place**'s attractions are behind the Chinese Theater and to the left of the Animation Courtyard. Between Pixar Place and the Animation Courtyard is **Mickey Avenue** with its two minor attractions.

Still farther to the rear is a limited-access area consisting of soundstages, technical facilities, wardrobe shops, administrative offices, and sets. These are accessible on a guided tour by tram and foot.

## FASTPASS+ ATTRACTIONS IN DISNEY'S HOLLYWOOD STUDIOS

LIKE EPCOT, THE STUDIOS implements tiering (see page 90) to restrict the number of FastPass+ reservations you can have at its headliner attractions:

**TIER A** *(Choose one per day)*
- *Beauty and the Beast—Live on Stage*
- *Fantasmic!*
- Rock 'n' Roller Coaster
- The Great Movie Ride
- Toy Story Midway Mania!

**TIER B** *(Choose two per day)*
- *The American Idol Experience* (closes January 2015)
- *Disney Junior—Live on Stage!*

- Indiana Jones Epic Stunt Spectacular!
- *Jim Henson's Muppet-Vision 3-D*
- *Lights, Motors, Action! Extreme Stunt Show*
- Star Tours—The Adventures Continue
- The Twilight Zone Tower of Terror
- *Voyage of the Little Mermaid*

**ENTERTAINMENT & PARADES**
- *The Comedy Warehouse Holiday Special* (seasonal)

These restrictions mean that having a good touring plan is essential to avoid long lines. The good news is that while FastPass+ is offered at more than a dozen Hollywood Studios attractions, there are really only four that you need to worry about most of the year. Here's why:

It's no surprise that our print and online plans emphasize FastPass+ for **Toy Story Midway Mania!** Families with children too small to ride Rock 'n' Roller Coaster or Tower of Terror make a beeline to Toy Story Midway Mania! first thing in the morning, and lines grow quickly. Waits at Toy Story can reach 90 minutes or more on a busy day—in fact, the lines grow so fast that in about one-third of our touring plans, we recommend getting a FastPass+ reservation for 9 a.m.–10 a.m., even when Toy Story is the first step in the plan. The two benefits to doing this are that (1) you'll shave off at least 10 minutes of waiting, and (2) you don't have to line up as early at park opening to join the mad rush to Toy Story.

Next, like Peter Pan's Flight in the Magic Kingdom, **Star Tours** isn't going to be anyone's first choice to visit. For teens and adults especially, the initial morning priorities will be Toy Story, Rock 'n' Roller Coaster and Tower of Terror, possibly with The Great Movie Ride while they're in the area. This makes Star Tours a great choice for a mid- or late-morning FastPass+ reservation.

We really like how our touring plan software places **The Twilight Zone Tower of Terror** in the evening in many of our touring plans: generally from 7 p.m. to 8 p.m. This allows you to focus on other attractions in the morning, which reduces your waits in line, and it makes for a short walk to *Fantasmic!* after you ride Tower of Terror at night.

Finally, our software thinks **The Great Movie Ride** is a good Fast-Pass+ choice for afternoon touring plans, especially if you can't get reservations for Toy Story or Rock 'n' Roller Coaster.

So why isn't **Rock 'n' Roller Coaster** among our four musts? Because it's in the same FastPass+ tier as Toy Story Midway Mania!, and you may choose only one of them. Since Toy Story almost always has the longer waits, it should be your FastPass+ choice. If you can get Fast-Pass+ reservations for Toy Story, Star Tours, and Tower of Terror, our touring plan software will usually make Rock 'n' Roller Coaster your first stop, where you'll find the shortest waits of the day.

FastPass+ kiosk locations at the Studios are as follows:

- At the MyMagic+ Service Center, immediately to the left once you get past the entrance turnstiles
- At the wait-times board on the corner of Hollywood and Sunset Boulevards
- Outside *Voyage of The Little Mermaid,* in Animation Courtyard
- Outside the Tower of Terror, to the left of the entrance
- At Guest Relations outside the park

## DINING IN DISNEY'S HOLLYWOOD STUDIOS

COUNTER-SERVICE RESTAURANTS in DHS are profiled in Part Ten, starting on page 455. For full-service profiles, see the section starting on page 457.

# DISNEY'S HOLLYWOOD STUDIOS ATTRACTIONS

## HOLLYWOOD BOULEVARD

THIS PALM-LINED THOROUGHFARE re-creates Tinseltown's main drag during the Golden Age of Hollywood. Most service facilities are here, interspersed with eateries and shops. Merchandise includes Disney trademark items, movie-related souvenirs, and one-of-a-kind collectibles obtained from studio auctions and estate sales.

Hollywood characters and roving performers entertain on the boulevard, and other happenings pass this way.

## The Great Movie Ride *(FastPass+)*   ★★★½

| APPEAL BY AGE | PRESCHOOL ★★★ | GRADE SCHOOL ★★★½ | TEENS ★★★½ |
| YOUNG ADULTS ★★★½ | OVER 30 ★★★½ | | SENIORS ★★★★ |

**What it is** Indoor movie-history ride. **Scope and scale** Headliner. **When to go** Before 11 a.m., during dinner, after 8 p.m., or use FastPass+. **Special comments** Elaborate, with several surprises. **Authors' rating** Unique; ★★★½. **Duration of ride** About 19 minutes. **Average wait in line per 100 people ahead of you** 2 minutes; assumes all cars operating. **Loading speed** Fast.

### DISNEY DISH WITH JIM HILL

**A "GREAT" TIME FOR A REDO**  The Great Movie Ride is in need of updating, but what to update it with was the big question. The Imagineers thought they'd finally hit upon an idea: replace all of the non-Disney content currently on display with scenes from all of the great franchises Disney has acquired over the past decade—e.g., Pixar, the Muppets, *Star Wars*, and *Iron Man*. The one hitch in this plan is that Universal has an exclusive on using the Marvel characters in a theme park setting in Florida. So The Great Movie Ride 2.0's proposed action-packed finale—right in the middle of *The Avengers'* battle–for–New York sequence—is being rethought.

**DESCRIPTION AND COMMENTS**  Entering through a re-creation of Hollywood's Chinese Theater, guests board vehicles for a fast-paced tour of soundstage sets from classic films, including *Casablanca, Tarzan, The Wizard of Oz, Alien,* and *Raiders of the Lost Ark.* Each set is populated with Disney audio-animatronic characters, as well as the occasional human, all augmented by sound and lighting effects. One of Disney's larger and more ambitious dark rides, The Great Movie Ride encompasses 95,000 square feet and showcases some of the most famous scenes in filmmaking. Life-size animatronic sculptures of stars, including Gene Kelly, John Wayne, James Cagney, and Julie Andrews, inhabit some of the largest sets ever constructed for a Disney ride.

A Tennessee reader thinks the attraction needs some freshening up:

*As someone who attended the grand opening of DHS in 1989, I think The Great Movie Ride is stuck in the '80s.*

A teenage girl from Fanwood, New Jersey, agrees (with attitude):

*A big suggestion for Disney: Update The Great Movie Ride, for goodness' sake! Start by getting rid of scenes from movies no one remembers or knows—Footlight Parade? What?—and put in scenes from recent films that are sure to become tomorrow's classics:* The Dark Knight, Slumdog Millionaire . . . *I could very easily go on.*

**TOURING TIPS**  It's rare to see a wait of more than 30 minutes at The Great Movie Ride except during peak season. Part of the reason is that it's an interval-loading, high-capacity attraction, and part of the reason is that the films (as the previous reader asserts) probably don't ring a bell with anyone under age 40. For what it's worth, actual wait times usually run about one-third shorter than the times posted.

## SUNSET BOULEVARD

EVOKING THE 1940s, Sunset Boulevard—the first right off Hollywood Boulevard—provides another venue for dining, shopping, and street entertainment.

## Fantasmic! (FastPass+)  ★★★★½

**What it is** Mixed-media nighttime spectacular. **Scope and scale** Super-headliner. **When to go** Check *Times Guide* for schedule; if 2 shows are offered, the 2nd is less crowded. **Special comments** Disney's very best nighttime event. **Authors' rating** Not to be missed; ★★★★½. **Duration of presentation** 25 minutes. **Probable waiting time** 50–90 minutes for a seat, 35–40 minutes for standing room.

**DESCRIPTION AND COMMENTS** Off Sunset Boulevard behind the Tower of Terror, this mixed-media show is staged on an island opposite the 7,900-seat Hollywood Hills Amphitheater. By far the largest theater facility ever created by Disney, the amphitheater can accommodate an additional 2,000 standing guests for an audience of nearly 10,000.

*Fantasmic!* is the most innovative outdoor spectacle ever attempted at any theme park. Starring Mickey Mouse in his role as the Sorcerer's Apprentice from *Fantasia,* the production uses lasers, images projected on a shroud of mist, fireworks, lighting effects, and music in combinations so stunning you can scarcely believe what you're seeing. The plot is simple: good versus evil. The story gets lost in all the special effects at times, but no matter; it's the spectacle, not the storyline, that's powerful.

A mom from Pearland, Texas, found *Fantasmic!* too intense for her young child:

*Fantasmic! should come with a warning label. The characters' larger-than-life laser visages, the loud and ominous music, and the thundering explosions with flashes of light, fire, and sparks sent hordes of parents with screaming children fleeing for the exits.*

We don't receive many reports of young children being terrified by *Fantasmic!,* but the reader's point is well taken. Spend some time preparing your kids for what they will see. You can mitigate the fright factor somewhat by sitting back a bit. Also, hang on to your kids after *Fantasmic!* and give them instructions for regrouping should you get separated.

**TOURING TIPS** *Fantasmic!* is presented one or more times each evening, but Disney has been known to change the schedule, so verify before you go. *Fantasmic!* is to the Studios what *IllumiNations* is to Epcot. While it's hard to imagine a 10,000-person stadium running out of space, that's just what happens almost every time the show is staged. On evenings when there are two shows, the second will always be less crowded. If you attend the first (or only) scheduled performance, then arrive at least an hour in advance; if you opt for the second, arrive 50 minutes early.

Disney offers FastPass+ for *Fantasmic!,* but we don't think it's useful. For one thing, your reservation doesn't guarantee you a seat: You must still arrive 30–60 minutes beforehand to be guaranteed a good spot. Arrive 5 minutes before the show starts, and you're likely to be turned away even with FastPass+. Also, there's no special section reserved for FastPass+ guests, as there is for guests who've booked the *Fantasmic!* Dining Package (see next page). Finally, using FastPass+ at *Fantasmic!* prevents you from using FastPass+ at Toy Story Midway Mania! and Rock 'n' Roller Coaster.

From a Yorktown, Virginia, mom:

*You seriously underestimated the time when people should arrive to see* Fantasmic! *if they want to get a seat. The stadium was already full when we arrived, 45 minutes before the show was scheduled to start, and the remaining seats filled up quickly—and this was during the off-season on a slow day.*

A Cross Junction, Virginia, woman offers this tip:

*It's a good idea to buy deli sandwiches outside the park, pack them with snacks and water in your backpack, and get a seat early.*

A multigenerational family from Barrie, Ontario, makes this suggestion for guests who are short on nature's upholstery:

*Bring pillows or towels to sit on. We were sitting on those benches from 6 p.m. for the 7:30 show, and boy, did our rears hurt by the end!*

Rainy and windy conditions sometimes cause *Fantasmic!* to be cancelled. Unfortunately, Disney officials usually don't make a final decision about whether to proceed or cancel until just before showtime. We've seen guests wait stoically for over an hour with no assurance that their patience and sacrifice will be rewarded. We don't recommend arriving more than 20 minutes before showtime on rainy or especially windy nights. On nights like these, pursue your own agenda until 10 minutes or so before showtime, then head to the stadium to see what happens.

A Franklin, Tennessee, family of five describes what you might be in for on a rainy night and offers Disney a suggestion:

*The week we were there, it rained every afternoon for several hours, and the audience had to sit in the rain for 60–90 minutes until Disney figured out whether they would do the show. Most times, it was cancelled. With Fast-Pass+, this wait is unnecessary—just go to kiosks at your convenience during the day, put in your pass, and get a "reservation" for* Fantasmic! *Then you can enjoy the park or choose to stay dry until 15–20 minutes before showtime, giving Disney time to make announcements about the show's status.*

Exiting *Fantasmic!* via the show's single exit can be hair-raising, as this retired elementary-school teacher attests:

*It was like a cattle stampede, but at a snail's pace! Twice I almost ran over toddlers whose mothers didn't have the sense or energy to carry them.*

From a veteran of both Disneyland and Walt Disney World:

*I visit Disneyland a lot, and their [crowd-control] cast members push the throngs of guests through the park like clockwork, even when it's bursting at the seams. At Disney World, it's basically every man for himself at the end of the spectacles as the cast members retreat, leaving very tired, very cranky guests to duke it out. Such is the case at* Fantasmic!*—while I was very happy to see a backstage corridor wide open for a quick reroute, the presence of cast members was extremely rare. I was stunned!*

Finally, a couple from Alberta, Canada, sums it up for all of us:

*For a show so deservedly hyped, I would hope WDW finds ways to make seeing it less stressful.*

**FANTASMIC! DINING PACKAGE** If you eat lunch or dinner at **Hollywood & Vine, The Hollywood Brown Derby,** or **Mama Melrose's Ristorante Italiano,** you can obtain a voucher for the members of your dining party to enter *Fantasmic!* via a special entrance and sit in a reserved section of seats. In return for your patronage of the restaurant, you can avoid 30–90 minutes waiting in the regular line to be admitted. If you know you're going to eat dinner at one of these locations, the dining package is a better way to see *Fantasmic!* than using FastPass+.

You must call ☎ 407-WDW-DINE (939-3463) 180 days in advance and request the package for the night you want to see the show. *Note:* This is a real reservation, not an Advance Reservation, and it must be guaranteed with a credit card at the time of booking. There's no additional charge for the package itself, but there is a $10 charge for canceling a reservation with less than 48 hours' notice.

Included in the package are fixed-price menus for all three restaurants as follows; respective prices are for adults and kids ages 3–9: *Hollywood & Vine:* buffet dinner, $36/$20; *The Hollywood Brown Derby:* lunch and dinner, $57/$17; *Mama Melrose's:* lunch and dinner, $38/$13. Nonalcoholic drinks and tax are included; park admission and gratuity are not. Prices fluctuate according to season, so call WDW-DINE to find out the exact price for a particular date.

You'll receive your vouchers at the restaurant. After dinner, report to the Highlands Gate on Sunset Boulevard—between Theater of the Stars and the Once Upon a Time store—30–45 minutes before showtime. A cast member will collect your vouchers and escort you to the reserved-seating section of the amphitheater. Though you're required to arrive early, you can be seated immediately. The reserved seats are in the center of the stadium; you won't have assigned seats—it's first-come, first-served—so arrive early for the best choice. Finally, understand that if *Fantasmic!* is canceled due to weather or other circumstances, you won't receive a refund or even a voucher for another performance.

Weather notwithstanding, a Waldorf, Maryland, couple thinks the dinner package is the only way to go:

> *We booked dinner at Hollywood & Vine, got our passes for the package, and waltzed on in to the show. It made us feel like VIPs, even though we just had a regular dinner under our meal plan. We've booked the* Fantasmic! *Dining Package every trip since. It's so much more relaxed to see the show without the rush of the crowds.*

## Rock 'n' Roller Coaster *(FastPass+)*  ★★★★

**APPEAL BY AGE  PRESCHOOL ★★  GRADE SCHOOL ★★★★½  TEENS ★★★★★
YOUNG ADULTS ★★★★½  OVER 30 ★★★★½  SENIORS ★★★½**

**What it is** Rock music–themed roller coaster. **Scope and scale** Headliner. **When to go** First 30 minutes the park is open or use FastPass+. **Special comments** 48″ minimum height requirement; children younger than age 7 must ride with an adult. Switching-off option provided (see page 341). Note that this attraction has a single-rider line. **Authors' rating** Disney's wildest American coaster; not to be missed; ★★★★. **Duration of ride** Almost 1½ minutes. **Average wait in line per 100 people ahead of you** 2½ minutes; assumes All trains operating. **Loading speed** Moderate–fast.

**DESCRIPTION AND COMMENTS** Exponentially wilder than Space Mountain or Big Thunder Mountain in the Magic Kingdom, Rock 'n' Roller Coaster is an attraction for fans of high-speed thrill rides. Although the rock icons and synchronized music add measurably to the experience, the ride itself, as opposed to sights and sounds along the way, is the focus. Rock 'n' Roller Coaster's loops, corkscrews, and drops make Space Mountain seem like It's a Small World. What really makes this metal coaster unusual, however, is that first, it's in the dark (like Space Mountain, only with Southern California nighttime scenes instead of space), and second, you're launched up the first hill like a jet off a carrier deck. By the time you crest the hill, you'll have gone from 0 to 57 mph in less than 3 seconds. When you enter the first loop, you'll be pulling 5 g's—

2 more than astronauts used to experience at liftoff on a space shuttle.

Reader opinions of Rock 'n' Roller Coaster are predictably mixed, colored invariably by how the reader feels about roller coasters. First, from a mother of two from High Mills, New York:

*You can't warn people enough about Rock 'n' Roller Coaster. My daughter and I refused to go on it at all. My 9-year-old son, who had no problems with any ride, including Tower of Terror, went on with my husband first thing in the morning. My son came off so shaken he was "done for" the rest of the day. My husband just closed his eyes and hoped for the best.*

And from a Longmont, Colorado, dad:

*Rock 'n' Roller Coaster: The first 15 seconds of this ride are spectacular. I've never experienced anything like the initial take-off.*

From an Australian couple who traveled a long way to ride a coaster:

*My wife and I are definitely not roller-coaster people. However, we found Rock 'n' Roller Coaster quite exhilarating—and because it's dark, we didn't always realize that we were being thrown upside down. We rode it twice!*

**TOURING TIPS** Rock 'n' Roller Coaster is not for everyone—if Space Mountain or Big Thunder pushes your limits, stay away.

Expect long lines except in the first 30 minutes after opening and during the late-evening performance of Fantasmic!. Ride as soon as possible in the morning, or use the single rider line or FastPass+.

A good strategy for riding Rock 'n' Roller Coaster, Toy Story Midway Mania!, and Tower of Terror with minimum wait is to make a midmorning FastPass+ reservation for Toy Story Midway Mania! and an evening FastPass+ reservation Tower of Terror up to 60 days in advance. Then, when you visit, rush first thing after opening to ride Rock 'n' Roller Coaster. If you can't make FastPass+ reservations before you arrive, ride Rock 'n' Roller Coaster or Toy Story Midway Mania! first, then find the nearest FastPass+ kiosk to make the other reservations.

## Theater of the Stars / *Beauty and the Beast—Live on Stage* (FastPass+) ★★★★

| APPEAL BY AGE | PRESCHOOL ★★★★½ | GRADE SCHOOL ★★★★½ | TEENS ★★★★ |
|---|---|---|---|
| YOUNG ADULTS ★★★★ | | OVER 30 ★★★★ | SENIORS ★★★★½ |

**What it is** Live Hollywood-style musical, usually featuring Disney characters; performed in an open-air theater. **Scope and scale** Major attraction. **When to go** Anytime; evenings are cooler. **Special comments** Performances are listed in the daily *Times Guide*. **Authors' rating** Excellent; ★★★★. **Duration of presentation** 25 minutes. **Preshow entertainment** None. **When to arrive** 20–30 minutes before showtime.

**DESCRIPTION AND COMMENTS** Theater of the Stars combines Disney characters with singers and dancers in upbeat and humorous Hollywood musicals. The *Beauty and the Beast* show, in particular, is outstanding. The theater offers a clear field of vision from almost every seat. Best, a canopy protects the audience from the Florida sun (or rain), but the theater still gets mighty hot in the summer.

**TOURING TIPS** Unless you visit during the cooler months, see this show in the late afternoon or the evening. The production is so popular that you should show up 25–35 minutes early to get a seat.

## The Twilight Zone Tower of Terror
*(FastPass+)* ★★★★★

**APPEAL BY AGE** PRESCHOOL ★★★ GRADE SCHOOL ★★★★ TEENS ★★★★½
YOUNG ADULTS ★★★★½ OVER 30 ★★★★½ SENIORS ★★★★

**What it is** Sci-fi-themed indoor thrill ride. **Scope and scale** Super-headliner. **When to go** First or last 30 minutes the park is open, or use FastPass+. **Special comments** 40″ minimum height requirement. Switching-off option provided (see page 341). **Authors' rating** Walt Disney World's best attraction; not to be missed; ★★★★★. **Duration of ride** About 4 minutes plus preshow. **Average wait in line per 100 people ahead of you** 4 minutes; assumes all elevators operating. **Loading speed** Moderate.

**DESCRIPTION AND COMMENTS** The Tower of Terror is a different species of Disney thrill ride, though it borrows elements of The Haunted Mansion at the Magic Kingdom. The story is that you're touring a once-famous Hollywood hotel gone to ruin. As at Star Tours, the queuing area immerses guests in the adventure as they pass through the hotel's once-opulent public rooms. From the lobby, guests are escorted into the hotel's library, where Rod Serling, speaking from an old black-and-white television, greets the guests and introduces the plot.

The Tower of Terror is a whopper, at 13-plus-stories tall. Breaking tradition in terms of visually isolating themed areas, it lets you see the entire Studios from atop the tower . . . but you have to look quick.

The ride vehicle, one of the hotel's service elevators, takes guests to see the haunted hostelry. The tour begins innocuously, but at about the fifth floor things get pretty weird. Guests are subjected to a full range of eerie effects as they cross into the Twilight Zone. The climax occurs when the elevator reaches the top floor—the 13th, of course—and the cable snaps.

The Tower of Terror is an experience to savor. Though the final plunges—yep, plural—are calculated to thrill, the meat of the attraction is its extraordinary visual and audio effects. There's richness and subtlety here, enough to keep the ride fresh and stimulating after many repetitions. Disney has also programmed random lift-and-drop sequences into the mix, making the attraction faster and keeping you guessing about when, how far, and how many times the elevator will fall.

A senior from the United Kingdom tried the Tower of Terror and liked it very much, writing:

*I was thankful I had read your review of the Tower of Terror, or I would certainly have avoided it. As you say, it's so full of magnificent detail that it's worth riding even if you don't fancy the drops involved.*

The Tower has great potential for terrifying young children and rattling more-mature visitors. If you have teenagers in your party, use them as experimental probes. If they report back that they really, really liked the Tower of Terror, run like hell in the opposite direction.

**TOURING TIPS** If you're on hand when the park opens and you want to ride Tower of Terror first, be aware that about 65% of the folks walking down Sunset Boulevard head for Rock 'n' Roller Coaster. If you're not positioned on the far right of the street, it will be hard to move through the crowd to make a right turn into Tower of Terror.

To save time once you're inside the queuing area, when you enter the library waiting room, stand in the far back corner across from the door where you entered and at the opposite end of the room from the TV. When the doors to the loading area open, you'll be the first admitted.

If you have young children (or anyone) who are apprehensive about this attraction, ask the attendant about switching off (see page 341).

Our touring plan on page 834 incorporates an optimal strategy for riding Tower of Terror, Rock 'n' Roller Coaster, and Toy Story Midway Mania! with minimum waits.

# ECHO LAKE

AN ACTUAL MINIATURE LAKE near the middle of the Studios, to the left of Hollywood Boulevard, Echo Lake pays homage to its real-life California counterpart, which served as the backdrop to many early motion pictures. It also provides a visual transition from Hollywood Boulevard's retro theming to Streets of America's film-set ambience.

## *The American Idol Experience\* (FastPass+)* ★★★½

| APPEAL BY AGE | PRESCHOOL ★★★ | GRADE SCHOOL ★★★★½ | TEENS ★★★★ |
| YOUNG ADULTS ★★★½ | | OVER 30 ★★★½ | SENIORS ★★★★ |

*\*Disney announced in the summer of 2014 that this attraction will close permanently in January 2015. We've left the profile in place for this edition.*

**What it is** Theme park version of the long-running TV talent show. **Scope and scale** Major attraction. **When to go** Anytime. **Special comments** Guests must be at least age 14 to perform. **Author's rating** Even if you don't watch the show, you'll find someone to cheer for; ★★★½. **Duration of presentation** 20 minutes for daytime preliminary shows, 40 minutes for the nighttime finale. **When to arrive** 20–30 minutes before showtime.

**DESCRIPTION AND COMMENTS** Based on the television talent search, *The American Idol Experience* is your chance to unleash your song stylings on the world. Your path to superstardom goes like this:

Guests audition a cappella in front of a judge, just as in *American Idol's* first shows of the season. Those who make the cut move on to a second audition and sing, karaoke-style, to a prerecorded track. The judges' picks from this round get to perform in one of the preliminary shows, held several times a day.

During the preliminaries, each contestant repeats his or her song from the second audition in front of a live audience of theme park guests. As with *Idol*, three judges—in this case, Disney cast members—provide feedback. For the most part, the panel uses gentle humor to tell you not to quit your day job, although the judge who stands in for former *Idol* host Simon Cowell does let fly the occasional zinger ("I can picture you on the cover of *Rolling Stone* . . . standing next to someone who can sing on-key").

Audiences decide the preliminary winners, who meet for one last showdown at night. The winner of the finale gets a "Dream Ticket"—a front-of-the-line pass to try out for *American Idol* in his or her hometown.

**TOURING TIPS** The last show of the day offers (ostensibly) the best talent but runs twice as long as the daytime shows. If you don't want to commit to the entire show inside the auditorium, the final show (usually scheduled around 7 p.m.) can be viewed from outside on a Jumbotron screen. This is a wise option (as is catching one of the daytime shows) for those who have to leave for a dinner reservation or line up early for *Fantasmic!*

Erin Foster, a coauthor of our *Unofficial Guide to Disney Cruise Line,* blogged about her daughter's *American Idol Experience* tryout at **tinyurl .com/americanidolmom.** While the attraction is still open, see **tinyurl .com/aiexperiencefaqs** for details on auditioning and eligibility.

## Indiana Jones Epic Stunt Spectacular!
### (FastPass+)  ★★★½

**APPEAL BY AGE**  PRESCHOOL ★★★½   GRADE SCHOOL ★★★★½   TEENS ★★★★½
YOUNG  ADULTS  ★★★★      OVER  30  ★★★★      SENIORS  ★★★★

**What it is** Movie-stunt demonstration and action show. **Scope and scale** Headliner. **When to go** First two shows or last show. **Special comments** Performance times posted on a sign at the entrance to the theatre. **Authors' rating** Done on a grand scale; ★★★½. **Duration of presentation** 30 minutes. **Preshow entertainment** Selection of "extras" from audience. **When to arrive** 20–30 minutes before showtime.

**DESCRIPTION AND COMMENTS** Educational though somewhat unevenly paced, the popular production showcases professional stunt men and women who offer behind-the-scenes demonstrations of their craft. Sets, props, and special effects are very elaborate. At press time, rumors were circulating that the *Stunt Spectacular* will close in 2015 along with *The American Idol Experience;* check **touringplans.com** for updates.

**TOURING TIPS** The Stunt Theater holds 2,000 people; capacity audiences are common. The first performance is always the easiest to see. If the first show is at 10 a.m. or earlier, you can usually walk in, even if you arrive 5 minutes late. For the second performance, show up about 15–20 minutes ahead of time; for the third and subsequent shows, arrive 20–30 minutes early. If you plan to tour during late afternoon and evening, attend the last performance of the day. To beat the crowd out of the stadium, sit on the far right (as you face the staging area) and near the top.

To be chosen from the audience to be an "extra" in the stunt show, arrive early, sit down front, and display unbridled enthusiasm. A woman from Richmond, Virginia, explains:

*After the first performance, I realized the best way to get picked was to stand up, wave my arms, and shout when the "casting director" called for volunteers. (Sitting toward the front helps, too.)*

## Jedi Training Academy  ★★★½

**APPEAL BY AGE**  PRESCHOOL ★★★★   GRADE SCHOOL ★★★★½   TEENS ★★★½
YOUNG  ADULTS  ★★★½      OVER  30  ★★★★      SENIORS  ★★★★

**What it is** Outdoor stage show. **Scope and scale** Minor attraction. **When to go** First 2 shows of the day. **Special comments** To sign up your children to go on stage, visit the ABC Sound Studio building early in the morning; spots are first-come, first-served. **Authors' rating** A treat for young *Star Wars* lovers; ★★★½. **Duration of show** About 15 minutes. **When to arrive** 15 minutes before showtime.

**DESCRIPTION AND COMMENTS** *Jedi Training Academy* is staged several times daily to the left of the Star Tours building entrance, opposite Backlot Express. If you want your young Skywalkers-in-training to appear on stage, visit the sign-up area at the ABC Sound Studio building (across from Star Tours) as early in the morning as possible. Spots go quickly and are first-come, first-served.

A Windham, New Hampshire, mom describes a common conundrum:

*I'm guessing many families will have to choose between racing to Toy Story Midway Mania! to ride or racing to sign up for Jedi Training Academy (children MUST be present at sign-up). We hopped on TSMM, then crossed the park to sign up for JTA. By the time we got there, we were pushed to the 2:20 p.m. show, which eliminated the possibility of leaving for a nap after lunch.*

Once on stage, these miniature Jedi are trained in the ways of The Force and do battle against Darth Vader. If all this sounds too intense, it's not—Storm Troopers provide comic relief, and just as in the movies, the good guys always win.

**TOURING TIPS** Surprisingly popular, given that Disney hasn't promoted it at the same level of hype as other shows. If you plan to watch during summer afternoons, grab drinks at Backlot Express, right next door, about 20 minutes before the show starts.

## Star Tours—The Adventures Continue
*(FastPass+)* ★★★½

| APPEAL BY AGE | PRESCHOOL ★★★★ | GRADE SCHOOL ★★★★½ | TEENS ★★★★½ |
|---|---|---|---|
| YOUNG ADULTS ★★★★½ | OVER 30 ★★★★½ | SENIORS ★★★★½ | |

**What it is** Indoor space-flight-simulation ride. **Scope and scale** Headliner. **When to go** Before 10 a.m., after 6 p.m., or use FastPass. **Special comments** Expectant mothers and anyone prone to motion sickness are advised against riding. Too intense for many children younger than age 8; 40" minimum height requirement. **Authors' rating** A classic adventure; not to be missed; ★★★½. **Duration of ride** About 7 minutes. **Average wait in line per 100 people ahead of you** 5 minutes; assumes all simulators operating. **Loading speed** Moderate–fast.

Motion Sickness

**DESCRIPTION AND COMMENTS** Based on the *Star Wars* movie series, this was Disney's first modern simulator ride. Guests ride in a flight simulator modeled after those used for training pilots and astronauts. You experience dips, turns, twists, and climbs as your vehicle goes through an intergalactic version of the chariot race in *Ben-Hur.* The ride film is projected in high-definition 3-D and has more than 50 combinations of opening and ending scenes. You could ride Star Tours all day without seeing the same film segment twice.

An interactive show, *Jedi Training Academy* (see previous page), is staged several times daily to the left of the Star Tours building entrance.

**TOURING TIPS** Try to ride before 10 a.m., or use FastPass+. If you have young children (or anyone) who are apprehensive about this attraction, ask the attendant about switching off (see page 341). Watch for throngs arriving from performances of the *Indiana Jones Epic Stunt Spectacular!* If you encounter a long line, try again later.

## STREETS OF AMERICA

FORMERLY A WALK-THROUGH back-lot movie set, Streets of America is now a themed area that's home to four attractions. The street sets remain intact and serve as the primary pedestrian thoroughfare.

### DISNEY DISH WITH JIM HILL

**A GALAXY FAR, FAR AWAY GETS A LITTLE CLOSER** If all had gone the way the Imagineers intended, the Studios' new *Star Wars* land (planned for the vicinity of Streets of America and Mickey Avenue) would already be under construction. But Disney CEO Bob Iger was supposedly concerned that the screenplay for the next movie wasn't up to snuff, so he ordered a rewrite and pushed back the release of the film to the 2016 holiday season. As a direct result, the start of construction on DHS's new themed area got pushed back to 2015. But don't worry—it won't be long now till you can stroll down the streets of Tatooine and ride a Speeder Bike through the forests of Endor.

## American Film Institute Showcase ★★★

**APPEAL BY AGE** PRESCHOOL ★★★ GRADE SCHOOL ★★ TEENS ★★★★
YOUNG ADULTS ★★★½ OVER 30 ★★★½ SENIORS ★★★½

**What it is** Display of movie props and costumes. **Scope and scale** Diversion. **When to go** After the Studio Backlot Tour. **Authors' rating** Interesting for film buffs; ★★★½.

**DESCRIPTION AND COMMENTS** At the exit to the Studio Backlot Tour (see page 632) is a series of exhibits and a gift shop collectively known as the American Film Institute Showcase. See movie paraphernalia such as a Darth Vader costume from *Star Wars*.

**TOURING TIPS** Tour anytime. Note that you can enter the gift shop without taking the Studio Backlot Tour—look for this entrance across the street from Studios Catering Co.

## Honey, I Shrunk the Kids Movie Set Adventure ★★½

**APPEAL BY AGE** PRESCHOOL ★★★★½ GRADE SCHOOL ★★★★½ TEENS ★★½
YOUNG ADULTS ★★½ OVER 30 ★★½ SENIORS ★★★

**What it is** Small but elaborate playground. **Scope and scale** Diversion. **When to go** Before 11 a.m. or after dark. **Special comments** Opens an hour later than the rest of the park; kids must be age 10 or younger to play. **Authors' rating** Great for young children, more of a curiosity for adults; ★★½. **Duration of presentation** Varies. **Average wait in line per 100 people ahead of you** 20 minutes.

**DESCRIPTION AND COMMENTS** This elaborate playground appeals to kids age 10 and younger. The story is that you've been "miniaturized" and must make your way through a yard full of 20-foot-tall blades of grass, giant ants, lawn sprinklers, and other oversize props. There are also tunnels, slides, and rope ladders to play on. All areas are padded, and cast members are on hand to maintain some semblance of control.

**TOURING TIPS** While this attraction undoubtedly looked good on paper, it has problems that are hard to "miniaturize" in practice. First of all, it's nowhere near large enough to accommodate all the kids who would like to play. Only 240 people are allowed "on the set" at a time, and many of these are supervising parents or curious adults who hopped in line without knowing what they were waiting for. Frequently by 10:30 or 11 a.m., the playground is full, with dozens waiting outside (some impatiently).

Also, kids get to play as long as parents allow. This creates uneven traffic flow and unpredictable waits. If it weren't for the third flaw—that the attraction is poorly ventilated (read: as hot and sticky as an Everglades swamp)—there's no telling when anyone would leave.

A Tolland, Connecticut, mom found the playground exasperating:

*We let the kids hang out here because we thought it would be relaxing. NOT! You have three choices: (1) Let your kids go anywhere and hope if they try to get out without your permission, someone will stop them. (2) Go everywhere with your kids—this takes a lot of stamina, some athleticism, and a high tolerance for humiliation (you look pretty stupid coming down those slides). (3) Try to visually keep track of your kids. This is impossible, so you'll be either on the edge of or in the middle of an anxiety attack the whole time you're there.*

If you visit during warmer months, get your kids in and out before 11 a.m.—by late morning, this attraction is way too hot and crowded for anyone to enjoy. Access is via Streets of America or Pixar Place.

## Jim Henson's Muppet-Vision 3-D (FastPass+) ★★★★

**APPEAL BY AGE** PRESCHOOL ★★★★  GRADE SCHOOL ★★★★  TEENS ★★★★
YOUNG ADULTS ★★★★  OVER 30 ★★★★  SENIORS ★★★★

**What it is** 3-D movie starring the Muppets. **Scope and scale** Major attraction. **When to go** Anytime. **Authors' rating** Uproarious; not to be missed; ★★★★. **Duration of presentation** 17 minutes. **Preshow entertainment** Muppets on television. **Probable waiting time** 12 minutes.

**DESCRIPTION AND COMMENTS** *Muppet-Vision 3-D* provides a total sensory experience, with wild 3-D action augmented by auditory, visual, and tactile special effects. If you're tired and hot, this zany presentation will make you feel brand-new. Arrive early and enjoy the hilarious video preshow.

A New Brunswick, Canada, reader thinks the Muppets are heaven-sent:

*I think Muppet-Vision 3-D is a godsend for five reasons: (1) It NEVER has a line (even on our visit on New Years' Day). (2) Everyone ages 1–100 gives the show high marks. (3) Between the preshow and the movie, it's half an hour seated comfortably in an air-conditioned theater. (4) Between the live actors and animatronics, it's so much more than just another silly 3-D movie. (5) IT'S THE MUPPETS! Who doesn't love these hysterical creatures and their 3-D shenanigans?*

**TOURING TIPS** This production is popular, but the theater's capacity is almost always sufficient. Waits peak around lunchtime, and it's unusual to see a wait of more than 20 minutes except during holidays. Watch for throngs arriving from performances of the *Indiana Jones Epic Stunt Spectacular!* If you do encounter a long line, try again later.

## Lights, Motors, Action! Extreme Stunt Show (FastPass+) ★★★½

**APPEAL BY AGE** PRESCHOOL ★★★★  GRADE SCHOOL ★★★★½  TEENS ★★★★½
YOUNG ADULTS ★★★★  OVER 30 ★★★★  SENIORS ★★★★

**What it is** Auto stunt show. **Scope and scale** Headliner. **When to go** Anytime. **Authors' rating** Good stunt work, slow pace; ★★★½. **Duration of presentation** 25–30 minutes. **Preshow entertainment** Selection of audience volunteers. **When to arrive** 25–30 minutes before showtime.

**DESCRIPTION AND COMMENTS** This show, which originated at Disneyland Paris, features cars and motorcycles in a blur of chases, crashes, jumps, and explosions. The secrets behind the special effects are explained after each stunt sequence, with replays and different camera views shown on an enormous movie screen; the replays also serve to pass the time needed to place the next stunt's props into position. While the stunt driving is excellent, the show plods between tricks, and you'll probably have had your fill by the time the last stunt ends. Expect about 6–8 minutes of real action in a show that runs 25–30 minutes.

**TOURING TIPS** At the end of the Streets of America, *Lights, Motors, Action!* presents two to five shows daily. It's popular, but its remoteness—it's the most distant attraction from the park entrance—helps distribute and moderate the crowds. Seating is in a 3,000-person stadium, so it's not difficult to find a seat except on the busiest days. However, a family of four from Mount Pleasant, South Carolina, notes that it's easier to get into the stadium than out:

*When we exited the arena (which was full the day we visited), it was horrible! The cast members directed us all to the same exit, and it was a HUGE bottleneck that took us 20 minutes to break free from.*

## Studio Backlot Tour ★★★½

**What it is** Combination tram and walking tour of modern film and video production. **Scope and scale** Headliner. **When to go** Before noon or after 5 p.m. **Special comments** Use the restroom before getting in line. **Authors' rating** Educational and fun; ★★★½. **Duration of presentation** About 30 minutes. **Preshow entertainment** A video before the special-effects segment and another video in the tram boarding area.

**DESCRIPTION AND COMMENTS** A substantial part of the Studios was a film- and TV-production facility, although no actual production takes place these days. Nonetheless, visitors to DHS can take a backstage tour to learn about production methods and technologies.

The tour begins on the edge of the back lot with the special-effects walking segment, then continues with the tram segment. To reach the Studio Backlot Tour, turn right off Hollywood Boulevard through the Studio Arch into the Animation Courtyard. Bear left at the corner where *Voyage of the Little Mermaid* is situated. Follow the street until you see a redbrick warehouse on your right. Go through the door and up the ramp.

The first stop is a special-effects water tank where technicians explain the mechanical and optical tricks that "turn the seemingly impossible into on-screen reality." Included are rain effects and a naval battle.

A prop room separates the special-effects tank and the tram tour. Trams depart about once every 4 minutes on busy days, winding among production and shop buildings before stopping at the wardrobe and crafts shops. Still seated on the tram, you look through large windows to see craftspeople at work.

The tour continues through the back lot, where western desert canyons exist side by side with New York City brownstones. The tour's highlight is **Catastrophe Canyon,** an elaborate special-effects movie set where a thunderstorm, earthquake, oil-field fire, and flash flood are simulated.

A reader from Cherry Hill, New Jersey, found the tour lacking:

*I was extremely disappointed to discover how much the Studio Backlot Tour has been shortened. The tram ride is hardly worth the time, as most of the back lot is now gone. Catastrophe Canyon is tired and in need of refurbishment.*

**TOURING TIPS** Because the Studio Backlot Tour is one of Disney's most efficient attractions, you'll rarely wait more than 15 minutes (usually less than 10). Take the tour at your convenience.

### DISNEY DISH WITH JIM HILL

**NEARER MY GODZILLA TO THEE** Over the years, the Imagineers have come up with plenty of weird concepts for attractions at the Studios. But among the absolute weirdest had to be a proposed "Scream Actors Guild" attraction: a horror-themed spoof of award shows with an ending where the hosts present a lifetime-achievement award to . . . Godzilla. After Big G had been invited to come on down and accept his award, dimensional sound and in-theater effects would have made it feel as if Godzilla were stomping through the Studios, heading for the theater. And the end gag was supposed to have the terrible lizard literally bring the house down, as a life-size Godzilla foot stomped through the roof and splintered the stage.

## PIXAR PLACE

THE WALKWAY BETWEEN *Voyage of the Little Mermaid* and the Studio Backlot Tour holds the popular **Toy Story Midway Mania!** attraction. To emphasize the importance of the *Toy Story* franchise, this section of the park is called Pixar Place.

### Toy Story Midway Mania! *(FastPass+)*   ★★★★½

**APPEAL BY AGE**   PRESCHOOL ★★★★½   GRADE SCHOOL ★★★★★   TEENS ★★★★½
YOUNG ADULTS ★★★★★   OVER 30 ★★★★★   SENIORS ★★★★½

**What it is** 3-D ride through indoor shooting gallery. **Scope and scale** Headliner. **When to go** As soon as the park opens or use FastPass+. **Authors' rating** Not to be missed; ★★★★½. **Duration of ride** About 6½ minutes. **Average wait in line per 100 people ahead of you** 4½ minutes. **Loading speed** Fast.

**DESCRIPTION AND COMMENTS** Toy Story Midway Mania! ushered in a whole new generation of Disney attraction: the "virtual dark ride." Since Disneyland opened in 1955, ride vehicles have moved past two- and three-dimensional sets often populated by audio-animatronic (AA) figures. These amazingly detailed sets and robotic figures defined the Disney Imagineering genius in attractions such as Pirates of the Caribbean, The Haunted Mansion, and Peter Pan's Flight. Now for Toy Story Midway Mania!, the elaborate sets and endearing AA characters are gone. Imagine long corridors, totally empty, covered with reflective material. There's almost nothing there . . . until you put on your 3-D glasses. Instantly, the corridor is full and brimming with color and activity, thanks to projected computer-graphic (CG) images.

Conceptually, this is an interactive shooting gallery much like Buzz Lightyear's Space Ranger Spin (see page 530), but in Toy Story Midway Mania!, your ride vehicle passes through a totally virtual midway, with booths offering such games as ring tossing and ball throwing. You use a cannon on your ride vehicle to play as you move along from booth to booth. Unlike the laser guns in Buzz Lightyear, however, the pull-string cannons in Toy Story Midway Mania! take advantage of CG image technology to toss rings, shoot balls, even throw eggs and pies. Each game booth is manned by a *Toy Story* character who is right beside you in 3-D glory, cheering you on. In addition to 3-D imagery, you experience vehicle motion, wind, and water spray.

The ride begins with a training round to familiarize you with the games, then continues through a number of "real" games in which you compete against your riding mate. The technology has the ability to self-adjust the level of difficulty, and there are plenty of easy targets for small children to reach. *Tip:* Let the pull-string retract all the way back into the cannon before pulling it again.

Finally, and also of note, a 6-foot-tall "living character"—Mr. Potato Head—interacts with and talks to guests in real time in the queuing area (similar to *Turtle Talk with Crush* at Epcot).

**TOURING TIPS** Because it's a ton of fun and it has a relatively low rider-per-hour capacity, Toy Story Midway Mania! is the biggest bottleneck in Walt Disney World, surpassing even Test Track at Epcot. The only way to get aboard without a horrendous wait is to be one of the first through the turnstiles when the park opens and zoom to the attraction. Another alternative is to obtain FastPass+ reservations for Toy Story Midway Mania! But you'll need to act fast: Even on days of moderate attendance, all reservations for the day are usually gone by 11 a.m.

Families with children too small to ride Rock 'n' Roller Coaster or Tower of Terror make a beeline to Toy Story Midway Mania! first thing in the morning, and lines grow quickly. Waits at Toy Story can reach 90 minutes or more on a busy day. In fact, the lines grow so fast that in about a third of our touring plan variations, we recommend getting a FastPass+ reservation for 9 a.m.–10 a.m., even when Toy Story is the first step in the plan. The two benefits to doing this are that you'll shave off at least 10 minutes of waiting, and you don't have to line up as early at the park entrance to join the mad run to Toy Story.

Readers generally love the ride but hate the wait. This effusive praise from a Fanwood, New Jersey, reader is typical:

*Toy Story Midway Mania! is the best ride at Disney—well worth the 70-minute wait. Five stars from one teen and two over-30s!*

A Nashville, Tennessee, mom was mostly positive:

*Toy Story Midway Mania! was already swamped fairly early in the day. We had to resort to getting some of the last FastPass+ reservations, and it extended our day to wait until our return time came up. But oh my gosh, it was worth the wait!*

But a woman from Aberdeen, Washington, was mostly frustrated:

*We decided to risk the 70-minute wait for Toy Story Midway Mania! because my family loves Pixar. The line is a nightmare—it took 2 hours to complete, because for every 5 regular-line people let into the ride, 40–50 FastPass+ people are let in. (Yes, I counted.) It was incredibly irritating to be in such a slow-moving line. I highly recommend riding this only if you have FastPass+.*

## MICKEY AVENUE

MICKEY AVENUE HOSTS two minor attractions on the pedestrian promenade that connects Pixar Place and the Animation Courtyard.

## The Legend of Captain Jack Sparrow ★★½

| APPEAL BY AGE | PRESCHOOL ★★★ | GRADE SCHOOL ★★★ | TEENS ★★★½ |
| --- | --- | --- | --- |
| YOUNG ADULTS ★★½ | | OVER 30 ★★★ | SENIORS ★★★ |

**What it is** Interactive film. **Scope and scale** Minor attraction. **When to go** After dinner. **Authors' rating** Promising technology but not much story; ★★½. **Duration of presentation** Around 10 minutes. **Probable waiting time** 20–30 minutes.

**DESCRIPTION AND COMMENTS** This interactive walk-through attraction takes guests through pirate adventures, including a confrontation with skeleton pirates and a summoning of the squidlike Kraken. Virtually all of the presentation takes place in a room designed like a pirate's cave lair and populated with animatronic figures and other props. A talking skull, recognizable from Pirates of the Caribbean at the Magic Kingdom, narrates each scene. Finally, an impressive holographic Jack Sparrow leads guests in a pirate oath, cementing their commitment to kidnapping, ransacking, and not-giving-a-hoot-ing.

That said, we wonder whom Disney thinks is the target audience for this attraction. Guests are instructed at various times to chant, roar, and stomp their feet in order to vanquish each threat, as if they were 3-year-olds taking part in *Dora the Explorer Meets the Pirates of the Caribbean;* on the other hand, the skeletons, monsters, and shooting are scary enough to frighten many small children. Still, if you can ignore the juvenile dialogue, the holographic Jack Sparrow and Johnny Depp's new scene are worth the few minutes you'll spend here.

A woman from Rahway, New Jersey, wasn't impressed:

*I can't believe we waited in line 45 minutes for this. I spent the entire time thinking there HAD to be something more exciting about to happen. I'm convinced it's there only because they needed to fill some empty space.*

**TOURING TIPS** May not open until late morning or noon; check the *Times Guide*. Because it's next to Toy Story Midway Mania!, *Jack Sparrow* tends to draw guests who have either just finished riding or who balked at getting in Toy Story's long line. If the wait for *Sparrow* is more than 20 minutes, try later in the day.

## Walt Disney: One Man's Dream ★★★

| APPEAL BY AGE | PRESCHOOL ★★★ | GRADE SCHOOL ★★★½ | TEENS ★★★½ |
|---|---|---|---|
| YOUNG ADULTS ★★★★ | | OVER 30 ★★★★½ | SENIORS ★★★★½ |

**What it is** Tribute to Walt Disney. **Scope and scale** Minor attraction. **When to go** Anytime. **Authors' rating** Excellent; ★★★. **Duration of presentation** 25 minutes. **Preshow entertainment** Disney memorabilia. **Probable waiting time** For the film, 10 minutes.

**DESCRIPTION AND COMMENTS** Launched in 2001 to celebrate the 100th anniversary of Disney's birth, *One Man's Dream* consists of an exhibit area showcasing Disney memorabilia and recordings, followed by a film documenting Disney's life. On display are a replica of Walt's California office, various innovations in animation developed by Disney, and early models and working plans for Walt Disney World as well as various Disney theme parks around the world. The film provides a personal glimpse of Disney and offers insights regarding both his successes and failures.

**TOURING TIPS** Give yourself some time here. Every minute spent among these extraordinary artifacts will enhance your visit, taking you back to a time when the creativity and vision that created Walt Disney World were personified by one struggling entrepreneur.

## ANIMATION COURTYARD

THIS AREA IS TO THE RIGHT of the big blue sorcerer's hat in the middle of the park. It holds two large theaters used for live stage shows, plus a separate attraction focusing on Disney animation and several character-greeting locations. We think it's just a big swath of asphalt in desperate need of some landscaping or a water feature.

## Disney Junior—Live on Stage! (FastPass+) ★★★★

| APPEAL BY AGE | PRESCHOOL ★★★★★ | GRADE SCHOOL ★★★★ | TEENS ★★★ |
|---|---|---|---|
| YOUNG ADULTS ★★★ | | OVER 30 ★★★ | SENIORS ★★★½ |

**What it is** Live show for children. **Scope and scale** Minor attraction. **When to go** Per the daily entertainment schedule. **Special comments** Audience sits on the floor.

**Authors' rating** A must for families with preschoolers; ★★★★. **Duration of presentation** 20 minutes. **When to arrive** 20–30 minutes before showtime.

**DESCRIPTION AND COMMENTS** The show features characters from the Disney Channel's *Sofia the First, Doc McStuffins,* and *Jake and the Never Land Pirates,* among others. *Disney Junior* uses elaborate puppets instead of live characters on stage. A simple plot serves as the platform for singing, dancing, puppetry, and audience participation. The characters, who ooze love and goodness, rally throngs of tots and preschoolers to sing and dance along with them. All the jumping, squirming, and high-stepping is facilitated by having the audience sit on the floor so that kids can spontaneously erupt into motion when the mood strikes. Even for adults without children, it's a treat to watch the tykes rev up.

*Disney Junior* will be the highlight of a preschooler's day, as this Florida mother of a 4-year-old attests:

*My daughter absolutely LOVED the Disney Junior show! If you have preschoolers, this is a must!*

**TOURING TIPS** Staged in a huge building to the right of The Magic of Disney Animation. Get here at least 25 minutes before showtime, pick a spot on the floor, and take a breather until the action begins.

## The Magic of Disney Animation   ★★½

| APPEAL BY AGE | PRESCHOOL ★★★½ | GRADE SCHOOL ★★★½ | TEENS ★★★½ |
|---|---|---|---|
| YOUNG ADULTS ★★★½ | OVER 30 ★★★★ | | SENIORS ★★★★ |

**What it is** Overview of Disney animation process, with limited hands-on demonstrations. **Scope and scale** Minor attraction. **When to go** Anytime. **Special comments** Opens an hour later than the rest of the park. **Authors' rating** Better as a self-guided experience; ★★½. **Duration of self-guided tour** 20–50 minutes.

**DESCRIPTION AND COMMENTS** The consolidation of Walt Disney Animation Studios in Burbank, California, has left this attraction without a story to tell. Park guests get a general overview of the Disney animation process but do not see the detailed work of actual animators, as was possible in previous versions.

Now a self-guided tour, The Magic of Disney Animation includes a small theater presentation starring Mushu, the dragon from *Mulan,* covering the basics of Disney's animation processes and history. Afterward, guests have the option of exiting the attraction, meeting characters, participating in interactive games, or attending the Animation Academy (see below). Various art from memorable Disney films decorates the walls throughout.

Interactive games include **The Sound Stage,** where you add music and sound effects to a short movie scene; **Digital Ink and Paint,** where you add digital color to an uncolorized Disney movie scene; and **You're a Character,** a short quiz to help identify which Disney character you're most like.

**Animation Academy** is an interactive mini-attraction: a drawing class led by a Disney-trained artist. Guests learn to sketch a Disney character, and they get to keep the artwork they create.

This is by far the most interesting part of the attraction, but it's not designed for all guests. The animator works quickly, which seems to frustrate kids who need more time or assistance. For those who can keep up, this part demonstrates how difficult hand-drawn animation really is.

If you don't want your artwork to get wrinkled badly during the rest of the day as you tour the park, a cast member at the attraction's store may be able to provide a bag for it.

TOURING TIPS Some days, Animation doesn't open until 10 or 11 a.m., by which time the park is pretty full. Character greetings take place throughout the day. If you want to meet characters without taking the tour, go through the Animation Gallery gift shop and head to the back of the store. A path leads directly from the shop to the characters.

## Voyage of the Little Mermaid *(FastPass+)* ★★★½

| APPEAL BY AGE | PRESCHOOL ★★★★ | GRADE SCHOOL ★★★★ | TEENS ★★★½ |
|---|---|---|---|
| YOUNG ADULTS ★★★½ | OVER 30 ★★★★ | | SENIORS ★★★★ |

**What it is** Musical stage show featuring characters from the Disney movie *The Little Mermaid*. **Scope and scale** Major attraction. **When to go** Before 9:45 a.m., just before closing, or use FastPass+. **Authors' rating** Romantic, lovable, and humorous in the best Disney tradition; ★★★½. **Duration of presentation** 15 minutes. **Preshow entertainment** Taped ramblings about the decor in the preshow holding area. **Probable waiting time** Before 9:30 a.m., 10–30 minutes; after 9:30 a.m., 35–70 minutes.

DESCRIPTION AND COMMENTS *Voyage of the Little Mermaid* is a winner, appealing to every age. Sweet but not saccharine, the *Little Mermaid* show is the most tender and romantic entertainment offered anywhere in Walt Disney World. The story is simple and engaging, the special effects impressive, and the Disney characters memorable.

We get a lot of mail from Europeans who complain about the "soppy sentimentality" of Americans in general and of Disney attractions in particular. These comments of a man from Bristol, England, are typical:

*Americans have an ability to think as a child and so enjoy the soppiness of* The Little Mermaid. *English cynicism made it hard for us at times to see Disney stories as anything other than gushing, namby-pamby, and full of stereotypes. Other Brits might also find the sentimentality cloying. Maybe you should prepare them for the need to rethink their wry outlook on life temporarily.*

TOURING TIPS Except during the busiest holiday periods, it's unusual for anyone in line not to be admitted to the next showing of *Mermaid*. Typical waits are under 25 minutes most of the year.

When you enter the preshow lobby, stand near the doors to the theater. When they open, go inside, pick a row of seats, and let 6–10 people enter the row ahead of you. The strategy is twofold: to obtain a good seat and be near the exit.

Finally, a Charlotte, North Carolina, mom takes exception to our fright-potential assessment:

*The* Guide *let me down on the* Little Mermaid *show—the huge sea witch portrayed in laser lights, cartoon, and live action TERRIFIED my 3-year-old. Your description led me to believe it was all sweetness and romance.*

# LIVE ENTERTAINMENT *at* DISNEY'S HOLLYWOOD STUDIOS

THE STUDIOS' LIVE-ENTERTAINMENT ROSTER includes theater shows, musical acts, roaming bands of street performers, and *Fantasmic!* (see page 622), a nighttime water, fireworks, and laser show that draws rave reviews. Of all of these, the theater shows, musical acts, and street performers are generally as good as or better than comparable acts at the other Disney parks. We'd be remiss if we didn't tell you to catch a show of **Mulch, Sweat, & Shears** (★★★½), a group of landscaping "brothers" who make up a cover band that plays everything from AC/DC to Journey. Guests standing near the front may be invited into the act.

**AFTERNOON PARADE (★★★½)** Disney canceled the Studios' latest afternoon parade in 2013. We hear a new, smallish parade may be coming shortly.

**DISNEY CHARACTERS** Donald, Daisy, Goofy, and Pluto are usually found in front of the Sorcerer's Hat. *Toy Story*'s Buzz and Woody are in Pixar Place in front of Toy Story Midway Mania!, while Mike and Sulley from *Monsters, Inc.*, are a little farther down the same walkway, near Backlot Tour. Mickey and Minnie Mouse hold court near the Magic of Disney Animation, along with characters from recent Disney films. Other Disney Junior stars are in Animation Courtyard, too, near *Disney Junior—Live on Stage!* Disney Channel's Phineas and Ferb, plus the cast of Pixar's *Cars* franchise, are found along the Streets of America. Check the *Times Guide* for times and locations of character appearances.

**STREET ENTERTAINMENT (★★★½)** The Studios has one of the best teams of roving street performers in all of Walt Disney World. Appearing primarily on Hollywood and Sunset Boulevards, the cast of characters includes Hollywood stars and wannabes, their agents, directors, and gossip columnists. Keep in mind that the performers aren't shy about asking you to join in their antics.

**OSBORNE FAMILY SPECTACLE OF DANCING LIGHTS (★★★★½)** During the holidays, the Streets of America are transformed into the Osborne Family Spectacle of Dancing Lights. More than 5 million lights of many colors adorn the facades that replicate New York and San Francisco. These lights periodically "dance" by blinking in time to music that fills the area, and guests are periodically dusted with suspiciously soaplike "snow" from the rooftops. What started as a traffic-snarling eyesore in Arkansas is now one of Disney's premier holiday attractions.

The Osborne Lights draw heavy crowds, causing the Streets of America to be as crowded as the real streets of Manhattan during rush hour. The lights go on at dusk (normally 6 p.m., accompanied by a short ceremonial flipping of a light switch with characters). You can loiter to be among the first to see the lights, or visit during a *Fantasmic!* show or shortly after the park has officially closed.

The lights usually operate evenings from around the end of the first week of November to around the end of the first week of January.

# DISNEY'S HOLLYWOOD STUDIOS TOURING PLAN

TOURING THE STUDIOS CENTERS primarily around Toy Story Midway Mania! and the fact that it simply cannot handle the number of guests who want to ride. A wonderful attraction for small children, it's therefore the first choice for families with young kids.

## "Not a Touring Plan" Touring Plans

For the type-B reader, these touring plans (see page 820) avoid detailed step-by-step strategies for saving every last minute in line. For DHS, these "not" touring plans include advice for adults and parents with one day in the park, for anyone with two days, and for anyone with an afternoon and a full day to tour.

## BEFORE YOU GO

1. Call ☎ 407-824-4321 or visit **disneyworld.com** to verify the park's hours.

2. Buy your admission and make FastPass+ reservations before you arrive.

3. Make lunch and dinner Advance Reservations or reserve the *Fantasmic!* Dining Package (if desired) before you arrive, by calling ☎ 407-WDW-DINE (939-3463).

4. The schedule of live entertainment changes from week to week and even from day to day. Review the handout daily *Times Guide,* available free throughout Disney's Hollywood Studios.

## DISNEY'S HOLLYWOOD STUDIOS ONE-DAY TOURING PLAN *(page 834)*

WITH DISNEY INTRODUCING FASTPASS+, we've listed the approximate FastPass+ return times for which you should attempt to make reservations. (The touring plan should work with anything close to the times shown.) In case Disney changes FastPass+ rules, we've listed in the plans the attractions most likely to need FastPass+, too. Check **touringplans.com** for the latest information.

# PART FIFTEEN

# UNIVERSAL ORLANDO

WHEN UNIVERSAL STUDIOS FLORIDA **(USF)** opened in 1990, it competed directly with Disney's Hollywood Studios. Both parks offered movie- and television-themed rides and shows, while other attractions provided an educational, behind-the-scenes introduction to the cinematic arts. And both had working film- and television-production facilities.

In the summer of 1999, Universal launched its second major theme park, **Universal's Islands of Adventure (IOA),** which competes directly with the Magic Kingdom. Universal Studios Florida, Islands of Adventure, the four Universal hotels, and the **CityWalk** dining, nightlife, and shopping complex are collectively known as **Universal Orlando** and are profiled in the next two chapters.

The parks have gone in different directions since then. Whereas Disney's Hollywood Studios essentially abandoned its production facilities long ago, at Universal there is test-marketing of television pilots to guests, along with actual filming. Then there are the attractions, the most famous being the groundbreaking **Wizarding World of Harry Potter–Hogsmeade** at Islands of Adventure. As if to prove this was no one-hit wonder, Universal opened the equally ambitious **Wizarding World of Harry Potter–Diagon Alley** at Universal Studios Florida in 2014.

In contrast, only one truly innovative attraction has opened at Disney's Hollywood Studios in the past decade: 2008's Toy Story Midway Mania! Not even the most ardent Disney supporter would argue that Disney is as invested in the Studios as Universal is in its parks.

Even hardcore Disney fans, such as this Moncton, Nebraska, reader, are beginning to pay attention:

> I'm a huge fan of all things Disney, so it pains me a little to say that the highlight of our most recent trip was actually Universal Orlando. Not because Disney World isn't spectacular—it always is—but because Universal's themed Harry Potter experience is by far the most immersive I've ever had. Disney has to be a little nervous. Responding to Pottermania with an Avatar land just doesn't seem like a good move—Disney on the defensive! But hey, a little competition is healthy.

# *A* UNIVERSAL PRIMER

## UNIVERSAL ON THE WEB

IF, JUDGING FROM THE PLENITUDE of independent Disney World websites, you expect a similar number of such sites for Universal, you'd be wrong. Though some of the Disney sites mentioned in Part One (see pages 34 and 35) cover Universal in some (usually minimal) way, independent Universal sites, especially for Universal Orlando, are practically nonexistent. Of the independent Disney sites that deal with Universal, we recommend **mousesavers.com** for hotel and admission bargains, as well as touring tips for The Wizarding World of Harry Potter. For more-comprehensive information and discussion, try **park scope.net** and the discussion boards dedicated to Universal at **orlando united.com**. For crowd projections and touring tips, check our own **touringplans.com**. News and theme park developments are available at **orlandosentinel.com** and **orlandoweekly.com; jimhillmedia.com** offers insider information on attractions, new technologies, and changes in the parks. Finally, there's the official Universal Orlando website, **universal orlando.com**.

Universal also offers a free smartphone app for Apple and Android devices that displays wait times and interactive maps while you're inside the parks, using the resort's free Wi-Fi (connect to **xfinitywifi** and accept the legal terms to access).

## COST

UNIVERSAL'S ADMISSION POLICY largely emulates Disney's Magic Your Way program (see page 54). A one-day, one-park Base Ticket is on par with those at the Disney parks; multiday single-park Base Tickets, however, are significantly less expensive at Universal. Park-hopping (or "Park-to-Park," in Universal parlance) passes can be much more expensive at Disney, where, for example, a four-day Park Hopper ticket costs a little over 50% more than what you'd pay at Universal.

Be aware that you *must* have Park-to-Park admission to ride the Hogwarts Express train between IOA and USF; single-park tickets may be upgraded at Guest Services or the train stations.

As at Disney, passes expire 14 days after the first use. Prices listed on page 644 are what you'd pay at the gate and include tax; unlike Disney, however, Universal offers discounts when you purchase passes online at **universalorlando.com,** including $20-per-pass discounts on multiday tickets plus other time-limited specials. Passes purchased online are printable, can be used at the turnstiles, and are good for 14 days beginning with the day of first use. Although Universal discounts multiday tickets online, one-day admissions are slightly more expensive than at the gate; nevertheless, they're probably worth it for the convenience.

**Undercover Tourist,** a ticket discounter (**undercovertourist.com**), offers the most deeply discounted Universal tickets we're aware of to subscribers of **MouseSavers** (**mousesavers.com**). Tickets purchased through the MouseSavers newsletter include tax and free shipping.

*Continued on page 644*

## Universal Orlando

Turkey Lake Rd.

Universal's Cabana Bay Beach Resort

The Wizarding World
of Harry Potter–
Hogsmeade

Universal's
Islands of
Adventure

Adventure
Way

To Tampa &
Walt Disney
World

4

Hollywood Way

Universal's Royal Pacific Resort

Universal Blvd.

International Dr.

Parking Garages

Kirkman Rd.  435  435

4  To
↓ Orlando

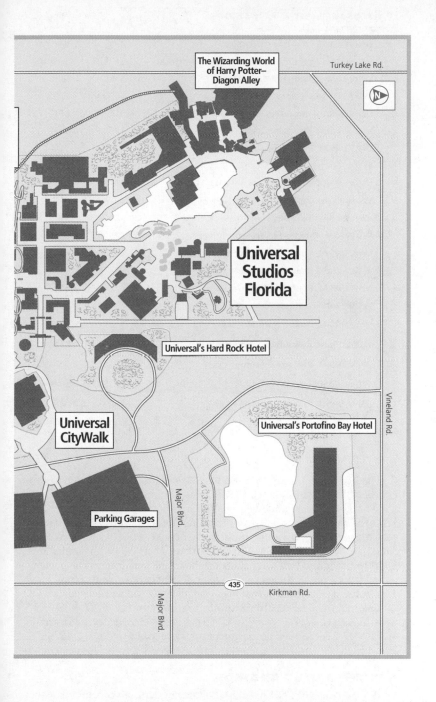

The Wizarding World
of Harry Potter–
Diagon Alley

Turkey Lake Rd.

Universal
Studios
Florida

Universal's Hard Rock Hotel

Universal
CityWalk

Universal's Portofino Bay Hotel

Vineland Rd.

Parking Garages

Major Blvd.

435    Kirkman Rd.

Major Blvd.

| UNIVERSAL VS. WDW ADMISSIONS *(prices include tax)* | | ADULTS | AGES 3–9 |
|---|---|---|---|
| **BASE TICKETS** | UNIVERSAL One-Day Base Ticket | $102 | $96 |
| | WDW One-Day Base Ticket (Magic Kingdom) | $105 | $99 |
| | UNIVERSAL Two-Day Base Ticket | $166 | $155 |
| | WDW Two-Day Base Ticket | $299 | $186 |
| | UNIVERSAL Three-Day Base Ticket | $177 | $165 |
| | WDW Three-Day Base Ticket | $292 | $272 |
| | UNIVERSAL Four-Day Base Ticket | $187 | $175 |
| | WDW Four-Day Base Ticket | $313 | $292 |
| **PARK-HOPPING** | UNIVERSAL One-Day Park-to-Park Ticket | $145 | $138 |
| | WDW One-Day Park Hopper | $143 | $136 |
| | UNIVERSAL Two-Day Park-to-Park Ticket | $209 | $198 |
| | WDW Two-Day Park Hopper | $252 | $239 |
| | UNIVERSAL Three-Day Park-to-Park Ticket | $219 | $207 |
| | WDW Three-Day Park Hopper | $344 | $324 |
| | UNIVERSAL Four-Day Park-to-Park Ticket | $230 | $217 |
| | WDW Four-Day Park Hopper | $377 | $356 |
| **ANNUAL PASSES** | UNIVERSAL Power Annual Pass | $229 | $229 |
| | WDW Florida Resident Seasonal Pass | $340 | $340 |
| | UNIVERSAL Preferred Annual Pass | $314 | $314 |
| | WDW Annual Pass | $675 | $675 |
| | UNIVERSAL Premier Annual Pass | $463 | $463 |
| | WDW Premium Annual Pass | $803 | $803 |

*Continued from page 641*

The five-park, 14-day **Orlando Flex Ticket** allows unlimited entry to Universal Studios Florida (USF), Universal's Islands of Adventure (IOA), SeaWorld, Aquatica, and Wet 'n Wild and costs $307 for adults and $291 for children ages 3–9, tax included. The six-park, 14-day **Orlando Flex Ticket Plus,** providing unlimited entry to USF, IOA, SeaWorld, Aquatica, Wet 'n Wild, and Busch Gardens, costs $349 for adults and $330 for children. Buy the tickets online at the websites of the participating parks, or get them at a discount at **officialticketcenter.com.** Flex Tickets are a good deal only if you visit all of the parks covered.

The main Universal Orlando information number is ☎ 407-363-8000. Reach Guest Relations at ☎ 407-224-4233; order tickets by mail at ☎ 407-224-7840. The numbers for Lost and Found are ☎ 407-224-4244 (USF) and 407-224-4245 (IOA); press 2 to be connected.

## A WORD ABOUT CROWDS

YOU'VE PROBABLY READ ABOUT the huge crowds that inundate the Wizarding World outposts at both Universal parks. The reports are true, but they present an unbalanced view of the crowds at the Universal parks overall. To get a quantitative grip on crowding, let's look at attendance figures compared with the size of the parks. On a day of average attendance, USF sees about 140 guests per acre, while Disney's Hollywood Studios sees about 203. Because both parks contain almost the same number of attractions, this means Disney Studios is 45% more crowded on an average day than USF. Contrasting the Magic Kingdom with IOA, the latter averages 200 guests per day, per acre, while the Magic Kingdom—the attendance leader of all the world's theme parks—registers a whopping 460 guests per day, per acre. Depending on how you define attractions, however, the Magic Kingdom has about 31, versus 22 at Islands of Adventure. Even so, there are still more than twice as many guests for each Magic Kingdom attraction as for each IOA attraction.

## HOW MUCH TIME TO ALLOCATE

TOURING UNIVERSAL STUDIOS FLORIDA, including one meal and a visit to Diagon Alley, takes about 10–12 hours. One reader laments:

*There's a lot of "standing" at USF, and it isn't as organized as DHS. Many of the attractions don't open until 10 a.m. We weren't able to see nearly as many attractions at Universal as we were at DHS during the same amount of time.*

As the reader observes, some USF attractions don't open until 10 a.m. or later. Most theater attractions don't schedule performances until 11 a.m. or after. This means that early in the day, all park guests are concentrated among the limited number of attractions in operation.

As a postscript, you won't have to worry about any of this if you use our Universal Studios touring plans. We'll keep you one jump ahead of the crowd and make sure that any given attraction is running by the time you get there.

## LODGING AT UNIVERSAL ORLANDO

UNIVERSAL HAS FOUR RESORT HOTELS. The 750-room **Portofino Bay Hotel** is a gorgeous property set on an artificial bay and themed like an Italian coastal town. The 650-room **Hard Rock Hotel** is an ultracool "Hotel California" replica, and the 1,000-room, Polynesian-themed **Royal Pacific Resort** is sumptuously decorated and richly appointed. All three are on the pricey side. The retro-style **Cabana Bay Beach Resort,** Universal's newest and largest hotel, has 1,800 moderate- and value-priced rooms, plus amenities (bowling alley, lazy river) not seen at comparable Disney resorts.

Like Disney, Universal offers a number of incentives for visitors to stay at its hotels. Perks available that mirror those offered by the Mouse include delivery to your on-site hotel room of purchases made in the parks, tickets and reservation information from hotel concierges, priority dining reservations at Universal restaurants, and the ability to charge purchases to your room account.

Universal charges a $20-per-night self-parking fee ($27 for valet) at its luxury resorts ($10 per night at Cabana Bay, self-parking only); day guests pay significantly more. Free buses and water taxis serve Universal Studios Florida, Islands of Adventure, CityWalk, SeaWorld, Aquatica (SeaWorld's water park), and Wet 'n Wild. Hotel guests (except for those at Cabana Bay) may use the Universal Express program without limitation all day long and are also eligible for "next available" table privileges at CityWalk restaurants and similar priority admission to Universal Orlando theme park shows. The most valuable perk to most Universal resort guests, however, is admission to The Wizarding World of Harry Potter–Hogsmeade at Islands of Adventure and The Wizarding World of Harry Potter–Diagon Alley at Universal Studios Florida 1 hour before the general public.

## ARRIVING AT UNIVERSAL ORLANDO

UNIVERSAL ORLANDO CAN BE ACCESSED from eastbound I-4 by taking Exit 75A and turning left at the top of the ramp onto Universal Boulevard. If you're traveling westbound on I-4, use Exit 74B and then turn right on Hollywood Way. There are also entrances off Kirkman Road to the east, Turkey Lake Road to the north, and Vineland Road to the west. Universal Boulevard connects the International Drive area to Universal via an overpass bridging I-4. Turkey Lake and Vineland Roads are particularly good alternatives when I-4 is gridlocked.

Two multistory parking garages hold 20,000 cars; signs from all four entrances route you to the parking structures. Parking is $17 for cars and $22 for RVs, trailers, and other large rigs. Regular parking drops to $5 between 6 p.m. and 10 p.m. and is free after 10 p.m. Preferred parking is offered during the day for $22, but we've scored spaces just as good or better using the regular parking, especially when we've arrived before 10:30 a.m. An advantage of preferred parking, however, is that you'll park faster because the ratio of cars choosing preferred to regular is about 1 to 13. In addition to the garages, valet parking is available at CityWalk for $15 for a visit of up to 2 hours or $30 for longer than that. If you're a Universal hotel guest, park in the hotel lot and walk, take a free water taxi to CityWalk, or catch a shuttle bus to the parking garages' central hub.

The two rectangular garages lie along a north–south axis, with the pedestrian walkways leading to the theme parks running along the west, or long, side of each building. Because the garages are two-thirds as wide as they are long, the farther your parking place is from the west side, the worse it will be. This is why preferred parking is often not as close as regular parking—with the former, you'll be closer to the covered walkways to the parks, but if your particular space is toward the east side of the garage, you'll end up farther away than a guest who chose regular parking and was assigned a space closer to the west side of the structure.

We strongly recommend that you take a photo of the name and number of your section, level, and row. Sections are named for movies—Jurassic Park, King Kong, and the like. The first numeral of the number following the section name tells you what deck level you're on, and the remaining numbers specify the row. So if a sign tells you that you're on King Kong 410, you're in the King Kong section on the fourth floor in Row 10.

From the garages, moving sidewalks deliver you to CityWalk. From here, you can access the main entrances of both Universal Studios Florida and Islands of Adventure. Unlike at Disney parks, there are no trams, so depending on where in the garage your car is parked, you'll have an 8- to 20-minute hike to the theme park entrances even if you use the (sometimes) moving walkways.

If you're staying at Walt Disney World and you don't have a car, **Mears Transportation** will shuttle you from your hotel to Universal and back for $20. Pickup and return times are at your convenience. To schedule a shuttle, call ☎ 855-463-2776.

## UNIVERSAL EXPRESS

SIMILAR TO DISNEY WORLD'S FASTPASS+, Universal Express is a system whereby any guest can schedule an appointment to experience an attraction later in the day with little or no waiting. Unlike FastPass+, Universal Express is not free. Two versions are available, both of which require you to cough up more money beyond your park admission:

*unofficial* **TIP**
Universal Express is not valid at the headliner Harry Potter attractions, **Forbidden Journey**, **Escape from Gringotts**, and **Hogwarts Express**.

Universal Express is free to guests at all Universal hotels except Cabana Bay Beach Resort; they may use the Express lines all day long simply by flashing the pass they get at check-in. This is especially valuable during peak season.

Guests staying at Cabana Bay or a non-Universal hotel can purchase Universal Express for an extra $30–$110 (depending on the season), which provides line-jumping privileges at each Universal Express attraction at a given park.

You can purchase Universal Express for one or both parks and for either single (one ride only on each participating attraction) or unlimited use. The number of Express passes is limited each day, and they can sell out. Increase your chances of securing passes by buying and printing them at home off Universal's website. Speaking of participating attractions, more than 90% of rides and shows are covered by Universal Express, a much higher percentage than those covered by FastPass+ at Walt Disney World.

You can also buy Universal Express at the theme parks' ticket windows, just outside the front gates, but it's faster to do so inside the parks. At Universal Studios Florida, it's available at Super Silly Stuff; at Islands of Adventure, you can buy Universal Express at Jurassic Outfitters, Toon Extra, and the Marvel Alterniverse Store. It's also available up to eight months in advance at **universalorlando.com.** You'll need to know when you plan on using it, though, because prices vary depending on the date.

A New York mom had a trouble-free experience but questions the value of the investment:

*We bought Universal Express, but it was neither necessary nor consistently effective. By arriving at park opening, we were able to see many attractions right away without needing the passes at all. They helped on about three attractions between the two parks—a poor* *return for an investment of $156, but it was like life insurance: good to have just in case. On Dudley Do-Right, we still had to wait 30 minutes even with Express, whereas with Disney's free FastPass+ we never waited more than 5 minutes for an attraction. The only aspect of UE that was better than FP+ is that touring order was unaffected: UE could be used whenever you first approached an attraction instead of your having to come back later.*

**IS UNIVERSAL EXPRESS WORTH IT?** The answer depends on the season you visit, hours of park operation, and crowd levels. Attendance has jumped at both parks since the opening of each Harry Potter land, especially at Universal Studios Florida now that Diagon Alley has opened. However, the big-ticket rides in Hogsmeade and Diagon Alley don't participate in Universal Express, so you don't get to cut in line at Universal's most in-demand attractions. Still, if you want to sleep in and arrive at a park after opening, Express is an effective, albeit expensive way to avoid long lines at the non-Potter headliner attractions, especially during holidays and busy times.

If, however, you arrive 30 minutes before park opening and you use our touring plans (see pages 835–838), you should experience the lowest possible waits at both USF and IOA. We encourage you to try the touring plans first, but if waits for rides become intolerable, you can always buy Express in the parks.

Finally, you'll want to devise a convenient way to keep track of your pass, as this Bluffton, Indiana, dad found out a little too late:

*I wish I'd known ahead of time to bring a lanyard to hang our Universal Express pass on.*

**UNIVERSAL EXPRESS FOR RESORT GUESTS** This program allows guests at all Universal resorts except Cabana Bay to bypass the regular line anytime and as often as desired by simply flashing a pass they get at check-in. This perk far surpasses any benefit accorded to guests of Disney resorts. Be aware that neither Harry Potter and the Forbidden Journey nor Pteranodon Flyers at IOA is a Universal Express attraction, nor is Harry Potter and the Escape from Gringotts at USF or the interpark Hogwarts Express train. Again, however, all Universal hotel guests, including those staying at Cabana Bay, may enter both parks' Wizarding World outposts 1 hour before they open to the public. Which park you may enter on any particular day, and which attractions will be operating, are at Universal's discretion and may rotate among the hotels to manage demand.

A father from Snellville, Georgia, did the math and discovered that it was cheaper for his family to stay at a Universal resort than buy Universal Express:

*The benefits of staying on-property are worth it, with early entry to The Wizarding World and unlimited Express privileges at both parks. We got a room at the Royal Pacific Resort for $349 on a Saturday night, which allowed us to use Universal Express Saturday and Sunday. The room cost $43.63 per person per day, while an [à la carte] Express pass this same weekend would have cost $56 per person per day, and we still would have had to pay for a hotel.*

### How Universal Express Affects
### Crowd Conditions at Attractions

This system dramatically affects crowd movement (and touring plans) in the Universal parks. A woman from Yorktown, Virginia, writes:

> *People in the Express line were let in at a rate of about 10 to 1 over the regular-line folks. This created bottlenecks and long waits for people who didn't have the Express privilege at the very times when it's supposed to be easier to get around!*

## SINGLES LINES

ANOTHER TIME-SAVING OPTION is the singles line. Several attractions have this special line for guests riding alone. As Universal employees will tell you, this line is often just as fast as the Express line. We strongly recommend using the singles line whenever possible—it will decrease your overall wait and leave more time for repeat rides or just bumming around the parks. Note, though, that some queues (particularly Forbidden Journey's and Escape from Gringotts') are attractions in themselves and deserve to be experienced during your first ride.

## U-BOT

THIS RIDE-RESERVATION SYSTEM works much like Disney's FastPass+ but incorporates the small U-Bot device. Guests can purchase access to the device at any Express kiosk (buying access online is currently not an option). Once you have your U-Bot, you can use it to reserve ride times for any Universal Express attraction, but note that you can make only one reservation at a time. The U-Bot will vibrate and display a message telling you when it's time to ride. Next, you take your U-Bot to the ride's Express entrance, where the attraction greeter will scan your device and admit you to the Express queue. U-Bot costs considerably less than an Express Pass (usually by about $20).

## LOCKERS

UNIVERSAL ENFORCES A MANDATORY locker system at its big thrill rides. Lockers outside these attractions are free for an amount of time that depends on the length of the standby line. So if the line is 30 minutes, for example, and the ride itself is 10 minutes, you get 40 minutes plus a small cushion of about 15 minutes. The lockers then cost $3 for each hour after that, with a $20 maximum.

The locker banks are easy to find; each bank has a small computer in the center. When the sun is bright, the screen is almost impossible to read, so have someone block the sun or use a different computer. After selecting your language, you press your thumb onto the keypad and have your fingerprint scanned. We've seen people walk away cursing at this step, having repeated it over and over with no success. Don't press down too hard—the computer can't read your thumbprint that way. Instead, take a deep breath and lightly place your thumb on the scanner.

After your do your thumb scan, you'll receive a locker number. Write it down! When you return from your ride, go to the same kiosk machine, enter your locker number, and scan your thumb again. At Guest Relations, family-sized lockers are available for $10 for the entire day, but remember that only the person who used his or her thumb to get the locker can retrieve anything from it.

## UNIVERSAL, KIDS, AND SCARY STUFF

ALTHOUGH THERE'S PLENTY FOR YOUNGER CHILDREN to enjoy at the Universal parks, most major attractions can potentially make kids under age 8 wig out. At Universal Studios Florida, forget *Disaster!*, Hollywood Rip Ride Rockit, Men in Black Alien Attack, Revenge of the Mummy, The Simpsons Ride, *Terminator 2: 3-D*, Transformers: The Ride 3-D, and *TWISTER . . . Ride It Out*. The first part of the E.T. Adventure ride is a little intense for a few preschoolers, but the end is all happiness and harmony. There are some scary visual effects on both the Hogwarts Express train that runs between the two parks and the Gringotts dark ride–roller coaster, but both are billed as family rides. Interestingly, very few families report problems with *Beetlejuice's Graveyard Mash-Up* or *Universal Orlando's Horror Make-Up Show*. Anything we haven't listed is pretty tame.

At Universal's Islands of Adventure, watch out for The Amazing Adventures of Spider-Man, Doctor Doom's Fearfall, Dragon Challenge, Harry Potter and the Forbidden Journey, The Incredible Hulk Coaster, Jurassic Park River Adventure, and *Poseidon's Fury*. Popeye & Bluto's Bilge-Rat Barges is wet and wild, but most younger children handle it well. Dudley Do-Right's Ripsaw Falls is a toss-up, to be considered only if your kids like water-flume rides. The *Eighth Voyage of Sindbad Stunt Show* includes some explosions and startling special effects, but again, kids tolerate it well. Nothing else should pose a problem.

**CHILD SWAP** "Switching off" at Universal is similar to Disney's version. The entire family goes through the whole line together before being split into riding and nonriding groups near the loading platform. The nonriding parent and child(ren) wait in a designated room, usually with some sort of entertainment (for example, Forbidden Journey at IOA shows the first 20 minutes of *Harry Potter and the Sorcerer's Stone* on a loop), a place to sit down, and sometimes restrooms with changing tables. At any theme park, the best tip we can give is to ask the greeter in front of the attraction what you're supposed to do.

## BLUE MAN GROUP

BLUE MAN GROUP GAVE UNIVERSAL its first large-scale introduction to that nebulous genre called "performance art." If the term confuses you, relax—it won't hurt a bit. Blue Man Group serves up a stunning show that can be appreciated by folks of all ages. The 1-hour, 45-minute production was updated and reimagined in 2012 to reflect cultural changes in the use of technology in daily life.

The three blue men are just that—blue—and bald and mute. Wearing black clothing and skullcaps slathered with bright-blue grease paint, they deliver a fast-paced show that uses music (mostly percussion) and multimedia effects to make light of contemporary art and life in the information age. The Universal act is just one expression of a franchise that started with three friends in New York's East Village. Now you can catch their zany, wacky, smart stuff in New York, Las Vegas, Boston, Chicago, and Berlin, among other places.

Funny, sometimes poignant, and always compelling, Blue Man Group pounds out vital, visceral tribal rhythms on complex instruments (made of PVC pipes) that could pass for industrial intestines, and makes seemingly spontaneous eruptions of visual art rendered with marshmallows and a mysterious goo. The weekly supplies include 25½ pounds of Cap'n Crunch, 60 Twinkies, 75 gallons of Jell-O, 996 marshmallows, and 9½ gallons of paint. If all this sounds silly, it is, but it's also strangely thought-provoking and deals with topics such as the value of modern art, the ubiquity and addictive nature of smartphones, DNA, the persistence of vision, the way rock music moves you, and how we're all connected. (*Hint:* It's not the Internet.)

A live percussion band backs Blue Man Group with a relentless and totally engrossing industrial dance riff. The band resides in long, dark alcoves above the stage. At just the right moments, the lofts are lit to reveal a group of pulsating neon-colored skeletons.

Audience participation completes the Blue Man experience. The blue men often move into the audience to bring guests on stage. At the end of the show, giant glowing balloons drop from the rafters for the audience to bat around like beach balls. And a lot of folks can't help standing up to dance—and laugh. Magicians for the creative spirit that resides in us all, Blue Man Group makes everyone a co-conspirator in a joyous explosion of showmanship.

This show is decidedly different and requires an open mind to be appreciated. It also helps to be a little loose, because, like it or not, everybody gets sucked into the production and leaves the theater a little bit lighter in spirit. If you don't want to be pulled onstage to become a part of the improvisation, don't sit in the first half-dozen or so rows.

The Universal Box Office (☎ 888-340-5476 or 407-224-3200) is open 7 a.m.–7 p.m. EST, or you can buy tickets online at **universal orlando.com.** Advance tickets at the Universal Orlando website run $60–$95 for adults, $30–$47 for children; tickets purchased at the box office cost $10 more. The show is staged in the Sharp Aquos Theatre, which can be accessed from inside or outside Universal Studios theme park. We recommend seats at least 15 rows back from the stage.

## UNIVERSAL ORLANDO DINING PLAN

UNIVERSAL HAS DONE AWAY WITH its all-you-care-to-eat Meal Deals, replacing them with a **Quick Service Dining Plan** that provides one counter-service meal, two soft drinks, and one snack. The cost is $20 for adults and $13 for kids age 9 and younger, plus tax. It's valid at most counter-service eateries in both parks (including Three Broomsticks at The Wizarding World of Harry Potter–Hogsmeade and Fast Food Boulevard in Springfield U.S.A.) and a smattering at Universal CityWalk, but not at the hotels.

Universal claims the plan can save you up to 30%, but unless you order the most expensive eligible items—a few, like whole pizzas, aren't covered—you'll probably just break even, especially with an Annual Pass discount. You can buy the plan on-site at any participating restaurant after you've read the menu. A full-service dining plan is also offered to on-site hotel guests buying vacation packages, but it's an even worse bargain.

# PART SIXTEEN

# UNIVERSAL'S ISLANDS *of* ADVENTURE

WHEN UNIVERSAL'S ISLANDS OF ADVENTURE (IOA) opened in 1999, it provided Universal with enough critical mass to actually compete with Disney. Doubly interesting is that the second Universal park is a direct competitor to Disney's Magic Kingdom, the most-visited theme park in the world. How direct a competitor is it? See below for a comparison.

And though Universal played second fiddle to Disney for many years, times have changed: Universal's Islands of Adventure is a state-of-the-art park competing with a Disney park that is more than 35 years old and did not add a new super-headliner attraction for many years until the Fantasyland expansion begun in 2010 launched in phases, from 2012 to 2014.

> *unofficial* **TIP**
> Roller coasters at Islands of Adventure are the real deal—not for the faint of heart or for little ones.

Incidentally, 2010 marked IOA's coming-out party. In one of the greatest seismic shifts in theme park history, Universal secured the rights to build a Harry Potter–themed area within the park. Harry P. is possibly the only fictional character extant capable of trumping Mickey Mouse, and Universal has gone all-out, under J. K. Rowling's watchful and exacting eye, to create a setting and attractions designed to be the envy of the industry.

Disney and Universal officially downplay their fierce competition, pointing out that any new theme park or attraction makes Central Florida a more marketable destination. Behind closed doors, however, the two companies share a Pepsi-versus-Coke rivalry that keeps both working hard to gain a competitive edge. The good news is that all this translates into better and better attractions for you to enjoy.

| IOA AND THE MAGIC KINGDOM AT A GLANCE | |
| --- | --- |
| **ISLANDS OF ADVENTURE** | **MAGIC KINGDOM** |
| • Seven "islands" (includes *Port of Entry*) | • Six "lands" (*includes Main Street*) |
| • Two adult roller-coaster attractions | • Two adult roller-coaster attractions |
| • A Dumbo-type ride | • Dumbo the Flying Elephant |
| • One flume ride | • One flume ride |
| • Toon Lagoon character area | • Main Street, U.S.A. character greeting |

## BEWARE OF THE WET AND WILD

ALTHOUGH WE'VE DESCRIBED Universal's Islands of Adventure as a direct competitor to the Magic Kingdom, know this: Whereas most Magic Kingdom attractions are designed to be enjoyed by guests of any age, attractions at Islands of Adventure are created largely for an under-40 population. The roller coasters at Universal are serious with a capital *S*, making Space Mountain and Big Thunder Mountain look about as frightening as Dumbo. In fact, seven of the top nine attractions at IOA are thrill rides; of these, three will not only scare the crap out of you but will also drench you with water.

For families, there are three interactive playgrounds as well as six rides that young children will enjoy. Of the thrill rides, only the two in Toon Lagoon (described later) are marginally appropriate for little kids, and even on these rides your child needs to be fairly hardy.

# GETTING ORIENTED *at* UNIVERSAL'S ISLANDS *of* ADVENTURE

BOTH UNIVERSAL THEME PARKS are accessed via the Universal CityWalk entertainment complex. After crossing CityWalk from the parking garages, bear right to Universal Studios Florida or left to Universal's Islands of Adventure.

Islands of Adventure is laid out much like Epcot's World Showcase—arranged in a large circle surrounding a lagoon—but it evinces the same thematic continuity present in the Magic Kingdom. Each "land," or "island" in this case, is self-contained and visually consistent in its theme.

You first encounter the Moroccan-style **Port of Entry,** where you'll find Guest Services, lockers, stroller and wheelchair rentals, ATM banking, lost and found, and shopping. From the Port of Entry, moving clockwise around the lagoon, you access **Marvel Super Hero Island, Toon Lagoon, Jurassic Park, The Wizarding World of Harry Potter–Hogsmeade, The Lost Continent,** and **Seuss Landing.** There is no in-park transportation to move you between lands.

## DECISIONS, DECISIONS

WHEN IT COMES TO TOURING IOA efficiently, you have two basic choices, and as you might expect, there are trade-offs. The Wizarding World of Harry Potter–Hogsmeade sucks up guests like a Hoover. If you're keen to experience **Harry Potter and the Forbidden Journey**

*Continued on page 656*

Universal's Islands of Adventure

↑ To Universal Studios Florida

The Wizarding World of Harry Potter–Hogsmeade

The Lost Continent

Jurassic Park

Toon Lagoon

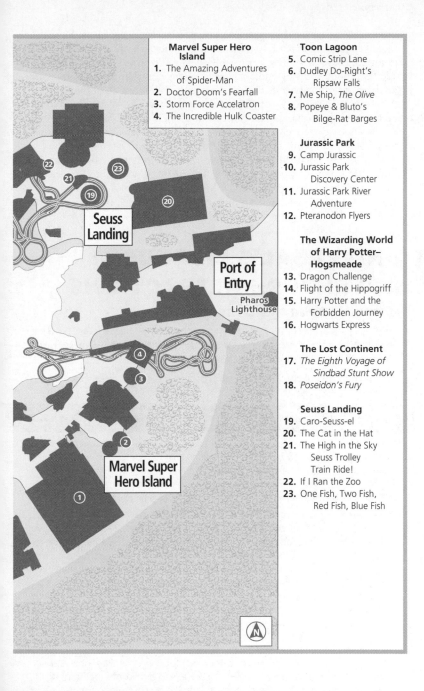

**Marvel Super Hero Island**
1. The Amazing Adventures of Spider-Man
2. Doctor Doom's Fearfall
3. Storm Force Accelatron
4. The Incredible Hulk Coaster

**Toon Lagoon**
5. Comic Strip Lane
6. Dudley Do-Right's Ripsaw Falls
7. Me Ship, *The Olive*
8. Popeye & Bluto's Bilge-Rat Barges

**Jurassic Park**
9. Camp Jurassic
10. Jurassic Park Discovery Center
11. Jurassic Park River Adventure
12. Pteranodon Flyers

**The Wizarding World of Harry Potter– Hogsmeade**
13. Dragon Challenge
14. Flight of the Hippogriff
15. Harry Potter and the Forbidden Journey
16. Hogwarts Express

**The Lost Continent**
17. *The Eighth Voyage of Sindbad Stunt Show*
18. *Poseidon's Fury*

**Seuss Landing**
19. Caro-Seuss-el
20. The Cat in the Hat
21. The High in the Sky Seuss Trolley Train Ride!
22. If I Ran the Zoo
23. One Fish, Two Fish, Red Fish, Blue Fish

Seuss Landing

Port of Entry

Pharos Lighthouse

Marvel Super Hero Island

*Continued from page 653*

without suffering 1–2 hours in line, you need to be at the turnstiles waiting to be admitted at least 30 minutes before the park opens. Once you're admitted, move as swiftly as possible to The Wizarding World and then ride Forbidden Journey and Dragon Challenge, in that order. If you can get them out of the way in about an hour, you'll find much of the remainder of the park sparsely populated. Come back to The Wizarding World later in the day to explore Hogsmeade and the shops. Even if you're the first day guest to arrive, you'll find Hogsmeade already occupied by hotel guests, but it's the least crowded the land will be until late in the day.

If you can't be at the park when it opens, skip Potterville first thing and enjoy other attractions in IOA. The good news is The Wizarding World usually clears out in the last hour even on busy days, so you can ride Forbidden Journey with a minimal wait if you get in the queue 10 minutes before closing.

# UNIVERSAL'S ISLANDS *of* ADVENTURE ATTRACTIONS

## MARVEL SUPER HERO ISLAND

THIS ISLAND, WITH ITS FUTURISTIC AND RETRO-FUTURE design and comic-book signage, offers shopping, dining, and attractions based on Marvel Comics characters.

### The Amazing Adventures of Spider-Man  ★★★★★
### *(Universal Express)*

| APPEAL BY AGE | PRESCHOOL ★ | GRADE SCHOOL ★★★★★ | TEENS ★★★★★ |
|---|---|---|---|
| YOUNG ADULTS ★★★★½ | | OVER 30 ★★★★½ | SENIORS ★★★★★ |

**What it is** Indoor adventure simulator ride based on Spider-Man. **Scope and scale** Super-headliner. **When to go** During the first 40 minutes the park is open. **Special comments** 40" minimum height requirement. **Authors' rating** One of the best attractions anywhere; not to be missed; ★★★★★. **Duration of ride** 4½ minutes. **Probable waiting time per 100 people ahead of you** 5 minutes. **Loading speed** Fast.

**DESCRIPTION AND COMMENTS** The Amazing Adventures of Spider-Man—covering 1½ acres and combining moving ride vehicles, 3-D film, and live action—was enhanced in 2012 with a complete high-definition digital upgrade. Thirteen reanimated 3-D scenes fuse almost seamlessly with the actual sets and props, so that in many instances guests cannot tell until the action begins whether they're looking at a movie screen or an actual brick wall. The total package is astonishing—frenetic yet fluid, and visually rich. The ride is wild yet very smooth. Although the attractions are not directly comparable, Spider-Man is technologically ahead of The Twilight Zone Tower of Terror at Disney's Hollywood Studios—which is to say it will leave you in awe.

The storyline is that you're a reporter for the *Daily Bugle* newspaper (where Peter Parker, a.k.a. Spider-Man, works as a mild-mannered photographer), when it's discovered that evildoers have stolen—we promise we're not making this up—the Statue of Liberty. You're drafted on the spot by your cantankerous editor to go get the story. After speeding around and being thrust into a battle between good and evil, you experience a 400-foot "sensory drop" from a skyscraper roof all the way to the pavement. Because the ride is so wild and the action so continuous, it's hard to understand the plot, but you're so thoroughly entertained that you don't really care. Plus, you'll want to ride again and again. Eventually, with repetition, the storyline will begin to make sense.

**TOURING TIPS** If you were on hand at park opening, ride after experiencing Harry Potter and the Forbidden Journey, Dragon Challenge, and The Incredible Hulk Coaster. If you elect to bypass all the congestion at Forbidden Journey, ride after Dragon Challenge and the Hulk. If you arrived more than 15 minutes after park opening, skip Wizarding World attractions and ride Spider-Man after the Hulk.

## Doctor Doom's Fearfall *(Universal Express)*   ★★★

| APPEAL BY AGE | PRESCHOOL ★ | GRADE SCHOOL ★★★★½ | TEENS ★★★★½ |
|---|---|---|---|
| YOUNG ADULTS ★★★★ | | OVER 30 ★★★½ | SENIORS ★★ |

**What it is** Vertical ascent and free-fall. **Scope and scale** Headliner. **When to go** First 40 minutes the park is open. **Special comments** 52" minimum height requirement. **Authors' rating** More bark than bite; ★★★. **Duration of ride** 40 seconds. **Probable waiting time per 100 people ahead of you** 18 minutes. **Loading speed** Slow.

**DESCRIPTION AND COMMENTS** Here you are (again), strapped into a seat with your feet dangling and blasted 200 feet up in the air and then allowed to partially free-fall back down. Imagine the midway game wherein a macho guy swings a sledgehammer, propelling a metal sphere up a vertical shaft to ring a bell—on this ride, you're the metal sphere.

That prospect sounds worse than it actually is. The scariest part of the ride by far is the apprehension that builds as you sit, strapped in, waiting for the ride to launch. Blasting up and falling down are actually pleasant.

**TOURING TIPS** We've seen glaciers that move faster than the line for Doctor Doom's Fearfall. If you want to ride without investing half a day, be one of the first to ride. If you're on hand at opening time, being among the first isn't too difficult (mainly because the nearby Wizarding World, Hulk, and Spider-Man attractions are bigger draws).

Fortunately, as this reader discovered, Doctor Doom also has a singles line that's nearly always open:

*If you ask a staff member for the single-rider line, they'll send you through the exit in the arcade. Then just follow the signs.*

## The Incredible Hulk Coaster *(Universal Express)* ★★★★½

| APPEAL BY AGE | PRESCHOOL ★ | GRADE SCHOOL ★★★★½ | TEENS ★★★★★ |
|---|---|---|---|
| YOUNG ADULTS ★★★★★ | | OVER 30 ★★★★½ | SENIORS ★★ |

**What it is** Roller coaster. **Scope and scale** Super-headliner. **When to go** During the first 40 minutes the park is open. **Special comments** 54" minimum height requirement. **Authors' rating** A coaster-lover's coaster; not to be missed; ★★★★½. **Duration of ride** 2¼ minutes. **Probable waiting time per 100 people ahead of you** 9 minutes. **Loading speed** Moderate.

Motion Sickness

**DESCRIPTION AND COMMENTS** There is, as always, a storyline, but for this attraction it's of no importance whatsoever. What you need to know about this attraction is simple. You'll be shot like a cannonball from 0 to 40 mph in 2 seconds, and then you'll be flung upside down 100 feet off the ground, which will, of course, induce weightlessness. From there it's a mere six rollovers punctuated by two plunges into holes in the ground before you're allowed to get out and throw up.

Seriously, the Hulk is a great roller coaster, one of the best in Florida, providing a ride comparable to that of Montu (Busch Gardens) with the added thrill of an accelerated launch (instead of the more typical uphill crank). Plus, like Montu, this coaster has a smooth ride.

**TOURING TIPS** Arrive before park opening. When admitted, ride after experiencing Harry Potter and the Forbidden Journey and Dragon Challenge. If you want to stay clear of the crowds at Forbidden Journey, ride after Dragon Challenge. If you arrived more than 15 minutes after park opening, skip the Wizarding World attractions and ride the Hulk first thing. Universal provides electronic lockers near the entrance of the Hulk to deposit any items that might depart your person during the Hulk's seven inversions.

When you reach the boarding area, note that the Hulk has a separate line for those who want to ride in the first row. There's also a singles line, but you may not notice it at first, as this reader attests:

*The single-rider line is kind of hard to find—ask where it is. I stood in the standby line for 20 minutes before I realized my mistake.*

## Storm Force Accelatron *(Universal Express)* ★★½

| APPEAL BY AGE | PRESCHOOL ★★★★★ | GRADE SCHOOL ★★★½ | TEENS ★★★ |
|---|---|---|---|
| YOUNG ADULTS ★★★½ | | OVER 30 ★★½ | SENIORS - |

**What it is** Covered spinning ride. **Scope and scale** Minor attraction. **Special comments** May induce motion sickness. **When to go** During the first hour the park is open. **Authors' rating** Spiffed-up teacups; ★★½. **Duration of ride** 1½ minutes. **Probable waiting time per 100 people ahead of you** 21 minutes. **Loading speed** Slow.

**DESCRIPTION AND COMMENTS** Storm Force is a spiffed-up version of Disney's nausea-inducing Mad Tea Party. Here, you spin to the accompaniment of a simulated thunderstorm and swirling sound and light. A storyline loosely ties this midway-type ride to the Marvel Super Hero Island area, but it's largely irrelevant and offers no advice on keeping your lunch down.

**TOURING TIPS** Ride early or late to avoid long lines. If you're prone to motion sickness, keep your distance.

## TOON LAGOON

THIS LAND TRANSLATES cartoon art into real buildings and settings. Whimsical and gaily colored, with rounded and exaggerated lines, Toon Lagoon is Universal's answer to the old Mickey's Toontown Fair in the Magic Kingdom—only you have about a 60% chance of drowning at Universal's version.

### Comic Strip Lane

**What it is** Walk-through exhibit and shopping and dining venue. **Scope and scale** Diversion. **When to go** Anytime.

**DESCRIPTION AND COMMENTS** This is the main street of Toon Lagoon. Here you can visit the domains of such vintage Sunday-funnies favorites as Beetle Bailey, The Family Circus, and Blondie and Dagwood—in other words, intellectual property that Universal could get for cheap. (The characters, though classic, are probably unrecognizable to anybody younger than Generation X.) Shops and eateries tie in to the comic strip theme.

**TOURING TIPS** This is a great place for photo ops with cartoon characters in their own environment. It's also a great place to drop a few bucks in the diners and shops—but you probably already figured that out.

## Dudley Do-Right's Ripsaw Falls (*Universal Express*)
★★★½

| APPEAL BY AGE | PRESCHOOL ★½ | GRADE SCHOOL ★★★★½ | TEENS ★★★★ |
|---|---|---|---|
| YOUNG ADULTS ★★★★ | | OVER 30 ★★★★½ | SENIORS ★★★★ |

**What it is** Flume ride. **Scope and scale** Major attraction. **When to go** Before 11 a.m. **Special comments** 44" minimum height requirement. **Authors' rating** A minimalist Splash Mountain; ★★★½. **Duration of ride** 5 minutes. **Probable waiting time per 100 people ahead of you** 9 minutes. **Loading speed** Moderate.

**DESCRIPTION AND COMMENTS** Inspired by the *Rocky and Bullwinkle* cartoons, this ride features Canadian Mountie Dudley Do-Right as he tries to save Nell from the evil Snidely Whiplash. Storyline aside, it's a flume ride, with the inevitable big drop at the end. Universal claims this is the first flume ride to "send riders plummeting 15 feet below the surface of the water." Actually, though, you're just plummeting into a tunnel.

The only problem with this attraction is that everyone inevitably compares it to Splash Mountain at the Magic Kingdom. The flume is as good as Splash Mountain's, and the final drop is a whopper, but the theming and the visuals aren't even in the same league. Taken on its own terms, however, Dudley Do-Right is a darn good flume ride.

**TOURING TIPS** This ride will get you wet, but on average not as wet as you might expect. If you want to stay dry, however, arrive prepared with a poncho or at least a big garbage bag with holes cut out for your head and arms. After riding, take a moment to gauge the timing of the water cannons that go off along the exit walk. This is where you can really get drenched. Ride after experiencing the Marvel Super Hero rides.

## Me Ship, *The Olive*   ★★★

| APPEAL BY AGE | PRESCHOOL ★★★★★ | GRADE SCHOOL ★★★★½ | TEENS ★★ |
|---|---|---|---|
| YOUNG ADULTS ★★ | | OVER 30 ★★½ | SENIORS ★★ |

**What it is** Interactive playground. **Scope and scale** Minor attraction. **When to go** Anytime. **Authors' rating** Colorful and appealing for kids; ★★★.

**DESCRIPTION AND COMMENTS** *The Olive* is Popeye's three-story boat come to life as an interactive playground. Younger children can scramble around in Swee'Pea's Playpen, while older sibs shoot water cannons at riders trying to survive the adjacent Bilge-Rat Barges.

**TOURING TIPS** If you're into the big rides, save this for later in the day.

## Popeye & Bluto's Bilge-Rat Barges (*Universal Express*)
★★★★

| APPEAL BY AGE | PRESCHOOL ★½ | GRADE SCHOOL ★★★★★ | TEENS ★★★★½ |
|---|---|---|---|
| YOUNG ADULTS ★★★★ | | OVER 30 ★★★★ | SENIORS ★★★★ |

**What it is** Whitewater-raft ride. **Scope and scale** Major attraction. **When to go** Before 11 a.m. **Special comments** 42" minimum height requirement. **Authors' rating** Bring your own soap; ★★★★. **Duration of ride** 4½ minutes. **Probable waiting time per 100 people ahead of you** 5 minutes. **Loading speed** Moderate.

**DESCRIPTION AND COMMENTS** This whitewater-raft ride includes an encounter with an 18-foot-tall octopus. Engineered to ensure that everyone gets drenched, the attraction even provides water cannons for nonparticipants ashore to fire at those aboard. The rapids are rougher and more interesting, and the ride longer, than Animal Kingdom's Kali River Rapids. But Bluto doesn't surpass Disney's raft ride for visuals and theming.

**TOURING TIPS** If you didn't drown on Dudley Do-Right, here's a second chance. You'll get a lot wetter from the knees down on this ride, so use your poncho or garbage bag and ride barefoot with your britches rolled up. This ride often opens a hour after the rest of the park. Experience the barges in the morning after the Marvel Super Hero attractions and Dudley Do-Right. If you've forgotten your wet wear, you might want to put off riding until last thing before leaving the park. Most preschoolers enjoy the barges. Kids who are frightened react more to the way the rapids look than to the roughness of the ride.

## JURASSIC PARK

JURASSIC PARK is a Steven Spielberg film franchise about a theme park with real dinosaurs. Jurassic Park at Islands of Adventure is a real theme park (or at least a section of one) with fictitious dinosaurs.

### Camp Jurassic  ★★★½

| APPEAL BY AGE | PRESCHOOL ★★★★★ | GRADE SCHOOL ★★★★½ | TEENS ★ |
| --- | --- | --- | --- |
| YOUNG ADULTS ★★ | | OVER 30 ★★★ | SENIORS ★★ |

**What it is** Interactive play area. **Scope and scale** Minor attraction. **When to go** Anytime. **Authors' rating** Creative playground, confusing layout; ★★★½.

**DESCRIPTION AND COMMENTS** Camp Jurassic is a great place for children to cut loose. A sort of antediluvian Tom Sawyer Island, it allows kids to explore lava pits, caves, mines, and a rainforest.

**TOURING TIPS** Camp Jurassic will fire the imaginations of the under-13 set. If you don't impose a time limit on the exploration, you could be here awhile. The layout of the play area is confusing and intersects the queuing area for Pteranodon Flyers.

### Jurassic Park Discovery Center  ★★½

| APPEAL BY AGE | PRESCHOOL ★★★ | GRADE SCHOOL ★★★★ | TEENS ★★★ |
| --- | --- | --- | --- |
| YOUNG ADULTS ★★★ | | OVER 30 ★★★ | SENIORS ★★★ |

**What it is** Interactive natural-history exhibit. **Scope and scale** Minor attraction. **When to go** Anytime. **Authors' rating** Definitely worth checking out; ★★½.

**DESCRIPTION AND COMMENTS** This interactive educational exhibit mixes fiction from the movie *Jurassic Park,* such as using fossil DNA to bring dinosaurs to life, with skeletal remains and other paleontological displays. One exhibit lets guests watch an animatronic raptor being hatched. Another allows you to digitally "fuse" your DNA with a dinosaur's to see what the resultant creature would look like.

**TOURING TIPS** Cycle back after experiencing all the rides or on a second day. Most folks can digest this exhibit in 10–15 minutes.

### Jurassic Park River Adventure *(Universal Express)*
★★★★

| APPEAL BY AGE | PRESCHOOL ★ | GRADE SCHOOL ★★★★ | TEENS ★★★★ |
| --- | --- | --- | --- |
| YOUNG ADULTS ★★★★ | | OVER 30 ★★★★½ | SENIORS ★★★★★ |

**What it is** Indoor-outdoor river-raft adventure ride based on the *Jurassic Park* movies. **Scope and scale** Super-headliner. **When to go** Before 11 a.m. **Special comments** 42″ minimum height requirement. **Authors' rating** Better than its Hollywood cousin; not to be missed; ★★★★. **Duration of ride** 6½ minutes. **Probable waiting time per 100 people ahead of you** 5 minutes. **Loading speed** Fast.

**DESCRIPTION AND COMMENTS** Guests board boats for a water tour of Jurassic Park. Everything is tranquil as the tour begins, and the boat floats among large herbivorous dinosaurs such as brontosauruses and stegosauruses. Then, as word comes in that some of the carnivores have escaped their enclosure, the tour boat is accidentally diverted into Jurassic Park's maintenance facilities. Here, the boat and its riders are menaced by an assortment of hungry meat-eaters led by the ubiquitous T-Rex. At the climactic moment, the boat and its passengers escape by plummeting over an 85-foot drop.

**TOURING TIPS** Though the boats make a huge splash at the bottom of the 85-foot drop, you don't get all that wet. Once you're under way, there's a little splashing but nothing major until the big drop at the end of the ride. Fortunately, not all that much water lands in the boat.

A Honolulu reader thinks Jurassic Park doesn't pass the smell test:

*The Jurassic Park ride is a lot of fun—so fun, in fact, that you won't realize how truly HEINOUS the water that drenches you during the climactic splashdown is until much later. We sat in the front row for the ride and got soaked. Three hours later, my girlfriend and I realized we reeked.*

Young children must endure a double whammy on this ride. First, they're stalked by giant, salivating (sometimes spitting) reptiles, and then sent catapulting over the falls. Unless your children are fairly hardy, wait a year or two before you spring the River Adventure on them.

Because the Jurassic Park section of IOA is situated next to The Wizarding World of Harry Potter–Hogsmeade, the boat will experience heavy crowds earlier in the day. Try to ride before 11 a.m.

## Pteranodon Flyers ★★

| APPEAL BY AGE | PRESCHOOL ★★★½ | GRADE SCHOOL ★★★★ | TEENS ★★★★ |
|---|---|---|---|
| YOUNG ADULTS ★★★½ | OVER 30 ★★★ | | SENIORS ★★★★ |

**What it is** Slow as Christmas. **Scope and scale** Minor attraction. **When to go** When there's no line. **Special comments** Adults and older children must be accompanied by a child between 36″ and 52″ tall. **Authors' rating** All sizzle, no steak; ★★. **Duration of ride** 1¼ minutes. **Probable waiting time per 100 people ahead of you** 28 minutes. **Loading speed** More sluggish than a hog in quicksand.

**DESCRIPTION AND COMMENTS** This is Islands of Adventure's biggest blunder. Engineered to accommodate only 170 persons per hour, the ride dangles you on a swing below a track that passes over a small part of Jurassic Park. We recommend skipping this one. Why? Because the Jurassic period will probably end before you reach the front of the line! And your reward for all that waiting? A 1-minute-and-15-second ride.

**TOURING TIPS** Photograph the pteranodon as it flies overhead. You're probably looking at something that will someday be extinct.

## THE WIZARDING WORLD OF HARRY POTTER–HOGSMEADE

IN WHAT MAY PROVE TO BE the competitive coup of all time between theme park archrivals Disney and Universal, the latter inked a deal with Warner Brothers Entertainment to create a "fully immersive" Harry Potter–themed environment based on the bestselling children's books by J. K. Rowling and the companion blockbuster movies from Warner Brothers. The books have been translated into 68 languages, with more than 450 million copies sold in more than 200 territories around the world. The movies have made more than $7 billion worldwide, making Harry Potter the largest-grossing film franchise in history. The project was blessed by Rowling, who is known for tenaciously protecting the integrity of her work. In the case of the films, she demanded that Warner Brothers be true, to an almost unprecedented degree, to the books on which the films were based.

The 20-acre Wizarding World is an amalgamation of landmarks, creatures, and themes that are faithful to the films and books. You access the area through an imposing gate that opens onto **Hogsmeade,** depicted in winter and covered in snow. This is The Wizarding World's primary shopping and dining venue. Exiting Hogsmeade, you first glimpse the towering castle housing **Hogwarts School of Witchcraft and Wizardry,** flanked by the **Forbidden Forest** and **Hagrid's Hut.** The grounds and interior of the castle house part of the queue for the super-headliner **Harry Potter and the Forbidden Journey.** Universal has gone all-out on the castle, with the intention of creating an icon even more beloved and powerful than Cinderella Castle at Disney's Magic Kingdom.

### "What a Long Strange Trip It's Been"

That Grateful Dead lyric is awfully appropriate when recounting the evolution of The Wizarding World–Hogsmeade. A Harry Potter theme park (or themed area) has been the chop-licking dream of the amusement industry for a decade. First, of course, there were the books, which against all odds trumped texting and TV to lure a broad age range of youth back to the printed page. Next came the movies. In securing the film rights, Warner Brothers, along with several unsuccessful suitors, learned the most important thing about exploiting the Harry Potter phenomenon: J. K. Rowling is boss.

As the Potter juggernaut took the world by storm, entertainment conglomerates began approaching Rowling about theme park rights. When she spurned a Universal Studios Florida concept for a show based on the Potter characters, industry observers were certain that she had struck a deal with Disney. In fact, Disney was in talks with Rowling about a standalone Harry Potter theme park. For her part, Rowling had no problem visualizing what she wanted in a theme park, but from Disney's point of view, what Rowling wanted was operationally problematic, if not altogether impossible. Never an entity to concede control, Disney walked.

Universal caught Rowling on the rebound and brought her to Orlando to tour Islands of Adventure. Among other things, they squired her around the Lost Continent section of the park, impressing her with its detailed theme execution and showing her how with a little imagination it could be rethemed. Rowling saw the potential but wasn't much more flexible with Universal than she was with Disney. From her perspective, getting a themed area right couldn't be any harder than getting a movie right, so she insisted that Stuart Craig, her trusted production designer for the films, be responsible for faithfully re-creating sets from the movies. Universal, on fire to land Harry Potter, became convinced that the collaboration could work.

But theme parks and movies are two very different things. With a film, a set has to look good only for a few moments and then it's on to something else. With a theme park, a set has to look good 12–16 hours a day, in all manner of weather, and with tens of thousands of tourists rambling through it in need of food, drink, restrooms, protection from rain, and places to rest. With The Wizarding World–Hogsmeade, Rowling's insistence on authenticity occasioned conundrums not anticipated by the theme park designers, who, for example, logically assumed that guests would like to see the interior of Hagrid's Hut. No problem—a walk-through attraction will serve nicely. Of course, there's the Americans with Disabilities Act, so we'll need ramps both in and out of the hut. No way, say the movie people: Hagrid's Hut in the films had steps, so the theme park version must have them, too.

## Bone Up

We don't have room to explain all the Potter allusions and icons incorporated into The Wizarding World. Because they so accurately replicate scenes from the books and films, it helps immeasurably to be well versed in all things Harry. If it's been a while since you've seen one of the movies or read one of the novels, you can brush up by watching the first four flicks in the series, in particular *Harry Potter and the Goblet of Fire* and *Harry Potter and the Sorcerer's Stone* (*Harry Potter and the Philosopher's Stone* outside of India and the United States). For an easy memory jog, check out the films' trailers at **YouTube.** If you know nothing at all about Harry Potter, you'll still have fun, but to truly appreciate the nuance and detail, we suggest you hit the books.

## Getting In

Crowds are certainly larger during summer and holidays, but because of The Wizarding World's overwhelming popularity, you'll encounter lines even at slower times of year. In the summer of 2014, guests were allowed through the turnstiles 30–60 minutes before official opening time. Universal hotel guests formed a line on the right side of Port of Entry (IOA's main entrance plaza) and were admitted to The Wizarding World through the Hogsmeade main gate; day guests (the general public) were directed left to The Wizarding World's border with Jurassic Park. Here, on the Jurassic Park side of the bridge leading to The Wizarding World, day guests could obtain a pass to enter The Wizarding World later.

Wizarding World crowd management has been a work-in-progress for Universal. Now, with five years of operation under its belt, Universal has settled on a flexible system with three basic crowd-control options predicated on the expected level of attendance for any given day. (Similar procedures are in place at Diagon Alley; see Part Seventeen.) No matter the crowd level, if you're staying in one of Universal's four on-site hotels and you have early-entry privileges for The Wizarding World, use them, arriving as early during the early-entry period as possible.

**CROWD-CONTROL OPTION ONE** is for off-season and slow days. On these days you can enter and depart The Wizarding World–Hogsmeade as you please. The waits for the rides will still be more than an hour at times, but gaining entry to the themed area itself is not an issue.

Sometimes Option One will be in force in the morning, transitioning to Option Two as crowds build over the course of the day.

**CROWD-CONTROL OPTION TWO** is for days when the park is nearly full to capacity—during spring break, for example, or on the days before or after a major holiday. At this level, barricades are placed at both entrances to The Wizarding World–Hogsmeade once the area reaches maximum occupancy. You can then go to touchscreen ticket kiosks outside the Jurassic Park Discovery Center and obtain a free return ticket (not unlike the old paper Fastpass at Walt Disney World) to come back at a designated time. At the specified time, return to the Lost Continent entrance and present your pass to the barricade crew.

*un*official **TIP**

If you leave The Wizarding World while the entrance barriers are in place and you wish to return, you'll either have to wait in line to get another pass (provided they haven't all been distributed) or wait until late in the day, when the barricades come down as crowds disperse.

Note that guests arriving on the Hogwarts Express disembark outside of Hogsmeade, and must still retrieve a ticket before entering.

Once admitted to The Wizarding World–Hogsmeade, you'll still have to wait for each ride, store, and concession, as well as for the area's one restaurant. It's common when Option Two is in effect for the entrance barricades to be removed during the last hour or two the park is open, thus presenting the opportunity to come and go as you please.

**CROWD-CONTROL OPTION THREE** is for when the park is at full capacity, usually during major holidays. On these days, the barricades around The Wizarding World–Hogsmeade are in place all day, and the demand to get in is much higher.

On an Option Three day, you'll be directed toward the Jurassic Park entrance to The Wizarding World. There, you can obtain a pass with a designated return time as described under Option Two. On these peak days, a standby queue may also be erected in the waterfront landing behind the Jurassic Park Discovery Center; since more guests can enter only as others leave, this line can be painfully slow, so a return ticket is strongly suggested.

Be forewarned that on Option Three days, return passes are fully distributed by noon or earlier. This means that if you aren't in line to enter IOA before the park opens, you might not be able to enter The Wizarding World at all. You must arrive an hour before opening on these days and, once admitted, immediately obtain a return pass.

On Option Two and Option Three days, don't leave The Wizarding World until you've done and seen everything of interest. Don't defer anything for later in the day or depend on being able to get back in. Eat before or after you visit.

**VARIATIONS** On days when the park is projected to be at or close to full capacity, day guests are sometimes admitted to the park before official opening and directed clockwise around the lagoon to obtain a return ticket. On days when attendance is less than expected, Universal might start the day running Option Two and later remove the barricades, allowing for free access.

The return time on your pass depends on crowd conditions and how many Universal resort guests are in The Wizarding World–Hogsmeade before the park opens to the general public. Another factor that will affect your wait is how well Harry Potter and the Forbidden Journey is operating, since this is what those in line are waiting for. If the ride comes up on schedule and runs trouble-free, everything runs smoothly. If Forbidden Journey experiences problems, though, especially first thing in the morning, it gums up the works for everyone.

Crowds finally dissipate between 7 and 8 p.m., except on Option Three days. A bonus of visiting late is enjoying the exquisite lighting and magical nighttime personality of The Wizarding World. Forbidden Journey will accommodate anyone already in line at park closing, and many of the Hogsmeade shops stay open awhile after closing.

However complicated, it's all doable, as a multigenerational Grosse Pointe, Michigan, family attests:

> *Convinced of your rectitude, we went without fear to Universal. We made it to Harry Potter by 8:05, were out of the Forbidden Journey and on the Hippogriff by 8:30, and had our Butterbeer by 9.*

## Ladies and Gentlemen, Start Your Broomsticks

The Wizarding World–Hogsmeade is in the northwest corner of Islands of Adventure, between The Lost Continent and Jurassic Park. From the IOA entrance, the most direct route there is through Port of Entry then right, through Seuss Landing (staying to the left of Green Eggs and Ham) and The Lost Continent, to the Hogsmeade main gate. The alternative route is to cross the bridge connecting The Lost Continent with Jurassic Park, then turn right after entering the latter area. Note that the bridge is closed on slower days.

For the moment, though, let's begin our exploration at The Wizarding World's main entrance, on the Lost Continent side. Passing beneath a stone arch, you enter the village of **Hogsmeade.** The **Hogwarts Express** locomotive sits belching steam on your right. The village setting is rendered in exquisite detail: Stone cottages and shops have steeply pitched slate roofs, bowed multipaned windows, gables, and tall, crooked chimneys. Add cobblestone streets and gas street lamps, and Hogsmeade is as reminiscent of Sherlock Holmes as of Harry Potter.

Your first taste—literally—of the Harry Potter universe comes courtesy of **Honeydukes.** Specializing in Potter-themed candy

*un*official **TIP**
The only restrooms in The Wizarding World at IOA, labeled PUBLIC CONVENIENCES, are in the middle of Hogsmeade. Remember where they are—especially if you're planning to ride Forbidden Journey or Dragon Challenge and you're prone to motion sickness.

such as Acid Pops (no flashbacks, guaranteed), Tooth Splintering Strong Mints, and Fizzing Whizzbees, the sweet shop offers no shortage of snacks that administer an immediate sugar high. There's also a small bakery inside; while we highly recommend the Cauldron Cakes, the big draw is the elaborately boxed Chocolate Frogs. The chocolate inside isn't anything special, but the packaging looks as if it came straight from a Harry Potter film, complete with lenticular wizard trading card.

Next door to Honeydukes and set back from the main street is **Three Broomsticks,** a rustic tavern serving English staples such as fish-and-chips, shepherd's pie, Cornish pasties, and turkey legs; kids' fare includes the obligatory mac-and-cheese and chicken fingers. To the rear of the tavern is the **Hog's Head** pub, which serves a nice selection of beer as well as The Wizarding World's signature nonalcoholic brew, Butterbeer (see nezt page). Three Broomsticks and the Hog's Head were carved out of The Lost Continent's popular Enchanted Oak Tavern, which was Potterfied pretty effectively in its reincarnation, although a good deal of seating capacity was sacrificed. To dine at Three Broomsticks anytime from its opening until roughly 8 p.m., you'll have to wait in a long queue during busier times of year. In the summer of 2014, waiting times for Three Broomsticks were upwards of 70 minutes much of the day (though additional capacity was added in 2013 by replacing space-hogging booths with tables). This, coupled with the facts that (1) one usually can't reenter The Wizarding World without starting over and (2) no other food is available in the themed area save some meager vendor snacks, means that many guests are left without a practical alternative for getting something to eat.

Roughly across the street from the pub, you'll find benches in the shade at the **Owlery,** where animatronic owls (complete with lifelike poop) ruffle and hoot from the rafters. Next to the Owlery is the **Owl Post,** where your can have mail stamped with a Hogsmeade postmark before dropping it off for delivery (an Orlando postmark will also be applied by the real USPS). The Owl Post also sells stationery, toy owls, and the like. Here, once again, a nice selection of owls preens on the timbers overhead. You access the Owl Post in either of two ways: through an interior door following the wand-choosing demonstration at Ollivanders (see below), or through **Dervish and Banges,** a magic-supplies shop that's interconnected with the Owl Post. You can't enter through the Owl Post's front door on busy days, when it serves exclusively as an exit. Because it's so difficult to get into the Owl Post, IOA sometimes stations a team member outside to stamp your postcards with the Wizarding World postmark.

Next to the Owl Post is the previously mentioned **Ollivanders** (★★★★), a musty little shop stacked to the ceiling with boxes of magic wands. Here, following a script from the Potter books, you can pick out a wand or, in an interactive experience, let it pick you. This is one of the most truly imaginative elements of The Wizarding World: A Wand-keeper sizes you up and presents a wand, inviting you to try it out; your attempted spells produce unintended, unwanted, and highly amusing consequences. Ultimately, a wand chooses you, with all the attendant special effects. It's great fun, but the tiny shop can accommodate only about 24 guests at a time. Usually just one person in each group gets to be chosen by a wand, and then the whole group is dispatched to the Owl Post and Dervish and Banges to make purchases. Wand prices range from $25 for a no-frills model to $45 for an interactive gizmo that triggers special effects hidden inside shop windows throughout Hogsmeade. The wand experience is second in popularity only to Harry Potter and the Forbidden Journey—lines build quickly after opening, and there's little to no shade. If Ollivanders is a priority, go there first thing in the morning or after 7:30 p.m. The average wait time during summer and other busy periods is 45–85 minutes between 9:30 a.m. and 7:30 p.m. If you're just looking to buy a wand without the interactive experience, a cart is usually set up between Filch's Emporium of Confiscated Goods and the Flight of the Hippogriff exit, with little to no wait.

At the far end of the village, the massive **Hogwarts** castle comes into view, set atop a rock face and towering over Hogsmeade and the entire Wizarding World. Follow the path through the castle's massive gates to the entrance of Harry Potter and the Forbidden Journey. Below the castle and to the right, at the base of the cliff, are the **Forbidden Forest, Hagrid's Hut,** and the **Flight of the Hippogriff** children's roller coaster. In the village, near the gate to Hogwarts Castle, is **Filch's Emporium of Confiscated Goods,** which offers all manner of Potter-themed gear, including Quidditch clothing, magical-creature toys, film-inspired chess sets, and, of course, Death Eater masks (breath mints extra).

In keeping with the stores depicted in the Potter films, the shopping venues in The Wizarding World–Hogsmeade are small and intimate— so intimate, in fact, that they feel congested when they're serving only 12–20 shoppers. With so many avid Potter fans, lines for the shops develop most days by 9:30 or 10 a.m., creating a phenomenon we've never seen in our 28 years of covering theme parks: The lines for the shops are longer than the lines for Dragon Challenge and Flight of the Hippogriff—at 11 a.m., there was frequently a 30- to 40-minute wait to get into the shops, but a less-than-20-minute wait to ride the coasters. Filch's Emporium is the only shop in The Wizarding World that you can enter during high season without waiting in line; problem is, it doubles as the exit for Forbidden Journey. As throngs of riders flow out continuously, trying to enter Filch's is not unlike swimming upstream to spawn; still, it's a whole lot better than standing in lines for the other shops. Because the stores are so jammed, IOA sells some Potter merchandise, including wands, through street vendors and in Port of Entry shops.

At the end of the village and to the left is the walkway to **Jurassic Park,** the themed area contiguous to The Wizarding World.

## The Butterbeer Craze

**Butterbeer** is a nonalcoholic, cream soda–like beverage served from a tap, with a butterscotch-y head that's added after the drink is poured. There's also a frozen version that's sort of like a slushie. Both were invented for The Wizarding World and had to meet J. K. Rowling's stringent specifications, which, among other things, required natural sugar (don't ask for Butterbeer Lite). We didn't expect to like it but were pleasantly surprised: It's tasty and refreshing, albeit *really* sweet. Twelve ounces of the soda in a plastic cup goes for $4.49 while the frozen version is $4.99. The same soda in a Harry Potter souvenir cup sells for $9.50.

*unofficial* **TIP**

At J. K. Rowling's request, no brand-name soft drinks are available in The Wizarding World—if you want a Coke, you'll have to go to The Lost Continent or Jurassic Park.

It seems everyone in the park is dead-set on trying Butterbeer, as confirmed by Universal's sale of its five millionth cup in December 2013. Unfortunately, the ambrosial liquid is sold only at **Three Broomsticks,** at the **Hog's Head** pub, and by two street vendors—and that means, once again, long waits. Many guests buy from the outside vendors, waiting 30 minutes or more in line to be served. We recommend that you try your luck at the Hog's Head—the wait here is generally 10 minutes or less, and often there's nobody in line, even when the outdoor carts have lines 30 people deep only 20 feet away. Once served, you can relax with your drink at a table in the pub or out on the rear patio.

## Wizarding World Entertainment

Nearly every retail space sports some sort of animatronic or special-effects surprise. At **Dervish and Banges,** the fearsome Monster Book of Monsters rattles and snarls at you as Nimbus 2001 brooms strain at their tethers overhead. At the Hog's Head pub, the titular porcine part, mounted behind the bar, similarly thrashes and growls. Street entertainment at the Forbidden Journey end of Hogsmeade includes the **Hogwarts Choir** (★★★), accompanied by frogs sitting on pillows, and the **Triwizard Spirit Rally** (★★★½), showcasing dancing, martial arts, and acrobatics. Performances run about 15 minutes.

## Harry Potter and the Forbidden Journey ★★★★★

| APPEAL BY AGE | PRESCHOOL ★ | GRADE SCHOOL ★★★★½ | TEENS ★★★★★ |
| --- | --- | --- | --- |
| YOUNG ADULTS ★★★★★ | | OVER 30 ★★★★★ | SENIORS ★★★★★ |

Motion Sickness

**What it is** Motion-simulator dark ride. **Scope and scale** Super-headliner. **When to go** Immediately after park opening. **Special comments** Expect *long* waits in line; 48" minimum height requirement. **Authors' rating** Marvelous for Muggles; not to be missed; ★★★★★. **Duration of ride** 4¼ minutes. **Probable waiting time per 100 people ahead of you** 4 minutes. **Loading speed** Fast.

**DESCRIPTION AND COMMENTS** This ride provides the only opportunity at Universal Orlando to come in contact with Harry, Ron, Hermione, and Dumbledore as portrayed by the original actors. Half the attraction is a series of preshows, setting the stage for the main event, a dark ride. You can get on the ride in only 10–25 minutes using the singles line, but everyone should go through the main queue at least once.

From Hogsmeade you reach the attraction through the imposing Winged Boar gates and progress along a winding path. Entering the castle on a lower level, you walk through a sort of dungeon festooned with various icons and prop replicas from the Potter flicks, including the Mirror of Erised from *Harry Potter and the Sorcerer's Stone.* You later emerge back outside and into the Hogwarts greenhouses. Cleverly conceived and executed, with some strategically placed mandrakes to amuse you, the greenhouses compose the larger part of the Forbidden Journey's queuing area. If you're among the first in the park and in the queue, you'll move through this area pretty quickly. Otherwise . . . well, we hope you like plants. The greenhouses are not air-conditioned, but fans move the (hot) air around. Blessedly, there are water fountains but, alas, no restrooms.

Having finally escaped horticulture purgatory, you reenter the castle, moving along its halls and passageways. One chamber you'll probably remember from the films is a multistory gallery of portraits, many of whose subjects come alive when they take a notion. You'll see for the first time the four founders of Hogwarts: Helga Hufflepuff holding her famous cup, Godric Gryffindor and Rowena Ravenclaw nearby, and the tall, moving portrait of Salazar Slytherin straight ahead. The founders argue about Quidditch and Dumbledore's controversial decision to host an open house at Hogwarts for Muggles (garden-variety mortals). Don't rush through the gallery—the effects are very cool, and the conversation is essential to understanding the rest of the attraction.

Next up, after you've navigated some more passages, is Dumbledore's office, where the chief wizard appears on a balcony and welcomes you to Hogwarts. The headmaster's appearance is your introduction to Musion Eyeliner technology—a high-definition video-projection system that produces breathtakingly realistic, three-dimensional, life-size moving holograms. The technology uses a special foil that reflects images from HD projectors, producing holographic images of variable sizes and incredible clarity. After his welcoming remarks, Dumbledore dispatches you to the Defence Against the Dark Arts classroom to hear a presentation on the history of Hogwarts.

As you gather to await the lecture, Harry, Ron, and Hermione pop out from beneath an invisibility cloak. They suggest you ditch the lecture in favor of joining them for a proper tour of Hogwarts, including a Quidditch match. After some repartee among the characters and a couple of special-effects surprises, it's off to the Hogwarts Official Attraction Safety Briefing and Boarding Instructions Chamber—OK, we made up the name, but you get the picture. The briefing and instructions are presented by animated portraits, including an etiquette teacher. Later on, even the famed Sorting Hat gets into the act. All this leads to the Room of Requirement, where hundreds of candles float overhead and you board the ride.

After all the high-tech stuff in your queuing odyssey, you'll naturally expect to be wowed by your ride vehicle. Surely it's a Nimbus 3000 turbo-broom, a phoenix, a hippogriff, or at least the Weasleys' flying car. But no, what you'll ride on the most technologically advanced theme park attraction in America is . . . a *bench*? Yep, a bench.

A bit anticlimactic, perhaps, but as benches go, this one's a doozy, mounted on a Kuka robotic arm. When not engaged in Quidditch matches, a Kuka arm is a computer-controlled robotic arm similar to the kind used in heavy manufacturing. If you think about pictures you've seen of automotive assembly plants, Kuka arms are like those long metal appendages that come in to complete welds, move heavy stuff around, or fasten things. With the right programming, the arms can handle just about any repetitive industrial tasks thrown at them (see **kuka-robotics.com** for more info).

Bear with us for a moment; you know how we *Unofficials* like techno-geekery. When you put a Kuka arm on a ride platform, it provides six axes—six degrees of freedom, with synchronized motion that can be programmed to replicate all the sensations of flying, including broad swoops, steep dives, sharp turns, sudden stops, and fast acceleration. Here's where it gets really good: Up to now, when Kuka arms and similar robotic systems have been employed in theme park rides, the arm has been anchored to a stationary platform. In Forbidden Journey, the arm is mounted on a ride vehicle that moves you through a series of action scenes projected all around you. The movement of the arm is synchronized to create the motion that corresponds to what's happening in the film. When everything works right, it's mind-blowing.

When the ride was being designed, it was assumed that Kuka's robotic programming could easily produce the various movements called for in each scene. What nobody considered, however, is that the program was designed for maximum industrial efficiency. If, to correspond to the action in a given scene, the Kuka arm had to simulate 22 different motions, the software—not knowing a theme park ride from a diesel assembly line—would think, "OK, let's knock these 22 movements down to 13 and save half a minute." Because this would throw the timing of everything out of whack, Universal ended up having to create a program that would behave as it was told and not be so anal about efficiency. For you, the practical implication of all this is an extraordinary attraction with more gremlins than inhabit the dark-arts lab.

High-tech troubles aside, is the attraction itself ultimately worthy of the hype? In a word, *yes!* Your 4½-minute adventure is a headlong sprint through the most thrilling moments from the first few Potter books: You'll soar over Hogwarts Castle, narrowly evade an attacking dragon, spar with the Whomping Willow, get tossed into a Quidditch match, and fight off Dementors inside the Chamber of Secrets. Scenes alternate between enormous physical sets, complete with animatronic creatures, elaborate lighting effects, and high-definition video-projection domes that surround your field of view, similar to Soarin' or The Simpsons Ride. Those Kuka-powered benches really do "levitate" in a manner that feels remarkably like free flight, and while you don't go upside down, the sensation of floating on your back or being slung from side to side is certainly unique.

The seamless transitions between screens and sets, and the way the domes appear to remain stationary in front of you while actually moving (much like Dreamfinder's dirigible in the original Journey into Imagination at Epcot) serve to blur the boundary between actual and virtual better than any attraction before it. The greatest-hits montage plotline may be a bit muddled, but the ride is enormously effective at leaving you feeling like you just survived the scariest scrapes from the early educational career of The Boy Who Lived.

Having experienced Forbidden Journey for ourselves, we have two primary bones to pick. First, Islands of Adventure team members rush you through the queue. To understand the storyline and get the most out of the attraction, you really need to see and hear the entire presentation in each of the preshow rooms. This won't happen unless, contrary to the admonishments of the team members, you just park yourself and watch a full run-through of each preshow. Try to find a place to stop where you can let those behind you pass and where you're as far away from any staff as possible. As long as you're not creating a logjam, the team members will leave you alone as often as not.

Another alternative is to tell the greeter at the castle entrance that you want to take the **castle-only tour.** This self-guided experience lets guests who don't want to ride view the many features of the castle via a different queue. You can pause as long as you desire in each of the various chambers and savor the preshows without being herded along. At the end, if you decide to ride, ask to be guided to the singles line—using this strategy, you'll maximize your enjoyment of the castle while minimizing your wait for the ride. Note that the castle-only tour is often unavailable on peak-attendance days.

Another gripe: The dialogue in the preshows is delivered in English accents of varying degrees of intelligibility, and at a very brisk pace. Add an echo effect owing to the cavernous nature of the preshow rooms, and it can be quite difficult for Yanks to decipher what's being said. This is especially evident in the staccato repartee between Harry, Ron, and Hermione in the Defence Against the Dark Arts classroom.

**TOURING TIPS** Harry Potter and the Forbidden Journey has quickly become the most popular attraction at Islands of Adventure, and one of the most in-demand theme park attractions in America. The only way to ride without a prohibitive wait is to be one of the first through the turnstiles in the morning or to visit after 7:30 or 8 in the evening.

Upon entering Forbidden Journey's outside queue, you have two choices: left line or right line. They are unmarked, but the left line is for those who have bags or loose items and therefore require a locker (no charge). Our wait-time research has shown that in some cases, not needing a locker can save you as much as 30 minutes of standing in line. If you do need to stow your stuff, be aware that the Forbidden Journey locker area is small, crowded, and confusing. It may make more sense to pay the $3 to stash your things in the lockers beside Dragon Challenge.

Universal warns you to secure or leave behind loose objects, which most people interpret to mean eyeglasses, purses, ball caps, and the like. However, the ride makes a couple of moves that will empty your trousers faster than a master pickpocket—ditto and worse for shirt pockets. When these moves occur, your stuff will clatter around like quarters in a slot-machine tray. Much better to use the small compartment built into the seat back for keys, coins, phone, wallet, and pocket Bible. Be prepared, however: Team members don't give you much time to stow or retrieve your belongings.

The single-rider line is likewise unmarked, as relatively few guests use it. Whereas on most attractions the wait in the singles line is one-third the wait in the standby line, at Forbidden Journey it can be as much as one-tenth. Because the individual seating separates you from the other riders whether your party stays together or not, the singles line is a great option. To get there, enter the right (no-bags) line and keep left all the way into the castle. Past the locker area, take the first left into the singles line.

If you see a complete iteration of each preshow in the queue and then experience the ride, you'll invest 25–35 minutes even if you don't have to wait. If you elect to skip the preshows—the Gryffindor Common Room, where you receive safety and loading directions, is mandatory—and use the singles line, you can get on in about 10–25 minutes at any time of day. At a time when the posted wait in the regular line was 2 hours, we rode and were out the door in 15 minutes using the singles line.

Universal has toned down the Kuka programming to help reduce motion sickness, but we nonetheless recommend that you not ride on an empty stomach. If you start getting queasy, fix your gaze on your feet and try to exclude as much from your peripheral vision as possible.

If you have a child who doesn't meet the minimum height requirement of 48 inches, a child-swapping option is provided at the loading area.

The seats accommodate a wide variety of body shapes and sizes. Each bench has specially modified seats at either end. Though these allow many more people to ride, it's possible that guests of size can't fit in them. The best way to figure out whether you can fit in a regular seat or one of the modified ones is to sit in one of the test seats outside the

*unofficial* **TIP**
Even if your child meets the height requirement, consider carefully whether Forbidden Journey is an experience he or she can handle—because the seats on the benches are compartmentalized, kids can't see or touch Mom or Dad if they get frightened.

queue or just inside the castle. After you sit down, pull down on the safety harness as far as you can. One of three safety lights will illuminate: A green light indicates you can fit into any seat, a yellow light means you should ask for one of the modified seats on the outside of the bench, and a red light means the harness can't engage enough for you to ride safely.

In addition, IOA team members select guests of all sizes "at random" to plop in the test seats, but they're really looking for large people or those who have a certain body shape. Team members handle the situation as diplomatically as possible, but if they suspect you're not the right size, you'll be asked to sit down for a test. For you to be cleared to ride, the overhead restraint has to click three times; once again, it's body shape rather than weight (unless you're over 300 pounds) that's key. Most team members will let you try a second time if you don't achieve three clicks on the first go. Passing the test by inhaling sharply is not recommended unless you can also hold your breath for the entire 4½ minutes of the ride.

With The Wizarding World and especially Forbidden Journey soaking up so many guests in IOA, waits for attractions in the other themed areas are minimal up to around 11 a.m., so there's no reason to pay the big extra bucks for Universal Express.

## Dragon Challenge (*Universal Express*) ★★★★

| APPEAL BY AGE | PRESCHOOL ★ | GRADE SCHOOL ★★★★★ | TEENS ★★★★½ |
| --- | --- | --- | --- |
| YOUNG ADULTS ★★★★★ | | OVER 30 ★★★★½ | SENIORS ★★★ |

**What it is** Roller coaster. **Scope and scale** Headliner. **When to go** Immediately after Harry Potter and the Forbidden Journey. **Special comments** 54″ minimum height requirement. **Authors' rating** As good as the Hulk coaster; not to be missed; ★★★★. **Duration of ride** 2½ minutes. **Probable waiting time per 100 people ahead of you** 9 minutes. **Loading speed** Moderate.

**DESCRIPTION AND COMMENTS** Dragon Challenge, formerly Dueling Dragons and part of The Lost Continent, was renamed and incorporated into The Wizarding World in 2010. The storyline is that you're preparing to compete in the Triwizard Tournament from *Harry Potter and the Goblet of Fire.* As you wind through the long, long queue, you pass through tournament tents and dark passages that are supposed to be under the stadium. You'll see the Goblet of Fire on display and hear the distant roar of the crowd in the supposed stadium above you.

Riders board one of two coasters—Chinese Fireball or Hungarian Horntail—that are launched moments apart on tracks that are closely intertwined. The tracks are configured so that you get a different experience on each. The trains are dispatched sequentially instead of simultaneously, so it looks as if one train is chasing another.

Because this is an inverted coaster, your view of the action is limited unless you're sitting in the front row. Regardless of where you sit, there's plenty to keep you busy. Dragon Challenge is the highest coaster in the park and also claims the longest drop at 115 feet, plus five inversions. As on the Hulk, it's a smooth ride all the way.

Coaster fans argue about which seat on which train provides the wildest ride. We prefer the front row on either train, but coaster loonies hype the front row of Fireball and the last row of Horntail.

**TOURING TIPS** Use the restrooms before getting in line. The queuing area for Dragon Challenge is the longest, most convoluted affair we've ever seen, winding endlessly through a maze of faux subterranean passages. After what feels like a comprehensive tour of Mammoth Cave, you finally emerge at the loading area, where you must choose between Chinese Fireball or

Hungarian Horntail. Of course, at this critical juncture, you're as blind as a mole rat from being in the dark for so long. Our advice is to follow the person in front of you until your eyes adjust to the light.

Waits for Dragon Challenge, one of the best coasters in the country, rarely exceed 30 minutes before 11 a.m. Ride after experiencing Harry Potter and the Forbidden Journey. Even if there's no line to speak of, it takes 10–12 minutes just to navigate the passages and not much less time to exit after riding. If lines are short, however, park employees will open special doors marked REENTRY TO CHINESE FIREBALL or REENTRY TO HUNGARIAN HORNTAIL (depending on which coaster you just rode) that allow you to get right back to the head of the queue and ride again. Finally, if you don't have time to ride both coasters, the *Unofficial* crew unanimously prefers Chinese Fireball.

## Flight of the Hippogriff *(Universal Express)*   ★★★

| APPEAL BY AGE | PRESCHOOL ★★★½ | GRADE SCHOOL ★★★★ | TEENS ★★★ |
|---|---|---|---|
| YOUNG ADULTS ★★½ | OVER 30 ★★★½ | | SENIORS ★★★ |

**What it is** Kiddie roller coaster. **Scope and scale** Minor attraction. **When to go** First 90 minutes the park is open. **Special comments** 36" minimum height requirement. **Authors' rating** A good beginner coaster; ★★★. **Duration of ride** 1 minute. **Probable waiting time per 100 people ahead of you** 14 minutes. **Loading speed** Slow.

**DESCRIPTION AND COMMENTS** Below and to the right of Hogwarts Castle, next to Hagrid's Hut, the Hippogriff is short and sweet but not worth much of a wait. Fortunately, waits usually don't exceed 20 minutes, even in the non-Express line.

**TOURING TIPS** Have your kids ride soon after the park opens while older sibs enjoy Dragon Challenge. Check out Hogwarts Castle from the cliff bottom and Hagrid's Hut above the path for the regular line.

## Hogwarts Express   ★★★★½

| APPEAL BY AGE | PRESCHOOL ★★★★ | GRADE SCHOOL ★★★★★ | TEENS ★★★★ |
|---|---|---|---|
| YOUNG ADULTS ★★★★½ | OVER 30 ★★★★½ | | SENIORS ★★★★½ |

**What it is** Transportation attraction. **Scope and scale** Super-headliner. **When to go** Immediately after park opening. **Special comments** Expect lengthy waits in line. **Authors' rating** Not to be missed; ★★★★½. **Duration of ride** 4 minutes. **Probable waiting time per 100 people ahead of you** 7 minutes. **Loading speed** Moderate.

**DESCRIPTION AND COMMENTS** See Part Seventeen, page 700, for a full review.

**TOURING TIPS** Because the Hogsmeade Station doesn't include the cool Platform 9¾ effect found at the King's Cross end, expect waits for the one-way trip to be shorter here. A Park-to-Park ticket is required to board, and all guests exit at Universal Studios Florida outside of the London Waterfront, so the train isn't a shortcut into Diagon Alley.

The Hogsmeade Station lies within the footprint of the Dragon Challenge roller coaster and provides pedestrian access to Hogsmeade and IOA's Lost Continent themed area. On days of low-to-average attendance, disembarking guests will be allowed directly into Hogsmeade, less than a minute's walk away. On days of heavy attendance, they'll be directed to the bridge between The Lost Continent and Jurassic Park, where they'll have to either queue to enter Hogsmeade or obtain a free timed-entry ticket to visit The Wizarding World at a specified time.

If you wish to experience the train, make it your first stop of the day, but remember that you must wait in a slow standby line to take a same-day return ride.

# THE LOST CONTINENT

## The Eighth Voyage of Sindbad Stunt Show
### (Universal Express) ★★

| APPEAL BY AGE | PRESCHOOL ★★ | GRADE SCHOOL ★★★½ | TEENS ★★★ |
|---|---|---|---|
| YOUNG ADULTS ★★★ | | OVER 30 ★★½ | SENIORS ★★½ |

**What it is** Theater stunt show. **Scope and scale** Major attraction. **When to go** Any time on the daily entertainment schedule. **Authors' rating** Lame-o; ★★. **Duration of presentation** 17 minutes. **Probable waiting time** 15 minutes.

**DESCRIPTION AND COMMENTS** A story about Sindbad the Sailor is the glue that (loosely) binds this stunt show featuring water explosions, 10-foot-tall circles of flame, and various other eruptions and perturbations. Not unlike an action movie that substitutes a mind-numbing succession of explosions, crashes, and special effects for plot and character development, the production is so vacuous and redundant (not to mention silly) that it's hard to get into the spirit of the thing. When our researchers went to review *Sindbad,* one team member passed, explaining that the show is like a colonoscopy—once every 10 years is enough.

**TOURING TIPS** See *The Eighth Voyage* after you've experienced the rides and the better-rated shows.

## Poseidon's Fury (Universal Express)   ★★★½

| APPEAL BY AGE | PRESCHOOL ★★ | GRADE SCHOOL ★★★★ | TEENS ★★★★ |
|---|---|---|---|
| YOUNG ADULTS ★★★★ | | OVER 30 ★★★★ | SENIORS ★★★★ |

**What it is** High-tech theater attraction. **Scope and scale** Headliner. **When to go** After experiencing all the rides. **Special comments** Audience stands throughout. **Authors' rating** ★★★½. **Duration of presentation** 17 minutes, including preshow. **Probable waiting time** 25 minutes.

**DESCRIPTION AND COMMENTS** In the first incarnation of this story, the Greek gods Poseidon and Zeus duked it out, with Poseidon as the heavy. Poseidon fought with water, and Zeus fought with fire, though both sometimes resorted to laser beams and smoke machines. In the current incarnation, the rehabilitated Poseidon now tussles with an evil wizardish guy—named Lord Darkenon, of all things—and they fight with fire, water, lasers, and smoke machines. As you might have inferred, the story is somewhat incoherent, but the special effects are still amazing, as is the theming of the preshow area. The plot unfolds in installments as you pass through a couple of antechambers and finally into the main theater. Though the production plods a bit at first, it wraps up with quite an impressive flourish. *Poseidon* is far and away the best of the Islands of Adventure theater attractions (it only has to compete with *Sindbad*).

**TOURING TIPS** If you're still wet from Dudley Do-Right, the Bilge-Rat Barges, or the Jurassic Park River Adventure, you might be tempted to cheer the evil wizard's flame jets in hopes of finally drying out. Our money, however, is on Poseidon—it's legal in Florida for theme parks to get guests wet, but setting them on fire is frowned upon.

Frequent explosions, dark, and noise may frighten younger children. Catch *Poseidon* after getting your fill of the rides.

As impressive as the facade of *Poseidon's Fury* is, this Massachusetts mom of a family of four thinks the attraction itself is a letdown:

*The one ride we all wished we'd skipped was* Poseidon's Fury. *The posted wait time was 10 minutes—after waiting for 30 minutes, we were ushered into a*

*series of rooms with no chairs to watch a set of poorly executed special effects.
I'm 5 feet tall and saw none of it since everyone was standing and the floor was
poorly slanted. At the end, we were all tired and we wanted to go home.*

## SEUSS LANDING

THIS 10-ACRE THEMED AREA is based on Dr. Seuss's famous children's books. Buildings and attractions replicate his whimsical style, with exaggerated features, bright colors, and rounded lines. Seuss Landing has four rides; **If I Ran the Zoo,** an interactive play area populated by Seuss creatures; and ***Oh, the Stories You'll Hear!,*** a live musical show.

### Caro-Seuss-el *(Universal Express)*  ★★★

| APPEAL BY AGE | PRESCHOOL ★★★★★ | GRADE SCHOOL ★★★★ | TEENS ★★★ |
|---|---|---|---|
| YOUNG ADULTS ★★★ | OVER 30 ★★★½ | | SENIORS ★★★★ |

**What it is** Merry-go-round. **Scope and scale** Minor attraction. **When to go** Before 11 a.m. **Authors' rating** Wonderfully whimsical; ★★★. **Duration of ride** 2 minutes. **Probable waiting time per 100 people ahead of you** 9 minutes. **Loading speed** Slow.

**DESCRIPTION AND COMMENTS** Totally outrageous, this full-scale, 56-mount merry-go-round is made up entirely of Dr. Seuss characters.

**TOURING TIPS** Even if you're too old or you don't want to ride, Caro-Seuss-el is worth an inspection.

### The Cat in the Hat *(Universal Express)*  ★★★½

| APPEAL BY AGE | PRESCHOOL ★★★★½ | GRADE SCHOOL ★★★★ | TEENS ★★½ |
|---|---|---|---|
| YOUNG ADULTS ★★½ | OVER 30 ★★½ | | SENIORS ★★★ |

**What it is** Indoor adventure ride. **Scope and scale** Major attraction. **When to go** Before 11:30 a.m. **Special comments** 36" minimum height requirement. **Authors' rating** Dr. S. would be proud; ★★★½. **Duration of ride** 3½ minutes. **Probable waiting time per 100 people ahead of you** 5 minutes. **Loading speed** Moderate.

**DESCRIPTION AND COMMENTS** Guests ride on "couches" through 18 different sets inhabited by animatronic Seuss characters, including The Cat in the Hat, Thing 1 and Thing 2, and the beleaguered goldfish who tries to maintain order in the midst of bedlam.

**TOURING TIPS** This is fun for all ages. Try to ride early. The ride recently had its energetic spinning greatly dampened, and a new height minimum was imposed, reducing its appeal for both tykes and teens.

### The High in the Sky Seuss Trolley Train Ride!
*(Universal Express)*  ★★★½

| APPEAL BY AGE | PRESCHOOL ★★★★★ | GRADE SCHOOL ★★★½ | TEENS ★★★ |
|---|---|---|---|
| YOUNG ADULTS ★★★ | OVER 30 ★★★ | | SENIORS ★★★★ |

**What it is** Elevated train. **Scope and scale** Major attraction. **When to go** Before 11:30 a.m. **Special comments** A relaxed look at the park; 34" minimum height requirement. **Authors' rating** ★★★½. **Duration of ride** 3½ minutes. **Probable waiting time per 100 people ahead of you** 9 minutes. **Loading speed** Molasses.

**DESCRIPTION AND COMMENTS** Trains putter along elevated tracks while a voice reads a Dr. Seuss story over the train's speakers. As each train makes its way through Seuss Landing, it passes a series of animatronic characters in scenes that are part of the story being told. Little tunnels and a few mild turns make this a charming ride.

There are two tracks at the station. As you face the platform, to your left is the Beech track, which is aquamarine; to your right is the Star track, which is purple. Each track offers a different story.

**TOURING TIPS** The trains are small, fitting about 20 people, and the loading speed is glacial. Ride at the end of the day or first thing in the a.m.

### One Fish, Two Fish, Red Fish, Blue Fish
*(Universal Express)* ★★★

| APPEAL BY AGE | PRESCHOOL ★★★★★ | GRADE SCHOOL ★★★½ | TEENS ★★½ |
|---|---|---|---|
| YOUNG ADULTS ★★★½ | OVER 30 ★★★ | | SENIORS ★★★ |

**What it is** Wet version of Dumbo the Flying Elephant. **Scope and scale** Minor attraction. **When to go** Before 10 a.m. **Authors' rating** Who says you can't teach an old ride new tricks?; ★★★. **Duration of ride** 2 minutes. **Probable waiting time per 100 people ahead of you** 9 minutes. **Loading speed** Slow.

**DESCRIPTION AND COMMENTS** Imagine Dumbo with Seuss-style fish instead of elephants and you've got half the story—the other half involves yet another opportunity to drown. Guests steer their fish up or down 15 feet in the air while traveling in circles. At the same time, they try to avoid streams of water projected from "squirt posts."

**TOURING TIPS** We don't know what it is about this theme park and water, but you'll get wetter than at a full-immersion baptism.

# DINING AT UNIVERSAL'S ISLANDS *of* ADVENTURE

OF IOA'S GUSTATORY OFFERINGS, we like **Three Broomsticks,** The Wizarding World of Harry Potter's counter-service restaurant, which serves Boston Market–style rotisserie chicken, plus fish-and-chips, shepherd's pie, and barbecue ribs. The **Hog's Head** pub, a short walk from Three Broomsticks, serves beer, wine, mixed drinks, and the obligatory Butterbeer. We're also fond of the gyros at **Fire Eater's Grill** and the sandwiches at **Blondie's.** Finally, we'd be remiss if we didn't tell you to skip the green eggs at the **Green Eggs and Ham Cafe.**

IOA has two sit-down restaurants: **Confisco Grille,** in Port of Entry, and **Mythos Restaurant,** in The Lost Continent. Confisco is fine for pizza and drinks. Despite its Hellenic-sounding name, Mythos isn't a Greek restaurant; rather, like a typical Applebee's or Chili's, it serves something-for-everyone fare, including Italian risotto, Asian noodles, and Mexican fish tacos, plus steaks and burgers. Nothing on the menu stands out as either very good or very bad, so stick with appetizers and drinks.

# UNIVERSAL'S ISLANDS *of* ADVENTURE TOURING PLANS

### ROLLING THE DICE WITH HARRY POTTER

THE WIZARDING WORLD, and Harry Potter and the Forbidden Journey in particular, create some real challenges when trying to develop an optimum touring plan for IOA. Some of this will sort itself out over time, but for The Wizarding World's fifth year:

- The 20-acre section of the park will be completely overrun by crowds.
- Because of Forbidden Journey's several preshows, it takes about 25 minutes to experience, even if you don't have to wait.

If you try to enjoy Forbidden Journey first thing after the park opens, and if the ride operates as designed, you're golden. You'll be off to other must-see attractions before the park gets crowded. If, on the other hand, the ride suffers technical difficulties, you may be stuck in line a long while, during which time the crowds will have spread to other areas of IOA. By the time you exit the Forbidden Journey, there will be long lines for all of the park's other popular attractions.

If The Wizarding World is your top priority, experience it early in the morning and take your chances with crowds in the other parts of the parks later on. If Harry isn't such a hot button, skip The Wizarding World and enjoy short waits at IOA's other top attractions.

Following are what the first two alternatives look like in the first five steps of a touring plan:

| PLAN A: HARRY POTTER OR BUST | PLAN B: EASY TOURING |
|---|---|
| **1.** Harry Potter and the Forbidden Journey | **1.** The Incredible Hulk Coaster |
| **2.** Dragon Challenge | **2.** Spider-Man |
| **3.** The Incredible Hulk Coaster | **3.** Dr. Doom's Fearfall |
| **4.** Spider-Man (*skip Dr. Doom's Fearfall*) | **4.** Dudley Do-Right's Ripsaw Falls |
| **5.** Popeye & Bluto's Bilge-Rat Barges | **5.** Popeye & Bluto's Bilge-Rat Barges |

## UNIVERSAL'S ISLANDS OF ADVENTURE ONE-DAY TOURING PLAN *(page 835)*

THIS TOURING PLAN is for groups of all sizes and ages and includes thrill rides that may induce motion sickness or get you wet. If the plan calls for you to experience an attraction that doesn't interest you, simply skip it and go to the next step. Be aware that the plan calls for some backtracking. If you have young children in your party, customize the plan to fit their needs and take advantage of switching off at thrill rides.

## THE BEST OF UNIVERSAL STUDIOS FLORIDA AND ISLANDS OF ADVENTURE IN ONE DAY *(page 837)*

THIS TOURING PLAN is for guests with a one-day, two-park pass who wish to see the highlights of USF and IOA in a single day. It assumes that Universal hotel guests will be allowed into both parks an hour before day guests. The plan uses Hogwarts Express to get from IOA to USF; you'll walk back to IOA in the evening. A one-day, two-park plan doesn't leave time for sit-down meals, so eat a good breakfast, and snack as you go. Finally, the plan leaves IOA's water rides for last, so you're not walking around wet all day.

# PART SEVENTEEN

# UNIVERSAL STUDIOS FLORIDA

UNIVERSAL CITY STUDIOS INC. HAS RUN a behind-the-scenes tour and movie-themed tourist attraction in Hollywood for nearly 50 years, pre-dating all Disney parks except Disneyland. In the early 1980s, Universal announced plans to build a new theme park complex in Florida. But while Universal labored over its new project, Disney jumped into high gear and rushed its own studios and theme park into the market, beating Universal by more than a year.

Universal Studios Florida (USF) opened in June 1990. At the time, it was almost four times the size of Disney's Hollywood Studios (which today is the larger of the two parks), and much more of the facility was accessible to visitors. USF is spacious, beautifully landscaped, meticulously clean, and delightfully varied in its entertainment. Rides are exciting and innovative and, like many Disney attractions, focus on familiar and/or beloved movie characters or situations.

While these rides incorporate state-of-the-art technology and live up to their billing in terms of creativity and uniqueness, some lack the capacity to handle the number of guests who frequent major Florida tourist destinations. If a ride has great appeal but can accommodate only a small number of guests per ride or per hour, long lines form. (It isn't unusual for the wait to exceed an hour and a quarter for E.T. Adventure, for example.) Happily, most shows and theater performances at USF take place in venues that accommodate large numbers of people. Since many shows run continuously, waits usually don't exceed twice the show's performance time (15–30 minutes).

USF is laid out in a P-configuration, with the rounded part of the P sticking out disproportionately from the stem. Beyond the main entrance, a wide boulevard stretches past several shows and rides to the park's New York area. Branching off this pedestrian thoroughfare to

| NOT TO BE MISSED AT UNIVERSAL STUDIOS FLORIDA | | |
|---|---|---|
| • Harry Potter and the Escape from Gringotts | • Men in Black Alien Attack | • *Terminator 2: 3-D* |
| • Hogwarts Express | • Revenge of the Mummy | • Transformers: The Ride 3-D |
| • Hollywood Rip Ride Rockit | • The Simpsons Ride | • *Universal Orlando's Horror-Make-Up Show* |

the right are four streets that access other areas of the park and intersect a promenade circling a large lake. The area of USF open to visitors is a bit smaller than Epcot.

The park is divided into eight areas: **Hollywood, New York, Production Central, San Francisco, Woody Woodpecker's KidZone, World Expo, Springfield U.S.A.,** and **The Wizarding World of Harry Potter–Diagon Alley.** Except for Diagon Alley, where one area begins and another ends is blurry, but no matter. Guests orient themselves by the major rides, sets, and landmarks and refer, for instance, to "New York," "the waterfront," "over by E.T.," or "by Mel's Diner."

Because the majority of USF attractions really aren't thematically integrated into the areas of the park in which they reside, we present them alphabetically rather than by area.

Opened in 2013, **Springfield U.S.A.,** the setting of the long-running animated sitcom *The Simpsons,* is a themed area—more like window dressing for a once-sterile part of the park—with **The Simpsons Ride** as its centerpiece. Rounding out that attraction are a spinning ride and several *Simpsons*-themed restaurants, including a real-life Moe's Tavern.

In diametric contrast, the new **Wizarding World of Harry Potter–Diagon Alley** is an immersive themed area whose scope and scale exceed those of its older sibling at Islands of Adventure. We discuss Diagon Alley and its attractions in their own section, starting on page 694.

Services and amenities include stroller and wheelchair rental, lockers, diaper-changing and infant-nursing facilities, car assistance, and foreign-language assistance. Most of the park is accessible to disabled guests, and TDDs are available for the hearing-impaired. Almost all services are in the **Front Lot,** just inside the main entrance.

# UNIVERSAL STUDIOS FLORIDA ATTRACTIONS

## *Animal Actors on Location* (Universal Express)   ★★★½

| APPEAL BY AGE | PRESCHOOL ★★★★ | GRADE SCHOOL ★★★★ | TEENS ★★★ |
|---|---|---|---|
| YOUNG ADULTS ★★★ | | OVER 30 ★★★ | SENIORS ★★★★ |

**What it is** Animal-tricks and comedy show. **Scope and scale** Major attraction. **When to go** After you've experienced all rides. **Authors' rating** Cute li'l critters; ★★★½. **Duration of presentation** 20 minutes. **Probable waiting time** 25 minutes.

**DESCRIPTION AND COMMENTS** This show integrates video segments with live sketches, jokes, and animal tricks performed onstage. The idea is to create eco-friendly family entertainment. Several of the animal thespians are veterans of TV and movies; many were rescued from shelters. What sets *Animal Actors* apart is the use of varied and unusual kinds of animals, and the opportunity to see the animals being trained on stage. Audience members can participate as well—where else will you get the chance to hold an 8-foot albino reticulated python in your lap?

**TOURING TIPS** Check the daily entertainment schedule for showtimes. You shouldn't have any trouble getting in.

*Continued on page 682*

## Universal Studios Florida

1. *Animal Actors on Location*
2. *Beetlejuice's Graveyard Mash-Up*
3. *The Blues Brothers*
4. *A Day in the Park with Barney*
5. *Despicable Me Minion Mayhem*
6. *Disaster!*
7. *E.T. Adventure*
8. *Fear Factor Live*
9. *Fievel's Playland*
10. Harry Potter and the Escape from Gringotts
11. Hogwarts Express
12. Hollywood Rip Ride Rockit
13. Kang & Kodos' Twirl 'n' Hurl
14. *Lucy—A Tribute*
15. Men in Black Alien Attack
16. Revenge of the Mummy

17. *Shrek 4-D*
18. The Simpsons Ride
19. *Terminator 2: 3-D*
20. Transformers: The Ride 3-D
21. *TWISTER . . . Ride It Out*
22. *Universal's Cinematic Spectacular* (seasonal)
23. *Universal Orlando's Horror Make-Up Show*
24. Woody Woodpecker's Nuthouse Coaster, Curious George Goes to Town

**Parade Route:** ● ● ● ● ● ● ● ● ● ● ● ●

To Universal's
← Islands of
Adventure

**New York**

**Production Central**

5th Ave.

57th St.

7th Ave.          7th Ave.

Plaza-of-the-Stars

8th Ave.

South St.

Nickelodeon Way

Hollywood Blvd.

Rodeo Dr.

**Hollywood**

**Main Entrance**

*Continued from page 679*

## Beetlejuice's Graveyard Mash-Up *(Universal Express)*
★★★

| APPEAL BY AGE | PRESCHOOL ★★★★ | GRADE SCHOOL ★★★★ | TEENS ★★★★ |
|---|---|---|---|
| YOUNG ADULTS ★★★½ | | OVER 30  ★★★½ | SENIORS ★★★ |

**What it is** Rock-and-roll stage show. **Scope and scale** Almost major attraction.
**When to go** At your convenience. **Authors' rating** Capable of waking the dead;
★★★. **Duration of presentation** 18 minutes. **Probable waiting time** None.

**DESCRIPTION AND COMMENTS** *Beetlejuice's Graveyard Mash-Up* features Dracula, the Wolfman, and Frankenstein and his bride singing pop music from the 1980s, such as Michael Jackson and Mötley Crüe hits, with a few recent pop songs thrown in for the kids. Beetlejuice, the title character from the 1988 film of the same name, serves as the show's emcee, adding monster jokes, groan-worthy puns, and pop-culture references between songs. New characters were added when the show was updated in 2014, including Cleopatra, a female mummy; Phantasia, a female Phantom of the Opera; and a quartet of ghoulish backup dancers.

This is far from Orlando's best theme park show, though the new version is better than the last. The performers don't play any instruments, so the show seems a little like a Halloween-themed karaoke party, minus the booze. But the new cast gives its all in executing the energetic, nonstop choreography, and several of the actors have stellar vocal chops.

In response to concerns from parents, Beetlejuice's formerly risqué dialogue has been made more family-friendly; still, keep an eye on BJ in the background for some snarky sight gags.

While the show runs around 20 minutes, there is almost no break between any of the songs (or mash-ups), so sitting through a set can be something of an ordeal. The pyrotechnics are less percussive but more frequent than before, and the soundtrack is still cranked to 11, making for an audio assault on the audience.

**TOURING TIPS** The show is staged in a covered theater and participates in Universal Express. Its proximity to Diagon Alley ensures large audiences.

## The Blues Brothers   ★★★½

| APPEAL BY AGE | PRESCHOOL ★★★ | GRADE SCHOOL ★★★½ | TEENS ★★★½ |
|---|---|---|---|
| YOUNG ADULTS ★★★½ | | OVER 30. ★★★★ | SENIORS ★★★★ |

**What it is** Blues concert. **Scope and scale** Diversion. **When to go** Scheduled showtimes. **Special comments** A party in the street. **Authors' rating** Energetic; ★★★½.
**Duration of presentation** 12 minutes. **Probable waiting time** None.

**DESCRIPTION AND COMMENTS** Held on the corner of the New York area, across from the lagoon, *The Blues Brothers* show features Jake and Elwood performing a few of the hit songs from the classic 1980 movie musical, including "Soul Man" and "Sweet Home Chicago." The brothers are joined on stage by Jazz the saxophone player and his girlfriend, Mabel the waitress, who belts a cover of "Respect" to start the show.

**TOURING TIPS** Check the daily entertainment schedule for showtimes. The audience stands on the street during the 12-minute show, without cover or shade.

## *A Day in the Park with Barney* (*Universal Express*)  ★★★

| APPEAL BY AGE | PRESCHOOL ★★★★★ | GRADE SCHOOL ★★★ | TEENS ★★ |
|---|---|---|---|
| YOUNG ADULTS ★★★ | OVER 30 ★★★ | | SENIORS ★★★ |

**What it is** Live-character stage show. **Scope and scale** Major children's attraction. **When to go** Anytime. **Authors' rating** A great hit with preschoolers; ★★★. **Duration of presentation** 20 minutes, plus 5-minute preshow and character greeting after the show. **Probable waiting time** 15 minutes.

**DESCRIPTION AND COMMENTS** The cuddly purple dinosaur of public-TV fame leads a sing-along with the help of the audience and sidekicks Baby Bop and BJ. A short preshow gets the kids lathered up before they enter Barney's Park (the theater). Interesting theatrical effects include wind, falling leaves, clouds and stars in the simulated sky, and snow. After the show, Barney poses for photos with parents and children in the indoor playground at the theatre exit.

**TOURING TIPS** If your child likes Barney, this show is a must. Unfortunately, we heard rumors at press time that Barney may be calling it quits at USF in the near future.

## Despicable Me Minion Mayhem (*Universal Express*) ★★★★

| APPEAL BY AGE | PRESCHOOL ★★★★ | GRADE SCHOOL ★★★★ | TEENS ★★★★ |
|---|---|---|---|
| YOUNG ADULTS ★★★★ | OVER 30 ★★★★ | | SENIORS ★★★★ |

**What it is** Motion-simulator 3-D ride. **Scope and scale** Major attraction. **When to go** The first hour after park opening or after 5 p.m. **Special comments** Expect *long* waits in line. **Authors' rating** Great fun; ★★★★. **Duration of ride** 5 minutes. **Average wait in line per 100 people ahead of you** 7 minutes; assumes all simulators in use. **Loading speed** Moderate–slow.

Motion Sickness

**DESCRIPTION AND COMMENTS** This motion-simulator system premiered as the Funtastic World of Hanna-Barbera when the park opened in 1990; was used again in Jimmy Neutron's Nicktoon Blast, which replaced the former in 2003; and is being retained for the attraction's third incarnation as Despicable Me Minion Mayhem, which opened in summer 2012.

As with the former attractions, Despicable Me Minion Mayhem involves the motion simulators moving and reacting in sync with a cartoon projected on an IMAX-like screen. Though the simulators have been updated, the most significant upgrade is incorporated in the projection system, which employs high-definition 3-D digital technology.

The story combines elements from the animated movie *Despicable Me,* starring Gru, the archvillain, along with his adopted daughters and his diminutive yellow Minions. During the queue and preshow, you visit Gru's house and are then ushered into his lab, where you're turned into a Minion. The ride ends with a 3-minute dance party that you join as you exit.

**TOURING TIPS** The ride is just inside the USF main entrance, making crowding a problem. If you're on hand at park opening and you ride Despicable Me first, you'll have a short wait. However, you'll set yourself up for a long wait at nearby Hollywood Rip Ride Rockit. If the coaster is a priority for you, ride it first and then return to Despicable Me immediately afterward. If by that time the wait is intolerable, try again in the late afternoon. Stationary seating is available for those prone to motion sickness and for children less than 40 inches tall.

## Disaster! *(Universal Express)*  ★★★½

| APPEAL BY AGE | PRESCHOOL ★★★ | GRADE SCHOOL ★★★★ | TEENS ★★★★ |
| --- | --- | --- | --- |
| YOUNG ADULTS ★★★★ | | OVER 30 ★★★★ | SENIORS ★★★★ |

**What it is** Combination theater presentation and adventure ride. **Scope and scale** Major attraction. **When to go** In the morning or late afternoon. **Special comments** May frighten young children. **Authors' rating** Shaken, not stirred; not to be missed; ★★★½. **Duration of presentation** 20 minutes. **Loading speed** Moderate. **Probable waiting time** 18 minutes.

**DESCRIPTION AND COMMENTS** Guests are recruited for roles in a film called *Mutha Nature,* directed by the overbearing and conceited Frank Kincaid (Christopher Walken) and starring an unnamed actor you'll recognize as Dwayne "The Rock" Johnson. After the recruiting, the audience enters a soundstage where a number of seemingly random scenes are filmed starring the guests-cum-volunteers. The filming demonstrates various techniques for integrating sets, blue screens, and matte painting with live-action stunts. Next, guests board a faux subway where they experience a simulated earthquake. Following the quake, while the subway returns to the station, guests view a finished cut of *Mutha Nature* that incorporates all the soundstage shots.

**TOURING TIPS** Experience *Disaster!* after tackling the park's other rides.

## E.T. Adventure *(Universal Express)*  ★★★½

| APPEAL BY AGE | PRESCHOOL ★★★★ | GRADE SCHOOL ★★★★ | TEENS ★★★ |
| --- | --- | --- | --- |
| YOUNG ADULTS ★★★ | | OVER 30 ★★★★ | SENIORS ★★★★ |

**What it is** Indoor adventure ride based on the beloved movie. **Scope and scale** Major attraction. **When to go** During the first 90 minutes the park is open. **Special comments** 34" minimum height requirement. **Authors' rating** A happy reunion; ★★★½. **Duration of ride** 4½ minutes. **Average wait in line per 100 people ahead of you** 5 minutes. **Loading speed** Moderate.

**DESCRIPTION AND COMMENTS** Guests aboard a bicycle-like conveyance escape with E.T., The Extra-Terrestrial, from earthly law enforcement officials and journey to his home planet. Concerning the latter, where E.T. is reunited with family and friends, Len Testa likens it to *The Wizard of Oz*'s Technicolor scene, only reenacted with a cave full of naked mole rats. (C'mon, Len, where's the love?) The attraction is similar to Peter Pan's Flight at the Magic Kingdom, only longer and wilder.

A Baton, North Carolina, reader with perhaps too much time on his hands got to wondering:

*Why do the inhabitants of E.T.'s home planet, who presumably have never visited Earth, speak better English than he does?*

**TOURING TIPS** Most preschoolers and grade-school children love E.T. We think it's worth a 20- to 30-minute wait, but no longer than that. Lines build quickly after 10:30 a.m., and waits can be more than 2 hours on busy days. Ride in the morning or late afternoon.

## Fear Factor Live *(Universal Express)*  ★★½

| APPEAL BY AGE | PRESCHOOL ★ | GRADE SCHOOL ★★ | TEENS ★★★★ |
| --- | --- | --- | --- |
| YOUNG ADULTS ★★★ | | OVER 30 ★★★ | SENIORS ★★ |

**What it is** Live version of the gross-out-stunt television show. **Scope and scale** Headliner. **When to go** 6-8 shows daily; crowds are smallest at the first and second-to-last shows. **Authors' rating** *Ewwww;* ★★½. **Duration of presentation** 30 minutes. **Probable waiting time** 25 minutes.

**DESCRIPTION AND COMMENTS** *Fear Factor Live* is a stage version of the uniquely stomach-turning reality show that ran on NBC from 2001 to 2006 and again from 2011 to 2012. In the theme park iteration, six volunteers compete for one prize; this varies but is always a package that contains Universal goodies ranging from park tickets to T-shirts. Contestants must be 18 years or older (with a photo ID to prove it) and weigh at least 110 pounds. Those demented enough to volunteer should arrive at least 75 minutes before showtime to sign papers and complete some obligatory training for the specific competitive events. Anyone who doesn't wish to compete in the stage show itself can sign up for the Critter Challenge or the Food Challenge. With an adult's permission, volunteers as young as age 16 can compete in the latter.

The stage show is performed in a covered theater and consists of three different challenges. In the first, all six contestants are suspended two-and-a-half stories in the air and try to hang on to a bar as long as possible. The difficulty is compounded by heavy-duty fans blasting the contestants' faces (as you can imagine, this stunt requires exceptional upper-body strength). Only four people go on to the next round, and the person who hangs on to the bar the longest gets to choose his or her partner for the next event.

Once the first two contestants are eliminated, it's time for a brief inter-mission called the Desert Hat Ordeal. This involves a brave audience mem-ber–lunatic who has signed up for the Critter Challenge. Prepared with eye goggles and a mouthpiece, the volunteer is put in a chair with a glass case over his or her head. A wheel is spun to determine what will be crawling over the volunteer's head; the creepy-crawly choices include spiders, snakes, roaches, and scorpions. The only incentive to participate is a free photo of the ordeal for contestants to take to their therapists.

Back at the main competition, the four remaining contestants are split into two teams to compete in the Eel Tank Relay. This consists of one team member grabbing beanbags out of a tank full of eels and throwing them to his or her partner to catch in a bucket. Audience members drench the contestants with high-powered water guns, further spicing up the event. The duo who buckets the most beanbags wins, going on to compete against each other in the final round for the $400 prize package.

As the stage is prepared for the finale, the folks who volunteered for the Food Challenge are split into two teams and invited to drink a mixture of curdled milk, mystery meat, and various live bugs that are all blended to-gether on stage. The team that drinks the most of the mixture within the time limit wins a glamorous plastic mug that says, "I Ate a Bug," a conve-nient euphemism for "I have the brain of a nematode."

The last event has the two remaining contestants scramble up a wall to retrieve flags, jump into a car that is lifted in the air, then jump out of the car to retrieve more flags. When the required climbing, jumping, and flag-grabbing are accomplished, the first player to remove a rocket launcher from the backseat of the car and hit a target on the stage wall wins.

**TOURING TIPS** If you've ever wanted a chance to test your mettle (sanity?), *Fear Factor Live* may be your big chance. Participants for the physical stunts are chosen early in the morning and between performances outside the theater, so head there first thing if you want to be a contestant. The contestants for the skeevier stunts, like the bug-smoothie drinking, are chosen directly from the audience. Sit close to the front and wave your hands like crazy when it comes time for selection. Finally (and seriously), this show is too intense and gross for kids age 8 and under.

## Fievel's Playland ★★★

**What it is** Children's play area with waterslide. **Scope and scale** Minor attraction. **When to go** Anytime. **Authors' rating** A much-needed attraction for preschoolers; ★★★. **Probable waiting time** 20–30 minutes for the waterslide; otherwise, no waiting. **Loading speed** Slow for the waterslide.

**DESCRIPTION AND COMMENTS** This whimsical playground in Woody Woodpecker's KidZone features ordinary household items reproduced on a giant scale, as a mouse would experience them. Preschoolers and grade-schoolers can climb nets, walk through a huge boot, splash in a sardine-can fountain, seesaw on huge spoons, and climb onto a cow skull. Most of the playground is reserved for preschoolers, but a combo waterslide and raft ride is open to all ages.

**TOURING TIPS** Most of Fievel's Playland requires no waiting, so you can stay as long as you want. Younger children love the oversize items, and there's enough to keep teens and adults busy while little ones let off steam. The waterslide–raft ride is open to everyone but is extremely slow-loading and carries only 300 riders per hour. With an average wait of 20–30 minutes, the 16-second ride isn't worth the trouble. Also, you're highly likely to get soaked.

Lack of shade is a major shortcoming of the entire attraction—the playground is scorching during the heat of the day.

## Hollywood Rip Ride Rockit (*Universal Express*) ★★★★

**What it is** High-tech roller coaster. **Scope and scale** Headliner. **When to go** Immediately after park opening. **Special comments** 51″ minimum height requirement; expect long waits in line. **Authors' rating** Woo-hoo! Not to be missed; ★★★★. **Duration of ride** 2½ minutes. **Average wait in line per 100 people ahead of you** 6–8 minutes. **Loading speed** Moderate.

Motion Sickness

**DESCRIPTION AND COMMENTS** Opened in the summer of 2009, Hollywood Rip Ride Rockit is USF's candidate for the most technologically advanced coaster in the world. Well, we know how long that distinction lasted, but for sure this ride has some features we've never seen before. Let's start with the basics: Rip Ride Rockit is a sit-down X-Car coaster that runs on a 3,800-foot steel track, with a maximum height of 167 feet and a top speed of 65 miles an hour. Manufactured by German coaster maker Maurer Söhne, X-Car vehicles are more maneuverable than most other kinds and use less restrictive restraints, making for an exhilarating ride.

You ascend—vertically—at 11 feet per second to crest the 17-story-tall first hill, the highest point reached by any roller coaster in Orlando. The drop is almost vertical, too, launching you into Double Take, a loop inversion in which you begin on the inside of the loop, twist to the outside at the top (so you're upright), and then twist back inside the loop for the descent. Double Take stands 136 feet tall, and its loop is 103 feet in diameter at its widest point. You next hurl (no, not that kind of hurl!) into a stretch of track shaped like a musical treble clef. As on Double Take, the track configuration on Treble Clef is a first. Another innovation is Jump Cut, a spiraling negative-gravity maneuver. Usually on coasters, you experience negative gravity on long, steep vertical drops; with Jump Cut you feel like you're in a corkscrew inversion, but you never actually go upside down. Other high points include a 95-degree turn, a downhill into an "underground chasm" (gotta love those Universal PR wordsmiths!), and a final incline loop banked at 150 degrees.

The ride starts in the Production Central area; weaves into the New York area near *TWISTER . . . Ride It Out,* popping out over the heads of guests in the square below; and then storms out and over the lagoon separating Universal Studios Florida from Islands of Adventure.

Each train consists of two cars, with riders arranged two across in three rows per car. Each row is outfitted with color-changing LEDs and high-end audio and video technology for each seat. Like Rock 'n' Roller Coaster at Disney's Hollywood Studios, the "Triple R" features a musical soundtrack, but in this case you can choose the genre of music you want to hear as you ride: classic rock, country, disco, pop, or rap. When it's over, Universal flogs a digital-video "rip" of your ride, complete with the soundtrack you chose, that you can upload to YouTube, Facebook, and the like.

From a Whalton, England, mom:

*A fabulous, gut-wrenching coaster that thrilled the socks off my 8- and 9-year-olds. (Mum found it a bit too brutal to repeat.)*

A perhaps-jaded Easton, Connecticut, coaster aficionado offers this:

*The loud music blasting in our ears cancelled out the sound of the coaster. If only they had a "None of the Above: Silence" selection. The singles-line hint was a real time-saver.*

When Hollywood Rip Ride Rockit premiered in 2009, it was pretty smooth. Alas, the wheels on the cars haven't held up well in the hot Florida sun. While perfectly safe, Rip Ride Rockit now subjects you to a lot of side-to-side jarring. To crib a phrase from Tina Turner, some folks like it easy . . . and some folks like it *rough.*

**TOURING TIPS** Rip Ride Rockit can put more trains on the tracks simultaneously than any other coaster in Florida, which means on paper that it should be able to handle about 1,850 riders per hour. In practice, you'll wait about 6–8 minutes for every 100 people in the queue ahead of you, indicating an hourly capacity of 1,500 riders. Because the ride is so close to the USF entrance, it's a crowd magnet, creating bottlenecks from park opening on. Your only chance to ride without a long wait is to be one of the first to enter the park when it opens.

## Kang & Kodos' Twirl 'n' Hurl   ★★★

| APPEAL BY AGE | PRESCHOOL ★★★★ | GRADE SCHOOL ★★★ | TEENS ★★★ |
|---|---|---|---|
| YOUNG ADULTS ★★★ | | OVER 30 ★★★ | SENIORS ★★ |

**What it is** Spinning ride. **Scope and scale** Minor attraction. **When to go** After The Simpsons Ride. **Special comments** Rarely has a long wait. **Authors' rating** The world's wittiest spinner; ★★★. **Duration of ride** 1½ minutes. **Probable waiting time per 100 people ahead of you** 21 minutes. **Loading speed** Slow.

**DESCRIPTION AND COMMENTS** The Twirl 'n' Hurl is primarily eye candy for Springfield U.S.A., USF's new *Simpsons*-themed area. Think of it as Dumbo with Bart's sense of humor: Guests ride around in little flying saucers while the alien narrators, Kang and Kodos, hold pictures of Simpson characters for you to blast away at with a ray gun. All the while, Kang exhorts you (loudly) to destroy Springfield and makes insulting comments about humans. Preschoolers enjoy the ride, while older kids crack up over the upchuck, um, gags.

**TOURING TIPS** You can dig the narration from the sidelines rather than queue up for this slow-loading midway ride. If you have folks who are hot to ride, get them on whenever there are 50 or fewer guests in line.

## Lucy—A Tribute ★★★

| APPEAL BY AGE | PRESCHOOL ★ | GRADE SCHOOL ★★ | TEENS ★★ |
|---|---|---|---|
| YOUNG ADULTS ★★★ | | OVER 30 ★★★ | SENIORS ★★★ |

**What it is** Walk-through exhibit about Lucille Ball. **Scope and scale** Diversion. **When to go** Anytime. **Authors' rating** A touching remembrance; ★★★. **Probable waiting time** None.

**DESCRIPTION AND COMMENTS** The life and career of Lucille Ball are spotlighted, with emphasis on her role as Lucy Ricardo in *I Love Lucy*. Well designed and informative, the exhibit succeeds admirably in recalling the talent and temperament of the beloved redhead.

**TOURING TIPS** See Lucy during the hot, crowded midafternoon.

## Men in Black Alien Attack *(Universal Express)* ★★★★½

| APPEAL BY AGE | PRESCHOOL ★★ | GRADE SCHOOL ★★★★★ | TEENS ★★★★★ |
|---|---|---|---|
| YOUNG ADULTS ★★★★★ | | OVER 30 ★★★★★ | SENIORS ★★★★ |

**What it is** Interactive dark thrill ride. **Scope and scale** Super-headliner. **When to go** During the first 90 minutes the park is open. **Special comments** May induce motion sickness; 42″ minimum height requirement. Switching-off option provided (see page 341). **Authors' rating** Buzz Lightyear on steroids; not to be missed; ★★★★½. **Duration of ride** 4½ minutes. **Average wait in line per 100 people ahead of you** 5 minutes. **Loading speed** Moderate–fast.

**DESCRIPTION AND COMMENTS** Men in Black Alien Attack brings together Will Smith and Rip Torn (as Agent J and MIB director Zed) for an interactive sequel to the hit film. The storyline has you volunteering as a Men in Black (MIB) trainee. After an introduction warning that aliens "live among us" and articulating MIB's mission to round them up, Zed expounds on the finer points of alien spotting and familiarizes you with your training vehicle and your weapon, an alien "zapper." You then load up and are dispatched on an innocuous training mission that immediately deteriorates into a situation where only you can prevent aliens from taking over the universe. If you saw the movie, you understand that the aliens are mostly giant bugs and that zapping them involves blasting them into myriad gooey body parts. Thus, the meat of the ride (pardon the pun) consists of careening around Manhattan in your MIB vehicle and shooting aliens. The technology at work is similar to that used in the Spider-Man attraction at Islands of Adventure, which is to say that it's both a wild ride and one where movies, sets, robotics, and your vehicle are all integrated into a fairly seamless package.

Men in Black is interactive in that your marksmanship and ability to blast yourself out of some tricky situations will determine how the story ends. Also, you're awarded a personal score (as at the Magic Kingdom's Buzz Lightyear's Space Ranger Spin) and a score for your car. There are about three dozen possible outcomes and literally thousands of different ride experiences determined by your pluck, performance, and, in the final challenge, your intestinal fortitude.

**TOURING TIPS** Each alien figure has sensors that activate special effects and respond to your zapper. Aim for the eyes and keep shooting until the aliens' eyes turn red. Also, many of the aliens shoot back, causing your vehicle to veer or spin; in the mayhem, you might fail to notice that another vehicle runs beside you on a dual track. At a certain point, you can shoot the flashing "vent" on top of this other car and make its occupants spin around. Of course, they can do the same to you.

Avoid a long wait and ride during the first 90 minutes the park is open, or try the single-rider line if you don't mind splitting your group. You can reride by following the signs for the child swap at the top of the exit stairs.

## Revenge of the Mummy *(Universal Express)*   ★★★★½

| APPEAL BY AGE | PRESCHOOL ★★ | GRADE SCHOOL ★★★★ | TEENS ★★★★★ |
|---|---|---|---|
| YOUNG ADULTS ★★★★½ | | OVER 30 ★★★★ | SENIORS ★★★½ |

**What it is** Combination dark ride and roller coaster. **Scope and scale** Superheadliner. **When to go** The first hour the park is open or after 6 p.m. **Special comments** 48" minimum height requirement. **Authors' rating** Killer! Not to be missed; ★★★★½. **Duration of ride** 3 minutes. **Average wait in line per 100 people ahead of you** 7 minutes. **Loading speed** Moderate.

**DESCRIPTION AND COMMENTS** It's hard to wrap your mind around this attraction, but trust us when we say you're in for a very strange experience. Here, quoting Universal, are some of the things you can look forward to: "authentic Egyptian catacombs"; "high-velocity show-immersion system" (Huh? quickie baptism?); "magnet-propulsion launch wave system"; "a 'Brain Fire' [!] that hovers [over guests] with temperatures soaring to 2,000°F"; and "canopic jars containing grisly remains."

When you read between the lines, Revenge of the Mummy is an indoor dark ride based on the *Mummy* flicks, where guests fight off "deadly curses and vengeful creatures" while flying through Egyptian tombs and other spooky places on a high-tech roller coaster. As far as special effects go, they're pretty good: video effects, animatronics, lighting, and enough fire-spewing gas vents to rotisserie a chicken. The endings (yes, plural) are pretty clever.

The queuing area serves to establish the storyline: You're in a group touring a set from the *Mummy* films when you enter a tomb where the fantasy world of film gives way to the real thing. Along the way, you're warned about a possible curse. The visuals are rich and compelling as the queue makes its way to the loading area where you board a clunky, jeeplike vehicle. The ride begins as a slow, very elaborate dark ride, passing through various chambers, including one where flesh-eating scarab beetles descend on you. Suddenly your vehicle stops, then drops backward and rotates. Here's where you're shot at high speed up the first hill of the roller coaster part of the ride. We won't divulge too much, but the coaster part of the ride offers its own panoply of surprises (there are no barrel rolls or upside-down stuff, however). And though it's a wild ride by anyone's definition, the emphasis remains as much on the visuals, robotics, and special effects as on the ride itself.

**TOURING TIPS** The newer Hollywood Rip Ride Rockit and Despicable Me Minion Mayhem have diminished the early-morning crowds. Nevertheless, try to ride during the first hour the park is open. If lines are long, one fallback is to use the singles line, which is often more expedient than Universal Express. Concerning motion sickness, if you can ride Space Mountain without ill effect, you should be fine on Revenge of the Mummy. Switching off is available (see page 341). Finally, note that the Mummy's queue contains enough scary stuff to frighten little kids all on its own.

### Shrek 4-D *(Universal Express)* ★★★½

| APPEAL BY AGE | PRESCHOOL ★★★★ | GRADE SCHOOL ★★★★★ | TEENS ★★★★★ |
| YOUNG ADULTS ★★★★★ | | OVER 30 ★★★★★ | SENIORS ★★★★★ |

**What it is** 3-D movie. **Scope and scale** Headliner. **When to go** The first hour the park is open or after 4 p.m. **Authors' rating** Warm, fuzzy, sometimes smelly mayhem; ★★★½. **Duration of presentation** 20 minutes. **Probable waiting time** 16 minutes.

**DESCRIPTION AND COMMENTS** Based on characters from the hit movie, the preshow presents the villain from the movie, Lord Farquaad, as he appears on various screens to describe his posthumous plan to reclaim his lost bride, Princess Fiona, who married Shrek. The plan is posthumous since Lord Farquaad ostensibly died in the movie, and it's his ghost making the plans, but never mind. Guests then move into the main theater, don their 3-D glasses, and recline in seats equipped with "tactile transducers" and "pneumatic air propulsion and water spray nodules capable of both vertical and horizontal motion." As the 3-D film plays, guests are also subjected to smells relevant to the on-screen action (oh boy).

Technicalities aside, *Shrek 4-D* is a mixed bag. It's frantic, laugh-out-loud funny, and iconoclastic. Concerning the last, the film takes a good poke at Disney, with Pinocchio, the Three Little Pigs, and Tinker Bell (among others) all sucked into the mayhem. But the video quality and 3-D effects are dated by today's ultra-HD standards, the storyline is incoherently disconnected from the clever preshow, and the franchise's relevance has faded since the lackluster fourth film. On the upside, in contrast to Disney's *It's Tough to Be a Bug!*, *Shrek 4-D* doesn't generally freak out kids under age 7.

**TOURING TIPS** Universal claims it can move about 2,400 guests per hour through *Shrek 4-D*, but the show's location at the front of the park and directly across from Despicable Me Minion Mayhem translates to heavy traffic in the morning. If you see lines longer than 20 minutes, try visiting during mealtimes or in the last 2 hours the park is open. There's not much in the film or preshow to scare small children.

### The Simpsons Ride *(Universal Express)* ★★★★

| APPEAL BY AGE | PRESCHOOL ★★ | GRADE SCHOOL ★★★★ | TEENS ★★★★ |
| YOUNG ADULTS ★★★★ | | OVER 30 ★★★★ | SENIORS ★★★½ |

**What it is** Mega–simulator ride. **Scope and scale** Super-headliner. **When to go** During the first hour the park is open. **Special comments** 40" minimum height requirement; not recommended for pregnant women or people prone to motion sickness. Switching-off option provided (see page 341). **Authors' rating** Despicable Me with attitude; not to be missed; ★★★★. **Duration of ride** 4 minutes and 20 seconds, plus preshow. **Average wait in line per 100 people ahead of you** 5 minutes. **Loading speed** Moderate.

Motion Sickness

**DESCRIPTION AND COMMENTS** The Simpsons Ride is based on the Fox animated series that is now TV's longest-running sitcom. Featuring the voices of Dan Castellaneta (Homer), Julie Kavner (Marge), Nancy Cartwright (Bart), Yeardley Smith (Lisa), and other cast members, the attraction takes a wild, humorous poke at thrill rides, dark rides, and live shows "that make up a fantasy amusement park dreamed up by the show's cantankerous Krusty the Clown."

Two preshows involve *Simpsons* characters speaking sequentially on different video screens around the line area. Their comments help define the characters for guests who are unfamiliar with the TV show. The attraction is a simulator ride similar to Star Tours at DHS and Despicable Me Minion

Mayhem (see page 683), but with a larger screen more like that of Soarin' at Epcot. The visuals aren't as sharp as Soarin's, but they're sharp enough.

The storyline has the conniving Sideshow Bob secretly arriving at Krustyland, the aforementioned amusement park, and plotting his revenge on Krusty and Bart, who, in a past *Simpsons* episode, revealed that Sideshow Bob had committed a crime for which he'd framed Krusty. Sideshow Bob gets even by making things go wrong with the attractions that the Simpsons (and you) are riding.

Like the show on which it's based, The Simpsons Ride definitely has an edge, and more than a few wild hairs. Like *Shrek 4-D,* it operates on several levels. There will be jokes and visuals that you'll get but will fly over your children's heads—and most assuredly vice versa.

**TOURING TIPS** Though not as rough and jerky as its predecessor, Back to the Future—The Ride, it's a long way from being tame. Skip it if you're an expectant mom or prone to motion sickness. Some parents may find the humor too coarse for younger kids.

## Terminator 2: 3-D *(Universal Express)*   ★★★★

| APPEAL BY AGE | PRESCHOOL ★★★ | GRADE SCHOOL ★★★★ | TEENS ★★★★ |
|---|---|---|---|
| YOUNG ADULTS ★★★★★ | | OVER 30 ★★★★★ | SENIORS ★★★★ |

**What it is** 3-D thriller mixed-media presentation. **Scope and scale** Super-headliner. **When to go** After 3:30 p.m. **Special comments** One of the nation's best theme park theater attraction; very intense for some preschoolers and grade-schoolers. **Authors' rating** Furiously paced and not to be missed; ★★★★. **Duration of presentation** 20 minutes, including 8-minute preshow. **Probable waiting time** 20–40 minutes.

**DESCRIPTION AND COMMENTS** The evil "cop" from *Terminator 2* battles Arnold Schwarzenegger's T-100 cyborg character. In case you missed the *Terminator* flicks, here's a refresher: A bad robot arrives from the future to kill a nice boy. Another bad robot—who has been reprogrammed to be good—pops up to save the boy. The bad robot chases the boy and the good robot, menacing the audience in the process.

The attraction, like the films, is all action, and you really don't need to understand much. What's interesting is that it uses 3-D film and a theater full of sophisticated technology to integrate the real with the imaginary. Images seem to move in and out of the film, not only in the manner of traditional 3-D, but also in reality: Remove your 3-D glasses a moment, and you'll see that the guy on the motorcycle is actually onstage.

**TOURING TIPS** The 700-seat theater changes audiences about every 19 minutes. Even so, because the show is popular, expect to wait about 30 minutes. We suggest that you save *Terminator* and other theater presentations until you've experienced all the rides. Families with young children will be relieved to know that the violence characteristic of the movie series is largely absent from the attraction—there's suspense and action, but not much blood and guts.

## Transformers: The Ride 3-D   ★★★★★

| APPEAL BY AGE | PRESCHOOL ★★★ | GRADE SCHOOL ★★★★★ | TEENS ★★★★★ |
|---|---|---|---|
| YOUNG ADULTS ★★★★★ | | OVER 30 ★★★★★ | SENIORS ★★★★ |

**What it is** Multisensory 3-D dark ride. **Scope and scale** Super-headliner. **When to go** First 30 minutes the park is open or after 4 p.m. **Special comments** Must be 40" tall to ride; single-rider line available. **Authors' rating** Not to be missed; ★★★★★. **Duration of ride** 4½ minutes. **Loading speed** Moderate–fast.

**DESCRIPTION AND COMMENTS** Hasbro's Transformers—those toy robots from the 1980s that you twisted into trucks and planes—have been, well, transformed into director Michael Bay's recent movie franchise. In 2013, Transformers fans at Universal Studios Florida finally received a theme park attraction befitting their pop-culture idols. Recruits to this cybertronic war enlist by entering the N.E.S.T. Base (headquarters of the heroic Autobots and their human allies). Inside, in the queue, video monitors catch you up on the backstory. Basically, the Decepticon baddies are after the Allspark, source of cybernetic sentience. Your job is to safeguard the shard. The highly vexing evil Megatron and his pals Starscream and Devastator threaten the mission, but don't worry—we have Sideswipe and Bumblebee on the bench to back us up.

Transformers harnesses the same traveling simulator system behind Islands of Adventure's Amazing Adventures of Spider-Man ride, and it ups the ante with photorealistic high-definition imagery, boosted by dichroic 3-D glasses that produce remarkably sharp, vivid visuals. The plot amounts to little more than a giant game of keep-away, and the uninitiated will likely be unable to tell one meteoric mass of metal from another, but you'll be too dazzled by the debris whizzing by to notice. The ride's mix of detailed (though largely static) set pieces and video projections bring these colossi to life in one of the most intense, immersive thrill rides found in any theme park.

**TOURING TIPS** This ride draws crowds—your only solace is that The Wizarding World of Harry Potter–Diagon Alley draws even larger throngs. Follow our touring plan to minimize waits. The single-rider line will get you on board faster, but as singles lines go, this is the pokiest we've seen. Finally, it's hard to focus on the fast-moving imagery from the front row; center seats in the second and third rows provide the best perspective.

### TWISTER . . . Ride It Out (Universal Express) ★★★½

| APPEAL BY AGE | PRESCHOOL ★★ | GRADE SCHOOL ★★★★ | TEENS ★★★★ |
| --- | --- | --- | --- |
| YOUNG ADULTS ★★★★ | | OVER 30 ★★★★ | SENIORS ★★★ |

**What it is** Theater presentation featuring special effects from the movie *Twister*. **Scope and scale** Major attraction. **When to go** Should be your first show after experiencing all rides. **Special comments** High potential for frightening young children. **Authors' rating** Gusty; ★★★½. **Duration of presentation** 15 minutes. **Probable waiting time** 20 minutes.

**DESCRIPTION AND COMMENTS** *TWISTER* combines an elaborate set and special effects, climaxing with a five-story-tall simulated tornado created by circulating more than 2 million cubic feet of air per minute.

**TOURING TIPS** The wind, pounding rain, and freight-train sound of the tornado are deafening, and the entire presentation is exceptionally intense. Schoolchildren are mightily impressed, while younger children are terrified and overwhelmed. Unless you want the kids hopping in your bed whenever they hear thunder, try this attraction yourself first.

### Universal Orlando's Horror Make-Up Show (Universal Express) ★★★★½

| APPEAL BY AGE | PRESCHOOL ★★★ | GRADE SCHOOL ★★★★ | TEENS ★★★★ |
| --- | --- | --- | --- |
| YOUNG ADULTS ★★★★ | | OVER 30 ★★★★ | SENIORS ★★★★ |

**What it is** Theater presentation on the art of makeup. **Scope and scale** Major attraction. **When to go** After you've experienced all rides. **Special comments** May frighten young children. **Authors' rating** A gory knee-slapper; not to be missed; ★★★★½. **Duration of presentation** 25 minutes. **Probable waiting time** 20 minutes.

**DESCRIPTION AND COMMENTS** The *Horror Make-Up Show* is a brief but humorous look at how basic monster-movie special effects are done. The show includes on-stage demonstrations of effects such as blood-spurting fake knives and rubber limbs, plus how mechanical effects are combined with rubber masks to transform human heads into wolf-shaped skulls. Film clips are interspersed throughout the presentation, showing how computer-generated special effects are blended into live-action films. This may be Universal's most entertaining live show. While there's plenty of fake blood thrown around, the script is mostly funny. The hosts' running commentary about horror-film making is interspersed with plenty of pop-culture jokes for the kids.

**TOURING TIPS** The *Horror Make-Up Show* is the sleeper attraction at Universal. Its humor and tongue-in-cheek style transcend the gruesome effects, and most folks (including preschoolers) take the blood and guts in stride. But it's the exception that proves the rule, as this reader relates:

> *My 7- and 9-year-olds had no problem with* Terminator *but were scared by the* Horror Make-Up Show *(despite my telling them the guy really was not cutting anyone's arm off!). We ended up leaving before the show was over.*

## Universal's Cinematic Spectacular: 100 Years of Movie Memories ★★★½ *(seasonal when park is open late)*

| APPEAL BY AGE | PRESCHOOL ★★★ | GRADE SCHOOL ★★★★ | TEENS ★★★½ |
|---|---|---|---|
| YOUNG ADULTS ★★★★ | OVER 30 ★★★★ | | SENIORS ★★★★ |

**What it is** Fireworks, dancing fountains, and movies. **Scope and scale** Major attraction. **When to go** 1 show a day, usually at park closing. **Authors' rating** Good effort; ★★★½. **Special comments** Movie trailers galore. **Duration of presentation** 15–20 minutes. **Probable waiting time** None.

**DESCRIPTION AND COMMENTS** This is USF's big nighttime event, designed to cap your day at the park. Shown on the lagoon in the middle of the park, the presentation runs through film clips and music from the first 100 years of Universal's biggest movies. The scenes are projected onto three enormous "screens" made by spraying water from the lagoon into the air (similar to *Fantasmic!* at Disney's Hollywood Studios). Fireworks and colored lights are also used to good effect throughout the presentation, which is narrated by God himself—well, actually, Morgan Freeman. It's an enjoyable way to end your day at the park.

The show premiered in May 2012, with reviews generally either mixed or positive. This mother of two liked it:

> *My family really enjoyed the show. It didn't have the same emotional impact as [Disney's]* Wishes, *but it was entertaining. There were so many great movies we hadn't thought about in ages!*

If you've been experiencing USF attractions throughout the day, you've already been exposed to most of the characters and memorable scenes referenced in the nighttime show. Reliving them again so soon becomes tedious after a few minutes—and the show lasts nearly 20.

**TOURING TIPS** The ends of the lagoon are not recommended for viewing. The best spot is directly across the lagoon from Richter's Burger Co., where the sidewalk makes a small protrusion overlooking the water. Because acquiring a spot here can be very difficult, we recommend arriving at least 45 minutes ahead of time.

Before the show begins, realize that not all of the movie clips may be suitable for young viewers. The horror montage, for example, mixes excerpts from hoary black-and-white monster movies with potentially fright-inducing clips from films like *The Birds, Halloween, Psycho, The Silence of the Lambs,* and *Tales from the Crypt.*

Finally, just as Disney does with *Fantasmic!,* Universal offers a dinner package for the *Cinematic Spectacular.* As of now, the only restaurant option is Lombard's Seafood Grille; the cost is $45 for adults and $13 for kids, including tax and tip. After the meal, you'll go to a special seating area to watch the show and enjoy a dessert buffet. It's a decent option if you're in the mood for seafood and you planned to see the show anyway. Reservations are required and can be made online (**tinyurl.com/cinematicspectaculardining**) or by phone (☎ 407-224-7554, Monday–Saturday, 7:30 a.m.–10 p.m. Eastern time; until 9 p.m. on Sunday).

## Woody Woodpecker's Nuthouse Coaster and Curious George Goes to Town ★★½

| APPEAL BY AGE | PRESCHOOL ★★★★ | | GRADE SCHOOL ★★★½ | TEENS – |
|---|---|---|---|---|
| YOUNG ADULTS | – | OVER 30 | – | SENIORS – |

**What it is** Interactive playground and kids' roller coaster. **Scope and scale** Minor attraction. **When to go** Anytime. **Authors' rating** *The* place for rambunctious kids; ★★½. **Average wait in line per 100 people ahead of you** 5 minutes for the coaster. **Loading speed** For the coaster, *slooow.*

**DESCRIPTION AND COMMENTS** These two kid-friendly attractions reside, along with Fievel's Playland (see page 686), in Woody Woodpecker's KidZone. The Nuthouse Coaster is small enough for kids to enjoy but sturdy enough for adults, though its moderate speed might unnerve some smaller children (the minimum height to ride is 36 inches). Adjacent is Curious George Goes to Town, an interactive playground that exemplifies the Universal obsession with wet stuff; in addition to innumerable spigots, pipes, and spray guns, two giant roof-mounted buckets periodically dump a thousand gallons of water on unsuspecting visitors below. Kids who want to stay dry can mess around in the foam-ball playground, also equipped with chutes, tubes, and ball-blasters.

**TOURING TIPS** Visit after you've experienced all the major attractions. Rumor has it that the KidZone may be closing in the near future.

## THE WIZARDING WORLD OF HARRY POTTER–DIAGON ALLEY

WHEN UNIVERSAL opened The Wizarding World of Harry Potter at Islands of Adventure, it created a paradigm shift in the Disney–Universal theme park rivalry. Not only did Universal trot out some groundbreaking ride technology, but it also demonstrated that it could trump Disney's most distinctive competence: the creation of infinitely detailed and totally immersive themed areas. To say that The Wizarding World was a game-changer is an understatement of the first order.

It was immediately obvious that Universal would build on its Potter franchise success—but how and where? Universal's not sitting on 27,000-plus acres like Disney, so real estate was at a premium. If Potterville was going to grow, something else had to go. Conventional wisdom suggested The Wizarding World expansion would gobble up the Lost Continent section of Islands of Adventure, and that may happen yet. But looking at the ledger, it was clear that the older Universal Studios Florida theme park could use a boost.

It just so happened that a substantial chunk of turf at USF was occupied by the aging JAWS ride and its contiguous Amity themed area. The space would allow for substantial development; plus, its isolated location—in the most remote corner of the park—was conducive to creating a totally self-contained area where Potter themes could be executed absent any distraction from neighboring attractions. In short, it was perfect.

So how would the new Potter area tie in to the original at IOA? And what Harry Potter literary icons could be exploited? It was pretty clear that a new suburb of Hogsmeade wasn't going to cut it. Turns out the answer was virtually shouting from the pages of the Harry Potter novels, which observe a clear dichotomy of place—plots originate in London and then unfold at distant Hogwarts.

Two London sites that figure prominently in the Potter saga brim with attraction possibilities: Diagon Alley, a secret part of London that is a sort of sorcerers' shopping mall; and the King's Cross railroad station, where wizarding students embark for the train trip to Hogwarts.

Following much deliberation and consultation with Warner Bros. and author J. K. Rowling, the final design called for a London-waterfront street scene flanking Universal Studios Lagoon. The detailed facades, anchored by the **King's Cross** railroad station on the left and including **Grimmauld Place** and **Wyndham's Theatre,** recall West London scenes from the books and movies. **Diagon Alley,** secreted behind the London street scene, is accessed through a secluded entrance in the middle of the facade. Like Hogsmeade at IOA, Diagon Alley features shops and restaurants in addition to three attractions and live entertainment.

Diagon Alley covers 20 acres—about the same area as the Hogsmeade original—but offers about two-and-a-half times the pedestrian space, since it doesn't have space- (and people-) eating outdoor roller-coasters. With only one high-capacity ride (**Harry Potter and the Escape from Gringotts**), along with an enlarged version of the **Ollivanders** wand-shop experience in Hogsmeade and the **Hogwarts Express** train connecting the two Wizarding Worlds, the new area's increased elbow room is canceled out by a relatively reduced hourly attraction capacity, making the maximum comfortable occupancy more or less a wash.

In the attraction department, Universal once again came out swinging for the fences. As before with Harry Potter and the Forbidden Journey, the headliner attraction for the expansion is high-tech and cutting-edge—and once again a dark ride, but this time of the roller-coaster genre. The labyrinthine passages and caverns of Gringotts Wizarding Bank, the financial institution of choice for the wizarding set, are the setting of this plot-driven 3-D dark ride–coaster.

Though the Gringotts attraction is Diagon Alley's headliner, the most creative element in the two-park Potter domain is the Hogwarts Express, which re-creates the train trip from London to Hogwarts and vice versa. Serving as both an attraction and transportation between USF and IOA, the Express unifies the two disparately located Wizarding Worlds.

## Diagon Alley in Detail

Diagon Alley and its London Waterfront are sandwiched between the San Francisco and World Expo areas of the park, about as far from Universal Studios Florida's main entrance as you can get. From the park entrance, turn right on Rodeo Drive to Mel's Diner; from here,

**WIZARDING WORLD WHISPERS WITH JIM HILL**

**KEEP YOUR TIME-TURNER HANDY**  Which Harry Potter movies are celebrated in The Wizarding World? Depends on where you are. Hogsmeade appears in the middle of *Harry Potter and the Goblet of Fire,* just before Harry attempts the first task. If you're entering Diagon Alley through the back wall of the Leaky Cauldron, the setting is *Harry Potter and the Sorcerer's Stone,* where Harry and Hagrid first enter the wizarding center of London. The queue for Harry Potter and the Escape from Gringotts recalls the part of *Harry Potter and the Deathly Hallows* in which Harry, Ron, Hermoine, and Griphook break in to the Lestrange family vault to retrieve the Horcrux. And if you stop to shop at Weasleys' Wizard Wheezes at Diagon Alley, you're in one of the settings of *Harry Potter and the Half-Blood Prince.*

circumnavigate the lagoon counterclockwise, keeping it to your left until you reach the entrance to the London Waterfront, where wrought-iron fencing surrounds a parklike promenade. You can also access the London Waterfront from the San Francisco area by walking clockwise around the lagoon and then taking a shoreline bypass along the embankment to the World Expo side of the Potter themed area. Here you can access London through the gateway closest to the *Fear Factor Live* stadium. A third option is to take the Hogwarts Express from Islands of Adventure—exit the London Waterfront–Diagon Alley area into San Francisco.

Having arrived at the London area, take a moment to spot Kreacher (the house elf regularly peers from a second-story window above 12 Grimmauld Place) and chat with the Knight Bus conductor and his Caribbean-accented shrunken head. Also notable are snack and souvenir stands and a towering statue-topped fountain.

Now enter Diagon Alley next to the Leicester Square marquee in the approximate center of the building facades. As in the books and films, the unmarked portal is concealed within a magical brick wall that is ordinarily reserved for wizards and the like. (Unfortunately, the wall doesn't actually move, due to safety concerns.) However, the endless queue of Muggles (plain old humans) in shorts and flip-flops will leave little doubt where that entryway is.

Once admitted, look down the alley to the rounded facade of **Gringotts Wizarding Bank,** where a 40-foot fire-breathing Ukrainian Ironbelly dragon (as seen in *Harry Potter and the Deathly Hallows: Part 2*) perches atop the dome. To your left is the **Leaky Cauldron,** the area's flagship restaurant, serving authentically hearty British pub fare like bangers and mash, cottage pie, and Guinness stew. You order and get your drinks at a counter; then you're seated with a candle that helps servers deliver food direct to your table. You can top off your meal with potted chocolate and sticky toffee pudding for dessert, or you step around the corner to **Florean Fortescue's Ice Cream Parlour** for Butterbeer soft-serve or unusual hard-pack flavors like clotted cream, Earl Grey and lavender, and chocolate chili. If all that eating makes you thirsty, a variety of alcoholic and virgin novelty drinks are poured at **The Hopping Pot** and **Fountain of Fair Fortune.** Try the Wizard's Brew (a heavy porter) or Dragon Scale (a hoppy amber), or the Fishy Green Ale (mint boba tea with balls of blueberry juice) or Gillywater, which can be spiked with four different flavored elixirs. Of course, you can also get your Butterbeer or Pumpkin Juice fix.

Shopping is a major component of Diagon Alley in Potter lore; while Hogsmeade visitors went wild for the few wizardy shops there, Diagon Alley is the planet's wackiest mall, with a vastly expanded array of enchanted tchotchkes to declare bankruptcy over. Shops include **Weasleys' Wizard Wheezes,** a joke shop with many of the toys previously found in Hogsmeade's Zonko's, plus new gags like Skiving Snackboxes and Decoy Detonators. Look up through the three-story store's glass ceiling for fireworks. **Wiseacre's Wizarding Equipment,** at the exit of Escape from Gringotts, sells crystal balls, compasses, and hourglasses. **Madam Malkin's Robes for All Occasions** stocks school uniforms, Scottish wool sweaters, and dress robes for wizards and witches. Adopt a plush cat, rat, owl, or hippogriff from the **Magical Menagerie. Shutterbutton's** will film your family in front of a green screen and insert your into a DVD of Potter scenes (about $70); **Quality Quidditch Supplies** sells golden snitches and jerseys for your favorite teams; and **Scribbulus** carries quills, notebooks, and similar school supplies. You can pay for all this loot in Gringotts bank notes, which you can purchase inside a money exchange overseen by an imperious interactive animatronic goblin, then spend it anywhere within Universal Orlando (think Disney Dollars). In general, Diagon Alley's stores are larger and more plentiful than the tiny shops over in Hogsmeade, with carefully planned external and internal queues to corral waiting customers.

To the right of Escape from Gringotts is **Carkitt Market,** a canopy-covered plaza where short live shows are staged every half-hour or so. *Celestina Warbeck and the Banshees* (★★★★) showcases the singing sorceress swinging to jazzy tunes titled and inspired by J. K. Rowling herself, and *Tales of Beedle the Bard* (★★★½) recounts the Three Brothers fable from *Deathly Hallows* with puppets crafted by Michael Curry (*Festival of the Lion King, Finding Nemo—The Musical*).

Intersecting Diagon Alley near the Leaky Cauldron is **Knockturn Alley,** a labyrinth of twisting passageways where the Harry Potter bad guys hang out. A covered walk-through area with a projected sky creating perpetual night, it features spooky special effects in the faux shop windows (don't miss the creeping tattoos and crawling spiders) and **Borgin and Burkes,** which sells objects from the dark side of magic (watch out for the mummified hand!).

With the opening of Diagon Alley, Universal also introduced interactive wands ($45) to the parks, supplementing the nonfunctional replica wands ($35) that continue to be sold at **Ollivanders** (see page 701) and in the smaller selection at **Wands by Gregorovitch.** Medallions embedded in the ground designate a couple dozen locations spilt between the two Wizarding Worlds, where hidden cameras in storefront windows can detect the waving of these special wands and respond to the correct motions with special effects both projected and practical. You might use the swish-and-flick of Wingardium Leviosa to levitate one object or the figure-four Locomotor spell to animate another. It's a much more thematically satisfying form of interactivity than the gimmicky games found at the Magic Kingdom, but it can take some practice to get the hang of spell-casting; wizards will supposedly be stationed at windows to coach novices and supply loaner wands, but it's easy to imagine how demand for the experience may prove unmagically unmanageable at peak times. A map provided with each wand purchase details the location and movement for most effects, but there are some secret ones to discover on your own.

*Discover* is an important word in Diagon Alley, because this overwhelmingly intricate area actually feels like a place you can explore and get lost in, much like, say, Epcot's Morocco Pavilion or Disneyland's New Orleans Square. We can't overstate how seamlessly Diagon's designers have rendered the illusion of a living world, topping even Disney California Adventure's Cars Land. *Immersion* is an often-overworked buzzword in themed entertainment, but the new Wizarding World exemplifies it, enveloping fans in Potter's world to a degree that far exceeds Hogsmeade's high standards. And even if you aren't a follower of the franchise, you may find yourself falling for the fictional universal after experiencing Universal's incarnation.

## Diagon Alley Attractions

### Harry Potter and the Escape from Gringotts  ★★★★★

| APPEAL BY AGE | PRESCHOOL ★★ | GRADE SCHOOL ★★★★ | TEENS ★★★★★ |
| --- | --- | --- | --- |
| YOUNG ADULTS ★★★★★ | | OVER 30 ★★★★★ | SENIORS ★★★★ |

**What it is** Super-high-tech 3-D dark ride with roller-coaster elements. **Scope and scale** Super-headliner. **When to go** Immediately after park opening. or just before closing **Special comments** Expect *looong* waits in line; 42″ minimum height requirement. **Authors' rating** The ultimate realization of "Ride the Movies"; not to be missed; ★★★★★. **Duration of ride** 4½ minutes. **Probable waiting time per 100 people ahead of you** 4 minutes. **Loading speed** Moderate–fast.

**DESCRIPTION AND COMMENTS** Owned and operated by goblins, Gringotts is the Federal Reserve of the wizarding economy, and the scene of memorable sequences from the first and final Potter installments. It's known for its toppling column facade, chandelier-adorned lobby, and bottomless caverns, and the heart-stopping rail carts running through them. The theme park adaptation is the centerpiece of Diagon Alley, and the ultimate expression of the "virtual reality" rides Universal has been refining since IOA opened.

Like Forbidden Journey at IOA, Harry Potter and the Escape from Gringotts incorporates a substantial part of the overall experience into its elaborate queue, which (like Hogwarts Castle) even nonriders should experience. You enter through the bank's lobby, where you're critically appraised by glowering animatronic goblins. Your path takes you to a "security checkpoint" where your photo will be taken (to be purchased afterwards as an identity lanyard in the gift shop, natch), and past animated newspapers and office windows where the scenario is set up.

Unlike Forbidden Journey, Gringotts doesn't rush you through its queue, but rather allows you to experience two full preshows before approaching the ride vehicles. In the first, goblin banker Blordak and Bill Weasley (Ron's curse-breaking big brother) prepare you for an introductory tour of the underground vaults. Then you're off for a convincing simulated 9-mile plunge into the earth aboard an "elevator" with a bouncing floor and ceiling projections. All this is before you pick up your 3-D glasses (identical to those at Transformers: The Ride 3-D) and ascend a spiral staircase into the stalactite-festooned boarding cave where your vault cart awaits.

Also unlike Forbidden Journey, and indeed all the rest of The Wizarding World, Gringotts is not set in a nebulous "moment frozen in time" where incidents from various stories simultaneously coexist. Instead, visitors enter the bank at the exact moment that Harry, Ron, Hermione, and Griphook have arrived to liberate the Hufflepuff Cup Horcrux from Bellatrix Lestrange's vault. Only in this retelling of Deathly Hallows Part 2's iconic action scene, you (as Muggles opening new bank accounts) are ingeniously integrated into the action. Familiar film moments featuring the vaults' guardian dragon play out in the ride's background as Bellatrix and Voldemort appear to menace you with snakes and sinister spells, whereupon the heroic trio pauses its quest to save your hapless posteriors. The storytelling, which is much more coherent than Forbidden Journey's hodgepodge approach, may disorient scholars of the Potter canon, but it's an intelligent way to allow fans to relive a favorite adventure without merely rehashing the plot.

Gringotts' ornately industrial ride vehicles consist of two-car trains, each holding 24 people in rows of four. The ride merges Revenge of the Mummy's indoor-coaster aspects with Spider-Man's seamless integration of high-resolution 3-D film (the finale dome completely surrounds your car) and massive sculptural sets (some of the rockwork inside is six stories tall), while adding a few new tricks like independently rotating cars and motion-simulator bases built into the track.

The result is a ride that, though it doesn't break completely new ground as Forbidden Journey and Spider-Man did, combines favorite innovations from its predecessors in an exhilarating new way. It isn't quite the perfect attraction some might be anticipating. The visuals are sometimes murky and the dialogue difficult to discern. And it's slightly disappointing that no animatronic figures, moving set-pieces, or actual pyrotechnics appear in the ride, though you will get spritzed with water, blasted with warm air, and sprayed with fog—this is Universal, after all. Finally, though Helena Bonham Carter and Ralph Fiennes reprised their screen roles, Daniel Radcliffe and Emma Watson did not. Harry and pals' CGI stand-ins look OK, as they're never seen up close, but Hermione's voice double is dreadful.

Nitpicks aside, whether Escape from Gringotts is the greatest themed thrill ride of all time or merely one of the greatest can be happily debated by park fans until the next great leap forward comes along.

**TOURING TIPS** Gringotts is the pot of gold at the end of Universal's rainbow that a kazillion crazed guests are racing toward. Though the interior line is gorgeous and air-conditioned, the mostly unshaded outdoor extended queue holds 4,000 guests—you don't want to be at the end of it. If you're a Universal resort guest and you qualify for early entry, use it. Otherwise, arrive at the turnstiles, admission in hand, 35–45 minutes before park opening and be ready to haul butt. On most days you will need to retrieve a return-time ticket (see page 702) before attempting to enter Diagon Alley, then queue up again for Gringotts. As an alternative, try the attraction at the very end of the day. As long as you're inside the entrance before closing time, you should be allowed to ride as long as it hasn't broken down. But be warned that, as with any ride this advanced, Gringotts can be expected to experience some downtime almost daily, at least during its initial months of operation.

As far as physical thrills go, Gringotts falls somewhere between Seven Dwarfs Mine Train and Space Mountain, with only one short (albeit unique) drop and no upside-down flips. It was designed to be less intense (read: less nauseating) than Forbidden Journey and therefore more appealing to families, with fewer height, weight, and size restrictions. The restraints are similar to the Mummy's, with bars across your lap and shins, but slightly more restrictive. Use the test seat to the left of the front entrance if you're unsure, and request the third or sixth row for additional legroom.

The ride feels noticeably different depending on which row you're seated in. The front is closest to the action and has the scariest view of the drop; 3-D effects look better farther back. The sixth row gets the most coaster action, especially from the initial fall, but the screens are slightly distorted. Row three may be the sweet spot.

As is the case with most of Universal's thrill rides, you must leave your bags in a free locker. Luckily, unlike at Hogwarts Express, the lockers were separated from the attraction entrance, greatly improving guest flow. Universal Express is **not** currently accepted at this attraction. If you don't have bags and don't mind breaking up your group, the singles line will greatly cut your wait, but you'll skip all the preshows past the lobby. If you want to see the queue but not ride, ask an attendant if a "bank tour" is available.

## Hogwarts Express   ★★★★½

APPEAL BY AGE   PRESCHOOL ★★★★   GRADE SCHOOL ★★★★★   TEENS ★★★★
YOUNG ADULTS ★★★★½      OVER 30 ★★★★½      SENIORS ★★★★½

**What it is** Transportation attraction. **Scope and scale** Super-headliner. **When to go** Immediately after park opening. **Special comments** Expect lengthy waits in line. A Park-to-Park pass is required to ride. **Authors' rating** A moving experience; not to be missed; ★★★★½. **Duration of ride** 4 minutes. **Probable waiting time per 100 people ahead of you** 7 minutes. **Loading speed** Moderate.

**DESCRIPTION AND COMMENTS** Part of the genius of creating Diagon Alley at USF is that it's connected to Hogsmeade at Islands of Adventure (see Part Sixteen) by the Hogwarts Express, just as in the novels and films. The counterpart to Hogsmeade Station in IOA is Universal Studios' King's Cross station, a landmark London train depot that has been re-created a few doors down from Diagon Alley's hidden entrance. (It's important to note that King's Cross has a separate entrance and exit from Diagon Alley: You can't go directly between them without crossing through the London Waterfront.)

The passage to Platform 9¾, from which Hogwarts students depart on their way to school, is concealed from Muggles by a seemingly solid brick wall, which you'll witness guests ahead of you dematerializing through. (Spoiler: The "Pepper's Ghost" effect creates a clever but congestion-prone photo op, but you experience only a dark corridor with whooshing sound effects when crossing over yourself.)

Once on the platform, you'll pass a pile of luggage (including an owl cage with an animatronic Hedwig) before being assigned to one of the three train cars' seven compartments. The train itself looks exactly authentic to the $n$th degree, from the billowing steam to the brass fixtures and upholstery in your eight-passenger private cabin. Along your one-way Hogwarts Express journey, you'll see moving images projected beyond the windows of the car rather than the park's backstage ares, with the streets of London and the Scottish countryside rolling past outside your window. The screen isn't 3-D, but it's slightly curved to conceal the edges and create a convincing illusion of depth. Even more impressive are the frosted-glass doors you enter through, which turn out to be amazing screens that makes it seem as if someone is standing on the other side. You experience a different presentation coming and going, and in addition to pastoral scenery there are surprises appearances by secondary characters (Fred and George Weasley,

Hagrid) and threats en route (bone-chilling Dementors, licorice spiders), augmented by temperature and sound effects in the cars.

Hogwarts Express isn't an adrenaline rush in the same way that Escape from Gringotts is, but for those invested in Potter lore, it may be even more emotionally thrilling. And unlike most Potter attractions, it can be experienced by the whole family, regardless of size.

**TOURING TIPS** Universal was somehow surprised by a survey that showed guests considered the Hogwarts Express an attraction rather than merely a means to get back and forth between the two Wizarding Worlds. This "revelation" threw the creative team into a tizzy about how they could increase the capacity of the train—a task made all the more difficult because the stations and track were already under construction.

There's a capacity-versus-authenticity issue front and center with the Hogwarts Express—and if you know J. K. Rowling's reputation for perfectionism where adaptations of her books are concerned, you know the sticky wicket this presented for Universal. The train cars from the films and novels are divided into private compartments that seat eight, but replicating those compartments means fewer seats and longer loading times (and longer queues, too).

As a result, not everyone in one or the other park will be able to experience the train, because its carrying capacity is relatively small and the track can accommodate only two trains, each moving in a different direction and passing one another in the middle of the journey. This leaves Universal with a few crowd-mitigating options:

First, because using the train for a one-way trip involves park-hopping, one-way passengers will need a valid two-park ticket. Disembarking passengers must enter the second park and, if desired, queue again for their return trip. You'll be allowed (nay, encouraged) to upgrade your 1-Park Base Ticket at the station entrance.

Second, Universal Express is, ironically, unavailable for the Hogwarts Express, at least for the time being.

Third, you are permitted only one ride per day. If you wish to take a same-day return trip, you'll be relegated to an secondary queue that promises to be exponentially slower than the already glacial standby queue.

Fourth, on days of peak attendance, Universal could close off the entry to King's Cross from outside the London Waterfront and mandate a timed-return ticket for entry, as with Diagon Alley (see page 702).

Park-to-park ticket-purchasing Potterphiles should make the train their first attraction of the day. If, for example, Diagon Alley is your top priority of the day, enter Islands of Adventure as early as possible and line up at the Hogsmeade Station for the train to London King's Cross. Then get a return ticket (if necessary) to reenter the London area.

Guests exiting in Hogsmeade have a chance to take a photo with the locomotive before it backs out for its next run. Guests departing from Hogsmeade should pose with the static train outside the station before they queue up.

## Ollivanders   ★★★★

| APPEAL BY AGE | PRESCHOOL ★★★★ | GRADE SCHOOL ★★★★★ | TEENS ★★★★ |
|---|---|---|---|
| YOUNG ADULTS ★★★★ | | OVER 30 ★★★½ | SENIORS ★★★½ |

**What it is** Combination wizarding demonstration and shopping op. **Scope and scale** Major attraction. **When to go** After riding Harry Potter and the Escape from Gringotts. **Special comments** Audience stands. **Authors' rating** Enchanting; ★★★★. **Duration**

**of presentation** 6 minutes. **Probable waiting time per 100 people ahead of you** 7 minutes.

**DESCRIPTION AND COMMENTS** Ollivanders, located in Diagon Alley in the books and films, somehow sprouted a branch location in Hogsmeade at IOA (see page 666). Potter purists pointed out this misplacement, but the wand shop stayed put and became one of the more popular features of The Wizarding World. It also became a horrendous bottleneck, with long lines where guests roasted in an unshaded queue. In the Diagon Alley version, Ollivanders will assume its rightful place, and with much larger digs. At IOA, only 24 guests at a time can experience the little drama where wands choose a wizard (rather than the other way around). At USF, the shop has three separate choosing chambers, turning it from a popular curiosity into an actual attraction. As for the IOA location, it continues to operate.

**TOURING TIPS** If your young 'un is selected to test-drive a wand, be forewarned that you'll have to buy it if you want to take it home.

## Touring Strategy

The Wizarding World of Harry Potter–Diagon Alley is the queen of the hop in the theme park world in 2014 and beyond. Because of the crowds, experiencing Diagon Alley without interminable waits is a challenge—if you visited The Wizarding World of Harry Potter–Hogsmeade during its first three years at IOA, you know of which we speak. Hogsmeade opened with three rides and Ollivanders; now it has four rides plus the wand shop. As discussed earlier, Diagon Alley has another Ollivanders and only two rides, one of which, Hogwarts Express, it shares with Hogsmeade in IOA. Because only half of each day's total train passengers can board at the USF station, Diagon Alley in essence has only one-and-a-half rides, plus Ollivanders and the various shops, to entertain the expected masses. In other words, it's crazy, folks.

*un**official** **TIP***
The earlier you obtain your ticket, the sooner you'll be admitted to Diagon Alley. It remains imperative, therefore, that you arrive at the USF turnstiles 35–45 minutes before opening.

Once again, Universal resort guests are admitted an hour before the general public; which hotels are eligible on each day is at Universal's discretion. Early entry is a tremendous perk if you're staying on-property, but you'll still be competing with thousands of other resort guests, so arrive at least 40 minutes before early entry starts. If you're a day guest, Diagon Alley will already be packed when you arrive.

As at IOA, Universal has multiple operational options for allowing guests into USF's Wizarding World. On low-attendance days, you may be able to stroll in and out of Diagon Alley without restriction—expect days like this to be vanishingly rare for at least the next year. On most days, barricades will limit access to the London waterfront all day, and timed-entry return tickets specifying when you can visit will be distributed from touchscreen kiosks located between Men in Black and *Fear Factor Live*. Guests are given a selection of 1-hour return windows, assuming any are still available. Once your time comes, report to the gates at the end of London near *Fear Factor Live*. On the busiest days, a return ticket may be required not only to enter Diagon Alley but also to ride the Hogwarts Express, and if you leave the London area you'll need a new ticket to reenter. At any time, you may experience an additional wait after being admitted to the London plaza before being permitted to pass through the portal into Diagon Alley.

Circling the lagoon clockwise to the waterfront is the shortest route to the Hogwarts Express, but it's also the route that about 70% of guests take. Hustling to the waterfront counterclockwise through the Simpsons area is the most direct path to the ticket kiosks.

On the upside, the rush to Diagon Alley diminishes crowds and waits at other attractions. The downside to that upside: Those who can't enter Diagon Alley right away spread to nearby attractions, particularly *Disaster!,* Men in Black Alien Attack, and to a lesser extent The Simpsons Ride and Revenge of the Mummy. Diagon Alley spillover affects wait times at these attractions all day, so experience them as early as possible.

In addition to guests flocking to Diagon Alley from the Universal Studios Florida entrance, about 168 passengers arrive from IOA's Hogsmeade Village station every 7–8 minutes on the Hogwarts Express—making it an even tougher ticket than Gringotts. Heading first to The Wizarding World–Hogsmeade at IOA and lining up for the Express may be the best way to experience both the train plus Gringotts in the least amount of time. Hogsmeade won't be hit with a morning inundation comparable to that of USF, and the queue there isn't slowed by a Platform 9¾ effect, so waits for the train from there should be less onerous. You'll want to grab a Diagon Alley return ticket from the opposite end of the area immediately upon arrival. If you're among the first on the train in the morning, you shouldn't be too far behind the first wave of guests who entered USF directly.

# LIVE ENTERTAINMENT *at* UNIVERSAL STUDIOS FLORIDA

IN ADDITION TO THE SHOWS PROFILED PREVIOUSLY, USF offers a wide range of street entertainment. Costumed comic book and cartoon characters (Shrek, Donkey, SpongeBob SquarePants, Woody Woodpecker) roam the park for photo ops supplemented by look-alikes of movie stars, both living and deceased, plus the towering, talking Transformers cyberstars, which can be said to be neither. Musical acts also pop up.

In 2012 USF introduced the Disney-like **Universal's Superstar Parade** (★★★½), featuring dancers and performers, four large and elaborate floats inspired by cartoons, and a very mixed bag of street-prowling Universal characters. The parade stops twice for a highly choreographed ensemble number. Though impressive in its scope and coordination, the performance is well-nigh impossible to take in from any given viewing spot. The same floats are trotted out individually at various times of day for mini-shows and character meet-and-greets.

The parade begins at the gate between Louie's Pizza, in the New York area of the park, and *Beetlejuice's Graveyard Mash-Up,* in San Francisco. From there it proceeds along 5th Avenue, past Revenge of the Mummy. At the end of 5th Avenue, the parade takes a left onto Plaza of the Stars and heads toward the front of the park, where it makes another left onto Hollywood Boulevard, from whence it disappears backstage across from Mel's Diner. The best viewing spots are along 5th Avenue, on the front steps of faux buildings in New York.

If you miss part of the parade in the New York area, you can scoot along the waterfront to Mel's Diner and catch it as it comes down Hollywood Boulevard. If after watching the parade on the New York streets you plan to leave the park, you can use the same route to access Hollywood Boulevard and the park exit before the parade arrives.

# DINING *at* UNIVERSAL STUDIOS FLORIDA

USF'S FAST FOOD is utterly unremarkable: burgers, pizza, pasta, chicken fingers, sandwiches, and salads. The mediocre food is matched by the predictable theming: American diner? Check. New York Italian? Got it. We're a little surprised that there's not a Chinese-takeout place next to a laundry in the San Francisco section. We're a *lot* surprised that the food quality isn't better, given the enormous competition coming from Disney. That said, for something quick, there's usually a **Nathan's Famous Hot Dogs** stand at Central Park in the New York area of the park, and for milkshakes made the old-fashioned way, try **Schwab's Pharmacy** on Hollywood Boulevard.

*un*official **TIP**
We advise heading to Universal CityWalk (see page 413) if you're looking for good-quality food.

The debut in 2013 of the **Springfield U.S.A.** themed area brought a number of wacky *Simpsons*-inspired eateries, including **Krusty Burger, The Frying Dutchman** for seafood, **Cleatus' Chicken Shack, Luigi's Pizza, Lard Lad Donuts, Lisa's Teahouse of Horror, Bumblebee Man's Taco Truck,** and **Moe's Tavern.** Serving sizes are large, and the food quality is consistent with that in the rest of the park.

An Ambler, Pennsylvania, couple sampled the offerings:

> The doughnuts at Lard Lad were fresh, flavorful, and surprisingly delicious. (Mmm . . . doughnuts.) The Flaming Moe is an overpriced glass of orange soda with dry ice on the bottom—for $8, it should have some alcohol in it or be larger. The queuing for Krusty Burger was frustrating during the lunch rush—they let only a few guests up to the food-court area at a time—but once you go through the line and pay, an employee shows you to a table. Lunch for the four of us cost $88 with two beers and that one overpriced Flaming Moe. Duff beer was essentially a less-delicious Heineken. My husband's Krusty Burger was pretty good; my chicken-and-waffle sandwich was excellent but had too much sauce on it.

USF's two sit-down restaurants are **Finnegan's Bar and Grill,** in New York, and **Lombard's Seafood Grille,** in San Francisco. Finnegan's serves typical bar food—burgers and wings—as well as fish-and-chips and other takes on Irish cuisine. Stick to the burgers. Lombard's is the better restaurant, but it's not in the same league as Disney's Hollywood Brown Derby.

At the **Superstar Character Breakfast,** guests dine with characters from *Despicable Me, Spongebob SquarePants, Hop,* and *Dora the Explorer.* Cost is $26 for adults and $11 kids. Call ☎ 407-224-7554 for reservations, or book at **universalorlando.com.**

There's also a weekly character breakfast at **Jake's** in the Royal Pacific Resort ($27 adults, $15 kids); reserve online at **opentable.com**.

# UNIVERSAL STUDIOS FLORIDA TOURING PLAN

## BUYING ADMISSION TO UNIVERSAL STUDIOS FLORIDA

ONE OF OUR BIG GRIPES ABOUT USF is that there are never enough ticket windows open in the morning to accommodate the crowds. Therefore, we strongly recommend that you buy your admission in advance. Passes are available online or by mail from USF at ☎ 800-711-0080; at the concierge desks or attractions box offices of many Orlando-area hotels; and through Guest Services at the DoubleTree Universal hotel (☎ 407-351-1000), at the intersection of Major Boulevard and Kirkman Road.

Many hotels that sell Universal admissions don't issue actual passes. Instead, the purchaser gets a voucher that can be redeemed for a pass at the theme park. Fortunately, the voucher-redemption window is separate from the park's ticket-sales operation. In addition, tickets bought online can be printed at home and contain a bar code that can be read at the turnstiles.

## UNIVERSAL STUDIOS FLORIDA ONE-DAY TOURING PLAN *(page 836)*

THIS PLAN IS FOR DAY GUESTS without early entry or Park-to-Park tickets and assumes that a return-time ticket is required to enter Diagon Alley. If a ride or show is listed that you don't want to experience, skip that step and proceed to the next. Move quickly from attraction to attraction and, if possible, hold off on lunch until after Step 10.

## THE BEST OF UNIVERSAL STUDIOS FLORIDA AND ISLANDS OF ADVENTURE IN ONE DAY *(page 837)*

SEE PAGE 677 for a description of this plan.

# PART EIGHTEEN

# SEAWORLD ORLANDO

SEAWORLD IS A WORLD-CLASS marine-life theme park near the intersection of I-4 and the Beachline Expressway (FL 528). It's about 8 miles east of Walt Disney World. Open daily at 9 a.m. and closing between 6 and 11 p.m. depending on the season, SeaWorld charges about $97 for adults and $92 for children ages 3–9 at the gate (prices include tax). If you buy online at the website below, the same tickets will save you about $10, plus other online-only promotions are offered seasonally. Several multipark tickets are available as well, including the six-park **Orlando Flex Plus Ticket,** which includes admission to SeaWorld, Aquatica, Universal Studios Florida, Islands of Adventure, Wet 'n Wild, and Busch Gardens. Parking is $15 per car, $20 per RV or camper; preferred parking costs $20 For additional information, call ☎ 407-351-3600 or 888-800-5447, or visit **seaworld.com/orlando.**

*unofficial* **TIP**
You can't take prepackaged sandwiches or drinks into SeaWorld or Aquatica.

SeaWorld offers a front-of-the-line pass called **Quick Queue Unlimited.** For $19 and up depending on the season, you can bypass the regular lines at Manta, Kraken, Antartica: Empire of the Penguin, Journey to Atlantis, *TurtleTrek,* Sky Tower, and Wild Arctic. The pass is good all day and can be used multiple times on any participating attraction. For an additional $19 and up, you can score reserved seats for theater and stadium shows with **SeaWorld Signature Show Seating.** Four venues are included, and you can view one performance in each.

Figure on 8–9 hours to see everything, 6 or so if you stick to the big deals. **Discovery Cove** (see page 710), another SeaWorld park, is directly across Central Florida Parkway.

SeaWorld is about the size of the Magic Kingdom and requires about the same amount of walking. In terms of size, quality, and creativity, it's unequivocally on par with Disney's major theme parks. Unlike Walt Disney World, SeaWorld primarily features stadium shows and walk-through exhibits. This means you'll spend about 80% less time waiting in line during 8 hours at SeaWorld than you would for the same-length visit at a Disney park.

Because lines, except those for Journey to Atlantis, Kraken, and Manta (see next page), aren't much of a problem at SeaWorld, you

*unofficial* **TIP**
If you don't purchase your admission in advance, take advantage of the automatic admission machines to the right of the main entrance. If you have a credit card, the machines are faster than standing in line at the ticket windows.

can tour at almost any time of day. If you visit in the morning, arrive early. Morning arrivals tend to create long waits at the ticket windows, so consider buying your admission in advance. Like those at other area parks, SeaWorld's turnstiles often open at either 8:30 a.m. or 8:45 a.m., depending on the season, which means you can enter the park before the scheduled 9 a.m. opening.

A mother of two correctly points out that crowds at SeaWorld on some days can be as daunting as those at the Disney parks:

> *Your reference to crowds at SeaWorld should be changed. We were there on a Sunday and it was extremely crowded, so crowded that we were not able to see everything, even the major attractions. Waits were way too long for us to consider the rides.*

A daily entertainment schedule is printed on a place mat–sized map of the park. The featured shows are as follows:

- *A'Lure: The Call of the Ocean* (Cirque du Soleil–type revue)
- *Blue Horizons* (whale, dolphin, and bird show)
- *Clyde and Seamore Take Pirate Island* (sea-lion, walrus, and otter show)
- *One Ocean* (Shamu and killer-whale show)
- *Pets Ahoy!* (show with performing domestic animals)
- *Shamu Up Close* (behind-the-scenes killer-whale training and habitat)

Trying to sort out a game plan for seeing the shows while you're on the run is somewhat exasperating. A better alternative is to visit **seaworld.com/orlando** and, under "Park Info," click on "Theme Park Hours and Show Schedules." Here you can see the show roster for the day of your visit and plan your touring itinerary in advance.

Much of the year, you can get a seat for the stadium shows by showing up 10 or so minutes in advance. When the park is crowded, however, you need to be at the stadiums at least 20 minutes in advance (30 minutes in advance for a good seat). All of the stadiums have "splash zones," specified areas where you're likely to be drenched with ice-cold salt water by whales, dolphins, and sea lions. Trust us when we say you should take these seriously. You don't have to be in the tank for Shamu to douse you.

In 2013 SeaWorld introduced **Antarctica: Empire of the Penguin,** at 4 acres the largest expansion in SeaWorld history, and *TurtleTrek.* Empire of the Penguin features a trackless, high-tech ride and the largest artificial penguin habitat in the world, populated with four different species. *TurtleTrek* combines a domed 3-D theater presentation about the life of sea turtles with an outdoor tour of alligator, manatee, and turtle habitats.

**Journey to Atlantis, Kraken,** and **Manta** are SeaWorld's entries into the theme park super-attraction competition. Occupying the equivalent of six football fields, Journey to Atlantis is the world's first

| STAR RATINGS FOR SEAWORLD ATTRACTIONS | |
|---|---|
| ★★★★★ | Manta (roller coaster) |
| ★★★★½ | Antarctica: Empire of the Penguin |
| ★★★★½ | One Ocean (high-tech Shamu and killer-whale show) |
| ★★★★ | Kraken (roller coaster) |
| ★★★½ | Clyde and Seamore Take Pirate Island (sea-lion, walrus, and otter show) |
| ★★★½ | Shamu's Happy Harbor (children's play area) |
| ★★★½ | Shamu Up Close (killer-whale training and habitat) |
| ★★★½ | Shark Encounter |
| ★★★½ | Wild Arctic (simulation ride and Arctic-wildlife viewing) |
| ★★★ | A'Lure: The Call of the Ocean (Cirque du Soleil–type presentation) |
| ★★★ | Blue Horizons (whale, dolphin, and bird show) |
| ★★★ | Pacific Point Preserve (sea lions and seals) |
| ★★★ | Pets Ahoy! (show with performing birds, cats, dogs, and a pig) |
| ★★★ | TurtleTrek (3-D film about sea turtles; animal habitats) |
| ★★½ | Journey to Atlantis (combination roller coaster–flume ride) |
| ★★½ | Stingray Lagoon |
| ★★ | Sky Tower (400-foot-tall observation tower) |

attraction to combine elements of a high-speed water ride and a roller coaster. (By the way, you'll get soaked.) Kraken is currently the second-longest roller coaster in Orlando.

Opened in 2009, Manta is a steel coaster that arranges riders four across, lying facedown and parallel to the track, beneath the expanse of a giant manta ray–shaped carriage. The coaster is said to emulate the movements of a manta ray, but if that's the case, it's a mighty frisky ray. The coaster soars and swoops through a pretzel loop, a 360-degree inline roll, and two corkscrews—not to mention a first drop of 113 feet. Manta reaches a height of 140 feet and speeds of more than 55 mph. But don't worry: Lying facedown puts you in the perfect position to throw up. Actually, the ride is very smooth. If you get sick, it'll be from the bugs you pick out of your teeth (keep your mouth closed at all times—you're supposed to be a ray, not a bat). The queuing area is a stunning underwater exhibit featuring 300 rays from five different species; several fish keep the rays company. Manta is a huge hit—roller-coaster buffs almost unanimously rank it as the top coaster in Florida. Catch all three rides just after the park opens, or prepare to wait.

SeaWorld offers quite a few guided tours. Most include the major shows, a glimpse behind the scenes, rides (without waiting) on Journey to Atlantis and Kraken, and interacting with seals, rays, penguins, or dolphins. The tour guides, both personable and well informed, are a font of interesting and useful information. We learned on a recent tour, for example, that in the United States, more people are killed each year by vending machines than by sharks. Think about that next time you buy a Coke.

# DISCOVERY COVE

ALSO OWNED BY SEAWORLD, this intimate park is a welcome departure from the hustle and bustle of other Orlando parks. Its slower pace could be the overstimulated family's ticket back to mental health.

The main draw at Discovery Cove is the chance to swim with an **Atlantic bottlenose dolphin** from among the 45 here. The 50-minute experience (30 minutes in the water) is open to visitors age 6 and up who are comfortable in the water. The experience begins with an orientation led by trainers and an opportunity for participants to ask questions. Next, small groups wade into shallow water to get an introduction to the dolphin in its habitat. The experience culminates with two to three guests and a trainer swimming into deeper water for closer interaction with the dolphin.

*unofficial* **TIP**
With a focus on personal guest service and one-on-one animal encounters, Discovery Cove admits only 1,300 guests per day.

Other exhibits at Discovery Cove include the **Grand Reef,** the **Freshwater Oasis,** and the **Explorer's Aviary.** Snorkel or swim in the Grand Reef, which houses thousands of exotic fish as well as an underwater shipwreck and hidden grottoes. The Freshwater Oasis is a swimming and wading experience where you can get up close and personal with otters and marmosets. In the Explorer's Aviary, you can touch and feed gorgeous tropical birds. The park is threaded by the **Wind-Away River,** in which you can float or swim, and dotted with beaches that serve as pathways to the attractions.

All guests are required to wear flotation vests when swimming, and lifeguards are omnipresent. You'll need your swimsuit, pool shoes, and a cover-up. On rare days when it's too cold to swim in Orlando, guests are provided with free wet suits. Discovery Cove also provides fish-friendly sunscreen samples; guests may not use their own sunscreen.

Discovery Cove is open 8 a.m.–5:30 p.m. daily. Admission is limited, so purchase tickets well in advance; call ☎ 877-557-7404 or visit **discoverycove.com.** Prices vary seasonally from $244 per person to $425, including tax (no children's discount). Florida residents receive a discount. Admission includes the dolphin swim, self-parking, Continental breakfast, a substantial lunch, snacks and drinks, and use of beach umbrellas, lounge chairs, towels, lockers, swim and snorkel gear, and unlimited admission to SeaWorld and Aquatica water park (see page 732) for 14 days surrounding your visit to Discovery Cove.

For an additional $59 per person, you can experience **SeaVenture,** a 25-minute underwater stroll on the bottom of the Grand Reef aquarium. Participants wear diving helmets (large enough to accommodate eyeglasses), and no experience or scuba certification is necessary. Minimum age is 10 years.

# PART NINETEEN

# BEHIND *the* SCENES *at* WALT DISNEY WORLD

IF YOU'RE INTERESTED IN THE MOUSE'S INNARDS—um, make that inner workings—a number of guided tours offer a glimpse of what goes on behind the scenes. Reservations must be guaranteed with a credit card, and you need to cancel at least 48 hours in advance if you want a full refund. Many tours require that you buy park admission separately; we've noted where it isn't mandatory. Prices listed include sales tax; discounts on some tours are available to Walt Disney World Annual Pass holders, Disney Vacation Club members, and Disney Visa Card holders.

*unofficial* **TIP**
The walking tours involve a considerable amount of walking, standing, and time spent outdoors (depending on the tour).

Certain tours are available only on certain days of the week (see the chart on the next two pages for specifics). For reservations and more information, call ☎ 407-WDW-TOUR (939-8687). Customized VIP tours are also available; call ☎ 407-560-4033 for details.

## MULTIPARK TOURS

THE 7-HOUR **Backstage Magic** tour ($249) goes behind the scenes at all the WDW parks. Includes lunch; guests must be at least 16 years old to participate. Park admission is not required.

**Disney's Holiday D-Lights** (5 hours, $209) and **Disney's Yuletide Fantasy** (3½ hours, $89) explore the myriad ways in which Walt Disney World transforms for the Christmas season. Neither tour requires park admission; guests must be at least age 16. Call ☎ 407-WDW-TOUR for 2015 tour dates; the holiday tours fill up quickly.

## BEHIND *the* SCENES *at the* MAGIC KINGDOM

AS ITS NAME MAKES CLEAR, **Disney's Keys to the Kingdom** takes guests behind the scenes at the Magic Kingdom. This fascinating guided tour provides a detailed look at the park's logistical, technical, and operational sides. Included are the parade-assembly area, the waste-treatment

## Behind-the-Scenes Tours at Walt Disney Wor

| | TOUR LENGTH | COST | MINIMUM AGE |
|---|---|---|---|
| **MULTIPARK TOURS** | | | |
| Backstage Magic | 7 hours | $249 | 16 |
| Disney's Holiday D-Lights | 5 hours | $209 | 16 |
| Disney's Yuletide Fantasy | 3½ hours | $89 | 16 |
| **THE MAGIC KINGDOM** | | | |
| Disney's Family Magic Tour | 1½–2 hours | $36 | None |
| Disney's Keys to the Kingdom | 4½–5 hours | $79 | 16 |
| Disney's The Magic Behind Our Steam Trains | 3 hours | $54 | 10 |
| Pirates and Pals Fireworks Voyage | 1–3 hours | $59 age 10+, $34 ages 3–9 | None |
| Walt Disney: Marceline to Magic Kingdom Tour | 2–3 hours | $30 | 12 |
| **EPCOT** | | | |
| Behind the Seeds at Epcot | 1 hour | $20 age 10+, $16 ages 3–9 | None |
| Dolphins in Depth | 3 hours | $199 | 13 |
| Epcot DiveQuest | 3 hours | $175 | 10 |
| Seas Aqua Tour | 2½ hours | $150 | 8 |
| The UnDISCOVERed Future World | 4 hours | $59 | 16 |
| **DISNEY'S ANIMAL KINGDOM** | | | |
| Animal Kingdom Lodge Night Safari (hotel guests only) | 1 hour | $70 | None |
| Animal Kingdom Lodge Sunrise Safari (Club Level guests only) | 3 hours | $75 age 10+, $40 ages 3–9 | None |
| Backstage Safari | 3 hours | $77 | 16 |
| Wild Africa Trek | 3 hours | $201 | 8 |
| Wild by Design | 3 hours | $64 | 14 |
| **DISNEY'S BOARDWALK** | | | |
| BoardWalk Ballyhoo Guided Tour | 45 minutes | Free | None |
| **FORT WILDERNESS CAMPGROUND** | | | |
| Disney's Wilderness Back Trail Adventure | 2 hours | $96 | 16 |

plant, and the utilidor network beneath the park. The program ($79 per person) includes lunch and runs about 4½–5 hours; children must be at least 16 years old to participate. For those interested in the tour, a reader from Ludington, Michigan, warns:

> *Keys to the Kingdom is not for the faint of heart. This is a 4-hour walking tour with only one 15-minute break, plus a few minutes to sit awhile on Pirates of the Caribbean or The Haunted Mansion.*

| FOCUS | DAYS AVAILABLE |
|---|---|
| Peeks behind the scenes at every Disney World park | M, some Th, F |
| Close-up look at Disney World holiday spectacles | Seasonal |
| Another look at holiday productions | Seasonal |
| Following clues in a sort of treasure hunt | Daily |
| Park's logistical, technical, and operational sides | Daily |
| Steam locomotives of the Walt Disney World Railroad | M–Sa |
| Cruise around Seven Seas Lagoon | F–Tu (varies seasonally) |
| Examination of Walt Disney's career and vision | M, W, F |
| Vegetable gardens in the Land Pavilion | Daily |
| Visiting the dolphin-research facility at The Seas | Tu–Sa |
| Swimming with the fish at The Seas | Tu–Sa |
| Swimming in the main tank at The Seas | Tu–Sa |
| The history of Epcot | M, W, F |
| After-dark tour of the lodge's savannas with night-vision goggles | M, W |
| Sunrise ride on Kilimanjaro Safaris (see page 599) and breakfast; **must have valid park admission to participate** | Th, Su |
| Observing how the animals are housed and cared for | M, W, Th, F |
| Enhanced safari and adventure activities with meal | Daily |
| Inside look at the creation of Animal Kingdom | M, W, Th, F |
| Tour of BoardWalk and discussion of its historical inspiration | Daily |
| Segway romp on campground trails and paths | Tu–Sa |

**Disney's The Magic Behind Our Steam Trains,** a 3-hour tour for children age 10 and up, takes a backstage look at the steam locomotives of the Walt Disney World Railroad. Cost is $54 per person. A less costly tour is **Disney's Family Magic Tour,** an interactive romp through the park following clues in a sort of treasure hunt. The 1½- to 2-hour tour is offered daily for $36. **Walt Disney: Marceline to Magic Kingdom Tour** (2–3 hours, $30 age 12 and older) is a guided walking tour that interprets the Magic Kingdom as a "walking time line" of Disney's life (Marceline, Missouri, was his childhood hometown).

The Contemporary Resort's **Pirates and Pals Fireworks Voyage** (1–3 hours, $59 age 10 and older; $31 ages 3–9) offers sailings with a unique view of the Magic Kingdom fireworks from Seven Seas Lagoon; the days offered vary seasonally but typically include Friday–Tuesday. Your guide, Patch, sings pirate songs and delights the kids with Disney trivia. On select nights, the voyage also includes a viewing of the Floating Electrical Pageant.

# BEHIND *the* SCENES *at* EPCOT

A TOUR CALLED **The UnDISCOVERed Future World** traces the history of Epcot, including Walt Disney's original concept. The tour takes guests to backstage areas and lasts a bit over 4 hours. The cost is $64; guests must be at least 16 years old to participate.

**Behind the Seeds at Epcot** is shorter and takes guests to vegetable gardens and aquaculture farms in the Land Pavilion. The quality of the experience—a cross between science lecture and Willy Wonka factory tour—depends heavily on the tour guide's presentation and enthusiasm. You're not permitted to touch or sample the plants shown on the tour, but it's hard to resist the urge. Behind the Seeds requires same-day reservations; make them on the lower level of The Land (next to the entrance to Soarin'). The cost of the hour-long tour is $20 for adults and $16 for children ages 3–9.

**Disney's Wilderness Back Trail Adventure** ($96) is a 2-hour Segway romp on the trails and walking paths of Fort Wilderness Campground. Guests must be at least 16 years old and weigh 100–250 pounds.

## EPCOT DIVEQUEST

THE SOGGIEST BEHIND-THE-SCENES experience available anywhere is **Epcot DiveQuest,** in which open water scuba–certified divers (age 10 and up; kids age 12 and younger must be accompanied by an adult) can swim around with the fish at The Seas with Nemo & Friends Pavilion. Offered twice a day, Tuesday–Saturday, at 4:30 and 5:30 p.m., each tour lasts about 3 hours, including a 40-minute dive. Cost is $175 per diver and includes all gear, a souvenir drawstring bag, and a dive-log stamp. For recorded information, call ☎ 407-560-5590. Theme park admission is not required, but proof of dive certification is.

## DOLPHINS IN DEPTH

THIS TOUR (FOR GUESTS AGE 13 AND OLDER) visits the dolphin-research facility at The Seas with Nemo & Friends. There you'll witness a training session, then wade into the water for a photo (but not a swim) with a dolphin. Cost for the 3-hour experience is $199; children under age 18 must be accompanied by an adult; expectant mothers may not participate. Theme park admission is not required. Wet suits are provided. Only eight guests per day can participate; call ☎ 407-WDW-TOUR when you're ready to book.

If you really dig dolphins, keep in mind that for $229–$419 (tax included), you can visit SeaWorld's **Discovery Cove** and actually swim with a dolphin. Though the experience is only about 30 minutes long, the ticket entitles visitors to an entire day at Discovery Cove. For more information, see page 710.

## SEAS AQUA TOUR

THIS TOUR IS SORT OF a watered-down (rim shot) version of Epcot DiveQuest. The 2½-hour tour lets you swim with goggles, a mini–air tank, and a flotation vest in the main tank for 30 minutes and explore backstage areas at The Seas with Nemo & Friends. It costs $140, accepts guests as young as 8 years old, and doesn't require separate park admission. Children under age 12 must be accompanied by an adult; children ages 12–17 must have a parent or guardian sign a waiver. Gear and a souvenir drawstring bag are included.

# BEHIND *the* SCENES *at* DISNEY'S ANIMAL KINGDOM

IN THE 3-HOUR **Backstage Safari** tour, animal keepers and vets discuss conservation, animal nutrition, behavioral studies, and medicine, among other topics. Limited to guests age 16 and older, the Backstage Safari costs $77. You'll see animal enclosures, feed bins, medical facilities, and labs, but not many animals.

**Wild by Design** offers an inside look at the creation of Animal Kingdom, explaining how architecture, functionality, habitats, themes, and storytelling are combined to provide a complete theme park experience. The tour also runs 3 hours and costs $64 per person; it's open to guests age 14 and older.

The **Wild Africa Trek** takes groups of up to 12 on to newly created forest hiking trails, on suspension bridges high above hippo and crocodile pools, and on a private safari complete with a gourmet camp meal. Possibly our favorite tour of the last couple of years, the Wild Africa Trek lasts 3 hours and costs $201 per person. Open to guests age 8 and older. Extensive walking is required, and guests must weigh 45–310 pounds and be at least 48" tall for the safety gear. A host of other warnings applies, so call Disney for details.

The **Night and Sunrise Safaris** are offered only to guests of Animal Kingdom Lodge & Villas. The Sunrise Safari must be booked by calling ☎ 407-938-4755; Animal Kingdom Lodge guests can book the Night Safari through the concierge.

# PART TWENTY

# *The*
# WATER PARKS

---

# YOU'RE SOAKING *in* IT!

DISNEY HAS TWO WATER PARKS, and there are two competitive water parks in the area. At Disney World, **Typhoon Lagoon** is the more diverse splash pad, while **Blizzard Beach** takes the prize for the greater number of slides and the more bizarre theme. Outside the World are **Wet 'n Wild** and **Aquatica by SeaWorld,** both on International Drive.

At both Disney water parks, the following rules and prices apply: One cooler per family or group is allowed, but no glass or alcoholic beverages allowed; towels are $2; lockers are $7 small, $9 large (includes $5 refundable deposit); parking and life jackets are free.

Guests can use automated ticket-vending machines to purchase admission at Blizzard Beach and Typhoon Lagoon. These machines use touchscreen technology and are intended to reduce the amount of time spent standing in line at ticket windows. Admission, including tax, runs $57 for adults and $48 for children ages 3–9.

## WATCH THE WEATHER

IF YOU BUY YOUR WALT DISNEY WORLD admission tickets before leaving home and you're considering the **Water Park Fun and More (WPFAM)** add-on (see page 55), you might want to wait until you arrive and have some degree of certainty about the weather during your stay. You can add the WPFAM option at any Disney resort or Guest Relations window at the theme parks. This is true regardless of whether you purchased your Base Tickets separately or as part of a package.

We get a lot of questions about the water parks during cold-weather months. Orlando-area temperatures can vary from the high 40s to the low 80s during December, January, and February. When it's warmer out, these months can serve up a dandy water-park experience, as this Batavia, Ohio, reader confirms:

> *Going to Blizzard Beach in December was the best decision ever! We went on December 12, and there was no one there. They told us at the entrance that if the park didn't reach 100—yes, I said 100—people by noon, they would be closing. I guess they got to 101, because it stayed open but was virtually empty. There was no wait for anything*

*all day! In June we waited in line for an hour for Summit Plummet, but in December it was just the amount of time it took to walk up the stairs. We had the enormous wave pool to ourselves. We did everything in the entire park and ate lunch in less than 3 hours. It was perfect. The weather was slightly chilly at 71 degrees, and overcast with very light rain, but the water was heated, so we were fine.*

## EXTRA MAGIC HOURS

WHILE DISNEY ONCE OFFERED morning and evening Extra Magic Hours at its water parks, it's been a couple of years since we last saw them on the operating schedule. It's Disney's prerogative to change its mind, however, especially during summer, so check the operating schedules a couple of days before you plan to go.

# BLIZZARD BEACH

BLIZZARD BEACH IS DISNEY'S MORE EXOTIC water-adventure park and, like Typhoon Lagoon, it arrived with its own legend. This time, the story goes, an entrepreneur tried to open a ski resort in Florida during a particularly savage winter. Alas, the snow melted; the palm trees grew back; and all that remained of the ski resort was its Alpine lodge, the ski lifts, and, of course, the mountain. Plunging off the mountain are ski slopes and bobsled runs transformed into waterslides. Visitors to Blizzard Beach catch the thaw—icicles drip and patches of snow remain. The melting snow has formed a lagoon (the wave pool), fed by gushing mountain streams.

Like Typhoon Lagoon, Blizzard Beach is distinguished by its landscaping and the attention paid to executing its theme. As you enter Blizzard Beach, you face the mountain. Coming off the highest peak and bisecting the area at the mountain's base are two long slides. To the left

*unofficial* **TIP**
Picnic areas are scattered around the park, as are pleasant places for sunbathing.

of the slides is the wave pool. To the right are the children's swimming area and the ski lift. Surrounding the layout like a moat is a tranquil stream for floating in tubes.

On either side of the highest peak are tube, raft, and body slides. Including the two slides coming off the peak, Blizzard Beach has 17 slides. Among them is **Summit Plummet,** Disney World's longest speed slide, which begins with a 120-foot free fall, and the **Teamboat Springs** water-bobsled run, 1,200 feet long.

One reader reports that the Blizzard Beach slides picked her husband's pocket:

*Our family absolutely loved Summit Plummet, but it claimed all four of our park passes/room-key cards as its victims. My husband had the four cards in an exterior pocket of his swimsuit, secured closed by Velcro AND a snap. But after doing Summit Plummet and Slush Gusher twice apiece and Teamboat Springs once, he looked down, noticed the pocket flapping open, and found all four cards missing! So we had to cancel all the cards (they had charging privileges) and couldn't purchase any food or drinks while we were there (we didn't bring any cash because we planned to charge with our cards)!*

## BLIZZARD BEACH Attractions

**CHAIRLIFT UP MT. GUSHMORE Height requirement: 32 inches.** Great ride even if you only go up for the view. When the park is packed, use the singles line.

**CASTAWAY CREEK No height requirement.** Lazy river circling the park; grab a tube.

**DOWNHILL DOUBLE DIPPER Height requirement: 48 inches.** Side-by-side tube-racing slides. At 25 mph, the tube zooms through water curtains and free falls. It's a lot of fun, but rough.

**MELT-AWAY BAY No height requirement.** Wave pool with gentle, bobbing waves. Great for younger swimmers.

**RUNOFF RAPIDS No height requirement.** Three corkscrew tube slides to choose from. The center slide is for solo raft rides; the other two slides offer one- or two-person tubes. The dark, enclosed tube makes you feel as if you were flushed down a toilet.

**SKI PATROL TRAINING CAMP Height requirement: 60 inches for T-Bar.** A place for preteens to train for the big rides.

**SLUSH GUSHER Height requirement: 48 inches.** A 90-foot double-humped slide. Ladies, cling to those tops—all others, hang on to live.

**SNOW STORMERS No height requirement.** Three mat-slide flumes; down you go on your belly.

**SUMMIT PLUMMET Height requirement: 48 inches.** A 120-foot free fall, at 60 mph. Needless to say, this ride is very intense. Make sure your child knows what to expect. Being over 48 inches tall doesn't guarantee an enjoyable experience. If you think you'd enjoy washing out of a 12th-floor window during a heavy rain, then this slide is for you.

**TEAMBOAT SPRINGS No height requirement.** 1,200-foot group whitewater-raft flume. Wonderful ride for the whole family.

**TIKE'S PEAK 4 feet and under only.** Kid-sized version of Blizzard Beach. This is the place for little ones.

**TOBOGGAN RACERS No height requirement.** Eight-lane race course. You go down the flume on a mat. Less intense than Snow Stormers.

A couple from Bowie, Maryland, came away with battle scars:

*Summit Plummet gave me a bunch of bruises. Even my husband hurt for a few days. It wasn't a fun ride, and we both agree that it wasn't worth waiting in line for. Basically, you drop until you hit the slide, and that is why everyone comes off rubbing their butts. They say you go 60 mph on a 120-foot drop. I'll never do it again.*

For our money, the most exciting and interesting slides are the **Slush Gusher** and Teamboat Springs on the front right of the mountain, and **Runoff Rapids** on the back side of the mountain. Slush Gusher is an undulating speed slide that we consider as exciting as the more vertical Summit Plummet without being as bone-jarring. On Teamboat Springs, you ride in a raft that looks like a children's round blow-up wading pool.

Runoff Rapids is accessible from a path that winds around the far left bottom of the mountain. The rapids consist of three corkscrew tube slides, one of which is enclosed and dark. As at Teamboat Springs, you'll go much faster on a two- or three-person tube than on a one-person tube. If you lean so that you enter curves high and come out low, you'll really fly. Because we like to steer the tube and go fast, we much prefer the open slides (where we can see) to the dark, enclosed tube. We thought crashing through the pitch-dark tube felt disturbingly like being flushed down a toilet.

The **Snow Stormers'** mat slides on the front of the mountain are fun but not as fast or as interesting as Runoff Rapids or **Downhill Double Dipper** on the far left front. The **Toboggan Racers** at the front and center of the mountain consists of eight parallel slides where riders are dispatched in heats to race to the bottom. The

*un*official **TIP**
The more people you load into the raft, the faster it goes. If you have only a couple in it, the slide is kind of a snore.

ride itself is no big deal, and the time needed to get everybody lined up ensures that you'll wait extra-long to ride. A faster, more exciting race venue can be found on the side-by-side slides of the undulating Downhill Double Dipper. Competitors here can reach speeds of up to 25 miles an hour.

A ski lift carries guests to the mountaintop (you can also walk up), where they can choose from Summit Plummet, Slush Gusher, or Teamboat Springs. For all other slides at Blizzard Beach, the only way to reach the top is on foot. If you're among the first in the park and don't have to wait to ride, the ski lift is fun and provides a bird's-eye view of the park. After riding once to satisfy your curiosity, however, you're better off taking the stairs to the top. The following attractions have a minimum height restriction of 48 inches: Slush Gusher, Summit Plummet, and Downhill Double Dipper.

The wave pool, called **Melt-Away Bay,** has gentle, bobbing waves. The float creek, **Cross Country Creek,** circles the park, passing through the mountain. The children's areas, **Tike's Peak** and **Ski Patrol Training Camp,** are creatively designed, nicely isolated, and, like the rest of the park, visually interesting.

Like Typhoon Lagoon, Blizzard Beach is a bit convoluted in its layout. With slides on both the front and back of the mountain, it isn't always easy to find a path leading to where you want to go.

At the ski resort's now-converted base area are shops; counter-service food; restrooms; and tube, towel, and locker rentals. Blizzard Beach has its own parking lot but no lodging, though Disney's All-Star and Coronado Springs Resorts are almost within walking distance. Guests at Disney resort hotels can commute to the park aboard Disney buses.

Because it's novel and has popular slides, Blizzard Beach fills early during hotter months. To stake out a nice sunning spot and to enjoy the slides without long waits, arrive at least 35 minutes before the official opening time (check **disneyworld.com** for hours before you go).

# TYPHOON LAGOON

TYPHOON LAGOON is comparable in size to Blizzard Beach. Eleven waterslides and streams, some as long as 420 feet, drop from the top of a 100-foot-tall man-made mountain. Landscaping and an aftermath-of-a-typhoon theme add interest and a sense of adventure to the wet rides.

Guests enter Typhoon Lagoon through a misty rainforest, then emerge in a ramshackle tropical town where concessions and services are situated. Special sets make every ride an odyssey as swimmers encounter bat caves, lagoons and pools, spinning rocks, formations of dinosaur bones, and many other imponderables.

## TYPHOON LAGOON Attractions

**BAY SLIDES  Height requirement: 60 inches and under.** A miniature two-slide version of Storm Slides, specifically designed for small children. Kids splash down into a far corner of the Surf Pool.

**CASTAWAY CREEK  No height requirement.** Half-mile lazy river in a tropical setting. Wonderful!

**CRUSH 'N' GUSHER  Height requirement: 48 inches** Water roller coaster where you can choose from among three slides: Banana Blaster, Coconut Crusher, and Pineapple Plunger, ranging from 410 to 420 feet long. This thriller leaves you wondering what exactly happened—if you make it down in one piece, that is, it's not for the faint of heart. If your kids are new to water-park rides, this is not the place to break them in, even if they're tall enough to ride.

**GANG PLANK FALLS  No height requirement.** Whitewater-raft flume in a multi-person tube.

**HUMUNGA KOWABUNGA  Height requirement: 48 inches.** Speed slides that hit 30 mph. A five-story drop in the dark rattles the most courageous rider. Women should ride this one in a one-piece swimsuit.

**KEELHAUL FALLS  No height requirement.** Fast whitewater ride in a single-person tube.

**KETCHAKIDDEE CREEK  Height requirement: 48 inches and under only.** Toddlers and preschoolers love this area reserved only for them. Say "splish-splash" and have lots of fun.

**MAYDAY FALLS  No height requirement.** Wild single-person tube ride. *Hang on!*

**SHARK REEF  No height requirement; kids under age 10 must be accompanied by an adult.** After you're equipped with fins, mask, snorkel, and a life vest, you get a brief lesson in snorkeling. Then off you go for about 60 feet to the other side of the saltwater pool, where you swim with small, colorful fish; rays; and very small leopard and hammerhead sharks. If you don't want to swim with the fish, visit the underwater-viewing chamber anytime during the day. Surface Air Snorkeling, a scubalike pursuit involving a "pony" tank, small regulator, and buoyancy vest, is also offered. Participants must be at least 5 years old. To sign up and get more information, visit the kiosk near the entrance to Shark Reef.

**STORM SLIDES  No height requirement.** Three body-slides down and through Mount Mayday.

**SURF POOL  No height requirement.** World's largest inland surf facility, with waves up to 6 feet high. Adult supervision is required. Monday–Friday, in the early morning before the park opens (hours vary), surfing lessons are offered (surfboard provided). Cost is $165 for 2½ hours; minimum age is 8; class size is 12. Call ☎ 407-WDW-PLAY (939-7529). The price doesn't include park admission.

Typhoon Lagoon has its own parking lot but no lodging. Disney resort guests can commute to the water park on Disney buses.

If you indulge in all features of Typhoon Lagoon, admission is a fair value. If you go primarily for the slides, you'll have only 2 early-morning hours to enjoy them before the wait becomes prohibitive. Speaking of crowds, a Maryland family tried a little experiment and reports the following:

> We did Typhoon Lagoon one morning and it was fun. So we theo-rized that since it was crowded midday, that maybe it clears out late afternoon. My wife took our oldest there at 3 p.m. on Friday and said it was wide open—they rode waterslides without any wait at all for 2 hours and loved it.

Typhoon Lagoon provides water adventure for all ages. Activity pools for young children and families feature geysers, tame slides, bubble jets, and fountains. For the older and more adventurous are the enclosed **Humunga Kowabunga** speed slides, the corkscrew **Storm Slides,** and three whitewater-raft rides: **Gang Plank Falls, Keelhaul Falls,** and **Mayday Falls.** Billed as a "water roller coaster," **Crush 'n' Gusher** consists of a series of flumes and spillways that course through an abandoned tropical fruit–processing plant. It features tubes that hold one or two people, and you can choose from three different routes: Banana Blaster, Coconut Crusher, and Pineapple Plunger, ranging between 410 and 420 feet long. The minimum height requirement is 48 inches. Of all the Typhoon Lagoon slides, only Crush 'n' Gusher and the Humunga Kowabunga speed slides (where you can hit 30 miles an hour) have a minimum height requirement of 48 inches.

A Waterloo, Ontario, mom found Typhoon Lagoon more strenuous than she'd anticipated:

> We visited Typhoon Lagoon for the first time with our two kids, ages 12 and 10. I wish I'd been prepared for the fact that we'd have to haul the tubes up the stairs of the Crush 'n' Gusher. My daughter was not strong enough to carry hers, so I had to lug them up by myself. I was EXHAUSTED by the end of the day, and my arms ached for a couple of days afterwards. Had I known that was the case, I would have started lifting weights several months before our trip in preparation!

Slower metabolisms will enjoy the scenic, meandering, 2,000-foot-long **Castaway Creek,** which floats tubers through hidden grottoes and rainforests. And, of course, the sedentary will usually find plenty of sun to sleep in. Typhoon Lagoon's **Surf Pool** and **Shark Reef** are unique, the former being the world's largest inland surf facility, with waves up to 6 feet high (enough, so Disney says, to "encompass an ocean liner"). Shark Reef is a saltwater snorkeling pool where guests can swim among real fish.

## SHARK REEF

FINS, MASK, SNORKEL, AND WET-SUIT VEST are provided free in the wooden building beside the diving pool. After you obtain the proper equipment (no forms or money involved), you shower and then report to a snorkeling instructor. After a brief lesson, you swim about 60 feet to the other side of the pool. You're not allowed to paddle aimlessly but must traverse the pool more or less directly.

*unofficial* **TIP**
Try Shark Reef in the morning—afternoons can get crowded, and you may be ushered out of the pool more quickly than in the early hours.

The reef is fun in early morning. Equipment collection, shower, instruction, and the quick swim can be accomplished without much hassle. Also, because few guests are present, attendants are more flexible about your lingering in the pool or making minor departures from the charted course.

Later, as crowds build, it becomes increasingly difficult and time-consuming to provide the necessary instruction. The result is platoons of would-be frogmen restlessly awaiting their snorkeling lesson. Guests are grouped in impromptu classes with the entire class briefed and then launched together. What takes four or five minutes shortly after opening can take more than an hour by 11 a.m.

By far the most prevalent species in the pool is the dual-finned *Homo sapiens*. Other denizens include small, colorful tropical fish; some diminutive rays; and a few very small leopard and hammerhead sharks. In terms of numbers, it would be unusual to cross the pool and not see some fish. On the other hand, you aren't exactly bumping into them.

It's very important to fit your diving mask on your face so that it seals around the edges. Brush your hair from your forehead and sniff a couple of times once the mask is in place, to create a vacuum. Mustaches often prevent the mask from sealing properly. The first indication that your mask isn't correctly fitted will be salt water in your nose.

If you don't want to swim with fish early in the morning or fight crowds later in the day, visit the underwater viewing chamber, accessible anytime without waiting, special equipment, showers, instruction, or water in your nose.

## SURF POOL

WHILE BLIZZARD BEACH and Wet 'n Wild have wave pools, Typhoon Lagoon has a Surf Pool. Most people will encounter larger waves here than they have in the ocean. The surf machine puts out a wave about every 90 seconds (just about how long it takes to get back in position if you caught the previous wave). Perfectly formed and ideal for riding, each wave is about 5–6 feet from trough to crest. Before you join the fray, watch two or three waves from shore. Since each wave breaks in almost the same spot, you can get a feel for position and timing. Observing other surfers is also helpful.

The best way to ride the waves is to swim about three-fourths of the way to the wall at the wave-machine end of the Surf Pool. When the wave comes (you'll both feel and hear it), swim vigorously toward the beach, attempting to position yourself one-half to three-fourths of a body length below the breaking crest. The waves are so perfectly engineered that they will either carry you forward or bypass you. Unlike an ocean wave, they won't slam you down.

*unofficial* **TIP**
*A final warning:* The Surf Pool has a knack for loosening watchbands, stripping jewelry, and sucking stuff out of your pockets. Don't take anything out there except your swimsuit (and hang on to that).

A teenage girl from Urbana, Illinois, notes that the primary hazard in the Surf Pool is colliding with other surfers and swimmers:

*The Surf Pool was nice except that I kept landing on really hairy fat guys whenever the big waves came.*

A reader from Somerset, New Jersey, alerted us to yet another problem:

*Typhoon Lagoon is a great family water park—our unexpected favorite. However, please tell your readers not to sit on the bottom of the wave pool—I got a horrible scratch/raspberry and saw about five others with similar injuries. The waves are stronger than they look.*

Sitting on the bottom also disturbs the hippos.

The best way to avoid collisions while surfing is to paddle out far enough that you'll be at the top of the wave as it breaks. This tactic eliminates the possibility of anyone landing on you from above and assures maximum forward visibility. A corollary to this: The worst place to swim is where the wave actually breaks. You'll look up to see a 6-foot wall of water carrying eight dozen screaming surfers bearing down on you. This is the time to remember every submarine movie you've ever seen . . . Dive! Dive! Dive!

On weekdays in the early morning before the park opens (hours vary), you can take surfing lessons, with an actual surfboard. Practice waves range from 3 to 6 feet tall. Most of the school's students are first-timers. Cost is $165 per person, and equipment is provided. For reservations and information, call ☎ 407-WDW-PLAY (939-7529).

# TYPHOON LAGOON *versus* BLIZZARD BEACH

*unofficial* TIP
If you're into slides, Blizzard Beach is tops among the Disney water parks.

MANY WALT DISNEY WORLD GUESTS aren't interested in leaving the World. For them, the question is: Which is better, Typhoon Lagoon or Blizzard Beach? Our readers answer.

A mother of four from Winchester, Virginia, gives her opinion:

*At Blizzard Beach, the family raft ride is great, but the kids' area is poorly designed. As a parent, when you walk your child to the top of a slide or the tube ride, they're lost to your vision as they go down because of the fake snowdrifts. There are no direct ways down to the end of the slides, so little ones are left standing unsupervised while parents scramble down from the top. The Typhoon Lagoon kids' area is far superior in design.*

A couple from Woodridge, Illinois, writes:

*We liked Blizzard Beach much more. It seems like they took everything from Typhoon Lagoon and made it better and faster. Summit Plummet was awesome—a total rush. Worth the half-hour wait. The toboggan and bobsled rides were really exciting—the bobsled really throws you around. The family tube ride was really good—much better and much longer than the one at Typhoon Lagoon. Tube rides were great, especially in the enclosed tube. If you have time to go to only one water park, go to Blizzard Beach.*

A hungry reader from Aberdeen, New Jersey, complains:

*At Blizzard Beach, there's only one main place to get food (most of the other spots are more for snacks). At lunchtime, it took almost 45 minutes to get some sandwiches and drinks.*

# WHEN *to* GO

THE BEST WAY TO AVOID STANDING IN LINES is to visit the Disney water parks when they're less crowded. Our research, conducted over many weeks in the parks, indicates that tourists, not locals, make up the majority of visitors on any given day. And because weekends are popular travel days, the water parks tend to be less crowded then. In fact, of the weekend days we evaluated, the parks never reached full capacity; during the week, conversely, one or both parks closed every Thursday we monitored, and both closed at least once every other weekday. We recommend going on a Monday or Friday.

From a mom from Manlius, New York, here's what *crowded* means:

**un*official* TIP**
During summer and holiday periods, Typhoon Lagoon and Blizzard Beach sometimes fill to capacity and close their gates before 11 a.m.

*Because we had the all-inclusive pass, we also visited Typhoon Lagoon, arriving before opening so we could stake out a shady spot. The kids loved it until the lines got long (11 a.m.–noon), but I hated it. It made Coney Island seem like a deserted island in the Bahamas. Floating on Castaway Creek was really unpleasant. Whirling around in a chlorinated, concrete ditch with some stranger's feet in my face, periodically getting squirted by water guns, passing under cascades of cold water, and getting hung up by the crowd is not at all relaxing for me. My husband and I then decided to "bob" in the Surf Pool. After about 10 minutes of being tossed around like corks in boiling water, he turned a little green around the gills, and we sought the peace of our shady little territory which, in our absence, had become much, much smaller. The kids, however, loved the body slides and the surf waves.*

A visitor from Middletown, New York, had a somewhat better experience at Typhoon Lagoon:

*On our second trip to Typhoon Lagoon, we dispensed with the locker rental (having planned to stay for only the morning when it was least crowded), and at park's opening just took right off for the Storm Slides before the masses arrived—it was perfect! We must have ridden the slides at least five times before any kind of line built up, and then we were also able to ride the tube and raft rides (Keelhaul and Mayday Falls) in a similar uncrowded, quick fashion because everyone else was busy getting their lockers! We also experienced the Shark Reef, snorkeling three times with minimal crowds that day, because, I think, most people overlook this attraction. Shark Reef is fun and a great way to cool off since their water temp is well below the wave pool's.*

If your schedule is flexible, a good time to visit the swimming parks is midafternoon to late in the day when the weather has cleared after a storm. The parks usually close during bad weather. If the storm is prolonged, most guests leave for their hotels. When Typhoon Lagoon or Blizzard Beach reopens after inclement weather has passed, you almost have a whole park to yourself.

# PLANNING YOUR DAY
## *at* DISNEY WATER PARKS

DISNEY WATER PARKS ARE ALMOST AS LARGE and elaborate as the major theme parks. You must be prepared for a lot of walking, exercise, sun, and jostling crowds. If your group really loves the water, schedule your visit early in your vacation. If you go at the beginning of your stay, you'll have more flexibility if you want to return.

To have a great day and beat the crowds, consider:

**1. GETTING INFORMATION** Call ☎ 407-WDW-MAGIC (939-6244) or check **disneyworld.com** the night before to verify when your chosen park opens.

**2. TO PICNIC OR NOT TO PICNIC** Decide whether you want to carry a picnic lunch. Guests are permitted to take lunches and beverage coolers into the parks. However, alcoholic beverages and glass containers of any kind are forbidden.

**3. GETTING STARTED** If you're going to Blizzard Beach or Typhoon Lagoon, get up early, have breakfast, and arrive at the park 40 minutes before opening. If you have a car, drive instead of taking a Disney bus.

**4. FOLLOW A GOOD TOURING PLAN** We've got two touring plans designed to help you avoid the crowds and bottlenecks at the Disney water parks (see pages 839 and 840). If you're attending on a day of moderate-to-heavy attendance (see the Crowd Calendar at our website), consider using one of these battle-tested plans. More are available at **touringplans.com**.

**5. ATTIRE** Wear your bathing suit under shorts and a T-shirt so you don't need to use lockers or dressing rooms. Regarding women's bathing suits, be advised that it's extremely common for women of all ages to part company with the top of their two-piece suit on the slides. Wear shoes. Paths are relatively easy on bare feet, but there's a lot of ground to cover. If you have tender feet, wear your shoes as you move around the park, removing them when you raft, slide, or go into the water. Shops in the parks sell sandals, Reef Runners, and other protective footwear that can be worn in and out of the water.

**6. WHAT TO BRING** You'll need a towel, suntan lotion, and money. Since wallets and purses get in the way, lock them in your car's trunk or leave them at your hotel. Carry enough money for the day and your Disney resort ID (if you have one) in a plastic bag or Tupperware container. Though nowhere is completely safe, we felt very comfortable hiding our plastic money bags in our cooler. Nobody disturbed our stuff, and our cash was much easier to reach than if we'd stashed it in a locker across the park. If you're carrying a wad or you worry about money anyway, rent the locker.

A Canadian reader offers another option if you don't feel comfortable stashing your valuables:

> As our admission was from an all-inclusive ticket, I was concerned about our multiday passes being stolen or lost, yet I didn't want the hassle of a locker. Once inside, I noticed several guests wearing small plastic boxes on strings around their necks, and was pleased to find these for sale in the gift shop. They're waterproof and available in two sizes for around $5, with the smallest being just big enough for passes, credit cards, and a bit of money. I would've spent nearly as much on a locker rental, so I was able to enjoy the rest of the day with peace of mind.

**7. WHAT NOT TO BRING** Personal swim gear (fins, masks, rafts, and the like) isn't allowed. Everything you need is provided or available to rent. If you forget your towel, you can rent one (cheap!). If you forget your swimsuit or lotion, they're for sale. Personal flotation devices (life jackets) are available at no cost.

**8. ADMISSIONS** Buy your admission in advance or about 45 minutes before official opening. If you're staying at a Disney property, you may be entitled to a discount; bring your hotel or campground ID. Guests staying five or more days should consider the **Water Park Fun and More** add-on, which provides admission to both Disney swimming parks.

**9. LOCKERS** Rental lockers are $7 per day for a small one and $9 per day for a large, $5 of which is refunded when you return your key. Small lockers are roomy enough for one person or a couple, but a family will generally need a large locker. Though you can access your locker freely all day, not all lockers are conveniently located.

Getting a locker at Blizzard Beach or Typhoon Lagoon is truly competitive. When the gates open, guests race to the locker rental desk. Once there, the rental procedure is somewhat slow. If you aren't among the first in line, you can waste a lot of time waiting to be served. We recommend you skip the locker. Carry only as much cash as you'll need for the day in a watertight container you can stash in your cooler. Ditto for personal items including watches and eyeglasses. With planning, you can manage nicely without the locker and save time and hassle in the bargain.

*un*official **TIP**
When lines for the slides become intolerable, head for the surf or wave pool or the tube-floating streams.

**10. TUBES** Tubes for bobbing on the waves, floating in the creeks, and riding the tube slides are available for free.

**11. GETTING SETTLED** Establish your base for the day. There are many beautiful sunning and lounging spots scattered throughout both Disney swimming parks. Arrive early, and you can almost have your pick. The breeze is best along the beaches of the surf pools at Blizzard Beach and Typhoon Lagoon. At Typhoon Lagoon, if there are children younger than age 6 in your party, choose an area to the left of Mount Mayday (ship on top) near the children's swimming area.

Also available are flat lounges (nonadjustable) and chairs (better for reading), shelters for guests who prefer shade, picnic tables, and a few hammocks.

The best spectator sport at Typhoon Lagoon is the bodysurfing in the Surf Pool. It's second only to being out there yourself. With this in mind, position yourself to have an unobstructed view of the waves.

If you've got money to burn, a handful of private covered seating areas are available at both Disney water parks for up to six guests at $319 per day. That includes your own lounge chairs, tables, towels, private lockers, a refillable drink mug, and a cabana boy who'll be at your beck and call. These seating areas are first-come, first-served.

**12. A WORD ABOUT THE SLIDES** Waterslides come in many shapes and sizes. Some are steep and vertical, some long and undulating. Some resemble corkscrews; others imitate the pool-and-drop nature of whitewater streams. Depending on the slide, swimmers ride mats, inner tubes, or rafts. On the body slides, swimmers slosh to the bottom on the seat of their pants.

Modern traffic engineering bows to old-fashioned queuing. At the waterslides, it's just one person, one raft (or tube) at a time, and the swimmer on deck can't go until the person preceding him or her is safely out of the way. Thus, the slides' hourly capacity is limited compared with the continuously loading rides in the major theme parks. Because a certain interval between swimmers is required for safety, the only way to increase capacity is to increase the number of slides and rapids rides.

Though Typhoon Lagoon and Blizzard Beach are huge parks with many slides, they're overwhelmed almost daily by armies of guests. If your main reason for going to Typhoon Lagoon or Blizzard Beach is the slides, and you hate long lines, be among the first guests to enter the park. Go directly to the slides and ride as many times as you can before the park fills.

For maximum speed on a body slide, cross your legs at the ankles and cross your arms over your chest. When you take off, arch your back so almost all of your weight is on your shoulder blades and heels (the less contact with the surface, the less resistance). Steer by shifting most of your upper-body weight onto one shoulder blade. For top speed on turns, weight the shoulder blade on the outside of each curve. If you want to go slowly, distribute your weight equally as if you were lying on your back in bed. For curving slides, maximize speed by hitting the entrance to each curve high and exiting the curve low.

Some slides and rapids have a minimum height requirement. Riders for Humunga Kowabunga at Typhoon Lagoon and for Slush Gusher and Summit Plummet at Blizzard Beach, for example, must be 4 feet tall. Pregnant women and persons with back problems or other health difficulties shouldn't ride.

**13. FLOATING STREAMS** Disney's Blizzard Beach and Typhoon Lagoon, Aquatica, and the independent Wet 'n Wild offer mellow floating streams. A great idea, the floating streams are long, tranquil inner-tube rides that give you the illusion that you're doing something while you're being sedentary. For wimps, wussies, and exhausted people of all ages, floating streams are an answered prayer.

Disney's streams flow ever so slowly around the entire park, through caves, beneath waterfalls, past gardens, and under bridges. They offer a relaxing alternative to touring a park on foot.

Floating streams can be reached from several put-in and take-out points. There are never lines; just wade into the creek and plop into one of the inner tubes floating by. Ride the current all the way around, or get out at any exit. It takes 30–35 minutes to float the full circuit.

Predictably, there will be guests on whom the subtlety of floating streams is lost. They'll be screaming and splashing. Let them pass, stopping a few moments, if needed, to distance yourself from them.

**14. LUNCH** If you didn't bring a picnic, you can buy food. Quality is comparable to fast food; prices (as you might expect) are a bit high.

**15. MORE OPTIONS** If you really are a water puppy, consider returning to your hotel for a heat-of-the-day nap and coming back to the water park for some early-evening swimming. Special lighting after dusk makes Typhoon Lagoon and Blizzard Beach enchanting; crowds tend to be lighter, too. If you leave the park and want to return, keep your admission ticket and have your hand stamped. If you're staying in a hotel served by Disney buses, older children can return on their own to the water parks, giving Mom and Dad a little private quiet time.

**16. BAD WEATHER** Thunderstorms are common in Florida. On summer afternoons, storms can be a daily occurrence. Water parks close during a storm. Most storms, however, are short-lived, allowing the water park to resume normal operations. If a storm is severe and prolonged, it can cause a great deal of inconvenience. In addition to the park's closing, guests compete aggressively for shelter, and Disney resort guests may have to joust for seats on a bus back to the hotel.

*unofficial* **TIP**
Because Florida is so flat, approaching weather can be seen from atop the slide platforms at the swimming parks. Especially if you're dependent on Disney buses, leave the park early when you see a storm moving in.

We recommend you monitor the local weather forecast the day before you go, checking again in the morning before leaving for the water park. Scattered thundershowers are to be expected, but moving storm fronts are to be avoided.

**17. ENDURANCE** The water parks are large and require almost as much walking as one of the theme parks. Add to this wave surfing, swimming, and all the climbing required to reach the slides, and you'll be pooped by day's end. Unless you spend your hours like a lizard on a rock, don't expect to return to the hotel with much energy. Consider something low-key for the evening. You'll probably want to hit the hay early.

**18. LOST CHILDREN AND LOST ADULTS** It's easier to lose a child or become separated from your party at one of the water parks than it is at a major theme park. Upon arrival, pick a very specific place to meet should you get separated. If you split up on purpose, set times for checking in. Lost-children stations at the water parks are so out of the way that neither you nor your lost child will find them without help from a Disney cast member. Explain to your children how to recognize cast members (by their distinctive name tags) and how to ask for help.

# WATER-PARK TOURING PLANS

ONE-DAY TOURING PLANS for Blizzard Beach and Typhoon Lagoon can be found on pages 839 and 840, respectively. These plans are for parents with small children; touring plans for adults, along with our online reader survey, can be found at **touringplans.com**. We'd love to hear from families who've tried these plans.

The plans presented here include all the slides, flumes, and rides appropriate for kids in both parks. Having brought our own children to these parks, we've also included tips on which slides to try first in case this is your child's first water-park experience. For example, at Typhoon Lagoon we suggest the family whitewater-rafting ride Gang Plank Falls as the first attraction. If your child enjoys that, we list Keelhaul Falls as the next step up in waterslides. If that seems a bit much, however, the touring plan recommends the Ketchakiddee Creek play area as an alternative.

# WET 'n WILD

**unofficial TIP**
Wet 'n Wild, though clean, is cluttered and not very appealing to the eye.

WET 'N WILD (on International Drive in Orlando, one block east of I-4 at Exit 75A; ☎ 800-992-WILD or 407-351-1800; wetnwildorlando.com) is a non-Disney water-park option. Unlike Typhoon Lagoon and Blizzard Beach, in which scenic man-made mountains and integrated themes create a colorful atmosphere, Wet 'n Wild's only themes appear to be concrete, plastic, and water. Fortunately, the thrill, scope, and diversity of its rides make Wet 'n Wild an excellent alternative to the Disney swimming parks. Besides, contrary to what some Disney execs might believe, their water isn't any wetter.

**Mears Transportation** operates a shuttle to Wet 'n Wild that stops three times a day at Disney hotels. It's the same shuttle that commutes between Walt Disney World and Universal Orlando. Cost is $20 for guests age 3 and older. If you're staying in Walt Disney World, in Lake Buena Vista, or along US 192, you'll need a car. If you're staying on International Drive, you can take the **International Drive trolley** (visit iridetrolley.com for schedules and fees). If you drive, a large Wet 'n Wild parking lot charges $12 per day for cars and vans and $16 for RVs. Parking is ample; just be sure to hold the kids' hands when crossing the street.

You can buy your Wet 'n Wild tickets at the main gate or at **wetn wildorlando.com/tickets.** Prices are about $56 for adults and $51 for children ages 3–9, and $58 for weekday season passes, but call or check online for special deals and discounts. For the same price as a single-day ticket, Wet 'n Wild offers a Length of Stay pass on its website that is good for 14 consecutive days. Ticket prices are similar to those of the Disney parks, but if you attend during the summer, the park is open late (hours vary, from 9:30 a.m. until 9 p.m. at the latest; call or visit the website for details), allowing visitors to hit the slides in the morning, go back to their hotels for lunch and a nap, and then return for a dip at night. Disney water parks typically close by 6 or 7 p.m.

When you get hungry, the main food pavilions are the centrally located **Bubba's BBQ, Manny's Pizza,** and **Surf Grill,** together offering such staples as burgers, pizza, and barbecued-pork sandwiches as well as more-nutritious (and nontraditional) items such as veggie burgers and tabbouleh. Wait times are long, and prices are high but not outrageous. For guests whose budgets and impatience thresholds are less flexible, feel free to bring in a cooler of lunch fixings (remember, glass containers and alcoholic beverages are prohibited, but you can purchase beer inside).

All the slides outside the **Blastaway Beach** kids' park have a 48-inch height requirement except for multipassenger slides, for which the minimum height is 36 inches if an adult accompanies the short rider; the only exceptions to this are the rides at the **Wake Zone,** with a height requirement of 51 inches (The Wild One) and 56 inches (Knee Ski and Wake Skating).

## BODY AND MAT SLIDES

*unofficial* **TIP**
Although ride attendants say that all three of the Mach 5 slides are equal, the center slide appears to be the zippiest route to the bottom.

SLIDES AT WET 'N WILD INCLUDE **Aqua Drag Racer, Mach 5, The Bomb Bay, Der Stuka,** and **The Storm.** Six stories tall, Aqua Drag Racer propels guests through four lanes of head-to-head competition at 15 feet per second. The Mach 5 tower, to the left of the park entrance, consists of three mat slides. The mats increase your speed and eliminate the chafing often experienced on body slides. To go even faster, try to get a newer mat with a smoother bottom. They're easily distinguishable: The new mats have white handles, while the old mats have blue ones.

Among the body slides (those without mats or rafts) are The Bomb Bay and Der Stuka, twin speed flumes with pitches up to 79 degrees that descend from the top of a six-story tower. On The Bomb Bay you stand on a pair of doors that open, dropping you into the chute. You have to work up the nerve to launch yourself on Der Stuka. The lack of a fully enclosed tube (such as the one on the Humunga Kowabunga speed slide at Typhoon Lagoon) adds the (perhaps justifiable) fear of falling off the 250-foot slides, but their ability to float your stomach somewhere near your teeth is a pretty unforgettable thrill.

The Storm body slide, near The Bomb Bay and Der Stuka, is a hybrid ride: half slide, half toilet bowl. The steep slide creates enough momentum to launch riders into a few laps around the bowl below before they begin slipping toward the hole in the center, eventually falling into a 6-foot-deep pool. The ride is exhilarating and disorienting; when the lifeguard at the ending pool begins hollering, just stumble toward his voice and give him a thumbs-up.

## RAFT AND TUBE RIDES

THE HEADLINERS AT WET 'N WILD are the raft and tube rides, including **Brain Wash, Disco H2O, The Surge, The Black Hole,** the **Bubba Tub, The Flyer,** and **The Blast.** Brain Wash is an extreme six-story tube ride with a 53-foot vertical drop into a 65-foot funnel; tubes hold two or four riders. Disco H2O holds up to four people in one raft, ushering them down a long tube into a 1970s-era nightclub complete with lights, music, and a disco ball. The basic design of the ride is similar to that of The Storm (a long tube into a bowl), only not as frantic and disorienting; the disco theme, coupled with the fluidity of the ride, makes it a main draw.

The Surge launches from the same tower as Disco H2O and uses the same four-person rafts. Riders spin down the open-air course, drifting high onto the walls on each banked corner. To reach the top of the walls, try to go with a full raft—as with all raft rides, the more riders squeezed in, the faster you'll all go. Directly across from The

Surge's splashdown pool is the entrance for The Black Hole. Bring a partner for this one; The Black Hole requires two riders on each raft, and honestly, who wants to embark into endless murk without some company? As impressive as the ride seems from afar, the anxiety created by the gaping entrance is the most exciting part of the ride. Yes, it's dark—a piece of green track lighting runs the length of the entire course—but besides the darkness, the ride lacks the dips and turns found on the other slides. If you're claustrophobic and scared of the dark, this isn't the ride for you; if tight spaces and inky blackness don't give you a rush, then this ride isn't for you either.

The three gentler raft rides are The Flyer, The Blast, and the Bubba Tub. The first two launch from the same tower as the Mach 5, but their entrance is accessible through the Blastaway Beach kids' area. At the base of the entrance are one- and two-person rafts; these are only for The Blast, so don't carry them up to the tower to the Flyer entrance. The Flyer is a calmer, toboggan-style ride in which riders sit one behind the other; it's suitable for families with smaller children. The Blast is a themed ride, like Disco H20, and is the wettest you can get without swimming. The theme of The Blast appears to be a broken waterworks, complete with spinning dials and broken pipes, all painted in comic book red and yellow. From mist to falling water to spraying pipes, this is the best way to cool off at Wet 'n Wild. The Bubba Tub, across the park from The Flyer and The Blast, is a long, straight track with three hummocks to impede momentum, but with a full tube of four people, you hit the "tub" at a pretty good clip.

## OTHER ATTRACTIONS

THE CENTRAL FIXTURE at Wet 'n Wild, the **Surf Lagoon** wave pool, is on par with Blizzard Beach's. Unlike at Typhoon Lagoon, there's no surfing in this wave pool, but you can rent tubes at the main rental stand or go bobbing with your body. The wave-making machine takes long breaks every day, so when you walk by and see waves, be sure to wade in.

Another any-time-of-day option is the **Lazy River**. Don't be fooled by the name, though: The circuit is short, the current fast—nothing lazy about it. Don't even bother trying to walk upstream to catch a tube; it's better to swim down the river or wait patiently until one passes within reach.

Wet 'n Wild's 1-acre **Blastaway Beach** is a small-fry version of the adult menu. It's to the left of the main gate; look for the oversize sand castle capped off with a big blue bucket. The bucket actually fills with water and tips over, soaking the people in front of the castle. Blastaway Beach is the largest water-park playground in Florida. The giant sand castle alone spans two pools (upper and lower), covering over 15,000 square feet with over 85,000 gallons of water powering over 100 soakers, jets, waterfalls, and water cannons; 15 slides; and the aforementioned bucket.

## WAKE ZONE

THE MOST DISTINCTIVE OFFERING AT WET 'N WILD is the Wake Zone, on a lake that's roughly the same size as the rest of the park and offering three different activities: wakeboarding, kneeboarding, and tubing. The lines can be considerable, especially since the attraction only runs from noon to dusk and is open on weekends only from mid-March to June, daily during the summer, and weekends only from September to mid-October. Be sure to call before going to Wet 'n Wild to see if the area is open that day. To avoid lines, wander over to the Wake Zone at least 20 minutes before noon.

At the boarding area, you can choose either a wakeboard or a kneeboard. Helmets and life jackets, provided free at the entrance, are required; the height requirement is 56 inches. The ride is basically a cable with hanging towlines that, like a T-bar at a ski resort, pull riders along the half-mile loop. You board from a slightly submerged dock where you grab the towline as it passes overhead. Brace yourself—towlines have a tendency to jerk. Keep your arms rigid and the nose of the board up. There are no instructors, so watch the other riders and chat up the good ones for tips while you're in line. If you fall down while riding, get out of the cable's path and swim to shore. If you fall where no dock is nearby, a Jet Ski will come and pick you up.

The name of the tubing ride is **The Wild One.** For an extra fee ($6 per person), a Jet Ski will pull you around the lake while you sit in an inner tube. The ride lasts five minutes, but it's worth the money if you've never been tubing before.

# ■ **AQUATICA** *by* **SEAWORLD**

AQUATICA IS ACROSS INTERNATIONAL DRIVE from the back side of SeaWorld. From Kissimmee, Walt Disney World, and Lake Buena Vista, take I-4 east, exit onto the Central Florida Parkway, and then bear left on International Drive. From Universal Studios, take I-4 west to FL 528 and from there exit onto International Drive. Admission prices are actually a little higher than those of the Disney water parks if you purchase at the gate: $60 for adults and $54 for kids. Tickets purchased online are $10 cheaper, and off-season specials available online can reduce admission to as little as $20. Standard parking is $12 ($16 for RVs, $16 for preferred parking, $25 for valet parking). If you don't want to wait in a queue to purchase tickets, buy them in advance at **aquatica byseaworld.com,** or use the credit-card ticket machines to the left of Aquatica's main entrance.

Aquatica is comparable in size to the other water theme parks in the area. Attractively landscaped with palms, ferns, and tropical flowers, it's far less themed than Disney's Typhoon Lagoon and Blizzard Beach but much greener and more aesthetically appealing than Wet 'n Wild. Promotional material suggests that Aquatica is unique by virtue of combining SeaWorld's signature marine-animal exhibits with the expected water-park assortment of wave pools, slides, and creek floats. Marine exhibits, however, start and end with a float-through tank of tropical fish and a pool of black-and-white Commerson's dolphins. Print, web, and television ads for the park show guests viewing the dolphins while descending through a see-through tube on the

**Dolphin Plunge** body slide—a corkscrewing romp through a totally dark tube until you blast through the clear tube at the end. The reality, however, is that you're flushed through the clear tube so fast, and with so much water splashing around your face, that it's pretty much impossible to see anything. At Aquatica, the best option by far is to view the dolphins from the walkway surrounding the exhibit or from the subsurface viewing windows.

A Yorkshire, England, woman reacted to the Dolphin Plunge:

> *The slide had the longest queue in the park. We queued for the best part of an hour and all agreed that it was a waste of time! You can barely see through the* transparent *part of the tube where the dolphins are (if you're lucky!), the slide is short, and the see-through bit lasts about 2 seconds!*

SeaWorld's promotion hype, coupled with the location of the Plunge just inside the park entrance and the slide's low carrying capacity (about 280 persons per hour), ensures that the slide stays mobbed all day. To experience the slide without a long wait, be on hand at park opening and ride first thing.

The first new slide at Aquatica in years, **Ihu's Breakaway Falls** artfully blends hanging (without a noose) and being flushed down a really big toilet. But first you have to climb the equivalent of 10 stories of stairs. Once you haul yourself to the top of the tower and are revived, you step into one of three tubes with Plexiglas doors. At some undetermined time (Aquatica staff dither around to build your anxiety), a trapdoor opens under you, gallowslike, and down you go. Each tube offers a different ride, but all three include big vertical drops, pitched drops, and corkscrews (the toilet part). A fourth tube at the top of the tower provides a wild but less intimidating ride, with the usual sit-down-and-off-you-go launch.

**Omaka Rocka** is a wide-diameter, one-person enclosed tube ride. The name derives from the wave action inside the tube, which washes you alternately up one side of the tube and then the other.

Other slides include **Tassie's Twisters,** in which an enclosed tube slide spits you into an open bowl where you careen around the bowl's edge much in the manner of the ball in a roulette wheel. Close to the Dolphin Plunge, Tassie's Twisters should be your second early-morning stop. Next, head over to **Walhalla Wave** and **HooRoo Run,** both on the park's far right side. Both slides use circular rafts that can accommodate up to three people. Walhalla Wave splashes down an enclosed twisting tube, while HooRoo Run is an open-air run down a steep, straight, undulating slide. The same entrance serves both slides. Line up for Walhalla Wave (vastly more popular) on the right, for HooRoo Run on the left. Make Walhalla Wave your third slide of the day, followed by HooRoo Run.

Then pass along the right side of the children's adventure area, **Walkabout Waters,** to **Taumata Racer,** the park's highest-capacity slide with eight enclosed corkscrewing tubes. The remaining slide is **Whanau Way,** all the way across the park to the left of the entrance. Sporting one corkscrew and a few twists, Whanau Way employs tubes that can carry one or two people. Because it's hard to see from the park entrance, Whanau Way doesn't attract long lines until midmorning.

Taken as a whole, the slides at Aquatica are not nearly as interesting, thrilling, or imaginative as those of its competitors, and aside from whisking you through a dolphin tank, they don't break any new ground. Also, all the slides except HooRoo Run have you launching yourself down a black hole, making every ride seem like the one before it. Dark slides are an essential part of every water-park lineup, but to have all slides dark save one makes for a very homogenized experience.

In addition to the slides, Aquatica offers side-by-side wave pools, **Cutback Cove** and **Big Surf Shores.** This arrangement allows one cove to serve up body-surfing waves while the other puts out gently bobbing floating waves. A spacious beach arrayed around the coves is the park's primary sunning venue. Shady spots, courtesy of beach umbrellas, ring the perimeter of the area for the sun-sensitive.

**Loggerhead Lane** and **Roa's Rapids** are the two floating streams. The former is a slow and gentle tube journey that circumnavigates the Tassie's Twisters slide. Its claim to fame is a section of the float where a Plexiglas tunnel passes through the Fish Grotto, a tank populated by hundreds of exotic tropical fish. Unique to Aquatica, Roa's Rapids is a much longer course with a very swift current. (The other water parks have floating creeks, but most are leisurely affairs where you can fall asleep in your tube.) Buoyancy vests are available, but most adults float or swim the stream. The name notwithstanding, there are no rapids, but the flow is constricted from time to time, considerably increasing the already fast speed of the current. There's only one place to get in and out, so if you miss the takeout, you're in for another lap.

When it comes to children's water attractions, Aquatica more than equals the other area parks. In the back of the park, to the right of the wave pools, is **Kata's Kookaburra Cove,** featuring a wading pool and slides for the preschool crowd. But the real pièce de résistance is **Walkabout Waters.** If you have children under age 10, this alone may be worth the price of admission. In a calf-deep 15,000-square-foot pool, it's an immense three-story interactive playground set with slides, stairs, rope bridges, landings, and more. Water sprays, spritzes, pulsates, and plops at you from every conceivable angle. Randomly placed plastic squirting devices allow kids to take aim at unsuspecting adults, but the kids disperse quickly when either of two huge buckets dumps hundreds of gallons of water down on the entire structure. It's impossible not to get wet. It's also impossible not to have fun.

As at the other water parks, there are lockers, towels, wheelchairs, and strollers to rent, gift shops to browse, and places to eat. The three restaurants are **WaterStone Grill,** offering specialty sandwiches, fried fish, wraps, and salads; **Banana Beach,** an all-you-can-eat venue dishing up burgers, hot dogs, and chicken; and **Mango Market,** a diminutive eatery serving pizza, wraps, and salads. WaterStone Grill and Mango Market serve beer.

# PART TWENTY-ONE

# BEYOND *the* PARKS

## DOWNTOWN DISNEY, *a.k.a.* DISNEY SPRINGS

DOWNTOWN DISNEY IS A SHOPPING, dining, and entertainment development strung along the banks of Village Lake. In the years since the nighttime-entertainment venues at Pleasure Island were closed, the powers-that-be have struggled to formulate an overall vision for Downtown Disney. After several fitful attempts, Disney decided in 2013 on an expansion with a Florida-waterfront-town theme. Called **Disney Springs,** it will comprise the current three Downtown Disney areas and add a fourth. Pleasure Island will become **The Landing.** As the name implies, it lies along the lake on one side and faces a new area, **Town Center,** on the opposite side of the development's namesake springs, the centerpiece of the expansion. Town Center will be built out toward the parking lot.

To the east of Town Center and The Landing is the **Marketplace,** with an expanded World of Disney store. It's connected by bridge to Disney's Saratoga Springs Resort & Spa. Anchoring the opposite end of the complex is the **West Side,** featuring elevated observation platforms, restaurants, shops, a bowling venue, and a Cirque du Soleil show. In addition to pedestrian walkways, West Side, The Landing, and Marketplace will be connected by water taxi. Scheduled for completion in 2016, Disney Springs will expand from 75 to more than 150 shopping, dining, and entertainment venues.

Downtown Disney–Disney Springs is a Disney bus hub and transfer point. It's also accessible by boat from Port Orleans French Quarter and Riverside, Saratoga Springs and Treehouse Villas, and Old Key West. Boats depart every 20 minutes 10 a.m.–4:30 p.m. and every 10 minutes 4:30–11:30 p.m. A new pedestrian bridge will span the waterway between Saratoga Springs and Marketplace, shortening the walk.

Turn the page for a sneak peek at Disney Springs post-redevelopment; see pages 754 and 755 in Part Twenty-Two for a current map of the area's shopping opportunities.

## Disney Springs: A Sneak Preview

*Village Lake*

Amphitheater

The Landing

West Side

Observatory

## MARKETPLACE

ALTHOUGH THE MARKETPLACE OFFERS interactive fountains, a couple of playgrounds, a lakeside amphitheater, and watercraft rentals, it's primarily a shopping and dining venue. The centerpiece of shopping is the 50,000-square-foot **World of Disney,** the largest store in the world selling Disney-trademark merchandise.

At **Disney Design-a-Tee** you can create customized T-shirts, and **Mickey's Pantry** offers Disney home and kitchen products, including the Donald Duck Press (joke!). Another noteworthy retailer is the **LEGO Imagination Center,** showcasing a number of huge and unbelievable sculptures made entirely of LEGO "bricks." Spaceships, sea serpents, sleeping tourists, and dinosaurs are just a few of the sculptures on display. **Once Upon a Toy** is a toys, games, and collectibles superstore. Rounding out the selection are stores specializing in resort wear, athletic attire and gear, Christmas decorations, Disney art and collectibles, and handmade craft items. Most retail establishments are open from 9:30 a.m. until 11:30 p.m. Detailed coverage of shopping opportunities follows in Part Twenty-Two.

**Rainforest Cafe** and **T-REX** are the headliner restaurants at the Marketplace. The others are **Earl of Sandwich,** for deli Dagwoods; **Wolfgang Puck Express Cafe;** and **Ghirardelli Soda Fountain & Chocolate Shop.** A small **Starbucks** opened next to World of Disney in 2014, along with a much larger location on the West Side. Downtown Disney's full-service restaurants are profiled in Part Ten, Dining In and Around Walt Disney World.

## THE LANDING

THROUGH 2014 AND INTO 2015, The Landing will be a construction zone, albeit with a promenade that connects the West Side and Marketplace on opposite ends of the expansion. When complete, The Landing will feature shops, restaurants, and docks.

## TOWN CENTER

WHEN FINISHED, Town Center will feature "one-of-a kind" shopping opportunities as well as several restaurants. Like The Landing, it will be a work-in-progress well into 2015. The architecture in the concept art seems more Mission style than the announced Florida-waterfront theme. The gateway and grand entry to Disney Springs will include a signature water tower.

## WEST SIDE

WEST SIDE OFFERS a broad range of entertainment, dining, and shopping. Restaurants include the **House of Blues,** which serves Cajun specialties (**The Smokehouse,** attached to the main restaurant, is a walk-up barbecue joint); **Planet Hollywood,** offering movie memorabilia and basic American fare; **Bongos Cuban Café,** serving Cuban favorites; and **Wolfgang Puck Grand Cafe,** featuring California cuisine. All four West Side restaurants are profiled in Part Ten, Dining In and Around Walt Disney World.

The West Side's new **Food Truck Park** features gourmet truck fare from four franchises. **Namaste Café** serves Indian-inspired cuisine such as butter chicken and tandoori shrimp; **Superstar Catering** serves meatballs (turkey, lamb, and beef) in a variety of sandwiches; **Fantasy Fare** has ham-and-cheese sandwiches, corn dogs, and noodle salads; and the **World Showcase of Flavors** offers beef sliders, a lobster roll, and pierogis. Prices range from around $8 to $12.

West Side shopping is some of the most interesting in Disney World. For instance, there's **Pop Gallery,** selling high-end paintings and sculptures, and **D-Street,** offering "cutting edge" (that is, bizarre) apparel and Vinylmation figurines (see page 750). Other shops include a **Harley-Davidson** showroom; **Fit2Run,** selling running gear and fitness apparel; and a designer-sunglasses studio.

In the entertainment department are **DisneyQuest,** an interactive theme park contained in a building; **House of Blues,** a concert and dining venue; and a 24-screen **AMC** movie theater. Opened in 2012 is **Splitsville,** an upscale bowling, billiards, and dining venue covering 45,000 square feet on two levels. Prices are astronomical at $15–$20 per person. If you feel like getting high, try **Characters in Flight,** where you ascend 400 feet over Downtown Disney in a tethered balloon (the characters are painted on the balloon—don't expect to float around up there with Br'er Fox). The weather-dependent ride operates 8:30 a.m.– midnight, lasts 8–10 minutes, and costs $18 for adults (age 10 and up) and $12 for kids (ages 3–9). It's also wheelchair-accessible.

The West Side is also home to **Cirque du Soleil** *La Nouba,* an amazing production show with a cast of more than 70 performers and musicians. The House of Blues concert hall and *La Nouba* are described in Part Twenty-Three, Nightlife In and Out of Walt Disney World. A discussion of DisneyQuest follows.

## DISNEYQUEST

THE LARGEST BUILDING IN DOWNTOWN DISNEY besides the Cirque de Soleil arena is the five-floor DisneyQuest, on the West Side. Billed as a virtual theme park, it was supposed to be the first of many DisneyQuests throughout the country. Unfortunately, the travel industry tanked in the early 2000s, and Disney found it too expensive to update attractions that rely heavily on both technology and parts that get a lot of wear and tear from guests.

These days, most of DisneyQuest is a quaint game museum. Your smartphone probably has better graphics and more computing power than most of the games, and nostalgia is more common than cutting-edge technology.

### DisneyQuest Tickets

You have multiple options for admission. A DisneyQuest visit is bundled with the **Water Park Fun and More** admission add-on (see page 55) and the **Premium Annual Pass** (see page 56). Everyone else must purchase separate admission. Adult admission to DisneyQuest is $48, and kids 3–9 years old pay $42. Frankly, we find the cost out of proportion to the entertainment value offered.

### DisneyQuest Discounts

The best discount for DisneyQuest admission for people who haven't bought the WPFAM option is to buy in advance from **Undercover Tourist** (see page 59). Regular Annual Pass holders and Disney Vacation Club members receive a gate discount; if you arrive close to closing, you may be offered a discount may be offered as well. Surprisingly, Disney does not offer DisneyQuest tickets for advance purchase on its website.

## Recommended Attractions

Visitors arrive at the **VenturePort,** the third floor of the building, by elevator; from here, they can then either take the stairs or another elevator to the other floors. Dining options are on the fourth and fifth floors.

We enjoy the attractions that are truly interactive. **CyberSpace Mountain** (on the second floor, in the **Create Zone**) lets you design and ride your own virtual roller coaster, and, while it isn't as advanced as the very similar Sum of All Thrills at Epcot (see page 559), it's still pretty fun. Despite graphics that are rather primitive by today's standards, **Virtual Jungle Cruise** and **Pirates of the Caribbean—Battle for Buccaneer Gold,** both in the first floor's **Explore Zone,** score points with us for active (and sometimes exhausting) physical interaction. Kids will enjoy **Mighty Ducks Pinball Spin,** and **Buzz Lightyear's AstroBlasters** is a fun take on bumper cars, with the added bonus of shooting basketballs at your opponents' (protected by a cage) car.

Anyone who remembers changing dollar bills for quarters at the mall will enjoy the classic video games and air hockey in the **Replay Zone** (floors five and three; all games are set for free play). We've even played games we've never seen before, like very fun head-to-head **Pac-Man** and **Tetris,** with up to four players on a large screen. Hidden among the classics is a one-of-a-kind, real-life **Fix-It Felix Jr.,** from the Disney animated movie *Wreck-It Ralph*.

We don't recommend any of the virtual-reality games that require you to wear VR goggles, such as **Aladdin's Magic Carpet Ride** and **Ride the Comix.** The graphics are rudimentary at best and have a strong likelihood of inducing motion sickness in even the strongest of stomachs.

While nearly every game at DisneyQuest can be played at no charge, there are a few exceptions. Claw-type games where you try to retrieve a prize have a charge. Also, nearly everything in the second-floor **Create Zone** is free to play but flogs a souvenir you can buy later, such as a recording or drawing. You may want to keep this in mind if you're trying to keep costs down.

## Crowds and Hours

DisneyQuest opens for business at 11:30 a.m. and closes around 10 or 11 p.m., before the rest of Downtown Disney closes. Rainy or exceptionally hot days will bring out guests to enjoy some indoor, air-conditioned fun, but for the most part, crowds are light and there's not much queuing for the more popular games.

*un*official **TIP**
Weekday mornings are the least crowded times to visit DisneyQuest.

Note that several major attractions at DisneyQuest have a height requirement of up to 51 inches. Smaller kids will appreciate the console games and the air hockey tables, made especially for them to be able to reach.

Reader response to DisneyQuest is very mixed, as evidenced by the following comments.

From a Pennsylvania family with kids ages 11 and 13:

*Our only really big disappointment was DisneyQuest. My husband and daughters paid $48 to get in because the guy at the window told us that fee covered nearly all the experiences. Once inside, they found that at least half the stuff they wanted to do cost mega-extra-bucks. It's truly offensive deal for people who have already spent scads in their darned parks.*

But for a Cleveland family of five, DisneyQuest was a slam dunk:

*If you have right-brained (creative) kids, you can't miss at DQ. Your book said 2–5 hours for the experience. We had dinner reservations that forced a cutoff at 7 hours, otherwise we could have pulled an all-nighter! The interactive stuff was fascinating. I think DQ provides parents the best chance to see their kids' brains and personalities in action.*

A family from Columbia, Maryland, offers this advice to parents with babies and toddlers:

*Alert your readers to bring a baby carrier–backpack to DisneyQuest. You're there for several hours, and absolutely no strollers are allowed in the entire building. [Authors' note: There is a coat check on the first floor where you can leave your stroller.]*

# ESPN WIDE WORLD *of* SPORTS COMPLEX

THIS 220-ACRE, STATE-OF-THE-ART competition and training center consists of a 9,500-seat ballpark, a fieldhouse, and dedicated venues for baseball, softball, tennis, track and field, beach volleyball, and 27 other sports. From Little League Baseball to rugby to beach volleyball, the complex hosts a mind-boggling calendar of professional and amateur competitions.

In late winter and early spring, the complex is the spring-training home of the Atlanta Braves. While Disney guests are welcome at the ESPN Wide World of Sports as paying spectators (prices vary according to event), none of the facilities are available for guests unless they're participants in a scheduled, organized competition. To learn which sporting events, including Major League Baseball exhibition games, are scheduled during your visit, call ☎ 407-939-GAME (4263) or check the online calendar at **disneyworldsports.com.**

The complex is also home to Orlando's Major League Soccer team, the **Orlando City Soccer Club.** Orlando City's schedule usually runs February–mid-September. Tickets start around $23.

Admission is $17 adults, $12 children ages 3–9 (prices include tax). Some events carry an extra charge. There's a restaurant, the **ESPN Wide World of Sports Grill,** but no on-site lodging.

Off Osceola Parkway, on Victory Way, the complex has its own parking lot and is accessible via the Disney transportation system.

# *The* DISNEY WILDERNESS PRESERVE

ABOUT 40–60 MINUTES SOUTH of Walt Disney World is the Disney Wilderness Preserve, a wetlands-restoration area operated by The Nature Conservancy in partnership with Disney. At 11,500 acres, this is as real as Disney gets. There are hiking trails and an interpretive center. Trails wind through grassy savannas, beneath ancient cypress trees, and along the banks of pristine Lake Russell.

More than 1,000 species of plants and animals call the preserve home. Birds include the bald eagle, red-cockaded woodpecker, Florida scrub-jay, wood stork, sandhill crane, northern harrier, and crested caracara. Other wildlife includes the southeastern big-eared bat, Sherman's fox squirrel, the eastern indigo snake, and the gopher tortoise. The Florida panther has been spotted here as well.

The preserve is open Sunday–Friday, 9 a.m.–5 p.m., except for major holidays; admission is free, but donations are welcome. For more information and directions, call ☎ 407-935-0002 or visit **tinyurl.com /disneywildernesspreserve.**

# WALT DISNEY WORLD SPEEDWAY

ADJACENT TO THE TRANSPORTATION AND TICKET CENTER parking lot sits the Walt Disney World Speedway, a 1-mile tri-oval course. It's home to the **Richard Petty Driving Experience,** where you can ride in a two-seater stock car for $144 (3 laps) or learn to drive one for $449 (8 laps), $849 (18 laps), $1,299 (30 laps), or $2,099 (50 laps); tax isn't included, but a $39 driver-release fee is. There's also a teen (ages 14–19) ride-along for $31 when a parent purchases the full-price riding option. For information call ☎ 800-BE-PETTY (237-3889) or check out **drivepetty.com.**

Also at the speedway is the **Indy Racing Experience.** Usually starting in the afternoon when the Richard Petty folks have finished, this experience features sleeker, faster open-wheeled cars like those seen in the Indianapolis 500. You can ride in a modified two-seat Indy car or drive one of the single-seat cars. The cost is $425 (tax included) for eight laps. For information call ☎ 317-243-7171, ext. 106, or 888-357-5002, ext. 106, or visit **indyracingexperience.com.**

For either driving course, you'll be paired with an experienced instructor who'll show you how the car handles, how the various gauges and pedals work, and most importantly, where to change into the flame-retardant driving suit you'll be wearing. If you choose to drive, the instructor will drive a pace car ahead of you and (we're told) will happily go as fast as you can demonstrate you're comfortable with—up to 180 mph in the Indy cars.

Both the Richard Petty and Indy experiences are by reservation only. Plan on arriving an hour before your appointment to fill out paperwork and go through an orientation session. To drive any of these cars, you must be age 18 or older, have a valid driver's license, and be able to operate a stick shift; for the Indy course, you must also be shorter than 6 feet 5 inches and weigh less than 250 pounds. Richard Petty riders must be at least age 14; Indy riders must meet the same age, height, and weight requirements as drivers. The Indy Racing Experience is closed around some major holidays and when Disney hosts PGA golf events, so check the website for schedules before you go.

For those more interested in how cool they look than how fast they go, there's the **Exotic Driving Experience,** which takes you six laps around the 1-mile track and incorporates the high banks of the speedway plus a Formula One–style street course. Prices range from $208 to $458 (including driver-liability release fee) plus tax, depending on the car; choices include a Ferrari 458 Italia, two variations on the Lamborghini Gallardo, a Porsche 997 S, and an Audi R8. Drivers must be age 18 or older, but there's a $99 ride-along option for those age 14 and older. For more information and online reservations, call ☎ 855-822-0149 or go to **exoticdriving.com.**

# WALT DISNEY WORLD RECREATION

MOST WALT DISNEY WORLD GUESTS never make it beyond the theme parks, the water parks, or Downtown Disney. Those who do, however, will discover an extraordinary selection of recreational opportunities ranging from guided fishing adventures and water-skiing outings to hayrides, horseback riding, fitness-center workouts, and miniature golf. If you can do it at a resort, it's probably available at Walt Disney World.

Boat, bike, and fishing-equipment rentals are handled on an hourly basis. Just show up at the rental office during operating hours and they'll fix you up. The same goes for various fitness centers in the resort hotels. Golf, tennis, fishing expeditions, water-ski excursions, hayrides, trail rides, and most spa services must be scheduled in advance. Though every resort features an extensive selection of recreational options, those resorts on a navigable body of water generally offer the greatest variety. Also, the more upscale a resort, the more likely it is to have such amenities as a fitness center and spa. In addition, you can rent boats and other recreational equipment at Downtown Disney Marketplace.

# WALT DISNEY WORLD GOLF

RECENT YEARS HAVE BROUGHT a stream of big changes to Walt Disney World golf, and this upheaval shows no sign of slowing down. In late 2011, after four decades, Disney stepped back from golf operations, turning maintenance and supervision of all its courses over to Arnold Palmer Golf Management. Visitors will notice little change, but Disney is hoping to increase visibility for its golf offerings with Palmer at the reins—an Orlando resident, he's among the most famous and well-liked athletes in the history of the sport.

As for Disney's golf venues themselves, the **Magnolia** and **Oak Trail Golf Courses,** across Floridian Way from the Polynesian Resort, envelop the recreational complex of the Shades of Green military resort, and the pro shops and support facilities adjoin the hotel proper.

The **Palm Golf Course,** in the same complex, underwent a major renovation by Arnold Palmer in 2013. Updates include modernized bunkers (94 of them!) and tees, and completely rebuilt greens. Some of the fairway grass is still rough in places, but that should even out once the grass gets a full growing season in. The updated Palm is 7,011 yards from the blue tees, 5,262 from the reds.

It's business as usual for the **Lake Buena Vista Golf Course** at Saratoga Springs Resort & Spa, near Downtown Disney Marketplace and across the lake from the redeveloping Pleasure Island.

The really big news is the reimagining of Disney's Osprey Ridge Golf Course as **Tranquilo Golf Club at Four Seasons Orlando.** Opened in September 2014, the course—which is also a certified Audubon wildlife sanctuary—will be shared by the new Four Seasons Resort Orlando (see hotel profile on page 251) and Golden Oak, a Disney-owned luxury residential development. Tom Fazio, who designed the original 1992 course, is also supervising the redesign, which involves contouring the greens and renovating/adding bunkers. A new par-3 hole (#16) will feature deep bunkering and sand and minimal greens. New club cars will make use of GPS technology; the updated clubhouse will have a pro shop and a restaurant called Plancha, serving casual Cuban-American fare in a lakeside setting. The course will be open to the public, not just Four Seasons guests and Golden Oak residents. Though Tranquilo is no longer an official Disney golf course, we've included it here due to its proximity to the World.

Back at Walt Disney World, the Magnolia has undergone substantial renovations and upgrades over the past few years. Oak Trail is a nine-hole, par-36 course for beginners. The other Disney courses are designed for the midhandicap player and, while interesting, are quite forgiving. All courses are popular, with morning tee times at a premium, especially from January through April. In addition to the golf courses, there are driving ranges and putting greens at each location.

*unofficial* **TIP**
To avoid the crowds, play on a Monday, Tuesday, or Wednesday, and sign up for a late-afternoon tee time.

Peak season for all courses is January–May, and off-season is May–October. Off-season and afternoon twilight rates are available. Carts, required at all courses except Oak Trail, are included in the greens fee. Tee times may be reserved 90 days in advance by Disney resort guests and 60 days in advance by day guests with a credit card. Proper golf attire, including spikeless shoes, is required. A collared shirt and Bermuda-length shorts or slacks meet the requirements.

Besides the ability to book tee times farther in advance, guests of Walt Disney World–owned resorts get other benefits that may sway a golfer's lodging decision. These include discounted greens fees, club rental, and charge privileges. The single most important, and least known, benefit is the provision of free round-trip taxi transportation between the golf courses and your hotel, which lets you avoid moving your car or dragging your clubs on Disney buses. (Cabs are paid with vouchers supplied to hotel guests.) Perhaps as a sign of tough economic times, Walt Disney World introduced discounted two-day, two-round passes at its four championship courses, taking about 30% off rates that are already good values.

The following chart summarizes prices for daily play at all Disney golf courses except Oak Trail; the cost of replaying the same course on the same day (if space is available) is half the full rate.

| TYPE OF ADMISSION | OPENING–3 P.M. | 3 P.M.–4 P.M. | 4 P.M.–CLOSING |
|---|---|---|---|
| Resort guest | $95 | $59 | $45 |
| Resort guest, 2-round pass | $120 | $120 | $120 |
| Day guest | $90 | $55 | $55 |
| Day guest, 2-round pass | $125 | $125 | $125 |

For more information, call ☎ 407-938-GOLF (4653); to book a tee time online, go to **golfwdw.com.**

## Lake Buena Vista Golf Course ★★★

**ESTABLISHED 1971   DESIGNER Joe Lee   STATUS Resort**

2200 Club Lake Dr., Lake Buena Vista, FL 32830; ☎ 407-938-GOLF

**TEES**

- BLUE: 6,745 yards, par 72, USGA 72.3, slope 133
- WHITE: 6,281 yards, par 72, USGA 70.1, slope 130
- GOLD: 5,910 yards, par 72, USGA 68.5, slope 125
- RED: 5,177 yards, par 72, USGA 69.7, slope 119

**FACILITIES** Pro shop, GPS, driving range, practice green, locker rooms, snack bar, food and beverage cart, and club and shoe rentals.

**COMMENTS** There are several memorable holes here, but this layout is the only one at Disney with housing on it—a lot of housing—which detracts from the golf experience. Nonetheless, the course itself is relatively pristine and was certified by Audubon International as a Cooperative Wildlife Sanctuary. The setting is geographically unique among the other layouts, tucked behind Saratoga Springs, and has a swampy feel reminiscent of the area's pre-Disney wetlands, with trees dripping Spanish moss. Narrow fairways and small greens emphasize accuracy over length.

## Magnolia Golf Course ★★★½

**ESTABLISHED 1970   DESIGNER Joe Lee   STATUS Resort**

1950 W. Magnolia/Palm Dr., Lake Buena Vista, FL 32830; ☎ 407-938-GOLF

**TEES**

- BLACK: 7,516 yards, par 72, USGA 76.0, slope 141
- BLUE: 7,073 yards, par 72, USGA 74.0, slope 137
- WHITE: 6,558 yards, par 72, USGA 71.6, slope 130
- GOLD: 6,027 yards, par 72, USGA 69.0, slope 121
- RED: 5,127 yards, par 72, USGA 69.6, slope 126

**FACILITIES** Pro shop, GPS-equipped golf carts, driving range, practice green, locker rooms, food and beverage cart, and club and shoe rentals.

**COMMENTS** Another fine Joe Lee creation, Magnolia is Disney's longest course and features a whopping 97 bunkers, including the famous one in the shape of Mickey Mouse's head. But the layout is slightly less challenging than the Palm's. Ten holes were lengthened and all greens resurfaced with TifEagle turf in 2005 as part of an "extreme makeover." This refurbishment added 300 yards to the already long course, and at more than 7,500 yards, it will be the longest most guests ever have the opportunity to play. Like the Palm, this course long hosted the PGA Tour (until 2012).

## Oak Trail Golf Course ★★½

**ESTABLISHED 1980  DESIGNER Ron Garl  STATUS Resort**

1950 W. Magnolia/Palm Dr., Lake Buena Vista, FL 32830; ☎ 407-938-GOLF

**TEES**
- WHITE: 2,913 yards, par 36
- RED: 2,552 yards, par 36

**FEES** Adult, $38; junior (age 17 and under), $20. Pull carts, $6 (course is walking only). Replaying the course costs an additional $19 for adults and $10 for junior players.

**FACILITIES** Pro shop, driving range, practice green, locker rooms, food and beverage cart, and club and shoe rentals.

**COMMENTS** This Ron Garl nine-holer is a "real" course, not an executive par-3 like many nine-hole designs. Geared toward introducing children to the game, it also makes a good quick-fix or warm-up before a round, and the walking-only layout is the only such routing at Walt Disney World.

## Palm Golf Course ★★★★

**ESTABLISHED 1970  DESIGNER Joe Lee  STATUS Resort**

1950 W. Magnolia/Palm Dr., Lake Buena Vista, FL 32830; ☎ 407-938-GOLF

**TEES**
- BLUE: 7,011 yards, par 72, USGA 73.7, slope 131
- WHITE: 6,479 yards, par 72, USGA 71.4, slope 125
- GOLD: 6,006 yards, par 69.2, USGA 71.4, slope 118
- RED: 5,262 yards, USGA 70.5, slope 126

**FACILITIES** Pro shop, driving range, practice green, locker rooms, food and beverage cart, and club and shoe rentals.

**COMMENTS** Completely renovated in 2013, with more-difficult bunkers and undulating greens. The greens play medium-fast to fast, so either go with a lot of spin and loft or try to bounce your shot on. Carts have GPS screens. Staff service is excellent. Beware the noise from the nearby Richard Petty Driving Experience raceway . . . and the alligator in the water at #9 (not kidding).

## Tranquilo Golf Club at Four Seasons Orlando

**ESTABLISHED 2014  DESIGNER Tom Fazio  STATUS Resort**

10100 Dream Tree Blvd., Golden Oak, FL 32830; ☎ 800-267-3046

**TEES** To be determined.

**FEES** To be determined.

**FACILITIES** Pro shop, driving range, practice green, locker rooms, restaurant, and club and shoe rentals.

**COMMENTS** See summary on page 744.

# ■ MINIATURE GOLF

YEARS AGO, THE DISNEY INTELLIGENCE PATROL (DIP) noticed that as many as 113 guests a day were sneaking out of Walt Disney World to play Goofy Golf. The thought of those truant guests making instant millionaires of miniature-golf entrepreneurs on International Drive was enough to give a fat mouse ulcers.

The response to this assault on Disney's market share was **Fantasia Gardens Miniature Golf,** an 11-acre complex with two 18-hole dink-and-putt golf courses. One is an "adventure" course, themed after Disney's animated film *Fantasia*. The other, geared more toward older children and adults, is an innovative approach-and-putt course with sand traps and water hazards.

Fantasia Gardens is beautifully landscaped and creatively executed. It features fountains, animated statues, topiaries, flower beds, and a multitude of other imponderables that you're unlikely to find at most mini-golf courses.

Fantasia Gardens is on Epcot Resorts Boulevard, across the street from the Swan resort; it's open daily, 10 a.m.–11 p.m. To reach the course via Disney transportation, take a bus or boat to the Swan. The cost to putt, including tax, is $15 for adults and $13 for children ages 3–9. In case you arrive hungry or naked, Fantasia Gardens has a snack bar and gift shop. For more information, call ☎ 407-wdw-play (939-7529).

In 1999, Disney opened **Winter Summerland,** a second miniature-golf facility next to the Blizzard Beach water park. Winter Summerland offers two 18-hole courses—one has a "blizzard in Florida" theme, while the other sports a tropical-holiday theme. The Winter Summerland courses are much easier than the Fantasia courses, which makes them a better choice for families with preteen children. Operating hours and cost are the same as for Fantasia Gardens.

Our favorite minigolf in Orlando is **Hollywood Drive-In Golf,** in Universal CityWalk next to Universal Orlando's parking garage (just off the walkway to the parks; 6000 Universal Blvd.; ☎ 407-802-4848). One hole has the Creature from the Black Lagoon spitting water over the walkway you need to pass through; another hole has a huge alien ship that you need to walk through and for which you need to press a button so that a door opens, *Star Trek*–style, to let you out. It's a nonstop barrage of clever in-jokes, insanely well-designed holes, and unique lighting elements. There's also an iPhone app for keeping score and misting fans for keeping cool. Open daily, 9 a.m.–9 p.m.; cost is $14 for adults, $12 for children ages 3–9.

# PART TWENTY-TWO

# SHOPPING
## *in and out of*
# WALT DISNEY WORLD

## ▌ HEY, BIG SPENDER

THE UNOFFICIAL GUIDE aims to help you see as much as possible, not buy as much as possible. But we acknowledge that for many people, a vacation is an extended shopping spree. If you're among these shoppers, you'll love exploring the stores at and around Walt Disney World. You'll notice that our touring plans keep you on track to see attractions, dissuading you somewhat from shopping. However, to give you a notion of what shopping means to an enthusiast, we share this letter from a Los Angeles couple:

> *Although your book discourages it, the shopping is a divine experience at WDW for those who like to shop. One doesn't shop in WDW for bargains (that's what flea markets, garage sales, and Target are for), but Disney buyers obtain a large selection of above-average to excellent-quality merchandise, much of it not available anywhere else (not even at a Disney Store or in a catalog). They're marketing geniuses! Not even the largest shops have all the merchandise they have to offer, hence, a shopper can make little discoveries in almost every shop. That, coupled with congenial, helpful Disney staff and services like complimentary hotel delivery, makes shopping an attraction of its own at WDW.*

And a woman from Suffolk, Virginia, advises:

> *Let readers know if they're into shopping to allot at least 6 hours for Downtown Disney Marketplace and West Side.*

Central Florida is a shopper's Mecca. With more than 52 million square feet of retail space, Orlando now has nine first-rate malls and three top shopping outlets, and millions of visitors from around the globe have retailers scrambling to keep up with demand.

Beyond the ubiquitous mouse ears and T-shirts, avid shoppers can find a wide array of items, from hard-to-find imports at Epcot's World Showcase to designer bargains from hundreds of off-price outlets. We figure you haven't come to Orlando *just* for the shopping, so we'll whittle down our lists to the best of the best. We'll take a look at all four Disney theme parks and Downtown Disney, then head for the other shopping hot spots around Central Florida.

There are too many shops to mention every single one, but we'll tell you what's special and point out the smart buys—along with the overpriced merchandise. We'll also tell you where to locate hard-to-find goods. If a shop has a special, not-to-be-missed quality, we've marked it with a ★.

## PIN MANIA

CALL IT A HOBBY OR AN OBSESSION—serious pin traders show up at the theme parks decked out in vests, hats, and sashes decorated with collectible Disney pins, always on the lookout for the one that got away. The mania started in October 1999 with the launch of Disney's Millennium Celebration, and today Disney churns out thousands of pins annually at its resorts around the world. The pins generally sell for around $8–$20, with one for every occasion, from new attractions to special events. The spot for the largest collection of pins is **Disney's Pin Traders** at Downtown Disney Marketplace.

There's a real camaraderie in the chase. Most agree there's no great monetary gain in the trade, just lots of fun. But there is "pin etiquette" (see "Disney Pinformation," below). For instance, pins must be cloisonné, semicloisonné, or hard-enamel metal and must be traded one at a time, hand-to-hand.

---

### DISNEY PINFORMATION

Since pin trading is such a serious business, here's a primer on Disney's pin-trading etiquette, courtesy of **disneypins.com:**

**1.** Pins should be in good, undamaged condition.

**2.** You can trade pins only one at a time. The back of the pin must be attached.

**3.** Guests may trade a maximum of two pins per cast member.

**4.** Don't touch a cast member's, or another individual's, pins or lanyard. If you want a closer look, just ask.

**5.** Pins must represent a Disney event, location, character, or icon.

**6.** "Name pins" cannot be traded with cast members.

**7.** If the cast member already has the same pin that you want to trade, don't even bother trying.

**8.** You may trade only one pin of the same style with a particular cast member.

**9.** Don't try to buy a pin from a cast member—not acceptable.

**10.** Pins from other business units of The Walt Disney Company, such as ABC, ESPN, and Disneyland, are accepted for trade as well.

---

Many Disney cast members wear lanyards festooned with the ubiquitous pins and happily trade with park visitors. Cast members wearing pin-trading lanyards can be found at all four theme parks, Downtown Disney, and some resorts.

A Michigan mom has the pin-trading thing figured out:

*I'm both a bargain geek and a Disney geek. I got a grab bag of 20 tradable pins for $1 each on eBay, plus I learned a trading tip this year: At Guest Services at every park, there's a book with many pages of pins to look at. My daughter scored a hard-to-find Perry the Platypus pin!*

And a Bloomfield Hills, Michigan, reader suggests:

*If you're buying pins to trade, buy a set. The per-pin price is much cheaper.*

## VINYLMATION

ANOTHER DISNEY COLLECTING CRAZE involves 3-inch vinyl figures in the shape of Mickey Mouse. Some are completely blank, allowing you to make your own design with markers and stickers. Others are already decorated with a variety of motifs, representing the Disney parks, Disney movie characters (from Mr. Incredible to WALL-E), and even an "urban" theme. The limited-release 3-inch figures are sold in opaque boxes, so you don't know what you get until it's opened. (For this reason, you can't return limited-edition Vinylmation merchandise.) There are 10–12 3-inch figures in each series, and the last design is kept a secret, adding to the intrigue of the collectible. Much like the pins, guests can trade Vinylmation with other guests and cast members. Though Vinylmation is sold throughout the parks, the biggest and most comprehensive selection is available at **D-Street** in Downtown Disney West Side, where you can also spend time at the Vinylmation Creation Station decorating your own blank figure with pens, markers, stickers, jewels, and more.

# SHOPPING *in* WALT DISNEY WORLD

## TIPS FOR DISNEY SHOPPING

AFTER EXHAUSTIVE RESEARCH in all four Disney theme parks, water parks, and resorts, we can assure you that Disney-brand merchandise is pretty much the same wherever you go. In fact, maybe too much the same, as a Denver family laments:

*unofficial* **TIP**
Beyond Epcot, shopping is hit-and-miss in the other three theme parks. You'll find the same basic Disney merchandise everywhere, with specialty items for each park tossed in. Nevertheless, amid all the Disney goods are some unusual shops.

*One problem is the homogenization of merchandise throughout the resort. This not only undermines the opportunity to find truly unique gifts and products in the shops, but it also dilutes or destroys critical theming—the dinosaur stores in DinoLand U.S.A., for instance, now contain very little actual dinosaur merchandise.*

The only big differences are a handful of items with logos for specific resorts or theme parks. So if you're short on time, save your shopping spree for one favorite theme park or for the **World of Disney** shop in Downtown Disney Marketplace, the largest Disney-character shop in the world.

Much like the merchandise, prices rarely differ across Disney property. A beach towel, for instance, was the same price at every location we checked. Ditto for sale merchandise: If it's on sale at one store, it's on sale in all stores (though you may not be able to find it at all locations).

**THEME PARK SHOPS WITH THE BEST DISNEY STUFF**

**THE MAGIC KINGDOM**
- **Emporium** Main Street, U.S.A. (largest selection at Magic Kingdom)

**EPCOT**
- **MouseGear** Future World (largest selection at Epcot)

**DISNEY'S ANIMAL KINGDOM**
- **Island Mercantile and Disney Outfitters** Discovery Island
- **Serka Zong Bazaar** Asia

**DISNEY'S HOLLYWOOD STUDIOS**
- **Animation Gallery** Animation Courtyard
- **Mickey's of Hollywood** Hollywood Boulevard

If you're staying at a Disney hotel, you can have your packages delivered to your resort from any of the four Disney parks. Packages will be delivered to your hotel's gift shop by noon of the following day, so this service is unavailable if you're checking out of your room the same day. Same-day pickup inside the theme parks is available. For a nominal charge, you can ship items to your home.

A New Brunswick, Canada, reader spread the news:

> So often I've seen beleaguered parents loaded like Sherpas, and I can't help but wonder how well known the parks' delivery services are. In Epcot I overheard two shoppers discussing whether they should buy a large pint glass; a major point of discussion was, "How would we get it home?" I chimed in to tell them all about Disney's Package Pick-Up service.

If you remember on your flight home that you forgot to buy mouse ears for your nephew, call Walt Disney World Mail Order Merchandise on weekdays at ☎ 877-560-6477, e-mail **merchandise.guest .services@disneyparks.com,** or visit the Disney Catalog online at **disney parks.com/store.** Most trademark merchandise sold at Walt Disney World is available.

## DOWNTOWN DISNEY

*unofficial* **TIP**
Except for specialty items and resort-specific merchandise, you can find a little bit of everything at Downtown Disney.

IF SHOPPING IS AN ESSENTIAL PART of your Disney vacation, we recommend that your first stop be Downtown Disney, which comprises four shopping areas, each with its own special feel: the **Marketplace, Town Center, The Landing,** and **West Side.** For the moment, The Landing and Town Center are the site of the three-year Disney Springs expansion project (see page 735 for a discussion). Both are being carved out of the former Pleasure Island nightlife district and will offer only limited shopping and dining until the project is completed.

Downtown Disney stretches along the shore of Lake Buena Vista at the intersection of Buena Vista Drive and Hotel Plaza Boulevard. It's a pleasant walk from the Marketplace on the east end to the West Side. The West Side has smaller shops with trendy merchandise; the Marketplace is loaded with Disney merchandise and a smattering of non-Disney products. So what you're shopping for determines the best place to park—free parking on a surface lot spreads from one end to the other.

| I NEED . . . |
| --- |
| Where at Walt Disney World is the best selection of a particular item? Here are a few recommendations: |

**BATHING SUITS**
- **Bou-Tiki,** Polynesian Resort
- **Curl by Sammy Duvall,** Downtown Disney West Side

**MEN'S CLOTHING**
- **D-Street,** Downtown Disney West Side   • **ESPN Club,** BoardWalk
- **Mouse About Town,** Disney's Hollywood Studios
- **Team Mickey,** Downtown Disney Marketplace

**WOMEN'S CLOTHING & ACCESSORIES**
- **Summer Lace,** Grand Floridian   • **Tren-D,** Downtown Disney Marketplace

**SPORTSWEAR**
- **Fit2Run,** Downtown Disney West Side
- **Team Mickey,** Downtown Disney Marketplace

**JEWELRY**
- **House of Good Fortune,** China Pavilion, Epcot (costume jewelry)
- **Uptown Jewelers,** Magic Kingdom
- **World of Disney,** Downtown Disney Marketplace (Disney-themed jewelry)

### The Marketplace

Hours at the Marketplace vary among shops, but most stores open at 9:30 a.m. Beat the crowds by arriving right when everything opens—it's usually nearly empty then, so you'll have at least an hour or two to enjoy the shops without the lines or flocks of other shoppers. There are more than 20 shops and 8 places to eat, including **Rainforest Cafe** and **T-REX.** Wheelchair and stroller rentals are available at Guest Relations (near Team Mickey). It's a comfortable place to stroll and people-watch. Near the central area is a carousel that runs daily; it's decorated with hand-painted renderings of the Marketplace shops. Cost is $2 per ride (there's also a kiddie train ride for around $2). If you don't mind the kids getting wet, check out the free "Fun Fountain" in the back of the Marketplace. Streams of water squirt out of the spongy sidewalk, soaking energetic youngsters on hot summer days.

The Marketplace is accessible by Disney bus or boat.

Longtime Marketplace shoppers have complained that the merchandise is "too Disney" and that all the unusual shops have disappeared and been replaced with Disney shops. You'll still find non-Disney merchandise (like clothes and swimwear), just not in the abundance of the old Marketplace.

## TOP SHOPS AT THE MARKETPLACE

**ARRIBAS BROTHERS** There's beautiful (and expensive) glassware and crystal at every turn, including an area dedicated to sparkling Swarovski pieces. *Not* the place to take rambunctious kids.

**THE ART OF DISNEY** Sells pricey original Disney art, from pottery to personalized sketch art, with a few affordable souvenirs in the mix.

**BASIN** Browse among wooden tubs filled with soaps and lotions, then scoop your own bath salts or build your own gift basket. All the store's products are chemical-free and made with natural ingredients.

**DISNEY DESIGN-A-TEE**  A store where guests can create custom T-shirts and personalized merchandise. Next door is **Disney's Wonderful World of Memories,** which offers stationery and scrapbook materials, as well as customizable ear hats—themes include sports, princesses, brides, grooms, and more.

★ **DISNEY'S DAYS OF CHRISTMAS**  This shop is just plain fun, with hundreds of holiday decorations from ornaments to stockings to stuffed animals wearing their Christmas Day best. We especially like the station for ornament personalization. A hot seller in all the Christmas shops is the Disney monorail train (also carried at some toy stores).

**DISNEY'S PIN TRADERS**  The spot for the largest collection of pins, with tables for trading and two Internet stations for visiting the official pin-trading website (**disneypins.com**).

**GOOFY'S CANDY CO.**  An interactive show kitchen with lots of sweets!

**GHIRARDELLI SODA FOUNTAIN AND CHOCOLATE SHOP**  You can smell the chocolate when you walk in, and most of the time a cast member is on hand to dole out free samples. Chocolate souvenirs abound, but treat yourself to a "world famous" sundae topped with the decadent hot fudge made daily at the shop. The line for ice cream often winds out the door—it's that good.

★ **LEGO IMAGINATION CENTER**  This is an ideal rest stop for parents, and you don't even have to go inside the store. A hands-on outdoor play area has bins of LEGOs that the kids can go crazy with while Mom and Dad take a break. Inside is all the latest LEGO paraphernalia. Check out the "sea monster" across from the store "swimming" in Lake Buena Vista.

**LITTLEMISSMATCHED**  Little fashion plates will have fun browsing the selection of funky printed socks, bags, and clothes. Socks are sold three to a pack in different patterns that you can mix and match.

**MARKETPLACE CO-OP**  Six shops-within-a-shop: **Beautifully Disney,** for makeup, fragrance, and beauty products (*Maleficent* lip gloss, anyone?); **Cherry Tree Lane,** for women's accessories; **D-Tech on Demand,** featuring

*Continued on page 756*

# Downtown Disney Shopping & Dining

**West Side**

**Town Center**
*(opens 2016)*

**Parking**

1. Cirque du Soleil *La Nouba*
2. DisneyQuest
3. Curl by Sammy Duvall/Fit2Run
4. Splitsville
5. House of Blues
6. Wolfgang Puck Grand Cafe
7. Bongos Cuban Café
8. AMC Downtown Disney 24 Theatres
9. *Specialty shopping:*
   Blink by Wet Seal
   Disney's Candy Cauldron
   D-Street
   Hoypoloi Gallery
   Orlando Harley-Davidson
   Pop Gallery
   Something Silver
   Sosa Family Cigars
   Sunglass Icon

10. Characters in Flight
11. Planet Hollywood
12. Paradiso 37
13. Raglan Road/Cookes of Dublin
14. Portobello
15. Fulton's Crab House
16. T-REX
17. LEGO Imagination Center
18. World of Disney/Bibbidi Bobbidi Boutique
19. *Specialty shopping:*
    Arribas Brothers
    Basin
    Ghirardelli Soda Fountain & Chocolate Shop
    Marketplace Co-op
    Tren-D

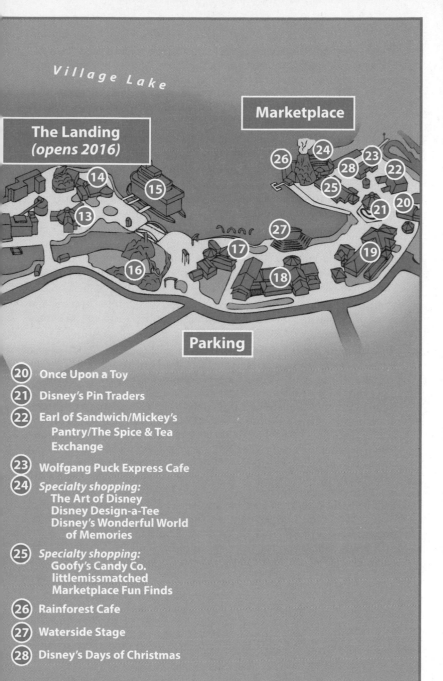

Village Lake

**Marketplace**

**The Landing**
*(opens 2016)*

**Parking**

20 Once Upon a Toy

21 Disney's Pin Traders

22 Earl of Sandwich/Mickey's
Pantry/The Spice & Tea
Exchange

23 Wolfgang Puck Express Cafe

24 *Specialty shopping:*
The Art of Disney
Disney Design-a-Tee
Disney's Wonderful World
of Memories

25 *Specialty shopping:*
Goofy's Candy Co.
littlemissmatched
Marketplace Fun Finds

26 Rainforest Cafe

27 Waterside Stage

28 Disney's Days of Christmas

*Continued from page 753*

phone cases and other electronic accessories that you can have personalized on-site; **Disney Centerpiece,** for fun home goods with that Disney touch (think *Enchanted Tiki Room* appetizer bowls and ceramic replicas of Dole Whip swirls); **The Trophy Room,** specializing in vintage-look sports apparel and collectibles; and **Zoey and Pickles,** where tween girls can find the latest fashions just for them.

**MARKETPLACE FUN FINDS** Disney-character merchandise organized into price points, including plush toys, clothing, and housewares.

**MICKEY'S PANTRY** A small shop with Disney home products, kitchen gadgets, and cookbooks. Also home to the **Spice & Tea Exchange,** which offers an assortment of one-of-a-kind teas and gourmet seasonings created and blended in Orlando.

**ONCE UPON A TOY** Five rooms of toys, from build-your-own Mr. Potato Heads and light sabers to a room dedicated to video games. Several favorites, including *Star Wars, Toy Story,* and *Transformers* toys, are on the shelves. Also for sale are miniature play sets of Cinderella Castle; plush animals; and plenty of pirate, princess, and fairy items.

**TREN-D** A fun, hip, urban-inspired boutique with fashion apparel and accessories, plus exclusive items from cutting-edge designers and Disney merchandise you won't find anywhere else.

★ **WORLD OF DISNEY** It's a superstore with 12 rooms—50,000 square feet—stacked with Disney merchandise. World of Disney is also home to one of Disney World's two **Bibbidi Bobbidi Boutiques,** sort-of salons that can turn your snot-nosed tomboy into a little princess (the second location is inside Cinderella Castle in the Magic Kingdom). At the boutique, girls can try on various princess costumes before repairing to the beauty parlor for hairstyling, makeup, a manicure, and even a princess gown, depending on which of the three packages you choose. Girls can choose between three hairstyles—Disney Diva, Pop Princess, or Fairytale Princess. At 2 p.m. daily, the newly minted princesses and divas are invited to participate in the Princess Parade. Holding onto a rope adorned with bells, the girls are walked from World of Disney to the carousel in Downtown Disney and given a personalized certificate. Call the boutique at ☎ 407-WDW-STYLE for more details.

Bibbidi Bobbidi Boutique costs a bundle, but this Northport, Alabama, mother of a 4-year-old thought it was worth it:

*Yes, we spent $200, but the look on my daughter's face was priceless as she walked to the castle to eat. Everyone spoke to her, calling her "Princess." There hasn't been a day in three months since we've been home that she has not asked to go back.*

If you don't have $200 in loose change lying around, there are alternatives, as a dollar-conscious Kalamazoo, Michigan, mom explains:

*The tip that tickled me the most in your book is taking little girls to the* **Harmony Barber Shop** *[on Main Street, U.S.A.] to get their hair done. I think I spent about $12, including tip. You don't need reservations, and in my opinion they do a better job than Bibbidi Bobbidi Boutique. They put my daughter's hair into a teased bun and use*

*brightly colored paints and colorful confetti to match whatever prin-
cess dress she had on. I understand that Disney doesn't want the barber shop to compete with the BBB, so I don't know if I want you telling anyone this great secret or not!*

### Downtown Disney West Side

The West Side opens daily at 10:30 a.m. This is the hip extension of the
Marketplace, with shops full of unique fashions and fun tchotchkes.

## TOP SHOPS ON DOWNTOWN DISNEY WEST SIDE

**BLINK BY WET SEAL**  The latest in denim for young women.

**CURL BY SAMMY DUVALL**  Offers men's, women's, and children's summer clothing, along with watches, sunglasses, and lots of bathing suits.

**DISNEY'S CANDY CAULDRON**  Watch as gooey treats are made in the
open kitchen. You can buy everything from jelly beans to caramel apples
and cotton candy—more than 200 sweets are on the shelves.

**D-STREET**  This shop offers an eclectic mix of urban-chic apparel for men
and women. It also houses the largest and most extensive collection of
Vinylmation figurines, apparel, and accessories, plus a Vinylmation Creation Station where you can customize blank figures with markers.

**FIT2RUN**  Running gear and RunDisney merchandise.

★ **HOYPOLOI**  Not a set of mouse ears in sight, but one of our favorite
shops, with one-of-a-kind pieces of art from various regions of the
United States—Zen water fountains, contemporary art, blown glass,
wooden boxes, and Judaica including mezuzahs and menorahs.

**ORLANDO HARLEY-DAVIDSON**  Sit on a real Harley and shop for Harley
outerwear, including men's and women's T-shirts and (of course) leather
jackets. You can even customize your own leather vest.

**POP GALLERY**  The sister store to Hoypoloi, this gallery-like shop features a wide variety of contemporary art, including limited-edition
sculptures and paintings, high-end gift items, and even a small collection
of inexpensive souvenirs such as art-instruction kits and brightly painted
ceramic piggy banks.

**SOSA FAMILY CIGARS**  They hand-roll 'em here and feature premium
imports, including Arturo Fuente, Cuesta-Rey, Diamond Crown, La
Gloria Cubana, Macanudo, Puros Indios, Padrón, Partagas, and Sosa.
A walk-in humidor stores the top brands.

**SPLITSVILLE**  This luxury bowling spot includes a large gift shop with
themed merchandise for bowling enthusiasts.

**SUNGLASS ICON**  Designer sunglasses and eyewear.

## THE MAGIC KINGDOM

BECAUSE THE MAGIC KINGDOM is usually the most crowded
theme park, you're best off browsing the shops in the early afternoon,
when attractions are crowded. Much of the non-Disney merchandise
that was once available here has disappeared from the shelves. For
instance, longtime visitors may remember Liberty Square's Olde World
Antiques, which sold unique brass, silver, and pewter, but today it's a

shop full of Disney Christmas ornaments. Or remember when The Yankee Trader stocked soufflé dishes and escargot holders? Now it's mostly generic Disney-themed kitchenware.

**MAIN STREET, U.S.A.** Because this area stays open an hour after the official park closing, you could save your shopping time until the end of the day; just be prepared for crowds. Two shops here are of note: If you want a monogrammed mouse-ears hat, ★ **The Chapeau on Main Street** has scores of them, along with a nice selection of other Disney-themed hats. At **The Emporium,** a Disney superstore, you can browse among four huge rooms categorized by kids' apparel, adult apparel, toys and costumes, and souvenirs. It's one-stop shopping if time is of the essence.

*unofficial* **TIP**
Store your purchases in lockers at the Main Street rail station while you tour, or have them forwarded from shops to Package Pick-Up and retrieve them when you leave the park.

Fun for browsing is **Crystal Arts.** Glassblowers entertain, and the merchandise includes jewelry, swords, Disney figurines, and traditional glass and crystal. Occupying prime real estate on the corner of Town Square, **Main Street Confectionery** is the biggest candy shop in all four theme parks, with every sweet imaginable. Watch as cast members make fudge and dip apples in caramel. For expensive jewelry, lots of Disney pins, and Lenox and Armani figurines, as well as some handbags and accessories, check out **Uptown Jewelers.** Lots of parents bring babies and toddlers to the **Harmony Barber Shop** (open daily, 9 a.m.–6 p.m.; make reservations in advance by calling 407-WDW-PLAY) for their first haircut, but anyone can stop in for a trim. For interactive spending, let the artists at **The Shadow Box,** a tiny kiosk in the alcove between Crystal Arts and Uptown Jewelers, snip your silhouette out of black paper (similar kiosks can be found in Liberty Square). Inside the Main Street Cinema you'll find yet another **Art of Disney** that replicates the merchandise found in the other Art of Disney stores around the parks, including the collectible fad Vinylmation (see page 750). **Box Office Gifts,** inside Town Square Theatre near the entrance to the park, sells a small selection of pins, as well as film and photo supplies, including picture frames and scrapbooks. It's also where you purchase the photos cast members take of you and your family as you enter the park.

**ADVENTURELAND** Across from The Magic Carpets of Aladdin, **Agrabah Bazaar** and the adjacent **Zanzibar Trading Co.** specialize in safari-themed clothing and toys, Aladdin merchandise, and moderately priced imports from Africa. The shops are worth a look solely for their wide selection of beautifully handcrafted African sculptures, masks, and pottery. Near Pirates of the Caribbean, the **Plaza del Sol Caribe Bazaar** carries an ample selection of Pirates merchandise, including costumes, play sets, men's and women's T-shirts, swords, eye patches, and Jack Sparrow dreadlocks. Young pirate wannabes can join Captain Jack's crew at **The Pirates League** in the same plaza, where three packages offer buccaneer makeovers and souvenir portraits (call ☎ 407-WDW-CREW). **Island Supply Company,** across from the Swiss Family Treehouse, carries men's and women's clothing from such designers as O'Neill, Roxy, and Quiksilver.

**FRONTIERLAND** The **Frontier Trading Post** has been converted into a Disney pin-trading and Vinylmation shop; **Big Al's,** a small kiosk across the way, sells a very limited selection of frontier-themed items. Those who forget to try the fudge at the Main Street Confectionery have another chance at the **Prairie Outpost,** a small bakery and candy shop. **Briar Patch** is a small store that sells apparel and hats for the whole family. **Splash Mountain Shop** sells Magic Kingdom merchandise.

**LIBERTY SQUARE  Ye Olde Christmas Shoppe** is a repeat of the holiday shops in all the other Disney parks. **The Yankee Trader Gourmet Shop,** near The Haunted Mansion, stocks primarily housewares such as character aprons, plates, and picture frames.

**FANTASYLAND** Shops are themed to the attractions, like **Hundred Acre Goods** at The Many Adventures of Winnie the Pooh. **Bonjour! Village Gifts,** in Belle's Village, sells apparel, plush toys, and other souvenirs. A favorite of little girls is ★ **Castle Couture,** with a large selection of princess costumes—Belle, Snow White, Cinderella, and others. A second **Bibbidi Bobbidi Boutique** is in the breezeway of Cinderella Castle. Reservations are strongly recommended; call ☎ 407-WDW-STYLE.

**TOMORROWLAND** The sci-fi stock in **Merchant of Venus** is limited to items with a Disney tie-in. You'll find a sampling of *Star Wars* products and other toys. A corner of the store is occupied by a photo station, where guests can have their faces transplanted onto a character from a favorite *Star Wars* or Disney scene. The adjacent **Mickey's Star Traders** is a general Walt Disney World souvenir shop. While the decor has a Tomorrowland theme, there's no space- or future-themed merchandise here. Neither shop is a must-see unless you're killing time. **Space Mountain Shop,** at the exit of the iconic attraction, features apparel and accessories and a large selection of cell-phone, tablet, and e-reader accessories.

## EPCOT

WE ENJOY WANDERING IN AND OUT of the shops in the 11 World Showcase pavilions, looking for unusual finds and bargains. Often you'll see sale items, especially in the shops in France and Italy, but most of the imported merchandise is relatively expensive. However, the Epcot shops may be among the few places in the United States that carry some of the merchandise found here.

Aside from World Showcase, two stores in Future World are worth a mention: **MouseGear,** on the east side of Future World, is the biggest Disney shop in any of the four theme parks. You can find almost any Disney merchandise here, and there's an enormous selection of adult and children's clothing. Prices and selection are about the same as at other Disney merchandise shops. On the other side of Future World is **The Art of Disney,** featuring framed artwork, Giuseppe Armani and Lenox figurines, and character models.

Walking clockwise around World Showcase, you'll find:

★ **MEXICO** The **Plaza de los Amigos** is a lovely re-creation of a charming Mexican city at dusk; here, a live mariachi band often entertains passersby. Carts and kiosks are piled with blankets, sombreros, paper flowers, animal sculptures, and tambourines. Sure, the merchandise may be cheaper south of the border, but these prices aren't bad: Piñatas are wildly popular, starting at about $10, while blankets start at about $20. Or pick up a good bottle of tequila or hot sauce to pack home. Two shops along the perimeter are **La Princesa Cristal** (a small crystal shop) and an unnamed store that sells leather handbags, wallets, and jewelry. **La Cava del Tequila** is a bar serving more than 70 varieties of tequila, plus margaritas and appetizers. For those who want to take home some spirits, tequila is sold by the bottle in the nearby kiosk, though the selection is mostly low-end.

★ **NORWAY The Puffin's Roost** is a series of small shopping galleries with popular imports such as trolls (from $15) and wooden Christmas ornaments ($4 and up). Other hard-to-find imports include Scandinavian foods and candies, Laila perfume and body lotion, and Helly Hansen and Dale of Norway clothing, including thick woolen sweaters. You'll also find sterling-silver jewelry, butterfly pins, and classic Viking hats (with or without braids).

★ **CHINA** This pavilion features one of our favorite shops, piled with imports from real silk kimonos to cloisonné and thick silk rugs. **House of Good Fortune** is more like a rambling department store than a shop. You'll find everything here from silk fans to $4,000 jade sculptures to antique furniture. The silk dresses and robes are competitively priced in the $100 range. Darling handbags are $10 and up, and silk ties are around $20. We always admire the handwoven pure-silk carpets, starting around $300 for a 2-foot rug and topping out around $2,500 for a 4 x 8–foot rug. The prices are comparable to what you'd pay in a retail shop—if you could find one that imports carpets like these.

**Village Traders,** a shop between China and Germany, sells African woodcarvings that are as unusual as they come. Every day, an artist carves new creations using a special tool called a *ngomo*. Another specialty here is beautiful bead jewelry, crafted in Uganda from repurposed Disney paper products such as old handout guides.

★ **GERMANY** Shops interconnect on both sides of the cobblestoned central plaza and purvey an impressive collection of imports. Tiny **Das Kaufhaus** stocks a nice selection of Adidas sportswear. Next door is **Volkskunst,** where the walls are covered with Schneider cuckoo clocks and the shelves are stocked with limited-edition steins and glassware. Next is **Der Teddybär,** featuring Engel-Puppen dolls and Steiff plush toys, among other delights for kids. Across the plaza, **Kunstarbeit in Kristall** carries a fabulous collection of Swarovski crystal, including pins, glassware, and Arribas Brothers collectibles (check out the limited-edition $37,500 replica of Cinderella Castle, blinged out with more than 20,000 Swarovski crystals). Next is the **Weinkeller,** with nearly 300 varieties of German wine. Step through the door to **Die Weihnachts Ecke,** where Christmas ornaments and handmade nutcrackers are on display year-round. Anyone with a sweet tooth will go crazy just smelling the most delicious addition to Germany's lineup, **Karamell-Küche.** Treats are made in-house with Werther's Original caramel, from caramel apples to cookies and candies made or drizzled with caramel. You'll also find an impressive selection of Werther's Original candies.

★ **ITALY Il Bel Cristallo** showcases Puma sportswear, Bulgari and Emilio Pucci fragrances, Giuseppe Armani figurines from Florence, elaborate Venetian masks, and a small selection of Christmas decorations in the back room.

**THE AMERICAN ADVENTURE Heritage Manor Gifts** carries patriotic gifts with a twist, such as American-made candy, and regional souvenirs.

★ **JAPAN** A US branch of Japan's 300-year-old **Mitsukoshi Department Store** stretches along one entire side of the pavilion. Kid-friendly merchandise—Hello Kitty, Naruto, and Yu-Gi-Oh!—fills the front, with kimonos, slippers, handbags, and lots more at the back of the store. Mitsukoshi's expanded culinary display includes a sake-tasting bar, along with chopsticks, pretty rice bowls, a large variety of teas and teapots, and imported snacks. Pricey Mikimoto pearls (rings, necklaces, earrings, and bracelets) are showcased in a separate room. And tourists line up for an oyster guaranteed to have a pearl in its shell (pearls are polished for you by the salesperson).

★ **MOROCCO** Several shops wend through this pavilion: **Tangier Traders** sells traditional Moroccan clothing, shoes, and fezzes; **The Brass Bazaar** features brass, of course, and ceramic and wooden kitchenware (not dishwasher safe); **Casablanca Carpets** offers a wider variety of Moroccan rugs, as well as decorative pieces such as abstract-shaped lamps, sequined pillows, and incense holders; and **Medina Arts,** which as of late appears to be an extension of the merchandise sold at the Brass Bazaar, stocks larger pottery and ceramic pieces.

★ **FRANCE** We always find a few moments to browse in **Plume et Palette,** a perfume shop with more than 100 imports. You'll find scents by Dior, Chanel, Givenchy, and other top names. Famed design house **Givenchy** recently opened a 300-square-foot cosmetics shop here—the only retail location in the United States to offer the full line of Givenchy makeup and skin-care products, as well as a large selection of fragrances. Cross over to **Les Vins de France** and **L'Esprit de la Provence,** two stores in one, with a wine room and a small selection of Provençal goods. At the back of the pavilion, **Souvenirs de France** offers T-shirts, traditional berets, *Aristocats* merchandise, and Eiffel Tower collectibles.

★ **UNITED KINGDOM** A handful of interesting imports is scattered throughout a half-dozen small shops. **The Toy Soldier** stocks costumes, books, and plush toys featuring English characters from favorite films, as well as British rock and roll–themed items, including Beatles merchandise. You'll find plenty of Alice in Wonderland, Peter Pan, and Winnie the Pooh merchandise here. Stop in **The Crown & Crest** to look up your family name in the coat-of-arms book, and the shop will create your family's insignia in a beautiful frame of choice. At the adjacent **Sportsman's Shoppe,** you'll find plenty of football (soccer) apparel, balls, and books.

Across the street, you'll find **The Queen's Table,** a gift shop with UK-themed clothing, glassware, and more. **Lords and Ladies,** a quaint store, offers lotions, soaps, scarves, jewelry, and perfume from the United Kingdom. **The Tea Caddy** stocks Twinings tea, biscuits, and candies.

Speaking of which, a Cambridge, England, reader found a little piece of heaven in Central Florida:

> You can buy English chocolate at [The Tea Caddy]. This is impossible to buy in America, and so I was over the moon!

★ **CANADA** There's not much shopping here, but **Northwest Mercantile** has a wide selection of merchandise, including NHL jerseys, T-shirts, sweatshirts, aprons, and pajamas. Bottles of ice wine and maple syrup make nice souvenirs for foodies.

## DISNEY'S ANIMAL KINGDOM

THOUGH DISNEY MERCHANDISE DOMINATES, Animal Kingdom has a fair selection of animal-themed items. The largest cluster of shops is in the centrally located Discovery Island: **Disney Outfitters** carries men's, women's, and children's clothing and animal-themed items, as well as a selection of Disney souvenirs. Check out the carved animal totem poles in the center of the room. **Island Mercantile** offers more (yawn) Disney-character merchandise.

In Africa, ★ **Mombasa Marketplace** and the adjoining **Ziwani Traders** showcases reasonably priced African-themed pottery, musical instruments, South African wines, and housewares, plus plenty of plush animal toys and a large selection of Animal Kingdom–themed merchandise. Asia has several open-air kiosks, but the main attraction in shopping is the ★ **Yak & Yeti Bhaktapur Market,** next to Yak & Yeti Restaurant. The venue is small but packed with extraordinary themed merchandise, including cast-iron teapots and tea sets; sushi kits and Asian cookbooks; bonsai kits; origami; and some beautiful Southeast Asian–inspired clothing and shoes. At Expedition Everest's exit is **Serka Zong Bazaar,** where the merchandise is more interesting than that of most post-attraction shops. Although mostly Disney-branded, the goods don't scream "Mickey Mouse." The selection is mostly Everest- and Yeti-themed, with T-shirts, sweatshirts, accessories, collectibles, and historical books and videos for those interested in the legend of the Yeti.

**Chester & Hester's Dinosaur Treasures** in DinoLand U.S.A. is worth a look simply to check out the amusing architecture. The atmosphere inside is reminiscent of a kitschy roadside stand—the merchandise is a mix of apparel, hats, coffee mugs, toys, DINOSAUR-themed toys, and Disney-branded souvenirs. **The Dino Institute Shop** has more dino-themed clothing, dinosaur figurines, books, and toys.

## DISNEY'S HOLLYWOOD STUDIOS

ON HOLLYWOOD BOULEVARD, on the right side of the street, shops include **The Darkroom,** for cameras, film, and accessories, and **Celebrity 5 & 10,** with men's, women's, and children's T-shirts and other small souvenirs. **Adrian & Edith's Head to Toe** has an embroidery station where you can get any Disney item embroidered with a name, phrase, or character of your choice. (One caveat: The item needs to have been purchased on Disney property and be unworn.) On the left side of the street, **Mickey's of Hollywood** carries plush toys, watches, T-shirts, hats, sunglasses, and more—virtually none without a Disney logo—while **Keystone Clothiers** offers an array of Disney wear for grown-ups. There's plenty to look at but not much to recommend.

On Sunset Boulevard, **Sunset Club Couture** carries a sizable stock of clothing and Disney collectibles. **Mouse About Town** features apparel and accessories. The **Planet Hollywood Shop** sells merchandise related to that franchise. **Legends of Hollywood,** also on the boulevard, is home to souvenirs and other gifts. **Rock Around the Shop,** at the exit of the Rock 'n' Roller Coaster, offers a selection of music-themed apparel and souvenirs like drumsticks.

Elsewhere in the park: ★ **Animation Gallery** in the Animation Courtyard carries an impressive collection of paintings, sculptures, and other artwork. You'll pay the same price here as in all the other Disney art galleries. You can pick up a hat or trench coat just like Harrison Ford's, or an Indy-style T-shirt, action figure, or Mickey plush at the **Indiana Jones Adventure Outpost** outside the amphitheater. **Stage 1 Company Store** carries a wide variety of Muppet- and *Phineas and Ferb*–themed merchandise; *Star Wars* fans will eat their hearts out at ★ **Tatooine Traders,** where everything from light-saber key chains to $200 glass light-saber collectibles is for sale. **In Character,** next to *Voyage of the Little Mermaid,* is the best spot in the Studios for Disneyprincess dress-up clothes and accessories for little ones. **Toy Story Dept.,** across from Toy Story Midway Mania!, offers *Toy Story* and Disney-Pixar souvenirs and toys.

# DISNEY OUTLET STORES

ORLANDO IS HOME TO TWO **Disney's Character Warehouse** stores at each of the **Orlando Premium Outlets (premiumoutlets.com/orlando)**— one at 4951 International Dr. (☎ 407-354-3255) and another at 8200 Vineland Ave. (☎ 407-477-0222). The I-Drive location (in the complex's Mall 1) gets liquidation merchandise directly from Walt Disney World stores, so you never know what you'll find. The Vineland location has even more sale-price souvenirs of similar selection and vintage.

# SHOPPING *beyond* WALT DISNEY WORLD

## CELEBRATION

"THE TOWN THAT DISNEY BUILT," near Walt Disney World off US 192 (**celebrationfl.com**), gets its fair share of tourists who like to stroll the sidewalks. No one shop is worth going out of the way for, but you'll find good restaurants here (including Italian, Spanish, and American), as well as a two-screen theater and a handful of shops. Because Celebration is an upscale community, the shops are all high-end.

Celebration residents often gather on the patio of **Starbucks** for a freshly brewed cuppa joe. Specialty stores include **Market Street Gallery,** with year-round Christmas décor, candles, jewelry, and gifts for the home; **Sanrio Surprises,** dedicated to all things Hello Kitty; **Woof Gang Bakery,** which sells fun items for furry friends, including fresh-baked treats; **Confetti,** a monogramming and personalized-stationery store that also sells candies and other snacks; **Soft as a Grape,** offering casual clothing for the whole family; **Jewel Box,** featuring fine jewelry, diamonds, and watches; and **Kilwin's Chocolates & Ice Cream,** an extraordinary confectionery.

## UNIVERSAL CITYWALK

WHILE DOWNTOWN DISNEY is 120 acres (with a strolling area equivalent to about 10 city blocks), CityWalk (**citywalk.com**) comprises

30 acres in a relatively compact area between the two Universal theme parks. It's undergoing expansion in 2014.

*unofficial* **TIP**
CityWalk is open 11 a.m.–2 a.m. (although some stores may close earlier). Parking, though plentiful in the Universal garage, costs a steep $17 before 3 p.m. but only $5 in the evening.

At both destinations, the shopping complements the restaurants and clubs. Without question, Disneyphiles will prefer Downtown Disney, where at least a third of the shops are Disney-themed. CityWalk is most comparable to the West Side at Downtown Disney—fun for browsing and impulse buys. Our favorites include **Fresh Produce,** featuring swimwear and loungewear for women, kids, and infants, bags and accessories, and more; **Quiet Flight Surf Shop,** with merchandise from beachy brands such as Billabong, Element, Hurley, Nixon, Oakley, Quiksilver, Reef, Rip Curl, Roxy, Volcom, and Von Zipper; and **The Island Clothing Company,** featuring upscale resort wear from designers such as Lacoste, Lilly Pulitzer, and Tommy Bahama.

Up for some ink? CityWalk also has a branch of **Hart & Huntington Tattoo Co.** For jewelry, **Fossil** has a notable collection of watches, as well as sunglasses and leather goods. **The Universal Studios Store** offers one-stop shopping for all theme park merchandise.

## INTERNATIONAL DRIVE

"I-DRIVE" IS THE HEART OF CENTRAL FLORIDA'S tourist district, jammed with hotels, motels, discount stores, and restaurants. Locals generally avoid the area except for the outlet malls (which we'll discuss separately).

On the more refined south end of International Drive is **Pointe Orlando** (9101 International Dr.; ☎ 407-248-2838; **pointeorlando .com**), with a handful of stores. This complex gets a lot of its business from the convention center, less than a mile away, rather than from locals. Hours are Monday–Saturday, noon–10 p.m. October–May, until 9 p.m. other months; Sunday, noon–8 p.m. (Bars and restaurants stay open later.)

Clothing stores include **Chico's; Armani Exchange; Hollister; Tommy Bahama; FLOW; Design by U,** with custom-embroidery options; and **Victoria's Secret.**

Among the specialty shops are **Charming Charlie,** an accessories and handbag shop; **Tharoo & Co.** jewelry boutique; **Image Leather,** featuring Italian-lambskin leather goods; **Sunglass Hut,** offering shades from Ray-Ban and Prada; and **Bath & Body Works.**

## OUTLETS

LIKE EVERY MAJOR TOURIST DESTINATION in the United States, Central Florida has hundreds of factory-outlet stores, most of them situated near major attractions. Having spent many hours checking prices and merchandise, we generally conclude that at most stores you'll save about 20% on desirable merchandise and up to 75% on last-season (or older) stock. Some stores in the outlet malls are full retail or sell a few brands at a 20% discount and the rest at full price.

**Orlando Premium Outlets–International Drive** (4951 International Dr.; ☎ 407-352-9600; **premiumoutlets.com/orlando;** open Monday–Saturday, 10 a.m.–11 p.m.; Sunday, 10 a.m.–9 p.m.), on the north end of I-Drive, features 175 of the world's hottest designers and brand names, among them **BCBG Max Azria Factory Store, Hugo Boss Factory Store, Kenneth Cole, Michael Kors, Saks Fifth Avenue OFF 5TH, Sean John, St. John Outlet, Tommy Hilfiger, Under Armour, Victoria's Secret,** and the only **Neiman Marcus Last Call** in Central Florida.

★ The second location, **Orlando Premium Outlets–Vineland Avenue** (8200 Vineland Ave.; ☎ 407-238-7787; **premiumoutlets.com/orlando;** open Monday–Saturday, 10 a.m.–11 p.m.; Sunday, 10 a.m.–9 p.m.), is off I-4 (Exit 68) at Vineland, near Lake Buena Vista. An impressive array of 150 stores includes **Banana Republic Factory Store, Barneys Warehouse, Brooks Brothers, Fendi, Armani Outlet, Joe's Jeans, Nautica, Nike Factory Store, Polo Ralph Lauren Factory Store, Salvatore Ferragamo, 7 For All Mankind,** and **Tory Burch.**

> *unofficial* **TIP**
> If you're picky, a major department store's end-of-season sales often yield deals as good as or better than an outlet store's.

Another popular outlet center is **Lake Buena Vista Factory Stores** (15657 S. Apopka–Vineland Rd.; ☎ 407-238-9301; **lbvfs.com**), on FL 535 near Walt Disney World. Hours are Monday–Saturday, 10 a.m.–9 p.m.; Sunday, 10 a.m.–7 p.m. We think the inventory is underwhelming, and the discounts are mostly in the 10–20% range. Key tenants include **Aéropostale, Crocs, Eddie Bauer, Gap Outlet, Justice, Levi's, LOFT Outlet, Nike Factory Store, Nine West, Old Navy, Oshkosh B'Gosh, Samsonite, Tommy Hilfiger,** and **Under Armour.**

## TRADITIONAL SHOPPING

THE PREMIER SHOPPING EXPERIENCE in Central Florida is **The Mall at Millenia** (☎ 407-363-3555; **mallatmillenia.com**), anchored by **Bloomingdale's, Macy's,** and **Neiman Marcus.** Other stores include **Anthropologie, Burberry, Cartier, Coach, Crate & Barrel, Gucci, Guess?, J.Crew, Kate Spade, Louis Vuitton, lululemon athletica, Tiffany & Co., Tory Burch, Urban Outfitters,** and **Versace.** Hours are Monday–Saturday, 10 a.m.–9 p.m.; Sunday, 11 a.m.–7 p.m.

★ **The Florida Mall** (☎ 407-851-6255; **simon.com/mall/the-florida -mall**) is the biggest in the area, with about 200 shops, including **Coach, Macy's, M•A•C Cosmetics, Nordstrom, H&M, Gymboree,** and **Sephora.** Go early and park near one of the major stores you want to explore. The mall is at 8001 S. Orange Blossom Trail, at the corner of Sand Lake Road (FL 482) and South Orange Blossom Trail (US 441); hours are Monday–Saturday, 10 a.m.–10 p.m.; Sunday, 12–8 p.m.

# PART TWENTY-THREE

# NIGHTLIFE
## *in and out of*
# WALT DISNEY WORLD

# WALT DISNEY WORLD
# *at* NIGHT

DISNEY SO CLEVERLY CONSPIRES to exhaust you during the day that the thought of night activity sends most visitors into shock. Walt Disney World, however, offers much for the hearty and the nocturnal to do in the evenings.

### IN THE THEME PARKS

EPCOT'S MAJOR EVENING EVENT is *IllumiNations,* a laser and fireworks show at World Showcase Lagoon. Showtime is listed in the daily entertainment schedule (*Times Guide*).

In the Magic Kingdom are the popular evening parade(s); *Celebrate the Magic,* in which a high-tech light-and-video show is projected onto Cinderella Castle; and the *Wishes* fireworks show. Consult the *Times Guide* for performances.

On most nights, Disney's Hollywood Studios features *Fantasmic!,* a laser, special-effects, and water spectacular (see page 622).

Disney's Animal Kingdom currently offers **Harambe Nights,** a summer event combining a retelling of the *Lion King* story with an outdoor party featuring food and live music (see page 595 for more information).

### AT THE HOTELS

A SORT OF MAIN STREET ELECTRICAL PARADE on barges, the **Floating Electrical Pageant** stars creatures of the sea. This nightly spectacle, with background music played on a doozy of a synthesizer, is one of our favorite Disney productions. The first performance of the short but captivating show is at 9 p.m. off the Polynesian Resort docks. From there, it circles around and repeats at the Grand Floridian at 9:15 p.m., heading afterward to Fort Wilderness Resort & Campground, Wilderness Lodge & Villas, and the Contemporary Resort–Bay Lake Tower.

For something more elaborate, consider a dinner theater. If you want to go honky-tonkin', the Buena Vista Palace, Hilton, and B Resort hotels at the Downtown Disney Resort Area have lively (all right, all right, *relatively* lively) bars.

Speaking of bars, Disney hotels, the BoardWalk, and Downtown Disney have them, too. Be prepared, however, for an odd wrinkle, as described by this reader:

*I understand Disney is all about kids, but we tried to go into a resort bar at 8 p.m. for some drinks, and there were three children running wild playing Duck-Duck-Goose. This would not fly in any bar at home, but we were told there was nothing to be done, as "It's Disney."*

If you're into family films, all Disney resorts offer outdoor movies each evening. The largest, most permanent screen is at Fort Wilderness Resort & Campground; other resorts use inflatable screens set up near their pools. Movie schedules are available at the front desk.

**AT ANIMAL KINGDOM LODGE** For children, there's African storytelling around a campfire each night, followed by a movie shown by the pool. In addition, kids can march around the lobby each evening at 8 p.m. during the **Zawadi Primal Parade.** Finally, guests can view animals after dark using night-vision goggles.

**AT THE BOARDWALK Jellyrolls** features dueling pianos and sing-alongs. **Big River Grille & Brewing Works** is Disney's first and only brewpub (see page 464). Completing the BoardWalk's entertainment mix are the **ESPN Club,** a sports bar; the **Atlantic Dance Hall,** an upscale but largely deserted dance club; and several restaurants. Access is by foot from Epcot, by ferry from Disney's Hollywood Studios, and by bus from other Disney World locations. The *Unofficial Guide* research team rates Jellyrolls as its second favorite of all Disney nightspots (**Raglan Road Irish Pub & Restaurant** at Downtown Disney is our top pick). It's raucous, frequently hilarious, and positively rejuvenating. The piano players are outstanding. Best of all, it's strictly for adults.

**AT CORONADO SPRINGS RESORT** Perhaps Disney's hippest nightspot is the 5,000-square-foot **Rix Lounge,** a Vegas-ultralounge clone. DJs spin dance tracks 6 p.m.–12 a.m.; a percussion band performs on select evenings. Few locals or resort guests have discovered Rix, so the place is frequently dead unless there's a big meeting or trade show at Coronado Springs. Also at this resort is the **Laguna Bar,** a romantic outdoor-terrace affair arrayed alongside the lake.

**AT FORT WILDERNESS RESORT & CAMPGROUND** The free nightly campfire program begins with a sing-along led by Chip 'n' Dale and progresses to cartoons and a Disney movie. For Disney lodging guests only. For the grown-ups, there's **Crockett's Tavern,** near Pioneer Hall.

## AT DOWNTOWN DISNEY

**PLEASURE ISLAND** Walt Disney World's nighttime-entertainment complex cashed in its chips in 2008. Gone for good are the BET Soundstage Club, Mannequins Dance Palace, Motion, 8 TRAX, the Comedy Warehouse, and the much-loved Adventurers Club. All the Pleasure Island restaurants survived, though, and have been incorporated into the new **Landing** and **Town Center** sections of the **Disney Springs** expansion (see page 735 for more info on this redevelopment). For now, the only live-music venues are **Raglan Road Irish Pub & Restaurant** (see page 487) and, occasionally, **Paradiso 37** (see page 485).

**MARKETPLACE** There's no nightlife here, but it's flog-your-wallet every night, with stores open until 11 p.m. Sunday–Thursday and 11:30 p.m. Friday and Saturday.

**WEST SIDE** This 70-acre shopping, restaurant, and nightlife complex is to the left of the Landing and Town Center sections. This area features a 24-screen **AMC** movie complex; **DisneyQuest**, a pay-for-play virtual theme park (see page 739); a permanent showplace for **Cirque du Soleil**'s extraordinary *La Nouba* (see profile below); **Splitsville**, an upscale bowling, billiards, and dining venue; and a **House of Blues.** concert hall with a seating capacity of 2,000. Dining options include **Planet Hollywood;** a Cajun restaurant at **House of Blues; Wolfgang Puck Grand Cafe;** and **Bongos Cuban Café,** owned by Gloria and Emilio Estefan. The complex is accessible via Disney buses from most Disney World locations.

## Cirque du Soleil *La Nouba* ★★★★★

**APPEAL BY AGE** Under 21 ★★★★  21–37 ★★★★★  38–50 ★★★★  51 and up ★★★★½

**Type of show** Circus as theater. **Tickets and information** ☎ 407-939-7600; **cirque dusoleil.com/lanouba. Admission cost** *Golden Circle*: $159.75 adults, $133.13 children ages 3–9; *Category Front & Center*: $145.91 adults, $120.34 children; *Category 1*: $129.93 adults, $106.50 children; *Category 2*: $101.17 adults, $83.07 children; *Category 3*: $82 adults, $67.09 children; *Category 4*: $67.09 adults, $55.38 children. All prices include tax. **Cast size** 72. **Night of lowest attendance** Thursday. **Usual showtimes** Tuesday–Saturday, 6 p.m. and 9 p.m. **Authors' rating** ★★★★★. **Duration of presentation** 1 hour, 45 minutes (no intermission) plus preshow.

**DESCRIPTION AND COMMENTS** *La Nouba* is a far cry from a traditional circus but retains all the fun and excitement of it. It is whimsical, mystical, and sophisticated, yet pleasing to all ages. The action takes place on an elaborate stage that incorporates almost every part of the theater. The original musical score is exotic, like the show.

*Note:* In the following paragraphs, we get into how the show *feels* and why it's special. If you don't care how it feels, or if you're not up to slogging through a boxcar of adjectives, just trust us when we tell you that *La Nouba* is great. See it.

*La Nouba* is a most difficult show to describe. To categorize it as a circus doesn't begin to cover its depth, though its performers could perform with distinction in any circus on earth. *La Nouba* is more, much more, than a circus. It combines elements of classical Greek theater, mime, the English morality play, Dalí surrealism, Fellini characterization, and Chaplin comedy. *La Nouba* is at once an odyssey, a symphony, and an exploration of human emotions.

The show pivots on its humor, which is sometimes black, and engages the audience with its unforgettable characters. Though light and uplifting, it is also poignant and dark. Simple in presentation, it is at the same time extraordinarily intricate, always operating on multiple levels of meaning. As you laugh and watch the amazingly talented cast, your mind enters a dimension seldom encountered in a waking state. The presentation begins to register in your consciousness more as a seamless dream than as a stage production. You're moved, lulled, and soothed as well as excited and entertained. The sensitive, the imaginative, the literate, and those who love good theater and art will find nothing in all of Disney World that compares with *La Nouba*.

Thus far, as the following comments suggest, we have not received one negative comment about *La Nouba*.

From an Exeter, England, reader:

*It should be almost criminal not to see Cirque du Soleil on a visit to WDW!*

The comments of a mom from Kansasville, Wisconsin, whose teens reluctantly consented to attend the show:

*Even my hard-to-impress MTV-generation teens were awestruck.*

Finally, from an Andover, Massachusetts, mother:

*One of the true highlights of the trip was seeing Cirque du Soleil. The ticket prices were a bit steep, but I thought it might be enjoyable for my non-Disney-loving husband and decided it was no more expensive than the rest of the trip. In fact, we all loved it, and it was the best money we spent.*

**TOURING TIPS** Be forewarned that the audience is an integral part of *La Nouba* and that at almost any time you might be plucked from your seat to participate. Our advice is to loosen up and roll with it. If you don't want to get involved, politely but firmly decline to be conscripted. Then fix a death grip on the arms of your chair. Tickets for reserved seats can be purchased in advance at the Cirque box office or over the phone, using your credit card. Don't wait until the last minute; book well in advance from home.

## House of Blues

**Type of show** Live concerts with an emphasis on rock and blues. **Tickets and information** ☎ 407-934-BLUE (2583); **hob.com. Admission cost with taxes** About $8–$95, depending on who's performing. **Nights of lowest attendance** Monday and Tuesday. **Usual showtimes** Vary between 7 p.m. and 9:30 p.m., depending on who's performing.

**DESCRIPTION AND COMMENTS** House of Blues, developed by original Blues Brother Dan Aykroyd, features a restaurant and blues bar, as well as the concert hall. The restaurant serves Thursday–Saturday, 11:30 a.m.–11 p.m., and Friday and Saturday, 11:30 a.m.–1 a.m., which makes it one of the few late-night-dining options in Walt Disney World. Live music cranks up every night at 10:30 p.m. in the restaurant–blues bar, but even before then, the joint is way beyond 110 decibels. The music hall next door features concerts by an eclectic array of musicians and groups. During one visit, the show bill listed gospel, blues, funk, ska, dance, salsa, rap, zydeco, hard rock, groove rock, and reggae groups over a two-week period.

**TOURING TIPS** Prices vary from night to night according to the fame and drawing power of the featured band. Tickets ranged from $8 to $62 during our visits but go higher when a really big name is scheduled.

The music hall is set up like a nightclub, with tables and bar stools for only about 150 people and standing room for a whopping 1,850 people. Folks dance when there's room and sometimes when there isn't. The tables and stools are first-come, first-served, with doors opening an hour before showtime on weekdays and 90 minutes before showtime on weekends. Acoustics are good, and the showroom is small enough to provide a relatively intimate concert experience. All shows are all ages unless otherwise indicated.

Sunday night at the House of Blues is Service Industry Night (a.k.a. SIN), when hospitality-industry employees (read: Disney cast members) get in free; other folks are welcome but pay a cover of $8 (age 21 and older). A Florida Gen Y reader describes it:

*Ahh, SIN night . . . there's always a DJ who will play club music, and all the times I went it was packed. It's more of a club atmosphere, and both floors are open for people to dance and mingle, but it's still a great time for tourists if they want to stay on-property and dance all night. Basically, each Sunday night is a huge party there.*

## WALT DISNEY WORLD DINNER THEATERS

SEVERAL DINNER-THEATER SHOWS play each night at Walt Disney World, and unlike other Disney dining venues, they make hard reservations instead of Advance Reservations, meaning you must guarantee your reservation ahead of time with a credit card. You'll receive a confirmation number and be told to pick up your tickets at a Disney-hotel Guest Relations desk. Unless you cancel your tickets at least 48 hours before your reservation time, your credit card will still be charged the full amount. Dinner-show reservations can be made 180 days in advance; call ☎ 407-939-3463. While getting reservations for the *Spirit of Aloha Dinner Show* isn't terribly tough, booking the *Hoop-Dee-Doo Musical Revue* is a trick of the first order.

*unofficial* TIP
To make reservations for the *Hoop-Dee-Doo Musical Revue,* call as soon as you're certain of the dates of your visit. The earlier you call, the better your seats will be.

A couple from Bismarck, North Dakota, explains:

> *I'm glad we made our reservations so early (a year in advance). I was able to reserve space for us at* Spirit of Aloha *at the Polynesian and the* Hoop-Dee-Doo Musical Revue. *At both of these, they seat you according to when you made your reservation. At the Hoop-Dee-Doo Musical Revue, we had a front-center table. We were so close to the stage, we could see how many cavities the performers had!*

If you can't get reservations and want to see one of the shows:

1. Call ☎ 407-939-3463 at 9 a.m. each morning while you're at Disney World to make a same-day reservation. There are three performances each night, and for all three combined, only 3–24 people total will be admitted with same-day reservations.

2. Arrive at the show of your choice 45 minutes before showtime (early and late shows are your best bets) and put your name on the standby list. If someone with reservations fails to show, you may be admitted.

Borrowing a page from Vegas strip joints where nearsighted old coots are charged extra to sit way up front, Disney offers tiered seating for the *Hoop-Dee-Doo Musical Revue* and the *Spirit of Aloha Dinner Show.* The best seats are in Category 1. Next comes Category 2, with seats off to the side or behind Category 1. Finally, Category 3 seats are at the Orlando Greyhound station, where you watch the show on a video feed. Just making sure you're still with us—actually, they're farther still to the side or back, or on another level from the stage. For both the *Spirit of Aloha Dinner Show* and the *Hoop-Dee-Doo Musical Revue,* there's a good view from almost all seats, so you can decide if sitting closer to the action is worth the extra bucks.

### Hoop-Dee-Doo Musical Revue

**Pioneer Hall, Fort Wilderness Campground** ☎ 407-939-3463. **Showtimes** 4, 6:15, and 8:30 p.m. nightly. **Cost** *Category 1:* $66–$70 adults, $34–$36 children ages 3–9.; *Category 2:* $59–$63 adults, $29–$31 children; *Category 3:* $55–$59 adults, $28–$30 children. Prices include tax and gratuity. **Discounts** Seasonal. **Type of seating** Tables of various sizes to fit the number in each party, set in an Old West–style dance hall. **Menu** All-you-can-eat barbecue ribs, fried chicken, corn, and strawberry shortcake. **Vegetarian alternative** On request (at least 24 hours in advance). **Beverages** Unlimited beer, wine, sangria, and soft drinks.

**DESCRIPTION AND COMMENTS** Six Wild West performers arrive by stagecoach (sound effects only) to entertain the crowd inside Pioneer Hall. There isn't much of a plot, just corny jokes interspersed with song or dance. The humor is of the *Hee Haw* ilk, but it's presented enthusiastically.

Audience participation includes sing-alongs, hand clapping, and a finale that uses volunteers to play parts on stage. Performers are accompanied by a banjo player and pianist who also play quietly while the food is being served. The fried chicken and corn on the cob are good, the ribs a bit tough though tasty. With the all-you-can-eat policy, at least you can get your money's worth by stuffing yourself silly.

Traveling to Fort Wilderness and absorbing the rustic atmosphere of Pioneer Hall augments the adventure. For repeat Disney World visitors, an annual visit to the revue is a tradition of sorts. Plus, warts and all, the revue is all Disney, and for some folks that's enough. The fact that performances sell out far in advance gives the experience a special aura.

Most of our readers enjoy the *Hoop-Dee-Doo Musical Revue,* but not all, as this letter from a Texas family attests:

*What is all the hoop-dee-doo with the* Hoop-Dee-Doo Musical Revue? *The food was OK, if "gut busting" fare is your idea of a fine night out, and the entertainment was pleasant. As a dinner theater, however, our family of three found it unexceptional in every respect but its cost. Had your review of the Revue tempered its enthusiasm (much as you present its Polynesian counterpart), we probably would've canceled our reservation, pocketed the $100, and spent the evening joyously stunned by another glorious light-and-fireworks spectacle.*

More typical are the remarks of a Cambridge, Massachusetts, mom:

*The kids in our group (ages 3–8) thought the* Hoop-Dee-Doo Musical Revue *was just terrific. They watched intently the whole time, laughing hysterically. With them having such a good time, how could the adults not enjoy themselves? But I wouldn't recommend the show for adults on their own. One thing we adults appreciated was the lack of commercialism: no movie tie-in, no merchandise sales. The entire experience, including its setting in the rustic Fort Wilderness campground, brought us back to simpler days and gave the kids exposure to entertainment before there were special effects.*

If you go to *Hoop-Dee-Doo,* allow plenty of driving time (about an hour) to get there. Or do as this California dad suggests:

*To go to the* Hoop-Dee-Doo Musical Revue *at Fort Wilderness, take the boat from the Magic Kingdom rather than any bus. This is contrary to the "official" directions. The boat dock is a short walk from Pioneer Hall in Fort Wilderness, while the bus goes to the main Fort Wilderness parking lot, where one has to transfer to another bus to Pioneer Hall.*

Disney ferry service may be suspended during thunderstorms, so if it's raining or it looks as if it's about to rain, Disney will provide bus service from the parks.

## Mickey's Backyard BBQ

**Fort Wilderness Campground** ☎ 407-939-3463. **Showtimes** Thursday and Saturday at 5, 6:30, and 7 p.m. **Cost** $60 adults, $36 children ages 3–9. Prices include tax and gratuity. **Type of seating** Picnic tables. **Menu** Baked chicken, barbecue pork ribs, burgers, hot dogs, corn, beans, mac and cheese, salads and slaw, bread, and watermelon and ice-cream bars for dessert. **Vegetarian alternatives** On request. **Beverages** Unlimited beer, wine, lemonade, and iced tea.

**DESCRIPTION AND COMMENTS** Situated along Bay Lake and held in a covered pavilion next to the site of the old River Country swimming park, *Mickey's Backyard BBQ* features Mickey, Minnie, Chip 'n' Dale, and Goofy, along with a country band and line dancing. Though the pavilion gets some breeze off Bay Lake, we recommend going during the spring or fall, if possible. The food is pretty good, as is, fortunately, the insect control.

The barbecue was previously offered only seasonally, from March through December, but is now year-round. Even so, dates are usually not entered into the WDW-DINE reservations system until about six months in advance. Once the dates are in the system, you can make an Advance Reservation for anytime during the dinner show's season.

The easiest way to get to the barbecue is to take a boat from the Magic Kingdom or from one of the Disney resorts on the Magic Kingdom monorail. Give yourself at least 45 minutes if you plan to arrive by boat. Ferry service may be suspended during thunderstorms, so if it's raining or it looks like it's about to rain, Disney will provide bus service from the parks.

## Spirit of Aloha Dinner Show

**Disney's Polynesian Resort** ☎ 407-939-3463. **Showtimes** Tuesday–Saturday, 5:15 and 8 p.m. **Cost** *Category 1:* $70–$70 adults, $36–$40 children ages 3–9.; *Category 2:* $63–$67 adults, $31–$33 children; *Category 3:* $59–$63 adults, $30–$32 children. Prices include tax and gratuity. **Discounts** Seasonal. **Type of seating** Long rows of tables, with some separation between individual parties. The show is performed on an outdoor stage, but all seating is covered. Ceiling fans provide some air movement, but it can get warm, especially at the early show. **Menu** Tropical fruit, roasted chicken, island pork ribs, mixed vegetables, rice, and pineapple bread; chicken tenders, PB&J sandwiches, mac and cheese, and hot dogs are also available for children. **Vegetarian alternative** On request. **Beverages** Beer, wine, and soft drinks.

**DESCRIPTION AND COMMENTS** This show features South Seas–island native dancing followed by an all-you-can-eat "Polynesian-style" meal. The dancing is interesting and largely authentic, and the dancers are attractive though definitely PG-rated in the Disney tradition. We think the show has its moments and the meal is adequate, but neither is particularly special.

The show follows (tenuously) the common "girl leaves home for the big city, forgets her roots, and must rediscover them" theme. The performers are uniformly attractive ("Studmuffins!" said a female *Unofficial* researcher when asked about the men), and the dancing is very good. The story, however, never really makes sense as anything other than a slender thread between musical numbers. Our show lasted for more than 2 hours and 15 minutes.

The food does little more than illustrate how difficult it must be to prepare the same meal for hundreds of people simultaneously: The roasted chicken is better than the ribs, but neither is anything special. We conditionally recommend *Spirit of Aloha* for special occasions, when the people celebrating get to go on stage. But go to the early show and get dessert somewhere else in the World.

A well-traveled couple from Fond du Lac, Wisconsin, comments:

*Spirit of Aloha was a beautiful presentation, better than some shows we have seen in Hawaii! The food, however, lacked in all areas. Better food has come out of Disney kitchens. During our visit, the fruit platter was chintzy, the honey-roasted chicken was a bit fatty, and the pineapple cake was dry.*

And from a Middletown, Delaware, reader:

*I booked Spirit of Aloha using two dinner credits each. Having enjoyed the show throughout the 1980s and in 1998 with my parents and siblings, you can imagine my disappointment at how it is now. The food was decent, but the crowd noises was deafening. We still remember fondly the conversations we had around the table in the 1980s from the show. Now with the "cafeteria" so full, my husband and I couldn't even have a conversation! The show itself was overly long for all the young children in the audience. The performers were talented, but we won't go again, and I've told my extended family to skip it*

# UNIVERSAL CITYWALK

CITYWALK WAS UNIVERSAL ORLANDO'S ANSWER to Pleasure Island. Now, with Pleasure Island defunct, CityWalk takes its place as the preeminent nightlife venue. Clubs include **CityWalk's Rising Star,** a karaoke joint where singers are backed by a live band; reggae at **Bob Marley—A Tribute to Freedom;** a **Pat O'Brien's** dueling-pianos club; **Fat Tuesday,** specializing in New Orleans–style daiquiris; a **Hard Rock Cafe** and **Hard Rock Live** concert venue; **Jimmy Buffett's Margaritaville;** the **Red Coconut Club,** a two-story upscale cocktail lounge with live music and dancing; and a dance club called **the groove,** with high-tech lighting and visual effects.

If you do decide to dine at CityWalk, your options include **Anto-jitos Authentic Mexican Food, Bubba Gump Shrimp Co., Bob Marley—A Tribute to Freedom, CityWalk's Rising Star, Emeril's Orlando, Hard Rock Cafe, Jimmy Buffett's Margaritaville, NASCAR Sports Grille, NBA City, Pat O'Brien's, Red Oven Pizza Bakery,** and **Vivo Italian Kitchen.** (For more on CityWalk restaurants, see pages 413–415.)

There's no admission charge to enjoy the shops, restaurants, and street entertainment. As for the clubs, you can buy a **CityWalk Party Pass** for about $12 that admits you to all of them, or if you prefer, you can pay a cover charge (usually about $7) at each club you visit. In addition to the clubs, shops, and restaurants, there's a 20-screen **AMC Universal Cineplex** movie theater. Add a movie to your pass for a total cost of $15.

# APPENDIX

# READERS' QUESTIONS
## *to the* AUTHORS

FOLLOWING ARE QUESTIONS AND COMMENTS from *Unofficial Guide* readers. Some frequently asked questions are addressed in every edition of the *Guide*.

**QUESTION:**

*When you do your research, are you admitted to the parks free? Do the Disney people know you're there?*

**ANSWER:**

We pay the regular admission, and usually the Disney people don't know we're on-site. Similarly, both in and out of Walt Disney World, we pay for our own meals and lodging.

**QUESTION:**

*How often is the* Unofficial Guide *revised?*

**ANSWER:**

We publish a new edition once a year, but we revise every time we go to press, usually twice a year.

**QUESTION:**

*Where can I find information about what's changed at Walt Disney World in between published editions of the* Unofficial Guide?

**ANSWER:**

We post important information online at **touringplans.com.**

**QUESTION:**

*Do you write each new edition from scratch?*

**ANSWER:**

Nope. When it comes to a destination the size of Walt Disney World, it's hard enough to keep up with what's new. Moreover, we put a lot of effort into communicating the most useful information in the clearest possible language. If an attraction or hotel has not changed, we're reluctant to tinker with its coverage for the sake of freshening the writing.

## QUESTION:

*I've never read any other* Unofficial Guides. *Are they all as critical as* The Unofficial Guide to Walt Disney World?

## ANSWER:

What some readers perceive as critical we see as objective and constructive. Our job is to prepare you for both the best and worst of Walt Disney World. As it happens, some folks are very passionate about what one reader calls "the inherent goodness of Disney." These readers might be more comfortable with press releases or the *Official Guide* than with the strong consumer viewpoint represented in our guide. That said, some readers take us to task for being overly *positive*.

## QUESTION:

*How many people have you surveyed for your age-group ratings regarding the attractions?*

## ANSWER:

Since the first *Unofficial Guide* was published in 1985, we've interviewed or surveyed almost 53,000 Walt Disney World patrons. Even with such a large survey population, however, we continue to find certain age groups underrepresented. Specifically, we'd love to hear more from seniors about their experiences with coasters and other thrill rides.

## QUESTION:

*Do you stay in Walt Disney World? If not, where?*

## ANSWER:

We stay at Walt Disney World lodging properties quite often. Since we began writing about Walt Disney World in 1982, we've stayed at all the Disney resorts and more than 100 different properties in various locations around Orlando, Lake Buena Vista, and Kissimmee.

## QUESTION:

*Bob, what's your favorite Florida attraction?*

## ANSWER:

What attracts me (as opposed to my favorite attraction) is **Juniper Springs,** a stunningly beautiful stream about 1½ hours north of Orlando in the Ocala National Forest. Originating in a limestone aquifer, the crystal-clear water erupts from the ground and begins a 10-mile journey to the creek's mouth at Lake George. Winding through palm, cypress, and live oak, the stream is more exotic than the Jungle Cruise, and alive with birds, turtles, and alligators. Put in at the Juniper Springs Recreation Area on FL 40, 36 miles east of Ocala. The 7-mile trip to the FL 19 bridge takes about 4½ hours. Canoe rentals and shuttle service are available at the recreation area. Call ☎ 352-625-3147 for more information.

# ◾ READERS' COMMENTS

OUR READERS LOVE TO SHARE TIPS. From a St. Louis mom:

*When dining at Downtown Disney, it's best to arrive before 7 p.m. We ate there twice and had no problem getting seated immediately, but after 7 p.m. everywhere was packed.*

And from an Ann Arbor, Michigan, mother of three:

*Even though we stayed on Disney property, we stopped off on US 192 and loaded up on the local freebie visitor magazines and coupon books. We estimate they saved us over $200, mostly on food.*

An Iowa City, Iowa, couple offers this observation about being in touch with your feelings:

*We didn't build rest breaks into our plans but were willing to say, "OK, I'm just not having fun right now—we should leave the park," and go on to something else (like a water park, hotel pool, or shopping trip to Downtown Disney). This is a skill I would like to see more people develop. I can't count the number of people or families I saw who were obviously not having fun.*

A woman from Suwanee, Georgia, offers a suggestion for the perfect Disney vacation:

*Your book made our trip a much more successful one. It also frustrated our male adults, who erroneously believed this was a trip for their enjoyment. We followed your advice to get up early and see as much as possible before an early lunch. But the men refused to go back to the hotel for a nap and a meal outside the park, so we fought the crowds until 3 or 4 p.m., by which time everyone was exhausted and cranky. My mother and I decided our next trip will include your guidebook and the children—but no men!*

From a Greenville, Kentucky, mom who wasn't able to take advantage of the free-admission promotion on her daughter's birthday:

*We were disappointed that a birth certificate was the only acceptable ID for my daughter. We had certified shot records, and they still wouldn't accept them.*

A Norwalk, Ohio, mom searched for happy feet:

*On the subject of footwear, support is just as important as comfort. On one trip I wore Keds—big mistake. My shins ached unbelievably before the end of the second day. From then on I was a die-hard tennis-shoe girl, until I discovered FitFlops [go to **fitflop.com** for stores]. You get the support of a tennis shoe with the comfort of a flip-flop.*

A reader from Crofton, Maryland, discovered that the best bargains on Disney merchandise can turn up in unexpected places:

*People who want to save $$$ on Disney trinkets and aren't fussy about selection really should go to the Disney shop at Orlando Premium Outlets. I bought a talking Goofy doll for my nephew and was very pleased with the $19.99 price, which was significantly lower* *than the list price. However, the VERY SAME doll was only $9.99 at (of all places!) Publix grocery store! In fact, Publix has loads of cute dolls, T-shirts, keychains, and other gifts at great prices!*

A Midwestern mom loved getting in the game, writing:

*It was a thrill for me to stand behind the ropes and wait till the park officially opened—to hear the music and announcements, then hurry with the throngs to the first ride. It was so exciting! My husband wasn't so thrilled. He teased me for days about running over old ladies and little children—I didn't run! I was speed-walking!*

A woman from Mount Gretna, Pennsylvania, had some questions about theme park attire:

*I don't believe there was a section that addressed whether or not you could wear dresses on the rides. Quite a few amusement parks have security straps or bars that come up between one's knees, making it very difficult and immodest to wear dresses or skirts. Many women want to wear dresses for convenience, comfort, or cultural/religious convictions. I was concerned as I was packing whether this would limit any rides I could get on. I was quite pleased that it did not.*

Henry Ford famously said, "You can have any color car you want, as long as it's black." A hungry (and persistent) Fairfax, Vermont, reader found that mindset alive and well at his Disney resort's food court:

*The real difficulty of our stay began when I made the ill-advised decision to request a hamburger at the food court. I was first given a cheeseburger. I then informed the cast member that I requested a hamburger. She placed the burger back under the heat lamp, and I proceeded to watch the person at the grill place cheese on all 14 burgers that had just been put on the grill. Sensing my unease, another cast member asked me what I had ordered. I informed him that I was waiting for a hamburger. He then reached under the heat lamp and proceeded to give me the original cheeseburger. Had I realized that, at that very moment, fate had determined that I was not to enjoy a hamburger on this night, then I would have given up. Sadly, I did not come to this realization at that time. Instead, I chose to "spit into the wind" and insist on getting my hamburger. Thus, I watched as another 14 burgers were placed on the grill. I could almost taste the reward for my patience . . . until I saw the cast member delicately place cheese on each and every one of the new burgers. Alas, my quest for a burger ended, and my call to Pizza Hut delivery was made.*

A Fenton, Missouri, woman evidently took her banker with her:

*Love your book! Our last trip was with eight people total: Grandma, Grandpa, my sister and her husband and two sons (ages 4 and 12), and my finance and me.*

A Widnes, England, dad knows who butters his bread:

*While we didn't make the early starts, the Guide still managed to advise of enough short-cuts that enabled us to keep everyone happy. (Let's face it—I'm talking about my wife.)*

A Yardley, Pennsylvania, woman of few words sums up the Walt Disney World experience thus:

*Expect to wait for everything—except the bathroom!*

A Nashville, Tennessee, family of three report a tough reentry:

*My wife and I were so depressed when we had to adjust to reality after a week of being in Disney's alternate universe. We think Disney needs to offer some sort of debriefing or transition program to ease its visitors back into the real world. Perhaps they could send Mickey and Minnie over to make blueberry pancakes the morning after you return.*

An Atlanta reader relates the story of a dirty bird and a solicitous cast member:

*While riding Splash Mountain, a mother and teenage son in our boat had brought ponchos (smart move), and the son took his off before we got out of the boat . . . just in time for a bird to poop on him. He went to buy a clean shirt in the gift shop, and when the cast member found out what had happened, he gave the kid a free shirt. I thought that was very nice!*

A Rockville, Maryland, woman offers a recipe for relaxation:

*The true secret to our enjoyable experience was the cocktails at Planet Hollywood. I started the evening with Blazing Saddles and finished it off with Gorillas in the Mist. I didn't taste a lot of alcohol, but they sure helped me relax after a day of following a 7-year-old around a theme park. When the stress of a Disney vacation is starting to get to you and you feel like you're ready to strangle that sweet little angel by your side, this place is a must.*

From a Clarksville, Maryland, family:

*Your book should include a review of Legoland. We took a side trip there, and it was awesome—perfect for kids ages 4–12, with a very affordable water park for only $12 extra.*

We devote an entire chapter to Legoland, including touring plans, in *Beyond Disney: The Unofficial Guide to Universal Orlando, SeaWorld, and the Best of Central Florida.*

A Columbia, Missouri, woman offers advice for wives with anxious husbands:

*A smartphone is the best thing in the world for keeping your husband busy in line. As long as mine had that phone, he could check e-mail, check dinner plans, and take and send pictures of the kids to family back home. He never complained about waiting in line, ever.*

A Denver reader bursts our bubble (we thought we were Disney's favorites):

*WDW cast members have an interesting reaction to the Guide. In one case, with the book in hand, we got an almost vampire-vs.-holywater reaction from one CM (who then asked if he could take a quick peek).*

A mom from Brighton, Michigan, was searching for quiet in all the wrong places:

> *Disney is so much flash and sparkle without a lot of time for reflection. They had to fill every quiet minute throughout the park with noise, music, talking, animation, flashing lights, etc.—as if they were afraid we'd get bored if we stopped to think. Next year we plan to go to Costa Rica instead.*

There's just no pleasing some people—this London bloke, for example:

> *Why, oh why is Toy Story Midway Mania! rated so highly? It's like playing crummy Wii games as someone pushes you around on your sofa.*

From an exhausted mother:

> *Make sure moms are prepared for the fact that their kids will throw tantrums . . . and so will their husbands. Disney is a magical, wonderful thing, but it was also the most exhausting thing I have ever done. It required more patience than I've needed so far as a parent.*

A Scottsdale, Arizona, woman found the silver lining (and we agree):

> *I listen to podcasts and read various Disney websites, and the one thing I find amusing is that no one seems to spend much time on how truly beautiful the Disney resorts are. The rooms themselves are adequate, but the grounds are spectacular. If these hotels weren't affiliated with the theme parks, they would be destination resorts (provided the food was substantially improved).*

All for the love of Mom, writes a woman from Haddon Heights, New Jersey:

> *I was traveling with my mother, who has an artificial knee, a herniated disc, and bad feet. My mantra was, "Try not to kill your mother." Without the book, I would have undoubtedly come home an orphan.*

From a husband and wife from Atlanta:

> *My brother-in-law Pat and his wife were planning a trip to Disney for the first time with their 4-year-old daughter. My other brother-in-law Robert, who has three kids and has taken them to Disney twice, asked Pat if he had taken the Disney test: Take a $100 bill, throw it in the toilet, and flush. If you can do this without flinching, you're ready for Disney.*

A mom from Flower Mound, Texas, boils our windy 850-page guide down to one paragraph, and she's pretty much right-on:

> *If you get just the following two things from the Guide, they're worth the cost of the entire book—especially when you put them together: (1) Get to the parks early. You won't believe what a difference it makes. The parks are wonderful in the morning. (2) The afternoon break is essential! I wouldn't even consider a WDW trip without it. If your kids are under 10 years old, turn out the lights, shut the curtains, and make them sleep. It's the difference between disaster and delight!*

A Texas woman never says never:

*As I walked out of the Magic Kingdom for the last time, I promised I wouldn't wait so long to visit again.*

This Hawaii woman either is a record-holder of some sort or forgot to proofread before she hit SEND:

*We've used the book for more than 90 years and love it. Keep up the good work!*

From an opinionated Georgia family of four:

*My 13 year old son's one-word description of Space Mountain: "Awesome." My husband's one-word description: "Hell." My 10-year-old's best comment: "Hey Mom, here's a Disney motto that no one talks about: 'Bleed 'em dry.' My 13-year-old's best comment as I was trying to get everyone to stop and pose in front of the topiaries: "Keep movin', Mom! There's no time for memories!"*

No drugs needed for an Asheville, North Carolina, mom:

*I have recommended the* Guide *to everyone who has asked me about our trip and is impressed that I made it back without a prescription for lithium!*

Finally, a Somerville, Alabama, woman is succinct if nothing else:

*Everything, other than my husband, was perfect.*

And so it goes. . . .

# ACCOMMODATIONS INDEX

*Note:* Page numbers of profiles are in **boldface** type.

*See also* the Restaurant Index on pages 788–791 and the Subject Index on pages 792–819.

*See also* the Restaurant Index on pages 788–791 and the Subject Index on pages 792–819.

*See also* the Restaurant Index on pages 788–791 and the Subject Index on pages 792–819.

*See also* the Restaurant Index on pages 788–791 and the Subject Index on pages 792–819.

*See also* the Restaurant Index on pages 788–791 and the Subject Index on pages 792–819.

*See also* the Restaurant Index on pages 788–791 and the Subject Index on pages 792–819.

*See also* the Restaurant Index on pages 788–791 and the Subject Index on pages 792–819.

# RESTAURANT INDEX

*Note:* Page numbers of restaurant profiles are in **boldface** type.

*See also* the Accommodations Index on pages 781–787 and the Subject Index on pages 792–819.

*See also* the Accommodations Index on pages 781–787 and the Subject Index on pages 792–819.

*See also* the Accommodations Index on pages 781–787 and the Subject Index on pages 792–819.

*See also* the Accommodations Index on pages 781-787 and the Subject Index on pages 792-819.

# SUBJECT INDEX

*Note:* Attractions at non-Disney parks are labeled; those at Disney parks are unlabeled.

See also the Accommodations Index on pages 781–787 and the Restaurant Index on pages 788–791.

*See also* the Accommodations Index on pages 781–787 and the Restaurant Index on pages 788–791

*See also* the Accommodations Index on pages 781–787 and the Restaurant Index on pages 788–791.

*See also* the Accommodations Index on pages 781–787 and the Restaurant Index on pages 788–791.

*See also* the Accommodations Index on pages 781–787 and the Restaurant Index on pages 788–791.

*See also* the Accommodations Index on pages 781–787 and the Restaurant Index on pages 788–791.

*See also* the Accommodations Index on pages 781–787 and the Restaurant Index on pages 788–791.

See also the Accommodations Index on pages 781–787 and the Restaurant Index on pages 788–791.

*See also* the Accommodations Index on pages 781–787 and the Restaurant Index on pages 788–79

*See also* the Accommodations Index on pages 781–787 and the Restaurant Index on pages 788–791.

*See also* the Accommodations Index on pages 781–787 and the Restaurant Index on pages 788–791

See also the Accommodations Index on pages 781–787 and the Restaurant Index on pages 788–79

*See also* the Accommodations Index on pages 781-787 and the Restaurant Index on pages 788-791.

# TOURING PLANS

## "Not a Touring Plan"
# TOURING PLANS

BELOW ARE THE SIMPLE RULES we use when friends ask us for touring plans that don't sound like a space-shuttle launch checklist. Use these when you don't want the regimentation of a step-by-step plan but you do want to avoid long waits in line. Skip attractions that don't suit you, and use FastPass+ if waits seem too long.

### MAGIC KINGDOM

**FOR PARENTS OF SMALL CHILDREN WITH ONE DAY TO TOUR, ARRIVING AT PARK OPENING** *Note:* Use FastPass+ wherever you can get it. See Fantasyland first, starting with *Enchanted Tales with Belle* and Seven Dwarfs Mine Train. See Frontierland and some of Adventureland, then take a midday break. Return to the park and complete your tour of Adventureland. Next, meet characters at the Town Square Theater and tour Tomorrowland. End on Main Street for parades and fireworks.

**FOR ADULTS WITH ONE DAY TO TOUR, ARRIVING AT PARK OPENING** *Note:* Use FastPass+ for attractions in the late morning and midafternoon, especially in Frontierland and Tomorrowland. See Seven Dwarfs Mine Train and Peter Pan's Flight in Fantasyland, and then head to Liberty Square. Tour Frontierland, Adventureland, and Tomorrowland next. End on Main Street for parades and fireworks.

**FOR PARENTS AND ADULTS WITH TWO DAYS TO TOUR** *Note:* Day One works great for Disney resort guests on Extra Magic Hour mornings. Use FastPass+ where you can. Start Day One with Seven Dwarfs Mine Train in Fantasyland, then tour Liberty Square and Frontierland before leaving the park around midday. Begin Day Two in Tomorrowland, then tour Adventureland. End on Main Street for parades and fireworks.

**FOR PARENTS AND ADULTS WITH AN AFTERNOON AND A FULL DAY** *Note:* The full day works great for Disney resort guests on Extra Magic Hour mornings. For the afternoon, tour Adventureland, Frontierland, and Tomorrowland (get FastPass+ reservations for Splash and Space Mountains). On your full day of touring, see Fantasyland, Liberty Square, and Tomorrowland again for any missed attractions there from the previous afternoon. End on Main Street for parades and fireworks.

### EPCOT

**FOR PARENTS AND ADULTS WITH ONE DAY TO TOUR, ARRIVING AT PARK OPENING** Ride Test Track, then Mission: SPACE Orange (FastPass+ suggested start time: 9 a.m.). Next, ride Sum of All Thrills, Soarin'

(FastPass+ suggested start time: 11 a.m.), and Spaceship Earth; tour other Future World East and West attractions as you come to them and as you desire. Then tour World Showcase clockwise, starting in Mexico (FastPass+ suggested start time for Maelstrom in Norway: 2 p.m.). End the day with *IllumiNations*.

**FOR PARENTS AND ADULTS WITH ONE DAY TO TOUR, ARRIVING LATE MORNING** Tour Future World West except for Soarin'. Tour World Showcase counterclockwise, starting in Canada (FastPass+ suggested start time for Maelstrom in Norway: 3 p.m.). Tour Future World East, then ride Spaceship Earth. Now ride Soarin' (FastPass+ suggested start time: 6:30 p.m.)—or, if FastPass+ is unavailable for that, try to get reservations for Test Track instead. End the day with *IllumiNations*.

**FOR PARENTS AND ADULTS WITH TWO DAYS TO TOUR** On Day One, start with Test Track and Mission: SPACE Orange (FastPass+ suggested start times: 9 a.m. and 10 a.m., respectively), then ride Sum of All Thrills. See the rest of Future World as desired, then tour Mexico through the United States in World Showcase (FastPass+ suggested start time for Maelstrom in Norway: 2 p.m.). On Day Two, ride Soarin' (FastPass+ suggested start time: 9 a.m.), then tour Canada through Japan in World Showcase. End the day with *IllumiNations*.

## DISNEY'S ANIMAL KINGDOM

**FOR PARENTS AND ADULTS ARRIVING AT PARK OPENING** Obtain FastPass+ reservations for Expedition Everest in Asia, then begin a land-by-land counterclockwise tour of the park, starting in DinoLand U.S.A. Work in shows as you near them, but leave *Finding Nemo— The Musical* for last.

**FOR PARENTS AND ADULTS ARRIVING LATE MORNING** Get FastPass+ reservations for Kilimanjaro Safaris, then begin a counterclockwise tour of the park starting in Africa, saving Kali River Rapids and Expedition Everest for last.

## DISNEY'S HOLLYWOOD STUDIOS

**FOR ADULTS ARRIVING AT PARK OPENING** Obtain FastPass+ reservations for Toy Story Midway Mania! (suggested start time: 10 a.m.), then begin a counterclockwise tour of the park with Rock 'n' Roller Coaster, Tower of Terror, The Great Movie Ride. Work in shows as you near them. End the day in Animation Courtyard for Voyage of the Little Mermaid and The Magic of Disney Animation. End the day on Sunset Boulevard for *Fantasmic!* (If you're staying for the show, FastPass+ for Tower of Terror in the last hour the park is open would work well.)

**FOR PARENTS AND ADULTS ARRIVING LATE MORNING** Try to get FastPass+ reservations for Star Tours or Tower of Terror, plus Toy Story Midway Mania! Start a clockwise tour of park with the Studio Backlot Tour, working in shows as you near them. If you obtained FastPass+ reservations for Toy Story Midway Mania!, use those at the appropriate time; otherwise, save it for last, grab a bite to eat, and see *Fantasmic!*

## The Magic Kingdom

## MAGIC KINGDOM ONE-DAY TOURING PLAN FOR ADULTS

1. Arrive at the Magic Kingdom entrance 50 minutes (Disney resort guests) to 70 minutes (non–Disney resort guests) before opening. Get guide maps and the *Times Guide*.

2. As soon as the park opens, head to Fantasyland and ride Seven Dwarfs Mine Train.

3. Ride Under the Sea: Journey of the Little Mermaid.

4. Ride The Many Adventures of Winnie the Pooh.

5. In Frontierland, ride Splash Mountain.

6. Also in Frontierland, ride Big Thunder Mountain Railroad.

7. See *Walt Disney's Enchanted Tiki Room* in Adventureland.

8. Eat lunch.

9. In Fantasyland, see *Mickey's PhilharMagic*.

10. Ride Peter Pan's Flight.

11. In Liberty Square, see The Haunted Mansion.

12. Experience *The Hall of Presidents*.

13. In Liberty Square, ride the *Liberty Belle* Riverboat.

14. Ride It's a Small World in Fantasyland.

15. Ride Buzz Lightyear in Tomorrowland.

16. See *Walt Disney's Carousel of Progress*.

17. Ride Space Mountain.

18. Ride the Tomorrowland Transit Authority PeopleMover.

19. See *Monsters, Inc. Laugh Floor*.

20. Eat dinner.

21. In Adventureland, play A Pirate's Adventure.

22. Ride Pirates of the Caribbean.

23. Explore the Swiss Family Treehouse.

24. In Frontierland, see *Country Bear Jamboree*.

25. Take the Jungle Cruise in Adventureland.

26. See the evening parade on Main Street.

27. See the evening castle light show and fireworks on Main Street. A good viewing spot is somewhere between The Plaza Restaurant and Tomorrowland Terrace.

You can customize this touring plan and get real-time updates while you're in the park! See **touringplans.com** for details. **Suggested start times for FastPass+ reservations:** Big Thunder Mountain Railroad, 9:30 a.m.; Peter Pan's Flight, 12 noon; Space Mountain, 3:30 p.m.

# The Magic Kingdom

## MAGIC KINGDOM AUTHOR'S SELECTIVE
## ONE-DAY TOURING PLAN FOR ADULTS

1. Arrive at the Magic Kingdom entrance 50 minutes (Disney resort guests) to 70 minutes (non–Disney resort guests) before opening. Get guide maps and the *Times Guide*.

2. As soon as the park opens, head to Fantasyland and ride Seven Dwarfs Mine Train.

3. In Frontierland, ride Big Thunder Mountain Railroad.

4. Ride Splash Mountain.

5. Take the Jungle Cruise in Adventureland.

6. Ride Pirates of the Caribbean.

7. Eat lunch.

8. In Liberty Square, see The Haunted Mansion.

9. In Fantasyland, ride Peter Pan's Flight.

10. See *Mickey's PhilharMagic*.

11. Ride It's a Small World.

12. In Liberty Square, ride the *Liberty Belle* Riverboat.

13. Experience *The Hall of Presidents*.

14. In Tomorrowland, see *Monsters, Inc. Laugh Floor*.

15. Ride the Tomorrowland Transit Authority PeopleMover.

16. Back in Fantasyland, ride The Many Adventures of Winnie the Pooh.

17. Explore the Swiss Family Treehouse in Adventureland.

18. See *Walt Disney's Enchanted Tiki Room*.

19. In Frontierland, see *Country Bear Jamboree*.

20. In Adventureland, play A Pirate's Adventure.

21. Eat dinner.

22. In Tomorrowland, ride Space Mountain.

23. Ride Buzz Lightyear's Space Ranger Spin.

24. In Fantasyland, ride Under the Sea: Journey of the Little Mermaid.

25. See the evening parade on Main Street.

26. See the evening castle light show and fireworks on Main Street. A good viewing spot is somewhere between The Plaza Restaurant and Tomorrowland Terrace.

You can customize this touring plan and get real-time updates while you're in the park! See **touringplans.com** for details. **Suggested start times for FastPass+ reservations:** Peter Pan's Flight, 11:40 a.m.; The Many Adventures of Winnie the Pooh, 3:30 p.m.; Space Mountain, 6:30 p.m.

*The Magic Kingdom*

## MAGIC KINGDOM ONE-DAY TOURING PLAN
### FOR PARENTS WITH SMALL CHILDREN
*(Review the Small-Child Fright-Potential Chart on pages 332–335.)*

1. Arrive at the Magic Kingdom entrance 50 minutes (Disney resort guests) to 70 minutes (non–Disney resort guests) before opening. Rent strollers before the park opens. Get guide maps and the *Times Guide*.
2. As soon as the park opens, head to Fantasyland and ride Seven Dwarfs Mine Train.
3. Ride The Many Adventures of Winnie the Pooh.
4. Ride The Barnstormer.
5. Ride Dumbo the Flying Elephant.
6. Ride Under the Sea: Journey of the Little Mermaid.
7. Ride Peter Pan's Flight.
8. Take the Jungle Cruise in Adventureland.
9. In Liberty Square, see The Haunted Mansion.
10. Ride It's a Small World in Fantasyland.
11. Eat lunch and take a midday break.
12. In Frontierland, take the raft over to Tom Sawyer Island. Allow at least 30 minutes to explore the island, Fort Langhorn, and the barrel bridges.
13. In Frontierland, see *Country Bear Jamboree*.
14. In Tomorrowland, see *Monsters, Inc. Laugh Floor*.
15. Ride Buzz Lightyear's Space Ranger Spin.
16. Eat dinner.
17. Meet Mickey Mouse at Town Square Theater on Main Street.
18. See *Enchanted Tales with Belle* in Fantasyland.
19. See *Mickey's PhilharMagic*.
20. In Adventureland, explore the Swiss Family Treehouse.
21. Ride Pirates of the Caribbean.
22. See the evening parade on Main Street.
23. See the evening castle light show and fireworks on Main Street. A good viewing spot is somewhere between The Plaza Restaurant and Tomorrowland Terrace.

You can customize this touring plan and get real-time updates while you're in the park! See **touringplans.com** for details. **Suggested start times for FastPass+ reservations:** Peter Pan's Flight, 10 a.m.; Buzz Lightyear's Space Ranger Spin: 5 p.m.; *Enchanted Tales with Belle*, 7 p.m.

*The Magic Kingdom*

## MAGIC KINGDOM TWO-DAY TOURING PLAN: DAY ONE

1. Arrive at the Magic Kingdom entrance 50 minutes (Disney resort guests) to 70 minutes (non–Disney resort guests) before opening. Get guide maps and the *Times Guide*.

2. As soon as the park opens, head to Fantasyland and ride Seven Dwarfs Mine Train.

3. Ride The Many Adventures of Winnie the Pooh.

4. Ride Under the Sea: Journey of the Little Mermaid.

5. Meet Goofy and Donald at Pete's Silly Sideshow.

6. Take the Jungle Cruise in Adventureland.

7. In Frontierland, ride Splash Mountain.

8. Ride Big Thunder Mountain Railroad.

9. Eat lunch.

10. Ride Peter Pan's Flight In Fantasyland.

11. See *Mickey's PhilharMagic*.

12. Ride It's a Small World.

13. In Liberty Square, see The Haunted Mansion.

14. Ride the *Liberty Belle* Riverboat.

15. Experience *The Hall of Presidents* in Liberty Square.

16. In Frontierland, see *Country Bear Jamboree.*

17. In Frontierland, take the raft over to Tom Sawyer Island. Allow at least 30 minutes to explore the island, Fort Langhorn, and the barrel bridges.

18. In Adventureland, play A Pirate's Adventure.

19. Ride Pirates of the Caribbean.

20. See the evening parade on Main Street.

21. See the evening castle light show and fireworks on Main Street. A good viewing spot is somewhere between The Plaza Restaurant and Tomorrowland Terrace.

You can customize this touring plan and get real-time updates while you're in the park! See **touringplans.com** for details. **Suggested start times for FastPass+ reservations:** Big Thunder Mountain Railroad: 10:30 a.m.; Peter Pan's Flight, 12 noon; The Haunted Mansion, 1 p.m.

*The Magic Kingdom*

## MAGIC KINGDOM TWO-DAY TOURING PLAN: DAY TWO
*(Note that Day Two does not require FastPass+.)*

1. Arrive at the Magic Kingdom entrance 50 minutes (Disney resort guests) to 70 minutes (non–Disney resort guests) before opening. Get guide maps and the *Times Guide*.
2. In Tomorrowland, ride Space Mountain.
3. Ride Buzz Lightyear's Space Ranger Spin.
4. In Adventureland, explore the Swiss Family Treehouse.
5. Take the Jungle Cruise in Adventureland. (If you want to ride Splash Mountain and/or Big Thunder Mountain again today, make Fast-Pass+ reservations for sometime in the afternoon.)
6. See *Walt Disney's Enchanted Tiki Room*.
7. Return to Tomorrowland to see *Monsters, Inc. Laugh Floor.*
8. Ride the Tomorrowland Transit Authority PeopleMover.
9. See *Walt Disney's Carousel of Progress*.
10. Eat lunch.
11. Tour Main Street, U.S.A., and meet any characters that interest you (check the *Times Guide* for locations and times). Or shop, see live entertainment, or revisit favorite attractions.

You can customize this touring plan and get real-time updates while you're in the park! See **touringplans.com** for details.

# The Magic Kingdom

## MAGIC KINGDOM DUMBO-OR-DIE-IN-A-DAY TOURING PLAN
## FOR PARENTS WITH SMALL CHILDREN
*(Review the Small-Child Fright-Potential Chart on pages 332–335.*
*Interrupt the plan for meals, rest, and a cocktail or two.)*

**1.** Arrive at the Magic Kingdom entrance 50 minutes (Disney resort guests) to 70 minutes (non–Disney resort guests) before opening. Rent strollers before the park opens. Get guide maps and the *Times Guide*.

**2.** As soon as the park opens, head to Fantasyland and ride Seven Dwarfs Mine Train.

**3.** Ride Under the Sea: Journey of the Little Mermaid.

**4.** Ride Dumbo the Flying Elephant. Ride again, if desired. (*Tip:* Have one parent stand in line about 48 people behind the other parent and child. When the first parent is done riding, hand the child to the second parent in line.)

**5.** Ride The Barnstormer.

**6.** In Tomorrowland, ride the Astro Orbiter.

**7.** Take the Jungle Cruise in Adventureland.

**8.** Return to Fantasyland to ride Peter Pan's Flight.

**9.** In Liberty Square, see The Haunted Mansion.

**10.** Ride It's a Small World in Fantasyland.

**11.** Eat lunch and take a midday break of at least 3 hours outside the park.

**12.** In Frontierland, take the raft over to Tom Sawyer

Island. Allow at least 30 minutes to explore the island, Fort Langhorn, and the barrel bridges.

**13.** In Adventureland, ride Pirates of the Caribbean.

**14.** Ride The Magic Carpets of Aladdin.

**15.** See *Walt Disney's Enchanted Tiki Room*.

**16.** In Frontierland, see *Country Bear Jamboree*.

**17.** In Fantasyland, see *Mickey's PhilharMagic*.

**18.** Eat dinner.

**19.** Ride Buzz Lightyear in Tomorrowland.

**20.** Take a spin on the Tomorrowland Speedway.

**21.** Back in Fantasyland, ride the Prince Charming Regal Carrousel.

**22.** See *Enchanted Tales with Belle*.

**23.** Ride The Many Adventures of Winnie the Pooh.

**24.** Meet Mickey Mouse at Town Square Theater on Main Street.

**25.** See the evening parade on Main Street.

**26.** See the evening castle light show and fireworks on Main Street. A good viewing spot is somewhere between The Plaza Restaurant and Tomorrowland Terrace.

You can customize this touring plan and get real-time updates while you're in the park! See **touringplans.com** for details. **Suggested start times for FastPass+ reservations:** Peter Pan's Flight: 10:30 a.m.; Buzz Lightyear's Space Ranger Spin, 6:30 p.m.; *Enchanted Tales with Belle,* 7:30 p.m.

*Epcot*

## EPCOT ONE-DAY TOURING PLAN FOR ADULTS

1. Arrive 40 minutes before opening. Get guide maps and the *Times Guide*.
2. As soon as the park opens, ride Soarin' in The Land.
3. Ride Living with the Land.
4. In Future World East, ride Test Track.
5. Ride Sum of All Thrills.
6. Ride Mission: SPACE Orange.
7. Experience *Ellen's Energy Adventure*.
8. Eat lunch (we recommend Sunshine Seasons in The Land).
9. Ride Spaceship Earth.
10. See The Seas with Nemo & Friends and *Turtle Talk with Crush*.
11. In the Imagination! Pavilion, experience Journey into Imagination with Figment.
12. Tour Canada and see *O Canada!*
13. Tour the United Kingdom.
14. Play a game of Agent P's World Showcase Adventure. Sign up between the UK and France Pavilions.
15. Visit France and see *Impressions de France*.
16. Tour Morocco.
17. Explore Japan.
18. See *The American Adventure*.
19. Visit Italy.
20. Tour Germany.
21. Eat dinner.
22. Tour China and watch *Reflections of China*.
23. Ride Maelstrom and visit the stave church in Norway.
24. Tour Mexico and ride the Gran Fiesta Tour.
25. See *IllumiNations*. Prime viewing spots are along the lagoon between Canada and France. You could also try for a lagoon-side table at La Cantina de San Angel or La Hacienda de San Angel in Mexico (Advance Reservations needed at the latter), or Spice Road Table in Morocco.

You can customize this touring plan and get real-time updates while you're in the park! See **touringplans .com** for details. **Suggested start times for FastPass+ reservations:** Test Track, 9:15 a.m.; Mission: SPACE Orange, 10:15 a.m.; Spaceship Earth, 1 p.m.

*Epcot*

## EPCOT AUTHORS' SELECTIVE ONE-DAY TOURING PLAN FOR ADULTS

1. Arrive 40 minutes before opening. Get guide maps and the *Times Guide*.
2. As soon as the park opens, ride Soarin' in The Land.
3. Ride Living with the Land.
4. In Future World East, ride Test Track.
5. Ride Sum of All Thrills.
6. Ride Mission: SPACE Orange.
7. Experience *Ellen's Energy Adventure*.
8. Eat lunch (we recommend Sunshine Seasons in The Land).
9. Ride Spaceship Earth.
10. See *Captain EO*.
11. See The Seas with Nemo & Friends and *Turtle Talk with Crush*.
12. Tour Canada and see *O Canada!*
13. Tour the United Kingdom.
14. Visit France and see *Impressions de France*.
15. Tour Morocco.
16. Explore Japan.
17. See *The American Adventure*.
18. Visit Italy.
19. Tour Germany.
20. Eat dinner.
21. Tour China and watch *Reflections of China*.
22. Ride Maelstrom and visit the stave church in Norway.
23. Tour Mexico and ride the Gran Fiesta Tour.
24. See *IllumiNations*. Prime viewing spots are along the lagoon between Canada and France. You could also try for a lagoon-side table at La Cantina de San Angel or La Hacienda de San Angel in Mexico (Advance Reservations needed at the latter), or Spice Road Table in Morocco.

You can customize this touring plan and get real-time updates while you're in the park! See **touringplans .com** for details. **Suggested start times for FastPass+ reservations:** Test Track, 9:15 a.m.; Mission: SPACE Orange, 10:15 a.m.; Spaceship Earth, 1 p.m.

Epcot

## EPCOT ONE-DAY TOURING PLAN FOR PARENTS WITH SMALL CHILDREN

*(Review the Small-Child Fright-Potential Chart on pages 332–335.)*

1. Arrive 40 minutes before opening. Rent strollers if needed. Get guide maps and the *Times Guide*.

2. As soon as the park opens, head to the Epcot Character Spot in Innoventions West.

3. Ride Soarin' in The Land.

4. See *The Circle of Life*.

5. In the Imagination! Pavilion, experience Journey into Imagination with Figment.

6. See *Captain EO*.

7. Ride Spaceship Earth.

8. Eat lunch and take a midday break back at your hotel.

9. Experience *Ellen's Energy Adventure*.

10. See The Seas with Nemo & Friends and *Turtle Talk with Crush*.

11. Ride Living with the Land.

12. Play a game of Agent P's World Showcase Adventure. Sign up on the east side of the main walkway from Future World to World Showcase.

13. Eat dinner.

14. See *The American Adventure*.

15. Ride Maelstrom and visit the stave church in Norway.

16. Tour Mexico and ride the Gran Fiesta Tour.

17. See *IllumiNations*. Prime viewing spots are along the lagoon between Canada and France. You could also try for a lagoon-side table at La Cantina de San Angel or La Hacienda de San Angel in Mexico (Advance Reservations needed at the latter), or Spice Road Table in Morocco.

You can customize this touring plan and get real-time updates while you're in the park! See **touringplans .com** for details. **Suggested start times for FastPass+ reservations:** Soarin'*, 9 a.m.; Maelstrom, 8 p.m.; Spaceship Earth, 11 a.m.

*Epcot*

## EPCOT TWO-DAY EARLY-RISER TOURING PLAN: DAY ONE

*(Parents with young children should review the*
*Small-Child Fright-Potential Chart on pages 332–335.)*

1. Arrive 40 minutes before opening. Rent strollers if needed. Get guide maps and the *Times Guide*.

2. As soon as the park opens, see The Seas with Nemo & Friends and *Turtle Talk with Crush*.

3. In the Imagination! Pavilion, experience Journey into Imagination with Figment.

4. See *Captain EO*.

5. Ride Soarin' in The Land.

6. See *The Circle of Life*.

7. Eat lunch (we recommend Sunshine Seasons in The Land).

8. Ride Living with the Land.

9. Tour Canada and see *O Canada!*

10. Tour the United Kingdom.

12. If you have small children, sign up for Agent P's World Showcase Adventure between the UK and France. Ask for a mission in either of those pavilions.

13. Visit France and see *Impressions de France.*

14. Tour Morocco.

15. If time permits, tour Innoventions West.

You can customize this touring plan and get real-time updates while you're in the park! See **touringplans .com** for details. **Suggested start times for FastPass+ reservations:** Soarin', 10 a.m.

Epcot

## EPCOT TWO-DAY EARLY-RISER TOURING PLAN: DAY TWO
*(Parents with young children should review the*
*Small-Child Fright-Potential Chart on pages 332–335.)*

1. Arrive 40 minutes before opening. Rent strollers if needed. Get guide maps and the *Times Guide*.

2. As soon as the park opens, ride Test Track.

3. Ride Sum of All Thrills.

4. Experience *Ellen's Energy Adventure*.

5. Ride Mission: SPACE Orange.

6. Tour Innoventions East.

7. Ride Spaceship Earth.

8. Eat lunch.

9. Tour Mexico and ride the Gran Fiesta Tour.

10. Ride Maelstrom and visit the stave church in Norway.

11. If you haven't already done so, try Agent P's World Showcase Adventure in Norway or China. Register at the Norway Pavilion,

between the UK and France, or on the east side of the main walkway from Future World to World Showcase

12. Watch *Reflections of China*.

13. Tour Germany.

14. Visit Italy.

15. See *The American Adventure*.

16. Explore Japan.

17. See *IllumiNations*. Prime viewing spots are along the lagoon between Canada and France. You could also try for a lagoon-side table at La Cantina de San Angel or La Hacienda de San Angel in Mexico (Advance Reservations needed at the latter), or Spice Road Table in Morocco.

You can customize this touring plan and get real-time updates while you're in the park! See **touringplans.com** for details. **Suggested start times for FastPass+ reservations:** Test Track, 9 a.m.; Mission: SPACE Orange, 10 a.m.; Spaceship Earth: 11 a.m.

# Disney's Animal Kingdom

## DISNEY'S ANIMAL KINGDOM ONE-DAY TOURING PLAN

1. Arrive 30–40 minutes prior to opening. Get guide maps and the *Times Guide*.
2. Experience Expedition Everest in Asia.
3. In DinoLand U.S.A., ride TriceraTop Spin if you have young children in your group.
4. Ride Primeval Whirl.
5. Follow the signs to DINOSAUR and ride.
6. Ride Kali River Rapids.
7. Take the Wildlife Express Train from Africa to Conservation Station and Rafiki's Planet Watch. Tour the area and take the train back to Africa.
8. Eat lunch.
9. See *Festival of the Lion King* in Africa.
10. See *It's Tough to Be a Bug!* on Discovery Island.
11. Walk the Maharajah Jungle Trek in Asia.
12. See *Flights of Wonder*.
13. Earn a couple of badges playing Wilderness Explorers.
14. See *Finding Nemo—The Musical* in DinoLand U.S.A.
15. Walk the Pangani Forest Exploration Trail.
16. Explore the trails and exhibits around The Tree of Life.
17. Ride Kilimanjaro Safaris in Africa

You can customize this touring plan and get real-time updates while you're in the park! See **touringplans.com** for details. **Suggested start times for FastPass+ reservations:** DINOSAUR, 9–10 a.m.; Kali River Rapids, 10–11 a.m.; Kilimanjaro Safaris, 5:45–6:45 p.m. or the last hour the ride is open.

*Disney's Hollywood Studios*

## DISNEY'S HOLLYWOOD STUDIOS ONE-DAY TOURING PLAN

1. Arrive at the park 30–40 minutes before official opening time. Get guide maps and the *Times Guide*.
2. As soon as the park opens, ride Rock 'n' Roller Coaster.
3. Ride The Great Movie Ride.
4. In Echo Lake, ride Star Tours—The Adventures Continue.
5. Ride Toy Story Midway Mania! in Pixar Place.
6. Take the Studio Backlot Tour.
7. See *Walt Disney: One Man's Dream*.
8. Eat lunch.
9. Work in *Disney Junior—Live on Stage!* if you have small children.
10. Take the Magic of Disney Animation tour. If time is short and you have small children, choose between this and *Disney Junior*.
11. See *Voyage of the Little Mermaid*.
12. See *Beauty and the Beast—Live on Stage*.
13. See *The American Idol Experience* while it's still open (closes January 2015).
14. See the *Lights, Motors, Action! Extreme Stunt Show*.
15. See the *Indiana Jones Epic Stunt Spectacular!*
16. Explore the Streets of America on the way to *Jim Henson's Muppet-Vision 3-D*.
17. See *Muppet-Vision 3-D*.
18. Eat dinner.
19. Ride The Twilight Zone Tower of Terror.
21. Enjoy *Fantasmic!* Plan on arriving about 1 hour early to get good seats, or 30 minutes early for standing-room-only.

You can customize this touring plan and get real-time updates while you're in the park! See **touringplans.com** for details. **Suggested FastPass+ reservation times:** Star Tours, 9 a.m.; Toy Story Midway Mania!, 10 a.m.; Tower of Terror, 6:30 p.m.

## Universal's Islands of Adventure

## UNIVERSAL'S ISLANDS OF ADVENTURE ONE-DAY TOURING PLAN

1. Call ☎ 407-363-8000 the day before your visit for the official opening time.

2. Arrive at least 60 minutes before opening time, and pick up a map and daily entertainment schedule.

3. Line up at the turnstiles. Ask if any attractions are closed; adjust touring plan accordingly.

4. As soon as the park opens, ride The Incredible Hulk Coaster on Marvel Island.

5. Ride Doctor Doom's Fearfall.

6. See The Amazing Adventures of Spider-Man.

7. Continue clockwise and ride Dudley Do-Right's Ripsaw Falls in Toon Lagoon.

8. Take the Jurassic Park River Adventure in Jurassic Park.

9. Pass through The Wizarding World–Hogsmeade on your way to The Lost Continent. If the wait for Dragon Challenge in Wizarding World is less than 15 minutes, ride now.

10. Experience *Poseidon's Fury* in The Lost Continent.

11. Continue clockwise and ride The Cat in the Hat in Seuss Landing.

12. Ride Popeye & Bluto's Bilge-Rat Barges in Toon Lagoon.

13. Eat lunch.

14. See the *Eighth Voyage of Sindbad Stunt Show* in The Lost Continent.

15. Head to The Wizarding World of Harry Potter. Explore Hogsmeade and ride Harry Potter and the Forbidden Journey.

16. Ride Dragon Challenge if you've not already done so.

17. Revisit favorite rides and check out attractions you may have missed.

*Universal Studios Florida*

The Wizarding World of Harry Potter–Diagon Alley

## UNIVERSAL STUDIOS FLORIDA ONE-DAY TOURING PLAN
*(Assumes: Day guest without Universal Express; 1-Day Base Ticket)*

1. Buy your admission in advance and call ☎ 407-363-8000 the day before your visit for the official opening time.

2. Arrive 60–90 minutes before opening and pick up a map and entertainment schedule. Confirm with a park worker whether you'll need a timed-return ticket (TRT) to Diagon Alley.

3. Line up at the rightmost open turnstile. Ask if any rides or shows are closed, and adjust touring plan accordingly.

4. If you need TRTs to enter Diagon Alley, send one member of your party to obtain them: Turn right on Hollywood Boulevard and walk toward Men in Black: Alien Attack. Look for the Diagon Alley timed-return kiosks between Men in Black and the *Fear Factor Live* arena. Get a TRT for the earliest available time slot. Interrupt the touring plan when you're able to enter Diagon Alley (steps 18–20), then resume the plan when you're done.

5. Ride Despicable Me Minion Mayhem in Production Central.

6. Ride Hollywood Rip Ride Rockit.

7. Experience Transformers: The Ride 3-D.

8. Ride Revenge of the Mummy in New York.

9. See *TWISTER . . . Ride It Out*.

10. Experience *Disaster!* in San Francisco.

11. Work in *Beetlejuice's Graveyard Mash-Up* **(11a)** and *Fear Factor Live* **(11b)** around lunch and your Diagon Alley return time, according to the daily entertainment schedule.

12. Ride Men in Black Alien Attack in World Expo.

13. Ride The Simpsons Ride in Springfield U.S.A.

14. Ride E.T. Adventure (expendable if there are no young kids in your group) in Woody's KidZone.

15. See *Shrek 4-D* in Production Central.

16. See the *Universal Horror Make-Up Show* **(16a)**, *Animal Actors on Location* **(16b)**, and *Terminator 2: 3-D* **(16c)** according to the daily entertainment schedule. If time is short, skip *Animal Actors on Location*.

17. Eat dinner.

18. Enter Diagon Alley and ride Escape from Gringotts.

19. Tour Diagon Alley. Browse the shops, and if you're hungry, try the Leaky Cauldron or Florean Fortescue's Ice Cream Parlour.

20. See the *Celestina Warbeck* and *Tales of Beedle the Bard* shows.

21. If time permits, see *Universal's Cinematic Spectacular* at the lagoon.

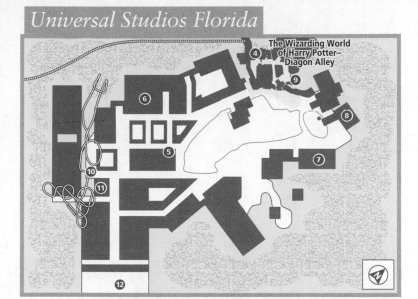

*Universal Studios Florida*

The Wizarding World of Harry Potter–Diagon Alley

## THE BEST OF UNIVERSAL STUDIOS FLORIDA AND
## ISLANDS OF ADVENTURE IN ONE DAY

1. Call ☎ 407-363-8000 the day before your visit for the official opening times.
2. Arrive at Universal's Islands of Adventure 60 minutes before opening, and pick up a map and entertainment schedule. *(See map on next page.)*
3. Line up at the turnstile. Ask if any rides or shows are closed, and adjust touring plan. *(See map on next page.)*
4. As soon as the park opens, walk quickly to The Wizarding World of Harry Potter–Hogsmeade and take the Hogwarts Express train to The Wizarding World of Harry Potter–Diagon Alley. *(See map on next page.)*
5. Once off the train, experience Transformers: The Ride 3-D in Production Central.
6. Ride Revenge of the Mummy.
7. Ride The Simpsons Ride.
8. Ride Men in Black Alien Attack.
9. Ride Harry Potter and the Escape from Gringotts, eat a quick lunch, and tour Diagon Alley.
10. Ride Hollywood Rip Ride Rockit.
11. Ride Despicable Me Minion Mayhem.
12. Exit Universal Studios Florida and walk to Islands of Adventure.

*(Continued on next page)*

*Universal's Islands of Adventure*

### THE BEST OF UNIVERSAL STUDIOS FLORIDA AND ISLANDS OF ADVENTURE IN ONE DAY
*(Continued from previous page)*

**13.** Ride The Incredible Hulk Coaster on Marvel Super Hero Island.

**14.** Ride The Amazing Adventures of Spider-Man.

**15.** Experience *Poseidon's Fury* in The Lost Continent.

**16.** Eat a quick dinner.

**17.** Ride Dragon Challenge in The Wizarding World–Hogsmeade.

**18.** Ride Harry Potter and the Forbidden Journey.

**19.** Take the Jurassic Park River Adventure.

**20.** Ride Dudley Do-Right's Ripsaw Falls.

**21.** Ride Popeye & Bluto's Bilge-Rat Barges

**22.** Repeat any missed attractions or revisit favorites as time permits.

## Blizzard Beach

### BLIZZARD BEACH ONE-DAY TOURING PLAN
### FOR PARENTS WITH SMALL CHILDREN

1. Arrive at the park entrance 30 minutes before opening. Take care of locker and towel rentals at Lottawatta Lodge, to your left as you enter the park. Find a spot to stow the remainder of your gear, noting any nearby landmarks to help you find your way back.

2. Take the chairlift up Mt Gushmore to the Green Slope. *Note:* It might be faster—but more tiring—to walk to the top.

3. Raft down Teamboat Springs. Repeat as much as you like while the park is still uncrowded.

4. If your kids are up for it, try the Toboggan Racers.

5. If the kids enjoyed the Toboggan Racers, try the Snow Stormers next.

6. Visit the Ski Patrol Training Camp.

7. Ride Tike's Peak.

8. Grab some tubes and ride Cross Country Creek.

9. Swim in Melt-Away Bay's Wave Pool as long as you like.

You can customize this touring plan and get real-time updates while you're in the park! See **touringplans.com** for details.

*Typhoon Lagoon*

## TYPHOON LAGOON ONE-DAY TOURING PLAN
## FOR PARENTS WITH SMALL CHILDREN

1. Arrive at the park entrance 30 minutes before opening. Take care of locker and towel rentals at Singapore Sal's, to your right after you've walked along the winding entrance path and emerged into the park. Find a spot to stow the remainder of your gear, noting any nearby landmarks to help you find your way back.

2. Ride Gang Plank Falls as many times as you like.

3. If your kids enjoyed Gang Plank Falls, try Keelhaul Falls if it seems appropriate.

4. Enjoy the Ketchakiddee Creek kids' play area.

5. Grab some tubes and ride Castaway Creek. A complete circuit takes 20–25 minutes.

6. Swim in the Surf Pool as long as you like.

7. Ride the Bay Slides in the Surf Pool.

8. Repeat your favorite attractions as desired.

You can customize this touring plan and get real-time updates while you're in the park! See **touringplans.com** for details.

# MAGIC KINGDOM TOURING PLAN COMPANION

### ATTRACTION | RECOMMENDED VISITATION TIMES | AUTHOR'S RATING

**Ariel's Grotto** | Before 10:30 a.m., in the 2 hours before closing, FastPass+ | ★★★

**Astro Orbiter** | Before 11 a.m., in the hour before closing | ★★

**The Barnstormer** *(FastPass+)* | Before 11 a.m., during parades, in the 2 hours before closing, FastPass+ | ★★

**Big Thunder Mountain Railroad** *(FastPass+)* | Before 10 a.m., in the hour before closing, FastPass+ ★★★★
    *Special comments* 40" minimum height; expectant mothers should not ride

**Buzz Lightyear's Space Ranger Spin** *(FastPass+)* | First or last hour the park is open, FastPass+ | ★★★★

**Captain Jack Sparrow's Pirate Tutorial** | Check *Times Guide* for showtimes | ★★★½

**Casey Jr. Splash 'N' Soak Station** | Anytime | ★½

*Country Bear Jamboree* | Anytime | ★★★½

**Dumbo the Flying Elephant** *(FastPass+)* | Before 10 a.m., after 3 p.m., FastPass+ | ★★★½

*Enchanted Tales with Belle* *(FastPass+)* | At opening, in the 2 hours before closing, FastPass+ | ★★★★

*Frontierland Shootin' Arcade* | Anytime | ★½

*The Hall of Presidents* | Anytime | ★★★½

**The Haunted Mansion** | Before 11 a.m., in the 2 hours before closing | ★★★★ | *Special comment* Fright potential

**It's a Small World** *(FastPass+)* | Before 11 a.m., during parades, after 7 p.m., FastPass+ | ★★★½

**Jungle Cruise** *(FastPass+)* | Before 10:30 a.m., in the 2 hours before closing, FastPass+ | ★★★

*Liberty Belle* **Riverboat** | Anytime | ★★½

**Mad Tea Party** *(FastPass+)* | Before 11 a.m., after 5 p.m., FastPass+ | ★★ | *Special comments* Expectant mothers
    should not ride; motion-sickness potential

**The Magic Carpets of Aladdin** *(FastPass+)* | Before 11 a.m., after 7 p.m., FastPass+ | ★★½

**The Many Adventures of Winnie the Pooh** *(FastPass+)* | Before 10 a.m., in the hour before closing, FastPass+
    ★★★½

**Meet Merida at Fairytale Gardens** | Check *Times Guide* for schedule | ★★★½

*Mickey's PhilharMagic* *(FastPass+)* | Before 11 a.m., during parades, FastPass+ | ★★★★

*Monsters, Inc. Laugh Floor* *(FastPass+)* | Before 11 a.m., after 4 p.m., FastPass+ | ★★★½

**Peter Pan's Flight** *(FastPass+)* | First or last 30 minutes the park is open, FastPass+ | ★★★★

**Pete's Silly Sideshow** *(FastPass+)* | Before 11 a.m., in the 2 hours before closing, FastPass+ | ★★★½

**A Pirate's Adventure: Treasure of the Seven Seas** | Anytime | ★★★½

**Pirates of the Caribbean** | Before 11 a.m., after 7 p.m. | ★★★★

**Prince Charming Regal Carrousel** | Before 11 a.m., after 8 p.m. | ★★★

**Princess Fairytale Hall** | Before 10:30 a.m., after 4 p.m. | ★★

**Seven Dwarfs Mine Train** *(FastPass+)* | At park opening, FastPass+ | ★★★★

**Sorcerers of the Magic Kingdom** | Before 11 a.m., after 8 p.m. | ★★★

**Space Mountain** *(FastPass+)* | At opening, FastPass+ | ★★★★ | *Special comments* 44" minimum height;
    expectant mothers should not ride

**Splash Mountain** *(FastPass+)* | At opening, during parades, just before closing, FastPass+ | ★★★★★
    *Special comments* 40" minimum height; expectant mothers should not ride

*Stitch's Great Escape!* | Before 11 a.m., during parades, after 6 p.m. | ★★★ | *Special comments* Fright potential;
    40" minimum height

**Swiss Family Treehouse** | Anytime | ★★★ | *Special comments* Fright potential due to height

**Tom Sawyer Island and Fort Langhorn** | Midmorning–late afternoon | ★★★

**Tomorrowland Speedway** *(FastPass+)* | Before 10 a.m., in the 2 hours before closing, FastPass+ | ★★
    *Special comments* 54" minimum height requirement for kids to drive unassisted

**Tomorrowland Transit Authority PeopleMover** | Anytime, but especially during hot, crowded times of day
    (11:30 a.m.–4:30 p.m.) | ★★★½

**Town Square Theater Meet-and-Greets** *(FastPass+)* | Before 10 a.m., after 4 p.m., FastPass+ | ★★★★

**Under the Sea: Journey of the Little Mermaid** *(FastPass+)* | Before 10:30 a.m., in the 2 hours before closing,
    FastPass+ | ★★★½

*Walt Disney's Carousel of Progress* | Anytime | ★★★

*Walt Disney's Enchanted Tiki Room* | Before 11 a.m., after 3:30 p.m. | ★★★

**Walt Disney World Railroad** | Anytime | ★★½

## DINING INFORMATION—Counter Service
**RESTAURANT | LOCATION | QUALITY | VALUE**

**Aloha Isle** | Adventureland | Excellent | B+ | *Selections* Ice cream, sorbet, fresh fruit

**Be Our Guest Restaurant** | Fantasyland | Excellent | B+ | *Selections* Tuna niçoise salad, *croque monsieur* (grilled ham-and-cheese sandwich), carved turkey or roast beef sandwiches, braised pork with bacon mashed potatoes, veggie quiche, quinoa salad

**Casey's Corner** | Main Street, U.S.A. | Fair | B | *Selections* Hot dogs, hot-dog nuggets, fries

**Columbia Harbour House** | Liberty Square | Good | B | *Selections* Grilled salmon, fried fish and shrimp, chicken nuggets, sandwiches, soups, salads, kids' meals

**Cosmic Ray's Starlight Cafe** | Tomorrowland | Good | B | *Selections* Burgers (veggie available); rotisserie chicken and ribs; hot dogs; Greek salad; chicken, turkey, or vegetable sandwiches; some kosher

**Friar's Nook** | Fantasyland | Good | B | *Selections* Hot dogs, specialty mac and cheese, homemade potato chips, chicken Caesar salad, frozen drinks

**Gaston's Tavern** | Fantasyland | Good | C | *Selections* Roast pork shank, hummus with chips, cinnamon rolls, chocolate croissants, LeFou's Brew (frozen apple-juice drink)

**Golden Oak Outpost** | Frontierland | Good | B+ | *Selections* Chicken nuggets, fried-chicken sandwiches, fries, cakes and cookies

**The Lunching Pad** | Tomorrowland | Good | B– | *Selections* Hot dogs, dessert pretzels, frozen sodas

**Pecos Bill Tall Tale Inn & Cafe** | Frontierland | Good | B | *Selections* Burgers, barbecue-pork sandwiches, steak-and-chicken platter, taco salad, chili, kids' meals

**The Pinocchio Village Haus** | Fantasyland | Fair | C | *Selections* Personal pizzas, meatball sub sandwiches, chicken nuggets, salads, kids' meals

**Tomorrowland Terrace Restaurant** *(open seasonally)* | Tomorrowland | Fair | C | *Selections* Burgers, lobster rolls, chicken sandwiches, pasta, kids' meals

**Tortuga Tavern** *(open seasonally)* | Adventureland | Fair | B | *Selections* Tacos, taco salad, chicken Caesar salad, burritos, quesadillas

## DINING INFORMATION—Full Service
**RESTAURANT | MEALS SERVED | LOCATION | PRICE | QUALITY | VALUE**

**Be Our Guest Restaurant** | D | Fantasyland | Moderate | ★★★★ | ★★★★
*Selections* Pan-seared salmon, New York strip, shrimp and scallops in puff pastry, mussels Provençal

**Cinderella's Royal Table** | B-L-D | Fantasyland | Expensive | ★★★ | ★★
*Selections* Beef tenderloin, Major Domo's Favorite Pie (beef in Cabernet sauce, mashed potatoes, and puff pastry), bone-in pork, fish of the day, kids' menu

**The Crystal Palace** | B-L-D | Main Street, U.S.A. | Moderate | ★★★½ | ★★★
*Selections* Buffet (items change often); best dining value in the Magic Kingdom

**Liberty Tree Tavern** | L-D | Liberty Square | Moderate | ★★★ | ★★★
*Selections* Roasted meats, sandwiches, salads; all-you-can-eat family-style dinner

**The Plaza Restaurant** | L-D | Main Street, U.S.A. | Moderate | ★★ | ★★
*Selections* Sandwiches, salads, ice cream

**Tony's Town Square Restaurant** | L-D | Main Street, U.S.A. | Moderate | ★★★ | ★★
*Selections* Sausage-and-pepper flatbread, pasta, New York strip; gluten-free options

*Advance Reservations recommended for Magic Kingdom full-service restaurants; call*
☎ *407-WDW-DINE (939-3463) or visit* disneyworld.disney.go.com/reservations/dining.

## GOOD REST AREAS IN THE MAGIC KINGDOM
**PLACE | LOCATION | NOTES**

**Covered porch with rocking chairs on Tom Sawyer Island** | Frontierland
Across the water from the Liberty Belle Riverboat dock; bring refreshments from Frontierland; closes at sunset

**Cul-de-sac** | Main Street, U.S.A. | Between the china shop and Main Street's Starbucks on right-hand side of street as you face the castle; nearby refreshments

**Quiet seating area** | Tomorrowland | Near restrooms on the right as you approach Space Mountain—look for pay phones, and there's a covered seating area farther back of that corridor; refreshments nearby

**Picnic tables** | Fantasyland | Near the *Tangled*-themed restrooms, between Peter Pan's Flight and The Haunted Mansion. Outdoors but has phone-charging stations.

**Upstairs at Columbia Harbour House** | Liberty Square | Grab a beverage and relax upstairs. Restrooms available upstairs too.

**Second floor of train station** | Main Street, U.S.A. | Refreshments nearby; crowded during fireworks and parades

# EPCOT TOURING **PLAN COMPANION**

## ATTRACTION | RECOMMENDED VISITATION TIMES | AUTHOR'S RATING

**Agent P's World Showcase Adventure** | World Showcase, various pavilions | Anytime | ★★★★

*The American Adventure* | United States, World Showcase | Anytime | ★★★★

*Captain EO (FastPass+)* | Imagination! Pavilion, Future World | Anytime | ★★★

*The Circle of Life* | The Land, Future World | Anytime | ★★★½

**Epcot Character Spot** *(FastPass+)* | Innoventions West, Future World | Before 11 a.m., FastPass+ | ★★★

*Gran Fiesta Tour* | Mexico, World Showcase | Before noon, after 5 p.m. | ★★½

*Impressions de France* | France, World Showcase | Anytime | ★★★½

**Innoventions East and West** | Future World | Second day or after major attractions | ★★★½

**Journey into Imagination with Figment** *(FastPass+)* | Imagination!, Future World | Anytime | ★★½

**Living with the Land** *(FastPass+)* | The Land, Future World | Before 11 a.m., after 1 p.m., FastPass+ | ★★★★

**Maelstrom** *(FastPass+)* | Norway, World Showcase | Before 1 p.m., after 7 p.m., FastPass+ | ★★★

**Mission: SPACE** *(FastPass+)* | Future World | First hour the park is open, FastPass+ | ★★★★
   *Special comments* 44" minimum height; expectant mothers should not ride; motion-sickness potential

**The "Mom, I Can't Believe It's Disney!" Fountains** | Future World | When it's hot | ★★★★

*O Canada!* | Canada, World Showcase | Anytime | ★★★½

*Reflections of China* | China, World Showcase | Anytime | ★★★½

**The Seas Main Tank and Exhibits** | The Seas with Nemo & Friends, Future World | Before 11:30 a.m., after 5 p.m. | ★★★½

**The Seas with Nemo & Friends** *(FastPass+)* | The Seas with Nemo & Friends, Future World Before 11 a.m. after 5 p.m., FastPass+ | ★★★

**Soarin'** *(FastPass+)* | The Land, Future World | First 30 minutes the park is open, FastPass+ | ★★★★½
   *Special comments* 40" minimum height; motion-sickness potential

**Spaceship Earth** *(FastPass+)* | Future World | Before 10 a.m., after 4 p.m., FastPass+ | ★★★★

**Sum of All Thrills** | Innoventions West, Future World | Before 10:30 a.m., after 5 p.m. | ★★★★
   *Special comments* 48" minimum height, 54" for coaster-track designs with inversions

**Test Track** *(FastPass+)* | Test Track, Future World | First 30 minutes the park is open, just before closing, FastPass+ | ★★★★ | *Special comments* 40" minimum height; expectant mothers should not ride

*Turtle Talk with Crush (FastPass+)*| The Seas with Nemo & Friends, Future World | Before 11 a.m., after 5 p.m., FastPass+ | ★★★★

**Universe of Energy:** *Ellen's Energy Adventure* | Future World | Anytime | ★★★½

## DINING INFORMATION—Counter Service

### RESTAURANT | LOCATION | QUALITY | VALUE | SELECTIONS

**L'Artisan des Glaces** | France, World Showcase | Excellent | C | *Selections* Ice cream, sorbet

**La Cantina de San Angel** | Mexico, World Showcase | Good | B | *Selections* Chicken and beef tacos, nachos, cheese empanadas, margaritas

**Crêpes des Chefs de France** | France, World Showcase | Excellent | B+ | *Selections* Dessert crêpes, ice cream, specialty beer, espresso

**Electric Umbrella Restaurant** | Innoventions East, Future World | Fair–good | B– | *Selections* Burgers, chicken nuggets, veggie flatbread, Caesar and Greek salads, kids' meals

**Fife & Drum Tavern** | United States, World Showcase | Fair | C | *Selections* Turkey legs, pretzels, ice cream, frozen slushes, beer

**Fountain View** | Future World Plaza | Fair | C | *Selections* Disney-themed Starbucks with all the usual suspects: coffee drinks, breakfast sandwiches, and pastries

**Katsura Grill** | Japan, World Showcase | Good | B | *Selections* Beef, chicken, or salmon teriyaki; noodles; sushi; miso soup; beer, sake, green tea

**Kringla Bakeri og Kafe** | Norway, World Showcase | Good–excellent | B | *Selections* Pastries, sandwiches, vegetable torte, rice cream, beer

**Les Halles Boulangerie Patisserie** | France, World Showcase | Good | A | *Selections* Pastries, niçoise salad, cheese plate, sandwiches, quiches, soups

**Liberty Inn** | United States, World Showcase | Fair | C | *Selections* Burgers, barbecue-pork sandwich, hot dogs, chili, chicken nuggets, New York strip steak, salads, kids' meals, some kosher

**Lotus Blossom Cafe** | China, World Showcase | Fair | C | *Selections* Egg rolls, pot stickers, fried rice, orange chicken, noodle bowls

**Promenade Refreshments** | World Showcase Promenade | Fair | C | *Selections* Meatball subs, pretzels, popcorn, ice cream, beer

**Refreshment Cool Post** | Between Germany and China | Good | B– | *Selections* Hot dogs, ice cream, coffee and tea, beer

**Refreshment Port** | Near Canada | Good | B | *Selections* Croissant doughnuts, chicken nuggets, flavored coffees, hot chocolate ice cream

## DINING INFORMATION—Counter Service *(continued)*
### RESTAURANT | LOCATION | QUALITY | VALUE | SELECTIONS

**Rose & Crown Pub** | United Kingdom, World Showcase | Good | C+ | *Selections* Fish and chips, Scotch egg, British Bulldog (split sausage stuffed with mashed potatoes, bacon, and cheese), beer

**Sommerfest** | Germany, World Showcase | Good | B– | *Selections* Bratwurst and frankfurter sandwiches, curried bratwurst, Reuben sandwich, baked mac and cheese, beer and wine

**Sunshine Seasons** | The Land, Future World | Excellent | A | *Selections* Rotisserie meats, salads, sandwiches, soups, Asian noodle bowls and stir-fries; quick breakfast

**Tangierine Cafe** | Morocco, World Showcase | Good | B | *Selections* Chicken and lamb shawarma, lentil and couscous salads, hummus, wraps, kids' meals, wine and beer

**Yorkshire County Fish Shop** | United Kingdom, World Showcase | Good | B+ | *Selections* Fish and chips, shortbread, draft ale

## DINING INFORMATION—Full Service
### RESTAURANT | MEALS SERVED | LOCATION | PRICE | QUALITY | VALUE

**Akershus Royal Banquet Hall** | B-L-D | Norway, World Showcase | Expensive | ★★★ ★★★★ | *Selections* *Koldtbord* (Norwegian buffet), pork tenderloin, pan-seared salmon)

**Biergarten** | L-D | Germany, World Showcase | Expensive | ★★ | ★★★★ *Selections* Buffet with schnitzel, sausages, spaetzle, roast chicken

**Le Cellier Steakhouse** | L-D | Canada, World Showcase | Expensive | ★★★½ | ★★★ *Selections* Canadian Cheddar cheese soup, steaks, seafood

**Les Chefs de France** | L-D | France, World Showcase | Expensive | ★★★ | ★★★ *Selections* Duck à l'orange, braised beef short ribs, French onion soup, crêpes

**Coral Reef Restaurant** | L-D | The Seas with Nemo & Friends, Future World | Expensive | ★★ | ★★ *Selections* Creamy lobster soup, steaks and seafood, kids' menu

**Garden Grill Restaurant** | D | The Land, Future World | Expensive | ★★ | ★★★ *Selections* Beef filet, fish of the day, kids' menu with chicken drumstick, sweet potatoes, and broccoli

**La Hacienda de San Angel** | D | Mexico, World Showcase | Expensive | ★★★½ | ★★½ *Selections* Soft-taco appetizer, shrimp tacos, grilled tilapia with roasted corn and cactus leaves

**Monsieur Paul** | D | France, World Showcase | Expensive | ★★★★½ | ★★★ *Selections* Black-truffle soup, red snapper in potato "scales," roasted duck breast à l'orange

**Nine Dragons Restaurant** | L-D | China, World Showcase | Moderate | ★★★ | ★★ *Selections* Roasted Beijing chicken, shrimp and steak, five-spiced fish, noodles, veggie stir-fry

**Restaurant Marrakesh** | L-D | Morocco, World Showcase | Moderate | ★★½ | ★★ *Selections* Bastilla (minced-chicken pie), lemon chicken, roast lamb, couscous

**Rose & Crown Dining Room** | L-D | United Kingdom, World Showcase | Moderate | ★★★½ | ★★ *Selections* Fish and chips, bangers and mash (sausage and mashed potatoes), cottage pie

**San Angel Inn** | L-D | Mexico, World Showcase | Expensive | ★★★ | ★★ *Selections* Mole poblano (chicken in chile-chocolate sauce), tacos, tostadas, quesadillas

**Spice Road Table** | L-D | Morocco, World Showcase | Moderate | ★★★★ | ★★★ *Selections* Mediterranean-style small plates; frozen drinks, cocktails, wine, beer; specialty ice creams

**Teppan Edo** | L-D | Japan, World Showcase | Expensive | ★★★★ | ★★★ *Selections* Chicken, shrimp, beef, scallops, and veggies stir-fried on teppanyaki grill

**Tokyo Dining** | L-D | Japan, World Showcase | Moderate | ★★★★ | ★★★ *Selections* Grilled meats and seafood, tempura, sushi, and sashimi

**Tutto Italia Ristorante** | L-D | Italy, World Showcase | Expensive | ★★★★ | ★★★ *Selections* Pasta, steak, cheese polenta with braised short ribs and meatballs

**Via Napoli** | L-D | Italy, World Showcase | Moderate | ★★★½ | ★★★ *Selections* Wood-fired pizzas, pastas, salads, sandwiches; best pizza in Walt Disney World

*Advance Reservations recommended for Epcot full-service restaurants; call* ☎ *407-WDW-DINE (939-3463) or visit* disneyworld.disney.go.com/reservations/dining.

## GOOD REST AREAS IN EPCOT
### PLACE | LOCATION | NOTES

**Benches** | The Seas with Nemo & Friends, Future World | Air-conditioned

**Benches** | Innoventions East and West, Future World | Air-conditioned; usually not crowded

**Rotunda and lobby** | United States, World Showcase | Ample room; air-conditioned; refreshments nearby; usually quiet unless singers are performing

**Benches** | Mexico, World Showcase | Inside the pavilion against the inside of the wall that forms the walking ramps down to the retail space; air-conditioned

**UK Rose Garden benches** | United Kingdom, World Showcase | Behind the UK Pavilion is a small town square and manicured gardens; several outdoor benches are available

**Japan gardens** | Japan, World Showcase | To the left of Katsura Grill is a set of tables overlooking a lovely garden and koi pond. Outdoors but shaded, with refreshments nearby.

# DISNEY'S ANIMAL KINGDOM **TOURING PLAN COMPANION**
## ATTRACTION | RECOMMENDED VISITATION TIMES | AUTHOR'S RATING

**The Boneyard** | Anytime | ★★★

**Conservation Station and Affection Section** | Anytime | ★★★½

**DINOSAUR** *(FastPass+)* | Before 10:30 a.m., after 4:30 p.m., FastPass+ | ★★★★
    *Special comments* Fright potential; 40" minimum height; expectant mothers should not ride

**Expedition Everest** *(FastPass+)* | Before 9:30 a.m., after 3 p.m. | ★★★★½
    *Special comments* 44" minimum height; expectant mothers should not ride

*Festival of the Lion King* *(FastPass+)* | |Before 11 a.m., after 4 p.m., FastPass+ | ★★★★

*Flights of Wonder* | Anytime | ★★★★

**Kali River Rapids** *(FastPass+)* | First or last hour the park is open, FastPass+ | ★★★½
    *Special comments* You'll get wet; 38" minimum height; expectant mothers should note that ride is bouncy

**Kilimanjaro Safaris** *(FastPass+)* | At opening, in the 2 hours before closing | ★★★★★

**Maharajah Jungle Trek** | Anytime | ★★★★

**Meet Favorite Disney Pals at Adventurers Outpost** *(FastPass+)* | First thing in the morning, after 5 p.m., FastPass+ | ★★★½

**The Oasis** | Anytime | N/A

**Pangani Forest Exploration Trail** | Anytime | ★★★★

**Primeval Whirl** *(FastPass+ )* | First or last hour the park is open, FastPass+ | ★★★
    *Special comments* 48" minimum height; expectant mothers should not ride

**Theater in the Wild/***Finding Nemo—The Musical* | Anytime | ★★★★

**The Tree of Life/***It's Tough to Be a Bug!* **(FastPass+)** | Before noon., after 4 p.m., FastPass+ | ★★★★
    *Special comment* Fright potential

**TriceraTop Spin** | Before noon, after 3 p.m. | ★★

**Wilderness Explorers** | Sign up first thing in the morning and complete activities throughout the day. | ★★★★

**Wildlife Express Train** | Anytime | ★★

## DINING INFORMATION—**Counter Service**
### RESTAURANT | LOCATION | QUALITY | VALUE

**Flame Tree Barbecue** | Discovery Island | Excellent | B– | *Selections* Barbecue-pork sandwich; ribs; smoked-chicken salad; jumbo turkey legs; fruit plate; child's plate of baked chicken drumstick, hot dog, chicken sandwich, or PB&J sandwich; beer and wine

**Kusafiri Coffee Shop and Bakery** | Africa | Good | B | *Selections* Pastries, bagels, yogurt, coffee, cocoa, juice

**Pizzafari** | Discovery Island | Fair | B | *Selections* Cheese, pepperoni, and veggie pizzas; salads; kids' meals; beer and wine

**Restaurantosaurus** | DinoLand U.S.A. | Good | B+ | *Selections* Burgers, mac-and-cheese hot dog, chicken nuggets, chocolate mousse, cheesecake, kids' meals, beer

**Royal Anandapur Tea Company** | Asia | Good | B | *Selections* Hot and iced teas, coffee, lattes, pastries

**Tamu Tamu Eats & Refreshments** | Africa | Good | C | *Selections* Quinoa or roasted-chicken salad, chicken or vegetable curry

**Yak & Yeti Local Food Cafes** | Asia | Fair | B | *Selections* Crispy honey chicken with steamed rice, beef lo mein, sweet-and-sour chicken, Mandarin chicken salad, Asian chicken sandwiches. Kids' menu: chicken tenders or cheeseburger with applesauce and carrots.

## DINING INFORMATION—**Full Service**
### RESTAURANT | MEALS SERVED | LOCATION | PRICE | QUALITY | VALUE

**Rainforest Cafe** | B-L-D | Park entrance | Moderate | ★★ | ★★ | *Selections* Pasta, turkey wraps, coconut shrimp, ribs, brownie cake; breakfast served at this location

**Tusker House Restaurant** | B-L-D | Africa | Moderate | ★★★ | ★★★
    *Selections* Rotisserie chicken, couscous, curry, roasted meats; character breakfast

**Yak & Yeti Restaurant** | L-D | Asia | Expensive | ★★½ | ★★ | *Selections* Seared miso salmon, glazed duck, tempura shrimp

*Advance Reservations recommended for Animal Kingdom full-service restaurants; call* ☎ *407-WDW-DINE (939-3463) or visit* disneyworld.disney.go.com/reservations/dining.

## GOOD REST AREAS IN DISNEY'S ANIMAL KINGDOM
### PLACE | LOCATION | NOTES

**Walkway between Africa and Asia** | Between Africa and Asia | Plenty of shaded rest spots, some overlooking streams; refreshments nearby; a favorite of *Unofficial Guide* researchers

**Gazebo behind Flame Tree Barbecue** | Discovery Island | Follow the path toward the water, along the left side of Flame Tree Barbecue; gazebo has ceiling fans

**Outdoor covered benches near exit from DINOSAUR** | DinoLand U.S.A. | Gazebo-like structure with nearby water fountain

**Seating area adjacent to Dawa Bar** | Africa | Refreshments nearby. Outdoors and can be noisy from street performers.

# DISNEY'S HOLLYWOOD STUDIOS **TOURING PLAN COMPANION**

### ATTRACTION | RECOMMENDED VISITATION TIMES | AUTHOR'S RATING

**American Film Institute Showcase** | After the Studio Backlot Tour | ★★★

*The American Idol Experience (FastPass+)* | Anytime | ★★★½ | *Closes January 2015*

*Disney Junior—Live on Stage! (FastPass+)* | Per entertainment schedule | ★★★★

*Fantasmic! (FastPass+)* | Check *Times Guide* for schedule; if 2 shows are offered, 2nd show will be less crowded. | ★★★★★

**The Great Movie Ride** *(FastPass+)* | Before 11 a.m., during dinner, after 8 p.m., FastPass+ | ★★★½

**Honey, I Shrunk the Kids Movie Set Adventure** | Before 11 a.m., after dark | ★★½
    *Special comment* Kids must be age 10 or younger to play

*Indiana Jones Epic Stunt Spectacular! (FastPass+)* | First 2 shows or last show | ★★★½

*Jedi Training Academy* | First 2 shows | ★★★½

*Jim Henson's Muppet-Vision 3-D (FastPass+)* | Anytime | ★★★★

*The Legend of Captain Jack Sparrow* | After dinner | ★★½

*Lights, Motors, Action! Extreme Stunt Show (FastPass+)* | Anytime | ★★★½

**The Magic of Disney Animation** | Anytime | ★★½

**Rock 'n' Roller Coaster** *(FastPass+)* | First 30 minutes the park is open, FastPass+ | ★★★★
    *Special comments* 48" minimum height; expectant mothers should not ride; kids under age 7 must ride with an adult

**Star Tours—The Adventures Continue** *(FastPass+)* | Before 10 a.m., after 6 p.m., FastPass+ | ★★★★
    *Special comments* Fright potential; 40" minimum height; expectant mothers should not ride; motion-sickness potential

**Studio Backlot Tour** | Before noon, after 5 p.m. | ★★★½

**Theater of the Stars/Beauty and the Beast—Live on Stage** *(FastPass+)* | Anytime | ★★★★

**Toy Story Midway Mania!** *(FastPass+)* | At opening, FastPass+ | ★★★★½

**The Twilight Zone Tower of Terror** *(FastPass+)* | First or last 30 minutes the park is open, FastPass+ | ★★★★★ | *Special comments* 40" minimum height; expectant mothers should not ride

*Voyage of the Little Mermaid (FastPass+)* | Before 9:45 a.m., just before closing, FastPass+ | ★★★★

*Walt Disney: One Man's Dream* | Anytime | ★★★

## DINING INFORMATION—Counter Service
### RESTAURANT | LOCATION | QUALITY | VALUE

**ABC Commissary** | Echo Lake | Fair | B− | *Selections* Asian salads (chicken or salmon), Angus cheeseburger with fried shrimp, chicken club sandwich, shrimp platter, couscous salad, kids' meals, some kosher

**Backlot Express** | Echo Lake | Fair | C | *Selections* Cheeseburgers with fries or carrot sticks; Southwest salad with chicken; grilled turkey-and-cheese sandwich; hot dogs; salads; desserts; child's plate with chicken nuggets, PB&J, or grilled-veggie sandwich

**Catalina Eddie's** | Sunset Boulevard | Fair | B | *Selections* Pizzas, sandwiches, salads, banana parfait, vanilla cake with chocolate custard

**Fairfax Fare** | Sunset Boulevard | Fair | B | *Selections* Breakfast: egg-and-cheese English muffins, pastries, cereal, yogurt, fruit cup. Lunch: barbecue chicken, ribs, and pulled-pork sandwiches; "designer" hot dogs; salad with roasted corn, peppers, cheese, and tortillas

**Min and Bill's Dockside Diner** | Echo Lake | Fair | C | *Selections* Italian sausage, jumbo turkey legs or pork shanks, hot dog on a pretzel roll, shakes, beer, chips, cookies

**Pizza Planet** | Streets of America | Good | B+ | *Selections* Pizza, subs, salads, cookies

**Rosie's All-American Cafe** | Sunset Boulevard | Fair | C | *Selections* Burgers (veggie available), fries, child's turkey sandwich or chicken nuggets

**Starring Rolls Cafe** | Sunset Boulevard | Good | B | *Selections* Sandwiches, salads, sushi, pastries, baked goods, coffee

**Studio Catering Co.** | Streets of America | Good | B | *Selections* Veggie sandwiches, chicken Caesar wraps, buffalo chicken sandwiches, kids' meals

**Toluca Legs Turkey Company** | Sunset Boulevard | Good | B | *Selections* Smoked turkey legs, coffee, and soft drinks

## DINING INFORMATION—Full Service

RESTAURANT | MEALS SERVED | LOCATION | PRICE | QUALITY | VALUE

**50's Prime Time Cafe** | L-D | Echo Lake | Moderate | ★★★ | ★★★
*Selections* Meat loaf, pot roast, fried chicken

**Hollywood & Vine** | B-L-D | Echo Lake | Moderate | ★★★ | ★★★
*Selections* Chilled salads, fish of the day, carved and grilled meats, vegetables and pasta, fresh fruits and breads, dessert station with chocolate fountain; character breakfast and lunch

**The Hollywood Brown Derby** | L-D | Hollywood Boulevard | Expensive | ★★★★ | ★★★
*Selections* Cobb salad, crispy spiced duck breast, grapefruit cake, herb-roasted rack of lamb, Thai noodle bowl, crab spring-roll appetizer. New patio lounge serves cocktails and small plates.

**Mama Melrose's Ristorante Italiano** | L-D | Streets of America | Moderate | ★★★ | ★★
*Selections* Caesar salad, crispy calamari, penne alla vodka, charred strip steak, pork osso buco, grilled tuna, four-cheese flatbread

**Sci-Fi Dine-In Theater Restaurant** | L-D | Commissary Lane | Moderate | ★★½ | ★★
*Selections* Sandwiches, burgers, salads, shakes; pasta, ribs, steak

*Advance Reservations recommended for DHS full-service restaurants; call* ☎ *407-WDW-DINE (939-3463) or visit* disneyworld.disney.go.com/reservations/dining.

## GOOD REST AREAS IN DISNEY'S HOLLYWOOD STUDIOS
PLACE | LOCATION | NOTES

**Covered seating behind Toluca Legs Turkey Company** | Sunset Boulevard | Refreshments nearby; ample seating

**Studios Catering Co.** | Backlot | Ample covered seating; refreshments nearby

**Benches along Echo Lake** | Echo Lake | Some are shaded; refreshments nearby

**Tune In Lounge** | Echo Lake, next to 50's Prime Time Cafe | Air-conditioned bar; nonalcoholic drinks and food from 50's Prime Time Cafe also available. (Thanks to Matt Hochberg of **studioscentral.com** for this tip.)

**Animation Building** | Animation Courtyard | Benches in and around the Magic of Disney Animation attraction; refreshments nearby.